Anonymus

Irish Society and London companies (Irish estates)

Anonymus

Irish Society and London companies (Irish estates)

ISBN/EAN: 9783742811134

Manufactured in Europe, USA, Canada, Australia, Japa

Cover: Foto ©Suzi / pixelio.de

Manufactured and distributed by brebook publishing software (www.brebook.com)

Anonymus

Irish Society and London companies (Irish estates)

REPORT

FROM THE

SELECT COMMITTEE

ON

IRISH SOCIETY AND LONDON COMPANIES (IRISH ESTATES);

WITH THE

PROCEEDINGS OF THE COMMITTEE,

MINUTES OF EVIDENCE,

AND APPENDIX.

Ordered, by The House of Commons, to be Printed,
24 July 1890.

LONDON:
PRINTED BY HENRY HANSARD AND SON;
AND
Published by Eyre and Spottiswoode, East Harding-street, London, E.C.,
and 32, Abingdon-street, Westminster, S.W.;
Adam and Charles Black, North Bridge, Edinburgh;
and Hodges, Figgis, and Co., 104, Grafton-street, Dublin.

IRISH SOCIETY AND LONDON COMPANIES (IRISH ESTATES).

Ordered,—[*Wednesday*, 14*th May* 1890]:—THAT a Select Committee be appointed to Inquire as to the Terms of the Charters or other Instruments by which their Estates in Ireland were granted to the Irish Society and to the London Companies, and as to the Trusts and Obligations (if any) attaching to the Ownership of such Estates, and as to the mode in which the Sale of their Estates has been effected, or can be effected consistently with such Trusts and Obligations as may be shown to have existed or now exist.

THAT the Committee be nominated of—

Mr. Clancy.	Mr. Lawson.
Lord Elcho.	Mr. Lea.
Sir John Ellis.	Sir William Marriott.
Mr. John Ellis.	Mr. John Morley.
Mr. Elton.	Mr. Sexton.
Mr. T. M. Healy.	Sir Richard Temple.
Colonel Laurie.	

THAT the Committee have power to send for Persons, Papers, and Records.

THAT Five be the Quorum of the Committee.

Ordered,—[*Tuesday*, 8*th July* 1890]:—THAT the Select Committee on Irish Society and London Companies (Irish Estates) have leave to hear Counsel (to such extent as they shall think fit) upon the matters referred to them.

REPORT.

THE SELECT COMMITTEE appointed to inquire as to the Terms of the CHARTERS or other INSTRUMENTS by which their ESTATES in *Ireland* were granted to the IRISH SOCIETY and to the LONDON COMPANIES, and as to the TRUSTS and OBLIGATIONS (if any) attaching to the Ownership of such ESTATES, and as to the mode in which the Sale of their ESTATES has been effected, consistently with such TRUSTS and OBLIGATIONS as may be shown to have existed or now exist;——HAVE considered the matters to them referred, and have agreed to the following REPORT:—

YOUR Committee have examined numerous Witnesses upon the matters referred to them, and have heard arguments by Counsel, but as it will not be in their power to conclude their investigation in the present Session, they have agreed to report the Evidence already taken, and to recommend that a Committee on the same subject should be appointed at an early date in the next Session of Parliament.

24 *July* 1890.

PROCEEDINGS OF THE COMMITTEE.

Thursday, 15th *May* 1890.

MEMBERS PRESENT:

Mr. Lawson.
Mr. Sexton.
Sir William Marriott.
Mr. Clancy.
Mr. John Morley.
Lord Elcho.
Mr. T. M. Healy.
Sir John Whitaker Ellis.
Sir Richard Temple.
Mr. Lea.
Mr. John Ellis.
Mr. Elton.
Colonel Laurie.

Motion made, and Question proposed, "That Mr. John Morley do take the Chair"—(*Mr. Lea*).—Amendment proposed to leave out the words "Mr. John Morley," in order to insert the words "Sir William Marriott"—(*Sir John Whitaker Ellis*).—Question put, That the words "Mr. John Morley," stand part of the Question.—The Committee divided:

Ayes, 8.	Noes, 5.
Mr. Clancy.	Sir John Whitaker Ellis.
Lord Elcho.	Mr. Elton.
Mr. John Ellis.	Colonel Laurie.
Mr. T. M. Healy.	Mr. John Morley.
Mr. Lawson.	Sir Richard Temple.
Mr. Lea.	
Sir William Marriott.	
Mr. Sexton.	

Main Question, put, and *agreed to*.

Mr. JOHN MORLEY, in the Chair.

The Committee deliberated.

[Adjourned till Tuesday next, at Three o'clock.

Tuesday, 20*th May* 1890.

MEMBERS PRESENT:

Mr. JOHN MORLEY, in the Chair.

Sir John Whitaker Ellis.
Mr. Lea.
Mr. John Ellis.
Mr. Elton.
Colonel Laurie.
Lord Elcho.
Sir Richard Temple.
Mr. Clancy.

The Committee deliberated.

[Adjourned till Thursday, 5th June, at Twelve o'clock.

Thursday, 5th June 1890.

MEMBERS PRESENT:

Mr. JOHN MORLEY, in the Chair.

Sir William Marriott.	Lord Elcho.
Sir John Whitaker Ellis.	Mr. John Ellis.
Colonel Laurie.	Mr. Lea.
Mr. Sexton.	Mr. Elton.
Sir Richard Temple.	Mr. Lawson.

Dr. *Freshfield* made an application on behalf of the Mercers' Company, that they might be heard by Counsel before the Committee.

Mr. *Rose*, on behalf of the Salters' and Skinners' Companies, made a similar application.

Mr. *Marsh*, on behalf of the Irish Society, made a similar application.

Motion made, and Question proposed, "That on all Questions involving legality of title, counsel be allowed to appear"—(*Sir John Ellis*).—Amendment proposed, to leave out all the words after the word "That" to the end of the Question, in order to add the words, "the Question of the appearance of counsel upon legal points be deferred until the Committee has before it copies of the charters, and other instruments referred to in the terms of reference to the Committee," instead thereof—(Mr. *John Ellis*).

Question put, "That the words proposed to be left out stand part of the Question."—The Committee divided:

Ayes, 4.	Noes, 6.
Sir John Ellis.	Lord Elcho.
Colonel Laurie.	Mr. John Ellis.
Sir William Marriott.	Mr. Elton.
Sir Richard Temple.	Mr. Lawson.
	Mr. Lea.
	Mr. Sexton.

Words added.

Main question, as amended, *agreed to.*

Motion made, and Question, "That the evidence of all witnesses examined before this Committee (except those who shall be exempted by special resolution) shall be taken upon oath, in accordance with the powers conferred upon Committees of the House of Commons by 34 & 35 Vict. c. 83"—(*Sir William Marriott*),—put, and *agreed to.*

Rev. *R. H. F. Dickey*, Rev. *H. B. Wilson*, D.D., and Rev. *John Mark*, were sworn, and examined.

[Adjourned till Monday next, at Twelve o'clock.

Monday, 9th June 1890.

MEMBERS PRESENT:

Mr. JOHN MORLEY, in the Chair.

Mr. Lea.	Sir Richard Temple.
Mr. John Ellis.	Mr. Clancy.
Lord Elcho.	Sir William Marriott.
Mr. Sexton.	

Rev. *N. M. Brown*, and Rev. Dr. *Jordan*, were sworn, and examined.

[Adjourned till Thursday next, at Twelve o'clock.

Thursday, 12*th June* 1890.

MEMBERS PRESENT:

Mr. JOHN MORLEY, in the Chair.

Mr. Sexton.
Mr. John Ellis.
Sir John Whitaker Ellis.
Mr. Lea.
Colonel Laurie.
Mr. T. M. Healy.
Sir William Marriott.
Sir Richard Temple.
Mr. Clancy.
Lord Elcho.
Mr. Lawson.

Mr. *Murrough O'Brien* was sworn, and examined.

[Adjourned till Monday next, at Twelve o'clock.

Monday 16*th June* 1890.

MEMBERS PRESENT:

Mr. JOHN MORLEY, in the Chair.

Sir John Ellis.
Mr. Sexton.
Mr. Elton.
Mr. Lea.
Sir Richard Temple.
Sir William Marriott.
Sir John Whitaker Ellis.
Colonel Laurie.
Mr. Clancy.
Mr. T. M. Healy.
Mr. Lawson.

Lord Justice *Fitzgibbon* was sworn, and examined.

[Adjourned till Thursday next, at Twelve o'clock.

Thursday, 19*th June* 1890.

MEMBERS PRESENT:

Mr. JOHN MORLEY, in the Chair.

Mr. John Ellis.
Mr. Sexton.
Mr. Lea.
Mr. Clancy.
Sir Richard Temple.
Mr. T. M. Healy.
Colonel Laurie.

Mr. *Murrough O'Brien* was re-called, and further examined.

Mr. *William* [illegible] was sworn, and examined.

Monday, 23rd *June* 1890.

MEMBERS PRESENT:

Mr. JOHN MORLEY, in the Chair.

Sir John Whitaker Ellis.
Colonel Laurie.
Mr. Sexton.
Mr. John Ellis.
Mr. Lea.
Sir William Marriott.
Mr. Lawson.
Sir Richard Temple.
Lord Elcho.
Mr. Clancy.
Mr. T. M. Healy.

Mr. *Aaron Baxter* (Mayor of Londonderry), Sir *William Miller*, and Mr. *Thomas S. Magee*, were sworn, and examined.

[Adjourned till Thursday next, at Twelve o'clock.

Thursday, 26th *June* 1890.

MEMBERS PRESENT:

Mr. JOHN MORLEY, in the Chair.

Sir John Whitaker Ellis.
Mr. Sexton.
Mr. Clancy.
Mr. Lea.
Mr. John Ellis.
Mr. Elton.
Mr. T. M. Healy.
Colonel Laurie.
Sir Richard Temple.

Mr. *Percival C. Gaussen*, and Dr. *Robert Henderson Todd*, were sworn, and examined.

[Adjourned till Monday next, at Twelve o'clock.

Monday, 30th *June* 1890.

MEMBERS PRESENT:

Mr. JOHN MORLEY, in the Chair.

Mr. Clancy.
Lord Elcho.
Sir John Whitaker Ellis.
Mr. Lawson.
Colonel Laurie.
Mr. T. M. Healy.
Mr. Lea.
Sir William Marriott.
Mr. John Ellis.
Mr. Sexton.
Sir Richard Temple.

Dr. *Robert Henderson Todd* was further examined.

Mr. *W. H. M'Cormack* was sworn, and examined.

[Adjourned till Monday next, at Twelve o'clock.

Monday, 7th July 1890.

MEMBERS PRESENT:

Mr. JOHN MORLEY, in the Chair.

Mr. Lea.
Mr. Clancy.
Sir William Marriott.
Colonel Laurie.
Mr. John Ellis.
Mr. Sexton.
Lord Elcho.
Sir Richard Temple.
Mr. T. M. Healy.
Mr. Lawson.

Mr. *Joseph Ballintine*, and Mr. *John Walary*, were sworn, and examined.

[Adjourned till Thursday next, at Twelve o'clock.

Thursday, 10th July 1890.

MEMBERS PRESENT:

Mr. JOHN MORLEY, in the Chair.

Sir William Marriott.
Mr. Sexton.
Mr. John Ellis.
Sir John Whitaker Ellis.
Mr. T. M. Healy.
Sir Richard Temple.
Lord Elcho.
Mr. Clancy.
Colonel Laurie.
Mr. Lea.

Mr. *Edward A. Hamilton*, Rev. *E. Loughrey*, P.P., and Rev. *J. Quinn*, P.P., were sworn, and examined.

[Adjourned till To-morrow, at Twelve o'clock.

Friday, 11th July 1890.

MEMBERS PRESENT:

Mr. J. MORLEY, in the Chair.

Mr. Lea.
Mr. John Ellis.
Colonel Laurie.
Sir William Marriott.
Lord Elcho.
Sir John Whitaker Ellis.
Mr. Clancy.
Mr. T. M. Healy.
Mr. Lawson.
Sir Richard Temple.

The Rev. *J. Quinn* P.P., re-called, and further examined.

Mr. *John Wrench Towse*, F.R.G.S., and Sir *Owen Roberts*, F.S.A., were sworn, and examined.

[Adjourned till Monday next, at Twelve o'clock.

Monday, 14th *July* 1890.

MEMBERS PRESENT:

Mr. JOHN MORLEY, in the Chair.

Sir William Marriott.	Mr. T. M. Healy.
Sir John Whitaker Ellis.	Mr. Clancy.
Colonel Laurie.	Sir Richard Temple.
Mr. John Ellis.	Mr. Sexton.
Mr. Lea.	Mr. Lawson.
Lord Elcho.	

Sir *Owen Roberts*, F.S.A., re-called, and further examined.

Mr. *Herbert Clifford Saunders*, Q.C., and Mr. *Edward Herbert Draper*, were sworn, and examined.

[Adjourned till Thursday next, at Twelve o'clock.

Thursday, 17th *July* 1890.

MEMBERS PRESENT:

Mr. JOHN MORLEY, in the Chair.

Sir John Whitaker Ellis.	Mr. Elton.
Mr. John Ellis.	Lord Elcho.
Sir William Marriott.	Mr. T. M. Healy.
Sir Richard Temple.	Mr. Sexton.
Mr. Lea.	

Sir *Henry Hervey Bruce*, Bart., Mr. *John Glover*, Mr. *William Philip Sawyer*, and Sir *William Cunyngham*, were sworn, and examined.

[Adjourned till To-morrow, at Twelve o'clock.

Friday, 18th *July* 1890.

MEMBERS PRESENT:

Mr. JOHN MORLEY, in the Chair.

Sir John Whitaker Ellis.	Sir William Marriott.
Colonel Laurie.	Mr. Sexton.
Mr. Lawson.	Sir Richard Temple.
Mr. Lea.	Mr. T. M. Healy.

The Very Rev. Dr. Andrew F. *Smyly*, Dean of Derry, the Rev. *R. Ross*, Mr. *R. L. Moore*, and Mr. *Thomas Bedford Montgomery*, were sworn, and examined.

[Adjourned till Monday next, at Half-past Eleven o'clock.

Monday, 21st July 1890.

MEMBERS PRESENT:

Mr. JOHN MORLEY, in the Chair.

Mr. Lea.
Sir William Marriott.
Sir Richard Temple.
Lord Elcho.
Mr. John Ellis.
Mr. T. M. Healy.
Mr. Sexton.
Sir John Whitaker Ellis.
Mr. Elton.
Mr. Laurie.
Mr. Clancy.

Mr. *Walker*, Q.C., was heard on behalf of the Receivers of Charities in county of Londonderry.

Mr. *George Harris Lea* was heard on behalf of several religious societies in the county of Londonderry.

[Adjourned till Wednesday next, at Half-past Eleven o'clock.

Wednesday, 23rd July 1890.

MEMBERS PRESENT:

Mr. JOHN MORLEY, in the Chair.

Lord Elcho.
Mr. Elton.
Mr. John Ellis.
Sir John Whitaker Ellis.
Mr. Lea.
Sir William Marriott.
Mr. Sexton.
Mr. Lawson.
Sir Richard Temple.

Mr. *Latham*, Q.C., was heard on behalf of the Mercers' Company; also for the Salters', the Drapers', the Grocers', the Fishmongers', and the Clothworkers' Companies.

[Adjourned till To-morrow, at Half-past Eleven o'clock.

Thursday, 24th July 1890.

MEMBERS PRESENT:

Mr. JOHN MORLEY, in the Chair.

Mr. John Ellis.
Mr. Lea.
Mr. Elton.
Colonel Laurie.
Mr. Lawson.
Mr. Sexton.
Sir Richard Temple.

Mr. *Latham*, Q.C., was further heard on behalf of the several London Companies for which he appeared.

Mr. *Rigby*, Q.C., was heard on behalf of the Skinners' Company.

Mr. *Bosser*, Q.C., was heard on behalf of the Irish Society.

Mr. *Pollard*, Q.C., was heard on behalf of the Corporation of London.

Draft Report brought up, read the first and second time, and *agreed to*.

Ordered, To Report, together with the Minutes of the Evidence, and an Appendix.

EXPENSES OF WITNESSES

Profession or Condition.	From whence Summoned.	Number of Days absent from Home, under Orders of Committee.	Allowance during Absence from Home.	Expenses of Journey to London and Back.	Total Expenses allowed to Witness.
			£ s. d.	£ s. d.	£ s. d.
Clergyman - - -	[illegible], County Londonderry.	5	[illegible]	[illegible]	10 [illegible] -
Clergyman - - -	Cookstown, County Tyrone.	5	[illegible]	[illegible]	10 9 -
Clergyman - - -	[illegible], County Londonderry.	5	[illegible]	[illegible]	10 [illegible] -
Clergyman - - -	Limavady, County Londonderry.	6	[illegible]	[illegible]	11 10 -
Clergyman - - -	[illegible], County Londonderry.	5	[illegible]	[illegible]	10 [illegible] -
Endowed School's Commissioner.	10, [illegible]-square, Dublin.	[illegible]	[illegible]	[illegible]	[illegible]
Irish Land Commissioner.	64, Upper [illegible]-street, Dublin.	[illegible]	[illegible]	[illegible]	14 [illegible] -
Mayor - - -	Londonderry - -	5	[illegible]	[illegible]	10 9 -
Physician - - -	Londonderry - -	5	[illegible]	[illegible]	[illegible]
Stockbroker - -	Londonderry - -	5	[illegible]	[illegible]	[illegible]
Barrister - - -	Magherafelt, Londonderry.	[illegible]	[illegible]	[illegible]	[illegible]
Solicitor - - -	Londonderry - -	15	[illegible]	[illegible]	[illegible]
J. P. - - - -	Londonderry - -	4	[illegible]	[illegible]	[illegible]
Builder - - -	Londonderry - -	4	[illegible]	[illegible]	[illegible]
Secretary to Harbour Commissioners.	Londonderry - -	4	[illegible]	[illegible]	[illegible]
P. P. - - -	Dungiven, Londonderry.	5	[illegible]	[illegible]	10 [illegible] -
P. P. - - -	Magherafelt, Londonderry.	5	[illegible]	[illegible]	10 [illegible] -
Dean of Derry - -	[illegible] - -	[illegible]	[illegible]	[illegible]	[illegible]
Presbyterian Assembly	Londonderry - -	4	[illegible]	[illegible]	[illegible]
Gentleman - -	Londonderry - -	5	[illegible]	[illegible]	11 4 [illegible]
Solicitor - - -	Londonderry - -	[illegible]	[illegible]	[illegible]	[illegible]
Agent to Irish Society	Londonderry - -	[illegible]	[illegible]	[illegible]	[illegible]
				TOTAL - - £.	[illegible]

LIST OF WITNESSES.

MINUTES OF EVIDENCE.

Thursday, 5th June 1890.

MEMBERS PRESENT:

Lord Elcho.
Sir John Ellis.
Mr. John Ellis.
Mr. Elton.
Colonel Laurie.
Mr. Lawson.
Mr. Lea.
Sir William Marriott.
Mr. John Morley.
Mr. Sexton.
Sir Richard Temple.

THE RIGHT HONOURABLE JOHN MORLEY, IN THE CHAIR.

Dr. *Freshfield*, on behalf of the Mercers' Company, applied that (the question involved being for the most part a legal question, namely, as to the trusts and obligations of the Companies) the Mercers' Company might be represented by Counsel.

Mr. *Rees*, on behalf of the Skinners' Company and the Saddlers' Company, and Mr. *Maitland* on behalf of the Irish Society, made a similar application.

The Committee-room was cleared.

After some time the parties were again called in.

The *Chairman* stated that the Committee, having considered the applications to be heard by Counsel, had determined that the question of the appearance of Counsel upon legal points be deferred until the Committee had before it copies of the charters and other documents referred to in the Order of Reference.

Mr. *Elton*, at the request of the Chairman, read out the following list of documents which the Committee desired might be furnished to them:—

1. Charter of James I.
2. Licence in mortmain following thereon.
3. Proceedings in the Star Chamber, 1634 to 1637, so far as they relate to the subject-matter of this inquiry.
4. Petitions to Parliament, about January 1641.
5. Report to Committee of Parliament, 24th August 1642.
6. Acts of Parliament or Ordinances of the Commonwealth, about 1653.
7. Charter of the Protector Cromwell.
8. Grant of Cromwell to one of the Companies.
9. Charter of Charles II.
10. Release to the Mercers' Company.
11. Copies of Indemnities given by the Companies to the Irish Society on the sale of their estates.
12. Disclaimer given by the Society to the Companies of their rights to timber, in June 1741.

3 June 1890.

The Reverend R. H. F. DICKEY, M.A., sworn; and Examined.

Mr. *Lea.*

1. You are, I think, a double gold medallist of the Queen's University?—Yes.

2. And also a graduate of Edinburgh?—I am a graduate in divinity of Edinburgh University.

3. And you are minister of the Presbyterian Church at Maghera?—Yes.

4. Since you have been there, have you taken a very prominent part in all educational and political movements?—Yes.

5. And you have taken a great interest in the London companies?—Yes.

6. Do you know the feeling of the people of the district in which you live?—Yes, pretty well.

7. Have you any authority or commission from your church, or from the people, to appear here?—I have no official commission from the Presbyterian Church; but the ministers affected throughout the county of *Derry* have given me all the information that they can, and have requested me to come before the Committee.

8. Instead of appearing separately, they have authorised you to state their case?—Yes.

9. You have studied the history of the companies in the county of Derry?—Yes, slightly.

10. From all the documents that you have been able to obtain?—Yes.

11. You know the charters under which the estates were granted to the London companies?—

Dr. *Freshfield* inquired whether he would be at liberty to cross-examine this witness, inasmuch as the Committee were now going directly into the question of the companies' legal title.

The *Chairman* stated that the Committee was in exactly the same position in which the corresponding Committee was last Session, and that it took that position until their next meeting, at all events; and that, therefore, they could not accede to Dr. Freshfield's desire, either to cross-examine this witness himself, or to employ counsel to do so.

Dr. *Freshfield* asked whether it might be understood that this witness would be forthcoming, so that he might be cross-examined in the event of the Committee deciding that the companies might be represented by Counsel.

The *Chairman* stated that that was a point upon which the Committee could not at present give any opinion.

Mr. *Lea.*

12. (To the *Witness.*) You are not a lawyer?—No.

13. I do not propose to ask you the legal bearings of the question; but you know the popular opinion with regard to these charters?—Yes; certainly.

14. And the popular opinion of the district may be taken as strongly impregnated with the idea that they constitute a trust?—Yes; we all believe that the companies are trustees, as well as the Irish Society, under whom they hold.

Mr. *Lea*—continued.

15. And the action of the companies in the past has rather confirmed that idea?—Yes.

16. The popular idea is that the charter has bestowed these estates upon London companies for the religious and moral well-being of the community?—The companies hold by deed, under the charters, and the popular opinion is that the companies are under the same trusts as the Irish Society were under, under whom they hold.

17. The companies have given considerable sums, have they not, to public works in the district?—Yes; mostly for religious and educational objects.

18. We have had before us evidence with regard to the Episcopal Church of Ireland; can you give us any evidence with regard to the grants to Presbyterian ministers, given by the companies in the past?—Yes. We have two Synods represented in County Derry, with seven presbyteries, and 47 congregations, and 8,469 families in them.

19. Does it extend into County Tyrone as well?—Yes, part of County Tyrone comes into it; almost the whole of County Derry and part of County Tyrone.

20. You have received grants from the London companies to a considerable extent, have you not?—Yes; 646 *l.* has been given annually by the London companies; but of this sum 371 *l.* 10 *s.* has been withdrawn. I can give the particulars, if required.

21. Will you state them?—The first presbytery, taking them in alphabetical order, is the Presbytery of Aboghill. The congregation of Boveedy is under the Mercers' Company. There are 64 families, and they receive a grant of 10 *l.* annually, and that is continued. The congregation of Churchtown is also under the Mercers' Company. There are 110 families in it. A grant has been given recently to this congregation for building purposes, but no annual grant is given. The second presbytery affected is the Coleraine Presbytery. The first congregation is Aghadowey. There are 395 families, and 10 *l.* is given to it by the Ironmongers' Company. Castlerock was under the Clothworkers' Company. It never received a grant; but when the Clothworkers' Company sold out, this congregation received 100 *l.* as an endowment. There are 42 families in it. Coleraine-terrace-row was under the Clothworkers' Company. There are 245 families, but no grant is given. A grant was at one time given, but I do not know what the amount of it was. I think it was 10 *l.*

Chairman.

22. Up to when was it given?—It has not been given for many years. Crossgar under the Ironmongers' Company received 10 *l.*; but some time ago it was reduced to 5 *l.* There are 78 families in it. First, Dunboe was under the Clothworkers' Company. There are 310 families in it, and it received 20 *l.*, and when the company sold out in 1873 the congregation received an endowment of 200 *l.*, and Sir Harvey Bruce, the purchaser of the estate, was bound to continue the charities to education on the estate. That 20 *l.*,

Chairman—continued.

of course, has been withdrawn. The second congregation of Dunboe has 110 families, and it received 10 *l.* under the Clothworkers' Company. This is withdrawn, but the congregation received as an endowment 100 *l.* at the time of the sale. First, Garvagh has 175 families, and it received 10 *l.* from the Ironmongers' estate, but that has been reduced recently to 8 *l.* Second Garvagh congregation has 150 families, and it received 10 *l.*, but that has been recently reduced to 5 *l.* under the Ironmongers' estate.

Mr. *Sexton.*

23. Could you not give the time of the reduction more precisely?—First Garvagh has been reduced for the last two years; second Garvagh was reduced in 1887; and third Garvagh has been reduced for the last two years; third Garvagh has 85 families, and it received 10 *l.* This has been reduced also to 8 *l.* within the last two years under the Ironmongers' Company. The congregation of Macosquin has 140 families, and it received 10 *l.* This has been reduced to 8 *l.* under the Ironmongers' Company. The congregation of Moneydig has 146 families. It receives 10 *l.* as yet from the Ironmongers' Company. It received 10 *l.* from the Mercers' Company, but that has been withdrawn; it was only received for one year. Ballylintagh received 10 *l.* from the Ironmongers' Company, but that has been withdrawn about eight years ago in consequence of the congregation going down. The next presbytery is Glendermot. The congregation of Banagher has 167 families, and it receives 10 *l.* from the Fishmongers' Company, but that has been withdrawn at the time of the sale.

Mr. *Lea.*

24. Are there many more of these details?—Yes.

25. Last year, when we were dealing with the representatives of the Episcopal Church, they put in a statement with regard to these details, and gave us the total; could you put in a similar statement?—I can give you the amount of the grants given to the presbyterian, if you wish for that.

Chairman.

26. You will, perhaps, do better to put in, in the form of a table, the figures which you have prepared as to the amount of the grants made for these various purposes in the various parishes, and the present sums, if any sums are still contributed; and any lump sums given in commutation of what have hitherto been annual sums?—Yes. Perhaps I could give to the Committee now the sums given as compensation by the companies who sold out. The Fishmongers' Company, when they sold out, gave three years' purchase of the annual grant to the ministers on their estate.

Mr. *Lea.*

27. I do not propose to ask you questions upon the history of the companies, in consequence of what has occurred at the Committee to-day; but I think you understand clearly that the charter states that it was given for the religious and moral elevation of the people, and it is so viewed in the district?—Yes.

Mr. *Elton.*

28. Have you a copy of that charter with you?—I have not.

29. Do you know what the words of it are?—I have seen extracts from it. I have a copy of the "Concise View."

Mr. *Lea.*

30. You have a copy of the "Concise View," which gives the charter?—Yes.

31. And you have read the charter in that copy?—Yes.

32. The "Concise View" was represented last year as an authorised statement of the Irish Society's affairs, and of that you have a copy?—Yes.

33. Have the companies generally recognised what you consider to be their obligations under the trust?—They have in part, so far as grants to religion and education are concerned, but not so far as the tenantry and the country generally are concerned.

34. You gave us a statement of the grants made to Presbyterian bodies; how does that compare with grants given to other bodies?—They are altogether out of proportion to what has been given to the Episcopal Church.

Mr. *Sexton.*

35. When you say that they are out of proportion, do you mean that they are much too little?—Much too little.

Mr. *Lea.*

36. The Presbyterian grants, I think, have been given for 50 or 60 years?—Some of the grants on the Mercers' and Drapers' estates were given in 1817 or 1818.

37. Have you seen a copy of the book of a deputation of the committee of the Drapers' Company which visited their estates in 1818?—I have seen it.

38. It was in consequence of that committee's report that grants were given to the Presbyterian church at Moneymore, to the Presbyterian church at Lissan, and to the Presbyterian church at Tobermore?—Yes.

39. Those grants had been continued up to that date?—The grant to Moneymore is continued to the present date, but the grants to Lissan and Tobermore have been withdrawn.

40. Have you the dates?—The grant to Tobermore was withdrawn in 1884 when the Rev. Mr. Robinson died; it was not continued to his successor. The grant to Lissan was withdrawn at the death of the Rev. Mr. Wilson.

41. At what date?—I am not quite sure of the date, but it was about four years ago, I think.

42. Some of the companies have been selling their estates?—Upon the Drapers' estates a great many grants have been withdrawn at various times. The grant to Coagh was withdrawn some years ago, during the life of the present minister. The grant to First Cookstown was withdrawn four years ago. The grant to Second Cookstown was withdrawn four years ago. The grant to Claggan was reduced to 5 *l.* five years ago.

43. These grants have been withdrawn chiefly since the companies proposed to sell their estates?

Mr. *Lea*—continued.

—Some were withdrawn before, and some have been withdrawn since.

44. Do you know whether there is any understanding, since the companies have been selling their estates, to withdraw their grants?—None of the companies, so far as I am aware, have given any intimation of that with the exception of the Skinners' Company lately to the minister of Lower Cumber. They intimated to him (I have the letter here) that his grant of 20 *l.* would be withdrawn in consequence of the sale of the estate.

Mr. *Sexton.*

45. Have you the letter with you?—I have got his memorial to the Skinners' Company on the withdrawal of his grant and the company's replies. (*The same were delivered in.*)

Mr. *Lea.*

46. What is the reply in general terms?—The reply is to the effect that the grant would not be continued, inasmuch as the company had sold the portion of their estate on which the congregation resides.

47. Is that the only reason given?—That is the only reason given; they do not intend, they say, to continue this donation.

48. The general feeling in the district is that as the estates are sold the grants there will be withdrawn?—There is an uneasy feeling to that effect, unless something is done.

49. Have not grants to schools been withdrawn upon the death of the schoolmaster?—Yes, some grants have been withdrawn from schools by the Salters' Company, who have sold. There are three schools, or two at any rate, from which the grants have been withdrawn. There is one from which a grant has been threatened to be withdrawn; 5 *l.* has been withdrawn from one school and 5 *l.* from another, and 10 *l.* has been threatened to be withdrawn.

50. And the teachers of those schools have suffered that diminution of salary?—Yes.

51. Is it impossible to raise the amount in the district to recoup the schoolmasters?—Yes.

52. And those grants have been withdrawn since the companies have sold their estates?—They have.

53. Do you know the Rainey School at Magherafelt?—Yes.

54. That is an intermediate school, is it not?—It was established under the will of Hugh Rainey in the early part of the seventeen hundreds, about 1712 I think, as a Presbyterian school.

55. Did the Salters' Company support that school?—When the Salters' Company came into possession of their estate in 1854 they made an application to the Lord Primate to have this school taken over, and made more efficient; and for that purpose they went into Chancery in 1864, and got a Bill in Chancery under which the Lord Primate was appointed the Governor of the school. He had previously, under an Act of Parliament, been trustee for the property. The Salters' Company at that time took over the old school building and 16 Irish acres, and erected a new school on the site of the old school at a cost of, say 1,500 *l.* In conjunction with the Lord Primate they appointed a schoolmaster, Mr. Kincaid. Mr. Kincaid was always paid by the Salters' Company. The original endowment brought in 165 *l.* or 167 *l.*, and the Salters' Company supplemented that by 180 *l.* annually, and Mr. Kincaid and his assistants were paid out of those two amounts by the Salters' Company. When the Salters' Company sold out, they made an application to the Education Commissioners to formulate a scheme for the Rainey School, and they proposed at first under this scheme to hand over the markets in Magherafelt to the Governors of the school, to be appointed under a scheme. The Education Commissioners were dissatisfied with this arrangement, and thought it would be a bad thing for the school as the Governors could not realise very much out of the markets. They accordingly suggested to the Salters' Company that they should create a rent charge on the markets and give that over to the Governors of the school, so that they would not have anything to do with the management of the markets. The Salters' Company did so and created a rent charge of 180 *l.*; but subsequently this 180 *l.* was divided, 66 *l.* to go to Rainey's school and 54 *l.* to the *Roman Catholics*; so that the Salters' Company left 66 *l.* a year to the *Rainey* school in lieu of the 180 *l.* which they had been accustomed to give, and they left to Mr. Kincaid, an English gentleman and an M.A. of Cambridge, whom they had appointed in 1864, a pension or retiring allowance to be paid out of the Salters' Company's endowment.

56. Which leaves less than nothing to the school? Yes.

57. Is there great lack of intermediate education in the county?—There are very few schools in the county. The Skinners' Company had a school in Dungiven which has gone down. The Drapers' Company have a school in Moneymore. Then there is this Rainey's school, and there is an intermediate school in Maghera, which is entirely a private school, and none of the companies contribute to it. An application was made to the Mercers' Company to contribute to this school, but no reply has been received from them yet. The companies might have done much more for intermediate education than they have done; in fact it is neglected in the county.

58. They have assisted primary education a good deal, I understand?—Yes, but with regard to that, the people are very much dissatisfied with the class of teachers that they appoint. The appointment of teachers until recently turned on the question of religion.

59. What do you mean by its turning on the question of religion?—It was almost a *sine qua non* that the teachers should be Episcopalians. I can give an example.

60. But that does not bear on the question of the London companies?—It is the London companies that had the appointment of these teachers. Recently that has not been so much the case; the companies have been a little fairer; but in some cases they have mismanaged the school for the purpose of having Episcopalian appointments. There was one glaring case lately on the Mercers' estate where there was a fine school, and should have been an efficient one. They advertised for a first-class teacher, and it was required that he should be able to teach elementary classics, Latin and Greek. A teacher of my

own

Mr. *Lea*—continued.

was applied for the situation, a first-class teacher under the National Board and a graduate of the Royal University, but he was passed over in favour of a third-class teacher who was an Episcopalian.

61. You complain of the theological preference?—Yes; but this applies more to times gone by than to the present time.

Chairman.

62. When was this?—The appointment that I am speaking of was about four years ago.

Mr. *Sexton*.

63. They have become more liberal in that sense, have they, as they have begun to reduce or withdraw the grants?—Yes.

Mr. *Lea*.

64. Did they support dispensaries in olden days?—They did; they supported a dispensary in Kilrea. Dr. Clarke, of Kilrea, got up to his death an annual grant from the Mercers' Company. The Mercers' Company also supported a doctor and dispensary in Swatragh, Dr. Mullan being the doctor.

65. Was there a dispensary at Drapers Town?—There was.

66. Have the Drapers' Company continued that?—The grant of the Drapers' Company I think has been discontinued.

67. What comparison do the London Companies bear to private landowners in the country?—As landlords they have acted pretty much in the same way; in some respects a little better; in other respects a great deal worse.

68. Your complaint is that if the whole of the money is paid to the Companies in London there is no landlord and no private gentleman who will replace the London Companies?—The county would not suffer very much from the withdrawal of the companies in that way, because the companies were always absentees. Of course they have their agent on the estate, but the moneys accruing from the lands in county Derry were not spent in the country; they were spent in London largely, with the exception of these grants.

69. Have you a statement of the grants made by the companies in the county?—Yes.

70. Can you give me some statement as regards the Salters' Company as landlords?—In 1757 they leased their estate to the Batesons for 100 years. There were two leases, the first for 160 *l.*, but that lease was surrendered and a new lease given for 100 years at 600 *l.* a year. During those 100 years the Salters' Company never spent a shilling upon the estate. At the beginning of that time there was no town of Magherafelt. The Batesons gave long building leases, and at the termination of the lease the town of Magherafelt was built to a considerable extent by the tenants themselves. The valuation of the town of Magherafelt at the end of the lease was 3,800 *l.* The rental of the town of Magherafelt was about 310 *l.*

71. Have you a statement of what the rental of the Salters' Company was at the beginning and end of such lease?—At the beginning of the lease it was thought that the rental was about 300 *l.*; we do not know definitely.

Mr. *Kenrick*.

72. When the lease expired, what was the rental?—When the lease expired the rental of the whole estate was 15,000 *l.* from property entirely created by the tenants.

Chairman.

73. How long was the lease?—One hundred years. It expired in 1857.

Mr. *Lea*.

74. During that time had the Salters' Company done anything for the improvement of the tenants?—Nothing.

75. You stated just now, did you not, that the town of Magherafelt was built entirely by the tenants?—Yes.

Mr. *Dixon*.

76. You are not a very old man, and you are speaking of 1757?—Yes.

Mr. *Swain*.

77. Your point is that the tenants built the houses?—Yes; and if you want any confirmation of it, I have a question which was asked in the House of Commons, and the answer of the Chief Secretary, and it appears from the Chief Secretary's answer that the rental of the town in 1855 was 307 *l.*, and an increase was then made of 410 *l.* by the Company, making a total of 717 *l.*

Mr. *Lea*.

78. Without any expenditure on the tenants' houses?—Certainly.

79. Was a memorial presented to the Salters' Company after that?—Yes, afterwards. The poor law valuation was 2,942 *l.*, and in 1885 the rental had been further augmented by 814 *l.*; but this small increase was due to an outlay by the Company of nearly 6,000 *l.* That is what Lord Naas says, but the tenants give an explanation of this 6,000 *l.*, which I can submit to the Committee, which it is said was spent upon the estate. It was not spent upon the town houses, the rents of which they were raising; it was spent in building churches. They spent some money on building an Episcopalian church and some money on building a Presbyterian church.

80. These rents that you said were raised from 300 *l.* to 700 *l.* in the town of Magherafelt, were rents raised entirely upon buildings erected by the tenants?—Yes.

81. And the money spent by the Company was spent in building churches?—Yes, and in other public works, or on buildings of their own for which they received rent.

82. That was the answer of the Salters' Company to the tenants' memorial. Then that was explained by the tenants afterwards?—Yes.

83. Was any reply received by the tenants from the Salters' Company?—Yes; but I have not come to that yet. There was 314 *l.* of increase made in 1865. In 1867 notices to quit were served upon the townholders with a view to increasing the rents to 1,220 *l.* The matter was then brought before Parliament, and in 1883, or about that time, the tenants memorialised the companies. I have got one of the memorials here, but I can give the Committee a book in which the whole correspondence is contained

Mr. Lea—continued.

tained. This memorial is in response to the assertions of the company.

Chairman.

84. Was there an answer sent to that memorial?—There was, but it was a short answer.

85. What was the answer?—The company could not answer it.

86. Have you got the answer there?—Yes; I have got the whole of the correspondence here.

87. Have you any other memorials?—I have another memorial with regard to tenant-right. The company tried to destroy tenant-right on the estate by limiting it to 10 *l.*, and the tenants sent up to them a memorial.

Mr. Lea.

88. Did they receive an answer to that memorial also?—I have not got the answer to it. I cannot find out whether there was an answer sent to it or not.

89. You put in these two memorials and the answers?—I do. (*The same were delivered in.*)

90. The general effect was that the rental was raised on the Salters' estate from 400 *l.* to about how much?—The rent of the whole estate was raised from 15,000 *l.* at the termination of the lease to between 17,000 *l.* and 18,000 *l.*; but it was afterwards reduced under Mr. Gladstone's Land Bill, and then the company sold out, and realised 240,000 *l.*

91. But what the tenants (I mean the clergy as well as the agricultural tenants) and the people of the town of Magherafelt complained of was, that they had built their houses, and reclaimed their land entirely without the assistance of the companies, and that then they paid the companies the value of their own buildings and improvements?—Yes.

92. It is pretty universally acknowledged, is it not, that the tenants do all the improvements? —Certainly.

93. Have you seen this book of the Drapers' Company?—Yes.

94. Did you notice this paragraph, which is an alleged expression of opinion by the Drapers' Company, at page 11, "And by the same universal practice, all rates and taxes are borne by the tenant as well as the universal practice of the county being that repairs and new buildings of all sorts are executed at the expense of the tenant"?—That refers to the Drapers' Company, but it is true of all the companies.

95. What you contend is, that the inhabitants of the country have bought that which is practically their own property, and they contend that, if it is a Trust, the benefit of that Trust should be extended and belong to the country?—Yes; we hold, moreover, that the tenants should have got the land on easier rents.

96. Can you tell us what sort of rentals the tenants pay?—Here is a lease dated 1760. The rent under this lease was 3 *s.* 6 *d.* an acre, and now the rent of the same land would be between 25 *s.* and 30 *s.* per acre.

Mr. Sexton.

97. A lease by whom?—This is a sub-lease under the lessee. The lessee of the estate was Bateson, and he gave a lease to the tenant, and that tenant made this sub-lease, and the rent under the sub-lease is 3 *s.* 6 *d.* per acre.

98. Bateson holding from the company?—Yes. Here is another lease on the Vintners' estate, made by Sir Thomas Conolly, and the rent is about 3 *s.* 4 *d.* per acre.

Mr. Lea.

99. Did the tenants consider that under the terms of the charter they were to pay any rents?—Yes.

100. What sort of rents have they paid?—They have paid rack-rents; rents on their own improvements.

101. Have any of the companies done anything to encourage manufactures in the district?—No, they have discouraged manufactures in every way. There are no manufactures on the companies' estates in county Derry.

102. Have any attempts been made to establish manufactures?—I can give you one or two cases where leases were asked for, for the purpose of establishing manufactures, and where the companies refused, if the Committee desire to have them. There was a gentleman called Thomson Bryan, who lived in Rose Cottage. He built it under lease.

Chairman.

103. Can you give us the date of all this?—I am not quite sure of the date; it is about 20 years ago, or it might be a little more.

Mr. Lea.

104. Do you know that it is a fact?—Yes. He said to the company, because they would not give him a lease long enough to start a mill. It was a flax mill, and he had to go to county Antrim, where he established a factory, and employs about 100 hands. That is at Ballymena, in county Antrim.

Mr. Sexton.

105. Did they refuse the lease because he wanted to start a mill?—None of the companies would give long leases.

Mr. Lea.

106. Not sufficiently long to warrant him in expending a large sum of money in building a mill; is that the case?—Yes, that is the case. A man had a coach factory at Magherafelt, and he paid 14 *l.* to 15 *l.* a week; Montgomery was his name. The company would not keep it in repair, or give him a lease, and he removed to Omagh, where he has been doing a great deal of business; consequently, Magherafelt lost that on account of the company's action.

107. Can you give the date of that?—It was not long ago; five or six years ago.

108. You give that as a proof that the company did nothing to encourage manufactures?—Yes, and there are a great many other cases.

109. With regard to the public rentals, and the public spirit of the company, I have in my hand a copy of Mr. Stannus' report to the Drapers' Company. Mr. Stannus was agent to the Drapers' Company, was he not, in 1820?—Yes.

110. And

Mr. Lea—continued.

110. And he made a report to the company in 1880, of which you have a copy?—Yes.

111. He wished, of course, to obtain the largest possible income for the Drapers' Company, I suppose?—Yes.

112. And in doing so, did he throw what rates and taxes he could on the county?—He did.

113. On page 18 you will find what Mr. Stevenson says: "I allude chiefly to opening up the estate by a new line of road, and by attending at the presentment sessions and assizes, and, after considerable discussion and opposition, inducing the grand jury, with all the members of which I am personally acquainted, to place upon the county, and keep in repair, roads that had been, many years ago, laid out by Drapers' Company." That did not show great liberality on the part of the Drapers' Company?—No; but would you please go on a little further.

114. "But which, from want of attention on the part of the tenants themselves, and want of repairs, had almost become impassable." So that the Drapers' Company threw on the county what they, as landlords, ought probably to have borne?—Yes.

115. Then again, on the next page, the same report says, with regard to the town of Moneymore: "The thatched-roof cottages have almost entirely disappeared, and the little narrow footpaths, in many places broken away, and at most not two feet wide, have been replaced by handsome footways from seven to nine feet in width; made at a cost to the county of nearly 800 *l.*" Is that correct?—Yes.

116. So that in that case the Drapers' Company threw on the county what they, as large landowners, might have been expected to bear themselves?—Yes.

117. Have the proceedings of the company in selling and about selling been such as to give the impression that they wanted to take away the largest possible sum, as the value of their estates?—Yes; the action of the Salters' Company gives us good ground for that belief in their shabby treatment of the Rainey's School.

118. Is Sir Robert Fowler the Master of the Salters' Company?—I do not know.

119. Are you aware that he wrote a letter to the "Times" on the part of the Salters' Company, and he said that one of the advantages to the company would be that, in selling their estates there, subscriptions would cease?—I did not see that, but I have no doubt of it.

Mr. Sexton.

120. They have secured that advantage at any rate in some cases?—Yes.

Sir William Marriott.

121. You said that the Salters' Company came into their property in 1854; what did you mean by that?—The lease terminated, and they took the property into their own hands at the termination of the lease.

122. They were the freeholders before, but the lease terminated; they did not come into the property then?—They leased the estate, and at the termination of the lease they resumed possession.

Sir William Marriott—continued.

123. But it had been their property for 100 years before I suppose?—They were the lessors for 100 years.

124. They did not come into their property then, but the lease that they had upon their property ceased?—Yes.

125. You said something, did you not, about a sum of over 100 *l.* which was paid by them, of which 54 *l.* was now paid to the Catholics?—To the Rainey's School they gave 160 *l.*, but it is now reduced to 66 *l.*

126. What becomes of the rest of the money?—£. 54 of the 120 *l.* goes to the Roman Catholics.

127. They pay the same amount, but it is divided differently?—There was 160 *l.* paid to the Rainey's School before the sale. At the time of the sale they created a rent-charge upon the markets of 120 *l.*, and that 120 *l.* was divided. The Roman Catholics put in a claim under the scheme, and the Salters' Company gave them 54 *l.* and 66 *l.* was given to the school to supplement the Rainey endowment.

128. So that they pay 40 *l.* less than they did?—It is more than that, a great deal. It was reduced from 160 *l.* to 66 *l.* for the Rainey's School.

129. But they give 54 *l.* to the Catholics, I understand?—Yes, but not to the Rainey's School.

130. But the amount that they give is 40 *l.* less than it was?—It is 66 *l.* now, but it was 160 *l.* before the sale, so that the school is the loser.

131. But they still give 120 *l.*?—They give 120 *l.* to all denominations.

132. And before that they gave 160 *l.*, you say?—To the Rainey's School.

133. The Rainey's School got what other denominations now get, and the Rainey's School are jealous of the Catholics I suppose?—Rainey's School got more than is now given to all the denominations. The governors of Rainey's School do not object to the Roman Catholics getting the endowment at all.

134. But they would sooner have the 54 *l.* than let it go to the Roman Catholics?—They think that the Rainey's School ought to be maintained in its efficiency, and they object, especially when the company put the pension of their own masters on the endowment.

135. But the complaint really of the Rainey's School is, that instead of the company giving 160 *l.*, they now give 120 *l.*, and that out of that 120 *l.* the Rainey's School only gets 66 *l.*, and the Catholics get 54 *l.*?—No, they do not complain that the Catholics get 54 *l.*

136. They would not mind, I suppose, if they got the same amount?——

Colonel Lewis.

137. You said, I think, at first, that out of 604 *l.* given to the Presbyterian Church in your district 271 *l.* per annum was withdrawn?—Yes.

138. Did you include in the 271 *l.* those subscriptions which had been replaced by capital sums?—There were no capital sums handed over, with the exception of the three years as a compensation to the ministers on the Fishmongers' estate. The General Assembly applied

Colonel *Lawrie*—continued.

to the companies at the time of disestablishment for an endowment to the Sustentation Fund. I have the correspondence here.

139. But in reading out your list just now you stated that in some cases 10 *l.* had been withdrawn, but that a sum of 100 *l.* had been given; did you include in the 371 *l.* those annual grants of 10 *l.* that had been replaced by capital sums?—No; that 371 *l.* is just the sum of all the annual grants that were withdrawn.

140. As against that, a certain sum of money has been handed to your endowment funds, and you have not brought that into the account in any way?—I wish to explain that what has been handed over is an endowment to the Presbyterian Church.

141. You told us in evidence here that certain sums had been withdrawn, and that a capital sum of, say, 100 *l.* or 200 *l.* had been given by the companies when they sold their property; have you included in the 371 *l.* those subscriptions that have been replaced by a capital sum?—Certainly.

142. Then you have not given credit in any way for the capital sums that were given in lieu of the annual grants when the company sold their estates?—But the capital sums were only 30 *l.* each to the ministers on their estate.

143. You told us that there were sums of 100 *l.* to 200 *l.*, given when the subscriptions were withdrawn?—That was on the Clothworkers' estate. On the Clothworkers' estate there was 200 *l.* given to one minister, and 100 *l.* given to another minister, in compensation for the withdrawal of annual grants of 20 *l.* and 10 *l.*

144. But you have not brought those into the account?—No.

145. And therefore that 371 *l.* that has been withdrawn includes those sums for which a certain amount of compensation has been given?—Yes, certainly.

146. You said just now, in speaking of the companies' estates and the public feeling, the people in the neighbourhood dislike the money going to London?—Yes.

147. Do they take into account the historical fact that the whole of the money expended in planting and cultivating Ulster in the first place came from London?—Yes; and they take into account the fact that half-a-million was taken for timber by the London Companies.

148. Was not that timber absolutely planted with money which came from London?—No; the timber was there before they came.

149. You cannot tell that, I am afraid, from personal knowledge. However, the money that was spent in planting Ulster came from London?—Yes.

150. You said just now, did you not, that the industries were discouraged by the City Companies?—Yes.

151. Do you say that they deliberately discourage industries?—Perhaps that is too strong an expression; I should have said that no encouragement is given to industries.

152. That is different altogether, but we are reasonable people here, and you can hardly imagine that people administering a large estate would discourage what would very much add to the value of their property?—The effect was discouragement.

153. That may be so, but you are not prepared to say that they deliberately discouraged industries?—I would not say that they deliberately discouraged industries.

154. There is one other point. You have just mentioned what you describe as a case of illiberality; that some roads made on the Drapers' Company's estate had been thrown, perhaps rather unfairly, upon the county rates?—Yes.

155. Is it usual in your county for the highways to be maintained by a county rate, or by the landlords?—Generally by a county rate.

156. Therefore there was nothing very unusual, was there, in roads which had been made by the Drapers' Company being handed over to the county, for them to keep in repair?—But Mr. Stannus, the agent, asserts that he had handed over those roads to be made by the county, which would have been made otherwise by the Drapers' Company, thereby saving them the expense of making them. It is not our assertion, it is the assertion of Mr. Stannus, the agent of the company.

157. But I understood that the roads had been made, and had been handed over to the county to maintain?—Yes.

158. Is it customary, when roads have been made, in a county, that they should, when completed, be handed over to the jurisdiction of the county?—Yes.

159. Therefore there is nothing very unusual in roads on the property of the Drapers' Company being handed over to the county authority to maintain in repair?—That is generally done.

Mr. *Sexton.*

160. About the Rainey School: the Catholics and Presbyterians together only receive about two-thirds of what the Presbyterians alone received formerly?—No; the Presbyterians and the Episcopalians came in under a scheme for the Rainey School; they received 60 *l.*, and the Roman Catholics received 64 *l.* to themselves.

161. What did they receive before?—They had nothing to do with the school formerly; the money was left for a Presbyterian school.

162. The complaint is that the total amount has been unduly reduced?—Yes.

163. Have you any letter from the company which you would like to put in?—Here is the correspondence which took place upon the sale of the Clothworkers' estates. I think what is material I can describe in a few words. The Clothworkers' Company sold to Sir Hervey Bruce, in spite of the protests of the tenants, in 1872; the tenants sent a deputation to London to get the estates sold to them under the clauses of the Land Act, and the company refused to do so. The tenants offered 165,000 *l.*, and this is the correspondence on the subject.

164. I think we had better have it put in. I understand you to say that the Presbyterian Communion, by comparison with the Episcopalian Church, in Ulster had not been fairly treated?—They complain of it.

165. Have

Mr. *Sexton*—continued.

165. Have they always felt it?—They have never asserted it in public, but they have always felt it.

166. Could you by any table give the Committee a precise idea of the unfair treatment that you consider the Presbyterian Communion have suffered in comparison with the Episcopalian Church?—I can.

167. Will you do so?—I will.

168. Would you say that there was a policy in recent years of a withdrawal or reduction of grants and charities by the companies?—Certainly; especially to Presbyterians.

169. Within what period?—The last five or six years.

170. In consequence of the projected sales?—There have been a great many withdrawals in consequence of sales. The Grocers' Company have withdrawn all theirs without compensation.

171. Was there any other reason, or was that the sole reason for this new policy?—Yes, the grants were withdrawn when the sales were made. They were withdrawn on the Grocers' and Clothworkers' estates; three years' compensation was given upon the Fishmongers' estate when they were withdrawn, and a notice has been given to the minister of Lower Cumber that his grant will be withdrawn in consequence of the company selling out their estate.

172. You consider, taking the companies you have named, that there are clear signs of a policy to evade what in the public opinion, and by their own action, has been hitherto their obligation?—Certainly.

173. What did the Salters' Company get 240,000 *l.* for, for their whole estate?—For their whole estate.

174. Was that the same estate in respect of which they had paid 3,000 *l.*, at the beginning, to the Corporation Society?—Yes, 3,333 *l.*

175. The estate for which they obtained 240,000 *l.* was the estate in connection with which they had paid 3,000 *l.* Colonel Lawrie says 3,000 *l.*?—No, I do not admit that they paid 3,000 *l.* for the estate.

176. As I understand, the general course has been this: They have not taken the mere value of the property, but the companies have appropriated the value of the improvements by imposing rack-rents?—Yes.

177. And they have either sold the estate upon the basis of the rack-rent, or propose so to sell?—Yes.

178. You used the word "discouragement" in relation to manufacturing enterprise?—Yes.

179. What was the length of lease that the companies were willing to grant for any purpose. I understand that the refusal of a lease for a certain period operated as a discouragement?—Yes, they would have given 61 years' leases, but they would not give a perpetual lease such as manufacturers would need.

180. Was it represented to the companies in these cases, and in other such cases, that a longer lease was necessary in order to enter into manufacturing enterprise?—Certainly, that was the reason why the negotiations were broken off; the company would not give a longer lease.

181. You think you may describe that as a discouragement?—Yes, the result was discouragement, as you say.

182. Are you aware that the original charter of James the First was intended to promote not only religion and education, but the general prosperity of Ulster?—Yes.

183. By reason of that you give it in evidence that there has been discouragement of manufactures?—Yes.

Mr. *Lawson*.

184. Your people have always, whether rightly or wrongly I understand, considered that the companies possess their land under different conditions to those under which individual landlords own land?—Yes.

185. You said in your evidence that in some way you thought they had behaved worse than the average landlord?—Yes.

186. Did you refer solely to cases of leasing land for industrial buildings, or did you speak generally?—I can give a distinct case in which the company refused to do what a private landlord would do. The case of the Claudy river, which divides the Vintners' estate from the Mercers' estate. There are two townlands belonging to the Vintners' Company upon one side of the river, one townland was sold to Mr. Beresford, and the other was sold to Mr. Alexander. The country is very level, and this river floods the whole of it. The Mercers' Company were applied to for a grant to straighten the river, and Mr. Alexander and Mr. Beresford were also applied to for grants; Mr. Alexander and Mr. Beresford gave sums of money; Mr. Alexander gave 50 *l.*, and Mr. Beresford gave 25 *l.*; and the tenants gave 40 *l.*; but the Mercers' Company refused to give anything.

187. The Mercers' Company's was the largest interest?—Yes, they occupy all the other side of the river, and they had a great many tenants whose property was destroyed by the floods, but in consequence of the Mercers' Company refusing, the river was not properly straightened; parts were straightened and parts were not straightened: the parts that were not straightened are now blocking up the parts that were straightened so as to render the work that was done useless; I produce a map of the Claudy river.

188. Dealing with the question of leasing for industrial purposes, is it the custom in your part of the country to grant perpetual or very long leases of 999 years?—Yes; the general rule in Ireland is perpetuity leases for linen manufacturers.

189. You are speaking of the north?—Yes, in the north.

190. Chief-rents, or dues, or whatever you call them?—The usual rents for manufacturing purposes.

191. Did the City Company take an exceptional course in refusing to give these perpetuity leases?—Yes, there was no reason why they should not have given them, and it would have been for the benefit of the country.

192. They tried to introduce the London system of short leases?—They gave no leases at all, but every 31 years they raised the rent; that was their rule.

193. And they give no agreement for lease?—No agreement.

194. These

Mr. Lawson—continued.

194. These manufactories were held from year to year?—I am speaking of ordinary leases, there were no manufactories on the estate.

195. And by refusing to give leases, they prevented the establishment of manufactories?—Yes.

Mr. Sexton.

196. In those two cases where industry was diverted from the Salters' Company's estate to Belfast, in one case, and to Omagh in another, did the company offer leases?—Their offer was not satisfactory, and the negotiations were broken off.

197. Their practice was to give no lease?—They would have given a short lease.

198. Their practice was to give no lease?—Their practice was to give no lease, but for this purpose they offered a lease, but not a sufficient lease.

Mr. Lawson.

199. Was the Clothworkers' case not before the Land Act?—About that time.

200. The Ulster custom would have obtained in the case of agricultural land, but it never extended to towns or manufacturing premises?—No.

201. Therefore they took advantage of this break in the custom to prevent the establishment of manufactories by refusing to grant leases; whereas in the case of agricultural land there would have been a security for improvement, there was none in the case of manufacturing premises?—We have no leases for agricultural improvements.

202. No; but you could not, under the Ulster custom, get any compensation or any security for expenditure upon machinery fixtures, or anything of that sort, in a building used as a manufactory?—No.

Mr. Sexton.

203. Is the Ulster custom purely agrarian?—Yes.

Mr. Lawson.

204. In negotiations of this kind, with whom have you had to deal?—We first applied to the agent, and then sent a memorial to the company through the agent.

205. Has the company sent a committee of inspection in the same way as the Irish Society has?—Very often a deputation is sent down.

206. Do those deputations consist of the master and some of the other members?—I have never seen the deputations from the companies.

207. Do they go round to the land?—The Drapers' Company's deputation comes to Moneymore and visits Draperstown.

208. And they hear complaints?—Yes, they do.

209. Is it a ceremonial or business visit that they pay; do they go into the different cases?—They receive complaints, but they take the complaints away. They do not discuss them then and there.

210. Is there a good deal of festivity while they are there?—They have a dinner.

211. For themselves or the tenants?—For themselves.

Mr. Lawson—continued.

212. Has there been an attempt in those cases of hardship which you have mentioned to appeal from the agent to the company?—We always considered it better to have the agent with us in those cases.

213. But when you had him not with you, did you try to go behind him?—In the case of grants we have gone direct to the company when we knew the agent was against us.

214. Has the company generally taken the agent's view or yours?—Sometimes the agent has been set aside. There was one case in which Dr. Pettigrew applied for a grant from the Fishmongers' Company. The agent had arranged that he should get 50 *l.*; but he went to London and saw the company, and in the result he got 100 *l.*

215. You sometimes find that the company are more tender-hearted than the agent?—Yes.

216. In the cases that you mentioned, where subscriptions have come to an end, has there been a direct appeal to the company?—Yes, I believe so.

217. As well as to the agent?—I could not say rightly. This memorial of Mr. Johnson's is directed to "The Worshipful Company of Skinners, London."

218. It has gone straight to the company?—Yes.

Mr. Elton.

219. These companies, from your evidence, appear to have acted very much like private landlords?—Yes.

220. As far back as people can remember?—Yes; as far back as their leases were.

221. A very long time back?—In the case of the Salters' estate, it would be about the year 1854.

222. A little earlier?—The case of the Drapers' Company was about 1817.

223. Whenever they have been in possession of an estate they have acted as private landlords?—Yes.

224. And not as public trustees, apparently?—They have acted as public trustees in giving these grants; but as private landlords in relation to their tenants.

225. I understand they were rather shabbier than private landowners; not more liberal than private landowners?—Yes; to the tenants.

226. And the tenants occasionally made protest?—Yes. Upon the Mercers' estate there was a protest against the rise of rents. The rents were raised to 14,000 *l.*, and they protested against the rents being raised by public meetings, and decrees were issued against some of the tenants; and the tenants were beaten, and Lord Selborne had to interfere in the matter.

227. Still the companies went on acting as if they were the owners of the estates?—In regard to their tenants they did, but not in regard to the grants.

228. I quite understand your exception. You think that some of the companies went on so far as to discourage trade and industry by refusing leases to those who wanted to take them in perpetuity?—In other parts of Ireland persons would have been willing to give a rent for leases for the establishment of these manufactories.

229. If

Mr. Ellis—continued.

229. If they had been trustees they could not have appropriated the property?—I do not call it appropriation to give a long lease or to let on a reasonable rent.

230. A perpetuity lease. I speak of the old 60 years' lease?—They could give 999 years.

231. Do they ever give that in your part of the country?—Yes, there are leases for 999 years.

232. They are very rare, are they not?—They are not rare for a manufactory.

233. You mean they are rare, and so are manufactories rare?—Yes, except in Belfast.

234. It would be rather unusual, would it not, for a company to give a 999 years' lease; it is not the customary form?—They ought to have granted leases and so encouraged manufacturers, seeing that they were from London.

235. But the company were willing to give a 60 years' lease instead of a perpetual lease?—Yes.

236. Have you any other instance of their discouraging trade and manufacture?—There is a case quoted in this pamphlet.

237. Do you know anything of it yourself?—No.

238. What is the name of the pamphlet?—It is on the Clothworkers' Estate.

239. If you do not know anything about it I will not trouble you?—I have no personal knowledge of it.

Sir Richard Temple.

240. You said that one of the companies sold for 240,000 *l.* a property which they bought for 3,000 *l.*?—I did not say they bought it for 3,000 *l.*

241. I understood you to give an answer in the affirmative to the question of one of the honourable Members opposite?—We would not concede that this was purchase-money for the estate.

242. Would it, or would it not, be correct, in your opinion, to say that the company sold for 240,000 *l.* that which they bought for 3,000 *l.*?—It would not be correct, because I hold that they did not buy it at all.

243. What is the date of this 3,000 *l.* transaction?—About 1617 or 1618.

244. When you said that the company gave certain grants in their capacity as public trustees, were not those grants given in their capacity as private owners?—No, we always regarded them as trustees giving those grants; private landowners never give such grants in Ireland as they give, at least, to our Church.

245. Then in what way did those grants given by the company differ from ordinary grants given by landowners?—The ordinary landowners of the company give grants to the Episcopalian Church, but they never give grants to the Presbyterian or Roman Catholic Churches. We thought it was evidence of their being trustees that they gave grants to the Presbyterian and Roman Catholic Churches.

246. In that case, is there great liberality on the part of these companies as compared with ordinary owners?—Yes, so far as the grant is an evidence of liberality; but perhaps it would be hardly fair to describe the administration of a trust estate as liberality.

247. Do you mean to say if a landowner chooses to give a grant, that if the landowner has tenants belonging to several religious persuasions, and he gives a grant to each of the persuasions, he ceases to act as a landowner, and becomes a public trustee?—We take it in connection with the charters and history of the London companies, and hold that the one is evidence of the other; we hold the grants as evidence of what we believe the history of the companies and the charters is.

248. When the companies sell their estates, why do not the purchasers continue the charity; by "the charity," I mean, including the grant for educational purposes?—The tenants under the companies would have been unable to exist under the higher rents, and even with purchase they will have a hard struggle to exist as it is.

249. I ask, when the companies sell their estates, why do not the purchasers continue the grants and charities for educational purposes?—The purchasers are very small holders of about 10 or 15 acres, or 20 acres; and, of course, they could not continue the grants which the rich London companies were giving.

250. Do I infer from you that the maintenance of the schools and charities depends upon the existence of rich landlords?—The rich landlords can and do give grants; but the London societies, being trustees, were bound to provide for the education of the country.

251. But without the companies as landlords, these charities cannot be maintained?—I would not altogether say that; very independent people will do it, but we object to the societies taking away all these moneys which should be spent upon the maintenance of charities and grants.

252. Then, as a matter of fact, these charities and schools can be maintained by the independent action of the people?—Not so well as if they got the grants from the London companies.

253. But they can be maintained?—There are a great many schools that could be established, if the London companies gave us some of the money accruing from the purchase of their estates. I think they should establish intermediate schools over the whole of the country; there is great need for them; the people are badly educated.

254. They have no education rate?—They have no education rate.

255. Then in that respect are they more favourably situated than the people in Great Britain?—Certainly not; education suffers from want of educational endowments, teachers are not so well paid in Ireland as they are in England.

256. But I speak of the people?—And the people consequently suffer.

257. The people have no rate to pay?—They have to pay school fees.

258. But no education rate?—We have not free education in Ireland.

259. I understand

Mr. *John Ellis.*

259. I understand that you come before us here in a representative capacity?—I do not officially represent any body, but I represent fairly the ministers and the tenant farmers of County Derry.

260. What justifies you in saying that; had you any meeting or was any resolution passed, or has it been talked of amongst your neighbours?—If it were necessary to have meetings we could have meetings, but as yet we have had no public meetings, but I have had private meetings with prominent ministers and laymen. I had one in Moneymore, one in Magherafelt, one in Kilrea, and one in Garvagh, and I have had letters from almost all the ministers whose congregations are affected by the estate.

261. You have taken great pains to satisfy yourself of the general feeling: you do not come here merely as an individual?—That is so.

262. You can speak the mind of a large number of people in the north of Ireland?—Yes, I can quote from letters.

263. Have you lived long there?—I have been there more than 10 years, nearly 11 years.

264. Are you a native of the district?—No, but I am a native of an adjoining district; I am a native of County Donegal.

265. Can you give the Committee any idea of the number of people or the population, and the area for which you wish to speak without going much into detail?—I know South Derry and the constituency of South Derry very well, the whole of it.

266. Can you give the Committee the population?—I am not sure of the population, but there are about 11,000 Parliamentary voters in it.

267. You come here to represent six figures of people; may I take that from you?—Yes.

268. You think you would speak the sentiments of from 100,000 to 200,000 people?—I cannot give the figures.

269. You tell us distinctly, as I understand you, that there is a popular opinion that these London companies hold their property upon trust?—Yes.

270. That in short their title has grown to some extent from the performance of certain obligations?—Yes.

271. Can you tell the Committee whether that popular opinion, whatever it is worth, has been handed down by tradition, or whether it has arisen within your lifetime?—There is a tradition, but the people were ignorant of it until recently, and it is only since these grants were withdrawn that an inquiry has been made into the state of affairs, and the people are exceedingly interested in the question, and ministers and prominent laymen have read up all that is to be read up upon the subject.

272. The recent action of the companies has led to a much more wide-spread interest and inquiry into the subject?—Yes.

273. I speak of these grants; you do not consider these subscriptions at all in the light of subscriptions by private individuals?—No.

274. You regard them as, so to speak, a charge upon the landowners, part of the obligation to be performed to secure their title?—We look upon it as part of the administration of the trust.

Mr. *John Ellis*—continued.

275. They have been diminishing the grants?—Yes.

276. And you think that great inconvenience and difficulty will arise to education if they are discontinued entirely?—Yes.

277. Has there been any other grants other than those for education purposes given by the companies?—For religious purposes.

278. Not merely educational but religious?—Yes; our ministers get the annual grant that I have mentioned; but we never got anything for our sustentation fund, with the exception of 250 *l.* from the Ironmongers' Company; that was at the time of the disendowment; all the companies were approached, but none of them gave anything but the Ironmongers' Company; they gave us 250 *l.* for the sustentation fund, and the interest of it was to be divided amongst eight congregations.

279. Have there been any other purposes served than religion and education for which financial grants have been made?—Not that I am aware of.

Mr. *Sexton.*

280. Has there not been something given for highways?—Yes, and they have made drains for tenants.

Mr. *John Ellis.*

281. That would be in order to continue or maintain the value of the land?—Yes.

282. Have there been any grants to public objects, such as buildings and laying out of market places or building court houses?—Yes, they built court houses, I know, in Draperstown, Kilrea and Magherafelt, but they charged pretty good rents for them.

283. How do you know; do you know one case where they were built within your own time?—They are of long standing.

284. They were built years ago?—Yes.

285. You cannot say that you saw them built?—No; they have also spent large sums in building churches, they have built some Presbyterian churches and some Episcopalian churches; the Presbyterian Church of Draperstown and the Presbyterian Church of Moneymore were both built by the companies, and they built one manse that I heard of.

286. I understand you to say that when the particular purchaser by name, Sir Hervey Bruce, bought his property of one of these companies, he was bound to continue his subscription?—It was understood for 10 years.

287. Do you know whether it was a part of the arrangement, that it was expressed in written terms?—It was given in evidence at the last meeting of the Committee, and it is reported through the country, and as a matter of fact the grants were discontinued at the end of 10 years.

288. Do you know any other case of the kind in which the purchaser has been bound to continue subscriptions or grants?—Not any that I remember.

289. Now with regard to the town of Magherafelt, what is the population of that place?—The population so far as I can remember now is about 1,200 or 1,300.

290. Do

Mr. John Ellis—continued.

290. Do you know what the rental of that place was at different periods?—It gives it in these answers of Lord Naas, who was Chief Secretary for Ireland.

291. I want it from you; have you got the figures?—It was 307 *l.* in 1835, it was then increased to 717 *l.* in 1865, and it was then increased by 314 *l.*, that is 835 *l.*, and then it was increased to about 1,250 *l.*

292. What date was the last increase?—In 1867, two years afterwards.

293. Was that property, the rental of which you have just quoted, bought by the tenants?—The property was built by the tenants.

294. Was it bought by the tenants?—The tenants were settled there under the plantation.

295. That is not my point; was ever any purchase and sale effected as between the tenants and the owner?—Not that I am aware of.

Mr. Lea.

296. As I understand you, the tenants bought it from the Salters' Company as part of the 540,000 *l.*?—Yes, it was so. I am speaking of the Salters' estate of Magherafelt.

Mr. John Ellis.

297. I refer to the town of Magherafelt, where there 1,200 or 1,500 people live; did they buy it?—Yes, they bought it.

298. Upon what rental did they buy it?—They bought it at about 20 years' purchase of the rent.

299. Which rent had been derived from the property which they created themselves?—Yes. As to the withdrawal of these grants from one or two particular congregations in which the Presbyterian Church has been unfairly treated as compared with the Episcopalians, may I give in a statement to that effect.

Chairman.] Yes, certainly.

Mr. Lea.

300. Upon that I understand that there have been complaints not that the Episcopalian Church received too much, but that the Presbyterian Church received too little?—We make no complaint against the Episcopalian Church, we think they have got a fair share, but not too much, and we should like to get in proportion to them if this is declared to be a trust.

The Rev. Hamilton Brown Wilson, D.D., sworn; and Examined.

Mr. Lea.

301. Where do you live?—At Cookstown, County Tyrone.

302. How long have you been there?—Forty-four years.

303. How far is it from the estate of the company?—Some half a mile from the boundary of the Drapers' estate.

304. Have you been in receipt yourself of any grant?—Yes, I received 10 guineas a year, and my predecessor received it, and his predecessor received it.

305. And you have been there 44 years?—Yes.

306. And you have had all that time 10 guineas a year?—Not all that time; a year or two at the first I did not have it; but I had it up to 1858; the last payment was in May 1858.

307. It was withdrawn in 1858; why was it withdrawn?—No reason was given for the withdrawal. I have not much cause to complain of them in one way, because I have but few families connected with my congregation on my estate, but they withdrew it also from a minister living beside me who has few families also.

308. What was the reason given?—We had no reason given at all, further than that when it did not come we inquired, and the agent told us that it had not been voted to us; it was given by an annual vote.

309. Do you believe it was withdrawn because they intended selling the estate, or were selling the estate?—I believe it was withdrawn with the intention of cutting off all vested rights when the estate would be sold.

310. Most of the companies have been selling their estates, have they not?—The whole of the companies have sold their estates now except the Mercers' Company. Of course, I do not refer to the Irish Society.

311. What effect will the departure of the companies have?—So far as the tenants go, I think the selling of the farms to them is an advantage, undoubtedly to their advantage; but it will be very injurious to the benevolent objects and to the charities and education generally. There is one point that I would add to Mr. Dickey's evidence; that is to say, the Drapers' Company, for example, gave liberally to dispensaries; we have a dispensary at Moneymore, and they gave the doctor 100 *l.* a year, a free house, and 30 *l.* for a horse, and supplies of medicine to be sent to the poorer classes of the tenantry, and they did the same at Draperstown; both of those have stopped.

Mr. Sexton.

312. When were those stopped?—The Moneymore grant was stopped 15 years ago on the retirement of Dr. Maxwell. The Draperstown was stopped a few years after that upon the removal of Dr. Morewood; the house was continued free to his son, and upon the death of the son Dr. Heggarty was appointed, and he gets nothing whatever.

313. The retirement or death of a particular medical practitioner was made a pretext for the withdrawal of the grant?—It was.

Mr. Lea.

314. What action have the general assembly of your church taken?—In the year 1871, when we found it necessary to try and get a sum given to us, we sent a deputation, but in the year 1887, when the companies were about to sell, our general

Mr. Lea—continued.

general assembly appointed a deputation to wait upon the companies, and ask that we should get certain rights, as we thought.

315. Were you one of that deputation?—I was the moderator of the assembly as well as of the deputation.

316. Were you received?—No.

317. They refused to see you?—In the first instance, we happened to be over here at the Jubilee; we saw a clerk of the company, and were courteously received; but we put in a formal application, and got a formal letter of refusal to receive us as a deputation.

318. They would not hear what you had to say?—No.

319. Was that the time when the Lord Primate and the Duke of Abercorn were refused also?—Yes; it was one of the reasons assigned to us that they could not consistently receive us, having refused the others.

320. What else did they say?—They said that they had made arrangements with the companies associated with them, and that they could not depart from the rule that they had adopted. It was the Skinners' Company.

321. Would anything that you would have said have altered it?—I think it would if we had had an opportunity considering that we had to do with very capable men, and men that were fair-minded, I think we had a very strong case: taking the Protestant element of our tenantry, we held that the Presbyterians paid three-fourths of the rent, and had always done so, and have never got a proportionate share of the grants; we asked to put forward that statement, but we were not allowed to do so.

322. Have you any documents which you wish to put in?—No, I have not.

Chairman.

323. What is the proportion of Presbyterians and Episcopalians compared with Catholics among the tenants?—I think in some districts the Roman Catholics are the most numerous, but towards Derry the Presbyterians are the most numerous; there the Presbyterians are the largest farmers and pay the most rent.

Mr. Lea.

324. What class of farmers have you living in County Derry?—In some districts, as between Limavaddy and Derry, they are a large class of farmers about Maghera, and about Kilrea they are very small farmers, the people there holding small patches of land of the Mercers' estate, and at small rents.

325. What is the average of their holdings?—Most of them are as small as 6 to 10 acres, some 20 acres, and some 30 acres. I should not like to average it at above 20 acres.

326. Would they find it easy to keep up the charities and schools?—Of course they would find it very difficult, especially with schools. It would be a great drawback to the education of that class. We are very much in want all over Ulster of better arrangement for intermediate education.

Chairman.

327. Have the Catholics kept up their charities and schools?—Yes, they have, they are building fine churches and erecting splendid buildings, but they are making as much money as they like, and we cannot.

Mr. Sexton.

328. How is that?—There is a leverage that we do not possess. If we had power, there is no doubt that where there is a will there is a way.

329. In the part of the county where you are, with regard to the population, have you not got the leverage there?—In the town I live in the wealth of the place is very much Presbyterian.

330. And you have the leverage?—That is not the leverage I refer to. I cannot compel my people to give.

Mr. Lea.

331. You mentioned just now you had expectations of success with the companies, why?—The ground that we intended to argue was that as our people gave a great portion of the rents we were entitled to a larger sum than we were getting. For example, we understood they gave liberal grants to the Episcopalians towards their sustentation fund, and we thought they should not leave the country and take their money with them without giving us something to make our grants perpetual.

332. In what light did you look upon the companies in the past?—We have always looked upon the companies in the light of being trustees; if they are ordinary proprietors I hold they have dealt very liberally with us, but if they are trustees I think they should give us more than they do; and whether there is any legal basis for the opinion or not, the opinion has always existed that they were trustees, and so far as I can read the ordinary English language, I arrive at the same conclusion myself.

333. Did you give evidence before Lord Derby's Commission?—I did not; but I have read a good deal of what is there said about the lawsuit between the Skinners' Company and the Irish Society, in which the Master of the Rolls and Lord Lyndhurst have very freely expressed their convictions.

334. We will not ask you upon that; we shall have the judgments before us. All I want to ask you about is that the opinion generally held by the ministers of your church?—No doubt of it; all over our church we are very much interested with the decision in the case of the Skinners' Company, and that has very much decided our opinion.

335. You gave evidence before the Endowment Commission with regard to Rainey's scheme?—Yes.

336. Do you consider the Rainey schools greatly crippled by the action of the Salters' Company?—I do not know that they are. We, as the assembly, have been always much dissatisfied with the action of the Salters' Company with regard to that, because it has deprived us as Presbyterians of the control of the Rainey endowment.

337. Lord Fitz-Gibbon will give evidence about the Rainey scheme?—Lord Fitz-Gibbon and I do not agree. My representation is that

if

Mr. *Lea*—continued.

if the Salters' Company had not touched this, Lord Fitz-Gibbon must admit that it was purely a Presbyterian endowment, and that they must have continued it as such; but, inasmuch as the Salters' Company added their endowment to it, we cannot get it ourselves.

338. They appointed their own master?—They appointed a master, and by the words of the will it was left for purely Presbyterian purposes, they appointed the Lord Primate as the channel for conveying the funds, and as the treasurer; we hold that that is not the correct thing to appoint a Protestant Archbishop to have control over a Presbyterian endowment.

339. You hold that certain of the tenantry have created this large property of the London companies?—Yes, that applies to all the tenants in Ulster.

340. Farms and town holdings?—Farmers as a rule have created many improvements upon their farms.

341. But that applies to the town tenants equally?—No; I think the case of Magherafelt is exceptional. As a rule, we get good building leases in Ulster.

342. That is not owned by a London company?—It is not; but in the town where I live the regular lease is 999 years. Take a town of the size that Belfast has grown to be. Belfast has grown to be what it is simply owing to the action of the Marquess of Donegall. Every man who builds gets a lease in perpetuity. In Derry that could not be had until within the last 25 years, and the Irish Society are now freely giving perpetuity leases; and not only that, but they are allowing people to buy up the head rent, so that it becomes a fee.

343. In the town of Magherafelt they give 61 year leases, do they not?—Yes.

344. And that cripples building?—It stopped building. With regard to all the companies, they were good landlords as regards their agricultural tenants; but they mistook the wish of the people in giving short leases for building purposes. Now, on the other hand, we have a fund in our church called the Church and Manse Fund, the object of which is to aid weak congregations in building their manses and their churches. But we have one rule, that we never give a grant to any congregation unless it has a perpetuity lease. The result is, that, as a rule, over the estates of these companies there were no manses till lately. It is still true that on the Mercers' estate there is not a single manse, because we will not give a grant unless there is a perpetuity lease. I remember we had a contest at Limavady. We were willing to give a grant of 100 *l.* if the company would give a lease. They would not give a lease, and they gave the grant themselves rather than do so. In Moneymore they were left 1,300 *l.* to build a manse, and could not get a site for it, because the lease must be in perpetuity.

345. The bridge which the tenants have built for the improvement of the town of Magherafelt was built by the inhabitants, and not by the Salters' Company?—Yes.

346. The London companies are popularly held to be trustees of these large properties, and you maintain that the money should be kept in the country where it was created?—I maintain that all the produce of the land of county Derry held under charter ought to be impounded, and expended upon the plantation.

Sir Richard Temple.

347. I understand you to say that you think your people have certain rights as against the companies?—Yes.

348. Do you consider those rights to be legal or moral?—I would think it very extraordinary if they are not legal, but I am certain they are moral.

349. You believe they are legal?—Yes, I do.

350. May I ask why has the Presbyterian Church never tried their legal rights; if they believe the rights to be legal, why has the Church not tried them by law?—The Presbyterians have no more rights than the Episcopalians or any other denomination, but we have only had our attention called to the point when the companies began to sell their estates and take the money with them. We hold that London is not the place in which to expend the produce of Ulster.

351. If you have a legal right, why do not you try it at law?—We never have thought of trying it, and I am sure we will not, because we would not have the means of going to law with the London companies. Rather to be poor and be defrauded than make ourselves bankrupt in an attempt of that sort.

352. Then you have refrained from taking legal action from dread of the expense?—As a matter of fact, the point has never been before us.

353. It was not from any doubt as to the legal validity of the case?—I am not a lawyer, but I have read, for example, that King James gave the charter on certain conditions; those conditions I hold gave no personal right to members of the company. I think it is a wise man and a wise church who keeps out of law as much as possible.

354. Have you refrained from taking action by law proceedings from any doubt as to the legal validity of the case?—I look upon the decision in the Skinners' Company's case as virtually deciding it, and I believe it would be so held if we were to go to law.

Mr. *Sexton.*

355. I should like to get your view clearly. I understand from you that you think the capital value of these estates ought to be devoted to public use?—Yes; Lord Lyndhurst's decision was that it was held in trust for public purposes.

356. You think the companies should not be allowed to take the capital value of their estates out of the country?—The trust rested upon the land, and now rests upon what the land produces, and descends through centuries upon it; it is not a terminable trust at all.

357. Without endeavouring to enter into any legal discussion, you think the equity of the case is that this money ought to be applied in Ireland?—Yes, to take it away from us would be oppress-

ing

Mr. *Sexton*—continued.

ing the best interests of Ireland, and constituting an Irish grievance in reality.

358. Are the schools you speak of what we know as national schools?—Till lately the schools I know the history of were not national, but now they are national, that is to say, we have in Moneymore an intermediate school which is not national, but we have also male and female national schools in connection with the Drapers' Company.

359. When you speak of the reduction or withdrawal of grants from primary schools you mean national schools?—I do.

360. Does not the reduction or withdrawal of a grant, in the case of a national school, inflict upon you a damage beyond the amount of the grant withdrawn or reduced?—Of course, as regards those contributory schools, to that extent it would.

361. By so much as you reduce the local aid, you reduce your claim to the final third?—Yes.

362. Do the Roman Catholics receive any benefit from this system of the London companies?—I think they have received less than the Protestant denominations. They do receive a portion. The priest at Moneymore is getting 30 *l.* a year.

363. I believe the benefit they receive is infinitesimally slight?—It is very much slighter.

364. Upon what principle do you go, when you say that the Presbyterian community has been damnified or injured by the relative distribution; do you refer to rent, or do you speak of population?—I do not so much blame the companies as I blame the fact that it is always an episcopal agent that is appointed, and where you have an episcopal agent you may say that you have episcopacy down to the bailiff. There is an atmosphere of episcopacy pervading the whole place, and we suffer in consequence of that.

365. What is your claim as a communion; do you say that you ought to get back a proportionate amount of the grants corresponding to the amount of rent that you pay, or that it ought to follow the relative population?—We should prefer that it should follow the amount of the rent, because then we should get much more; but we would be even content if it followed the population. I will take the Salters' estate. I have ascertained, by pretty careful inquiry, that on the Salters' estate the rental, speaking only of the Protestant rental, is three-fourths Presbyterian. The grants to Episcopalians are four times as much as to Presbyterians.

366. So that they get 12 times as much as they ought to get relatively?—Yes.

Chairman.

367. Do you mean three-fourths of the whole of the Protestant tenantry, or of the tenantry altogether?—On the Salters' estate three-fourths of the Protestant rents are Presbyterian rents, whilst the Episcopalians get four times as much help from the grants as we do. I will not say that it is the fault of the company, but it arises from the fact that the company always has an Episcopalian agent with us.

Mr. *Sexton.*

368. What arrangement would satisfy you?—I think we ought to get a larger proportion. We do not want to reduce the Episcopalian grants, but I think we ought to get more ourselves, and I think there ought to be an arrangement made that that should be permanent, and that it should not be dragged over to London.

369. Do you think that the Roman Catholics ought to have a finger in the pie at all?—I question very much whether, as regards giving to religion, that would be in harmony with the charter; but I think they ought to share in every respect otherwise.

370. Secularly?—Yes.

371. In education and in what is called general prosperity?—Yes. I think that they ought to give us waterworks and things of that sort, and to let one denomination drink as much as the other and as pure.

Colonel *Laurie.*

372. I think you said just now that you had some complaint: that the contributions to the Presbyterian denomination were smaller in proportion than to other religious bodies?—Yes.

373. I think you also said that, in your part of the county, the Presbyterians were the most prosperous part of the community?—They pay the most rent.

374. Do you not think that that might have influenced the companies to some extent in the amount that they contributed towards Presbyterian objects?—I do not believe that it did.

375. And that they might perhaps have contributed more to less prosperous denominations?—That involves more charity and regard to common-sense than I give credit for; I believe it is simply because their case was better presented to the company; I am sure of it.

376. You have lived all your life probably in Ireland?—I was born in the County of Derry, and I have lived for 44 years within half-a-mile of it.

377. I daresay you knew Ireland before there was a poor law at all?—I did.

378. Do you remember when the Poor Law Act was passed there?—Yes. It was passed in 1844, and I am 70 years of age now.

379. Do you not think that those payments by the Drapers' Company for doctors and medicines were probably given before the Poor Law Act was passed?—They were.

380. And that the necessity for them did not exist after that Act had been passed?—Yes. I admit that.

381. It would have been candid to have said so at first, because it looked very much at first as if you were complaining that the companies had been guilty of very great injustice?—I think there is fairness in that. It was given before that. I only mentioned it as an example of the withdrawal of grants.

382. But the necessity for the grants had ceased owing to legislation?—If the company had turned it into other channels where there was a necessity for it and not put it into their own purses it would have been a different matter.

383. That is not the question. Is it not the fact

Colonel Laurie—continued.

fact that it was in consequence of the poor law having been passed in Ireland that those contributions became unnecessary, and that that is why they ceased, and not from any want of liberality on the part of the companies?—It is the fact that it was in consequence, I am sure, of the passing of the poor law; but at the same time the doctor that is there complains. I had a conversation with him last week, and I know it to be a fact that he complains that the poorer class of the tenantry were trained to get medical treatment for nothing, a class above those that would get it from an ordinary dispensary, and that therefore they felt the want of it now.

384. But it was primarily in consequence of the poor law having been passed in Ireland that the grants were withdrawn?—No doubt.

The Rev. John Mark, sworn; and Examined.

Mr. Lea.

385. You have lived, have you not, on the Clothworkers' estate?—Yes.

386. For how many years?—Twenty-three years.

387. You know a good deal about the sale of the Clothworkers' estate to Sir Hervey Bruce?—I do know something about it.

388. Will you state what you know about it?—I think the sale of the estate was carried out in the year 1871. I was a member of a deputation at that time sent over to seek to purchase the estate on behalf of the tenants, our object being to approach the Clothworkers' Company and put the claims of the tenants before the Court, so as to obtain for them the liberty of purchasing. When we came to London we were denied access to the Court, and were given to understand that the Company of Clothworkers were not favourable to permitting the tenants to become the owners of their holdings, although I understood that they offered some 25,000 *l.* more for the estate than Sir Hervey Bruce actually paid.

389. Were the tenants afraid of an increase of rent?—They were afraid of an increase of rent, and an increase of rent took place. On Sir Hervey Bruce getting possession of it he raised the rent on an average 25 per cent.

Chairman.

390. The date of all this was 1871?—It was.

391. How would the tenants have got the money to purchase with?—Under Bright's clauses of the Land Act, the 1871 Act.

Mr. Lea.

392. The tenants were not allowed to purchase, I think you said?—They were not; Sir Hervey Bruce purchased the estate and raised the rents 25 per cent. on the average, and in some cases as high as 90 per cent., and perhaps over. Then there came in Mr. Gladstone's Acts, which reduced the rents somewhat, but the average rental of the estate is higher than it was at the time Sir Hervey Bruce purchased, notwithstanding the Land Courts and the Land Acts.

393. When was the rent reduced by the Land Court?—That was a process which extended over several years.

394. But about when would it be?—Mr. Gladstone's Act was passed in 1881. Then it went on for five or six years, and is going on still. The tenants did not all go into the Court at one time. Some went at first, and some tried to make terms and failed, and then went again.

395. But for 14 years they paid the increased rent?—Yes; they paid the increased rent from the time it was raised until the court reduced it.

396. Are you aware whether any arrangement was made with Sir Hervey Bruce about continuing the grants to ministers?—The congregation of my church were wont to receive from the Clothworkers' Company 20 *l.* per annum for their minister. This was applicable to my predecessor as well as to myself. For example, Mr. Lyle, my immediate predecessor, got this money for many years, not during the whole of his life, from the Clothworkers' Company. There was an occasion which I think it right to refer to. In the year 1836 or 1837 the estate had for a length of time been let to a middleman, named Mr. Alexander. The tenants held their farms by lease, at the same time, but unfortunately their leases fell before Mr. Alexander's lease fell. Then he had only a few years of the lease to run, and he increased the rents enormously; he quadrupled them in some instances. Then as soon as his lease fell, the Clothworkers' Company came into possession. On their coming into possession the bad times came, the years of famine, and a reduction was made upon the enormous increase that had been made by Mr. Alexander; but on the years of famine passing away the Company again demanded the old rent.

Chairman.

397. You mean that they demanded the rent as enhanced by Mr. Alexander?—Yes. The tenants held a meeting to petition the company against this rise of rent. Mr. Lyle, my predecessor, presided at that meeting, and for a number of years his 20 *l.* grant was taken away because he presided at that meeting.

398. What year was this?—It would be about the year 1858.

Mr. Lea.

399. But after that the 20 *l.* was again given to him?—Yes.

400. And it has been continued to you?—It has. There was a deputation appointed at that time to approach the Clothworkers' Company with this memorial of the tenants against this rise of rent. When they came over to London they were refused access to the court absolutely, and not only so, but on their return to Ireland the three members were all served by the agent with notices to quit for coming to London upon that

Mr. Lea—continued.

that errand. They got the alternative of leaving or of making an apology. One of the three apologised and was permitted to live on the estate. The other two did not see their way to apologise; they were privileged to sell, but they had to leave the estate. Of these two, one was the minister of Terrace row, Coleraine, and the other was a tenant, Mr. Kerr, father of the Reverend Matthew Kerr, of Cork.

401. Has the 20 *l.* a year been continued to you since then?—The 20 *l.* a year was continued for some 10 or 12 years. The understanding was, I believe, at the time of the sale, that Sir Hervey Bruce should continue to pay these endowments to religion, education, and charity, for a period of 10 years. I think he paid them for 10 or 12 years, but it has ceased now.

402. But you understand that the Clothworkers' Company sold on the condition that the grant should be continued for 10 years?—Yes.

403. And it was continued by Sir Hervey Bruce for that time?—Yes, for fully that time.

404. Had you a grant for schools as well?—We had.

405. How much?—Several of the school teachers received 5 *l.* twice a year from the grant. I think that a grant of 5 *l.* twice a year is paid perhaps to the majority of them even yet. I heard last week before leaving home, and I understand it to be a fact, that one of the teachers has been notified that this grant will be withdrawn.

406. Have any of them been withdrawn?—One has.

407. Have you a grant of 10 *l.* for schools?—There were several schools of which my predecessor was patron. By the action of the agent of the Clothworkers' Company on the death of my predecessor, the management of all these schools was taken from the Presbyterians and from the church of which I am minister, and was appropriated by the then agent of the company. He himself constituted himself manager and patron of these schools. You see, being the donors of a grant of this kind they thought they should have a larger hand in the management of the schools than they had had, I presume, and they appropriated the whole thing to themselves.

408. Your predecessor was the manager of those schools?—Of more than those; of about six schools.

409. Does the National Education Board require a manager to be appointed within a certain time?—Perhaps that is so; I am not sure.

410. Your church takes a certain time before appointing a successor?—Yes, because our ministers are called by popular election, and it takes a little time to do that.

411. In the meantime the agent of the Clothworkers' Company had himself appointed, being a donor to these schools?—Yes.

412. And therefore he took the management of the schools out of the hands of the Presbyterian church?—Yes.

413. Who built the school houses?—In the first instance they were largely erected by the Presbyterians, but it is right to say that afterwards the company, in conjunction with the Board of Works, rebuilt the most of them, indeed I think the whole of them.

414. When the Clothworkers' Company was a landlord how did it act?—We would think that they acted to the tenants in a way that was not encouraging, but the very opposite; and whilst thankful for certain gifts that they made to religion and charity and education, we think that these gifts were distributed in a way which was not at all in keeping with equity or justice.

415. You mean that ecclesiastically they did not treat your church equally with the others?—They did not, especially where the vast majority of the tenants, perhaps 80 or 90 per cent. of them, were Presbyterians.

416. And you have never obtained the management of these schools since then?—We have never obtained the management of the schools since then. I should think it right to say that on selling the estate they gave large endowments to the Episcopalian Church, whilst the endowments granted to us were very small indeed. £. 20 given to myself and 10 *l.* to a neighbouring clergyman have been withdrawn.

Chairman.

417. Is anything given to Catholics?—I think they have been helped always in erecting churches and things of this kind, and one of the schools has passed over into the management of the parish priest.

Mr. Lea.

418. Have you many children in that school?—We have 50 children on the rolls.

419. Do you look upon the London companies as landlords of an ordinary character?—We do not, and the idea is very prevalent that they are not landlords of an ordinary character, and that whilst they act in a very high-handed way with their tenantry as has been indicated, yet they acted in a way that was not in keeping with the terms of the Charter under which they are said to hold. By way of indicating how they acted in the way of improvements I may say that Judge Greer, who was a tenant of the Clothworkers' Company at a certain point of his life, wanted to erect a building somewhat in keeping with his social position. He made application to the Clothworkers' Company for the purpose of obtaining a lease. The Clothworkers' Company would not grant him a sufficient long lease of his farm, but they divided the farm into two, and gave him a lease of 60 years of a portion of it, upon which he was to erect this dwelling-house, binding him in that lease with very many restrictions, that there should be no shop opened upon it, and no manufactory of any kind started upon this portion of the ground attached to the house, and things of that kind; so that when the Land Act came out this portion of the farm was declared not to be an agricultural holding at all, but a building lease.

420. What induced the companies to sell these estates for 25,000 *l.* less than they could have obtained from the tenantry?—I can only give you the reason that was given by one of the members of the company to myself at the time of the sale. He said that he did not believe that it would be desirable to root the Irish in the soil.

421. Did

Chairman.

421. Did you know the member of the company who said that?—Yes, I can give his name. I said: "If these be the sentiments of the English, thank God I am an Irishman."

Mr. *Lea.*

422. Was it the arrangement with Sir Hervey Bruce that for 10 years he should keep up your charities?—I cannot say that, but Sir Hervey Bruce said that now that the relationship between landlord and tenant had been so vastly altered he thought there was no necessity for his paying these endowments.

Colonel *Lewis.*

423. Is it not a fact that when the Clothworkers' Company sold this property they set aside a sum of money for the permanent endowment of some of the religious or charitable bodies in that district?—Yes, they gave to the Episcopalian Church 1,600 *l.*, paid down, according to the evidence of Canon Babington. That was in relation to the Castlerock Church; while to the Killowen Episcopalian Church they gave 500 *l.* also.

424. But they gave nothing to the Presbyterians?—It is stated here correctly that they gave 800 *l.* to the managers of the church of which I am minister, and they gave 100 *l.* to the managers of a neighbouring church; but that church in Castlerock to which they gave an endowment in perpetuity of 80 *l.*, is not built upon their estate at all; whereas there is a Presbyterian church built upon their estate adjoining that one which never received any endowment except a gift of 100 *l.*

425. Do you complain of their having sold that property?—Yes, I complain that they did not permit the tenants to become the purchasers, and the tenants complain of the same thing too.

426. You do not complain of the sale *per se*, but you think it desirable that the City companies should sell to their Irish tenants?—I think the tenants would be desirous of the City companies selling to them, but they would desire also that the City companies should not carry off the spoil.

427. But there is no real objection, on your part, to their selling to their Irish tenants?—There is a great desire that they should sell to their Irish tenants.

428. You do not think that the Clothworkers' Company did behave with liberality?—I really do not.

429. They imposed certain conditions upon Sir Hervey Bruce, besides giving these sums of money which you mentioned just now?—I do not know very well what the conditions were; the whole thing has been kept largely secret from us.

430. He has kept up a large number of subscriptions, has he not?—Yes, but they have now ceased.

431. Perhaps these payments may have been in some shape a consideration for their taking 25,000 *l.* less from him. If he gave 25,000 *l.* less than the Irish tenantry would have given, and he had conditions imposed upon him of that sort, that was part of the bargain, was it not?—I do not know anything of that at all.

Colonel *Lewis*—continued.

432. But it may be so?—I do not know what may be.

433. I thought you said just now that for 10 years he had been bound to keep up certain subscriptions?—Yes.

434. That was part of the bargain. If he gave 25,000 *l.* less than the Irish tenants would have given, he has given a certain annual income for 10 years, and that is the reason, I take it, why the company may have been disposed to accept from him a smaller sum of money than the Irish tenants were prepared to give?—I have heard it stated that even long since the sale the company made him a concession on condition that these things should be continued for a time; but I do not know whether it is true or not.

435. You complained just now that they had sold the property to Sir Hervey Bruce for 25,000 *l.* less than the Irish tenants would have given; but they imposed certain conditions upon Sir Hervey Bruce, which made a difference in the value to him?—We complain, first, that we could not under any circumstances get access to the company at all; secondly, we complain that when we called upon individual members they gave us to understand that, in their opinion, it would not be good to root the Irish in the soil, making them owners; we complain, in the third place, that the estate was sold over our heads, though we offered 25,000 *l.* more than the purchaser gave, and we complain, lastly, that they carry off the money to London.

436. But the Irish tenants would have not taken over those serious liabilities that Sir Hervey Bruce took over, would they?—I do not know whether they would or not.

Chairman.

437. Could you tell us about how much Sir Hervey Bruce's contributions came to for each of the 10 years?—20 *l.* to myself annually; 10 *l.* to the minister of Second Dunboe annually; 10 *l.* to be given out in charity to the needy and deserving poor in connection with my church annually; 5 *l.* to be given to the needy and deserving poor in connection with the second Presbyterian Church annually; and 5 *l.* to eight or ten teachers of the national schools twice annually.

438. Do you mean that 50 *l.* a year would be about the total of Sir Hervey Bruce's subscriptions under the agreement to purchase?—Yes, to religion and charity, with additional grants to schools as already stated.

Colonel *Lewis.*

439. I have it here that, as a matter of fact, Sir Hervey Bruce is keeping up the charities beyond the 10 years?—I have intimated that he paid it fully 10 years and more, but it has now ceased to the Presbyterian churches.

Mr. *Lawson.*

440. It is also said by Canon Babington that Sir Hervey Bruce came and said, "I will take care of these parishes," at the time of sale; that you contend he has not done?—He has not, so far as we are concerned.

441. What was the official reason given by the Clothworkers' Company for their preference for Sir

Mr. *Lawson*—continued.

Sir Hervey Bruce as a purchaser, to their own tenants?—I think that will be brought out in the correspondence which has been handed in here to-day. The official reason, however, as stated by the clerk of the company to myself, was this: That before the tenants came on the scene at all they had had a sort of honourable understanding with Sir Hervey Bruce, and although it was not in a legal shape and the sale was in no sense perfected, yet they did not feel disposed to retire from the position.

442. But the difference in price is so astounding, even allowing for those subscriptions, not very considerable in amount, to continue for 10 years, that I am tempted to ask whether Sir Hervey Bruce had anything to do with this company?—Nothing whatever. I think the whole thing arose from the company being inimical to letting the Bright's Clauses of the Land Act have any application to Ireland at the time.

Mr. *Sexton*.

443. Who were they that said that it was not a good thing to root the Irish people in the soil?—A member of the Clothworkers' Company. When we were refused access to the Court, we called upon some of the members to see if we could interest them on our behalf to espouse our cause.

Mr. *Lawson*.

444. Were you one of those who saw these gentlemen?—I was.

445. And therefore that is not hearsay?—No; I know that it happened myself.

446. Had it been the custom of the company to refuse to receive deputations?—Yes; and it is so still. Lately I have been over here seeking to have an interview with the Clothworkers' Company, but I would not be permitted. They are inaccessible.

447. You can only see them through their agents?—We can see the agent, and by courtesy when we call at the office Sir Owen Roberts will receive us graciously.

448. As they have no property there now your interview with them was, I presume, with reference to some past transactions?—No. We thought that though they have no property there now they had the value of the property, and considering that it was Presbyterian energy and industry that had made their estate a thing so marketable as it was, we thought we ought not to have been left out in the cold, by an arrangement such as they effected.

449. And they refused to see you?—They refused to see us. I need not say "they;" Sir Owen Roberts, the clerk of the company, refused to see us.

Mr. *Sexton*.

450. To what do you attribute this recent policy of the reduction of grants; is it altogether due to the impending sales?—No. Sir Hervey Bruce's own statement is that owing to the altered relationship existing between landlord and tenant in Ireland he felt no longer bound to pay these moneys.

451. Was the refusal of the companies to continue these grants partly due to the reduction of rent under the Act of 1871 and partly due to the prospect of selling out?—So long as the company held the property they did pay a certain proportion.

452. I understand from some of the witnesses that reductions began to be made before they sold?—Yes, but not in relation to this particular estate upon which I am being examined.

453. I am not examining you upon any particular estate?—That is so.

454. How soon did they begin to reduce the grants?—I would not say that it was as soon as the rents began to be reduced. It was with the prospect of selling that they began to get rid of certain encumbrances.

455. But even before they approached the question of sale did they not make the reduction in the grants in consequence of the Act of 1881?—I can only speak immediately for my own company. I have not been taking the same wide interest as Mr. Dickey, the former witness has been taking. I have been living in my own house and managing my own affairs.

456. When did they say that it was not a good thing to root the tenants in the soil?—In 1871, immediately after the passing of the first Land Act, with Bright's Clauses in it.

457. That was at a time when they could get others than the tenants to purchase?—Yes.

458. It is not so now, is it?—The tenants would be most anxious to purchase if they had an opportunity.

459. Did this company sell?—Yes, they sold to Sir Hervey Bruce.

460. In what year?—In 1871.

461. Then this observation, that it was not good to root the Irish tenants in the soil, was given as a reason for selling to Sir Hervey Bruce rather than to the tenants?—Yes.

462. That was a remark that was made to you, as I understand, by several members of the Company?—I would not say that. It was the result of our interview.

Colonel *Lewis*.

463. With how many members; two or three?—Half-a-dozen, or perhaps more. We called upon several of them, but it was in the year 1871, and I was younger then than I am now, and was just beginning public life, and I did not think of noting down these things.

Mr. *Sexton*.

464. Nevertheless, it made an impression upon you?—Yes. That statement that I have quoted was made by Mr. Bloxam. I had the pleasure of meeting him on one occasion, when he came over to Coleraine as a member of a deputation, and I knew him personally; and I waited upon him at his office here, and that was his statement to myself in his office.

465. Did you share the view of Dr. Cook that the capital value of the estates ought equitably to be appropriated to Irish public uses?—I did not know that that was Dr. Cook's opinion, but it is my own opinion.

466. That relates to sale; but in the event of some of these companies retaining what may be styled for the moment the ownership of these properties, what would you consider satisfactory; would you consider it satisfactory that the Episcopalian grants remaining as they are, the grants

Mr. *Sexton*—continued.

grants to your own communion, and possibly to the Roman Catholic communion, should be made to correspond?—I think decidedly they should.

Mr. *Elton*.

467. You said that it was a complaint of yourself, and of gentlemen whom you represent, that when you did get to see the companies you had that remark made to you about its being a bad thing to root the Irishman in the soil; have you ever known it made by any member of the company except this Mr. Gibson that you have mentioned?—I would not say that I have, but that was the impression that we received everywhere.

468. When you told us the story first, I think you said that one gentleman told you that, and you remembered it very well, and you remembered the answer, and you said, "I can give his name;" and then in the course of the succeeding examination that gentleman seemed to grow into a good many?—I have not said that, but I have said that that was the gist of the opinion of those with whom we came into contact.

469. But it was not expressed except by one gentleman?—Quite so.

Mr. *Sexton*.

470. I suppose it struck you when you went home from London at the time that the conclusion that it was a bad thing to root the Irish in the soil of Ireland was a strange result of the old plantation policy?—It left a very disagreeable impression on my mind all over.

Mr. *Elton*.

471. Where did this gentleman make that remark which has left that impression upon your mind?—In his own office in 1871.

472. In his private house?—In his private house; in his own office.

Monday, 9th June 1890.

MEMBERS PRESENT:

Mr. Clancy.	Sir William Marriott.
Lord Elcho.	Mr. John Morley.
Mr. John Ellis.	Mr. Sexton.
Mr. Lea.	Sir Richard Temple.

THE RIGHT HONOURABLE JOHN MORLEY, IN THE CHAIR.

The Reverend NATHANIEL MACAULAY BROWN, D.D.; Examined.

Mr. Lea.

473. You live at Limavady, in North Derry?—I do.

474. And you are the Presbyterian minister of Limavady?—I am.

475. And you appear here to represent the feelings and wishes of the community living in that part of the county?—I do.

476. You know something about estates of the London companies, rather different from those which we have hitherto dealt with, I think?—I know the history of those that come nearest to my town best of all; that is to say, the companies of the Fishmongers and the Skinners.

477. How many years have you been at Limavady?—I have been there upwards of 40 years.

478. You have therefore had a long experience of the London companies?—A considerable experience.

479. Are you willing to give the Committee your opinion with regard to them?—Yes, I have no objection to do so.

480. Which are the two companies that you chiefly know?—The Fishmongers and the Skinners.

481. Have they sold?—The Fishmongers have sold; the Skinners have partially sold.

482. When did the Fishmongers sell?—They sold, I think, the year before the Ashbourne Act.

483. To whom did they sell?—They sold to the tenants.

484. Under what Act?—It must have been under the Act of 1881; I think, between 1881 and 1885.

Mr. Sexton.

485. There were sale clauses in the Act of 1881, and also in the Act of 1870. Can you state under which of the Acts they sold?—I am not quite sure; but it was before the Ashbourne Act, because they did not get all the money.

Mr. Lea.

486. Did the tenants find a proportion of the money themselves?—They did.

487. Do you know from whom they obtained that proportion?—Some of them borrowed, and some of them were able to pay their own proportion.

Mr. Lea—continued.

488. Did they borrow it from money lenders?—No; They borrowed from their neighbours.

489. Then you say that the Skinners' Company have partially sold?—They have sold partially.

490. You mean that they have sold a part of the estate?—Yes.

491. When did they sell?—They have not sold the whole of it yet, but they sold a portion of it about two or three years ago.

492. Was that the end next the city of Derry?—It was.

493. Which part of the Skinners' estate has not yet been sold?—The part about the town of Dungiven is not yet sold.

494. Have they offered it to the tenants?—They expect to sell it to the tenants. I understand that there are some sales in the neighbourhood of Dungiven also, but it is not entirely sold off there.

495. You mean that they are selling off their estate in patches?—They are.

496. Why is that?—They cannot get the people all to agree; and I suspect that the people imagine that instead of the price rising it will rather fall.

497. They are hanging back?—They are hoping for better terms.

498. Have these two companies continued their grants to the localities since they sold?—They have withdrawn some of them already, and some of them they have not. The Fishmongers have withdrawn all, but the Skinners have not. The price at which the Fishmongers sold was some 15 or 16 years' purchase.

499. Do you know the amount of money that it came to?—The rental was about 10,000 *l.*, and that multiplied by 15 would give the sum.

500. Do you know how much the Skinners' Company sold for?—They sold nominally at 19 years' purchase, but they made an abatement of a year and a half, I think; that is the rent that

Mr. *Lea*—continued.

that they did not take up at the close; 17½ years' purchase, I think, was about the real price.

501. What was the total of that purchase-money?—That, multiplied by about 13,000 *l.*, would give the whole of it, if it were all sold.

Mr. *Sexton.*

502. Did they add a year and a-half of arrears to the purchase-money to make up those 19 years?—I think it was nominally 19, and they did not take up a year and a-half at the close.

503. They included a year and a-half of arrears in the purchase-money; did the tenants pay 19 times the rent?—I think not; I think it was 17½ times the rent.

Mr. *Lea.*

504. You do not know the total of the purchase-money of those two estates?—No, except by multiplying the amount of the rental by the years.

505. Do you know anything about any other companies?—Yes, I have heard of them all.

506. We have heard nothing before about the Haberdashers' Company; do you know anything about them?—I know a good deal.

507. Have they sold?—They have sold.

508. When did they sell?—They sold, I think, to an Earl of Tyrone, who was a progenitor of the family of Lord Waterford. Lord Waterford was the proprietor, lately, of the estate, and he is partially the proprietor of that estate just now.

509. When did they sell?—They sold, I think, in 1685. It is very far back.

510. The Haberdashers' Company sold to a private owner?—They did.

511. What sort of landlords have the private owners been there?—They raise the rents always upon the tenants' improvements from period to period. Their period was rather longer than the ordinary period. The ordinary period for most of the companies was about 21 years; their period was about 25 years.

512. What do you mean by "period?"—The period between two valuations; and a valuation in those days always meant a rise of rent because they valued the tenants' improvements.

513. Is the Haberdashers' estate in the hands of private owners now?—It is partly in the hands of the tenants that bought. I myself was one of those that bought.

514. Whom did you buy from?—From the Marquis of Waterford.

515. When did you buy?—In 1871.

516. Under the Bright's Clauses?—Yes.

517. What number of years' purchase did you pay?—Only 23½.

518. Is there any other information about the sale of the estate of the Haberdashers' Company that you can give to the Committee?—At the time it was sold about one-third was bought by the tenants; about one-third was bought by private owners or new landlords; and a third was retained in the Waterford family. They have been trying to sell that off latterly piecemeal, one farm after another, just as they can agree with the people.

519. About how many years' purchase do they get?—They got upon an average above 20 years' purchase at the time at which I bought.

520. That is not quite the question; about how many years' purchase do they get now?—They are quite content now to take about 17 or 18 years' purchase.

521. Then the fall in land in that district would appear to be the difference between 17 or 18 and 23 or 20 years' purchase?—Yes. I remember after the sale, that the tenants of two townlands asked me, inasmuch as I had aided the people in purchasing it, to communicate with the Marquis of Waterford with regard to the two townlands that were not bought by the tenants. I communicated with him and asked him how much he would take for those townlands that had been bought in. His Lordship said that he did not understand the meaning of the word "bought in," but that if I meant the townlands that were purchased by Lord Charles Beresford, he begged to tell me that Lord Charles Beresford was so well satisfied with his purchase that he was not inclined then to sell. I would have given him in the name of the people, and on behalf of the people, nearly 30 years' purchase.

522. When was that?—That was a little after the public sale in 1871; about the beginning of 1872.

Dr. Freshfield stated that the Haberdashers' Company sold in the year 1687.

Mr. *Lea.*

523. (*To the Witness.*) I think you said that they sold about 1685?—Yes; there is two years' difference between us.

Chairman.

524. Who then were the vendors in 1871, in the transaction of which you have just been speaking?—The Marquis of Waterford.

Mr. *Sexton.*

525. His ancestor, the Earl of Tyrone, I understand, had purchased from the Haberdashers' Company?—Yes.

Mr. *Lea.*

526. We have heard a good deal about the Clothworkers' Company; have you any special knowledge of the Clothworkers' Company?—Yes; I know a little about them. The property was let to a middleman of the name of Jackson.

527. We have had evidence as to the Clothworkers' Company from Mr. Mark the other day; have you read the evidence given by Mr. Mark with regard to the Clothworkers' estate?—I saw a couple or three sentences, but only that.

528. So far as regards the estates, what sort of landlords have the London companies been, as a rule, in your district?—For a long time I had a strong prejudice in their favour from the fact that for public objects, and for useful purposes of a social kind, we would have got a little occasionally from them, and we got very little from private landlords; but latterly, since I have understood their history better than I formerly did, I have not thought so highly of their administration.

529. In what respect do you think less highly of their administration?—Because I thought at

our

Mr. *Lea*—continued.

one time that they were as they represented themselves, the real owners, and that as real owners they were more liberal than some other real owners: whereas I find now that they were only trustees.

Chairman.

530. How were they more liberal than real owners; what did they do in the way of liberality that exceeded the liberality of real owners?—They gave donations to the clergy of different denominations.

531. You mean, I suppose, to the Presbyterian and Episcopalian clergy only?—To the Roman Catholics also.

Mr. *Lea*.

532. And they made grants to the schools, did they not?—They did.

533. And what else?—To dispensaries they gave a trifle, and sometimes to poor people they gave a few shillings. Sometimes they had old pensioners that they gave 1 *s.* or 2 *s.* by the week to.

534. Did they give donations for public objects like markets and court houses?—They gave donations and subscriptions to those sometimes.

535. Did they do anything in the way of making roads and public improvements?—They did aid the tenants sometimes in making byeroads, say to turf bogs and places of that kind.

536. In those respects you think they were better than other landlords?—They were rather better, so far as donations to public objects of that kind were concerned; but I do not say that they were much better in the way of making private roads than other landlords.

537. I cannot ask you any question as to your opinion whether they are trustees, but I think I may ask what is the popular opinion as to their being trustees?—I do not think that there are 10 intelligent men in the county that believe they are anything but trustees.

538. How long has that opinion prevailed?—I think since the suit between the Skinners' Company and the Irish Society; and more light has been coming in I may say from different sides in these later days.

539. Has the sale of the estates by the companies had anything to do with it?—I think that that made the people inquire considerably more than otherwise they would have done; but I think that if they had been left in the possession of the small donations which were only crumbs which fell from the rich man's table, they would not perhaps have said much about it in the meantime.

540. Now they are enlightened a bit?—They are considerably enlightened and are getting more light from day to day.

541. What have the companies done for their tenants?—They have done nothing in the way of improving the property.

542. Did they build any houses?—No; I have often heard it reported that they built houses, and that they have expended large sums of money, but for my part I never could see the expenditure, and I think the general opinion is that the expenditure was very small.

Mr. *Lea*—continued.

543. The expenditure was not in improving their agricultural district?—No such thing. The tenants did that entirely themselves.

544. But the rent was raised all the same every 20 or 30 years?—Periodically it was raised upon the tenant's improvements.

545. Then I suppose there is a certain amount of indignation felt that when the rent has been raised constantly for so many years, the whole of the purchase-money received by the London companies for their estates should be taken away from the district?—The people are uncommonly indignant at these late sales. They look upon it as a great robbery of the country, and I have heard very strong language used about it, namely, that the administration of these companies, I may say through their whole history was a great imposition and a gigantic swindle. I would not use that language myself, but I have heard it uttered.

546. Have you seen statements that when they have been withdrawing grants of 5 *l.* or 10 *l.* from your schools they have given 60,000 *l.* to objects (no doubt good objects) in the East-end of London?—We saw that, and it intensified the indignation.

547. They have given grants to religious objects and to schools, have they not?—They have.

548. We will take the *Fishmongers'* Company first; do you know what amount they gave for religious objects or for schools?—They gave 20 *l.* a year to seven schools.

549. What did they give for religious objects so far as you can tell?—They gave 20 *l.* a year each to about six clergymen, so far as I know; Presbyterian and Roman Catholic clergymen. I think, in one case that I know, it was only 10 *l.*, because it was an adjoining estate that the house of worship was on. That was Lower Cumber.

550. Did the *Fishmongers'* Company ever build any churches or schools?—They built Ballykelly Church, and I understand they built the church at Banagher. These two churches they built early after they came into possession of the estate after 1820, when the lease fell in.

551. Did they give sums of money to rebuild Catholic and Presbyterian churches?—They gave a trifle for the building of such churches as those.

552. Have they withdrawn any of those grants to churches of all kinds?—They have withdrawn them all, I understand.

553. Do they now give anything to the building of churches of all kinds?—They give nothing. They cut off the clergy by paying three years' purchase, and that was the close.

Sir *William Marriott*.

554. Three years' purchase of the 20 *l.*?—Yes.

Mr. *Lea*.

555. You say that they gave to seven schools 20 *l.* each?—So I understand.

556. Are those grants continued?—No; the grants are not continued, but the schools are left in possession of the people.

557. What did they do in the way of contributions?

Mr. *Lea*—continued.

mutation; did they give any compensation?—Not that I am aware of.

558. Was not the three years' purchase that they gave to the church continued to the schools at all?—No.

559. That was cut entirely off?—Yes; they acted very unkindly towards certain farmers that they had denuded of portions of their farms in the famine year of 1846. In that year they took portions of farms from farmers that they might plant gorges and places that were not well cultivated. They took rough lands from farmers and planted these for the purpose of making work, and they did not compensate the farmers from whom they took these portions of farms. But at the sale they sold these portions of the farms, sometimes to the farmers from whom they took them, and charged them the full price as if those portions had belonged to themselves from the first, although they had taken them from the farmers without compensating them at the beginning; and, in some instances, if the farmer would not pay as well as they wanted, they sold to a stranger.

560. How many years' purchase did they get for the woods?—They got as much as they could sell them for. They did not run the woods at 15 or 18 years' purchase as they did the arable land; but they offered them for sale to the tenant first from whom they had taken them. If he bought them well and good; if not, they sold them to a stranger at the highest figure they could get.

561. They tried to pocket everything they could?—They did to the uttermost farthing.

562. Coming back to the grants, they gave nothing to the schools, but simply cut off the 150 *l.*, or the 180 *l.*?—They did.

563. I suppose you cannot tell me what proportion they gave in commuted sums to the churches here to the whole purchase-money of the estate?—I could not. They gave three years' purchase of all the endowments or donations, and that was the end.

564. They took away at least 9-10ths of the property then?—I should think so.

565. Then the Skinners' Company, you say, have sold part of their estate, and are trying to sell the rest?—Yes.

566. What did they give in grants to churches?—I think they gave fully as much to the clergy as the other company, but not so much to schools.

567. You mean so much a year?—They gave 20 *l.* a year to four or five clergy, and they gave 30 *l.* a year, I think, to the Roman Catholic clergyman of Dungiven; but they did not generally run the Episcopalian clergyman with the other two clergy; they generally kept the Episcopalian clergyman by themselves, as they did in the Fishmongers' case. In the Return to Lord Derby's Commission, I see that they never brought in the Episcopalian clergyman, and his endowment, along with the Roman Catholic clergyman and the Presbyterian clergyman. They kept these two together, and they kept the other separate by itself.

568. When the Skinners' Company sold, did they give any sum to the religious bodies or to the schools?—They seemed to be cutting the thing clean off without allowing as much as the Fishmongers. The Fishmongers' Company gave three years' purchase. They have withdrawn their donations from some of the clergy, at least one that I know, by giving them notice, "This is the last donation you shall receive." That is Lower Cumber.

569. Did they give any reason?—They said, in effect, "We have sold that portion of the estate; it is your people that attend your congregation that have bought, and we have done with you all."

570. As they sell they take that course?—I suspect they will do the same thing when they sell the district round Dungiven.

571. The Haberdashers' Company sold a good many years ago; have they ever given any grants to religious bodies or schools?—No; they and their successors kept up a semblance of administering a trust for a number of years by keeping a school alive in every parish; but it was only a semblance; it was a mere trifle of 8 *l.* or 10 *l.* that they gave, and before the Marquis of Waterford sold off, the schools were a wreck and a ruin. In fact, the schools were given up.

572. Then there is nothing given now?—Not a halfpenny.

573. You said just now that the Skinners' Company sold part of the estate; do you know what was the reason that they have not sold the rest of the estate?—I think they are anxious to sell, and the people if they could buy at a fair rate I think are anxious to buy; and why they have not sold I cannot exactly say.

574. Have the Skinners' Company negotiated with anybody else to buy the estate?—I have not heard of that. I believe they considered that the tenants would be the best purchasers because I think in these later days outsiders do not care about purchasing land.

575. I thought I had seen in the papers something about a syndicate; is there any idea of selling to a syndicate?—I have not heard anything of that kind, but it is quite possible. Where the people delay, they sometimes talk about syndicates and all the rest of it to frighten the people.

576. To make them buy?—Quite so. There is one thing that I would say with regard to that section that they sold. A gentleman was acting for them in the way of selling the estate for them, and in fact he is a friend of mine, a gentleman I know very well, a man of ability, and a man of probity and honour, and for the purpose of inducing them to purchase he said that all these outgoings, these donations and privileges, would be continued to the tenants after they purchased; and I find now by the testimony of a gentleman who travelled 40 or 50 miles to tell me the tale before I left, and who is a magistrate and a man of character and standing who would not deceive me or anybody else, that they have not implemented and carried out what that gentleman who was their legal agent had promised to the people. They understood that all the donations and privileges that had been accorded to them hitherto would be continued; but they are cut off. The matter of bog is one thing, and the matter of that donation to the Presbyterian congregation of Lower Cumber is another. That 30 *l.* was cut off most unceremoniously without any

Mr. *Lea*—continued.

any notice whatever. The gentleman who was there had not been long in the place, but he was endowed for at least one year, and after he had got that year's payment he was told that he need not expect any more, and that that was the last.

Mr. *Sexton.*

577. What company is this?—The Skinners'.

Mr. *Lea.*

578. You referred to a bog just now; have they sold the bog as well as the holdings?—They have retained that, I understand. When the Marquis of Waterford sold his estate, for a long time he did not know what to do with the bog. For a time he very properly believed that the right thing to do was to allocate a portion of the bog to certain lots on the lower ground; but he found that that would be difficult, and some of his friends advised him just to throw the bog in as a lot by itself. He did that, and inasmuch as the Government valuation of the bog was very low, some outsiders came in and bought the bog, and are making a good thing of it now, for they are charging 4 *l.* an acre for that bog to the tenants below.

579. You said just now that the Fishmongers' Company had made attempts to create bits of woodland; have the Skinners' Company done anything of the same kind?—I have not heard of anything of the kind of them.

580. Are you aware that the Irish Society a good many years ago arranged with the London Companies to reafforest some of the districts?—I heard something of it, but I do not know much of the history of that point.

581. You know the Reverend Mr. Johnston; had he a grant of 20 *l.*?—He has lost his endowment.

582. Which company is that?—That is the Skinners' Company.

583. You do not know how many of the Skinners' Company's grants have been withdrawn?—I think there is only one, so far as I know, as yet.

584. You mentioned the town of Dungiven just now, has that been sold to the tenants?—They have not sold much of it. I think there is some of it agreed to be sold to the tenants.

585. How was that town formed; who built it?—The people.

586. Entirely?—Yes; the company built a few houses, but they charged the full rent for them.

587. Upon what basis are they selling it now?—They are selling the houses at the best price they can get and the land at 17½ years; but they raised the rents enormously after they came in 1872.

588. Did the tenants consider that the houses that they built were built under the Ulster Custom?—I think they must have done so.

589. Why do you think they must have done so?—Because they were nearly all holders of pieces of land, town-parks, and the like of that, and they looked upon themselves as entitled to the same privileges as their neighbours.

590. But now they are buying those houses that they have erected at 17 or 18 years' purchase?—I think so. They generally kept their rentals in three separate compartments; that is to say, ordinary agricultural holdings, town-parks, and houses, but town-parks and houses sometimes were run together; that is to say, the same man held sometimes a house in the town and a town-park.

Mr. *Sexton.*

591. When you say houses you mean houses in the town?—Yes.

Mr. *Lea.*

592. I thought I had heard of considerable indignation in Dungiven with regard to the way in which the Skinners' Company were increasing the rents, and selling what they could the tenants' own property?—Yes, they raised the rents when they came in, that is after Mr. Ogilby's lease was out. They raised the rents 12½ per cent., I think, upon ordinary agricultural holdings, 20 per cent. upon town-parks, and 25 per cent. upon the houses.

593. Have the Skinners' Company given large sums for other public purposes besides charities?—No, they have not.

594. But they have helped railways, I suppose?—Yes; they give 5 per cent. upon 20,000 *l.* for 22 years.

595. That is to say, they have guaranteed 5 per cent. upon 20,000 *l.*?—Yes.

596. Did they give any land as well for the making of the railway?—I think they did; I think they gave what land it ran through.

Mr. *John Ellis.*

597. You used the word "think"; do you know?—I have not had any communication with them, but from the testimony of those that know, the testimony of those I can trust, I know.

Mr. *Lea.*

598. That you consider is a mark of their sense of responsibility, I suppose?—Yes; and they considered, I am sure, that they were serving themselves materially by opening up the little town of Dungiven to a railway.

599. Is there any other information that you can give to the Committee on the sale of the estates?—If any gentleman round the table asks me any question, I will be very happy to answer it.

Sir *William Marriott.*

600. Are the tenants the chief purchasers?—On these two estates they are.

601. Are they willing purchasers?—They are willing purchasers.

602. The tenant in Ireland, I believe, likes owning his own land, like the tenants in many other places?—They are uncommonly anxious for it, and therefore it was that upon the Haberdashers' estate we purchased at 20 years' purchase, rather than want it.

Mr. *Lea.*

603. Do you mean the Haberdashers' estate?—Yes, the Marquis of Waterford's.

604. The

Sir William Marriott.

604. The Haberdashers' Company sold to the Marquis of Waterford's ancestor in 1685, and the Marquis of Waterford has since sold to his tenants?—Yes; not the whole of the estate, but about one-third of it.

605. But the Haberdashers' Company do not get the profit of it; but Lord Waterford does?—Of course.

Chairman.

606. Were the Haberdashers' Company out of the whole transaction in 1685 or 1687?—I think they must have been.

607. Then why do you speak of it as the Haberdashers' estate?—Because I think that all the estates of the companies that were sold were sold liable to whatever conditions the companies held under; and I understand that the four companies that sold out gave a bond of indemnity to the Irish Society.

Sir William Marriott.

608. That is another matter; but as a matter of fact, do you know how many years' purchase the Haberdashers' Company sold for to Lord Waterford's ancestor?—I understand that it was a very small thing: I have heard that it was 1,200 *l.*, but I am not certain of that. They sold to the Earl of Tyrone, I think it was.

609. How much land had the Haberdashers' Company to sell?—About 36,000 acres.

610. Do you know what Lord Waterford gave for it?—Lord Waterford gave nothing for it. He inherited it from his progenitor.

611. But how did it get back into his hands?—I think the Earl of Tyrone bought it all from the Haberdashers' Company.

612. When was that?—In 1685.

613. Then, as I understand, it is now back in the hands of Lord Waterford?—Only a portion of it; one-third of it he holds still.

614. But are the Haberdashers' Company themselves selling to the tenants directly?—The Haberdashers' Company have nothing to do with it now. One-third was bought by the tenants, one-third by the new landlords, and one-third was bought in, and therefore retained by the Waterford family.

615. When was that?—In 1871.

616. Who was the owner in 1871?—The present Marquis of Waterford.

Mr. Sexton.

617. Did the Haberdashers' Company sell the whole estate in 1685?—They sold the whole.

618. Has any part of it ever come back into their hands since?—No.

Sir William Marriott.

619. We understand that they have given 30 years' purchase to Lord Waterford; how many years' purchase have the tenants given to the companies?—As I have already stated, they have given 16 or 18 years' purchase on the estate of the Fishmongers' Company, and 17½ years and on the other estate.

620. Then it is a fact that the companies have sold to the tenants at a very much reduced rate as compared with what Lord Waterford sold at?—But I think that is from the general depreciation of property.

621. I am not asking your opinion, but the fact?—They have; and the Marquis of Waterford is getting no more for what remains in his hands.

622. At the present time he is not?—No; he is getting just the same as the others are getting.

623. The tenants, I suppose, would sooner be their own landlords than have the companies as landlords?—Yes, they would.

624. What do they want from the companies?—They want them to leave the endowments and a great deal more.

625. They want all the money, I suppose?—If they can get it, and they think they are justly entitled to it.

626. They would like to get the land for nothing, I suppose?—No, they want only what is fair.

627. What is fair?—Well, the companies themselves, as appears from the charters, got the land at a very easy rate, at about 1½ *d.* an acre, and they were instructed that they were to let to their tenants at a similarly easy rate; and then in 1623 that easy rate was determined, in the time of Charles I., by its being put down at 9 *d.* an acre for those who held as freeholders.

628. You say that the tenants want what is fair; I, on the part of the Committee, should like to know what the tenants think is fair?—As land is generally sold, it is not sold too high. I think the tenants are pretty well pleased with that, but they are not pleased with the fact that the companies are carrying away the money out of the country.

629. The tenants, if I understand you aright, want to sell the land to the company on the condition that the company should invest the money in Ireland; is that so?—Yes.

630. How are they to invest it?—For public and useful purposes.

631. You mean for public and useful purposes in Ireland?—Yes.

632. And the companies are to have no advantage?—The companies may be recouped for anything they laid out in the beginning. I would not cheat any man or number of men or syndicate.

633. Why are the companies to be different from other landlords?—They are not different from other landlords, ordinarily speaking, but in this case I think they are.

634. Why?—I suppose we are touching now the legal point. I think they are not holding for private purposes at all, but for public purposes.

635. What do you call public purposes?—It was for the establishment of religion and morality, and good order and loyalty.

636. Those are established now, are they?—Well, partially.

637. I only want to get to know how you would have them spend this money that they have got. You say that they are selling at a very moderate price, and therefore the price given is not too much for the tenants; what are they to do with the money now that they have it?

 There

Sir William Marriott—continued.

There is no doubt, I understand, that the tenants would prefer keeping the land?—I would not give it to the treasury; I would let a portion of it go for the county cess; I would let a portion of it go for poor rates, and I would let a portion of it go for the education of the people of the country. I would pay so much for primary schools, and so much for intermediate schools, and that would require very much because the Intermediate School Act for Ireland has done very little for us; it has done a great deal for the large public schools, but it has done nothing whatever for the small towns like the town of Limavady; and I think if we had a donation, of say 100 *l.* a year for the purpose of establishing a school in such a town as Limavady, where there are about 3,000 inhabitants, it would be a very great matter for the county.

638. But I am not mistaking your view when I say that your idea is that it would be a very good thing for the companies to sell to the tenants, the purchase money to be spent entirely in Ireland for public purposes?—I would not say that it should all go in that way; I would have them be honest to the parties from whom the small sums of money came in the first instance.

639. If they are not carrying out their legal trusts you can make them do it?—And I have no doubt that the time will come when the people will possess so much money and so much courage as will make them.

640. In your opinion there are trusts; you used the word "trustees"; you say that there are not 10 sensible men who do not think that the companies are trustees. Trustees for what? In what way do you use the word "trustees"?—For the plantation for one thing.

641. But that is completed now?—But not by them.

642. By whom?—By the people themselves. They have not expended a shilling upon what might be called the development of the country or the progress of agriculture.

643. Then what do you propose to do in a court of law; what trust would you make them perform?—I do not understand you.

644. What trusts have they neglected to carry out that you could make them perform in a court of law?—They have not in my opinion carried out any of their trusts.

645. Has anybody tried the case in a court of law in Ireland?—As I have said already, it is only latterly that we are turning our attention to the matter, and it is only latterly that we have got the proper amount of light that will enable us to take proceedings.

646. Have any of those very able men, called solicitors, been consulted upon the subject?—Yes, we have able men amongst us.

647. Do they say that you could enforce this claim in a court of law?—I am sure that that is the opinion of many.

648. That it could be enforced in a court of law?—Yes; and I have no doubt that it will be tested before all is over, but it requires some courage, and it requires perhaps more money.

649. I do not know that it requires courage to go to law. A good many people go to law in England?—But in Ireland, you know, we are a cautious people.

650. We thought you were rather impetuous. You are thinking of the Presbyterian Church in Scotland; they are always supposed to be very cautious you know?—They have a spice also of caution.

651. The Skinners' are the worst company, are they?—I think upon the whole they deserve their name.

652. They skin the people?—They do.

Mr. *Sexton*.

653. I understand you to refer to some record of the sale by the Haberdashers' Company to Lord Tyrone, and to say that they sold 36,000 acres for 1,800 *l.*?—That is my opinion, from documents that I have seen, but not lately.

654. That is about 8 *d.* an acre?—Yes; I suppose it would not be more than that; and the people have improved it enormously, so that the Marquis sold at a very large figure.

655. You have been asked by the right honourable gentleman whether the tenants like to buy their holdings; I presume you would say that they like to buy if they can buy at a fair price?—They would all buy if they could buy at a fair price.

656. I should like to understand what you mean by 17½ years' "net" in the case of the sale of the Skinners' estate?—I think there is what is called a running term, and during the time that they were negotiating a year's rent accumulated, and they did not charge for that last year's rent. I think they gave it to them without calling upon them to pay for the last year.

657. Do you mean that if they had charged the last year the rate would have been 18½?—It would have been 18. It was nominally 18, but really 17½.

658. The right honourable gentleman has referred to the great difference between the price obtained by the Marquis of Waterford in 1871, and the price now obtained by the companies?—Yes, but the Marquis of Waterford can get no more than the companies for the remnant of his estate, and he is uncommonly anxious to sell the remnant of his estate.

659. Is the difference in price between you now due to any liberality on the part of the companies?—Not at all.

660. It is due to circumstances beyond their control?—Certainly.

661. I should like you, if you can, to compare the total rental and the total public expenditure upon these two estates of which you have special cognisance. First you say that the total rental of the Fishmongers' estate is about 10,000 *l.* You know the whole estate very well?—I do.

662. Out of that rental of 10,000 *l.* per annum what amount did they expend in Ireland for what you call the purposes of their trust?—I saw a return which was made to Lord Derby's Commission, in which they say that they have expended about half of the 10,000 *l.* for these purposes; but neither I nor any man in my neighbourhood knows where that 5,000 *l.* went which they say they expended upon the estate.

663. You

Mr. Sexton—continued.

663. You spoke of certain schools and clergymen; could you sum them up again?—They do not give them, I am sorry to say in minute details. They group things, and therefore we do not know what they mean when they say "improvements," "building farm-houses," and "conducting a scutch mill," between 1,870 *l.* and 2,820 *l.* Now a scutch mill is a money-making thing, instead of a losing thing, for I never heard that they kept a scutch-mill to scutch the flax of the community for nothing.

664. How much to your knowledge did they give in any year, by what you call grants?—They gave 20 *l.* a year for schools to seven schools.

665. That is 140 *l.* a year?—Yes.

666. What else?—They gave I think about 180 *l.* for Roman Catholic clergymen and Presbyterian clergymen; and they gave I think about 80 *l.* a year for two or three dispensaries.

667. That makes a total of 380 *l.* a year?—Yes.

668. Do you know of any more than the 380 *l.* a year?—There are other things that the outside world do not know much about, little donations to the poor, and things of that kind, that never see the light very much; but things were grouped in that return in such a way that no human being could make anything of them.

669. So far as religion and education are concerned you are not aware that the Fishmongers' Company in any year gave more than 380 *l.*?—That is all that came before the public. That is in one neighbourhood.

670. And all that has now ceased?—Yes. There was a time when, for a year or two, a gentleman from London, Mr. Towse, junior, acted as the agent, and he acted with very much judgment and kindness and good taste, and became uncommonly popular with the people, for it was a novelty to have such a man over them. He did something for public purposes outside the estate. He, for example, came into the town of Limavady and opened an intermediate school there; and he got a donation from the Fishmongers' Company of some 10 *l.* to aid that school; and if he had been left among us he would have done more good I have no doubt, for he got 50 *l.* from the company to aid in building a sea-wall that had been blown down in 1884 upon the property of the Irish Society.

671. I should like you to say at what you estimate per annum the total expenditure of the Fishmongers' Company when they did expend anything out of their 10,000 *l.* a year of rent?—As I have said already there are a number of small things, such as blankets and things like that at Christmas, which I could not estimate the value of; but so far as public things that come before the public eye are concerned I have given you a general account of them.

672. How much is the Skinners' Company's rental?—About 13,000 *l.*

673. How much would you say they gave per annum in grants?—They gave for schools a miserable amount. I have a return here in which it is said that they only gave about 40 *l.* altogether for their schools. They gave 50 *l.* a year for a time for an intermediate school in Dungiven, but that died out in the course of two or three years.

674. Is it just to say that the public grants were a miserable fraction of the rental?—They were uncommonly miserable.

675. I suppose the view you take in Ulster is that the companies were subject to the same Trusts as the Irish Society from which they derive?—That is the impression of everybody.

676. And that they ought to have acted in like manner?—And that they ought to have acted in like manner.

677. Did they?—No; the Irish Society are acting very fairly now. The companies have never done justice to the people, but the Irish Society are acting very generously now, compared with what they did some twenty-five years ago, I think.

678. If we could apply to the companies the principles of conduct voluntarily adopted by the Irish Society, the result you think would be satisfactory?—I think the result would be nearly satisfactory because if the Irish Society improve, as they have been doing the last 25 years, we would not wish to see it disendowed and disestablished. I would almost go as far as that.

679. Could you draw into one answer in a few words the various public objects to which the companies are bound by their own action and practice?—I have mentioned already two things that would relieve the public considerably that is the payment of the county cess and the poor rates.

680. But they have not done that hitherto?—The Fishmongers' Company paid a part of those.

681. Then we have had schools, churches, the building of churches, the maintenance of clergymen, the building of schools, the maintenance of teachers, the construction of highways, pensions to certain persons; can you add anything else?—I think intermediate education and technical education.

682. Have the companies ever contributed to those objects?—They have given a little to intermediate education. I have said that the Skinners' Company gave 50 *l.* a year for two or three years for a school in the town of Dungiven; but it died out at last.

683. Have they ever assisted technical education?—No, never.

684. I understand that the special need of technical education lies in the fact that the department is starved by an inadequate grant?—We feel it, and we are very little more benefited now by the Act, than when we had no Act, because we have to send our boys and girls even away to schools at a distance, whereas if we had intermediate schools in towns like Limavady in which I live, they could be educated at home and at a much cheaper rate.

685. Your notion is that the companies should get back the full amount that was levied upon them at the outset by the Irish Society?—I think that everybody ought to be just to companies and to syndicates as well as to single individuals.

686. You go so far as to say that you would allow them a fair profit upon the original money that

Mr. Sexton—continued.

that they gave to the Irish Society?—I would not object.

687. But the balance of the purchase-money, or the rent as the case may be, ought to go to public purposes in Ireland?—I think so; and that was the opinion of Lord Langdale, when he gave his opinion in the case of the Skinners' Company, against the Irish Society. He said the trusts were local as well as the property, and that anything that would be carried out of Ireland as a matter of course, would not be just to Ireland.

688. The trusts are secular as well as religious?—Yes.

689. They refer to prosperity as well to religion?—Yes.

690. Do you concur in the complaint that the Presbyterian Church has been unfairly treated as compared with the Episcopal Church?—I am not come to complain about it, but I am prepared to state the facts. In the city of Derry, for example, they are the majority, and they only get one-fifth of the endowment there; and upon both of the estates I speak of, the Skinners and Fishmongers, the Presbyterian Church has not received so much as the Episcopalian. They did not like to make a return of the Episcopalian along with the Roman Catholic and Presbyterian clergy, because they are afraid it would be noticed, and would engender complaints from those who are receiving the smaller sum.

691. The Episcopalian clergymen receive much more?—Yes.

692. And I suppose the Roman Catholics are still worse treated in comparison with their income and numbers?—They are not any better off than the Presbyterians.

693. Might you not go a little farther than that; what is the total amount you have known to be given to Catholic men?—I know they are put on a par with Presbyterians and Episcopalians in the neighbourhood of Dungiven, and indeed all over the estate; that is so far as schools are concerned. In one case they receive a larger donation for Roman Catholic purposes than the Presbyterian minister receives; that is in the town of Dungiven. There he gets 80 *l.* instead of 20 *l.*; but the Roman Catholics have three times as many as the Presbyterians in numbers.

694. They have about three times the number of people, but they receive about the same as the Presbyterians?—They receive a little more than they do there, but in other places only the same.

695. Taking the Episcopalian grant as the basis, do you think if the Roman Catholics and Presbyterians were put in the same position as that which the Episcopalians now hold that would be satisfactory?—I do not say the Episcopalians receive too much; in fact I would say they are entitled to a larger grant from the trustees than they have got; but I would certainly bring up the two other denominations to be on a par with them.

696. You do not envy the Episcopalians, but you desire equal treatment for yourself?—Just so.

Mr. Sexton—continued.

697. Now let me ask you what have the Skinners' Company done with the bog; I understand you to say they have retained the bog?—Yes.

698. What have they done with it?—They promised through the gentleman who had the carriage of the sale, and who is a gentleman of probity and honour, that the endowments and donations should be continued as usual; but they find now, when it has come to working, instead of sixpence for a permit to cut peat in the bog, they are now increasing that, and asking a shilling; and the people are refusing to pay that, because they think it would be a breach of the engagement, and they are afraid perhaps it would be 5 *s.* next year, or 10 *s.*, or 20 *s.*, before long.

699. The Skinners' Company have sold the estate and hold the bog, and are charging the occupying purchasers for the turf much higher rates than they charged to the tenant formerly?—Yes, although the gentleman who had the carriage of the sale for them, and who was acting, I may say, for both sides, and who is a friend of my own, promised the people, when he was about to make the conveyance to them, that no change would be made in those donations and endowments.

700. Instead of continuing the donations and endowments they have discontinued them, and now they are making fresh exactions as regards the bog?—They cut off the endowments from the minister whose congregation is paying 1,850 *l.* a year into their funds, without a moment's notice; when they paid the last donation they merely said, This is the last.

701. That is in addition to making fresh exactions, as regards the price of the turf; that is, they charge a higher price than formerly, do they not?—They do. I understand this gentleman, who is a friend of my own, but whom I have not seen for a long time, will likely appear before this Committee, and I would be very happy that some gentleman round this table would ask him to explain about that.

702. Who is the gentleman you refer to?—Dr. B. H. Todd of Londonderry; he is a solicitor, a very able man, and a man of probity and honour.

Sir Richard Temple.

703. With regard to your answer to a question put as to a certain allowance being made to the company on the sale of its estate for its legitimate profit on the transaction, suggesting that the balance should be reserved for local charities in Ireland, to which you assented, can you give me any concrete example of how that would work?—There is a civic impost in the first instance upon the freemen of London raising a certain sum. The first was 20,000 *l.* that they raised and the whole of it was about 40,000 *l.* If the representatives of those who paid that money are still to be found, I would allow them to be justly compensated and paid for that sum which they first paid for the purpose of establishing a plantation.

704. Then the balance of the purchase-money you would apply for local charities in Ireland?—Certainly.

705. In

Sir *Richard Temple*—continued.

705. In that case how would you assess the difference between the 20,000 *l.* or 40,000 *l.* in the reign of Charles the First, as compared with the value of money at the present time?—That would not depend upon me; that would be the work of an actuary.

706. You would allow that calculation to be made, would you?—I would allow the basis to be taken of the moneys paid in the first instance for the establishment of the plantation.

707. I mean a calculation of the difference between 20,000 *l.* now as compared with 20,000 *l.* in King Charles the First's time?—I suppose we could not refuse to take it in that way.

708. Do you suppose, after such a calculation as that, there would be much balance remaining?—I think a great deal; because they have been pocketing all along enormous sums, until the time they sold, and they have been paying very little of that back to Ireland, and I suppose that is added to their property.

709. But the enormous sums they pocketed, I presume, represented current income?—They represented rent latterly, and the heavy fines which they received from middlemen to, whom they let their estates for a time. They all let the estates for a time upon a heavy fine. Some of them received as much as 25,000 *l.* for a fine, and they let to middlemen for 1,500 *l.* a year.

710. The fines occurred in the century before last, I presume?—No; in this century. In 1803 the Skinners' Company let their estate to Mr. Ogilby for 41 years, I think, and three lives. They raised 25,000 *l.* for a fine, and 1,500 *l.* a year rent; and then, when they came in after the fall of the lease, they sent out valuators, and they raised what they were getting, 1,600 *l.* a year to 13,000 a year.

711. Was not the rent calculated with regard to the amount of the fine?—I am telling you the amount of the fine, and the amount of the rent.

712. You do not mean that instead of charging, say, 6,000 *l.* a year rent, they charged 1,500 *l.* a year rent and a fine?—Mr. Ogilby paid 25,000 *l.* cash down to the company.

713. I understand that; but what I ask is this, was the rent diminished; was he charged 1,500 *l.* a year rent instead of 3,000 *l.* or 3,600 *l.* a year rent, in consideration of having paid this fine?—I suppose in some cases that was so.

714. If that were so, how can you say that the fine was pocketed; would not the fine be merely a payment in advance upon the rent?—They have got the fine appropriated, and put it to their own uses.

715. Certainly; but the question is, was the amount of rent adjusted in regard to the fine, or was the full rent charged, plus the fine?—I think they insisted upon the full rent; although I am not prepared exactly to say whether the rent was not reduced in consequence of the fine.

716. If the rent was not so reduced, why should the purchaser have been so weak as to pay the fine, unless he got some benefit from it?—Because he knew that he had a power to raise the rent enormously upon the tenants, upon their own improvements, from the hour that he got possession, and recoup himself four or five times over, or perhaps even 10 times over.

717. Then I presume, when he paid the fine, he considered he was paying only the current value of the property?—I think the company did not want to be troubled with the management of it, and they let it off to a man who was on the spot, and let him make the best or most of it; and they thought they would look in when the lease went up, and take advantage of all the improvements that were made in the meantime.

718. What I am asking you is, what the purchaser conceived when he paid the fine and the rent; did he not conceive that he was paying only the current value of the property?—I suppose he made the best bargain that he could. It would not be easy telling how they felt or how he felt. They thought it was of advantage to them to let, and he thought it was of advantage to him to take.

Mr. *Clancy.*

719. You said that the Skinners' Company promised, on the sale of their estates, that certain privileges which their tenants had hitherto enjoyed would be continued under the new ownership?—So I was told by a magistrate who travelled 50 miles to mention the fact to me.

720. Would you mention what those privileges are?—The payment of the donations that they gave to the clergy, and particularly the Presbyterian clergy, because I know more about them than I do about the two other denominations, and also the small permit they had to pay for the privilege of cutting peat in the bog. Both of these have failed; that is, the promise is not carried out and implemented.

721. Whatever these privileges are, do you think, or are you aware, that the promise that they would be maintained under the new ownership induced the contract?—I am almost certain of it.

722. Do you believe that the tenants, in other words, would not have given 17½ years' rent, unless they were assured, or felt assured before, that the privileges would be maintained?—They would not.

723. You consider therefore that the burden, so far as the schools are concerned, was taken up under false pretences?—That is public opinion; but I do not really throw any blame upon the gentleman who was acting for them; I wish to guard myself against that.

724. You consider that the blame lies at the head-quarters in London?—I think so.

725. You were asked about the expenditure of some of these companies, with which you were acquainted; have you ever prepared, or have you with you now, any figures upon the subject?—I could furnish figures. I have seen figures; I have read them not long since, and if I had time to go minutely over them now, which I have not, I think I could furnish the figures. I am not prepared this year to state them now.

726. You said, in addition to the money which the companies originally paid for this land, you would give them interest upon their money?—Yes, I would give them whatever was just.

727. I want

Mr. *Clancy*—continued.

727. I want to know exactly what you would consider just; you said you would be willing to give them a certain interest or profit upon the money which they advanced originally, in addition to giving them their money back?—I do not think that I would give them anything like what the compound interest would amount to now; that would be a large sum.

728. Why should they get any interest?—I would fall in with that suggestion very readily.

729. Have they not been getting interest, and compound interest, all along?—That is my opinion.

730. In the shape of these enormous rents? —Yes.

731. Earned by their tenants' improvements? —I think they could not complain if they got their own money back.

732. It is upon the tenants' improvements?— Yes, in every case.

733. Of course these London companies never effected any improvements themselves upon the tenants' holdings?—Not at all; in fact they did not know anything about the management of the land, and it was left to a local agent, and he mismanaged everything usually.

734. In addition to the rents, they have been getting fines?—Yes.

735. Do not you look upon that as a sort of compound interest also?—I think so; they have got the money in hand.

736. You were asked by Sir Richard Temple whether the rents were not lowered where the fines were paid; is it not the fact that the rents were also raised in many cases?—I think in some cases they were.

737. You were asked why a man should pay a fine for no consideration; was not the lease a consideration?—It was, and particularly when that lease enabled them to raise the rent upon the tenants enormously by it at once.

738. That was at a time when landlords could evict capriciously?—Yes.

739. And raise the rent capriciously?—Yes.

740. You are aware that on the company's estate in Derry, as well as elsewhere in Ireland, tenants have paid more rent than the land justified in order to obtain security of tenure?— They have. There was a time when they had to pay their rents out of weaving in that district.

741. And other employment, I suppose, outside ordinary agricultural industry?—Yes, quite so.

742. You were asked by Mr. Sexton with regard to the bog, and as to making an additional charge upon the tenants after the sale; but did not the company sell some of the bog altogether? —Some of it may have gone in some of the farms.

743. I understand you to state that they sold some of it to outsiders, who were making 4*l.* an acre of it?—That was Lord Waterford; that was upon the Haberdashers' Estate.

Chairman.

744. You mean the Waterford estate?—Yes, the Waterford estate.

Mr. *John Ellis.*

745. As I understand, you wish the Committee to infer that you hold the opinion strongly that the Irish Society and the London companies hold these properties upon trust?—I do; I am of that opinion, and everybody else in my neighbourhood.

746. You have formed that opinion, as I have gathered, mainly for two reasons: in the first place, upon the terms of their charters and other instruments, and secondly, upon their action; is that so?—Yes.

747. Now, not to go this morning into the charters and instruments, of which we shall hear a great deal hereafter, can you give any other illustrations of their action, other than those which you have given to Mr. Sexton, as regards contributions to a number of public objects?— Do you mean with regard to their being trustees?

748. Yes, and that which leads you to think they are trustees?—I am led by the fact that their case has come up frequently before law courts and before commissions; and in no case has the decision been contrary to our impression.

749. But leaving the legal aspect of the case for a moment this morning, can you give us any other illustration of their action that leads you to that conclusion?—From their action we have come to the conclusion that they have either given too much or too little. If they are private landlords, they have acted a generous part; if they are trustees, they have acted a miserable part, a part, in fact, that makes us think they are not just.

750. That is rather a general assertion; can you give any other illustrations, other than those you gave to Mr. Sexton, of their contribution to public objects; can you give any specific instances of their action other than those you have given? —They have contributed for public objects, occasionally for asylums and hospitals, and paying a part of the poor rate, and a part of the county cess, and things of that kind, which no private landlord ever does.

751. Then the general impression of their action upon the minds of those whom you wish to represent here this morning is, that they are trustees?—Yes.

752. In regard to the management of their property, you mentioned circumstances with regard to the planting of some waste land in 1848; can you give us any other illustrations; you considered that a grievance, I think, to the tenants from whom that land was taken?—Yes; the land was taken without compensation; then it was sold to them afterwards, even to the men from whom it was taken.

753. I understand that. That happened in 1848 or thereabouts, I think?—Yes.

754. Can you give us any other illustrations of the same sort of thing since that time?— Nothing occurs to me at this moment.

755. You have no other illustrations of a grievance of that kind, at all events?—No.

756. Now with regard to this matter of sale, which is one of the matters in regard to which this Committee has to inquire, you have mentioned 17½ years; was that 17½ years on judicial rent

Mr. John Ellis—continued.

rent or non judicial?—Some of the tenants have taken the company, I think, into the Land Court, and therefore these must have been under judicial rent; others have not.

757. Do you remember at all the percentage of reduction in these cases?—It was very considerable.

758. Would it be 20 per cent.?—I believe it was.

759. Would it be 15 per cent.?—They raised it when they got it from Mr. Ogilby, and they thought Mr. Ogilby had charged enough, they raised it 12½ per cent., 20 per cent., and 25 per cent.

760. Would you say in the majority of instances the sales were effected on non-judicial rents?—I am not sure whether it would be the majority of cases, but in some cases it was not upon the judicial rent.

761. Are you aware of any cases of sales on so many years' rental in which application by the would-be buyer (the tenant) was pending before the Land Commission, but had not been adjudicated upon?—No, I do not know of any case of that kind.

762. Have there been any disappointments at all in your district as to the delay of the Land Commission in deciding upon the judicial rent?—Yes. But they were not buying; and so they were not so very anxious.

763. I am speaking of cases of buyers and sellers?—I think some of the buyers have been aggrieved.

764. Seeing the reductions on the same land in their immediate district, they thought afterwards that if they had obtained the judicial rent they would have obtained better purchase terms?—Yes, I think so.

765. With regard to some of the questions asked by the honourable Member on my left, Sir Richard Temple, I suppose you would say, with the Bessborough Commission of 1881, that, practically, there has not been freedom of contract in your district, that is, as between buyer and seller; would you say that?—Do you mean as between the companies selling to the tenants now?

766. No; I mean during the last 20 years. Let me put it this way: the companies being in possession, have they had certain legal rights over property, the value of which has been created by the tenants?—From about 1869 down to 1872 there were serious disputes between the Fishmongers' Company and their tenants, from the fact that the Fishmongers' Company was forcing upon them, through their agent, new terms; in fact, a new lease that utterly destroyed the tenant right at the end of the lease.

767. That was in 1872. Coming a little later, has there been any pressure used by the companies in the way of increasing rents, or asking for arrears, or of any kind which would quicken the desires of the occupiers to buy?—In 1873 they had to surrender to the tenants the rights that the tenants claimed; they were not able to force that very bad lease upon their tenants. Then the tenants took the new lease, and consequently they could not disturb that in the meantime, and they sold under that lease; that was the reason they only got 15 or 16 years' purchase, because they were afraid when the lease went up, if they were taken into the Land Court, the rents would be considerably reduced.

768. Then, practically, the tenants achieved a victory in 1873, and have been in a better position since?—They got a smaller number of years' purchase because the company thought that if they had gone into the Land Court the rents would be considerably reduced.

769. You use the expression "willing purchasers"; do you mean in the sense of being willing to give what was asked, or eager to buy the property they had created?—Eager to buy.

770. Eager to buy the property, they had created, do you take it?—No; but they would have been very anxious to buy the property of the landlord; but they were obliged to buy the property they had created along with that, or they could not buy at all.

771. You used the expression that the tenants wanted nothing but what is fair; do you mean by that that they object to being rented on the value they have created, that they object to pay rent on their own improvements?—They objected all along, but they could not defend themselves.

772. But they are perfectly willing to pay for that which they believe belongs to somebody else; is that so?—They are willing to buy because they cannot buy at a lower rate.

Mr. Lea.

773. I think Sir Richard Temple asked you a question about the balance of the purchase money. The question, I think, was whether it would be applicable to local charities in Ireland?—Yes.

774. I presume by "local" charities you do not confine it to the county of Derry if Parliament thought just; you might extend it to the whole plantation districts, the six counties?—I would be disposed to say so. I think the bulk of the money ought to come into the county of Derry, but I would not confine it to it, certainly.

Chairman.

775. I only wish to ask a couple of questions; the first question is this: are the purchasing tenants, in consequence of the more advantageous position, in which they have been placed by the purchase, able to make up in any way for those subscriptions that have been withdrawn by the company?—They are greatly hampered at the present time from that fact.

776. From what fact?—That they have lost the donations; they have to make them up out of their own pocket now.

777. My point is that their own pocket is fuller now, because their purchase annuity is less than the rent that they were paying?—Rather less.

778. Is it not so much less that they may be expected to make good the deficiency caused by the withdrawal of the company's subscriptions?—No.

779. You are clear upon that?—Yes.

780. Then one question with regard to the local agents; you spoke of the local agents employed by the companies to carry on their affairs; do

Chairman—continued.

do you consider that the agents have been left with a tolerably freehand?—We had very few that were popular men.

781. That is another matter; but did the agents represent that they were obliged to refer to head-quarters for instruction as to this point or that?—Yes; and it was not very easy for the tenants to get at head-quarters. They found that the agent was not a good medium of communication with head-quarters; for it has been ascertained by facts from history that if they stated their case to the local agent, sometimes he never sent forward the memorial to head-quarters at all. If they believed that was the case, and took the liberty of sending their memorial to head-quarters, immediately at head-quarters they inquired of the local agent, "What about this?" and he, finding that he was superseded, or rather that they had got over his head and had not consulted him before the application, almost invariably reported against them, and said they were troublesome people.

782. Am I to understand that the tenants were in the hands of the agents, and that the companies were content to see through the eyes of their agents?—I think so, invariably.

783. When the tenants, as you have just described, sent memorials to head-quarters, the companies referred them back to the agents?—Yes.

784. And the agent, in some cases, punished them for having tried to get over his head?—Almost invariably. They were afraid, in fact, to make any application whatever at last. As regards this company, the Fishmongers, they were very much aggrieved after 1820. The tenants sent a deputation of three individuals to head-quarters in London here, and they were so aggrieved because they took the liberty of coming and telling their own tale before the Fishmongers' Court here in London, that these three men were ejected and cast out of their place and off the estate altogether; so that the tenants were afraid to make any application whatever.

Mr. *Clancy*.

785. Do you know anything about the Salters' Estate?—I do not know much of it.

786. Do you know, with regard to the estates of which you have given evidence, of any threats being used by the companies in order to induce their tenants to buy?—I think there are not so much threats as inducements, the statement being made that things would be just as well as they were.

787. You have given us evidence about that already?—Yes; the case I have referred to already, with regard to the bog, and with regard to the endowments not being taken away.

Mr. *Sexton*.

788. It has been suggested to you that you might have these trusts made effectual, by resort to courts of law. I wish to ask you whether you adopt the view that as these trusts, or alleged trusts, sprang out of Imperial action, by Royal Charter, and so, on the one hand, with a number of wealthy corporations, and on other hand, a great community of hundreds of thousands of persons, you would consider it the duty of the Legislature to intervene and secure the execution of these trusts?—I think so; and that would relieve the people considerably; because they do not want to resort to courts of law, if they can get justice in any other way.

Mr. *Clancy*.

789. You said you expected that once they would have money enough to contest the question in the courts; how can you expect anything of that kind in the case of the tenantry of the Drapers' Company, who are so poor?—I would expect the tenantry under all the companies, and, perhaps, even beyond the companies, would contribute the money to bring forward a test case and have the question decided once for all.

790. You are not clear as to what the expense would be?—No, I am not; and if other people had clear views of what the expense would be, the law matter might have been taken up before now.

Sir *Richard Temple*.

791. Did it never occur to you to take counsel's opinion upon your case; that would not be very expensive, would it?—I have no doubt counsel have been consulted.

Mr. *Clancy*.

792. Of course counsel's opinion would not have determined anything?—No, it would not.

The Reverend THOMAS JORDAN, D.D., sworn; and Examined.

Mr. *Lea*.

793. You are the Rector of Magherafelt?—Yes.

794. And Prebendary of Armagh Cathedral?—Yes, I am one of the prebendaries.

795. How many years have you lived at Magherafelt?—About 11.

796. What is the chief estate that you have had to do with?—The Salters' Company.

797. Have they done much for your church?—They have done a great deal indeed for the church. The church is a very fine edifice indeed. It was built about 45 years ago, and I understand that they were very liberal towards the building of it, and until they left us, they

Mr. *Lea*—continued.

were very liberal in maintaining it, and they still give, for the churches on their estates, a yearly contribution to the different churches of 345 *l.*

798. Is that continued now?—It is; it is a yearly vote. We should be glad to have some guarantee for the future; but it is a yearly vote, I understand. It is continued.

799. What did they give for the building of the church?—I really could not say; but I think it must have been a very considerable sum, because it is a very noble church.

800. What is your population on the Salters' Estate?—The entire population upon the Salters' Estate is something over 10,000. The Church

discontinued, at all events?

egard to National schools, chools have you?—I have

Mr. Lea—continued.

National schools are discontinued according to the principle that I ventured to mention where the teacher is changed. These persons called upon me as a friend of education, and to represent their case, if I could help them.

825. Are there other local charities?—Would you allow me to explain that when a grant is discontinued to a National school it causes a direct and an indirect loss also; because the Commissioners of National Education pay one moiety of the result fees absolutely, and the second moiety is contingent on the local contribution. The withdrawal of the local contribution will no doubt lead to the loss of the second moiety of the result fees in some cases.

Mr. Sexton.

826. I should like to understand that quite clearly. Suppose the first moiety is 20 *l.*, and suppose the local contribution, instead of being 20 *l.* reaches only 15 *l.*, then the other moiety is only 15 *l.*, and you lose double the amount withdrawn?—I think in that case it would be all paid, because the 20 *l.* in your case, earned as the result fees, would be divided into 10 *l.* and 10 *l.*

827. Take it as 10 *l.* if you like; I am speaking of the moiety payable immediately upon the result of the examination. Take that as 20 *l.*; supposing the local contribution which had been 20 *l.* is lowered to 15 *l.* by reason of the withdrawal of 5 *l.*, then the second moiety from the Government is 15 *l.* instead of 20 *l.*?—The first moiety is paid absolutely; they would only pay the second moiety up to the amount of the local contribution; in the case you put 15 *l.* would be paid.

Mr. Lea.

828. Have you any other information with regard to the schools which you wish to give us?—As a friend of my neighbours there, I feel it very hard, as they have added so very materially to the value of the estate, that they should suffer in the matter of intermediate education, and still harder upon my poorer neighbours, that they should suffer in this matter of the elementary National schools.

829. Now, I understand, you have done with the schools. Are there any other charities, in the shape of dispensaries or anything of that sort, where the grants have been discontinued?—As to dispensaries, I really do not know with regard to them; but there are small local charities, for instance, there is a small grant given to me to help a Sunday school; and that has been continued. There was a small grant given to me for a winter clothing fund, that has been discontinued. We always were profited by even a small contribution in that way, because it was made into a nucleus for a collection for the purpose.

830. What was understood by the purchasers on the Salters' estate when they bought their holdings?—The purchasers in many cases made inquiries from the people who were accredited by the Salters' Company, as to the continuance of the grant to churches and schools, and in several cases which I know of they completed their purchase on being satisfied on that point.

831. That the grants would be continued?—Yes.

832. Who told you that?—In 1887 there was a correspondence in the London "Times" upon the subject, and when this correspondence was going on, three of my neighbours, who are farmers, called upon me, and they stated that that was what they understood; that the grants would be continued to the churches and the schools, and that they completed their purchase on that understanding.

833. Have they made declarations to that effect?—The three called upon me, and I took down what they said. Each of their statements ends with the words, "I have no objection to make an affidavit to the above effect at any time I am called on to do so;" "signed in my presence, *Thomas Jordan*, Magherafelt Rectory, 25th August 1887."

834. That is, they understood they had a promise from the company that if the estate was bought by the tenants those grants would be continued?—Yes.

Mr. Sexton.

835. Had you not better read the statement made before you?—"James Ferguson; Townland of Ballinagarve, about 18 Irish acres. When about to purchase my farm from the Salters' Company, I called with Dr. Todd, who was carrying out the sale, and in conversing with him I said I would sign the agreement of purchase if I was satisfied that the grants to the sustentation fund of the church, and the grants to the schools were continued, and if I were satisfied as to what I wished about the bog. Dr. Todd said he could not answer these questions, but that he would have an answer on that day week."

Chairman.

836. Dr. Todd was the agent of the Salters' Company, was he?—He was their solicitor; that is, he was acting as between the purchaser and the Salters' Company as solicitor. "In pursuance of this I called on that day week, and he said here was a letter from the company's clerk, and he satisfied me about the bog, and said that the grants to the church and to the schools would be continued so long as we paid rent. I have no objection to make an affidavit to the above effect at any time I am called on to do so.—*James Ferguson.*" The statement signed by Alexander Bennett, holding 45 acres, is in the same spirit and in the same tenour. The third one, signed by James Bennett, holding 20 Irish acres, is in the same spirit, and each ends with the words, "I have no objection to make an affidavit to the above effect at any time I am called on to do so."

837. What do you understand by the expression "so long as we paid rent"?—What I understood was that it meant so long as half-yearly payments for their purchase annuity went on.

838. That they meant purchase annuity, and not rent?—Yes.

839. Dr.

Mr. Lea.

639. Dr. Todd is referred to there; was there a promise from any other gentleman, so far as you know?—About the same time when the correspondence in the London "Times" was going on, Mr. William Ash Hanson, of Ballyronan House, one of the county magistrates, put his letter into the London "Times," saying he bought two farms, having been satisfied by the agent of the company, and also by the solicitor, that the grants would be continued.

640. Who do you mean by the agent of the company?—Sir Henry Cartwright, then Mr. Cartwright.

641. The present Sir Henry Cartwright?—Yes.

642. He was the authorised agent of the company?—Yes.

643. But the Salters' Company have discontinued many grants despite of that?—Yes, they have, to the schools. Archdeacon Hamilton had a document which he referred to in his letter, signed by six purchasers who were school teachers, of the same tenour and spirit as those statements made in my presence.

Chairman.

644. You speak of his letter; was that referred to in the evidence given by Archdeacon Hamilton last year before this Committee?—I do not know; but I refreshed my memory by looking into his letter which appeared in the London "Times" about that date; and it states that six purchasers and school teachers signed a statement of that sort. The date of his letter in the London "Times" is September the 6th, 1887. Archdeacon Hamilton says: "I have now before me a document signed by six purchasers and school teachers, in which they say they hereby assert, and are prepared to declare upon oath, that we have had on different occasions most emphatic promises from Dr. Todd and Mr. Cartwright, that the educational grants which we had hitherto been receiving would be continued, and on these conditions, both expressed and understood, many of the tenants completed their purchase." That is a quotation from the Archdeacon's letter.

645. That is probably the letter referred to by Archdeacon Hamilton in his answer to Question 658. He was there asked by Mr. Lea whether he remembered "that when the master of the Salters' Company was informed of the view that the public took of his liabilities, he used in reply, the words that it was a 'novel view,'" and the Archdeacon said "Yes," and I replied to that by answering that others had taken that view. My letter is in existence, I think, in the columns of "The Times." I suppose that is the letter?—I think that would be what he refers to.

Mr. Lea.

646. From your knowledge of the feeling in the district should you think there was an expectation of the continuance of the grants when the tenants purchased their holdings?—I would think so.

647. Do you know that that is the feeling?—I know it is the feeling in the mind of those persons who have said so, and it certainly was the feeling in my own mind.

Mr. Lea—continued.

648. Have you anything else to say with regard to the Salters' estate?—The improvements I know on the Salters' estate were made by the tenants, and, as I said before, the people feel very strongly their loss with regard to these educational grants.

649. With regard to the Drapers' Company, do you know any of their parishes?—Yes. I was rector of the parish of Arboe for seven years, and some of the town lands of the Drapers' Company are in that parish. I had a grant from the Drapers' Company of 10 *l.* for the school at that time, which has been withdrawn; and there was a grant after the Church Act passed to the church funds of 15 *l.*, which has ceased also. So that there is a loss there to that parish which I know very well (and indeed there cannot be a poorer place at all) of 25 *l.* a year in grants.

650. Is that a very poor parish?—It is extremely poor; there cannot be a poorer place at all.

651. About the same time that the Drapers' Company withdrew their grant from the poorest parish you know this company gave 60,000 *l.* to the People's Palace in the east of London?—They have been very generous to the east of London.

652. Were they very generous to the poor parish of Arboe?—They have withdrawn 25 *l.* from it.

653. Have there been any other grants withdrawn on the Drapers' estate that you know of?—In Lissan parish they have withdrawn 10 *l.* from the school, and there was 5 *l.* allowed for, I think, a reader of the Holy Scriptures; that is 15 *l.* Those two grants have been withdrawn.

654. Then with regard to Cookstown, have any grants been withdrawn?—In the parish of Cookstown there was a grant by the Drapers' Company of 25 *l.* to their church, and that, I understand, is reduced to 15 *l.* There was a grant of 10 *l.* to the school at Cookstown, which has been reduced to 5 *l.*

655. Then with regard to Tamlaght?—There was a grant there by the Drapers' Company of 16 *l.*, which I understand has been discontinued. The Drapers' Company's grants to churches up to 1884 have been 140 *l.* a year, and since 1884 they have been reduced to 100 *l.* a year.

656. Is that because they have sold, or are selling, their estate?—Well, I do not know indeed what the reason of it is, but I presume it is because they look forward to withdrawing from the estate.

657. And getting away with all the money they can?—Well, that may be.

658. What is the prevailing notion in the district that you know with regard to the property in the trusts?—That it was impressed with trusts in the minds of the people is a sure truism; that is the universal idea.

659. What do the people think of their withdrawing in this way?—Their feeling is very strong against the way in which they have been treated.

660. Their feeling of confidence in the trust rested on the charters and other things they had heard

Mr. *Lea*—continued.

heard of?—The people generally have heard of the charters; they have heard of them in publications and in speeches of various sorts, in which reference has been made to these documents, to the charter of James I., and to the correspondence of James with the Lord Lieutenant of Ireland.

661. That is confirmed by the large grants they have given to your churches in times past?—Yes.

662. The clergy of the Presbyterian Church who have been witnesses here have represented that the value of the estate has been made by the occupiers' improvements: do you, as a clergyman of the Episcopal Church of Ireland, agree with the opinion that the occupiers' improvements have formed the increase of the property?—I think so. The Salters' Company no doubt had agents who were good men of business, and under the skill of those men as directors, the estate was improved; but I think the increased value, the increment of value of the estate, in a very great measure is owing to the tenants themselves.

663. That is to say the money of the company was spent on churches and other objects, and not in improving the tenants' holdings?—The Salters' Company were very good as to public buildings, I think, and as to plantings and things of that sort; but, as to farms and as to agricultural holdings, my observation was that the increment of value on those was in a great measure owing to the farmer himself.

664. Is there a strong feeling in the district about it?—Yes, there is a very strong feeling indeed. I wanted just now to refer, when Mr. Lea asked me about the Salters' Company having given contributions to building churches, to a pamphlet that I got some days ago from a gentleman in Belfast, where it is stated, on page 33, that the Salters' Company's own return for religious and charitable objects in the year 1879–80 was 1,983 *l.*

665. I only asked you with regard to the feeling of the district; you say that there is a feeling of very strong indignation?—There is a feeling of very strong indignation that such a thing should have been done.

Mr. *Cleary*.

666. You have referred to some correspondence in the London "Times"?—Yes.

667. What was that correspondence about?—The grants to churches and schools being continued.

668. Was it denied that certain promises were made beforehand; was there a controversy on the subject?—Yes, there was a controversy on the subject.

669. Could you get that correspondence for us?—I could get some copies of the London "Times" in which some of the letters are.

Chairman.

670. Could you give us the date?—Yes; I have some of the dates here, and I can give them; and I could also give some of the copies of "The Times" in which the letters appeared. The letter of Mr. William Ash Gunning, of

Chairman—continued.

Ballyronan House, Magherafelt, appeared in "The Times" of the 31st of August 1887; the letter of Archdeacon Hamilton, which has been referred to already, appeared in "The Times" on 6th September 1887.

671. It was in fact in the autumn of 1887 that the correspondence went on?—It was.

Mr. *Cleary*.

672. Have you said, or do you now say, that the promises made to the tenants when they were about to purchase these holdings, that those grants would be continued in aid of churches and schools, induced the contract?—In certain instances it did.

673. In the great majority of instances?—I cannot say from knowledge in the great majority of cases. As regards the impression on my own mind, I may say the clergy had several conferences upon the subject, and often at my house the clergy of the Church of Ireland put their views forward to the company through the agent of the company; and in the interviews that I had from time to time with the agent of the company upon the subject of the continuance of the grants, there was always a favourable impression left on my mind with regard to the great probability of their being continued.

674. In fact you were under the distinct impression that they would be continued?—The impression always was that there was a very great probability of that being so.

675. Who were the persons, do you say, who made those promises?—The clergy of the Church of Ireland always acted through Sir Henry Cartwright, the agent; and as regards anything that was agreed upon on the subject, I would call upon him and speak over the matter with him.

676. I thought you said Dr. Todd also had made those promises?—So I was informed by those three neighbours of mine; but I never had any conversation on the subject with Dr. Todd myself.

677. Did the companies or the agents of the Salters' Company, either Dr. Todd or Sir Henry Cartwright, or anybody else, in addition to inducements, hold out any threats to induce the tenants to purchase?—I am not aware of any.

678. Did you ever hear of any letter from Dr. Todd, threatening proceedings in the name of the company for the recovery of rents and arrears of rent against unwilling purchasers?—I really could not say with regard to that. My course in the whole matter was to confine myself as much as I possibly could to the matter of grants to churches and schools.

679. Did you ever see that notice before (*handing a paper to the Witness*). Will you read what it purports to be—the last paragraph, and by whom it was signed?—I am not aware of having seen it before; I may have; I could not swear that I have not. I have no distinct impression of my attention having been called before to it, but I may have seen it, very possibly.

680. Will you explain what that document is to the Committee?—"Notice. The Salters' Company

Mr. *Clancy*—continued.

Company is now prepared to sell to the general public several farms which the tenants have refused to purchase"——

881. You need not read the whole of it; it is a notice to the tenants, is it not, for the purchase of their holdings?—Yes.

882. By whom is it signed?—"H. B. Cartwright, Agent."

883. It is dated from the Manor House?—It is dated, Manor Office, 2nd February 1886.

884. Will you now read the last paragraph?—"After to-morrow the company will make no allowances, but will insist upon immediate payment of all arrears of rent and interest due."

885. If you were in the position of a tenant who owed arrears of rent, and were not willing to purchase, would you look upon it as a threat to induce you to purchase?—I think so.

886. What would be the consequence, broadly speaking, of withdrawing all these grants to charities and churches, such as the Salters' Company, as I understand, have practically done?—It would be most hurtful to the churches and schools.

887. Do you think that the whole educational system of that district would break down?—It certainly would be greatly marred by it.

888. Now, coming to the Rainey school, what compensation do you say they have given, or have they given anything to the support of the school; you spoke of a sum of 66 *l.*?—Yes.

889. Is that to be given to the Rainey school?—Yes, it is to be given as a grant in future; and that will be in lieu of the yearly grant of 150 *l.* formerly given.

890. Are you aware that as against that, some years ago the Salters' Company got a farm that belonged to the school when they got the management of the school?—I have heard people at Magherafelt make some reference to that farm, but the history of it I really do not know. I gave my information from the monumental stone which is in the school-house: "This house was re-built by the Salters' Company in 1864."

891. We will get that information from some person who knows about it. The Salters' Company seems to have acted a particularly shabby part towards the head master of the Rainey school; have you heard how they treated him?—Yes; he has been there a very long time.

892. He came over there, did he not, as their servant?—He came over there upon the strong recommendation of the Salters' Company, but, as regards the technical ground, he was appointed by the Primate of Armagh.

893. But he was practically their servant, was he not?—Yes.

894. He was the servant of the company?—I think that was so indeed.

895. They brought the school, they were the managers of the school, were they not?—Yes.

896. He was their servant, and now, in his old age, he is shut on to a new governing body, which, I understand, has not money enough to pay him?—A scheme for the future management of the school has been formulated by the Education Commissioners, and will probably come into effect in due course, and, of course, the chief master and the second master will come under the new scheme.

Mr. *Clancy*—continued.

897. I thought I understood you to say that you do not know where the funds are to come from?—I say so still. I was just going to add on to my answer that we do not know how we will carry on the school, except it be handed over to be put under the new educational scheme, free of debt and free from incumbrances.

898. You spoke of some withdrawals of grants by the Drapers' Company; have you heard of any recent threats of withdrawals of further grants in addition to those you have mentioned?—I have not.

Mr. *Sexton.*

899. What was the amount of the Salters' Company's rent?—Indeed, I do not know.

900. Have you no idea?—I think I heard it stated at 16,000 *l.*

901. Have they sold the whole estate?—I think it is all sold, with the exception of, perhaps, some very small fragment.

902. Do you agree with those witnesses who say that the practice was periodically to value the tenants' improvements, and to charge a rack-rent upon the value of the improvements?—I agree with them in this way; that on the farms being valued again, there was usually a rise of rent; I believe that to be so.

903. Because those improvements had been effected since the last valuation?—Yes. The improvements were no doubt under the management of the agent; he gave his intelligence and his guidance; but the improvements were made in a very great measure by the occupiers themselves.

904. Substantially, would you say that the increased value of the land, since the time of the original grants (apart from the value by social development), the increased value due to the changes in the soil itself, was due to the tenants?—I would say, as I have ventured to say already, that in a very great measure the increment of value is due to the occupiers.

905. Would you say substantially?—Yes.

906. Then the rents from time to time were so raised as to represent the value of those improvements?—Yes, that would be so.

907. And then the purchase-money was calculated upon those rents?—Yes, I suppose so.

908. Then do you agree, that the companies, where they take away this purchase-money so calculated, take away from Ireland, not only the capital value of the original grant, but also the capital value of all the labour of the tenants for the generations in the meantime in the permanent improvement of the soil?—I think, in substance, that is so, and that is the reason of our strong moral feeling against such a very large sum of money being carried away from the country.

909. Does that appear to you to deserve the name of public plunder?—Well, I would not express it in that way; I said that it caused a feeling of moral indignation in us.

910. Without taking so brief a phrase as "public plunder," would you say that it amounts to the appropriation of the value of property created by others?—Well, I do not understand agriculture very well; but there is no doubt, as I said

Mr. *Sexton*—continued.

I said before the improvements, I hold, were mainly made by the occupiers.

911. You said that the Salters' Company's rents were about 16,000 *l.*, I think?—I could not really say accurately, but my impression is that is what I have heard.

912. I only want an approximation?—Quite so.

913. What do you say, from your knowledge, was the annual amount expended by the Salters' Company under the trusts, which, as you say, were impressed upon the property?—I could add up what I know, if you wish.

914. Could you give a general approximate idea; was it 1,000 *l.* out of the 16,000 *l.*?—I really do not know how much was given to the Presbyterian body, nor do I know how much was given to the Roman Catholic body.

915. Take your own body, the Episcopalian body; how much do you get per annum on that estate?—We are getting at present 245 *l.* for our churches as a yearly vote, and 43 *l.* is paid to two of my school teachers, and there is 6 *l.* paid to the Protestant Orphan Society, and there is 6 *l.* paid for the working of the Sunday school.

916. About what was the total when it was at the maximum for your ecclesiastical body upon the estate?—I could make it out after a little calculation.

917. I only want a general estimate?—Generally I would say, to our ecclesiastical body, to our churches and our schools, there would be 245 *l.* first, and then there would be 45 *l.*; that would be, say, nearly 300 *l.*; and then there would be grants to other schools. I would say it would not exceed 800 *l.* to the Church of Ireland, and to our churches and schools on the estate.

918. You are one third of the whole population; and you are the body who are best treated by the companies; is that not so; compared with the other bodies you receive the most, do you not?—I suppose that would be so.

919. Some of your answers suggested a contrast between the 60,000 *l.* given to the East End of London by the Drapers' Company and the treatment of the parish of Arboe, where they have starved out education; what will be the effect of that conduct upon the school at Arboe; is it a National school?—Yes.

920. Do you know it?—Yes.

921. How many children attend there?—I really do not know; but I was manager of that school when I was rector there, and my friends were very kind to me when I was there. I have not been able to go to them since; so that I do not know what the number would be, but it must have, at all events, 30 children, or it would not have the payment from the National School Commissioners of Ireland.

922. What was about the total income of the teacher, including the 25 *l.* a year from the Drapers' Company?—There was a good master when I was there, and I suppose it would be about 70 *l.*, perhaps.

923. Taking into account the contingent loss upon the second moiety of the result fees as due to the withdrawal of the 25 *l.*, what would his income, which was 70 *l.*, come to now?—I do not know who is the teacher now.

Mr. *Sexton*—continued.

924. No matter who he is; what would his income come to?—Besides, it was only a grant to a school there of 10 *l.*, and, of course, the effect of that would depend upon the amount of the results he had earned, and he might lose a moiety of his results fees from the loss of that grant.

925. It brings him down to 50 *l.* from 70 *l.*, does it not?—I would not think it would have so great an effect as that.

926. Does not the loss of 10 *l.* of local aid carry with it probably the loss of 10 *l.* contingent result fees?—In that way it would.

927. I understand you complain of the very meagre provision for intermediate education generally in Ireland?—Yes, I do; I think that is a very great loss indeed; and I think my neighbours there have a very great and strong and well-grounded complaint with regard to that.

928. This Rainey School was one of the few good intermediate schools that you had?—It was the only intermediate school we had.

929. The company gave you 180 *l.* a year?—They gave us 180 *l.* annually; they were very helpful with regard to it till they went away.

930. Now you get 66 *l.*, as I understand?—We are to have it when we get under the new scheme; we have not got it yet.

931. That is the most you will get?—Yes; unless they see their way to help us more with regard to it.

932. Is it true that they have charged even this 66 *l.* with a pension for the teachers; we have been told they intended to charge this 66 *l.* with the pension of Mr. Hincmid, the teacher?—I think that is not the case; I did not hear anything of that at all.

933. Unless the income is charged with the pension, how is this gentleman, whom they have brought over to Ireland, to be provided for when he retires?—I think they may take a more generous view of a very deserving case.

934. Do you find in the facts any presumption to lead you to expect that?—I have applied to them in the strongest way I could.

935. I understand that certain grants have been continued after the sale of the estate?—It is so.

936. Does that appear to you to be significant as conveying a recognition by the companies of the trusts impressed upon the property when they held it?—I think it does go to show that.

937. I mean this: an ordinary landed proprietor, who held his property subject to no trust, if he sold his estate, would not continue to make grants; but the companies do continue?—That is so.

938. I understand you also to say that people bought their holdings on being satisfied that the grants would be continued after the purchase?—Yes.

939. Was that belief general?—I would not like to say that it was general; but it was so in those cases that I have pointed out, and the impression left upon my mind, as I have said to the gentleman upon my right, in my interviews, which were many, with the agent, was always a favourable one with regard to the great probability of the continuance of the grants.

940. Did

Mr. Sexton—continued.

940. Did not the occurrence of this correspondence, and the giving of these pledges become a matter of public knowledge at the time, and did not it influence the transactions of sale and purchase on these estates?—I presume it would.

941. Do you think that unless the tenants had believed that the old system would have been followed in regard to the public trust, they would have been so ready to buy and conclude bargains with the companies?—Those purchasers to whom I referred have stated that they certainly held that view; and those others than Archdeacon Hamilton has referred to, and Mr. Chambers, one of the magistrates of the county, held that view; and, as I said myself, my own view was that also. But in the trouble that we had to go through in this whole matter, I confined myself as rigorously as possible to churches and to schools, and I tried to have as little to do with the agricultural matters and troubles as possible.

942. To come to the conclusion, was there not a general knowledge, at the time of these pledges, that the grants would not be withdrawn in the event of the purchase; was not that general knowledge?—That notion was very much before people's minds, no doubt.

Mr. Clancy.

943. How much did the Salters' Company get for their estate?—The popular voice says 240,000 *l.*

944. Have you calculated the capital value of what they have left?—No, I have not.

945. Could you let us have that estimate before you go?—Yes, I will.

Mr. Lea.

946. Mr. Clancy referred to the correspondence in "The Times" just now; you wrote to "The Times," did you not?—Yes.

947. In your letter you stated that a deputation was intended to be sent by the Diocesan Councils of Armagh and Derry?—Yes.

948. Was that deputation sent?—It was sent by the two councils.

949. Did the Salters' Company receive them?—No, they did not; they informed us they were not able to receive us.

950. They would not see them?—They informed us so. The Primate, who is the head of the Church of Ireland, and the Moderator of the General Assembly, were members of the deputation, and some very influential laity.

951. The Duke of Abercorn was one, I think?—The Duke of Abercorn was one.

952. Did you wind up your letter to "The Times" with this: that you hoped that the "matter will be reconsidered, and that we will be saved from our churches and schools in many cases being left decaying monuments of a great London company so long and so generously known in this part of Ulster"?—Those are my words.

953. That is your view of what will result?—Yes.

Mr. Clancy.

954. You were a witness, I think, at the recent investigation before the Privy Council with regard to the scheme for the government of Rainey School?—Yes.

955. Did Lord Ashbourne, in your hearing on that occasion, express any opinion upon the subject of the treatment by the company of Mr. Kincaid, and of the treatment generally of the schools under their control?—Yes.

956. Would it be true to say that Lord Ashbourne expressed a very hostile opinion, hostile, I mean, to the company?—Lord Ashbourne was chairman of the Privy Council that day, and he certainly expressed himself very strongly with regard to the large sum of money that was being carried away for the sale of this estate, and so little being done for the school.

957. And as to the disastrous effects of taking away all this money on the charities and schools in the district?—His Lordship was speaking with regard to this particular school, the Rainey School.

958. And also as to the treatment by the company of Mr. Kincaid, the head master?—Yes; his Lordship seemed to think that something generous ought to have been done for him.

959. He seemed to think that they ought to provide for him?—Yes.

960. And that they ought to provide for the school?—Yes.

Chairman.

961. Were you present when Lord Ashbourne made these remarks?—Yes; I was present on behalf of the Rainey School.

962. Is there any printed report of them?—It appeared in the Dublin newspapers the next morning, and in the Belfast newspapers, I think.

Thursday, 12th June 1890.

MEMBERS PRESENT:

Mr. Cleary.	Mr. Lawson.
Lord Elcho.	Mr. Lea.
Sir John Ellis.	Sir William Marriott.
Mr. John Ellis.	Sir John Mowbray.
Mr. T. M. Healy.	Mr. Sexton.
Colonel Laurie.	Sir Richard Temple.

THE RIGHT HONOURABLE JOHN MORLEY, IN THE CHAIR.

Mr. MURROUGH O'BRIEN, sworn; and Examined.

Chairman.

963. You are in the office of the Land Commission in Dublin?—I am.

964. What is the exact position which you hold in that department?—I am their Inspector under the Land Purchase Acts.

965. Under the Land Purchase Act of 1885?—Yes.

966. You had also been inspector in regard of the operation of the purchase clauses of the Act of 1881?—Yes.

967. And before then had you experience of purchase transactions?—Since 1870 I had been engaged in similar work for the Church Commission down to the year 1881; after that under the Irish Land Commission; and since 1885 under the Purchase Commission.

968. Then your experience covers a considerable number of years?—About twenty years.

969. Can you inform us what amount of land the London companies have sold under the Purchase Act of 1885?—Under the Purchase Act of 1885, four companies only have sold their estates. They have not sold the whole, but they are in process of sale. The Salters' Company, the Fishmongers' Company, the Skinners' Company, and the Drapers' Company have all sold, or are selling.

Mr. T. M. Healy.

970. Do you mean under the Ashbourne Act? All under the Act of 1885.

Chairman.

971. Can you tell us the number of holdings that have been dealt with by those transactions?—2,196 holdings have been sold.

972. What has been the amount of money?—The price advanced by the Land Commission in respect of those holdings is 578,303 *l.* That is the capital sum advanced.

973. Do you mean by that, that the whole of that 578,303 *l.* has been actually paid, or that it has been sanctioned?—It has been paid.

974. Has all been paid that has been sanctioned?—In addition to the amount paid, there are 173 cases where loans have been sanctioned on the Fishmongers', Skinners', and Drapers' estates.

975. That is to say, 173 over and above the 2,196?—Yes.

976. What is the amount?—The amount of purchase money sanctioned in these cases is 37,860 *l.* Perhaps I had better give you the details of the sales on each company's estate. The Salters' Company have sold 990 holdings, obtaining an advance of 240,598 *l.* The Fishmongers' Company have sold 310 holdings, receiving 120,465 *l.* The Skinners' Company have sold 565 holdings, receiving 132,125 *l.* The Drapers' Company have sold 331 holdings, receiving 85,116 *l.*

Mr. Sexton.

977. Would you subdivide the amounts sanctioned between the four companies in addition to the amounts paid?—The amounts sanctioned and not paid, are four holdings on the Fishmongers' Company's estate, amounting to 884 *l.*; 75 holdings on the Skinners' Company's estate, amounting to 13,140 *l.*; and 94 holdings on the Drapers' Company's estate, amounting to 23,836. On the Salters' Company's estate there are no cases sanctioned and not paid.

Chairman.

978. That is in effect the return which the Committee desired the Land Commissioner to hand in?—Yes.

979. How much property do you estimate is now left in the hands of the London Companies, deducting the properties dealt with by these transactions?—I am only able to form a very rough estimate by taking the rateable value of the property held by these companies. The Skinners' and Drapers' having only partially sold, I am unable to say how much remains to be sold of those estates; but the following companies appear to hold property in Londonderry, and have not yet sold. The estate known as the Ironmongers' Estate, has been recently divided among the Corporation of London, the Carpenters',

Chairman—continued.

ters', the Scriveners', the Barbers', and the Brewers' Companies. They have given notice of sale.

980. When you say that the estate has been divided, what do you mean by that?—These companies were associated with the Ironmongers, and up to the present time the Ironmongers have been known as the owners of the estate; but within recent years a division has been made giving each company their proportion of those estates. A number of the minor companies are associated with the great companies in the original grants.

Mr. T. M. Healy.

981. Was that partition done by deed, or how how was it done?—The partition was done by deed, I believe, within the last five or six years.

982. They could not, I apprehend, divide more than the cash accruing out of the rents; they could not divide the land?—I apprehend that they have divided the land, because each of these companies has lodged a preliminary statement of their title with a view of carrying out sales to the tenants. I take the whole lot in bulk, and their notices give us a number of 403 tenants paying 5,476*l*. Besides the Ironmongers, the Mercers' hold an estate in the county Derry, which is rated at 11,740*l*. They have given no notice of sale.

Chairman.

983. How many tenants have they?—I have no information as to the tenants on the Mercers' estate. The Irish Society hold estates which are rated at 11,386*l*.

984. Are those agricultural estates, or do they include the town property in Londonderry and Coleraine?—The rating would extend to all, but I do not know to what extent the rating discloses their actual property; I do not think it is a reliable figure. The Vintners' Company have an estate which is rated at 6,457*l*; I believe a portion of that has already been sold, but not under the Act of 1885.

985. Under what Act has it been sold; under the clauses of the Act of 1881?—Under previous Acts, or privately.

Mr. Sexton.

986. You have not stated whether the Irish Society have given notice of sale or not?—They have given no notice of sale. I reckon roughly that, taking the sales at the price that has been realised for the proportion sold, the capital value of the estates in Derry might vary from one million to a million and a-half.

Chairman.

987. Do you mean the capital value of the property belonging to them, sold and unsold?—No; sold under the Act of 1885, or remaining unsold.

988. You have given us the figures of some of the Companies' annual returns; have you a rough estimate of the capital value of what remains unsold?—I have only a rough estimate, because owing to the partial sales of the Skinners' and Drapers' Companies I am quite unable to say what remains unsold.

Mr. Sexton.

989. By deducting the amount paid or sanctioned from the total estimate, could you not arrive at the amount which remains unsold?—Yes.

Chairman.

990. Are you personally conversant with any transactions on any of these estates?—The estate which I am personally conversant with, is the Drapers' estate. I have visited some of the other estates, but not to an extent which would enable me to give the Committee much information about the details of the sales.

991. Then the estate, as to which you are in a position to give us information as to details, is the Drapers' estate?—The Drapers' estate I visited on several occasions by the direction of the Land Commission, and I am more conversant with the proceedings on it than with those on any of the other estates.

992. Did you find the tenants on the Drapers' estate anxious to purchase?—The tenants on the better land of the Drapers' estate were all most anxious to purchase on terms resulting from negotiations between the tenants and the company. The tenants on the poorer lands were not at all anxious to purchase at the price at which their holdings were offered; but they are very anxious to obtain the fee-simple of their holdings if they can do so.

993. Did the tenants and the company come to terms, and if so, when?—The Drapers' Company began negotiations with their tenants in the years 1885 and 1886, but it was not till the year 1889 that the first sales were completed.

994. There was an interval then of three years between the initiation of the transaction and its completion?—There was an interval of fully three years.

995. Was there any difficulty in coming to terms, and carrying out the sales?—The terms were very quickly arranged, I think on the better portion of the lands known as the Moneymore division; but the greatest difficulty arose afterwards in completing those sales. The Land Commission had to complain very much of the delay, and the delays that occurred were very injurious and prejudicial to the tenants and to the Commissioners, so far as it affected their security for the loans that they made.

996. Can you explain to us the circumstances of those three years delay?—The delays arose in this way: Applications were lodged with the Land Commission towards the end of 1886. There were sundry requisitions from the Land Commission to the company, as to certain requirements that they asked for. The result was that after the conveyances had been settled by the Land Commission the delay still continued. The Land Commission then found that the company were delaying the sales for the purpose of recovering very heavy arrears of rent, of which the Land Commission had no cognizance at the time that they sanctioned the agreements.

997. Do you mean that when the Land Commission sanctioned the agreements, the heavy liabilities of the tenants were not disclosed to them?—The Commissioners were aware that there were arrears of rent, but they did not know that

Chairman—continued.

that they amounted to such a very large sum as afterwards appeared; and as the sales were delayed so long the company claimed interest from the tenants from the date of the agreement up to the date of the sale.

Mr. T. M. Healy.

998. At what rate?—I could not say whether it was 3½ or 4 per cent. The tenants had entered into these agreements, having been assured verbally by the persons who negotiated for the company that no rent or interest would be demanded after the year 1885. The tenants further had letters from the company, one dated the 10th of August 1886, in which the price was stated to be 18 times the rent.

Chairman.

999. Have you a copy of the letter?—I have the letters.

1000. Perhaps you had better read us the letter unless it is very long?—It is very short. It is a letter dated the 10th of August 1886 from Mr. W. T. Sawyer.

1001. Is he the clerk of the Drapers' Company?—I believe so. It was addressed to Mr. Benjamin Barefoot, the tenant who was the principal medium of negotiation: "The terms of sale will therefore stand thus: Purchase money, a sum equal to 18 times the rent. All arrears of rent to the 1st November 1885 to be paid in cash, and no rent to be demanded after that date. The company to pay the costs of the sale as between them and the tenants."

1002. Will you put that letter in?—Certainly. (*The letter was handed in.*)

Mr. Sexton.

1003. There is a printed heading to the letter, is there not?—"Drapers' Hall, London, E.C."

Chairman.

1004. How did that letter come before the Land Commission?—That letter came before me in the process of my inquiry, when I was sent down by the Land Commission to report upon the estate.

1005. At what date?—In May 1889. There is another letter which I should like to read of the 3rd of January 1887 from Mr. W. T. Sawyer to Mr. Benjamin Barefoot: "The Drapers' Company have had under consideration your letter of the 18th ultimo. They are sorry that there should still be any difficulty in the way of tenants purchasing their holdings, but they cannot think that they are called upon to make fresh concessions in the matter. As the terms now stand, purchasing tenants will be called upon to pay neither rent nor interest from the 1st of November 1885."

1006. This is a repetition, in fact, and a reassurance of what he had said in his previous letter?—With the addition that no interest would be asked for either.

1007. No rent and no interest after the 1st November 1885?—No.

1008. Will you give us the particulars of your action when you went down to investigate the circumstances of this transaction for the Land Commission?—The Land Commission having made repeated efforts to get the company to close, came to the conclusion that these sales were being delayed in order that the company might recover arrears of rent and interest. The Land Commission inquire into the security in the first instance, as to the circumstances of the tenants, that is to say, their debts, and whether there are any mortgages on their farms; and they apprehended that their security would be endangered by a delay of the proceedings which involved the tenants in litigation and in payments which the tenants had not anticipated when they entered into these agreements.

1009. Will you be kind enough to tell us what litigation you are referring to: did litigation take place in regard to a claim for rent, interest, or for arrears?—After the sales were sanctioned, the company, in spite of the letters which I have read, and in spite of the understanding which the tenants had, that no rent or interest was to be paid after the rent for the year 1885 was satisfied, took proceedings and recovered in a court of law interest as well as rent, involving the tenants in money costs. The way that that decision was obtained, perhaps, should be explained.

1010. It was a decision of what court?—A Division of the High Court of Justice.

Mr. T. M. Healy.

1011. They sued Mr. Barefoot personally, I understand?—They sued Mr. Barefoot personally.

1012. In spite of this letter?—In spite of this letter. Mr. Barefoot was the tenant who persuaded the tenants to agree to the company's terms; he thought that he was responsible, and he allowed his case to be put forward as a test case. But since the agreements for sale were executed the Purchase of Land Amendment Act of 1888 passed, and it provides that the vendor may recover from the vendee interest in lieu of rent between the date of the agreement and the date of the completion of the sale, unless the parties have otherwise agreed.

Chairman.

1013. Then are we to understand that the company availed themselves of the clause in the Act of 1888, to throw over the assurance which they had given in these letters?—They recovered judgment against the tenants, but whether it was in consequence of that particular clause, or in consequence of a decision of a majority of the judges of the High Court of Justice in Ireland, I am unable to say. There was a decision irrespective of this clause, that where an agreement was silent as to the payment of interest between the date of the execution of an agreement and its completion, the vendor was entitled to recover interest.

1014. What was the amount of the arrears and interest claimed and recovered or decreed?—I have a return furnished by the company to the Land Commission as to the amount they claimed from the tenants, and the amount paid. Some slight confusion arose which prevents my being able to give you the exact figures. But from about 800 tenants on this division of the estate,

Chairman—*continued.*

estate, about 7,500 *l.* was recovered. I am unable to divide it into rent and interest.

1015. What was the purchase money involved in the transactions with these 200 tenants?—About 70,000 *l.*

Mr. Sexton.

1016. The letter said that the company would not claim after the 1st of November 1887; up to what date did the rent or the interest run?—The return of the company merely gives the amount claimed up to the 1st of May 1889, but some of that amount claimed was no doubt rent that was due in 1888.

Chairman.

1017. Then this transaction, I suppose, besides the 7,500 *l.* of arrears and interests, involved the tenants in pretty heavy costs?—It involved several tenants in costs.

1018. The tenants whose cases were made test cases?—Besides that there were proceedings taken of various kinds, ejectments in which the tenants paid costs; but the whole proceedings are governed by the decision in Mr. Barefoot's case, after which the tenants surrendered and paid up as quickly and as well as they could.

Mr. Clancy.

1019. How many years' rent?—I have given you the amount, but I cannot tell you how many years' rent were claimed.

Chairman.

1020. The commissioners fearing for their security, and having failed to get the companies to complete the sales, sent you down to examine into the circumstances of the holdings of the tenants, did they not?—Just so.

1021. Will you give us any particulars of your action; when did you go down?—I went down in April 1889. I found that the tenants on this division of the estate were most anxious to get the sale closed, that was the Moneymore division. They complained bitterly of the company having departed from the assurance given in those letters, and from the verbal statements made by their agents; but they accepted the situation and paid as far as they could; but the result was that many tenants sold their stock, some borrowed money on mortgage on their farms and incurred expenses in that way which made their position in respect of security to the Land Commission very different from what it would have been if the sales had been closed within six months after the execution of the agreements.

Mr. T. M. Healy.

1022. A number of them gave bills to the company, did they not?—The Land Commission were able to stop that proceeding.

1023. Was there not litigation over a number of the bills?—Not on that estate. The company proposed that promissory notes should be given, and that then they would close the sales; but the Land Commission objected to those promissory notes.

Chairman.

1024. How did they notify that objection, through you or otherwise?—It was done by correspondence.

1025. You have no further remark to make as to what you found among the purchasing tenants in the matter of delay?—Nothing beyond the loss to them arising out of the delay, tenants having in many cases to borrow money at a high rate of interest, and pay costs in connection with that loan. For instance, I may mention one woman whose case came under my notice, whose purchase money was 863 *l.* In order to settle with the company and get her case closed, she had to borrow 63 *l.* at 6 per cent.

1026. What had she to borrow that for?—To pay the company.

1027. To pay them what?—Arrears.

1028. And costs?—I could not say about costs in that case; but the loan in that case involved her in 30 *l.* costs in raising the money. She had to raise the money by a mortgage on her interest in her farm.

1029. Did you feel as the representative of the Land Commission that this action had to some extent weakened your security?—Certainly.

1030. Were there any other complaints either by the Land Commission or from the tenants?—The Land Commission then required the company to close the sales forthwith, and remit all outstanding accounts.

1031. When you say "then" do you mean in the autumn of 1889?—In May 1889. The company's reply to that was, "If the Land Commission will not lend the money we will not carry out the sales except to those tenants who choose to pay the cash themselves." The result was that as the tenants were most anxious to complete, the Land Commission practically had to give way, and the sales were then not closed till October.

1032. Was there any communication or remonstrance made to the Land Commission from the tenants?—There was no remonstrance against the decision of the Court, which they all accepted.

1033. But was there any remonstrance as to the delay or other matters?—There were various remonstrances as to the delay in that particular case.

1034. Did they make any formal communication to the Land Commission embodying those remonstrances?—They did, but I have not got it with me. They made a formal communication to the Commissioners, asking them to close the matter as quickly as they could.

1035. Was there any complaint or remonstrance in this petition or address, or was it merely a request that they should quickly close?—It did not seem to me that it bore upon the case at all, except so far as the delay was concerned.

1036. Can you give us the substance of the report which you made to the Land Commissioners after your visit?—My report was a recital of the facts that I have stated to the Committee as to the delay.

1037. Have you the report before you?—I have.

1038. Is it long?—I am afraid it is rather long.

Chairman—continued.

long, and it deals with a lot of irrelevant matter; but my conclusion was that "It appears to me that for the protection of the Commissioners' security it would be wise to require all outstanding cases to be closed at once and that all rent, interest, and costs unpaid should be released. The long delay has caused infinite discontent, has made the tenants dissatisfied with the purchase, and to a great extent destroyed the pleasure which they would have felt at being created freeholders."

1039. That was the substance of your report?—That was the substance of my recommendation to the Commissioners.

Mr. T. M. Healy.

1040. What is the date of that report?—16th April 1888.

Chairman.

1041. Can you give us any instances that came under your own observation upon which you founded your report?—I have mentioned one instance of a woman who borrowed 53 *l.* at 5 per cent., and was involved in 80 *l.* costs in connection with that loan as well. In another case where the purchase money was 311 *l.*, also a woman, the amount due by her to the company was 111 *l.*, she had to raise that money, and her farm was practically devoid of stock at the time of my visit. Another woman, whose purchase money was 199 *l.*, owed 20 *l.* to the company; and I should like to mention that case as an illustration of the readiness with which these people paid. The case was to come before the Land Commission for their decision in four days after my visit to this woman. She had no crop on her farm, every item had been sold out, but she told me that she had 20 *l.* of money in the house. I said to her that she had better hold that money until the case had been heard by the Land Commission, as it might affect those payments. Her reply to me was, "I promised Mr. Glover that he should have the money tomorrow, and he shall have it."

1042. Mr. Glover is the agent on the spot of Drapers' Company?—Yes.

1043. Have you any other instances?—Those are the only instances with regard to that Moneymore division of the estate.

Sir John Ellis.

1044. You say that the purchase money was 311 *l.*, and that there was 111 *l.* due to the company; was this 111 *l.* the subject of a claim, contrary to the spirit of these letters, as alleged; did it spring out of what the tenants considered was a misunderstanding at least? In other words, was the 111 *l.* arrears after the year 1885?—I am unable to divide that amount of 111 *l.* into rent and interest. In that case the tenant's rent was 17 *l.* 14 *s.* 6 *d.*

> Mr. *Percival A. Nairne*, on behalf of the Drapers' Company, said that he assumed that an opportunity would be given to the Drapers' Company of tendering rebutting evidence on these points, because they did not admit that this was an accurate representation. He also stated that the letters in question had formed the subject of judicial decision in Dublin.

Chairman.

1045. Is there a difficulty in giving us the names of these cases?—There is no difficulty as regards the cases that I have mentioned, but there are other cases on the estate where I think it would be very unadvisable to give the names.

1046. But those are not cases that you have mentioned to us?—They are not.

1047. Then the only question is whether you consider that you are at liberty to give us the names of the cases of which you have given us some particulars?—I am quite ready to give the name of the woman who owed 111 *l.* 6 *s.* 10 *d.* to the company. The name is Esther Crookes. The return made by the company's agent is, that this amount was recovered since May 1887, leaving a balance of 4 *l.* 17 *s.* 8 *d.* still due.

1048. In the other case of the woman, whose purchase-money was 383 *l.*, what was the name of the woman?—The name of the woman, whose purchase-money was 383 *l.*, is Elizabeth Johnson.

1049. Can you still further specify what townland she was on?—I can; she was on the townland of Ballymoyle. The third one is Elizabeth McCullagh, of Ballymoyle.

1050. What view did the Land Commission take of your report?—The Land Commission required the company to close the sales forthwith, remitting what balance of interest and costs remained due. They considered that the relation of debtor and creditor between the two parties should cease, inasmuch as the security for their loans was being endangered by these proceedings, as well as by the long delay. The company's answer to that was, that they would withdraw from the sales, and the result was that the sales were closed, but not till October and November 1889, and then disposed of that division of the estate.

1051. Did the Commissioners, or any of them, give any public utterance to their views?—Mr. Commissioner Lynch made a judgment on the subject, which I can put in if it is desired.

1052. You had better put it in, and perhaps tell us what the drift of it is?—I am afraid that that judgment is rather long.

1053. But there must be operative sentences in it, which will show us whether we need have it put in or not?—

> Mr. *Nairne* asked that the whole judgment might be put in.

> (*Chairman.*) The Committee will consider that, and determine it for themselves.

> *Witness.*] I will read the concluding part, which seems to me all that is material of this report. Mr. Venables, the solicitor for the tenants, appeared before the Land Commission, asking that the sales should be carried out, in spite of the Land Commission having said that they would not lend the money except under those conditions. Mr. Commissioner Lynch, in concluding his judgment, said: "Mr. Venables has put the case of the tenants with great ability, and with moderation and perfect candour. He admitted the great advantages which the Moneymore tenants would obtain by our-

Chairman—continued.

clearing of the advances we sanctioned. He tells me that the great majority of the tenants on his division are thriving and industrious, and he gave instances of the very high rates at which tenants' interests have sold in that district; and the reports which I have received from our inspector fully confirm his statements. He admits, on the other hand, that there are a good many of these tenants who have been, and are, in straitened circumstances. There are improvident persons to be found amongst all classes; but there are others who through no fault of theirs were not so well able as the rest to battle with adverse seasons and the markets, who were in arrears in November 1883, and who have had to pay these arrears with costs and interest, and who have been crippled by their efforts to make these payments; or who have still hanging over them, as appears by this schedule, the balance of their indebtedness. But Mr. Venables urges upon me that the alternative offered by Mr. Glover's circular of the 17th of June, if the door is closed to the completion of these sales, might result in ruin to some of these tenants by remitting them to the position of indebtedness as tenants for rent, with only credit for the payments they have made since May 1887. While therefore I shall make no advance in any case where I believe our security for the punctual payment of the instalments which, under the order I now propose to make, would accrue, due on the 1st of May next, may be weakened, I am prepared to rescind this ruling" (that is the ruling that he would not advance except upon the terms of the interest being remitted) "of 16th April, so as to enable those who have paid, or are prepared to pay, the interest to which the company is there entitled, to settle with the company by the 1st of October, so as to have their conveyances completed and the advances closed by the 31st October next. Their indebtedness to us would, in such cases, commence from the 1st of November." That is, I think, all that is material.

1054. Will you put that judgment in?—Yes. (*The Judgment was handed in.*)

1055. I see, if this is a correct report which I have in my hand, that Mr. Commissioner Lynch uses some very direct language as to the course taken by Mr. Glover. Mr. Glover is the solicitor for the Drapers' Company, is he not?—Mr. Glover is the solicitor for the Drapers' Company, but I am not sure what that report is which you have in your hand.

1056. This is a report from the "Freeman's Journal," printed in June; is it not the report that you have been reading from?—No, I think not. That was another case upon which judgment was given on the same day, which we shall come on to later. The other judgment should be put in, I think. There was another judgment on the other division of the estate. The judgment from which I have read refers only to what is

Chairman—continued.

known as the Moneymore division, which is the richest part of the estate.

1057. Will you tell us about the other division, if there is anything to tell?—The other divisions of the estate comprise a large quantity of very much poorer land, mountainous land, with very small and poor holdings. There have been great delays in carrying out the sales on that part of the estate, and still greater dissatisfaction was caused by the quantity of ejectments served before these agreements were entered into. The tenants on that portion of the estate presented a petition to the Land Commission.

1058. Have you that petition?—I have the petition here.

1059. Will you read it?—"We, the undersigned tenants of the Ballynascreen and Brackaslievegallion portions of the Drapers' estate, in the County of Londonderry, humbly beg to submit to your consideration the terms of purchase and circumstances under which the tenants of this division have been forced to sign agreements to buy out their holdings from the Drapers' Company. We do this in order that you, as public servants of the Government, may be able, while there is yet time, to judge of the security the company are offering you for the enormous advance of cash you are called upon to make to them out of the funds allotted to you for the purposes of the Purchase of Land (Ireland) Acts, 1885-7. We do this, also, in order that you may have a clear knowledge of the facts and be able to judge of the probable consequences before approving of these purchases, and if the tenants, by force of circumstances, which it is very easy to foresee are sure to occur in the course of a very short time, shall not be able to fulfil their obligations to the State, they are not to be told the fault is their own, and that they entered into their engagements voluntarily and with their eyes open, or with a fraudulent intention of never fulfilling them. In the year 1883 the Drapers' Company offered their estate for sale to the tenants at a price of 18 years' purchase upon the rental as it then stood; the arrears to be paid up. About one-third of the tenants who live on the fat and fertile lands in the district of Moneymore, and scarcely any of whom were in arrear of rent, then agreed to purchase at the company's terms. The remaining two-thirds, on whose behalf this petition is humbly presented, and who live in a wild, rugged mountain district, were all in a considerable arrear of rent, averaging from two to five years, and in a state of extreme poverty. Their land is not one-fourth the value of that in the Moneymore district, and was rack-rented to an extent which the tenants were absolutely unable to meet. In order to force these tenants on the Draperstown portion of the estate to fall into line with the tenants on the Moneymore division, and buy out on the same terms as they, Messrs. Glover and McGuckin, solicitors for the company, issued 350 ejectment processes for non-payment of rent against them in the month of October 1887 and in January 1888, and obtained in all these cases decrees. Three hundred and twenty of these tenants served notices under the provisions of the Land Law Act, 1887, to have fair rents fixed

Chairman—continued.

fixed before John C. Neligan, Esq., Q.C., Recorder of Londonderry; and at the time the ejectment decrees were obtained they got an average reduction of 20 per cent., and then offered the company 18 years' purchase on the judgment rents as fixed by the Recorder. The Drapers' Company refused this offer, and insisted upon selling upon the basis of the old and impossible rents. In order to coerce the tenants into buying out at the old rents, the law agents for the company then served upon about 250 of the tenants of the Draperstown division notices of eviction under the 7th section of the Land Act, 1887, and subsequently brought summonses to the petty sessions of Draperstown, and obtained warrants for possession against the greater number of these tenants. Besides these ejectment proceedings, ordinary civil bills for 'use and occupation' were issued against all the tenants against whom ejectment decrees had been obtained in October 1887, and ordinary civil bills were also served in January 1888 for the year's rent of 1887. These latter numbered about 150, and there were then two sets of decrees, with the necessary costs in each, against nearly all the tenants. In November 1888 the sheriff, with bailiffs, horses, and carts, came out amongst the tenantry and seized under the ordinary civil bill decrees, and took all the chattels they could obtain from the tenants for the purpose of satisfying them, and in the next month, December 1888, Mr. Glover, solicitor for the company, came with the sheriff, emergency-men, battering rams, and all the other resources of the law, to carry out evictions after the tenants had been left almost destitute by the execution of the civil bill decrees for rent. The tenants were then driven to one of two alternatives, to sign the agreements to purchase at the terms dictated by the company, and add the arrears of rent to the purchase money and pay up all the costs, or leave for the workhouse. Rather than adopt the latter course they signed the agreements which you are now called upon to approve. They were forced to pay costs, varying in most cases from 5 *l.* to 3 *l.*, and nearly all the tenants have lost any credit that remained to them, and were unable to meet this emergency. Those, however, who could either beg or borrow, by that means strove to bridge over the difficulty and stave off the day of eviction. We verily believe that we shall not be able to carry out the contracts made in this manner and upon these terms. We humbly submit these facts to you, and if you consider the security good enough, and that you are justified under the circumstances in approving of the purchases then do so. The future will condemn or justify the act."

1060. What is the date of that petition?—11th of November 1888.

1061. Then it was after that petition that you went down; three months after?—Yes.

1062. Did your inquiries on the spot corroborate these allegations?—Yes, in general terms. I am unable to verify the details as to the number of the evictions, but I am aware that a very large number of evictions were served; civil bill processes for rent and caretaker notices;

Chairman—continued.

those were exhibited to me at most of the tenants' houses that I visited in May 1889.

1063. You saw the documents, receipts, ejectment notices, &c.?—I visited at that time 84 holdings, in the case of which agreements had been lodged, and which were scattered over the whole of this division of the estate, and taking them as samples I believe that the statements in the petition are substantially correct; I found the prices excessively high. There was no doubt that the agreements had been signed when the tenants were under eviction. In some cases the arrears amounted to six, seven, and eight years, and I found from examining the tenants' receipts for rent, that arrears and costs had been added to the prices which the tenants had in the first instance refused to buy at. I may explain that by an illustration. In this case I prefer not giving the names of the tenants. Many of these people are still tenants of the company, and I never in all my experience met Irish tenants in such abject terror of those who had the management of the estate. I will take as an illustration of the position a case where the rent arranged by the company in 1862 was 6 *l.* 10 *s.* The tenant had a fair rent fixed by the Recorder of Derry at 3 *l.* 5 *s.*

1064. £. 6 was the original rent; or a judicial rent?—No, it was a rent fixed by the company in 1889, when they took about 15 per cent. off rents which had been raised in 1875.

1065. When did they take it off?—In 1875 there had been a revision of the rents on this estate.

Mr. T. M. Healy.

1066. Leasehold in 1875?—I do not know.

Chairman.

1067. £. 6 10 *s.* in 1868; what next?—The fair rent was fixed by the Recorder of Derry at 3 *l.* 5 *s.* The price in the agreement lodged with the Land Commission was 133 *l.*, which would be about 25 times the fair rent, but this tenant held receipts for the payments he had made for rent and interest, and in the course of my business to verify the statements made by the tenants, I required them to show me these documents. I found that the price of his holdings stated in the receipts for interest on the purchase money which he had paid pending the sale was 113 *l.* 10 *s.*; that four years' rent had been added to the price.

1068. £. 100 was the purchasing price, and 23 *l.* had been added?—£. 21 had been added. He held receipts from the company for 18 *l.* 15 *s.* Three years' rent due November 1886, less an abatement of 7 *l.* 16 *s.*, leaving a net amount of 10 *l.* 19 *s.*; 3 *l.* 1 *s.* 8 *d.* costs were added to that, making 14 *l.* 0 *s.* 8 *d.* On the back of that receipt was marked, "added to purchase." He then held a second receipt for 7 *l.*, two years' interest to the 1st of November 1888 on the purchase money of 113 *l.* 10 *s.*, and on the back of that it was indicated that this was also added to the purchase. That tenant's application was refused by the Land Commission, and now, although he holds receipts for these moneys, he is sued for rent for which he holds receipts.

1069. How

Chairman—continued.

1069. How can that be?—I do not know how it can be, because the case has not come on for hearing, but I met this tenant last week, and, as a great many of his neighbours are, he is sued for back rent, although he holds receipts. Of course it might be pleaded that the money was never paid. That is the reason I do not wish to mention his name, because he is now in litigation with the company.

Mr. Sexton.

1070. The agreement for sale was not executed?—The agreement for sale was executed and lodged with the Land Commission.

1071. But never carried out?—The Land Commission refused to lend the money under the circumstances, because they thought they had no security.

1072. The man is still a tenant then?—Yes.

Chairman.

1073. He is still a tenant, and he is at this moment the subject of legal proceedings?—Yes.

1074. Have you any other instance which came under your observation?—Another case is one where the old rent was 6 *l.*; the fair rent was fixed at 4 *l.* 10 *s.*, and the price 135 *l.* Six years' rent were due in January 1889. In such a case the instalment payable to the Land Commission when a tenant purchased would be in excess of the judicial rent.

1075. What would the instalment be on 135 *l.*; it is 4 per cent., is it not?—Yes.

1076. It would be just over 5 *l.* 8 *s.*?—Yes. Another case among the same tenants was a rent of 7 *l.* 13 *s.*, reduced by the Recorder of Derry to 5 *l.* 15 *s.* The price in the agreement 164 *l.* The annuity on that would be 6 *l.* 11 *s.* 2 *d.* 25 *l.* 18 *s.* 10 *d.* had been added to the price of 18 years' purchase originally proposed. This tenant was seven years in arrear with his rent at the time he purchased. That is sufficient in the way of illustration of my statement, and of the statement in the petition.

1077. These cases are illustrations of your proposition, and the proposition of the petition that rent and costs were added to prices of purchase originally proposed; is that so?—Yes, to the price originally proposed and refused by the tenants, until under the influence of these proceedings they agreed.

1078. That is to say, they agreed to the inclusion of these arrears over and above the original price proposed, because they wished to escape eviction and the workhouse?—Yes.

1079. And it was under duress that they assented to this arrangement?—The company had a legal right to recover the rents, but when rents run six or seven years in arrear they are practically irrecoverable; and they were an engine by which the company could do exactly what they liked, and the tenants in those cases when matters were brought to a point, submitted like sheep.

1080. Is it the practice of the Land Commission to require that agreements for sale should disclose the judicial rent?—Certainly. They should set out the true rental, and the setting down in the agreement for sale of a rent which was no longer the legal rent, and had ceased to be the legal rent for one or two years, was practically a fraud.

1081. Is it a rule of your department; I am only asking for information; to require an agreement for sale to disclose the judicial rent?—The legal rent should be put down.

1082. In the agreements which were sent up to you between the Drapers' Company and their tenants was a judicial rent disclosed?—It was not; neither the Land Commission nor any of their officials had any idea whatever that judicial rents had been fixed, and they accepted these agreements understanding that the prices were 18 years' purchase on the existing rents.

1083. The Commissioners understood that?—The Commissioners understood that.

1084. Did they express any opinion when your report was sent in?—Mr. Commissioner Lynch gave a judgment which I have here also.

1085. What is the date of it; I want to see whether it is the same as this which I have been reading?—31st July 1889.

1086. Could you read to us his remarks upon the evidence that you have just given us?—Perhaps I may read the concluding part of the report I made: "I conclude from my examination these cases that the contracts entered into were obtained by intimidation and undue influence, and that they were entered into under duress; and that they were presented to the Land Commissioners in a misleading aspect by the omission or concealment of judicial rents, and by the inclusion in the prices of arrears and costs for which the tenants hold receipts. If the Commissioners are satisfied that the facts are as I have stated, I venture to suggest that they should give publicity to the facts of this case and their opinion of them. It would be very prejudicial to the operation of the Purchase Acts that tenants should think that loans could be obtained under such circumstances to stave off immediate peril of threatened eviction, or that landlords, agents, or solicitors should procure the signature to contracts by such means."

1087. That is the conclusion of your report to the Commissioners?—That was the substance of my report to the Commissioners.

1088. What remark did they make upon it?—Mr. Commissioner Lynch in giving judgment upon the 31st of July 1889 said, in conclusion: "It appears that in 42 out of these 51 cases judicial rents had been fixed by the Recorder of Derry before the signing of the agreement for sale, but in the preparation of these agreements, notwithstanding our rule, notwithstanding the instructions on the face of the agreements which were printed by and used for the Drapers' Company and in gross violation of our rules, the solicitors in this case deliberately inserted in the agreements the rents fixed in 1883 and described the tenants as ordinary tenants from year to year at these rents, instead of setting the out true rents which were the judicial rents; and they got the tenants to sign and verify by affidavit these erroneous statements. And what is the explanation now offered by the solicitors. In their letter dated 17th July they say, 'after the tenants got fair rents fixed they insisted

Chairman—continued.

sisted they had a right under the company's offer to buy at 18 years of those fair rents. This the company refused to accede to, and in order to prevent any misunderstanding as to the terms of sale, and having regard to the tenant's contention, it was considered better to insert the rent of 1882, leaving it open to the company when the inspector came round to explain the matter to him by a statement in the form now sent.' It was stated voluntarily by Mr. John Glover, when he was examined before me last Friday, that this course was adopted by the direction of the company: I can only say that if this direction was given the company, it was a most improper one; it was a course which the solicitors should have refused to follow at the suggestion of their client, and that they should never have allowed tenants, many of them illiterate, to verify these agreements, which it now appears are false in this material respect. Assume the case of any ordinary mortgage. The owner of an estate is seeking for a loan, he furnishes a rental to the mortgagee as evidence of value, and he verifies it by a declaration. What would be said if he "inserted" in that rental, instead of the existing judicial rents, former rents which were 20 or 25 per cent. higher? And this is what was done in the present cases, leaving it to our officer to discover the suppression (or the company to volunteer the explanation) now given. They say they sold at 18 years' purchase in a former rent. In the first place the purchase money named in many of the agreements is not 18 times the rent, but a great deal more, the figures being now explained by the tacking on of arrears; but in the next place we do not ask to be told the number of years' purchase; 18 years' purchase of one rent might be a very high rate, while 25 years' purchase of another rent might be moderate. What we do require to know is the existing rent and how it has been created, and the capital sum which the landlord and tenant have mutually agreed upon as the price to be paid by the tenant for the landlord's interest, and it is then for us to satisfy ourselves as to the sufficiency of the security; and it matters not to us the number of years' purchase within which the prices may range provided the contract is a free contract, and that the State has ample security for the money we are asked to advance. I can only say that in my opinion these agreements have been most improperly prepared, in violation of our rules, and that they cannot be now regarded as agreements upon which advances might be made." If I am to put in the report, it is unnecessary perhaps to read more.

1089. Yes, I think you have read enough to give us the drift of it. Will you be kind enough to tell us what is the rule which the Commissioner in his judgment says was violated?—I am afraid I could not do that. It is a direction on the form of application.

1090. But it is in print somewhere or other, is it not?—It is.

1091. You have not got it with you?—I have not.

1092. If you are here next Monday, which is probable, would you be good enough to bring it?—Certainly.

1093. So that we may see exactly what the rule is which was violated?—Yes.

Mr. Sexton.

1094. And which appears, as I understand, printed on every form of application?—So Mr. Lynch's judgment states, and I am sure he is accurate.

Chairman.

1095. Who acted for the companies in all these transactions, Mr. John Glover?—Messrs. Glover & McGuckin are solicitors to the company. Mr. John Glover is the agent, I believe, at present.

1096. Was any notice taken by any legal authorities in Ireland of the conduct of Mr. Glover?—Not with reference to the facts I have referred to here. There was another question, where agreements lodged with the Land Commission were found not to have been signed by the parties who purported to have signed them.

1097. That is another matter, but not with regard to this matter?—Nothing whatever.

1098. Did the companies or Mr. Glover, after Mr. Commissioner Lynch delivered this judgment and this criticism of their action, attempt any defence; had they anything to say for themselves?—The company then sent a circular to the tenants of those divisions of the estate.

1099. After Mr. Commissioner Lynch's judgment?—No, after they became aware that these facts were known to the Commission. I could not say the exact date of the issue of the circular. The circular is dated the 20th June 1889. In it the company informed all the tenants on that estate that they decline to alter the terms of sale, but are prepared to cancel any or all the agreements which have been entered into by tenants to purchase their holdings, and that any purchasing tenant who may wish to do so may cancel his agreement by signing the form of the letter enclosed. The company say that it is entirely a matter for the discretion of the tenants whether or not they accept the terms of sale offered to them, but if they elect to remain tenants they must be prepared to fulfil the obligations of their tenancies.

1100. That is to say, in plain language, to pay up their arrears?—To pay up their arrears. They further say, "For some time past it has been apparent to the company that a number of tenants of these divisions of the estate have combined to withstand the payment of rent, and being determined not to yield to an illegal combination of this kind, the company have been compelled to take proceedings at law in many cases."

1101. Did you find from your inquiries that there was a combination in existence?—I do not think there was anything like a combination among the tenantry. They are scattered over a great extent of country. I suppose it is 20 miles from one end of the estate to the other. It is a very rugged and mountainous country; the circumstances of the tenants are such that some are well off and some excessively poor. My impression

Chairman—continued.

version from conversations with the tenants, from the facts and documents presented to me, would show me that there was nothing like combination.

1102. You believe that in making that statement the company had been misinformed?—I think they were misinformed, so much so, that some of these tenants were evicted, and were out of possession, and I am informed that they applied to the National League for assistance. The National League refused to give them assistance because they had it on the admissions of the tenants themselves that any money granted for the support of evicted tenants would simply be used to pay rent, and get themselves reinstated. The result to my mind was, that there was no combination within the estate, and that no external pressure was brought upon the tenants from any part whatever to combine together for the purpose of refusing to pay rent, as alleged there.

1103. This circular came from London, of course, or from the agent's office on the spot?—I think it is issued by the agent.

1104. Therefore, under these circumstances, the offer, or rather the invitation in the circular to the tenants to use their discretion, was a mere farce?—I think it was.

1105. They had no alternative?—They had no alternative except to pay up these arrears, which were exceedingly heavy in most of the poorer cases.

1106. What is the state of things now; are sales going on, or are there sales pending, or has the whole operation come to an end?—The sales are still proceeding, but very slowly, and the same complaints of delay are being made. I have had to visit the estate several times, and I found numbers of tenants scattered all over the estate who told me that they signed agreements to buy which have never been lodged with the Land Commission. We are aware at the Land Commission that this is the case, because agreements are continually brought in long out of date; in fact they are executed by tenants; they then go to the solicitor's office, and come to London to be sealed. They lie an indefinite time in these offices.

1107. Which offices; in the offices of the solicitors at Magherafelt?—Yes, and in London.

1108. Then they come to London?—Yes, for the company to seal them.

1109. To the office of the company; and then they go back?—Then they go back, and are not lodged in the Land Commission until it suits the managers of the estate. Between the signing of the agreement by the tenant, which is the date of the application, arrears of rent are demanded from them, and until these are paid the agreement is not lodged with the Land Commission.

1110. In short, what is the object of holding over the agreement?—To enable the company to recover arrears and costs, I believe, because the agreement states that the price is inclusive of all arrears; but on applying to the company to know why the agreements were not lodged at the proper date, and why sums were recovered from the tenants after the date of the agreement, I was informed that the company considered the date of the agreement to be the date of the lodgment with the Land Commission.

1111. What is your rule at the Land Commission as to the date of lodgment?—That it must be lodged within two months of execution. As an illustration of those delays, when I was on the Drapers' estate last week a number of agreements were handed to me to know if I would inspect the holdings, so as to facilitate the sales, the tenants being anxious to close them; I found they were executed in December last. They have not been lodged up to the present day.

1112. Though executed six months ago?—Yes.

1113. Does that failure vitiate the agreement to the Land Commission; do they consider it voids it?—It involves the tenants in expense, because the agreements are not received without a special application to the Land Commission. They may be rejected, and although the company have agreed to pay all the costs of the sale, the tenants are put to those expenses.

1114. Do you mean by the last remark that the prices in the agreement include all the expense of purchase?—That is a provision in most of the agreements, if not in all, on the Drapers' estate, and is the usual agreement in all agreements under the Land Purchase Acts.

1115. And yet in spite of that agreement these extraneous expenses of purchase are added?—Applications to the Commissioners in consequence of delay put the tenants to a great deal of expense.

1116. The agreements allege, do they not, that the price is inclusive of all the rent up to the last gale day?—Yes.

1117. What rent is it that the company demands; what rent can be due; how can rent accrue due?—The results of proceedings which have been taken on the Drapers' estate, and the vast amount of arrears that have accumulated, and the remission by the company of some part of the arrears (I believe it is the year that is due, 1886), is that the tenants are in such confusion that they really do not know what they owe. It is my business when I visit these holdings to make myself acquainted with what arrears are due. I found it most difficult to ascertain it. I have applied to the tenants' solicitors, and they have told me in the same way that they are unable to ascertain it except by asking the company's agents. I might give you an illustration of one such case where it appears to me that money was taken in contravention of the provisions in the agreement for sale. There is a tenant whose rent is 3 l. 8 s. on 8th January 1885; he received an ejectment for 19 l. 4 s. On 31st March 1887 he received an ejectment for 21 l. 9 s. 8 d. On 10th January 1888 he received an ejectment for 17 l. 11 s. 3 d. He holds receipts, one dated 29th August 1886, 10 l. on account of two years' rent due May 1885. That was paid when the sheriff was at his door. On 25th January 1889 he received two receipts, 3 l. 5 s., balance of rent due May 1886, and 5 l. 15 s., two years' interest to 1st May 1888. On 27th February 1890 he received a receipt for 3 l. 5 s. 8 d., the balance of rent due November 1885. That last payment of rent due November

1885

Chairman—continued.

1886 was taken after he had agreed to buy his holding in 1882.

1118. These cases illustrate what?—They illustrate the fact that the tenants are now reduced to that state of submission that they are ready to pay, and do pay, amounts which they are not legally liable for if they are asked.

1119. It occurs to me that there must be a tremendous harvest of costs out of these proceedings, an amount sufficient to impair enormously the boon which it is the policy of the Act to confer on the purchasing tenant?—In the cases I have mentioned there were three ejectments served, and apparently no rent paid, or very little rent paid, and in each case there were probably costs paid. The amount paid by the tenants on this estate generally has been for the last few years very large indeed, but I am not able to give any estimate of it.

1120. You do not happen to have the amount of the costs in this one case, do you; could you give us one or two instances of the lawyers' bills?—I have not got any estimate in this particular case where the tenant made a payment of rent due in 1883 after he had signed an agreement to buy in the year 1880; I merely have his statement that, in addition, he paid 7 *l.* for costs.

1121. Does the company readily give the Commission all the information it wants with respect to these transactions?—No; they have refrained from giving the information about the judicial rents, as I have said, and after the Commissioners made a difficulty and disallowed these costs for duress, and for improper preparation of the agreements, I find it rather difficult to obtain information from anybody except the solicitor to the company, because the bailiffs and other people, I think, do not like to meddle in a quarrel, and perhaps get into hot water with the company.

Mr. T. M. Healy.

1122. The solicitor is willing to give information?—The solicitor is willing to give information.

Chairman.

1123. Now, on another side of the matter, as to expenditure by the company; we are still confining ourselves to the Drapers' Company. Does the estate look, to your very experienced eye, as if it had had much money, or any money, laid out upon it by the company?—I do not see any signs of money having been laid out by the company on the improvement of farms or farm buildings. I believe the company spent a very large sum in building the town of Moneymore.

1124. In the petition which you have put in, which was sent to the Land Commission, you, no doubt, have noticed this passage: "About 50 years ago, before the tenants had any recognised interest in their holdings, the company were in the habit of advancing sums of money, varying with the value of the holdings, to the tenants, for the purpose of making permanent improvements, by way of buildings, &c., and the interest upon these advances was charged in the books of the company, and in the books of the company alone, as interest, and added to the rent on the tenants' holdings"?—I did not read that because it did not bear on the question we were talking of.

1125. Does this, which the petition admits or alleges to have been done 50 years ago, affect your judgment or not, from your observation, that money had not been laid out by the company?—I could not discern by my eye what had been done, but from all the inquiries I have made, and from it not being the custom of the country, I should think that the company has not laid out money, as a rule, upon the improvement of farms or farm buildings. I believe they have laid out money on planting; making plantations which have latterly been sold to a large extent to timber merchants. They have laid out money, I believe, on roads and main drains, but as to the improvement of farms, I should not think, from my observation, and from the inquiries I have made, that they were in the habit of doing that.

1126. Does the estate show any evidence of improvement?—The estate is vastly improved, and is in process of improvement. This is a mountainous country, and a great deal of land has been reclaimed.

1127. If the estate bears evidence of improvements, and if, so far as you can observe, those improvements have not been made by the company, they must have been made by the tenants?—I think there would be no question about that. It would be admitted that the company took possession of the estate in 1817, after the dropping of a middleman's lease. The report of a deputation mentions it as the universal practice of the country that help is not given for farm buildings or improvements, either in land or materials, by the landlords, and I fancy that that system has been the prevalent one, as it is throughout the rest of Ireland.

1128. You do not consider that that statement and that view of yours is at all impaired by the fact that 50 years ago the companies expended sums of money for which they charged interest afterwards to the tenants?—I do not think so. But I could not discern simply by observation such matters.

1129. Was the Drapers' Company in the habit of raising the rents?—The Drapers' Company has, I believe, like the other companies, raised the rents from time to time. It was claimed, as being part of the custom of the country, that rents should be revised every 21 years. Of course revision generally meant raising.

1130. That was the custom both on private estates and company estates?—I think the custom was more regular on the company's estates than on private estates, because the management was more systematic.

1131. It is not merely an inference from the custom of the country, but do you know, as a matter of fact, that the company did raise its rents periodically?—I know that the rents on this estate were raised in 1876.

1132. What amount of rise?—From a report of a former agent I find that 1,500 *l.* was added to the estate in that year.

1133. That increase must have been upon the tenants' improvements, I presume, as the expenditure referred to in the petition was 50 years ago?—I should think so. I should add, with regard

Chairman—continued.

gard to that, those years were very prosperous, and landlords all over Ireland, where they thought themselves justified in doing so, raised the rents although they might have made no improvements.

1134. We will leave the agricultural holdings and go to Moneymore; will you tell us what happened there; Moneymore is a little town, is it not?—Moneymore is a small and very prettily situated village. I believe it has been entirely built by the Drapers' Company.

Mr. John Ellis.

1135. In what county is it?—Londonderry.

Chairman.

1136. Can you tell us anything about the circumstances of Moneymore?—The expenditure by the company in building the village has not been a success in any way. At present there is in Moneymore no trade, practically, or business of any kind. My observation shows me that.

1137. Will you first tell us what the company did at Moneymore?—They built the whole village.

Mr. John Ellis.

1138. When?—After 1817. They refused to give grants of land for building purposes, and preferred to do all the building in the village themselves. That did not suit the habits of the people in the country. They did not wish to carry on business when they were simply yearly tenants to a company like this, whom they could not approach, and of whom they knew nothing except through their agents and bailiffs. The result has been that, while all the villages and small towns round Moneymore are comparatively prosperous and thriving, there is no business whatever done in Moneymore. Here is a report from a former agent of the company, made in 1851, saying, at page 9, "There being no trade and very little employment for labourers in Moneymore or the neighbourhood, the occupiers of the cottages are in many cases almost in abject poverty, and it is a marvel how they can subsist, having no visible means of support." It did not suit people to enter into business when they were subject to be dispossessed, or subject to the rules of a company, and, in fact, where they had no tenure of their place of business. That is the explanation why Moneymore, with several advantages, with all this money spent by the company, is absolutely devoid of any trade or business.

Chairman—continued.

1141. Are those prosperous places under the Drapers' Company?—The town of Magherafelt belonged to the Salters' Company's, and is a business town; but there not only were leases given, but, subject to certain office rules, the property in the houses built by the tenants was recognised by the company, although they had no legal right.

1142. Then the Drapers' Company at Moneymore were, if I may use the word, harsher than the Salters at Magherafelt?—I do not know that they were.

1143. I am only interpreting your own account of things?—Having built the town they were perfectly entitled to keep the occupiers of the houses under such conditions as they chose to prescribe. They have another village on their estate, Draperstown. They have built, or lent people money to build, houses there, and they built market sheds which were of use for many years, but since these difficulties about the sale have turned up the company have shut up the market sheds, and would, but for the action of the magistrates of the district, have converted it into a pound.

Mr. Sexton.

1144. With regard to Magherafelt we have been told it was an exception as regards prosperity; are you aware that the company leased that place in the 18th century for about 100 years to Sir Robert Bateson, and it was owing to the grant of a tolerably long lease by Sir Robert Bateson and his family that the town of Magherafelt was built?—I am aware that the whole of the town of Magherafelt has been built by the occupiers, and the houses sold from time to time, some under a leasehold tenure, and some under yearly tenures; but the property being admitted by the company in the parties who had built the houses, or their successors.

1145. But this building progress took place during the period when the company had no control; when it was held by the Bateson family?—I am not aware; but it may have been so.

Chairman.

1146. One or two more questions I must trouble you with, which your evidence suggests to me as to the practice of the Land Commission. Does your estimate of security before you sanction an advance, either in the case of the Drapers' company or other transactions, include the consolidated interest of the landlord and the tenant?

Chairman—continued.

1148. You do not go behind that?—No.

1149. What one of these purchasing tenants buys is, I suppose, the landlord's interest in the land, whether it is a charge or an estate, or however we may describe it; what he purchases is the landlord's interest?—Certainly.

1150. Then price and security are not equivalent?—Not at all.

1151. And bear no necessary proportion to one another?—No; there are cases where the tenant's interest is largely in excess of the landlord's.

1152. But when we were told that in some of these transactions the price has been so many years' purchase, that means purchase of the landlord's interest?—Certainly.

1153. Therefore, if we are told that the price has been 18 years' purchase, that is solely the price of the landlord's interest, and does not describe the value of the holding?—No, it does not; 18 years' purchase means 18 years' purchase of the landlord's rent. That really explains nothing of the value of the holding. It may be 18 years' purchase of a fictitious rent, as in some of these Drapers' cases; it may be 18 years' purchase of a very high rent, or it may be 18 years' purchase of a very low rent, in which case the tenant would have a large interest himself.

1154. If the tenant did not have an interest in the land over and above the price, your advance would not be regarded as safe?—It would not be regarded as safe, and it ought not to be made.

1155. The tenant's interest is an indispensable cover in the view of the Land Commission?—Certainly.

Sir William Marriott.

1156. You gave us the list, in the first instance, of the holdings of the different companies and their value: you gave us the Salters and the Fishmongers; where do you get those from?—That is the list of sales completed; I got this from the Land Commission Office.

1157. There are returns which I suppose we could have?—You have them.

1158. All that first part of your evidence, then, was simply the contents of some returns which we have?—Certainly.

1159. Then after you had given them you said that the value of the land held by the companies was from a million to a million and a half?—I said that as a very rough estimate, and as the best I could form, taking the returns of the rateable value of the property of the company.

1160. It is rather rough; there is a difference between half a million and a million?—It is; I do not think any better estimate could be formed without a detailed rental.

1161. What made you arrive at that opinion?—I thought I had explained that I had merely taken the figures of the property for which the companies are rated in the county.

1162. Would not that give it you pretty well exactly?—No, because there are some properties held by the company for which they do not appear rated as immediate lessors.

1163. When the rating is not a good test?—For instance, in the case of a large part of the

Sir William Marriott—continued.

Irish Society's property in Derry and Coleraine, I do not believe the Irish Society would appear as the rated lessors at all.

1164. I suppose somebody pays the rates?—Somebody pays the rates. I fancy the Irish Society have let land for building purposes in Derry, and the person who built the house would probably appear as the lessor, and the Irish Society, though the owner of the ground, would not appear at all.

1165. As I understand you with regard to the Drapers' estate the tenants in the better part are willing to buy, and in the poorer part not willing; is that so?—That is so generally.

1166. Do not the poorer tenants wish to own their own land?—Very much, but not at the price asked by the company.

1167. They wish it, but the terms asked are too much for them?—Yes.

1168. What terms do they want?—I have not asked them. My business was merely to advise the Commissioners whether they should lend or not lend.

1169. Is the 18 years' purchase looked upon as exorbitant?—The 18 years' purchase which has been referred to was 18 years' purchase of rents which have not been paid, and in some cases of rents which do not exist.

1170. I mean 18 years' purchase of the fair rent; is that excessive?—Until that fair rent is fixed, and it has not been fixed or disclosed in many cases, I cannot say.

1171. Assuming that the rent is a fair rent, is 18 years' purchase an excessive price?—Yes, in some cases it would be, in the case of lands badly situated. Just as the same rate of purchase would not apply to property in the slums and property in a good part of London, so the same rate of years' purchase of fair rents fixed by the Land Court would not apply to the best land, situated in accessible positions and with a good climate, and to very poor bad lands lying 500 or 600 or 700 feet up a mountain side.

1172. I am afraid your example from the slums of London is not a happy one, because I think the number of years' purchase is just as much; it depends on the rental; very often you get in the slums a larger number of years' purchase. In England (I do not know the rule in Ireland) the number of years' purchase depends on the security you get for your rent?—The security of the bad farms in this district would not be good for 18 years' purchase.

1173. Anybody acquainted with London would tell you that it is as I say?—It is not the case in Dublin.

1174. How many years' purchase would you have in the poorer districts?—I am not prepared to lay down any general line, because each loan has to be looked upon as a separate transaction.

1175. In any of the properties you examined have you come to the opinion that 18 years is too much?—Of a fair rent.

1176. Yes, I mean the fair rent?—I do not think that is a question which admits of any answer, because a fair rent may be the full value of the property. Remember that if a tenant is living upon land, and the tenant through his own fault has injured that land, and made it of less value

Sir William Marriott—continued.

value than it formerly was, the fair rent might be in excess of the full value.

1177. Who is to suffer for the tenants' default, the landlord or the tenant?—It is not a question of landlord and tenant from my point of view, but merely of whether it is safe for the State to lend money.

1178. Now we are rather inquiring into the action of the Drapers' Company. Apparently they have not only been harsh but fraudulent; I am coming to that presently; it may be so, I do not know. If they are harsh the harshness is not in exacting too many years' purchase. I want to know if there is any single case in which they have asked too many years' purchase, assuming the rent is fair?—Certainly; I mentioned an instance where the price asked was 28 years' purchase of the rent.

1179. So it appears; but there may be some explanation of that; could you give the name of that case?—I can give it, but I explained the reason why I preferred not to mention that tenant's name.

1180. Because it might injure him?—It might injure the tenant, he being still a tenant, and in course of litigation with the company.

1181. What you have done with regard to the Drapers' Company is, you have said their action amounted to fraud; it may be true, but it is a serious accusation; you said it was practically a fraud, and that was after giving instances; you gave the names of Esther Crooks, and Elizabeth Johnson, and Elizabeth M'Killick?—I do not think it was with regard to those cases; the only case where I may have used the expression was where the rental named by the agreement was not the legal rent, but a rent of 25 or 30 per cent. higher.

1182. Not the judicial rent?—Yes.

1183. The explanation, as I understand, given in the letter was, that the solicitor, Mr. Glover, I presume, in coming to terms with them, had agreed to take the rental of 1879, and to give 18 years' purchase; that was the explanation?—That was the explanation.

1184. That would not be a fraud, would it?—Certainly not; but the explanation was not furnished till these applications for loans had been investigated.

1185. Have you got an application form which you could show us?—I have not got one here.

1186. In what particular was there any fraud on the part of the Drapers' Company?—I do not attribute fraud to any particular person in the matter, but I do think that it appears in the nature of a fraudulent transaction to represent a different rent as being evidence of the value of the property from that which really exists; it is misleading.

1187. Suppose they put 6 *l.* as the rental, were they at that time receiving 6 *l.*?—As far as payment goes, I think they were receiving nothing.

1188. But they were supposed to receive 6 *l.*?—All they could recover was 5 *l.*

1189. Do you know when a judicial rent in these cases was fixed?—The judicial rents were fixed at various times, but they were fixed before these agreements were sent to the Land Commission, and before they were executed.

1190. Were they fixed before the offer was made?—I should think probably not. I am unable to say when the offer was made, because the offer was made at various times.

1191. Therefore, what they put in the application was really the terms of the agreement between them and the tenants; there is no misleading the tenants?—I have nothing to do with the tenants' view of the matter; my view is simply that of the person investigating the security. I say it was misleading to them.

1192. Take this case: the negotiations began in 1883. In 1887, let us say, the rent of 1882 was the only rent, call it 6 *l.* Then, perhaps, in 1888 a judicial rent is fixed, which we call 5 *l.* They had come to that agreement in 1887 to give 18 years' purchase of the 6 *l.* Was it fraudulent to put that down in the application to the Commissioners?—I do not think it can be said that they had come to the agreement at that time, because the agreement was non-existent; in fact, it was refused by the tenant until after the judicial rents were fixed.

1193. Is that so?—Certainly.

1194. In all cases?—Not in all cases, because these negotiations have been going on for four or five years.

1195. Do you know what delayed the negotiations?—I do not know what delayed the negotiations. I have explained what delayed the completion of the sale after the agreements were executed, but as to any previous negotiations I have no knowledge.

1196. Who was the immediate agent of the company who acted for them; was it Mr. Glover?—The company have had several agents. A Mr. Sawyer, I believe, has been over to Moneymore occasionally.

1197. Have you seen any of these gentlemen; do the Land Commissioners see any of them?—I believe Mr. Lynch has had interviews with Mr. Sawyer. I never had, but I have seen Mr. Glover.

1198. Have these gentlemen ever had any opportunity of giving their explanation of the matter?—Certainly; they came before the Land Commission on the occasion when these judgments were given.

1199. It was after hearing them that Mr. Commissioner Lynch made the remarks in his judgment?—Mr. Lynch, as I believe, had interviews with them more than once.

Chairman.

1200. It was upon Mr. Glover's evidence that Mr. Lynch made those remarks?—Yes.

Sir William Marriott.

1201. You yourself have not asked Mr. Glover or Mr. Sawyer with regard to these matters?—I do not think I have ever seen Mr. Sawyer, but I have seen Mr. Glover often.

1202. Did you bring to his notice that he had put in applications at the wrong rent?—I brought it to the notice of Sir William Cunningham, who was agent of the company, when I discovered it, merely because he happened to be at Moneymore at the same time that I was.

1203. What explanation did he give?—He gave

Sir William Marriott—continued.

gave me no explanation, nor did I expect any from him, because the agreements were not prepared by him.

1204. You mentioned it to Sir William Cunningham, who did not prepare the agreement, but not to Mr. Glover, who did; is that so?—Mr. Glover does not reside at Moneymore, and I had no opportunity of seeing him, nor would it be right for me to mention the matter till I had brought it before the Commissioners. I believe I did mention it to Sir William Cunningham.

1205. But never to Mr. Glover?—No.

1206. Mr. Glover never had an opportunity of giving his version, whatever it might be?—It was not to me he was to give explanations, but to the Land Commission. I am only a subordinate officer of the Land Commission.

1207. There were, I see, several lawsuits, one especially against Mr. Beresford; in what courts were they?—In the High Court of Justice.

1208. They gave their decision in favour of the Drapers' Company?—They did.

1209. I suppose we can have a copy of those proceedings, and they can explain themselves?—I should think so.

1210. This case of Mr. Beresford, as I understand, settled all the others?—I believe so. Mr. Beresford was a prominent tenant on that part of the estate.

1211. In your opinion, were the Drapers' Company very harsh in their proceedings?—No; I do not accuse the Drapers' Company of harshness in respect to the fixing of these prices, but I think, in the face of these letters, it was very natural for the tenants to resist the payment of interest.

1212. The first letter is dated 10th August 1886, and it says: "Referring to our interview on the 26th July last, I beg to inform you that the Court of Assistants of the Drapers' Company have had under further consideration the question of the sale of the estate to the tenants, and will modify the terms, as communicated to you by me at the interview, by substituting the payment of one year's rent in cash for the proposed promissory notes, and remitting all rent to purchasing tenants from the 1st November 1885. The terms of sale will therefore stand thus: purchase money, a sum equal to 18 times the rent; all arrears of rent to the 1st November 1885 to be paid in cash and no rent to be demanded after that date; the company to pay the costs of the sale as between them and the tenants. These terms must be considered as finally and definitely settled, so far as the company are concerned, and no further modification will be made in them. They will stand good for one month from this date, and the company will not be bound by them after that time." So you see these terms only stand good to 10th September 1886; you had not noticed that at all?—Yes; but I believe the agreements were executed before the time. The delay arose from the company not completing the procedure necessary before the Land Commission.

1213. What was the company's object in that; they were willing to then?—I do not know what the object was. I know they did not do so.

1214. Do you mean to say the allegation against the company is this: here, in August, 1886, they offer certain terms which must be taken up within a month's time, or they fall through, and then that the company cause delay to cause them to fall through?—I can give you one reason for their delay. It is not a question I could go into, as it involves a great many questions of procedure. They offered to sell the tenants the fee-simple of their farms. When they came to lodge the draft conveyance, it was found they had not the fee-simple. There was a reservation to the Irish Society, and the release from the Irish Society which was part of the company's title was not produced till 1888.

1215. Pardon me. If this letter were accepted within the month ulterior delay would not affect it. All this letter says is, that the terms are to be accepted within a month; were they accepted in this case?—I believe so.

1216. This is in writing, and it would be binding. Do you mean to say they were accepted within the month, and that the Drapers' Company has since departed from them?—It is my belief that they did.

1217. What I want to get at is, the allegation against the Drapers' Company, so that the Drapers' Company may know what to answer. You say that, though they gave these terms on 10th August 1886, and they were accepted before 10th September 1886, they then departed from them?—I do not know what you would call the acceptance. I should deem the acceptance merely the signature of the contract.

1218. The acceptance of the terms?—I believe they did that at once.

1219. That is quite sufficient to form a contract. Mr. Healy will tell you so, I think. I want to know what the allegation against them is. Do you know that these terms were accepted within the month?—I do not know. I believe they were. The tenants were most anxious to buy. There was a subsequent letter, I think.

1220. The contract may have been varied then. There is no other correspondence, except the letter of the 3rd January 1887, and that letter I may read again, because the whole of it was not read. "Drapers' Hall, London, E.C., 3rd January 1886. Dear Sir,—The Drapers' Company have had under consideration your letter of the 13th ultimo. They are sorry that there should still be any difficulty in the way of tenants purchasing their holdings, but they cannot think that they are called upon to make fresh concessions in the matter. As the terms now stand, purchasing tenants will be called upon to pay neither rent nor interest from the 1st November 1885. The company confidently anticipated that many purchases would have been completed before the 1st November 1886; but as matters stand, several weeks must yet elapse before any purchase-money is paid over to the company. This delay is, of course, a serious loss to them, and, if it continues, may compel them to further consider the terms of sale, but not in the direction which you suggest." I suppose the terms of sale being made rather onerous?—No; I think it refers to the collection of interest, because the company had no power to withdraw

Sir William Marriott—continued.

withdraw from the sale or alter when once the contract was signed.

1221. But this looks as though that were not arranged, because this is January 1887?—The agreements were signed before then, I think.

1222. At what date were the agreements signed, do you know; if you could give us that it would put the matter right?—Unless I am to take it by inference from Mr. Commissioner Lynch's judgment, I could not speak of my own knowledge without inspection of the documents.

1223. With regard to the arrears, according to this they could get no arrears after 1885. Are you aware of any case where they demanded arrears after 1885?—No, it was the interest they recovered after 1885.

1224. Not arrears, but interest of purchase money?—I believe so.

1225. Then there is no charge that they got arrears after 1885, but that they charged interest on the purchase money?—Certainly.

1226. In one case where a poor woman had receipts for the rent you said they were still going to sue her for that. How could that be? You said that though she had got receipts for the rent which she had paid, they were still going to sue her for the same amounts?—That is on another part of the estate, and does not refer to this lawsuit at all. Shall I explain that now?

1227. Yes, I should like to know very much.—It is admitted that these receipts were given to the tenants, although no money was paid.

1228. Then why were they given?—The consideration given by the tenants for those receipts was the execution of a contract to buy.

1229. The tenants had not paid any rent. The agent for the Drapers' Company gave them receipts as though they had, and the consideration was that they should enter into a contract. Was that it?—Yes; on entering into the contract they received receipts for rents which were not paid in cash.

1230. If they entered into the contract, surely the Drapers' Company could not sue in a court of law. In those cases the agreements are not going to be carried out?—No.

1231. Therefore the receipts are presumed to be worthless?—Yes.

1232. With reference to this place, Moneymore, to which you have referred, there, as I understand, the company built all the houses themselves?—So I understand.

1233. The custom elsewhere is to let on lease, on what length of lease are the other villages let; is 99 years the length of a lease?—In the neighbouring town of Cookstown I believe the land is held on leases for ever. In the town of Magherafelt I am not aware, but it has all been sold now.

1234. They like the leasehold system better than the freehold system and keeping it in their own hands?—I think the occupiers would prefer to own the freehold.

1235. What tenures are the villages or towns in Ireland generally built on?—On so many various tenures that I do not think I can tell you. There are many cases where towns have been built on yearly tenures by the occupiers, and the custom has been permitted of their selling those houses as if they held the fee-simple, although there is no legal protection. I believe such a custom exists in some places in England; I have heard of it in Scotland.

1236. In Moneymore the company built the houses, and will not sell them; is that so?—Oh, they will sell them.

1237. What is the complaint against them with regard to it?—I have no complaint against them as regards that; but they are so anxious to sell that, having offered two of their houses in Moneymore to the occupants, and the occupants declining to buy them on those terms, they served them with a notice to quit.

1238. Then they want to sell?—Yes.

1239. Are there any willing buyers or not?—Certainly there are many willing buyers. In those two cases the tenants agreed to the company's terms rather than leave their houses. Of course, in the towns the occupiers have no protection from the various Land Acts.

1240. Is it that the terms they ask in this particular case of Moneymore are too high?—I did not refer to the town of Moneymore at all as to the prices they were asking or getting.

1241. I rather gathered from what you said that Moneymore was in a bad position on account of the tenure of the houses; that in most villages they had had a leasehold system which had answered, and in Moneymore the Drapers' Company, getting it to themselves, and not letting it out in leases, the tenants had no hold on the property, and therefore they could not manufacture or carry on a shop business?—I think the result of the Drapers' Company expenditure there has been to prevent the existence of trade.

1242. And that is because they will not grant leases?—I think so; but now there is no complaint. I am sure they spent the money there with the best intentions. I think they made a mistake, and now they are selling, or have sold, the greater part of the house property in Moneymore.

1243. I think you said the tenant's interest in the land you can take as a commissioner's security for the money advanced?—Yes.

1244. If it belongs to the tenant; if it is not sold or mortgaged before?—Even if it is mortgaged.

1245. You can still take it?—Yes.

Colonel *Lewis*.

1246. When you were asked as to complaints against the Drapers' Company you said there was a difficulty in obtaining information from them, and when the Chairman asked you afterwards further about it, you said the only complaint you made was that they did not tell you what the judicial rents on their property were; is it not a fact that the judicial rents are perfectly well known; they are public property, are they not?—The Land Commission take the statement of the rental and the area of the tenancy which are set out in the contract to buy as being true.

1247. I am asking you as to judicial rents; they are published?—Yes.

1248. They

Colonel *Laurie*—continued.

1248. They are public property?—Yes.

1249. Therefore that information is to be obtained from other sources than the Drapers' Company?—It can be.

1250. Is it not rather an unfair complaint against them that they have not furnished that information?—I do not think it is an unfair complaint, because they are bound not only by the rules of the Land Commission court, but by the ordinary principles of business to set out the rents of the property on which they want a loan, and the complaint I make is that they did not do it. I understand their explanation perfectly, but I think they presented the contracts in a misleading aspect to the Land Commission.

1251. The Land Commission have the information as to the judicial rents. You are an officer of theirs; you therefore are in possession of this information. Is it not a somewhat unfair complaint to make against the Drapers' Company that they have not supplied you with information, which is within the knowledge of your own department?—I do not think it is. An officer of a court with a great many branches like ours cannot be acquainted with the records of judicial rents which extend to some thousands of cases.

1252. There was a complaint as to the cost to which the small tenants were put by the action of the Drapers' Company. You mentioned one case in which Elizabeth Johnson had to borrow 80 *l.*, and the cost of taking it were 20 *l.*?—Yes.

1253. Is that a usual sum for raising a small loan of 80 *l.*?—I think it was rather heavy. I gave you that not from inspection of the bill of costs, but from the statement of the party who lent her the money.

1254. The Chairman just now used the expression, "A rich harvest of costs." £. 20 for obtaining 80 *l.* would seem to me in England a very large sum to pay. It would be hardly usual in Ireland, I think?—I have frequently known such sums paid, but that had nothing to do with the Drapers' Company.

1255. You complained that they had placed this burden on the backs of the small tenants?—I gave it as an instance of the way in which the commissioners' security had been impaired by the long delay which has led to these loans.

1256. Do you consider the Drapers' Company responsible for this very exorbitant bill of costs?—Not in the least. I do not think the Drapers' Company had anything to do with it. I did not mention it as against the Drapers' Company, but as an illustration of the loans borrowed by the tenants to pay off these unexpected calls.

1257. As regards the expenditure of money on the agricultural farms of the Drapers' Company, we have it of course in the petition that 50 years ago they did expend money themselves, and charge interest in the way usual in England. I believe under the old Ulster law it was impossible to rack-rent tenants upon their own improvements. They were entitled to the value of their own improvements, were they not?—I do not think it was in the least impossible to do it. It was because it was so very easy that the Act of 1881 was passed.

1258. In Ulster, even before that Act, there was a system of Ulster tenant-right, was there not, which practically protected tenants from being rack-rented for their own improvements?—I do not think it did at all. The Act of 1870 gave a tenant the right to claim compensation for certain improvements, but he had a very long and costly lawsuit, with a doubtful issue, to stand before he could do it; therefore he generally accepted the landlord's terms, and agreed to whatever rent he was asked to pay.

1259. Of course you considered it was to the advantage of the tenants if the Drapers' Company as the landlords expended the money and charged a moderate rate of interest for a permanent improvement?—Certainly, but I think that the expenditure in that way was not very large. We find in the first report of the deputation, that the expenses of the estate are agency and management only, as by universal custom of the country, repairs and new buildings of all sorts are done and executed at the expense of the tenant without the landlord contributing either material or workmanship.

1260. That is the system?—That was the custom in 1817, when the Drapers' Company first got control of this estate.

1261. Then the statement in that petition is not absolutely accurate, I suppose. Fifty years ago takes us back to 1840?—I have not dealt with that statement at all, because I do not know anything about it.

1262. The tenants themselves state that, and probably they know more about it than you yourself do?—Certainly.

Mr. *T. M. Healy*.

1263. Colonel Laurie has suggested that the Land Commission having in their possession their own records, might have found out whether these tenants were judicially rented or not. Is it not the case that the lists of judicial tenancies number 200,000 or 300,000 tenants, and that they are not indexed in any way, and that there is no means of getting to know on the Land Commission without a search of weeks or months for information which the company ought to have furnished?—A search is necessary.

1264. It is absolutely impossible for the Land Commission to find out without at least a month's search, whether A. B. is a judicial tenant or not?—Oh, with a shorter search than that; but the commissioners, relying on the accuracy of the statement furnished with the contracts for sale, dispensed with the obligation previously enforced upon applicants of supplying copies of the judicial orders on the ground of the difficulty and expense of these searches.

1265. Have the Land Commission any handier means of getting information as to whether a man is a judicial tenant than any Member of this House has from the Returns presented to Parliament?—Nothing except that the books are in the House.

1266. Are these books indexed in any way alphabetically, or are they all higgledy-piggledy?—They are prepared in counties.

1267. To each county is there a particular year and a particular month?—Yes. They are indexed under the names of the landlords.

1268. It

Mr. T. M. Healy—continued.

1368. It has been suggested that the Ulster tenant right prevented the raising of rents upon improvements; is that so?—I do not think it did at all.

1369. Was there any machinery known to the law by which any landlord in Ulster would be prevented from raising his rents under the Ulster tenant right?—None that I am aware of, if he chose to run the risk of a law-suit with his tenant for compensation for improvements.

1370. But before the Act of 1870?—None whatever.

1371. The Ulster tenant was no more protected from the imposition of rent for improvements than any other tenant?—No.

1372. Sir William Marriott has asked you with regard to certain prices whether 18 years' purchase was fair or not. I should like to ask whether I correctly understand you as giving us the fact that in numbers of cases the instalments which the tenants would have to pay under the 18 years' purchase would be heavier than the judicial rents?—In some cases the instalments which the tenants would have had to pay on the prices for which the contracts were lodged would have been in excess of the judicial rents, and in addition the tenant would have been liable for a proportion of poor rate for which he is not liable now.

1373. What inducement would a tenant have to buy if his instalment of purchase was higher than his judicial rent?—None; he would have no inducement whatever, except to escape from the ejectment proceedings.

1374. Then we may infer from that that if it was not for the pressure of the ejectment proceedings such a tenant would not dream of buying?—Certainly not.

1375. And there is no other explanation except coercion and duress for such a purchase?—In this case none; the tenants were, I believe, quite unwilling to buy at the prices asked.

1376. May I take it that it is possible to use the Land Purchase Act, the Ashbourne Act, as an engine of oppression?—Where there are very large arrears of rent the tenants have the alternative of ejectment for the arrears of rent, or agreeing to the landlord's terms.

1377. If a landlord makes his instalments higher than the judicial rent, he can compel the tenant to purchase. If the tenant does not choose to purchase, the landlord can compel the tenant to adopt his terms?—If there were arrears of rent he could practically.

1378. Then the Ashbourne Act in certain cases is an engine of oppression?—I think it is not due to the Ashbourne Act. There is no doubt that arrears may be used to compel people to buy who do not wish to buy upon the terms on which they are asked.

1379. You may by means of the Ashbourne Act compel the tenant who has a judicial rent fixed to pay a higher rent to the State?—I would not say that it is by means of the Ashbourne Act, but by the fact of the existence of large arrears.

1380. But the fact is that you could compel a tenant holding at 4 *l.* to adopt a course involving him in a 5 *l.* a year liability?—Certainly; any man who has the means of exercising an undue influence of that kind over a tenant may induce him to agree to the purchase at a price which would be in excess of what would be fair and what would be safe for the State to lend upon.

1381. With this scandal before their eyes what steps have the Land Purchase Commissioners taken, whether by rule or otherwise, to prevent this kind of oppression going on; the cancelling of a particular agreement, is not sufficient, is it?—I am not aware that they have done anything on the Drapers' estate, except to give the judgments that I have put in, and the dismissing of all cases where they considered the security was insufficient.

1382. The Land Commission would have known nothing of this matter on the Drapers' estate if the tenants had not sent up that round robin?—They would not except through that, and the inquiries of their inspector.

1383. Has the action of the Land Commission been confined to cancelling the particular agreement on the Drapers' estate, or have they done anything by rule to prevent the Ashbourne Act being utilised in this way?—I do not think they could do anything except direct all persons who advised them as to the security to institute these inquiries, or to alter or frame their rules and their forms in such a manner as to prevent it. This action of the Drapers' Company has led to some changes in the form of application and in their rules.

1384. There are still pending, as I understand, in the Land Commission office a number of agreements from the London City companies to be dealt with?—Yes.

1385. Would it not be possible for the Land Commission to adopt a rule to have no agreements unless the agreement contained on the face of it a release from all arrears?—The agreement in use at present, which, I believe, was brought into use on account of such instances occurring, does that. It recites that the price is inclusive of all arrears of rent up to the last gale day.

1386. Does it go on to recite that none of the purchase money and none of the consideration of purchase has been agreed upon on account of arrears of rent?—I do not think it could do that.

1387. You do not think it is the business of an official like yourself to inquire and report upon that fact?—I make inquiry if I have any reason to suspect anything of the kind, but my business is simply to advise the Commissioners as to whether in my opinion the security offered, including the landlord's estate and the tenant's estate, is sufficient to cover their loan.

1388. I want to know whether the Land Commission have now adopted any rule whereby such scandals as we understand have arisen in this case will be prevented in future?—The framing of their application form, as I have explained, I think does that.

1389. But as I gather it does not prevent the fact that the arrears of rent may be added on to the purchase money?—No, I believe it does not.

1390. And it does not protect the tenant in respect

Mr. *T. M. Healy*—continued.

respect of the interest to be charged?—Yes, it does. One protection to both parties is that these contracts should be as definite as possible. The form of agreement now has a clause by which the tenant binds himself to pay interest from the date of the execution of the agreement to its completion.

1291. Did not the Land Commission, after the courts had decided that $3\frac{1}{2}$ per cent. was the legal interest, continue to allow 4 per cent. to be exacted?—I am not aware, but it is very possible.

1292. We have been hearing about Moneymore, and you told us that the tenants of the Moneymore division of the estate were the rich tenants who were willing to purchase; that is so, is it not?—Yes.

1293. As to the Ballinascreen portion, you described those and you said you never saw more abject serfs in the tenants of any country; that is the poorer portion?—The poorer parts of that division, because that division contains good as well as bad land.

1294. I think I am right in saying that the Moneymore division is the Protestant division, and that Ballinascreen is the Catholic?—I think you would be right in saying that the occupants of the poorer land generally are Catholics; but it is not my business to inquire into the religion of the people I visit, and I have not done so.

1295. We may take it as consequent upon that that the incident of oppression and hardship has fallen to a larger extent in this case on the Catholics than on the Protestants?—I think it is possible, but you must not take me as giving any statement as to the religion of the people, because I do not go into that question.

1296. It is the fact that the Catholics are on the bogs and the hills and the Protestants on the good lands?—It is very probable.

1297. You mentioned certain bill transactions. Mr. Benjamin Barefoot I understand did sign certain bills or promissory notes?—If there was any suggestion, as there was, made that these arrears should be settled by the tenants giving a promissory note it never came to anything. I believe such a suggestion was made.

1298. Did not a number of the companies when the tenants found themselves unable to pay the arrears of rent or arrears of interest compel them to sign promissory notes to the amount?—I do not know whether they compelled them or not, but the case you referred to was on the Salters' estate.

1299. Was not Mr. Benjamin Barefoot sued on a promissory note?—Not that I am aware of.

1300. In the second action. He was the hero of two cases?—I am not acquainted with the circumstances.

1301. What was the Salters' case of a promissory note?—I am very imperfectly acquainted with it; but I know promissory notes were given by some tenants for arrears due and not paid at the completion of the sales.

1302. Was it not brought under the notice of the Land Commission that one of the London companies had contemporaneously running side by side with their agreements a kind of pocket transaction with the tenants in the shape of promissory notes that they should pay not only their instalments to the Government, but that they should pay sums from time to time on promissory notes to the company?—These promissory notes were given, the sale was completed, and therefore, after the annuity began to the Land Commission the tenants would still be liable for the promissory notes. The matter was the subject of an action in Dublin, but I am not acquainted with the particulars.

1303. Would not that also impair the security of the Government for the purchase-money?—I think it is very desirable that the Land Commission, when they make a loan, should at any rate start with a man unencumbered by any such claims for previous debts.

1304. Now I go back to my former inquiry. You stated that the existing forms of the Land Purchase Commission provide that all arrears of rent are settled for. Does that recital prevent the existence of what I may call pocket transactions in the shape of promissory notes?—I am not able to give an answer to that question. It would be a question of law. Wherever the Land Commission find that promissory notes have been given, and are in existence at the time of the sale, they have required, in many cases, such promissory notes to be sent up to their office, and cancelled.

1305. You have justified the existing form of the Land Commission, which recites that all arrears of rent are settled for. You have stated that the Land Commission have prevented for the future any scandals by adopting that form?—I did not say so. I say they have adopted this form for the purpose, as far as they can, of preventing such transactions.

1306. Is there anything to prevent a company which recites to the Land Commission that all arrears of rent are satisfied, getting at the same time from the tenant, under the same species of coercion, a promissory note for those arrears which his agreement says have been satisfied for?—I do not think there is anything to prevent it being got, but I suppose the same question would arise if they sued upon those promissory notes, as in the case of suing tenants in the case mentioned for arrears of rent for which they hold receipts.

1307. Have not they successfully sued tenants on those promissory notes in the courts?—They recovered judgment in the Salters' case.

1308. On a promissory note?—Yes; but I am not prepared to speak about that. In fact, I only know of that matter by hearsay.

1309. We may take it generally that in spite of this recital on the Land Commission contract that all arrears of rent are extinguished, they have still been successfully recovered on a promissory note?—No, not in spite of it; because the form of agreement now in use was not in use then.

1310. Do you think that in those cases the agreements ought to deal in any way with the question of the subsequent accrual of interest; do you think that would prevent hardships?—I think that when an agreement is entered into the sale should be closed with as little delay as possible.

1311. Is it not the interest of the landlord to

delay

Mr. T. M. Healy—continued.

many cases, where the law gives him interest in the meantime, where he is certain to get the purchase money also, to delay the transaction; is it not a premium on delay?—No; I think in most cases the landlord is anxious to complete, but the law's delays and the delays incident to a public office are a cause of great hardship both to landlords and tenants; because both parties, as a rule, want to close the matter as soon as possible.

1312. What is the longest period the Drapers have taken to close a transaction?—Three years.

1313. Do you consider that reasonable?—Certainly not; I think there was great cause for complaint of delay in the case of the Drapers' estate.

1314. Do you not think it would be recoverable if a rule were adopted to prevent interest accruing during that terribly long period?—I do not think it would be reasonable; I think the reasonable thing would be to provide, as is done by a proceeding under a vesting order, by the 15th Section of the Act of 1887, for the quick termination of the relation of debtor and creditor between the two parties, and then if the delay is on the part of the landlord in completing his title he alone suffers because his money lies there, and he cannot get it until he has completed his title; but the transaction, as far as vesting the land in the tenant, is completed, and the landlord is delivered from the necessity of collecting the interest.

1315. That is rather an expensive process, is it not?—I do not think it is more expensive than proceeding by conveyance.

1316. Why in the case of the Drapers' Company was it not suggested that they might have proceeded by vesting order?—I am unable to say. It was not supposed that in the case of a company who presumably had a good title, there would be any such delay at all; and therefore it was unlikely that any suggestion was made to them as to expediting the matter at first.

1317. Will you give us what is the total balance of the Drapers' estate remaining to be dealt with?—I have no information on the subject.

1318. You have no information either as to the total number of uncompleted transactions now pending before the Land Commission?—Yes; there are 140 cases of agreements lodged by the Drapers' Company, many of which have been nearly lodged a year. These were delayed because the lands cannot be inspected until maps of those lands are furnished, and those maps never have been furnished.

1319. Whose fault is that?—I think it is the fault of the company. The Land Commission took these agreements on account of the strained relations between the tenants and the company in the hope that they might expedite the sales; and, therefore, they took them in the first instance without maps, those maps never having been lodged, although they have been asked for over and over again; nothing has been done in those cases.

1320. The tenant in the meantime has been paying interest on this money?—He is liable to interest; and not only that, but in cases where they have signed agreements some of them are asked to enter into an arbitration that is pending, and for that purpose to pay up 1½ years rent and costs to the Drapers' Company.

1321. Are the Land Commission absolutely helpless to prevent a scandal of that kind?—Except by cancelling the agreement.

1322. And letting the tenant go back without any redress whatever to his former position?—Except on those grounds I think the Land Commission would have long ago cancelled a number of agreements that are in their office.

1323. May we take it that a State Department affected by commiseration for the tenants is doing things that it would not do in a normal condition of affairs?—I think it is a very natural thing for them to do. If the tenants represent that they are anxious to complete those sales, I think it is very proper of the Land Commission not to dismiss the agreements for the delay of the company. The great difficulty is to bring such power to bear upon the company in these particular cases, and as to this particular detail, as to expedite the matter.

1324. My point is that as the rules now stand the Land Commission could not punish the company's default without punishing the tenants. Could no means be adopted by a rule which would prevent the punishing of the tenants, and would punish a defaulting landlord?—I do not suppose the Land Commission want to punish either one party or the other, but they want to get their business through.

1325. Would not the owner of interest in these great delays be an inducement to sellers to complete transactions?—I think it would be much better to expedite the proceedings by vesting the holding in the tenant at once on the agreement being approved of. As you spoke about delays, I should like to give you an illustration. Here is a tenant who presumably has agreed to buy his holding, for he receives a receipt for 9 *l.* 6 *s.* 3 *d.*, two years' interest on his purchase money, 149 *l.* 17 *s.*, up to the 1st November 1888. He also receives a receipt for 8 *l.* 8 *s.* 6 *d.*, a year's rent to the 1st November 1885, to the Drapers' Company. There is an abatement of 3 *l.* 7 *s.* 6 *d.* off that, and costs, 3 *l.* 1 *s.* 6 *d.*, added. That agreement has never been lodged in the Land Commission office, and those sums appear to be added to the purchase. The receipts are marked on the back "To purchase." That tenant tells me he has entered into an agreement to buy. He is asked to pay a year's rent and 1 *l.* on account of costs, if any, due to the company, and to attend an arbitration.

1326. You stated, I think, that Sir William Cunningham was the agent at one time?—Yes.

1327. He had the reputation of being a kindly gentleman, I believe?—Very much so.

1328. And was well regarded in the district?—So I understand.

1329. Why did the company dismiss him?—I am not aware whether the company have dismissed Sir William Cunningham or not; but on the occasion of my last two visits to Moneymore he has not been resident there. What his relations with the company are I do not know.

Mr. *T. M. Healy*—continued.

1330. He has ceased to be the agent?—Mr. Glover is at present the acting agent, I believe.

1331. Have expressions of opinion fallen from the Land Commissioners, in a number of cases, as to the inconvenience resulting to a tenant from the same gentleman being solicitor and agent?—I am not aware.

1332. You do not think it in any way affects the piling up of costs in the collection of rent?—It is said to do so; but that is not a subject which I have considered, at any rate with reference to this particular inquiry.

1333. You have stated that it is only fair to Mr. Glover to say that he was most willing to give you information?—Mr. Glover has given me information whenever I have had occasion to apply to him. As regards the insertion of the rents improperly in the agreement, we have it in Mr. Glover's own evidence that that was done by the direction of the company. That is stated in Mr. Commissioner Lynch's judgment, but I have no knowledge of it myself.

1334. It is only fair to Mr. Glover that the statement should go forth that at any rate he was in no way reluctant to give you information?—Not at all; he has not been reluctant.

Mr. *T. M. Healy*—continued.

1335. You stated that in your experience you never met with any such miserable and terror-stricken population as the Ballinascreen portion?—I do not think they are miserable, but they are very poor. They are farming poor land, lying at a great elevation; and agriculture in such a situation is very precarious.

1336. I believe they are uneducated also?—They have shown a great deal of ignorance in this matter.

1337. Did you notice a great many schools erected amongst them by the Drapers' Company?—There are schools, but the number I could not say, built by the Drapers' Company, I believe, and I believe also to some extent endowed by the Drapers' Company; when I say "endowed" I mean they receive grants.

1338. Have the Land Commissioners at all taken into account in the purchase transactions the fact that in the matter of price the companies have been in the habit of giving grants for religious and educational purposes which are now stopped?—It had nothing to do with the Commissioners' business in the transaction.

Monday, 16th June 1890.

MEMBERS PRESENT:

Mr. Clancy.
Sir John Ellis.
Mr. John Ellis.
Mr. Elton.
Mr. T. M. Healy.
Colonel Laurie.
Mr. Lawson.
Mr. Lea.
Sir William Marriott.
Mr. John Morley.
Mr. Sexton.
Sir Richard Temple.

THE RIGHT HONOURABLE JOHN MORLEY, IN THE CHAIR.

The Right Honourable LORD JUSTICE FITZGIBBON, Examined.

Chairman.

1339. BESIDES being a Judge of the Court of Appeal in Ireland, you are, I believe, a member of the Endowed Schools Commission?—I am one of the two Judicial Commissioners, under the Act of 1885, for the reorganisation of Educational Endowments.

1340. And you have also been a Commissioner of National Education, have you not?—I have, since 1884.

1341. And you have been a member of the Endowed Schools Commission since 1878?—I was a member of the Parliamentary Commission appointed in 1878 which reported in 1880.

1342. You have been concerned in inquiries into the Ulster endowments, have you not?—Yes, on two occasions. The first Commission was a commission of inquiry only, appointed by the Lord Lieutenant, of which Lord Rosse was the chairman. It was appointed, I think, on the motion of Lord Randolph Churchill in the House of Commons, and it inquired into all the educational endowments of Ireland at that time, and reported in 1880. The Commission of 1885 was constituted by Act of Parliament as an executive Commission to frame schemes for the future management of endowments, and it reports annually to Parliament, but its duty is principally executive.

1343. What was the nature of the inquiries in which you have been concerned?—The earlier Commission visited the North of Ireland, and took evidence as to the nature, state, condition, and history of the endowments, in fact, it only carried on the Report of a previous Commission which had sat from 1854 to 1858, and had published a very elaborate Report, giving a full history of all the existing endowments at that time.

1344. Was that a Report to Parliament?—It was a Report to Parliament, and was presented in 1858.

1345. You say that the Commission of 1885, of which you are a member, is an executive Commission; what does it do?—First, I may, perhaps, tell the Committee the constitution of the Commission. There are two Judicial Commissioners. The original Judicial Commissioners named in the Act were myself and the Right Honourable John Naish, at that time ex-Chancellor; he became Chancellor again afterwards. Since that he has been an additional Judge of the Court of Appeal. He and I were the Judicial Commissioners until unfortunately at the beginning of this year he was obliged to resign from ill-health. There are also three Assistant Commissioners, one a member of the Church of Ireland, one a Roman Catholic, and the other a Presbyterian. The three Assistant Commissioners take part in all the proceedings of the Commission, down to the final settlement of the scheme, and every scheme has to be signed by both the Judicial Commissioners, so that they must concur in any plan that is passed. When they sign the scheme it goes before the Lord Lieutenant in Council, and after a period being allowed for objections it is provisionally approved by the Lord Lieutenant, and then, if no petition is presented to Parliament against it, or no Resolution of either House is passed against it, it is finally approved by the Lord Lieutenant and becomes a statute.

1346. When approved it has the force of a Statute?—When approved it has the force of a Statute, but not until then. But the Act provides that every scheme, when finally approved, shall be deemed to be within the powers of the Commission, so that substantially it is a legislative Commission.

1347. I think it will be convenient if we divide the evidence which you are prepared to give to the Committee under three heads. First, anything that you can tell us as to the Irish Society; secondly, as to the London companies generally; and, thirdly, as to a specific case, which we have heard a great deal about both this year and last, the case of Rainey's School at Magherafelt. First, as to the Irish Society, what dealings has your Commission had with transactions in which the Irish Society was concerned?

Chairman—continued.

cerned?—We were obliged to consider how far the grants for the Irish Society came under our Act. The procedure prescribed to us is that we shall first hold a preliminary inquiry in the case of any endowment as regards which we contemplate framing a scheme; and that we shall then, after that preliminary inquiry, which is to be a public inquiry, on due notice, prepare a draft scheme which must lie for two months for objections. The objections are then considered, and if the objections are important, we hold a further public inquiry to examine into them; and those inquiries have always been conducted in the localities. Accordingly the Commission having been started in 1885, in October 1886 we went to the north of Ireland and visited all the Royal schools and the schools in receipt of grants from the Irish Society.

1348. The Royal schools are the Royal free schools which were established by James I.?—The Royal schools are the five existing schools which were founded as part of the Plantation of Ulster by King James I.

1349. Then I suppose the question that came before you when you went to the north of Ireland, and that you had to consider was, whether the grants of the Irish Society were, or were not, of the nature of endowments?—Yes; we took a great deal of evidence at Londonderry and at Coleraine on the first occasion; that is, on the preliminary inquiry. Those were the only places in the county of Londonderry where the Commission sat at that time, in October 1886; and we had before us, of course, the report of the case of the Skinners' Company *v.* the Irish Society, in 12 Clarke and Finnelly, in the House of Lords, of which I have no doubt the Committee has heard.

1350. Was that the case in the year 1845?—Yes; we also had the Report of the previous Commission of 1858, and of the Commission of 1820 to go some. I have brought with me the passages in those previous Blue Books bringing the matter down to the time when we proceeded to our inquiry. We found this on p. 185 of the Report of 1858: "In 1854 the Commissioners who were appointed to inquire into the Corporation of London investigated, as a part of their duties, the history and constitution of the Irish Society." They reported at that time that "From the constitution of the Irish Society, and in consequence of its being managed by a board sitting in London, we cannot expect that in the management of educational trusts in Ireland it should possess the important assistance which personal observation and careful supervision can alone supply;" and that Commission recommended (p. 281): "(1) That immediate steps should be taken in order that all the funds devoted to education under the charter of the Irish Society should assume a definite form, and be placed under a system of efficient management; and with this view, that the scattered funds of the society should be secured for and concentrated on a limited number of endowed schools on this foundation in the county of Londonderry. (2) That in the event of the recommendations of the Commissioners on the Corporation of London being carried into effect, and the Irish Society dissolved, the townlands of Ronnagallagh and Gransha should be set apart for a Royal free school for the county of Londonderry. (3) That in case the society shall not appoint local patrons and managers, and put their primary schools under the proposed Board of Endowed Schools, or under the Board of National Education, a local board ought to be established in the county, which should have the management of the schools supported from such funds of the society as may be allocated to educational purposes."

1351. Then, in short, the purport of those recommendations which you have read was to dissolve the Irish Society, and define the trusts?—Yes; those recommendations seem, however, to have required legislation to give effect to them.

1352. What do you mean by dissolving the Irish Society?—That proposal seems from another portion of the Report to have reference to a Report of 1854 of a Committee or Commission on the Corporation of London. I should mention also that the second paragraph is important with regard to those two townlands that are spoken of, which they sought to make an endowment for the Royal Free School in Londonderry. Foyle College was receiving large grants from the Irish Society; it had originally been a diocesan school under the Statute of Queen Elizabeth: and that passage relates to certain lands held by the Irish Society which the Commissioners thought were lands that had been allotted originally for the purposes of a Royal free school in Londonderry. There is a schedule to this Report containing the endowments that then existed as endowments in operation (vol. 3, page 588). There were then 110 endowed schools in the county of Londonderry. Of these 110, 88 schools were aided by the Irish Society, the grants amounting to 1,434 *l.* 10 *s.* per annum; 56 *l.* 10 *s.* was paid for schools in Donegal, and 10 *l.* for a school in Tyrone. All these grants are described as "Annual applications of funds as parts of the trusts of their estates;" and the total is 1,501 *l.*

1353. Will you state the special facts with regard to Foyle College?—Its endowments are described at page 600 of vol. 3. It is stated to have been founded under the Statute of Elizabeth. That is the Statute founding the diocesan free schools. They had nothing but a money endowment, and the money endowment consisted entirely of a tax upon the incomes of the clergy.

1354. In that Report they speak of Foyle College as a diocesan free school, do they not?—They do.

Mr. *Sexton*.

1355. What was this Commission?—It was a Commission appointed by Royal Warrant in 1854, and inquired into all the educational endowments in Ireland and produced four large Blue Books. They were called the Endowed Schools Commission of 1854, and they reported in 1858. They describe amongst the endowments of Foyle College "the Irish Society's annual application of funds from 1818." They then refer to some of earlier Acts of Parliament, and to an Order of the Lord Lieutenant in Council of 1824; and then, "Grand Jury presentment with donations

Mr. Sexton—continued.

from some of the London Companies and Corporation, and subscriptions, together amounting to 12,923 *l.* 1 *s.* 6 *d.*, expended on building about 1814," on a site granted by the Bishop of Derry.

Chairman.

1356. That is the enumeration of the sources of income of Foyle College?—Yes; the sources from which the funds by which the building was erected were derived, and, secondly, of its annual income. Its annual income at the time consisted almost entirely of grants from the Irish Society and a voluntary grant from the Bishop of Derry, and the clergy fees under the Statute of Elizabeth. The Report, at page 168, sets out the expenditure of the Irish Society in support of education for the five years before the Report.

1357. Is that all for intermediate education?—No; a great number of the grants, the great majority of them, were small sums annually paid to primary schools. As I have already stated there were 110 schools in the county, of which 88 got grants from the Society.

Mr. Sexton.

1358. What is the total annual grant from the Society?—The total annual grant as given in the Report of 1838 is 1,501 *l.* I should mention with regard to Foyle College that the account of its endowments is found at page 167, and it was shortly this. In the early years of the plantation lands were stated to have been intended to be allotted for a Royal free school in the county of Londonderry, as they were in other counties also. They never were allotted.

Chairman.

1359. They were allotted in the other counties but not in Londonderry?—They were, but not in Londonderry. In 1624 there was an Order by the King to the Corporation of London that the 700 acres intended by His Majesty for the maintenance of a school within that city, if it be possible, might be found out; and the Corporation made answer that for the 700 acres intended for the free school they knew not in whose possession the same were, but they desired they might be examined and found out, whereby they might be freed from 20 marks per annum, which they were obliged to pay. The Crown pressed them again, and the Privy Council in 1683 ordered that the surveyor of Ireland should be written to concerning these 700 acres. The Corporation replied, praying that the surveyor of Ireland might be writ to find out these 700 acres. When the inquiry took place they did not appear to have discovered the 700 acres; but 300 acres are stated to have been allotted; and the case made by the Commission in 1868 was that 300 acres of the Irish Society's property lies on the east side of the Foyle, and only 300 acres. According to their own grant all their property ought to be on the west side of the Foyle, and the Commission seek to identify these two townlands which are mentioned in that Report as being the townlands set apart for a Royal free school, which ultimately became Foyle College.

Chairman—continued.

1360. What is the drift of that, so far as the Irish Society is concerned?—The drift of it seems to have been for the purpose of showing that if defined trusts were attached to the property of the Irish Society, there should be at least those 300 acres specially set apart for Foyle College. In page 19 of the Assistant Commissioner's Report, he says that even if those lands cannot be identified, Foyle College itself, the Free School of Londonderry, has a strong claim upon the Irish Society in consequence of the length of time that they have been assisting it and supporting it; he says that, "independently of this special claim on the part of the Foyle College to a specific allotment of an endowment of land, it appeared to have a general claim on the funds of the Irish Society to a more liberal support than it had as yet received. The school was for a long period of time mainly dependent on the liberality of the Bishops and Corporation of Derry and the twelve London Companies having property in the neighbourhood, and received until later times little assistance from the Irish Society. The support of the London companies was a precarious resource for a public school as appears from the changes which have taken place in the list of donations within the last 40 years. The following donations have altogether ceased:—Corporation of Derry, 80 *l.*; Fishmongers' Company, 100 *l.*; Ironmongers', 50 *l.*; Carpenters', 5 *l.* 5 *s.*; Barbers', 5 *l.*; Grocers', 100 *l.*; Drapers', 100 *l.*; Skinners', 100 *l.*; Cooks', 10 *l.*; Brewers', 5 *l.*; Pewterers', 5 *l.* The Mercers' gave 105 *l.*; they now give 50 *l.*, but nominate two boarders who pay 10 *l.* each, but for whom the regular charge is 79 *l.* 16 *s.*"

1361. All these donations from the companies are reported by the Commission of 1834 as having ceased at that time?—Yes. I am reading from the Report of the Assistant Commissioner, Dr. Ferguson, afterwards Registrar of the Court of Chancery.

1362. What is the meaning of that with regard to the Mercers' Company?—It means that they gave 50 *l.*, and that they got nominations which, if the boys were charged the full fees, would be worth 79 *l.* 16 *s.* They made a profit therefore of 9 *l.* 16 *s.* They gave 50 *l.*, and each boarder paid 10 *l.*, but the regular charge was 79 *l.* 16 *s.*

Mr. Sexton.

1363. Then 70 *l.* was granted, and 159 *l.* would be the charge upon the college?—I think not; I suppose that the 79 *l.* 16 *s.* would be the stipend for the two boys. "The Irish Society has increased its grant from 110 *l.* 13 *s.* 4 *d.* to 420 *l.*; but the school has, notwithstanding, lost an annual income of 486 *l.*, and is reduced to a state of very great destitution."

Chairman.

1364. That is to say, so far back as 1834 the Commissioners reported that this educational institution of Foyle College was suffering severe detriment by the withdrawal of those contributions by the London companies and others?—The grants from the London companies and the Corporation, of about 486 *l.*, had been withdrawn,

Chairman—continued.

drawn, but the Irish Society had increased its grant to 480 *l.*

1365. Was the increase of the Irish Society's grant equal to the withdrawal of their grants by the Companies?—Apparently not. The Irish Society's grant was increased at that time to 480 *l.*, and the withdrawn grants are stated to have been 190 *l.* I did not work out the arithmetic, but it is all to be made out from that passage.

Mr. Sexton.

1366. From what sum did the Irish Society grant an increase to 480 *l.*?—From 110 *l.* 15 *s.* 4 *d.* to 480 *l.*

Chairman.

1367. Then it was an increase not of 480 *l.*, but of 810 *l.*?—Yes. It states in the body of the Report that the Irish Society's grants had gone on from 1812. Of course they varied in amount, but they had been continued for that length of time. I have given you now the Report of 1858. I propose now to give you the facts in brief from the subsequent Report. In the Report of 1880, at page 166, the expenditure of the Irish Society is given for the five years before the Report. This is the Commission of which I was a member, and which was appointed in 1878. I was not a judge at the time. I need hardly trouble the Committee with more than one year, I suppose; the average is about the same. In 1878-9 the expenditure of the Irish Society in support of education is stated to be 3,518 *l.* 10 *s.* 6 *d.* That is more than double what it was in 1858.

1368. It was 1,201 *l.* in 1858?—Yes. With regard to Foyle College the report is to be found at page 167. It was stated by the Commission that at their inquiry the Presbyterian witnesses had given evidence that the proportion of the grants made to them by the society was not satisfactory, and they contrasted the grants made to the Londonderry Academical Institution with the much larger grants made to Foyle College.

1369. The Londonderry Academical Institution, I presume, is Episcopalian?—No; the Londonderry Academical Institution was founded shortly before this Report by voluntary effort on the part of the inhabitants, and it is under a mixed governing body, of which the majority is Presbyterian. It was established by voluntary effort, but largely supported by the Irish Society. "A Roman Catholic resident of Londonderry stated that half of the population of the city was Roman Catholic, and that the necessity for higher education having greatly increased, the bishop had erected St. Columb's College, at a cost of about 10,000 *l.*, collected from the Catholics, as a middle-class seminary for the Catholic population of Derry and the surrounding country; that the college which when finished would, he believed, be as free to Protestant pupils as the academical institution was, had no endowment beyond its site and buildings, and that no application had been made to the Irish Society for a grant. He stated that the society contributed 10 *l.* annually to St. Eugene's Schools, which were conducted by the Sisters of Mercy, and which were in connection with the National Board, and St. Columbkill's Male and Female National Schools, which were substantially Catholic, got 21 *l.* in 1877; and that these were the only sums given by the society to Roman Catholic schools in the parish of Londonderry. He stated that one of the greatest grievances under which the Roman Catholics laboured was the exclusion of their schools from the grants of the society. He did not blame the society, but thought the conditions of the charter too stringent, which, as he understood, obliged them not to contribute to Catholic purposes." The whole of the details are given in the schedule to the Report.

1370. How much of the 3,518 *l.* went to Foyle College?—Foyle College got a much larger part of it than any other institution. There were, at that time, 86 endowments in operation in the county of Londonderry.

1371. Do you mean endowments from the Irish Society?—No; there were 86 endowments in operation in the county, corresponding to the 110 which I gave you on the former occasion. Of these 73 were in receipt of grants from the Irish Society.

1372. That is to say as against 89 which received grants previously?—Yes; and the difference is pretty nearly accounted for by schools having failed, and things of that kind. The grants to these 73 schools amounted to 2,901 *l.* 0 *s.* 6 *d.*, and there was 66 *l.* for schools in Donegal; the 10 *l.* in Tyrone seems to have dropped out. Foyle College was in a very different position from what it was in in 1858. Dr. Hime, who had been previously head master of the Monaghan diocesan school, had been appointed head master of Foyle College in 1877; that was the year before this Report. He stated that all the pecuniary support of Foyle College was, at the date of the inquiry, derived from the Irish Society, and that the society regarded the schoolhouse as their property. His salary was paid by them, and the repairs and additions were executed at their expense.

1373. This was in 1877?—The date of the Report is 1880; the Commission was issued in 1878. Mr. Hime made a curious arrangement with the Society. He asked for a larger salary for the beginning of his service than at the end of it. The previous head master had got 500 *l.* a-year. Mr. Hime stated that at the time of his appointment the school was not in a particularly prosperous condition. I have read to you from the former Report that it was in a state of destruction. There seemed to be some difficulty also with the previous master about religious matters. Mr. Hime petitioned the Irish Society for an increase of salary for eight years, by which time he thought the school would be on a satisfactory basis. "The society, in consequence of the low condition to which the school had sunk, agreed to give him 850 *l.* a-year for the two first years of his mastership, and thenceforward to reduce his salary by 50 *l.* every successive year until it should be brought down to 500 *l.* a-year, the former stipend; they also undertook to pay the taxes, amounting to about 60 *l.* a-year, formerly borne by the head master."

1374. Then the more successful he was the less he was to get; if he succeeded his salary

fell?

Chairman—continued.

…ll?—The more successful he was the more profitable the school would be, of course, as an institution, and the school has been very successful under him. There were 105 pupils in it at the time of this Report, and it is now getting on extremely well.

1375. It was surely a very extraordinary arrangement, was it not?—It seems to me to have been a very sensible one, because he had raised the Monaghan diocesan school from nothing at all to a very good school, and wanted a larger salary at first while working up Foyle College also.

Sir John Ellis.

1376. On their examination were not the Commissioners satisfied with the course pursued?—Yes; and Dr. Hime seemed to be perfectly satisfied, and the arrangement seems to have worked very well because he is there still, and the school is still successful.

Mr. Sexton.

1377. *How many boys has he now?*—I think about the same number, about a hundred.

Chairman.

1378. What was the next step?—With those Reports before us, the Educational Endowments Commission under the Act of 1885, the Executive Commission, went to Londonderry on the 7th October 1886, to hold a preliminary inquiry. We had not, at that time, undertaken the preparation of any draft scheme for any of the Ulster schools; we wanted to see first what the state of affairs was in Ulster. "Mr. R. H. Lowe, solicitor, appeared on behalf of the governing body of Foyle College, and also of the Irish Society, and claimed that Foyle College was exempt from the jurisdiction of the Commissioners. He referred to Foyle College Act, 1874, and submitted that as originally Foyle College was built out of moneys to a great extent, if not altogether, obtained by voluntary subscriptions, the endowment was exempt under the provisions of the Educational Endowments (Ireland) Act, 1885, sect. 7, sub-section 3, that the only portion that could be an endowment within the Act, was that which consisted of lands and buildings. The grants and subscriptions of the Irish Society were purely voluntary. He also submitted that the Act of 1874, having been recently passed, and the governing body being a representative body, and the school worked in a satisfactory manner, the Commissioners should not interfere with the existing arrangements."

1379. His contention was that so far as the Irish Society were immediately concerned, as their contributions were voluntary, they were not technically endowments, and therefore were outside of your jurisdiction?—Our Act of Parliament defines endowments as "property dedicated to charitable uses and which has been applied or is applicable in whole or in part, whether by the declared intention of the founder or the consent of the governing body or by custom or otherwise to educational purposes." That, of course, would take in nearly everything, but section 7 exempts a number of classes of endowments, and amongst the rest, sub-section 3 exempts any endowment which in the discretion of the governing body may be wholly applied to other than educational purposes; sub-section 4 exempts any endowment given to charitable uses at any time after the passing of the Act; and sub-section 5 exempts any endowment consisting of voluntary subscriptions or accumulations, or investments thereof, unless the governing body signify their consent in writing to our dealing with them. The moment they do that, we have jurisdiction; but until they do we have not, where the endowment is voluntary or where it can be withdrawn from educational purposes.

1380. The representative of the Irish Society and the governing body of Foyle College protested against your jurisdiction?—Yes, they claimed exemption. Foyle College is now regulated under a statute passed in 1874, which made a governing body for it, consisting of the Bishop of Derry and Raphoe for the time being, the governor of the Honourable Irish Society for the time being, the deputy governor of the Honourable Irish Society for the time being, the moderator of the General Assembly of the Presbyterian Church for the time being, and the worshipful the mayor of the city of Londonderry. They are made a body corporate and they are made trustees. The general agent in Ireland for the time being, of the Irish Society, is made the treasurer, and they have power to make bye-laws; and the right of nominating the head master is vested in the bishop and the governor of the Irish Society. These two, out of the body of five, have the power of dismissing the master and of appointing him; but what we should call the governing body of the school consists of five members, of whom two are members of the Irish Society, one the mayor of Londonderry, and two ecclesiastics, the bishop and the moderator, and they were the body for whom Mr. Lowe appeared. We decided, that inasmuch as the school-house had been erected at an expense of 13,000 *l.*, of which a considerable portion was raised from taxation by the grand jury, we could not hold all the endowments to consist of voluntary subscriptions. We also pointed out that the question of buildings erected by voluntary subscriptions, and afterwards devoted to educational purposes, being treated as investments, was one on which we had an opinion rather adverse to the contention that they would be exempt, and also we said, "There is again a question whether the money given by the Irish Society to Foyle College, is not an endowment coming within the jurisdiction of the Commission. That depends upon whether the property of the Irish Society is legally applicable, and has been legally dedicated to educational purposes. The mere fact that the society gives it, or has given it, for a certain time, would not constitute it an endowment, if there was no obligation to do so; but if given under an obligation, it would then be an endowment. We shall hear any evidence on the subject that may be offered."

1381. But you did not open the question whether there was an obligation or not?—We said we would take evidence upon that point.

1382. Did you get any evidence?—We did. Dr. Hime was examined, and the agent of the

Chairman—continued.

Irish Society, Mr. Montgomery, was examined. He stated that the total amount applied during the last year in aid of education in Londonderry, speaking from recollection, was about 4,500 l.; and that out of that Foyle College got 500 l. a-year for the head master; that they gave 310 l. a-year to the Academical Institution, and that they gave 125 l. a-year to St. Columb's. Speaking roughly he said that their net rental was about 12,000 l. a-year; and then he said; "My view of the matter is that Dr. Hime receives his salary during the pleasure of the court to give it. All these grants are during the pleasure of the court."

1383. He meant the court of the Irish Society?—Yes. Again, he was asked whether there were other grants in the same position, and he said, yes.

1384. But I presume you only regarded that as the dictum of a layman; there was no authority in it?—That was all; but he gave us also the procedure by which these grants were obtained. Substantially every application for a grant had to go through the agent. Some of them were given for fixed periods of years, such, for example, as the one to Dr. Hime, which I have already referred to. Others had to be applied for each year, and were re-granted each year. We asked him to give us a full list of them, which he did, and it will be found at p. 308, setting out all the schools which got grants; and he accompanied it with this letter: "8th October 1888.—I forward herewith, agreeably to the request of the Educational Endowments Commission, a list of schools and educational institutions in receipt of aid from the Honourable Irish Society. Many of these institutions have been from time to time assisted by supplemental donations. You will please understand that all these grants are made during the pleasure of the court of the Honourable Irish Society, and can be modified or withdrawn as circumstances may render desirable."

1385. Did you express any view upon the contention that was laid before you?—We did. We presented an interim report to the Chief Secretary, and we afterwards presented it to Parliament.

Mr. Sexton.

1386. Was there any evidence given in favour of the view that the grants are endowments?—There was evidence given that they had been received for a long time, and were relied upon. But I may tell you that the result that we arrived at was this: that we acted, in fact, upon the judgment of the House of Lords in the Skinners' case in 1845, where Lord Lyndhurst says distinctly that the Irish Society "are public officers invested with a public trust, having a right to apply those funds in discharge of that public trust, and they therefore cannot be accountable in a suit of this kind by the companies of London or by any particular company as if they were trustees for private purposes and private objects." But he says that, "they have a discretion to exercise as to what extent they will apply those funds, and to what objects." That appeared to us to make it impossible for us to treat those funds, under our Act, as dedicated to educational purposes, or as being funds that might not be withdrawn from educational purposes; and accordingly we were of opinion that we could not settle a scheme dealing with them compulsorily unless we got the consent of the Irish Society.

Chairman.

1387. Because you could not, under the decision of the House of Lords in 1845 regard them as endowments, which for their specific destination they were bound to make?—They were trust funds, the particular destination of which might or might not be educational; and the discretion whether they should or should not be educational rested with the Irish Society, and we could not take it from them.

1388. Then you came to the conclusion that you had nothing to do with the Irish Society with reference to Foyle College?—Not altogether that. We framed schemes for the Royal Schools, for Magee College, for Coleraine Academical Institution, and for Londonderry Academical Institution, giving the Irish Society representation on some of the governing bodies, and giving those bodies power to receive and expend whatever monies the Irish Society gave them; but of course we could not fix the amount of those grants for the reason I have mentioned. When we returned from Ulster, where we spent nearly a month going round the Royal schools, on the 30th of November 1888, we addressed a memorandum to the Chief Secretary, stating as the reason for our doing so, that we were now in a position to commence the preparation of draft schemes for the future management of the endowments hitherto administered by the Commissioners of Education in Ireland, a body constituted in 1813, who had the property of the Royal schools vested in them; but that having regard to the evidence before us, as to the existing provision and demand for intermediate education in Ireland, we had thought it our duty to address that communication to the Chief Secretary, before publishing any draft scheme affecting the public endowments which were within the scope of our Commission. We called attention to the unsatisfactory condition of the existing Royal schools at the time, and we stated the amount of the endowments, which all taken together could scarcely be expected to produce more than about 5,000 l. a year net for the whole of the Royal free schools; and we said that the first question which met us was, whether we were to extend those endowments beyond the limits of Ulster. We stated that the amount of property available beyond question could be fully utilised in Ulster, and that we should have no difficulty in thus localising the benefits of the existing endowments, if any corresponding provision were made for the other provinces; but we pointed out that if the Royal school estates were to be the only public endowments available for distribution under our Act, we feared that if we restricted them to Ulster, great disappointment would arise in those parts of the country which would be left unprovided for, while if we extended them to the whole of Ireland, the amount would be quite insufficient to be of any appreciable use; and that in either alternative the be-

nefits

Chairman—continued.

nefits expected from the work of our Commission would in a great measure fail to be realised. We stated that we believed Ireland to be the only country possessing a system of public education in which the public provision for intermediate instruction was entirely disproportionate to that made for university and primary education.

1389. And that is your deliberate judgment?—Distinctly so, from the figures which we gave: "The University of Dublin possesses an endowment of public origin, amounting, we understand, to about 38,000 *l.* per annum, the Royal University has an endowment from the Church surplus of 20,000 *l.*" (that is Irish money), "and the Queen's Colleges receive 21,000 *l.* per annum from the Consolidated Fund, making for university education in Ireland a total public annual endowment of 79,000 *l.* In addition, very large grants have been annually voted, and the existing buildings and appliances represent a vast outlay."

1390. *L.* 79,000 for higher or university education?—Yes. Then the grant for primary education amounted in the year of this Report to 881,336 *l.*; I believe it is now nearly a million, exclusive of 1,300,000 *l.* allocated from the Church surplus for the pensions of national school teachers. We also said that no provision had been made for intermediate education, except the Royal school endowments, a few scattered local grants of small amount from municipal bodies, and the sum of 33,000 *l.* per annum derived from the Church surplus, and administered by the Intermediate Education Board. We pointed out the advantages of this intermediate education, and mentioned the cases of the schools of Erasmus Smith, and of the Incorporated Society, with regard to both of which we said that the governing bodies were contending strenuously that they were denominational in their character, and private in their origin; and we referred to the promise made in the House of Lords, by Lord Cairns, Lord Granville, Lord Spencer, and Lord O'Hagan, that if girls were brought in upon the million originally intended for the boys, another half-million at least should be provided for them; and we mentioned also that of the money given to the National Board 38,777 *l.* was given to model national schools alone; and then there is this passage on page 29, "In the course of our inquiries in the north we have found that several of the London companies, which have at all times devoted considerable sums to educational purposes, have sold, or are now selling, their estates, without, so far as we know, making any provision for the schools which have been hitherto dependent upon them. The position of the Irish Society also has been brought before us. That society has been declared by the House of Lords to hold its property upon trust for public purposes, and especially for education. 'They have to superintend and take care of the education of the inhabitants of the district, and have also to perform other public duties of great importance'" (that is a quotation from Lord Lyndhurst). "The grants of the Irish Society for education during the year 1886 amounted to 3,030 *l.*, and those made by the London companies were also of large amount; but all these grants were in form voluntary, and in the absence of any specific statutory obligation devoting some definite property to educational purposes we have hitherto been unable to treat such grants, however long continued, as endowments within the scope of our Commission; unless Parliament should intervene much of the property we have mentioned is likely to be withdrawn from those general obligations under which it has hitherto been largely devoted to educational purposes."

1391. You reported to that effect and in those words to the Lord Lieutenant, did you not?—Yes; on the 30th November 1886.

1392. There was a Report to Parliament afterwards, was there not?—Yes; that Report we appended to our annual Report, which we are bound to present to Parliament, on the 12th November 1887; and in the body of that Report we stated that "The endowments available for intermediate education in Ireland are wholly inadequate, and are so unequally distributed that the majority of the people, and large districts of the country are without adequate provision for higher instruction." We stated that we had sent this memorandum to the Chief Secretary, and called attention to the arguments in support of the demand for additional aid for such education. We referred to that communication, and observed that if the scheme which we were then about to propose for utilising the Royal school endowments were adopted, the efficacy of the provision made for a defined district would strengthen the claim of the rest of Ireland to similar assistance from public sources. "Even a moderate endowment," we said, "judiciously applied would prove most useful, and with such a provision we still believe that through the Educational Endowments Acts, 1885, the arrangements for intermediate education throughout Ireland might now be placed on a satisfactory basis, but we are convinced that without it the benefits expected from the work of our Commission will in a great measure fail to be realised."

1393. Therefore you had made a report to that effect to the Lord Lieutenant, and you had made a report to Parliament which appeared in the Blue Book; was anything done?—Nothing was done. I do not know how far the appointment of this Committee may be taken as doing something. We stated in the body of the report the principles upon which we proposed to deal with the Royal school endowments, viz., to appoint two local governing bodies in each district; to confine the endowments to the districts for which King James had granted them; to let one local body represent all denominations of Protestants, and to let the other local body represent the Roman Catholics; each of these bodies to be incorporated with power to hold any property, and to administer any endowments, that they could get from other sources.

1394. You have prepared schemes for Magee College, and for the Coleraine and Londonderry Academies, have you not?—Yes, and also for the Royal schools.

1395. To go back to Foyle College, which is the case immediately before us, did you prepare a scheme for Foyle College?—We did not. On the 28th April 1887, nothing being done on this report, we postponed the issuing of a scheme for

Chairman—continued.

Foyle College until the Commissioners had a further opportunity of considering how the claims of the several religious denominations in the locality could be satisfied. The reason we did that was because the only public property that Foyle College had, apart from the Irish Society grant, was its buildings, and if we had taxed its resources in any way to give other people a share in the value of those buildings, we should have damaged Foyle College, and we should not have had enough money to make any substantial advance to others. We therefore thought it better to call attention to the fact that there was no endowment to meet other claims.

1396. What are now the endowments of Foyle College?—It has the buildings and land which were originally provided largely by subscriptions from individuals as well as from the London companies and the Irish Society.

1397. And from the grand jury?—And largely also from the grand jury. That, and the grant from the Irish Society, are its present only endowments.

1398. Where do its annual supplies now come from?—The 500*l.* a year for the head master comes from the Irish Society, and they also appear to be very liberal in giving considerable sums for assistant masters and for the repairs of buildings; and Dr. Hime, on all occasions when we have examined him, has seemed satisfied with the money that he receives. The dissatisfaction is on the part of those who do not get so much.

1399. You made further inquiries in 1888, did you not?—In October 1888 we made an inquiry at Coleraine, where there was a very important school. The Irish Society have only one set of schools directly under their own management, and these are called the Irish Society Free Schools at Coleraine. These are primary schools, and the condition of them is described in the 4th Report, page 76. The Irish Society's Free Schools at Coleraine have an attendance of about 600 pupils. They consist of a boys' school, a girls' school, and an infants' school, all under the National Board; and they were, in consequence of disagreements about religious instruction and other matters, placed by the Society under the management of a committee appointed under a plan that they drew up purporting to represent all the religious denominations in the place. This committee consisted of the general agent and the clergymen of all denominations officially connected with the town of Coleraine.

1400. What do you mean by "officially connected"?—Mr. Montgomery, the agent of the Society, was not able to attend and give evidence, but Mr. Bailey, who appeared for him, said that the committee consisted of the general agent and the clergymen of all denominations officially connected with the town of Coleraine, including rectors, curates, ministers, assistant ministers, and all clergy of all denominations and degrees engaged in clerical work in the town; and that associated with these were twelve gentlemen resident in the place, the Town Commissioners appointing four, the Harbour Commissioners four, and the Irish Society four. There was a good deal of dissatisfaction about the working of the committee.

Chairman—continued.

1401. What was the ground of dissatisfaction?—The Church people were dissatisfied because they had presented a memorial to the Society complaining that they had not got a sufficient number of teachers of their own denomination, and sufficient facilities for teaching, and they asked the Irish Society to divide the grant and to separate the buildings. The Roman Catholics did not attend the schools at all, except two or three of them, and they were dissatisfied. The managers of the other National schools in the town and in the neighbourhood which got no grants, or very small grants, were also dissatisfied; and it appeared furthermore that the more advanced pupils in the town went to the model school.

1402. Will you tell the Committee, as it may be useful to some Members of the Committee, what a model school is?—A model school is a National school which only differs from other National schools in this: that the actual management and appointment of teachers is kept by the Commissioners in their own hands. The other National schools have local managers who can appoint and remove the teachers. In a model school they are appointed by the Commissioners, and the rule of the Commissioners is that the number of the teachers of the various religious denominations is to be more or less proportionate to that of the pupils; and the result is that they are regarded as mixed schools, and the greater number are principally attended by Protestants.

Mr. *Clancy*.

1403. They approach rather to intermediate schools?—They do; they were not so intended originally. They have usually a better staff and better buildings than ordinary primary schools.

Chairman.

1404. Did you express or form any view as to the substance of those complaints with regard to the Irish Society's free schools?—We were quite satisfied that the Irish Society were doing their best to please everybody, with the usual result. We thought the money might probably be more usefully applied if they had left it to the management of the people themselves.

Sir John Ellis.

1405. Upon that answer I should like to ask, do you think by the constitution of the committee which you have just given us, they did not leave it in the hands of the people themselves?—The point was that the committee did not appear to satisfy anybody except one party, and that was the party that had the majority upon it.

1406. Could you suggest a committee more representative?—No; but the suggestion was to divide the money and have several committees.

Mr. *Sexton*.

1407. Of each denomination?—Of each denomination.

Sir John Ellis.

1408. Are you aware that a Committee has been

Sir John Ellis—continued.

here formed which is representative, and appears at the present moment to satisfy all the grievances?—I am very glad to hear that. The memorial presented to the Society and brought before us is in our report. It really turned upon the question that is turning up everywhere in Ireland, the denominational question.

Chairman.

1409. As a general result of all that you have said upon this first head of your evidence, namely, the relations of the Irish Society to education in the North of Ireland, I gather that you formed an opinion which was not different from that of the Commissioners of 1854, namely, that if the educational part of the Irish Society's funds were defined and set apart, and placed under the management, as you have just said, of the local bodies, that would be a better arrangement?—We did come to that conclusion. It was in one sense an extra-judicial conclusion, as it was one we could not give effect to. It seemed that the small grants were given directly to the managers of the schools, without the Society having any means of ensuring the efficiency of the school, except by getting a report from their agent once a year. As regards the large grants I have told you about, such as Foyle College and the *Irish Society's* schools, what the various contending parties appeared to wish was that each side should have its own share, and manage it independently. Our view was, and we had every reason to concur in that view with the Commission of 1854, that the most efficiently managed schools in Ireland are those managed by local bodies as distinguished from any central or absentee bodies.

1410. Then you would say, first of all, what most of us are aware of, that the funds for intermediate education in Ireland are extremely inadequate; and secondly, and therefore, that it would be greatly to be regretted if the companies, when they sell their estates, withdrew any portion of what is now contributed by them, for the purposes of intermediate education?—There is no doubt of that at all. The withdrawal of money at any time is unfortunate, and it would be particularly unfortunate to withdraw money that has been applied and is required for the purposes of education.

1411. It would be a withdrawal of money that has been of great value for meeting a public need, and if it is withdrawn, that need will be deeper even than before?—I have no reason to believe that the Irish Society could withdraw their funds. Their funds are bound by public trusts, so far as I can make out, on the authority of the House of Lords. The only difficulty we had was to find our authority to define the trusts, that is, to fix the destination of any particular portions of the funds.

Mr. Sexton.

1412. That is to say, what particular part of the income should be devoted to a particular use?—It appeared that they were trustees of the whole estate, but could withdraw the whole income from one charity and give it to another; for instance, say, to hospitals, or to other public purposes; and, if they could withdraw the whole, they could alter the amount they gave for education.

Chairman.

1413. When you say "public purposes," I presume you mean public purposes in Ireland, and in that part of Ireland?—Lord Lyndhurst speaks of the public purposes of the district; and the district is the counties of Coleraine and Derry, as they were originally; the county of Londonderry, as it is now.

1414. As regards the second division of your evidence in respect to the London companies generally, you find there, I suppose, the same reasons exist as in the case of the Irish Society, precluding your dealing with the grants of the London companies as endowments?—The same reason applied exactly, assuming them to be trustees, but over and above that there was the contention on the part of the London companies that they were not trustees at all.

1415. That is to say, the Irish Society clearly were trustees by the judgment of the House of Lords in 1845, but the London companies insisted that their possessions were not impressed with the trusts of the Irish Society?—The Skinners' Company's case gave us no help upon that point; because, in the Skinners' Company's case, it is curious that the argument was exactly inverted.

1416. I will put it in this way: would you tell us what arguments presented themselves to your mind as regards the whole of the London companies in the first place?—The first argument is one which was used by their own counsel, which you will find in the *Report* in 12 Clark and Finnelly, namely, that, inasmuch as all this property was originally granted to the Irish Society, if any part of it was bound by a trust the whole of it was; and they relied upon the fact that large portions of the estates had been allotted to them in severalty, to show that those portions held in severalty were not bound by a public trust, and therefore that what was retained by the Irish Society was not bound by a public trust; and the Lords, in deciding that what was retained by the Irish Society was bound by a trust, had not before them the case as to the portions held in severalty, and therefore the decision did not affect that point, and was no guide to us.

Sir William Marriott.

1417. The Irish Society were allowed, by their Charter, to grant such lands to the companies as were not required by them for the trusts with which they were impressed?—I have not got the terms of the Charter before me. I was merely giving the argument used by counsel for the Skinners' Company in that case in 1845; not the decision of the House of Lords. The argument used was that there was no trace of a distinction between the purposes on which one part of the estate was granted and another, that what they had in severalty they held as their own, and that therefore the surplus land, after discharging the Irish Society's trust, belonged equally to them.

Chairman.

1418. You are not, as I understand, arguing the case; you are merely stating to the Committee

Chairman—continued.

niston the views presented to the Commissioners, yourself, and your brother Commissioners, by counsel, or by witnesses?—Yes. We had no counsel before us, but there were views presented by the witnesses, and considerations which we had to take into account.

1419. You first took into account those considerations for the companies?—Yes.

1420. Then other arguments, no doubt, presented themselves to your mind against the views stated for the companies?—Yes. The great argument against the trust was the long possession which the companies had had, and the different modes in which the different companies had dealt with their estates.

1421. All the companies, I understand, got all their lands from the Irish Society?—The best account I know of (I am not going to the original documents, for I have no means of doing so) is the Report of House of Lords Cases (11 Clark and Finnelly); and there it is stated that the whole property was granted to the Irish Society in 1614, but after that the Irish Society executed deeds, in 1616 and 1617, granting separately to each of these companies its share, as it was called, of the property, in severalty. Then, in 1632, on an information by the Attorney General, the Star Chamber cancelled the Charter of the Irish Society altogether.

1422. By information filed against the Irish Society?—Yes. They appear to have treated them very strongly; they fined them 70,000 *l.*, and they cancelled their Charter. Then afterwards it appears, according to the Report, that the Attorney General filed an information against the individual companies; but that was never proceeded with. Then Cromwell renewed the Charter by patent, and Charles II. gave the Society the new one which they have now. That patent again included all the property in severalty, and in 1621, or thereabouts, new deeds were executed by the Irish Society re-granting to the companies their estates. From that date down we had no trustworthy evidence we could rely upon as to the existence of any trust, because we found that the different companies had dealt differently with their estates; some have sold the fee a hundred years ago; some have let them and re-let them, others have kept them in their own hands, and others have got them into their own hands recently. On the whole, it is better for me to say that the one ground upon which we went was that if the Irish Society was exempted from our jurisdiction, the London companies were also to be exempted; but even if the Irish Society was not exempt, there was a formidable case behind that again with regard to the London companies.

Mr. Sexton.

1423. Would it rest upon the ground that, supposing there was a trust, it was not in your discretion to say to which particular part the trust applied?—That applies both to the Irish Society and to the London companies. On that ground the companies were exempt, and therefore we saw, in that case as well as the other, that we could not proceed to treat the property of these companies as being endowments within our jurisdiction.

Chairman.

1424. The view of the companies was further pressed upon you, I understand, in this way: The argument was laid before you that the money originally paid by the companies seems to have been rather levied as a poll-tax on individual members?—It appears in the Report that it was not the companies' corporate money, but money raised, under some of the powers they had, as a poll-tax upon individual members of the companies themselves. I cannot give you the details, but can only speak from what appears in the Report, in Clark and Finnelly, where it is called a poll-tax.

1425. The contention argued before you was, that on the sale of their Irish property the proceeds of those sales, so far as they consisted, at all events, of what it is now the fashion to call unearned increment, should be applied in Ireland, and that they will be wanted to make up for the withdrawal of the annual grants?—That is a matter not so much of law as of feeling. There can be no doubt, I apprehend, speaking extra-judicially, if they are, as I suppose they are, trustees for charitable purposes in England, that within their general charitable purposes any part of the property that represents Irish money might be very well spent, and a good deal of it has been spent, in Ireland, the Skinners' Company, for example, giving scholarships to the Alexandra College in Dublin, and a scholarship in Londonderry. In fact, in the Report of 1858, there are three schools which have grants from the Clothworkers' Company, two each from the Ironmongers', Grocers', and Drapers', and one each from the Weavers', Mercers', and Salters', making 10 schools altogether in Londonderry then receiving grants as endowments from those companies. In the later Report of 1880 there are two each from the Grocers', Clothworkers', and Salters', and one from the Skinners', making altogether seven. The principal ones are the Coleraine Academical Institution, which got a large building grant from the Clothworkers' Company, and is administered under our scheme, and the Rainey School at Magherafelt, which got its building and also an annual endowment from the Salters' Company; and there are scholarships for girls founded by the Skinners' Company in Dublin and Derry, and the Magee College has a scholarship founded by the Ironmongers' Company. In the Moore College the scheme has now been administered for a long time under a body formed by us.

1426. The general result, so far as you, the Endowment Commissioners, are concerned, was that you could do nothing beyond enabling the existing institutions to receive and apply anything that the companies might voluntarily give, or that Parliament might eventually set apart as an endowment?—We can do nothing compulsorily; but if we got a written consent, as occurred afterwards in the case of the Salters' Company, a written declaration that they were willing to set apart any sum of money, our Act of Parliament provides (if I may say so without advertising ourselves) about the cheapest and most effectual way of securing its useful administration.

1427. In order to give this admirable Commission

Chairman—continued.

mission plenty of room and means, you would not be sorry if Parliament were to pass an Act setting apart some of these funds?—Personally, I am afraid I should not be glad, for we have been working for the past four years at this; but of course we should be very glad if there were more funds for intermediate education, because they are badly wanted.

1428. Now, coming to a long story which we have heard a great deal about in this Committee, and which we look to you to clear up for us, that is, the story of the Rainey School at Magherafelt, in which the Salters' Company is concerned, perhaps it would be best if you could conveniently begin by giving us very shortly the history of the endowment?—I am afraid this case will give you some idea of the trouble it is to settle these points in Ireland. I will shortly give you the history of the foundation. This school was founded by a man named Hugh Rainey. By will on the 11th of April 1707 he gave all his worldly concerns (the will is a most amusing document, but I will not trouble you with the whole of it) upon trust to lay out the same on the purchase of a freehold estate to produce 400 *l.* a year; half of that estate to go to his family, and the other half to erect a schoolhouse in Magherafelt. The plan of the schoolhouse was that it was to be for 24 boys, each to be kept three years, eight boys to be taken in at each Martinmas, each eight after staying three years to be put out, keeping 24 boys always at the school. These boys were to be fed, clothed, taught trades, and put out as apprentices; and when they had done their three years, they should "each be bound in such trade or occupation as should be judged most fit for his genius," and each was to get a fee of 50 *s.* when he went away. If the income of half the estate was not enough, then the number of boys was to be reduced. So far it was a plain question enough. Then comes the inevitable religious question. His direction upon that was that "two old, grave, and good men, known Christians, such as really feared God, well qualified to read the Scriptures, sing psalms and pray morning and evening, and who should take pains to instruct the boys," "should be also maintained" (that, of course, means maintained in the house on the charity), "and that if any of such old men should be found defective or unable to perform such duties, he should be outed, and another wrote for to the Presbytery of Ulster, who should be found very capable and fit to be an instrument of youth."

1429. There is no other mention of Presbyterians except that reference, is there?—The Presbytery of Ulster, we were informed, was at that time the governing body of Presbyterians in all that part of Ireland. The testator directed that these old men should also instruct the boys, getting clothes and diet. He appears from other things in the will to have been a Presbyterian; he gave legacies for Presbyterian purposes, and there are other things of that kind. Then the will contained this provision, that "if either the old men or the boys did not behave as expected, it should be in the power of his executors, or such as were only life renters of his estate, to turn them out and put in such as should be deserving." That he recommended what, unfortunately, wrecked the whole thing, namely, that the executors should take proceedings for confirming his will by a short Act of Parliament, "in order that it might be out of the power of any that should be entrusted with his property to misapply the same." According to the principles we go upon, if it was a modern will, we should have treated that as being a will that did indicate that the governing body of the place was to be Presbyterian, and that the instruction was to be Presbyterian in character. We are bound to have regard to the intentions of the deceased, and we would take that fact, if it were a new will, as being a sufficient indication.

1430. Did they apply for a short Act of Parliament?—They did get an Act of Parliament in 1738.

1431. That is the 11th of George II.?—Yes. It is an Act of Parliament as to which there was a good deal of misapprehension on the part of some witnesses before us, and I daresay, also, before this Committee. The 11th of George II. was a private Act of Parliament. That Act of Parliament did really only two important things. It first of all gave the charity, instead of a moiety of the estate, a fixed rent charge of 175 *l.* a year (Irish) on the estate; so that it deprived the charity altogether of any prospect of increase in the value of the estate; but at the same time it gave it, if the estate should become less valuable, a fixed income.

1432. Was 175 *l.* then the moiety of the estate?—Possibly it was; because it appears from the Act they bought the property partly with borrowed money, and the property was worth about 400 *l.* a year; that is a rough figure, and it is probable that the sum named did represent the moiety. The estate now produces 4,000 *l.* a year, so that it was a bad bargain for the charity.

1433. What was the next step?—It vested that yearly rent-charge of 175 *l.*, and the right to recover it, in the Archbishop of Armagh as sole trustee.

1434. Although the appointers of the old men and boys were the Presbytery of Ulster?—Yes; but (and this is what there was a misapprehension about) it did not enable the Primate to manage the school at all. The Act of Parliament will be found in our Second *Report*, at page 313. It vested the property in the Archbishop under the trusts and subject to the nomination declared in the will.

1435. What was the governing body left by the Act of Parliament?—They would be the testator's life renters of his estate and his executors, and they would be bound by the trusts of the will, whenever they wanted to remove the old men, to go to the Presbytery. The trusts of the will, however, were expressly recognised by the Act of Parliament, and it was apparently because the testator's relations at the time may not have been Presbyterians that the Act was passed under which the Archbishop of Armagh was to hold the property.

1436. What was the next step in the history of the school?—The next step was that the last male representative of the founder died, and his family expired in 1847, long afterwards, you will observe.

1437. The

Chairman—continued.

1437. The family had not anything to do with the school, had they?—Yes, they had, under the will. The old men and boys were to be nominated by his executors, or such as were only life renters of the estate. They appear down to 1847 to have, from time to time, more or less looked after the place; but in 1847 the last of them disappeared, and then the primate of that day got a legal opinion from Serjeant Warren, a very eminent Irish lawyer at the time, that the trusts had devolved upon him, as they plainly had. The property was vested in him; there were no managers, and he therefore would become trustee.

1438. How had the school been getting on meantime?—Very badly. The school was reported in 1858 to be no longer at all capable of maintaining 24 boys. The fall in the value of money alone would have prevented that. It was reported at page 186 of the Report of 1858 that it was not in a satisfactory state. "The circumstances which interfere with its efficiency arise from causes that deserve particular attention, because, we regret to say, they exist and operate in many other schools. The principal of these is the present inadequacy of the endowment to carry out the views of the founder, which, moreover, as expressed in his will and confirmed by an Act of the Legislature, had reference to a state of things very different from that which now exists. The rent-charge of 175 *l.* late Irish currency, at which the endowment was fixed by the Act of George II., is of course wholly insufficient to maintain, clothe, and educate 24 boys, as directed by the testator; and even the 10 boarders now on the foundation can be supported only by the diversion of their time and attention from a course of instruction to the cultivation of a farm of 12 acres, which the master cultivates by permission of the trustee, his Grace the Lord Primate." "The schoolhouse is falling into ruin, having no fund for its repair. The premises are held at will only; but it appears that the landlords, the Salters' Company, have expressed their willingness to build a new schoolhouse, and to aid the school in other ways."

1439. Will you explain what the Salters' Company had to do with the matter?—The Salters' Company were the owners of the manor of Magherafelt, and the school was on their estate; so far as I can see they had no other connection but that.

1440. The Salters' Company did intervene about 1852, as I understand?—Yes; a point was made afterwards about that farm. In 1858 there were 12 acres of land held by the Archbishop of Armagh as sole trustee, as tenant-at-will, to the Salters' Company. It is stated in the Report of 1858 that that land was held at a high rent, and practically that the school had no interest in it; but on the other hand it was contended before us at Magherafelt that the land was town parks and valuable land, and that something might have been made of it if it had been kept.

1441. Was not there a Chancery scheme with regard to the school?—There was; and the present question really turns principally upon that Chancery scheme. It will be found in our Second Report at pages 318 and 319. The Primate left the management of the school to the rector of the parish, and the Primate and the rector presented a petition to Chancery which contains an offer by the Salters' Company, on which I think a good deal may now turn. The petition was presented on the 24th of April 1852. It is suggested "That the existing dilapidated schoolhouse should be surrendered to the Salters' Company, on whose property it stands, and that the farm held in connection with it from the said company, and who have given notice to determine the yearly tenancy thereof, should no longer be retained." Then it contains this recital: "That the Salters' Company have generously offered to defray the expense of erecting a suitable building for the school on an eligible site in the town of Magherafelt, and to execute a declaration of trust or otherwise secure the use of such building for the objects of the said charity, so long as the same shall be administered in accordance with the scheme prayed for in this petition, or any altered scheme to which the said company can give their concurrence, and the said endowment or rent-charge" (that is, Rainey's bequest) "shall be applied for the support thereof. That in the new schoolhouse so to be erected by the Salters' Company free education should be given to 30 boys as day pupils, such being the greatest number contemplated by the testator participating of his bounty. That besides instruction in the usual elementary parts of useful learning, the pupils, in accordance with the testator's wishes, should be instructed in the Sacred Scriptures, and that 15 of the boys who are to be admitted to receive a free education shall be nominated by the Lord Primate, and 15 by the Salters' Company; that is, one-half of the number admitted by each of them. That the boys be clothed out of the funds of the charity as enjoined by the testator, and that books and other school requisites be provided for them free of charge. That a highly qualified teacher, to be nominated by the Lord Primate, be employed at a competent salary, and that, if the funds permit, provision be also made for the support and payment of a pupil teacher, and for apprenticing one of the scholars every year. That, in order to make the charity as extensively useful as possible, the school shall be open for the education of other scholars besides those on the foundation, on the payment of school fees, to be regulated by the Lord Primate." On that petition, Mr. Litton, Master in Chancery, settled a scheme for the management of the school, and he reported to the Lord Chancellor, and an order was made, confirming the Report, that the offer of the Salters' Company should be accepted and the building proposed to be erected should be erected, and should be duly conveyed to trustees or otherwise legally secured for the use of the school in perpetuity, or so long as the school should be conducted according to the provisions of the scheme. The school was to be changed to being a day-school only, and 30 boys were to be admitted free, 15 nominated by the Primate, and 15 by the Salters' Company; and that was all carried out, except the conveyance.

1442. The present school, in conformity with that,

Chairman—continued.

that, was erected, and the head master appointed?—Yes; and the Commission of 1880 describes the condition of the school then at page 225. There were at that time 30 boys on the foundation; the rector of the parish was a visitor of the school in conjunction with the agent of the Salters' Company.

1443. Who had made the rector of the parish the visitor?—The Primate had made him visitor while he was sole trustee. Magherafelt is in the archdiocese of Armagh, although it is in the county of Derry. The Archbishop of Armagh is the local prelate. He was so far away that I suppose he appointed the rector the visitor, and the Salters' Company appointed the agent.

1444. The visitor and the agent practically managed the school?—Yes, they practically managed the school. I have documents here from the old Commission of 1880 which rather bear upon the subject. The old Commission went down there in October 1878, and I hold in my hand a return to the Commission, which was accompanied by a letter of Mr. Cartwright, now Sir Henry Cartwright, the agent of the Salters' Company. It is signed by Mr. Kincaid, but in Mr. Cartwright's letter he says he has sent it in, and the answers I am going to read are most of them in Mr. Cartwright's handwriting.

1445. On what point are these letters?—On the point of the part taken by the company in the management and support of the school, and how far they carried out the manifest intention of the Chancery scheme that they should take part in supporting the school. The condition to which the school was reduced was because the means were insufficient; and it is plain the intention was that the means should be increased, because there were only seven boys in it at the end of the old regime, and the pupils were to be 30 under the scheme. Then a master was appointed at a handsome salary, and from that time to 1887 the company supported the school. The statement in the return was that besides the Rainey's rent-charge, "The amount received from the endowment has been hitherto voluntarily supplemented by the Salters' Company, at an expense of about 200 *l.* per annum;" and it is also stated in the return that the master was appointed by the Salters' Company and the Lord Primate of all Ireland as co-trustees, and the appointment of the under masters is vested in the Salters' Company and the Lord Primate. Mr. Cartwright wrote in October 1879 to the secretary of the Commission, not being able to attend himself, saying, "The Salters' Company provide all the cost of the school beyond the amount of the endowment, which you have stated in the return I made upon your printed forms. They have this year approved with the Primate of our making the school entirely open to all denominations, and giving all ministers of religion equal right of access for religious teaching to pupils of their persuasion, and the school has been placed under the Intermediate Education Act, thus giving the town the full advantages of that Act. There are at present attending the school, 17 Church, two Roman Catholic, and 11 Presbyterian scholars." That was the condition of the school at that time.

1446. Then, did the company proceed to take any action, to make any grants?—The company published papers which they handed in, stating that the school was to be called "The Rainey Foundation School," and this inscription was put on the school: "Rainey's Foundation School. Rebuilt, A.D. 1864, by the Worshipful Company of Salters, London. For the education of Thirty boys, free of all charge, to be styled 'Foundation Boys,'" and it was placed under the management of a Mr. Kincaid, who is still the master, who was an English graduate, and recommended by the company to the Primate; he was appointed at a salary of 150 *l.* a year; his house, and some allowances, and his right to the school fees made his place altogether worth about 280 *l.* or 340 *l.* a year, he told us.

1447. I understand that the Salters' Company gave 1,333 *l.* in 1864 for building, and also an annual contribution?—From that time down Rainey's Endowment was handed over by the Primate to the agent of the Salters' Company, and the agent paid the entire expenses of the school.

1448. Do you know the amount?—Yes; I think I referred to it. We held an inquiry at Coleraine on the 9th of October 1886 into this matter.

1449. Was that at Coleraine or at Magherafelt?—The first was at Coleraine, and we afterwards went to Magherafelt. About 200 *l.* a year over and above what they got from the Rainey Endowment was the average expenditure.

1450. About 318 *l.* in all?—From that to 400 *l.* The company's grant varied from 150 *l.* to 300 *l.*; it was not fixed in any way. The whole expenditure was borne by the company.

1451. Will you tell us what the proceedings of your executive Commission were; you say you went to Coleraine on 9th October 1886?—We went to Coleraine, and at the inquiry there evidence was given that the company had so far supported the school, and Mr. Cartwright was examined, and we came back to Dublin, the company indicating an intention at that time of continuing to do something for the school.

1452. Did they indicate their intention in a correspondence with you?—Yes; both in the correspondence and at interviews. The first letter of importance on the matter, which Mr. Cartwright sent us, is on the 4th of November 1886, after we came back. It enclosed a return of expenditure for 14 years on the school, showing that the rent-charge had been very regularly paid; it varied a pound or two in the different years; but the company had spent altogether on the school 3,000 *l.*, in addition to what they got from the rent-charge. Mr. Cartwright wrote describing the endowment, and said: "It was endowed with 175 *l.*, late Irish currency, vested in the Primate, on whose authority the rector of Magherafelt administered the school. The Salters' Company agreed with the Primate" (this is manifestly the agreement that took place at the time of the Chancery scheme) "that they would pay the increased expense if the school were placed on an enlarged basis to improve local education, by making it capable of receiving 60 boys, 30 of whom were to receive clothing, so that

Chairman—continued.

that the poverty of boys should not exclude them from attending. The Salters' Company built a good school and dwelling, at a cost of 1,332 *l.*, and have maintained it in perfect condition; but no interest has ever been charged on that outlay." Then they say they wished it "to be worked as an intermediate school, provided the Salters' Company continued their payment to as large an amount at least as the trust fund. This was done, and children of any denomination were admitted, the vacancies being filled by competitive examination; but Dr. Jordan" (who was the rector) "retained his right to half the presentations, if he wished to exercise it, on behalf of the children of his church. In other words, the Primate was willing to have the school extended in numbers, provided the rector retained a share equal to the original endowment of 150 *l.* a year, and under the scheme by which the school has been worked this share would be about one-half. All religious denominations were on perfect equality under the competitive examination system," and he gives the numbers. He says on the 1st of January 1886 the 30 boys were thus represented, 15 Church, 8 Presbyterians, and 7 Roman Catholics. He then says that Dr. Jordan "is entirely in favour of the school being open to all denominations, as it is, and as it has been entirely since 1878. A school of this sort would, no doubt, attract greater interest if managed by a local committee, selected from the various religious denominations; but if the Salters' Company discontinued their subscriptions, could the trust fund be diverted from the present trustee?" He said there was a prescriptive right "of 100 years in his behalf. On this account I think the local committee should be external to, and not touching on this right." Sir Henry Cartwright sent us that letter, and when we had got it with the return, he came up to Dublin, and we saw him, and he conveyed to us that the company were just about selling their estates, that he had been very active in promoting the sale, and that they had also disposed of all the primary schools they had been supporting, and given them to the various denominations, and he was anxious to do something for the Rainey School also before the company left the place.

1453. By doing something for them, I suppose he meant giving them the fabric?—Yes, giving the fabrics of the primary schools. I do not know whether there was any money given to them or not. However, we wished him to put it in writing, and he wrote to me on the 14th of December 1886 the letter which is at page 321 of our Report: "In reference to the Rainey Foundation School, I beg to enclose, for your Lordship's perusal, a copy of a letter I have written to the Lord Primate, Dr. Knox, asking for his acceptance of such a scheme as I understand from you the Commissioners had in contemplation to frame, provided I can induce the Salters' Company (as I fully hope to succeed in doing) to settle an endowment for the future maintenance of the school in at least undiminished usefulness." The letter to the Primate told him of what had occurred at our meeting, that the Presbyterian body had put forward a claim to the endowment under Rainey's will, and he spoke of the liberality with which it had been previously managed. He said, "The Royal Commissioners will, I believe, be disposed to frame a scheme by which the advantages of the intermediate education may continue to children of all denominations, with a board of management at which the Church will be fairly protected in the direct interest it has, without excluding the Presbyterians or Roman Catholics, though in practice the latter will take no part in the management, and I have just given over to them (R. C.'s) schools male and female of their own. On these principles I shall propose to my company to meet the wishes of the Royal Commissioners, and endow the school with the entire buildings, and a subsidy to maintain its usefulness unimpaired. The advantages this will secure to the district for advanced education will, I feel sure, attract your Grace's adherence to the scheme, and will save all trouble of contention or possible litigation." He sent the letter I have read to me in December 1886, and the Primate and the Commissioners both wrote to the company. I do not know how far the Committee think these letters material.

1454. I think they are material. They disclose, or at all events the letters of Mr. Cartwright disclose the view the company then took of their obligation: I do not know whether the further letters go in the same direction?—There are a vast number of letters with other people. I have the letters on which we formed the belief that the Salters' Company intended to continue to this school the same amount of money they had previously given.

1455. I do not think you need trouble to read the other letters, if you say they point all in the same direction; that is to say, the recognition by the Salters' Company of an obligation?—I will read only the most material letters. Our secretary wrote to the company's agent, saying it was important we should know what the intention of the company was.

1456. Mr. Cartwright being the recognised agent of the company?—He was the agent; but we wrote also to their clerk in London, and he, on the 5th of March, wrote us an official letter. He told us that the court had had the letter from the Archbishop of Armagh under consideration; but "after deliberation, and having due regard to the interest which the company has taken in the school for so many years, and being unwilling to restrict in any way the usefulness of the school, as at present constituted, the court have resolved to create a supplementary endowment, in addition to the existing rent-charge, &c., by vesting in the future properly constituted authorities of the school the following premises: First, the school buildings, and then the markets now held by the market trustees of Magherafelt, which he set out, and the rent of which he gave, and which set out the total gross amount of the proposed endowment as annually 184 *l.* Those market premises consisted of two sets of grain stores and one set of flax stores, and two markets, one a butter market and the other a general market yard or place.

1457. That, I understand, was to be the source of their contribution; the source of the income?—Yes, it is so stated; it is stated that these were rented at so much, and that that made a total of 184 *l.* per annum, which would have been

Chairman—continued.

within a few pounds, if not quite as much as they had been previously giving. That letter is dated 5th of March 1887. There then arose a question about the constitution of the governing body which was to manage the school.

1458. I suppose that arose from the point of view of what you have told us in Ireland is inevitable, the question of religious denominations?—Yes, but it arose in a curious way. We got a letter first from the solicitors to the Archbishop telling us that the Primate had sent them a letter from the clerk of the Salters' Company, saying that they "desire to nominate his Grace a trustee for the purpose of assigning to him certain property to be held in trust for the future maintenance of the school. His Grace is already the sole trustee, and we see no objection to this property being vested in him for the purposes of the trust." We sent a copy of that letter at once to Sir Henry Cartwright, calling his attention to the inconsistency of this proposal "with those hitherto entertained by the Commission for the constitution of a representative governing body which the Commissioners understood from you" (that is, Sir Henry Cartwright) "had the approval of the Salters' Company." He answered that by saying, "All I can do now is to forward your letter to the Salters' Company, but what I understood as the intention of the company was, that, having the desire, which has always distinguished them, for the advancing of the education of the young, they would make the arrangements proposed by the contemplated scheme of the Education Commissioners, viz., that a joint board of governors should be appointed, composed of representatives of the Church of Ireland and the Presbyterian Church, but open for children of all denominations, with the Lord Primate as chairman, to which board of governors the Salters' Company would convey an endowment which was defined in their letter, capable with the present endowment of maintaining the school in at least its present usefulness and efficiency."

1459. Catholic children were to be admitted to the school, but no Catholics were on the governing body?—Up to the present they had told us that there was to be a governing body representing the different denominations. The Primate said he was to be the sole trustee, and Sir Henry Cartwright said it was to consist of representatives of the two Protestant churches only. We had understood from Sir Henry Cartwright that the Salters' Company contemplated the incorporation of a board of representative governors, and we wrote this letter to the clerk to the Salters' Company on the 6th of July 1887, to ask what they meant: "I am directed by the Commission to inquire whether your company wish that their endowment to be given to the above-mentioned school should be administered by a board which shall be exclusively Protestant, or by a board on which all denominations shall be represented."

1460. That was your letter to the company?—Yes; and their answer of the 12th of July 1887 says, after referring to the other correspondence, "I am directed to point out to you that a misunderstanding has evidently arisen in the minds of the Lord Primate and of Messrs. Dobbie and Company, as to the wishes and intentions of the Salters' Company with regard to the school, and to inform you that the Court quite endorse Sir Henry Cartwright's reply, dated the 30th of July 1887, to your letter which fully expresses their views and intentions on the subject. Under these circumstances I need scarcely lay before the company your inquiry of the 6th instant." The letter referred to spoke of two Protestant denominations only, and Mr. Scott, the clerk to the company, said that he did not see he was bound under the circumstances to lay before the company the question about the Roman Catholics. Of course we pressed the question, and I need not go through all the very long correspondence; it ended in a letter telling us they would not interfere. We pressed the question, and on the 14th of July we wrote again through our secretary, "I am now directed to inquire whether it is the wish of the Salters' Company that the board to be constituted for their administration of their endowment should be an exclusively Protestant board. The Commission find it necessary to ascertain the wish of the company in this respect, inasmuch as they are required under their Act of Parliament in preparing a scheme for the administration of any endowment to have regard to the spirit of the founder's intentions." The answer to that letter was on the 26th of July: "I have submitted your letter of the 14th instant to the Court of Assistants of the Salters' Company, and I am directed to inform you that the company desire to remain neutral in the question raised by you with regard to the religious denomination of the members of the proposed board for the administration of Rainey Foundation School endowment."

1461. That made it, I suppose, impossible for you to deal further with the matter so far as the Salters' Company were concerned?—We then thought we were bound to settle the scheme for Rainey's endowment only, and our reason for doing that was because we did not consider that a school would be open to all denominations on fair terms if the governing body exclusively belonged to either Protestants or Catholics, as the case might be.

1462. You resolved to confine your draft scheme to Rainey's endowment?—Yes.

1463. Was that scheme prepared and published?—We then published a draft scheme for Rainey's endowment only.

1464. When was that?—The draft scheme was published on the 18th of August 1888. There was a good deal of correspondence went on in the meantime. The company stopped their subscriptions altogether. Mr. Jordan, the manager of the school, was in great straits for money, and was pressing the Salters' Company to give him money, and we pressed them also. The head master's salary was due, and the funds that they drew upon for the purpose of keeping up the school was a sum of 300*l.* or 400*l.* or accumulated rent-charge, which had been recovered from a defaulting agent of the former Primate, and that has been since spent in carrying the place on. In the meantime, before we published the scheme, the Roman Catholic parish priest, Canon Donnelly, put forward his claim.

Chairman—continued.

He objected to taking part in a mixed school, and, above all, objected that the mixed school should be exclusively under a Protestant governing body. The upshot of the whole thing was that we published this scheme in 1888 for Rainey's endowment only.

1465. What was the frame of the scheme?—The frame of the scheme was to form a governing body, half Presbyterian and half Church, with the Primate as chairman, with power for the subscribers of the school to elect additional governors. The Salters' Company were out of it.

1466. Who else was on the governing body besides the Primate?—One governor was to be elected by the Diocesan Council, which is a Church body, and another by the vestry, which is a parochial body, and two by the Presbytery. There were to be four *ex-officio* governors, the Protestant Archbishop of Armagh, the moderator of the General Assembly, the incumbent of the parish, and the minister of the parish.

1467. I do not understand why you put no Roman Catholic on?—Because we had only Rainey's endowment to deal with, and we considered that as a Protestant endowment. If the Salters' Company gave money for all denominations, we would have represented all the denominations; but we wrote to them to say that we regarded Rainey's endowment as a Protestant endowment.

1468. Admitting Roman Catholic children?—Yes, with a conscience clause; but probably there would not be many. We also added six governors (I think that was the number), to be elected by subscribers. We introduced that power of adding to the governing body, and provided that the Salters' Company might, as subscribers, appoint representatives on the governing board, if they so chose.

1469. The Salters' Company did take action, did they not?—When we published the scheme, the Salters' Company executed a deed which requires some explanation. They declared a trust of the market property for Rainey's School as at present constituted, but not to take effect until the scheme had come into force. The trust was "for the accommodation, use, and benefit, and for the purposes of the said school in same manner as heretofore, and as a perpetual endowment therefor." They sent us a copy of that deed in September 1888.

1470. Was it a draft deed?—It was an escrow, as we lawyers call it. It was delivered to the solicitor of the Representative Church Body on the condition that it was not to take effect if our scheme did not deal with the endowment to their satisfaction.

Mr. Healy.

1471. In doing that, were they not thereby sealing and executing the deed?—I do not think they understood at the time the effect of the deed, but we wrote and called attention to it at once, and then they sent it in another way, as you will see; we then got objections to the draft scheme from everybody in Magherafelt, and accordingly we went to Magherafelt once more at a later stage in the autumn of 1888. The Primate objected, and Mr. Jordan objected, to being deprived of the power they had; the Presbyterians objected. It is right to say that some of the Presbyterians, in fact, all but one, accepted the mixed board, but they objected to the chairmanship of the Primate, as they thought it would give a majority against them. We accordingly went down to Magherafelt, and we held a further inquiry which rather raised more difficulties. I must tell you exactly what happened. We went down on the 22nd of October 1888. Having had all these objections from the various denominations, we wanted first to see what the property was.

Chairman.

1472. That is to say, this property of the markets, and so forth?—Yes. The Salters' Company wrote us a letter wishing to leave the scheme so framed as to dispose of these markets; they wanted to throw no obstacle in our way. It turned out that this property was all in their own hands; it was not let at any permanent rent, and there were no patents for the markets; they were markets held in yards, which of course would go on as very good markets as long as there were no competing markets. But they were managed by a market committee appointed by the inhabitants of the town, and this market committee was under an agreement to pay, I think, 96 *l.* a year to the Salters' Company out of the proceeds of the market; but they used to get back about 30 *l.* of that by way of allowances. The upshot of the thing was that some of the stores were let from time to time for small quantities of grain brought in, and things of that kind; others were let half-yearly and quarterly; and the net rental altogether so far as we could make out was only at the outside about 136 *l.* or 137 *l.* a year.

1473. Instead of 104 *l.*, as was mentioned?—Yes; furthermore, it was not a secure rental; and it struck all of us that it was property which the school committee could not manage at all.

1474. The school committee would have had to administer these markets?—A number of witnesses came forward and said that if the proceeds of these markets were to go to a school only open to two denominations they would set up markets of their own, they would not go to these markets, and they would not pay tolls; and everybody was dissatisfied with the Salters' endowment. After hearing all this we came to the conclusion that we could not deal with the Salters' endowment at all, "in consequence of their having granted it only upon a condition which cannot take effect until after the scheme has come into force, and also in consequence of the inconsistency of the conditions, that the school shall be under exclusively Protestant government, and shall be available for all denominations." And also on the ground that we considered we could not form any school body that would be able to manage market property of that kind. We had therefore to reconsider the scheme, and proposed to confine it altogether to Rainey's School. Further correspondence then followed, which was very long indeed, between us and the company, and the company ultimately declared its intention to make the market property subject to a rent-charge of 190 *l.* a year, which was the sum the market committee had told us they were willing to pay,

Chairman—continued.

and to give the rent-charge as an endowment. Among other difficulties was the fact that the market committee were only what I may perhaps call a scratch body; they had no legal existence; they were only certain inhabitants of the town, managing the markets; but they said they were willing to pay 120*l.* a year for them.

1475. Were they to remain as tenants of the company?—Yes, they were to become tenants of the company; and the company finally called upon us to say whether if they did become tenants of the company, subject to 120*l.* a year, we would settle the scheme for the management of the rent as an endowment. Of course we said we would, and we did; and the last letter they wrote to us of any importance was a letter in which they told us that they wished to provide that endowment, but to divide it, and to give 66*l.* a year, to be applied to Rainey's School, and 54*l.* a year for the benefit of the Roman Catholic education of the town and neighbourhood.

1476. Was that to be given to some other school?—They only said for the benefit of Roman Catholic education in the town. They told me that the figures of 66*l.* and 54*l.* were ascertained in proportion to the number of inhabitants representing the two denominations in the town or on their estate; I forget which it was.

1477. What is the date of the letter informing you of their intention to give 66*l.* to the Rainey School and 54*l.* to the Roman Catholics?—The 16th of April 1889; it is an important letter. What they said was, "The company are, therefore, prepared to vest the property in the markets committee of Magherafelt, subject to an annual payment of 120*l.* by way of rent-charge, to be secured upon the premises, the members of the markets committee entering into covenants by which they are made individually and collectively responsible for the payment of this rent-charge. They shall further covenant to hand over the property, subject, of course, to this rent-charge, and any profits that may accrue in the course of its management, to the Town Commissioners, if and when constituted, and in the meantime they shall devote any such profits to the maintenance of the property and improvement of the town. Having regard to the company's wish that the Commissioners should declare such trust of the property as they may consider just in the interests of the inhabitants of the town, irrespective of creed and of any limits of the original trust of Rainey's Foundation, I am directed to state that the company are prepared to consent to avail themselves of the jurisdiction" (that is the jurisdiction of our Commission by consent) "to which you refer in your letter of the 2nd of March 1889, and I am, therefore, to request the Commissioners to take the necessary steps for the application of the rent-charge proposed to be secured upon the markets, &c., as hereinbefore described, to the undermentioned purposes, namely, 66*l.* per annum to be applied to Rainey's Foundation School; 54*l.* to be applied to the educational requirements of the Roman Catholic body of the town and neighbourhood. The company are given to understand that the above figures represent the proportion, or thereabouts, of Protestants to Roman Catholics on their late estate. The company hope that they have now removed all obstacles to the settlement of this matter." We then wrote to them, and told them of course that we would do what they desired, but we wrote: "The Commissioners understand that the creation of the rent-charge and the arrangements with the lessees will be carried out by the company by deed, as it could not be done by a scheme under our Act." We then re-cast our scheme and finally signed it.

1478. Was that at the beginning of this year?—On the 11th of January 1890. The Company declined to appoint any members of the governing body.

1479. Your scheme had then to go before the Privy Council?—Yes. The form of the governing body was the same as before; there was an alteration as regards the chairman; we yielded to the Presbyterian objection to this extent: that we made the existing Primate chairman during his life, and after his death or in his absence the chairman was to be appointed by rotation, and the body was to be half-and-half between the two denominations so long as they did not subscribe, but members of either denomination might qualify as subscribers and elect additional governors. We thought that the only chance of keeping the school going.

1480. When the scheme was submitted to the Privy Council, were any objections taken by the Presbyterians?—All the objections we had had before us disappeared, except those of the Presbyterians. After we had been to Magherafelt the General Assembly, the central body, sent us a deputation claiming to have Rainey's Endowment entirely to themselves, and pressed much more forcibly than anybody else their desire to separate Rainey's Endowment. The three reasons for the view which I and my brother judicial Commissioner took (our colleagues hardly agreed, and we did our best to come to a fair agreement) were, first, that because all the successful schools which we had met with in the north of Ireland, almost without exception, were under bodies representing all denominations of Protestants, we thought that a mixed body would be more likely to succeed. We also thought that Magherafelt was entirely unable to support two schools for Protestants; there were not boys enough, and we thought they would be much better taught in one school. And also another reason which weighed with us was this: whatever Rainey's Endowment might have been originally, neither when the Act of Parliament was passed nor when the Chancery scheme was got, nor at any time for a period of nearly 200 years, had the Presbyterians done anything to assert their rights; therefore, we thought we could not exclude the Church people altogether. If we admitted them at all we came to the conclusion that it was better to admit them in equal numbers, because if one was in a minority there would be friction. We gave both parties a compensating power of subscribing so as to get a majority on the governing body by earning it. That went before the Privy Council.

1481. I understand

Chairman—continued.

1481. I understand the claim of the Presbyterians was a sort of sudden revival under Rainey's will?—It is hardly right, I think, to call it a sudden revival. When we were first in Magherafelt there was one gentleman for whose evidence we had great respect, namely, Dr. Wilson, who presented that view; but the local clergyman and the Presbytery of Magherafelt quite accepted putting it under a mixed body in equal proportions. The Presbyterians, however, always objected to giving the Church of Ireland the chairmanship. We said to them, you must have a casting vote of some sort, because if you are dividing two and two, and there is no casting vote, no business will ever be done, and if, on the other hand, you draw lots, or take it turn and turn about, you will have different decisions alternately day by day. We pressed them to accept our proposal, and ultimately the decision was confirmed by the Privy Council.

Mr. Sexton.

1482. Giving the Church the majority?—No, we left the existing Primate chairman during his life, but after his death, and in his absence, the chair is to be taken in a rotation settled by themselves.

Chairman.

1483. The scheme passed in the Privy Council, and was provisionally approved by the Lord Lieutenant, I understand?—The Presbyterian objections were overruled by the Privy Council, but you may still have it all up again in Parliament; there is a power to petition Parliament for two months. I may say that we have never had a petition against us in Parliament yet, and this will be the first time if a petition comes.

1484. It was approved by the Lord Lieutenant on the 19th of May, this year; perhaps you would like to say a word or two as to the present condition of the school, and as to whether the endowments including the contributions to be expected from the Salters' Company are sufficient?—It is perfectly impossible that the school can be continued with its present funds as it was hitherto. The original endowment was about 400 *l.* a year in addition to the buildings. The head master had a salary of 150 *l.*; his assistant was paid also, I think, 80 *l.*; the second assistant got some 30 *l.*, and the master had other emoluments bringing his post up to be worth about 240 *l.* The whole income now is Rainey's rent-charge of 175 *l.*, late Irish currency, equal to about 161 *l.* English, and the 65 *l.* from the Salters' Company.

1485. That is to say they get 65 *l.* now from the Salters' Company instead of nearly 200 *l.*?—Yes, 200 *l.*

1486. From previous witnesses we have heard reference to Mr. Kincaid, the head master; it appears that he had a great grievance?—Mr. Kincaid appeared on the second occasion of our going to Magherafelt; he was examined on the first occasion, but the question of his personal rights was not then raised. On the second occasion he told us that as soon as he heard of the sale of the property being impending, he had gone to Sir Henry Cartwright and had represented his position to him. He said, in his evidence before the Commission, "About a month before he left I went into his office and said to him 'as the Salters' Company are now parting with their estate what will be my position?' 'Oh,' he said, 'you will be all right; you will have your salary as long as you live.'" Then Dr. Traill asked him, "He did not say from whom?" and Mr. Kincaid says, "He did not." (Mr. *Graham.*) Did you ever look to the Primate at any time as your master?—(*A.*) Never. (*Q.*) You always dealt with the company?—(*A.*) Yes. (*Q.*) Was your knowledge of the Salters' Company one of the things that led you to accept the position of head master?—(*A.*) Oh, yes, for I had always known of the London companies and believed that their conduct would be most generous. I have at all times received from the Salters' Company the greatest personal kindness and consideration." After taking that evidence we told all parties that we would delay the signing of the scheme until we could bring it before the Salters' Company, both on Mr. Kincaid's case and also on the future support of the school. We sent them this important evidence, and they answered us by stating that Sir Henry Cartwright disputed the accuracy of Mr. Kincaid's statements, and also, that they themselves would not take any further responsibility with regard to the school, except as regards the 120 *l.* I have previously explained. We sent Mr. Kincaid that letter, and he pointed out in a further letter that he had been on oath in giving his evidence, and said that he had a memorandum of his conversation with Sir H. Cartwright, made at the time, which he was prepared to produce. He also sent a letter to the Company, I believe. We were obliged to tell him that we could only deal with the endowment we had. There was a statement made here about his pension which was entirely a misapprehension. We put into our scheme the ordinary provision enabling the governing body from any funds at their disposal to superannuate the masters; but as regards Mr. Kincaid there are no funds out of which he could now get a pension, except by starving the school. As far as his legal position is concerned he holds his office at Rainey's School at the pleasure of the Primate.

1487. I do not think we need ask you any more questions about Mr. Kincaid; my honourable friend Mr. Lea has received two telegrams, which are by no means irrelevant to the subject of this inquiry, from Magherafelt this morning. The first is a telegram from Magherafelt (I do not know who sends it): "Rainey's School write me willing to advance 1,000 *l.* to credit of the school account." The second, sent off a few minutes later, is from Mr. Kincaid: "Much pleasure in informing Committee, Salters' Company have promised to consider my position favourably"?—I am very glad to hear that. He certainly appeared to us to have a very strong moral claim against the company, and also, if his evidence before us were correct, he had had direct

representations

Chairman—continued.

representations made to him by Sir H. Cartwright that his position was secure.

Dr. Freshfield.] Would you allow the representatives of the Salters' Company to say one word.

Mr. E. L. Scott.] It is only that the telegram should have stated 100 *l.*, which is what the Salters' Company have agreed to, instead of 1,000 *l.*

Chairman.] Is it 100 *l.* down or 100 *l.* every year?

Mr. E. L. Scott.] It is 100 *l.* advanced for the present to enable the school to be carried on.

Witness.] I have said they only had about 340 *l.* of the old accumulations, and these have been all exhausted during the correspondence in trying to keep the place up; I presume 100 *l.* will only carry them on for about six months more.

Sir William Marriott.

1488. I see, at the end of your examination, you say that intermediate education in Ireland is very ill provided for; I suppose that is a fact about which there is no possible doubt?—I do not think there can be any question.

1489. The great question is as to how to raise the money to provide for it?—Yes.

1490. With regard to the companies, in your opinion is there any legal claim upon them to provide for it?—I could not give a legal opinion upon that subject; I have never had the materials for forming it.

1491. If there was a legal claim, are there not means in Ireland for enforcing it?—Certainly.

1492. If there are any trusts in deeds by which the land was conveyed two centuries ago to the London companies in Ireland, there are competent courts in Ireland to enforce them, are there not?—Of course.

1493. So far as you know, up to the present has any attempt been made to enforce such trusts?—None. I may explain, and I think I have stated already, we have never had any documents before us, with regard even to the Irish Society itself, which contain any express trusts.

1494. As I understand it, it is only general; there are trusts in the Charter or Deed of the Irish Society, but they are not defined?—Yes.

1495. But in the conveyances to the City companies there is this difference, is there not, that there are no trusts defined?—I have never seen any of the conveyances; I speak merely from the Report which I have mentioned; I believe they are conveyances from the Irish Society, therefore, strictly, if the Irish Society were trustees at the time those deeds were executed, the trusts might have been enforced then if they existed.

1496. You mean to say that the Irish Society could not grant land free from trusts?—No trustee can get land into the hands of another person free from trust unless that person is a purchaser for value and without notice.

1497. If there were trusts in the deeds to the

Sir William Marriott—continued.

Irish Society, and the Irish Society had gone beyond their powers, and tried to give the property without the trusts, those trusts could be enforced?—Certainly; if it was done in time, and I understand from the Report that an information was filed for the purpose and not proceeded with.

1498. Practically this question, with regard to the trust, is a legal question?—Yes; or rather all trust questions are equitable.

1499. No doubt there is a moral aspect also. The general idea, as put by witnesses before us, seems to be that because the companies have subscribed a certain amount, they ought to continue their subscriptions?—We had evidence that the companies have subscribed considerably, but all the subscriptions proved before us were more or less variable in amount, and appeared to be given now and again; we had no evidence of any subscriptions that we could treat as permanent.

1500. There were no subscriptions you could enforce as a duty upon them?—Apparently not; but of course we had not to consider that question, because the decision in the case of the Skinners' Company seemed to put an end to our jurisdiction in the matter on the other ground altogether; there are several schemes of ours under which the contributions of the companies are administered. For instance, the Ironmongers' Company gave 1,000 *l.* to found a scholarship at Magee College.

1501. Putting aside the legal questions, assuming there is no legal liability, what would it be fair for the companies to do?—I could hardly say what I think to be fair. Any money that the companies offer they can have devoted to the trusts under this Commission which I represent.

1502. Is it fair that when they sell the property they ought to leave ample provision to keep up the subscriptions they have given?—I am sure that the localities would be delighted.

1503. They do not want anything beyond that, do they?—We have never taken any evidence upon that point, but so far as I can understand they would be very well satisfied if they were assured in the future what they have had in the past. In the case of the Salters' Company, all that was ever expected, and all that was promised, as I think it was by those letters, was such an income as had kept the school in its present state of efficiency; that would be 200 *l.* a year.

1504. Do you think that those letters formed a contract binding them legally to continue that grant?—It is very difficult to find a consideration in them.

Sir John Ellis.

1505. With regard to the donations which the Irish Society give, I understand you to say they were given without restriction, and you seemed to have some objection to their being given without restriction?—I was quoting from one of the former Reports. It was not that they were given without restriction, but that a great number of small sums were given to schools by way of subscriptions without the Society being able to see to their application.

Sir John Ellis—continued.

1506. But then in another part of your evidence you mention that you thought local control was the best?—Certainly, for schools.

1507. That is what the Irish Society afford opportunity for; they give without restriction, and therefore local control comes in?—Yes, that is so, with regard to any schools that have a sufficiently large endowment, except the Irish Society's own school in Coleraine: there the managing committee is a voluntarily formed body; they have no legal status.

1508. It is a local committee?—Yes, it is a local committee requested to act by the Irish Society.

1509. I think you say that you have not read the charters and legal documents under which the Irish Society and companies hold?—I have got a general knowledge of them, but I have never seen the originals.

1510. You have never studied them?—No.

1511. Does not it strike you that these grants were made for services rendered and for something done, and have you not heard that surveys were made to see whether these services were performed, and the consequence was that the charter was re-granted?—I never went into that question, because the decision of the House of Lords in the case of the Skinners' Company was accepted by us as final, and it disposed of our jurisdiction.

1512. May I take it that you do not express an opinion upon that point?—Certainly not.

1513. You do not now express an opinion upon that point?—I do not; I have never had occasion to study the matter sufficiently to form one.

Colonel Laurie.

1514. I understand you to say that this case of Balsey's School was the only case of complaint against the City companies you have to make?—It was the only case that came before us of the withdrawal of a grant.

1515. You have no other complaint to make against the companies, I understand; in other dealings you found them fairly liberal?—We have no dealings other than that. In all the other cases we dealt with funds already given.

1516. I presume you have had cases of the endowment of schools come under your notice; have you had any complaint in those cases?—No. Of course there were a number of complaints of inequality in the amount given to the different denominations.

1517. May I take it that most of the difficulties arose from religious differences among those who received the money?—Yes, religious differences and the difference in the amounts that the different religious bodies got.

1518. It was not so much as regards the conduct of the companies?—No; and also the view was pressed very often upon us that the difference was as stated in the old Report in consequence of the restriction of their charter.

Mr. Sexton.

1519. How many governors of Balsey School are there, including the Chairman?—At present, under the scheme, there are eight.

1520. Has the chairman a casting vote?—Yes.

Mr. Sexton—continued.

There are four *ex-officio* governors and four representative governors, making eight altogether.

1521. The arrangement, as I understand, is that during the life of the present chairman the Church party has a majority, and afterwards it goes to each body alternately?—The Church have a majority only when the present Primate is present; we kept it a personal privilege. The provision in the scheme is this: "So long as the most Reverend Robert Knox, D.D., shall hold the office of Archbishop he shall be the chairman of the governors. The governors at their first meeting, and from time to time afterwards when necessary, shall fix an order of rotation in which each governor shall be entitled to take the chair, in the absence of the above-named chairman, or after he shall have ceased to hold office." We had to deal with the claim on the part of the Primate to retain a majority, as well as with that of the Presbyterians, who objected to their being even equally numbered.

1522. It appears in the Reports from which you quoted, that there were considerable reductions in the grants by the companies for the purpose of education in Ireland, even before they proceeded to sell?—There is a statement in the Report of 1858 of a reduction to the extent of 496 *l.* per annum in the grants to Foyle College alone.

1523. Then we know there have been several reductions since they began to sell?—The only case that came before us was Balsey's case. Of course there were a great number of subscriptions that did not come before us; subscriptions to churches and other charities; we had nothing to do with anything except schools.

1524. The grants for educational purposes have been restricted from time to time?—I believe so; not in the case of the Irish Society, I think; they seem to have been rather increased.

1525. It is so, I gather, in the case of the London companies. You quoted a Report of the Commission of 1878, I think it was, of which you were a member, in which it is suggested that the funds of the Irish Society applicable to education should be placed under efficient management?—That was in the Report of 1858.

1526. Do you confirm that suggestion?—The Report of 1858 says: "We feel that immediate steps should be taken in order that all the funds devoted to education under the Charter of the Irish Society should assume a definite form, and be placed under a system of efficient management." That refers to the statement that they were an absentee body, and that local governing bodies were best for the schools.

1527. Do you consider that an appropriate suggestion?—We have certainly thought everywhere we went that local committees managing the schools were the best, and the Royal schools in Ireland seem to be an instance of that.

1528. You agree that local management is the most efficient, and that the trusts ought to be defined?—Yes; but the Irish Society do not appear to be the managers of any schools, except their schools in Coleraine. They give the money to the governing bodies, but they are not themselves the governing body.

1529. You

Mr. *Sexton*—continued.

1529. You think, also, I gather, that where members of the various denominations exist in sufficient numbers to attend different schools, the schools of the denominational bodies would be the most efficient schools?—Certainly.

1530. Would you apply to the companies generally the suggestion you have adopted from the Report with regard to the Irish Society?—So far as funds have been given for educational purposes, I would. But the principal grants made were grants of lump sums of money.

1531. But you conveyed to the Committee that those sums in the case of the Irish Society and also of the companies are used very much indiscriminately, in various places, without local knowledge or efficient examination of the schools?—The impression conveyed to me was that the Irish Society had so many applications that they gave money to everybody all round.

1532. Without any efficient means of inquiry as to whether the grant for education was required?—Except that they were mostly National schools; they would have that guarantee. It is right to say Mr. Montgomery stated he was obliged to furnish a report annually that the schools to which the money went were properly managed; but he rather conveyed to us he was not able to make any investigation, but just satisfied himself that the school was at work, and in fact no visitor could do more.

1533. Would you wish to suggest anything further than to say that the education trusts had better be defined as to their extent and that the schools are better managed under local management?—I cannot suggest anything more than to say that if there was a defined sum of money available for educational purposes in those localities, each denomination that would not work harmoniously with the others should have its own school, but I entertain the strongest opinion from our inquiries that all the Protestant denominations will work very much better together than they would separately. There was a strong corroboration of that in our first scheme for the Royal schools. The objection was put forward by the Church people that we had put them upon a mixed board in Armagh, and the Privy Council altered our scheme, or rather, they sent it back to us with the declaration that we were to establish what was practically an exclusively Church board in Armagh, and an exclusively Presbyterian board in Tyrone. The moment that was published objections were sent in from all quarters, and we have now the scheme sent back from the Privy Council, with a declaration that we are to restore it as it was at first, putting each county under a mixed governing body, and giving the majority to that branch of Protestants who are in a majority in the place.

1534. I followed you with very great lucidity in your elucidation of the question of the trusts, and I gathered from you referring to the judgment in the House of Lords in the Skinners' Company's case you found the Irish Society's property impressed with a public trust, but having a discretion as to portions of their income which they were to apply to the various purposes, and therefore you did not feel that you were entitled to question their discretion as to the amount they should apply to education as compared with other purposes?—Quite so; for instance, if we had framed a scheme for Foyle College declaring that the Irish Society should subscribe 500 *l.* a year in perpetuity, I believe that would have been outside our jurisdiction, because they could reduce it to 400 *l.*, or increase it to 600 *l.*, as they thought fit. And also if we had defined the amount, it would probably have led to their withdrawing the grant altogether.

1535. The trust being admitted, the amounts applicable to the various uses were left to the discretion of the society?—They hold the money on trust to divide, and are therefore responsible for the division, and the power of division rests with them; we have, under our Act, no power to make the division for them.

1536. Therefore, even if the whole of the income were avowedly applicable to trust uses, you could not say what part should be devoted to a particular purpose?—Precisely. I think the whole income is declared by Lord Lyndhurst to be subject to trust. Our Act does not apply to any endowment which the governing body may withdraw from educational purposes, except with their consent. If they wrote a letter and said, we will appropriate so much for a certain educational purpose, then we could settle a scheme at once, as we did in Rainey's case. The 54 *l.* mentioned in Rainey's case we dealt with by the same scheme as the other, by declaring that it was to be managed by Roman Catholics, by the local Roman Catholic body for the diocese of Armagh, unless a local body is framed by some future scheme; in the meantime they may depute the management of it to the Roman Catholic parish priest and two resident laymen appointed by him, for intermediate education.

1537. You said the Irish Society could not convey their property from themselves divested of the trust?—A trustee cannot convey property impressed with a trust divested of the trust, except to purchasers for value, without notice.

1538. Any trust obligation on the Irish Society would attend to the companies?—They would by law, except in the hands of a purchaser for value without notice. I apprehend that the question is, whether there was any trust affecting property not wanted for the general purposes of the Irish Society. However, I cannot really give any legal opinion upon a matter of that kind.

Chairman.

1539. You do not go behind the judgment of Lord Lyndhurst in 1845?—Quite so.

Mr. *Sexton.*

1540. Assuming the same trust lay upon the companies, you would apply the same principles you did apply to the Irish Society, as you could not, without consent, undertake the division of the funds?—My Commission could not, and for the same reason. Besides, we had hardly any instance except this of the Salters' Company, where there was any defined income paid for any number of years. Large sums, of 1,000 *l.* for instance, were given for buildings or scholarships, and

Mr. Sexton—continued.

and there are some in buildings or investments, which are dealt with under our schemes.

1541. I think your Commission warned the Irish Government some years ago, did they not, that the interests of education might suffer in consequence of the sale of those properties?—We have no right to warn anybody; we informed both the Government and Parliament.

1542. That is a more courteous way of putting it; you also conveyed a similar intimation to Parliament?—Yes; we attached a copy of the memorandum to our report to Parliament in 1887, and repeated the substance of it in the body of the report.

1543. You apprehended that what has happened would be the result?—The evidence on our original inquiry disclosed the danger of those grants being withdrawn.

1544. Did the Irish Government ever make any communication to you on that report?—We could hardly expect any communication upon it except by action in Parliament, and so far as I know there has been none.

1545. So far as you know there has been no action by the Government?—I am not aware of any.

1546. You have also discussed in your report the application of the income from the Royal Schools estates to intermediate education for districts in Ulster?—Each of those estates was granted under the old plantation arrangement for the benefit either of the diocese or the county, and there was a confusion in some of the old papers whether it was the diocese or the county, and we formed what we called a district, a sort of combination of the two. We confined them to six counties. We brought in Monaghan, which was in the diocese of Clogher, and to those six counties we confined the Royal School endowment. We proposed originally that one-third of the money should go among all the schools in proportion to their work. The Privy Council struck out that provision, and declared that each endowment should be divided in its own district, half and half between Protestants and Roman Catholics. The scheme has not yet been finally approved; it was sent back the other day to have another provision restored; but that part of it has not been objected to. In fact every one of the denominations preferred a bird in the hand to the indefinite provisions framed by us to ensure that the schools should be efficiently managed.

1547. We may take it that the produce of the Royal Schools estate has gone wholly to districts in Ulster?—Yes, and each to its own original district in full. The effect is that Fermanagh has much the largest amount, and the Donegal endowment is scarcely worth anything, owing to the changes in the circumstances of the estate. Fermanagh is worth nearly 3,000*l.* a year, and Donegal is not worth 200*l.*

1548. Are these endowments for an education of intermediate character?—The Royal Schools were all intended to be grammar schools at the beginning, and we have done our best to secure that the money shall go not only to grammar schools, but to large and efficient schools. We had made elaborate provisions for this in the original scheme, and we have kept all those provisions, although they are no longer worked by way of results.

Chairman.

1549. According to the Report of the Royal Commission of 1857, to which you referred, did they not say with regard to the Foyle College, that there was more than a colour of probability that the Irish Society intercepted the endowment intended for the Royal free school?—Yes, I mentioned that. Those two townlands mentioned there, those 300 acres of land, are very fairly identified to be the 300 acres which were allotted for the Royal Free School of Londonderry; they are now the property of the Irish Society, and have been so from the commencement, although they are not in the charter.

1550. The point is that they intercepted this endowment intended by King James for free schools, and used it for their own purposes?—Yes; but on the other hand there is no evidence that the society ever gave less to Foyle College than those two townlands produced. Latterly they gave much more. The present value is about 350*l.* a-year. We considered the question of dealing with those two townlands, but we saw that Foyle College would lose by it, because at present it is getting more from the general funds of the Irish Society than the town lands would produce.

Mr. Sexton.

1551. What is meant by finding those 300 acres?—If you look at the history of those days, you will see that people were often sent to find lands, which it was apparently very often very difficult to identify. There seem to have been some 700 acres in 1616, altogether outside the Irish Society grants, which were intended to be allotted. The King intended to found in Londonderry a school identical with those founded at Dungannon, in Tyrone, and Cavan, and elsewhere. That land never was allotted; and, so far as the evidence goes, nobody ever had the 700 acres in his possession. The King made the Corporation of London pay 20 marks a-year for this school until the land should be set out, and they pressed him to be relieved from the payment. They sent over surveyors, one of whom was Matthias Springham, who appears to have been one of the founders of Foyle College, and they allotted 300 acres. Those 300 acres are supposed to be those two townlands on the east of Foyle River, which produce now 350*l.*, or thereabouts.

1552. Those townlands are in the hands of the Irish Society?—Yes.

1553. The Irish Society has given, you say, to this particular college for which those lands were designated, an amount equal to the income of the land?—Yes, and more; latterly much more; they have from 1616 to the present time always contributed largely to Foyle College.

1554. I was struck by an observation in your report, that if the income of the Royal School estate was devoted to districts in Ulster, the rest of Ireland in regard to intermediate education would be placed at a disadvantage?—We thought so.

1555. The intermediate educational system is very poorly endowed, and now the southern and western portions of Ireland are at a disadvantage?—Yes, they are at a disadvantage; and the intermediate endowment itself under the Intermediate Education Act really does not produce

Mr. *Sexton*—continued.

done to any school so much as it costs. It is 34,000 *l.* a year altogether, and the amount of expenses of examinations and what goes to the pupils, and so on, is very large, and what goes to the teachers in result fees varies from 7,000 *l.* or 8,000 *l.* to, perhaps, 10,000 *l.* a year. The expense is very considerable; the schools have to get well qualified teachers and pay for expensive books, and so on; so that none except a very large school can earn what it costs.

1556. The system started very strongly, did it not, a few years ago, but it has been falling off?—I do not think it has fallen off.

1557. Has not the number of candidates fallen off?—The number of candidates has fallen off that year, because there has been an attempt to prevent primary schools from sending in a large number of candidates. Personally, I think it is a great mistake that this fund is not strictly confined to really intermediate education, because the money is too small.

1558. Would not the falling off in the number of candidates be accounted for by the fact that the managers cease to send in candidates because they find it prohibitory, except a few cases?—I do not see that any of the good schools that have been successful are withdrawing their candidates. It is a very singular fact, that very nearly 40 per cent., as we reported, of all the boys of all denominations that passed the intermediate examinations three years ago were educated in the Christian Brothers' Schools.

1559. Do you think that the intermediate system is very ill-treated in comparison with the primary and university education?—I do; I think it wants a larger endowment than university and smaller than primary education, because the expense ought to diminish with the number to some extent. Of course, the expense of a university would be much larger, but the number of pupils very much smaller, and intermediate education wants at least twice as much as it has now.

1560. If any funds were available, you think the most useful application of them would be to supplement intermediate education?—I think it is there that it is wanted most, because the primary grant is practically unlimited; the money is voted by Parliament; the intermediate grant is practically limited, and it is not Imperial money at all; it is the Church surplus, nothing else.

1561. You think that Irish money for such a purpose might be appropriately supplemented by a declaration of the trusts attached to these estates?—I only make the remark that there is no Imperial endowment for intermediate education at all; there is no Vote.

Mr. *Lawson.*

1562. Have charges been brought of sectarian preference in this manner of grants for education on the part of the Irish Society as well as of the City companies?—A great many charges were put forward that the subscriptions to the Roman Catholic and Presbyterian schools were proportionately smaller than those to the Church schools.

1563. In the case of the Irish Society as well?—Yes.

1564. Do you think those charges well

Mr. *Lawson*—continued.

founded?—I thought there was certainly a very much smaller proportion given to the Roman Catholics and a small proportion to Presbyterians; but the reason given was, the terms of the charter.

1565. Was the case so glaring in the case of the Irish Society as in the case of the City companies?—In the case of the City companies we had very few instances brought before us, indeed none except the Rainey School.

Mr. *Elton.*

1566. You cannot say whether there was a glaringness in either case?—There was a very great difference.

1567. The honourable Member asks whether it was so glaring in the case of the City companies as in the case of the Irish Society; I understand it was not brought before you in the case of the City companies?—The contrast was conspicuous and remarkable.

1568. I wish to ask you one or two questions, so as to make your evidence a little more clear upon one or two points. With regard to the special case of Magherafelt, I understand when you came to examine into the matter there did not appear to be a real market there at all?—There was no patent for the market. There were two market places.

1569. The Salters' Company did not, as lords of the manor, have the right of taking a toll?—We asked whether there was any patent, and no evidence was given that there was any. At the same time the markets were perfectly well established markets, and unless there was an agitation got up against them they would probably go on all right. We were pretty confident that if the town was incorporated under the Town Improvements Act, they would go on; but we were almost equally certain that if an agitation were got up against them they would not go on.

1570. Were there tolls?—Yes; not strictly market tolls, but weighing tolls and stallages. There were enclosed yards, and one of them, I may say, was enclosed by a very high wall that appeared very likely to fall, and we thought the school might very likely have to spend a couple of hundred pounds to build it up.

1571. Was it a franchise that belonged to the Salters' Company by prescription or otherwise, or was it simply the usual modern substitute, that is to say, a stallage payment of so much per head?—There is nothing a lawyer finds harder to prove than a legal market. There was no evidence that there was a legal market in the place, but the evidence showed that it had been used as a market for years. It appeared to be what you call the usual modern substitute. It was used as a market by the lords of the manor, but without a patent.

1572. Do you know whether it has been reported upon by the Markets Commission?—I fancy not; I have not heard of it. The titles of several of these markets have come up in the courts. There was no statement to us by anyone on the part of the company that there was any patent for a market there, in fact, as they held their property originally by grant from the Irish Society, I apprehend the patent would

have

Mr. *Elgie*—continued.

have had to be a separate document. There was no evidence that there was one.

1573. We shall have the grant before us. With regard to this school, I understand you to say that the history of it indicated that the Primate at first seemed to be a bare trustee?—Yes.

1574. But that he by some means obtained or exercised power as if he were an active trustee?—When the testator's family died out, he took a legal opinion and he was informed that the trusts had devolved upon him. That was in 1848, I think.

1575. Apparently by some means he exercised the authority of active trustee?—They were perfectly legitimate means.

1576. He could not make himself into an active trustee, could he?—He could not help himself; he was made trustee of the property by Act of Parliament. The present trustees are the Representative Church Body.

1577. I understood you to say that the Presbyterian body had the management of it, according to the will?—The passage in the will was that the two men who were to be the teachers, the managers, inspectors, and overseers of the boys were to be appointed by the Presbytery of Ulster.

1578. The management appeared to be in the Presbytery of Ulster?—The appointment of the two old men was in them.

1579. You told us that after having this authority, he appointed the rector as "visitor." I presume you did not use the word in its technical sense, but in its general sense?—Quite so; in the printed advertisement the agent of the Salters' Company and the rector were described as visitors.

1580. The Archbishop would strictly be the visitor?—He was the patron himself; he was the trustee. It was not in the technical sense that the word visitor was used, but in the popular sense.

1581. He managed it, and the Salters' Company's agent helped him to manage the property?—Yes, the Salters' Company's agent seems to have managed all the temporal affairs, and the rector looked after the school.

1582. You explained the whole question most clearly, but so far as I could make out, it was an isolated single question depending upon declarations of trust supposed to have been made by the Salters' Company of their particular position as lords of this manor. I take it it is not a case that governs the whole question at issue?—No, it was a perfectly exceptional case. They came forward apparently as owners of the property at the time the school was going to ruin, and entered into an arrangement with the Primate at the time of the Chancery scheme.

1583. We cannot draw any general rules from that case?—Certainly not.

1584. One question with regard to the other maxim you mentioned once or twice; you alluded to the general maxim that a trustee cannot get rid of property which he holds upon trust; of course you did not mean to say anything against the doctrine that a trustee is allowed to grant land for plantation purposes to persons who would not be trustees?—Of course a trustee for plantation purposes could grant to planters or settlers.

1585. According to the report of the Skinners' Company's case, their business, I see, includes establishing a city, and we may take it, they could make a grant in fee, for instance, or create a manor?—I believe that is so, historically; but I think the question is, whether the companies took as grantees in the ordinary sense, or whether they took as trustees. That depends upon matters upon which I can really express an opinion. I have never had any legal evidence as to the terms upon which their money was paid.

1586. I tried to keep away from that question, because it was different from what I was asking; I did not want a false impression to arise from your evidence. Although a trustee could not ordinarily alienate property without its carrying on the trust, you have pointed out that a trustee for plantation purposes might do so?—He might alienate it for plantation purposes, but we require to see what they were.

1587. The person to whom he alienated it might take it unburdened with the trust?—That would depend altogether upon the circumstances of the particular case.

1588. And partly no doubt upon the documents before us?—The documents would be the root of the title.

1589. You have not given your mind to those particular documents?—I have not; I have not had any of them before me at all.

1590. You have been good enough to tell the honourable Member opposite so clearly about the trusts of the Irish Society that I have very little to ask; but may I take it that amongst the trusts which are imposed upon the Irish Society was one for the education of the inhabitants of the district?—Lord Lyndhurst says so expressly.

1591. And you agree with him?—Yes.

1592. Then they could not in their position of trustees say that no part is to be so appropriated?—I do not think that they could, and I do not think that they ever pretended to say so. A large part of their funds has always gone for education, but, as I have already said, my official difficulty in dealing with them as a member of the Commission, was that there was no specific part dedicated either for education in general or for any particular school.

1593. But there was some part, a little undefined, for education?—Yes.

1594. Did you not consider that practice and usage pointed out the part which they had dedicated to education in a particular case like Foyle College?—Even in the case of Foyle College there was no fixed sum by practice. It had varied from one hundred and odd pounds a year 60 years ago up to 850*l.* in one sum to the head master, besides the other expenses. There were large grants from time to time for repairs and for building.

1595. So that on the general trusts of the Irish Society there was great difficulty in saying what should be their educational endowments for that college?—It was impossible, so far as we could see.

1596. It was a totally separate difficulty, was it

Mr. Elton—continued.

it not, that it might be that the college had a trust to itself outside the trusts of the Irish Society in these two townlands?—Outside these two townlands, the college was certainly one of the institutions that from the commencement the Irish Society had supported, but it had other supports. It was a diocesan school, it was built by grand jury money, and it had other sources of endowment besides that.

1597. It might be that the college was not in the general trusts of the Irish Society at all there?—It is quite possible that there was a separate trust as regards those townlands, in addition to its being one of the institutions that would come under the general trusts.

1598. But the existence of a separate endowment would naturally diminish their chance of getting anything more if it was a sufficient separate endowment?—It would; and there never was a Royal Free School in Londonderry established at all as there was in the other counties. The property was intended to be given for it, but, apparently, instead of establishing a Royal Free School, the property was given to the Irish Society, and they contributed to the school already existing there under Queen Elizabeth's Act, and so it became a sort of compound institution. A free school does not mean a school where no fees are paid, but one open to all.

1599. It generally means, in England, free from the jurisdiction of the ordinary?—Yes.

1600. From what you have told us it looks as if there was still some doubt about whether this endowment of the two townlands is of Foyle College; I suppose it is not too late to find them now?—The townlands are there, but I think nobody wants to put off Foyle College with those two townlands only; it would be better off without them.

1601. Would it be better off with what it receives from the Irish Society?—Much better now, and for many years past.

1602. But it is precarious?—I have no reason to suppose that it is.

1603. The reason that you could not deal with it was that it was precarious in amount?—It varied in amount; they could withdraw it all; and Foyle College at one time, as is mentioned in one of these reports, was brought very low. Religious differences got up, and the Academical Institution was established as a competing school with Foyle College. They thought the clergyman who was then head master belonged to the High Church party, and some amusing evidence was given by Dr. Hime. One of the conditions on which he was appointed was that he should have the chapel that was in Foyle College de-consecrated, whatever that means.

1604. You have shown us, of course, that circumstances might arise in which it would have been better to have even the two townlands; however, it is not too late, as a matter of fact, so far as you know, for the identification of the lands subject to that trust?—No, the lands are capable of identification; all the evidence with regard to the identity of them is in the first Report of 1838. It is more or less circumstantial evidence, but it is very strong.

1605. As to the division of the property between the London companies, there was one point that was not quite clear to my mind; you spoke of the division of the property among the companies; you did not mean to say that there was not an exception from the property to be divided?—I referred to the grants in severalty that were made on two occasions by the Irish Society.

1606. You did not mention that part of the general property was excepted for the purposes of the Irish Society, and never divided amongst the companies?—It was not divided, but the case that the Skinners' Company made was that it ought to have been divided.

1607. But it failed, and the documents mentioned in that case, I think, go so far as this, do they not, that there was a partition of the estates except the city of Londonderry?—Those parts which were not granted away were the subject-matter of the suit in 1845.

1608. They were shown by the result of that suit not to have been property divisible amongst the companies, were they not?—They were not divided.

1609. An honourable Member asked you and you answered as to the educational trusts in relation to the London companies; of course, understand that you did not give any opinion as to whether there are any such educational trusts in the case of the London companies as there are in the case of the Irish Society?—I have no material upon which to form any opinion with regard to them.

1610. You were asked a question about these educational trusts, and you answered it without diminishing their existence?—Lord Lyndhurst's authority goes to this extent, that amongst the general trusts of the Irish Society there is an educational trust.

1611. You did not mean to carry that on to the London companies in any way?—No, I disclaimed giving any opinion, or having any material for forming one, as to how far they are trustees at all.

Mr. Cherry.

1612. You sent, on the 30th November 1888, a very valuable memorandum to the Chief Secretary; you had no communication in reply?—No.

1613. Have you any means of ascertaining the amount of grants made for educational purposes, withdrawn since that date from such purposes?—I have no materials for saying whether any were withdrawn except the Salters' grant to Rainey's School. No other school from which any annual grant had been withdrawn came before us.

1614. You referred to certain correspondence between Sir Henry Cartwright and your Commission; has that correspondence been printed in any public form?—We have printed almost all the letters that I quoted. I have brought some few with me that have not been printed and I can hand them in. There are, I suppose, 300 letters besides those that I referred to. We had a long correspondence with Canon Donnelly and with Mr. Jordan and the Markets Committee, and we spared no trouble over it, because we thought we might get something for the school out of it in the end.

Mr. *Channing*—continued.

1615. You have stated, I have no doubt, what became of the Rainey School Farm?—The Rainey School Farm was surrendered to the Salters' Company under the Chancery scheme, but it was stated in the petition that it was under notice to quit at the time.

Mr. *T. M. Healy.*

1616. Would you be glad to see the Educational Endowments Act so amended as to enable it to capture these fluctuating grants?—I should hardly like to undertake the process of capturing fluctuating grants. I do not know that it could be done by an amendment of our Act. The Act is an Act of executive procedure to which it would be very hard to tack on a general capturing clause.

1617. I understand that the reason why you think your power did not apply in the case of particular grants, was that those grants were of a fluctuating and precarious character?—That they were not definitely appropriated to education.

1618. Although for centuries these grants had been given to education?—Quite so.

1619. The mere fact that it was in the volition of the donor to give or withhold, you thought, expressly withdrew them from the Educational Endowments Act?—Because the Act expressly says that it is not to apply to any grants which can be withdrawn by the donor, even though their amount may be laid for charitable purposes. If it can be applied to any other charitable purpose than education, our Act does not apply to it, unless the donor gives his consent in writing.

1620. Would it not be possible by an amendment of the Act to capture what you might call fluctuating endowments?—It would be quite possible to pass an Act that we should inquire and ascertain what sum of money had for a certain number of years been given to educational purposes, and that the sum of money so ascertained should be regarded as an educational endowment, or something of that kind; but I am afraid that the question of voluntary subscriptions would remain still.

1621. If the attention of Parliament had been attracted to the existence of these subscriptions, and they were of a fluctuating character, and your Act, as originally passed, did not apply to them, would you not consider it very likely that during its passage through Parliament it could have been properly drafted with that object?—At the time of that Act I do not know that this question had been raised at all. We hardly thought it a likely thing, but we thought the chances were good enough to make it worth while to call the attention both of the Government and of Parliament to it, and to state that unless Parliament did intervene this property was in danger of being withdrawn.

1622. Why did not your Commission inquire into the existence of these grants, with a view of seeing if you could capture them?—We did, in the case of every school that we had to deal with, ascertain what income it had received; but we considered that the decision of the House of Lords made it impossible for us to put these grants into schemes, except by written consent.

Mr. *T. M. Healy*—continued.

1623. Did you at all consider that the decision of the House of Lords is weighted with this defect: that it is what I may call a kind of *consent* decision; that is to say, that both sides, both the Skinners' Company and the defendants, the Irish Society, tried their positions, and that neither had any interest from the public point of view, which, indeed, was not put forward at all?—The Attorney General was a party to the proceedings.

1624. But that was only nominal, I presume?—He made an objection that he was brought in too late.

1625. Is not the House of Lords' decision weighted with this defect: that the public view in no sense was put forward?—I am afraid I am not at liberty to suppose that there is any defect in a House of Lords' decision.

1626. May the Committee not take it that the House of Lords' decision was based on a view put forward by the litigants in the case, who, of course, had no interest in presenting what I may call the public view?—But I understand that the public view was the one that was defended by the Irish Society. Remember that that litigation dealt only with the surplus lands; it did not affect the companies' lands at all. As regards the whole of that property, I understand that the decision goes to this: that, subject to the expenses of management, it is all trust property for public purposes. Beyond that, I do not see that the public could expect anyone to go.

1627. But that only touches the property in the hands of the Irish Society?—What the trusts were, of course, was not involved at all, and that would have to be ascertained, if necessary, by filing an information against the Irish Society alleging default in the execution of their trusts. But there again the decision took away our power of doing anything, because it decided that the discretion to apply any part, and what part, of its funds to education rested with the Society.

1628. But the decision does not in any way show what the trusts are?—No; except that they are public trusts, and that these include education.

1629. You mentioned, a moment ago, that the lapse of time might be a difficulty in the way of the courts ruling on this question?—The lapse of time would be, of course, a difficulty if the companies have been dealing with the property so as to afford evidence of a title under the Statute of Limitations. It would be very difficult to get behind the lapse of time except by an express trust.

1630. Would the fact of the Attorney General filing an information against the companies in the time of Charles I. and the Star Chamber appear to show that in the view then there prevailed those were public bodies with a trust?—The Star Chamber proceeding was of the same character with the one against the Irish Society that was set aside.

1631. But the proceedings were merely abandoned because of the political fluctuations of the times; does not the fact that the Attorney General in the reign of Charles I. took a particular view seem to show that at the time that

Mr. T. M. Healy—continued.

that those trusts were established the Law Officers of the Crown deemed that there was a particular duty attaching to these properties?—Of course it does at that time, but that proceeding not having gone on, and the other proceeding having been cancelled, would go to weaken it.

1632. But a fine was set upon the companies for failure of duty?—Not, I understand, on the companies. A fine of 70,000 *l.* was put upon the corporation, and then an information was filed against the companies for the purpose of fining them and cancelling their grants, but that was not proceeded with; I do not think that there is any record that the companies were fined. As a prophet, I should have no doubt at all that if the information had gone on against the companies, they would have met with exactly the same fate as the Irish Society.

1633. It was decided in the Skinners' case that the Irish Society is a public body, and holds for public purposes. Lord Campbell, in his judgment, says that Lord Cottenham "stated the question at once to be whether the Irish Society are to be considered as merely private trustees, or trustees for public purposes." He then gives his opinion that they were trustees for public purposes. When the case came before Lord Langdale, he, after great deliberation, came to the same conclusion. I concur in the opinion which those eminent judges have pronounced. Does that declaration in your opinion also attach to the property of the companies as well as to that of the Irish Society?—The property that was held in severalty by the companies was not the subject of the suit at all, and therefore if he meant to speak of that property he was really speaking of something that was not before him. There is a passage in Lord Lyndhurst's judgment at p. 41, in which he says that the intention of the charter of Charles II. was to replace the parties in their former position precisely in the same way as if nothing had been done. "Then it went on to convey again and confirm those lands to the Irish Society, to re-incorporate the Irish Society, and to carry out the stipulations and conditions of the former charter as far as they were applicable, in consequence of the lapse of time which had occurred since the grant of the former charter." Therefore, I take it that whatever proceedings had been taken in the Star Chamber were treated as entirely put an end to.

1634. But, assuming that the companies hold as grantees from the Irish Society, and the Irish Society being declared to be holding for public purposes, would it not seem as if there were a trust attaching also to the lands and moneys in the hands of the companies?—It certainly would be evidence upon that side of the question. At that time, unless they could give some other explanation, they would be *primâ facie* affected by, I suppose, the same trusts; but it is right to say that they put it in their argument that the grants to them were under the plantation trust, that is to say, that they were treated just like other owners in fee, and having regard to the length of time, I do not think any court could shut it out of view, if they were found to have dealt ever since with the property as being private property. I say if they were (I have not the facts before me), you could hardly separate the effect of that evidence from the fact that there was no trust declared in the deeds.

1635. Do you think it is a convenient thing that the funds for a body like Foyle College should be left to the mere fluctuating discretion or indiscretion of a London body?—I do not.

Mr. John Ellis.

1636. Are you the sole judicial Commissioner now?—No; there are two judicial Commissioners. Mr. Justice O'Brien has taken Lord Justice Naish's place, and not only that, but one judicial Commissioner has no authority whatever.

1637. Was this land which was left by one Rainey, in 1707, his freehold?—He directed all his worldly possessions to be laid out in the purchase of a freehold estate, and that was done. They bought a freehold estate in the county of Down, producing 400 *l.* a year as he directed; but they had to borrow about 2,000 *l.* to complete the purchase-money, and that property is now producing 4,000 *l.* a year.

1638. I think you mentioned that the Salters' Company came in connection with the Chancery scheme?—For the first time.

1639. Will you give us the date of the Chancery scheme?—I think the 21st of January 1863 was the date of the scheme. The proceedings began in 1862.

1640. Then I think I gathered from you that the Salters' Company stopped their contributions in or about the year 1887?—In the year 1887 they wrote a letter saying that they would not contribute any more.

1641. To your Commission?—No; they wrote first to Mr. Jordan, who wrote to us; and then they also wrote to us. We wrote to them about it. These are among the letters that I did not think it necessary to read.

1642. Did they write to you in the year 1888?—We were in constant correspondence with them from the time it began in 1885 down to a few days ago.

1643. Did they write any specific letter declining to make further contributions?—They wrote several letters; and even when Mr. Jordan pressed them, saying that the master had no funds they said that they would pay one quarter more, and I think they did even that a second time; but I believe they ultimately and finally declined to pay any more in 1887.

1644. In this letter they gave certain reasons, I presume?—No; they gave no reason except that they had sold their estates, and were discontinuing their contribution.

1645. That was their reason, that they were discharged of all responsibility?—Yes; they wanted to substitute for their former contributions this market property.

Mr. Lea.

1646. You said just now, did you not, that there were no schools allotted to the county of Londonderry?—No Royal free school.

1647. Why was that?—Apparently because they took the diocesan school instead; but that is

Mr. *Lea*—continued.

is all lost in obscurity. The Report of 1858 shows that it was not clearly ascertained.

1848. Would it be because they expected the London companies to maintain the Royal free school?—Apparently the 300 acres were allotted for the Royal free school, and appropriated to the school that was there already, and then the land went to the Irish Society. I think there is pretty clear proof of that, and, therefore, Foyle College had an endowment through the Irish Society; and very probably on that ground they did not establish a second school.

1849. The Foyle College acts as a school for the whole county of Londonderry, I suppose?—Certainly. Foyle College is quite equal to any of the Royal schools.

1850. The London companies, I think you have told the Committee, withdrew their grants in 1854?—The Report of 1858 states that the grants mentioned had been withdrawn within the previous 40 years; I think that was the time that was given.

1851. We will put it before 1854?—Within the last 40 years is the time that they give. "The support was a precarious resource as appears from the changes which have taken place in the list of donations within the last 40 years." That is printed in 1858, and the number of grants withdrawn from Foyle College then amounted to 496 *l.* in all.

1852. If Foyle College acts for the whole county of Londonderry, why should the London companies have withdrawn their grants?—I am afraid I cannot answer that question.

1853. They did withdraw them did they not?—They did: so it appears by this report. Foyle College is both a boarding-school and a day-school, and until the establishment of the Academical Institution and St. Columb's College, as far as I know it was the only intermediate school in the city of Londonderry. The day boys are of course from the city and county; but it has always had a considerable number of boarders from other parts of Ireland.

1854. The Irish Society's grants, you told us, were given from 1813?—1813 is stated in the schedule to the Report of 1858 as the date from which they commenced.

1855. Do you know when the rest of the 496 *l.* of the London companies dated from?—No; that does not appear.

1856. Is the Academical Institution chiefly Presbyterian?—The Academical Institution was really founded by subscribers. They got a large sum from the Irish Society and from some of the companies, I think, too; but their principal means of establishment were voluntary subscriptions. They formed a body under deed, of whom the majority were Presbyterians; but there were a number of members of other denominations. There were no Roman Catholics on it, but there were a considerable number of Church people; and with their own consent we framed a scheme for them, which provides for a mixed body with a Presbyterian majority, I apprehend.

1857. So much has been said about Lord Lyndhurst's judgment that I do not want to trouble you upon that; but I think that action was commenced through the Attorney General; would you explain that?—I do not think it was commenced by the Attorney General; it began in 1832, and in the Report, 13th Clark and Finnelly, the Attorney General certainly appeared, and I think he made a point that he had been only joined as a party defendant by amendment in the course of the proceedings.

1858. Must an information be laid by the Attorney General?—An information for a breach of any public trust, or of any charitable trust, must be brought by the Attorney General, who represents the public interest. But this was not a suit of that kind. This was a suit by the Skinners' Company to claim the property as their own private property; and they made the Attorney General a defendant for the purpose of establishing against him that it was not public property.

Mr. *T. M. Healy.*

1859. He did not argue the question?—No; but if the Irish Society, as defendants, made the case that the whole property was attached by a public trust, the Attorney General could only be in the same interest. Of course, whether they performed their trust or not, would be the subject of a different suit by him.

Mr. *Lea.*

1860. Would the only way of acting be through the Attorney General?—There are other ways, but that is the usual and the most effective way.

1861. You said that the Irish Society had been declared a public trustee; are you acquainted with Lord Derby's Commission, which I think holds all the London companies as trustees?—I am not.

1862. I think you said that the Dalnoy school was the only intermediate school from which grants had been withdrawn?—The only one that came before my Commission.

1863. What other intermediate schools have you in the county of Londonderry?—There is a very fine one at Coleraine; the Coleraine Academical Institution is one of the best schools in Ireland.

1864. That I think receives its money from the Irish Society?—It receives something; but it was principally founded by voluntary contributions, and it has also had a scheme framed under our Act, which is at work, and it is also under a mixed governing body.

1865. Do you know any other intermediate school which receives its support from the London companies exclusive of the Irish Society?—The Skinners' Company have made grants for scholarships for girls to the Alexandra College in Dublin and to a school in Londonderry, and there is an Ironmongers' scholarship in the Magee College. The Clothworkers have made some provision in Coleraine, I think, for a permanent scholarship as well as a provision for building; that is to say, they have given a sum of money which is vested in the corporate body, and held in trust for the school.

1866. Is that exclusive of any grants given through Sir Hervey Bruce?—I think so; I could tell you by reference to the scheme. There is a statement about the Coleraine Academical Institution, in the body of the scheme, that it was erected at the cost of 7,800 *l.*, which sum was obtained by means of subscriptions and donations from the Irish Society and from the Clothworkers' Company, and from the inhabitants

Mr. Lea—continued.

Coleraine and the neighbourhood; and that it is maintained by the pupils' fees, grants, subscriptions and donations from the Irish Society and others; and on the 4th September 1873, the Clothworkers' Company granted them 1,000 *l.* to found a Clothworkers' scholarship, and provisions as to how it is to be competed for, and everything of that kind, are contained in the scheme.

1667. Is there any fixed endowment from Sir Hervey Bruce?—I think not.

1668. With regard to the Rainey School, I think you said that Rainey was a Presbyterian, and that it was obviously intended to be a Presbyterian school?—We argued that he was a Presbyterian, from the fact that he directed these old men to be sent for to the Presbytery, and also that he gave 5 *l.* a year, I think, to the Presbyterian minister, and things of that kind. It was evidence that we had acted upon in many other cases for other denominations, as being quite sufficient to show what the testator was.

1669. Was the executor a Presbyterian, too?—I cannot tell; but the will, which is an extremely inartificial document, mixes up the executors with the life-owners of his estate, and it is very hard to tell who were to be the patrons of the school. Whoever they were I strongly suspect that they became Church people or were Church people. They certainly were so at the date of the Act, I should say from the framing of it. Nearly all the documents that I have quoted are already in the Blue Books, to which I have given the references. The will of Rainey is printed, and so is the Act of Parliament. The provision of our Act is that unless a petition is presented to either House within two months from the date at which the Lord Lieutenant finally approves of the scheme it becomes law. If a petition is presented, a Resolution of either House will nullify any portion of the scheme to which it relates; but we have not as yet had any such case.

1670. I think you said that Sir Henry Cartwright stated that liberal provision had been made for primary schools?—He said so in his letter; but the provision appeared to consist of assigning the existing school buildings to the managers; I do not know of any pecuniary provision at all.

1671. Are you aware that the Salters' Company are withdrawing their grants from primary schools?—I rather understood from those letters that all they were doing was giving up the buildings to the managers.

1672. With regard to the Rainey School, the market tolls were entirely outside the rest of the Salters' property?—I do not know that there were any market tolls in the strict sense. This property consisted of the market yards, which, with the buildings I understood to be in the hands of the Salters' Company themselves down to the time when they sold the rest of the estate. I may be wrong, but I thought that the so-called market trustees were only a committee appointed at that time, and the resident sub-agent (Mr. Bailey, I think, was his name) was really managing the place.

1673. Was this market or were these market tolls easily saleable?—I should be very sorry to buy them.

1674. Do you know that they took away [illegible] *l.* for their estate?—We heard that, but we had no particulars of the sale.

1675. Then where was the liberality to the Rainey School or to the primary schools?—I did not say there was any liberality; they gave 120 *l.* a year, of which the Rainey School got 68 *l.*, charged on the market tolls, instead of previous grants averaging 200 *l.* a year. The 120 *l.* is a rent-charge on that market property; but, of course, if the markets do not produce it, the endowment will not be there.

1676. You stated, did you not, in answer to the Right honourable gentleman, that there would be a feeling of satisfaction if the previous grants given by the companies were continued?—I was speaking of those that came before us.

1677. But if there is any right to further grants or further property, there is no reason for stopping at the previous grants, I presume?—I suppose not.

1678. You say that intermediate education demands further grants?—It certainly wants more money.

1679. And if I understand you rightly, it wants it immediately?—Yes.

1680. And you think that Parliament ought to take immediate action with regard to this matter?—If I might refer again to that memorandum of ours, you will find that we state that even 15,000 *l.* a year in addition to what is spent now, would produce a very sensible result, for the intermediate schools are many of them extremely badly off for money, and a very small sum of money is of importance to them. To some of them in some of the southern and western parts of Ireland particularly, even 50 *l.* or 100 *l.* a year, they have told us, would be the means of keeping their schools going.

1681. If these London companies' money is an Irish fund, it could be very well spent in intermediate education in Ireland?—Certainly it could.

1682. And especially in the county of Londonderry, to which it is supposed to belong?—Yes.

Thursday, 19th June 1890.

MEMBERS PRESENT:

Mr. Clancy.	Mr. Lea.
Mr. John Ellis.	Mr. John Morley.
Mr. T. M. Healy.	Mr. Sexton.
Colonel Lawrie.	Sir Richard Temple.

THE RIGHT HONOURABLE JOHN MORLEY, IN THE CHAIR.

Mr. MURROUGH O'BRIEN, re-called; and further Examined.

Mr. *Sexton.*

1683. You have stated, I think, that four of the companies have wholly or partly sold?—That is so.

1684. Can you state the terms of sale in regard to the several companies?—I am unable to give you any other terms of sale, except those stated in the return which has been put in which gives the rental and the gross purchase money. The rate at which holdings are sold may have varied between the holdings; there is not in all cases a uniform rate.

1685. But the return has been put in?—It has.

1686. Were the sales usually upon judicial or non-judicial rents?—I am unable to say as regards all the sales that have taken place on the companies' estates. I apprehend that there were cases on every estate where judicial rents had been settled, but in the majority I fancy they had not.

1687. Can you state whether the number of years' purchase upon those estates would have varied according as the rents were judicial, or non-judicial, or was a uniform number of years' purchase imposed?—I do not think that there was a uniform rate of purchase.

1688. As to the number of years?—As to the number of years.

1689. You are unable, I believe, to state what part of the property remains in the hands of the companies in those cases where they have partly sold?—I am unable to say.

1690. Have you any means of ascertaining that?—Except by obtaining the rental from the companies, I have not.

1691. Do you suggest that we might obtain that from the companies?—It could be obtained from the companies.

1692. Could we obtain a detailed rental?—Yes.

1693. You have paid to the companies from your commission 578,000 *l.*, and you have sanctioned a further payment of 37,000 *l.*, making a total of 615,000 *l.*; can you state in addition what sum has been applied for by any or all of those companies, and not yet sanctioned?—I am unable to give you any figures as to the loans applied for and not yet dealt with, except in the case of the Drapers' Company as to which I mentioned that there are 140 cases awaiting settlement in the office of the Land Commission.

Mr. *Sexton*—continued.

1694. After your return to Dublin, could you send in a statement that would give us the precise amount involved in the cases now depending before you?—I should have thought that the proper course would be to ask the Land Commission to furnish such information.

1695. Then if we communicate with the Land Commission, no doubt they will furnish it?—I have no doubt that they will.

1696. Taking the total amount paid or sanctioned at 615,000 *l.*, I understood you to say that the rateable valuation indicates that the total value of the properties held, including those sold, was between a million and a million and a half. Can you get any nearer than you did on the last day of your examination to the value of the unsold residue?—I do not think it would be possible to form an estimate of the value of the companies' estates in Derry without obtaining from them a detailed rental. An estimate could be made from that of the capital value of those estates.

1697. When you say "in Derry," you do not convey that there are any estates elsewhere?—The London Companies, so far as I am aware, hold estates in no other county but Derry.

1698. When you say "in Derry," you mean all the estates?—All the estates.

1699. You raise the point that the companies are not lessors in some cases; that I understand to be where the land has been used for building?—Yes.

1700. But they have a substantial interest as owners in all the agricultural land?—They have.

1701. Did you give us the rateable valuation as between the companies that still retain the land. I believe those are the Irish Society, the Mercers', the Grocers', and a combination lately formed under the flag of the Ironmongers'?—No; the companies I mentioned are the only ones I know of who hold estates in Derry, or who appear rated as lessors of property in that county.

1702. You give us, I think, the rateable valuations

Mr. Sexton—continued.

tion of the Irish Society, the Ironmongers', and I think, the Mercers'; did you give the rateable valuation of the Drapers', or have you got it?—I have not got it.

1703. With regard to the Moneymore division of the Drapers' estate, a delay, you said, of three years (I think it was rather more) intervened between the making of the agreements and the completion of them?—About three years, I said.

1704. The negotiations began, did they not, in 1885?—The first loans were sanctioned by the Land Commission in December 1886, and the first payments were made in October 1889.

1705. So that, between the time when the matter came formally before you and the time when the contracts proceeded to sale, there was an interval of three years?—It would not be quite three years from the date when the applications were sanctioned, which was in December 1886.

1706. But, of course, there was some time consumed previous to that in the negotiations between the company and the tenants?—Certainly.

1707. Have you known such delay as that to occur in any other case?—That is a part of the Land Commission business with which I am not very conversant, but such a very long delay is unusual, except in the case of very complicated titles.

1708. This was not a case of complicated title, was it?—I am not able to give an opinion as to the companies' title.

1709. You have conveyed to the Committee that it was found that they had not the fee simple, but that they had to procure a release from the Irish Society; that appears to have been the only question that arose upon their title so far as I could learn from your evidence?—That would have been a natural cause of delay, but the delays complained of arose out of other circumstances, which I explained. In February 1889 a letter was written to the company, in which the Commissioners concluded by saying: "The Commissioners cannot permit proceedings to be indefinitely retarded by the vendors." That was written after repeated efforts had been made to get these transactions closed.

1710. I gather from the phrase "indefinitely retarded," that there was quite an exceptional and extraordinary delay?—I think the delay was quite exceptional in this case.

1711. Can you tell us what is the ordinary interval between the execution of an agreement and the completion of the sale, where the length of the interval depends upon the Land Commission itself, and not upon circumstances relating to the vendor or the vendee?—I could not.

1712. You cannot say what is the usual course?—Any statement of an average time would be misleading, because some cases are closed very rapidly, and others are delayed for various reasons.

1713. You have been twenty years an officer of the Irish Purchase Department under its various names, and you have great experience; and it would be valuable to us to know if this company caused delay which was never caused before. Have you known any such delays then to occur in any other case?—The legal part of the proceedings is not a branch of the business with which I have very much to do. My business is chiefly advising the commission as to the security upon which they lend.

1714. No doubt that is your function, but you take an intelligent interest, I should say, in the whole of the proceedings of the department?—I do.

1715. And you are probably aware, generally, of the length of the interval between the time when the proceedings are initiated on a property, and the time when the sales are concluded?—I am quite unable to give you any figure as to the average time taken in carrying a sale through the Land Commission.

1716. You have conveyed to us that this delay was protracted by the company in order to give them time to recover arrears of rent and interest and costs; is not that so?—That was the conclusion to which the Land Commission came, because they were prepared to close these sales; they had approved of the draft deeds, and there was no obstacle to the sales being closed at a very much earlier date.

1717. They were driven, in fact, to the conclusion, there being no other motive apparent, that the period of delay was being deliberately prolonged in order to enable the company to recover certain moneys?—They ascertained that as a matter of fact.

1718. To recover moneys in violation of the pledges given in the letters of 1886 and 1887?—I do not say that the whole amount which they sought to recover was recovered in violation of the statements made in the letters which have been put in, but all the interest which was recovered appears to have been recovered in spite of the declarations in those letters.

1719. You are doubtful in regard to how much rent was recovered, but in regard to the interest, it is clear, I should say, that any interest recovered must have been recovered in violation of the pledges in the letters of 1886 and 1887, which promised that no interest should be charged?—That is so if the pledge was binding upon the company, as it naturally appeared to country farmers.

1720. When you say "binding," you mean binding in law. Of course, every man can judge for himself how far it was binding in honour?—The tenants were unable to form an opinion as to the legal obligations arising out of those letters until the suits against them were concluded.

1721. They took it naturally as a valid pledge?—Certainly.

1722. You referred to a decision of the High Court, which you summarised in this way: that where an agreement was silent as to the recovery of interest in lieu of rent, during the period between the execution of the agreement and the completion of the sale, it might be recovered?—That, I believe, was a decision in some early cases where such difficulties arose between landlords and tenants.

1723. Can you say whether it was held under that decision that an agreement referred simply to the document lodged with the Commission, and that such pledges as those given in the letters of

Mr. Sexton—continued.

of August 1886 and January 1887 would not be operative in law?—In the case of the Drapers' Company, I understand that the Court could not receive these letters or oral evidence as to the negotiation in explanation of the contracts lodged with the Land Commission on which the tenants were sued.

1724. So that although the pledges were contained in the letters the absence of them from the contracts put the tenants out of court, or rather subjected them to an adverse decision?—If the statements in the letters had been embodied in the contracts I do not think any question could have arisen.

1725. But the circumstance that although they were in those letters they were not embodied in the contracts exposed the tenants to liability for the payment of the monies which the letters said they were not to be asked to pay?—I think so.

1726. I understand you to convey, but I should like to have it clearly, that in addition to the other misleading characteristics in reference to these contracts between the company and the tenants, they kept the Commission in ignorance of the amount of the arrears which you considered you had a right to have made known to you?—The Commissioners were not aware of the amount of arrears due by the Drapers' Company's tenants; but as the proceedings went on they called for a return from the company of the amounts due by the the tenants and claimed by the company.

1727. But has the Commission any right or reason to expect that that information should have been given to them voluntarily by the company?—I do not think they had.

1728. Then what did you intend to convey by saying that the Commissioners were misled through their ignorance of the amount of arrears?—Perhaps you will kindly refer me to the question.

1729. I cannot refer you to the particular question; but I understand you to say that the Commissioners were misled by reason of not being informed of the amount of arrears at the time of the conclusion of the contract?—The Commission were not aware that such a large claim would be made upon the tenants, because the long delay in the sales of course caused the interest to accumulate as well as the rent that was due up to the year 1885 on the Moneymore division. The Commissioners have made a rule that after a loan is sanctioned, no claim can be made upon a tenant, except for six months' interest on his purchase money. They made that rule in order to protect themselves and the tenants.

1730. No matter how long the period between the agreement and the sale may be, only six months' interest is to be charged?—Where a sale is closed the vendor can only recover six months' interest on the purchase money, in consequence of the rule made by the Land Commission.

Mr. Clancy.

1731. When the agreement is signed, you mean?—No, when the sale is closed; that is to say, the payment of the money.

Mr. Sexton.

1732. Supposing that this three months' interval had passed between the agreement and the sale in the case of this company, would you, under your present rules, have permitted the company, when once the sale was closed, to recover the six months' interest?—Yes, that is so.

1733. That rule was not in operation, then, when this company got the money?—The payments had been made to the Drapers' Company at various times; but I believe the rule was in operation. But in this case the rent and the interest were recovered to a large extent before the sales were closed.

1734. As you have said already, the company prolonged the delay previous to the conclusion of the sales, and used that interval to recover the money?—That is how it appeared to the Land Commission.

1735. You are unable to divide the 7,500 l., which they recovered from the tenants by the law suits into money which they might have recovered without reference to the pledge in the two letters, and money which was recovered in violation of that pledge; but would you indicate any proportion of it which was recovered in violation of that pledge?—I could not.

1736. I noticed that in one case 111 l. was recovered from a tenant whose yearly rental was 17 l.; does that seem to indicate to you that the bulk of the indebtedness arose after 1885, and was recovered in violation of the pledge, because it seems to indicate a recovery of six years' rent or interest?—That figure of 111 l. is returned by the company as the amount received in May 1887.

1737. The annual rent in that case was 17 l., and as the interest could scarcely be more than the rent, does it not seem to indicate that the money recovered covered a period of six years or so?—The annual rent was 17 l. 14 s. 6 d.

1738. Then if the company recovered a total of 111 l., the annual rent being 17 l., would you conclude, upon these figures, that a considerable part of that sum must have accrued after November 1885, and therefore must have been in violation of the pledge?—I have not come to any conclusion upon the matter at all, because I have no information as to what part of that sum might have been arrears due before 1885. The company, I believe, did not claim the rent, and did not recover the rent due in November 1885. That was part of the arrangement, I believe.

1739. But they recovered interest in lieu of it?—I am quite unable to divide the sum recovered into rent and interest.

1740. At any rate, in order to assume that their recovery of that sum was allowable under the pledge of 1885, you have to assume that there was six years' rent due and recovered up to November 1885, have you not?—I have not assumed anything at all. I have merely given you the figures returned by the company.

1741. But they amount to six times the annual rent, do they not?—About that.

1742. You learnt by personal inspection that many of these tenants on the Moneymore division had sold crops and even stock, and had borrowed money upon mortgage, and at oppressive rates of interest, in order to discharge their indebtedness?

Mr. Sexton—continued.

debentures?—I do not think I said anything about oppressive rates of interest. The case I mentioned was one where money was borrowed at 6 per cent. Where the security is not very good, I do not consider that rate of interest oppressive.

1743. The security may not be good, but surely the fact that the security is not good does not render a high rate of interest less oppressive upon the man who borrows?—It is the same to him; but I think where a security is bad a lender is entitled to ask for a larger rate of interest than if he lent on very first-class security.

1744. If by the word "oppressive," you think that I reflected upon the lender, I substitute the word "burdensome"?—A country farmer who has to borrow money can rarely borrow it at less than 5 per cent.

1745. But 6 per cent. at any rate is considerably higher than the interest that he has to pay to the State?—Very much higher.

1746. Can you tell us whether the Land Commission in an ordinary case would think it satisfactory for the State to start out upon a term of 49 years as the creditor of small farmers who have been obliged to sell their stock or to borrow the money upon mortgage at 6 per cent., and who were to continue subject to that liability at the same time that they were debtors of the State?—The Commission's inquiries into the security on which they lend extends to the tenant's personal circumstances as well as into the saleable value of his farm; and if they think that their security is in any way endangered either by the circumstances of the tenant or by his being loaded with debt they decline to lend.

1747. In this case, Mr. Commissioner Lynch said, did he not, that these tenants had been crippled by the conduct of the company?—He said that some of them had been, I believe.

1748. Do I rightly interpret the final action of the Commission in sanctioning these sales when I say that they apprehended that if the sales were not sanctioned in consequence of the embarrassed condition of the tenants, the tenants by being given back into the hands of the company might be driven to ruin?—I do not think they apprehended that, on the division of the estate of which you are speaking, the Moneymore division, where the tenants were most anxious to close the matter, and the Commissioners were satisfied that the security was good in all cases where they had lent.

1749. But did not Mr. Commissioner Lynch say (I quote his words in the judgment which referred to this part of the estate, the Moneymore division), that although the security of the tenants had been affected by the litigation with the company, the Commissioners were moved by the consideration that if the agreement were not ratified it might result in the ruin of the tenants; was not that the expression used?—I have not the words of the judgment before me, because I have handed it in.

1750. From your own examination of the Moneymore division, do you think that if the agreements had not been sanctioned by the Commission, the position of the tenants would have been extremely precarious in regard to the tenure of their holdings?—Some few of the tenants who were heavily in debt to the company, I imagine, would have been sold up unless they had settled with the company on easier terms; but taking the Moneymore division as a whole, the security was considered perfectly good.

1751. Do I drive the conclusion too far when I say that the Land Commission strained a point in this case in order to save the tenants from remaining in the hands of the company?—I do not think they did; I think the tenant-right on the Moneymore division was sufficient cover for the security of the Commissioners' loans in every case.

1752. It was nothing to you that the tenants' interest might be confiscated; you simply considered whether the State had security for the advance, even on that which was the property of the tenant himself?—The cover for the Commissioners' loans, as a rule, is the tenants' interest, because if their security was only the interest which the tenant purchased they would have no cover.

1753. What I am driving at is this: It does not matter how far the money liability, which the tenant accepts, for the purchase of the landlords' interest encroaches upon or consumes his own interest, so long as it leaves any substantial share of his own interest as your security?—It can hardly be said to encroach upon the tenants' interests, because the operation of the Purchase Acts, in nearly all cases, is to make the annual payment, to which the tenant becomes liable, less than the rent. Therefore, it does not encroach upon the tenant's interest.

1754. In some of the cases on this estate we have heard that the annual instalment was higher than the judicial rent?—I thought you were speaking only of the Moneymore division. On the poorer parts of the estate, I said that the instalments, payable to the Land Commission, on the prices which were agreed upon, but which the Commissioners refused to lend, would have been, in some cases, higher than the judicial rent; and taking into account the additional poor-rate that the tenants would have had to pay as owners, it would have been practically higher in other cases.

1755. But taking these Moneymore cases and all the circumstances together, even though the instalments to the State may have been somewhat lower than the former rent, the former rent, I understand, was not judicial in the Moneymore division?—I believe not.

1756. The judicial rents have never been fixed there?—They had made an arrangement with the company as to a reduction of rents in 1882, and the sales were based upon those rents. The tenants might have gone into Court if they had chosen.

1757. But those rents of 1882 were still, in the poorer division of the estate at least 20 per cent. higher than the judicial rents fixed by the Recorder of Derry, were they not?—Yes, perhaps I am confusing you by speaking of both divisions of the estate together. I should like to separate them.

1758. I am separating them in my own mind, but

Mr. *Sexton*—continued.

but I am only drawing an inference, that if the tenants upon one portion of the estate got a reduction of 20 per cent. when they went into Court, I suppose we may presume that the tenants of the other division, if they had gone in would have obtained some reduction?—I could not say. The Moneymore division was very much the best, and tenants there were perfectly ready and willing to buy on the rents fixed in 1881.

1759. Is the willingness of a tenant to buy in the prospect of a reduction of his annual payment any conclusive proof that his rent is not one which ought to be reduced in Court?—Not at all; but in this case the tenants might have gone into Court if they had chosen. They preferred, instead of entering into litigation about the rent, to buy upon the terms that the company offered.

1760. Take the circumstances that the rents were not judicial and that in order to meet the liability caused by this litigation they sold stock and borrowed money at high rates of interest; does it not occur to you that their position was not satisfactory in regard to security, and that as Mr. Commissioner Lynch said a point was strained to sanction the purchase rather than subject some of those tenants to the chance of ruin?—The point that Mr. Commissioner Lynch referred to as being strained was that he varied a judgment which he had given to the effect that he would dismiss the cases on account of delay unless they were closed at once; by at once I mean within a month. They were not closed for three or four months.

1761. Mr. Commissioner Lynch having decided to rescind his former judgment, disallowing sales, and to allow sales, when he called upon the company to close their accounts with the tenants they replied, I think, by what amounted to a defiance of the Commission?—They declined to deal with the Commission on the terms mentioned in Mr. Lynch's requisition.

1762. That is to say they insisted upon doing what the Commission said should not be done if the sales were to proceed?—In Mr. Commissioner Lynch's judgment he said that he thought the relation of debtor and creditor should cease at once between the vendors and the tenants, and that all rent and interest, and costs then due by the tenants should be remitted.

1763. This the company refused to do?—They did not close the sales till October.

1764. And they did not remit the sums which the Commissioner desired them to remit?—The Commission had no power to order them to remit the sums. It was only that they had to give them the alternative of dismissing the cases or closing on the terms which the Commission suggested. That was the substance of Mr. Commissioner Lynch's first requisition to the company.

1765. If the tenants upon the Moneymore division had been unwilling to buy as the tenants upon the Ballynascreen division were unwilling to buy, it is obvious, I think that the sales upon the Moneymore division would never have been concluded in consequence of the refusal of the company to comply with the requisition of the Commissioners that they should close the accounts with the tenants?—I think that they would not have been closed because it was at the tenants' request, made formally in court to the Land Commission, that the sales were closed.

1766. Out of consideration for the tenants they waived their own requisition upon the company?—It was at the tenants' request. If you mean by consideration that the Commissioners did it out of charity, I do not think it was a case for charity. It was done at the tenants' request.

1767. The upshot of the matter was that after the Commission had said that they would not sanction those sales except upon certain terms, the company had their own way as against the Commission, and the sales in the result were sanctioned?—I am unable to say to what extent the company had their own way, because I do not know what sums they recovered after that judgment, but they could have had their own way completely.

1768. They did go on recovering?—I am unable to say to what extent.

1769. The final requisition of Mr. Commissioner Lynch, as I understand, was that all accounts between the company and the tenants should be closed say in October, in order that the sales might be ratified in November?—His requisition was that they should be closed in May if I am not mistaken; certainly not in October.

1770. I understand his judgment to be that the first instalments from the tenants to the State would fall due in May, and then as the half year began in November, the tenants would have to start with a clear slate in November, so as to have no conflicting liability. You withheld the name of a tenant in the Moneymore division at one point of your evidence; what was the reason of that?—I stated at the time that as that tenant is now in litigation with the company I thought it would be unfair to disclose his name.

1771. In the Moneymore division?—In the Ballynascreen division.

1772. You did not withhold any name in the Moneymore division?—I withheld no name in the Moneymore division, but I think I ought to have done so.

1773. Why?—Because those tenants may for all I know still be in debt to the company. I am not aware that they are, but I have not satisfied myself that they are not.

1774. Even though they be indebted to the company, what then?—The company is a very powerful body; these are very poor farmers, and I do not think it would be right for me to give the Committee the names of those tenants, because the company might infer that the tenants had asked me to mention their cases. Now none of the tenants have done anything of the kind.

1775. I am very glad to have given you the opportunity of saying that, and I entirely sympathise with your motives. Do you apprehend that the Drapers' Company of London, upon discovering that a tenant had given information to a public officer would subject the tenant to

vindictive

Mr. *Sexton*—continued.

vindictive proceedings?—The Drapers' Company in London act through a great number of agents, and I think that the tenants in litigation with the company might be placed in a very unpleasant position if it was thought that they had in any way made hostile representations to this Committee through me.

1776. You think that the company being in London, and transacting its business through local intermediaries of different degrees of discretion, possibly the tenants might be ill-treated?—A large company like that at a distance must act upon general rules, and upon a system which private individuals may be able to dispense with by a consideration of each particular case.

1777. But action upon a system is one thing and special persecution of an individual because he has given information to a public officer is another thing?—I do not think that the Drapers' Company would specially persecute a tenant on the ground of his having given me any information.

1778. But upon the whole, looking to the circumstances as you have stated them, you considered it desirable not to give information that you could withhold as to names?—It would have been very desirable if all the names of the tenants had been withheld.

1779. Have you any special reason for saying that?—The company of course have a perfect right to collect anything in the shape of costs or other debts that are due by the tenants; but I think that it would have been very reasonable for a powerful and wealthy company like this to have shown some consideration in the matter, and if they think there has been any mismanagement or misunderstanding, they might very well have remitted some of the costs that arose out of these suits. Here is a letter to a tenant whose name has been mentioned, and therefore I will mention him again, Mr. Benjamin Barefoot. The letter says: "However willing you may have been to further negotiation between the company and the tenants for the sale of the estate, your resistance to the company's claim for rent and interest, a claim against which you had neither legally nor morally the smallest defence, has caused them considerable trouble and expense. The company are unable to see any reason why they should remit any part of the sum for which you are still indebted to the company, and they cannot entertain your request that they should do so." That is dated 26th April 1889, Drapers' Hall, London, signed by W. T. Sawyer, Clerk.

Mr. *T. M. Healy.*

1780. How long was that letter dated after Mr. Sawyer's previous letter?—The date of that letter is the 26th April 1889; I have not the date of the other letter.

1781. Have you copies of Mr. Barefoot's replies to those letters?—I have not.

Mr. *Sexton.*

1782. Was it before or after the effort of the Commission to close the accounts between the company and the tenants that the company endeavoured to obtain promissory notes for the indebtedness of the tenants?—I am not aware of the company having endeavoured to obtain any promissory notes. Some such suggestion was made, but it never came to anything.

1783. I should like to have that more precisely if you could give it?—It is a matter which did not come before me, and on which therefore I am not prepared to answer.

1784. But you spoke of correspondence. Was there a correspondence between the company and the Commission on the subject?—If so, I am not acquainted with it.

1785. I should wish to pass from the Moneymore division to the Ballynascreen division, that is, from the division where the tenants desired to buy to the division where they did not desire to purchase?—I should like to explain, with regard to that, that I only stated that the tenants on the poorer part of the Brackaghslievgallion division were unwilling to buy at the prices named. There are good lands as well as bad in that division, and the tenants on the good lands were in the same position as the Moneymore tenants, and their sales have, to a large extent, been closed.

1786. But the petition addressed to the Land Commission proceeded, I think, from the great majority of the tenants upon the poorer division, and declared very emphatically their unwillingness to buy upon the terms pressed upon them by the company?—That petition referred only to the poorer parts of the estate.

1787. Were they the majority of the tenants?—I am unable to give the number.

1788. Were you not on the estate?—I was several times, but I have not got complete statistics dividing the tenants into poor and rich.

1789. What proportion of them would you say, generally, were what you call the very poor in that division?—I could not answer you that.

1790. Not the majority?—I could not say.

1791. What rents would "very poor" indicate?—I do not think poverty necessarily means a very small holding. What I mean by "poor" is the inferior and higher-lying lands. The occupants of those holdings were, I considered, poor, and the cases that came before Mr. Commissioner Lynch for the judgment put in from that part of the estate were 53 in number; but they were scattered all over it; they were not 53 lying together, and they may be taken as a fair sample of the poorer part of the estate.

1792. They said in their petition that they were in a state of extreme poverty, and I gathered from you that you had, by your visit, verified their statements; in general, did you find them in a state of extreme poverty?—Some of the tenants on the estate are in a state of extreme poverty.

1793. And had been so?—I was not acquainted with their circumstances before 1889.

1794. You would have inferred, from the state in which you found them, that they had been so?—I should.

1795. Could you give us in brief sequence the stages by which the Drapers' Company imposed the agreements upon those tenants; about when did the company offer to sell these Brackaghslievgallion farms at 18 years' purchase of the old rent?—I am not able to go into the question

Mr. *Sexton*—continued.

question of dates, because those agreements have been lodged from time to time with the Land Commission, and I have no knowledge at what time the preliminary negotiations between the tenants and the company commenced.

1796. The company having made those offers in October 1887, served 150 ejectments, did they not?—I do not pledge myself to the number of ejectments. No doubt the company could tell you that, but they served a great number of ejectments.

1797. After that they served notices, under Section 7 of the Land Act (what is commonly known as the "Ejectment made easy" section) to turn the tenants into caretakers?—The petition states that caretakers' notices were served upon the tenants. That I know to be the case, because I saw some of those notices in the tenants' houses; but my acquaintance with this part of the estate dates from the time that I was first sent down by the Commission to report upon that part.

1798. But you saw various documents?—When I visit I make it my business to obtain or verify all the statements made to me by examining the tenants' receipts for rent; and in the course of my examination of the receipts for rents I saw so many ejectments among their papers that I took to examining them, because I thought that the first case I visited was perhaps an exceptional case.

1799. Was this the sequence of events: Following the notices of eviction there were summonses for possession and issue of warrants, then there were civil bills served for use and occupation; then civil bills in January 1888, for the 1887 rent; then, in midwinter of 1888, in November, the the sheriff, upon the civil bill, seized the chattels, and, in the following month, December, he came to eviction; and the matter, having reached that final stage, the tenants were about to be evicted, and then, after a struggle of three years, they yielded to the terms imposed by the company?—I am unable to say whether that statement, including the dates, is correct. I made a report to the Land Commission, part of which I read, and that gives all the information that I collected in a general way.

1800. You generally verified the statement in the petition, and you have no reason to doubt, I presume, that this account in the petition is inaccurate?—I had never seen the petition when I visited the estate. I simply went down by the direction of the Commissioners to inspect 53 holdings, and then these facts transpired. When I came back to Dublin having heard that the petition had been sent up, I looked for it and found it; but it had not come under my notice before I visited the estate.

Chairman.

1801. The petition was dated the 11th of November 1888, and you went down three months afterwards?—I was very frequently absent from the Land Commission Office, and it may have come in and not come under my notice.

Mr. *Sexton*.

1802. After this proceeding under section 7, the result was that the tenants having at first refused to buy at 18 years of the old rent were obliged to agree to buy at 18 years of the old rent, and to add to the purchase money the heavy arrears of rent and costs which you have described in your evidence; was not that so?—The prices at which the tenants had at first refused to buy were increased by the addition of rent, interest, or costs.

1803. At the end of that series of events they had to accept terms much worse than they had refused at the beginning?—Yes, by the addition of rent, and in some cases of costs.

1804. When were the judicial rents fixed upon the Brackaghalorgallon divisions?—They were fixed at different dates, but they were fixed before the execution of the agreements to which I have referred in my report to the Commissioners, and in my statement to the Committee.

1805. About how long before?—I am unable to say; but they were fixed.

1806. Was it weeks or months, or was it a considerable period?—A considerable period. I will not bind myself to accuracy; but I believe it was a year before in some cases. You must remember every case dealt with is the subject of a separate agreement, and all the agreements are not entered into at the same date; therefore any general statement may not be applicable to the whole division.

1807. But the company inserted in the agreements a rent which had ceased to exist about a year before in most cases?—It had ceased to exist before the agreements were signed.

1808. The agreements containing those four statements, as they were described by the Commissioners, were verified upon oath, were they not?—They were; and that is alluded to in Mr. Commissioner Lynch's judgment, which I have put in.

1809. Who verified the four statements upon oath on the part of the company?—I do not think the agreements are verified by the company. The person making the application, that is, the tenant, verifies the application by an affidavit.

1810. Does not the landlord pledge himself to the truth of the statements?—Not by affidavit.

1811. How then?—I am not aware, without examining one of the Commissioners' forms.

1812. But the company procured perjury?—Mr. Commissioner Lynch blamed the company for having got men who, in many cases, were illiterate; who even, if they were able to read and write, were quite incapable of reading and understanding a long document like this, to make these affidavits.

1813. Apparently so much the worse for the persons who induced the illiterate person to commit perjury?—I should hardly call it perjury, because the company have the explanation which I have given, that their negotiations with the tenants were intended to arrive at prices equal to eighteen times the old rent, and the tenants wished to buy at eighteen times the judicial rent; and the company (I suppose to deliver themselves from bargaining with the tenants) left the old rent standing.

1814. Let me read the explanation: "This is what Mr. Glover said: "After the tenants

got

Mr. Sexton—continued.

got fair rents fixed, they insisted they had a right, under the company's offer, to buy at 18 years of those fair rents. This the company refused to accede to, and in order to prevent any misunderstanding as to the terms of sale, and having regard to the tenant's contention, it was considered better to insert the rent of 1882, leaving it open to the company, when the inspector came round, to explain the matter to him by a statement in the form now sent." Would the insertion of the rent of 1882 have prevented any misunderstanding? Did not the tenants perfectly well understand what was going on? You have told us that the judicial rent had been fixed about a year before these agreements were entered into, and the rents inserted in the agreement were rents which had ceased to have a legal existence a year before these documents were executed?—That is what was wrong in the agreements; that a non-existent and higher rent was inserted in agreements instead of the rent that had been judicially fixed.

1815. So that, in fact, instead of preventing misunderstanding, the insertion of the rent of 1882 in these documents produced a misunderstanding; it misled the Commission?—I had no idea till I visited the farms that the rents stated in the agreements were anything but the legal rents to which the tenants were still liable.

1816. They were rents which had long ceased to exist. The letter I have just read says, it was considered better to insert the rent of 1882, leaving it open to the company, when the inspector came round, to explain the matter to him. You went round; was it explained to you by the company?—It was not. But I did not ask the company; I reported myself to the agent at Moneymore, and then I went to visit the estate; and until I examined the tenants of the farms, I was not aware that these judicial rents had been fixed; and that return which you refer to there was not sent to me or the Land Commission until after my visit.

1817. You had to find it out for yourself?—I did.

1818. Do you consider that there is any point in the explanation of Mr. Glover?—I think there is; there is an explanation of what occurred; but I do not think there is any justification.

1819. Does the law, as administered by the Land Commission, provide any power to punish for making false statements and procuring their confirmation by affidavit?—I am not enough of a lawyer to answer that question.

1820. We asked you when you last gave evidence, whether you could give us a copy of the form of application; first, I should like to see such a form of application as these tenants of the Drapers' Company signed?—The applications from the Drapers' Company have been coming in at different dates and on different forms since the year 1886; and therefore I do not think I could say that the form of agreement now in use would represent the forms which the company used.

1821. No, I quite understand the contrary from your own evidence. I understand from your evidence, that in consequence of the misconduct of this company, you have been obliged to make changes in your forms and in your rules?—And in consequence of Acts passed since. The Act of 1877 and the Act of 1888 made it necessary for the Commissioners to change their forms.

1822. I should like to know the changes you have been specially induced to make by reason of what occurred in the transactions with the Drapers' Company, if you could indicate them in a few words?—I could not.

1823. Can you give the Committee the form of application upon which these agreements, referred to in the so-called explanation of Mr. Glover were made, and also the form of the agreement now in use; that would enable us to obtain a comparative view of what the agreement was then and what it is at present?—It appears that the company got special forms printed for themselves, and there were some slight variations from the form in use in 1888, which perhaps would make it misleading to put in any of the ordinary forms that I have got here.

1824. I think we should need, at all events, to have put in one of the forms actually used by the tenants of the Drapers' Company in the Brackaslievgallon division?—Would it not be better to apply to the Land Commissioners for anything you want, which I am not able to speak about personally.

1825. Certainly, if you have not got any of the forms here?—I have not.

1826. How are the tenants on this whole division situated now; have any of them completed the sales?—The Land Commissioners refused all the cases where they considered the security insufficient; and in the first instance after my visit, and after having investigated the fifty-four cases I referred to on the Brackaslievgallon division, the Land Commissioners rejected them all, writing a letter in these terms to the company; shall I read the letter?

1827. No, it will be sufficient to say that they rejected them, unless there is any matter in the letter which you think would be valuable to the Committee?—It explains their reasons, and merely confirms the statement that I have made to the Committee.

1828. Then I think it need not be read. I understand that they are still delaying the proceedings of these sales; they have not lodged certain maps, and the period allotted by the Land Commissioners to elapse between the agreement and the lodgment of it is still continually exceeded by the company?—There are quite inexplicable delays still. Some cases are not proceeded with because the maps have not been lodged; but a letter I have here from the solicitor acting for the tenants will explain the nature of the delays. He sent me six agreements which had not been lodged in the Land Commission, I being at that time at Moneymore.

Chairman.

1829. When was this?—On the 5th of June 1890. He wrote me a letter asking me if I could expedite the dealing with these agreements by inspecting that land. He says: "These agreements

Chairman—continued.

ments were signed by the tenants in November, December and January last, but were held over by the company without being sealed, and were sent to me long after the stipulated time for lodging them had expired, reckoning from the date on which they were signed by the tenants, in consequence of which they have not been lodged, and will not be until after a special application is made to the Land Commission Court."

Mr. *Sexton*.

1830. This special application involves the tenants in increased cost, I suppose?—I presume an application would not be made to the Land Commission by a solicitor unless he was paid for it.

1831. Do the company insist upon regarding the date of the agreement as the date when the period begins to run?—The date inserted in the application is the date as to which the rule of the Land Commission would apply as to lodgment; it must be lodged within two months after that date.

1832. As a rule it is not lodged within that period, I understand; but you have found numbers of cases outstanding after six months?—A number of cases; and I am informed that there are a number of cases that have been signed by the tenants where no attempt has been made to lodge them as yet.

1833. What is the reason of this systematic violation of your rules by the company?—I am unable to say. It is not a violation of the Commissioners' rules if they get another one executed and bring it within the prescribed date. It is entirely a matter for the tenants if they choose to proceed against the company, which of course they could not, and have it lodged and claim to be remunerated for any delay incurred, if it is incurred by holding them over in the company's offices.

1834. To get an agreement signed and then to withhold it and attempt to lodge it after a year or so, is a breach of your rules, is it not?—It cannot be lodged without coming under the Commissioners' rules; but I think it is very unfair and hard upon these country farmers to deal with them in such a way.

1835. It subjects the tenants to special expense, does it not?—It has been a cause of expense to a number of them.

Mr. *Morton*.] May I ask, Sir, whether we may understand that all the forms of the Land Commissioners from time to time will be sent over and put in, together with the dates when they came into operation?

Chairman.] We will consider what forms we will send for.

Sir Richard Temple.

1836. (*To the Witness*.) The letter which you described in your evidence as constituting a pledge, is the letter printed in the minutes signed by Mr. Sawyer of the 3rd of January 1887, is it not?—Yes; that is the letter I have put in.

Sir Richard Temple—continued.

1837. Does this letter constitute a pledge, do you think?—I am unable to say, not being a lawyer, whether it constitutes a legal contract, or whether it ought to be read into the contract entered into.

1838. Is it a moral pledge?—I think it is, morally, and would be interpreted so by simple people like country farmers.

1839. A pledge to what effect?—That no interest would be demanded from the tenants after they had satisfied the year's rent due in 1885.

1840. Neither rent nor interest?—So the letter states.

1841. But do you observe this passage at the end of it: "The Company confidently anticipated that many purchases would have been completed before the 1st November 1886," and then they go on to say, "This delay is, of course, a serious loss to them, and, if it continues, may compel them to further consider the terms of sale"?—So I understand.

1842. Did the delay continue?—The delay appears to me to have arisen on the part of the company. It was not a delay in accepting the terms; because the tenants and the company agreed to sell and to buy, and lodged the agreement with the Land Commission. It then remained with the company, who were to pay all the costs of sale, to carry the sale through.

1843. But as regards the moral pledge, does not the sentence imply that unless the sales were quickly completed the company would revise the terms?—I do not think it affects the pledge in the least; because the delay appears to have arisen from the action of the company.

1844. But then if this letter is taken as a pledge, or as amounting morally to a pledge, does not that sentence imply that the company said that they would not be bound by those terms of charging neither rent nor interest unless the sale were quickly completed?—I do not think it would affect their obligation if they were the parties who caused the delay.

1845. But still does not that sentence amount to an indication on their part that they would revise?—I think it might be pleaded as such in a court of law; but I cannot understand the company or a landlord dealing with the tenants, varying the pledge given in the first part of the letter, on account of that sentence at the end.

1846. Then, as a matter of fact, did they collect rent and interest after the 1st of November 1885?—Yes. I have a return from the company of the amounts claimed up to May 1889. That must have included interest, because rent admittedly ceased in 1885.

Chairman.

1847. But in Question 1016, Mr. Sexton put this question to you: "The letter said that the company would not claim after the 1st of November 1885; up to what date did the rent or the interest run?" and the answer that you gave is not quite clear as I read it, you said: "The return of the company merely gives the amount claimed up to the 1st of May 1889," which is much as you say now. Did they or did they not claim rent after the 1st of November 1885?—I do

Chairman—continued.

do not think they claimed any rent due after 1885, but they claimed interest.

1848. They claimed no rent after the 1st of November 1885, but they claimed interest on what?—On the purchase money.

1849. What rate is the interest at; would it be 5 per cent.?—I am unable to say whether it was $3\frac{1}{2}$ or 4 per cent.

Sir Richard Temple.

1850. When they say neither rent nor interest, does interest, in that sentence, mean interest on the purchase-money?—That is the way I understand it.

1851. "Neither rent nor interest upon the purchase-money," is that the way you think it should be read?—Certainly.

1852. Did you say they did claim rent after 1885?—They did not claim rent, nor could they have done so.

1853. But they did claim interest upon the purchase-money?—Certainly.

1854. Was that interest claimed on the ground of delay in the completion of the sale?—It was claimed and recovered under a decision of the High Court of Justice in Ireland; and the amounts so given in in a return to the Land Commissioners, to which the tenants were liable, are set down as received or claimed up to the 1st of May 1889, about which time it was intended and hoped that the sales would be closed.

1855. If they recovered the interest under a decision of the High Court of Justice, could that properly be said to be in violation of the pledge?—I think to have sued the tenants at all was certainly a departure from the perfectly plain meaning of that letter. The tenants felt themselves very much aggrieved by it, and the law is not always consistent with what is morally right.

1856. Do you know upon what ground the company claimed?—I am not sufficiently a lawyer to tell you for certain, but I have explained to the Committee already that a decision of the High Court of Justice was given, which was to the effect that where the agreement for these sales was silent as to the interest, interest was payable for the period pending the completion of the sale. But further, the Purchase of Land Amendment Act of 1889 had passed, while these sales were pending, and section 3 provides that the vendor may recover from the vendee interest in lieu of rent for the period between the date of signing agreement and the date of the completion of the sale, unless the parties have otherwise agreed.

1857. Was this letter laid before the court, do you know?—I understand it was precluded from being before the court. A rule of law prohibits a letter of that kind being laid before a court in interpretation of the contract which was the subject of litigation.

1858. Do you know whether the substance of this letter was pleaded on behalf of the tenants?—I am unable to say.

Mr. *Nairn.*] We would ask again, Sir, that these proceedings before the High Court should be put in.

Chairman.] We will consider for ourselves whether we will have them put in. It will be a matter for the companies to consider hereafter. It is understood, and perhaps my repeating it now will prevent the recurrence of these interruptions, that the companies are to have a full chance of rebutting any evidence that is laid before us, or applying when their turn comes for the production of material to elucidate their case. In the meantime it must be remembered by the gentlemen on the other side of the table that they are not before the Committee.

Sir Richard Temple.

1859. I just want to clear up this point. The substance of this letter, I gather, was not pleaded before the court?—I am unable to speak as to any pleadings in the court. I merely state the fact of the letter, and the interpretation that seems obvious to me, and I think it would be to most persons.

1860. Did the tenants urge the existence of this letter upon the company as a reason why the claim should not be made?—It was because of that letter that the tenants, instead of paying, refused to pay, and were in consequence sued and defeated.

1861. Then there was a correspondence between the company and the tenants about this letter, I presume; there must have been?—I do not think there must have been, because the tenants go to pay their rent personally to the agent.

1862. What I am trying to arrive at is this: do you know what was the ground upon which the company alleged that they had a right to claim, notwithstanding this letter?—I am unable to say.

1863. Do you know what their answer was, when this letter was urged as a reason why the claim should not be made. Do you know what in substance was the rejoinder of the company?—I cannot imagine there being any rejoinder or any reason given, except that the company had the right under the law to recover the interest; and they got it.

1864. You do not think they urged what is indicated in the last sentence of the letter, namely, that the delay absolved them from the pledge?—I ought not, perhaps, to speak merely of what I think; but I think the delays arose on the company's part. The tenants naturally did not think they were responsible for the delay, and refused to pay.

1865. Did the company claim, or did they allege, that the delay was owing to the tenants?—I am unable to say what the company thought.

1866. Nor what they alleged?—Nor what they alleged.

Mr. Clancy.

1867. Referring to the last sentence in the letter referred to by Sir Richard Temple: "This delay is, of course, a serious loss to them, and, if it continues, may compel them to further consider the terms of sale, but not in the direction which you suggest;" that seems to be a perfectly

Mr. *Clancy*—continued.

audacious statement, considering the delay was entirely their own?—I do not think I could give an opinion as to the audacity of it.

1868. You have given the opinion that the delay was entirely their own?—So I believe.

1869. Therefore, for the company to express a regret, or a complaint, that delay was caused, was an extraordinary thing to do under those circumstances, was it not?—I think it was.

1870. You were asked by Sir Richard Temple why the tenants were sued, and why the rent was recovered in spite of this letter. You are aware, of course, of the rule of law, that where you have a written contract you cannot give evidence of any document adding to, or varying, or taking away from, the terms of the contract? —That was the ground upon which, as I understand, the letter was excluded.

1871. Therefore, the thing could not be pleaded at all?—Quite so.

1872. Sir Richard Temple has asked what was the letter to which this was a reply?—I have not got the whole correspondence.

1873. This letter could not be put in evidence at all?—Not without calling Mr. Barefoot, to whom that letter was addressed.

1874. You could not put it in evidence at all, because it is an agreement for which there is no consideration, and which could not be enforced at all. That is evidently the meaning of the fact that in spite of it the interest was recovered?—The letter, I imagine, was not taken into consideration in interpreting the contract in any way.

1875. It could not be. Now, have you stated how much interest was recovered up to May 1890?—I am quite unable to give any division of the sums recovered or claimed from the tenants in the way of rent or interest; they were furnished in bulk to the Land Commissioners.

1876. Referring to the question of arrears, are landlords obliged, or are tenants obliged, to make the Land Commissioners acquainted with the amount of arrears due?—The Land Commission forms state the price to be inclusive of all arrears of rent due up to the last gale day; that practically settles the question of what arrears are included in the price.

1877. Therefore, practically, they are bound to disclose the total amount of the arrears?—No, I cannot say that the agreement discloses the amount of arrears. This agreement simply discloses the price. The Commissioners, if they think necessary, direct the inspector to inquire how the rent has been paid in the past. That is one of the evidences of the value.

1878. When you go down to inspect a holding, and see whether the security is sufficient or not, you would ask, no doubt, what the *former* rent was, and how much of it was due?—It is part of the duty of the Commissioners' inspectors to acquaint themselves and inform the Commissioners what rent was due when the agreements were signed.

1879. In cases in which you discovered that the amount of arrears was not accurately disclosed, you would not sanction the agreement to purchase?—It is not disclosed in the agreement at all.

Mr. *Clancy*—continued.

1880. It is practically, is it not, because they agree upon a price which is to be inclusive of all arrears?—Those arrears, if they existed, may have been forgiven by the landlord altogether. We deal with nothing but the lump sum. The vendor agrees to sell a holding, say, for 100*l.*; the Commissioners' investigation is directed to whether the holding is sufficient security for the loan they are asked to make.

1881. As I understand, your practice is to ask as to the amount of arrears that were forgiven from the rent?—It is the practice of the Commissioners' inspectors to do so; but the agreement does not disclose all that information.

1882. I quite understand that. Would you also ask whether promissory notes were in those cases given for arrears of rent?—It is the duty of the Commissioners' inspectors, by the Commissioners' direction, to ascertain everything that bears in any way upon the security.

1883. Therefore you would ask whether promissory notes were given for arrears?—Such a transaction has been very uncommon.

1884. But is it not common enough on the Drapers' Estate?—I am not aware that any promissory notes are given on the Drapers' Estate.

1885. I thought you said you were able to put a stop to that transaction?—I said there was a suggestion that some arrears should be settled by promissory notes; but whether that suggestion came from the company or the tenants, whatever it was, the Land Commissioners said they would not allow any such transaction or carry out any sales on those terms.

1886. Did the tenants speak to you at all of any promises on the part of the company that if they bought, those grants which the company were in the habit of making would be continued?—I never heard any such proposal mentioned.

1887. You referred to the costs; you mentioned in one case 7 *l.*; costs being incurred in the case of an ejectment; were those ejectments brought in the High Court or in the county court?—I think they were brought in the county court.

1888. You spoke of a rule a while ago, that after a sale is concluded and the money paid over, only six months' interest could be recovered; would you tell us when that rule was made?—I could not say when that rule was made.

1889. Was it in operation when you inspected the Drapers' Estate?—It was.

1890. Did you enquire at all into the expenditure by the Drapers' Company upon their estate in Derry?—I made no enquiry; that is not part of my business; I have, in fact, made no enquiry upon the subject.

1891. You do not know anything about that? —No.

1892. It is the business of the Land Commission to see whether there is sufficient security given to the State for the money they advance, as I understand?—That is one of the chief functions of the Land Commission.

1893. In arriving at a conclusion upon that subject, you take into account the whole value of the holding?—Certainly. The Land Commission do not enter into the consideration of what or who has made the holding valuable.

1894. Therefore,

Mr. *Clancy*—continued.

1894. Therefore, in many cases, the tenant may be paying for his own property over again?—I do not see that.

1895. Take this Ballinascreen division of the Drapers' Estate; is it not the fact that there the tenants have made all the improvements?—I judge that the tenants are the persons who made the buildings, and have done what reclamation there is visible; but beyond its being a general practice in the country that the tenants do these things, I am unable to say, from any information I had before me, who had done it on that estate.

1896. Supposing the tenants did it, it is quite obvious then, I should say, that their interest in the place was greater than that of the landlord?—There are some cases where a tenant's interest will fetch in the market as much as the tenants are paying to the landlord.

1897. And even more?—Even more, sometimes.

1898. Therefore, in estimating the value of the holding as a security to the State for the money advanced by the State, it is quite conceivable, if not certain, is it not, that the tenant would be paying for his own property?—I cannot see that; because the tenants' property is whatever interest he has over the rent. Now, in all the transactions in the way of sale that have come before me, the tenant by buying is subject to a smaller annual payment than the rent.

1899. Whether the payment of the tenant be higher or lower, it may be estimated on his own property, may it not?—Under the Purchase Act it is not the business of the Commissioners to go into that. The more improvements a tenant has made the better is the security.

1900. I know it is not the business of the Commissioners to go into that; I am only asking your opinion; have you any statistics as to evictions on this estate?—I have no information as to the number of ejectments served.

1901. Has your department, the Land Commission, any opportunity of getting the returns of evictions for recent years?—None whatever.

Mr. *John Ellis*.

1902. As I understand, you do not come before us as a gentleman learned in the law, but as an official of the Land Commission; is that so?—I am not a lawyer.

1903. Then I will only put one question to you with regard to this letter which has been mentioned so much. What I understand you to wish to convey is this: that the company gave an honourable pledge upon a certain point in this letter, and that when the matter came before the Court, by the rule of the Court, or by the laws of evidence, this letter could not be put in?—So I understand.

1904. In your opinion, having great experience of agricultural matters, and knowing the circumstances of these poor tenants, you think that the company gave a pledge to them morally not to do certain things which afterwards they did?—I think so. That letter was only confirmatory of what the tenants understood from the verbal negotiations which took place on

Mr. *John Ellis*—continued.

several occasions, and at different places on the estate.

1905. With regard to your visits to this estate, how many official visits have you made?—I think I have visited the estate four times, and probably spent three or four weeks there; but I have been acquainted with the district for many years.

1906. Can you give us the dates of those visits?—I am afraid I could not without referring to my note books, which I have not got here.

1907. I asked you about this point before, in Questions 1051 and 1052; but as it is not quite clear, perhaps you will explain it. In Question 1050, the date "11th of November 1888," occurs with respect to a certain petition, and in Question 1051, you state you went down three months after that; that would be at the beginning of this year?—I think 1888 is a misprint; it should be 1889. My first visit to this estate was in February or April 1889.

1908. Have you known these districts otherwise than as an official?—I have visited this district several times during the 20 years I have been employed in connection with the sale of land under the Church Commission and under the Land Commission of 1881.

1909. I may take it that any opinions you have formed or given in any official reports, are derived from an acquaintance with the district extending over many years?—Certainly, I have had occasion to visit this district very often.

1910. You have used two words, "tenants" and "farms," will you give us some idea, as many people will read this evidence who are not so familiar with the matter as you are, as to what you mean by "tenants" and "farms"; will you briefly describe the sort of persons and the sort of land you referred to?—What question do you refer to?

1911. I am not referring to any particular question, but you have used the two terms in your evidence; what sort of person do you mean by a tenant; in England a tenant might be a man who had 200 or 300 acres; do you mean anything like that?—The tenant farmers on the Drapers' Estate are almost without exception men paying from 5 *l.* to 20 *l.* rent.

1912. Something like a superior agricultural labourer in some districts in England?—In a country of small farms like Ireland we count them farmers.

1913. Do any of these men come over to this country to perform agricultural labour?—Yes; I have met some cases where the tenants of these farms were frequently working in England, visiting it every year, or going there for the harvest.

1914. You used the expression "illiterate" with respect to some of them; you do not mean, I presume, that they are unintelligent in connection with their own affairs, but that probably they do not understand these written documents?—That is so.

1915. Could you give us any illustration of the injury done to the tenants by the delay you have mentioned?—I cannot give you any illustration of the injury done by delay. I can explain what the injury was, that it has deferred the commencement

Mr. *John Ellis*—continued.

ment of the tenant's farm as a freeholder, that it has put him to some costs, and that during the period of the delay he of course was in a state of unrest, and therefore was liable to be distracted from cultivating his farm properly.

1916. Will you now turn, if you please, to Question 1192. There is no foundation whatever, I may take it, for the statement that the agreement was signed before the judicial rent was fixed?—I am satisfied that in the cases that I have referred to the judicial rent was fixed before the agreements were signed.

1917. And the company were perfectly aware therefore of the existence of the judicial rent?—Certainly.

1918. In Question 1127 you used the expression "deputation"; are you acquainted with this book (*handing a book to the Witness*)?—That is the book from which I took the extract I read.

1919. Will you kindly read the title page of that book?—"Two Reports of a Deputation, who, in pursuance of the resolutions of the Court of Assistants of the Drapers' Company, of the 23rd January 1817, and 3rd August 1818, visited the estates of the company in the county of Londonderry in Ireland, in those years; and which were ordered by the Court to be printed for the use of its members—London, 1818."

1920. Now will you refer to page 10 of that book?—Yes.

1921. Will you read any sentence you may find there to which you alluded in your evidence?—What I alluded to was this statement. "By the universal practice of the country, repairs and new buildings of all sorts are done and executed at the expense of the tenant, without the landlord's contributing either materials or workmanship."

1922. Will you refer now to page 68, if you please; does that bear any signatures?—"Signed, Nathaniel Stonard, Master; William Hammond, Master Warden."

1923. That is the official report of the deputation, and that is the deputation to which I understand you to have alluded in answer to Question 1127?—Yes.

1924. From your own observation, would you say that what is there described as the "universal practice" has been maintained since?—I think it is the universal practice in the country; but I made an exemption in the case of the Drapers' Estate in mentioning that they had spent a very large sum of money upon the town of Moneymore.

1925. Then with respect to the use made of arrears, would you wish us to infer that, from your observation, arrears have been made use of to extract more onerous terms from the tenants; perhaps you will explain the view you take upon that point?—I think that a tenant who is largely in arrear may be induced by his landlord to agree to buy at a higher price than he otherwise would; but it is one of the chief functions of the Land Commission to see that the security for their loan is perfect; and in such cases they would probably, if not certainly, reject the loan.

1926. But may we take it from you that the Land Commission have no regard to the equity between the landlord and the tenant; they simply and solely regard the value of the property as security for any advance they may sanction?—I think the Land Commission have some regard to the equity of the proceedings between landlord and tenant; because the Drapers' Company's case is one in point. The Land Commissioners there refused to sanction loans obtained under threats of eviction. But their principal duty is the examination of the security; and the case of the Drapers' Estate is an illustration. They reject all those cases where they consider the security insufficient; and have done so throughout all their proceedings. They have refused to sanction 3,000 applications since they began operations, where the purchase money amounted to over one million and a quarter, on the ground that the security was insufficient, or other similar reasons.

1927. The present state of things, as I gather, on this Drapers' estate is, that there is great delay at the present moment in concluding a number of the purchases?—Yes. I explained to Mr. Sexton the nature of the delays at present.

1928. The whole of that delay, I gather from you, rests not with the Land Commissioners or the tenant, but with the Drapers' Company in withholding sufficient information?—The cases at present pending before the Land Commissioners have not been able to be proceeded with because the information required from the company, has not yet been furnished.

Mr. *Lea*.

1929. I want to correct one little point; you stated that the whole of these lands were in the county of Derry; Mr. Miller, in his evidence here on the first day, stated that they also extended into Tyrone. You were not aware of that?—I am not aware that any part of the company's estates are situated in Tyrone.

1930. You told us that the company's estates sold under the Ashbourne Act, or remaining unsold, amounted to about one million or a million and a half; is that so?—I estimated, as well as I could, taking the very imperfect materials before me, the property as being worth between one million and one million and a half.

1931. Are you aware that under the Bright Clauses of the Land Act of 1870, under the Act of 1881, considerable portions of the Company's estates have been sold?—I am not aware that under the Act of 1881 there were sales to any extent. I believe under the Bright Clauses of the Act of 1870 there were some sales, but not many by the companies.

1932. Other companies have sold to private owners, have they not?—Some of the companies sold estates in the last century.

1933. Do you know the Clothworkers' Company?—I have been on part of their estate, which was bought, I think, by Sir Harvey Bruce, and afterwards re-sold to the tenants under the Bright Clauses of the Act of 1870.

1934. Under what Act was the Clothworkers' Estate sold to Sir Harvey Bruce; it was not sold under any Land Purchase Act at all, was it?—Certainly not; it was sold in the ordinary course of business, I suppose.

1935. Do you know the amount it was sold for?—I do not.

1936. Have you heard it was sold for 140,000 *l.* or 160,000 *l.*?—I have no recollection; I may have read of it.

1937. We

Mr. *Lea*—continued.

1937. We have evidence to that effect. You have not included that in the amount of your valuation?—No.

1938. Nor the purchases under the 1870 Act?—Those have long ago ceased to belong to the company as have other very large estates which were alienated by the companies, I believe with the consent of the Irish Society in the last century.

1939. You have not included any of those cases in your total of a million to a million and a-half?—I doubt if the capital value of all the property sold under the Land Purchase Acts and remaining unsold exceeds a million and a-half.

1940. You do not include land sold to private owners like Sir Harvey Bruce?—No; I say sold under the Land Purchase Acts.

1941. Would it be impossible for the total of the London companies' estates sold during the last couple of centuries to amount in value to two millions or more?—Very much more; I should say to several millions.

1942. You referred in answer to Question 870 to the Ironmongers' Estate being cut up among five companies?—Yes.

1943. Are you aware that when it was first granted it was given to seven different companies?—I am not aware.

1944. You did not mention the Coopers' and the Pewterers' Companies?—I merely gave you the names of the companies which have lodged agreements of sale with the Land Commissioners.

1945. You know nothing about the Coopers' and the Pewterers' Companies?—No.

1946. I think you say that the Land Commission has one-fifth of the purchase money lodged with them: is the whole one-fifth now in the hands of the Land Commission?—The Commissioners by law are obliged to retain one-fifth; but I apprehend the money never came to them; it is a mere book transaction, and as they obtain their money from the Treasury, the one-fifth for the guarantee deposit does not actually lie in their hands; it is arranged for by account between them.

1947. And in a certain time the companies claim that one fifth, do they not?—Certainly, after seventeen and a-half years.

1948. They have not claimed any of it at present?—They could not until that amount of capital has been paid off by the tenants' instalments.

1949. We have heard complaints about the tenants giving promissory notes; I think you said there were none on the Drapers' estates that you knew of?—I am sure that no promissory notes are given on the Drapers' estates for arrears of rents.

Mr. *Healy*.

1950. So far as you are aware?—So far as I am aware.

Mr. *Lea*.

1951. Have you heard any complaints of their being given on the Fishmongers' Estate?—I have not. I am not prepared to answer any questions upon the subject, because, really, I have no information on the subject, I have seen cases which came before the courts in the newspapers, but I really know nothing about them personally.

Mr. *Lea*—continued.

1952. On the Fishmongers' Estates, do you mean?—I do not know what estate, but I know there have been cases of promissory notes being sued for.

1953. With regard to the Salters' Company, have you heard complaints of their taking promissory notes?—I know there were some proceedings; but I am not acquainted with the circumstances under which the notes were given or sued for, nor do I know what the decision of the court was in the matter.

1954. Do you know Badger's case?—I do not.

1955. You are aware, perhaps, that a trial was before the courts, the Salters' Company against Badger, upon a promissory note?—When you mention the name, I think I do recollect that there was a case of that kind.

1956. Who inspected the land for the Land Commission in the case of the Salters' Company's sale?—I can only speak of myself. I inspected a portion of the Salters' Company's Estate round the town of Magherafelt, about 1,000 acres, known as the town parks of Magherafelt.

1957. Not the agricultural district?—I did not visit any part of the agricultural holdings.

1958. Somebody did from the Land Commission, I suppose?—No doubt.

1959. You do not know who it was?—I do not know who it was.

1960. Was the town of Magherafelt built by the tenants?—So I understood in the course of my inquiries there; all, or nearly all, of the houses were built by the tenants or their predecessors.

1961. Do you know how many years' purchase they paid for these houses built by themselves to the Salters' Company?—I do not think it would be right to say they paid so many years' purchase for the houses; because they were paying ground rents for the houses, and although they may have made complaints as to the amounts of the ground-rents, all they bought from the company was the ground-rents.

1962. The tenants bought from the Salters' Company at their full rents, I presume?—I presume they did; they extinguished their rents by purchase.

1963. They practically bought the houses they had erected?—They bought up the term of their leasehold rent and the company's reversion.

1964. You referred to a number of tenants who had not yet bought, on the Skinners' Estate?—Yes; there are a good many holdings I believe still unsold on the Skinners' Estate.

1965. Do you know why that is?—I presume the tenants have not yet come to an agreement with the company as to terms.

1966. Are you aware that on that part of the estate the tenants settled their judicial rents without going into the Land Court?—I do not know that to have been the case; but it is a very common occurrence in Ireland.

1967. And the company want them to buy upon this present rental?—I do not see any hardship in that; because after all what the vendor and his tenant have to do is to agree upon a lump sum in pounds, and whether it is 10 years' purchase of a high rent, or 25 years' purchase of a low rent really has nothing to do with the question. It is not as if Parliament had fixed some uniform

Mr. *Lea*—continued.

uniform rate of purchase; then there might be a dispute about the rent.

1968. Do you think that it is upon that basis that these tenants have not purchased their holdings?—Do you mean because they have been, or think they have been, asked too high a rate upon too high a rent? I do not know that to be the case.

1969. I think the question was asked you whether you knew anything of a syndicate for the purchase of that part of the estate?—I have not heard of it.

1970. A question was asked in Parliament, as perhaps you are aware, upon this point?—I did not notice it.

1971. If it is to be sold it ought to be sold to the tenants, ought it not, and not to a syndicate?—Certainly, if the tenants will buy it; but I should think it would be very difficult to sell it to a syndicate.

1972. You are not aware that there is any talk of a syndicate, or that one is being formed for the purpose of buying it?—No, I should not have thought it was possible to form one for such a purpose.

1973. Coming to the Drapers' estate, as Mr. Ellis has asked so many questions, I will only ask you two or three about it. Mr. Lynch said it was a gross violation of the rules of the Land Commission that caused the trouble there?—Yes.

1974. Do I understand that new rules have prevented any hardship being inflicted in future?—The rules of the Land Commission are directed to facilitating the procedure. The question of hardship can only arise in exceptional circumstances, as a landlord being in the position, owing to large arrears of rent, to compel his tenant to agree to terms which the tenant would otherwise refuse.

1975. Is it your experience that those cases of hardship are very exceptional?—In my experience I have met with absolutely nothing at all like the proceedings on the Drapers' estate.

1976. You referred to Mr. Glover?—I think the Court took a strong view of Mr. Glover's inadvertence; was he suspended for twelve months from acting as a solicitor in consequence?—Mr. Glover was suspended. But it always appeared to me a not unnatural mistake to have been made in a crowded office with a number of tenants coming in to sign these agreements; it was technically a grave mistake, but it was not an unnatural one to make.

1977. And he paid heavily for it?—He did.

1978. Do you know the arrangements which the companies make with their agents in selling their estates?—I do not.

1979. Do you know whether they are paid a commission upon the amount realised?—Do you mean their law agents who negotiate the sales, or the land agents?

1980. Either?—I am not aware.

1981. You are not aware of anybody who is paid a commission on the amounts realised?—I presume some one is; but I know nothing about the negotiations between the companies and their agents.

1982. Is it on the total amount realised?—I do not know anything about it.

1983. If it were so, would it not tend to obtaining of the biggest prices possible?—Certainly. If a commission is paid of course it would be paid on the amount for which the estate was sold.

1984. You mentioned to my honourable friend, Mr. Ellis, these reports of a deputation; I want to ask you one question with regard to them. On the second page of this report, it states that the maps and surveys of the company "are not always to be relied upon for accuracy as to quantity, and that since the last survey was made much land which was then in a state of mountain, and bringing but little profit, has been brought into a state of cultivation." That was evidently done by the tenants, was it not?—If you are reading from the report of the Drapers' deputation, taken in connection with the statement I quoted, I should presume it was so.

1985. The maps were wrong because the tenants had cultivated mountain land?—That is a process that is continually going on, and is going on at the present day on the Drapers' estate.

1986. You referred also to Mr. [illegible]' report of 1880 on the Drapers' estate?—Yes.

1987. This report was, that he placed in the county, and kept in repair, roads that had been many years ago blocked out by the Drapers' Company; do you remember that?—I have read the report, but I have not paid special attention to that point.

1988. I will give you the report if you like. He also says that "little narrow footpaths, in many places broken away, and, at most, not two feet wide, have been replaced by handsome footways from seven to nine feet in width, made at a cost to the county of nearly [illegible] *l.*" That is in his report; will you accept that, or would you like to see it for yourself?—I do not know what question you are going to put to me on that.

1989. He boasts that he has put upon the county the repairs of roads and footpaths, up to that time borne by the Drapers' Company?—Yes, he says so.

1990. Who pays the county cess?—The occupants, as a rule, in Ireland pay the county cess.

1991. Then, practically, it is putting upon the tenants the repairs of those roads which had hitherto been made by the Drapers' Company?—Certainly.

1992. That is an equivalent way of raising rent, is it not?—It would add to the burdens of the tenants; but it would be a very proper proceeding, because the county authority is the right one to take charge of the roads and their repairs.

1993. You stated, in Question 1183, that the companies had spent large sums of money in building Moneymore; do you know any public objects for which they spent other large sums of money?—I believe they gave grants to schools, but to what extent I do not know.

1994. I meant public objects, and not religious or educational objects?—I am not aware of any in Ireland.

1995. Do you know whether they lent or gave large sums for making railways?—I presume they took some part in the construction of the Draperstown Railway, which is some eight or

Mr. Lea—continued.

or nine miles long; but I am unable to say what they gave.

1997. Were these sums spent a good many years ago?—Moneymore has, I presume, been entirely built since 1817, but the expenditure must have been made at intervals.

1998. Has they have not spent much in these objects in the last 20 years?—I cannot say that I see any signs of any public buildings or repairs during a very recent date.

1999. Does not that look as though they were much more liberal half a century ago than they have been of late years?—I am quite unable to form an opinion as to what their liberality was half a century ago.

2000. Short leases have been referred to in the evidence as stopping the building of manufactories: has that been so in your experience of the Drapers' Company's estate?—My statement was with regard to the town of Moneymore, where the houses, having been all built by the company, the tenure was different from what it is in other towns where the landlord has frequently let for building, and the tenant becomes the owner of the house at a ground-rent and security for a long term of years.

2001. Are there no manufactories about Moneymore?—Moneymore appears to me to be as described in Mr. Simmons' report, without trade, and with a good many labourers in a state of abject poverty.

2002. Would manufacturers build factories on short leases?—I do not think it would pay them to do so.

2003. Would the refusal to give long leases tend to prevent manufactories in the district?—Certainly.

2004. In your answer to Question 1214, you say: "There was a reservation to the Irish Society, and the release from the Irish Society which was part of the company's title, was not produced till 1888." Can you tell me is it the practice for vendor companies to send any abstract or statement of title to the Land Commissioners?—I am informed by the solicitor who was acting for the tenants on the Moneymore division that the release from the Irish Society was not furnished to him until July 1888. But as I have nothing to do with the legal proceedings, I am not able to give you any information except that.

2005. The Irish Society then is made a party to each of the conveyances from the companies; is that so?—I do not know exactly what form the release has taken; but the reason for its requirement was that the company offered to sell the tenants the fee simple of their holdings; it was then found that mines, minerals, woods, and other similar reservations were made from

Mr. Lea—continued.

had; it was merely a question of what the tenants had agreed to buy.

2006. But the Irish Society had to join in the conveyance?—I said I could not tell you what form the release which they gave of their rights took.

2007. Is the statement of title a public record; do you know whether it is available?—I could not say, but I should think there would be no difficulty in inspecting it.

Colonel *Laurie*.

2008. Just now you said that the entire holding of the City companies' property in Londonderry was worth "millions;" do you mean 10 millions, or five millions, or two millions, or what do you mean by the expression "millions"?—The territory originally granted to the City of London.

2009. No; that is not the question that was put to you. The question was, what was the property in the county of Londonderry belonging, or which had belonged to the City companies, and you said "millions;" I want you to be a little more definite?—If you will allow me to answer the question in my own way, the original grant to the Corporation of London was the whole territory between the Foyle and the Bann.

2010. I admit that; but I want you to answer my point. You were asked whether the property belonging to the City companies was worth much, and you said it was worth millions; I want to get it a little more definitely?—I think that if you take the present value of the whole territory between the Foyle and the Bann, or that of the original portion belonging to the 12 great companies, taking in lands which are known to have sold, it will amount to seven or eight millions at least.

2011. Excluding Londonderry and Coleraine, and the rights of the Irish Society?—Yes, some of the estates have been sold for nearly half a million.

2012. Which company's estate has been sold for that money?—The Waterford estate, which comprised principally the Haberdashers' proportion, sold for very nearly half a million.

2013. Was that a more valuable property than the Salters'?—Not a bit; it was property very similar to the Salters'.

2014. The Salters' property fetched 230,000 *l.*, did it not, the other day?—No doubt you would be right there.

2015. I have a method of arriving at what the value was, but what I wanted to know was what you valued it at. We have it in evidence that the Salters' Company's property fetched 230,000 *l.* I think it was, or perhaps 240,000 *l.*;

Colonel *Laurie*—continued.

About that, I have no materials before me at present, or in my head, to give you any other estimate than what I have given, which would be that there are 12 companies, and their estates are very much of the same extent so far as I am aware, and that the value of these 12 propositions would run at least to three millions and a half.

2019. I thought you said five or six millions just now?—Yes, but I referred to the area originally granted.

2020. I wanted to correct the somewhat exaggerated ideas of the value of these companies' estates in the public mind. You know that the Merchant Taylors' was sold 100 years ago?—Yes.

2021. I presume they did not get anything like that price?—Certainly not; because the property has increased enormously in value.

2022. Do the Vintners' hold any property?—The Vintners' may hold rents; but they are not the immediate lessors of any property in Derry, I believe.

2023. Have you any idea of what the value of the property is to them?—It has been divided up among different people, I believe.

2024. To small companies?—No, but private owners.

2025. Has it been sold?—I believe they gave leases for ever, and that these have become divided; but if you take the whole territory between the Foyle and the Bann, I do not think that ten millions would be an over estimate.

2026. That may be so, taking Londonderry into account; but that was not the question asked you when you used the word "millions." I take it that something like three millions is nearer the amount in your opinion now?—I think that would be under the mark, if it were possible to define the territory originally granted; some of it no doubt has been lost.

Mr. Healy.

2027. How have the companies dealt with the question of turbary in selling their estates?—In the Moneymore division the company agreed to give the tenants whatever turbary rights they held at the time of the sale, and I believe that has been done. But taking the estate as a whole the turbary is very nearly exhausted.

2028. I see here in this Drapers' Company's report of the year 1817, which has been referred to, the company say, "No turbary is let as appurtenant to any land; the tenants took their fuel only by sufferance; this power was reserved over them to insure their votes at county elections"; is that continued in any way?—Turbary is not of sufficient value to enable it to be used as any such engine at present, for a great number of tenants on the estate get their turf on other estates.

2029. I may take it that the turbary is nearly cut out?—Mostly.

2030. It would form no ingredient in putting pressure upon them for the purposes of purchase?—None whatever.

Chairman.

2031. In answer to Question 1066, you read to the Committee a portion of your report upon this estate after your visit; will you put in the whole of that report?—Certainly. (*The same was handed in.*)

Chairman—continued.

2032. Will you tell us what action, if any, was taken in consequence of that report?—The Commissioners, having gone into the merits of each application, refused them in a letter addressed to the agent of the company in the following terms: "18th May 1889.—*Re* Estate of the Drapers' Company. Sir,—The Irish Land Commissioners have caused the 54 holdings on what is known as the Brackaghlislea division of the estate, and which are comprised in the agreements in the schedule herein named, to be inspected. These agreements appear to have been executed within the following dates: six in October and 25 in December 1888; 20 in January and three in March 1889. It appears that in the vast majority of these cases judicial rents had been fixed by the county court judge prior to the execution of the agreements, and that the original rents were in such cases inserted in the agreements as being the rents payable by the tenants, and that all information as to the existence of orders fixing judicial rents was withheld from the Commissioners. It further appears that at the date of, or subsequent to, the signing of these agreements, receipts were given by the solicitors for the company to many of the tenants for arrears of rent due prior to 1st November 1885, and for costs, and also receipts for two years' interest to 1st November 1888, on defined sums of money described in the receipts as 'the purchase money,' and apparently calculated at eighteen times the original rent. The total of the sums of unpaid costs treated in these receipts, when added to the purchase-money mentioned in the receipts so given for interest, appears to amount to the price named in the agreements for sale. Without entering into any question which might arise as to the impoverished condition of some of these tenants, the amount of arrears due, and the ejectment proceedings pending at the time of the execution of the contracts for sale, or to irregularities in the execution of two of these contracts, and without reference to the sufficiency of security, the Commissioners are not prepared to entertain applications for advances based upon agreements so prepared and entered into. The Commissioners are, however, further of the opinion that, with the exception of about 10 cases, the holdings do not offer adequate security for the advances applied for, and that in the excepted cases the agreements did not disclose the existence of judicial rents. Under these circumstances the Commissioners decline to sanction any of the advances applied for under the present agreements. Having regard to the facts now disclosed, the Commissioners, before directing an inspection on the Draperstown division, desire to be informed if judicial rents have been fixed on that section of the estate in any of the cases in which agreements have been lodged. Your obedient servant,—*John H. Franks.*"

2033. That letter, of course, is an acceptance by the Commissioners of your report?—Yes; it was based on my report.

2034. You would like the Committee, I gather from your answer to Mr. John Ellis, to take that as illustrating the practice of the Commission to take duress into account; although their immediate object is only a work of security, they do take duress into account?—Certainly.

2035. When

Chairman—continued.

2035. When it is likely to invalidate the security?—I think the Commissioners would dismiss any case in which they were aware that duress had been exercised, even if they thought the security was sufficient.

2036. As we are upon that point, I should like to ask you to say whether you would take a decision of one of the Commissioners, Mr. MacCarthy, of the day before yesterday, as illustrating the same temper in the minds of the Commissioners?—Mr. MacCarthy's decision was, I think, reported in nearly all the papers yesterday.

2037. Will you tell us in a sentence what the purport of it was, as bearing upon this point only; we have, of course, nothing to do with the decision as bearing upon the merits of the case; but only as illustrating the practice to which you referred in your evidence, of regarding the circumstances of the security outside its mere value?—Mr. MacCarthy's statement was to the effect that he would not sanction loans where persons had been placed in the possession of farms in the place of evicted tenants.

2038. That is to say, they would not sanction advances where old tenants had been evicted, and their places taken by those who are called planters or emergency men?—Just so; on the ground that it might lead to large evictions and the introduction into those holdings of a number of persons who might be merely adventurers, or who, at all events, were not *bonâ fide* farmers; and that the spirit of the Land Act would be transgressed by the Commissioners being parties to a proceeding which would practically lead to a state of disturbance and social disquiet in the neighbourhood.

2039. That is the drift of Mr. MacCarthy's decision?—That is my interpretation of his statement.

Mr. *John Ellis.*

2040. Is that judgment anything in the nature of a new departure?—I gather from Mr. MacCarthy's statement that a decision to that effect has not been given, but that he has acted upon that principle before now.

Chairman.

2041. You think that the Land Commission does rigorously refuse all cases where for any reason they regard the security for repayment to the Exchequer as insufficient?—Certainly; they consider that one of their principal functions.

2042. Was the number of refusals which you mentioned to Mr. Ellis the total number of applications refused since 1885, or what was the number?—I am unable to give you the total number, because applications are made in different forms, but the refusals have considerably exceeded 3,000 in number.

Mr. *Healy.*

2043. And how much did they represent in value?—Over a million and a quarter in value.

Chairman.

2044. Of course, what the Land Commissioners are thinking of in their condemnation of your Report, among other things, is this; that to include arrears in purchase is to enable the landlord or the vendor to recover bad debts at the risk of the Exchequer?—Certainly; it is to get an advance of a bad debt from the Land Commission and let them collect it.

2045. The attempt, therefore, was to make the Exchequer pay off those irrecoverable arrears, and then let the Exchequer take its chance of getting the money back again?—I think that is what the transaction would have amounted to if it had passed.

2046. That is to say, under the cover of enabling the tenants to buy the landlords' interest, proceedings of that kind really enabled the landlord to get arrears which otherwise he would have lost?—Yes.

2047. That, of course, would be to make the Purchase Bill an Arrears Recovery Bill?—The Commissioners have frustrated that in that and, I believe, in all other cases.

Mr. *Healy.*

2048. You say in all other cases; are you acquainted with the decision of the Commissioners in the case of Walsh against Lord Waterford, reported in the "Irish Law Times"?—I am not.

Mr. William Eccles, called in; sworn; and Examined.

Chairman.

2049. You are, I believe, Town Clerk of Coleraine?—Yes.

2050. Do you hold any other office?—I am Secretary to the Harbour Commissioners.

2051. You have held those offices for some time?—For the past 14 years.

2052. Why do you attend here?—I have been directed by those boards to submit resolutions which have been passed by each of them.

2053. Which boards do you refer to?—By the Town Commissioners and by the Harbour Commissioners.

2054. They passed two resolutions, I understand?—Yes.

2055. What was the effect of those resolutions?—The resolution of the Town Commissioners was passed on the second day of the present month, and is as follows: "That inasmuch as the Court of the Honourable the Irish Society of London acknowledge their trusts in connection with the city of Derry and the town of Coleraine, and are endeavouring to discharge their duties with due regard to local interests: *Resolved*, That this board strongly deprecate any change which would divert the funds for purposes other than those to which the revenue of the Society is at present liable."

2056. Was that the resolution of both those boards or of only one?—That was the resolution of the Town Commissioners.

2057. What was the resolution of the Harbour Commissioners?—The resolution of the Harbour Commissioners was passed on the 10th instant, and is much in similar terms: "That as the Court of the Honourable the Irish Society of London acknowledge their trusts in connection with

Chairman—continued.

with the city of Derry and the town of Coleraine, and have endeavoured to discharge their duties with due regard to local interests, contributing, among other grants for public purposes within recent years, a total sum of 37,340 l. towards the improvement of the navigation of the River Bann, and inasmuch as further sums are still required to complete these works; it is hereby resolved, That this Board strongly deprecate any change which would divert the income of the Society for purposes other than those for which their revenue is at present liable."

2058. You are here, as I take it, for two purposes: first of all, to commemorate the services of the Irish Society up to this point, and secondly, to deprecate any action which would induce them to discontinue those benefactions?—Yes.

2059. I should like to hear a little about those benefactions; what grants has the Irish Society made in connection with Coleraine, apart from those mentioned in the second resolution, which I will come to presently?—The first grant which the Society seem to have made for public purposes in Coleraine was made in the year 1858.

2060. Had they made any grants for religious and charitable purposes before 1858?—I have no information as regards that, but, excluding charitable and religious or educational grants, that was the first.

2061. You know nothing about the grants for religious, charitable, or educational purposes before 1858?—I am not aware of any educational grants or grants for religious purposes.

2062. They did exist, you believe?—They did.

2063. But they did not come within your cognizance?—I have no information about them.

2064. Your information, as I understand, relates to grants for public purposes?—Simply.

2065. What was the first public grant?—The first grant was a grant of 1,000 l. towards the erection of a town hall in Coleraine.

2066. What was the next?—The next grant was in 1877, and was a grant of 1,000 l. towards providing a public cemetery.

2067. Were there any more grants?—In 1883 there was a grant of 2,500 l. towards providing a town water supply.

2068. Of course, these are small sums compared with the sum of 37,340 l. mentioned in the Harbour Commissioners' resolution; would you explain to the Committee what the circumstances of that grant were?—The navigation of the River Bann was very bad prior to 1877, and in the year 1879 the Town Commissioners, who were then the harbour authorities, promoted an Act of Parliament, and obtained power to borrow a sum of 36,000 l. for the navigation, and a new board was constituted, the Harbour Commissioners then acting for the first time separate from the Town Commissioners. An application was made to the Irish Society.

2069. By whom?—By the then existing harbour authority, who were the Town Commissioners; and prior to the passing of the Act they agreed to have incorporated in the Bill a clause providing for a grant of 30,000 l. towards the improvement of the navigation.

2070. That is to say, as I understand, this body wished to raise a loan of 66,000 l., and then they went to the Irish Society, and did the Irish Society promise them 30,000 l. more?—They wished to raise 36,000 l. upon security of the river dues, and the rateable security of the town and the adjoining district; and, in addition, to obtain 30,000 l. from the society as a free grant.

2071. What did the Irish Society say?—They agreed to have that clause embodied in the Bill, and it was so passed.

2072. What was the clause, exactly?—That the Irish Society would contribute a sum of 30,000 l. for the improvement of the navigation of the River Bann.

2073. Can you give us the reference to the Act?—The River Bann Navigation Act, 1879.

2074. You have not got that Act, with the clause affecting the Irish Society, here?—I have not.

Mr. Healy.

2075. It was a Private Bill, was it not?—Yes.

Chairman.

2076. That Act was passed?—Yes; enabling the Irish Society to raise the sum of 30,000 l., and contribute that amount to the Harbour Commissioners.

2077. Do you know how the Irish Society raised that amount?—By bonds, repayable, I think, by drawings in a certain number of years.

2078. Repayable, of course, from their own resources?—Yes.

2079. They contributed 30,000 l., and the Town Commissioners raised by loan 36,000 l.?—Yes.

2080. I understand you have some wish to distinguish between two systems of effecting this improvement in the navigation, and that the distinction affects the subject before this Committee; is that so?—Certainly; there are two systems of navigation on the Lower Bann; the one a combined system of drainage and navigation, designed by Mr. M'Mahon in 1842.

2081. I do not know that we need go into that. After all, whether the Irish Society and the Harbour Board chose the right or the wrong system does not affect the inquiry before the Committee?—No; I do not wish to give evidence with regard to the combined system of navigation and drainage, but simply to distinguish it from the other; to distinguish the portion of the river on which the Harbour Commissioners have expended their money as separate from that portion of the river where the Board of Works have completed the drainage and navigation.

2082. I think that does not affect us here; all you have got to tell us as to the Irish Society, as I gather, is that they made certain grants for religious and charitable purposes, to the best of your belief (though you have no personal cognizance of it), before 1858; that in 1858 they made a grant of 1,000 l. for town works; in 1877 they made a grant of another 1,000 l.; and in 1883 they gave 2,500 l. for town works as well. Then you say they subscribed 30,000 l. for the navigation; but if it was only 30,000 l., why does the resolution of your Harbour Board talk of

Chairman—continued.

of 37,240 *l.*; how is the difference made up?—Prior to the passing of the Act, they contributed 33,000 *l.*, and subsequently to the passing of it they contributed 4,240 *l.*

2083. In all they have contributed 37,240 *l.*?—Just so.

2084. Speaking on behalf of these two representative boards, who have passed these resolutions, you wish to affirm on their behalf, that the feeling of the people in the town of Coleraine towards the Irish Society, is what?—Fairly good.

2085. They are fairly content with what has been done?—Yes.

2086. But they are looking forward with confident expectation to the continuance of those benefactions?—They hope so.

Mr. Lea.

2087. The money you have mentioned for the Bann drainage has been spent below the town entirely, has it not?—Yes, northwards of Coleraine; between Coleraine and the sea.

2088. What length of leases have the Irish Society given in Coleraine as a rule?—I believe four-fifths of the property in Coleraine would be held under perpetuity leases; I should think so.

2089. Have there been complaints among the religious bodies of how the charitable donations are given; the donations are not exclusively given to one body?—No; I do not hear of any special cause of complaint.

2090. Have there been any complaints?—In regard to educational grants I do not think the Roman Catholics have received any.

2091. Are they given to all the churches, the Catholic, the Presbyterian, and the Episcopal Church?—I have a general statement of the receipts and expenditure of the society, and for the two years preceding 1889 (the past year's statement has not yet been printed) I find no grants for educational purposes given to the Roman Catholics. During the past 18 months a new parochial house and schools have been built by the Catholics, and I think the society have made a grant; on what conditions I am not quite sure.

Mr. Clancy.

2092. Have you got that document with you?—I have a general statement of the receipts and expenditure (*handing the same to the honourable Member*).

Mr. Lea.

2093. I am only asking if they give grants generally to all religious denominations so far as you know?—I think until last year the Roman Catholics, so far as I am aware, received none.

Chairman.

2094. Have they never received any?—Not within my knowledge for educational purposes.

Mr. Lea.

2095. What you contend, as I gather, is that the Irish Society's money should be spent in Coleraine and Derry?—Yes, in accordance with the trusts.

Mr. Lea—continued.

2096. That is the sum of your evidence?—Yes.

2097. Do you know anything about the other London companies?—Not specially. The Clothworkers' property is partly situated in the town of Coleraine, but I have no special information that I think would be of assistance to the Committee.

Mr. John Ellis.

2098. Have the resolutions of these two bodies which you have read to the Committee, been communicated to the Irish Society?—They have not.

2099. You merely passed those resolutions, and you, as the clerk of the two bodies, bring them here?—Yes, I bring them before the Committee.

2100. What reason have you for the fear that is expressed in those resolutions?—At different times views have been put before the public that the trust funds of the Irish Society should be used for some more general purpose than the application to the city of Derry and the town of Coleraine.

2101. Has any communication been made to these two public bodies you represent that would lead you to fear any change?—Not recently.

2102. Will you explain what you mean by the word "recently"?—Some years ago the affairs of the society were under public discussion, and in Parliament the matter was frequently referred to in regard to the diversion of the funds for purposes more general than what they are at present applicable for.

2103. There is no question apparently, from these resolutions, as to the acknowledgment by the Irish Society of their trusts, or of this particular trust?—Just so. The society admit that.

Mr. Healy.

2104. You represent specially, I suppose, the Commissioners who obtained this Bann Navigation Bill of 1879?—And the Town Commissioners.

2105. I see they are very limited, a very select body indeed?—Yes, the board is appointed by nomination, by the Town Commissioners, and by the guardians of the Poor Law Union.

2106. I see they must be persons rated at not less than 50 *l.* a year?—Yes, or payers of dues.

2107. Which would be still more restrictive, would it not?—It makes the constitution of the Harbour Board certainly not by any means so representative as the constitution of the Town Commissioners Board.

2108. We may safely say, may we not, that there is not a more select body in Ireland than the body you represent?—I should think there are many.

2109. I presume you took office under this Act?—Yes, prior to the passing of the Act I held office under the Town Commissioners, who were then the Harbour Commissioners.

2110. You first obtained office under the Harbour Commissioners under the Act of 1879?—Yes, to the Harbour Commissioners.

2111. You said there were certain moneys advanced on the security of the tolls; will you kindly tell me the exact amount of the tolls you

Mr. Healy—continued.

have got under the navigation of the River Bann?—Taking the average of the last three years, I should say about 1,300 *l.* per annum.

2112. Have you formed any estimate of the amount of land that was flooded in order to enable you to get this grant?—The portion of the river over which the Harbour Commissioners have jurisdiction is not flooded.

2113. Could you give an estimate of the amount of damage done to the rest of the country in order to get this grant?—I would not acknowledge that there was any damage, because the improvement of the drainage of the rest of the river would not injure the navigation.

2114. What is the clause in this Act under which you say the Irish Society comes?—It is towards the end of the Act, and there is the form of mortgage bond provided in it.

2115. I see Clause 110 is: "It shall be lawful for the honourable the Irish Society to secure the repayment of all monies borrowed by them for the purpose of carrying out their proposed contribution of 20,000 *l.* towards the execution of the works in this Act mentioned by the issue of debentures," and so on. The society claimed all the fishings in the Bann, did they not. I observe that the Act is very cautious on the point; it does not in any way affirm your right. It says, "Whereas the governor and wardens of the new plantation in Ulster under and by virtue of letters patent," and so on, "claim to be seised and possessed of;" it does not say they are seised?—No, it is simply declaratory of an existing right; it does not give any right other than they at present possess.

2116. Can you give the total amount that the Irish Society make out of the fishings on the Bann?—I cannot say what amount they have rented the fisheries at; the amount is variable. The fishing has not been quite so good of recent years.

2117. Are the fisheries rented on lease or by precarious tenure?—They are rented upon lease. The same lessees seem to have been in occupation for a length of time.

Mr. Clancy.

2118. Do you represent to the Committee that in expressing the opinion of the Harbour Commissioners and the Town Commissioners of Coleraine you are expressing generally the opinion of the population?—I should think so, speaking broadly.

2119. What is the franchise upon which the town board is elected?—The town board is elected upon a franchise of upwards of 4 *l.* valuation.

2120. How many voters are there?—About 490.

2121. Out of a population of what?—Six thousand.

2122. Four hundred and ninety out of a population of 6,000 is not a very wide franchise?—A 4 *l.* valuation is not a very high franchise, I should think.

2123. It is not a very extended electorate?—In the clauses of the Town Improvements Act, under which the franchise is defined, I think there are provisions which are injurious to the

Mr. Clancy—continued.

voting interest. The length of occupation which is required, and other conditions, seem to be out of harmony with present legislation.

2124. You mean in addition to the restricted franchise the Registration Laws Act has a further restriction?—I do not think the franchise is so restricted, as, I think, the registration clauses in the Act make them more restricted than they should be.

2125. That is to say, the franchise is doubly restricted; first by the 4 *l.* valuation, and afterwards by the fact that it is difficult to get upon the register?—Very difficult; it requires two, and sometimes approaching three, years' occupation.

2126. In the face of these facts you could hardly contend, could you, that the Town Commissioners represent the general feeling of the population?—I should think fairly so. I think the Town Commissioners would indicate the pulse of the feeling in the community fairly well.

2127. How many Catholics are there on the Town Board?—Four.

2128. Out of how many?—Out of 18.

2129. What is the proportion of Catholics to Protestants in the town?—Something less than that upon the voting list.

2130. But I mean upon the general population?—I could not say quite so well with regard to that. There would be about one-eighth upon the voters' list, but I am not in a position to say what the actual percentage of the population would be.

2131. They would be more than one-eighth of the population, I presume?—Certainly.

2132. Are they not one half?—No, nothing like.

2133. Would they be one-third?—No, I should think not one-fourth.

2134. Have you a general idea of what the proportion of Catholics in Coleraine is to the general population?—I should say about a fourth, but I am speaking somewhat beyond my information in passing an opinion upon that.

2135. They are one-fourth of the general population, and only one-eighth on the voters' list?—I should think about one-eighth on the voters' list.

2136. They say in this resolution that the Town Commissioners are fairly satisfied with the administration of the funds by the Irish Society?—Yes, fairly so.

2137. I see an item in this general statement which you handed to me of 667 *l.* 14 *s.* 1 *d.* for "Visitation expenses, 1888, including cost of entertainments to public bodies and the tenantry;" are they satisfied with that. I suppose the Town Commissioners are always invited?—They are.

2138. I suppose a good deal of champagne is drunk at those entertainments?—Some complaints are made with regard to that part of the expenditure.

2139. By whom?—There are complaints with regard to its being rather unnecessary to expend annually so large a sum in that way.

2140. Is this sum of nearly 700 *l.* spent upon one banquet?—No, that would include a *déjeûner* in Coleraine and Derry, and perhaps some other

Mr. *Clancy*—continued.

expenditure which I am not very cognisant with.

2141. Two dinners, in fact?—I am not quite certain whether it includes perhaps some London expenses.

2142. What other expenses do you suggest are included under this head of visitation expenses?—If it is "Visitation expenses," it is confined entirely to expenses of that sort.

2143. That is to say dinners in Ireland?—Yes.

2144. In fact the 700 *l.* was spent upon two dinners?—There are two dinners in Derry, and one in Coleraine, I believe annually.

2145. May I take it the visitation expenses were the expenses of public dinners?—If it is so declared in the statement, no doubt it is so.

2146. No. They say here "Visitation expenses including cost of entertainments to public bodies and the tenantry"?—They may be personal expenses in connection with the members of the court visiting Ireland. I do not know how the details are made up; I have not access to the books of the society.

2147. But you come here to express satisfaction with the way in which the money is expended?—Yes, fairly; but with respect to these expenses that is a detail of which I cannot possess knowledge.

2148. This is a considerable item, it is nearly 700 *l.*?—Taking it broadly I should consider a high expenditure for such a purpose, but further than that I could not speak.

2149. Are the tenantry invited in a body?—Yes, the representative tenants, not all the tenants; such as the Irish Society might select.

2150. How many tenants have they got?—There would be about one hundred.

2151. How many are invited?—About a hundred sit down to dinner. There are more invitations than that, but there would be members who could not attend, and persons invited not able to be present.

2152. Do you say the company altogether numbers a hundred, or is that the tenants?—Those sitting down to dinner would be about a hundred to a hundred and twenty annually.

2153. How many of these are tenants?—Between eighty and ninety I should say roughly.

2154. Who selects the guests?—The court of the society; the invitations are sent out through the general agent in Derry.

2155. Are the same persons always invited?—Very much the same.

2156. The Town Commissioners and the Harbour Commissioners are always invited, I presume?—Yes.

2157. And they are very well satisfied, of course, with that part of the business?—I do not know that they are specially.

2158. Is that the reason they approve generally of the administration of the Irish Society's funds?—No; because I think there would be opposition on the part of some of the members of the board to the expenditure upon that item.

2159. I see the total income of the society, according to this statement you have handed in, is about 21,000 *l.*?—Yes; but that includes, I think, items of extra amount; I think the ordinary income of the society is between 17,000 *l.* and 18,000 *l.*

Mr. *Clancy*—continued.

2160. Would you point out the items here which go to form the permanent income of the society?—These figures would represent the permanent income: Received from "Derry and Liberties, 6,561 *l.* 16 *s.* 5 *d.*; Coleraine, 3,012 *l.* 8 *s.* 4½ *d.*; Culmore Fort and lands, &c., 764 *l.* 4 *s.* 3½ *d.*"; total, 11,343 *l.* 9 *s.* 1 *d.*; deduct "abatements to tenants, 336 *l.* 17 *s.* 0½ *d.*; balance, 11,001 *l.* 11 *s.* 6½ *d.*; for fisheries rent, 5,161 *l.* 15 *s.*; for rent of Lough Foyle Slobs, 700 *l.*; Quit rents from the Grocers,' Skinners,' and Ironmongers' Companies to 25th March, 1888, 34 *l.* 0 *s.* 11 *d.*"

2161. I understand these figures are already before us, so I will not ask you to go further into that. Do they practically spend all their permanent income in and about Coleraine and Derry?—Yes.

Colonel *Lewis*.

2162. There are no complaints on the part of the tenants about these dinners, I suppose?—There is a somewhat divided opinion. Some people of the town call it rather an unnecessary expenditure; some of them do not object much to it.

2163. Is it the custom in Ireland for landlords with large properties to give rent-day dinners to their principal tenants?—Not in that part of the country from which I come.

Chairman.

2164. Is it customary in any part of Ireland for landlords to give their tenants a feast?—Not to any extent that I am aware of.

Colonel *Lewis*.

2165. You were asked just now about the expenditure of the Irish Society in Coleraine; they contribute very handsomely to education there, do they not?—Yes.

2166. They maintain entirely one school?—Yes, they have free schools of their own.

2167. What are the schools called?—The Honourable Irish Society's Free Schools. They expend upwards of 800 *l.* annually on those schools.

2168. In fact they really pay the whole cost of maintenance?—They are under the National Board, so that the teachers have quite as much from other sources as they have from the Irish Society. They give them an annual allowance and then they have their salary and fees.

2169. The report states that this grant is dated from 1616; there have been grants to this school for nearly 300 years; is that within your knowledge?—Yes, I believe that to be correct. The charter to the town of Coleraine was in 1613, and in the same year the Society made a grant for free education in the town.

2170. And have maintained it ever since?—So I believe.

2171. The Act of Parliament produced just now was to give the Irish Society the necessary Parliamentary sanction, I presume, to raise the money by borrowing?—Quite so.

2172. That is the object so far as the Irish Society is concerned?—Yes, so far as regards the clause incorporated in the Bill.

Monday, 23*rd June* 1890.

MEMBERS PRESENT:

Mr. Clancy.
Lord Elcho.
Sir John Whittaker Ellis.
Mr. John Ellis.
Mr. T. M. Healy.
Colonel Laurie.
Mr. Lawson.
Mr. Lea.
Sir William Marriott.
Mr. John Morley.
Mr. Sexton.
Sir Richard Temple.

THE RIGHT HONOURABLE JOHN MORLEY, IN THE CHAIR.

Mr. AARON BAXTER, called in; and Examined.

Chairman.

2173. You are the Mayor of Derry for the present year, I believe?—Yes.

2174. How long have you been resident in Derry?—I have been 50 years resident in Derry.

2175. How long have you been a member of the corporation?—I have been a member of the corporation for 10 years.

2176. But you have been 50 years a resident?—Yes, in the city.

2177. During the whole of that time, or most of it, you have, no doubt, taken an interest in the affairs of the city?—I have.

2178. When was your corporation reformed?—I do not remember the date exactly.

2179. Looking at your charter and otherwise, in what position does the corporation regard itself as standing towards the Irish Society; or, if you like to put it the other way, how do they regard the Irish Society as standing to them?—We consider that they are entitled to give us assistance as a corporate body out of the funds of their trust.

2180. You do not regard them as lords of the manor are regarded; you regard them as trustees?—Yes, as trustees.

2181. You found that view of the Irish Society being trustees in respect of the corporation, I presume, on the judgment of the House of Lords in the Skinners Company's case in 1845?—Yes.

2182. You are aware that in that judgment the Lord Chancellor of the day said that the objects of the Irish Society "are public and important; and they were constituted for the purpose of carrying those objects into effect; that those objects are still in existence; that the funds of this district are applicable to those purposes; that they have a discretion to exercise as to what extent they will apply those funds, and to what objects." "The conclusion I come to," Lord Lyndhurst says, "appears to me to be irresistible; they are public officers, they have public duties to perform of an impersonal kind;" "they are to exercise their judgment as to what is necessary for the performance of their public duties, and after they have satisfied those duties, after they have applied to public objects what, in their judgment, in the fair exercise of that judgment, is necessary for those objects, then it is, and then only, that the surplus which remains, subject to their discretion, has been usually paid over to the companies." That, I suppose, is the kind of passage upon which the Derry Corporation found their view of the Irish Society being a trustee?—Yes, I believe it is.

2183. But are you aware that there are also passages in the official documents of the Irish Society which go further, and are even more specific; are you acquainted with what is called "The Concise View," a document published by the Irish Society?—No, I am not acquainted with it.

2184. Is not the Corporation of Derry acquainted with it?—I expect they are.

2185. Who is likely to be acquainted with it, if the mayor is not?—I expect the ex-mayor, who is to follow me, will give you some information about that.

2186. I suppose the ex-mayor, at all events, and probably other members of the corporation, are acquainted with this passage, where the Irish Society say that, "Notwithstanding the division of the estates amongst the 12 companies, such estates are to be considered still under the paramount jurisdiction of the Irish Society, and liable to contributions if necessary, in common with the indivisible estates in the Society's hands, towards supporting the civil government of the city of Derry"?—Yes; I believe the corporation entertain that idea; that is their view of the matter.

2187. That being their view of the matter, as you say, are you acquainted with any of the recommendations made by the Royal Commission which sat in 1854 upon the Municipal Corporation of London referring to the Irish Society?—No, I am not.

2188. You are not, in fact, well acquainted with the history of the relations between the Irish

Chairman—continued.

Irish Society and your corporation?—No, I am not thoroughly acquainted with it.

2189. We shall get that from Dr. Todd, I presume?—I expect you will.

2190. Do I understand the ex-mayor is to follow you here?—Yes; Sir William Miller.

2191. Have your corporation been in the habit of looking at the accounts of the Irish Society?—Yes, we have, from time to time.

2192. Has any fault ever been found with the expenditure and the account-keeping of the Irish Society?—The impression of some has been that they might be conducted at less expense, I believe; that is the expression I have heard expressed.

2193. That their expenditure is excessive?—It might be done for less.

2194. Are you acquainted with any public expression of those views?—Yes, I have heard it expressed.

2195. But have you heard any definite and public expression of those views?—No; it is just merely one and another mentioning it and making the remark.

2196. You do not remember a speech made by Sir Charles Lewis in 1875?—Yes, I remember he made a speech upon the subject.

2197. You do remember that?—Yes.

2198. Do you remember what the purport and drift of his speech was?—I think it was with regard to the expense.

2199. But you are not acquainted with it?—No.

2200. You say your corporation think some of the expenditure excessive; have they formed any view, for example, as to the cost of management of the Irish Society?—I cannot define any particular thing.

2201. Do you remember any memorial being drawn up in 1875 for abolishing the Irish Society.—Yes, I think there was such a thing.

2202. But you do not remember it with any accuracy?—No, not with any accuracy.

2203. You say you have looked into the accounts of the Irish Society; has anything been said in the meetings of your corporation, or among yourselves, as to the surplus which used to be handed over to the companies by the Irish Society?—I do not remember.

2204. Do you know how much the Irish Society now contributes to the funds of the city?—I have it here as 1,283 l. 10 s. 8 d.

2205. What year are you reading from?—This last year.

2206. The year 1888–89?—Yes.

2207. Is that the account from 1st February 1889 to the 8th February 1890?—Yes.

2208. Where did you get that figure from?—From our town clerk.

2209. What is the exact head under which it is put down; as I understand, there are two heads of contributions; the first is for public purposes?—Yes.

2210. And the second is for education?—Yes, education; but this is the amount contributed, as I understand, to the corporate funds.

2211. Do you say it is 1,283 l.?—Yes.

2212. It is in the account before me 1,300 l.; that is not a very marked difference. What do they contribute further in aid of public improvements, outside their contribution to the corporation?—They give large sums towards the public institutions in Derry.

2213. Can you give me the exact amount?—No, I cannot give the total amount.

2214. Does not the Mayor of Derry think it worth while to look into the accounts of the Irish Society?—Yes; but I did not know I would be asked on these points.

2215. If it would be more convenient to you to give your evidence in that way, would you read the paper you have got before you?—The first item is the term I have been living in the city of Derry, and the term I have been on the corporation. "The Irish Society contribute yearly towards the funds of the city 1,283 l. 10s. 8d., besides large annual payments towards public institutions in Derry and Coleraine."

2216. Have you no more definite statement than that they make large annual payments?—No, I have not the amount. Amongst others they have given us the toll-free bridge, and they contributed to our new water supply largely.

2217. How much did they give to the toll-free bridge, and when?—It is a number of years ago.

Mr. *Sexton.*

2218. Fifty or 60 years?—No; it is within the last 15 years, I should say.

Chairman.

2219. Do you know how much they contributed?—I have not the item.

Mr. *Sexton.*

2220. Is the town clerk here?—No, he is not here; he had, unfortunately, to leave.

Chairman.

2221. You spoke of the ex-mayor; is that Mr. Magee?—No; Sir William Miller.

2222. He, perhaps, will be able to give us the figures precisely?—I expect so.

2223. Are there any complaints, or any demands, or any suggestions, in the mind of your corporation as to the Irish Society to which you would wish to refer?—There has been a complaint years ago, that we did not get perpetuity leases; but during the last five or six years, or more, there has been a considerable change in our favour in that respect, especially under the governorship of Sir John Whittaker Ellis, and I hear few complaints now compared with what we have heard in previous years; there is general satisfaction as to the way in which the affairs of the Society are managed towards the city.

2224. There has been, you say, a long-standing opinion that leases ought to have been granted before?—Yes.

2225. Is there an opinion that the prosperity of Londonderry would have been more rapid if the tenure of land had been different?—Yes; I believe if they had been granted 30 or 40 years ago, the population, instead of being 35,000, would have been 50,000 by this time; I have no doubt of it.

2226. Would you explain the difference between the prosperity of Londonderry and that of

Chairman—continued.

of Belfast by the difference in the tenure?—Yes; I believe that what has tended to the prosperity of Belfast is that they got perpetuity leases there, and every encouragement for their action.

2227. That is to say, that Lord Donegal did more for Belfast than the Irish Society did for Londonderry; is that what you mean?—Yes, until lately.

2228. Until five or six years ago?—Yes.

2229. I will not ask you any questions as to the historical part of the case, or as to the accounts; but is there anything you particularly wish to bring before the Committee?—I have nothing that I particularly wish to say, unless it be that if there were greater encouragement given in the way of granting leases, and especially to parties building manufactories, who should especially be dealt with liberally, to encourage the prosperity of the city, I believe that would be a great advantage. They should be raised on liberal terms as regards the ground-rent for the erection, especially, of buildings for manufacturing purposes.

2230. Do you mean that the ground-rent charges are too high?—I have heard that stated by some parties.

2231. Is that your own opinion?—Yes.

2232. You have just said that the Irish Society would do well for the prosperity of your town if they charged lower ground-rents?—Yes.

2233. Assuming, of course, that they persisted in this policy of granting leases?—Yes.

2234. As to the disposal of the surplus funds, they have every year a surplus over and above their expenditure?—Yes.

2235. Have you any views as to the disposal of that surplus?—For educational purposes, I presume you mean.

2236. Does the corporation think that that surplus ought to be devoted exclusively to Derry purposes?—Yes; so far as the trust of the Irish Society exists with regard to the city.

2237. I do not think I quite understand your answer. Does or does not your interpretation of the trust you have told us of mean that the whole surplus ought to go to the purposes of the city of Derry and the town of Coleraine?—Yes.

Sir William Marriott.

2238. What kind of leases do they want?—Perpetuity leases.

2239. At a fixed ground-rent?—Yes.

2240. Will you tell me what ground-rent is it that is too high; do you know of any?—The only ground-rent in my recollection at present is round where the new municipal buildings are erected.

2241. Who is the lease to in that case?—It is only with regard to leases that have yet to be granted that I was speaking.

2242. I gathered from you that some of the ground-rents are too high, and I wanted an instance of it?—I do not suppose that those who have got perpetuity leases consider that they are too high, possibly they do not; but it is with respect to future leases that I am speaking.

2243. Then, as a matter of fact, there are no

Sir William Marriott—continued.

ground-rents at present which you know of that are too high?—No.

2244. It is only that you have a fear for the future?—Yes.

Sir John Whittaker Ellis.

2245. Suppose the whole of the leases which the Society granted some years ago had been perpetuity leases, and at very low ground-rents, what would have been the result to the revenues of the Society, which are expended in Derry and Coleraine?—I suppose it would have reduced their revenue somewhat.

2246. Therefore their opportunity for good would have been reduced in a like manner?—I do not know that I follow you.

2247. Supposing they had granted those leases, as is suggested, you know, at very low ground-rents, in point of fact at less than they ought to have granted them, those leases being in perpetuity, there would have been no increase whatever; whereas under the system adopted, now the leases have run out, they have increased the revenues of the Society some thousands a year, which is all spent in Londonderry and Coleraine?—Yes; but I refer to the ground which is now falling into your hands, which I think ought to be dealt with liberally.

2248. I will ask you upon that, are you aware that the Society always take the very best advice of the local people in the neighbourhood, and make personal inquiries as to the letting of other property?—I believe they do.

2249. And never ask more than they find is fairly to be charged; do you think that they would be fulfilling their trust, as you put it, if they let their property at less than what they find is the proper value of the citizens of Derry?—It depends upon the view the parties take of the matter. It is with the view to encourage the manufactories in Derry, which we want very much, that I think the leases granted should be granted as liberally as possible in such a case.

2250. I suppose you are aware, even by common knowledge, that there is a very large area of the property of the Society let upon perpetuity leases?—Yes.

Colonel *Laurie.*

2251. In the account of the Irish Society which I have before me for the year you were speaking of just now I find their income from the town of Derry amounts to 6,581 *l.*?—Yes.

2252. And there is Coleraine and the fisheries beside. I suppose you admit that if they spend in Derry the amount of the revenue derivable from Derry, Coleraine has a right to its share?—Yes.

2253. We have been told that the grant to schools from the Irish Society was 2,843 *l.* in Londonderry alone, and to other charities in Londonderry, 48 *l.* 10 *s.*; then the mayor and corporation receive, as you have told us, 1,223 *l.*, which makes up, in round numbers, taking the figures from the published accounts, 4,500 *l.*?—Yes.

2254. Then I find this item: "In aid of public improvements, building expenses, &c., in

Colonel *Laurie*—continued.

in Londonderry, Coleraine, and Culmore 5,823 l. 6 s. 1 d.?—Yes.

2255. How large a proportion of that 5,823 l. 6 s. 1 d. would you consider was expended in Londonderry; are the Irish Society spending money in public improvements and building in Londonderry?—They are.

2256. What proportion should you imagine of this 5,823 l. 6 s. 1 d. is being spent in Londonderry?—I could not give the figure. I know they give grants to Foyle College and to the Magee College and to the Academical Institution; they give about 400 l. a year at present. Some of the grants are terminable.

2257. Do you understand what I am asking; I am not asking what they spend in salaries for teachers, exhibitions, and scholarships, but I am asking what they are spending in public improvements and building expenses in Londonderry; may I take it from you that they are spending considerable sums?—Yes, they are.

2258. Do you imagine that out of the 5,800 l. a fair and reasonable proportion is spent in Londonderry?—I believe so.

2259. In that case it appears to me the whole of the money that is being received from Londonderry is being expended in the place itself? —Yes, I believe so, at least to a large extent it is.

2260. Then what surplus do you lay claim to. You have just told me that 4,300 l. was spent, in the year I have taken, on schools and charities in Londonderry, and that you get a fair proportion of the 5,823 l.; surely you are enjoying fairly the income received in the form of the company's rents in Derry?—I believe we are to a fair extent.

2261. You say that Coleraine is entitled to its share?—Yes.

2262. If you got your share you ought to be satisfied?—If we get our share we are satisfied.

2263. If the rents are smaller of course your advantages are smaller?—Yes.

2264. Then practically you have no complaint if the income is being practically spent in Londonderry?—No.

Mr. *Sexton*.

2265. The Irish Society formerly assumed a control over your Derry corporation?—I believe they did.

2266. Do they now exercise or attempt any control?—No.

2267. The only relations between you as a corporation and the Society, are your relations to them as landlords and as contributors to the civic funds?—Yes, as trustees.

2268. Has Coleraine been differently treated from Derry in the matter of perpetuity leases?—I am not aware.

2269. You said, in reply to Colonel Laurie, that you had no complaint with regard to the expenditure of the money; are you aware that there has been for a long time a very indignant feeling in Ireland in regard to the amount of the expenses of management?—I have heard it stated by parties that the expenses might be less.

2270. There was a predecessor of yours, Mr. Haslett, who was mayor of the city in 1843. I want to refer you to what he said on the subject of the expenses of management. He took the 23 years from 1817 to 1843, and he said this, if you will kindly listen to it: "Now observe the case the Society wish to make for themselves is this, that they are trustees, and that the primary object of their trust is to promote the interests of the City and County of Londonderry; yet during 23 years, the most favourable for them of the last 150 years of their total expenditure, very little more than one-fifth has been laid out for the promotion of those objects for which they say they were originally constituted, and are still continued." Do you think that observation might still be made with any force as against the Irish Society?—No, I think not.

2271. Do you think the observation might still be made that the expenses of management are higher than they need be?—That is the impression I have heard expressed.

2272. Are you aware of the complaint that the Society appropriated to themselves 1,300 acres of land which the city of Derry held itself to be entitled to by charter?—I am not aware of that.

2273. I wish to ask you one question with regard to a certain petition. In the year 18[illegible] a petition was presented to the House of Commons from the corporation of Derry, and the magistrates of Derry, the police committee, and the inhabitants, and I want to read you these words from the petition: "That from the nature of their constitution, the Society" (that is the Irish Society) "is incapable of rendering any permanent benefit to this country, as it is composed of merchants and tradesmen in the City of London, whose business requires their constant residence therein, whereby they are of course ignorant of the local circumstances and wants of the inhabitants of this district, and besides, being elected for only two years, cannot possibly acquire the information proper to qualify them for the due discharge of their duties." I want to ask you whether you consider that this trust of Irish territory for Irish uses would be better administered by Irish trustees, by local trustees resident in Ireland, than by a London body, such as is described in this petition emanating from your city?—Some are of opinion that it would be, and others not.

2274. You come here as a witness; what I want to know is your opinion?—We are satisfied with the manner in which the Society of late have been managing and distributing the trust; but I have heard it expressed that if the Society were so constituted that the members of it were for a longer time members of the Society (I think it is only two years they are elected for) they would have a better knowledge of the affairs in the city of Derry.

2275. But are you aware of any reason why Englishmen living in London should be better trustees of Irish trusts than Irishmen living on the spot?—No, I am not.

2276. You think that local trustees would be more efficient?—I have heard that expressed.

2277. But you very modestly refrain from giving your opinion; what do you think yourself?—

Mr. Sexton—continued.

self?—Possibly it would be better to be in the hands of local parties.

2278. You have said that the expenses of management are high?—Yes.

2279. Do you know any other bodies in which the expenses of management are so high as those of the Irish Society?—I am not aware.

2280. Does it occur to you that the expenses would be lower if the estates were administered on the spot?—Possibly.

2281. So that there would be more money available for local purposes?—It might be so.

2282. Where there would be greater knowledge of local circumstances?—Yes, it might be so.

Mr. Lea.

2283. Did you say that the Irish Society gave perpetuity leases in the city of Derry?—Yes; they have given them to some parties.

2284. The clerk to the Commissioners at Coleraine stated that four-fifths of the leases in Coleraine were perpetuity leases given by the Irish Society; is it so in Derry?—I am not aware that it is.

2285. The Irish Society has alone to do with the city of Derry; the other London companies have nothing to do with it, I understand?—I believe not, without they come round Derry.

2286. Is it the popular impression in Derry that the other London companies hold under the same tenure as the Irish Society?—It is.

Mr. Clancy.

2287. Do you know anything about the administration of the trusts of the Irish Society before your mayoralty?—No, I have no accurate knowledge.

2288. You can give no evidence as to the administration of the trusts?—No.

2289. You come here simply as expressing the satisfaction of the corporation of Derry with the present administration of the trust?—Yes.

2290. What is your municipal franchise in Derry?—£. 10.

Mr. Clancy—continued.

2291. How many voters have you in Derry?—I could not state the number.

2292. Are there 500?—More than that.

2293. Have you 1,000; cannot you give an approximate estimate?—There must be 700 or 800, I should say.

2294. Do you think the corporation fairly represents the citizens?—There is only one member of the Catholic Church a member of the corporation.

2295. How many Catholics are there in Derry?—About half the population; I should say nearly half.

2296. What is the population of Derry?—I should suppose now about 35,000.

2297. There are 17,000 or 18,000 represented by one person in the corporation of Derry?—Yes.

2298. In the face of that fact, you could hardly say that the corporation represents the general population in Derry, I should say?—Perhaps not.

2299. You are speaking the opinion of those who have had the benefit of this trust in the past?—Yes.

2300. They would like to have it continued to their party in the future?—I do not think there is any party feeling in the matter; they want it for the benefit of the city generally.

2301. Can you conceive no improvement which you could suggest in the administration of the trusts?—Nothing beyond what I have stated.

2302. You are not quite sure whether it could be managed better in Ireland than in England?—I am not quite sure.

2303. Or by residents in Derry?—I am not quite sure.

Mr. Sexton.

2304. I think you admitted that there might be certain advantages in Irish management?—It might be; it depends very much upon the parties appointed.

Sir WILLIAM MILLER, called in; and Examined.

Chairman.

2305. You have been Mayor of Derry, I believe?—Yes.

2306. When were you mayor?—I was mayor in 1875, 1876, and 1877, and again in 1886 and 1888.

2307. You have been mayor five years in all?—Yes.

2308. As mayor, did you make it your business to go into the accounts of the Irish Society?—I have read the published accounts; I know nothing further of them than that.

2309. Could you tell us a little more fully than the mayor was able to do, what are the items under the head of "Public improvements, building expenses, &c., in Londonderry"?—Do you mean as it is at present?

2310. Yes; this account before us is for the year 1886–88, and the amount under that head, in Londonderry, Coleraine, and Culmore, is

Chairman—continued.

5,823 *l.*; can you tell us on what objects that is expended?—At present there is a large expenditure for the new Guildhall going on. That is a grant that was made between three and four years ago, and I believe the total grant the Irish Society gave us was somewhere about 16,000 *l.*, and it is being given to us year after year as the building goes on. It is now completed.

2311. What other objects are there?—There was a considerable amount given to the enlargement of the Derry Cathedral and the embankment at Culmore, also at the Bannmouth, Coleraine.

2312. Culmore is not in the city of Derry, is it?—It is within four miles; it is included in the liberty.

2313. It is not within the boundaries, is it?—It is not within the municipal boundaries, but it is within the lower liberty of the city of Derry; the city itself.

2314. Can

Chairman—continued.

2314. Can you tell us what the liberties of Derry are; the item figures here as "Derry and liberties"?—It is a certain three miles round the city.

2315. But Culmore is not within the three miles, is it?—It is just outside; but I rather think there is a special arrangement with regard to it. I cannot tell you of my own knowledge. I know that although Culmore, geographically, is within the county of Donegal, it is within the county of Derry for taxation purposes.

2316. Are there any other objects?—There is the freeing of the Derry bridge.

2317. When did the freeing of the Derry bridge take place?—In 1878.

2318. How much did that cost?—I think it was 40,000 *l.*

2319. How much did the Irish Society contribute?—I should correct myself. The total sum for freeing it, I believe, was 80,000 *l.*, and the Society gave a moiety of 40,000 *l.*; it is being paid off gradually.

2320. If you were mayor in 1875 you were mayor when Sir Charles Lewis, if I may use the word, denounced the expenditure of the Irish Society?—I was.

2321. Did public opinion support that denunciation; did they think that the cost of management, for example, was excessive?—At that time I think public opinion did support that view.

2322. Is there any feeling that the cost of management is still excessive?—I believe it is.

2323. What is the ratio now, according to the accounts for 1888–89, of the cost of management to the total outlay; how much do you make it out to be?—It is between 20 and 25 per cent.; as well as I remember, I think it is over 4,000 *l.* out of an income of 20,000 *l.*

2324. Supposing it to be, as you say, from 20 to 25 per cent., is that supposed to be an excessive cost?—I think so.

2325. Have you any view as to the point at which the excess takes place, or what items they expend too much upon?—I think the general view is that the expenditure is too large.

2326. We have, for example, item of Visitation Expenses, including cost of entertainment to public bodies and the tenantry; does that mean the tenantry of Londonderry as well as Coleraine?—It does.

2327. What sort of entertainment to the tenantry is that?—Of late years there has always been a large dinner given.

2328. What, in your opinion, is the ordinary cost of managing an urban or town estate?—I believe an agent would be generally satisfied with five per cent.; I have heard it said so. Of course I do not know of my own knowledge.

2329. When you say five per cent., do you include the total cost of collecting, incidental law expenses, and bad debts?—No, I would not; I would be simply including the cost of collecting the rent only.

2330. Of course, in an ordinary case, there are no such items as visitation expenses?—No.

2331. It would seem to follow, in your view, that a more economical method of administering this estate would be to divest the Irish Society of its present position there; if its cost of management is, on your lowest estimate, 15 per cent. above what you would be inclined to think necessary, that would be a reason surely for reforming the expenditure of the Irish Society, or for putting in place of it a more economical body, would it not?—It would.

2332. Is it your view that a more economical body could be devised?—I should suppose it could be.

2333. You are aware, perhaps, as you have evidently followed the history of your town, that in 1854 there was a Royal Commission which sat upon the Corporation of London. I should like to ask your opinion at the present day upon a recommendation of this Commission which sat in 1854, which is a good many years ago?—I should say that that was before I took any part in public business.

2334. Quite so; but I want to know whether since you have taken part in public business, since 1873 for example, your experience confirms the view which this Royal Commission took in 1854. What that view was I will now tell you; "The leading advantages which formerly accrued from the connexion of the managing body with the Corporation of London have ceased; and their distance from the place where the estates are situated necessarily creates embarrassment in their administration as well as much additional expense. For these reasons we recommend that the Irish Society be dissolved, and its charter repealed, by Act of Parliament; and that its property be vested in a new set of trustees, whose number and character should be defined in the Act. We recommend further that the trustees be appointed by the Lord Chancellor of Ireland, and that he have power to fill up vacancies as they occur from time to time." You have gathered from that, I presume, what the recommendation of that Commission was?—Yes.

2335. Does your experience bear out the prudence of that recommendation?—Up to some few years' ago; but certainly not within the last few years.

2336. When you say "a few years ago," what is the date to which you refer?—Especially since the present Governor took office.

2337. That is seven years ago, I understand?—Yes.

2338. You think that within the last seven years such changes have been made as to no longer make it desirable to carry out this recommendation of the Royal Commission of 1854?—I would go so far as to qualify it in this way: that since Sir Whittaker Ellis took office the administration has been much more liberal towards the tenantry, and the tenantry are much better satisfied with the administration now than they were in former years.

2339. But on the point which we were talking about, namely, the cost of management, has there been a diminution in the percentage of the cost of management since 1883; because you said just now that the expense was 20 or 25 per cent.?—Yes.

2340. You seemed to think that this was excessive; I want to know if it was still more excessive

Chairman—continued.

expensive before 1863?—I have not the figures of 1863 in my recollection, and of course I can scarcely give an opinion about that. My opinion was more as to those previous years with regard to the question of the renewal of leases and the dealing with the tenantry in that way, than as to the expenses at that time.

2341. Do you think that the Commission of 1854 were wrong when they said that (because this fact of distance remains true) that "their distance from the place where the estates are situated" (that is to say, the distance of the Irish Society) "necessarily creates embarrassment in their administration, as well as much additional expense;" do you think that that consideration is still of weight?—Of course the distance question still exists; but it does not exist to the same extent as it did then, because the facilities for travelling are so much greater.

2342. Let me point out to you that in these accounts the expenses in England are very little short of being as great as the expenses in Ireland, in spite of this increased nearness?—Undoubtedly we do think the expenses in England are too large.

2343. Do you think them greatly too large?—Of course I cannot tell what all the expenses of England are for. Of course there must be law expenses in England as well as in Ireland, and necessarily with renewal of leases and different other proceedings in that way, I presume, there must be expenses in England which could not be avoided.

2344. Of course there is no item in the English expenditure so heavy as the item of 667 *l.* which goes to visitation expenses in Ireland?—No.

2345. But are you prepared to say that the changes since 1883, when Sir John Ellis became Governor, whatever those reforms may amount to, put an end to the value of the recommendation of the Commission of 1854?—No, I am not prepared to say that.

2346. You think there is still some force left in that recommendation?—I do.

2347. The reforms, as I gather, since 1883, have chiefly concerned the relation of the Irish Society with the tenants?—Not altogether. The reforms have been that they have been much more liberal in granting money for public improvements.

2348. They have been more liberal since 1883 in granting money for public improvements?—They have; and they have also been more liberal in granting leases to the tenantry; in both those respects they have been more liberal.

2349. Can you tell us how much more they give now than they did in 1883 for public objects. We can get the figure later; but if you chance to know it, it might be convenient to take it now?—I cannot exactly tell you, further than this; that I know the question of the new Corporation Hall or Guildhall was agitated frequently before Sir Whittaker Ellis' time; because for at least the past 25 years, since I became a member of the Corporation, it frequently was agitated and brought before the Society, altogether unavailingly; and after Sir Whittaker Ellis was appointed he took it up cordially; and the result was the grant of the site and 16,000 *l.* for the erection of the hall.

2350. Upon the other head, in regard to the more liberal terms to the tenants, would you kindly explain how the terms are more liberal now than they were?—In some cases when leases fell in, I understand they have disposed of the sites in perpetuity. It was one of the old grievances that leases could not be got in perpetuity in former years.

2351. Do you agree with the last witness, that it is owing to the refusal to grant those leases that Londonderry allowed Belfast to shoot ahead?—I do perfectly. I believe that if 70 or 80 years ago perpetuity leases had been granted, we in Derry would probably have been in the position in which Belfast now is.

2352. Then you agree with the last witness, that Lord Donegal acted better for his town than the Irish Society did for theirs?—At the time.

2353. Up till when?—Up to the last few years.

2354. Up to 1883?—Yes.

2355. I asked whether you agreed with the Commission of 1854 upon one passage which I have just read to you; now would you agree with this: "A control of this kind, maintained at the present day by the municipality of one town in England over another in Ireland, appears to us so indefensible in principle that our opinion would not have been changed even if it had been found that hitherto it has been conducted with discretion and forbearance." The Commission of 1854 there says it is not expedient or defensible in principle that an English municipality should have the control over an Irish municipality which the London Irish Society has over the Corporation of Londonderry?—Yes.

2356. You agree with that?—I do perfectly.

2357. You think in principle that the relation between the Irish Society and the Corporation of Londonderry is an indefensible relation in principle?—I do.

2358. You have been mayor for five years at one time and another, and in that capacity I presume you have the means of knowing the opinion of your townsmen; may we take it that your opinion is the opinion of most of your townsmen?—So far as this goes: I am merely dealing with the question as to the bye-laws made by the Derry Corporation, which require to be submitted for the approval and sanction of the Irish Society.

2359. That is by the terms of the Charter of Londonderry, is it not?—It is. The reason I give that opinion is this: that it causes an immense amount of delay in regard to the sanctioning of new bye-laws. I am not aware that any instance has occurred where the Irish Society have interfered or prevented our passing a bye-law; but it has caused considerable delay where we have found it necessary to pass new bye-laws dealing with certain questions, such as the management of the markets and things of that kind; and consequently it has interfered with us to a certain extent in that way.

2360. You would say not merely is this relation between the Irish Society and your Corporation

Chairman—continued.

Corporation indefensible in principle, but it does result in substantial and practical inconvenience?—Just so far as I have mentioned.

2361. The bye-laws are delayed and your city suffers inconvenience in consequence of the delay?—I am afraid I could not go so far as to give a practical instance of any inconvenience further than just that, that we think if we pass a bye-law there should not be a delay of perhaps five or six months.

2362. Has the Irish Society never interfered with any bye-law proposed by you?—I am not aware that they have.

2363. Then as to the power of interfering with the bye-laws, that has never, so far as you know, been used?—I am not aware it ever has.

2364. We have referred to the attack made by Sir Charles Lewis in 1875; was there not a memorial sent up from Londonderry in consequence of that attack?—There was.

2365. Whom was it sent to?—I think it was transmitted to Sir Charles Lewis. I am not positive, but so far as my recollection goes, it was sent to Sir Charles Lewis.

2366. Can you tell us what the drift of that memorial was, and what the signatories wanted?—I really cannot go into that now.

2367. You do not remember?—I quite remember there was a memorial. My impression is that my own signature was the first to it.

2368. You were then the mayor?—I was.

2369. But you cannot tell us whether or not the memorial is truly described as being "a memorial for appointing new trustees from local gentlemen who should be thoroughly independent men of high public character and standing, and that the new trustees should apply the whole of the funds, deducting the necessary expenses, for the benefit of the city of Derry, and the town of Coleraine;" you cannot say whether that is a true description or not?—No, I cannot.

2370. Have you any suggestion to make to the Committee as to making the relations between the Irish Society and your Corporation better; is there anything you think the Irish Society ought to do which they leave undone?—We would be delighted to get more money from them.

Mr. *Lea*.

2371. The Chairman has just asked with regard to Sir Charles Lewis' memorial; do you know why Sir Charles Lewis did not proceed any further with the matter?—I do not.

2372. From whence did the Irish Society derive its property?—I believe it was from the Crown.

2373. But where does its present income come from?—It comes partly from landed property, and partly from house rents in Derry, and a considerable amount of it comes from the fisheries.

2374. You consider it comes from the city of Derry?—And from the town of Coleraine.

2375. And it should be retained for Derry; is that your contention?—Certainly.

2376. You spoke of the agricultural tenants; has the society many agricultural tenants?—They have a considerable number.

Mr. Lea—continued.

2377. What have been their relations with the agricultural tenants generally?—Of course there has been a certain amount of dissatisfaction.

2378. Why?—I think the tenants thought they should have got their holdings at reduced rents, particularly since the Land Acts were passed.

2379. Have there been many cases in the Land Courts?—I believe there have.

2380. Were the rents reduced in the Land Courts by the Commissioners?—I rather think so.

2381. Then as regards agricultural leases, have leases been given to agricultural tenants?—They have, to a certain extent.

2382. Were they as short as the town leases?—I do not exactly understand the question.

2383. Were leases given to the tenants of the agricultural part of the Irish Society estate?—They were.

2384. Were those leases as short as the town leases?—They were shorter in the majority of instances. I am not aware that any perpetuity leases were granted to the agricultural tenants at all.

2385. Do you know anything about the agricultural tenantry?—Yes, I do; I happen to be an agricultural tenant myself.

2386. What were the terms of the leases given?—In some few instances there were long leases given. After the Royal Commission in 1834, my father and the late Mr. Anthony Babington, and the late Mr. William Moore of Mullenan, all got leases for 61 years.

2387. As agricultural tenants?—Yes.

2388. Did other tenants get those leases?—There may have been a few others; but I cannot give you the names, with the exception of those I have mentioned. I think the late Mr. Samuel Law Crawford got the same tenure of lease at that time.

2389. With regard to the agricultural tenants generally, when the leases came to an end was there a considerable advance in the rent?—I have been told there was; I do not know it of my own experience.

2390. Have you heard much complaint or have you heard of grievances on the part of agricultural tenants at the end of their leases?—I have.

2391. Can you tell me the reduction of the rentals in the courts?—I think to the best of my recollection it varies. There was a Mr. Harvey and also a Miss Mills who lived in the Upper Liberty, and I think they got reductions to the amount of about 25 per cent.; but I could not trust my memory to speak positively.

2392. Do you know a tenant of the name of Mr. Samuel Osborne?—Yes.

2393. Has he complained very much of the action of the Irish Society?—He has.

2394. Do you know whether he was greatly raised at the end of the lease?—I believe he was, but I should add that I believe he has got very large reductions since that.

2395. The Chairman asked you with regard to Belfast; do you know Mr. Harland's, now Sir Edward Harland's, shipbuilding yard in Belfast?—Yes.

Mr. Lea—continued.

2396. Do you know whether he applied to the Irish Society for a lease at Derry?—I have heard it stated. I do not know it of my own knowledge.

2397. If Messrs. Harland & Wolff had established their shipbuilding yard at Derry, what would have been the result?—It would have been an enormous improvement to the city of Derry.

2398. Is not the popular opinion that the Irish Society refused a sufficient length of lease to Messrs. Harland & Wolff?—I have heard it stated so.

2399. You do not know it as a fact?—I do not.

2400. Do you know whether the Irish Society possess the foreshore?—It is generally believed that they do.

2401. Are they willing to make grants of the foreshore?—I cannot state that positively. I have heard it stated that they do not; but I do not like to repeat what does not come under my own knowledge.

2402. With regard to the other London companies, do you know much about them?—Not a great deal.

2403. Is it considered that they hold under the same tenure as the Irish Society?—I have always understood so; and whatever the tenure of the Irish Society was, that in dividing the lands among the twelve companies they carried on the trust to them.

2404. And if the Irish Society spends all its money in Derry, the London companies ought to spend all their income in the estates where they are situated?—So we think.

2405. There is a strong impression to that effect?—There is.

Mr. John Ellis.

2406. With respect to the case of Mr. Osborne that has been mentioned, are you acquainted with his holding personally?—I am.

2407. Then you will be quite aware that a large portion of the rental value of the holding has been created by his outlay of capital?—I believe so.

2408. Have you been over it?—Yes, I have.

2409. You mentioned that he had received a large reduction of rent; was that received in the Land Court?—I have heard it stated that he settled with the society without going into the Land Court.

2410. Did he take any proceedings that induced them to make this reduction of rent?—I believe he did; he withheld his rent, he did not pay for a year or two. That was a most important proceeding.

2411. But he withheld his rent on the assumption, I presume, that the rent was not a fair one?—I presume so.

2412. Then after his so proceeding, the company made him a large abatement of rent?—So I have heard.

2413. You suggested to us that there had been a great change of policy on the part of the company in the direction of greater liberality in the year 1883?—Yes, since that time, commencing then.

Mr. John Ellis—continued.

2414. You connect that with the name of the honourable Member who is now the Governor, Sir John Whittaker Ellis?—Yes, I do principally; and, of course, I also connect with it the secretary's name, Mr. Dorie Miller.

2415. Would you wish us to assume that that change of policy arose from the personal ideas of those two gentlemen, the governor and the secretary?—I should think so to a considerable extent.

2416. They personally entertained a different view to that which some of their predecessors did as to the duties or action of the society towards their tenants?—That is the only conclusion I can draw from the change of policy.

2417. You come before us as a gentleman of very great experience, and that is your conclusion?—It is.

2418. Your opinion is that this policy largely rests upon the personal views of those gentlemen?—It is, for this reason: that they being permanent officials, have thoroughly, at their fingers' ends, all connected with the property, and I presume for that reason, being better acquainted with it, they see what will conduce to the prosperity of the property, and of course whatever conduces to it will be followed by an immense increase of outlay in the district, and conduce to our prosperity also.

2419. You would allow that their places might be taken by other gentlemen whose views were not the same, and that a change of policy to another sort might occur. That is possible, I suppose?—It is.

2420. Are you aware whether these gentlemen have any reasons outside the Society for this change of policy?—No.

2421. It was not brought about by any remonstrance or representation?—I have no doubt that, on each visitation of the society, remonstrances were lodged with the society, and I have no doubt that those two gentlemen, being intimately acquainted with the property, and inquiring into it, perhaps find that those remonstrances are well founded, and think it necessary to accede to them.

2422. But it was mainly in consequence of the zealous way in which they discharge their duties, and the enlarged view they took of their duties, that this change came about?—I would say so.

2423. Then we clearly apprehend from you that, in your opinion, if the management of these estates was entrusted to those living on the spot, given equal zeal and capacity, the result would be great economy and better correspondence with the wishes of those on the spot?—I am not prepared to advocate the change to local trustees.

Mr. Clancy.

2424. Would you like to see the property sold and the money carried away to England?—Certainly not.

2425. Would you like to see the property sold, and the money kept in Ireland?—I would.

2426. You are in favour of purchase?—I think everything tends that way.

2427. Are

Mr. Clancy—continued.

2427. Are you in favour of the compulsory purchase of this estate?—I cannot say I have ever considered that.

2428. Is it your personal regard for Sir Whittaker Ellis that prevents your giving an opinion upon that?—Not in the slightest degree.

2429. You said that your principal objection to the requirement that the bye-laws of the Corporation of Derry must be sanctioned by the Irish Society is that it causes delay?—Just so.

2430. Do you really object to it on no other ground?—I object to it altogether; I object to having to refer a bye-law over for consideration, because I think it is quite unnecessary.

2431. You do not see why a committee of the Londonderry Corporation should supervise the rules of the Corporation of Derry?—I do not.

2432. You object to that power altogether?—Yes.

2433. And you add to that, that it causes great delay?—It does.

2434. You said that the Irish Society, since the administration of Sir Whittaker Ellis began, has been more liberal in granting perpetuity leases?—Yes.

2435. Do you know anything of the terms upon which those leases have been granted?—I cannot say I know personally; all I know is from public report.

2436. Have fines been exacted?—I could not answer that question.

2437. Was a fine exacted in your own case?—I have no perpetuity.

2438. I thought you said you were one of the few tenants who got a 61 years' lease?—My father did, in the year 1854.

2439. Had he to pay a fine?—To the best of my recollection he had not; but he was bound by his lease to make certain expenditure in the way of building.

2440. Are you aware of the demand formerly made by the Society that renewal fines should be based on the improved value of the premises, instead of on the rental reserved in the lease?—I have heard it so stated, but I do not know it at all of my own personal knowledge.

2441. Within your experience, you do not know of any such demand having been exacted?—I have heard it stated.

2442. Are you aware, within your experience, of any such demand having been enforced?—I think that in former years there were certain premises held in the city of Derry on lives renewable for ever, and I believe that, as each life fell out, there was a fine demanded for a fresh life being inserted in the lease; at least, I have heard it so stated. I believe all those tenures are at an end.

2443. Are you aware that when the Renewable Leasehold Reversion Act passed, or before it passed, the Society made an attempt to get its property exempted from its provisions?—So I have heard.

2444. You are aware of it, I suppose?—I have no doubt it is the case; but all that occurred before I took any part in public business.

2445. Can you tell me how many leases in perpetuity have been given within your experience?—I could not give you the figures. There have been a considerable number given lately. A considerable amount of property in the chief business part of the city has fallen in within the last seven or eight years, and I know that some portions of it were in a very bad state of repair, and, on condition that new and improved buildings were put up, there were leases in perpetuity given in the district, in Foyle-street, for instance.

2446. Could you give me the number of such leases which have been granted in the last seven or eight years?—I could not give you the figure.

2447. Was an increase of rent demanded in those cases?—I believe there was.

2448. Were any fines exacted?—I never heard there were; but a considerable portion of it in the neighbourhood of Foyle-street was set at either a pound or a guinea a foot.

2449. Is it not a fact that only a few such leases have been given altogether; a dozen or so?—My impression is that there are more than that; I cannot give you the exact figure, but it is my belief that, from the number of holdings that fell in along Foyle-street, more than a dozen have been given.

2450. Within the last 10 years would you say more than 20 such leases have been given?—Possibly about that; but I cannot state exactly.

2451. Where is the great liberality you spoke of?—In former times there were no leases in perpetuity given at all. In 1760 there were a few leases in perpetuity given, and then after that it fell into disuse again, and no leases in perpetuity, I believe, were given at all.

2452. I think you are wrong in that; are you not aware that in 1773 it was a standing order in the Society that no leases should be renewed until within three years of their expiring?—Yes; but I stated leases in perpetuity.

2453. I would like you to define the liberality of which you have spoken?—What I allude to is the fact of getting perpetuity leases now at all, which, up to the last few years, we could not get.

2454. That is the sole ground upon which you speak of the increased liberality of the Irish Society?—It is the principal ground.

2455. I understand there were only 20 such leases given within the last 10 years?—I really cannot go accurately into the figures.

2456. I am only taking you generally; you said there were not more than 20 granted within the last 10 years?—It will be probably about that number, but I have no doubt the Society's own returns could correct my statement upon that point.

2457. Have any persons applied for perpetuity leases and been refused?—I am not aware.

2458. Have you never heard of that?—I cannot say that I ever did; that is to say, lately.

2459. I mean within the time during which you say perpetuity leases have been given for the first time?—It is quite possible there may have been.

2460. Does anybody get them who asks for them, or is it only in favour of a few?—No; my impression is that there is no favour shown in any way. I presume anyone who comes to terms with the Society will get them.

Mr. Clancy—continued.

2461. No doubt, when he comes to terms: but supposing that the Society asks a very heavy fine, and a very high rent, I suppose the tenant would hardly come to terms, would he?—I do not suppose he would.

2462. Are the agricultural tenants satisfied now?—I would not suppose they are.

2463. You are an agricultural tenant yourself, I understand?—Yes.

2464. Are you acquainted with their circumstances and their feelings as regards their landlord?—I think I am.

2465. Cannot you say whether they are satisfied?—I do not believe they are satisfied.

2466. Those are satisfied who have got leases, I presume, or do they want their leases broken?—No, they do not, but they would like to have their leases at a lower rent.

2467. Do you know how many have got leases?—I think the majority of the tenantry in the upper liberty have got leases.

2468. How many have got leases?—I cannot tell you accurately.

2469. You are speaking about agricultural tenants, I understand; about how many agricultural tenants are there?—I suppose from 60 or 70 to 100, probably.

2470. How many of them have got leases?—I really could not tell you accurately.

2471. Have any got them except the two or three you mentioned?—Yes, there are others.

2472. How many more; are there a dozen out of the whole 60 or 70?—I would think that perhaps a third of them have got leases, or possibly more; but really I cannot answer the question exactly, because it is a question I have never heard them discuss.

2473. I want to get at the liberality you spoke of; it seems to consist in these perpetuity leases, which, amongst the agricultural tenants, do not seem to have any existence?—Not among the agricultural tenants; but the public grants, the freeing of the bridge, and building a new town hall in Derry, are, of course, instances of the increased liberality.

Sir Richard Temple.

2474. When you spoke of the compulsory purchase of the Irish Company's estate, have you considered whether that Company possesses any rights on account of the transactions in the seventeenth century?—The only opinion that I can give about the matter is this; I have always understood, whatever powers the Society have themselves, that in dividing the property amongst the companies they transmitted those powers on to them, and whatever trusts existed in the one instance were passed on at the time of the division of the property among the companies.

2475. I am talking not of the companies' estate, but of the Irish Society's estate, as to compulsory purchase; did you not say, in reply to my honourable colleague who last questioned you, that you were in favour of compulsory purchase of the Irish Society's estate?—I do not think I did.

2476. Did you not answer that question in the affirmative?—I am not sure that I did.

Chairman.

2477. Some of the Committee understood you to say, in answer to Mr. Clancy, that you did not desire to see the Irish Society's estate sold; is that what you meant?—I understood Mr. Clancy to add to his question, "and the money taken away out of Ireland."

Sir Richard Temple.

2478. I understood Mr. Clancy also to ask you whether, if the money could be kept in Ireland, you would be in favour of the compulsory purchase of the estate, and you certainly did not dissent from that; do you assent to, or dissent from, that proposition?—If the money for the purchase could be kept in Ireland; under those circumstances I would not at all object to the estate being sold; this is, if the capital sum was kept for the benefit of the district.

2479. But the question was, whether you would be in favour of compulsory purchase; I ask you again, would you be in favour of the compulsory purchase of the estate if the money could be kept in Ireland?—I am not prepared to give an opinion.

2480. You are not prepared to assent to that proposition?—No, I am not prepared to give an opinion either one way or the other; I would rather not give an opinion upon that point.

2481. When you said that your people would be delighted to have more money from the Irish Society, did you consider where that money was to come from?—I cannot say I did.

2482. When you said that your people would like to get lower rents, did you consider whether the Irish Society would afford to take a lower rent?—The reason that made me give the answer was this: we look upon it that if we had lower rents there would be much more prosperity in the district, and, in that way, prosperity in the town.

2483. But what I ask is, did you consider whether the Society could afford to take less rent?—We consider that if the expenditure on the management was cut down they could afford to take less rent.

2484. Do you consider that the economy might be very considerable?—I would say that the expenditure might be one-half at least of what it is now; that it might be cut down from 20 to 10 per cent.

2485. About what amount in money would that reduction represent?—About 2,000 *l.* a year. The published accounts, as I understand them, state that the expense of management both in Ireland and England amounts to something over 4,000 *l.* a year.

2486. Then you think that that difference of 2,000 *l.* a year might be applied to the reduction of rent?—I do.

2487. When you said that you would be delighted to get more money from the Society, would you say that a portion of the money could be devoted to that object?—Yes, I should think it could.

2488. That is to say, you would distribute the 2,000 *l.* partly in the reduction of rent and partly in increased grants?—Yes, I think that would be a very good way; I think all the parties who at present benefit from the Society would be entitled

Sir Richard Temple—continued.

entitled to a share in any further funds that they had from the reduction in expenditure, and that they would be entitled to divide it among them.

2489. Have you considered in detail how that reduction of expenditure could be effected?—No, I have not, because I have no means of telling what the expenditure is entirely on. There are only general headings given in the published accounts, and I have no possible means of suggesting how they could be cut down, not knowing the different items.

2490. Are not the amounts given in considerable detail?—There is so much given for law expenses. It is given generally; they do not go into all the minute details.

2491. Can you put your finger upon any items where reduction would be possible?—There is one item of course that I have heard people talk about, and that is the cost of the entertainments to public bodies in Ireland.

2492. What does that amount to?—The visitation expenses of 1889, including the cost of entertainments to public bodies and the tenantry, are given as 614 l.

2493. Would you reduce the whole of that?—I do not know. The Irish are very fond of hospitality.

2494. And this 614 l. you say is spent upon that?—Not all of it; but I have no means of knowing what exact amount goes for entertainments.

2495. Have you any other item that you could criticise?—Of course we look upon the law and Parliamentary expenses as a heavy item. For instance in Ireland, the law expenses are put down as 239 l., and in England 465 l., being in round numbers nearly 700 l.

Colonel *Lewis*.

2496. May I ask what year that is which you are referring to now?—It is the last year: "The Honourable the Irish Society, being the produce of their estates from the 9th of February 1889 to the 11th of February 1890."

2497. It is for 1889–90?—Yes, up to February of the present year.

Sir *Richard Temple*.

2498. Do you think that the Irish Society could escape those law charges?—I do not know; I do not suppose they could, at least not the entire of them.

2499. Do you suppose that they would pay them if they could possibly help it?—I do not suppose they would.

2500. Is there any other item that you would suggest after the entertainments and the law expenses?—I do think that if instead of the grants to schools, 5 l. to this school and 5 l. to that, there were one or two good large schools, such as either a school for instructing in agricultural knowledge, or if technical schools were founded through the country, it would in a great extent be a better appropriation of the money than giving small doles to different small schools throughout the country.

Chairman.

2501. That does not concern the amount, but its distribution?—That would be so.

0.112.

Sir *Richard Temple*.

2502. Would that process save money on the whole?—Probably it would not; but it would be better expended.

2503. Could you suggest any reduction of expenses?—There is another item given there as "Incidental expenses of the court connected with the administration of the society's affairs during the year 1889–90." Of course I have no means of knowing what that expenditure is on.

2504. How much is that?—£. 484; and then there is in England "Salaries and gratuities, 820 l." Of course I have no means of knowing what the different items of this expenditure are, and I merely make the suggestion off-hand as you have asked me the question. I am not to be taken as finding fault with them if they are legitimate items of expenditure; but I merely suggest that possibly there might be savings effected in those items.

2505. But you apprehend that *primâ facie* savings would seem to be possible there?—I do; and I think also from what I have heard stated would be the expenses of the management of any large estate, that a number of those expenses would not exist in the management of large estates.

2506. Do I correctly understand you to say that the existence of perpetuity leases in Belfast, is the sole or principal cause of the greater prosperity of that city as compared with Londonderry?—I think it was the originating cause and the chief originating cause. Of course we must be permitted to acknowledge that Belfast is geographically better situated; but to counterbalance that it had a miserably small river, whereas we have a capital river. The harbour of Belfast has been created by the energy of its own inhabitants, whereas our harbour was naturally a good one.

2507. Is not the access to Belfast by the sea tolerably good now?—It is now; but it has only risen within the last quarter of a century.

2508. Does not the geographical advantage of Belfast vastly outweigh any advantage arising from the tenure of leases?—I would not say vastly. It is about six hours nearer to Liverpool than we are, and it is about three hours nearer to Glasgow.

2509. Does not that difference of time account for a great deal in such short distances?—It does, certainly.

2510. Are there no local causes besides those which may be looked upon as favourably affecting Belfast in comparison with Derry?—I am not aware that there are.

2511. Do all the materials for the Belfast manufactures come from a distance?—With the exception of the linen trade I would think so, but I cannot speak from personal knowledge; I can only speak from hearsay.

2512. Do the materials for the linen trade come from a distance or from the neighbourhood?—There is a very large cultivation of flax in the neighbourhood of Belfast and the surrounding districts.

2513. Is not that a cardinal circumstance in favour of Belfast as compared with Derry?—It is, of course, a great advantage.

2514. Then do not these two great advantages

R of

Sir Richard Temple—continued.

of maritime communication and proximity of raw material together, vastly counterbalances any difference of tenure between the two places?—I would not be prepared to admit the "vastly." Now-a-days, of course, with the size of Belfast and everything, it vastly counterbalances Derry, but I would not have said so before Belfast came to such a size.

2515. Could Derry, under any conceivable circumstances of leases or anything else, have had a chance of competing with Belfast in the linen trade?—I think it could. I have heard it stated by elderly people in Derry that about the beginning of this century we had quite as large a linen trade as they had at Belfast, if not larger. At the beginning of this century Belfast was much smaller than Derry, and, of course, it has far outstripped us.

2516. When Derry had a linen trade, where did she get the material from?—There was an immense amount of flax, I have been told, grown in the district round about Derry at that time. That growth has almost entirely disappeared; very little flax is grown in the neighbourhood of Derry now.

2517. Do you think that flax could now be profitably cultivated near Derry?—There being no spinning mills in Derry, I should suppose that it could not.

2518. If there were spinning mills do you think it could?—I should think so. In my younger days I remember two spinning mills in Derry.

2519. If there were perpetual leases, do you think there would now be spinning mills in Derry, notwithstanding the competition of Belfast?—I would not go so far as to admit that. I am afraid that the competition of Belfast would be too powerful.

2520. So Belfast has shot ahead, leases or no leases?—But they got perpetuity in Belfast; at least I have always understood so.

2521. But irrespectively of the leases or of the terms of the leases in the two places, has not Belfast shot much ahead of Derry?—It has enormously.

2522. So that Derry is completely distanced under any circumstances?—I am afraid I must admit that we are distanced.

Mr. Lawson.

2523. I understood you to say that the insecurity of tenure was a principal cause in the first place, not dealing with present conditions?—We have looked upon it as such.

2524. Since 1883, on the termination of the tenancies in the urban holdings, have perpetual leases been granted in every case where they have been asked for?—I am not prepared to give the exact figures.

2525. But so far as you know have these perpetual leases been granted when they have been asked for?—I believe so, but I only speak from my belief.

2526. Therefore, there is really a complete change of tenure in your city?—There is a change of tenure going on, but I should suppose there is a great deal more to be dealt with still.

2527. But for the first time now the manufacturers and the business men have a chance of getting some security of tenure?—A much improved chance.

Mr. Lawson—continued.

2528. You say that since 1883 the change has come about. Before that year, but within your own experience, had leases been granted for shorter terms?—I believe they had.

2529. For what sort of terms?—Do I understand you to mean the urban districts?

2530. I am talking of the urban districts?—I believe there were leases granted; for instance, of the ground upon which the Derry Branch of the Northern Bank was built, and also the Ulster Bank, I have heard it stated that there was a lease granted for 61 years.

2531. Is that the Irish Society's land?—I think so. I should add that the late Alderman Gilliland, of Derry, got a lease of, I think, a portion of the slob-land running down the river towards Culmore, and he embanked it and built a large mill upon it.

2532. Was there any formal statement made when this change of policy took place?—Not that I am aware of.

2533. Was it in consequence of the visitation of the Society?—I should suppose that it was.

2534. Was there a memorial, or what?—I suppose it was in consequence of representations made at some of the visitations.

2535. It is the custom, then, to make these representations when the Irish Society comes round at its annual visit?—It is.

2536. Do you think that these visitations do effect any practical good?—I think they effect some good; but we would feel rather better satisfied if the deputation gave their decisions on the spot.

2537. What do they do?—We do not get an account of the decision until after the court sits in London.

2538. Certain formalities have to be gone through, I presume?—Yes.

2539. I suppose this visitation is looked upon principally as an outing for the members of the Society?—I cannot say that.

2540. But is it not so looked upon in your own city?—I really could not say as to that. We are always very glad to see them, because we always expect to get something from them.

2541. It is looked upon as a holiday trip for the purpose of amusement?—We always expect to get something from them.

Mr. Sexton.

2542. Where is your agricultural holding situated?—It is about a mile from the city.

2543. Then the other agricultural tenants of the Society are your neighbours?—They are.

2544. Have you lived amongst them long?—I have lived in Derry all my life.

2545. Do the agricultural tenants wish to be freeholders?—Yes, I think so.

2546. I suppose you know that one of the original objects of the Charter was to promote the general prosperity of the district?—Yes.

2547. Would it promote the general prosperity of the tenants if they were freeholders?—I suppose we would think so.

2548. I suppose you would approve of any steps that Parliament might take to bring about that end?—I should think so.

2549. You have lived there so long; can you

Mr. *Sexton*—continued.

say whether the Society follow the ordinary practice of the London companies in regard to agricultural tenants; that is to say, at intervals of 21 years or so do they raise the rents upon their improvements?—I know very little about the different London companies.

2550. But you know about the Society; have they been a singular exception, or have they followed the practice of the London companies in raising the rents?—I believe that the rents have been raised at the expiration of the tenancies.

2551. Assuming that the estate was sold, do you think that the capital sum resulting from it ought to be administered in Ireland?—I do, and that it should be administered in the district for the city of Derry, the town of Coleraine, and the county Derry.

2552. And administered by the hands of persons locally resident?—I am not prepared to say that.

2553. But if the Irish Society ceased to be the owners, and if new trustees were appointed, in your opinion, what description of persons should they be?—I would not be prepared to give my opinion in favour of local trustees for this reason; I think that if there were local trustees administering a very large sum of money, local pressure might be brought to bear upon them to do things that they should not do.

2554. Would you extend that objection to all Irishmen, or do you think that the capital sum, the value of these estates, might properly and beneficially be administered by Irishmen for Irish benefit?—I would limit the benefit altogether to the district.

2555. But do you think that you could find in Ireland persons competent to administer that trust more beneficially than persons outside Ireland?—I would think that there could be no difficulty in finding suitable persons to administer it.

2556. In Ireland?—In Ireland. But if you will permit me to explain, I think our great objection is, in the first place, that the members of the Society hold office for much too short a period. They only hold office for two years, and we find it is a practical fact that, as soon as they become acquainted with the wants of the district, they go out of office and we never see them again. Then I think that if we had a much smaller body to deal with, for instance, if it was limited probably to three, in that way the expense of management might be greatly cut down, and I cannot see that there could be the slightest objection to a committee of three of the present Society, or a committee of three Irishmen if deemed right, being invested with power to administer the property, clothed with the sole condition that the trusts should be administered in the district for which they were originally intended.

2557. Does not the whole of that reply which you have just given go to show that, whether the estates are sold or not, the funds had better be administered in Ireland than by what I may call with regard to Ireland a foreign body; I mean outside the country?—I would rather not give an opinion upon that subject.

2558. But if you have an opinion you may as well give it?—It is a matter which I have not so fully considered that I would consider myself qualified at the present time to give an opinion upon the subject.

2559. I understood that in answer to the Chairman you agreed with the recommendation of the Committee of 1854?—Yes, certainly; that is as to the constitution being completely altered and new trustees being appointed.

2560. And that those trustees should be Irishmen; is there any reason in public policy why this Irish trust for Irish benefit should be administered by Englishmen living in London?—No, I know no reason why it should be.

2561. Do you know any other corporation in Ireland or in the world that has to have its bye-laws confirmed by a body of gentlemen in another country?—No, I do not.

2562. It may result, in fact, in injury by delay, may it not?—It is quite possible that it might.

2563. And it is humiliating, at any rate?—Well, we do not like it.

2564. Do you confirm the estimate given by the last witness as to the relative proportion of Catholics in the city of Derry; he said that it was about half; is it not more?—It was stated to be something more at the last census; but the town has greatly increased since then.

2565. And the Catholics have increased also?—I have no doubt that, following the natural course of Irishmen, they have.

2566. How many members have you in the corporation?—Twenty-four.

2567. And there is one Catholic amongst them?—Yes.

2568. To what extent have the Catholics of Derry participated in the benefit derived from the income of the Irish Society?—I cannot tell you exactly; but my belief is that they have not participated to any great extent.

2569. Not to any material extent?—No.

2570. You do not assume to speak for the Catholics in Derry to-day, do you?—I am happy to speak for all my fellow-townsmen.

2571. But do you assume that you are authorised to speak for them, and that you express their views?—In what way?

2572. In regard to the administration of the Irish Society?—I think, so far as I know, that I am expressing the views of the majority of the citizens.

2573. Do you think, then, that the Catholics of Derry are such peculiar persons that they are satisfied with an administration which has given them no material benefit, as you have said, out of an income of 17,000 *l.* or 18,000 *l.* a year?—Certainly not; but permit me to say that I have not stated for a moment that we are satisfied. I have said that we thought matters were being conducted much better than they had been; but I did not go so far as to say that we were completely satisfied.

2574. Have the Catholics in Derry, in your opinion, peculiar and special reason for dissatisfaction?—I think they have reasons for dissatisfaction; but I believe, at least I have always been told, that the reason of it was in consequence of what is laid down in the Charter of Incorporation.

2575. Surely you are aware that the London companies

Mr. Sexton—continued.

companies have in this century given grants to Catholics, even for religious purposes, as well as to other communions?—I believe they have.

2576. Do you consider that the Catholics of Derry would prefer that the estate should be administered locally, or by Irishmen?—I think they would certainly prefer that it should be administered by Irishmen.

2577. You have paid a compliment, no doubt well deserved, to the honourable Baronet near me (Sir Whittaker Ellis); how long has he been a governor of this Society?—Six or seven years.

2578. All the time?—Yes, all the time.

2579. You noticed a distinct improvement when he became governor?—Certainly.

2580. It was better than it was before his time?—It was.

2581. Does it not occur to you that it may become worse when he leaves?—Possibly it might; but we hope that that time is not approaching.

2582. But in these practical days we desire something more substantial than hope; do you think it is satisfactory that a public trust of 17,000 *l.* or 18,000 *l.* a year should be so administered that you have to depend upon the personal disposition of an individual?—No.

2583. You prefer something more certain?—Yes.

2584. I understand from your reply to my honourable friend opposite that the number of perpetuity grants in the town is very slight indeed; how many houses have you in the town?—I could not give you the exact number; they are increasing considerably.

2585. I suppose there would be some thousands, at any rate?—Yes, I have no doubt there would.

2586. How many of those urban perpetuity grants are there?—All the city within the walls, I believe, is held in perpetuity.

2587. What were those grants that you referred to then?—What I referred to is the property that fell out of lease within the last ten years or so.

2588. But the extent to which the perpetuity grants have been given had not been such, I understand, as to very materially affect the general welfare up to the present time?—It has affected the general welfare to this extent; that all the buildings that have been put up are really now a credit to the town.

2589. But they are few in consequence of the perpetuity grants?—As these places are falling out of lease all the new buildings that are being put up are more creditable to the town.

2590. But the number of those perpetuity grants is very small up to the present time, is it not?—I cannot give you the exact figure; but my impression is that in the business part of the town, that is, in Foyle-street, most of the ground there which has fallen out of lease within the last 10 years is being built upon on perpetuity leases; but I cannot speak from my own personal knowledge.

2591. You cannot give precise evidence on that point?—No, I cannot.

2592. Are you aware that we have had it in evidence before the Committee that the ordinary practice in Ireland is to give perpetuity grants in towns?—I believe it is.

Mr. Sexton—continued.

2593. We have heard that the town of Moneymore, which is under one of these London companies had been completely deprived of any opportunity of establishing trade by reason of the short terms; and that adequate leases have been refused. You have drawn an important distinction between the progress of Derry and that of Belfast; are you aware that the linen industry, the main motive power of Belfast, was chiefly developed by reason of the perpetuity grants given by the Donegal family at the end of the last century?—That has always been my impression.

2594. The main industries of Belfast are, I think, linen-making and distilling; is there any local reason why linen-making and distilling might not have been equally pursued in Derry?—None; we have a most flourishing distillery.

2595. And a very favourable site and an excellent harbour?—Yes.

2596. Then may I infer from the comparison between Derry and Belfast, the Marquis of Donegal being the landlord in the one case, and the Irish Society in the other, that your relations to the Irish Society have been a misfortune to Derry in regard to development of trade?—We are under the belief that it has interfered certainly with the development of the city and trade in the past.

2597. Your view is, that if you could have got perpetuity grants in Derry as they have in Belfast, Derry would be another Belfast now?—Yes, if that had begun some 70, or 80, or 90 years ago.

2598. You have been closely questioned about the possibility of reducing the expenses of this estate under Irish management; if the estate were managed in Ireland, would not the salaries be contracted, inasmuch as there need not be two sets of officials?—I suppose there would not; but I am afraid that that would not be satisfactory.

2599. Not to those who get the salaries now, but it would be to the public?—It would.

2600. If you had Irish trustees need you have those costly annual visitations that run up to nearly a thousand a year?—I suppose not.

2601. Do you consider it proper that there should be so much luxurious festivity associated with the administration of funds, the objects of which comprise education and even charity?—I cannot say that I do.

2602. With regard to law costs, where you have a body of gentlemen in another country, themselves ignorant of the conditions of the trust, and depending upon agents, has not that a tendency to generate excessive law costs?—I should suppose that it has.

2603. Then, taking it all together, if the recommendation of the Commission of 1854, to which the right honourable Chairman referred (and which recommendation you adopted, I think), were carried out, do you not think that, under the several heads of salaries, law costs, and expenses of visitation, there would be an increase of the funds available for public objects to the extent of, say, between 3,000 *l.* and 4,000 *l.* a year?—I certainly think that there would be an increase available, probably not to such an extent as that.

2604. I understood you to say that there would be a saving of 3,000 *l.* a year, and I do not

Mr. Sexton—continued.

not think you included in that the cost of [illegible] and the reduction of law costs?—I think I did.

2605. At any rate, there would be a reduction of [illegible] l. a year. Just one question in conclusion. Forty-seven years ago the magistrates of your city, the police committee, and the inhabitants in general, signed a petition to the House of Commons, in the last paragraph of which they declared, as follows, concerning the Irish Society: "That from the nature of their constitution the Society is incapable of rendering any permanent benefit to this country, as it is composed of merchants and tradesmen in the City of London whose business requires their constant residence therein, whereby they are, of course, ignorant of the local circumstances and wants of the inhabitants of this district; and besides, being elected for only two years, cannot possibly acquire the information proper to qualify them for the due discharge of their duties." Do the facts that they are merchants and tradesmen in the City of London, that they are by reason of their constant residence in London ignorant of the local circumstances and wants of the inhabitants of the district, and that they are elected for only two years, still continue; and in your view of it the same as that expressed by the inhabitants of your city in that petition?—It is. I think I have already answered that to a considerable extent. I quite go with it in objecting to the present constitution of the society, that they are too short a time in office.

2606. And too far away?—Yes. To a certain extent that is modified now by the rapidity of communication; but, of course, the objection does hold good.

2607. And they are still defective in local knowledge?—Yes, with the exception of those permanently in office. That was the reason that I mentioned that I thought the increased benefits that we were getting were to be chiefly attributed to those two gentlemen, whom I named as the permanent officials, namely, the governor and the secretary.

2608. The governor may go out at any time, may he not?—He may.

2609. And the members of the Society go out every two years?—They do.

2610. Just as they begin to learn something they are dismissed?—Yes.

Colonel Laurie.

2611. The purposes to which the income of the Irish Society is appropriated are for public objects in Londonderry, Coleraine, and the district, are they not?—So I have always heard.

2612. Then all the net income of the property is expended upon public objects?—Yes, I believe so.

2613. You have the accounts before you, I think?—Yes.

2614. I know it is so from the accounts which I have before me. You take the view that the Irish Society are trustees?—Certainly. I have always understood so.

2615. And I suppose the property in Londonderry is improving in value, and it has improved in value in the past?—It is certainly improving in value.

Colonel Laurie—continued.

2616. And is it likely to improve in the future?—Within the last 10 or 15 years the city has taken a great start, and is improving rapidly.

2617. The value of property has increased in the past, and, in your opinion, it is likely to increase in the future?—I should say so.

2618. I heard you say just now that a system of perpetuity leaseholds would be advantageous for the city of Londonderry?—We always look upon it so.

2619. Supposing that the Irish Society a hundred years ago had granted perpetuity leases at the then existing values, what would have been the present position of the city of Londonderry and of Coleraine, and of the whole of the district; what I wish to point out to you is, that the income to be expended for public purposes would be far smaller?—Yes, it would.

2620. Whereas as you say the value of property is increasing in Londonderry, if at existing rents you were to give perpetuity leases now in a wholesale way throughout the whole property, you would render it impossible in the future, would you not, that a larger income could be obtained for the city for public improvements?—That would be so; but perhaps I may be permitted to draw attention to the fact that the permanent sum which is granted by the society to Derry amounts to 1,[illegible] l.

2621. To the corporation?—Yes; there is only a part of that that goes to the officials of the corporation. More than half of it is granted to the corporation for them to expend upon public improvements.

2622. But whether for educational purposes or anything else that money is paid for public purposes in Londonderry, is it not?—It is.

2623. Therefore if you gave perpetuity leases now you would, according to your own showing, largely decrease the amount that would be available in the future for those public purposes?—It would prevent an increase.

2624. You are a public man in Londonderry; will you tell me whether you consider that the Irish Society, as trustees for the public good of Londonderry, would be doing right, in the interests of the community at large, to alienate their property by perpetual leases?—We do not look upon it that they would alienate their property; they would retain the head rents.

2625. But if the property is increasing in value, they could not possibly increase the amount available for public purposes, and I ask you now whether, as trustees for the public good, they would be justified in granting perpetual leases; I am entirely confining my question to perpetuity leases?—As I understand, the feeling is this; that we look upon it that if a person gets a lease for, say, 60 or 61 years, and lays out a large sum of money in building there, it would be a hardship upon his successors that when the lease fell in they should not get it renewed at the original rate, but that the value of the property which was created by the tenants should be assessed as the future rent. That is the reason why we were anxious to have perpetuity leases.

2626. It is obvious that you would have to fall back upon the rates, instead of getting the increased rentals for the community of Londonderry?—Yes.

Colonel *Laurie*—continued.

2627. Do you not think that the creation of perpetual leases might be rather a dangerous course, and might it not be abused to some extent, seeing that it is practically an alienation of your property for ever?—It is quite possible that it might be abused.

2628. Do you still think that, in spite of the objections which I have raised, perpetual leases are desirable in the interests of Londonderry, looking to the position of trusteeship in which the Irish Society are now placed?—Yes. I must still make the same answer.

2629. And, therefore, you think that they should alienate their property for ever, and rely upon the rating for the future expenses of the administration of the city?—We look upon it that the only effect of perpetual leases would be to prevent their income increasing, but that it would not diminish it, or would not act further than putting a drag upon the increase of their income.

2630. But if you were to place the Irish Society in such a position that they could not spend that 2,800 *l.* a year upon educational purposes, you would certainly increase the education rates?—We are in hopes that the expenditure that they are now making on public improvements will be so effectual and so permanent that we may not have such large demands upon us in the future.

2631. You look upon the *Irish Society* as a trustee; under their charter it would be difficult for them to support Roman Catholic charities, would it not, if you take the strong view of the trust?—I believe so.

2632. And that, possibly, is the reason that the Roman Catholic charities cannot be supported in the same way that the Episcopalian and Presbyterian charities are?—I have always heard it stated that that is the case.

2633. That is the answer, is it not, to the statement that the Roman Catholic charities do not figure, at any rate to any appreciable extent, in the accounts?—Yes.

2634. You said that since 1883, since my honourable friend has been governor, the Society has been better administered than it was before; can you tell me who the last governor was?—Sir Sydney Waterlow.

2635. Was it during the time that he was governor, or was it since, that this large sum of, I think you said, 40,000 *l.* was voted for the free bridge?—It was in Sir Sydney Waterlow's time that the bridge was made permanently free.

2636. £ 40,000 was expended on the free bridge, as I understand, by the Irish Society?—Just so.

Chairman.

2637. Was the total 40,000 *l.*, or was that the moiety?—The total was 80,000 *l.* and the moiety 40,000 *l.*

Colonel *Laurie.*

2638. Then there was some public spirit even in Sir Sydney Waterlow's time?—There was. It occurs to me that there was another thing that I should have mentioned that they contributed to largely, and that was the improvement of the harbour; I think, as well as my recollection serves me, they have contributed a sum of 10,000 *l.* a year for two years.

Colonel *Laurie*—continued.

2639. And the improvement of the river?—Yes; I think it is only fair to mention that.

2640. A considerable sum, 34,000 *l.*, I think, was expended upon the river?—Yes.

2641. Therefore there was some public spirit even before 1883?—Yes; but we think that the present governor is following largely in the right direction.

2642. I think in Lord Donegall's case in Belfast it was practically a private property?—So I have always heard.

2643. And not property held for public trust; and therefore Lord Donegall, if he gave perpetual leases, was simply dealing with that over which he had complete control?—Just so.

2644. And he had not to consider the population round him at all?—No.

Sir *John Ellis.*

2645. The Society has been in existence for a long while?—It has.

2646. In association with your corporation?—Yes.

2647. And your corporation has been made by the Society, and under its charters; has been remodelled upon the same frame as the Corporation of London?—I believe so.

2648. And they have gone on for many years together?—They have.

2649. And any suggestion that has been made by the corporation which was within the fair limits of discretion, finance, public advantage and possibility of accomplishment was generally carried out, I think?—Yes, I would say that.

2650. You have been asked a great many times whether you could not make a suggestion for the improvement of the Irish Society; do you think that there is any public body in the world that could not be improved; do you not think that the House of Commons, or the House of Lords, or the judicature, might be improved?—I am afraid it would be presumptuous for me to express an opinion upon such a point as that.

2651. You are not surprised that there is room for improvement even in the Irish Society?—No.

Mr. *Clancy.*

2652. Do you think that even the Corporation of Derry might be improved?—It is quite possible that it might.

Sir *John Ellis.*

2653. Possible, but not probable?—No.

2654. You heard read out to you the proposition of the Commission of 1854?—Yes.

2655. The Lord Chancellor of Ireland was to appoint trustees, with powers from time to time to re-appoint; do you think that you would like the Lord Chancellor's trustees; do you think that they would be business men like those who come to visit you every August?—I cannot possibly form an opinion as to that.

2656. I think there were other suggestions in that Report which were not quite consonant with the feelings of the Derry people; something about a widespread user of the funds for general purposes, and so on?—We would not approve of that at all. We would exert ourselves in every possible way to prevent it.

2657. It has been suggested to you that it is

Sir John Ellis—continued.

rather an anomaly for a town in England to be associated in the way that we are with a town in Ireland; but there are a great many anomalies in this world, are there not, which work exceedingly well?—There are.

2658. Does it suggest itself to you that the prosperity and peace of the north of Ireland has been to a large extent created by the association of the City of London with Londonderry?—I think it is very possible that it has.

2659. I believe that the memorial that has been referred to during Sir Charles Lewis's tenure of the membership was rather an election-eering affair, was it not; Sir Charles thought it a good thing to attack the Society?—That is a point upon which I am really not prepared to give an opinion.

2660. You are not prepared to give us Sir Charles Lewis's feeling on the subject; it is possible it may have been so, I suppose?—It is quite possible. But I may say in 1874, if my recollection serves me, there was no election pending.

2661. I should presume not; it would have been very unwise of Sir Charles Lewis if it had been so. Now as regards the expense, how many trustees would you appoint?—I think I am really not prepared to answer that; I have not considered the question; but I think three would be a very good number.

2662. Do you think those trustees could administer all the estates; first of all manage them and collect the rents, and make all the necessary arrangements, and afterwards distribute the money in a beneficial manner for the interests of the town; do you think that those three trustees, being official trustees, would render their services without payment?—Certainly not. I have no doubt they will require a secretary, and they will require a solicitor.

2663. I am speaking of the trustees alone; taking them first, you think they would require a solicitor and a secretary, and other officers; a considerable staff?—Yes; most undoubtedly.

2664. Did Lord Donegal, who has been referred to several times, live in the country?—I believe not; but I have heard so many histories as to that, that I do not know which is the correct one.

2665. All the income derived by the Irish Society is spent in the country, is it not?—I believe it is.

2666. Even a very large proportion of those expenses which have been talked of; the general agent resides in the country?—Yes.

2667. He is a useful man?—Very useful.

2668. You can send him about and make use of him, can you not, and that tends to great advantage?—We do.

2669. So that that money is not all abstracted?—It is not.

2670. So again, with regard to the visitation expenses of the Irish Society, the visitation expenses are spent in Ireland; they come over and keep the town alive for a little while?—Yes, they do; we get a good deal of the visitation expenses.

2671. The name of Mr. Osborne has been mentioned; I think we have had a great deal of trouble over that case?—I have heard so.

Sir John Ellis—continued.

2672. He is a difficult man to please, is he not?—So I have heard.

2673. You were asked about Mr. Hayland's having applied for a lease to the Society; is that within your knowledge?—No, it is not within my personal knowledge.

2674. If you were told that he had never applied to the Society, I suppose you would accept that as a fact?—Yes, I would.

2675. As regards charging rents upon the tenants' outlay, is it not a fact that the Irish Society have spent large sums upon almost all their tenancies, and wherever they have charged the full rent to the tenant it has always been because they have themselves made the outlay upon the property?—I am not in a position to say.

2676. May I take it you are not in a position to deny it?—I am not in a position to answer that question.

2677. I will not ask you anything about the local persons, because I think the general tenour of your evidence is that it would be inadvisable to hand it over to them, that there would be pressure brought to bear upon them, and it would be difficult to work?—It is my belief that it might be liable to abuses.

2678. And as regards the sale of the estates, I gather that you would rather see them where they are; you know you have got something, but if they were sold you could not tell what would become of the floating capital?—There is one thing that we are unanimous upon, and that is, that we would not at all like any of the funds to be diverted from the charities.

2679. You think that there is a possibility of that under the schemes that have been propounded?—There might be.

2680. That has been their tenour?—Yes.

2681. Now, with regard to this change of policy, may I ask you this: it has been contended that the organisation of the Society tends to a possible or probable change of policy; is there any public body that is not liable to the same thing?—No.

2682. The character of a public body is very much improved by its leader, is it not?—It is.

2683. And any possible human arrangement would hardly prevent that?—Certainly not.

2684. If you had a good Lord Chancellor, for instance, he would appoint good trustees, and if you had a man with strong prejudices, he might appoint different trustees?—Yes.

Mr. *Healy*.

2685. Who appointed you to come here?—I was summoned.

2686. I think you said you represented the Catholics of Derry?—No, I think not; at least what I meant to convey was, that I believe I represent the opinions of the great majority of the citizens.

2687. And the great majority are Catholics, are they not?—They are said to be in a slight majority.

2688. Have you at all referred to the Census Tables upon the point?—I have seen it stated that the Census of 1871 gave the population as 28,000 and some odd hundreds, and that the

Mr. *Healy*—continued.

Roman Catholics were then between 15,000 and 16,000, and the other denominations would be the remainder.

2689. Did you look at the Census of 1881 at all?—When I said 1871, I meant 1881.

2690. Would you kindly tell the Committee what position you hold in Derry?—I am physician and surgeon to the County Infirmary, medical officer to the Prison, and surgeon to the Londonderry Militia.

2691. Is that all?—Yes, that is all.

2692. You are connected with no other public or private body?—Yes; I beg your pardon, I am; I am medical officer to the Post Office.

2693. Are you still the head of the Apprentice Boys of Derry?—I never was at the head of them.

2694. Nor connected with them in any way?—I was connected with them.

2695. What position did you hold in connection with them?—As an ordinary member.

2696. Do you think it is likely that a gentleman holding that position would be entitled to speak for the majority of the population of Derry?—I have no reason to deny it.

2697. There is one Catholic on the corporation, is there not, out of the 24?—Yes.

2698. Does that fairly represent the number of Catholics among the population?—Not so far as numbers go.

2699. Would you be glad to see the franchise in Derry the same as the franchise in Belfast?—I should not have the slightest objection to it.

2700. Would you be glad to see the funds of the Irish Society transferred to the Corporation of Derry and the Corporation of Coleraine; would you think that would be a very good way out of the difficulty?—I am not prepared to say so.

2701. You would not care to see that?—I have already stated that I think if local bodies were entrusted with such large funds to administer, it is quite possible that pressure might be brought to bear upon them that they could not resist.

2702. The Corporation of Dublin, the Corporation of Waterford, and even the Corporation of London itself, have large funds, have they not?—They have.

2703. Do you think they are competently administered; say, for instance, in London, which we know is a model city?—I have heard it said that pressure could be brought to bear upon them.

2704. I gather you take the entirely altruistic view, that you would not like to have temptation thrown upon them?—If I was offered the trusteeship, I should hesitate greatly about accepting it.

2705. If the franchise in Derry were reduced, do you think that those representing the corporation under the reduced franchise would have any hesitation in expressing their opinion, in that sense, as to how the Irish Society ought to be dealt with?—I cannot form an idea about that at all; it would depend altogether upon who were returned to the corporation.

2706. You must live in very exclusive circles in Derry, if you are not able to form an opinion as to what the population there think?—My opinion is, if the franchise were reduced, it would make very little difference in the constitution of the corporation.

2707. You do not think it would follow the alterations that took place in the Imperial representation?—I am not prepared to say.

2708. I understood you to say, in answer to Sir John Ellis, that you got a good deal of the visitation expenses?—We do, in a certain way.

2709. *Per contra*, is it not?—In the way of eating and drinking.

2710. It was suggested by Colonel Laurie that the reason why there were so few grants to the Roman Catholics was because of the charter of the Irish Society; that is your view, is it?—No; I have merely heard it stated so, and I have seen it in the charter; but I have no means of knowing what their reason is for administering the funds as they do.

2711. Is it your opinion that the abolition of the State Church in Ireland, a generation ago, has not had in any way an effect upon the way in which the Irish Society distribute their funds?—I cannot see how I can connect the two together.

2712. You cannot at all form any view of State policy?—I cannot see how the abolition of the State Church could repeal the charter, if the charter has that effect.

2713. Supposing the Irish Society were to turn round and give all their grants to Catholics, how would they be restrained?—I cannot tell at all.

2714. You think it is simply a respect for the pious founder that induces them to give these grants to the Protestants?—I presume, in such a case, the other people would take the best legal advice they could to try and restrain them.

2715. Could you give us any idea, out of the entire estates of the Irish Society, how much goes to Protestants and how much to Catholics?—I cannot, at all. My belief is that a much larger quantity goes to the Protestants.

2716. We have a long list of schools in these accounts before us; I suppose those are nearly all Protestant; I see Lough Foyle College, the Presbyterian First Congregation School, the Presbyterian Female School, and so on: I suppose you would admit that the majority of the schools in this list are Protestant, though, of course, there are some Catholic schools amongst them; would you just look at that list (*handing the same to the Witness*) and just take a general glance at both sides; the vast majority of those schools are Protestant, are they not?—I have no doubt they are.

2717. Just tell me what proportion the Catholic schools bear to the Protestant schools?—With the exception of the schools of which the denomination is given here, I cannot give you an answer as to what the schools are. Where it is stated that they are Presbyterian schools or other schools, I may know them of my own personal knowledge; but I cannot tell you with regard to the others and the National schools that are given here, under what management they are.

2718. Should we have any difficulty in getting from Derry someone who would have more local knowledge

Mr. *Healy*—continued.

knowledge than yourself upon that point?—I think it is very probable you could.

2719. Do the Irish Society exempt the Catholics from the payment of rent?—I do not suppose they do.

2720. Do you think it is likely to be a satisfactory state of things where the majority of the population are Catholic that they should get practically no benefactions?—I should think it is not.

2721. Would you be glad to see it changed?—I should be glad to see any person who is entitled get a share of it.

2722. Would you be glad to see the Catholics receive a contribution in proportion to their number?—I would be glad to see them get a share.

2723. Would you be glad to see a distribution of the Society's funds in proportion to the number of Catholics within their domain?—I would not have the slightest objection.

2724. Do you think, in fact, seeing the Catholics get so small a portion, there is not just reason for dissatisfaction among them?—I have no doubt about it.

2725. When you say that you think you speak the views of the majority of the population of Derry, do you think that the majority of the population of Derry are satisfied with this state of things?—No; I have repeatedly said I do not think they are satisfied.

2726. How many agricultural tenants are there in the district?—I cannot give you the exact number; I think I have already said that I thought there might be about 60, but I cannot possibly give you the exact figures.

2727. Were you yourself at this meeting of tenants in October 1885, when this resolution was passed: "That we deprecate the conduct of the Honourable the Irish Society in forcing their tenantry to accept leases, with unusual and exceptional clauses, with the concealed intention of destroying our tenant right as by law established; and we also view with alarm their unprecedented and open attacks upon tenant right, by undue interference at the sale of holdings upon their estate"?—No, I was not; for this reason, that I was not a tenant at the time; because that meeting happened during my father's lifetime.

2728. Your father was then a tenant?—He was.

2729. Probably he was one of those who passed the resolution?—I do not think he was, for this reason, that he was between 80 and 90 years of age at the time.

2730. But you have no doubt that correctly represented the views then held?—I believe it did.

2731. Have there been any ameliorations since in the tenants' position apart from what the law gave them?—I am not aware that there has.

2732. Have the Irish Society dropped these objectionable covenants out of their leases?—I cannot tell; I have not seen or heard about any of the new leases given.

Mr. *Healy*—continued.

2733. Did you bring your own lease with you?—No.

2734. I suppose you hold under lease?—Yes; the lease was granted to my father some 30 years ago.

2735. For what term?—Sixty-one years.

2736. Then, I presume, it cannot be a very bad lease when you did not go into the court with it; you could have gone into court and broken your lease. I presume; that must be said for the credit of the Irish Society; surely you cannot object to the rent in your lease when you did not go into court with it?—I did not, of course, wish to enter into my private complaints at all.

2737. It seems to me if the Irish Society have given leases for over 100 years, or with 100 years still unexpired, and the tenants have not gone into court, that fact is to be registered to the credit of the landlord?—Of course, if you press me to go into private matters, I can do so; but of course I do not come to ventilate my private grievances.

2738. If this is a private matter that you would rather not have pressed for private reasons, I will not press it?—I have personally not the slightest objection to go into it. My reason was simply that if I enter into private matters, it may be thought I have come here to ventilate any grievance which I think I have.

Chairman.

2739. I do not suppose anybody would think that; you have given your evidence very straightforwardly and clearly?—I have no other objection to go into it.

Mr. *Healy.*

2740. What I was pointing out was that it seemed to be very creditable to the Irish Society (I should like to know what the facts were) if their tenants held under leases which would enable them to take them into court, and those tenants have not gone into court?—As you press me, I may state I have been for a considerable time past, and am, in correspondence with the Society; at least, up to within a few months ago.

2741. Do I understand that it would prejudice you in your negotiations with the society to go into it further?—No; so far as that is concerned, I may state that the private negotiations are at an end.

2742. Would you just speak generally, if you can, without touching on your own case; I take it it is a matter to the credit of the Irish Society that their tenants, if they have the power to go into court, have not yet done so; because the argument then is that their rents must be fair?—But the great majority of them have gone into the courts, and have got reductions.

2743. That is what I wanted to get at; and am I to understand that those who have not gone into court have been endeavouring to get the rent in their leases altered by private negotiation?—I can only speak for myself.

23 *June* 1890.

Mr. Thomas Scholes Magee, sworn; and Examined.

Chairman.

2744. Are you a member of the Corporation of Derry?—I am a member of the corporation, a councillor.

2745. And you know the town of Derry well?—I have been for eight years a member of the corporation, and I know the city very well.

2746. You wish, I understand, to tell us something as to the bad effect upon the prosperity of your town, of the land regulations of the Irish Society?—Yes; I think we have been considerably kept back by the failure on the part of the Irish Society to give perpetuity leases.

2747. It is no use saying that generally; perhaps you can give us one or more special instances?—I know that along the quays on both sides the slob lands were leased on terminable leases many years ago. Those leases have only, some of them, about 14 years to run, and all that land is now lying waste, with nothing on it but sheds, in the most important portion of the city.

2748. Why do you say lying waste?—Because the leases have only a few years to run under the terminable lease, which is unexpired. The society cannot interfere in those cases certainly, but what I say is that it is owing to the leases having been granted originally on those terms that the city is suffering, and is suffering very considerably.

2749. That seems to be rather the evil result of long leases, does it not?—It is the result of the terminable leases. At the time the leases were originally given, Derry was not sufficiently developed to make that portion of the city so important.

2750. You believe that if the lease had been a perpetuity lease, and not a terminable lease, the ground would not be in its present state; is that it?—Yes; all the land adjacent to the quays. If in place of terminable leases you had had perpetuity leases, the town would have been greatly improved in that direction.

2751. Is the part of the city which is in the society's own hands in the same condition as the other parts, in reference to occupation and prosperity?—There is very little of the city in the immediate possession of the Irish Society. As regards any that has been in their possession, or as regards most of it, at any rate, they have given perpetuity leases lately.

2752. But the perpetuity system only began when?—The greater portion, nine-tenths of the city, I may say, away from the business part, was granted in perpetuity in 1776; but all these were the portions reclaimed from the river, and he most important portions of the city.

2753. When was that land reclaimed?—During my lifetime, within the last 30 or 40 years.

2754. What do you say has been done there?—They are the most important portions of the city, most important to the prosperity of the city; and those lands cannot be utilised now because the present owners have only got terminable leases. I can give you an instance on the Gordon estate, which is lying there with only three dwelling-houses on it, that the tenants had to build under the terms of the lease. The ground is absolutely waste, and is just enclosed by a wall, whereas on the other side the same Gordon got some church lands in perpetuity, and when those lands were put up for sale that small portion of the Gordon estate sold for 4,000 *l.*, whereas this immense tract on the other side they could not get a purchaser for.

2755. Is it true that the church lands are very much sought after for occupation purposes?—Yes; very much indeed. That was the great advantage of the better use of the church lands for building purposes.

2756. You say, as I understand, that the church lands are built upon, and that the society's lands, which are very much in the same circumstances otherwise, are left unoccupied?—The particular portions of the Society's lands which I refer to are unoccupied, and they are the most important portions, that is, as I say, from the shipbuilding-yard up to the bridge.

2757. There have been industrial enterprises started of various kinds, have there not, in Derry especially shirt manufactories; they have been all built on perpetuity leases, have they not?—They have been built on perpetuity lands, but not in the position that would have been selected had they all been perpetuity lands. They were built at a distance from the quays, on old perpetuity grants no doubt. Take, for instance, the firm of Welsh and Margetson, an English firm; if they had been able to get land along the quay they would have spent their money there.

2758. What did Messrs. Welsh and Margetson, the English firm, do; did they choose an inconvenient site away from the city rather than go to a more convenient site upon the Irish Society's lands?—I do not think they could have chosen a more convenient site upon the Irish Society's land, because the Society's leases had not fallen in at that time.

2759. Can you give us any other instances to illustrate the advantage of the perpetuity system and the loss to the city through this other system?—Take, for instance, Messrs. M'Intyre, Hogg, and Company's very large shirt factory; that is built upon perpetuity church land in a very fair situation.

2760. Is there a strong feeling in your corporation in the direction of the evidence which you are giving?—Yes; there is a feeling on the part of the citizens that we should have perpetuity.

2761. I understand from Sir William Miller just now that since the accession of Sir Whitaker Ellis to the governorship of the Society all went well?—Yes; we acknowledge that Sir Whitaker Ellis' management has been very beneficial; but he cannot deal with the leases that have not fallen in, and which were originally given for a long term, but which are now unexpired with a short term running. Had those leases originally been given in perpetuity, the probability is that

those

Chairman—continued.

those lands to which I have referred would now have been covered by stores and manufactories.

2762. What you are complaining of is the effect of the past system of granting short leases upon the prospects of the city?—Yes.

2763. That is all you have to tell us upon that special point?—Yes, I think so.

2764. Then, on the general question, I think you heard the evidence of Sir William Miller?—Yes.

2765. I will ask you whether you do not think that the funds of the Irish Society would be more satisfactorily administered if they were administered by a body of gentlemen chosen as the memorial of 1875 said, men from the locality, thoroughly independent, and of high public character and standing; that is your view upon that question, is it?—I would not approve of its being placed in local hands; and if you refer back to the Report of the Royal Commission in 1854 you will see that they give a list of the members of the corporation who parcelled out the lands of the Society amongst themselves.

2766. If Parliament were to transfer the funds of the Irish Society to the Corporation of Londonderry, do you wish us to understand by your last answer that they would parcel it out amongst themselves?—No, I do not mean to say that they would; but that has happened in the past; and what has happened in the past may happen in the future. If you will refer to the report it gives the names of the members of the corporation, and what they have got; and as the result of those disclosures the Irish Society refused to renew a lease to the corporation which had a covenant to renew in it, or rather there was not a covenant, but there was a custom to renew; but, inasmuch as they had done away with part of those lands to some of the members of the corporation, with a *talis qualis* clause in the agreement when the lease fell in, the Irish Society would not renew, because it would not be going to the good of the city of Derry.

2767. Do you think that, although the corporation might be trusted with the funds that may be raised by the rates, and though they may be trusted to raise funds by the rates, and to look after the general purposes of local management, they are not to be so confidently trusted with the administration of these other funds as a body of gentlemen living in London?—There is this difference between the control of the local rates and the control of those funds of the Irish Society, that the system has grown up of giving these funds as doles from time to time, and it has demoralised the community, and most people think that they may get as much of them as they can, and they are not too scrupulous as to the means of getting a share. That is not the system of the corporation as regards the management of the rates; they are only elected for three years, and they know if they do anything that the community do not approve of they would not be re-elected.

2768. Are we to understand that your opinion is that the people of Derry are not to be trusted with the disposal of these funds?—I do not say that; I say they are honourable men, but I think it would not be desirable to bring the administration of the fund under local influence. I could mention any number of honourable men in Derry who would administer it properly; but I do not know who their successors would be, any more than I know who will be the successor of Sir Whitaker Ellis.

Sir John Whitaker Ellis.

2769. Do you, or do you not, know that nine-tenths of the property belonging to the Irish Society was, more than 100 years ago, leased in perpetuity?—I am perfectly aware of that.

2770. If those nine-tenths were leased 100 years ago, how can you possibly say that the non-leasing of the land in perpetuity has prevented the development of prosperity in Londonderry?—But we were in a very primitive state in Derry 130 years ago, and land was not valuable nor commerce developed in it; they were more agricultural leases; there was a tenement given in the city, with garden perhaps, but there was not commerce in the city.

2771. That does not affect the fact that nine-tenths of the property was leased in perpetuity?—But in course of time that property got incumbered, and people holding under perpetuity leases had no power to deal with them by letting them; and it is only lately, under the Settled Estates Act, that these people have had the power given them, and that they have been released.

2772. Why were they not able to deal with them?—Because of family incumbrances and wills, and so on.

2773. Had the Irish Society anything to do with family incumbrances?—No; but you wanted me to explain how it was that these perpetuities did not result in benefit to the tenants. My reply is, that the tenant could not improve his estate, and could not utilise the ground as it should be utilised, because during the last 160 years the property has got incumbered by wills and settlements and mortgages, and they were unable to deal with it; it is only lately, under the Settled Estates Act, that they were able to give perpetuity leases of this ground.

2774. The result of the perpetuity leases was that those who had perpetuity leases incumbered these lands in such a manner as to prevent their being made available?—Many of them are not available even now in later years when they are wanted; that difficulty, however, has been removed.

2775. Why is that?—You can make a title now through the Settled Estates Act to let it; and a few years ago you could not put it into the market at all.

2776. That had nothing to do with the Irish Society?—I know that.

2777. The Irish Society did what you asked them; they granted perpetuity leases?—Yes; we do not complain of that at all.

2778. You complained that they did not grant perpetuity leases; but it appears now that they did grant perpetuity leases?—I was simply confining myself to the slob land, which I defined as extending from the shipbuilding yard to the bridge downwards.

2779. That

Sir *John Ellis*—continued.

2779. That was all slob land 100 years ago?—Yes.

2780. It is all now fine handsome quays, is it not?—Yes; but take, for instance, the land between the quays and the Strand-road to Foyle College.

2781. The land below the shipbuilding yard is still slob towards the sea?—Up to the Asylum, with the exception of Rock Mill, is not covered with buildings, and those are the most valuable sites in Derry.

2782. Has there been any application for it, do you know whether there has been any application made to the Society to take that land?—Yes; I know from time to time there have been people anxious to use it, and they could not on account of its being only on a short lease.

2783. Do you know of any application to the Irish Society to take the land you refer to?—It is not in the hands of the Irish Society yet.

2784. How long will it be before it comes into their hands?—Forty-four years after this present time, I think.

2785. You are sure that this is not perpetuity land?—Certainly; the Gordon property.

2786. When will it fall in?—In 44 years after this.

2787. Has there been any application to the Irish Society to give an extension of the term, to warrant its being applied to any useful purpose?—No, not that I know of.

2788. Is that land ready for development at the present moment for any useful purpose, or is it the case that it is too far down the river, and the city has not yet extended to it?—Yes; but the city is extending in that direction, and has passed round it; it has passed round it like a horse-shoe.

2789. When it gets to it I suppose some arrangement will be made to enable buildings to be erected there?—Yes; there could be a reversionary lease granted by the Society to take effect from the end of the term.

2790. Or the holder of the term of 44 years could take a lease?—Yes, a reversionary lease, if the Society was willing to entertain the application.

2791. If there were any demand for it the Society could do that?—Yes.

2792. Do you know of any instance in which the Society has refused a perpetuity lease in recent times?—No; since 1883 the Society has been very liberal and altered its policy altogether, and has given satisfaction.

2793. I may sum up your evidence, may I not, thus: in olden days the Society granted perpetuity leases?—Yes.

2794. At the present day they grant perpetuity leases?—Yes.

2795. Yet I understand you to say that the non-granting of perpetuity leases is the cause of the non-prosperity of Londonderry?—No; I said between those two dates comes the fact that there were short leases given 70 years ago.

2796. Let us follow that up for a moment. At a certain period there were some short leases given?—Yes; and those lands, in consequence of their being short leases, are lying waste, whereas, if there had been perpetuity leases, they would have been used, I believe.

2797. Is that so; is it the case that the land of which short leases were given has not come back yet into the hands of the Irish Society?—Not yet.

2798. But a great deal has, has it not?—A good deal.

2799. Has not that been re-let by the Irish Society with great benefit to the town generally, with an improvement in the architecture of the city and the prosperity of the town?—A great improvement to the city, but they refused until now give to perpetuity leases.

2800. Has it not been for the benefit of Londonderry in general by reason of its larger income; according to your evidence, it appears to me that the Society have done everything; they have granted perpetuity leases and also short leases, which have greatly benefited the town and advanced your interest?—But you are skipping the 150 years between the two events. During that time they gave terminable leases; and it is these terminable leases that have had a great deal to do with keeping us back.

2801. I am not skipping that. I accept your position; I always try to accept the position of a witness, and see whether it will hold water. I accept your position; I take it that in the intermediate term there have been terminable leases granted, and I ask you whether those terminable leases have not fallen into the hands of the Irish Society, and whether the fact of their doing so has not been highly beneficial to the architectural appearance and the general prosperity of the town, and largely enhanced the revenue of the Society, who have been thereby enabled to effect large public works?—Yes, most undoubtedly that is the effect; but over and above that there is the fact that there are other leases which have not reached the Society's hand yet.

2802. Suppose a perpetuity lease is granted, is there anything to prevent that perpetuity lessee from granting a lease for a short period?—But I would see that perpetuity leases were not given to speculators.

2803. I will take your explanation in a moment if you will first answer my question; is there anything that would prevent a perpetuity lessee granting a short term?—You could not prevent that, unfortunately.

2804. He could do it, could he not?—Of course.

2805. Now I will go one step further; do you think there is anyone in Londonderry who, knowing that he could raise a large income by letting land held upon a perpetuity lease, would be so unjust to his family as not to take advantage of that power to get as much as he could by granting those short leases?—That is so in the case of a private owner who is unscrupulous; but the tendency of legislation is to prevent that, as is seen, *for example*, in the Town Holdings Commission. The Irish Society are trustees for the benefit of the community.

2806. I understand you are not yourself a tenant on the Irish Society's estate?—No.

2807. There

Colonel *Laurie*.

2807. There is a strong desire for perpetuity leases I understand you to say in Londonderry? —They will scarcely take anything smaller in Derry now, because there is so much land round about that can be got in perpetuity, but unfortunately it is not in the good districts.

2808. But perpetuity leases would be a valuable property, would they not? — Yes, to the lessee it would be of course.

2809. In that case as those lands according to the showing of the Corporation of Londonderry are public property, and used for public purposes, the holders of those perpetuity leases would be acquiring a valuable property at the expense of the community?—I am sorry to say they would be, but of the two evils I take the least.

2810. That of course would be the pleasantest and most agreeable side of the two to those who have leases?—It would be a great advantage to the community if those who get the perpetuities were obliged to build.

2811. At any rate it is the case, is it not, that the perpetuity leaseholder would have a valuable security at the expense of the community?—He would have a valuable security.

Mr. *Sexton*.

2812. Do you concur with the last witness in saying that perpetuity grants are the ordinary rule in towns in Ireland?—I have not a knowledge of many places outside Derry; but I have a very fair knowledge of Derry.

2813. You know, I suppose, that perpetuity grants greatly assisted the development of Belfast?—Undoubtedly.

2814. Have you studied this subject enough to be able to say whether those original grants were made to a few friends of the Irish Society in the town?—They would all be dead, and it is in the hands of the general public now.

2815. And they then farmed it out to occupiers?—Yes.

2816. But the occupiers could not get these leasehold grants themselves?—Not until lately; but the middlemen were worse in that respect than the society.

2817. But it sprang out of the action of the society that the middlemen used this power, and used it to the detriment of the society?—I think it arose, you may say, out of human nature.

2818. Could you define the period within which favourable terms to occupiers would have developed the prosperity of Derry, and those terms were not given, and in consequence Derry fell behind?—No; I say it is only now that we get the full advantage of it.

2819. During a certain period, as I understand, if you had got terms such as Belfast had, it would have developed your city; but you then did not get them, and now you got them too late?—In the particular portion to which I refer.

2820. As between Belfast and Derry, Belfast got those terms before you, and you were left behind?—Yes; but had Belfast not got the perpetuity leases they would have been left behind.

2821. The adoption of this policy, as I understand, by the Irish Society had a detrimental effect upon the prosperity of your city, as compared with Belfast?—The greater part of the city was granted in perpetuity by the Irish Society 100 years ago.

2822. But the occupiers had not those grants? —I fancy the lands were divided in small lots, and I fancy that each tenant was able to occupy his whole lot; for instance, a garden outside the walls and some acres in the country.

2823. Would you fix the period within which the policy of the society with regard to grants operated to the disadvantage of the town?—It is now we are beginning to feel that we have been kept back. Fifty years ago, if perpetuities had been freely given, it would have facilitated the progress of Derry.

2824. Could you fix the period within which the policy of the Irish Society has detrimentally affected the town, naming the beginning and the end; how far back did it reach, and how far forward does it come?—What we have suffered in that way may be shown by the statement that has been made here (of which I have no knowledge) that a portion of ground in Derry was refused for a ship-building yard. If that is so, and if this ship-building yard had come there, it is hard to say what the development would have been.

2825. Within what period did this disadvantage operate in Derry as compared with Belfast; what is the period within which the town would have developed if you had been well treated?—It was the general effect I was speaking of.

2826. For how long?—During the last 50 years.

2827. You appear to think the Corporation itself might be improved a little?—Whether I think it or not, I did not say it.

2828. I understand that you doubted whether they would be good administrators of these funds?—The Corporation was not mentioned at all I think; a local body was referred to.

Chairman.

2829. In my question I particularly referred to the Corporation, because that brought the thing to a point?—I beg your pardon; I thought you referred only to a local body. I would object to the administration of the funds being placed in the hands of any local body at all.

Mr. *Sexton*.

2830. Is it your opinion that in regard to the fund which, according to your argument, exists for the benefit of the city of Derry, Derry is so peculiar a city that in order to get the full advantage to the city the city ought to have the fund managed anywhere else than by the city. In fact, the city is the last place to manage it?—No, I do not say that. I only go on the principle that where there are two evils you should choose the least.

2831. The greatest evil of all is local administration in your opinion?—With money like this, and remember this is the case of money, a lot of which is given away in charity; the lives of the members of the local body would be pestered to death if they had the administration of it themselves.

2832. That applies to the administration of all funds, does it not. It applies to the administration by the Irish Society, and all the companies

Mr. *Sexton*—continued.

of their funds in England?—Are you speaking of a new state of things?

2833. I am speaking of the present state of things in England?—I do not know how they administer their funds in England.

2834. You have no control over the nomination and constitution of the Irish Society?—None whatever.

2835. Your corporation at present only represents half the citizens; it does not represent the Catholic half, does it?—I have among my supporters a large number of Catholics.

2836. That may be an exceptional fact; they have only one representative of their creed on the corporation?—One only.

2837. Suppose the corporation were improved in that regard by a widened franchise, do not you think a body of gentlemen, subject to scrutiny and re-election at the hands of the citizens of Derry, would be a very competent body to administer funds for the benefit of the city?—If you will allow me, the way I would like to see it done would be to capitalise the estates, and gradually pay off the public debt, and make Derry a free harbour. A ship coming into the harbour now cannot get a cargo, and must load with ballast. There is a debt of 800,000 *l.*, and if that were paid off there would be no loaves and fishes to fight about after that.

2838. Your preference is to sell the estate, if you had your way?—The agricultural portions I would sell under the Ashbourne Act in justice to the tenant. It does not matter if you sell the other, but you cannot realise it without selling.

2839. I understand your preference is that you would sell?—Rather than transfer it from the present management as at present managed.

2840. Even supposing it, with its present management, you would prefer that it should be sold?—No, I think they are doing a great deal for the city.

2841. You said you would prefer to have a free harbour?—Yes.

2842. Then assuming the estate to be sold, to what authority would you confine the use of the capital funds?—I would not define that; the Irish Society could do it as well as anybody.

2843. If Parliament were to sell the estate, what authority would you suggest?—The present authority, I fancy, would be the best; they have the machinery. I presume you would lay down in the Act of Parliament what they were to do with it.

2844. That is what I want your decision about. Would you have the Act say what is to be done with the money?—I cannot say.

Mr. *Lawson.*

2845. You would have it made what is called an express trust, I presume?—That would be the safest thing.

2846. In the case of the renewals of leases, as they fell in, on perpetual terms, I suppose, the rents charged were rack-rents?—Oh, dear no; they were very small rents; there were no rents at all, in fact.

2847. In the case of renewals, did they not charge the commercial value of the land?—No; they charge a septennial fine equal to a year's rent; or rather it was in this way: It was not a fine; but there was the ordinary rent paid, and a septennial rent, and the secretary's fees every seven years.

Mr. *Lawson*—continued.

2848. The rent was not raised?—No.

2849. What was the fine?—There was no fine, there was the ordinary rent and the septennial rent, and three guineas secretary's fees. Then, under the Renewable Leasehold Conversion Act, now, when it is converted into a grant, there is an annual sum substituted for these payments.

2850. I understand there were some urban properties which had been held on a short lease, and when the lease fell in there was a renewal granted in perpetuity?—Yes.

2851. I am talking only of leaseholds in Londonderry?—Yes, but all the land within the city walls was granted in perpetuity.

2852. You say that was not at a rack-rent?—No, it was at a very small rent.

2853. By the rack rent of course I only mean the full commercial rent?—It was not the full commercial rent.

Mr. *Cleary.*

2854. I do not know whether you answered this question before, but at any rate I wish you now to answer it distinctly: do you say that the present corporation of Derry is not to be trusted with the administration of the funds of the Irish Society?—I do not mean that for a moment.

2855. What do you mean?—I mean as a matter of choice. I would not transfer it to a local body.

2856. Why not?—Local people are liable to be pestered and annoyed when money is to be given away.

2857. Do you mean to say that they would not resist any pestering directed to an unjust administration of the funds?—Yes, they would, but the scope of the trust is very wide.

2858. Then you mean to say that the present corporation of Derry is not to be trusted; I ask you frankly to say yes or no?—I say it is to be trusted; but I should object to the corporation or any other body getting the funds to dispose of as the Irish Society are allowed to do; as for instance, giving to poor people, and giving to schools, and all that.

2859. If your corporation is to be trusted, may I take it it is to Irish control you object altogether, and not to local control?—I refer to local control.

2860. Do you see any reason whatever why 24 Londoners should manage the funds of the Irish Society, or have any control or connection with it?—Up to 1883 I could not see any reason, but from 1883 I did see that it was a great advantage to have the management in their hands.

2861. In what way?—As things stand now it is an advantage.

2862. This Irish Society is a body of trustees administering the funds for Irish purposes: is there any reason why they should continue to manage it rather than Irishmen?—The administration

Mr. *Clancy*—continued.

[illegible] by the Irish Society at present is very satisfactory.

2863. You said the greater part of the urban property in the city of Derry was given in perpetuity leases some years ago?—150 years ago.

2864. Do you know how many leases were given; to how many persons were grants made?—I suppose there were fully 150, but I cannot say that for certain.

2865. You said, in answer to the Right honourable Chairman, that the doles given from time to time by the Irish Society had demoralised the whole population?—That was what I referred to. That was my answer; that the people of Derry had been so used to look upon the Irish Society as a body from which they can get doles.

2866. Who got these doles?—You will see that in the returns.

2867. I am asking you what your impression is; what generally was the class of persons who got the doles?—Schools, and charitable institutions, and such like.

2868. I would like to know a little more about the doles, if you can tell us about them; did any individuals get private benefactions?—Not exactly in that shape. You will see in the account under Charitable Donations: "Widow Hampsey 8 *l.* 10 *s.*, Mrs. Campbell 4 *l.*, and W. Henry, late teacher Bohill School (pension) 15 *l.*"; and then there is also "Clothing for the Poor."

2869. Do you know of any doles given for private purposes?—Those are private pensions I should take it; they are gratuities given as I understand.

2870. What for?—For some services rendered. For instance, in this case of a teacher in a school a pension of 15 *l.* a year was given; in a case like that if it were under the management of local men they would be prepared to make it 25 *l.* perhaps.

Mr. *Healy*.

2871. Do you agree with the "no popery" aspect taken up by the Irish Society?—I do not think the Irish Society took up that aspect; it was the charter.

2872. Do you approve of the aspect in the charter?—I do not believe in the funds of the Irish Society being devoted to any denominational or sectarian purposes; I believe in its being given to public purposes such as I mentioned.

2873. Would you be glad to see the Society abolished?—I have no particular reason for wishing that.

Mr. *Lea*.

2874. You are afraid that the funds might be taken from Derry if the Irish Society were abolished; is that your reason?—Yes; if the Society were abolished there might be a scramble for the funds, and we would not get the full benefit.

2875. You contend it is a Derry fund?—Certainly, and I hold the London companies money belongs to the Society too.

2876. I presume you know nothing about the London companies outside the Irish Society?—Only that the Irish Society itself always held that the London companies derived from them.

2877. But I mean you have no experience of the dealings of the London companies, apart from the Irish Society?—No.

Thursday, 26th June 1890.

MEMBERS PRESENT:

Mr. Clancy.
Sir John Ellis.
Mr. John Ellis.
Mr. Elton.
Mr. T. M. Healy.
Colonel Laurie.
Mr. Lawson.
Mr. Lea.
Mr. John Morley.
Mr. Sexton.
Sir Richard Temple.

THE RIGHT HONOURABLE JOHN MORLEY, IN THE CHAIR.

Mr. P. C. GAUSSEN, sworn; and Examined.

Mr. *Clancy.*

2878. YOU are a member of the Irish Bar, I believe?—I am.

2879. You are connected by family with the county of Londonderry?—Yes.

2880. I believe as an Irish barrister you are connected with various legal proceedings in relation to the estates of the London companies?—In regard to the Drapers' Company's sales especially, I was counsel for the tenants there.

2881. What estates are you particularly conversant with?—As regards personal knowledge, I am more conversant with the Salters' estate; as regards the management of the sale, I am, of course, naturally more conversant with the sale of the Drapers' estate, where I was counsel for the tenants, and am so still.

2882. Have you got with you a copy of the memorial from the Mayor and Corporation of Derry to the Irish Society, dated 1858?—Yes, I have, among my papers; I will hand it in in a moment.

2883. What was the substance of the memorial?—The substance of the memorial was complaining against the manner in which the Irish Society managed the city of Derry, and specially as to refusing to give perpetuity leases, and contrasting the progress which Belfast had made under the long leases given by Lord Donegal's family with the progress of Derry, and dwelling upon the fact that it was owing to the refusal to give perpetuity leases.

Sir John Ellis.

2884. Had we not better have the memorial; have you got the memorial there?—I have it among my papers, and will find it presently if you will let me hand it in afterwards; perhaps you will allow me in the meantime to deal with the Salters' Company and the Drapers' Company. (*The same was afterwards handed in.*)

Mr. *Clancy.*

2885. Have you got a copy of the memorial dated the 10th of April 1867, signed by the tenants of the Salters' Estate?—Yes; I can put in the memorial from the tenants on the Salters' estate to the company, dated the 10th of April 1867.

2886. Will you tell us briefly (you can afterwards hand in the document if that is necessary) the substance of that memorial?—The memorial was the result of a meeting of the tenants of the Salters' estate, in consequence of the large increase of rent which was proposed, and afterwards insisted upon, by the Salters' Company upon their taking up the management of the estate, which had been up till then in the hands of the Bateson family.

2887. In the hands of the Bateson family as middlemen, I presume?—As middlemen.

2888. Did the tenants in that memorial make any statement as to the treatment they had received from the Bateson family?—Yes: if you will allow me I will read some of the salient points briefly. The first paragraph of the memorial states, "That after your worshipful company leased away the entire of your estate in the county of Londonderry, in 1754, to the grandfather of the present Sir Thomas Bateson, for 896 *l.* per annum, the greater portion of the town of Magherafelt was built entirely by the capital of the tenants, who had previously settled on the estate, under the articles published in the reign of James I., for the plantation of Ulster. (2.) That Mr. Bateson, disregarding his own private interests, from time to time leased off to the settlers on the estate the building lots on which the town of Magherafelt now stands for terms varying from 100 to 60 years, at fair ground rents. (3.) That in 1854, when the lease of 1754 expired, and your worshipful company entered upon the management of the estate, the value of the tenants' property in the town of Magherafelt was, according to the Poor Law valuation, 3,042 *l.*"

2889. You need not read the whole memorial; but if there are any explicit statements in the memorial as to an increase of rent enforced by the Salters' Company on the expiry of Sir Thomas Bateson's interest, will you read them?

Mr. *Clancy*—continued.

—The memorial states that the company "then trebled the rents of the town but confirmed to us" (that is, the memorialists) "at the same time the old and immemorial custom of the estate, to give the tenant full liberty to sell his improvements to the highest bidder. (5.) That in consideration of your leaving the old custom untouched, the town submitted to the increase of rent, though not without murmur and remonstrance. (6.) That inasmuch as you continued up to December 1863, to recognise this ancient custom, not only by allowing your tenants to sell to the highest bidder, but by yourselves purchasing, at full market value, the interest of several of your tenants in their holdings, we felt assured that we were safe in continuing to sink our capital and labour in the town, as we had been accustomed to do in times past. (7.) That we then learned, with feelings of great alarm, that you had resolved not only again to increase our rents, but to abolish our customary right to sell our property to the highest bidder. (8.) That these feelings were deeply intensified in April 1866, by the unexpected service of notices to quit on 58 tenants in the town, including many widows and orphans. (9.) That several of us who had very recently spent large sums of money in the purchase of old and ruinous tenements, and in making permanent and valuable improvements thereon, having memorialised your worshipful court for relief from our distressing condition, asking such an extension of term as would secure our outlay under the circumstances mentioned in our memorials, but we have not been able, after repeated petitioning for 12 months, to get any satisfactory replies."

2890. If the memorial is going to be put in, you had better tell us just the effect of it?—The effect of the memorial was to complain of the proposed increase of rent, and the proposed infringement upon the tenant right custom which then existed.

2891. They attempted to encroach upon it, and sought to destroy the tenant right custom?—Exactly.

2892. Will you hand in that memorial?—Yes. (*The same was handed in.*)

2893. Are there any specific instances given in the memorial of increase of rent?—There are no specific instances given in this memorial. There is a reply from the Salters' Company dealing with the memorial paragraph by paragraph.

2894. What is the date of that reply?—This reply is dated the 7th of May in the same year.

2895. What, briefly, is the reply of the Salters' Company?—It was briefly claiming that the estate was held by the Salters' Company unfettered by any fiduciary conditions.

2896. They claimed, I suppose, the right to do what they liked with their own?—It is claiming the right to make the proposed increases and stating the reasons why in their opinion it should not be considered unfair.

2897. They did not deny any of the statements in that memorial, did they?—The effect of their reply is rather to explain than to deny.

2898. Will you hand in that reply?—Yes. (*The same was handed in.*)

2899. Was there a supplemental memorial in answer to that reply of the Salters' Company?—Yes.

2900. Is there in that memorial any statement as to increased rents?—Yes.

2901. What is the date of that second memorial?—It was read and adopted at a public meeting held in the Court House, Magherafelt, on the 4th day of July 1867.

2902. Will you tell us if there are any specific instances there of increased rents. There is a table in that memorial, is there not, showing the increases; will you state the effect of it?—Before doing so, it would be well to state that in the supplemental memorial they did expressly set out the claim they are making at present, namely, that this is a trust estate derived from the conditions under which the property was originally obtained by the company. If you will allow me, I will read the first part of the supplemental memorial as showing that the claim which is made now by the tenants was made at that time, in 1867.

Chairman.

2903. Are you going to put that in?—Yes.

2904. Then you need not read it?—Very good. (*The same was handed in.*)

Mr. *Clancy.*

2905. Will you just tell us what it points to?—The general effect of the supplemental memorial is to point the attention of the company to certain matters connected with their title upon which the memorialists relied then, as showing that the tenure of the company in regard to the estate was affected by trusts.

Chairman.

2906. We do not want that; that does not concern us at this stage?—Then I will not go into that.

Mr. *Clancy.*

2907. What I am asking, is, are there any specific instances there of increase of rent?—There are; the table states that Mrs. M'Fall had been a tenant under Sir Thomas Bateson at a rent of 3 *l.* 10 *s.*; that the increased rent proposed by the Salters' Company was 19 *l.*; and that the term fixed by Mr. Gordon, who was then arranging for the Salters' Company, was to be 21 years from the 1st of November 1854.

Mr. *Sexton.*

2908. Was the rent increased in one operation from 3 *l.* to 19 *l.*?—Apparently.

Mr. *Clancy.*

2909. Is it alleged by whom the improvements on the holdings were made?—It is alleged that the purchase-money of the old premises (which, I take it, was the purchase-money that Mrs. M'Fall paid) was 295 *l.*, and the money expended by her was 1,000 *l.*; and the date of the expenditure was 1854.

2910. Is the extent of the holding mentioned?—It is not. I may say I have merely mentioned the first of the six cases given here, inasmuch as this memorial is put in, and it will, therefore, save time not to go more fully into the details.

2911. Do

Mr. Sexton.

2911. Do the other cases correspond to that of which you have given particulars?—I have also another list, which is a fuller list, giving the particulars for a number of tenants, which would go to show that the six cases mentioned in this supplemental memorial are not exceptional cases.

2912. Mrs. M'Fall's case is a typical case, you think?—So I would believe. I should add that I am not in a position to say that the increase was in one bound from 3*l.* to 10*l.*; but, from the statement in the memorial, I would so gather it. The company will be able to say with regard to that.

Mr. Clancy.

2913. Do the other cases in that table show any as large increase of rent?—So far as I can judge, the case I have mentioned, which is the first case, is practically typical of the other cases.

Chairman.

2914. What do you judge from?—From the figures. This other table which I put in is a table showing the comparative rental, and is evidently a fuller list than the six cases that are referred to in the memorial. This table, which I will now hand in, shows "the comparative rental of the various holdings in the town of Magherafelt. Under the late Sir R. Bateson, Bart., and the Marquis of Londonderry, with the increased rent charged by the Salters' Company of London, in coming into possession in the year 1854, and the further increase in 1867, together with the amount of the purchase-money of the several holdings, and the subsequent estimated expenditure in buildings."

Mr. Clancy.

2915. Are the totals given there?—There are parallel columns which purport to show the rental.

2916. If the totals are given will you read them?—There are two lists of cases. Taking the first list of cases, the first column shows that the total rental prior to 1854, under the late Sir Thomas Bateson and the Marquis of Londonderry, was 97*l.* 8*s.* 4*d.*; and it appears in the second column that the increased rent in 1854 brought it up to 285*l.* 16*s.*; that is to say, immediately on the company coming in, the 97*l.* 8*s.* 4*d.* became 285*l.* 16*s.*; and in 1867, upon a second increase of rent, this 285*l.* 16*s.* became 504*l.* 19*s.*, as is shown in the third column. Then in the last column the estimated expenditure of the tenants in buildings is put down as 10,900*l.*

2917. Is it alleged anywhere that the Salters' Company expended any money upon those buildings?—No; it is alleged generally and explicitly that the buildings were built by the tenants. The estimated expenditure by the tenants is put down here as 10,900*l.*, and the purchase-money, which, I take it, is the money that the tenants paid to their predecessors, is put down in the next column as 6,746*l.*

2918. Now will you hand in that table?—Yes. (*The same was handed in.*)

2919. Where did you get these documents

Mr. Clancy—continued.

which you have just handed in?—I got these documents from one of those tenants in Magherafelt, who was connected with the meeting which resulted in these memorials; these memorials were printed at the time.

2920. Were they printed in the public newspapers?—Yes.

2921. Have the statements in them ever been denied?—Not that I am aware of.

2922. As a matter of fact, I believe, these figures and the condition of these tenants were brought before the House of Commons?—Yes, I have before me the official documents of the House of Commons containing a notice of a question to be asked by Mr. Maguire, on the 14th of May 1867, of the Chief Secretary for Ireland.

2923. This question, I presume, was put by Mr. Maguire; have you got the Chief Secretary's answer?—No; I have not had an opportunity of looking it up. I may say that I did not think I should have been called first to-day, or I should have looked the matter up.

Chairman.] I find that the answer of the Chief Secretary for Ireland was given on the 20th of May 1867; but, looking to the form of that answer, I do not think we can have the question put in.

Mr. Clancy.

2924. Do you wish to refer to any other document in regard to these cases?—I would also like to put in two letters which were also printed at the time, which passed between the company's agent, Mr. Spotswood, and one of the tenants, in regard to his specific case.

Chairman.

2925. We do not want to overload our minutes with documents unless they have some real bearing upon the question we are considering. What is the point of the letters?—It is calling attention to his own case in particular, but also to the general management of the company.

2926. Will you let me look at them?—(*The letters were handed to the Chairman.*) I do not think these should be put in.

Mr. Clancy.

2927. Are you able to give any evidence regarding the regulations that have to be observed by each tenant on the company's estate; have they to sign any document, or anything like that?—Yes.

2928. Will you just state, as briefly as possible, the substance of it?—I have a pamphlet here, called "The Irish Land Question and the Twelve London Companies," which embodies the memorials I have put in, and also embodies what purports to be the regulations on the manor of Lizard, the property of the Ironmongers' Company; and amongst other conditions which the tenants had to observe on being admitted as tenants, is this: "In no instance shall any person now being or becoming tenant of the company's at any time underlet any portion of his farm or subdivide it to be occupied by any others, or make any assignment thereof; nor shall he erect any new building whatever upon the land without obtaining the previous consent in writing from the

Mr. Cleary—continued.

the company or their agent;" and then, again: "All directions given by the agent regarding improvements in tillage, draining, fencing, &c., shall be duly attended to by the tenants."

Chairman.

2929. I do not see how that bears upon this inquiry?—These apparently are the ordinary regulations (whether justifiable or not) on the estate; what is the point of reading them; the authorship of this pamphlet to which you refer is known, is it not?—Yes.

Mr. Cleary.

2930. By whom is it published?—It was published by the "Northern Whig" office. If I may refer to the Chairman's last question, the point, so far as it is material, is, that although it is recognised that large expenditures have been made by the companies on their estates, having regard to the principle on which that expenditure has been made, it has been felt that it has not proved productive of the same benefits that perhaps the company's expenditure would have produced had there been security of tenure given. In other words, to illustrate what I mean, upon the estates of the company practically, with the exception of Derry and Magherafelt, there are no towns that are in any sense commercial towns, that is where there is any commercial spirit.

Chairman.

2931. We have had a great deal of interesting evidence upon that point, but I do not see how this recital of the estate regulations of the Ironmongers' Company carries us any further?—Perhaps not.

Mr. Cleary.

2932. Now confining yourself to the sale of the Salters' estate, when did the negotiations commence for the sale of the Salters' estate?—I believe it was in 1883.

2933. Are you aware that promises were made by the Salters' Company, when they were negotiating the sale of their estate, that the grants they had been giving to churches and charities would be continued?—I am aware that the universal impression, I may say, on the minds of the tenants was, that the grants to churches and charities would be continued, and that they had that upon the authority of the company through their agents.

2934. Can you mention any particular agent?—Sir Henry Cartwright.

2935. Can you refer to any words Sir Henry Cartwright, or any other agent, used on the subject from which this impression might be derived?—Yes. I have before me a letter written by the late Mr. William Ash Gaussen, and what he states in that letter I also had from him personally.

Mr. Sexton.

2936. The late Mr. William Ash Gaussen is the gentleman who was referred to in Dr. Jordan's evidence here, and whose letter is referred to at Question 139?—Yes.

Mr. Cleary.

2937. Was Mr. Gaussen a relative of yours?—Yes, he was my uncle. He died recently.

2938. Will you just tell us the substance of the letter?—The substance of the letter is that Mr. Ash Gaussen there states, and he stated to me subsequently, that he went into Magherafelt to see Dr. Todd, who was then arranging the sale, amongst other things expressly to ascertain as to what the Salters' Company intended to do in reference to the continuance of the grants; that the position to be taken by the Salters' Company, so far as he personally was concerned, at all times was considered by him as a material circumstance in considering whether he would sign the agreement to sell.

2939. He himself was negotiating for the purchase of his own holding, was he?—He subsequently agreed to purchase, and at that time was considering as to whether he would accept the terms offered by the company or not. He states that he went in to see Dr. Todd and ask him as to whether any arrangements had been made. I had better, perhaps, read this part of the letter.

Chairman.

2940. Is it the letter that you are referring to or are you relating to the conversation?—Practically the conversation was the same as the letter.

2941. Will you tell us the conversation?—That Dr. Todd informed him that the Salters' Company were to continue the grants; that Dr. Todd suggested to him, or else that he suggested to Dr. Todd (which it was I am not quite certain) the advisability of seeing Sir Henry Cartwright personally upon the subject; that upon that day week he, with Dr. Todd, went in to Sir Henry Cartwright's office, and that Sir Henry Cartwright confirmed what he had already understood.

Mr. Cleary.

2942. Namely?—Namely, that the grants to the churches and the charities would be continued. He also informed me that had it not been for the belief which, under those circumstances, he entertained, he would not have joined in the sale, inasmuch as the continuance of his own church would mainly fall upon his own shoulders, he being the principal supporter of it at Ballyronan.

2943. You are speaking, as I understand, of what your uncle said to yourself?—Yes.

2944. Are you in a position to say that what your uncle felt and said upon the subject was felt and said by the other tenants?—Certainly. I have before me a letter from another tenant, a magistrate, Mr. Henry Church Mann, who practically states that the same impression was conveyed to him by Dr. Todd, and that if necessary he would give evidence.

2945. What is the date of that letter?—The 7th of June 1890. There was also a correspondence in 1887, one letter especially from Mr. Sparrow; I do not know whether it has been referred to.

2946. Do not read the letter, but tell us what is the substance of it?—The substance of it is that an express statement is alleged by him to have

Mr. Clancy—continued.

have been made by Sir Henry Cartwright in regard to the continuance of the grant.

2947. Is the statement quoted?—Yes.

2948. Will you read it?—He says, "I can only say, without wishing to attribute anything untruthful or ungenerous to anyone concerned in this matter, that Sir H. Cartwright on several occasions assured me, as he did the other local clergy, that the grants would be continued to our churches. On the occasion of his last visit at this rectory in the early spring of this year, he stated that, after several communications with the company, he had succeeded in securing the grants for at least three of the parishes on their estate, besides that for the Rainey School in Magherafelt."

2949. Whose words are those which you are reading?—Mr. Sparrow's, the rector of Moneymore.

2950. What is the date of the letter?—The date of the letter is the 17th of September 1887, and it appeared in a newspaper of the 19th of September 1887.

2951. What is the newspaper that it appeared in?—The "Belfast News Letter"; but it also appeared in the "Times."

2952. On what date did it appear in the "Times"?—I cannot say. All these letters practically appeared in the "Times." In consequence of the intimation from the company that they would not be responsible after that year for any further grants, these letters were written by the tenants to the "Times;" and the inference I would draw would be that in consequence of the correspondence in the "Times," and the articles therein, the grants have been continued up to the present. If you will allow me, I will just finish reading the paragraph in the letter, "In reply to my query as to the names of these parishes, he said they were Magherafelt, Woods, and Ballinderry, and he added that what he wanted was that the company should continue the grants to the other churches also."

2953. That will do; as a matter of fact, after the sale had been completed, were the grants discontinued?—As a matter of fact, after the sale was completed, an intimation was received that the grants would be discontinued; but the grants, as a matter of fact, have not yet been discontinued; they have been paid each year, but there has been an intimation from the company as to whether they consider themselves liable and responsible ever to pay them again.

Mr. Sexton.

2954. Were they discontinued and resumed on that estate?—There was an intimation of discontinuance and a subsequent payment.

Mr. Clancy.

2955. Have you got the letter intimating that they would be discontinued?—It would have been sent to the clergy, as a matter of fact.

Chairman.

2956. Have you got it?—No, I have not.

2957. Have you seen such a letter?—No.

2958. Do you know anybody who has ever seen it?—I know my uncle was aware of the discontinuance.

2959. But what we want to know is with regard to the letter; was a letter, to your knowledge, written and sent announcing the discontinuance?—As to the manner in which the intimation was given I cannot say.

2960. If you cannot say how the intimation was given, there is an end of that point?—Yes.

Mr. Lea.

2961. In answer to these letters, did you see a letter from Sir Robert Fowler in the "Times"?—I did.

2962. Did you read that letter?—I did.

2963. Sir Robert Fowler held an official position in the Salters' Company, did he not?—I understand he did.

2964. That letter was written in September 1887, was it not?—Yes; the same time as this correspondence, and in answer to some letters.

2965. Did Sir Robert Fowler say that one benefit they would get by selling their estate was that they would not have to continue the grants?—That is my recollection of what is in the letter. There is another I should like to refer to from Mr. Carter.

Chairman.

2966. What is it about?—It is on this point alone; it gives the names of certain tenants who say they are prepared to substantiate that these statements were given, and, in a subsequent letter from my uncle, he appends a sworn affidavit from a tenant, named Jared Derby, which purports to confirm the statements which he alleged had been made at the interview with Dr. Todd, in his first letter.

Mr. Clancy.

2967. Have you got a copy of that affidavit?—I have a printed copy here.

2968. Was it sworn?—It was a solemn declaration, I should think. As regards the only time which I remember personally discussing the grant at all with Sir Henry Cartwright, I remember upon one occasion talking to him about the Rainey School. The Rainey School was an institution in which I at the time took particular interest, and I understood from my uncle that the endowment was to be continued.

Chairman.

2969. This was merely a remark, as I understand, made by Sir Henry Cartwright in conversation with you; you made no contract in consequence; it was not a consideration for any contract?—Certainly not.

Mr. Clancy.

2970. Did Sir Henry Cartwright make these remarks to you for the purpose of having them conveyed to the tenants?—Certainly not. I should like to say, in regard to Dr. Todd, that subsequently to the sale, we have discussed the matter.

2971. Unless

Chairman.

2971. Unless you can bring forward some remarks made by Dr. Todd to induce you, or having the effect of inducing you, to do something, I do not conceive it affects this inquiry? —I should only like to explain that, in the evidence I have given, I do not impeach at all the *bona fides* of Dr. Todd or Sir Henry Cartwright; that the conversation with Dr. Todd was entirely consistent with his own letter, and that, from my personal knowledge of what occurred in the locality, I think the solution of the correspondence can be arrived at without impeaching the *bona fides* of either party. In other words, I think probably the strong expressions of opinion may perhaps have conveyed impressions that were not intended; but at the same time the impression undoubtedly existed; and, owing to that impression, some tenants certainly purchased who otherwise would not have purchased.

Mr. Clancy.

2972. We will now come to another point, if you can give any evidence upon that, namely, as to whether there were any threats made to tenants to induce them to buy; can you give any evidence upon that point?—No, I cannot give evidence of any threats to the tenants; but certainly some of the tenants were not anxious to join in the purchase at the terms arranged.

Chairman.

2973. Are you still dealing with the Salters' Company?—Yes.

Mr. Clancy.

2974. Have you any evidence to produce regarding threats for the recovery of rent, and of raising the rent, by Sir Henry Cartwright, in case the holdings were not purchased by the tenants?—I produce a circular of the 2nd February 1888, which is a notice signed by Sir Henry Cartwright, that "The Salters' Company is now prepared to sell to the general public."

Chairman.

2975. You are now on the point of alleged duress; does this circular bear upon that at all? —Yes.

2976. Will you just read the words, that did convey a threat?—"Threat" is a word I would prefer not to use; it is rather pressure on the part of the company, which from their point of view I can quite understand.

2977. Will you read the words, please, to which you refer?—"The Salters' Company is now prepared to sell to the general public the several farms which the tenants have refused to purchase. The Land Commissioners will lend half of the purchase-money to the purchasers, repayable by 49 annual instalments at the rate of 4 per centum, and the company will lend the other half of the purchase-money. Adjoining tenants who have purchased their own holdings will get the preference. The company reserves the right to enforce the contract of all tenants who have contracted to purchase their holdings. After to-morrow the company will make no allowances, but will insist on immediate payment of all arrears of rent and interest due."

2978. I ask you what sentences in that notice (there are only two so far as I can make out from hearing it read) do you regard as putting pressure upon the tenants; just read those sentences alone?—The last sentence: "After to-morrow the company will make no allowances, but will insist on immediate payment of all arrears of rent and interest due;" and the first: "The Salters' Company is now prepared to sell to the general public the several farms which the tenants have refused to purchase."

Mr. Clancy.

2979. Where did you get this notice; were they posted up?—Yes, at the time.

Mr. T. M. Healy.

2980. Have you this series of printed documents addressed by Dr. Todd to the tenants?—No, I have not.

Mr. Clancy.

2981. Have you any other evidence upon that point?—I have some copies of some letters which were written by Sir Henry Cartwright to the tenants, but it does not strengthen the circular. I should say that the interpretation that I put upon the circular is merely bearing upon the question of whether the sale was a bargain to the tenants, having regard to the fact that certain tenants did not wish to purchase unless they were pressed. I am not questioning the honesty of the company in any way.

2982. Have you any evidence upon any other points bearing upon the sale of the Salters' Company's Estate; if not, we had better come to some other point?—Perhaps I may read one letter from Sir Henry Cartwright.

Chairman.

2983. You just told us you considered there was nothing in the letter that carried us farther? —It is practically to the same effect.

Mr. Clancy.

2984. Are there in these letters any threats of legal proceedings, such as Sir Henry Cartwright intimated would be taken if the tenants did not buy?—Yes, in one of them; I will just read it: "Sir,—As you are one of the few who have refused the company's offer to sell to their tenants, and procure them the advantages of the Land Purchase Act, 1885, it is necessary to make other arrangements with regard to your holding; but before they are in a position to do so the company must have all rent to last gale day paid up. I have, therefore, to give you notice that the company require you forthwith to pay all rent due to 1st May last. If not paid before 8th July next I shall be reluctantly obliged to institute legal proceedings for its recovery, so that the company may be able without delay to deal with your holding. Yours faithfully, *H. E. Cartwright.*"

2985. What is the date of that letter?—The 25th of June 1888.

Mr. *Clancy*—continued.

2986. To whom is it addressed?—To one of the tenants; I think it was to Mr. Badger.

2987. Has it not upon it the name of the person to whom it is addressed?—I have only a copy of the letter here; I will find you the name.

Chairman.

2988. May I ask where you got it from?—I got it from the pleadings in the Salters' case against Badger.

Mr. *Sexton.*

2989. Was the letter addressed to Mr. Badger?—I believe so; it was in the brief.

Mr. *Clancy.*

2990. Did you copy it yourself; No, but I verified it.

Mr. *T. M. Healy.*

2991. Do I understand that it is on the files of the court?—I have got the brief here; it is in the brief.

2992. I thought you said it was the pleadings?—It is not in the pleadings; it is in the brief, I should have said.

Mr. *Clancy.*

2993. Was it proved at the trial; was it put in evidence?—My recollection is that it was.

Mr. *Ellis.*

2994. Were you counsel in the case?—No, but I was present.

2995. You say the original letter was put in?—My recollection is that it was: I was present in court.

Mr. *Clancy.*

2996. Is there any other evidence upon that point that you can give?—I think not to carry the matter further.

2997. I understand you came here to give evidence regarding the Rainey School?—Chiefly.

2998. I understand that, after the evidence given by Lord Justice FitzGibbon in regard to the Rainey School, the Committee do not desire to go into the matter further; I will therefore only ask you one question. You were yourself engaged as counsel in the case before the Privy Council when these questions affecting the Rainey School came before that body?—Yes.

2999. You listened to some observations made by Lord Ashbourne with regard to the treatment of the head master by the Salters' Company?—Yes.

3000. Will you just tell the Committee, in one sentence, the substance of what Lord Ashbourne said?—The purport of his observations was, that he expressed incredulity at learning that the Salters' Company purposed to treat the head master in the manner in which, as it came before the Privy Council, it was then proposed. He stated that the Salters' Company was the body to which Mr. Kincaid ought to apply; that the Privy Council had no funds of which they could have any disposing power in order to compensate him; but that his case was one that ought to be dealt with by the company.

Mr. *Clancy*—continued.

3001. Would it be going too far to say that he emphatically condemned the treatment of the head master by the Salters' Company?—I do not wish to use those words; but he said that the case was one which ought to be dealt with by the company.

3002. Can you give any information about the Drapers' Company's dealings with their tenants; have you read any of the evidence given already before this Committee in regard to that subject?—I have read the newspaper reports.

3003. Can you add anything to it?—No, I am not aware that I can.

Mr. *Lea.*

3004. Do you know the facts with regard to Badger's case, which you referred to?—Yes.

3005. Was it a case in which promissory notes were given for arrears of rent?—Yes.

3006. Over and above the amount paid to the Salters' Company?—Yes.

3007. Badger was sued upon those notes, was he not?—Yes, he was.

3008. And compelled to pay?—He was.

3009. He is, I suppose, a ruined man; has he been sold up since?—That I cannot say.

3010. Were there many other tenants in the same case as Badger?—There were a considerable number of tenants. There were two test cases taken; and, of course, having regard to the decision in Badger's case, no other tenants contested their liability.

3011. They have all paid their promissory notes, as far as you know?—So far as I know. I cannot give any personal evidence as to their position.

3012. Your uncle and your family have been tenants to the Salters' Company for a long time, I believe?—Yes; Ballyronan was practically built by my family.

3013. The evidence you gave was, that there was a strong general feeling in the district that the company would continue the grants to education and schools?—Certainly.

3014. Was that very strongly felt?—It was very strongly felt.

3015. If no actual promise was given, it was generally understood?—The impression undoubtedly existed, I may say, universally.

Mr. *John Ellis.*

3016. Have you any figures with respect to the rise or alteration of rental, other than those you have given us?—I have not.

Mr. *T. M. Healy.*

3017. Do you know anything about Benjamin Barefoot's case, which we have had under discussion?—Yes.

3018. Were you counsel in the case?—No but I recollect the proceedings.

3019. The matter arose here in this way: a letter was put in from the Salters' agent, making certain promises, and it was alleged by one of the witnesses (I think by Mr. Murrough O'Brien) that those promises were afterwards departed from, and the question was asked why this letter was not pleaded by Benjamin Barefoot; can you clear that point up?—Of course I am awa

Mr. *T. M. Healy*—continued.

of that letter, and I know the principle upon which the decision was grounded was, at the trial, that it appeared that the contingency that the sale might be delayed for a considerable period had not been considered by either party. That was, as I remember, the interpretation put upon that letter.

3260. Then the letter was pleaded, you think? —I believe the letter was referred to, but I cannot tell for certain.

Chairman.] Now I think the time has come when we may say something to Dr. Freshfield and the other gentlemen who represent the City companies here. We now certainly begin to see the end of the evidence which may be called, the evidence against the companies and the Irish Society. After that evidence is completed, which may be on Monday, or at the latest Thursday next, we should be glad to hear any evidence which the companies or the Irish Society think it worth their while to lay before the Committee with a view of rebutting the evidence which you, gentlemen, have listened to here. So it would be well if you could be ready with any evidence of that kind by next Thursday, or even possibly Monday.

Mr. *Healy.*] May I say, Sir, that two or three gentlemen, representing the Catholic interest, have made complaints to me which I should perhaps like to bring before the Committee. I did not think we were in sight of the termination of the evidence, and I hope I shall not be precluded from calling such evidence.

Chairman.] I did not mean to convey that we had necessarily come to the actual end of the evidence, but only that we are within sight of it, and it is fair to the companies and to the Irish Society to give them pretty abundant notice, in order that they may be ready, and that the Committee may not be kept waiting. On the other point, as to hearing the companies and the Irish Society by counsel, I may say, the view of the Committee is, that we should be willing to hear, not an examination by counsel of the evidence as to the administration, sales, and so forth, which has been laid before the Committee. The proper way for you to deal with that, in our judgment, is to deal with it by producing rebutting evidence, as I have already said. But as we are directed by the House to inquire into the terms by which the society and the companies hold their property, to inquire into the instruments and charters,—in order to guide the Committee in that matter, we are prepared to hear the view taken by the companies of their trusts, or their denial of the trusts, explained to the Committee by counsel. I do not mean any exhaustive or elaborate argument, such as might be addressed to a tribunal which had to decide, but simply their view explained to us. Then, either before or after that (and that is a point which the Committee will have to consider presently), we also propose to hear counsel setting out the opposite interpretation of the charters; that is to say, the view of those who contend that trusts are impressed upon the possessions of the companies. The point which the companies and the Irish Society will have to consider is whether the case of all the companies is not so nearly identical, that one counsel will probably be sufficient to present the whole of their view as to the interpretation of the instruments before us. That is the point which we should wish the companies and the society to consider before we meet again, or within some near period. It is to be understood that the counsel is only to address himself to an explanation of your view of the interpretation of the terms of the charters and other instruments.

Dr. *Freshfield.*] Might I submit this to you, Sir: the substantial part of the case against the companies has not yet, if I might say so, been touched upon at all; that is to say, the view which is taken against the view that we hold of the terms and conditions upon which we hold our property; and therefore, with very great submission, and knowing that you direct your proceedings according to your own will, what I would venture to suggest is, that we ought to know, by hearing the arguments beforehand, what it really is that our counsel is to answer.

Chairman.] I do not say that I accept that view, but what I meant to convey was that the Committee would consider presently the order in which we will hear counsel.

Dr. *Freshfield.*] I beg your pardon, Sir. All I said was really only in the interest of saving time. You would not want us to come afterwards to the Committee and say, "Permit us to answer this that and the other that has arisen in the arguments that we have just heard." May I refer to one other thing? By your kindness we are allowed to have the evidence supplied to us; but as a fact it so happens that we never get the evidence until the morning when we get here.

Chairman.] You mean you then get the evidence of the previous sitting?

Dr. *Freshfield.*] Yes.

Chairman.] Our own case is no more favourable than yours; we only get it the night before.

Dr. *Freshfield.*] The difference between your position and ours, if I may say so, is this, Sir, that you have nothing to answer, while we have. Therefore, if I only get the evidence at half-past ten on Monday morning, and you ask me to come in and be prepared to answer it an hour and a half later, it is rather sharp upon me.

Mr. *Sexton.*] But you get weeks to answer it.

Dr. *Freshfield.*] No, Sir, I think not; because the Chairman was good enough to say just now that he thought the evidence would be concluded either on Monday or Thursday next.

Chairman.] There will be no kind of precipitancy in the matter.

Dr. *Freshfield.*] Thank you, Sir. May I say one word upon the other point? We will consider what you have been good enough to say as regards counsel. As regards the two companies which I directly represent, the Mercers' Company and the Fishmongers' Company, they will probably

Dr. *Freshfield*—continued.

probably represented by the same counsel, and what you have said shall be represented to all the other companies.

Chairman.] It would save a great deal of time if that course could be adopted. It is subject to your own discretion, of course. But I cannot think there is such a diversity of interpretation of the charters and instruments as to make it impracticable. They are, so far as I can see, so identical that I do hope the companies will do their best to come to that view.

Dr. *Freshfield.*] You may rely upon it that we shall do our best, Sir, in the matter.

Mr. *Elton.*] I should suppose, Sir, if a number of gentlemen came to give to the Committee what appeared to be very much the same explanation, you would exercise your discretion, after hearing one, as to whether you would hear any others.

Chairman.] Quite so.

Dr. *Freshfield.*] So far as I have been able to gather, the case of the companies is totally distinct from the case of the Irish Society.

Chairman.] Quite true.

Dr. *Freshfield.*] And, therefore, I am not quite clear that it would be possible to have only one counsel.

Mr. *Sexton.*] As regards the calling of some Catholic gentlemen as witnesses, I presume their evidence would not be precluded, even although the rebutting evidence of the companies had begun.

Chairman.] Certainly not.

Mr. *Clancy.*] May I ask whether counsel are to be heard on the other side.

Chairman.] Certainly. That is what I wish to say. We are to hear the companies' views of the interpretation of their instruments, and, either after or before this (we will settle that afterwards among ourselves), we will hear the views of the other side.

Dr. *Todd.*] I may say, Sir, I have retained Mr. Walker to argue the case on behalf of the beneficiaries in Londonderry, and I have a telegram from him here asking at what date he will probably be wanted here.

Chairman.] I am not able to say at present; but I am very glad to hear that Mr. Walker will appear here.

Mr. *G. H. Lee.*] On behalf of the tenants, may I ask, Sir, are we to understand that the evidence on behalf of the companies will be put in before counsel is heard on either side.

Chairman.] That is the method of procedure that we intend to follow. We intend to finish the evidence as to administration, sales, and so forth, before we hear the legal argument as to the charter and the instruments.

Mr. *G. H. Lee.*] I understood that was so, but from some later remarks which have been made, I was not quite certain.

Mr. *Maton.*] The case of the Irish Society stands on somewhat different ground from that of the companies, and, as I understand, the same permission is granted to the society to appear by counsel.

Chairman.] Quite so, if they think it necessary.

Dr. *Freshfield.*] May I say one word as regards a remark which fell from the gentleman who spoke just now on behalf of the tenants. A great deal of our evidence is entirely documentary evidence, and when we call our witnesses here, in order to save time, what is proposed was not to call them twice, that is to say, not to call a gentleman to put in the documentary evidence and then to call evidence again to explain what you wish upon the subject of what you call the administration and sales, but let that one gentleman do everything. Supposing we had concluded our evidence, and then the counsel representing this gentleman raises points arising out of a certain document that we had not put in because we did not know that a question would be raised upon it, I must ask then to be allowed to recall that particular witness to put in the document.

Chairman.] We shall make no difficulty upon points of that kind if they should arise. I presume in all probability you will call, and if not probably the Committee will, certain official witnesses, such as the clerk to the Salters' Company, the clerk to the Drapers' Company, and the Secretary of the Irish Society, who gave evidence last year.

Dr. *Freshfield.*] I think you may assume that all the clerks of the companies will be ready to give evidence.

Chairman.] Of course there is no obligation to call your witnesses on next Monday or Thursday. I only thought it well to give notice, so that the Committee may lose no time.

Dr. *Freshfield.*] Thank you, Sir. We do not want any delay.

Chairman.] In order that I may not be misunderstood, I repeat that the only purpose for which we wish to hear counsel is as to the legal interpretation of the charters and instruments.

Dr. *Freshfield.*] Quite so, Sir.

Mr. R. H. Todd, LL.D., sworn; and Examined.

Chairman.

3021. You are a solicitor practising in Londonderry?—I am.

3022. For how long have you practised?—About 14 years.

3023. I believe that you acted for the tenants on certain companies' estates?—Yes, I did.

3024. In what transactions?—I acted for the tenants of the Skinners' Estate in having the rents fixed under the Act of 1881, and also for the tenants on various other estates in advising them as to purchase.

3025. Under what Act?—Under Lord Ashbourne's Act. I acted for the ordinary agricultural tenants on the Salters' Estate in carrying out the purchase under that Act.

3026. Did you also act for the tenants in transactions under the Arrears Act?—I did, chiefly on the Skinners' Estate.

3027. In the case of the Salter's Estate, as to which you have already heard some evidence, and as to which we have heard more, what was your position?—My position in the first instance was, solicitor to the tenants. I acted for the tenants in the sale of the ordinary agricultural holdings till completion of that. I acted for the company in selling to the general public the balance of the estate after the tenants' sale closed.

3028. You have read the Reverend Mr. Jordan's evidence, I presume?—Yes; the newspaper report of it.

3029. You have not read it in the printed notes of the evidence?—I think not.

3030. We will go into Dr. Jordan's evidence, to begin with, upon the Salters' Company's case. You have heard what Mr. Gamman said, and Mr. Gamman's evidence, on the whole, comes to very much the same as the evidence of the Reverend Mr. Jordan. The point is, that you made, on behalf of the Salters' Company, certain statements or inducements to the tenants to effect a purchase?—That is not accurate, to my the best of it.

3031. Before I go to that, you were acting for the tenants in previous transactions. Then you became the solicitor for the company, and it was as solicitor for the company that you made, or did not make, those promises which have been referred to by these two witnesses?—No. That is a mistake. I became solicitor for the company in the end of 1886, only with regard to the sale of timber, and with regard to the sale of the Manor House, and some outstanding holdings in the town of Magherafelt. That was in the end of 1888. From that time till the close of the sale I had no discussion with any tenant, or any person alive, so far as I recollect, as to the question of grants.

3032. Then you wish us to understand that you deny the statement that you, along with Sir Henry Cartwright, gave promises that the educational grants should be continued?—Absolutely.

3033. There is absolutely no foundation for it?—I will tell you exactly what occurred. There is no foundation whatever for the statement that I made any promise, or that Sir Henry Cartwright made any promise in my presence with regard to the continuing of the grants, either to schools or to churches. The sale of the estate commenced some time in 1884. I was instructed by the tenants to negotiate the sale for them. I had an interview with the committee of the company in London on the subject, and after arranging some preliminaries, I reported the result of that interview to the committee of tenants, consisting of two from each townland. At that meeting terms of purchase were settled between that committee and myself, and at the suggestion of, I think, the chairman of the committee, these terms were put in writing. Copies of these terms were printed by me, and handed to the committee, and the members of the committee got those instructions signed by the various tenants of the estate. I have here a copy of the instructions. In that there was no reference to religious grants, to no grants for schools, or to grants for charitable or any other purpose, and there was no discussion at that time, nor any intimation; nor any mention whatever, as to the question of grants, and that was not made part of the terms of purchase.

3034. It does not appear to be a long document, and if you will read it, it will bring us to the point?—The document is as follows: "We, the undersigned tenants of the Londonderry Estate of the Salters' Company hereby authorise and empower R. H. Todd, of Londonderry, solicitor, to negotiate and carry out the purchase by us of our several holdings from the Salters' Company on the following terms and conditions, and to sign for us and on our behalf the contract for purchase, in accordance with such terms and conditions: 1. The tenant in each case to obtain three-fourths of the purchase money, or as much thereof as he can, from the Land Commission on the terms provided by the Land Act of 1881." This was before Lord Ashbourne's Act was passed. "2. Where the tenant pays the balance of the purchase money in cash on the execution of the purchase deed, the price to be 19 years' purchase of the net Government valuation of the land, or of the rent in cases where the rent is less than the net valuation." Then there is an interlineation in writing. That is the way the third paragraph appeared when sent out by me, but when it was returned to me signed by the tenants, there was an intimation that Lord Ashbourne's Act would be passed, or the Act which afterwards was passed in the name of Lord Ashbourne's Act.

Mr. T. M. Healy.

3035. Kindly assure us on that point. Give us the month?—I cannot give you that.

3036. It is of great importance?—There was a discussion as to an enabling Bill at the time this scheme was sent out.

3037. That

Chairman.

3037. That was sent out when?—About the end of 1884. When these were returned to me, in all of them was interlined these words, "or such better terms as may be obtained from the Government."

Mr. T. M. Healy.

3038. You have used rather an important expression. You speak of it as Lord Ashbourne's Act?—I do not wish to mislead. There was a discussion at the time this was being signed as to whether there would be an amending Bill brought in and passed, giving more facilities to the tenants.

Chairman.

3039. There had been a Bill brought in in 1884?—It was in view of that Bill being brought in that this interlineation was put in, and it appears in all of them.

3040. You contend, and are prepared to inform the Committee, that you gave no promise whatever. Do you mean in reference to a continuance of the grants?—It was not even mentioned at this time at all.

3041. At this time. When was it mentioned?—I will come to that. After this was done I arranged the terms of sale with the company. I reported these terms of sale to the committee, and the committee approved of those terms of sale. The agreements then were prepared; these agreements embodied the terms of purchase, and in these agreements there is no reference to grants of any nature or kind. These agreements were then signed by the tenants at the end of 1884 and the beginning of 1885. Some casual agreements with some outstanding tenants were signed subsequently, but the body of them were signed at the end of 1884, or the beginning of 1885. Up to these agreements being signed, and returned to me, and lodged with the Land Commission, no mention whatever had been made of grants to churches or schools.

Mr. T. M. Healy.

3042. Will you continue the reading of that document?—Then, "4. The Company to buy up and redeem all permanent charges on the property before the sale to the tenants, and to pay Mr. Todd a percentage on the purchase-money to cover stamp-duty, registration, and all other necessary outlay. 5. Costs to be paid by the tenants to Mr. Todd for his trouble and professional services according to the following scale." Then the scale of costs is given, and that is all. Then the deeds were settled by counsel on behalf of the tenants; by counsel on behalf of the Land Commission, and by counsel on behalf of the company. Messrs. Thompson & Debenhams, of London, were acting for the company, I was acting for the tenants, and Mr. Browning was acting as solicitor for the Land Commission. All three solicitors had the draft deed through their hands; all three counsel had the draft through their hands, and that is important in this way, that in that deed there was inserted by the landlords' solicitors a clause providing that where arrears of rent were outstanding and promissory notes taken for these, that these should be good, notwithstanding the execution of the deed; that is to say, in the deed there was a covenant that the tenant should pay any promissory note that he had given for rent then due, notwithstanding the execution of the deed.

Chairman.

3043. What promissory notes were they?—At that time there was a certain amount of rent due. The company, though it is not in the concessions originally, ultimately, after negotiations I had with them, agreed to remit a year-and-a-half rent to each tenant. They also agreed to certain other points in favour of the tenants, over and above the contract that had been entered into, amounting to about 20,000 *l.*, which was remitted by the company to the tenants; but in some cases there was more than a year-and-a-half arrears due, and the company were asked by me, on behalf of the tenants, in case the tenants were not in a position to pay down the balance due in cash, to take promissory notes for that balance, payable in six months, so as to give time to the tenants who were not in a position then to make up the amount. They acceded to that request, and for the purpose of meeting that case, this clause was introduced into the deed, providing that those notes should be good, notwithstanding the execution of the deed. The Land Commission approved of that, and those were the notes that were afterwards sued on in Badger's case.

3044. The Land Commission knew of them?—Yes, and approved of the deed.

Mr. T. M. Healy.

3045. The Land Commission or the Land Purchase Commission?—The Land Purchase Commission; perhaps I might tell you the whole of the negotiations. Then the larger part of the deeds were executed without any mention being made of the grants to schools and churches.

Chairman.

3046. There was no mention of the grants?—No mention of the grants till a good many of the deeds were actually executed, stamped, and registered, and the purchase money paid over to the company.

Mr. Clancy.

3047. Do you mean mentioned in writing or at all?—At all; except on one occasion I will tell you of afterwards. Then for the first time some members of the committee asked me what my opinion was as to the disposal of the purchase money, and I gave them my advice, and referred them to the evidence I had given before Lord Derby's Commission.

Mr. Sexton.

3048. Fix that time precisely?—That was, I should say, some time at the beginning of 1886. I was asked my opinion as to the disposal of the purchase money, and I referred to my evidence before Lord Derby's Commission, in which I claimed that the estates were held in trust for public purposes in the locality, and I said, in my opinion, the whole of the proceeds of the estate should be devoted to public purposes in the locality.

3049. You

Mr. Sexton—continued.

3049. You said this to the tenants?—I did.

3050. Some of the deeds had not then been executed?—Some of them had not been executed. I also stated my opinion when I was asked by a few of the people, a very few.

Chairman.

3051. What opinion did you state?—I also stated my opinion that the company would make some provision with regard to schools and churches. I was speaking there to my own clients. They were consulting me as to what I thought; I was not discussing it in connection with terms of sale or part of the terms of the purchase of the holdings, but as a question of fact in the district, and they asked me my opinion, and I stated it freely that my own opinion was that the company would make some provision for the churches and schools, and I believe the company have.

3052. Is that the end of the history?—That is the end of the history so far as I am concerned. I might mention, perhaps, Mr. Gorman's case.

Mr. T. M. Healy.

3053. Would you tell us when you assumed that dual position of acting as solicitor for the tenant and for the landlord?—I was then asked at the end of 1886 to sell the timber on the estate, and to sell the manor house and some outstanding holdings to the general public, the sales to the tenants having concluded. I said I had no objection to do that, but I said the tenants who had not purchased should first get notice, to give them an opportunity of buying before it was on offer to the general public, and accordingly, with the consent of the company, I issued a letter to the tenants giving them that notice, and giving them a reasonable time to make up their minds whether they would or would not purchase.

3054. Was it while acting as solicitor to the tenants, or as solicitor for the landlord, or both, that this conversation about the churches and schools and the grants took place?—It was when I was acting as solicitor for the tenants that the discussion first took place. I have no doubt that that was repeated afterwards.

3055. Repeated afterwards when you were acting as solicitor for the company?—Not as the solicitor to the company.

Chairman.

3056. You were acting as solicitor for the company with regard to a certain part of the transaction?—I was acting as solicitor for the company with regard to the sale of a particular portion of the estate which had not been purchased by the tenants, and I discussed with any person who asked me the position of the company with regard to this trust, and I had my opinion from that day up to the present day, and I hold the same opinion at the present moment, and I have no hesitation in expressing it.

3057. Reference was made in the course of the Rev. Mr. Jordan's examination to a letter from you threatening proceedings in the name of the company for the recovery of rents and arrears of rents against unwilling purchasers. Have you any remark to make upon that?—I presume the letter he refers to is the letter at the conclusion of the sale to the tenants, giving notice to the tenants that the company would cancel the agreements if they did not carry out their bargain, and giving them a certain time to purchase before they offered the rest to the general public.

Chairman—continued.

3058. You did not tell us of that letter?—I was after mentioning it, because it was after the sales to the tenants had closed. After the sales to the tenants had closed, and after one part of the outside tenants refused to purchase, some of them had contracts for purchase but would not carry them out. When the matter was looked on as closed, the company, or Sir Henry Cartwright for the company, asked me if I would undertake the sale of the remaining portions of the estate. I said I would do so, but that the outstanding tenants should get notice of the fact that the company proposed selling the remaining portion of the estate, and accordingly, with Sir Henry Cartwright's consent, I sent a notice to the outstanding tenants, telling them that it was proposed to sell to the general public, but that they would have a certain time to make up their minds whether they would still purchase.

3059. Have you anything more to say as to the Salters' case?—That is all that occurs to me. Of course I shall be happy to answer any question, but I cannot recollect anything else.

3060. Then I will turn to the Skinners' Company's case, which is more important?—As I understand from Dr. Brown's evidence, there are two suggestions made.

3061. The position of the Skinners' Company is that they have sold part of their estates, and are trying to sell the rest at this moment?—Yes. That is not strictly the case. They are not trying to sell the remaining portion of the estate. What is done is this. They have actually given notice to the outstanding tenants that the sale is closed.

3062. Have you read Dr. Brown's evidence?—Yes, I have.

3063. Have you read it in a newspaper, or in the print of the evidence?—Only the newspaper report, but I have the substance of it.

3064. Dr. Brown said this, talking about the sale by the Skinners' Company: "A gentleman was acting for them in the way of selling the estate for them, and in fact he is a friend of mine"; then he speaks very well of his friend; "and for the purpose of inducing them to purchase, he said that all their outgoings, their donations, and privileges would be continued to the tenants after they had purchased." I suppose that gentleman is yourself?—That gentleman, I presume, is myself.

3065. Now did you, for the purpose of inducing tenants to purchase, say that all out-goings, donations, and privileges would be continued to the tenants after the purchase?—No, I did not. I put all my views on paper to the tenants. I sent a circular letter explaining the terms of sale to every tenant on the estate, and no reference was made to that, and no request was made from the tenants to me that that should be included in the terms of sale.

3066. And the subject of donations, and what the witness calls privileges, was never mentioned between you and the tenants?—I have no recollection

Chairman—continued.

lection of it except in the case of one person, and that was a gentleman named Johnson, a clergyman. He came to me complaining that the Skinners' Company were about to discontinue his grant. I advised him to send a memorial to the company. I believe he did send a memorial to the company, and the company refused to continue the grant. This was one of the transactions.

3067. You made no sort of promise?—On the contrary, I advised him to apply direct to the company. I said I had nothing to with that matter; I said I was concerned only with regard to the sales.

3068. Then you wish us to accept your assurance that you never mentioned the continuance of donations and grants as any inducement to purchase at all?—Yes.

3069. At any time, direct or indirect?—At any time, direct or indirect.

Mr. *Sexton*.] That question relates to the Skinners' Company.

Chairman.

3070. Now in connection with the matter of bog and turbary we were told this by Dr. Brown, which struck us as rather remarkable, I think. In answer to Mr. Sexton from Question 699 down to 702, he said that the Skinners' Company not only discontinued the donations and endowments, but that they actually made fresh exactions as regards the bog. You were referred to in those answers. Mr. Sexton said: "Then in addition to making fresh exactions as regards the price of turf, they charge a higher price than formerly;" to which the witness answered, "Yes," and said, "I understand this gentleman, who is a friend of mine, will most likely appear before the Committee, and will tell the Committee if they ask him to explain." I believe you are the person referred to, and will you be kind enough to explain to us this rather difficult-looking transaction?—I informed the tenants, with the consent of the company, that the company would hand over the whole of the bog on the estate for the benefit of the purchasing tenants to trustees without charging any extra price for it.

Mr. *Sexton*.

3071. Any price, you mean?—Anything.

Mr. *T. M. Healy*.

3072. Was the bog held in common?—A part of it was in the hands of the company, I believe, but some portions were on the holdings of tenants; some in common, and some in severalty. The company entrusted me with the carrying out of the arrangement. I informed the tenants that the company would transfer the bog to the trustees; that the trustees should manage it for the future as nearly as possible in the way the company had managed the bog in the past; that for the purpose of paying for the management of the bog for the keeping up and maintenance of the bog, roads and drains and so on, 1 *s.* in each case would be required to be paid to make up the necessary fund; that is after the company had parted with the estate that fund

Mr. T. M. Healy—continued.

would have to come out of some payment for management and maintaining the bog, and the plan I proposed was that each should pay 1 *s.* for a permit, and that on getting their permit a right to cut in a particular bog, as pointed out by the bailiff or bog agent, would accrue, and that the shilling would be devoted to the purpose of paying the bog agent, and for the maintenance of the roads and drains, and so on.

Mr. *Sexton*.

3073. In substitution for the 6 *d.* as paid formerly?—In substitution for the 6 *d.* as paid formerly. The company had maintained formerly and charged only 6 *d.*, but the company had been out of pocket something by that, and my desire was that there should be a sufficient fund to carry on the management in the same way as before.

Chairman.

3074. What was the difference. If they could manage it before for 6 *d.*, why did they want 1 *s.*?—The company paid the bog bailiff before, and made certain contributions towards roads and so on.

3075. What new charge was put on the company that they had to levy an extra 6 *d.*?—When the company were clearing out of the country altogether, they had no further connection with it.

Mr. *Ellis*.

3076. I think you said they had been out of pocket by the 6 *d.*?—Yes.

Chairman.

3077. The 6 *d.* did not pay?—Did not pay the full amount.

3078. And so for the future they determined they would not carry it on at a loss?—If the company once parted with the estate they would not carry it on at all; but they were handing over the turf to the tenants, and the object was to make a provision by which the management of the turbary should be carried on for the benefit of the whole of the tenants. The turbary is at present by two deeds, which I have, and can show to the Committee, transferred to three trustees for the sole benefit of the tenants. That is actually done, and was done some years ago. That deed I submitted to the Land Commission, and got their approval of it, and the whole of the clauses were discussed fully and carefully, and it was settled ultimately by counsel. The scheme was designed by me. I think it is a good scheme, and if there is any blame attached to it, the blame attaches to me.

Mr. *Sexton*.

3079. The trustees get the 1 *s.*?—No. The trustees collect the 1 *s.*, or the bog bailiff collects the 1 *s.*

Chairman.

3080. What becomes of the 1 *s.*?—That goes towards payment of the maintenance and management of the bog, which is the tenants' property.

3081. Who

Mr. Sexton.

3081. Who administer it?—The tenants' trustees. The company get nothing.

Chairman.

3082. The company have no concern with it?—None whatever. The trustees collect this shilling for the purpose of paying for the maintenance and management of the bog.

Colonel Lewis.

3083. The company have nothing whatever to do with it?—No, they have not, because it belongs absolutely to the tenants.

Mr. T. M. Healy.

3084. It is a pure matter of domestic administration after the sale?—Clearly.

Chairman.

3085. You had no personal share in any other transactions of sales, had you?—Except advising tenants; not with regard to the companies. On other private estates I have.

3086. With regard to the companies' estates, have you anything further to tell us with regard to sales?—Except this, if I might venture to make a suggestion: I think it would be advisable that in all cases the tenants should be separately represented.

3087. Have you had any experience, in your transactions of sales by the companies to their tenants, of duress or circumstances of that kind, which we have heard something of from the witnesses?—I cannot say anything except from hearsay.

3088. Nothing but hearsay?—No.

3089. We should be glad to hear your suggestion?—My suggestion is, that for the protection of both parties, and of the State, each tenant should be separately represented by his own solicitor, in the same way as an ordinary borrower is in the case of a bond.

3090. This is a general suggestion affecting all purchase transactions?—Yes, affecting all purchase transactions; and it is owing to my personal experience, and the difficulty of satisfying everybody.

3091. Have you any remarks to make on the Irish Society, as distinguished from the companies; you live in Londonderry?—Yes; and I have for the last 14 years. The Irish Society is not a popular body. The general feeling is that the Irish Society is an obsolete body.

3092. We want to get a little more than that. You were in the room the other day when we had the mayor from Londonderry, and Sir William Miller, and Mr. M'Gee, and you heard me ask them their opinion on the recommendations of the Royal Commission of 1854 that the Irish Society should be dissolved; and you heard their answers. What is your view with regard to that?—My view is that the Irish Society should be dissolved.

3093. Why?—Because the management of the trust estate is bad.

3094. In what respect?—They do not understand the necessities of the situation, living as they do in London. I do not impeach their *bona fides*, or their desire to do it rightly. Then, naturally, the expense of management is utterly out of proportion.

Chairman—continued.

3095. Illustrate, if you please, what you mean when you say they fail to understand?—The Irish Society is a fluctuating body, and they live in London.

3096. What do they do, or leave undone, in consequence of living in London?—They do nothing whatever except visit Londonderry once a year, and attend their two dinners.

3097. What is the failure; what have they failed to do that they ought to do?—In my opinion, they should apply the whole of the trust estate for beneficial objects, and they should not fritter away the trust estate on objects which are absolutely useless.

3098. Such as what?—Such as giving paltry grants to schools and churches that are of no value whatever.

3099. You mean they are not good judges of the proper distribution of their bounty?—I mean to say that it is in accordance with the amount of influence brought to bear on them in a particular manner what particular grants they make.

Mr. T. M. Healy.

3100. Where they dined the night before?—I would not go as far as that; but necessarily, going there only for a few days, they have little local knowledge.

Chairman.

3101. What else?—In taking up the Report of the Society you will see the cost of administration of an estate of 20,000 *l.* a year is upwards of 4,000 *l.* a year; you will see that if you refer to their accounts.

3102. Do you say that out of 20,000 *l.* they spend 4,000 *l.* in expenses of management?—Yes.

3103. Where do you get that figure from?—Their own return.

3104. Now, you heard some of the witnesses on Monday who were opposed to giving the control of these funds over to the corporation; can you explain that opposition?—Yes; the opposition arises from this, that the present corporation represents a limited body.

3105. You mean it is a high franchise?—The franchise is high, and the present corporation do not truly represent the feeling of the whole city; and the feeling of the present corporation is, that if the franchise is reduced the personnel of the corporation will be largely changed; and the desire is that the administration of the trust fund shall not go into the hands of the new corporation.

3106. They think if the franchise was reduced the personnel of the corporation would be changed; what kind of change are they afraid of?—The present corporation is largely conservative in its formation.

3107. To come to the point, we heard there was only one Catholic on it, for instance?—Only one Catholic. The feeling is that half, or thereabouts, would be Catholics on the new corporation; and the fear is that, this Irish Society's property being given for the purpose of converting Catholics, it would get into the hands of Catholics for purposes not favoured by Protestants.

3108. Do

Chairman—continued.

3108. Do you think that those fears are well founded?—I think the religious purpose is altogether obsolete, and I think the fears are unfounded as to the fact that the new corporation would not fairly and properly manage the property. An authority, such as a corporation, now-a-days, under the influence of public opinion, would fairly administer the trust.

3109. I see by your evidence before Lord Derby's Commission, that you had thought about these things. You know that when we went in for a Municipal Bill, about 1835, it was considered by Parliament, at that date, inexpedient that trust funds should be handed over to corporations. I express no opinion upon it myself; but supposing the Irish Society were dissolved, have you considered between the two courses which is preferable; to hand the funds over to the corporation, or hand them over to a body of local trustees, as has been suggested by some of the Londonderry people appointed to carry out the purposes of the trust?—I think that, so far as regards the property, that should be applied for the benefit of the city alone; that the corporation should have exclusive charge of that. There are two distinct portions of property. At the time the plantation scheme was first entered into the Irish Society entered into an agreement with the Crown.

3110. I think we had better not diverge into the history of it at this moment?—It is very short.

Mr. Sexton.

3111. The whole point is, that so much as is wanted for the city should be administered by the Corporation?—Exactly; what I say is so much as is required for the administration of the city should be in the hands of the Corporation; and so much as is applied to educational purposes, and to purposes of general public utility outside the city should be put in the hands of a properly constituted body of trustees who would be perfectly impartial.

Chairman.

3112. And those trustees local trustees?—Local trustees if possible.

3113. You will see that on your own trust theory, which I do not express an opinion upon at present, and which you advocated before Lord Derby's Commission in July 1882, there are under the name of "local" possibly four different competing claims. You may limit "local" to the particular estate, or you may extend it to the district; all these contentions have been actually made, as perhaps you are aware; or, thirdly, you may say that "local" may be extended to the whole province of Ulster; or, fourthly, to Ireland as a whole. Now, which of these do you favour? After you have got what you want for the Corporation for the purposes of Londonderry, do you favour the enlargement of this to the district, or still further to Ulster, or to Ireland as a whole?—I favour the district with a certain limitation; I should say in the first instance, I should not give the municipal property to Londonderry alone, but that Coleraine should also have all its municipal property; in fact the property originally provided for it by the scheme. One portion was to go to Londonderry, and another to Coleraine. Then the general property, the property outside, should be vested in trustees to apply for purposes of acknowledged utility in the district, but those purposes should be purposes that should be of general benefit, not to the district alone, but to as wide an area as possible.

3114. That is to say, you would not allow a penny of this to go outside the County of Londonderry?—I think that the trust, if I am right about the fact that there is a trust at all, limits it to the district, and I think the expenditure should be within the ambit of the County of Londonderry.

3115. If the Irish Society were dissolved and a body of trustees appointed to administer the funds, you think the fears that these funds would be dispersed over all Ulster, or even over all Ireland are groundless, and that the feeling of Londonderry would be in favour of limiting it to the district?—The unanimous feeling of the City and County of Londonderry, is that it should be limited to the district, and it is my own feeling, and I believe if am right in saying there is a trust, that trust is limited to the County of Londonderry. Furthermore, I do not think that the dispersion of the funds would be an advantage, because after you provide for Coleraine and Londonderry, and provide also for whatever may be considered vested interests, the general fund would be too small to distribute over the whole of Ireland to be of general advantage, but I think there are sufficient objects of public utility within the boundaries of Londonderry, in the effects of which the inhabitants of the Province of Ulster, and perhaps the whole of Ireland, would participate to exhaust the whole fund.

Mr. Sexton.

3116. Are you speaking of the Irish Society's estate?—And the companies' estates.

3117. That is very large?—Well, after providing for all, I suggest, in the first instance, you will find the residue not so large.

Chairman.

3118. You are against conveying these funds to a religious destination?—Altogether. I think that the religious destination at the present day is obsolete and useless. I think that the present incumbents, having regard to the fact that they came in under certain conditions to the incumbency, have an equitable claim to a certain consideration during their lives, but subject to that, I think the whole of the funds should be devoted to general public purposes, and not to the purposes of a particular sect.

3119. Now, as you took such a great interest in the Derby Commission, you no doubt are aware that when that Commission reported, they reported that the London Companies, so far as their English properties were concerned, at all events held their property upon trusts for localities. You no doubt hold therefore that the same principle ought to apply to the property of the London Companies in Ireland, and that as to the funds derived by the London Companies from Ireland,

Chairman—continued.

Ireland, they should be expended in Ireland, and belong to Ireland?—I do.

3120. By parity of reasoning, with the reasoning that led Lord Derby and his Commission to report as they did?—Certainly.

3121. You hold that in the two cases there is a duty; whether it is a legal, or a moral obligation only, is a point we will discuss in another way; but whether it is a legal obligation, or a moral obligation, the same obligation exists in respect of the property of the London Companies in Ireland as exists, and was held by Lord Derby to exist, in respect of their property in England?—Yes, that is, their corporate property. I think there is a paragraph in the Report of Lord Derby's Commission that equally allocates it to the particular districts. It is paragraph 8 of the recommendations on page 14, that is dealing with the London property only, and the recommendation is, that the London property should be devoted to objects of public utility. "We are of opinion that, having regard to the facts that (1) the Companies are connected with the municipality of London, (2) their wealth is, in the main, the result of the remarkable progress of London, the objects of acknowledged public utility to be promoted should be mainly metropolitan objects; but that, in cases in which a trade formerly carried on in London has established itself elsewhere, similar objects connected with the present place of the trade may properly be included." I think that that applies with equal force to the case of the Irish properties.

3122. You think you could affirm, with regard to their Irish property, what Lord Derby affirms here with regard to their London property?—I think so.

3123. That the companies are connected with the municipalities of Londonderry and Coleraine, and that their wealth is, in the main, the result of the remarkable progress, not of London, but of Londonderry, and the district?—Yes.

3124. As I have said, we do not ask you any question as to the legal obligation, but I would ask you one question which has been touched upon by previous witnesses. You take the view that there is a legal obligation upon the companies. Why do not you try that in a court of law?—I think there is a sufficient answer to that. In the first place it has been tried in a court of law, and decided.

3125. How so?—In the case of the Star Chamber proceedings, and the proceedings in Chancery following the Star Chamber proceedings, it is distinctly held that the companies are trustees for public purposes.

3126. I will not go into that. You say that you do not go into a court of law, because the Star Chamber decided something?—The Star Chamber decided what we should practically require to have decided in a court of law now.

3127. Is there any other reason, because that strikes me as rather an attenuated reason?—That is one reason, but I should like to say further, that the proceedings following the Star Chamber proceedings affirmed that.

3128. When?—A year or two after. I can give you the reference.

3129. We have in our Papers the *aide fociat* issued in consequence of a decree in 1641. Do you really mean to say, the reason why you do not take this matter into a court of law is, that something happened in the Star Chamber and in the Court of Chancery in 1641?—That is not the only reason.

3130. Let us have the practical reason?—There is a difficulty of course in the cost of conducting such a case. It is an extremely heavy contest, and there is no single individual sufficiently interested personally to embark the whole of his fortune, and the whole of his life practically in contesting with the City Companies through the various courts, the question whether there is a legal trust attached, or not.

3131. You think that the declaration by the House of Lords, of trusts in the case of the Irish Society, would not have been arrived at if a powerful company like the Skinners' Company had not been discreet enough to try the case themselves?—I think that the Irish Society would have claimed as the other companies now claim, that they are private owners, had it not been for that case, and had it not been for the fact that they had a powerful company to contend with. I may point out in connection with that, that up till that date of the case of the Skinners' Company against the Irish Society, the Irish Society took exactly the same position as the companies now assume.

3132. You think that the enormous cost of trying it, is a very good reason why the people of Londonderry should not take the thing before a court of law?—I think it makes it a practical impossibility. This might be done: A man of straw might be got, and there might be public spirit sufficient to contribute a sufficient sum for that purpose.

3133. What has a man of straw to do with it?—He might become the plaintiff, and a subscription might be got up to pay the costs, but the man of straw is liable to disappear at any moment by death, or otherwise. There is one point I think extremely important in connection with that. I do not think even if a court of law did decide that a trust attached to the estate legally, that would be a settlement of the question, and you would still have to come to Parliament to say, which of them were obsolete, and define the trusts which had to be carried out.

3134. What has got to be done first, is to establish the existence of the trust, but we are not going into that to-day. You take evidently very strong views as to the binding nature of these trusts on the companies, and you hold these trusts to be as binding on the companies as the House of Lords decided the trusts to be on the Irish Society?—In my opinion they are exactly in the same position.

3135. I will not ask you to go into that now, but perhaps you could tell us in one single answer, what series of instruments, in your opinion, we ought to have before us? We have our own view, but we should like to have yours too. Can you give us a short, or a long list of the instruments?—The first is: "The motives and reasons to induce the City to undertake the plantations."

Chairman—continued.

3136. What is the date of that instrument?—There is no date given, but it is prior to 1609. It is in the report of the case of the Skinners' Company against the Irish Society. Then the second is an order of the Crown to the Corporation of London to convene a meeting of the companies to consider the project. Then, third, an Order of the 14th July 1609, appointing a deputation to give the answer of the companies; fourth, a precept from the Corporation to the companies of the 22nd of July 1609; fifth, Report of the Commissioners of Plantations; sixth, the precepts to the companies to raise the necessary tax; seventh, the charter of James I.; eighth, the licenses in mortmain; ninth, the voluntary grants to the companies; and 10th, the charter of Charles II., incorporating that of James I.

3137. Now I want to ask you one or two questions as to your general view. You have told us something about the Irish Society, and about the companies, and before Lord Derby's Commission you were asked, on the 13th July 1882: "From your knowledge of the tenants on the company's Irish estates in the north of Ireland, do you think that those tenants would have been better off if they had been the tenants of private individuals instead of being tenants of the companies?" Then this is your answer: "With some private individuals they would have been better off, and with some worse." Then Lord Derby asked you: "On the average would they not have been materially worse off?" (*A.*) "On the average they are better off than with private landlords; I admit that freely, but I could give the names of landlords that are better landlords than the companies." Does that still remain your view?—That is still my view.

3138. You who have studied the history of the relations between the Irish Society and the companies and their tenants think that on the whole that has been as satisfactory a history as if their lands had been under private landlords?—So far as regards the relation of landlord and tenant I think it is.

3139. In other respects than outside of the relation of landlord and tenant?—In other respects the country has been somewhat better for the presence of the companies, because the companies have expended a proportion, and in some cases a large proportion, of their income on public objects in the locality, and they made a larger expenditure on the estates for public objects than was possible for private landlords to do.

3140. You make this statement, no doubt, after consideration. Have you followed any reports, for example, of deputations from the Irish Society and the companies?—I have.

3141. Have you them before you?—I have not them before me at the present moment, but I have read the reports.

3142. Are you aware that in the "Concise View," which you certainly are acquainted with, there are statements made by these deputations which shed a good deal of light, even in our own century, on the relations between the companies and their estates?—Certainly I am.

Chairman—continued.

3143. You have not got them before you?—Not at present, but I have read them recently.

3144. When you say you have read them recently you mean such passages as this taken from the report of the Society's deputation about the Clothworkers in 1836. Perhaps you will see whether these are the passages you refer to, and, if so, read one or two of the passages which you think most material for the consideration of the Committee?—These are the passages. I should say that at the time these reports were made, so far as I recollect, the company had sublet to middlemen, and all the companies did sublet to middlemen in the latter part of the 17th century and the beginning of the 18th century, and I was about to found an argument on that, but you have ruled that out.

3145. Do you find the passages that you refer to?—I think the report here from the Irish Society's deputation, stating what the condition of the companies' estates was at the time, is an accurate report, and fairly represents it.

3146. Read us one or two examples. Take the year 1836?—"Clothworkers (1836). Neither schools nor places of worship seem to have been attended to; the company are not interested in the present prosperity of the estate, nor can it be till it comes into their own hands." That is a case where it has been let to middlemen. Then (1841.) "This property was long in Chancery."

3147. This is still the Clothworkers?—This is still the Clothworkers. "During this period several of the tenants held favourable leases, and were correspondingly comfortable, those who did not hold leases were rackrented, and paid the highest amount that could be obtained from them. No schools erected by late lessee are seen; no dispensaries or charitable institutions occur." Then with regard to the Ironmongers in 1836, the deputation of the Irish Society reports: "The company seem heretofore to have treated the estate as a matter of merchandise, and the present owner, who never had a thought of residing in Ireland, bought it as such." Then in 1841 the deputation reports: "Let on lease for lives. The present owners seem only to have used this property for the purpose of making the most of it during the term of their lease."

3148. That is not material, because that is not the company but the middleman?—It is the middleman, but the objection I have to the companies' treatment is that they let it to middlemen, and allowed them to rackrent the tenants. Then as to the Fishmongers' estate in 1836, they report: "Since it came into the company's hands it has improved very little either in cultivation or the condition of the people. The rent has been suddenly raised; the company in many instances caused the gentry to quit their estate."

3149. I think you must read us, if you please, the Drapers'?—As to the Drapers in 1836, they report: "Since the estate came into the hands of the company, 1817, everything has been done that benevolence and good sense could dictate to spread education, morality, and industry among the

Chairman—continued.

the inhabitants. The company are stated to have expended their income largely on draining, planting, building, and other permanent improvements."

3160. We will not have any more; you say you were very much affected by passages of that kind; I do not see how that bears out your other position before Lord Derby's Commission, which you say you still hold, that they were no worse and no better than other landlords?—I spoke of the time when the companies resumed possession of their estates, and then they followed the ordinary custom of the country. They usually raised their rents, but were not so harsh in their dealings with their tenants as other landlords were, and they spent this large portion of their income on the estate, as I say, in acknowledgment of their trust, and as they say, on their own motion.

3161. I wonder if you have read the narrative of Mr. Slade's journey?—I have.

3162. It was in 1802 that Slade visited the north of Ireland. He was the secretary of the Irish Society, and made a report to the Society. Do you remember this passage: "The road from Down Hill to Coleraine goes through the best part of the Clothworkers' proportion, which was held by the Right Hon. Richard Jackson, who was the Society's general agent. It is commonly reported in the country, that, having been obliged to raise the rents of his tenants very considerably in consequence of the large fine he paid, it produced an almost total emigration among them to America, and that they formed," that is those emigrants, I suppose, "a principal part of that undisciplined body which brought about the surrender of the British Army at Saratoga." Do you remember that?—I remember that, and I have heard the same thing from other sources.

3163. Then there is this other passage where he says, "The first notice I received of my arrival on lands belonging to the Londoners (as they are there called), was at Kilrea, a market town situated on an eminence near the River Bann, which I learnt from the landlord of my inn was held by Mr. Stewart, uncle of Lord Castlereagh, under the Mercers' Company, and that it extended for more than six miles along the road over which I was to pass in my way to Londonderry. Inquiring into the reason of the want of accommodation and the apparent poverty of the place, the master of the inn observed: 'That it could not well be otherwise in a part of the country where they never saw the face of the owner of the soil, or even his under tenant;' and he mentioned this circumstance as a grievance which greatly prevails in Ireland, but particularly in all those parts situated in the north of the island which belong to any of the City companies. I felt," says Slade, the Secretary of the Irish Society, "the force of the observation, which impressed me with a greater degree of indulgence for the poverty, ignorance, and laziness of the lower order of the people, who toil for a miserable subsistence, and see the fruits of their labour carried off from time to time by an agent of their landlord, to be spent in a foreign country; while the very same description of people in England are cheered by a hospitable reception in the hall of their landlord when they wait upon him to pay their rent, derive benefit from his expenditure and example, and in case of petty disputes, find an honest magistrate, a kind landlord and a well-informed neighbour to reconcile their differences, and prevent little misunderstandings from growing into rancour and the desire of revenge. This want of example, assistance and consolation from the resident land owners, deprives the inhabitants of all inducement to exion, so that each family lives by itself, in a little cabin without a chimney, with a clay floor, and bed of straw or rags. A group of nearly naked figures are often seen at the doors, consisting of the wife and children. The husband finds the means by working at his loom to pay an extravagant price for four or five acres of land, on which a cow is kept for the family, and some potatoes and flax are grown. This, with a turf fire, kindled in the corner of their cabin, round which the family crouch, with some oatmeal for stirabout, constitutes all the wants, and whiskey the luxury of the Irish peasant; who, never looking beyond it, has no temptation to enterprise or exertion." Do you think that that is a good account of the administration of the Irish Society and the companies?—I think it is of that period.

3164. You think it is a true account?—I think it is a true account of the period, and I think the companies and the Irish Society are greatly to blame for allowing their land to be let to middlemen to fleece the tenants and ruin the country in the way they did at that period.

3165. Do you think there has been a very material alteration; would that sort of account be a very gross exaggeration of the state of things to-day?—It would, and chiefly for this reason; that the Land Act of 1881 interposed, and rents were fairly fixed.

3166. Up to the Act of 1881, you think that this bad state of things which the secretary of the Irish Society described at the beginning of the century was left untouched?—It was not quite so bad up to 1881, but I am bound to say it was not relieved so thoroughly as it should have been.

3167. Was it so bad up to 1881?—It was not worse, and barely so bad as on some neighbouring estates, but still the position of the tenants all round Londonderry, as well as elsewhere, was a very unsatisfactory one. The property they created by their own expenditure was appropriated by the landlords by increase of rent, and I am bound to say the companies followed the usual practice in the district, of increasing the rent on the tenants' expenditure.

3168. In short, though Mr. Slade had told them in 1802 that under the system that then existed, the Irish tenant under them had no temptation to enterprise or exertion; they never stirred a finger to better his condition?—They do not seem to have done very much except some expenditure they made on churches and schools.

Sir Richard Temple.

3169. When you recommend that the Irish Society should be abolished, does it occur to you that

Sir Richard Temple—continued.

that that Society may have some rights?—I think the Society has only the rights of trustees, and that has been judicially declared.

3160. Quite so; but still are those rights the rights of trustees in the ordinary sense of the term?—I do not understand what rights of trustees are. The rights are, I understand, rights to do something for their own benefit in connection with the administration of a trust estate.

3161. Does it occur to you that the Irish Society may have some rights?—Of what nature?

3162. When you speak of abolishing them, does it occur to you they may have some rights?—Of what nature?

3163. Rights derived from their position in the century before last?—They have the exact rights of ordinary trustees and no more and no less, as far as I see.

3164. Then are their rights to be taken away from them without their consent?—Certainly. In cases of ordinary trustees, if a trustee is a defaulter and does not carry out his trust, he is liable to be removed, and as they exist for particular purposes, which they do not carry out sufficiently, in my opinion, and they are not the best trustees, then it is perfectly competent for Parliament to intervene and say, we will appoint fresh trustees to administer this estate more efficiently, and more for the benefit of the public.

3165. Then they have no rights in the ordinary sense of the term "rights," you think?—Not rights in the sense of owners, they have the rights of trustees; they are the legal owners of the estate, as every other trustee is; they have no beneficial interest, if you mean that. If you mean they have power to appropriate to their own use any portion of the estate, or if you mean they are within their rights in spending the proceeds of the estate in entertainments, I do not agree with you.

3166. Did I understand you to say from some of your replies, that you think that grants to schools and churches are not of much use?—I think that the method of granting small donations to schools (I will take that in the first instance) that has been adopted both by the society and the companies, is a method that produces extremely little good. The only possible good I see so far as regards the public, is that it is certainly so much advantage by the increase of income to the individual who receives it, but in no instance that I know has there been a better teacher gained for the public, or a better school provided by means of these grants than there would have been without them.

3167. Do you mean to say that the grant to a school does no good to that school?—I only refer to the primary schools. They are under the National Education Board, and the same class of teacher exactly teaches in the companies' schools and the Irish Society's schools that teaches in any of the ordinary schools, and are paid by the State under the National Board. The grant of 10*l.* or 15*l.* a year to the particular teacher in a particular district has this effect, and it is the only effect, to give the patronage to the company's agent or the Irish Society's agent. It does not benefit the public in any way, but gives the patronage to the Irish Society's agent or the company's agent. It benefits the individual who receives it, and that is the only possible benefit it has, and the public money is being squandered and dissipated in these small grants, when if properly applied they would be of great use. May I say this, that if there was a large technical school established, and it was made an efficient school with the Irish Society's income or the companies' income, I think it would be a great public good; but I think that the method of distributing the school grants is a method that produces little or no good.

3168. Then it comes to this, that you think the grants should be concentrated?—I think so.

3169. Upon some particular institution?—I think that the State should provide for the primary education of the people, and that the money that is now taken from this trust for the purpose of providing education in the district, should be applied to providing technical education in the district, and to develop the district. For instance, develop the railways, improve the harbours, and do other works in the benefit of which everybody would participate.

3170. These are the general purposes to which you alluded in some of your previous replies?—They are.

3171. When you recommend that the trust or the property of the Irish Society should be made over to trustees, how do you consider those trustees should be appointed?—I should say the recommendation of the Commissioners of 1854 was a very good recommendation.

3172. What is the substance of that?—That the new trustees should be appointed by the Lord Chancellor for the time being.

3173. Not be elected by any body or any section of the community?—I should say not. I think it would be very undesirable that an education board, for a special purpose of this kind, or a board for the purpose of developing the country, should be elected in the ordinary way.

3174. I suppose you mean appointment by the Lord Chancellor of Ireland?—Yes.

3175. Would appointments of trustees by the Lord Chancellor of Ireland, for the time being, be more satisfactory to the people of Londonderry than the Irish Society?—I think so.

3176. Is not the Lord Chancellor a political officer?—I hope not; not strictly political.

3177. He changes from ministry to ministry?—He does.

3178. Would not these appointments be objected to on political grounds?—I do not think so, because I think that no Lord Chancellor would appoint gentlemen as trustees who did not occupy a pre-eminent position, and would not appoint any one who would not be looked on as conspicuously fair, and capable also of administering the trust.

3179. Would you have only one trustee?—I should say three or five.

3180. All to be appointed by the Lord Chancellor of the day?—Personally, I should have no objection to that.

3181. And

Sir Richard Temple—continued.

3181. And you have no apprehension?—I should have no objection to their being appointed by Parliament. Perhaps the best plan would be to appoint the first trustees by Parliament, and if the trusts were being defined by an Act, that the first trustees should be named in that Act. The successors to be appointed, in case a trustee died or resigned, by the Lord Chancellor for the time being.

3182. I did not understand what your answer with regard to the incumbents was; do I understand you to imply that the present incumbents of parishes or of cures should be got rid of?—No.

3183. What did you mean?—I say that the present incumbents have an equitable claim to have the grants continued during their incumbency, and on this ground; that they undertook that incumbency under the present circumstances, in which the grants are actually being made from year to year to them.

3184. And that their successors should have no claim?—I think that should exhaust the claim. I think that the support of the incumbencies in perpetuity would be a misappropriation of the public funds, on the ground that it is of little or no public advantage.

3185. One question about these trustees; supposing such appointments were made by the Lord Chancellor, might there arise no question about Protestants and Catholics?—I think Parliament might very well settle that.

3186. I am talking of the Lord Chancellor?—I mean, in settling the original scheme, Parliament could very well say that a certain proportion should be Catholic and a certain proportion Protestants. That is the ordinary tendency in the present day in dealing with all such matters.

3187. Would not questions arise among the Protestants, for instance, between the Presbyterian Church and the Church of England, and so on?—It is possible, but I think it would not be so objectionable as the present system, where all are Protestants and some are Catholics, and where none of them have any connection with the district, or any knowledge of the district, and where they spend 30 per cent. or upwards of the income in administering the trust, and spend at least two-thirds of the balance in objects that are of no public advantage.

Colonel *Lewis*.

3188. I think you have made a considerable study of this subject, have you not?—Yes.

3189. You gave a very confident opinion just now as to the trust, at any rate?—That has been my opinion.

3190. You have therefore, of course, studied it?—I have.

3191. I want to ask this question: before the negotiations were entered into with the City of London for the purpose of planting Ulster, did not King James offer the lands that were forfeited to certain others of his subjects?—He offered the land generally to certain classes of planters.

3192. In fact, he was desirous of settling the land with Englishmen and Scotchmen?—Yes.

3193. And establishing the Protestant religion?—Yes.

Colonel *Lewis*—continued.

3194. For that purpose he did offer to his subjects generally these lands?—Yes; either before or concurrently with the offer to the planters.

3195. Before?—I concede that.

3196. Did, as a matter of fact, any of his English and Scotch subjects accept the offer and establish themselves in this land?—Certainly.

3197. Do you consider that they were trustees?—I do not.

3198. Give your reasons?—Because they were simply subject to what is called the articles and conditions and nothing else. Those articles and conditions provided for the protection of the tenants, who were to be induced on favourable terms to come over and plant the lands. They provided for the tenure of those tenants, and for the care of those tenants in future, and that forms, as far as I know, the basis of what we call the Ulster custom of tenant-right. The Ulster custom of tenant-right springing from that was formed by gradual accretions owing to tenants' improvements.

3199. You do not consider holders of land under those conditions were trustees?—I say they were not trustees.

3200. Although they were sent there for precisely the same purpose that the Corporation of London were invited to go there?—By no means.

3201. They were not Irishmen, and not Catholics, and they went over for the purpose of establishing the Protestant religion, and to people the country with Englishmen and Scotchmen?—There is a clear distinction drawn between the individual planters and what are called the "Londoners," the Corporation and citizens of London.

3202. What is the distinction?—The distinction is drawn in the motives and reasons that he gave to the Londoners for undertaking the plantation of the county of Coleraine.

3203. I will not pursue that further; but has the result, at any rate, of the management of this large tract of country by the City companies been that the country is now prosperous?—Not so prosperous as I should like.

3204. But it is fairly prosperous?—Fairly prosperous.

3205. It compares favourably with the condition it was in when the companies first went there?—All parts of the country do.

3206. These especially?—I should not like to say that.

3207. You are not prepared to say the condition is prosperous; we have had that from other sources that it is prosperous?—Some parts are prosperous and some parts are not. There are certain parts of the estates all through the county that are prosperous, and less fertile parts of the estate that are not prosperous like the other portions of the estates.

3208. One question with regard to Londonderry: you just now spoke of the influence of middlemen being very disastrous in the county, and, in fact, in the management of these estates?—Yes.

3209. It has been suggested to us by witnesses from Londonderry that perpetual leases should be adopted; does not that really revive to some extent

Colonel *Laurie*—continued.

extent the principle of the middleman?—No; just the exact opposite.

3210. The same man cannot occupy either house or lands in perpetuity, can he; does not it involve the same principle; if you let land in perpetuity it must be demised in some way to somebody else?—Not necessarily at all.

3211. Unless there is a surrender?—I beg your pardon. What the Londonderry witnesses contended, or, at least, what they intended to contend, was, that the greater part of Londonderry being let on lease to middlemen, the middlemen farmed it out, and did not give perpetuities to the actual occupiers, and it was impossible to get perpetuities on which to build factories and other houses for the purpose of promoting industry in the city.

3212. It occurs to me, if you have perpetual leases you revive the same principle?—That is exactly the same principle on which the companies acted. They let their estates as a whole to one middleman; that middleman had complete power and control over the individual tenants, and he was able to raise the rents and fleece them at will, and actually did it.

3213. That is the same case with perpetual leases; if you take a perpetual lease of any land or property, it is impossible you can hold for ever; you must demise it in some way, either by reletting it or dealing with it in some way?—I draw a distinction, and the State has drawn a distinction, between a perpetual lease of an estate and of a plot occupied by the individual turning that plot to profitable advantage.

Mr. *Lawson*.

3214. Of course in the case of perpetuity it is not necessarily sublet by the grantee to another person, but is devised in the ordinary way as freehold property would be?—Certainly, that is what I contend. That is the reason I approved of the policy of the Land Purchase Acts, by which each tenant got absolute possession of his own holding, and could deal with it as he pleased.

3215. As a matter of fact the difference of tenure between perpetuities and long leases would have nothing to do with the creation of middlemen, unless it was handed over en bloc to one or two men?—Nothing.

3216. Generally I understand you to contend that the action of the companies and the Irish Society as landlords has been more or less according to the average standard of the time?—I speak as to the companies only. As to the Irish Society there are grave complaints that their dealings with their tenantry are not fair; and I am bound to say I agree with them in that.

3217. You believe that they have not differed substantially from the average of landlords?—Outside the Irish Society they differ substantially.

3218. For the worse?—For the worse; and very recently their policy has been extremely bad, and they have refused to sell to tenants under Lord Ashbourne's Act where the tenants offered large prices.

3219. I was not thinking of the amount on the sales of property, but rather of their treatment of the tenants in their ordinary dealings?—They have raised their rents, and kept them up at a time when they should have lowered them.

Mr. *Clancy*.

3220. I understand you to deny that any promise was made at the time of the sale of the Salters' estate, or before it, that the grants to churches and schools would be continued?—I do deny that there was any mention even of it at the time of sale. At the inception of the sale, before, or at the signing of the agreements of purchase, there was no mention of the grants.

3221. There was no mention in the documents?—Nor verbally.

3222. How are you able to say that?—From my own recollection of the facts. Nobody even alleges that, if you observe the statements made. I stated that in two letters to "The Times," and no one has ventured, up to the present moment, to contradict the fact.

3223. To-day Mr. Gaussen, and the Rev. Mr. Jordan on a previous day, and I think some other witnesses, spoke pretty confidently as to a widespread impression, amounting almost to a belief, that such a promise was made, and that on the faith of it a price was given for the lands that would not otherwise have been given; how can you account for that; I do not suppose you will impeach the evidence that such an impression existed?—Except as to date I would not.

3224. What is the point as to the date?—That there was no thought of the matter in the first instance at all, but that it began to be discussed, and there was a general impression that there would be a continuance of the grants.

3225. I understand the evidence of the Reverend Mr. Jordan and Mr. Gaussen to point to the time before the sales were completed?—You will observe they do not fix any date, and as a matter of fact it does not point to the date.

3226. I am forced to the inference that they refer to the time before, because one of the witnesses stated to me that this promise rather induced to the contracts?—I may say this with regard to Mr. Gaussen: Mr. Gaussen was not contemplating the sale originally at all; Mr. Gaussen was one of a few leaseholders.

3227. In the evidence of some previous witness there was a mention made of Mr. Gaussen?—In Mr. Jordan's evidence; he does not fix any date.

3228. I want to point out to you that he must have referred to the time before the contracts were entered into, because he said to me, I think, that the promise which he understood to be made induced to the contract?—I am bound to say that was an extremely disingenuous observation of Mr. Jordan's. Mr. Jordan was the rector of Magherafelt. He was the leading rector on the estate. He was in daily communication with Sir Henry Cartwright, the acknowledged agent of the company. He was seeing me from time to time during four years. I took out three conveyances for him, he being a tenant and a purchaser himself. He never up to this moment, from the inception of the sale to this moment, mentioned the question of grants to me; and he wrote to "The Belfast News Letter," when

this

Mr. *Cheney*—continued.

this controversy was going on, that Sir Henry Cartwright informed himself personally that the time was inopportune during the continuance of the sale to approach the company with regard to the grants, and that they were to wait until the sales were concluded before the question could be dealt with at all; and I consider that Dr. Jordan's evidence giving that statement was extremely improper evidence to give before the Committee.

3229. Do not you think what you have just said now, that Sir Henry Cartwright told him it was inopportune to speak of this matter, rather confirms his evidence?—No; on the contrary it shows that he had a discussion with Sir Henry Cartwright, the acknowledged agent of the company.

3230. About what?—About these grants; and that Sir Henry Cartwright told him the company had not made a promise, and had not dealt with the question, and that he must wait until the end of the sales, and that it was inopportune to ask leave to deal with the question.

3231. That shows, though he did not speak to you about it, he went to a higher authority?—I was not an authority at all until some time afterwards; and to tell the Committee here that I had made a promise when he was seeing me from day to day, I think is very extraordinary evidence to give.

3232. You do not deny, and I suppose you are not in a position to deny, that Sir Henry Cartwright may have made such a promise?—I cannot say what Sir Henry Cartwright did. I can only say what he did to myself. He made no promise to me.

3233. You are now giving some evidence that rather confirms the idea that he must have been talking to Sir Henry Cartwright on the subject?—He states so in the letter; and I do not think Sir Henry Cartwright denies the fact.

3234. I want to ask you to say frankly, if you think you are at liberty to say it, had you any conversation yourself with Sir Henry Cartwright on the subject?—I have no objection; and there is no reason why I should not say I had.

3235. I do not want to press you too far?—I have already stated in two letters to "The Times" exactly what I will state to you; that Sir Henry Cartwright's own opinion was that the company would do something with regard to these grants.

3236. He conveyed that opinion to you?—Yes, and, as a matter of fact, it has been done.

3237. Done, to what extent?—That I cannot tell exactly, I cannot give particulars, but probably the clerk of the company will give you that.

3238. The grants that have been given are still given?—Whether they are still given, or otherwise I cannot say.

3239. No grants have ever been withdrawn?—I have only heard what Mr. Gammon stated here.

3240. You have no knowledge yourself of any grants being withdrawn?—I have heard that none of the grants have been withdrawn, as a matter of fact; what may be the intention of the company I cannot say, but I have been informed on both sides that the grants have not been withdrawn.

3241. You stated you expressed the opinion to the tenants that the company would make provision for churches and charities as they had been accustomed to do?—I would not say as they had been accustomed to do, but I believed they would do something.

3242. Why did you express that opinion?—Because I believed it.

3243. What led you to express it?—The real reason I expressed it was this. It was only my private opinion, and so expressed. On various occasions during the progress of the sale, I made application to the company for remission of rent, and for other concessions to the tenants. Any representation I made, and that I could give reasonable grounds for, the company acceded to, and these representations resulted in a saving to the tenants of some 20,000 *l.* or upwards. I considered myself that this was reasonable, and that I could give good grounds to the company for a continuance of these grants in some form or other, and I had no reason to believe the company would not act in the same way in this matter as with regard to the other applications I made.

3244. Do not you think that an expression of opinion upon that subject did tend to make them enter into these agreements?—No, that is what I protest against; I do not mind what they thought about what the company would do, but I protest against the idea that they entered into these agreements in consideration of that at all, because the agreements had been entered into long before the question was raised or talked of.

3245. Not all?—Not all; but I should say nine-tenths of the money, and my conversations with individual tenants did not amount to conversations with half-a-dozen at the utmost, and was the expression of a private opinion, and not with regard to the terms of purchase at all, but with regard to a public question in which they were interested, and I was equally interested.

3246. Why did this expression of opinion come from you at that particular time, and not before?—Because it was not raised to me before.

3247. Do you mean to say the tenants then for the first time themselves thought of the matter?—My recollection is that some question was asked in the House of Commons about the appropriation of the funds, and about these schools and churches, and that that raised the question on the estate.

3248. Not until then?—Not, I believe, until then. Some public reference was made to the matter, and the question having been raised, some of them asked my opinion. I gave them that opinion, but that had no reference to the terms of sale of any kind.

3248*. Does not it strike you as curious that these gentlemen, like Mr. Jordan, should have sworn to a general impression existing on the subject without any word having been said about it?—The general impression, there is no question about it, did exist, but if you observe in Mr. Jordan's evidence, there is no date fixed.

3249. I am only asking you to account for this curious circumstance that this impression did undoubtedly exist generally, and yet, according to your evidence, the tenants never said a word to you about it?—The grants were going on at the

Mr. *Clancy*—continued.

the time, and had gone on for years and years. They never thought of questioning the matter at all. When the question was raised, no doubt they had a general impression that the grants would be continued in some form either during the life of the incumbents, or by some compensation. There were various suggestions which were made.

3250. The Rev. Mr. Jordan must have meant that the impression existed from the beginning?—Then I wish you had asked him that question. There was no expression either in writing or verbally at the time the sale took place, and the instructions are in writing dealing with the terms of purchase. I do not say the impression did not exist; but all I say is, that there was no reference to it in fixing the terms of sale, and that it was not a consideration in the terms of sale, and there was no verbal reference to it at the time.

3251. I only want you to explain how it was that such an impression as you say existed, could have existed without something having been said on the subject by somebody or other?—I could not say what took place, or what was in the minds of the episcopal clergy. There were, I believe, only two resident actually on the estate, but neither they nor any other episcopal clergyman ever spoke to me on the subject until quite recently.

3252. Now, to come to another matter; you are evidently not of the opinion of the gentleman sent here by the Corporation of Londonderry, with regard to the Irish Society and the administration of its funds?—I am not.

3253. You do not see any reason why 26 Londoners, to use the historical expression, should manage any affairs in relation to Londonderry?—I do not think they should; I think they are very admirable gentlemen in their own way, but I do not think they could manage our affairs as well as we could ourselves.

3254. You were here on the last day, when you heard the expression used, that if a local body were appointed to administer the funds, pestering would go on as to particular grants, and so on; according to you, that is exactly what has gone on under the present system?—That is exactly what has gone on.

3255. Do you mean to say that certain persons, in fact your evidence comes to this, might be more or less bribed by special favours conferred on them by the Irish Society from time to time?—From a certain point of view, you might say all these grants to churches and to all these teachers are in the form of bribes, but that is a method of expression one man might use and another would not.

3256. It is rather a strong expression?—Yes.

3257. Do I understand you to say that the reason, in your opinion, why the representatives of the Corporation of Londonderry object to the Corporation of Londonderry being entrusted with the administration of the Irish Society is, that they know that the position of parties in that body would not be maintained if the franchise were lowered?—There is a feeling amongst the Protestant population of Londonderry that this is a Protestant fund, and that on the reduction of the franchise there would be a Catholic majority in the corporation, and that if it went into the hands of the corporation, in which the majority were Catholic, the fund would not be administered in their interest.

3258. So that, when they come here to say that they are in favour of devoting these funds of this society to the general community, you do not think they are sincere?—I should not like to answer that question; I know the feeling exists, but I am bound to say this, that, in my opinion, if the people were polled, a large majority would go in favour of appropriating the funds to general public purposes.

3259. Have you any fear yourself that a Catholic majority in the Corporation of Londonderry would make any such misuse of the funds?—Not the slightest.

3260. You believe that they would distribute them fairly?—I believe a Catholic is as honest as a Protestant, and a Protestant as a Catholic, and I am of opinion that with the reduced franchise, care would be exercised by the ratepayers themselves that the funds should be properly administered.

3261. You were asked as to the danger of appointing local trustees, and that they would quarrel, and so on; are you aware that under the Educational Endowments Act, the Commission appointed under that Act have appointed in various parts of Ireland local bodies of trustees, who are working very well?—I am so aware.

3262. You do not know of a single instance in which they are not working well?—I do not.

3263. Are you in favour of the compulsory purchase of these estates?—I am.

3264. Do you know if that is the feeling in the district?—It is the universal feeling, I believe. Certainly among the occupiers it is the universal feeling.

Mr. *T. M. Healy*.

3265. I suppose the tenants did not care a button whether these grants were continued or not so long as they got the land?—I would not say that. I think they were more anxious about their land than about the grants. I do not think they were much interested in the grants.

3266. How many estates did you say you acted with regard to?—I acted for the tenants on the Salters' estate, and on behalf of the company, and the tenants on the Skinners' estate.

3267. Were they a majority of Protestants?—No, I think they were pretty well mixed.

3268. Half and half?—Quite half and half.

3269. Did the Episcopal clergy at all take any part in helping on the bargain, or did they intervene in any way?—They gave no assistance whatever.

3270. Did they go round amongst their flock and give them any help or counsel in the transaction?—None that I ever heard of.

3271. And then when the whole thing was over they intervened, and said they should get their grants?—Yes.

3272. The Skinners and the Salters?—Yes.

3273. The whole of the Salters' estate is sold, and the Skinners' partly, I understand?—The Salters' is all sold with the exception of eight agricultural

Mr. T. M. Healy—continued.

agricultural holdings, and a few holdings in town. As to the Skinners', I should say, two-thirds is sold and upwards.

3274. As to these grants to the parsons, do they do any good, much?—None whatever, except to the individual persons and their families.

3275. They did not do the public any good?—Not the slightest.

3276. There is no public ground for continuing them?—Except that a few people may think possibly they will have to pay the clergy a little if they do not get these grants. That is the only interest in the matter.

3277. Is it not a matter in which the public are concerned; it is not a public matter?—Not a public matter in the proper sense of the term at all in my opinion.

3278. It would be a different matter if the matter were one of houses, taking away the residence from a gentleman. That would be a different question?—That would be a very serious matter.

3279. Have any gentlemen, to your knowledge, lost their residences, either as schoolmasters or clergy?—None that I know of: I never heard of any instance.

3280. Have not they taken away the house of the priest of Dungiven?—No.

3281. Did you sell the Dungiven portion of the estate?—I did, to the priest.

3282. The Rev. Mr. Loughery?—Not at all, to his predecessor.

3283. What became of the house?—He devised it, I believe, to his sister's son.

3284. The priest did?—Yes.

3285. Did the company give him the house?—The position is this; he was tenant of a house and a small holding of about 12 or 15 acres of land.

3286. At a nominal rent?—At the ordinary agricultural rent. He purchased his holding like any other tenant on the estate purchased his holding, and then devised it to his relative. It is alleged the parish had an interest in the matter, but whether that is right or wrong I cannot say.

3287. That is not a matter the company has any concern in either?—Not the slightest.

3288. If the reverend gentleman parted with his interest to his family, that does not touch the company?—No, the company treated him exactly like any other tenant; he came in to me and signed his agreement like any other tenant. He was on the company's books as a tenant. It is alleged now that he was trustee for the parish, and that notwithstanding that, and in violation of his trust, he treated himself as private owner, and devised this property to his relatives.

3289. How is the company to blame for it?—I do not blame them at all.

3290. The suggestion is made to me that the company are in some way to blame because they took away the house from the clergyman?—I tell you the facts, and you can judge for yourself. The company had no knowledge of the matter at all.

3291. Was this house regarded as in any way having any kind of sacred character?—It was a holding held from year to year.

Mr. T. M. Healy—continued.

3292. Was it next door to the church?—It was close to the church.

3293. Would not the company be blameable in this way for allowing what was the residence of the parish priest to pass away into private hands?—The company might have been blameable provided they got notice of this; but the facts are these, that they let that house and the priest purchased from his predecessor and the predecessor purchased from his predecessor and each succeeded on the purchase. The allegation is that the purchase only covered the improvements and the tenant-right was not purchased and that the tenant-right was in the parish; but neither the agent of the company nor myself had any notice of the alleged trust whatever, and we considered him an ordinary tenant and treated him so, and he so represented himself; but I cannot see how the company could be possibly blamed for that.

3294. You think it is a grievance between the late priest and his congregation?—I do not think it; I know it.

3295. How long has the Rev. Father Loughery been in the parish?—He was installed within the last three months, I think.

3296. The fact that there is not a residence now is due to the conduct of his predecessor in alienating it?—That is so. As I understand, Father Loughery and the parish have offered to pay the relatives the same sum that the former priest paid for it, and the sister of the late priest refuses it, and the ground of her refusal is the advice of her solicitor that she holds in trust for a minor and she cannot divest it at all.

3297. You managed the Skinners' Estate partly under the Arrears Act?—I did.

3298. Did you act for the company or the tenants?—For the tenants.

3299. Were there large arrears?—Very large arrears, especially in the mountain districts.

3300. Did the existence of large arrears point to the existence of prior impossible rents in your opinion?—It did.

3301. I suppose it is in the Blue Book issued in connection with the Arrears Act. Can you give us roughly the total arrears wiped off by the Act?—I cannot from recollection.

3302. Was it distressing on the tenants; were they put to straits to make up the year's rent to qualify under the Arrears Act?—I could not say that. There are poor portions of the estate, and on these poor portions there were large arrears and they were wiped off. Beyond that I cannot tell you. The tenants are poor still, and I think their chronic condition would be poor.

3303. These are the people who have bought their estates?—These are the people who have not bought.

3304. Is each case is it true of the Skinners' Estate as of the Drapers', that it is poor remnant which is left?—That is so.

3305. Then would it equally be true of this estate as of the Drapers' Estate, that the rich tenants who bought would be Protestants and that those who are left are Catholics?—Not equally, but there would be a large proportion. I should say it would be pretty well half-and-half.

Mr. T. M. Healy—continued.

3306. It is the Catholics who are on the poor lands?—The majority of them are Catholics.

3307. You have told us about turbary; now was it your own device about holding the turbary in common after the company had cleared out, or was it suggested to you?—My own device.

3308. Did you provide by your deed what was to be done with it when the bog was cut out?—I myself am inclined to think the bog is on the tenants' holdings altogether. I was under a misapprehension. I was thinking of the Salters' bog and the tenants' bog together. The Salters' bog is in the hands of the company. The tenants' bog is all let to the tenants, and the turbary was reserved by the purchase deed to the company, and the company then granted to the trustees in trust.

3309. Do we understand there is bog still left on the hands of the company?—No. The Salters' bog was in their own hands at the time of the purchase, but they have also given their bog to the purchasers. The Skinners' bog had been let to the various tenants, and the turbary was within the ambit of the tenants' holdings; but all the bog on the Skinners' estate has been conveyed to trustees in trust for the tenants.

3310. Was the fact that this bog was retained in the hands of the company used as an instrument of coercion?—No, certainly not; I can speak positively as to that.

3311. You are speaking of the purchase transaction?—I am speaking of the purchase transaction.

3312. Then as to the previous condition of the tenants when under rent. Does not the fact that the bog is retained in the hands of the landlord, and not let to the tenants as a portion of their holdings, often used as an instrument of coercion and pressure?—I believe that is so very often, but not, as I say, as regards the particular estate in question.

3313. Do you think it was an advisable thing that you should have acted as solicitor for both landlord and tenant?—My opinion is that it is an objectionable practice, but I adopted the practice that the Land Commission favoured. In fact they provided for it.

3314. You would think now from your experience that every tenant should be represented by his own solicitor?—I do; and I thought so several years ago, and so wrote to the Land Commission and gave the reasons.

3315. Have you got with you the circulars you issued to the tenants?—I have some of them. Which estate are you referring to?

3316. I should like to have all three circulars. Were not the tenants threatened with litigation if they did not complete their purchases within a given date?—Which ones?

3317. By you in any case?—No, in no case.

3318. Was there not a threat that if they did not complete their purchases, actions for specific performance would be begun against them?—Sir Henry Cartwright, I believe, did send a letter to some of the tenants stating so.

3319. It was not done by you?—No.

3320. It was done by Sir Henry Cartwright?—Yes, on the Salters' estate; but I am bound to say that I think the circumstances justified it myself.

3321. Does it not point to the fact that the tenants were reluctant to buy?—No, they had bought at the time.

3322. That they were reluctant to carry out the sale?—They were reluctant to carry out the sale. There was a good deal of discussion going on at the time.

3323. Does not that point to the fact that they had given too big a price, or thought they had given too big a price?—That is so, but in my opinion they were misled about the matter.

3324. A man is the best judge of his own bargain. I only want to get at the fact that these tenants had purchased at a rate they thought was exorbitant, and had been threatened with legal proceedings to compel them to execute the conveyance?—I am bound to say that with regard to that they did not think it exorbitant in the first instance, and authorised me to carry it out; and I got better terms than they themselves fixed, and there was only a few on the estate that did object to carry out their purchases; and in my opinion it was from misrepresentation they were led to do that.

3325. Would circulars have been printed and distributed in most a few cases; if you have only one or two letters to write you do not get them printed?—I cannot remember whether it was printed or not, or whether it was a notice put up at particular places; but I recollect there were a number of statements wholly inaccurate that were circulated among the tenants, and they were misled, so misled that I felt it my duty to send a circular letter to the tenants explaining their position about it, explaining the facts of the purchase and the advantages of it.

3326. The Catholic clergy, as a rule, instruct themselves in their flock?—They do.

3327. Did, on this occasion, the Catholic clergy advise with the tenants in their transactions?—They did.

3328. The Protestant clergy held aloof from their flock?—They did; the Episcopal clergy did. I believe the Presbyterian clergy did advise with their people.

3329. Is it the case that this "concise view" was bought up and attempted to be suppressed by the Irish Society in the twenties?—It is so stated, and it is the current rumour. There were two editions, and it is said the first edition was bought up; whether it is true or not I do not know of my own knowledge. The first edition was thought to contain some damaging matter, and the first edition was suppressed, or attempted to be suppressed, and a second edition, with the damaging matter struck out, issued.

3330. What is the difference between the two editions?—I saw the two, but I cannot tell you now. I do not think they are materially different; at least, so far as regards the matter we are concerned in.

3331. Would you have any difficulty in putting your hand upon either of these printed circulars issued in connection with these estates?—I hunted up all I could get, and I have them here, and can hand them to you.

3332. Would the gentlemen who will be called, representing the companies, necessarily have copies?—No.

3333. They

Mr. T. M. Healy—continued.

3333. They would be in your custody?—They would be in my custody. In most cases there were a number left over after being issued, and in some cases not. Any that remained I have locked up.

3334. Through whose estates does the Londonderry Central Railway run?—It runs through part of the Mercers' estate, through part of the Salters' estate, through part of the Ironmongers' estate, and through part of what was the old Vintners' estate.

3335. The Londonderry Central Railway is a great convenience to the inhabitants of the entire county of Londonderry, or to a considerable extent a convenience?—In my private opinion it is a great blunder.

3336. Blunder or no blunder, did the companies take any trouble or pains to promote or build this line?—No, they did not promote it; but some of them gave some assistance towards it. I think they did; to some other railways they did. In my opinion they spent a large sum of money, which, if it had been properly spent, would have opened up the county; but at the present moment the county is practically without any railway accommodation. For instance, if I want to go from Londonderry to Draperstown, a distance by a proper line of 23 miles, I have to travel 75 miles, and spend the whole day travelling it, and that is where the London companies and the Irish Society are in existence for the purpose of developing the country and its resources. I think it is a standing disgrace to both the companies and the society.

3337. They have left the county practically derelict?—They have so far as that is concerned.

3338. And even so far as that roundabout line that has been constructed is concerned, you cannot tell us what amount of assistance they gave?—No, I cannot tell, but I am sure the clerks of the various companies will give you that. I see the Skinners' Company gave a large sum towards the Limavady and Dungiven line; if they had applied it to a proper railway scheme it would have been an advantage, but it is very little advantage as it is.

3339. The result of the roundabout manner in which the Londonderry Central Railway has been made is, that they can pay no dividend, and the Government do not get their interest on the loan?—The line is insolvent, and I believe all the lines promoted in that way are insolvent in the county; but if a proper line had been made it would have been a good paying line.

3340. So that both shareholders and Government are being robbed alike?—They are.

Mr. T. M. Healy—continued.

3341. It is your opinion that if these estates had been under local control, all these blunders would have been avoided in the county?—I believe so; but I believe the real cause why all these blunders were perpetuated was, that the companies' agents were all connected with the Northern Counties Railway, and the policy of the Northern Counties Railway was to get the grasp of the whole business to take it up to Belfast, the directors being all connected with Belfast interests.

3342. And the local interests and the interests of the general public were different?—I do not know about their interests; their views were different, and their policy was bad.

3343. At any rate we have it, so far as the companies are concerned, they have done nothing by making proper lines?—They might have done a great deal, but they did nothing of any use with regard to railway building. If they had applied the money that has been applied in the county to railway purposes in building a proper railway, the whole county would have been accommodated, and the line side of the county would have been brought into connection with the other side, and the city brought into connection with the whole county; whereas at the present you are obliged to go 75 miles instead of going 23 miles, and the centre of the county is utterly without railway accommodation.

3344. Had you any connection with any of the facts connected with Benjamin Barelon case?—Except by hearsay; I know the question involved.

3345. You deny that there was any illegitimate influence brought to bear on the tenants to induce them to purchase on the estates that you were connected with?—I do deny it utterly.

3346. As a matter of fact, was the landlord's interest in these holdings, assuming the tenant to be the owner of his own improvements, overpaid for; was the landlord's interest worth what the tenants gave for it?—If you mean, would the purchase-money have been so large had the tenants improvements been protected in all cases, my opinion is that it would not.

3347. Do not you think the tenants in most of the cases paid for their own improvements; bought their own improvements?—Just as they had been paying rent for their own improvements they bought them.

3348. Under the Ashbourne Act the tenant who has made the improvements has to pay the landlord for them?—And under the Act of 1881 he is paying the landlord for them, as you know.

Monday, 30th June 1890.

MEMBERS PRESENT :

Mr. Clancy.	Mr. Lawson.
Lord Elcho.	Mr. Lea.
Sir John Ellis.	Sir William Marriott.
Mr. John Ellis.	Mr. John Morley.
Mr. T. M. Healy.	Mr. Sexton.
Colonel Laurie.	Sir Richard Temple.

THE RIGHT HONOURABLE JOHN MORLEY, IN THE CHAIR.

Mr. G. H. Lee.] WILL you allow me, Sir, to make one observation arising out of what occurred on Thursday. I have been instructed, together with my friend, Mr. Stone, to appear and watch these proceedings by Mr. White, solicitor, of Belfast, on behalf of various tenants and bodies in the north of Ireland, who are much interested in the result of the proceedings here. We are now informed that Mr. Todd has instructed Mr. Walker to appear, and I need not say we are extremely glad so able an advocate will appear on the same side. At the same time I would ask you to allow us also to appear, as the interests of the persons whom I represent may be somewhat different to those represented by Dr. Todd. I do not think they will be materially different, and of course it will be subject to the remark made by Mr. Elton that there will be no repetition or needless argument.

Chairman.] I do not quite understand what you mean when you say "from Belfast." Is Mr. White of Belfast or of Londonderry?

Mr. G. H. Lee.] Mr. White, of Belfast; but he has a very considerable interest and is very well known in Londonderry, and he has been instructed by people in Londonderry. I have resolutions passed in Londonderry.

Chairman.] Your point of view is one that is not favourable to the administration of the companies, I understand.

Mr. G. H. Lee.] Certainly; it is on behalf of the tenants.

Chairman.] As against the companies as their landlords or vendors of their holdings.

Mr. G. H. Lee.] Against the companies as vendors of their holdings; and you will hear, as I gather, two or three counsel on behalf of the companies.

Chairman.] Let it be understood that we are going to hear counsel only on the interpretation of the instruments. That has been definitely laid down.

Mr. G. H. Lee.] That is clear.

Chairman.] We do not wish to hear, and shall not hear, counsel upon the administration of the estates.

Mr. G. H. Lee.] That I fully understand, Sir; and it will be merely so far as we may wish to add any observation on the construction of the instruments to anything that Mr. Walker may say (who will, of course, take the main part in the argument) that we desire to put in an appearance here.

Chairman.] When Mr. Walker has stated the case, if you think there is anything to be added by your counsel, we should not refuse to hear him; but, of course, it would be at your peril. It is very unlikely your counsel would discover points that have been neglected by Mr. Walker; but if there are such points there is no reason why they should not be presented. You understand, it is at your own peril, and that he will be liable to being interrupted by us at once.

Mr. G. H. Lee.] Certainly, Sir, I understand you will not hear irrelevant argument.

Chairman.] And no repetition of the same argument.

Mr. G. H. Lee.] I fully understand that, Sir; but there may be some different points of view which the tenants and the bodies in Londonderry, whom I represent, will take, from those taken by those represented by Dr. Todd.

Chairman.] I do not really see how that can be, because what counsel will put before is not the point of view taken by the tenants, but it will be the strictly legal point; it will not be interests that they will address us upon, but the principles of legal construction.

Mr. G. H. Lee.] That I understand, Sir.

Mr. John Ellis.

3349. In view of two or three questions that have been put to you, and your answers to them, I may put this question to you which I should not otherwise have put: are you a Protestant or a Catholic?—I am a Protestant.

3350. At the outset of your examination you mentioned that at the time you were acting for the company in the sale of timber and of the manor house, I think you were also acting for certain tenants, and with respect to what you called some outstanding holdings?—Yes; there were some outstanding holdings sold to the tenants where I was acting in the sale of the timber in a few cases.

3351. You were acting for both parties?—Yes.

3352. Could you say what was the number of the outstanding holdings?—I should say at that time there were about 40 altogether, and now there are about eight, as nearly as I can judge.

3353. You were acting on behalf of 40 tenants?—Yes.

3354. About what would be the acreage of their holdings, or the valuation; can you give us any idea?—I think they were, perhaps, just the average holding, and the holdings ran from 10 acres to 60 acres, and in a few cases above that; the average size of the holding, I should say, would be about 30 or 40 acres; perhaps 30 acres would be the average.

3355. Were these tenants ones who might be described, as we have heard some tenants described, as illiterate; that is to say, men not quite understanding legal documents?—I am not at all sure of that; I do not think that is possible in this case.

3356. Have they applied to the court for judicial rents?—Some of them have and some have not.

3357. Have any of them obtained judicial rents?—I think, perhaps, all obtained judicial rents; perhaps there may be some exceptions, but in most cases they have obtained judicial rents, either through the court or by agreement.

3358. In the case of those who have obtained them by agreement, was it after an application by the others to the court?—No; the greater part of the rents were fixed by agreement before there were any applications to the court, so far as I recollect.

3359. Can you tell us the percentage of reduction made, if there was reduction?—My recollection is (I am not quite sure) that there was 10 per cent. given. There had been 10 per cent. added at a particular period some years before, and that 10 per cent. was struck off again, and most of the tenants signed agreements for fair rents on those conditions. Those had been nearly all signed before I had anything to do with the estate at all.

3360. Can you give us the date when the agreements for fair rents were signed?—I should say in 1882 chiefly; after the passing of the Land Act of 1881.

3361. And the time when you were acting was

Mr. John Ellis—continued.

at the end of 1884 and the beginning of 1885, I understand?—Yes.

3362. You negotiated on their behalf on the basis of the judicial or fair rent?—I did not look upon the rents as exactly fair; I negotiated on the basis of the valuation of the land which I thought was nearer what was fair. In a few cases on a particular part of the estate, which had been at the time of the valuation looked upon as wheat land, the value there was depreciated more than the other land since the rents were less than the valuation, and in those cases, though the company did not at first consent they ultimately consented to a sale at the basis of the rental of the land; in other cases the valuation was less than the rent, and in those cases it was the basis of the purchase.

3363. In those cases you think the figures of the valuation afford some guide for the purchase basis?—It is not at all reliable.

3364. Have the 32 out of 40 who settled, as I understand, settled on the terms you advised?—Yes. I think in most cases there were some special concessions. There were some peculiarities in most of the outstanding cases: some of these lands for instance were subject to flooding; in others perhaps the rent was less fair than on the majority of the holdings; in most of those cases there were some exceptional circumstances. In those cases Sir Henry Cartwright made certain concessions and the sale was carried out.

3365. Can you tell us why the other eight tenants are still waiting for a settlement?—An application has been made by four or five of them, and is under consideration at present, and I think probably those will be settled. In other cases the tenants have very strong views as to the value of the holdings; they think the price is too high, and they are not disposed to purchase.

3366. You mentioned that the company proposed to sell those holdings to the outside public; but you advised that before that was done notice should be given to them, and I think you gave that notice?—Yes.

3367. Have you a copy of that notice with you?—No.

3368. Perhaps you could state to us the purport of it; what did it inform them of?—It informed the tenants that the sale was about to be closed, and that they must make up their minds within a certain time whether they would purchase, or, if they had an agreement to purchase, whether they would carry out the agreement; as otherwise the company would cancel the agreement, and dispose of the land otherwise, or keep them on as tenants, as the case might be; at any rate they would close the sale.

3369. Do you think that the mention of the disposal of the holdings otherwise had any influence in bringing the tenants to the point?—It is very difficult to answer that.

3370. Was it intended to have any such influence?—No; it was the formal notice given before the close of the sale.

Mr. John Ellis—continued.

3371. Referring to Question 3048, I gather that you thought it only fair those men should have fair notice that their holdings would be disposed of otherwise if they did not close the bargain?—That is so; and I have knowledge myself that the tenants were rather disposed to purchase, but they were holding out to see if they could get any further concession.

3372. They desired better terms if the delay would bring better terms?—They desired better terms, and they thought the delay would bring better terms; but they were determined even on these terms if they could get no better.

3373. Do not you think a notice of that kind, that outsiders might be appealed to if by a particular day the tenants did not close, might have some effect in making them close?—I should say it would induce the tenants to make up their minds to close if they intended doing so; but in most of these cases, if not all, there was some slight concession given beyond the terms, that is to say, the terms were made easier for them.

3374. Then the delay did to a certain extent improve their terms?—I am rather inclined to think not, for this reason, that in the meantime they were subject to rent; and I think they lost as much by the payment of rent if not more than they gained by the delay.

3375. Were they hoping for any action in Parliament?—I should say so; they were chiefly relying upon that, I think.

3376. Would the Act of 1887, if it had been then in existence, have affected them beneficially in any way?—I do not think so; I cannot see that it would have had any operation at all.

3377. I should like you to clear up the matter with regard to the bog on the Skinners' Estate; as I understand, the tenants have to pay a shilling where they formerly paid sixpence?—That is so.

3378. That goes to a fund to meet the expenses of managing the bog, does it not?—That is so.

3379. With which the company is now dissociated?—Exactly.

3380. Will you kindly tell me what consideration the tenants get for that extra sixpence; that is the point I want you to clear up?—They get the bog managed.

3381. Was the bog managed before at somebody else's expense?—It was managed at the company's expense of course, except so far as the sixpence went.

3382. Then the tenants are in a worse position now, are they not, if they have to do something at their own expense which before somebody else did at his expense?—I should say not, for this reason; that prior to the sale they had no legal right whatever to the turbary, and the turbary is a very valuable property on the estate. Now they have got that turbary absolutely to themselves without any payment, and the only thing they pay for is for the administration in their own interests. That may cost them a little more, and no doubt it will cost them a little more, because some part of the expense of management was not borne previously by them; but now they have an absolute vested right in the whole of the turbary on the estate, and no one can interfere and take it from them.

3383. This has been stated as a grievance, and I want to clear it up; you suggest that for the sixpence extra they get a valuable right?—A very valuable right, and I should add also that the tenants had express notice before the sale that the shilling would be charged and would be required; I have the circular letter showing that.

Mr. Lea.

3384. You were asked to give a list the other day of documents put in by you; I understand you have that list here to-day; do you consider that list an exhaustive list?—As at present advised, I do. I have the list here, and I will put it in now. (*The same was handed in.*) I should say, however, that I reserve to myself the right of putting in subsequently further documents, if counsel should so advise.

Chairman.

3385. I do not think that would be quite within your province. You told us that Mr. Walker was going to present this case; and that would be for him?—Exactly; I mean that, acting on his advice, I would put them in, with your permission.

Mr. Lea.

3386. In dealing with these estates what have the companies done with their timber?—They have sold the timber to the general public.

3387. Does that form part of the purchase money which has been mentioned; take the 344,000 *l.* for instance in the case of the Salters' Company; is it part of the money borrowed under the Land Acts?—No.

3388. That is an additional property which the company have obtained?—That is so.

3389. Have you any idea of the value of the property?—It is of very little value; a few thousands at least on the Salters' estate will cover the whole of it. I can give you the exact figure later on if you would like it.

3390. With all the companies that will be an addition, I understand?—I should say over the whole of the estates. If you refer to the six estates not purchased until after 1880 it would amount to probably about 20,000 *l.*

3391. What has been done with the land on which this timber was growing?—The land, I think, in the Salters' Company's case, was included in the tenant's holdings. No, I am wrong; I do not know exactly what has been done. I do not think anything has been done yet.

3392. I suppose, like some other companies, they still hold the land upon which the timber was growing?—I think they hold the land upon which the timber was growing, and I think they also hold the soil of the bogs, except some small portions; they are sold to the tenants to square the farms.

3393. This land may be an additional realisable asset in some cases?—Yes.

3394. You mentioned railways in your evidence the other day; can you tell me how much the London companies have contributed in the way, either of lending or giving, to railways?—The Skinners' Company, I believe, are paying interest on 22,000 *l.*; the Salters' and Drapers' Companies

Mr. *Lea*—continued.

Companies are paying some annual sums towards the Draperstown Railway; and I think the Salters', Drapers', Mercers', and Ironmongers' Companies are contributing to the Derry Central Railway. I cannot give you the figures with respect to them.

3395. Have they advanced money or guaranteed the interest?—I think they have guaranteed interest.

3396. In all cases?—I think in all cases.

3397. They took care these railways should go through their property, did they not?—The railways go through their property, but they are running in such a way that they are of very little real advantage. If the money which the Companies have applied to these railways had been properly applied to a railway through the centre of the county, it would be of vast advantage, but there is at present no railway through the centre of the county, and no access into the city from there; there is no direct railway connection between the far side of the county and the city.

Mr. *Sexton*.

3398. The city is on the extreme edge of the county, is it not?—Yes, it is on the extreme edge of the county, and the Northern Railway passes round the borders of the county and runs to Belfast; and the result is that the traffic goes rather to Belfast than to Derry.

Mr. *Lea*.

3399. The city of Londonderry is practically in Donegal?—It is on the Donegal side of the river.

3400. Would it not have been properly within the Donegal boundary?—Yes, it would.

3401. In Mr. Murrough O'Brien's evidence at Question 1314 there appears this statement: "There was a reservation to the Irish Society, and the release from the Irish Society which was part of the company's title was not produced till 1888." The Irish Society join in all the conveyances, I take it?—No, not in any case, where they purchase under the Land Purchase Act. The Irish Society did join in the conveyance in the case of the haberdasher's portion, and also the Vintners', and one or two other portions; they state so themselves in the concise view.

3402. The statement I have quoted was made with regard to the Drapers' Estate?—I think the Drapers' Company got a conveyance from the Irish Society of whatever interest they had, but the company themselves give a direct grant to the tenants.

3403. The Irish Society in some cases conveyed to the companies?—The Irish Society, I think, in all cases, have made a grant to the companies; they have either released their rights or made a direct grant.

Mr. *Sexton*.

3404. In the 17th century, you mean?—Yes, and they got a deed of indemnity from the companies.

Mr. *Lea*.

3405. In the case of the Drapers' Estate, it is stated in sworn evidence that some delay was caused by the Irish Society having to joined in the conveyance?—I am afraid I cannot give evidence as to that, because I have not seen any of the conveyances.

Chairman.

3406. Mr. Lea is asking with regard to conveyances of the other day, as it were, and you are answering with regard to the historical conveyances, I think?—With regard to the recent conveyances on the Drapers' Estate, Mr. Murrough O'Brien is a much more competent witness than I am; he knows the facts, and I have only heard something of them.

Mr. *Lea*.

3407. Did the Irish Society retain their rights to the minerals at all on these estates?—No, I do not think so.

3408. You are not aware of it?—I am not aware of it.

3409. Then when did they release their rights to the minerals?—I cannot give you the date.

3410. You know they have released their rights?—I believe they have; however you will get that direct from the Irish Society, I dare-say.

3411. We have distinct evidence here that the Irish Society joined in the conveyance to release their rights in the minerals?—Then of course that does release it. If that is evidence from Mr. Murrough O'Brien, I take it it refers to a particular estate which he has knowledge of and I have not.

3412. It refers to the Drapers' *Estate*?—Yes. In connection with that I would like to call attention to a passage on page 104 of the Concise View, in the edition which was published in 1842; it is under date 31st October 1810, and states as follows: "The master and wardens of the Goldsmiths' Company represented to the Society that they had agreed to sell their manor of Goldsmiths' Hall to the Right honourable the Earl of Shelburne for 14,100 *l.*; but being advised that they could not make a proper conveyance without the concurrence of the Society they requested the Society to join with them in making a title to the said Earl, which they consented to do upon being indemnified."

3413. So far as you know, there is no property in which the Irish Society has joined in the conveyance?—You mean, I presume, under the Land Purchase Act?

3414. Yes?—I do not think in any case they have directly joined in the conveyances, but they have given a release.

3415. A release to the tenant, do you mean?—No; a release to the Company before the Company granted to the tenant; the effect is the same.

3416. The copy of the release forms part of the tenant's security, I suppose?—Yes, of course.

3417. What do the Irish Society get for giving those releases?—I should say nothing at all.

3418. Do people generally give away any of their rights without something in return?—It is looked upon that the Irish Society and the companies are pretty well in the same position, and that whatever is done by one is approved by the other.

Mr. *Lea*—continued.

3419. If the companies were absolute owners, would it be necessary for the Irish Society to join or give any release at all?—Clearly not, except where there was a reservation of the minerals and mines, and it was intended to convey them.

3420. The mines and minerals belonging to the Irish Society, and being part of the trust property?—Yes.

3421. Then if the Irish Society has given away any mines and minerals to the other companies, it has parted with its property negligently, we may say?—Yes.

3422. If the mines and minerals in the county of Derry have been parted with by the Irish Society, they would properly belong to that part of Derry in which the Company's estates were situated and sold, would they not?—That is a question as to the legal construction of the trust, as to whether it applies to the particular estate or locality. I am afraid I am prohibited from going into that.

3423. If there were minerals on the Drapers' Estate, and the Irish Society joined in the conveyance of those minerals, would not that locality have a claim upon the Irish Society up to the value of those minerals?—Not any more than that locality would have a claim upon the proceeds of the whole estate, and then the question would arise as to whether there is a legal trust, or whether it is such a strong moral claim as Parliament would enforce, and if so, whether it is applicable to the particular estate, to the locality, or to the country generally.

3424. The minerals belonged to the Society, I presume, or they would not convey them?—Yes.

3425. With regard to the minerals on the Drapers' Estate, would not that locality have a claim upon the Irish Society through the Drapers' Estate?—I should say that the Irish Society, holding their estates for the general benefit of the plantation, any particular portions of the property they hold should be applicable to that purpose and not necessarily to the particular place where the property is situated.

Sir *William Marriott*.

3426. I think you said you had not seen the conveyances in the case of the Drapers' Company?—That is so. This is not a question of conveyancing at all, but a question as to the application of the proceeds of the sales, and, as to that, I have given my opinion generally.

Mr. *Lea*.

3427. Does it not go rather beyond that; is not the question whether the minerals are still retained by the Irish Society; having granted their estates to the companies, while the estates belong to the companies the minerals would seem to belong to the Irish Society, if they join in the conveyance to convey them?—If you look at the original grants from the Irish Society to the Company, I think you will see that they retained the timber, the mines and minerals, the fishing, and so on, and they had to release to the Company what remained in the hands of the Irish Society. You will see that from the conveyances.

Mr. *Lea*—continued.

3428. Last year the Irish Society conveyed the minerals on the Drapers' Estates to their tenants, did they not?—I do not know that as a fact, but Mr. Murrough O'Brien should know. I have had no connection with the sale of that estate, and cannot tell.

3429. With regard to your evidence on the Irish Society and the development of Derry, do you know whether Messrs. Harland & Wolff ever applied for a lease, with a view to establishing a shipbuilding yard at Derry?—I believe Messrs. Harland & Wolff did not apply, but I have heard that another firm did.

3430. Do you know that Messrs. Harland & Wolff did not apply?—I have heard so.

3431. Do you know the name of the firm that did?—I do not.

3432. Can you tell me whether the Irish Society possess the foreshore in Derry?—They do.

3433. Have they been willing to make grants of the foreshore?—Do you mean to occupiers?

3434. Yes?—They have refused to sell to occupiers altogether.

3435. Do they give long leases of the foreshore?—They do not. I should like, on that point, to refer to a statement made here on Thursday or Monday last, that nine-tenths of the society's property was given in perpetuity to individuals a century ago. So far as I can make out, that nine-tenths represented the whole property then in the hands of the Irish Society. They seem to have abdicated their functions of management altogether, and to have left it in the hands of a few private individuals to make or mar the city. The other tenth seems to have been reclaimed from the River Foyle and Lough Foyle since that time. That they have in their own hands and let on terminable leases.

3436. We have been asked why it is that the tenants do not take legal process proceedings to recover their rights under the trust; would any man risk his private fortune against the accumulated fortunes of the city companies?—I have a great interest in the matter myself, but I should be very sorry to risk a legal contest with the companies through all the courts, although I have a strong opinion that there is a legal trust binding the estates.

3437. No individual member of the companies would have any individual right in their property, of course?—I believe not.

3438. They would be fighting with the trust corporate funds?—Certainly.

3439. Which amount to three millions of money?—I should say about that sum.

3440. You gave evidence before Lord Derby's Commission, I think?—Yes.

3441. Were there any representatives of Ireland of any kind upon that Commission?—None.

3442. No Irishmen at all?—None at all; and there are certain statements in the Report with regard to the Irish case that are certainly inaccurate, and show that the Commission at that time were not in full possession of the facts.

3443. Had there been any Irishmen upon the Commission we might have had a very much better report with regard to the companies' estates?—I should think so.

3444. As regards the evidence you gave before Lord Derby's Commission, do you withdraw at all

Mr. *Lea*—continued.

all the statements that you made as to the tenants having created the great bulk of the property?—No; I believe my evidence in that regard is strictly accurate, and I do not think any person has tried to contest it at all.

3445. Have recent events, or your experience since then, corroborated that evidence?—I have no reason to think there is anything inaccurate in the statement I made then. Were I dealing with the legal question, I would put it differently now, but as regards the facts there stated with regard to the increase of rental and reclamation of land and the erection of the buildings by the tenants, I adhere to the statements I made.

3446. Then I want a few facts and figures; what was the value in 1609, when the estates were granted?—The valuation for taxation purposes was 1,800 *l.* yearly.

Mr. *Sexton.*

3447. How much an acre would that make it at the beginning; was it less than a shilling an acre?—I should say it was.

Mr. *Lea.*

3448. What would you say the rental is at the present time?—I should say it would average 10*s.*

3449. Will you give us the valuations at different periods from 1619 down to recent times?—The valuations of the estates given by Charter to the Irish Society was 1,800 *l.* per annum, that includes the Irish Society's estate, and the estate of the 12 London Companies. In 1697 the valuation was 9,150 *l.*; in 1738 the valuation was 20,000 *l.*; in 1858 it was 151,000 *l.*; and in 1883 I calculated the valuation to be 138,000 *l.*

3450. Now will you give us the figures for the rental?—The rental in 1635 was 2,190 *l.*; in 1737 it was 8,000 *l.*; in 1864 it was 124,000 *l.*; and in 1883 it was 180,000 *l.*

Colonel *Lockwood.*

3451. Is that for the same area?—Yes.

3452. Do you mean the estates in the hands of the company?—No; in the hands of the 12 City companies and the Irish Society.

3453. But the same area was not in the hands of the City companies in 1883 as originally?—No, there were six of the estates then sold. I include both the sold and unsold estates in that estimate; and the 2,190 *l.* in 1635 applied to the whole estate as well. In estimating the rent in 1883 at 180,000 *l.*, I may say that was prior to the fixing of rents under the Act of 1881, when the rental was somewhat reduced.

Chairman.

3454. What was the reduction?—It varies of course, but I should say on the average it would be 15 to 20 per cent. There were exceptional cases where the reduction would be 40 per cent., and upwards.

Mr. *Lea.*

3455. Do you know the quantity of land given by the charters of the companies?—I have that return somewhere, but I have not got it before me now. I know the amount that was intended to be given by the charters, or at least as stated by the documents.

Mr. *Sexton.*

3456. Do you know the total acreage dealt with by the charters?—I do not at the present moment, but I know the amount that the companies took possession of was very much larger than what the charter purported to give.

3457. That was one of the causes for the rescission of the grant?—Yes.

Mr. *Lea.*

3458. Do you understand that 90,000 acres more were taken by the companies than were supposed to be intended by the charter?—I believe that is accurate, but I have not the figures before me at the moment.

Chairman.

3459. Do you mean the companies hold 90,000 acres of land without a title?—The intention of the charter was to pass a certain portion, and according to the then survey it turned out that the amount that actually passed into the hands of the companies was some 90,000 acres more than was intended.

Mr. *Sexton.*

3460. Both the Star Chamber and the Court of Chancery held it to be proved, that instead of some 27,000 they got about 97,000 acres; was not that it?—Yes, and with the Chancellor was associated all the judges of the period in affirming that decision.

Mr. *Lea.*

3461. That was discovered some years after the taxation of the companies for about 3,000 *l.* each?—Yes.

3462. Can you tell me what quantity of land was supposed to be reclaimed by the tenants on their estates?—I could best answer that question by referring to my evidence before Lord Derby's Commission, because I looked up the point at that time, if you will allow me to read a portion from my statement there: "From the middle of the 17th century, when the estates were leased to middlemen up till recently, when they resumed possession of the estates, the companies do not seem to have spent a single penny in forwarding the work of the plantation. During the reign of the middlemen no assistance whatever was given the tenants in the reclamation or improvement of the estates. Since the estates came into the hands of the companies some of them have advanced money to the tenants to assist them in building and draining, but the sums advanced in this way would not amount in all to more than 16,000 *l.* or 20,000 *l.*, and nearly the whole of this was advanced by way of loan, the tenants paying in some cases 4, and in others 5 per cent. on the amount borrowed. The county roads are made and maintained out of the county cess, all of which is paid by the occupying tenants. The farm roads on the companies' estates have, with a few exceptions hardly worth mentioning, been made at the sole expense of the tenants. The farm houses, farm buildings, and all drains and fences on the various holdings on the companies' estates, have been made by the occupying tenants without any assistance, except what has been already mentioned. The tenants on the companies' estates, since the time of the plantation, have reclaimed at their own expense 130,000 acres

Mr. *Lea*—continued.

acres of waste lands. By their own labour and expenditure they have increased the annual value of the estates from 1,800 *l.* a year, which is the estimated value of the society's and companies' estates in 1608, to 160,000 *l.* which is in round numbers the present rental of the estates."

3463. That is enough for my purpose. What do you think would be the value of the tenants' property for reclaiming, per acre?—I think the value of the tenants' property would be worth the whole of the land reclaimed. I do not think the lands reclaimed in Derry, judging from my experience, would more than repay the cost of reclamation. I look upon the original value of the reclaimed land as practically nil.

3464. A large part of it was slob land, was it not?—No; that was the portion reclaimed from Lough Foyle at the time of the building of the railway; that is in the hands of the Irish Society. This land was chiefly mountain land, land that never did pay for reclamation.

3465. Can you tell me roughly the value of the companies' estates which were conveyed to them in 1609, now?—I should say about three millions.

3466. Of which how much would be created by the tenants, in your opinion?—I should say from half to two-thirds.

3467. You know the whole of the county; has it a large residential gentry population?—No, not large.

3468. Why not?—Because I think the greater part of the county was in the hands of companies, and they did not seem to favour the residence of country gentlemen except so far as regards the residence of their own agents. Complaints were made that country gentlemen could not get residences in perpetuity from the companies; what foundation there is for that I do not know, but I have heard that stated.

3469. Do you think in that respect the county has suffered a great deal?—That is a matter of opinion.

3470. Would not the expenditure of the incomes of land owners in the locality be very much better?—Supposing there were no absenteeism; supposing the gentlemen had been the owners of land and resided in the county, and had spent on the estate the rental of the estate, no doubt it would have been better.

3471. Practically the companies have induced absenteeism?—I believe the policy tended that way. I think it has been a serious injury to the county that a large part of the rental of the estates has been drained away yearly, the companies living in London and spending a great part of the income of the estates in London.

3472. Now I want to ask you with regard to two or three other estates; I will pass by the Drapers'; coming to the Skinners' estate, I want to ask if you have modified your opinion which you expressed before Lord Derby's Commission, when you said, "The Skinners' Company, I believe, is the worst managed estate in the north of Ireland without exception, and I know it intimately"?—That was correct, in my opinion, at the time I stated it.

3473. Then with regard to arrears, you stated with reference to the Skinners' Company's tenants, they are more in arrear than the tenants on any estates that you know of?—That was so.

3474. You said that they were very much more in arrear than on the estates of Lord Castlestuart and the Duke of Abercorn, for instance?—They were.

3475. The estate of the Skinners' Company was leased to Mr. Ogilvie for many years, was it not?—Yes.

3476. Can you tell me the rental that he paid for it?—I think 6,000 *l.* a year, and 20,000 *l.* for fine.

3477. That was in 1853, I think, when he got his lease; was that rental then raised to 16,000 *l.* a year on a fresh lease to Mr. Ogilvie?—No; it was raised to the tenants to 16,000 *l.*; Mr. Ogilvie raised the rents on the tenants to about 14,000 *l.*, and then the company came in 1872, and had a re-valuation, and the rental was then raised to about 16,000 *l.*

3478. Subsequently it was reduced again?—Yes, it was reduced again.

3479. The tenants on that estate have chiefly purchased, have they not?—I should say from two-thirds to three-fourths of the tenants have purchased; three-fourths, I should say.

3480. How many years' purchase did they pay?—Nineteen years' purchase.

3481. Upon what rents?—Upon the rents fixed by the Land Court.

3482. Did I understand you to say the other day that in some parts of the Skinners' estate they were impossible rents?—Certainly; before they were fixed by the court they were impossible rents; but those rents were very largely reduced by the court, some of them to the extent of 40 per cent.

3483. What will be done with the part that is not sold; is it being offered now?—No.

3484. There is no proposal to purchase it by a syndicate, that you know of?—I have heard it rumoured, but I know nothing of it whatever, and I have been informed by the clerk of the company that he knows nothing of it.

3485. Is there a strong feeling in the town of Dungiven with regard to the treatment by the Skinners' Company?—There certainly was a strong opinion before 1881.

3486. Has that strong feeling subsided at all?—I have not been in Dungiven for upwards of a year; but I should say that it has, owing to the purchase, or rather to the fixing of the rent in the first instance, and the purchase afterwards.

3487. Do they say they have bought their own buildings with their own improvements in the town of Dungiven and the district round?—I have not been so informed, but I have no doubt some hold that view.

3488. A great many, if I understand rightly?—I should not say a great many.

3489. With regard to the Skinners' grants, when the sale of the estate was arranged, was any promise given by them with regard to the grants?—No; the terms of purchase were put in writing in a circular letter sent to every tenant on the estate.

3490. Was the question never raised at all?—Mention was made of it in Mr. Johnstone's case, and I recommended Mr. Johnstone to send a memorial

Mr. *Lea*—continued.

memorial to the company, and I believe the company refused to continue the grant.

3491. Do you know Mr. M'Laughlin?—I know Mr. John M'Laughlin.

3492. Is he a magistrate?—Yes.

3493. Was he present when many of the agreements were signed?—He was.

3494. When hundreds of agreements were signed?—Probably that was so.

3495. If Mr. M'Laughlin contends that promises were made to the tenants in the first place, what should you say?—Made by whom?

3496. By the company?—I know of none.

3497. You made no promise?—I made no promise.

3498. You said, I presume, that you believed that the grants would be given?—On one occasion I believe Mr. M'Laughlin mentioned some rumours that the company were about to discontinue the grants, and I informed him that I had no information of that nature, and I had no reason to believe they would discontinue them.

3499. If Mr. M'Laughlin swears that you distinctly promised that all emoluments and privileges would continue as hitherto, and it was on that understanding the tenants purchased, and otherwise they would not have purchased, would you say that was incorrect?—I would say it is altogether incorrect.

3500. Would you say it is untrue?—I would say that Mr. M'Laughlin himself did not mean to state what was untrue, but probably my statement, in reply to his question that I had no information that the company intended to discontinue the grants, and no reason to believe they would be discontinued, may have been the foundation of what he writes you. However, that statement was only made to himself; I do not think there was any other person present when that statement was made to him; certainly it was not made to hundreds.

3501. If I understand Mr. M'Laughlin rightly he was present when hundreds of agreements were signed?—That is wholly a different point. Does he say that that statement was made in the presence of hundreds of persons?

3502. When each person was signing, I gather it would be?—Does he say so?

3503. I understand so?—That is a mistake. I had only two conversations with Mr. M'Laughlin on the subject. One was with himself, and, so far as I know, there were no tenants, and certainly not a number, and the only statement was that he told me that there was a rumour of the company intending to withdraw, and I said I had no knowledge to that effect, and that I had no reason to believe it. The other occasion when I had a conversation with Mr. M'Laughlin was when Mr. Johnstone was present, when I stated that personally I had no authority to make any statement upon the matter, but I recommended him to send a memorial to the company.

3504. Do you say that Mr. M'Laughlin's statement is incorrect?—It is true that Mr. M'Laughlin was present when a large number of tenants signed the agreements for purchase; it is not true that in their presence I made any statement or any reference whatever to grants. It is true that, in answer to Mr. M'Laughlin's query with regard to the rumour that the grants were to be withdrawn, I told him I had no reason to believe so, and I had no information upon the subject. It is also true that he and Mr. Johnstone, the clergyman, came to me subsequently and said the company proposed withdrawing the grants, and I recommended him to send a memorial, and informed him that I had no authority upon the subject myself.

3505. What happened to the memorial?—I have said already that I believe the prayer of that memorial was refused.

3506. Do you know the Lower Cumber grant has been withdrawn?—That is the grant I refer to.

3507. Now, with regard to the Fishmongers' estate, was that in the hands of the Beresford family at one time?—Yes.

3508. What rent did they pay; was it 400 *l.* a year?—Yes, I believe so.

3509. Did they get a rental of 4,000 *l.* a year from the tenants?—Yes, about that.

3510. It then came into the hands of the Fishmongers' Company in 1820, did it not?—Yes, 1820.

3511. What rental did they raise it to?—Are you reading from my former evidence?

3512. I have a note from your former evidence, and you stated then that it amounted to nearly 10,000 *l.* a year?—Then that is correct.

3513. You stated also that the Fishmongers' Company had not spent a single shilling upon the estate?—Upon the estate in agricultural improvements.

3514. Quite so?—Except by way of advancing money on loan; they did spend a considerable portion of their income on what they considered public purposes.

3515. The Fishmongers' Company were a liberal company with regard to schools and matters of that kind, were they not?—Yes; but I believe they have withdrawn all these grants now.

3516. The whole of them?—I believe the whole of them.

3517. To take two instances, was one rent on the Fishmongers' Estate 8 *l.* 15 *s.* 6 *d.* in 1820, and has it been raised since then to 66 *l.*?—That was so.

3518. Was another rent 7 *l.* 10 *s.*, and was that raised to 75 *l.*?—Yes, I recollect those cases; I have the receipts.

3519. That was when the Fishmongers' Company came into their estate. When the Fishmongers' Company sold, did they receive promissory notes for the balance of arrears?—I have a letter from a tenant stating so; personally I have no knowledge of the matter apart from that.

3520. If you have not any personal knowledge of it, I will not pursue that point?—I know the preliminary arrangements with regard to the sale of the Fishmonger's estate, but the transactions you refer to I only know from the letter that was sent to myself, and that contains a charge that in my opinion is unfounded, and I would rather say nothing about it.

3521. With regard to the Grocers' Company; do

Mr. *Lea*—continued.

do you know when they sold their estate?—I think in 1872.

3522. Have they continued any grants up till now?—I believe they made some provision by giving a lump sum to the parish church; but beyond that I think they have done nothing since.

3523. I just wish to ask one or two questions more with regard to the Salters' estate; I will not take you through the evidence previously given. You were agent up to a certain point?—No.

3524. Since a certain date, I should say; you acted for the tenants up to a certain date, and then as agent since then?—Then I acted for both.

3525. What portion of the Salters' estate is left?—There are I believe eight agricultural tenancies.

3526. What else?—A few houses in the town of Magherafelt; perhaps I can give you the number in a minute; I should say about 15.

3527. Could you give me a rough estimate of the value of what is left?—£. 4,000 or 5,000 *l.*, I should say.

3528. There were complaints that promissory notes were given by tenants to the Salters' Company for arrears?—There were promissory notes given.

3529. And a legal action was taken with regard to those promissory notes?—Yes.

3530. There was a case of a man named Badger?—Yes.

3531. Was he sued?—Yes, he was.

3532. On the promissory notes?—On the promissory notes.

3533. It came before a jury in Dublin, did it not?—Yes.

3534. What was the verdict?—The verdict was for the company.

3535. Did the jury add a recommendation of mercy as well?—I think the jury did, and I believe the judge (Judge Harrison) did. I was in the witness-box, and I concurred.

3536. What did the company do?—I think they have done nothing yet.

3537. Is Badger a ruined man at present; has he lost every penny he had got?—I cannot say that. I had some letters from him asking me to negotiate on his behalf with the Salters' Company.

3538. Has he been sold up since then?—I am not aware.

3539. But he is liable for very heavy costs, is he not?—Yes, the costs were very heavy. I think the poor man was misled; it is perfectly evident he was. He is a very worthy and decent man, and he was led into defending an action in which there was not the slightest ground for defence. The other tenants, I believe, promised to support him, and did advance some of the money, but the whole of the sum that was advanced was swallowed up in the costs of the defence, and now he is liable for the amount of the promissory notes and the costs of the company. I do not think the company have recovered the costs from him.

3540. Have they tried to?—I am not aware of it; I do not think so.

Mr. *Lea*—continued.

3541. He purchased his holding under the Act, did he not?—He did.

3542. And he paid the usual number of years' rental for it?—He did.

3543. Was not that sufficient for the company?—I am not sure that you heard my explanation of that before I gave it all at the last sitting of the Committee. The taking of the promissory notes was a special advantage, given to a number of tenants who were not in a position to pay cash for the rent.

3544. For arrears?—Arrears, if you like to say so. There was a year and a half or a year and three-quarters remitted to the tenants.

3545. If the Judge and jury recommended the company to take a lenient view of it, have they done so?—I am not aware; but my own opinion is that they should do so.

3546. Have they done so?—I cannot tell you.

3547. How long ago is it since the action was tried?—I should say four or five months, perhaps more.

3548. Is it not nearer 12 months?—Perhaps it is; I am not sure.

3549. Has not there been plenty of time for the company to make up its mind whether it would exact the last pound of flesh, or not?—I have no doubt there has. I am rather inclined to think if the company were properly approached they would deal leniently enough.

3550. What do you mean by "properly approached"?—I mean if it were put to them in a fair way. They were charged with acting fraudulently, and naturally enough they resented that charge; but, I think, if the poor man's circumstances were represented to them properly, and they were asked to do the thing as a favour, they would probably remit the costs, or do something for him.

Mr. *Clancy.*

3551. You mean, if they were appealed to do it as an act of mercy?—Exactly.

Mr. *Lea.*

3552. In the sale of all this trust property the companies have got as much as they could, have they not?—I do not think they should get any of it.

3553. But they have sold at the fair market price, have they not?—Yes.

3554. They got as much as the fair market price?—They got, as I considered, a fair market price.

3555. And that, in spite of the wording of the charter, that the lands were to be let at easy rents to the undertakers?—Yes.

3556. With regard to the evidence of Dr. Jordan, the Rector of Magherafelt, you were indignant on the last occasion at what he said?—I think justly so.

3557. Have you read his evidence?—Yes, I have.

3558. I will read question and answer, number 878, where is asked, "I thought you said Dr. Todd also had made those promises?" and his reply was this: "So I was informed by those three neighbours of mine, but I never had any conversation on the subject with Dr. Todd my-self."

Mr. Lea—continued.

self." He does not state that you had made any promise to him?—No, he does not.

3559. Why do you charge him with giving improper evidence?—Because he knew there was no promise made. He was the official representative of the church there; Sir Henry Cartwright was the official representative of the company; and he himself, over his own name, wrote a letter to the "News Letter," stating that Sir Henry told him that during the continuance of the sale the time was inopportune for applying for a renewal of the grants; and I think I am justified in being indignant at his suggesting that I made a promise when he knew I was not in a position to do so at all, and I think the only excuse for doing such a thing as that is that he is not a man of the world.

3560. Let me just hand you these letters; you have seen these letters from Dr. Jordan, the rector of Magherafelt; Mr. M'Creery, another rector; Dr. Carter, rector at Cookstown; and Mr. Sparrow, the rector of Moneymore (*handing the letters to the Witness*)?—Yes.

3561. Then we had Mr. Gunness here the other day who made the same statement?—Yes.

3562. In one of these letters there is a statement that six schoolmasters, I think, stated the same thing as these clergymen, and that was that you made promises that these grants should be continued?—As I stated before, that is wholly inaccurate; I wrote two letters to the "Times"——

3563. Is it the fact that these letters say so?—It is the fact that the letters say so.

3564. Six clergymen and six schoolmasters?—No; the clergymen do not say so themselves; on the contrary they say I said nothing whatever about it. They are the persons chiefly interested, and they say they have no knowledge of it, and then to bring a few people to say that I made a promise on behalf of the company, because I advised these gentlemen as a solicitor, is surely improper.

3565. You were acting, they say, for the company?—No, I was acting as solicitor for tenants. These gentlemen who were the persons interested knew that I made no promises, and they state that Sir Henry Cartwright had made no promises, but on the contrary warned them not to make any application.

3566. When the agreements were signed, you were agent for the tenants and not for the company?—Yes.

3567. When these letters were written, you were agent for the company and for the tenants? —I rather think I was agent for nobody at that time. At that time the sale was closed on both sides. Sir Henry Cartwright said the time was inopportune for applying for the continuance of the grants. That is clearly inconsistent with the promise being made, at least by me.

Chairman.

3568. May we not take it that you said all you desired to say upon this point in answer to my friend Mr. Clancy, in question 3239 and so forth, at the last sitting?—I have said it all before. There are only two of these clergymen resident on the estate. Both of these clergymen applied directly to Sir Henry Cartwright, the agent, and they state themselves they were informed by Sir Henry Cartwright that the time for making the application was inopportune and might be deferred to the conclusion of the sale. These two gentlemen knew I was acting for the tenants and not for the company. Why they should make this statement in the face of these facts I cannot understand.

Mr. Lea.

3569. You wrote a letter to the "Times"?—Yes, I will put in my two letters to the "Times" which describe the facts accurately.

3570. Would you kindly read that paragraph from your own letter which I have marked, which gave your opinion, I presume (*handing the same to the Witness*)?—Yes.

3571. Will you read it; that is your letter in September, 1887?—Yes. "It was at the instance of Sir Henry Cartwright, after the disestablishment of the Church, that most of these grants were made, and there is no doubt he earnestly desired their continuance, and believed he would be able to successfully press their continuance in some form on the company after the sale. I gladly admit that I was desirous, not only of seeing the grants continued, but anxious that every penny of the proceeds of the sale to be devoted to public purposes should be voluntarily given by the company to public objects in county Londonderry, and not expended in London." I adhere to that opinion.

3572. You do not go a fraction beyond that? —"I freely admit also that I stated my views on the subject to anyone who asked me, and that I expressed my belief that the grants would be continued in some form by the company. Before this correspondence commenced Sir Henry Cartwright and myself brought the subject before the company, and the company had not only arranged to endow an intermediate school for the benefit of the locality, but had under consideration the best way, in the public interest, of dealing with the question of religious grants." I adhere to all that.

3573. Might not your statement and Sir Henry Cartwright's statement, constantly renewed, that you believe these grants would be continued, and that the companies ought to continue them, be considered as a sort of promise?—I do not think it could be considered as a sort of promise; it might give rise to a belief; but what I protest against is the allegation or insinuation that these promises were given for the purpose of inducing the tenants to buy; because that question was not raised until after the tenants had actually bought; there was no question of that until after the tenants had actually bought.

3574. You said the other day that some liberal provision had been made by the Salters' Company to meet this question?—No, I did not say so so far as I recollect.

3575. You said that some provision had been made?—For what?

3576. For the continuance of these grants?—They have made some provision for the Rainey School, the particulars of which you have had before you already; they have not discontinued the

Mr. Lea—continued.

the grant, I am informed; those are the two facts I stand.

3577. Do you consider a provision of 60 *l.* a year or 66 *l.* a year for the Rainey School a liberal provision?—My view was, and I was pressing it upon the company, that the Rainey School should be converted into a high school, with a technical education department attached, and very liberally endowed, and made a thoroughly good school.

3578. Have they done so?—You have the particulars before you; you had better not press me upon that point.

3579. You said the other day that they had given some provision?—I said exactly what I say now; I said they had made some provision for the Rainey School; you have had the particulars of what they have done from Lord Justice Fitzgibbon; whether you consider that adequate, it is not for me to say.

3580. Are you aware that a list of withdrawals has been handed in with regard to many other schools?—I am not aware.

3581. At the time of this correspondence, did you see Sir Robert Fowler's letter in the "Times"?—No doubt I did, but I do not recollect it particularly.

3582. Are you aware that he stated that on the sale of the estate they would be relieved from continuing any of these grants?—He may have done so; I do not recollect it in the letter.

3583. He stated words to that effect, did he not?—I heard you put the question to another witness the other day, and I have no doubt it is accurate, but I have no knowledge of it myself.

3584. Do you know how the Salters' Company treated their old retainers?—I do not.

3585. Mr. Kincaid was, of course, the master of the high school?—I have heard complaints about his case, but I do not know exactly what they have done or what they intend doing.

3586. Do you know Mr. Young?—I do.

3587. Was he 40 years on the estate?—I do not know of my own knowledge; I have no doubt he was.

3588. Have they given him any pension?—I cannot say. You can get all that information better from the clerk of the company; I have no personal knowledge with regard to it.

3589. The policy of the companies has been to sell for as much as they could, I presume?—You must judge of that for yourself, I think.

3590. You know of the sales and surely you ought to have an opinion. I suppose you would say they ought to be treated as the Irish Society and spend all they get upon the districts?—That is my opinion; apart from the legal question I think there is a strong moral case on the part of the county to have whatever expenditure is made at all for public purposes made in the county of Londonderry.

Sir William Marriott.

3591. There is no doubt about your view?—I have always held the same view.

3592. You think that all the money ought to be spent in Ireland that is gained from the rents by these companies?—I hold that the companies stand in exactly the same position as the Irish Society.

3593. You think there is no difference between them?—I think not.

3594. Do they stand in the same position as what are called the undertakers?—No.

3595. Why not?—Because they hold under the charter that declares a trust, and because the motives and reasons in the correspondence between the Crown and Privy Council and the Common Council of London, show that the plantation of County Derry was undertaken for public purposes and not for private purposes.

3596. Let us just see about that. As regards the undertakers there were certain orders and conditions?—Yes.

3597. As regards the company there were certain motives and reasons?—Yes.

3598. Those motives and reasons were given for what object?—The orders and conditions were applicable to all the undertakings; the motives and reasons were expressed to the London Corporation alone and not to general undertakers.

3599. The object of the motives and reasons was to induce the City of London to undertake the plantation of the County Londonderry, was it not?—Clearly.

3600. And as a rule when you try to induce people, do you propose something for their individual benefit or something philanthropic?—It was for their own individual benefit.

3601. What was the inducement?—The inducement was the advancement of trade.

3602. Who was to benefit by the advancement of trade?—The individual trader, to start with. In the second place, it was to supply a place for settling the surplus population of London; and, in the third place, to supply a market for the goods of London; and fourthly, to please the Crown. All these were expressed in the motives and reasons.

3603. You have expressed a very strong opinion with regard to this being a trust; can you point to any portion of the companies' deeds which creates a trust?—I can.

3604. Where?—I will refer you to the Charter of James I.

3605. To what company?—To the Irish Society.

3606. That is not the question I asked; I say can you point to any of the companies' deeds?—That is the root of the title of the companies' deeds.

3607. Then I may take it that beyond what is in the Charter of James I. to the Irish Society, you can point to nothing in any of the companies' deeds and grants to them from the Irish Society that raises a trust?—I can.

3608. What?—The licenses in mortmain given to the 12 companies expressly state that the companies had undertaken the greater part of the burden of plantation. The burden of plantation was expressed on the face of the Charter to the Irish Society, and that is acknowledged in the licenses in mortmain given by the Crown to the 12 companies before they got their grants to the particular estates, and then the grants were made without consideration by the Irish Society to the companies in pursuance of the licenses in mortmain

Sir William Marriott—continued.

mortmain which expressed upon the face of it a trust and the fact of their having undertaken the fulfilment of the trust.

3609. Those are the words upon which you rely?—There is first the motives and reasons: secondly, the correspondence between the Crown and the Common Council of London: thirdly, the negociations between the Common Council and the companies; fourthly, the express words in the charter itself; and fifthly the licence in mortmain.

3610. Can you point to any words in the motives and reasons that create a trust?—The whole of it.

3611. I understand that the Committee do not wish to go into this question of law at present, so that I will not pursue that; but the question of trust is a purely legal matter, is it not?—Apart from the legal question of the trust I think that even if there were not a trust which the Court of Chancery would enforce, yet the expressions in the licences in mortmain and in the charters and those negotiations, all raise such a presumption in favour of an equitable claim on the part of the county that I think Parliament would be justified in dealing with the estates, and applying a large portion of the income to public purposes.

3612. When you say a trust, do you mean one that could not be enforced in a Court of Chancery or of law?—Yes; but if I am wrong in that I say there are sufficient indications, having regard to the expressions in the charter (which are the root of the title) and the negociations, as for instance the expression which I quoted from the licence in mortmain, as would justify Parliament in saying that they shall be applied to public purposes.

3613. Either there is a trust or there is not a trust; if there is not a trust Parliament may create one; I will not say anything about that; but I am asking do you say there is a trust now that can be enforced in a court of law or equity?—In my opinion I say there is, but I meet the other portion of the reference to this Committee by saying that I think these moral obligations are raised in those documents even if there were not a trust legally.

3614. You say they raise a trust that can be enforced by law?—I think so.

3615. I gather from the answers you have given that the reason those trusts are not enforced is because the tenants are poor people?—I think so.

3616. Do you mean to say really that if any strong body of men in Ireland were of opinion that they could get the whole of these three millions of money by enforcing the trust, they would not combine together, and subscribe a fund to enforce it?—I may say in answer to that, that a number of gentlemen consulted me as to taking proceedings for the purpose of enforcing this trust many years ago. There was a preliminary committee formed for the purpose; but on full consideration, having regard to the fact that public opinion was not so strong against the Irish Society and companies just then as it was at some former period, having regard to the fact that the companies and the society were spending a good portion of the income upon public purposes, it was thought that the game was not worth the candle, and it was better to wait until Parliament should deal with the matter.

3617. The tenants have got many friends in Ireland who would have funds at their disposal, have they not?—Yes, but the companies have got three millions.

3618. Could not some of the friends of the tenants, the Land League or some other body, raise this question on their behalf in a court of law?—Perhaps the Land League is not interested.

3619. Are there not funds in connexion with that society, or some other in this country, or in other countries, that could be used to help the tenants in such a case?—I am not a member of the Land League, and I cannot answer the question.

3620. Do you mean to say that the sole reason why the tenants have not tried to settle this question in a court of law has been for the lack of funds?—It is partly that, and partly because in the general opinion it is a question to be dealt with by Parliament and not in a court of law.

3621. That is what I want to get at; can a court of law deal with it?—I think a court of law can deal with it; I have already said so, but I think it would be so tedious and costly a proceeding, and even in the case of success so ineffectual, that the proper course would be to deal with it by Parliament at once.

3622. Is it your opinion that wherever there is a legal difficulty you should come to Parliament?—No; but this is a case of a great public trust. Some of the trusts are obsolete and others are not obsolete, and there must be a new definition of trusts and a new application of the funds, and that cannot be done without having recourse to Parliament. Why should any individual or body of individuals be put to the trouble of dealing with this question in a court of law, and be taken to the Court of Appeal, and ultimately up to the House of Lords? Why, I say, should an individual be bound to do that, when, after it was all done, you would have to come to Parliament in any case.

3623. Surely they would not have to come to Parliament if they were successful?—Yes, you must come in any case, because you must have the trusts defined. Circumstances have greatly changed since the charter was given.

3624. Are the estates managed by these companies worse than estates managed by private landlords?—I have already given my opinion.

3625. That they are better managed?—A good part of the income has been applied on the estates, of recent years at least, to public purposes; but the application of the money, in my opinion, has been very badly advised.

3626. In what way has it been badly advised?—The grants to churches and schools might be reconsidered in my opinion.

3627. You do not believe in grants to churches and schools?—I do not say that exactly.

3628. Is it a bad thing to grant money to schools and churches?—I think it is a mistaken policy to give public moneys to churches. I think such moneys should be applied to purposes by which the whole community would be benefited.

3629. In

Sir William Marriott—continued.

3629. In your opinion the companies were wrong in giving this amount to churches and schools?—The traditions were inherited by them, and naturally they acted upon them.

3630. You say the traditions were wrong?—The traditions were taken from the charter.

3631. You want the charter altered?—I have before given my opinion that the religious purposes are obsolete purposes.

3632. You made a remark about the improvement of the land; do you know what the land was an acre at the time that these charters were given; was there not an Act of Parliament in 1639 declaring the value of the land; do you know anything about that?—I do not.

3633. You are not aware that there was an Act of Parliament fixing 1,000 acres at 20 *l.*?—Do you mean generally all over Ireland?

3634. I refer to the land in this particular part of Ireland that was taken by the companies?—Do you mean the value for taxation purposes?

3635. No, for all purposes?—For rent purposes?

3636. Yes?—I am not aware.

3637. Was it valued at about 5 *s.* an acre?—No. I am not aware that Parliament declared the rent.

3638. You do not know what the companies subscribed to the fund and how much they got in return; take, for instance, the Mercers' Company; do you know what they paid?—To whom?

3639. To the general fund which was raised by the city, the 60,000 *l.* that was raised?—I think they paid about the same sum. I think the 12 companies paid about the same sum.

3640. How much?—At first it was only 3,000 *l.* odd. That was not money paid by the companies, however, I may say.

3641. Why not?—It was a tax raised from the citizens.

3642. In return for which they got what?—Who got?

3643. The companies?—They got the management of these estates.

3644. They got the estates?—No.

3645. You say they only got the management?—Certainly.

3646. You say they had no right in fee simple?—They had the legal title, the same as any other trustee would have.

3647. But they paid for it, did not they?—Oh no, they paid nothing for it. You will find the documents show that very clearly.

Sir John Whittaker Ellis.

3648. You say that they did not pay?—Clearly.

3649. And your whole argument is based on the assumption that they did not pay?—Not upon that alone.

3650. If you found they did pay then your answer would be a different one?—Not necessarily. That is not the only ground of my answer. The money was raised by the ordinary method of taxation. It was applied, not in payment to the Crown, or to any body for the estates, but applied in promoting plantation.

Sir John Whittaker Ellis—continued.

3651. I see, in your examination by the Chairman on Thursday last, you say that the Irish Society is an obsolete body?—Well, it should be.

3652. Did you ever look in the dictionary and see what the word "obsolete" means?—Not recently. Will you kindly define it for me first.

3653. I have been looking. The definitions are "worn out of use." Do you say the Irish Society is "worn out of use?"—It is useless.

3654. It is in full powers; it has all the officers, and all the machinery for conducting its business?—Yes, it has got too much machinery, and it costs too much.

3655. Do you say it is worn out out of use?—It is useless, and it performs no useful functions.

3656. It is not disused, is it?—No, it is in actual operation. It is not extinguished.

3657. Therefore, your answer does not come within those two definitions?—I admit the society is not extinct, but I think it should be.

3658. Then there is another definition, "unfashionable," perhaps that is what you intended?—I did not use the word "unfashionable."

3659. You did not, but you used the word "obsolete," and one meaning of "obsolete" is "unfashionable," and this is unfashionable, because the present fashion is to decry all existing institutions, and to endeavour to replace them with modern ones?—The present fashion is to decry all useless or effete institutions, and the Irish Society is both, in my opinion.

3660. You admit it is in existence?—I do.

3661. And you admit it is not disused?—Yes.

3662. When we come to the third definition "unfashionable," that is what you really mean by "obsolete," I suppose?—Do you mean unfashionable in a popular sense, or do you mean amid the community of Derry? It is certainly not popular in the City of Derry, if you mean that.

3663. That is your view, but there may be other views upon it?—I have no doubt.

3664. Are not the mayor and his colleagues of a different opinion?—The individuals who are getting the money will, I have no doubt, pay you a compliment.

3665. I see you say that they do nothing whatever except visit Londonderry once a year, and attend banquets; do you really mean that?—Not strictly that.

3666. Do you mean, honestly, as a resident of Londonderry, that you are not aware that the Irish Society have a very complete organisation; that they put that organisation into operation with very great care and great anxiety, and that they watch over the interests, so far as they are concerned in them, of the city of Londonderry with great consideration?—Of course, I do not know the anxiety of mind that you or the members of the society labour under, but I do know that according to your own statements the other day the society apportioned among a few individuals the whole of the property there in their hands, and practically abdicated their functions of managing the property. According to your own statement the other day, nine-tenths of the property of the Irish Society was apportioned out

among

Sir John Whittaker Ellis—continued.

among a few individuals a century ago, or thereabouts.

3667. You are talking about 160 years ago; I am not asking you about that; I am asking you about the society now; you said the other day they do nothing whatever, except visit Londonderry once a year?—Nothing; or nothing beneficial.

3668. You did not say "beneficial"?—Perhaps I did not.

3669. We will come to that presently, but what I want you to deal with is this; you said they do nothing?—I say they practically do nothing.

3670. Your answer is down here, "They do nothing;" now I say, are you not aware that they have an agent in Ireland; that they investigate all questions that arise upon letting their estates or upon giving away the money which they accumulate with great care for the purpose of advancing the interests of Londonderry, and are you not aware that they are in active performance of those duties at the present moment?—I do not think the question represents correctly the condition of matters, and if you will allow me I will tell you my reason for saying that.

3671. Are you not aware that the Irish Society have at the present moment an agent resident in Londonderry?—I am.

3672. And do you know that whenever any question arises either of tenancy or of any claim upon the society's finances, that in the first instance he is always called upon to investigate it?—I know there is a good deal of red tape without any effectual work.

3673. I did not ask you that; I asked you whether you knew that the agent was employed to investigate questions which arose with respect to the Irish Society's affairs?—The agent seems to have no authority or power whatever. He must consult the clerk in London.

3674. I did not ask you that; I only asked you whether he did investigate?—I cannot tell. I know that he writes letters to the society in London, and gets replies.

3675. In point of fact you are not aware what Irish Society do at all?—I am; I am aware that they do no good. That is my opinion, and I think it is my duty to express it.

3676. In your opinion they should apply the whole of the trust estate for beneficial objects, and they should not fritter away the trust estate on objects which are absolutely useless, such as giving petty grants to schools and churches that are of no value whatever; now, I will ask you this; are you not aware that this Committee is absolutely appointed on account of the very things that you say are frittering away the trust estate, and are absolutely useless; because the City companies are accused of not having continued these very things which you complain of?—The question is so long that I am afraid I do not catch it.

3677. Are not the petty grants you refer to the very things that this Committee is here to consider?—I think not.

3678. I see that in answer to a question of the Chairman (3105), you say the franchise is too high; will you tell me what the amount of the franchise is?—I did not say the amount of the franchise is too high; I expressed no opinion; I was not asked my opinion.

3679. In answer to a question by the Chairman, you say "The franchise is too high, and the present corporation do not truly represent the feeling of the whole society"?—Yes.

3680. Now, can you tell me what the franchise is?—At the present moment I cannot tell you exactly.

3681. Is it £10?—It is different from the Parliamentary franchise, very much higher.

3682. You advocate, as far as I can make out from your evidence, that the funds of the Irish Society should be allocated to the Corporation of Derry?—What I ventured to suggest was this, that the portion of the lands that were to be conveyed to the city of Derry under the original agreement between the corporation and the Crown should be now allotted to the city of Derry, and should be managed by the Corporation, that which was to be allotted to Coleraine under that agreement should now be allotted to Coleraine, and managed by Coleraine, and that the balance of the estates, both of the Irish Society and the companies' estates, should be applied for general public purposes in the locality, and that, subject to the claims of the clergy and the schoolmasters now in office, they should be applied, not to religious purposes, but to purposes of general utility in the benefit of which the whole community would participate.

3683. What I understand is that you advocate that there should be a new scheme altogether?—There should be a new scheme in my opinion.

3684. And you think that the corporation should be endowed with certain lands and properties?—I think the corporation should be able to manage their own municipal property, but I should prefer to see the land sold, and the funds invested, and to let them manage the fund.

3685. At Question 3136 you were asked by the Chairman: "You who have studied the history of the relations between the Irish Society and the companies and their tenants, think that on the whole that has been as satisfactory a history as if their lands had been under private landlords," and you answered: "so far as regards the relation of landlord and tenant, I think it is." In that respect you admit that the Irish Society have dealt fairly with their tenants?—I excepted the Irish Society.

3686. You say they have dealt fairly with their tenants?—No, I do not.

3687. Do you know what the custom of the Irish Society is in dealing with their tenants?—I do.

3688. Perhaps you will tell me?—I will. The Irish Society some years ago raised the rents, and endeavoured to confiscate the tenant-right of the tenants by giving them leases which would have been inconsistent with the existence of tenant-right. The tenants refused that, and after some contest, the leases were granted in some other form I believe. Now passing to the Act of 1881, the Irish Society endeavoured to settle with the tenants and failed, because the terms they proposed were not fair or just. The tenants to a very large extent went into the land courts and got very large reductions of rent. When the Act of 1887 passed, the Irish Society

Sir John Whittaker Ellis—continued.

Society said to the tenants, "Do not go in and have the rents fixed in court, and we will send a valuer over the estate, and deal equitably and fairly with you." They did send a valuer over the estate. They held over giving an answer to the tenants' application with regard to the rents for a considerable time; and then they proposed rents that were wholly inequitable towards the tenants, and they refused also to give them the abatements that they would have had had they entered the courts at the time the Irish Society made that application to them. The tenants, or the great majority of them, who held under leases then went into court refusing the rents that the Irish Society proposed, and the tenants got the rents reduced in court considerably below what the society proposed. The tenants proposed purchasing under Lord Ashbourne's Act and the Irish Society refused to sell to them under Lord Ashbourne's Act; so that as far as regards the tenants on the Irish Society's estate there is no single instance which they could point to of any generous or fair treatment of their tenants, and there are many instances in which it can be shown that the Irish Society treated their tenants badly.

3689. I wanted to elicit your view, because I shall have to show that that statement is not altogether in accordance with the facts?—It may be a little too wide in some particulars, but I am giving you generally what the facts were to my knowledge.

3690. Or, rather, what you believe to be the facts?—As a matter of fact I proposed to the Irish Society to purchase land, and was refused, and I know that various other tenants proposed to purchase, and were refused.

3691. Suppose you had an estate to manage for any of your clients, and you had first of all the interest of the tenant to consider, and next you had to consider the interest of the beneficiaries who were entitled to the income of the estate. Now that is the position of the Irish Society. They have the tenants to consider, but they have also to consider the interests of Londonderry and Coleraine. Now if you found that you had to sell your estate, and thus to reduce the opportunities of doing good for the beneficiaries you would be unwilling to sell, would you not, it not being a question of your own interest but a question of the interest of Londonderry and Coleraine?—Well, in my opinion the interests of Londonderry and Coleraine would be best served by a sale to start with. Secondly, I think that the keeping up of the rents of the estate, and keeping it in the hands of the society is the means simply of enabling a large part of the income of the society to be appropriated to other purposes than the trust purposes intended. If I were a trustee of an estate of 20,000 *l.*, and spent 4,000 *l.* a year in managing it I should probably be charged with dealing very unfairly and improperly.

3692. There is a question I want to ask you about, railways: If a railway is carried into any particular district is the landlord debarred by the Act of 1881 from increasing the rent of his tenants by reason of the improved value given by the railway?—No.

3693. Is there any clause to that effect in the Act?—No. That is a mistake of yours.

3694. If a railway were carried into a district and that increased the value of the land would the landlord be entitled to charge that to the tenant?—He would not be entitled to charge it to the tenant exactly, but the indirect benefit obtained by the tenant would be a reason for keeping rents higher than they otherwise would be. He would be entitled to give evidence of the fact that since the rents were fixed at a certain amount a railway had come into the locality, and that would be evidence on the part of the landlord to maintain the rent.

3695. It would be no bar against the landlord increasing the rent?—I know of my own knowledge it is accepted as evidence. I have heard such evidence given.

3696. There is no clause in the Act of 1881 to exclude it?—No; all the circumstances are to be taken into account. Of course, on the other hand, if a railway were guaranteed by the ratepayers that would be an element on behalf of the tenant to show that he was liable for that guarantee, and that it was built practically at his expense, together with other ratepayers, and not at the instance of the landlord.

3697. Would that entitle him to a reduction of the rent?—No; but it would be taken into consideration in fixing the rent. If the landlord says, "The rents should be higher because of the existence of this railway," the tenant might reply, "Oh, but that railway was built by me;" or, "by me and my fellows."

3698. That would entitle him to a favourable consideration?—The facts would be considered. If the landlord built the railways and improved the district he would probably be held entitled to increase the rent; if the tenant guaranteed the railway with others the landlord would not be held entitled to increase the rent.

3699. The railways have been laid out by the people of Ireland, and they have been influenced in their particular direction by the companies, have they not?—No. I am very much afraid it was owing to Irish advice that the railways have been built as they have been.

3700. You mean, your own advice?—No; I mean the advice of the agents of the companies.

3701. Are you prepared to prove that?—I assume it was for that reason the companies gave the money. It was certainly not my advice, because I strongly protested against it, and I still protest against it.

3702. It was not on the advice of the Irish Society, was it?—I do not say it was, but I do say I do blame the Irish Society for not taking an active interest in promoting or advocating the construction of railways in the centre of the county. I think if the Irish Society had used their influence with the companies that railway would have been built before now, and it is a very pressing public improvement required in the county.

3703. Where do you derive your figures from as to the rents?—I got them partly from Primer's survey, and partly from Sampson's survey, and various other public documents which I investigated at the time.

3704. Does it occur to you, if a tenant has possession

Sir John Whitaker Ellis—continued.

possession of his land at a nominal rent for a lengthened period, that that in some measure compensates him for any outlay he makes?—If that is the fact, it would. If he held a valuable property at a nominal rent, it certainly would tend to compensate him, but that is not so in the case we are dealing with.

3705. Were not all the undertakers put on nominal terms for that purpose?—The undertakers were brought over, and they got these inducements for coming over to plant the lands, but unfortunately the inducements held out to them were not performed, or only for a limited time.

Mr. WILLIAM HENRY M'CORRICK, sworn; and Examined.

Mr. Cherry.

3706. I BELIEVE you are one of the Catholic residents of Derry?—I am.

3707. And you are a magistrate of the city?—I am.

3708. You have lived there all your life?—I have.

3709. Can you speak as to the feeling of the Catholics of Derry as regards the management of the estates of the Irish Society?—Yes.

3710. It is a matter of public knowledge that the corporation have sent here three gentlemen who have given evidence before the Committee to the effect that the corporation, and they believe the general body of the citizens, were satisfied with the administration of the Irish Society's estates. Do you know whether that feeling is shared by the Catholics of Derry?—No, not at all.

3711. What is the feeling of the Catholics of Derry on the subject?—That they have been entirely neglected as a body by the Irish Society.

3712. Do you mean that the Protestant population of Derry have been favoured?—Yes, unfortunately the population are in two camps, and party feeling runs very high, higher I suppose than in any city in the world. One portion of the city is the Protestant party and they are considered to be always favoured by the Irish Society, while we as a body have received no favours whatever comparatively, though a small amount has been given lately.

3713. I would like you to substantiate by some facts or instances within your knowledge the statement you have just made: do you know anything about the money expended by Catholics in buildings in Derry?—In public buildings the Catholics have expended about 40,000 *l.* or 50,000 *l.* within the last 30 years, religious houses and schools.

3714. Have they ever got any aid from the Irish Society?—They have never got any aid from the Irish Society for this purpose.

3715. Have they got any free sites?—No, they have never got a free site.

3716. What has been the rent usually charged?—We had to buy from middlemen, and for one portion of what we built 1,850 *l.* was paid and 2,500 *l.* for another.

3717. Has it been a rule, without any exception, that although the Catholics build their own houses, they not only do not get any assistance from the Irish Society, but they are charged the full rent of the sites?—The houses were, I believe, mostly built on ecclesiastical land. We

Mr. Cherry—continued.

had to buy out the occupier. There is one site under the Irish Society. That is that in which the convent is built, I believe.

3718. Kindly confine yourself to the Irish Society's estates; how many buildings have been erected upon them at the sole expense of the Catholics?—I believe, I am not quite sure, the convent is built on the Irish Society's ground. But it is all in the city of Derry, and the ground of the city of Derry is looked upon as the property of the Irish Society.

3719. What was this estate on which you said 40,000 *l.* had been expended?—It was in the town of Derry. I do not know what estate it was.

3720. Had the Irish Society to do with it?—I think not. I think it belongs to the bishop's land; they may be head landlords.

3721. Do you know of any instance of an application having been made to the Irish Society for free sites for public buildings and which had been refused?—In the year 1872 there was a temperance society got up in Derry, and it increased very largely. There were, on the average, about 3,000 working men and about 3,000 women in the society. There was no public hall for them, and there was no place where they could meet, except occasionally in one of the religious houses or churches. This was considered to be a subject that the Irish Society would take into account when we asked for a site.

3722. You asked for a site for a hall?—Yes.

3723. Was the application granted?—The application was granted. It was the temperance society, properly speaking, that asked for the site for a hall. And the application was granted at 10 *l.* a year, with this condition in it, that if the hall was used for any but temperance purposes, the ground would revert back to the Irish Society.

3724. And the building with it, I suppose?—Yes, I suppose so. If the ground went the building would follow.

3725. Did the temperance society accept?—No. This condition was taken into consideration, because the temperance society itself was not able to build a large hall, and it was felt that that would be a very bad thing for them to do, because, if there was a public lecture or a ball given in it, or anything else of that nature, the society then had the power of taking it away from them; and they declined the offer on that ground, and asked them to take away that condition.

Mr. *Clancy*—continued.

dition. The society refused to withdraw the condition. We had, therefore, to decline. Then we bought another site for 1,250 *l.*, and commenced gathering funds to erect the hall.

3726. And you have erected it?—Well, with great struggling we did erect it. During the time of the building of the hall we asked the society for a grant in aid of the building.

3727. Did you get it?—The Irish Society declined to give any grant for the building, saying that they had given us so much in other ways that they could not afford to give anything to us, so that we finished the hall at an expense of 15,000 *l.*, and it is now used generally for the Catholics of Derry for temperance and amusement purposes and for teaching.

3728. Without any aid whatever from the Irish Society?—Without any aid at all from the Irish Society.

3729. Was there ever any assistance refused to the Catholics of Derry on the ground that the charter prevented such an application of the funds?—Yes; during the progress of the building of the cathedral, which cost about 30,000 *l.*, we took into consideration that it was right to apply to the Irish Society, and one of the principal citizens of our persuasion took the opportunity of asking a member of the deputation that came over here whether, if we should apply, it was likely that the request would be granted; and he stated, in reply, that such a thing could not be done, that it would be against the charter. So we declined to ask.

3730. Who was the Catholic who asked; do you know his name?—Yes, I will tell you his name if you wish.

3731. I think you had better give us the names on both sides?—It was Mr. Charles O'Neill. He is justice of the peace, harbour commissioner, and a member of the town council.

3732. Who was the member of the Irish Society who gave those answers?—I do not know.

3733. However, he was a member of the deputation?—He was a member of the deputation that came over on the annual visit.

Sir W. T. Marriott.

3734. What year was that?—I could not exactly say. I do not think it was more than seven or eight years ago.

Mr. *Clancy*.

3735. Do you know of any other application having been made for assistance by the Catholics of Derry, and having been refused?—We considered that, having got the information that it was against the charter to give the Catholics of Derry anything for religious purposes, it was no use applying.

3736. Have you any other instances to give of applications having been made?—No, we declined to make any application then.

3737. You thought it was of no use?—No use, because our bishop, the late Dr. Kelly, was very stiff in point of dignity. He would ask no favour from anybody at all unless he had a clear right to it.

3738. And he conceived he had no right to this?—He considered that they would not grant it; that it was outside the charter.

3739. The universal conviction was that there was no use in asking the Irish Society for anything for the Catholics of Derry?—No. We considered always that the office was against us, and there was another office in London.

3740. That is agent in Derry?—The agent in Derry and the agent in London.

3741. What would the Catholics of Derry wish to have done with the estate of the Irish Society?—We would like to see it turned into money, and one portion of it applied to pay off the debt that was incurred by the harbour commissioners for making the quays. That amounts to about 130,000 *l.*, or so, and another applied to reduce the debt of the corporation, which was incurred for improvement in drains and various other things; and then, I believe, the balance ought to be divided fairly among all the religious denominations, for I think that the Government of the country ought to be able enough to provide for education.

3742. Can you give me any other facts on the subject?—I would like to say a word upon the Foyle and Bann fisheries. They get 5,000 *l.* a year for the Foyle and Bann fisheries. The Foyle fisheries are the only part I wish to say a word upon. The Irish Society own the bed and soil of Lough Foyle, and all the fish in it, and it is divided into two parts. There is the lough, which is an expanse of water about 14 or 15 miles long, and nine or 10 miles wide; and then there is the river that goes from Culmore Fort up to Lifford Bridge, about 16 miles. Now the principal portion of the salmon are caught in the portion of the river from Culmore Fort up to Lifford Bridge; that is, the narrow part where the Irish Society's tenants have the fixed nets. The Irish Society have let these fisheries to tenants, but the wider portion of Lough Foyle is inhabited by county Donegal fishermen, and they fish in the Foyle and take all the fish out of it, except the salmon. They are prevented from taking out the salmon by the Irish Society's tenants, according to the Irish Society's directions, and they have a steamboat on the loch which attends every night to watch that the fishermen do not take any salmon. This has led to serious consequences. Sometimes gunshots have been fired, and this may eventually end in murder, so that in any arrangements to be made in the future I think it would be necessary that the Irish Society, for the peace of the country and for the benefit of the poor fishermen who live along the loch, should give these fishermen the privilege of taking the salmon from Culmore Fort to the sea, and that then the Irish Society could retain the privilege they now have of fishing in the Foyle from Culmore to Lifford Bridge, which is 16 miles, where the salmon are mostly all caught.

3743. Is there anything you would like to add?—I know it is the general feeling of the Catholic body of Derry that we have been very badly treated, and I may say also that I know some Catholic tenants in the neighbourhood, about a mile or a mile and a-half out of the town, in

Mr. Clancy—continued.

in what they call the Liberty, who have been obliged to leave their farms, either been led to sell them or had some trouble with the office, and that their places have been supplied by tenants of a different persuasion. I think the Irish Society has been more or less connected, or supposed to be connected, with the Apprentice Boys of Derry, and that has led to a very bitter feeling against the Irish Society from the Catholics, especially as they get no benefits. I should like to say a word with regard to the grant that they have given lately to the seminary. There was a large seminary in Derry and it is principally Catholic, and they applied for a grant, and they got a grant from the Irish Society of 125 *l.* a-year, but with this condition in it that it was to be during the Irish Society's pleasure. They thought that was rather stiff, considering the grants that they gave to the Foyle College and the Magee College of 1,000 *l.* and 250 *l.* a-year, and much more. In fact, they have treated the Protestant portion of Derry as children that were worth looking after, and they have treated the Catholic portion as orphans, I should say.

Sir John Whittaker Ellis.

3744. The Irish Society made a grant to the Roman Catholic Seminary of 25 *l.* a year?—Yes.

3745. You said it was given during pleasure?—During pleasure.

3746. Is it not the fact that that was a form used in the case of all the grants?—I cannot say; I would like to know.

3747. You may take it from me it is the case that all grants, under any circumstances, are always given in that way?—The sensibilities of the Catholics of Derry were wounded. They did not like what seemed to be an insult.

3748. They are always made either for a term of years or during pleasure, which really means unless anything very serious occurs?—I think if the society's property was sold, and every member of it got a service of plate for winding it up satisfactorily, it would be a very good thing. We should like to get this religious strife abolished, if we could.

3749. With regard to the salmon fishery, if what you ask were permitted, if the fishermen below Culmore were allowed to fish, do you think many salmon would get up the river?—I do. They fish now, only they poach, I believe.

3750. You think the salmon could give the fishermen the go-by?—They poach now.

3751. But they would poach a good deal more?—I do not think they would. The salmon would make its way up; the Foyle is very deep except in one part, and if they would give them the liberty at any part of the Foyle, it would be a charity, because the poor people cannot make a living by the white fish.

3752. Do you know that once, more particularly in the rivers in the south, there used to be a general fishery by fishermen until the fish were almost entirely destroyed?—It would be the upper reaches of the river that require to be guarded. You have 16 miles from Culmore to Lifford Bridge, and that is where they are all got nearly.

Sir John Whittaker Ellis—continued.

3753. Now as regards the temperance hall and the site of the building which we were anxious to assist, was not the condition that it should not be used for political purposes?—No, for nothing but temperance purposes; that would exclude a ball you know, and we have balls in it frequently.

3754. You are sure that it was not simply that it should not be used for political purposes?—Yes, I believe so.

Mr. John Ellis.

3755. How long have you been on the commission of the peace?—Between six and seven years.

3756. How long have you been resident in Derry?—About 63 years.

3757. And you came here considering yourself entitled and authorised to speak on behalf of the Catholics of Derry?—I have been commissioned by several of the most important of them to appear here to-day.

Mr. Lea.

3758. Evidence has been given here with regard to the Irish Society and the Corporation. If the Irish Society were dissolved, would you like the funds to be handed over to the Corporation of Derry to deal with?—Certainly, or also the interest of the funds yearly handed over to the Corporation.

3759. Do you think they would be a fair body to deal with it?—To be sure they would.

Mr. Clancy.

3760. Do you happen to know anything about the franchise of Derry?—The municipal franchise is high, 10 *l.*

3761. Does that exclude the great bulk of the Catholics?—Yes.

3762. And that accounts for the fact that there is only one Catholic on the town council of Derry?—Well, there are other reasons for that. There are societies, and one thing and another.

3763. Is that the main one?—That is the main one.

3764. The representatives of the Corporation who have been sent here have deprecated the idea of giving funds over to the management of the Corporation; but would you be willing to give it over, even under control of Parliament, to the Corporation of Derry?—Certainly.

3765. You have no fear that even the unreformed corporation would misuse the public funds?—They would not do so badly as the Irish Society have done with the funds in ancient times. I know latterly, within the last ten years, the society have turned over a new leaf. I think the general governor shows a good deal more sense than previous governors.

3766. Do you wish to withdraw your statement about the feeling of the Catholics of Derry?—No; it is deep-rooted. I would put the whole of the money in Sir John's pocket if the society was wound up; and I think he would act fairly with it.

3767. Rather than it should be in the hands of the Irish Society?—Oh, yes, the Irish Society, between

Mr. Cleary—continued.

between one office and another, never, I think, came to a correct conclusion.

3768. We have heard a good deal about dinners given by the Irish Secretary; who were invited to those dinners?—I never had the honour of being invited.

3769. Do you know of any Catholics who have been invited?—Mr. Charles O'Neill was the only one. There may have been one or two other Catholics; they would not amount to more than three or four, as far as I know.

Monday, 7th July 1890.

MEMBERS PRESENT:

Mr. Clancy.	Mr. Lea.
Lord Elcho.	Sir William Marriott.
Mr. John Ellis.	Mr. John Morley.
Mr. T. M. Healy.	Mr. Sexton.
Colonel Laurie.	Sir Richard Temple.
Mr. Lawson.	

THE RIGHT HONOURABLE JOHN MORLEY, IN THE CHAIR.

Chairman (to Dr. *Freshfield*).] WOULD you now find it convenient to inform the Committee of the course which you propose to take; I mean as regards the kind of evidence you propose to lay before the Committee, and the order of it?

Dr. *Freshfield*.] What we propose to do, Sir, is this. To-day we propose to offer to call Mr. Watney, the clerk of the Mercers' Company, the primary company, and Mr. Towse, the clerk of the Fishmongers' Company, which was the first company to sell after the Royal commission.

Chairman.] What have the Mercers and Fishmongers' Companies to say?

Dr. *Freshfield*.] Mr. Watney, the clerk of the Mercers' Company, will put in a statement which he has prepared, and which will be read if you think well. He will also submit to you the opinion that was taken by the company as to their title, and the relative documents, that is, the documents that were submitted to counsel in order to see what the condition of their title was. He will also submit to you one or two other supplemental documents for the information of the Committee. There will be the parcels in the Charters of King James and King Charles, which are omitted to be printed in the appendix to the Skinners' Company's case. In the two charters that have been put already into your hands, the parcels were omitted altogether. Probably at that time it was thought those parcels would not be material for the inquiry which was then going on; but they are material to the present inquiry. The other document will be the licence in mortmain in King Charles II.'s reign. The other document which you have had submitted to you, and which was printed in the Skinners' Company's case was the licence in mortmain granted by James I. to the companies. On the occasion of Charles II. granting a supplemental charter, he also issued to the companies a a licence in mortmain, which differs from the other, inasmuch as the Charter of King James speaks of the expenses which the company have been put to, and are going to be put to, whereas the Licence in Mortmain of King Charles II. merely speaks of the consideration of the expenses which the companies have already incurred.

Chairman.] But, in short, what the clerk of the Mercers' Company has got to say will all turn upon title, as I understand.

Dr. *Freshfield*.] Up to that point. But further than that, if it is your wish, the clerk of the Mercers' Company will be here prepared to give any information you may desire as to the management by the company of their Irish estates during the last 50 or 60 years.

Chairman.] Will he be prepared to tell us one fact, which is, perhaps, the only one which for the present I myself am curious about, namely, how much they have received from their Irish property, and how much they have been in the habit of annually expending in Ireland?

Dr. *Freshfield*.] The same course which would be followed by Mr. Watney would also, if you wish it, be taken by the clerk of the Fishmongers' Company; he will submit his statement.

Chairman.] Affecting the title of the company, I presume?

Dr. *Freshfield*.] Yes, affecting title, and carrying it generally down to the present time; because the difference between the Mercers' Company and the Fishmongers' Company is this: that the Fishmongers' Company have sold their property, and Mr. Towse's statement will give a general account of that. He will also be prepared to give you all the information you require as to the management of the estates and circumstances of the sale.

Chairman.] The management previous to the sale.

Dr. *Freshfield*.] Yes; and the circumstances of the sale if you wish it.

Chairman.] Very well. Is there anybody else you wish to call?

Dr. *Freshfield*.] We thought that that, Sir, would take up your time for to-day.

Chairman.] But could not you indicate the future course?

Dr. *Freshfield.*] I think that will save a great deal with you. The clerks of all the twelve companies are here, and with statements more or less similar to that which I have mentioned, not necessarily historical statements, but statements prepared more with the intention of giving you the fullest information, rather than any general evidence they could volunteer themselves, though, I believe, with regard to one or two points in respect of which you expressed a wish to hear evidence, they will come prepared with substantive evidence.

Chairman.] Substantive evidence on what points?

Dr. *Freshfield.*] The Drapers' Company, I believe, will wish to tender you some evidence in explanation. The solicitor to the Drapers' Company has met with an accident, and therefore I am here in a sense representing them. But, I understand, Mr. Sawyer will explain to the Committee what the Drapers' Company propose.

Mr. *Sawyer.*] The Drapers' Company would be much obliged if the Committee would let them tender the evidence of Mr. Glover, their Irish agent, who has acted in the matter of the sale of their Irish estates.

Chairman.] We expected that.

Mr. *Sawyer.*] If the Committee would wish to take the evidence of the agent of the company who was acting at the time the estate was sold, we will be prepared to produce him.

Chairman.] You mean Sir William Cunningham, I presume?

Mr. *Sawyer.*] Yes; and the company would also propose that I should attend as a witness, if the Committee desire my attendance. I may say that it would be a great convenience to the Drapers' Company if their evidence could be postponed until this day week; for, in consequence of their solicitor having met with an accident yesterday, they are not quite so prepared as they would like to be, and if their evidence could be taken this day week, it would be a great convenience.

Chairman.] Certainly. What will be done by the Irish Society?

Mr. *Maton.*] The Irish Society will ask that some evidence be heard by the Committee with regard to some general statements that have been made, and some specific allegations; but I do not think their evidence will take more than, perhaps, half-a-day. Their general agent will come over from Ireland, and, perhaps, there will be one or two witnesses from Derry to give evidence as to the mode in which the Society have been in the habit of dealing with the funds which they have had at their command, for the benefit of Londonderry and Coleraine. I do not think their evidence will take very long; and I do not wish to summon here our general agent, who is very busy in Ireland, before he is likely to be wanted.

Chairman.] The Committee will consider that. What is the name of the agent?

Mr. *Maton.*] Mr. Montgomery.

Chairman.] What day would suit Mr. Montgomery to attend?

Mr. *Maton.*] Monday next week, or Thursday next week.

Chairman.] Either Monday or Thursday?

Mr. *Maton.*] Thursday, if you please. If the Drapers' Company want to take their case on Monday, I would rather say Thursday for our evidence.

Chairman.] You think your evidence will take about half-a-day?

Mr. *Maton.*] About half-a-day.

Chairman (to Dr. *Freshfield*).] Have you any idea about how long the case of the Mercers' Company and Fishmongers' Company are likely to take?

Dr. *Freshfield.*] It would depend upon the gentlemen round the table.

Chairman.] But how long do you think the examination-in-chief will take?

Dr. *Freshfield.*] I should think about half-an-hour.

Mr. *Clancy.*] Each?

Dr. *Freshfield.*] It really depends. You will wish them, I suppose, to read their statements, and probably you would wish Mr. Watney also to read the opinion of counsel, to which I have referred; but you probably will not wish him to read the documents referred to in it, because they make up this bundle which I have in my hand. Mr. Watney's evidence will not take longer than half-an-hour, and probably Mr. Towse's evidence will not take longer than a quarter-of-an-hour. But then you, Sir, and other gentlemen will probably wish to ask them some questions.

Mr. *Rhodes.*] May I ask, on behalf of the Skinners' Company, that the clerk, Mr. Edward Herbert Draper, may also go into the chair and produce documents, and otherwise act in the same way as Dr. Freshfield has proposed with regard to the other companies.

Mr. *Draper.*] I wish to be allowed to say that the Skinners' Company would be glad, if you wish, in addition to myself, to call one of the members of the court, Mr. Herbert Saunders, Q.C., who was master of the company at the time the long lease of Ogilby's, which has been referred to, fell in, the reason being that our company is the latest that came into realisation of all these twelve companies; and Mr. Saunders took an active part in initiating the grants that were made by our company, and he also took an active part in connection with the railway company. I should like to ask that he may be tendered as a witness after the clerk.

Chairman.] Do I understand that the Skinners' Company propose three witnesses?

Mr. *Draper.*] No, Sir; only two: the clerk and Mr. Herbert Saunders. May I add that I should like to avoid the date of Thursday, the 17th, if possible.

7 *July* 1890.

Dr. *Freshfield.*] The Salters' Company propose to offer their clerk, Mr. Scott, and no other witness.

Mr. *Somers Smith.*] The Grocers' Company will be prepared to offer their clerk as a witness.

Chairman.] I do not know that the Grocers' Company have yet been mentioned in the matter. However, will you give us the name of their clerk?

Mr. *Somers Smith.*] The clerk to the Grocers' Company is Mr. Somers Smith. He would be prepared to put in a statement upon the question of title, and also to give evidence as to the dealings with the estate previous to the sale and the circumstances of sale.

Mr. *Goldney (City Remembrancer).*] I should like to make an application, Sir, on behalf of the Corporation to be put in the same position with regard to counsel as the companies are. Of course this Committee is aware of the position that the Corporation holds with regard to the Irish Society, and, as you have heard, questions of title very likely may arise on the charter.

Chairman.] How do you distinguish yourselves from the Irish Society; what is your *locus standi* apart from the Irish Society, which is, in effect, as I understand, a committee of the Corporation appointed by the Corporation, is it not?

Mr. *Goldney.*] No, Sir, it is not a committee of the Corporation; it is an entirely different body altogether.

Chairman.] It is a committee appointed by the Corporation, is it not?

Mr. *Goldney.*] The Corporation nominate the Irish Society every year.

Chairman.] They are the nominees of the Corporation?

Mr. *Goldney.*] Yes; but when once nominated they have an absolute and entirely independent existence.

Chairman.] Do you think that the Corporation have interests or rights apart from the Irish Society, which would make it desirable for them to appear here by counsel?

Mr. *Goldney.*] I think from the turn the inquiry has taken, it is extremely probable, and certainly possible, that questions of that character may arise.

Chairman.] Nothing has yet arisen?

Mr. *Goldney.*] Unless the Corporation retain counsel in sufficient time, it is impossible to get up the case, in order to answer any point that might arise suddenly, and one would hardly like to ask the Committee to postpone their meetings, because of the Corporation's counsel not being ready.

Chairman.] Yours is merely an application for a contingent hearing, as I understand?

Mr. *Goldney.*] Of course, Sir, when the time comes, it would be for the Committee to decide upon the particular points that arose, whether the counsel for the Corporation should be allowed to address the Committee; but unless we have permission, *de bene esse*, it throws the matter over for so long.

Chairman.] Then as to the Clothworkers' Company, who have been mentioned in some of our evidence, we have not heard anything about what witnesses they propose to tender.

Dr. *Freshfield.*] Sir Owen Roberts has expressed a wish to offer himself for evidence.

Chairman.] Sir Owen Roberts wrote to me and asked that the Clothworkers' Company should have a chance of appearing. He is not here, I think, at present?

Dr. *Freshfield.*] No.

Chairman.] He may desire to give evidence, I understand?

Dr. *Freshfield.*] I am sure he will, Sir.

Mr. *J. M. Stone.*] On behalf of the people for whom I appear here, namely, certain tenants and public bodies in Derry, it would be an assistance to us to have these statements printed and put into our hands at as early a date as possible.

Chairman.] What statements do you refer to?

Mr. *Stone.*] The statements of title that these gentlemen have been speaking about. Perhaps it would be fair to us, and enable us to see the position in which we stand.

Dr. *Freshfield.*] Do you appear for Dr. Todd?

Mr. *Stone.*] I am not appearing for Dr. Todd; I appear for J. C. White, of Belfast, with my friend, Mr. Lea, who happens not to be here at the moment.

Chairman.] Are you a solicitor?

Mr. *Stone.*] I am a counsel. My request is simply that we may have these statements of title as early as possible.

Chairman.] I think now I will ask for the room to be cleared, that we may consider what course we will take.

The Committee-room was cleared. After some time, the parties were again called in.

Chairman (to Dr. *Freshfield*).] The Committee have considered the course which you were good enough to indicate to us, and we have come to the conclusion that we do not desire to hear from the clerks or other agents of the Mercers, Fishmongers, or other companies, or the Irish Society, read or otherwise delivered statements of arguments. We do not propose to enter at this stage in any shape or form into the question of title. We have so far gone on the method of separating the question of administration and the circumstances of sale from the charters, instruments and other points of title generally. On the other hand, if the Mercers' Company, the Fishmongers' Company, and the other companies desire to put in documents and instruments which would form a ground for the arguments of counsel when we come to hear them for that purpose, we shall be very much obliged to them; but we do not wish to hear views or arguments of their own upon

points

points of title. What we do wish to hear from the representatives of the companies and the Irish Society is any evidence of any facts that they have to produce rebutting statements of fact that have been made before this Committee by the various witnesses whom we have already heard and whom you have heard. That distinction is in our minds is quite clear. It might happen that after we have heard counsel we might desire to examine the clerks of the various companies and the secretary of the Irish Society upon points as to which counsel have not been able to satisfy us. If that were so, we should then be glad to hear the clerks and the secretaries upon points that we might put to them. That is our general decision. We do not wish to hear evidence upon title, but we are willing to have put in through one any documents which may affect title. The application from the Corporation of the City of London to be represented here by counsel, we think a perfectly fair one, provided that it is thoroughly understood that we shall not hear the counsel for the Corporation of London, unless we are of opinion that some point has been raised as to which he would be able to satisfy us, and to inform us, but we should listen to any application he might make, and he may be here if he thinks fit. We propose to-day to begin by taking rebutment evidence from Londonderry; that of a gentleman from Londonderry, who has some evidence which he wishes to give, of which I have read the proof, and which I think it well we should hear. That probably will not take very long. After that, looking through the dates which the various gentlemen fixed as being most convenient to their principals, I am inclined to think we might this afternoon, after the Londonderry witness, take the evidence of the clerk of the Fishmongers' Company upon the circumstances under which they have sold their property, and then the evidence of the clerk of any other company.

Dr. Freshfield.] Do I understand that you do not wish to hear Mr. Watney, of the Mercers' Company, who is here?

Chairman.] There has been no attack, or rather I should say no criticism, so far as I know, upon the Mercers' Company. Has he anything to say as to the circumstances of the sale?

Dr. Freshfield.] No; the Mercers' Company have not sold.

Chairman.] They might, perhaps, be proposing to sell.

Dr. Freshfield.] No, they are not proposing to sell.

Chairman.] If he has anything to say with regard to the administration, we would hear him; only we should not wish to hear him upon title.

Dr. Freshfield.] The statements that Mr. Watney and I have prepared for the Mercers' Company, and which Mr. Towse and I have prepared for the Fishmongers' Company, were prepared merely with a view to help the Committee, to assist them, and to save them trouble when the legal argument comes to be heard. For instance, in the Fishmongers' Company's statement, we have referred at considerable length to the Calendar of State Papers. You referred just now to putting in documents. Of course, it would be impertinent to you to put in a Calendar of State authorities, and ask you to find out for yourselves those which bear upon this inquiry; but there are certain passages dealing with the history in the Calendar of State Papers, which we thought ought to be before the Committee, and we thought that what we had proposed would be a convenient mode for your own assistance. I assure you that the object of the companies has not been merely to help themselves in the matter, but to assist the Committee in the matter.

Chairman.] I am sure we are quite willing to accept that. But you see we would not allow Dr. Todd, and, so far as I could manage it, we would not allow other witnesses, to go into the question of title. One or two witnesses did indeed express an opinion, but it probably made no very serious impression upon the minds of the Committee. As I say, we declined to hear Dr. Todd's views, although we know he had taken great trouble to form his views. We remain in that frame of mind; we are going to hear counsel with minds entirely unbiassed and unaffected.

Dr. Freshfield.] May I say one thing more. I know perfectly what will happen. When Mr. Latham and the other gentlemen have addressed the Committee, there will simply appear upon the Notes, "Counsel here addressed the Committee"; nothing more will appear than that.

Chairman.] That, I suppose, depends upon the decision of the Committee. If the Committee thought otherwise, they could direct that the speeches of counsel should appear.

Dr. Freshfield.] All I meant was, that supposing you think it better not to accept the statements we put in because they deal with historical matters, so to speak, from which the title may be deduced, if Mr. Latham merely reads them, out to you, unless there is a minute taken of them, you will not have any record of where to look for them, and they will be forgotten altogether, or something of that sort.

Chairman.] When the time comes for us to hear counsel, there will be every disposition in the minds of every Member of the Committee to give the fullest hearing to the arguments; and as they are likely to be important historical arguments in connection with the possessions of the companies in Ireland, and perhaps important also in the history of Ireland, for myself, I should be very much inclined to preserve a record of the speeches of counsel.

Dr. Freshfield.] Very well, Sir. My only view is to do what will assist the Committee in the inquiry.

Chairman.] To-day, after the Londonderry witness is done with, I understand we shall have the Fishmongers' Company's witness or the clerk to the Mercers' Company.

Dr. Freshfield.] They are both here.

Chairman.]

7 July 1891.

(*Chairman.*] I may add that the Committee propose to sit on Mondays, Thursdays, and Fridays, because we are very anxious to get on with the business of the Committee. Therefore you ought to be ready, if you can make it convenient, on Friday next. Next Thursday we propose to take some Derry witnesses, and after that you can go straight on with your case without any interruption.

Dr. *Frankfield.*] Yes, Sir. Perhaps you would not mind Mr. Watney being heard to-day, because Friday is a day when he cannot attend.

(*Chairman.*] Then we will take Mr. Watney first after the Londonderry witness.

Dr. *Frankfield.*] If you please, Sir.

Mr. Joseph Ballantine, called in; sworn; and Examined.

Chairman.

3770. You are from Londonderry, I believe? —Yes.

3771. You are in business there?—Yes; I am a builder and contractor.

3772. How long have you been connected with Londonderry?—For about 34 or 35 years.

3773. What is the main point upon which you wish to give evidence before this Committee?—On the management of the property in Londonderry.

3774. You mean the property of the Irish Society in the town of Londonderry?—Yes.

3775. You have something to say, I believe, about the injury done to Derry by the refusal to grant long leases?—Yes; that is the principal evidence I wish to give.

3776. What do you wish to say upon that point?—When the property falls out in Londonderry it is not put up in the open market to be let at the highest possible penny to be obtained for it at the time it becomes vacant. That has been the practice for all my time in Derry.

3777. What do you say has been their practice when land has become vacant?—They do not put it into the open market and let it at the time it becomes vacant, but allow it to remain vacant for a number of years, to the loss of the trust, and to the loss in rates of the city, and to the inconvenience of the traders.

3778. Why do they do that?—I do not know; but they do it.

3779. Can you give us any cases in which they have done so?—Yes; when the old buildings were thrown down in Ship Quay-place where the northern bank and harbour offices are built; when that became vacant Mr. Alexander Black, a very extensive merchant in Derry, offered the Irish Society 100 *l.* a year for part of the block for the purpose of building there; and he would have expended 5,000 *l.* or 6,000 *l.* on building warehouses. His offer was not accepted.

3780. He offered them 100 *l.* a year, and offered to spend 5,000 *l.* or 6,000 *l.* in building upon it?—Yes.

3781. And they refused that offer?—They never accepted it, and they had not the courtesy to decline it; they did not write to Mr. Black declining the offer.

3782. They did not accept it?—No.

3783. What has happened to that block of land?—A portion of it is vacant from that day to this, although that occurred in 1872 or 1873.

Chairman—continued.

3784. Do you mean they gave no answer at all to Mr. Black's offer?—Yes; I had that from his own mouth on Saturday morning last. I called on him as I was coming away, and asked him the question.

3785. Have you any other case?—There was a similar block of buildings on the south side, where the buildings were thrown down in 1870, and the ground was never occupied until the new town hall, or what is called the New Guildhall, was built on it, though it remained vacant for 18 years. I would say that that block of building, if it had been let at the market value at that time, would have brought at least 400 *l.* or 500 *l.* a year, and consequently that money was lost to the trusts, and the rates on it were lost to the city.

3786. Did the Society make any communication to Mr. Johnston in that case?—The block that I refer to is not the block that Mr. Johnston resides on; this is the block known as Ship Quay-place. This is on the south side, whereas the first block of land which I referred to is on the north side.

3787. Is that land still vacant?—No; they have built the new Guildhall upon it; but it remained vacant for 18 years before the Guildhall was built.

3788. Do you give these cases as an illustration of the way in which the Society failed to make the best of their property?—Yes; private individuals who had similar property would have had it let in one or two years at the outside, because they would have let it at the highest penny obtainable at that time; but the Irish Society does not do that; they do not put it on the market and let the time it becomes vacant.

3789. Have you another illustration that you can give us?—Yes.

3790. What is it?—There was a field of 10½ acres known as Gilliland's Field, that lies between Mr. Tilly's residence and the Magee College. This 10½ acres was advertised to be let in the year 1858 to build one house upon the 10½ acres. This ground was all very eligible ground for the purpose of building streets and terraces of houses. It was within a stone's throw of the present shipyard. If that ground had been properly managed it would have, in my opinion, brought in an annual income of about 1,500 *l.* a year. It has been used for agricultural purposes up to the present time.

Mr. Cleary.

3791. Is that the Pennyburn field?—Yes.

Chairman.

3792. Are there any other cases you wish to refer to?—There are several blocks of buildings, but I will mention one that is on the Strand. That went out of lease in September 1888. The tenants occupying were taken on as quarterly tenants, that is to say, they were to leave on three months' notice. Although these men are extensive merchants, all requiring good business premises, nothing has been done with it from that time to this, and a large portion of the block is totally unutilised; that is, the portion facing Sackville-street, Great James-street, and Little James-street. In fact it is a disgrace to any civilised community to have it standing like that, and a total loss to the rates of the city and to the trade. With regard to the portion next the Strand, I do not believe it is a loss; because they have adopted the worst form that the middlemen adopts there, by continuing on the tenants at the highest rent obtainable in those dilapidated buildings.

3793. When you speak of middlemen, has the Society shown any desire to let to middlemen?—A number of years before my time they had let to middlemen.

3794. Up to what date?—Up to the beginning of the present century.

3795. But have they done so since?—There has not been any letting to middlemen in my time in perpetuity that I know of.

3796. You say not within your time: and your time is most important, of course; have you anything to say as to the rents demanded by the Society?—They are most exorbitant. That is the reason that the ground is not let. I will give you an illustration. Mr. Finlay Biggar, an extensive provision merchant in Derry, purchased the building ground thrown upon the market by the making of the new bridge, what was called the bridge approaches. He has all that ground let and built on many years ago. The Irish Society's ground on the Ship Quay was as good a place, and there were no lettings on it, whereas Mr. Biggar has let all his land. Mr. Biggar is not a man who, in the opinion of the people of Derry, is overburdened with zeal for the public good; his letting the land was purely for profit.

3797. Have you any other case of a tenant holding his business premises under the Society, and his prosperity being interfered with by the demands of the Society?—It has been utterly ruinous to some.

3798. Can you name one case?—Mr. Gamble, at the corner of William-street and Waterloo-place.

3799. What happened in that case?—He built on property that fell out of lease, paying an exorbitant head-rent, 80 *l.* a year, for the site he built upon, and he became bankrupt. He spent about 6,000 *l.* in building, and when the property was thrown on the market after the bankruptcy it would only realise 1,750 *l.*

3800. What were the terms he got?—He got it in perpetuity; but of course he was bound to put up a class of building ruinous to himself under

Chairman—continued.

the circumstances. It was the head-rent that ruined him; it was more than the commercial value. Take, for instance, the new buildings put up in Foyle-street; they have been entirely stopped, and there have been none built for the last year or two, and the class of buildings that would have been rebuilt is the sort of tumble-down buildings, covered with galvanised iron roofs.

3801. Why is that?—On account of the exorbitant head rent that is asked over the value that a man could be remunerated by building upon the ground.

3802. Do you mean the ground-rent?—The ground-rent is over the value. I mean the ground-rent, but it is commonly known as and called head rent with us.

3803. Have you some other instances?—Mr. Mitchell's has been a very unprofitable speculation, although he built a very fine building. Might I say, before passing from that Strand building, that in fact it is considered a disgrace to the city and the local press, a short time ago, as late as the 17th of April last, published a sketch and a description of the building which was on that site.

3804. You mean a woodcut?—Yes; here it is (*handing the same to the Chairman*). This is the very heart of the business part of Derry, opposite the Victoria Market.

3805. You attribute that state of things, as I understand, to the mismanagement of the Irish Society?—Yes; no private individual would afford to manage his property in that way.

3806. Are we to gather from you that one result of the management of the Irish Society is that, as I do gather from what you have said, in several of the best business parts of the city the houses are falling to pieces?—Yes; principally the houses that have been let on terminable leases; that is, let for a term of years.

3807. But we have heard from some other Derry witnesses that since the accession of Sir John Whittaker Ellis as Governor of the Irish Society there has been a great change, and that now they grant perpetual leases, and, in fact, the management has been so much improved that there is scarcely more to desire; what is your view as to that?—I do not notice any improvement in the management; it is the change of times mostly. Owing to the passing of the Church Act there was a lot of property put on the market, and the owners of it being private owners could let it in perpetuity; and there was a growing desire, owing to that, not to take terminable leases upon the part of people who were afraid to build upon land so held; the Church property being thrown in the market it forced the hands of the Irish Society, and forced them to give perpetuity leases the same as adjoining proprietors.

3808. Do you think that since the new Governor came into office in 1883 nothing has been left undone that ought to be done?—I think plenty has been left undone. For instance, as regards this block in the Strand, it is a disgrace to any management to have let it remain without striking it. It may be a profit to the Society, but it is a great loss to the city in rates, and to the trade.

3809. When

Chairman—continued.

3809. When the new governor came into office announcements were made that the society was willing to grant perpetuity leases; was that very well taken in the borough?—It was very well taken. The instance I referred to of a field of 10½ acres was the first intimation, in my opinion, that ever appeared in print in Derry that any land would be given in perpetuity.

3810. What did the Society do; did they advertise?—Yes, they advertised.

3811. That they were willing to grant perpetuity leases?—Yes, of that place; and afterwards there were perpetuity leases given and new buildings erected in Ship Quay-place and Foyle-street: in fact, generally there were perpetuity leases given of all the building land that they let where there were permanent buildings erected.

3812. You think that your complaints, which fill up the first part of your evidence, are still as strong against the management of the last seven years as they are against the management of the seven years before?—I do. Considering the advancement there should be more advantages given by the Society.

3813. Have you anything to say as to the local agents of the Society?—The management is principally done from London.

3814. Keeping, for the moment, to the local agents, have you anything to say with regard to them; do you mean that they have not powers enough?—They do not seem to have any power.

3815. They always refer to head-quarters, and do not use any power of their own; is that what you mean?—They always ask people to make offers which they will submit.

3816. You think that interposes an obstacle to the despatch of business?—I do.

3817. But do you not suppose that the local agent makes recommendations to head-quarters?—I suppose he would; but whatever recommendations are made, must be very seldom acted upon; because if there had been proper representations made, this ground would not have been vacant 18 years.

3818. Your view is, that though the Society knows less than its local agent, it prefers its own judgment, absentee as it is, to the advice of the local agent?—That is my opinion; because the local agent, being on the ground, must know what the wants and requirements of the place are.

3819. I suppose the Society and the agent never show any personal preferences; they show no unfairness in the management of the property?—I cannot say that. I think the people that go to them and work at what might be called backstairs' work, come out best in the end.

3820. You think there is a backstairs influence?—That is one of the complaints; that it is not thrown into the open market for everybody to compete alike.

3821. Do you mean that advantages are given as the result of backstairs' influence?—That is the general opinion in Derry.

3822. It may be general opinion; but can you give any evidence of it?—I cannot; but nine men out of ten in Derry would say that was the only way it could be got.

3823. But you cannot tell us any case?—No. I never made an application to them at any time.

3824. That is not the point of my question. You said there was backstairs' influence in getting unfair advantages on the ground of personal preference, or relationship, or I know not what else, and I ask you do you know of any case?—I do not; I cannot give you an instance of a case.

3825. We have heard something about the relations of the Society to the Harbour Commissioners; have you anything to say upon that?—Yes. The Society have, in fact, obstructed all the improvements that have been proposed at the port in my time.

3826. We shall have before us the Secretary of the Harbour Commissioners; so I will not trouble you about that matter. I think you have framed an estimate of the loss which has resulted to the trust, in your opinion, in consequence of the alleged mismanagement?—Yes. I believe that if it had been properly managed for the last 24 or 30 years at least, the income of the Irish Society would have been doubled.

3827. Cannot you give us more particulars; what do you suppose was the result of the loss in Mr. Black's case, for instance?—£. 100 a year.

3828. And in the case in the Strand-road that you referred to, what do you put the loss at?—Of course as regards the ground on the other side of Ship Quay-place, that is now being utilised for the new town hall; but there was a loss, for the 16 years it remained vacant, of 150 *l.* a year in my opinion.

3829. You put down 100 *l.* as the amount of the loss in Mr. Black's case, and 250 *l.* in the case of the Strand-road?—Yes.

3830. What else is there?—I consider the loss in the case of that field known as Gilliland's Field is at least 1,300 *l.* a year.

3831. You are an owner of house property, and therefore specially able to estimate this loss?—Yes, I am an expert in that; that is my business, and I have a knowledge of the value of the property.

3832. You still want a very big figure to make double the income of the Irish Society as you suggested. What else are they losing upon?—They lose in that block of buildings, at the present time, in Little James-street, and Great James-street, and Strand-road, and Sackville-street, in my opinion, about 500 *l.* a year.

3833. How much have you got it up to now?—That brings it to about 2,350 *l.*

3834. Is there anything else?—There are buildings in Foyle-street. It would take me a very long time to go on and enumerate all the buildings.

3835. I do not want you to do that?—The buildings in Foyle-street might be far better utilised than they are for profit. And, I believe, if the same principle which is recommended in the case of the building property were adopted as regards the fisheries there would be a much larger income from them.

3836. What same principle do you refer to?—Throwing

Chairman—continued.

Throwing the letting of it into the open market for competition.

3837. What is done with the fishery?—Nobody ever knew, that I am aware of, how it was let.

3838. I suppose the people who take it know how it is let?—Of course they do; and the Society knows.

3839. Who are the lessees of the fisheries?—Three or four families in Derry; Mr. Moore, Mr. Mann's family, and Mr. M'Corkell.

3840. I take it that what you mean is that it is let, by reason of partiality and personal preference, to favoured individuals, on lower terms than could be obtained in the open market?—I cannot say, because it has not been thrown into the open market. My opinion is that if it were, it would fetch a great deal more money annually than is done.

3841. How much more?—Nearly double.

3842. What is it at present?—I think it is 5,000 *l.* a year.

3843. Then you would have to add 5,000 *l.* for the fishery?—Yes, on behalf of the fishery. In my opinion there is a loss of 5,000 *l.* a year on the fishery, as compared with what it would be if it was properly managed.

3844. How is that largest figure made up?—It is a pretty large figure; but a gentleman connected with the fishery told me that his half share was valued at 1,500 *l.* a year.

3845. You are here to impute, as I understand, to the management of the Irish Society, a loss to the trust of something like 7,000 *l.* or 8,000 *l.* a year?—Yes; and perhaps that saving might be increased under good management.

3846. What would you do to avoid all this mischief, of which you are so convinced?—I would improve the management.

3847. How would you improve the management; you have nothing to do with it; the Irish Society manage as they think fit, do they not?—If they manage it in this way, it is a clear loss to the place.

3848. Have you any notion in your head of some other kind of management? I think local management that knew the wants of the place would be better.

3849. You think the management would be better, if it were in the hands of some local body?—Not local altogether; but if it was in the hands of some body appointed, that would know really the wants and requirements of the place, and how they could take the profits out of it.

3850. I want to get clearly at what you recommend as regards this local body; you say the body, whatever it might be, must be well acquainted with the local wants, and yet you say you object to a local body?—I do not object to a local body; but it would altogether depend upon how the local body were appointed.

3851. But are you in favour of a local body, if the local body could be properly constituted?—Yes, I am.

3852. Are you in favour, for instance, of handing the management over to the corporation; would you consider that a local body properly constituted for this purpose?—I would not.

Chairman—continued.

3853. If the franchise were lower, would you?—It would not.

3854. I understand you are against handing over, under any circumstances, the management of these funds (supposing Parliament agreed to it) to the corporation?—I would hand over to the corporation a portion of it; I would hand over to the corporation what was formerly known as the corporation lands for the benefit of the trust.

3855. What would you do with the rest?—The other portions of it should be managed, in my opinion, by some local men, but appointed say by either the Government or the Lord Chancellor of Ireland.

Mr. William Marriott.

3856. You are a builder residing at Derry, I gather?—Yes, and a saw-mill proprietor.

3857. You are the owner of house property?—Yes, and the owner of building ground as well.

3858. In your opinion, as I understand, the Irish Society do not get large enough rents for their property?—No; just the opposite; it is my opinion they do not let at the market price, but that they ask too much rent.

3859. They sell too low and get rents too high; is that it?—They sell too high, and ask too high rents for getting the ground let.

3860. But you said they might to make 8,000 *l.* more, as I understand?—Yes; so they should by using the property properly.

3861. That would be by increasing the rents, I suppose?—It would be using as building land the ground now used for agricultural purposes.

3862. But as to the 5,000 *l.* you spoke of, that would be from rents simply, would it not?—No; that is entirely management.

3863. Do they let out the fisheries?—Yes, they are leased.

3864. You think the rents charged are not high enough?—I do not know whether they are high or not, but if it was put into the market for open competition they would get more money.

3865. That is to say, they would get a higher rent?—Yes.

3866. Then it comes to this: that they do not let the fisheries at high enough rent?—It might be so. It is the principle of management that I object to.

3867. At present it is leased out, is it not?—Yes.

3868. And the lessees pay a certain rent?—Yes. I see by the Society's return that they pay about 5,000 *l.*

3869. In your opinion those lessees ought to pay 5,000 *l.* more?—I say, put it into the open market and then you will see the value of it.

3870. That is to say that the Irish Society are unique in Ireland in charging too low a rent for their fisheries?—Do not misunderstand me. I say that they do not get any rent at all; that is, they do not let, because they ask too high a rent.

3871. But as regards the fisheries, which are let for 5,000 *l.*, what do you say?—You would determine what its value was at once if it were thrown into the open market.

3872. You

Sir William Marriott—continued.

3872. You say they ought to let at 10,000 l.; you said they should get double the 5,000 l. they now get?—Yes.

3873. Then they do let these fisheries at 5,000 l. below the full market value of the rent, according to you?—What I object to is the principle, the way in which it is let, I say that the fisheries should be let in the open market.

3874. You object to the result, you object to their getting 5,000 l. instead of 10,000 l. a year?—If it is thrown into the open market it would at once determine its fair market value.

3875. What is the fair market value?—The largest sum you can get on it by letting, and that is the only way you can arrive at it. Nobody knows whether they get it or not, because it is not in the open market.

3876. You say they do not get it?—In my opinion I think it is let too low.

3877. That is to say, the rent is too low?—Yes; but in that case it is only a loss to the trust; it does not interfere with the prosperity of the city whether the fishery is let for nothing or whether it is let for 20,000 l.

3878. You spoke about backstairs' influence; did that apply to the fishery?—Certainly I think it would, if it was not let in the open market.

3879. Can you give me any proof of that?—Here is this let without being advertised in the ordinary way.

3880. Who has used backstairs' influence to get it?—That I cannot tell, because I was not in the secret: I was not in the swim at all.

3881. That is why you object perhaps?—Certainly, I object to it on the principle that everything should be done in the open market. The open market is the only way of determining the value of anything, land fisheries or anything else.

3882. Or rent or anything else?—Yes.

3883. Can you give me the name of anybody who you know has got property by backstairs' influence?—No.

3884. You you do not know any individual?—No.

3885. Or of any property given to any individual by backstairs' influence?—No.

3886. May I take it that it is a general opinion or rather a suspicion?—It is general opinion grounded upon general conversations about the society in Derry.

3887. What conversations can you refer to?—For instance, if you speak to a man in Derry about coming here to give evidence upon this matter, he would say to you, "I cannot do so because it would injure my interests with the Society." For instance, I spoke to two gentlemen within the last week.

3888. What are their names?—I prefer not giving their names.

3889. But if they declined to come it surely will not injure them with the Society?—It would injure them for this reason: they said that a large portion of their property was falling out on terminable leases, and in all likelihood if they would go to say anything objectionable as regards the management of the Society they would not get such good terms that is the general feeling.

3890. The general feeling is to keep in with them?—That is supposed to be the case; to keep in with the Society.

3891. When did the Strand leases fall into the Society's hands?—In 1884, I believe.

3892. Amongst those are there not a number of licensed houses?—Yes. In fact they are all licensed houses but one, I think; that is on the Strand front.

3893. Are they all public-houses?—Yes, they are all public houses.

3894. How many public-houses are there?—There are five houses out of the six, I think; but some of them are not public-houses in the ordinary sense of public-houses.

3895. What is your complaint with regard to that land?—That it is a very important centre of business, and that it should be better utilised.

3896. But are you aware that the corporation have memorialised the Society to get this land for a public bath?—Yes.

3897. And that that is now under consideration?—Yes.

3898. Are the corporation right, in your opinion, in presenting that memorial?—It would not occupy the whole ground, or anything like it.

3899. Would it occupy a large portion of it?—Certainly not; it would not interfere with the Strand frontage at all.

3900. What do you want them to do?—I want them to let it.

3901. Have you asked them to?—I have not asked them.

3902. You are a builder, are you not?—Yes.

3903. Would you like to have some of that land let to you?—No, I do not desire it at all; because I have no money to invest upon property of that sort, and I do not think it would be a wise investment. No man could make it pay only the man who is going to live and do his business there.

3904. If the company did what you wish with it, the company would suffer from making an unwise investment?—The man who was going to build.

3905. You would not mind his suffering?—I have no sympathy with him; it is a matter of necessity with him.

3906. Your complaint against the Irish Society with regard to this land is, that they will not let it to some unfortunate builder upon such terms as that, he must more or less come to grief?—No builder is asking for it.

3907. What do you want the Society to do?—To let it to the present occupiers.

3908. Are they willing to take it?—They are. Every man on the block is willing to take it; they are willing to take their own houses or to make a proper division; if six houses were divided into four, for instance.

3909. Have they applied to the Society for it?—Yes.

3910. What answer did they receive?—The answer that Alderman John B. Johnson got was that if he would arrange with the adjoining tenants they were quite willing to arrange with him.

3911. What else could the Irish Society do than that?—I consider under circumstances of that sort that they were shelving the first duties of a landlord. They should have made the arrangement themselves.

3912. Why?—

Sir William Marriott—continued.

3912. Why?—Because it is their duty as landlords to do so.

3913. Could they give it to one and not to the others?—They could divide it into any number of lots they wish.

3914. They wanted to deal with it as a whole, I suppose?—It would not be to their advantage to deal with the Strand front as a whole.

3915. Would Alderman Johnson come forward and make a complaint here?—I do not think he would; because if he did he would very likely get none of the property.

3916. Do you mean that they are afraid to come forward; that they are afraid of the Irish Society?—Yes; every person is frightened of the enormous influence they have.

3917. Has not a board been put up on the Ship-quay advertising the land to be let in perpetuity?—A board has been put up, advertising it; but not in perpetuity.

3918. I am instructed it is in perpetuity. Will you say it is not in perpetuity?—I never recollect seeing any board saying it was in perpetuity.

3919. *If it was in perpetuity that is just what you want, is it not?*—Here is the advertisement that was issued from the Irish Chambers, Guildhall-yard on the 24th June 1879.

3920. What does that say?—It says: "The honourable the Irish Society will be prepared to receive on the 6th day of August 1879 tenders for a lease or leases of plots Nos. one to nine of land belonging to them, situated in Ship-quay place, in the city of Londonderry, bounded on all sides by the public thoroughfares, for the term of 99 years from the 8th day of September 1879."

3921. Do you know the Ship-quay?—Yes; this is the Ship-quay.

3922. Do you say that there is no advertisement more recent than that?—There was an advertisement, but I do not remember anything about perpetuity.

3923. Was there not an advertisement offering to let in perpetuity?—I never mind seeing anything about perpetuity. I think I put up the board you refer to; but I have no recollection of there being anything about perpetuity upon it.

3924. When was that?—The board was put up about three years after this.

3925. What you read was in 1879?—Yes, 1879. No, it was not ten years; it would be put up in 1884 I should say.

3926. Is it the fact that they did offer to let the whole of this land in perpetuity and that they got no offers?—That was simply because the people knew it was no use offering because they would be asked such an exorbitant rent that it could not be taken.

3927. What rent did they ask?—I do not know.

3928. Then how do you know it was an exorbitant rent?—Take for instance, Mr. Black's rent. That should be the fair value, what he offered in 1872 or 1873, because it was the highest rent then obtainable.

3929. But we have now come to 1884; when I say they offered to let it in perpetuity, you want it to be let in perpetuity, as I understand?—Certainly, it should be let in perpetuity.

3930. They offered in the open market to let it in perpetuity; why was it not taken?—Because nobody knew what rent would be asked. It was not put upon the board in the ordinary way.

3931. Could not they ask what the rent was?—It is not business to go and dance attendance at the Irish Society's office to ask what the rent is. It should have been put up at so much; it might have been 1 *l.* or 30 *s.* a foot.

3932. If you are going to buy land in England (I do not know how it is in Ireland) have you not to go to the office and ask the value?—I do not know the practice in England; but with Englishmen in Derry I know what the practice is.

3933. What is it?—Take a large firm like Messrs. Welch, Margetson & Company; they have built an extensive building, a palatial building, in Carlisle-road; and they did not go to the Irish Society, but they went to the middleman, they took the ground from the middleman.

3934. I was asking whether, in answer to their advertisement, the Society got any offers, and you said, No, because they asked too much, and I say, how do you know that they asked too much. They have offered to let in perpetuity, have they not?—Yes.

3935. Why was not their offer accepted?—Because they asked too much rent.

3936. How much did they ask?—I do not know.

3937. Then how do you know they asked too much?—I know that Mr. Bigger's plot let off in two years freely.

3938. Is that your only reason for saying so, because other peoples' property has let and this has not?—I think it is a very sufficient reason.

3939. Is that the only reason?—That is the only reason.

3940. You do not know what they asked?—No; but if it had been properly managed it would have been let.

Mr. Healy.

3941. Do you consider that Sir William Miller and the Corporation of Derry represent the Catholics of that city?—Not at all; the Catholics of the city, so far as the corporation are concerned, are entirely without representation, because you cannot call Mr. Charles O'Neill's case representation, because he is in purely by favour of the party represented by Sir William Miller.

3942. He is elected by favour of the Conservative party?—Yes, certainly.

3943. Why do you object to the existing corporation having the management of the trust?—I do not think, from the indifference of the people of Derry in electing the corporation, that they are just the men that would manage the trust well. What I mean by the indifference of the corporation is, that there is a feeling amongst the business people that they cannot pay more than a 4 *s.* rate, and they cannot charge them any more, that is the limit by Act of Parliament. Among the other section of the community, they say, Let this matter stand

until

Mr. *Healy*—continued.

until we get Home Rule, and that will cure it, and they do not agitate. I mean the Roman Catholic population.

3944. If the franchise were lowered, do you think that would not improve matters?—I think it would. I think there would be more interest taken in corporation matters.

3945. As between the Corporation of Derry, whether a reformed corporation or the present corporation, would you rather have it or the Irish Society for management?—I would not have either a reformed corporation or the present one.

3946. Supposing you had to choose, which would you prefer?—I do not think it would be a wise thing to put it into the hands of such an extensive local body, considering the different local connections and the different interests there would be.

3947. Are you not aware that a great many of the local corporations manage large local estates?—Yes. I believe the Corporation of Dublin manage large local estates.

3948. And the Corporation of London, which controls to some extent the Irish Society, manage large estates, do they not?—In Derry, we have been watching the management of the Corporation of London, and we did not think that the control under the old board was good.

Mr. *Clancy*.

3949. What do you say is the feeling of the Catholics of Derry on this subject?—They do not think that they are going to get any benefit; in fact, they have not, as a rule, got any benefit.

3950. May I ask what your own religion is?—I am a member of the Church of Ireland, an Episcopalian.

3951. A Protestant?—Yes.

3952. Is it true that in Derry the Catholics think it useless to apply for favours to the Irish Society?—Certainly they do, for I am not aware of any favours that they ever got, except the grant that they got to St. Colomb's College, to which they got a grant of 125 *l.* a year.

3953. Is that the only grant that they ever got?—It is; and that was got, I believe, within the last six or seven years.

3954. And they constitute more than half of the population, do they not?—It is considered that they constitute about half the population, they are the poorest section of the community. The wealth is principally in the hands of the Presbyterians and Episcopalians.

3955. You were asked about improper dealing on the part of the local agents of the society, and you said that you could not recollect any instance of it?—I do not want to interfere. There have been some things talked about, old families, and about agents that are dead; but I would rather not say anything at all about them. I cannot give you facts from my own knowledge; it is only what is talked of in the place, and I would rather not say anything about it. It is more scandal than any substantial facts.

3956. But I do not know that I can excuse you if you know the facts. Did you ever hear of a Mr. Walter Green, a local agent of the society?—Yes; I have.

Mr. *Clancy*—continued.

3957. Did you ever hear of Mr. John Munn?—Yes.

3958. When was he agent?—He was agent before the Hon. Mr. Plunket's time.

3959. About how many years ago?—I suppose more than 20 years ago.

3960. As a matter of fact, is it not notorious that Mr. Munn got a grant of a plot of ground in Derry from the Irish Society?—I think he got a reversionary lease of a property situated at the back of this ground that I have been referring to as mismanaged ground.

3961. Could you indicate the locality?—It is on Foyle-street; it faces to Foyle-street and the public quays.

3962. Do you know what relationship existed between Mr. Munn and Mr. Green?—Mr. Munn was Mr. Green's father-in-law by his second marriage.

3963. Was Mr. Munn Mr. Green's father-in-law when he got this grant, or was it after he got the grant that Mr. Green married his daughter?—My recollection of it is that the marriage occurred afterwards.

3964. Do you know, as a matter of fact, whether Mr. Munn settled it upon his own daughter?—It was said so. I do not know.

3965. Was it a matter of notoriety in Londonderry?—It was. It was freely talked of at that time, and it has been talked of many times since.

3966. Do you know anything of the value of this plot of ground that was treated in this way?—I cannot give you the exact figures of it; but I may say that it was supposed by that stroke of business, in whatever way it was managed, that Mr. Munn made from 900 *l.* to 1,000 *l.* a year.

3967. That is to say, that Mr. Green, being the son-in-law of Mr. Munn, got a grant of this land for Mr. Munn, and that Mr. Munn afterwards settled it on his own daughter?—I cannot say whether Mr. Green was mixed up in the getting of it or not, but he got the reversionary lease, which increased the value by that amount.

3968. Do the old tenants of the society in Derry get any preference, or are they treated as strangers or outsiders?—As a general rule, they dealt with the immediate occupier at the time the lease falls out.

3969. When their leases expire, do the old tenants get any preference?—The one that is in occupation when the lease expires always gets the option, the first offer of building, if he is able to build.

3970. Those that are able to expend money?—Yes, those who were able to rebuild.

3971. Can you give any estimate of the number of tenants of the respectable mercantile class, who at present hold as half-yearly, yearly, or quarterly tenants?—I do not know of any that hold at less than yearly tenancies, only in this block of buildings that I referred to in the Strand-road.

3972. How many there do you think you know?—There are at least six or seven; perhaps altogether there might be about twelve on that block.

3973. Can you tell the Committee anything about the way in which the Society have dealt with the Harbour Commissioners?—The Har-

Mr. *Clancy*—continued.

bour Board has never in my opinion been fostered or encouraged in any way by the Honourable the Irish Society. So lately as the year 1863 the Harbour Commissioners went about reclaiming the ground where the present shipyard is now built. I was engaged on this work myself at the time, and the society got an injunction, and stopped them. It remained in that position from that time, down to, I think, 1874, and then the Harbour Commissioners went to Parliament for power to do what the Society refused, or restrained their doing, in 1863. The Society opposed that Act of Parliament, which cost the Harbour Trust a great deal of money, 4,000 *l.* or 5,000 *l.*; and it was not that loss alone, because if they had filled in the ground in 1863 it could have been done for half the money that it cost at the later time.

3974. About how much was the total loss altogether resulting from the opposition of the society to the projects of the Harbour Commissioners?—I believe the loss, if it was all put together, would come to [illegible] *l.*

3975. What was the final result?—The final result was, that Parliament granted the Harbour Commissioners the power, and the work has been successfully carried out by the Harbour Commissioners.

3976. These improvements therefore have been effected in spite of the Irish Society?—I may say almost in spite of them.

3977. First they restrained them by injunction, and then they opposed them in Parliament; what further could they do?—Yes; but they opposed the second Act, which was got in 1874, I think, also, in which they sought for increased rating powers.

3978. What were the improvements sought to be made on the first occasion?—The filling in of the slob land for the purpose of establishing a shipyard.

3979. Is that the slob land, which is now taken up by shipbuilding yards and other enterprises?—Yes.

3980. Do you mean to say, that if the Irish Society had their way, those enterprises would not exist in Derry to-day?—I mean to say, that if the Irish Society had had their way, they would not have been carried out. The Irish Society did not contribute properly to the doing of this work.

3981. Did they contribute anything?—They did; they gave 7,000 *l.*, or they gave 1,000 *l.* for seven years; but that was more than absorbed in the law expenses that they put the Harbour Commissioners to. And this was a very large thing. The Harbour Commissioners have expended about [illegible] *l.* on permanent improvements.

3982. And those improvements have added greatly to the progress of the city and its trade?—The port would have been nowhere, in my opinion, if they had not been so wise in their generation at an early stage as to go in for the dredging of the river, before the alteration in the ships carrying to the port came in. In 1865, the trade was principally done by what is known as East Coast vessels, vessels that only carried 300 and 800 tons. Now it is done by vessels carrying upwards of 3,000 tons. If these improvements had not been made previously to the change in the commerce, Derry would have been out of the ports for all-round chartering.

3983. Therefore it would not, you think, be going too far to say, that whatever prosperity has come to Derry, it is not due to the operations of the Irish Society at least?—In my opinion, it has not been due to them. Whatever prosperity the port has enjoyed has been principally owing to the lands that have been let to middlemen, and to the energy of the Harbour Commissioners, as now constituted, in developing the port.

3984. You were asked several questions by the right honourable gentleman about the rents at which the fisheries were let, and you said, did you not, that you did not think they were let at a sufficiently high rent?—I do not think they are.

3985. Why did they not let them at a sufficiently high rent, in your opinion?—I cannot give you any reason for it.

3986. Do you think that they do not want to let them to anyone indiscriminately?—If they did they would advertise it and let it to the highest bidder. The general feeling is that there are a few families that are favoured.

3987. And, of course, those families would not be favoured if the thing were put up to competition?—They would be likely to have to pay the full market value.

3988. Is that your opinion?—That is my opinion.

3989. Is that the general opinion in Derry?—It is the general opinion freely expressed.

3990. In fact, the policy of the Society has been, so far as I can gather from your evidence, to favour the wealthy few?—I think they have shirked their duties of management. They have given it to those individuals to save themselves the trouble of management, because if they allot out these things to half a dozen people, instead of dealing with a hundred people, that is more easily done.

3991. Whatever the cause may have been, the result is that only the wealthy few are favoured?—Undoubtedly, that is the fact. I would not suppose that they would take up a pauper and make a large middleman proprietor of him.

3992. What is your opinion as to the effects of the distribution of the grants of the Irish Society at the present time; is it good?—No; it is very bad. It has a very demoralising influence altogether on the entire community. In fact, in my opinion, it is only a system of bribery.

3993. You called it, I think, a system of bribery?—Yes. In my opinion it is a system of bribery, and a very degrading system on the people altogether.

3994. Everything being given as alms, too, has that effect?—In the Society's own report there is a sum given to Professor Leebody of 50 *l.*, which is put under the head of "Charitable Donations."

3995. What does Professor Leebody do?—He is a Professor in Magee College. In their own published report that is put down as a charitable donation given to a man of the attainments of Professor

Mr. *Cleary*—continued.

Professor Leebody. I think it is a very degrading thing. I think, also, it is a very degrading thing for a man like his Lordship the Bishop of Derry to have to go out in full episcopal dress to the Irish Society at Government House to beg a few pounds of them.

3996. Does he do that?—He does; I have seen him there myself.

3997. What do you mean by "full episcopal dress"?—An apron and gaiters, and all of that sort of thing. Especially in the case of a man of the attainments of his Lordship William of Derry and Raphoe; I think it is a most degrading thing.

3998. You think that he ought to be able to demand it as a right?—Certainly, I do. I think it should be given in some other way. You will see that this, which is given for cathedral purposes, is also put under the head of charitable donations, and is acknowledged, as all charitable donations are, through the public press; and advertisements are published that So-and-so got 2 *l.* or 3 *l.*, and So-and-so got so much, and they thank the Society.

3999. Do you know anything about the case of Mr. Macartney, an agricultural tenant of the society?—I do.

4000. Do you know the facts of that case?—I do not know them of my own knowledge, because I am not so much mixed up in agricultural land as in building land.

4001. Did Mr. Macartney tell you them himself?—He did; I have heard them repeatedly.

Mr. *Lea*.

4002. You referred to the fisheries just now; do you know whether there are complaints from the fishermen with regard to the Irish Society?—Do you mean from the present lessees?

4003. No; I mean from the fishing community?—Of course, every person looks upon that as a grievance, but it would be interfering with the Society's rights. The people on the shores of Lough Foyle think that the fishery should be free to everybody. That is the grievance which is generally talked of.

4004. Forty years ago the fishermen could fish for all kinds of fish, could they not?—Not to my knowledge. I think the salmon fishery has always been a separate fishery, and owned by the Irish Society.

4005. Do you know whether the Irish Society let the fishery to Mr. Allen some years ago?—I do not; but I mind Mr. Allen having the fisheries; Mr. Allen and Mr. Gordon.

4006. Do you know where that fishery extended from and to?—It was said at that time that it extended from the mouth of Lough Foyle to Lifford Bridge.

4007. But you are not personally acquainted with the fisheries?—No; I do not know the boundaries of them.

4008. You said just now, I think, that you did not wish that the corporation should have the administration of this money?—No; I think anybody constituted as the corporation is at present, or under an extended franchise, would not be the proper people to manage it.

Mr. *Lea*—continued.

4009. Do you think that there should be some trustees specially appointed?—Yes, I do.

4010. Should they be appointed by the Government?—By the Government or by the Lord Chancellor. Trustees appointed by the Government or the Lord Chancellor would not be so easily got at, I think, to be pestered or worried by people asking them for small grants.

4011. I think you said just now that the Irish Society had only given one grant to Catholics: was that so?—That is so.

4012. I see in their accounts handed in last year that they gave to the new Roman Catholic seminary classical master 50 *l.*, also to an English master 50 *l.*, and to an assistant-master 25 *l.*?—That is the 125 *l.* that I mentioned. But if you compare that with what is given to the Foyle College, or the Magee College, or the Academical Institution, they get about four times that amount.

4013. What were you saying just now about Mr. Biggar?—Mr. Biggar's management contrasted very favourably with the Irish Society's management. Mr. Biggar has let his ground, and is getting the rent from it, and the town is benefiting by the increased rates, as the property is now built over.

4014. Mr. Biggar is a large merchant in Londonderry, I believe, is he not?—He is, and a cute, shrewd business man.

4015. He has contributed a good deal towards the prosperity of Derry?—Any man who does anything of that sort contributes to the prosperity of the place he is in.

Colonel *Laurie*.

4016. You complained of the fisheries being let at insufficient rents; do you know, as a matter of fact, how they were let originally to the present tenants?—I do not; but I have no recollection of its being an open competition.

4017. You do not know whether they were let by tender?—They may have been, but in my opinion the tenders were not publicly advertised to allow all sections of the community to compete if they felt so disposed.

Mr. *Sexton*.

4018. I understand you to say that you think this system demoralising?—Undoubtedly it is.

4019. You think that the administration by the Irish Society is very wasteful?—I do; I think that money given away for purposes such as they give it away for is very wasteful.

4020. And you think that the money is not applied to the very best use?—Certainly not.

4021. And it is given in a form which is humiliating to public sentiment?—Very much so.

4022. You do not think that the administration of a public trust of this kind ought to involve public humiliation?—I think it should not, but I think it is a misapplication of it altogether to give it for these religious and educational purposes in the way it is given, because it creates a great deal of sectarian animosity amongst the community, one section getting a large portion and the other none.

4023. You think that religious hostility is excited

Mr. Sexton—continued.

excited by the way in which this trust is administered?—Yes, I do; and it should have been entirely done away with years ago.

4024. You think that the views of King James, with regard to one religion or another, have no relation to the present condition of Ireland?—Certainly they have not.

4025. And that these funds should be devoted to other uses?—I think they should be devoted to the improvement of the land and the reduction of taxation, and then the whole population would participate in the benefit instead of a few.

4026. Uses in which the whole community, without regard to creed, would have an equal interest?—Yes. And in doing that you would do away with a great deal of sectarian feeling which now exists in Derry.

4027. You think that the present system tends to perpetuate sectarian feeling?—Certainly it does. There is no doubt in my mind that it has that effect.

4028. And in that way probably it acts in a spirit contrary to the first intention of the charter?—I do not know about what the intention of the charter was; but, in my opinion, it has a bad effect at the present time. What views people had 200 or 300 years ago is a different matter altogether.

4029. The charter was intended to have only one sect; but if there are to be more sects than one, they ought not to be at variance?—If the charter meant that it has miserably failed.

4030. I understand you to say that you would have not local trustees but Irish trustees?—Yes; men that know the country, and know the requirements of it; because it is evident that the London Corporation and the Irish Society do not know it, from their mode of management.

4031. And they should be men who are so situated as to be drawn by local wire-pulling into jobbery?—Quite so.

4032. If Parliament, by Act of Parliament, were to revise and define these trusts afresh, would you have the first trustees' names in the Act of Parliament?—Certainly; in the usual way they should be named.

Mr. JOHN WATNEY, sworn; and Examined.

Sir William Marriott.

4033. You are Clerk, I think, to the Mercers' Company?—Yes.

4034. And you have been clerk for some 14 years, I think?—Yes.

4035. The Mercers' Company, I think, is the premier company, is it not?—Yes.

4036. I suppose you, as clerk, know all about the affairs of the company, and are here to answer any questions that may be put to you?—Yes.

4037. I believe the Mercers' Company are quite willing to give any information in their power as to the origin of their title, and also as to the management of their estates?—Quite so.

4038. You have prepared, I think, a printed statement with regard to not absolutely the title, but the history of how the company became possessed of their land?—Yes.

4039. I do not know whether you wish it to be put in now or not, until we hear the arguments of counsel?—I understood the Right honourable Chairman to say just now, that it was not desirable to put in the statement; I have the documents of title here.

4040. Are these the original documents?—No, these are prints of them.

4041. Was the statement simply a digest of these documents?—Partly a digest of them, and partly a short history of the company's dealings with their properties since they came into their possession.

4042. What was your intention in drawing up that statement?—It was drawn up for the use of the Committee, putting the facts into a short form.

4043. And you proffer it if the Committee choose to accept it?—Yes. I should say perhaps that that statement was not prepared for the purposes of this Committee; it was prepared some ten years ago for a totally different purpose, and it has been slightly altered; but such as it is, it is at the service of the Committee if they wish to have it.

Mr. T. M. Healy.

4044. Is there any objection to an individual member of the Committee reading it over, supposing the whole Committee do not have it?—I am of course in the hands of the Committee. If the honourable Member wishes to read it I have no objection.

Sir William Marriott.

4045. The Mercers' Company I understand have not sold any of their property?—No, excepting one small freehold.

4046. Whereabouts was that, and what were the circumstances?—I have a plan of the Company's estate marked on the Ordnance sheet. I thought perhaps the Committee would like to see it. This (*producing a map*) is the Ordnance sheet of the north-east part of Ireland, and it includes the whole of the county of Londonderry. Then I have a smaller map here on a larger scale (*producing another map*), which gives so much of the county as our property is situated in, and also shows the railway which has been mentioned.

4047. Is that the Mercers' property which is marked pink on that map?—The part coloured pink is the property which the company now hold, and the part coloured brown is the part that was allotted to them, and which they have since sold as freeholds.

4048. When was that sold?—At the time when it was allotted, in 1618, I think.

4049. There have been no recent sales?—No recent sales. I do not know whether the Committee would like to look at this plan (*producing a third map*); it is a map of the old plantation made for the purposes of that plantation in 1609.

4050. Do-

Mr. John Ellis.

4050. Does the brown in this map include all that has been sold by the company since the original allotment?—The company created freeholds on the original purchase, and the brown shows the freeholds which they created. There are seven of them.

4051. And it includes everything that they have parted with since their original allotment?—Yes, everything; it includes the whole of the original allotment.

4052. The pink and the brown taken together include all the property that they ever possessed?—Yes.

4053. And the brown is what the company have parted with at any time?—Yes; it was parted with, in fact, before they got their conveyance.

4054. Could you give me the relative acreage of the brown and the pink?—The pink represents 21,000 acres; I cannot tell you exactly the acreage of the brown; but, as you see, it is not very large.

Sir William Marriott.

4055. With regard to your not selling the property, are the tenants willing to buy, or do they wish to remain as they are?—There has been no representation on the part of the tenants of the company that they wished to buy.

4056. Have the company made any inquiries?—The company have never offered to sell.

4057. And I believe, so far as you know, it is not their intention to sell?—No; I believe not.

4058. They have no wish to sell?—Dr. Todd approached the company some years ago with reference to a sale, but the negotiations went off.

4059. Can you give us some information with regard to their method of managing their estate?—The company have been in possession of their estate since 1831, when the last long lease ran out.

4060. Then until 1831 the estates were leased, and the company did not take any personal part in the management of them?—They were leased until 1831, and after that the long lease fell in.

4061. Since 1831 have the company managed the estate themselves?—Yes.

4062. Will you give us some information with regard to that?—The way in which the company have managed the expenditure on their estate has been general, for the benefit of the whole of the estate, and not particular, with reference to particular farms.

4063. Have they spent much money on the estate since 1831?—Yes; in 60 years since 1831, they have spent 300,000 *l.* in one way and another on the estate.

Mr. Sexton.

4064. I think this will be the time to suggest the question whether the company wish to put in any accounts; have you any accounts to put in?—I can put in the accounts if the Committee wish.

Sir William Marriott.

4065. Have you any objection on the part of the company to showing the accounts?—No.

Mr. Sexton.

4066. Could you let us have an abstract showing the gross and net receipts, and also the expenditure for public purposes for each year since 1831, and for two or three years, a full copy of your accounts?—Yes, I have here a summary of the expenditure made for the purpose of giving evidence before the Land Commission about eight or nine years ago. It has been brought up to the present time, and that shows the expenditure.

4067. Does it show the receipts?—It does not show the receipts.

4068. I would ask you for an annual abstract from the period at which you took up the estates in 1831 till now, of the gross and net receipts, and of the expenditure for public purposes; and for the last two or three years a full copy of your accounts?——

Sir William Marriott.

4069. Would that be an easy thing to do?—It is difficult to know what the honourable Member means by "public purposes."

4070. What does this account, which you produce, show?—This (*producing an account*) is a summary of the expenditure upon the Irish estate from 1831 to 1889, inclusive. It gives various details, and shows a total expenditure of nearly 300,000 *l.*

Mr. Sexton.

4071. That is not the kind of return I mean. I mean a return showing for each year the gross receipts and the net receipts, that is, the receipts after deducting the expenses of management; and then the amount expended upon what you call public purposes?——

Sir William Marriott.

4072. This shows the amount expended; but it does not show the receipts?—It is taken in periods of 10 years.

4073. Could you give us a return in the same form as the Irish Society have given us?—Yes, I have no doubt that I can.

4074. Have the company any objection to give this return?—No, I am here to give any information that the Committee wish.

> *Mr. Sexton.*] I have defined the return which I think the Committee ought to have; a return enabling them to ascertain the gross and net receipts, and also the gross expenditure for what the company believe to be public purposes, as distinguished from their own profit.

Sir William Marriott.

4075. (*To the Witness.*) Could you supply that?—I should rather put in the expenditure as it is, the return that I have handed in. That shows the whole of our expenditure on the estate.

Mr. Sexton.

4076. I want the receipts, the income; is there any objection to our having that information?—No; there is no objection to that. I can tell you the income now.

Sir William Marriott.

4077. What is the income now?—The present income is 9,700 *l.* a year.

4078. What was the income in 1831?—The rental of our middleman, Stewart, was 9,203 *l.* To compare that with the present rental, you must add the agents' fees, and the turf and bog fees, which were 6½ per cent., that comes to 495 *l.* a year, and 720 *l.* tithes, which formerly were paid by the tenant, but which under an Act passed about 1833 were thrown upon the landlords, that makes 10,443 *l.* That was the rent in 1831 before we took possession.

4079. What is the rent now?—The rent now is 9,700 *l.*

4080. Then it is less now than it was in 1831?—To compare it with 1831 you must deduct from the 9,700 *l.*, say, 600 *l.* a year which is the proceeds of land, formerly bog land, which was cut out and let to the tenants since.

4081. Have the company at any time raised their rents?—They reduced their rents in 1831 by 1,843 *l.*, or 18½ per cent.

4082. When did they raise them?—The custom on the estate was to have a re-valuation every 21 years; and in about 1854 they had a re-valuation, and the rent was then fixed at 10,111 *l.*; that is about 18 per cent. increase.

4083. Have they had another valuation since then?—Yes; they had another one in 1874–75.

4084. What did that bring it up to?—That brought it up to 11,749 *l.* That rent was reduced under the Land Act to 9,700 *l.*

4085. Did you go to the court or did you reduce it by agreement?—The greater part of the rents were reduced amicably; but a certain number went into the court.

4086. And the result was that whether by agreement or by going into court there was a reduction from 11,749 *l.* to 9,700 *l.*?—Yes; a reduction of 20 per cent.

4087. From that you deduct a certain amount for the turf, do you not?—Yes; I take that at 500 *l.* a year. It is difficult to say exactly what it is. I should say that 500 *l.* a year is a very low estimate.

4088. What would you put the present rental at?—If you deduct that, it would put the present rental at 9,200 *l.*, as compared with the rental in Stewart's time.

4089. You said just now, did you not, that the company had spent something like 300,000 *l.* upon this property?—Yes.

4090. That was out of the rental, I suppose?—That was out of the rental.

4091. They have spent that 300,000 *l.* since 1831?—Yes.

4092. And the rental is less than it was in 1831, by nearly 2,000 *l.*?—It is.

Mr. Sexton.

4093. What is the yearly income after the expenses of management are paid?—About 5,600 *l.* a year.

4094. What is the net-rental after paying the expenses of management?—The net-rental last year was 5,600 *l.*

4095. And the gross rental is 9,700 *l.*?—The gross rental is 9,700 *l.*

4096. What do you deduct from that in order to get the 5,600 *l.*?—The expenditure on the estate.

Mr. Sexton—continued.

4097. I only want the expenses of management, the net-income, without including these grants?—I cannot tell you that just now; but I can give it to you.

4098. You do not know what it costs you to collect this rent?—Yes, the expenses of management would be about 1,100 *l.* a year.

4099. Then deducting that from 9,700 *l.*, we get a net income of about 8,600 *l.* a year?—Yes, if you put it in that way; but there are other things that have to be paid as well. We have guaranteed 500 *l.* a year to the Derry Central Railway.

4100. What are your expenses of management?—The expenses of management, that is to say, the agents' fees, and so on, would come to about 1,100 *l.* a year.

Sir William Marriott.

4101. As regards this 300,000 *l.*, which has been spent; this document, I think, tell us how it has been spent?—Yes.

4102. It is for the benefit of the whole estate chiefly, I understand?—Yes. There is a very small expenditure on individual tenants.

4103. It is on subscriptions and things that you think benefit the whole estate?—Yes, and for tithes, &c. That is the whole expenditure on the estate.

4104. Have you ever had any complaints from your tenants about their holdings?—Yes, occasionally.

4105. What class of complaints?—Of course when the rental has been under revision, there have been complaints that the rental has been too high.

4106. Have you suffered much from arrears?—No.

4107. Are there any arrears now?—Practically, none. The whole arrears on the estate, taking the year to end on 31st of October, at the present time are not more than half a year's rent.

4108. Of course, on your estates like all other estates in Ireland, you have tenant right?—Yes.

4109. What has been the value of the tenant right during the last five years?—I suppose about 20 years' purchase on the rent.

4110. That, I suppose, shows that it is a prosperous estate?—Yes. I have every reason to believe that it is a very prosperous estate.

4111. On the religious question, I do not know whether you have any Roman Catholic chapels on your estate or not?—Yes, we have two on the estate, and one just off it.

4112. What is the prevailing religion; is it Roman Catholic, Presbyterian, or Episcopalian?—It is rather difficult to tell, exactly; but so far as I can form an opinion, I think there are about two-fifths Presbyterians, two-fifths Roman Catholics, and one-fifth Episcopalians.

4113. How many schools are there on the estate?—There are seven schools.

4114. What do they cost the company?—They cost the company now 400 *l.* a year. We pay

Sir William Marriott—continued.

pay the whole expense of the schools except what is paid by the National Board.

4125. There is no school rate, I believe, in Ireland?—No.

4126. Have the company built any schools since 1831?—Yes; they have built four, and partially re-built three.

4127. Before the company came into possession, in 1831, did they pay anything towards the schools?—Yes: from 1806 to 1831 the company paid on an average 118 *l.* a year to the schools out of a rental of 450 *l.*

4128. In your knowledge, has the estate improved very much since 1831, when it came under the company's management?—Of course I cannot go as far back as that; but I have known the estate for 20 years, and in that time it has very much improved.

Colonel *Laurie.*

4129. I think the income you mentioned just now was the gross income, less the expenditure which you have in this table; and the income of the estate was 5,800 *l.*?—Last year.

4130. That is the gross income, less the charges which I see in this table?—Yes.

4131. And those charges in this table are such as any liberal landlord in England or elsewhere, who had the welfare of the people living on it at heart, would expend on his estate?—The difference between the two countries I understand to be this: that in Ireland all the buildings are in the first instance made and kept in order by the tenants; whereas in England the custom is for the landlord to erect buildings.

4132. But these various expenses which you have been pointing to, with the exception of the one you mention, are those that every liberal landlord would incur in the management of property in almost every country?—I think so.

Mr. *Sexton.*

4133. I should like to put some questions to you after I have had time to look over this elaborate return. How often do your company make up their accounts?—Every year.

4134. Do you publish a statement?—No.

Mr. *Sexton*—continued.

4134. By whom?—By the court.

4135. At a meeting or before?—At a meeting held for the purpose.

4136. Will you put in a copy of the accounts which have been submitted to the court and audited, say, for the last five years?—Yes.

4137. What was the rent of the estate when you sub-let it in the last century?—It has always been sub-let; it has always been let on long leases.

4138. At what rent did you first sub-let it?—At 300 *l.* a year in 1638.

4139. What fine did you take then?—£. 300.

4140. What was the next sub-letting?—The next sub-letting was in 1714.

4141. At what rent?—£. 430.

4142. And the fine?—£. 6,000.

4143. What was the next sub-letting?—The next sub-letting was in 1755.

4144. At what rent?—£. 450.

4145. And the fine was, what?—£. 16,300. That was a lease for 61 years and three lives. The last life dropped in 1831.

4146. And there was no further sub-letting?—No.

4147. What rent did you find the lessee in receipt of when the title dropped, the rental representing 450 *l.* at the beginning of the term?—Taking the agents' fees and tithes, it represented 9,205 *l.*, and 488 *l.*, the agent's fees; that is 9,693 *l.*

4148. Therefore the total rent that he imposed was 9,692 *l.*?—Yes. Then there were the tithes in addition, which the tenants paid at that time, and which they paid at the beginning of the lease, too.

4149. What had made the improvements upon the estate?—I do not know anything about the estate before 1831.

4150. Have you the records of the company that indicate that you made improvements before that time?—I do not suppose we did, because we were not in possession.

4151. What improvements do you say you have made since?—Directly we came into possession we built an agent's house, so as to have a resident agent there; we have contributed towards the Derry Central Railway; and we have spent a very large sum of money in roads and drains.

Mr. *Sexton*—continued.

4159. Is there anything else?—We have kept up the dispensary; and then there is the drainage.

4160. The drainage of the Bann you have referred to?—No; that is a different thing; I mean the drainage of the estate.

4161. Where shall I find it in this return which you have handed in?—Under the item "Drainage."

4162. I see for the 50 years it was 6,300 *l.*?—Yes.

4163. That is about 100 *l.* a year?—£. 126 a year.

4164. That would execute a very moderate amount of drainage, I should think; can you point to any other improvement?—We built a corn mill and two churches.

4165. In regard to what we understand in Ireland, or in other countries, I suppose, as agricultural improvements, such as buildings, out-buildings, fencing, general drainage, and so forth, would you say that kind of improvement has been executed by the tenants?—I told the Committee just now that the *system* of the company was not to help individual tenants, but to improve their estate.

4166. Quite so; and by that do you indicate such work as the drainage of the Bann, keeping up the dispensary, and so forth?—Yes; building churches and draining the estate, and keeping up the roads.

4167. But I pointed out to you that the drainage was a very moderate item; something over 100 *l.* a year?—I do not know that; 120 *l.* a year is a considerable sum to be spent in drainage.

4168. We are dealing with the case where the rental has increased in the course of a century from 400 *l.* to 9,000 *l.*?—Our rental, but not the rental of the estate.

4169. Your rental in the last century was 400 *l.*, and now it is 9,000 *l.*?—Our rental, but not the rental of the estate.

4170. From the period when you say it was in your hands until now, the rental has gone up from a few hundreds to 9,000 *l.*, has it not?—The rental has decreased by 1,200 *l.* a year since the estate came into our hands.

4171. I am speaking of the time that you had the estate originally?—We had it originally in 1613.

4172. Since the beginning have the improvements upon the agricultural holdings, which increased their letting value, been made or not by the tenants?—I cannot tell you.

4173. In recent years who have built the dwelling-houses and the out-buildings, and made the fences?—In the last 50 or 60 years the tenants have made all the improvements; that is to say, all the improvements in buildings, with the exception of some allowances for slates, and so on. The company were in the habit of giving slates to a tenant who built a two-storey house.

4174. With the exception of those allowances for slates, and the 100 *l.* a year, or so, for drainage, all the great improvements upon this estate, which you have described, have been accomplished by the tenants themselves?—That you say; but I should like to refer to the sheet, which shows you what we spent upon the place.

4175. We have gone through the sheet, and I do not think you have indicated anything else?—I went through part of it.

4176. Can you indicate anything to qualify the statement that what is understood as agricultural improvements on the holdings on the estate have been made by the tenants?—So far as the holdings of the tenants are concerned, the tenants have made the improvements. So far as the estate is concerned, the company has spent 310,000 *l.* upon it in 60 years.

Mr. *John Ellis.*

4177. Since when?—Since 1831, in one way or another.

Mr. *Sexton.*

4178. That gives an average of 5,000 *l.* a year?—£. 5,000 a year.

4179. Your rental during that time has always exceeded 8,000 *l.*, has it not?—No, not always, it began at 6,500 *l.*

4180. In 1831?—In 1833; we fixed the rental in 1833 at 6,500 *l.*

4181. You increased it next to 10,000 *l.* later on?—Later on.

4182. And in 1874, I think?—In 1875 to 11,600 *l.*

4183. And that you levied until the Land Act?—That we levied until the Land Act.

4184. As regards the expenses of management during that time, what have they averaged?—During the 60 years they averaged 1,347 *l.*

4185. So that after paying the expenses of management, your receipts have been from 8,000 *l.* to 10,000 *l.* a year?—Taking that item off, of course.

4186. Out of that 8,000 *l.* to 10,000 *l.* a year you have expended, on an average, 5,000 *l.* a year upon the estate?—Yes.

4187. How have you expended the balance?—It has gone into the company's general account.

4188. How is the general account applied?—I do not think I am prepared to answer a question of that sort.

The Committee-room was cleared.

After a short time the parties were again called in.

Mr. *Sexton.*

4189. The balance of your annual income from the Irish estate, after payment of the expenditure noted in this return, goes into the general account of the company, I understand?—Yes.

4190. Is any portion of that general account expended for Irish purposes?—I can hardly answer that question. We give donations for Irish purposes sometimes; but I am not prepared to answer the question off-hand.

4191. This is solely expenditure upon your Irish estates, I understand; do you make any grants or payments for public purposes in Ireland except those stated in this return?—No, not for public purposes.

4192. For any purposes?—As I said, I am not prepared to answer that question.

4193. Do

Chairman.

4193. Do you mean that you do not know?—I do not know at the moment. I can find out, I daresay, but at present I am unable to tell you.

Mr. Sexton.

4194. You cannot at present say whether or not any money is expended out of your general account for Irish uses?—I should think not; but I should not like to say so absolutely.

4195. Is your general account drawn upon for public or benevolent uses in England?—I think on that point I should like to refer the Committee to the accounts which were rendered to Lord Derby's Commission; and beyond that I have not come here to give any evidence as to what we do with our money in England.

4196. That was six years ago?—Yes.

4197. Have you no answer to give as to the period that has since elapsed?—I should prefer not to answer at present as to that.

4198. Do you mean that you refuse?—I should prefer not to answer.

Chairman.

4199. You could bring the account you submitted to Lord Derby' Commission in 1884 down to date, I presume?—It could be done, of course.

4200. If you saw no objection to laying that account before Lord Derby's Commission, what objection is there to giving it to us?—I did not lay it before Lord Derby's Commission; it was my company.

4201. I do not mean you personally; I mean your company?—I do not think I am justified in answering any questions with regard to what the company does with its money in England. I have come here to speak with regard to the Irish property.

4202. You said just now that your company had laid a certain account before Lord Derby's Commission; I ask you what possible objection your company can have to giving us the same account, brought up to date?—That is a question my company must answer, and not I.

4203. Are not you here to answer for your company?—Not on questions relating to the expenditure of their income.

4204. I am not asking you as to the expenditure of income, but as conducting the business of the Committee, I ask whether there can be any objection to producing the exact account which there was no objection to laying before Lord Derby's Commission, brought up to date. We were told this morning that you were coming here to speak for the company?—As regards their Irish estate.

4205. Certainly; and with regard to the facts bearing upon their Irish estate?—Yes.

4206. Reference has been made by yourself to that account which was tendered to Lord Derby's Commission; why should not we have that account brought up to date and produced here?—I shall be very happy to ask my company if they will put in such accounts, but I cannot do it myself.

4207. I think we may be content that you must ask your company to be kind enough to inform us upon that point?—Yes.

Mr. Sexton.

4208. You appear to forget already that you undertook, first of all, to hand in, for the information of the Committee, copies of the annual accounts which, for the last five years, were submitted to your court. Do you intend to revoke immediately the undertaking you have given us upon oath, to submit to us copies of the annual accounts of income and expenditure of the company submitted to the court of the company and audited, for the last five years, I mean the annual accounts of the income and expenditure?—I am not sure that I did not give an undertaking which I was not justified in giving. Upon that point I should like to ask my company's authority.

Chairman.

4209. Do you withdraw from the undertaking you gave?—I did not quite understand at the time the effect of the undertaking I gave, and I should like to consider that point, if the Committee will allow me.

Sir William Marriott.

4210. What did you mean when you said, in reply to Mr. Sexton, that you would give us the accounts of the last five years?—What I intended to give was a statement of the income in one line and a statement of the expenditure in another.

4211. Of what?—Of the Irish estates.

Mr. Sexton.

4212. Are there two sets of accounts submitted to your court every year, or one?—There is the Irish account. The Irish accounts are audited every year, and the balance of the Irish accounts goes into the general funds of the company. There is another set of accounts submitted, the general account of the company, including the balance of the Irish account.

4213. You have a regular account of income and expenditure for the Irish estate?—Yes.

4214. And also a general account?—Yes.

4215. Did you during your absence from the room consult with anyone?—I spoke to my master, who was in the room.

4216. What did you ask him?—I do not know that I asked him anything. I think he spoke to me.

4217. What did he say?—He said he thought it would not be desirable to give the details of the expenditure of our English property.

4218. That it was not desirable to give the information which you had just said you would give?—No, I beg your pardon; that is a very different thing.

4219. I asked you if you would furnish to the Committee the accounts of the income and expenditure submitted to your company, and you said you would; but now you say your master told you it would not be desirable?—No; I do not think we quite understand each other. What I undertook to do, as I understand it, was to give the Committee a statement of the income and expenditure on the Irish estate, and the way I should have done that would have been to have given the income in one line and the expenditure in another, in each year, and brought down the balance.

4220. You would simply have given the gross income

Mr. Sexton—continued.

income and gross expenditure, without any particulars?—Yes, of the Irish estate.

4221. You transfer the profit-balance every year, whatever it is, from the Irish account to the general account?—Yes.

4222. Can you inform the Committee upon what principle your court has classified the expenditure between the Irish account and the general account?—There is no classification of the expenditure at all.

4223. Do you arrive by any principle at the total amount of expenditure upon the Irish estate?—Yes; we have the other companies associated with us in the Irish estate, and we have to give them an account every year, and this table I have produced here to-day is the result of that account.

4224. Do they give you their accounts?—They have no accounts.

4225. I mean the other companies?—They have no accounts. We keep the accounts for them, and hand over the balance every year.

4226. You mean the companies associated with you in your particular estate?—Yes; that is what I said.

4227. But I wish, if possible, to obtain from you this information: you, having an income of 9,700 *l.* a year, upon what principle, if any, do you allot a part of the profit of that income to Irish uses, and the balance to uses which, so far as I can discover from you, are not Irish?—The balance of the income, after the expenditure made in Ireland, goes into the general funds of the company, and is spent in such a way as the company think fit.

4228. Out of Ireland?—In any way they please.

4229. Out of Ireland?—In any way they please.

4230. It is not spent in Ireland?—It is spent in any way the company please, whether in England or Ireland or anywhere.

4231. Is it spent in Ireland?—I told you just now that I am not quite prepared to answer you that now, from want of knowledge.

Chairman.

4232. That is a question absolutely vital to our inquiry. We are directed to inquire into "The trusts and obligations, if any, attaching to the ownership of such estates." Now, it is most germane to that inquiry that we should know, I do not say how you spend the funds in your general account, but that we should know what proportion of your receipts from Ireland is spent in Ireland. I mentioned that point, which seemed to me a clear one, to Dr. Freshfield before our proceedings began to-day. What Dr. Freshfield said is not binding on you, of course, but Dr. Freshfield saw no difficulty in it then, and I cannot conceive how you can suppose we are to inquire into the discharge of your duties, or alleged duties, in Ireland, if we are not to know what proportion of the funds received in Ireland has been expended in Ireland; and, therefore, I must really press you to answer that question; because it is not a question to which you objected?—I thought I had answered the question already by handing in this sheet.

Mr. Sexton.

4233. If that is so there is no difficulty before you?—Would you allow me to conclude my answer. I also said I was not prepared, from want of knowledge, to say exactly whether any other money had been spent in Ireland than is shown in this sheet. My impression is that if there is any, it is very small. The Committee shall have the evidence if they wish it, but at the moment I cannot give it.

4234. You rather think there is none, and if there is any, it is very small?—It is a small amount, I think; I could get the information, but I do not want to pledge myself to it.

Sir William Marriott.

4235. What is wanted is to know whether the 4,000 *l.* goes into the general fund as Irish or English?—Practically, English objects.

Mr. Sexton.

4236. Then out of this 9,000 *l.* about one-half only is spent in Ireland?—Yes; that is what it comes to.

4237. Do you consider, together with your associated companies, what proportion of your income ought to be spent in Ireland, or how do you fix the expenditure in Ireland?—The associated companies have each a very small interest in the estate that they do not interfere in any way with the management; they leave the management entirely to us.

4238. That is to say, the court?—Yes, the court.

4239. The general body of freemen does not interfere, I presume?—No; very little.

4240. How many members are there in the court?—The court is at the present time about seven or eight and twenty.

4241. How has it been the practice of the court to determine how much of this income they ought to spend in Ireland, and how much they ought to reserve for English uses?—Every matter that comes before them is dealt with on its merits.

4242–3. And they appropriate, therefore, their income from the Irish estate to Ireland, so far as the merits of the applications become apparent?—Yes; it is not all appropriated on application.

4244. They would not reject any application from Ireland that they thought meritorious?—I think not, from their estate; I do not know that I could say from Ireland.

4245. Did all your tenants go into the Land Court?—No; some of them went into the Land Court, and we settled with the others.

4246. What proportion had their rents fixed by the Land Court?—I should think, perhaps, a sixth; perhaps not so many; not more than a sixth, certainly.

4247. What reduction did the court direct in the rents?—I do not know; the reduction altogether was about 20 per cent.

4248. That confounds those who went in with those who did not, as I understand?—I have no means of telling them separately.

4249. Did the court give a larger reduction, in the cases before the court, than you did upon the other cases?—I think it was very much the same.

in

Mr. *Sexton*—continued.

in some cases it was, of course, a very much larger proportion, and in others less.

4250. Have you made any offers to sell?—No.

4251. Have the tenants made any overtures to buy?—No.

4252. None?—Dr. Todd made overtures.

4253. Was he authorised by the tenants?—We could not find out that he was; there was no application made by the tenants to buy.

4254. Are you willing to sell?—I cannot answer that question; the company have not the matter before them.

4255. Have they had it before them?—They have had it before them, once or twice, and they have refused to sell.

4256. What do you mean by "they refused to sell"?—Dr. Todd asked them to sell to him, and the company refused.

4257. The refusal was due, then, to the circumstance that they did not think him an authorised agent?—Yes; they did not think he was authorised by the tenants. The company's agent did not tell them there was any general feeling; in fact, he told them there was no general feeling among the tenants to purchase.

4258. If there were such a feeling, you would not be unwilling to negotiate?—I do not know.

4259. You sold one piece of freehold at one time, did you not?—We sold one of the freeholds. The owner sold it to his tenants, and he had to make a title, and he could not make the title without buying up the pound Irish, which we got for it.

4260. When was that?—The negotiation is just completed; the purchase has not actually been completed yet.

4261. Have you got the money?—No.

4262. How much of it?—A pound Irish, that is 18 s. 6 d., or something like that.

4263. I was going to ask whether you would put it into the general account; but if that is the amount I do not think it matters very much?—It is only a pound Irish.

Mr. *Clancy*.

4264. Why do you refuse to give an account of how all this which goes into the general account is spent?—I have said, practically, half the income is spent in England, and half in Ireland.

4265. I want to know how it is spent in England; is that knowledge within your procurement?—Of course; I am clerk to the company, and I have the company's books under my control.

4266. Are there materials in your possession to enable you to tell us how you spend that money which you say goes into the general account?—The books are in the company's possession, not in mine.

4267. Have you in your possession the materials for telling us how the money is spent which goes into the general account?—The materials are in the company's possession.

4268. Are they sufficient to enable you to give us the information we wish for on this point?—The company keep a proper account.

4269. Do you refuse to answer the question? —The company keep proper accounts of their receipts and expenditure.

Mr. *Clancy*—continued.

4270. Do you refuse to answer the question, whether there are materials in your possession sufficient to enable you to tell us how the money is spent that goes into the general account? —The accounts are in the company's possession, and not in mine.

4271. Are there materials in the company's possession?—No doubt.

4272. Sufficient materials?—No doubt.

4273. If that is so, does the company refuse to tell us how it is spent?—I very respectfully submit that that question is not before this Committee, and I have not come prepared to answer that question. I am unable to answer.

4274. Do you refuse to answer?—I am unable to answer.

4275. You do not know whether they will refuse or not?—I do not know.

4276. At all events, you refuse yourself?—I am unable to answer the question.

4277. If you had the information you would not give it us?—I have not the information.

Chairman.

4278. Will you tell us this much, and if you answer this (and I can see no difficulty in the way of your doing so) it will, perhaps, end this controversy. May we take it that the items of the general account are items of expenditure on public purposes?—Partly.

4279. But would you say mainly; what part would you say? I do not want you to give it as to a fraction, but pretty close?—I do not think that the Committee ought to press me upon that.

Mr. *Lawson*.

4280. Might I ask whether the surplus income from the Irish estate is ear-marked, and devoted to a particular purpose?—It is not.

4281. It is put into the general account?—Into the general account.

Mr. *Sexton*.

4282. Have you any objection to say whether the general account is mainly or generally devoted, not to uses of individual profit, but to what might be called either public or benevolent uses?—As I said before, partly it is.

4283. You would not say mainly?—I would rather say partly. I can give you the reference to the statement before Lord Derby's Commission if you wish it.

Sir *William Marriott*.

4284. Can you show us the return that was presented to Lord Derby's Commission?—I am not quite sure that I have that volume here; it is in the second volume, and I have only got the first volume here.

Chairman.

4285. We shall look into the form of account you laid before Lord Derby's Commission, and we shall certainly claim to have that account made up to date, and laid before us; because, if there was no reason why it should not be presented to Lord Derby's Commission, there can be no reason

Chairman—continued.

reason why it should not be laid before us; if it comes within our discretion, and we think fit to demand it?—The return is in the second volume.

Mr. *Clancy*.] Is it understood that we are to have a continuation of the account presented to Lord Derby's Commission.

(*Chairman*.) Yes, if we find that the account affects our inquiry.

Mr. Clancy.

4286. Can you tell us how the sum which you say is spent in Ireland is actually spent?—I have put in a sheet which shows that.

4287. Can you tell us generally?—I answered one of the Members of the Committee a similar question: we have built the agent's residence; we have contributed to the navigation of the Bann; we have spent money on a bathing infirmary, which was practically a cottage hospital; we have kept up the dispensary; I think I have given all that before.

Chairman.

4288. Will you hand in that statement which you have produced?—Yes. (*The same was handed in.*)

Mr. Clancy.

4289. Is there any money expended upon education or schools?—Yes.

4290. How much?—About 400 *l.* a year.

4291. Have you done anything to promote manufactures?—No.

4292. Have you ever?—We have only one manufactory on the estate; some flax mills which are held by a Mr. Clark; he built the mills himself. We have built a corn mill.

4293. You have done nothing to improve manufactures on the estate?—No.

4294. Have all your tenants held under the Ulster custom?—Yes; the farm tenants, certainly.

4295. Have there been complaints from the tenants that the Ulster custom was eaten into?—I do not remember that.

4296. How long have you been connected with the company?—For 14 years as clerk.

4297. During all that time there have been no complaints from tenants as to the tenant-right having been eaten into by the increase in rent in the rent, or the higher rent?—Whenever the rent has been increased, as I told the Committee, there have been complaints by the tenants, but they have always come in and paid.

4298. That is to say, they came in and paid when you threatened them with eviction?—I do not think it went so far as that.

4299. With writs of ejectment?—I do not think it went so far as that. We have always been on very amicable terms with our tenantry.

4300. Do you say you have been on very amicable terms?—Yes.

4301. Were the complaints very numerous?—No.

4302. Were they general?—No; I should say not. Of course, nobody likes to have his rent raised.

4303. Were there complaints of the tenant right having been eaten into by increases of rent or by higher rents, confined to a few cases?—None of the tenants liked to have their rents raised, but I cannot tell you how many people complained. I daresay a great many did, but they all came in and they all paid.

4304. Did you ever issue solicitor's letters for rent?—Yes.

4305. Frequently?—Yes, I should think so, on an estate of 1,200 tenants.

4306. Have you to do so in many cases?—We have to do so occasionally. I cannot say in how many cases.

4307. Have you had to do so every year?—Yes.

4308. Have you many cases on the average every year?—I cannot tell; that is a detail of management which does not come before me.

4309. Who is the officer of the society who could tell us that?—The company's agent could probably tell you.

4310. Shall we have him here?—If the Committee wish for him he could come over.

4311. Have writs for the recovery of rent or possession been frequent on the estate?—I do not think they have been frequent. If they have been frequent we should have heard of them in England.

4312. Are there some every year?—I have no doubt there are some every year. As I told the Committee, when you were absent, we have practically no arrears on the estate.

4313. Have you taken legal steps to have the rents collected year by year?—We have very little difficulty in collecting them in Ireland.

4314. Have you ever made any abatement of rent?—Not since the Land Act. The Land Act fixed our rents.

4315. Have there, since that time, been demands for abatement of rent?—No; I think not.

4316. None?—No.

4317. Not since 1882?—Not since the rents were fixed under the Land Act.

4318. Not even in 1886 when there was a general depression in agriculture?—I do not think so.

4319. Have there been no complaints at all as to the rents since 1882?—I do not think there have been any complaints that have come over to England.

4320. Are complaints made that are not transmitted to England?—I do not know; I cannot tell you.

4321. Is your agent bound to send such complaints over to England; has he a local discretion?—He would have to send over the complaints that were made, but if a man came into the estate office and complained about his rent, he would hardly send that over.

4322. Those are the complaints that I am asking about. You do not know how many of those complaints were made?—I cannot tell you.

4323. For all you know the tenants may be complaining one by one in that way, almost every one of them every year?—I do not know one way or the other.

4324. Then you can hardly say, can you, that you and your tenants are on very amicable terms?

Mr. Clancy—continued.

terms?—I think we are on very amicable terms, because we have no arrears.

4325. But it is quite possible not to be on amicable terms, and yet have no arrears. If you were a harsh landlord you know you would have collected very probably every penny of the rents?—Yes; but we are not harsh landlords.

Mr. Lea.

4326. We have heard very little evidence with regard to the Mercers' Company, I think, but there were one or two things I should like to have cleared up. With regard to leases, I think it was alleged you refused to give long leases; is that so?—I do not remember any allegation of that sort.

4327. What was the length of the leases you gave for building?—We are giving 99 years.

4328. Have you always given 99 years?—No; we used to give 61 years, I think.

4329. What did you do before that?—They are the only leases we have given.

4330. It was alleged, I think, that manufactures could not be established in consequence of the length of the leases; is that so?—I do not think that was alleged so far as our estate was concerned.

4331. It was also alleged that you refused to give leases for Presbyterian manses. Is that so?—I think not. I do not think that was alleged.

4332. Does the 500 *l.* a year cover the amount you give for railways, including everything?—£. 250.

4333. I thought you said you were liable for 500 *l.* a year?—Yes. I beg your pardon. It is 250 *l.* a year.

4334. Have you invested any money besides that in railways in Ireland?—No. The Derry Central is the only railway that comes anywhere near our property.

4335. One allegation was made with respect to the Mercers' Company about the drainage of the Clady river. Application was made by the tenants for drainage purposes. Did the Mercers' Company refuse to give a grant for the Clady river?—Yes.

4336. May I ask why?—I believe the reason was that they did not consider that anything could be done with that river until the obstructions lower down were removed, and that if these obstructions were removed there would be no difficulty in the water getting away.

4337. It was stated that two neighbouring landlords were willing to subscribe their share, but the Mercers' Company refused; is that correct?—Yes, that is correct.

4338. Is it the obstruction on the Bann that you refer to?—No, the obstruction is not on the Bann; it is in this little river between our estate and the Bann.

4339. Does not your estate go down to the Bann?—Not in that part.

4340. With regard to dispensaries, have you withdrawn any grants given to dispensaries on your estate?—At the time of the grant in 1830, or 1831, there was no medical man on the estate at all, and there was no Poor Law, and the company established two dispensaries in their villages for the benefit of their tenants. They paid a salary to two medical men to induce them to settle there, and to induce them to come to the estate. One of them retired from old age, and he was pensioned off; the other one died the other day after being, I think, between 50 or 60 years on the estate. Long before he died the Poor Law came into operation in Ireland, and now there are Poor Law doctors who look after the poor people on the estate.

4341. You think that does instead of a grant?—It does, to a certain extent. The company give a small grant to the successor of the gentleman I mentioned.

4342. Would not that be a fair way of spending the 5,000 *l.* a year you spend upon the estate?—I see no objection to spending it in that way, or any other way; one way is as good as the other.

4343. I think there were four associated companies, one of them being the Innholders?—Yes, there were four originally; but the Innholders dropped out in some way.

4344. Have you bought the interest of any of those four?—The Innholders dropped out; they paid the first instalment under the precepts from the City, but they did not pay anything more, and they dropped out in some way; the others are still going on.

4345. Are the Cooks one of the associated companies?—Yes, the Cooks, the Embroiderers, and the Masons.

4346. Does their share amount to about a fourth?—The Cooks paid 300 *l.*, the Embroiderers, 235 *l.*, and the Masons, 150 *l.*, that is 685 *l.* out of the 5,000 *l.*

4347. Do they receive a due proportion of the rent according to that sum?—Yes.

4348. Then do they acquiesce in all the expenditure of the money on the estate in Ireland?—They have never interfered with the management of the estate by the Mercers' Company.

4349. They are satisfied with your management?—They are satisfied.

4350. What have you done with regard to the timber on the Mercers' estate?—There is no timber there; there are a few trees which shelter the houses, and there are two or three copses; but I do not suppose there is 500 *l.* worth of timber on the whole estate.

4351. I suppose you consider it is acting fairly to spend half of the income on the Irish estate?—That is not a question which I can answer, and perhaps the Committee will excuse me from answering it.

4352. You do spend half on the Irish estate?—We spend half.

Mr. Clancy.

4353. Here is a statement which has appeared in print; will you tell me whether it is true or not: "The Mercers re-valued their estate in 1858, and again in 1878. On the latter occasion the tenants putting their trust in the Land Act of 1870, the provisions of which they hoped would protect their expenditure, resisted; 63 test cases were evicted by the company, and the defeated

Mr. Clancy—continued.

distressed tenant had to pay 831 *l.* costs." Is that true or not?—I cannot tell you off-hand.

4354. Who could tell us?—I could find out, but I cannot tell you off-hand.

Chairman.

4355. Will you kindly look into the matter of the account laid before Lord Derby's Commission before the next sitting of the Committee?—Would you wish me to send you that account?

4356. I think it would be just as well; perhaps you would also look up the answer to Mr. Clancy's last question?—I understand you wish me to take the instructions of my company as to whether the account is to be brought down to the present time?

4357. Yes; as to whether there can be any objection to presenting to us the same account that was laid before Lord Derby's Commission, brought up to date?—I will do so. I have some further documents here about which I do not

Chairman—continued.

wish to make my remarks; perhaps I may put them in.

4358. If you will give me a list of them I will look over it, and let you know next time?—Certainly.

Mr. Mates.] In relation to what was said this morning as to date when the Irish Society's case would be taken next week, I was under the impression that the evidence against the Irish Society was closed; but I understand that something was said about another witness coming here.

Chairman.] That is true. On Thursday we are to have more evidence, which will be, I take it, the last, as against the Irish Society. The case against the Irish Society, as I gather, will be closed on Thursday evening, so that it will be well if you can be ready on Friday.

Mr. Mates.] Thank you, Sir.

Thursday, 10*th July* 1890.

MEMBERS PRESENT:

Mr. Clancy.	Mr. Lea.
Lord Elcho.	Sir William Marriott.
Sir John Ellis.	Mr. John Morley.
Mr. John Ellis.	Mr. Sexton.
Mr. T. M. Healy.	Sir Richard Temple.
Colonel Laurie.	

THE RIGHT HONOURABLE JOHN MORLEY, IN THE CHAIR.

Mr. EDWARD A. HAMILTON, sworn; and Examined.

Chairman.

4359. WHAT body are you here to represent?—I am Secretary of the Londonderry Port and Harbour Commissioners.

4360. When was that body incorporated?—They were incorporated in the year 1854. I have been their secretary for the past seven years, and I have been connected with the board, in various capacities, since their incorporation in 1854.

4361. The Commissioners, I believe, took certain steps in regard to the river frontage; will you tell us what those steps were?—After I arrived in London, yesterday evening, I jotted down, for my own information, the leading features of the transactions between the Society and the Commissioners, and I think, if you would allow me just to state them to you, you would perhaps get the greater part of all the information I could give you, in the shortest possible time.

4362. Will you give us clearly what those statements, which you jotted down last night, point to?—They first of all state the Acts of Parliament and the power which the Commissioners have under them.

4363. You misunderstand me. I did not express myself clearly. I wanted to know what, in short, you would be driving at in this statement. Is it an account of the relations between the Harbour Commissioners and the Irish Society?—What I have jotted down shows the powers of the Commissioners, what they have done, and the assistance they have received from the Irish Society in carrying out the works.

4364. First of all will you tell us, with regard to the powers of the Commissioners?—The Commissioners were incorporated in the year 1854, by an Act, entitled, "The Londonderry Port and Harbour Act," and under that Act they were authorised to construct an uniform line of quays, docks, and various other works. All piers, jetties, lights, buoys, and other property belonging to the Ballast Office Committee, were vested in the Commissioners. For the purpose of laying up the river frontage and carrying out the works authorised by the Act, the Commissioners were authorised to borrow a sum not exceeding 150,000 *l.*, and they were authorised to levy rates on shipping, and on goods imported and exported, to pay the interest on the money borrowed, and to maintain the harbour and works. In the year 1874 the Commissioners procured another Act of Parliament. That Act of Parliament sets forth, "Whereas it would be for the advantage of trade and shipping resorting to the port, if the further powers in this Act contained were conferred upon the Commissioners." Accordingly further powers were conferred upon the Commissioners, and their borrowing powers were extended to 230,000 *l.*

Chairman—continued.

4365. Their borrowing powers were extended from 150,000 *l.* to 230,000 *l.*?—Yes. In the year 1883, another Act was obtained which conferred further powers, and authorised the leasing of the ship-building yard. Under the provisions of these Acts the Commissioners purchased land, built quays, docks, tramways, sheds, cranes and other cranes, offices, ship-building yard, and they dredged and improved the harbour, upon which altogether they expended a sum of 236,000 *l.*

4366. Within what period?—From their incorporation up to the 31st of December last.

4367. That is to say from 1854 to 1889?—Yes. The bond debt of the Commissioners on the 31st December last, which represents their sole liabilities, amounted to 180,000 *l.* The revenue of the board at present is about 13,000 *l.* per annum. As illustrating the progress of the port, I will just mention that in the year 1840 the registered tonnage of shipping entering the port was 64,000 tons, and last year it was 297,000 tons.

4368. That increase would of course have been impossible but for the expenditure by your Commissioners?—I should think so. A ship-building yard has been established, and is in successful operation at the present time, and has been for some years past, and very fine iron and steel ships are built there; at the present moment there is a steamer of between 3,000 and 4,000 tons ready to launch. One ship was launched about 10 days ago, and there are several others in course of construction.

Chairman—continued.

4369. We may take it, without going into details further, that the operations of the Commissioners have been very successful, and very conducive to the prosperity of Londonderry?—I have stated these facts for the purpose of showing that that is all I have got to say upon that matter. I then proceed to the next point, which is the assistance which the Society has given the Commissioners in carrying out these works. The first assistance was a grant of the Society's reversionary interest in the land for the quays and docks.

4370. Reversionary on the expiry of the leases, I suppose?—On the expiry of the leases. The Society stipulated in their grant that the tenants and the lessees of the Society should be compensated for their interest. Now, I believe I am safe in saying, in the majority of cases, the leases were in perpetuity, and consequently the compensation amounted to a very large sum.

4371. Consequently, also, the grant of the reversion on the perpetuity leases was not of very substantial value, I presume?—It was of very little value; that will appear afterwards. We paid altogether in compensation to the tenants of the Society 67,000 *l.* The Society at the same time made us a grant of 1,000 *l.* per annum for seven years after the passing of the Act of Incorporation.

4372. The grant of 1,000 *l.* for seven years was, I suppose, a grant at pleasure, given annually; or was it a grant promised for seven years from the start?—It was a grant promised for seven years.

4373. Not an annual grant?—It was a grant of 1,000 *l.* a year for seven years, paid annually. Immediately after the passing of the Act of 1854, the solicitor of the Society, Mr. Pearson, and the solicitor of the Harbour Commissioners, Mr. Crawford, entered into correspondence with a view of settling how the powers in the Act were to be carried out, and to what extent the Society would assist the Commissioners in doing so. A deputation also waited upon the Society at that time.

4374. A deputation from the Commissioners?—A deputation from the Commissioners. It was pointed out to the Society that it would be very unwise at that early stage to burden the trade of the port with heavy taxation; and the Society recognised this fact, and in consequence they gave the grant of 1,000 *l.* a year, which I have referred to. At that same time the Society agreed to give the Commissioners the reversionary interest that I have referred to, and they stipulated that the tenants and the lessees of the company should be compensated for their interest, that the compulsory powers of the Act should not be exercised against the Society, and that the works authorised by the Act should be carried out within the period allowed in the Act for their completion, and that otherwise the grant would be void. With the exception of the reclamation of the slob-land for ship-building purposes, the works were carried out within the period allowed by the Act. As regards the reclamation of the slob-land the time expired in 1864; that was 10 years after the passing of the Act.

4375. What do you mean by saying that the time expired?—There was a provision in the Act limiting the time within which the works were to be completed; and the period for the reclamation of that slob-land was 10 years, which expired in 1864. At that time the Commissioners had contracted for the reclamation of the ground, and the work was actually proceeding, when the Society notified the Commissioners that the grant of the land was void, they having failed to complete the works within the period; and they procured an injunction in Chancery, and stopped the works. The relations between the Society and the Commissioners consequently for some years were somewhat strained.

4376. After 1864?—After 1864. In 1873 the Commissioners considered that the progress of the port was being stopped, and that they would not submit any longer to such a state of things. Accordingly they applied to Parliament for compulsory power to take this slob-land from the Society, and to continue the works that had been stopped by the Society in 1864. That Bill was very strongly opposed by the Irish Society and by their fishery lessees.

4377. This request for Parliament to give the Commissioners the power of taking this slob-land against the will of the Irish Society was strenuously opposed by the Irish Society?—It was, and when it was before the Committee of the House of Lords, after the case had proceeded some length, the Chairman of the Committee said they had resolved to adjourn for a few days, and in the meantime they advised the counsel for the Society to meet the Commissioners and endeavour to come to some arrangement. That was done. A meeting was held, and the result of that meeting was that the Society agreed to convey to the Commissioners the slob-land that they requested for ship-building purposes, if the compulsory powers sought in the Act were withdrawn. Accordingly the clauses were withdrawn, and the conveyance of that slob-land was subsequently made to the Commissioners.

4378. In other words, the Irish Society granted in substance what was asked, but they granted it under a more agreeable form?—Yes.

4379. That operation, I suppose, involved your Commissioners in considerable cost?—Yes; that Bill cost us over 4,000 *l.*

4380. That was spent in attempting to make the Irish Society do what they afterwards agreed to do?—Yes. Of course there were other powers in the Bill besides the ship-building clauses. The Commissioners on obtaining that Act, proceeded with the reclamation of the ground, and built a ship-building yard upon it, which is now in successful operation, as I have already explained.

4381. Did the Commissioners get the power by this arrangement with the Irish Society to grant long leases?—We obtained power in the Act of 1882 to let the ship-building yards for the period of 31 years.

4382. But by the arrangement of 1874 you had

Chairman—continued.

had not that power?—No; the power was obtained in the Act of 1872.

4383. In connection with the Bill of 1882, did the Society again oppose the Commissioners?—They did.

4384. As in 1874?—Yes; they never appeared in the House, because we entered into negotiations, and the clauses of the Bill were amicably settled.

4385. You said that what happened in 1874 involved you in 4,500 *l.* costs; did the opposition of the Irish Society to the Bill of 1882 involve any expenditure?—Yes; 2,500 *l.* was the cost of that Bill. In that Act powers were taken for extensive improvements of the navigable channel, and particularly for the erection of a training wall for confining the tide at low water. This was a scheme which was strongly recommended by many eminent engineers, Sir John Hawkshaw among them. The obligations and restrictions upon the Commissioners introduced into the Bill, however, were such that, on looking into the matter subsequently, it was thought possible that heavy claims for consequential damage if this wall were constructed might arise, and the Commissioners were obliged to abandon the training wall altogether. They therefore abandoned the wall which was authorised by the Act of 1882.

4386. What else did your Commissioners do, besides this matter of wall-building that you have mentioned, under the powers of that Act; did they do any dredging?—The ship-building yard and extensive dredging have been carried out under the powers of that Act; but the training-wall (which is the principal feature, so far as the improvements went) was obliged to be abandoned, owing to the obligations that were placed upon the Commissioners in that Act.

4387. Let us see how far we have got, and how much the Irish Society have done. In 1854 they promised you 1,000 *l.* a year for seven years?—Yes.

4388. That grant, therefore, expired in 1861. What did they do after that in the way of grant or other aid?—No other aid.

4389. Did they give you no other aid?—No.

4390. Are we to take it that 7,000 *l.* was the whole contribution made by the Irish Society to these purposes?—Yes.

4391. You put the reversion in the lands down at something, I presume?—It is clearly very small. It has never been estimated to my knowledge.

4392. At all events, the total expenditure between 1854 and 1889 was 236,000 *l.*, as you have told us?—Yes.

4393. Towards that expenditure the Irish Society contributed a little over 7,000 *l.*?—Yes; and the object of that contribution was really not towards the works at all; it was for the purpose of keeping down taxation, and enabling the Commissioners to pay interest.

4394. On the other hand, by their opposition to measures in Parliament, the substance of which was conceded, they involved you in costs, as you have told us, of about 6,500 *l.*?—Yes.

4395. Which is, I suppose, a set off against the grant?—Yes; in 1886, when the ship-building yard was about completed and a contract entered into for the erection of a 80-ton crane, the Commissioners forwarded to the Society an estimate of the cost of these works, amounting to 19,000 *l.*, and they asked the Society to contribute towards the cost. The Society had that under consideration for a considerable time, and their reply was that, considering their obligations, they were not in a position to do so. I may say that the general opinion held in Londonderry is that practically the Society have done nothing for the Harbour Trust.

4396. Am I to understand that you are here to speak, not merely as the Secretary of the Commissioners, but you believe that you are speaking the opinion of all sections of the community of Londonderry?—Yes; a large number. I have been thoroughly acquainted with Londonderry and its inhabitants for the last 25 years, and I am here to give the fullest information I can with regard to the transactions between the Society and the Commissioners, so far as I know them.

4397. As regards this point of the relation of the Commissioners and the opinion of the community towards the Irish Society, will you tell us how your Board of Commissioners is elected?—Five members are elected annually by the ratepayers of the city of Londonderry.

4398. Of how many members does the Board consist?—There are 15 members on the Board.

4399. Where do the other 10 come from?—Five retire each year and are eligible for re-election, if qualified; and each Commissioner is elected for three years.

4400. There are 15 members of the boards you say, and five are elected by the ratepayers?—Yes; annually, for three years.

4401. But at any given moment there are 15 Commissioners?—Yes.

4402. Where do the other 10 come from?—They are all elected by the ratepayers; five being elected each year, for three years.

4403. Then originally, as I understand, 15 were elected by ratepayers?—Then originally 15 were incorporated by the Act.

4404. How were they removed?—After three years had expired, five were selected by ballot and retired, and their place was filled up by the electors.

4405. At this moment every one of the 15 Commissioners has been elected by the ratepayers?—Yes.

4406. Having been elected by the ratepayers they may be taken to represent the opinion of the ratepaying community?—Most undoubtedly they do.

4407. In expressing the opinion of the Commissioners you are expressing the opinion of gentlemen who have been elected by the community?—I think it is the best possible index to the feeling in Londonderry, considering the qualification that is necessary for the Commissioners and the voters.

4408. Is there any further point you wish to refer to?—I should like just to say that when the first deputation that I have referred to were before the Society, they made a report to the Harbour Board upon their return.

4409. In what year?—In 1866. I do not think

Chairman—continued.

think that report was altogether favourable or that it was very well received. The deputation reported that the Irish Society hesitated to grant them their interest in what was then known as the King's Quays, lest those quays should be appropriated for private purposes. I may say those were the only public quays in Londonderry at that time, inasmuch as the lease of that portion of the quays was for a short period; and I think the only one there was expired shortly, in 17 years or something of that kind. The Commissioners considered then, and have always felt, that the Society erred in holding such an opinion, and I think their conduct and management of the Trust since then shows that the Society did err. The Commissioners have all along felt that they could obtain nothing from the Society without the sacrifice of their independence, and they were not disposed to sacrifice that.

Sir John Ellis.

4410. Perhaps you will tell us at once in what way the Commissioners were asked to sacrifice their independence?—By the restrictions that were placed upon any grants; for instance, take the agreement of 1857, where our Parliamentary powers were restricted by the Society.

4411. Your Parliamentary powers were restricted by the Parliamentary Committee, were they not?—No; by the agreement with the Society. It is expressly stated in the agreement with the Society of 1857 that compulsory powers were not to be exercised against the Society.

4412. But you had everything granted to you; you had all the quays and docks granted to you, I understand, and therefore the compulsory powers would not practically have had any effect; is that so?—The Society bound us up by that agreement, and subsequently acted upon it in a manner that we considered exceedingly arbitrary, and one that in all probability would not have arisen but for that agreement with the Society.

4413. I suppose you are referring to the fact that the Society interfered and got an injunction with regard to the user you proposed to make of the slob lands?—Yes.

4414. Why was it that they got the injunction?—As I have already explained, because the time fixed in the agreement had expired; the land was not the Commissioners.

4415. Then I will ask this other question: Is it correct that shortly before the statutory powers expired, namely in 1864, the Commissioners applied to the Society to let them have, for other purposes, the land intended for a tidal dock. Is this a correct statement of what occurred: In support of their applications, the Commissioners brought their engineer, when, on discussion of the subject with him, it appeared that he did not at all approve of the plans proposed by the Commissioners, and considered the purposes for which they wanted the land unsuited to the requirements of the port. The Society thereupon refused to grant the lands for the purposes then asked for, but were willing to reserve them for the dock. Notwithstanding this, the Commissioners put out an advertisement for a contract for the construction of works which were not for a dock but for some other purposes, and then the injunction was obtained; is that correct?—I cannot speak with regard to any interview the engineer may have had with the Society, or as to what he may have said; but certainly the intention of the Commissioners all along was that the ground should be reclaimed for a ship-building yard and other purposes, timber ponds, and such like.

4416. But you represented that the Society attempted to withdraw the land from you on account of the period having expired?—Yes.

4417. But from the statement I have put to you, it would appear that it was not for that reason, but that it was because you were using it for some other purpose which your own engineer did not deem to be the most appropriate?—The notice I received to attend here was very short, and I have not had an opportunity of looking into this; but speaking from memory I think I could produce a letter from the Society giving as the reason that the Commissioners had failed to comply with a clause of the agreement.

4418. That is very likely. We often do that when we want somebody to do something which we think more advantageous for the public; we often put a little pressure on them, and say, for instance, "Your time has expired." You have often done that with your contractors, I dare say, when they are a little behindhand. I suppose that was the object of the Society. Do you mean seriously to say that the grant the Society made to you in 1854 was of no value at all?—No, I do not say that; but really on looking into it I cannot see that there is a great deal of value in the reversionary interest of the Society in the foreshore of the river which was leased in perpetuity to certain people in Londonderry, and whom we had to compensate for that interest. As I have mentioned, King's Quay, which was leased to Mr. Smith, and which was for a shorter period, was the only one which strikes me at the present time as being of very much value. That, as I dare say you are aware, has, since the time when the agreements were made in 1874, been leased to the Commissioners for 999 years at 1 l. per annum.

4419. Still you have very fine quays, have you not?—No doubt.

4420. And you have very fine water arrangements of every description; and all these you derived through the grant of the Irish Society; is that the fact?—If we had had to purchase the reversionary interest of the Society I do not know that it would have added a great deal to the amount of the compensation that we have paid.

4421. You never made a calculation of what the value of that grant was?—No.

4422. If you were told that it was very large, you would not deny it?—I would take exception to it if it were stated as anything very large, I think.

4423. Was it on the Bill brought before Parliament in 1874, that you spent 4,000 l.?—Yes.

4424. That was the whole cost of getting the Bill through Parliament?—Altogether.

4425. It had nothing to do with the opposition of

Sir *John Ellis*—continued.

of the Irish Society, had it?—Yes; the greater part of the cost was incurred in consequence of the opposition of the Irish Society. We should have procured that Bill, I think, for under 1,000 *l.*, if it had been an unopposed Bill.

4426. You think that the difference between the cost you might have incurred, if the Irish Society had not intervened, was the difference between 1,000 *l.* and 4,000 *l.*?—I should think something like that.

4427. Do you think that the intervention of the Irish Society improved the Bill generally?—No, I do not know that it improved the Bill. It improved it in this way certainly, so far as we are concerned, that we got the land that we required without compulsory powers, whereas if we had obtained and had exercised our compulsory powers, I dare say we would have had to pay for the ground.

4428. As to that I will give you evidence presently of what the fact were. Now, again, in 1882, that amount of 2,500 *l.* was the whole cost of the Bill, was it not?—Yes.

4429. Can you tell us what the proportion was that the Irish Society caused in that expense?—I cannot, except as a rough estimate, and it really is a very rough one. It strikes me that an unopposed Bill of the Harbour Commissioners should be obtained for a sum under 1,000 *l.*

4430. You think that the extra expense, by reason of the opposition of the Irish Society, was 1,500 *l.*?—Yes.

4431. Was there no improvement in that Bill, by reason of the consultation of the Irish Society with you and your engineer?—I am not aware of any improvement in it. I do not remember any.

4432. The result of your operations as Harbour Commissioners has been highly beneficial to the city, and has been very remunerative to the Commissioners, has it not?—It is not remunerative to any person; because whatever surplus money we have is applied to improvements. As you will observe, the total cost of works amounts to 233,000 *l.*, and the bond debt at the present moment is 180,000 *l.*, so that is somewhat upwards of 50,000 *l.*, that has been acquired by surplus revenue.

4433. In point of fact, yours is a prosperous concern?—Yes, it is.

4434. And does not want any assistance?—It would be very much better with assistance; for instance, the prosperity of Londonderry could be very materially advanced by a reduction in the rates. If the taxation of the trade of the port were reduced, it would be a matter of very great moment to the inhabitants in competing with the ports around.

4435. Has that been recently represented to the Irish Society; are your dues excessive?—Our dues are high, and if they were reduced, as I say, it would be of the greatest benefit to the city.

4436. That is a matter of opinion?—There can be no doubt about it.

Mr. *Healy.*

4437. You think you could survive your divorce from the Irish Society?—I think we could.

4438. Does the Irish Society claim the fishing down to Magilligan Point?—Yes, I believe they do.

Mr. *Healy*—continued.

4439. Is that nine miles down from the city?—Magilligan Point would be 20 miles from the city, I should think.

4440. That must affect what I may call the rural fishermen, to a great extent?—I think it is the salmon fishery which the Society leases; but, really, so far as the fishery is concerned, practically I know nothing about it.

4441. I presume the tide ebbs and flows all through?—Yes, it does.

4442. Have the Irish Society been in litigation with the poor fishermen during your experience?—I think I remember a lawsuit, but I really cannot give evidence upon that; I was in no way concerned with it, but I believe there was a lawsuit.

4443. Whatever rights there may be in the public and in the Society, the poor cod fishermen would be quite unable to cope in litigation with a powerful society like that?—Of course they would.

4444. Do you confirm the statement made here as to the mischief caused by the Society in refusing sufficiently long leases to enable the slob-lands along the quays to be built on?—I really cannot give any evidence as regards the tenants of the Society, because I have had no acquaintance with that matter at all. In fact, the only thing I know about the Irish Society is in connection with the Harbour Board.

4445. You have built the quays, I suppose?—We built the quays.

4446. And the public have to pay taxes for them in the city?—The shipping coming to the quays is taxed, and the goods imported and exported by the citizens are taxed.

4447. That must affect a far larger area than the city; it must affect the farms in Tyrone and in Derry county?—It affects the whole district served by the port of Derry.

4448. So that the dock dues in the Port of Derry affect an area of 20 or 30 miles around?—Yes, and even much further than that. It affects an area of 50 or 60 miles at least.

4449. So that the mischief of the exigences of the Society is not confined to Derry; it affects the whole of the north of Ulster?—If the rates of the port could be reduced, or if the Commissioners had received a larger amount of assistance from the Society, those rates might not have been so high, and if that were so, it would benefit the district served.

4450. It is not a purely local Derry question, but it affects the whole of Ulster?—Yes.

Sir *Richard Temple.*

4451. Are the dues of Londonderry higher than those of the competing ports?—They are much about the same as Belfast which is a competing port with us. Greenore is a competing port with us, and there, I believe, there are no dues at all; the harbour there, I believe, belongs to the London and North Western Railway Company, and I understand there are no dues there at all.

4452. What exactly is it that the Irish Society ought to do for Derry, from your point of view; what

Sir *Richard Temple*—continued.

what is it you want?—I cannot give the opinion of my board for I have not asked them on the point, but speaking personally, my opinion is that if the Irish Society were to devote a considerable portion of their funds or revenue to reducing the bond debt at present upon the port, the dues upon the shipping and trade there might be reduced, to the great benefit of the city of Londonderry and the surrounding district.

4453. What do you mean by a considerable portion; what is the amount you have in your mind roughly?—The total debt of the Harbour Commissioners is 180,000 *l.*, and I would be very glad to see the whole of that wiped out.

4454. Is that to be done by the Irish Society?—I am not sufficiently acquainted with the finances of the Irish Society to be able to say whether it could afford to do that or not.

4455. Then you are not prepared to find fault with the Irish Society after all?—Yes; I think the Irish Society should have assisted the Commissioners in carrying out the works that have been carried out; and if they had, the large debt at present on the port would not have been incurred.

4456. But what amount of assistance do you suggest?—As much as possible, up to 180,000 *l.*

4457. Is the Irish Society in a position to give you 180,000 *l.*?—I have just said I am not sufficiently acquainted with their finances to be able to say.

4458. If you are not so acquainted, how do you make out that they ought to have done more?—I say let the Society give as much as they can (and I presume they are acquainted with their finances) up to 180,000 *l.*; I do not ask them to go beyond that figure.

4459. Supposing they say they cannot afford it?—Then I say, give us as much as you can afford.

4460. But I understand you to have been finding fault with the Irish Society, do I not?—Yes; for not giving us more assistance.

4461. If you do not know the condition of their finances, how can you undertake to say that they ought to have done this, that, or the other?—I know the Irish Society have a large amount of property, and a certain income, and I think the Port and Harbour of Londonderry should have been the very first to receive consideration; it is the largest and most important trust upon their estates.

4462. Have they no other calls upon them?—They may; but I consider the Port and Harbour Trust should have been the very first to be considered.

4463. Would not the other interests say the very same thing on their own behalf?—Possibly. That is my opinion, and, I believe, the opinion of a good many others in Londonderry.

4464. I presume you speak solely for the Harbour Trust?—Yes, for the Harbour Trust.

4465. You stand up exclusively as regards the harbour interests?—Certainly. I am endeavouring to put forward their claim; and I think I am only putting forward what is fair and just, when I say that in my opinion, and in the opinion of many people in Londonderry, the Harbour Trust was deserving of the first consideration of the Society, and should have been the first to be considered, inasmuch as it was the largest and most important trust upon the estate of the Society, and the one that exercises the largest influence upon the prosperity of the city.

4466. Have the Society already done a good deal for the Harbour Trust?—The Society did nothing but what I have referred to, that I am aware of.

4467. Have they not given lands and leases?—Yes; that has been referred to. The Society have given the reversionary interest in certain foreshores of the River Foyle, and the lease of King's Quays, and a grant of the slob-land for ship-building and other purposes.

4468. Has it given any money grant?—They gave one money grant of 1,000 *l.* a year for seven years.

4469. Do not all these several things amount to something considerable?—We do not think they amount to a great deal.

Mr. *Healy*.

4470. Was it in your time that Messrs. Harland and Wolff, who afterwards settled in Belfast, made an application to the Irish Society, which the Irish Society rejected, for a space for a dock in Derry?—I cannot really say; but I presume it must have been in my time. I have been connected with the board since 1854.

4471. Are you acquainted with the grounds upon which the Irish Society rejected Messrs. Harland and Wolff's application, and compelled them to go to Belfast?—No.

Colonel *Lewis*.

4472. Do you know, as a matter of fact, that Messrs. Harland and Wolff even contemplated going to Londonderry?—I do not.

4473. You would not be surprised to hear that Sir Edward Harland denies that he ever had the slightest intention of going there?—I really do not know.

Mr. *Clancy*.

4474. Would you go so far as to say that in your opinion the best thing the Irish Society could do would be to clear out, and allow its estate to be managed, and its revenues to be administered by an Irish body?—That is a question rather outside the information I can give you. I am speaking solely from the point of view having regard to the Harbour Trust.

4475. Cannot you express your own opinion?—My own opinion is that if 180,000 *l.* were appropriated to paying off the harbour debt, if so much could be obtained, nothing better could be done with the funds of the Society.

Mr. *John Ellis*.

4476. As I understand, you come here as the secretary to this Harbour Trust, to represent to us that you are impeded and fettered in your operations for the benefit of the port of Derry by certain restrictions. Is that so?—I do not think I expressed myself in those words, or to that extent. I said that the Commissioners were of opinion that nothing was to be obtained from the Irish Society without loss of independence, and I referred to the agreement of 1857, where we got a grant of 1,000 *l.* a year for seven years,

Mr. *John Ellis*—continued.

and the reversionary interest of the Society in the lands; I referred to the conditions that were attached there as bearing out that view.

4477. I gather that, in your opinion, at all events, the existence of a body of gentlemen in London, called the Irish Society, with certain powers in relation to Derry, is a hindrance to the prosperity of the port of Derry. Is that so? —I did not say that. What I wished to convey was that I think the Society could and should have assisted the Commissioners more freely than they did.

4478. In fact, that the Society have not done all that they might have done to assist the Commissioners?—Precisely.

Mr. *Lea*.

4479. Are you acquainted with the fishery arrangements of the Irish Society?—I am not.

4480. You cannot tell me whether at one time the Irish Society only claimed the fishery down to Culmore Point?—No; I cannot tell you.

4481. You may have mentioned before, but I did not catch it, what was the cost of the Bill of 1854, to which you referred just now?—I cannot give you the cost of the 1854 Bill, because that was promoted by the Ballast Office committee, and was prior to the incorporation of the Commissioners, and I was not connected with the port at that time.

4482. What was the cost of the other Bill?—£. 4,000 was the cost of the 1874 Bill, and 2,000 *l.* was the cost of the third one in 1882.

4483. You think that about 6,000 *l.* was thrown away?—Those two Bills, as unopposed Bills, might be obtained for a couple of thousand pounds, 1,000 *l.* each.

4484. You stated that the dues are rather high in Derry; have you many complaints from merchants in regard to that?—Occasionally we have complaints; but they have been paying them so long now that they have ceased to say anything about it.

4485. Can you tell me what difference it makes, say, to the price of coal, taking dues, for instance, as an article of consumption?—I should think it would make a difference of about a shilling a ton in the price of coal.

4486. Coal is largely used in the manufactories in Derry, is it not?—Yes, there are very large imports of coal.

4487. Does Mr. Biggar of the new ship-building yard complain of the cost of material for his yard?—Yes; he complains of the dues upon the materials for building ships.

4488. On coal and iron?—On coal and iron.

4489. You have no surplus funds, I think, to divide amongst any shareholders or commissioners?—No, nothing of the kind.

4490. It is entirely for the public good?—It is entirely a debt due to the public. We borrow money from the public, and pay three and a-half per cent. upon our bonds.

4491. The Commissioners are simply trustees for the public good?—They are simply trustees.

Sir *William Marriott*.

4492. With regard to the cost of those Bills, you must have applied to Parliament in any event, I suppose?—Yes.

4493. That would have cost 2,000 *l.* you say? —I estimate 1,000 *l.* each.

4494. Were there no other opponents besides the Irish Society?—The fishery lessees opposed the Bill of 1874, and I think there was some opposition also from some landed proprietors along the shore of Lough Foyle in regard to that training wall.

4495. Then it would not have been an unopposed Bill in either case?—I doubt very much if the landowners would have come forward and opposed the Bill if it had not been already opposed by the Irish Society and the fishery lessees, as their opposition was very strong.

4496. We know, as a matter of fact, in these rooms, that whenever you apply for a Bill there is nearly always some opposition?—Generally speaking, it is so.

4497. I believe the money is well spent among counsel and solicitors?—It is pretty freely spent amongst those gentlemen.

The Reverend EDWARD LOUGHREY, sworn; and Examined.

Mr. *Healy*.

4498. You are parish priest of Dungiven, I believe?—Yes.

4499. And you are prepared to give evidence as to the action of the Skinners' Company in Derry?—Yes.

4500. And also with regard to the action of the Irish Society in the city of Derry?—Yes.

4501. You have been acquainted with the city of Derry and the county of Derry all your life? —Yes, all my life.

4502. Are you empowered, so far as the action of the Irish Society in Derry is concerned, to speak on behalf of the Roman Catholic Bishop of the Diocese, as well as upon your own account?—Certainly. I represent his views, and the views as well of some of the citizens, and the interests of myself and the tenants on the Skinners' Estate.

Mr. *Healy*—continued.

4503. I will take first the action of the Skinners' Company. You live at Dungiven, do you not?—Yes, presently.

4504. You are parish priest of that town?—Yes.

4505. Your attention has been called to the evidence given by Dr. Todd, the solicitor who conducted the negotiations for the sale of the Skinners' estate?—Yes.

4506. Dr. Todd was asked as to the manner in which the priest's house and land was sold by the Skinners' Company to a private individual, and the purport of his evidence was that there was no hardship whatever, and that practically all creeds were treated alike; will you please tell us what difference has been made by the Skinners' Company as regards the Roman Catholic priest's house and the Protestant priest's house,

Mr. Healy—continued.

in that respect?—I suppose I am right in beginning with how these parties came into possession of their respective places. It was under Mr. Oglsby, who was the lessee of the Skinners' estate, that the reverend rector and the reverend parish priest at that time each got a house and land. It was about 10 years since that the Skinners' Company came into occupation of that estate again. The Skinners' Company gave their estate to Mr. Oglsby about 60 years ago, and they came into occupation again somewhere about 1870. The rector and the parish priest, from time to time, enjoyed the possession of those places down to 1880.

4507. When the sale took place, what was done with regard to the parish priest, and with regard to the rector?—The late rector received, as we are informed, 500 *l.* as a donation or present from the company, and the place was then handed over free to the Church body for the benefit of the incumbent, from time to time, in years to come.

4508. They gave over the house and land in trust for the Church Society, and gave him an additional donation, as you believe, of 500 *l.*?—£. 500 was given to the late rector. The present rector, I believe, is in receipt for his time, as from time immemorial, of 40 *l.* a year.

4509. They have continued the grant of 40 *l.* a year?—Yes.

4510. I believe also in the case of Presbyterians in the locality assistance has been given?—They have received assistance in building the manse, and each of the two clergymen in the parish receive 30 *l.* a piece at present. How long it may be continued I cannot say.

4511. That grant has not been stopped?—Not so far as I know.

4512. Can you tell us what has been done by the Skinners' Company with regard to Roman Catholics?—At about the time they were coming into possession, they granted 25 *l.* to be divided between the four Catholic clergymen in the parish.

4513. Was that in 1872?—A little time after they came into possession in 1872. Before that we got nothing.

4514. Has that grant of 25 *l.* been stopped?—It has been notified as stopped.

4515. While the grant to Protestants and Presbyterians has been continued?—It has been continued.

4516. With regard to the house, did they make over the priest's house and glebe to the Catholics, as they did in the case of the Protestants?—No, it was made over to the late parish priest, who was in ill health, before he died, and not just as smart, perhaps, as a man in perfect health, and since he died it has fallen into the hands of his friends. But, at the same time, the solicitor, who apparently acted for both the tenant and the landlord, was quite aware of the position of the Catholic part of the trust, that it occupied the same place with the Catholics as the Protestant trust did with the Protestant bodies.

4517. In the case of the rector they bought the tenant-right and presented it to the incumbent?—The tenant-right was originally presented to the parish priest by Mr. Oglsby, who accepted the parish priest from time to time to be the owner of it; but it has now been treated as an ordinary tenancy.

4518. The net result is that your grant has been stopped and the house and land have passed into private hands, while the grants to Presbyterians and Protestants have been continued, and their houses put in settlement for the benefit of the religion to which they belong?—That is the fact.

4519. Did you, in that state of things, apply to the Skinners' Company that they should rent or sell you the manor-house that then became vacant?—Seeing how I stood, I wrote to Mr. Young, the new agent (for the old gentleman is not looking after anything at present), asking to have the manor-house, as it is called (it is the agent's house), and the garden given to me at a rent.

4520. Where do you live now?—I live in lodgings.

4521. Are you only able to get a single room?—A single sitting-room and a small bedroom. It is only a small place; there is not much choice in the town.

4522. You applied to the agent, and what did he say?—The agent told me it would not be rented, but it would be sold; and he advised me to write to the Skinners' estate office here in London, to ask to have it sold to me; and that I should make the proposal; and I asked them to grant it to me on the most reasonable terms they could, seeing the position in which I was placed. I did not get an answer to that application for some time, and then I was informed, and I suppose justly, that they could not decipher my writing in some parts of my letter, and the place in the meantime was sold to Mr. Oglsby, a descendant of the late lessee.

4523. That was the manor-house?—Yes; the manor-house is a large house and a garden.

4524. How have they treated you with regard to your schools?—The school is also handed over to the charge of Mr. Oglsby.

4525. That is a school to which Catholics go?—It is practically exclusively a Catholic school. There are only two families of Protestants, with four little boys attending the school.

4526. Mr. Oglsby is a Protestant, is he not?—Yes. You will understand I have no objection to Mr. Oglsby. It is only on principle I go.

4527. They did not hand over the Protestant schools to Catholics, did they? No. I think the Fishmongers' Company have given half-and-half to each denomination.

4528. At all events, they have handed the Catholic schools over to Mr. Oglsby, a Protestant gentleman?—Yes. I may mention that, so far as Mr. Oglsby is concerned, we are under many obligations to the family of the Oglsbys, and so are the tenants.

4529. In addition to the sums given to the Presbyterians and Protestant clergymen, they have given a grant of 10 *l.* to an outside clergyman, have they not?—Yes, to a clergyman who had only one tenant of theirs under his charge.

4530. He has only one tenant of theirs; so that for that one single tenant they have given 10 *l.* a year?

Mr. Healy—continued.

a year: they have not discontinued that, have they?—No.

4531. So much as regards their treatment of the tenants from the religious point of view. Now, can you say as to how they acted in 1878, when the Ogilby lease fell in. Did they send Messrs. Bassington and Gale, the well-known valuers, to value the estate?—They sent the valuators down upon the estate to make a valuation.

4532. They kept Messrs. Bassington and Gale's valuation secret, did they not, and never published it?—They never published it.

4533. Did they then raise the town tenants 25 per cent., and the agricultural tenants 18½ per cent.?—Yes.

4534. Were they compelled to pay those rents until the Act of 1881?—Yes, until it was again adjusted.

4535. I believe in order to qualify the tenants in town holdings for the power of sale under the Ashbourne Act, they added to their houses pieces of agricultural land?—Yes.

4536. But the prices asked were so high that the Government inspector refused to sanction the grants?—Yes. The people now are left worse than they were; they cannot buy it; they will not get the assistance, and they are not able to purchase from their own means.

4537. You mean those who have houses in the town?—Yes; they tried to qualify by getting the extent of land to make agricultural holdings; but the price was so high that the Government valuator would not sanction the grants.

4538. Is it the case that in making the sales under the Ashbourne Act some curious reservations of royalties have been maintained for the use of the Skinners' Company?—Yes.

4539. Have you the deed there?—I have the lease, which from its restrictions shows that there was not much inclination to encourage the tenants to build.

4540. Will you please read those curious reservations?—Perhaps you would like to read them, because I am a bad lawyer (*handing the lease to the honourable Member*). Before giving the lease the company made the tenants enter into an agreement binding them first to build and after building they gave them a lease, and put these restrictions in it.

4541. Those restrictions practically compel the tenants to surrender at any time the company like?—Yes, to surrender any portion of the building; they can enter into possession of it, and make them keep the rest at the valuation that is put upon it by the company, whether they like it or not.

4542. The lease you have handed to me is of a recent date, it is dated November 1882, between the Worshipful Company of Skinners' and Thomas Gwynne. I understand that you hand this in?—Yes (*the same was handed in*).

4543. I will not read the reservations now as the lease has been handed in. Do you conceive that the existence of covenants of that kind are an enormous restriction on the development of building on the estate?—Yes; it was for that purpose that I wished to have it brought before you.

4544. Have you, in addition, any documents reserving any royalties?—Yes, I have a conveyance here, under the late Act for purchasing.

4545. Would you let me see that?—Yes (*handing the same to the honourable Member*). You will see that in these cases where they are supposed to sell to the tenants all their interests, they reserve freestone quarries and pits, and so on.

Sir William Marriott.

4546. I observe the deed of 1888 says "Whereas, by agreement, dated 16th May 1879." So that there must be some agreement before this deed which you have handed in?—Yes, that was what I referred to. They entered into a plain paper agreement that they would build so-and-so, and the tenants did not get their lease till the building was up. That is the way of doing business.

4547. I see that there was a prior agreement from the deed; to make the case complete we ought to have the antecedent deed?—I do not know whether the company can give you that; we have not got it.

Mr. Healy.

4548. I observe that this indenture is made under the Ashbourne Act, between the Skinners' Company and the Land Commissioners and James M'Fey, with certain reservations. Of course, it is right to say, that as the Land Commissioners were parties to this deed it may be that the Skinners' Company had no power to give a greater grant than what they had themselves, and it may be that they are governed by their original grant?—May I say that there are other deeds of the same kind in which all the royalties are moved out and given to the tenant; but that case is likely to come up for litigation in future. The other tenants are going to take exception as to why one would get a royalty and the other not.

4549. I suppose those who have got the royalties are all Protestants?—No, there are some Protestants who have not got them. I may say there is no polemical spirit in this matter; we are all united. I represent Presbyterian and Protestant farmers alike as well as Catholic.

4550. This is the reservation in the deed of 1886: "All freestone and beds of freestone, freestone quarries and pits, as well opened as unopened, within, under, or upon the said lands, hereditaments, and premises, and with full right, power, and liberty to the vendors, their successors and assigns, to search for, sink, quarry, open, work, get, store, dress, make merchantable the said freestone," and so on; and then it also reserves certain other matters. You put in this deed, I understand?—Yes (*the same was handed in*).

4551. Is that as much as you wish to say with regard to the Skinners' Company?—I should only like to refer to the regulation of rents on the basis of the improvements made. The value of each holding is enhanced by so much as each party has expended; so that the rent is greatly higher, and the parties are paying on their own improvements.

4552. That is the general rule on all the estates; the tenants have bought their own improvements?

Mr. *Healy*—continued.

improvements?—I may tell you, so far as it is of any importance, that the tenants of all creeds and classes and denominations purchase on the understanding that all beneficiary interests are to be continued, and that is stated.

4553. Dr. Todd has denied that; are there in existence any letters or other documents from Dr. Todd or anyone else to that effect?—They are in existence to the extent of threatening people, if they would not purchase, that they would suffer.

Sir William Marriott.

4554. From whom are those letters; are they from Dr. Todd?—I suppose so. They would likely be here to-day. I have a telegram that Mr. John MacLaughlin, who was expected to be examined here, has the letters.

Mr. *Healy.*

4555. With regard to the Irish Society; you said you were empowered to express the views of the Roman Catholic Bishop of the diocese of Derry?—I am.

4556. Did the Catholics apply to the Irish Society for a site for their cathedral in the town?—Yes, they applied at various times.

4557. Was the application for a site within the walls of the city of Derry?—Yes. The first application was made some years ago for permission to build the new Catholic cathedral on the grounds occupied by the Convent of Mercy in Pump-street.

4558. A convent of nuns?—Yes.

4559. Although the existing convent was situated there, they were willing to use that as the site for the Catholic cathedral?—Yes.

4560. Was that application refused?—Yes.

4561. Were the Catholics forced to build the cathedral in an inferior position?—They were forced to go to Cow Bog, and there they got a site; I do not know from whom.

4562. Outside the walls?—Outside the walls.

4563. In consequence of the building of the cathedral ecclesiastical erection in the neighbourhood of Cow Bog, has that quarter, which was then a bog, become developed as a centre of commerce?—That, together with another cause, has made the whole city develope on that side. One cause is that, and the other cause is the property being in other hands than those of the society.

4564. At the time you went there, did the name of Cow Bog pretty accurately delineate the character of the place?—It was a low marsh; it was a part of the city which, in ancient times, was flooded when the tide ran in, so that it made an island of the town of Derry.

4565. What expenditure was made upon Derry Cathedral?—Close upon 50,000 *l.* upon the building; it is not completed as yet. I may say that the society were asked for a subscription to assist in that, but it was refused.

4566. That goes without saying; now, coming down to the time that Sir Sydney Waterlow was chairman, can you inform us as to the application for a site for a temperance hall?—Yes.

4567. Will you tell me what was the fate of that application?—It was not directly refused, but the conditions which were proposed to be embodied in the lease were such as made it utterly impossible to accept it. One question was asked at the outset as to whether it would be reserved to temperance business and nothing else; and the question was asked, whether, if a concert were held there for a charitable purpose, would that vitiate the conveyance. The question was put by the Reverend Mr. Dogherty, and I am informed that Sir Sydney Waterlow answered, "Decidedly."

4568. He held that it must be strictly confined to the discussion of temperance; what did the Catholics of Derry have to do then?—In order to get a site for a hall for the recreation of working men, they were obliged to purchase, from a private individual, a site in Orchard-street, which is in a backward part of the town.

4569. Did they get a site there?—Yes, at the cost of 3,000 *l.* and odd.

4570. Did they build a hall there?—They built a hall which has cost for building about 14,000 *l.*, but it is not completed yet. They expect it will cost about 20,000 *l.* when it is completed with all its appointments.

4571. Did you also ask the Society for a donation for that purpose?—There was a donation asked for, but it was refused.

4572. I believe, on the other hand, the Irish Society has largely subscribed to the re erection of the Protestant Cathedral?—They have been most liberal in all things pertaining to the Protestant grants. The Protestant Cathedral has been renovated, and they have assisted in that.

4573. I believe they have given 1,800 *l.* towards that?—It is believed so.

4574. And they have given a grant for a site for the Presbyterians?—They gave a grant for a Presbyterian Hall, and also for an Apprentice Boys' Hall, and a grant for building a hall for the recreation of Presbyterian young men, which is a most worthy institute, and they have granted a large donation in paying off the debt, and fitting it up.

4575. Will you just tell us the difference that they have made between Protestants and Catholics with regard to the schools?—The Catholics get, practically, nothing in comparison with the others. There is a school built in Bridge-street lately, at a cost of 1,500 *l.*, which is attended by about 800 little Catholic girls.

4576. That is under the National Board, is it not?—It is under the National Board. The Ladies of Mercy look after the poor children. For that there was no grant given by the Society when they were asked. Although it is usual for the Society to give grants to various schools under the National Board, they would give nothing to this, except that on two occasions they gave 80 *l.*, but on the third occasion when they were asked, the agent said the list of subscriptions was filled up, and they could give no more as regards that school.

4577. Now, coming to the other schools, will you give us their names?—There is the Long Tower School, and the Sheriff's Mountain School, and the Nuns' School, down in the Cow Bog; they get 10 *l.* each. Then there is one national school under Protestant management in the country,

Mr. *Healy*—continued.

county, quite a little rural school, the Molenan School, which gets 30*l.*, and other city schools, lower class schools, under the National Board, get the same generous donations.

4578. As regards those three schools you mention, the Long Tower, Sheriff's Mountain, and the Nuns' School, which get 10*l.* each, how many children do they instruct?—I suppose about an average of 150 as regards two of them, and the Nuns' School has about 600.

4579. And as regards this rural Protestant school, to which you referred at Molenan, how many scholars would be attending that?—I may be near the figure when I say 60 at the outside.

4580. I suppose all the other Protestant schools receive donations on a like scale?—Yes, on the same generous scale as the Molenan School, which is a rural school and gets 30*l.*

4581. Now, leaving the lower class education, let us take the middle class. There is a Catholic College called St. Columb's, is there not, which is a higher school?—Yes.

4582. What do the Society give to that?—They give 199*l.* in all. It is nine years since they gave the first.

4583. And then there is the Foyle College, which is a higher-class Protestant college, is it not?—Yes.

4584. What have the Society given there?—As near as I can tell, taking exhibitions and scholarships and professors, it comes to some 1,500*l.* a year, I believe; but I am instructed to say that you have those figures more accurate already in the returns which are before you.

4585. Then coming to the Magee College, which is a high class Presbyterian college; what did the Society contribute there?—To the Magee Presbyterian College and the academy connected with it, I estimate they give 800*l.* a year, but you will be able to correct that yourself in the returns before you.

4586. Now going outside Derry and taking the rural schools, there is a school in the parish of Eskaheen, is there not?—Yes.

4587. How are the Catholics and Protestants treated there?—In one national Catholic school under Catholic management they get 3*l.*, and in the other at Clonmenly the grant has been withdrawn.

4588. How have they treated the Protestants?—The Protestant school at Culmore cost the society 1,800*l.* to build it.

4589. They built it, did they?—Yes, and gave it a grant, so far as is known, of about 15*l.* or 80*l.* a year.

4590. Then there are two other small national schools which get the usual grants?—Yes.

4591. Did the parish priest, Father O'Neill, apply for a site for a school for Catholic children in that parish?—He informed me that he applied for a site, but it was refused, and that he had a petition signed by 34 of the Society's tenants which he handed to Mr. Montgomery the agent, and he refused to forward it.

4592. Mr. Montgomery is the local agent of the Society, is he not?—I believe so.

4593. Did Mr. Montgomery after refusing you a site for a Catholic school grant a site for an Orange hall?—Yes, they granted a site for an Orange hall, and assisted to build it.

Mr. *Healy*—continued.

4594. That is in Culmore?—Yes.

4595. Do other Protestant schools get donations in outside parishes?—Yes, in these parishes, and the national schools at Carnamoyle and Muff get the usual donation. I may say that any little sums that the Catholics get they report by letter and get it published; any little charity that the Catholics get they cause put in the papers; whereas it is not so generally with the other grants.

4596. They keep the Orange grants secret, but in the case of the Catholics they publish their benevolence by writing to the papers?—Yes; we would not object to that if everybody would publish their poverty and the charities they receive.

4597. I think there was one charitable lady who left to the Catholics a bequest of 10,000*l.* for a hall; what was her name?—Madame Waters left 10,000*l.* to erect a home for old ladies who had no means.

4598. Were they to be Catholic ladies?—I do not know whether there was even that restriction put in the will. I think it was simply for old ladies; any old ladies who wanted help.

4599. Did the Catholics apply for a site for that purpose?—The late bishop the year before he died, about two years ago I should say now, authorised Mr. O'Neill to ask for a site upon a place called Bluebell-hill.

4600. Is that a convenient place for such a home?—It is a very nice place, in an elevated position at the edge of the city.

4601. What was done?—That was all we heard about it; it came to nothing more. The site was not granted, and the old bishop died; but I hope it may be that on the present occasion they will grant it to us.

4602. At any rate the site was refused?—The site was refused.

4603. That was in the past 18 months?—Yes; in comparing the amounts given to the Protestants and the amounts given to the Catholics the numbers of the various tenants of the Society must be taken into consideration, and I suppose the Catholics would be far above the half. I suppose they would be close to 80,000 altogether, and their interests, taken collectively, would be more than the others.

4604. In addition to the treatment of the Catholics and the Catholic bishop which you have described, did the Irish Society persist in insulting the Catholic bishop by style and title up to recent years?—I believe until some time lately they usually addressed him as the Reverend Mr. Kelly. He considered that courtesy demanded that he should have the usual title and style adopted in addressing him.

4605. That insult was addressed to him until there came a Catholic sheriff, Sheriff Knill?—So I am informed; for that and other reasons the bishop thought it better not to attend some of their invitations.

4606. That is the evidence which you can give with regard to the discrimination made between the religious bodies by the Society?—Yes.

4607. Are you also prepared to give evidence with regard to the general progress of the town of Derry?—Yes.

4608. We have heard a good deal about that, and

Mr. *Healy*—continued.

and I do not know that we need go into it much. Do you concur with the statement as to the restriction placed upon the development of Derry by short leases?—Yes; I may remark also, as regards the leases and tenements of inside houses, that is, within the wall, when they were granted it was understood by the original charter or agreement, which is the authority of the Irish Society, that certain portions outside the walls would be granted to each house built inside the walls. It is a matter of complaint that it has come to pass that nearly all these pieces attached to houses inside the walls have been disconnected with the house property inside, and have become building grounds, which are producing benefit to the Society instead of to the owners of houses within the walls. There were long leases given many years ago, but within the last 50 or 60 years or so they have curtailed them down to short leases. They began, I think, with about 31 years.

4609. You agree that that has checked the growth of the city?—It has so far checked it that the people were compelled to get the worst possible form of house.

4610. You would agree that the existence of the Church land and the houses built on it have made a great improvement to the city, would you not?—That side of the city has been wonderfully improved, and there are very fine houses built upon that land.

4611. You consider that there are better buildings upon the Church land than upon the Society's land?—Yes.

4612. Is that because of the difference in the tenure?—Because of the leases.

4613. Can you speak as to the impression prevailing in the city with regard to the management of the Society?—Yes; the general opinion is that everything that could be done, as if directed to that end, was done to mar the progress of the city.

4614. Does the suspicion of favouritism attach to the Society's transactions?—Certainly. One instance which has been always in the minds of the general public for the last 30 or 40 years is the prevention of those celebrated ship builders coming to the Society to ask for permission to build a ship-building yard, and being only able to get a 30 years' lease as it was understood.

4615. We are told that Messrs. Harland and Woolf deny that, as I understand you say, that people believe that the Society's local management is not straight, and that there is favouritism shown?—That there is favouritism shown.

4616. Did the Catholics petition Parliament in the last couple of years upon that point?—They did; a petition, through Mr. M'Carthy, was presented to the House.

4617. Have you any evidence to give with regard to the prices charged for land for building purposes in the poorer portions of the city?—There is an objection on the part of the public to have exacted from them such high rents as the Society seem desirous to extract.

4618. What is the building charge per foot in the poorer part of the city?—I may say first that the improvements which have been made along the quays have been made at the expense of the city, and that the Society's property has no doubt been thereby improved very much at the expense of other people. Now, in the late arrangement of giving perpetuity leases, the Society put the whole total value, not only at present, but what ultimately may be accruing from such sites, and they sell their perpetuity leases upon that basis. That leaves no encouragement for speculation, black, blue, or white.

4619. What do they charge in the quarters where working men's dwellings might be supposed to be found; can you give the charges for frontage?—In a backward part of the city called Chamberlayne place, which is part of Cow Bog, it varies from 6 *s.* a foot, and there is an obligation to expend upon every house of, say, 16 feet frontage, a sum equal to at least 200 *l.* in building.

4620. Does that prevent the erection of workmen's dwellings and cottages?—If you calculate what would be the interest upon that to make a good basis for speculation you would not find anything left for the risk of building the houses and spending the money, and a poor man could hardly pay the amount of rent necessarily charged for such a house.

4621. In better quarters can you give us what the figures are?—In Foyle-street it ranges from 1 *l.* to 30 *s.* and 2 *l.* a foot.

4622. With what requirement as to expenditure on building?—They average 1,000 *l.* for a 30-foot house.

4623. So much with regard to the buildings. Was it in your time that the society put forward a claim for fisheries down as low as Magilligan Point?—Yes; there was a case against the fishermen there. I cannot say exactly the time, but I think it was about 11 years ago. The fishermen were prosecuted for trawling above Magilligan Point, and the fishermen claimed that they were entitled to Culmore, that that was the beginning of the river, and that the high seas began after that. That is as the River Foyle expands over a space of the extent in length or breadth of about 10 miles.

4624. The fishermen claimed to Culmore?—Yes, to Culmore.

4625. The company advanced the claim to Magilligan Point?—The lessees claimed down to Magilligan Point, which is a jutting point which goes across the river narrowing up the River Foyle at Greencastle, and making it a mile and a-half or two miles wide.

4626. And they took the poor fishermen into court?—I do not know whether it went into the higher courts of the country; but I need not tell you that the fishermen got the worst of it. They have had no means to fight the matter.

4627. Is there anything else that you would like to add?—I have nothing more to say, except that most people whose leases are falling out do not wish to make any complaint lest there might be a refusal to renew their leases. That is all I have to say upon the matter.

Sir John Ellis.

4628. You do not know much about the fisheries, I suppose?—In what way?

4629. As to how they are held or whom they belong

Sir *John Ellis*—continued.

belong to?—I know something about whom they belong to or who are the lessees at present. I know some of the gentlemen connected with them; but as regards the immediate terms on which they hold, I think I am like the public, that is kept a secret from me.

4630. But you do not know anything about the original deed of the fisheries, as to whom they belong to?—I suppose the Irish Society claim that they belong to them from the days of James, but I suppose he did not grant the whole of the high seas to the society. It is a question where the boundary begins and ends.

4631. You do not know that the society derive their title from the Crown, and that they pay an annual sum for it?—I know that they claim the title to it from the Crown, but the bone of contention is as to how far the Society's claim extends. The fishermen say that it is so far, and the Society say that it is so far.

4632. But you do not know anything about the original title of the fisheries?—I suppose that like the rest, you got them from King James, an absolute right of user and so on. It is a matter for lawyers and not for me to know how far your title goes.

4633. Now about the rents that are charged. You know what is done with the rents which are charged by the Irish Society, I suppose?—Certainly we do not know what they do with it; we only suppose; we hear that certain things are done.

4634. You have an account published every year. Do you know that they paid 1,200 *l.* to the Corporation of Londonderry?—I am aware that they gave something to the Corporation.

4635. Do you know that they subscribed half the amount of Londonderry Bridge?—I believe they did; but they were like the cow that gave a quantity of milk; when she was milked she kicked the pail over and away went the milk. So the society gave certain donations but they imposed certain obligations on the other side, and I think the obligations more than counterbalanced the donations.

4636. Do you know that they have assisted largely in the construction of the ports at Coleraine?—They have done something to that, but I think so far it is of very little avail.

4637. What I want to put to you is this: that if they took less rent than the property is fairly worth, they would not have the same means to carry out all those works, would they?—I admit that; but I hold on the other hand that if the Society had been as generous and as anxious to advance the value of their property as they might have been, their rents would be fourfold what they are.

4638. You mean generous with other people's money?—No; if they had let the people be generous with their own money. Derry would not have anything like the prosperity that it now enjoys but for two causes: the one is its natural position as the key to four counties; you cannot stop that in any shape or form; and if you took away from it the enterprise of the merchants of Derry, you would leave Derry a whole heap of bankruptcy and poverty. That is all you would have for the Society.

4639. Are you aware when application was made as we understand on behalf of Bishop Kelly by Mr. Neil, what the answers were that were given to him?—None at all so far as I am informed.

4640. You do not know what answers were given?—There was no grant given.

4641. Was there any answer to his application?—He was asked to get up out of his bed to go and see the deputation at Government House.

4642. Could not the Bishop have sent anyone else?—He might.

4643. Could he not have sent you?—He might if he had wished; but I think we are long enough paupers begging at your door.

4644. Until we know that something is wanted how can we send it?—It was put before you that a grant was required of a piece of ground to establish a home for a very beneficial object, and if you had any interest in the progress of the city you would have been glad to have seen that 10,000 *l.* expended in a permanent property; and there was no necessity to bring an old man of some 84 years above the roads or anybody to represent him. You were asked the simple question, and you might have said yes or no, but you said neither.

4645. Can you say that it was refused?—No, I cannot; I take it as a practical refusal.

4646. Many of the schools that the Society aid are national schools, are they not?—They are under the National Board.

4647. Model schools?—They are national schools under the National Board.

4648. They are open, are they not, to all denominations?—They are.

4649. To Roman Catholics as well as Protestants?—Yes. But you put it into my mind that when large schools are attended by various denominations it is usual for the managers to have, as far as possible, the master or mistress or monitors of the religion of a portion of the pupils, and you have taken care that you have none of them among our children.

Mr. *Cleary*.

4650. The teachers in the schools which the honourable baronet says are open to all denominations are all Protestants?—They are all Protestants, masters and mistresses and monitors.

Sir *John Ellis*.

4651. The Temperance Hall was a question of politics, was it not?—No.

4652. Did not the Society refuse to give a site for the Temperance Hall except on the condition that it was not to be used for political purposes?—You gave the site with the restrictions, an illustration of which I have put to you. A gentleman asked whether it would vitiate the conveyance to hold a public concert for any charitable object in the hall, and Sir Sydney Waterlow (whoever that gentleman may be) said, "Decidedly."

4653. That is your answer?—That is my answer.

4654. Let me take you a step further. Do you know that the application was made since I have been Governor of the Irish Society?—If you are Sir Sydney Waterlow I suppose so.

4655. But I am not Sir Sydney Waterlow?—I do not know. That is the gentleman whose

Sir John Ellis—continued.

name was given to me. He was the Governor, and I was told that he was Sir Sydney Waterlow.

4656. You do not know of any application since Sir Sydney Waterlow was Governor?—I do not know. We have the hall built.

4657. But you do not know of any application since Sir Sydney Waterlow was Governor; any application that has been made since is not within your knowledge?—There is Mrs. Waters's bequest.

4658. No; now we are talking of the Temperance Hall. Since that interview that you refer to, as having been had with Sir Sydney Waterlow, you are not aware of any other application?—How many applications there were I cannot say, but I know that in the correspondence between the parties, the conditions were such that they could not be accepted.

Mr. Lea.

4659. You referred just now to minerals on the Skinners' Estate; do I correctly understand that the tenants in buying resign their rights to minerals, and do not purchase the mineral rights?—Some of them it seems, have all the rights, unrestricted rights granted to them. In the deed which you have before you the company reserve certain rights to themselves; but the tenants understood, in purchasing, that all the rights of the company were to be vested in them and they were to be free of landlords for all time to come, except so far as the Crown was concerned.

4660. Do you know whether the company or the Irish Society hold the mineral rights?—I could not tell you, but the company say that they themselves have the right to enter upon the land. In the deed you will see that they have the right to enter upon the land.

4661. And they still retain that right?—In that deed which you have before you it is retained; but I am informed that some of the tenants have got all the rights without any restrictions whatever to game, minerals, mines, and everything.

4662. Do you know whether the Land Commission have been informed about this reservation?—I do not know.

4663. You cannot tell me why it is reserved, whether it is for the Irish Society or what?—It does not say that it is for the Society; it says for themselves, the Skinners' Company.

4664. There is a part of the Skinners' Estate which is not sold, is there not?—There is a portion not sold.

4665. What is being done with it?—It is just remaining *in statu quo*.

4666. Is there any attempt to sell it at the present moment going on?—I do not think there is; I think the tenants have come to the conclusion that they will see more clearly before they sign any more deeds, what will be the practical issue of the matters now in dispute.

4667. You mean partly with reference to this Committee?—Partly so, and partly with reference to what legal decisions may be made upon the various deeds that have been already granted.

4668. With regard to minerals?—With regard to minerals and game and so forth. They do not wish to have anybody over them hereafter.

Mr. Lea—continued.

4669. Do you know whether there has been any attempt on the part of the company to sell to a syndicate?—I did not hear anything further than what has been stated in the public press. So far as the company is concerned, I think the tenants on the whole are fairly satisfied with them.

4670. Is it the poorest district that is not sold at the present time?—That I could not say. There are some places where the valuable land is not sold, and some which you might call the poorer districts where the land is not sold.

4671. There was an intermediate school at Dungiven at one time, I think?—There was, but I think it has ceased.

4672. Did the Skinners' Company support that largely?—I do not know how much they gave to it; it had ceased to exist before I went there. But the Skinners' Company do give some assistance to the National schools round there; to some of them they give 10 *l.*, and to some of them 5 *l.*

4673. You stated just now, did you not, that the grants were withdrawn by the Skinners' Company from Catholic schools?—They have withdrawn some grants.

4674. They have also withdrawn grants from Presbyterian schools, have they not?—I am not aware.

4675. Are you not acquainted with the Lower Cumber School?—Yes, I have heard of that school.

4676. Are you not aware that a grant of 20 *l.* has been withdrawn from that school?—Yes; and I heard of their withdrawing the salary from the Presbyterian clergyman, and from the Catholic clergyman.

4677. Are you aware that Canon Babington, and the Reverend Edward Newland, last year gave instances of withdrawals of grants by the Skinners' Company from Protestant churches and Protestant schools?—I was not aware of that; I do not know where they are situated, or whether they have any interest.

4678. Do you know Donaghcady?—Yes; that is in county Tyrone.

4679. That is not in your neighbourhood; are you aware that the grant of 10 *l.* was withdrawn from that school by the Skinners' Company, and that a similar grant was withdrawn from the school at Dungiven?—Yes. What we claim is that they should not withdraw these grants, and that in the distribution of them they should treat all men alike, because we all claim to be tenants on the estate, and fairly good citizens, Presbyterian, Catholic, and Episcopalian.

4680. But they are treating all alike in the withdrawal of grants, are they not?—I do not say so. The major portion of these withdrawals will be falling on our heads, who are supposed to be the least able to bear them.

4681. The evidence points to all-round withdrawals; but of course all are equally indignant at the withdrawal of the grants?—All are equally indignant.

4682. It is a fund which you think has been greatly created in the district?—Nearly the whole of the enhancement has been created by the labour of the tenants occupying the property, and we hold that all surplus moneys should be

returned

Mr. Lea—continued.

returned to the advantage of the same, without any discrimination as to their political or other opinions.

4683. You consider that it is a local fund, created by the locality, and that it ought to be administered for the benefit of the locality?—We hold that as the companies are trustees as well as the Society, these funds ought to revert in some shape or other to those who are the objects of the trust.

4684. We cannot go into the question of title; but that is the popular feeling?—That is the popular feeling, that they should be administered by a disinterested body.

Mr. Clancy.

4685. You mentioned, did you not, in answer to the honourable Baronet that the late bishop, Dr. Kelly, refused to go to see the governor?—I do not say that he refused to go; he was not able to go.

4686. Was not that the same gentleman who was called "The Reverend Mr. Kelly"?—The same.

4687. The honourable Baronet asked you a question which implied that the grant would be made for the Temperance Hall, or free hall, if it were not to be used for political purposes?—So he said.

4688. Do you yourself see any reason why a grant should not be made for a hall that was intended to be used even for political purposes?—Certainly, I do not.

4689. Especially when they make grants for the erection of Orange halls?—I think the grants should be made without restriction to the parties requiring them, leaving it to the good taste and the good sense of the committee managing the institution to look after it.

4690. They do not exclude politics from Orange halls, I believe?—I have not had the honour of being present in any; but I think not.

4691. Have things improved so far as the Catholics of Derry are concerned since the accession to office of the present governor?—Some say they have and some say they have not. There is no material advance on the beneficial side of the question.

4692. Can you specify any improvement at all?—It is supposed that the present governor is a more civil and more urbane gentleman than those who preceded him.

4693. Because he called the bishop by his proper title?—I think a gentleman would do that anyhow. The general impression is that the sooner the Society go home to London and leave the property behind them to be managed by a properly established control the better.

4694. You agree that they ought to be cleared out?—They ought to be cleared out body and bone and sent home with a benediction. But they will not take the property with them if you please. We want that to be managed by some well-established arrangement.

Sir William Marriott.

4695. I did not quite understand with regard to the house; the Skinners' Company, in 1878, let the Protestant rector have his house and 500 *l.*; they let the Catholic priest also have his house, did they not?—He had it.

4696. And they have not disturbed him?—They have practically disturbed him.

4697. How so?—Because he has neither house nor habitation. They have treated his interest as if it were a simple tenancy.

4698. So far as I understand, the parish priest then in possession is dead, is he not?—He is dead and buried, and he was dead some years before he was buried.

4699. And his family have claimed the house?—His family have it.

4700. Then practically his family have been too sharp for the Skinners' Company?—The Skinners' Company, or the party acting for them knew what they were doing, and they did it with their eyes open, purposely to deprive me or whoever might hold my place of the convenience.

4701. Who is the agent of the company?—I understand that Dr. Tod was acting for them. I suppose he is acting for every side; he acted no doubt in that.

4702. He is not a partial man I suppose; he is a lawyer, is he not?—I am not quite sure.

4703. The Skinners' Company got no pecuniary advantage out of this arrangement, as I understand?—They benefit, themselves, by not giving the grant of 500 *l.*

4704. But they gain no advantage with regard to the house, do they?—Certainly, they do, because they got the purchase-money. They gave the rectory free and did not get anything for that.

4705. Then did the parish priest who was then in possession give money for the house?—It is bought under the Ashbourne Act, and they pay so much a year for so many years. It was built by the parish.

4706. Who bought it?—It was made over to the then parish priest first and in his name, and his friends now claim it and have it.

4707. Was money paid to the Skinners' Company from the parish priest?—Nothing more than the rent.

Mr. Healy.

4708. Of course the Skinners' Company got the price under the Ashbourne Act from the priest, but they did not get anything from the Protestant clergyman?—No, they got nothing from the Protestant. They gave it to him free, gratis, for nothing.

Sir William Marriott.

4709. Was the parish priest's house sold?—Yes; under the Ashbourne Act.

4710. What did they get for that?—So many years' purchase of the rent.

4711. What was the rent?—I think about 10 *l.* It was sold over, like any ordinary farm holding, to the representative of the gentleman who was lately living there. Nine generations of clergymen, both Roman Catholic and Episcopalian, have lived on these places, the Catholic clergyman on his place, and the Protestant on his.

4712. Did I correctly understand you to say that the Protestant rector got the house handed

Sir William Marriott—continued.

over to trustees for nothing?—For nothing; and he got 40 *l.* a year, and his predecessor got 500 *l.*

4713. And the parish priest did not get his house?—He did not.

4714. But his relatives have bought it?—The relatives have it now under the Ashbourne Act.

4715. At so many years' purchase?—Whatever the number of years agreed to is; and his successor is refused the continuation of the grant. I and those with me have lost the 25 *l.* a year, and the rector has his 40 *l.* a year continued to him and his successors after him.

Mr. Healy.

4716. With regard to those grants, I suppose the Catholics would be quite satisfied if the grants were abolished all round, except in so far as they may be evidence of a trust?—So far as the trust goes we wish to see the trust carried out; but in case it is to be carried out, we wish it to be carried out dispassionately, without relation to class or creed.

Mr. Healy—continued.

4717. The Catholics would be quite willing to see the grants abolished if they were abolished to Episcopalians and Presbyterians?—If they are all treated in the same way.

4718. The honourable Baronet asked you with regard to some matters affecting this Temperance Hall; was it in the time of the present Governor that the money was expended upon the Orange Hall and the Apprentice Boys' Hall?—The Apprentice Boys' Hall has been erected for a good many years, I should say 20 years.

4719. And the Orange Hall?—The Orange Hall was built about six or eight years ago.

4720. Did the body which objected to politics in the Catholic Hall make grants for the purpose of politics to an Orange Hall?—I would conclude that that is the principle upon which they acted. Taking it so far upon my own authority, I think I may say that any political body that wants the use of the Temperance Hall or the Assembly Hall will be quite free to have it. We will give every one entrance there.

The Rev. JOSEPH QUINN, sworn; and Examined.

Mr. Healy.

4721. You are a Roman Catholic Priest?—Yes.

4722. And you are a curate in the town of Magherafelt, in the county of Derry?—Yes.

4723. Whom do you represent here?—I have been asked by a number of representative Catholics in South Derry to represent them.

4724. I suppose you have lived for a considerable time in the county of Derry?—I am a native of Tyrone, adjoining the county of Derry, and I have also been under the Salters' Company for seven years. I have a more general knowledge of the southern portion of the county, and a more particular knowledge of the estates of the Drapers' and Salters' Companies.

4725. Are you prepared to give evidence here as to the treatment of the Catholics by the Drapers' and Salters' Companies?—Yes.

4726. Have you read the evidence that has been given already before the Committee?—Yes. Of course a great portion of the general evidence which has been given already affects that portion of the county, and I should be only repeating what has already been stated to the Committee if I were to go over it again.

4727. Have you read the evidence of Lord Justice Fitzgibbon?—Yes.

4728. And of the Presbyterian witnesses; the Rev. Mr. Dickey, Dr. Tod, and Dr. Jordan?—Yes; and many of the facts that each of them has given I could corroborate if necessary. With regard to the evidence of Lord Justice Fitzgibbon in the report that I have seen, I should like to add an extract from the Report of the Royal Commission for the year 1880–84 affecting the London companies. It is on page 23 of the introduction. "We think it our duty to mention another possible source of endowment. In the course of our inquiries in the north, we have found that several of the London companies which have at all times devoted considerable sums to educational purposes have sold or are now selling their estates without, so far as we know, making any provision for the schools which have hitherto been dependent upon them. The position of the Irish Society also has been brought before us. That Society has been declared by the House of Lords to hold its property upon trust for public purposes, and especially for education. 'They have to superintend and take care of the education of the inhabitants of the district, and have also to perform other public duties of great importance' (Skinners' Company *v.* The Irish Society, 12 Cl. and F. 486). The grants of the Irish Society for education during the year 1882 amounted to 3,610 *l.*, and those made by the London companies were also of large amount; but all these grants were in form voluntary, and in the absence of any specific statute of obligation devoting some definite property to educational purposes, we have hitherto been unable to treat such grants, however long continued, as endowments within the scope of our commission. Unless Parliament should intervene, much of the property we have mentioned is likely to be withdrawn from those general obligations under which it has hitherto been largely devoted to educational purposes."

4729. You desire to say that that represents the view and the feeling of the Catholics in Derry?—Yes.

4730. Are you acquainted with the conditions and the circumstances affecting the sale of the Drapers' and the Salters' Companies' estates?—Yes.

4731. After the passing of the Ashbourne Act were the tenants approached by agents representing the Salters' and the Drapers' Companies?—Yes; previously to the passing of that Act some of the tenants on the Salters' estate were anxious to purchase, and there had been some negotiations going on; but after the passing of

Mr. *Healy*—continued.

the Act a solicitor, who was sent to represent the tenants, negotiated with the Salters' Company, and the general terms upon which they were willing to part with their estate were 19½ years' purchase of the net Government valuation of the land.

4732. Was this Dr. Todd?—It was Dr. Todd.

4733. Dr. Todd was afterwards availed of by the companies to conduct the sale for them, was he not?—I cannot speak as to the fact.

4734. Was it not regarded as a grievance in the district that the tenants' solicitor should have been availed of by the landlord to complete or conduct negotiations on their behalf?—Yes; that was the feeling, but I cannot say whether, as a matter of fact, the Salters' Company employed him as their representative or agent as well as the tenants.

4735. At any rate, it is the case that the same gentleman who first acted for the tenants was afterwards employed to conduct the negotiations for purchase on behalf of the landlords?—Yes, it is the feeling, but I could not say whether it was a fact or not. Then I should mention that, although these were the general terms laid down by the company, inasmuch as some of the rentals were higher than that, the company agreed, in the course of the purchase, to take either 19½ years' purchase of the net Government valuation, or 19½ years' purchase of the rental, in cases where the rental was lower than the Government valuation. Proceeding under those terms, most of the estate was sold. I was informed, subsequently, that some of those lands were sold at a less number of years' purchase. With regard to the town parks, the terms were 18 years' purchase of the Government valuation, and the houses, from that down to 15 years' purchase, and even some of them as low as 12 years' purchase.

4736. Were those houses built by the tenants themselves?—Yes, with the exception of a few.

4737. And, therefore, the company picketed the purchase money for houses which were erected by the tenants?—I believe so.

4738. The Drapers' terms, I believe, were 18 years' purchase?—The Drapers' terms were 18 years' purchase of their rental.

4739. I believe, comparing the Salters' and the Drapers' Companies, you rather think that the Salters' Company acted more fairly than the Drapers' Company?—Yes, the Salters' Company's terms were made upon a valuation which was of a date prior to the date of any rental of their estate, or any neighbouring estate.

4740. You think that because they took the Government valuation they adopted a fairer basis?—Yes; there was not so much of the tenants' improvements included in the Government valuation as there would be in the case of the rental; because there were numbers of improvements made by the tenants subsequently to the date of the Government valuation.

4741. In the same way, on the Drapers' estate do you think that the Drapers' price included some of the tenants' improvements?—Yes. The Drapers sold their lands on the general terms of 18 years' purchase for all of their lands. It is well known that on their estate there are, roughly speaking, two classes of land. There is a good quality of land around the village of Moneygawn.

4742. That is a Protestant village, is it not?—It is.

4743. And the Protestants, we may take it, throughout are on the good lands?—Yes.

4744. And the portion of the land that is occupied by Catholics in the Ballinascreen division, a mountainous portion, is it not?—Yes. Sir William Cunningham, before the Cowper Commission, when asked as to those two districts, said that the land in the mountainous district would not be of so much value as the land in the Moneymore division.

4745. That was only another way of saying, I presume, that the Catholics were getting a worse bargain than the Protestants for the lands?—I suppose that would follow.

4746. Sir William Cunningham was the agent for the company?—He was.

4747. And he was a very much respected gentleman, I think?—Yes, he was respected by many.

Sir *William Marriott*.

4748. Of the Protestants?—I do not say that. So far as the question of purchase or rent is concerned, I do not think that the Protestants or the Catholics cared much who was the agent, supposing they got good terms.

Mr. *Healy*.

4749. At any rate Sir William Cunningham declared before the Cowper Commission that the land for which the Catholics were asked to give 18 years' purchase was not worth as much as the land for which the Protestants were asked to give 18 years' purchase?—Yes.

4750. And yet the company insisted upon the same price in both divisions?—Yes; the land about Moneymore is intrinsically good, so that it would produce good crops with a fair amount of labour; whereas the land in the other district is of such a quality that although the tenant is continually expending money and labour, and manure, the crops would be very poor; and, besides, the land lies so high that it is more affected by the weather, and the land is damp, and generally the crops are later, so much so that sometimes the tenants are not able to secure their harvests. It is a district in which the tenants have made a great portion of the improvements of the land because it is mountainous, and they reclaimed it. So that by selling it at 18 years' purchase the Drapers' Company would be insisting on the tenants paying for their own improvements.

4751. Can you give us some instances of inducement or pressure used by the Drapers' and Salters' Companies to get the tenants to buy?—A number of the tenants on the Drapers' estate came to me, hearing that I was coming here, and said that they were promised bog, which is very useful and serviceable for making peat for the purposes of fuel, especially on those farms on which there is no bog. The tenants would be inclined to give a higher price for the land if this bog was secured to them. Some of these tenants were promised that, and some also were promised portions of the various plantations that were on the estate.

Mr. *Healy*—continued.

In all those cases, so far as I have met the question, they have been refusal. That was after they had signed the purchase.

4752. It is right to say, in justice to the company, whose land the plantation was on, that the Land Commission refused in some way to facilitate the sale of the plantation to the tenants: I forget the reason why, but the company was hardly to blame as regards the plantation. Then as to arrears, was the existence of arrears on the buildings a main reason why the tenants were induced to give this high price?—On the Salters' estate, so far as I have been able to gather, the Salters' Company acted honourably, and never themselves interfered with the purchase. But there were some minor persons going about saying that if those tenants did not buy out at first, some other persons would purchase the fee-simple over them. I do not say that came from the company. I should say that the purchase went on more quickly on the Salters' estate than on the Drapers' estate, from the fact that in the case of the poorer tenants the Government valuation was lower than their rental, and did not include so much their own improvements; so that the poorer class of tenants on the poorer lands got better terms on the Salters' estate than on the Drapers' estate; and also on the Salters' estate a great number of tenants do not live altogether by farming, but are engaged in linen weaving, so that they would be better able to pay their instalments.

4753. Was the existence of arrears used as a force to compel the Drapers' tenants to pay up?—Yes, it was. I think, about the year 1884 or 1885, which was a time of depression, the tenants in these poorer districts saw that they were not able to pay their full rents; so they wanted the companies to give them what they considered a fair reduction. The company, I think, refused to give them so much as the tenants expected. The result was that many of those people who would have paid what was in their estimation a fair portion of the rent did not pay it at all, and the money went to other purposes. Then the next year they were, of course, almost worse, because the company would insist upon the two years. Then the company began to process them for their arrears, and after some cases had been gone through, it was arranged that the rents should be spread over a number of years. From one year to another, owing to this state of things, the arrears grew to be pretty large in some of the poorer districts, and then the company were pressing the tenants to either buy out at their terms, or to pay up all their arrears without giving them a reduction.

4754. To what do you attribute the difference between the action of the Salters' Company and the action of the Drapers' Company?—The Salters' Company had sold early, and the tenants were, I think, perhaps in better circumstances. Owing to this linen weaving, I suppose they would be better able to pay their instalments.

4755. Do you think that the Drapers' negotiations would not have dragged on so long if the price had not been so high?—In the poorer district, I am certain that they would not. Then I should say that certainly the Drapers' Company had been very pressing in some cases, to make those tenants buy who they thought should buy.

4756. By means of writs and processes?—Yes.

4757. Have you a number of writs and processes there?—Yes (*producing some documents*). This has been sent to me by a gentleman of the name of James M'Elhatton, on the Moneymore estate. It seems that in 1888, according to his own statement, there was two years' rent against him, and for that he was sued; I do not know by what process.

Mr. *John Ellis.*

4758. Was that rent a judicial rent?—No. The rental was about 13 *l.* or 14 *l.* That included the whole rent; that was not the judicial rent. Then the next year he was sued in law, and the costs that year were 8 *l.* 3 *s.* 9 *d.*

Mr. *Healy.*

4759. His old rent was 13 *l.* 10 *s.*, and then it was reduced to 8 *l.* 10 *s.*?—Yes, I think so.

4760. They first served him with a writ for two years' rent, 37 *l.*, in the Superior Court, and the Superior Court writs are always regarded with more terror, because of the costs?—Yes.

4761. That was dated on the 29th of November 1889, last year, and then they served an ejectment on the 28th of January 1890, for two years' judicial rent?—What I want to show is that there was not two years' judicial rent due at that time, but only one year's rent was due in November 1889; but notwithstanding that they served him with a writ of the Superior Court for two years' rent; that is to say, a year in advance of what was due, I suppose.

4762. The point is that within the one year they served him with an ejectment in the county court, for a higher rent than he was legally liable to be charged?—Yes; so that he was served with a writ of the Superior Court for the year ending November 1888, although paid.

4763. And you say that this rent was not due at the time?—It is not, because the receipts shows that the rent for one of the years was paid and the other was not.

4764. Are there any other cases of that kind?—There may be other cases, but I refer specially to that case. There are other cases of writs.

4765. With regard to the way in which the Catholics were treated on the estate, was a difference made between Catholic and Protestant tenants?—Yes; but I should say that my experience of the companies is this: that the Catholics looked upon them as good or bad landlords in proportion as the Catholics were fairly or otherwise treated. When the Catholics were treated with impartiality they looked on the companies as good landlords, although they might exact very high rents.

4766. That is to say, they did not look at them as being landlords?—They did not look on them as being landlords so much as from the point of view of impartiality, and some of the agents on the Drapers' estate were famous all the country round for their partiality towards Catholics.

4767. Wh

Mr. *Healy*—continued.

4767. Who were those agents who were known to be partial?—There were the Millers, of the Moneymore or Drapers' estate. The result of their policy was that they depopulated a whole townland of Catholics, or, at any rate, reduced them very much. The policy of those men that I allude to, so far as I have been able to gather, and as is well known, was, that in case a Catholic had any property to dispose of, he was not allowed to sell it to whomsoever he wished, but he had to go into the office, and then the agent would, if possible, get a Protestant to purchase it, and the tenant would be allowed only what the agent would say he should get.

4768. The agent compelled the Catholics to sell to Protestants at whatever price the Protestants cared to give?—Yes.

4769. What estate was this on?—On the Drapers' estate.

4770. That was Mr. Miller?—Yes; Rowley Miller. There was a number of them, but Rowley Miller was the most famous. That was only one of the circumstances. If he could not get a Protestant to buy it at the time, he would allow the tenant to hold it for some time. Then, if a Protestant was selling property, he got a Catholic to purchase it. The Catholic might get it in some cases, if the agent wished; but in that case the policy was, I was told, that a Catholic would not be accepted as a tenant for a length of time, sometimes up to two years; he would not be finally accepted as tenant, so that he could be set aside in the meantime if some more acceptable person turned up. This policy had a very demoralising effect upon the locality. It had a very demoralising effect upon the Catholics, because they had not confidence that they could get fair play on the estates, and it did not encourage them to work as they would have wished; and it also had a very demoralising effect upon the Protestants, because they would not give what would be a fair price in some cases.

4771. Were there other agents who treated the Catholics fairly?—Yes. I should say that there was an agent on the other company's estates who practised the same policy. Mr. Spottiswoode, on the Salters' estate, was said to carry out this policy too. I saw a case myself where there were two brothers; one of them had become somewhat reduced in circumstances, and he sold a portion of his land to his brother; but when they went into the office, the company's representatives did not agree to it for some time, and then they agreed to it. After the brothers had prepared the land for cropping, a Protestant turned up, and the agent deprived the Catholic brother of the property and gave it to his Protestant neighbour. Besides the demoralising effect of this course, it had the effect of stirring up discord among the members of the various religious denominations.

4772. Did Mr. Spottiswoode also refuse long leases to Catholics?—Yes, I was told that he did.

4773. And they were granted, on the other hand, to Protestants?—That I could not say. That is to show that the companies were very much in the hands of their agents. On the other hand, there were some very impartial agents; and amongst those I may mention Sir Henry Cartwright (then Mr. Cartwright), the late agent for the Salters' Company. I think he was for about 15 or 16 years the agent of the Salters' Company. He came as a successor to Mr. Spottiswoode, and the Protestants expected that they would be treated similarly, and that they would be favoured by him. A case arose soon after his coming, where a Protestant had been selling some property at a public sale, and a Catholic had bid the highest. After the sale the Protestant neighbour, who expected to get it, went into the agent, and asked that he should get this property. Mr. Cartwright said that he would not, and that if he wished for it he should have purchased it at the public auction, and that he would pursue the policy of treating all men alike, and impartially. That gave confidence to the Catholics that they could live on the Salters' estate. It also induced them to more improvements, because they would retain what they had.

4774. At any rate, the Catholics considered that gratitude was due from them for the fair treatment that they received on the Salters' estate?—Yes.

4775. They were grateful for bare justice?—Yes. In connection with this I may mention that those good agents had the effect of improving the estates, whereas bad agents had the effect of reducing the value of the estates. I think Mr. Cartwright helped in this respect to improve the value of the Salters' estates, because he not only acted impartially in this way, but took a lively interest in matters in connection with the estate and the improvement of the town. He started a building society, he established gasworks, and got the company to contribute towards; and he and the company treated the Catholics fairly in the matter of granting ground for a church. In the time of Mr. Spottiswoode the Catholics would get no ground for a church, except sites that were altogether inconsistent with the position of a church. In Sir Henry Cartwright's time the Catholics got a very fine site for a church.

4776. The inference which you wish to be drawn, as I understand, is that the same company, acting by different agents, pursued an entirely different policy?—Yes.

4777. And it shows that the company in London are entirely in the hands of their Irish agents?—Yes; that is the point.

4778. Now, will you give some instances of grants made by the companies?—The two estates with which I am most conversant are the Drapers' and the Salters'.

4779. I suppose the Catholics are at least 85 per cent. of the population?—The Catholics on the Drapers' estate are about 89 per cent., and the company grant to Catholic schools not a single penny; they give no money at all to Catholic schools. Heretofore they have been giving grants to one school, but they have discontinued it; and last year they would not even give coal.

4780. Had they been giving coal previously?—Yes.

4781. And they stopped the coal?—Yes; they stopped the coal, although, as I am informed, they

Mr. *Healy*—continued.

they continued the coal to the Protestant schools. I believe the only grant that they are giving on the estate to any Catholic purpose is 10 *l*. a year to two Roman Catholic clergymen.

4782. Have they stopped the grants to the Protestants?—I am not aware that they have. On the Salters' Company's estate they have acted more liberally.

4783. What have the Salters' Company done?—First, to speak generally, they have treated all fairly. They are giving grants to four Catholic schools of 5 *l*. each, and 20 *l*. to two Roman Catholic clergymen on the estate. Those are the grants that they have been making. With regard to those grants, so far as I can see, they are voluntary, and only to extend over the term of office, either of the teachers or of the clergymen.

4784. Have they made permanent grants?—The Drapers' Company, so far as I am aware, are making no permanent grants whatever. The Salters' Company have made permanent grants, first of all to education.

4785. We have heard about the Rainey School?—I should say that the Salters' Company have conveyed both the markets of the town of Magherafelt and the streets in trust; and, in the constitution of the board of trustees, they have treated the Catholics equally with the Protestants, putting an equal number of Catholics and Protestants on the board; and they have also conveyed the Fairhill and quarries, and some other property in the town; and the surplus of profit over the rent-charge of 120 *l*. for the purpose of schools is to be employed for the improvement of the town of Magherafelt.

4786. The Salters' Company have continued the grants for public purposes, whereas the Drapers' Company have entirely stopped them?—Yes; and the Salters' Company have been more liberal and generous in what they have done.

4787. Do you wish also to comment upon the way in which the dispensary doctor at Draperstown has been treated by the Drapers' Company?—Yes.

4788. What was done in his case?—As I was coming here he called upon me. He wished to come himself and tell you how he had been treated, but as he could not, he spoke to me about it. Previous to his time the dispensary doctor had received a free house in connection with the dispensary, and also a grant of 30 *l*. a year. When he came, he asked to get the same house, but it was refused to him; he even asked to get it at a rent, but he could not get it for any rent whatever.

4789. Was that because he was a Catholic?—They gave him 10 *l*. for a year or two. I think that was 1886 and 1887; and then they withdrew that. He told me that he believed one of the reasons why he was refused was because he was a Catholic.

4790. What was his name?—Dr. Hegarty.

4791. His predecessor was a Protestant?—Yes.

4792. As regards all this question of grants, I suppose the Catholics would be quite content if they were stopped, provided that the Protestants and Presbyterians were treated alike?—I saw in the evidence of Dr. Todd that he signified some opinion of that sort; I have been saying some people, and those I saw said they would be indifferent.

Mr. *Healy*—continued.

4793. The Catholics would take this position; they would be content that the grants should be stopped, provided that the Protestants and Presbyterians were treated in the same way?—They wish impartiality and all classes to be treated alike.

4794. I think one Catholic clergyman refused to take a grant?—Yes, a clergyman on the Salters' Company's estate who has been there 30 or 40 years would not accept it.

4795. And you are speaking on behalf of the Catholics generally when you say that, except so far as grants may be evidence of the public trust, you repudiate the desire to get grants for your community or religion, provided the Presbyterians and Protestants were treated in the same way?—I should think so. At the same time I would like that the grants should be continued for public and general purposes; for example, for the purpose of establishing technical schools in localities where they would be suitable, and intermediate schools in other places, and establishing scholarships obtainable by children even in national schools, whereby they would be enabled to prosecute their studies in a higher college.

4796. So far as the grants to clergymen are concerned, the Catholic clergy are quite content to see all the grants stopped, provided they are stopped all round?—I should think so.

4797. Will you explain why the Salters' Company have acted with more liberality than the Drapers' Company; is it because of the local manager being a differently-minded person, or is it due to the influence of the London management?—As regards the carrying out of the sale, and the management of the estate previous to that, I attribute it to the fact that the agent resided in the locality, and made his home there, and intended to remain there all his life.

4798. You mean the Salters' agent?—Yes. He took an interest in the locality and the management of the estate as if he were actually a local landlord.

4799. That was not the case with regard to the Drapers?—No, I think not; because their agents were changed so often.

4800. Do the Catholics concur with the Presbyterians and Protestants in considering that these companies hold their property in trust for the locality?—That is the general belief.

4801. And their desire and anxiety would be that the moneys of the companies should be devoted to some work of public advantage, such as education or something of that kind?—Yes; a large proportion at all events.

4802. Have you anything else you would wish to bring before the Committee?—I have just received a telegram since I came away with regard to some schools on the Drapers' estate. I may say that the proportion of Catholics as regards holdings is between 60 and 70 per cent.; and I should think as regards the population the proportion would be larger. The schools are scattered over the estate. If the companies continue those schools to the Protestants alone they will likely cause the ruin of these schools, because the Catholics can establish, and likely

will

Mr. *Healy*—continued.

will establish, schools of their own, and leave those schools so that they will not be able to have sufficient attendance to keep them up, except in Protestant districts, and those schools would be left as monuments in the locality. Seeing that this was the case, some persons who were believed to know something about the working of the Drapers' estate informed his Grace the Primate that one school in particular was considered superfluous for the Protestants, and he was told if he asked for it he would obtain it for the Catholics. He applied, and the answer made to him, so far as I can gather from this telegram, was that the sale of the estate was not yet completed, and therefore they could not give him a decided answer. I only gather that answer from the telegram.

4803. Do you conceive, generally speaking, that the Catholics have had fair play upon the estates of the London companies?—Where the agent was a liberal and impartial man they have; but those cases were not of too frequent occurrence.

4804. I want to know the result of your experience. Do the Catholics consider, taking it all round, that they are treated with impartiality and fairness on the estates of the London companies?—Speaking generally, they consider they are not; in particular cases they consider they are.

Mr. *Lea.*

4805. I want to correct one misapprehension. You said just now that the grants had been withdrawn by the Drapers' Company from the Catholics?—I did not say that; I said they were giving no grants whatever except to two clergymen of 10*l.* each; they had previously given one grant to one particular Catholic school, and I understand the grant in that case was withdrawn.

4806. I understood you to say that no grants had been withdrawn from Presbyterian schools?—I did not say that.

4807. Then I misapprehended you. I think you said you had read the evidence of Mr. Dickey, Dr. Jordan, and Dr. Todd and some of the other witnesses, I think?—Yes; some of it.

4808. And their general evidence with regard to the estate you agree with?—From the reports I have seen.

4809. You join with them and with men of all religions in trying to retain this property as a north of Ireland land property?—There are two or three things involved in that question. First, as regards retaining the property, of course the general opinion of all classes is that, considering the terms of the various charters, and also, considering the tradition and belief of the people of the north of Ireland on these estates that these were trusts, they consider that at least portions of these properties should be continued in trust. So far as the north of Ireland is concerned, I suppose the north would think they had the best right to it.

4810. So far as the county of Derry is concerned?—Yes.

Mr. *John Ellis.*

4811. I want to clear up this case of Mr. M'Elhatton about paying the rent, which you referred to. This man occupied a farm at a place called Coltrim and Drummont?—Yes.

4812. On the 28th of October 1889 he received a memorandum from the Drapers' Company, Number 314?—Yes; what he considered to be a receipt for rent.

4813. Did he receive this paper (*handing a paper to the Witness*)?—Yes; it bears the signature of the clerk in the company's office.

4814. That memorandum states that he "has left with me 8*l.* 10*s.* on account of the rent of the holding" in "Coltrim and Drummont for one year to 1st November 1888"?—Yes.

4815. He received also from the Drapers' Company a civil bill ejectment, dated the 29th November 1889?—Yes; it was subsequent to the date of paying.

4816. Did he not receive this blue paper, this civil bill ejectment?—He gave me all these papers and said he got these papers.

4817. In this blue paper it states that he holds the land at the yearly rent of 8*l.* 10*s.*, "and whereas the sum of 17*l.* of the said rent being one full year's rent and upwards due and ended on the 1st day of November last, became and is still due to the plaintiff, certain proceedings will be taken." How can you explain the case of this man having in his possession this memorandum, stating that he had paid the rent up to the 1st of November 1888, being sued in November 1889 for two years' rent then due?—It is for the company to explain it, not for me; I consider it a grievance of the greatest kind.

4818. You consider that the company sued him for rent which he had already paid?—Which he had already paid.

4819. Does the same case arise with regard to the same tenant of land at a place called Dunnabraggy?—The papers show that themselves; because you have the receipt there for the payment of money, and subsequently to that they were suing him in a summary court for two years' rent, whereas there was only one due.

4820. Can you tell us how that was?—I have not examined the papers or gone over them in that particular way; I can say nothing more about them, but what I have said and what the papers show.

4821. These papers were given to you, I understand?—Yes, these papers were handed to me because the man said he could not come himself, and as I was coming I said I would bring them and put them before you.

4822. You appear on his behalf and make this statement for him?—I simply undertook to convey them for him here. I do not go in for explaining them further than as I have said.

4823. The same thing applies to the farm at Dunnabraggy, does it not?—I can say nothing about that.

Mr. *Clancy.*

4824. I should like to find out whether the statement of the costs on this paper you have handed to us is correct?—I have only the man's evidence and the documents for it.

4825. The costs are given here for 1885 and 1886 as 6*l.* 6*s.*; for 1887, 2*l.* 3*s.* 9*d.*; for 1888, 17*s.* 6*d.*, and for 1889, 1*l.* 12*s.* 6*d.*; so that altogether for four years' rents the costs were 10*l.* 18*s.* 9*d.*?—Yes; so he said. They said that,

Mr. *Clancy*—continued.

that, inasmuch as they made a mistake in issuing this writ in the superior court for money than was already paid, they only charged him half the costs. Whether they had the right to make him pay half the costs or not is a question.

Mr. *Healy*.

4826. Was that to induce him to buy?—He said all this proceeding was to induce him to buy.

Mr. *Clancy*.

4827. It was persisted in for four years?—Or more, I think; proceedings were taken for four consecutive years.

4828. He has not bought yet, has he?—No.

Mr. *Healy*.

4829. Do you know anything about the Mercers' grant?—About the Mercers' Dr. Hegarty told me that the predecessor to the present Mr. Watney had exercised this policy

Mr. *Healy*—continued.

towards Catholics which was shown in these other two cases that I have mentioned; that is to say, excluding Catholics where they could.

4830. You say the predecessor to the present Mr. Watney; that is the brother of the gentleman who acts as clerk, I think?—He is an impartial man; but Dr. Hegarty said that his predecessor treated Catholics exclusively in this way; that when they wanted property they would not get it if another person could be found to take it.

4831. Do you mean Mr. Watney?—No; his predecessor. I think his name was Denman.

4832. He discriminated against the Catholics?—Yes; and Mr. Watney when he came pursued a policy of impartiality. That is what Dr. Hegarty told me.

4833. But with regard to the grants have the company pursued a policy of impartiality?—I cannot say for the Mercers' estate generally, but I know that they have given little or nothing for education.

Friday, 11th July 1890.

MEMBERS PRESENT:

Mr. Clancy.	Mr. Lawson.
Lord Elcho.	Mr. Lea.
Sir John Ellis.	Sir William Marriott.
Mr. John Ellis.	Mr. John Morley.
Mr. T. M. Healy.	Sir Richard Temple.
Colonel Laurie.	

THE RIGHT HONOURABLE JOHN MORLEY, IN THE CHAIR.

Rev. FATHER QUINN, re-called; and Examined.

Chairman.

4834. You desire, I understand, to correct one or two points in your evidence of yesterday?—To supplement them. In comparing the sales of the Salters' and the Drapers', I spoke of one of them as being more equitable than the other. In saying that, I did not wish to speak of the one as being fair or otherwise, because the general feeling of the people is, that the terms of both were higher than what is considered fair, and that in buying out their farms, especially in the case of reclaimed land, the tenants had to pay for a great portion of their own improvements. Another point is, that in respect of the grants made by the Drapers' Company to the Roman Catholic clergymen, I think I said that two Roman Catholic clergymen received 10 *l.* I have had a letter from one of the clergymen since, saying, that although the time for paying the last year's instalment, or subscription, or donation, has long gone past, he has not yet received it; so he understands they may have withdrawn giving him that grant. The reason he believes is, that they asked him to purchase his holding, and that he did not.

4835. You are now giving us what he says to you in his letter?—Yes, but I know some portion of this personally. They asked him to purchase his holding at a certain price, which he considered too high. A portion of it he was to pay down in cash, and the remaining portion he believed would be advanced under the Ashbourne Act. He considered the terms too high and refused to purchase. I understand that he was served by them with an ejectment process, and is now under ejection. This was, he believes, in order to press him to purchase at the terms they asked him. Another point I wish to mention is this.

4836. Is this the third point you wish to put right?—Yes. It is chiefly with regard to the way in which their officials rather than themselves treat their tenants. There was a tenant on this estate who was in some arrears, I think some £4 *l.*, and he has been served with an ejectment, and put out of his holding. He and his family immediately took fever, and were obliged to go to the infirmary.

Chairman—continued.

4837. What is the name of this person?—A Mr. Grant.

4838. What is his address and description?—I do not remember exactly now.

4839. However, he is on the Drapers' Estate?—Yes. They ejected him in the month of August. The result of this was that he was unable to save the crops that were on his land, and the company did not save them either, so that the crops were lost, and he was not reinstated until he agreed to purchase at their terms in the month of April following.

4840. In what year was this?—I should think it was 1889 he was reinstated.

4841. And you are sure it was April 1889?—Yes, and at such a time that it was very late for him to put in his crops. Then the fourth point is, speaking generally, as to the way the companies have treated the Roman Catholics.

4842. You are now here, as I understand, to correct what you said yesterday in some respects?—To put some amendments.

4843. What do you say on the fourth point?—I was going to put this as an amendment to what I have said, or rather as addition: it is that, speaking generally, the Roman Catholics have received but very small consideration in the way of grants from most of the Companies. In the case of the grants to the clergy they only gave it to one clergyman in the parish.

4844. You are speaking of the Roman Catholic clergy?—Yes; whereas in some of the parishes there were two, three, or four, but in the case of the clergymen of other religious denominations, most of whom had each a church of his own, they each received a donation.

4845. Then, is there any further point?—Yes; I said that the Roman Catholics considered that the companies were good or bad landlords as they treated them fairly or otherwise; of course, in saying that, I do not wish to imply that the Roman Catholics considered them good landlords when they have treated them harshly, though they may have treated them impartially in other respects.

Sir William Marriott.

4846. What made you think of these amendments?—I was afraid that I might have made a wrong impression on some of those points.

4847. What made you think you had made a wrong impression?—There was one new point arose about the clergyman's donation.

4848. But about the Catholics being hardly treated; what made you think of that and come with that amendment?—I thought I did not fully explain it yesterday.

4849. Have you had any talk with anybody since?—No.

4850. No talk?—No.

4851. It is entirely your own idea?—Yes; I did not expect to be called yesterday.

Sir William Marriott—continued.

4852. Between your examination yesterday and to-day you had no conversation with anybody on the point?—No.

4853. It is entirely your own opinion?—Yes.

4854. You have not spoken to anybody?—No, on this point.

4855. On any other of the points you have amended?—I got that letter.

4856. But putting aside that letter?—No; I had no opportunity of speaking to anyone on any of those points.

4857. It simply occurred to you in the night between yesterday and to-day?—They occurred to me, some of them, immediately after leaving here.

Mr. John Wrench Towse, sworn; and Examined.

Sir William Marriott.

4858. You are the clerk, I think, to the Fishmongers' Company?—Yes.

4859. And you are here to give any information which the Committee wishes, either with regard to the ancient history of the Fishmongers' Company or to their recent doings?—So far as I am able.

4860. I will not go into the ancient history, because that is rather beside the Committee; they have decided not to go into that at present. The Fishmongers' Company have sold their lands in Ireland?—They have.

4861. All of them?—All.

4862. When did they first decide to sell?—In 1883 they first passed a resolution stating that they would sell at a time which they thought would be convenient to themselves, and conducive to the interests of the tenants.

4863. Had they done anything to ascertain the view of the tenants with regard to the question of sale?—No. They have had some evidence from time to time, more particularly the evidence given before Lord Derby's Commission.

4864. The Commission of 1880?—Yes.

4865. Before that Commission reported, but after, I think, the Commission of 1880, they decided to sell their land if the tenants were willing to buy?—Yes.

4866. That Commission, I think, did not report till June 1884?—That was so.

4867. And it was in November of that year that the Court of the Fishmongers' Company decided to consider the question of sale?—Yes.

4868. Now what decision did the Fishmongers' Company come to in consequence of the Report of that Commission in the early part of 1885?—That they would offer the tenants their respective farms, the farms that they were occupying. Each man was to be offered the opportunity of purchasing the farm that he occupied.

4869. How many years' purchase did they offer them?—Twenty years' purchase on the net rent.

4870. Up to that time had the Fishmongers' Company been accustomed to subscribe to certain charities?—They had.

4871. Are you prepared to say how much they subscribed to Irish charities at that time?—I have a tabular statement here which gives the average.

4872. Let us see that?—There are two (*handing in same*).

4873. Why did you take the date from the year 1836?—We found it was most convenient.

4874. Had you had long leases before that which fell in?—No, the property fell in in 1820. I could supply the earlier details, if that is the wish of the Committee.

4875. I think the annual amount is very much higher in some years than in others?—Yes, it is so.

4876. The annual average is 4,777 *l.* 9 *s.* 4 *d.*?—Yes.

4877. That is the annual average of what has been given away by the Fishmongers' Company up to the present time?—Up to 1887.

4878. The donations were voluntary contributions to churches, chapels, schools, &c., and there is also the necessary expenditure upon the management of the estate; can you divide those two?—I think I can do it.

4879. That document would show it in itself?—Yes. It is only a matter of taking out the details; I can do that later on.

4880. Then what the Committee want to know is how much you gave each year in charities or public objects, separate from the expenditure on the estate; with regard to what you did spend whatever the amount may be upon these public objects, did the Fishmongers' Company in offering land to the tenants make any provisions for their continuation?—They did. They allowed for the half of the county cess which they had hitherto paid, and for draining, ditching roads, farm buildings, repairs, river banks, and sloh lands, and beyond that they took off a further percentage.

4881. How much was the percentage they took off?—They took off in all 25 per cent.

4882. Twenty years' purchase they gave?—Twenty years' purchase.

4883. And what did the 20 per cent. represent?—The 20 per cent. represented what I mentioned just now, the county cess, poor rate, draining, ditching roads, farm buildings, repairs, river banks, and sloh lands. Then there is a further 5 per cent. taken off as a round sum.

4884. What

Sir William Marriott—continued.

4884. What was that to represent?—That was to represent the depreciation perhaps in the value of the farms, and any other matter which they may have existed at the time of taking this into consideration.

4885. Was it 28 per cent. including that eight per cent.?—Twenty-eight per cent.

4886. Did they leave any special provision for the carrying on of the donations for schools and churches?—No.

4887. I think in the purchase they gave the tenants the option of three different ways of purchase, did they not?—That was so.

4888. What were those ways?—There were three schemes; Scheme A. was cash down.

Chairman.

4889. The whole cash down?—Yes, the net cash after the deduction of the 28 per cent. Scheme B., an annuity for 30 years, calculated at 6½ per cent. on the principal; that included interest and sinking fund. Then Scheme C., 25 per cent. cash down, and the balance by annuity for 30 years.

4890. On the same terms?—On the same terms.

4891. The 75 per cent. was to be paid by the annuity for 30 years?—Yes.

4892. At what interest was that?—The same, 5¼ per cent., including the interest and principal and the sinking fund.

Sir William Marriott.

4893. What percentage would that be?—About 3¼ths. It was calculated for the half-year, 1·816.

4894. These three modes of payment were offered to the tenants?—Yes.

4895. Did they take advantage of them?—They did; within about three weeks they expressed their willingness to accept the terms.

4896. How many tenants had you on the estate at that time?—About 400 in all.

4897. And did they all agree?—I may say they all agreed.

4898. What was the average acreage on the holdings of these 400 tenants?—They varied very much.

4899. What was the lowest and the highest?—The lowest would be about 10 acres and the highest about 250 acres.

4900. Have you got the rents per acre; I suppose they varied?—Very much; from 1 s. 6 d. to about 25 s.

Chairman.

4901. You say some of the holdings were 10 acres, and the highest was 250 acres; kindly tell us the rent of the 10-acre holding and the rent of the 250-acre holding; the highest in one case and the lowest in the other?—One of the lowest: I will not say that this is quite the lowest; but for a 9-acre farm the rent was 6 l. 5 s.

Sir William Marriott.

4902. Is there another of that size you have before you?—Yes, there is another of 9¾ acres; you might say 10 acres; 15 l.

4903. Now give us some of the bigger ones?—Yes, 284 acres, 294 l. The total rental upon that farm was 298 l., but that was owing to 4 l. being added for an advance for interest.

Chairman.

4904. Would you call it, generally, an estate of small holdings, 10-acre holdings, or large holdings?—Average holdings I should say; not large.

Sir William Marriott.

4905. What do you call the average?—I should say 20 to 30 acres would be the average. It is merely an hypothesis; I cannot say definitely.

Chairman.

4906. The details of the size of the holdings and the rentals were laid, I think, before Lord Derby's Commission?—I believe they were.

Sir William Marriott.

4907. Which of the three schemes did the majority of the tenants adopt: A., B., or C.?—The majority adopted B.; that was the annuity.

4908. I suppose those payments are going on now?—Lord Ashbourne's Act was passed in 1885, and then the majority of tenants asked the company to allow them to purchase under Lord Ashbourne's Act, but the company objected to alter the contract so recently entered into; but if the majority of the tenants wished to apply under Lord Ashbourne's Act for an advance to enable them to purchase their farms, the company were willing for the 25 per cent. to outstand as the guaranteed deposit; they all accepted the Company's terms, with a few exceptions, in 1885.

Chairman.

4909. What part of 1885?—April of 1885.

4910. They accepted most of them under Scheme B., in the spring of 1885?—Yes.

4911. What is the point of your reference to Lord Ashbourne's Act?—After they had signed the agreement for the purchase under the company's scheme, Lord Ashbourne's Act was passed, and then the tenants, considering the terms more favourable, and that they would have less to pay, and a longer period, of 49 years, they memorialised the company to allow them to purchase under that scheme or under that Act, instead of under the company's scheme.

4912. Then the transactions under the company's scheme, in fact, never came to anything?—Oh, yes, I beg your pardon, there were about 90 tenants completed under the company's scheme.

Sir William Marriott.

4913. Did those 90 get the benefit of Lord Ashbourne's Act?—No, it was their wish to continue under the company; they had the opportunity of taking either course.

4914. Did they determine to abide by the agreement made in 1885?—Yes.

Chairman.

4915. Lord Ashbourne's Act being August 1885?—Yes.

4916. You

Sir William Marriott.

4916. You could give, I suppose, the details of the sales in cash; the sales under scheme B.?—£. 17,833. 0s. 1d., under the Scheme B.

4917. And under the sales for cash?—Under scheme A., 9,691 l. 1s. 10d.

4918. And under the Land Commissioners?—£. 119,344. 0s. 6d., making altogether 146,668 l. 8s. 5d.

4919. That did not go into the hands of the Fishmongers' Company; there were deductions to be made?—Deductions were made.

4920. What were the deductions?—Legal expenses, 4,633 l. 16s.

Chairman.

4921. This is for all the transactions, both under Lord Ashbourne's Act and the Company's scheme?—All; the redemption of tithe, 10,482 l. 1s. 3d.; donations, grants, and sundry voluntary payments, 4,898 l. 3s.

4922. This was a commutation?—Yes, the donations and grants. The total was 20,012 l. 0s. 3d., leaving a nett sum of 143,656 l. 8s. 2d.

Sir William Marriott.

4923. What do the donations, grants, and sundry voluntary payments include, amounting to 4,800 l.?—Donations to the clergy, Presbyterian and Roman Catholic; schools, labourers, sub-agents, and others connected with the estates.

4924. Were these donations in any way in place of the subscriptions you had been giving before, so far as the clergy were concerned?—Yes.

4925. Can you give us any idea of what the amount of these donations was?—Three years upon the annual donation.

Chairman.

4926. You commuted as it were; you gave them a lump sum of three years of what the annual donation had been?—Yes.

4927. Did you do that with all the schools and churches you had subscribed to?—Not with the schools, only the churches.

Sir William Marriott.

4928. Did the Land Commissioners investigate the title?—They did.

4929. As vendors, I suppose?—As vendors.

4930. They passed it as good, I presume?—They did.

4931. At the present time, do any of the pensions that used to be paid stand good?—Yes, and others have been added since.

4932. What are those pensions?—They amount to about 500 l. per annum.

4933. And to whom were they paid?—Principally to labourers and people who had been on the estate.

4934. These are kept up now?—These are kept up now.

4935. Notwithstanding the Company has parted with the land, they still continue to pay them?—Yes.

4936. And they are paid up to the present date?—Yes; and they continue to pay during pleasure.

4937. In the Company's view it is a voluntary gift?—A voluntary gift.

4938. But they do pay it?—They do pay it.

Mr. Lea.

4939. I am not quite sure we had the total rental?—No, I did not give it.

4940. What was the total rental of the Fishmongers' Company's estate?—It was about 9,300 l.

4941. I mean when they sold it?—Yes. The gross total rental would amount to perhaps 9,800 l., but that included timber and other matters; 9,300 l. really is the correct amount.

4942. When you came into it in 1820, what was the rental you received in 1820?—Before 1820, 400 l. per annum.

4943. Who was it let to?—The Earl of Tyrone.

4944. Do you know what rents he received from the tenants?—No.

4945. Then what did you put the rental at when it came into your possession?—I believe the company ascertained then that it was about 8,000 l. a year, and they continued that rental and granted leases for 21 years.

4946. From the time that you had let it at 400 l. a year to the Earl of Tyrone up to the time you entered into it in 1820, had any expenditure been made on the estate by the Fishmongers' Company?—No.

4947. Then the total rental remained much the same from 1820 to the time you sold it?—Very much the same. In 1831 it was rather reduced by 800 l., owing to the great depreciation in agricultural produce.

4948. Had there been large reclamations of slob lands?—There had been.

4949. Who reclaimed the slob lands?—Undertakers appointed under the Act.

4950. When was this done?—Eighteen hundred and forty-seven to 1851, I believe.

4951. I see in the statement published in Lord Derby's Commission some very large increases in rent. Take the case of a tenant of the name of James Loughery whose rental was 8 l.; was that increased up to 20 l.?—I am unable to give you that information. I telegraphed for the information and have not received any reply yet. I was anxious to ascertain to whom Dr. Todd referred the other day.

4952. There is another tenant named William M'Keever whose rent was 2 l. and you raised it to 6 l. 5s. or an increase of 213 per cent.?—No, I do not recollect.

4953. Perhaps I ought to have put it in this form, that in 1878 the Fishmongers received a memorial from the tenants?—Yes.

4954. It is published here. Did the tenants allege that you wished to abolish the Ulster custom on the estate?—They did.

4955. Did you require at that time the purchasers of tenant-right to sign a covenant binding them to surrender their holdings at the end of the term without any claim of any kind whatsoever?—It was proposed in the draft leases, but I think the company were advised afterwards that there was no necessity to keep that clause in.

4956. How did they treat the memorial of the tenants?—The company considered that memorial, and obtained the opinion of two counsel, Mr. Leachman and the late Mr. Fraser, and it was by their advice that the clause relating to tenant-right was expunged.

4957. But

Mr. Lea—continued.

4957. But they still increased the rent enormously on the reclamations of the tenants?—I think not, if you will bear in mind that in 1820 it was 1,600 l., and in 1879 it only came up to 2,200 l., which included interest on loans.

4958. But some of the rents I see go up 212 per cent.?—Apparently, if you say so; but I think there must be an explanation of that, which I shall be very pleased to give to you.

4959. I think it is your return?—Very likely; but there may be an explanation about it which, unfortunately, I have not with me.

4960. Were there any arrears when the company sold their estates?—Yes, certainly.

4961. How did the Company treat those arrears?—They offered each tenant a reduction of 20 per cent., if they paid immediately.

4962. Is that in addition to the 20 per cent. referred to just now?—Quite apart from that; in addition; and they repeated that offer on more than one occasion.

4963. Was it accepted?—In most cases.

4964. Are there any arrears outstanding still?—There are one or two very minor cases.

4965. Did the Company take promissory notes for the arrears?—In some instances, about two or three.

4966. Only in two or three?—Yes, and I may say that they are not paid, and are not likely to be. The Company, in most cases, have written off the arrears.

4967. In 1838 a canal was made from Ballykelly to Lough Foyle?—Yes.

4968. This canal was used for the carriage of coal?—Yes.

4969. Did it make coal in the district much cheaper?—No; in fact, after a time it silted up, and although the company paid a considerable amount to deepen the canal they could never keep it open; there was not a sufficient depth of water.

4970. Could not they keep it open in their own time?—No.

4971. Is it since the sale it has silted up?—No; before. It has always been cleared out from year to year; but even then it silted up.

4972. I think the Company dredged the canal every year, did not they?—They cleaned it out; I will not say dredged it. The amount of gravel and sand that came down from the mountains was so great that perhaps in a day you would have a foot or more in.

4973. Still you cleared it out?—From time to time.

4974. And they were able to use it for boats of coal?—No, certainly not.

4975. Was it unusable when the Company sold their estate?—Perfectly.

4976. For years before?—Certainly.

4977. When the Company sold their estates, what did they do with regard to the minerals?—We have none.

4978. But I presume there were rights of minerals, at all events?—I do not think any reference was made to them.

4979. Were they conveyed to the tenants?—There being none, I do not think the Company took it into consideration as to what should be done in the event of minerals being found.

4980. Stones and slab, and gravel, and things of that sort; were there any of those?—No.

4981. I suppose, in conveying to the tenants all parties joined in the conveyance?—Certainly.

4982. And I presume the Irish Society joined?—No, certainly not.

4983. I see in the "History of the Irish Society" it is mentioned they joined in the conveyance to one or two companies?—I think there was a reason for that.

4984. Was there no reason in your case?—No.

4985. Had you given any bond or received any conveyance from the Irish Society beyond the original?—No, except a disclaimer of trees and timber.

4986. Except with regard to the timber?—Yes.

4987. And the Irish Society is not joined in the title at all as regards the sale of your estate?—No.

4988. I asked you because we have had it stated, with regard to the Drapers' Estate, that the Irish Society joined in the conveyance?—It is not so with the Fishmongers.

4989. With regard to the timber, what would be done with the timber?—We have sold most of it.

4990. What is the value of the remaining timber?—I may say that it is practically all sold.

4991. I think you did not tell Sir William Marriott what was the amount of money that you received in cash, the total in cash on the sale?—Yes, I think I did. If you would allow me, I will make this correction, that the Land Commission had in hand as a guarantee deposit the sum of 24,095 l.

4992. Would that be in addition to the cash you mentioned just now?—It would be deducted from that.

Chairman.

4993. Your figures represent the total advance made by the Purchase Commissioners?—The total agreed advance.

Mr. *Lea.*

4994. Was that the full value of the estate?—It is as much as the Company got for it.

Chairman.

4995. Got or will get when they get back the guaranteed one-fifth?—Yes. I do not think it is the value of the estate, because many of the farms have been sold since at very enhanced prices.

4996. Sold by the purchasers?—Sold by the purchasers.

Mr. *Lea.*

4997. But I presume they had a large tenant right upon that?—Taking that into consideration, even then the price was very large.

4998. You did not limit the tenant-right, did you, when you sold?—Not the least. When I tell you that one or two farms were sold at 50 years' purchase, I do not think the Company can be said to have limited the tenant-right.

Sir W. T. Marriott.

4999. The Company sold at 20 years' purchase?—Yes.

Mr. Lea.

5000. Tenant-right in Ulster sells for from 20 to 30 years' purchase very often?—This was 20 years' purchase.

Chairman.

5001. The tenant-right is merged in the fee now?—Yes, it is merged in the fee.

Mr. Lea.

5002. Do you say the purchasers sold the fee-simple without the tenant-right?—I think that Mr. Morley has put it correctly, that the tenant-right is now merged.

Chairman.

5003. There is no such thing as tenant-right?—No, there is no such thing.

Mr. Lea.

5004. You say that the purchasers have sold at a very much larger price since then. The purchasers were the tenants, were not they?—Yes.

5005. And in selling, they sold what they purchased from the Fishmongers' Company, and their own tenant-right?—I cannot say that. They have sold the fee-simple of their farms.

5006. Which includes the tenant-right?—That I cannot tell you.

5007. Do you know the value of the tenant-right?—It varies according to the size of the farm.

5008. Do you know that it is often sold for 25 to 30 years' purchase in Ulster?—It varies. It has been sold at five years up to, I may say 20; it varies according to the size of the farms. There is no value in the tenant-right at all, as a rule; it is a fictitious value.

5009. You said that the Company deducted 20 per cent. and 8 per cent. in selling?—In arriving at the net rental for the sale, 28 per cent. in all.

5010. That covered the poor rate?—The poor rate and county cess.

5011. How much would that be off the rental?—About 700 *l.*

5012. Of 9,000 *l.*?—Of 9,200 *l.*

5013. That would make a considerable hole in this 28 per cent.?—Certainly; I think it is about 8 per cent.; that is all.

5014. The Company expended 4,770 *l.* out of the 9,200 *l.*?—Yes, on the average.

5015. When they sold, did they consider how that ought to be made up to the district at all?—Certainly not.

5016. Did they think that in selling they could escape all these payments?—I do not understand you.

5017. In selling, did they think they could escape from all expenditure of this 4,770 *l.*?—They made provision for that in their allowance of the 28 per cent.

5018. Do they consider that 28 per cent. is anything like an equivalent proportion to 4,770 *l.* out of 9,200 *l.*?—They were selling a property, which I do not think it is necessary to make any payments on account of any anticipated payments. Whatever a landlord may have done, it is not necessary, I venture to submit, for him to continue to make payments.

5019. Did the Fishmongers care nothing about the education of the district when they sold their estate?—The Fishmongers' Company were fully aware that the National Board of Education had authority and control over the education of the children of Ireland.

5020. They thought they could place their alleged responsibility on to the National Board of Education?—No, I think you can hardly say that. I may say that up to 1884 the Company paid various sums amounting to about 1,200 *l.* a year for the education of their tenants' children, and if you refer to Lord Derby's Commission, I am open to correction, I think there is a statement in Dr. Todd's evidence that the Company were not compelled to pay that amount, and that instead of paying it to the education of children on the estate, it would be desirable to pay it towards improvements on the estate. Therefore the tenants, or the mouthpiece of the tenants himself, objected to the Company making this voluntary payment.

5021. Did the Fishmongers' Company consider how the schools could be carried on when they withdrew their grants?—Certainly.

5022. I have a letter from a school teacher named Connor on the estate; do you know him?—Very well.

5023. Mr. Dickey gave evidence here the other day that you had withdrawn a grant of 20 *l.* a year from that school?—That is so.

5024. I find that it is a total grant of 55 *l.*?—How is that.

5025. An assistant teacher, 18 *l.*; books and requisites, 10 *l.*; fuel, 3 *l.*; prizes for attendance, 4 *l.*?—I may say in reference to the staff, that if the school were of a sufficient size, the National Board of Education would provide the necessary staff.

5026. But you gave this 55 *l.* a year to the school?—Yes.

5027. When you sold you did not give it?—Certainly.

5028. That is to say that you retain the cash you had hitherto given?—Hitherto voluntarily given, if you will allow me to say so.

5029. These grants were discontinued in November 1884. I am told they were withdrawn summarily?—Not at all.

5030. One year's salary given to the teacher?—They did not lose their positions.

5031. But they were deprived of their grants; may I read what Mr. Connor says to me: "Most of these gave up good situations and came to the Company's schools expecting their grants would be permanent; this withdrawal has made a considerable change in the teachers' circumstances; it has also given a great check to the progress of education all over the estate"; did the Fishmongers' Company never consider that when they sold the estate?—They considered the matter very carefully and they have given to the Committees, which are now formed for the management of education on the estate, the schools and other premises free, for which they have received no payment.

5032. They

Mr. Lea—continued.

5032. They have taken out of the district, 118,000 *l.* you say; what was the total amount?—The total amount was 123,656 *l.*

5033. Was that the total amount of all the sales?—Yes.

5034. They took that out of the district though in 1820, they had only received 400 *l.* a year from the estate?—They received a fine from the Earl of Tyrone of 6,000 *l.*

5035. That is in addition to the 123,000 *l.*?—No; the Earl of Tyrone paid that in 1747.

5036. What did they do with that 6,000 *l.*?—Placed it to their corporate funds.

5037. For English uses?—Presumably.

5038. That 6,000 *l.* in 1747 is additional capital received from this estate to the 123,656 *l.*?—I cannot acknowledge that because the companies were originally at a very large expense.

5039. Expense in the purchase, do you mean, or in taxation?—Purchase, and other matters connected with the estates.

5040. But what did they expend besides their share. The Fishmongers' Company contributed 2,260 *l.*?—Yes, but they expended very much more than 2,260 *l.*

5041. How much more?—I am not prepared with the statement, but if you will refer to the "Concise History" you will see that the Companies paid over 120,000 *l.* in all at that time. Then they provided arms and accoutrements for the defence of Derry.

5042. You say the Fishmongers' Company did consider this question of the schools?—They did.

5043. But they did not consider it necessary to provide at all for them?—Not more than they have done.

5044. And what is that?—Giving the fee-simple of the school premises and grounds attached.

5045. And the grants to the churches and the clergy you gave, I think, three years' purchase of?—Yes.

5046. Is that in addition to the 123,656 *l.*; did they give it back out of the 123,000 *l.*?—*l.* 124,000 is the net amount.

Chairman.

5047. After that has been deducted?—After that has been deducted.

5048. Mr. Lea wants to know this, whether the total sum received by the Company for the holdings, the total figure given by you, did or did not include these deductions?—Yes, it included these; the 123,000 *l.* was the net sum after all these payments had been made.

Mr. Lea.

5049. Then the Fishmongers' Company did not consider how the churches of the various religious bodies were to be sustained, except by giving them three years' donation?—I think that you perhaps are not aware that the donations hitherto given to the clergy were not towards the maintenance of the churches, but they were in recognition of their services on the respective school boards of the Company.

5050. Did not they give any grants to churches at all?—Not annually.

Mr. Lea—continued.

5051. Did they give large sums for the building of churches?—They gave large sums for the building of churches.

5052. Did not they give certain clergymen so much a year?—Yes, for their connection with the school boards in their respective districts.

5053. When did they begin to give these grants?—From 1820.

5054. And continued them up to the time of sale?—Yes; the Company gave the manses and the grounds attached to the respective bodies without any consideration, and the farms which had been let to the respective ministers at a reduced valuation.

5055. That is all in addition to this capital sum you have named, of course?—Well, as no valuation was placed upon what they gave, of course, it is not included in this capital sum.

Mr. John Ellis.

5056. I wish to ask you a few questions arising out of this statement you have put in; I observe this comes down to the year 1887; is there any reason why we should not have it to the end of last year?—Practically it closed at the end of 1887.

5057. Your responsibility, and everything, as far as you are concerned, ceased then?—Yes.

5058. There you give us here 29 items, which are not very conveniently arranged; would you have any objection to classify these under the three heads, namely, capital outlay on the estate, revenue charges and management expenses, and donations and subscriptions to public objects?—I think I can supply you with those details.

Chairman.

5059. It is only a re-arrangement in fact?—I quite understand that; under donations and subscriptions to public objects do you include the schools?

Mr. John Ellis.

5060. Certainly; I include everything that is not either capital outlay or revenue charges on the estate; it is merely classifying those 29 items under three heads; the 43,220 *l.* is an expenditure for eight years, 1880 to 1887?—Yes.

5061. That is an average sum of 5,400 *l.* a year?—Yes.

5062. Is that all that was expended in Ireland by the Company during eight years?—Yes, on the management of the estate; that was the total.

5063. It is the entire sum out of the Company's revenue derived from Irish property which was expended in Ireland during those years?—Yes.

Chairman.

5064. It will be convenient if you will divide the cost of managing the Irish estate into two sub-heads; the cost of management in England, and the cost of management in Ireland?—The second tabular statement gives the English expenditure.

5065. What we want to get at, I take it, is the two figures; how much you received net from Ireland, and how much you gave back to Ireland?

Chairman—continued.

Ireland?—I think, if you kindly look at the second statement you will see it.

Mr. *John Ellis.*

5066. I understand that you refer to another tabular statement which is not put in; may I take it that this second one is put in?—If the Chairman is prepared to accept it.

5067. It is for you to say?—I have handed it in; I have no objection.

5068. Then the second statement, I gather from you, refers to expenditure in England?—Yes.

5069. Connected with the Irish estate?—Yes.

5070. Then perhaps you will follow the Chairman's suggestion to give us what has been expended from the revenue of the Company arising from their Irish estates in England and in Ireland?—I do not quite understand you; is it not there.

5071. Then we may take it that this is put in, and this shows what I have asked for?—Yes.

5072. Then may I take this average of 5,400 *l.* is all that was expended in Ireland on the Company's Irish estates?—Yes.

5073. But that there was expenditure in England which was derived from their Irish income?—According to the second statement.

5074. Then can you give me the total income for those eight years, from 1880 to 1887, as against this 43,200 *l.* of expenditure in Ireland, the gross income; what was the total sum that the Company received in those years from their Irish property?—I have not prepared it; it is only a matter of addition between one and the other.

5075. I think we should like to place side by side the two sums?—I will prepare that and submit it.

5076. For those eight years?—Yes.

5077. These are the last eight years that I understood the Company had the estate?—The last eight years.

5078. Can you give us any estimate of what that income was at all?—It would be about 8,320 *l.* a year, in round numbers.

5079. That is an average for the eight years?—Yes.

Chairman.

5080. That is the gross income?—Yes, that is the gross income in round numbers.

Mr. *John Ellis.*

5081. Can you give me the two or three heads from which that was derived; it was not all rental?—Yes, it was, with the exception of the timber and grazing from town parks.

5082. No other source of income than those three?—No; that is all.

5083. Sale of timber grazing in town parks and agricultural rental?—Yes.

5084. Then may I take it that 3,000 *l.*, the difference between the income and the expenditure, has been spent in England?—No; in England you will see the average expenditure was about 800 *l.* a year on the Irish estates. Then there was an average balance of about 2,800 *l.*, in round numbers.

5085. Has that gone into the general account, as the former witness said?—That has gone into the general account of the Company.

5086. Then there is nearly 3,000 *l.* (2,800 *l.*) out of 8,000 *l.*, the precise expenditure of which you do not place before us?—No; it has gone into the general account.

Chairman.

5087. You told us that the average gross income is between 8,400 *l.* and 9,000 *l.*?—Yes.

5088. Then to get the net you deduct the cost of management, both in England and Ireland; what does that come to, both here and on the other side, the annual average?—About 1,200 *l.* to 1,400 *l.*

5089. That leaves 7,600 *l.* as the net income, which you have told us you have paid over to the general account; therefore the difference between 8,200 *l.* and 7,600 *l.*, the net receipt, is what you spent in Ireland for public objects, that is, 4,700 *l.*?—Yes.

Mr. *Clancy.*

5090. I wish to ask you a few questions about this memorial that was presented to the Company by the Company's tenants in September 1879; did you ever make any answer to that memorial?—Certainly.

5091. Have you got it?—No, I have not.

5092. Can you produce it?—I think I could produce it; but I did not think you would call on me to produce it to-day; I am not prepared with it.

5093. Can you let us have it?—The tenants sent a deputation over to the Fishmongers' Company; I think they gave the deputation a reply.

5094. Is that reply in print?—No.

5095. Is it in manuscript?—In manuscript.

5096. Have you it yet?—I have not got it here; I believe there is one.

5097. Are you able to answer any of these allegations?—If you ask me a question I can say yes or no.

5098. For instance, this allegation: "That a few years ago the Company sought to abolish the Ulster custom on the estate by requiring the purchasers of tenant-right to sign a covenant binding them to surrender their holdings at the end of the term, without any claim of any kind or description whatsoever." Did you ask them to sign such a covenant?—I have not any knowledge that the Company made such a requisition.

5099. Are you able to deny that they did?—No.

5100. You are not able to deny it?—Not at present, without reference.

5101. Do I take it that you are not able to answer any of the questions which arise out of the memorial?—If you ask me I can say yes or no; and then I shall be happy to supplement my answer on another date, if the Committee wish to see me on it, by reference to the Company's books.

5102. Here is another allegation; "That the agreement which they have been recently required to sign, has renewed the apprehension that it is the desire of the Company to extinguish tenant-right on the estate." Was that second agreement ever in force?—No; I think I have already given evidence on that point.

5103. Do

Mr. Cleary—*continued.*

5103. Do you deny that there was such an agreement?—I have already given evidence before this Committee that the memorial was attended to and considered by the Company, and placed before counsel.

5104. I am asking you now about this particular agreement; were the tenants compelled to sign it?—They were not compelled. They memorialised the Company that the clause in the then proposed draft lease should be expunged, and that was done on the advice of Mr. Leachman and Mr. Fraser.

5105. What was expunged?—The clause relating to tenant-right.

5106. What was that clause in substance?—I cannot tell you. I have not got it here, and I should not like to give a garbled statement of a proposed clause.

5107. Is this right: "The agent requires our incoming tenants;" this relates to the year 1850; "or the assigns of old tenants to sign a deed resigning all claim to tenant-right"?—I prefer to look at the book first.

5108. I want to ask about the increase of rent when you succeeded to the estate, and on subsequent occasions?—What do you require to know.

5109. The various increases of rent exacted by the Fishmongers' Company in 1820, and downwards to the sale of their estate?—What is it you wish to know?

5110. I want to know all about them?—Will you kindly ask your question.

5111. I understand you are not able to answer that question?—I beg your pardon.

5112. Have you looked at the Appendices to the Report of Lord Derby's Commission relating to your estate in Volume 1. You denied, I think a while ago, that the increase of rent on the Fishmongers' estate was very exorbitant?—Yes.

5113. What was the total increase of rent exacted in 1820, when you came into your estate?—The Company had no notice whatever, nor can they compare the rents agreed to be paid by the tenants in 1820 with those paid to the Earl of Tyrone or to his representatives.

5114. How then can you say that the increase of rent was not large?—You are now alluding to 1820?

5115. Yes?—My answer you must please accept that we have no means of comparing the rents agreed to be paid by the tenants to the Fishmongers' Company with those paid originally by the same tenants to the representatives of the Earl of Tyrone.

5116. Then I ask you how you are able to say that the increase was not large?—I think I did not make such a statement.

5117. I understood that you did; what was your rental in 1820 after you came into the estate?—£. 7,897.

5118. When was the next increase in rent demanded?—The leases fell in in 1842, and the estate was then re-valued; but owing to agricultural depression, and famine, and distress in Ireland, tenants were allowed to go on with their rents till 1852.

5119.

Mr. Cleary—*continued.*

5119. There was no famine in 1842?—In 1846; they were allowed to go on till 1852.

5120. There was no increase of rent between 1820 and 1852?—No.

5121. None?—None.

5122. What was the increase of the rent in 1852?—Instead of an increase, there was a reduction of 897 *l.* 17 *s.*

5123. How much was it then?—£. 7,000.

5124. When did you re-value it next?—In 1872.

5125. What was the result of that re-valuation?—The increased rent then amounted to 9,900 *l.*, that is the total.

Chairman.

5126. The result of the increase was that the rental became 9,000 *l.* odd instead of 7,000 *l.*?—Yes.

Mr. Cleary.

5127. That is, you raised it 2,000 *l.*?—Yes. Then the Company has had to pay county cess and poor rate, which they did not pay in the previous years.

5128. What further amount would that be?—About 1,000 *l.*

5129. Then they did not bear those rates and taxes before?—No.

5130. Although all other landlords did?—I think not.

5131. The poor rate is paid in Ireland half by the landlord and half by the tenant?—Not originally, I think. It was after the famine, I think.

5132. I am not sure of the date, but for several years you had not been paying those taxes which were borne by all other landlords?—No; whatever taxes were borne by the other landlords, so far as they were applicable to the Fishmongers' Company, they paid.

5133. But as a matter of fact, you did not pay half the poor rate?—As a matter of fact I think we paid all that we were called on to pay.

5134. Did you pay half the poor rate before 1872?—My impression is that we did not.

5135. Did you pay any of the cess?—I believe it applies to that as well.

5136. You paid none of it. Did you contribute to the costs of any of the local institutions, gaols, bridewells, court-houses, lunatic asylums, infirmaries?—We had no gaols or court-houses on the estate.

5137. In the county of Londonderry they are not on every estate?—Undoubtedly we paid towards the farming societies.

5138. You have?—Undoubtedly.

5139. Do you mean to say you made direct grants for those purposes?—Why should we not.

5140. Did you, I say?—We did.

5141. Have you any record of them?—Not in print.

5142. Those institutions are maintained out of the county rates, and you did not contribute to the county rates all?—I beg your pardon.

5143. Not before 1872 you told me?—We may have had property in hand, and whatever the landlord at that date had to pay, of course the Fishmongers' Company paid, legally paid.

5144. I have to ask you again; did you contribute to the county cess before 1872?—Upon that which we had legally to pay, yes.

5145. What

Mr. Clancy—continued.

5145. What was that?—I am unable to tell you now without reference.

5146. I thought you told me a while ago you paid none of the county cess?—That which we had legally to pay, of course like other landlords, we should pay. I cannot say without any books what we paid prior to 1872.

5147. You were not legally bound to pay the county cess?—I gave you my impression just now, if you will kindly accept that.

5148. That is an occupier's tax and has always been so; you did not pay that, did you?—If you will kindly allow my answer to stand I shall be glad, until I have an opportunity of referring.

5149. Will you come prepared to answer about that matter on the next occasion?—If it is your wish.

5150. I see here in these appendices a statement as to increase of rent in particular cases about which I should like to ask you. Michael Creswell says that his rent at the time that the Beresfords held the estate was 8 *l.* or 9 *l.* 10 *s.* When the lease dropped the Company immediately raised the rent to 36 *l.* per annum. Are you able to say whether that is correct or not?—No.

5151. Are you able to deny this statement, that "Two or three years afterwards, the Company employed a surveyor and valuator to straighten the mearings and do away with rundale; by this we lost five Irish acres, and had our rent fixed at 33 *l.* 10 *s.* per annum"?—No, I am unable to say that, but I know that the Company straightened their farms and remodelled them through the offices of their then agent, the Rev. George Vaughan Sampson.

5152. I must take you through these statements?—I will answer them as far as I am able.

5153. Then the man further says, "a large portion of the farm was bog and waste, and at the taking of our present lease (1872) we had effected very considerable improvements, having reclaimed all the bog land and erected substantial buildings; our present rent was then fixed at 40 *l.* 5 *s.*" Then he goes on to say that the reclamation of 20 acres was effected altogether by his own expenditure; is that true?—That is probable, but he, like all other tenants, was allowed 5 *s.* per acre off the annual rent in consideration of the land he had reclaimed.

5154. I do not understand that, considering that the total rent was increased from 8 *l.* or 9 *l.* 10 *s.* to 40 *l.* 5 *s.*?—I have not the precise case, but I am now saying that generally.

5155. Confine yourself to these particular cases?—I am unable to give you that definitely.

5156. Take the case of John Kinkead. He says that he remembers his father "holding about 18 acres in Ballyhelly, 10 of which were under lease from the Beresfords, 'middleman holding under the Company of Fishmongers.' In 1820 the Fishmongers came into possession of the estate, and compelled my father to relinquish his lease. The boundaries of the farms were then straightened, and as a consequence my father lost his holding, but got instead, a few years after, a farm in Ballyking townland, which was previously held by a man named Wright, who had to leave, not being able to pay the rent;" and then he says that his rent was raised from 10 *s.* to 2 *l.* 1 *s.* per plantation acre; is that correct?—That I am unable to say.

5157. Then he says: "Of a number of tenants I remember Jack Creswell, Hamilton Irvin, Andrew Grey, and Robert Cowan having to quit their farms owing to excessive rents, they being industrious men. Distraints for rent were very frequent." Are you able to say whether that is correct or not?—What year is that.

5158. This statutory declaration is dated 5th July 1890?—All I can say is that distresses were very seldom served upon the tenants, that they were not called upon to quit their farms.

5159. You will not deny that these particular statements are correct?—I cannot without reference.

5160. Take another case, that of Henry Hyndman. He says the rent of his holding was 3 *l.*, Irish currency. "At the expiration of the lease the rent was raised to 3 *l.* 3 *s.* My father came into possession at my grandmother's death, and held under lease for lives and years, renewable at 3 *l.* 3 *s.* per annum to the death of King George in 1820, when the Fishmongers then coming into possession of the estate, compelled him to relinquish the lease, and raised his rent to 23 *l.*, and took the right of grazing from him on the mountain"?—I am unable, as I informed you just now, to compare the rents fixed by the Fishmongers' Company with those originally paid to the representatives of the Earl of Tyrone.

5161. Then he goes on, "In or about 1826 he straightened the boundaries of the farms; he then got an addition to his farm (making it in all about 25 acres plantation) at the rent of 30 *l.* I succeeded my father about 30 years ago, and in 1872 my rent was raised to 34 *l.*" You are not able to say whether that is right or not?—I can tell you that, as a result, 33 *l.* was the rent, and 16 *s.* was added for a lease.

5162. Then you confirm the statement of this tenant?—I confirm the rent in 1872.

5163. Then take another case of James Conners, of Sistrokeel; he says, that his family had under the Beresfords "a large portion of land adjoining Sistrokeel Mountain, at the yearly rent of 6 *l.* 6 *s.*, and one duty day for each tenant annually. They also occupied the right of grazing on the mountain. Immediately after the expiration of the lease we were deprived of the mountain, and our rents were raised to 37 *l.*" That is from 6 *l.* 6 *s.* to 37 *l.* Is that right?—I should say certainly not.

5164. But are you able to deny it?—There are two or three Conners, and I should be unable to deny it unless I knew the actual holding, but there is one Conner now paying 80 *l.* for 57 acres; another one paying 14 *l.* for 139 acres, and, therefore, I should say that that statement was wrong.

Chairman.

5165. Is there any Conner paying a rental of 37 *l.*, or whatever it is?—No; not in Sistrokeel. There is no such rent in Sistrokeel.

5166. "At

Mr. Clancy.

5166. "At the taking out of our present lease in 1878 we were still further raised to 60 l., our present rents?"—There is no such rent.

5167. As that of James Conway, raised to 60 l. in 1878?—There is no such rent.

5168. It is also incorrect, is it, to say, "We also lost a portion of our holdings for planting without any remuneration"?—If the value of the land can be taken at that time as being of any value, that is in 1878, they did not lose it. They may have lost some in previous years, but it would have only been hilly land or land not fit for cultivation, where it would have been an improvement to plant trees.

Mr. John Ellis.

5169. Was there an investigation into this memorial at the time?—There would be.

Mr. Clancy.

5170. Do you think you would be able to answer next time in detail every one of these allegations?—I think so.

5171. You were not, then, I presume, clerk of the Company?—No.

5172. It will be simply the production of some record?—I should have to refer to the books of the Company to see that.

5173. Just one question on the point of that agreement which you say was withdrawn; you were advised by some lawyers to withdraw the clause relating to the extinction of tenant-right. You are aware that the tenant-right can be extinguished in more ways than one?—I am not prepared at the present time to say.

5174. Tenant-right could be extinguished by exacting a very high rent?—The Company never went into that matter at all, nor were they anxious to take away from the tenants the interest they had acquired, but it was only to protect themselves as to any future transactions where the farmers had acquired no tenant-right.

5175. They proposed, however, in this agreement actually to take away the tenant-right?—No, I do not acknowledge that. It was only proposed that they should protect themselves, so that in the future the tenants should not acquire more than they then had. That I am prepared now to speak upon.

5176. Are you able to say yes or no, whether the Company or the tenants have made all the improvements on the estate?—The tenants have made most of the improvements so far as their respective farms are concerned in accordance with the Irish practice in contradistinction to the English.

5177. I want to ask you a few questions about the sale of this estate; in 1885, I believe, you sold it?—The proposals were in 1884.

5178. After you made the agreement to sell, and before you executed it, the Ashbourne Act became law?—That was so.

5179. Were the agreements signed and stamped before the Ashbourne Act came into force?—Some of them were.

5180. What proportion?—I am unable to give you the precise portion.

5181. Half?—I really cannot tell.

5182. This is of some importance, because the Commissioners under the Ashbourne Act could not advance money, except to tenants?—That has been very fully inquired into by the Land Commission and the whole of the transactions connected with the sale of the Company's estate were fully known to the Land Commission, and the Land Commissioners advised the Company upon the necessary action they should take.

5183. But I want to get at exactly what took place. In the case of these agreements to sell and buy, which were stamped and signed before the Ashbourne Act came into force, I take it, they had to be cancelled?—They had to be cancelled.

5184. And all these tenants who had agreed to buy, and had signed agreements to buy, signed other documents, becoming tenants again?—Certainly.

5185. Did all of them apply to the Land Commission?—The majority, but about 70 did not.

5186. Why did they not?—They elected to remain under the old scheme under the Company.

5187. Had you much arrears on the estate?—No.

5188. What did you do with the arrears?—We collected as much as we possibly could, but in order to induce the tenants to pay, the Company offered 20 per cent. reduction.

5189. Did you in any case add the arrears to the purchase-money?—In about two cases.

5190. Not more; are you sure?—Well, I will say under five, to be positive.

5191. Are you perfectly sure, in no more cases than five?—I believe I am correct in what I said just now.

5192. Did you represent to the Land Commission that you had added the arrears to the purchase-money?—I cannot say that, because I did not carry out the sale, but I believe the Land Commission knew it; and in one case in particular the Land Commission sent their surveyor to value the farm.

5193. In consequence of that?—I do not say that, because I had not the carrying out of the sale with the Land Commission; but in the case to which I particularly allude, as also in others, the Land Commission sent their surveyor to the farm; and they were perfectly satisfied with the amount that the Company had asked for the purchase-money.

5194. Did they know that you had added the arrears to the purchase-money?—I have answered that question; I said that I did not know.

5195. Could you find out for us before the next occasion. I want to know whether the Land Commissioners knew that in some few cases the arrears were added to the purchase-money.

Chairman.] I thought the witness told us that was not so.

Mr. Clancy.] He has admitted that, possibly, at the outside, in five cases that was so.

Chairman.

5196. In five cases out of something like 400 the arrears were added to the purchase price?—Yes, to the purchase price, at the request of the tenant.

Chairman—continued.

5197. It was disclosed to the Commissioners?—I anticipate it was so, but I am unable to state that, inasmuch as I did not carry out the sale.

5198. If it was only in five cases out of 400 it was not very important; we understand you are sure it was only in five cases?—Yes; 1,200 *l.* is the total arrears that we received.

5199. Do you mean you received in any form?—On the whole estate.

5200. But was the 1,200 *l.* added to the purchase?—Added to the purchase.

Colonel *Laurie.*

5201. Was the 1,200 *l.* added to the purchase?—In all I mean.

5202. You say not more than five cases; you do not bind yourself to five?—I do not bind myself to five.

5203. In not more than five cases they were added, but those arrears that were added did not amount to 1,200 *l.*?—£. 1,200 was the total of the arrears altogether.

5204. The five cases would not amount to 1,200 *l.*?—There was one very large arrear.

Mr. *Clancy.*

5205. In that case was the amount of arrears added to the purchase-money?—Yes.

5206. In that large case?—Yes.

5207. What was the amount of that?—£. 226.

Chairman.

5208. That was only 226 *l.*, and 1,200 *l.* was the total, and if you divided it among the five, it was not above the average?—I suppose not; I thought it was more.

Mr. *Clancy.*

5209. The rule of the Land Commission was, I believe, and is still, that unless landlords withdraw all claims against their tenants, they will not sanction the purchase?—This was fully known to the Land Commission, and the tenant was offered to purchase a farm cash down, and to pay the arrears.

5210. After you had come to an agreement to sell to your tenants; and after that agreement had been sanctioned by the Land Commission, did the Land Commission require you to withdraw or cancel all outstanding claims in respect of rent or interest?—That was done. There were no outstanding arrears, with the exception of this, that, according to the Company's terms, the tenant should pay five per cent. interest till the completion of the sale.

5211. Was there anything left for you to cancel?—No.

5212. Consequently, you did not cancel anything?—No; the arrears were added; but there may have been interest which had accrued, owing to the purchase not having been completed for one or two years afterwards.

5213. Was it in respect of that interest the promissory notes in the few cases were exacted?—Which interest.

Chairman.

5214. You mean interest on the price?—Of course it was in connection with the interest which had accrued due between the agreement and completion of the purchase.

Mr. *Clancy.*

5215. Was it in respect of the accruing interest that you exacted those promissory notes?—I cannot say we exacted; we asked for them.

5216. And you got them?—We got them.

Colonel *Laurie.*

5217. With regard to these promissory notes; we have heard a good deal about them; were they given by the tenants for arrears of rent, or for interest of money, or what were they given for?—For arrears of rent or interest.

5218. They were, I presume, taken by the Company to release the tenants from their obligations as between landlord and tenant?—Certainly.

5219. And, therefore, were a merciful consideration for the tenant's position, to enable them to deal with their holdings?—Certainly.

5220. They were in no sense a hardship on the tenants?—No, not the least.

5221. And by taking these you released them from the obligation of the tenant to the landlord?—Certainly we did.

5222. You are acquainted, I suppose, with the Report of the Royal Commission on the City Livery Companies of 1884?—Yes.

5223. On page 44 of their Report, you see it is signed by Lord Derby, the Duke of Bedford, Lord Sherbrooke, Lord Coleridge, Sir Sydney H. Waterlow, Mr. Albert Pell, Mr. Walter James, Mr. Bottomley Firth, and Mr. Burt?—Yes.

5224. Will you turn to page 38, under the head of the Benevolent and Public Objects. At the bottom of the page, speaking of the amount expended in benevolent and public objects by the City companies, they say, "Besides the contribution to churches, schools, and dispensaries in Ulster, which is frequently as we have stated included in the returns in the expenses of the management of these estates, the companies contribute largely to other Ulster charities, both religious and secular, and also have of late subsidised new railways by grants of land and loans. These sums taken together amount to a deduction from rent, greatly exceeding the sum annually contributed to such purposes by private landlords." Those are the words of that Report. Now, I have just to ask you from your experience of the affairs of your Company, whether, in your opinion, those words accurately describe the spirit and method of the Fishmongers' Company in dealing with their Irish estates?—I think they do.

Sir *William Marriott.*

5225. Will you bring all the papers you have been asked for next Monday?—Yes; will you allow me to make one correction, Mr. Clancy asked if the Land Commission had knowledge of the arrears with reference to the case I spoke of.

5226. The inclusion of the arrears in the purchase

Sir William Marriott—continued.

those prices?—They did have knowledge. They were informed in my presence. I have a memorandum here.

Mr. Clancy.

5227. Perhaps I might ask you one further question on the increase of rent. I see here a statement by Dr. Todd, given evidence before Lord Derby's Commission. Will you kindly say whether it is correct or not, because it traverses your own evidence. "The Fishmonger's estate was held by the Beresford family, who paid the company a rent of 400 *l.* yearly, and exacted 3,000 *l.* a year from the tenants. The last lease to the Earl of Tyrone expired in 1820; the company then resumed possession, revalued the estate, and raised the rental to nearly 10,000 *l.* a year"?—That is wrong.

5228. "The tenants who had most improved were subjected to the largest increases, some being raised as much as 1,000 per cent." Is that correct, or not?—I am totally unable, as I mentioned before, since I have been giving evidence, to say whether that is right or wrong. The company have no power, nor are they able to compare the rents paid to the representatives of the Earl of Tyrone, and those asked for by the company, on their coming into their estates in 1820. We have no record whatever.

Chairman.] I do not think you can get behind that.

Mr. Clancy.] The witness said that the rents in 1820 were about 7,800 *l.* a year, and Dr. Todd puts them down at 10,000 *l.* a year.

Witness.] £. 7,897. 17. is the estimated rental for 1820, and for 21 years afterwards.

Chairman.

5229. I only want to say this to you, that the way these two accounts you have handed in are made up, or are arranged, does not really shed any light on the points that the Committee are interested in. You must be kind enough, if you will, to arrange the items under the three heads that Mr. Ellis gave you?—I have them here; first, capital outlay on the estate; second, revenue charges; third, donations and subscriptions to public objects.

5230. What we want to distinguish for the purposes of this Committee is what really goes for public objects, as I may call them, such as a church, a school, or any other object that can be called public. We want them to be distinguished from what may fairly be called the charges for estate management?—Certainly.

5231. There are such items as draining, roads, falling fences, planting, farm buildings, cultivating slob land, and so on. All those charges incident to the possession of an estate we want to have distinguished from the other items of outlay, which may fairly be called charitable, if you like, or objects of a public character. It will give you very little trouble to classify them in that shape?—Certainly; you mean for the last eight years.

5232. We do not want any more figures than there are here. We only want the classification, and for them to be defined under those heads?—Certainly.

0.112.

Chairman—continued.

5233. Then I will only ask, you in re-arranging, to consider this point of view, that what we want to get at is the net figure which would cover your public objects. Then I may point out that the two tables are not conterminous, if I may so say. For instance, as to English expenditure, it is from 1879 to 1887. That is one column, but in the other table it is 1880 to 1887; they may just as well be made accurate. Then perhaps you will get them into that shape, with clear divisions or heads?—Yes.

Colonel *Lawrie.*] I should like a sub-division. The ordinary management of an estate, cost of agency, and legal expenditure, should be kept separate from road making, and so on.

Chairman.

5234. I think you may have expenses of management and then expenses of improving the estate?—Then you will allow four heads instead of three.

Chairman.] It is a sub-division of head two.

Colonel *Lawrie.*] Let the items be separate.

Sir William Marriott.

5235. With regard to the feeling of the tenants, has your attention been called to what Dr. Todd said before Lord Derby's Commission: "Would your Lordship allow me to explain one or two points. The main point is the claim made by the tenants to rebate from the purchase money or bonus over an ordinary purchaser. I think that feeling exists very generally, and that there is a very substantial basis for that feeling. It is what Mr. Dunn points out, that the tenants by purchasing will have to pay all the local burdens. That is a substantial basis to start with. If the landlord purchased he would have to bear a share of the local burdens." Was all that taken into consideration; were these the feelings of the tenants, to begin with?—Certainly. The company took into consideration what the tenant would have to bear as compared with that which was borne by the company while they held the estate.

5236. Was that the cause of the allowance they made?—Yes.

5237. Then Dr. Todd goes on: "But in case of purchase the tenants would have to support all the educational, religious, and charitable institutions to which the companies now contribute, and that a private purchaser might not assist in keeping up." Has your attention been called to that?—Yes.

5238. Was any promise made beyond what you have given to the tenants?—Not the least. I may mention this, that in a memorial which was presented to the company by the tenants, during the time that Lord Ashbourne's Bill was in the House, they there "thankfully recognise the careful equitable spirit in which the scheme of purchase has been framed, and they have no desire to disturb the arrangement further than the extension of time and reduction of interest."

Chairman.

5239. What are you reading from?—That is the printed memorial which was submitted to the company when the tenants asked for the extension

M M 4

Chairman—continued.

sion of these, or that the company would allow them to purchase under Lord Ashbourne's Act.

5240. There is one other question I should like to ask you. It is not strictly relevant to this inquiry, but you raised the point yourself, and I do not ask it for any controversial purpose, but for the sake of information. You said that of the purchasers from the Fishmongers' Company a certain number, I do not know whether a considerable number, had re-sold; that after they had acquired their holdings there was an advance from the Land Purchase Commission, though they had then parted with their holdings; do you know how many have done that?—No; some half dozen people in all.

5241. Then your point was that the price fixed by the Fishmongers' Company could not have been excessive, because they had been sold in these six cases at a considerable enhancement?—That is so.

5242. Do you know how much; what percentage of enhancement?—No, I have not worked that out, but I had three or four letters from Ireland calling my attention to the figures, and stating the astonishment of those there at the value given, and also calling attention to the lowness of the valuation set upon the company's estate.

5243. Then we may take it to be this, that of the 400 purchasing tenants in the course of six years or five years, only half-a-dozen have resold?—So far as I know.

5244. Do you know to whom they have sold? —Yes, to other tenants on the estate.

Mr. *John Ellis*.

5245. With regard to the accounts, will you kindly be careful in giving the income for the eight years, to distinguish between the rental and sale of timber and any other source of income?—That is for the last eight years.

Mr. *Lea*.

5246. I had not seen the accounts when I examined you. The 800 *l.* a year spent in England is practically in addition to the 4,700 *l.* spent in Ireland?—Yes.

Sir Owen Roberts, sworn; and Examined.

Chairman.

5247. I understand you are here to rebut and contradict sundry allegations made by the Rev. John Mark, of Dunboe, near Coleraine, on 5th June last, in regard to the Clothworkers' Irish Estate, and especially the circumstances attending its sale to Sir Harvey Bruce in 1871?—Yes.

5248. What are the points to which you wish especially to draw the Committee's attention?—The circumstances under which the sale to Sir Harvey Bruce took place, viz.: The question of sale was mooted in the autumn of 1870, when a deputation of the company, accompanied by myself, visited Coleraine, and, as a result of verbal negotiations, a letter was received from Sir Harvey Bruce on 27th January 1871, which I may take the liberty of reading.

5249. A deputation accompanied by you visited Coleraine?—Yes.

5250. And you had verbal negotiations with whom?—With Sir Harvey Bruce.

5251. And Sir Harvey Bruce wrote you a letter?—Yes, as follows: "Dear Sir. As the Clothworker's Company prefer my making an offer to their naming a price for their estates in the county of Derry, I hereby offer 120,000 *l.* (One hundred and twenty thousand) for them. I believe this to be, under present circumstances, a good offer if I am to live here as a resident landlord, and in harmony with my tenants, should they become mine. The Land Bill makes a considerable difference, and I might have felt able to offer a larger sum if it had not been for that. Perhaps you may have seen some of the decisions which threaten the stability of the landlords' position. Hoping the company may agree with me as to the offer, believe me, yours faithfully, *H. Harvey Bruce*."

5252. The Land Bill, to which he refers, is the Land Bill of 1870?—Yes.

Chairman—continued.

5253. What does he mean by saying it makes a considerable difference?—There were provisions in that Act I presume he meant (I can only speak inferentially), for giving compensations for disturbance, and matters of that sort.

5254. He felt that that would justify a low price?—He seems to say so.

5255. What does he refer to when he talks of "decisions which threaten the stability of the landlord's position"?—I imagine he refers to some decisions which had taken place in the early history of the Land Act of 1870, which seemed, by some expressions of the judges, to have that effect.

5256. Under the Act of 1870?—I imagine so.

5257. What did the Clothworkers' Company value the estate at when he offered 120,000 *l.*?—They came to the conclusion that it was at least worth 150,000 *l.*, and that they would not take less.

5258. What was the final agreement between Sir Harvey Bruce and the Clothworker's Company?—The company agreed to sell the estate for 150,000 *l.*, subject to certain conditions and rebates.

5259. What were those? — That 75,000 *l.* should remain on mortgage at 4 per cent. interest for a period of 10 years as from the 1st of May 1871, when the estate was sold, but that a reduction of 2,000 *l.* per annum for two years be made from the interest, if punctually paid.

5260. £. 75,000 was to remain on mortgage, at 4 per cent. for 10 years, but there was to be a reduction of 2,000 *l.* a year for two years from the interest?—From the mortgage interest. The interest would have been 3,000 *l.*, and, therefore, in the first two years, we only took a net 1,000 *l.* Then, for the succeeding eight years, 1,500 *l.* was to be deducted from the interest, subject to an honourable

Chairman—continued.

able understanding on the part of Sir Hervey Bruce, whereby payments, amounting to 242 *l.* per annum, should be continued by him, subject, however, to his general discretion.

5261. What form did that honourable understanding take; was it written down?—Yes; it was in this way. I wrote a letter, and he, through his solicitor, as far as I remember, agreed to it: there was nothing binding.

5262. Have you got the letter?—I cannot say that I have got it, but I have no doubt I could refer to it.

5263. As we are going to have Sir Hervey Bruce here, I think it is desirable you should have it in readiness?—I will take care to do so.

5264. You remember, I suppose, what the terms of it were generally?—Yes; I can give them to you. It was agreed that he should continue sums amounting to 242 *l.*, the particulars of which I will give.

5265. Two hundred and forty-two pounds per annum he was to give?—Yes.

5266. Was that the amount of the contribution that the company had been making?—To these particular objects and persons.

5267. What sort of items were they?—They were as follows; they have all been referred to in the evidence of Mr. Mark.

5268. Then, perhaps, you need only give us the total?—£. 242. To the *Episcopal* clergyman of Finmoyle, 30 *l.*; to Mr. Smillie, of Killowen, 20 *l.*; to Mr. Mark, the witness I have referred to, 20 *l.*; to Mr. Sturgeon, the second Dunboe Presbyterian minister, 10 *l.*; and to Father Doherty, Catholic priest, 10 *l.*

5269. That is to say, 90 *l.* in all for churches?—That is so.

5270. Fifty pounds to the Episcopalians; 30 *l.* to the Presbyterians, and 10 *l.* to the Roman Catholics?—That is so.

5271. Then with regard to the schools. Give us the totals but not the items?—£. 102.

5272. Was there anything else?—Also 50 *l.* to six parishes or districts on the estate for clothing the poor at Christmas time.

5273. That made in all 242 *l.*?—That is so.

5274. That had been up to the sale to Sir Hervey Bruce, the amount contributed by the Clothworkers' Company to these objects?—That is so.

5275. And Sir Hervey Bruce gave you an honourable understanding that he would keep that up?—For 10 years, during the time we made the rebate from his mortgage money.

5276. In making that arrangement with Sir Hervey Bruce, your company no doubt felt themselves under an obligation to serve these public purposes?—I should not put it so. What they did feel themselves under an obligation with regard to as they always do in all matters

Chairman—continued.

5277. Did you expect that their lives would all terminate in 10 years?—Yes, that they should either be dead or gone; and they all did, except one, I think.

5278. Has Mr. Mark who was here the other day?—He was the finest who survived, I suppose, and he was a young man. We did not reckon with him quite, and he remains.

5279. And with regard to the schools, did you think that the requirements of education would all cease in 10 years?—We thought the schoolmasters would.

5280. You say you thought only of the persons; did not you think at all of the objects?—No; we did not take the objects into consideration, except as connected with the persons.

5281. What brought the mind of the company to think of these persons at all; were their views entirely divorced from objects; was it simply from private attachment to these gentlemen?—No attachment, but a feeling of equity. They treated their agents and their under-agents in much the same way.

5282. I want to go further back; why did the company, in the first instance, make the grants, if it was not, as I suggest, from an attachment to the persons who were the incumbents of these offices, it must have been from a sense, at all events, of the desirability of promoting these objects?—No doubt; as landlords, taking an English view of the position, they considered, as good landlords, it was usual with good landlords to make grants of this description, but on ceasing to be landlords, of course, the grants ceased also.

5283. And did the Clothworkers take the English view of the position in all other respects; did they make all the improvements on the tenants' holdings?—Yes; I think you may say that the Clothworkers' estate was, generally speaking: of course there was the tenant-right, worked rather on the English system.

5284. Taking the English view, you gave these sums to public objects, and you arranged and took care, in fact, that Sir Hervey Bruce should carry them out for 10 years, and at the end of that time you thought your obligation, whatever it was, was discharged?—We considered that we, as a company, might take a more generous view of our position everywhere than a private person.

5285. When you say that, what is the breadth of your proposition: do you mean that your company alone does, or do all companies?—I believe the companies of London generally take that view of their position. Of course it is easier for a company, which does not live by its property, to take a generous view of the position than for a private individual. Sir Hervey Bruce, I have not the slightest doubt, would, and as a

Chairman—continued.

away from this place?—That is precisely what is done in other circumstances.

5288. Then it was not a large view, but an ordinary view, of any landlord?—But I may supplement that by some statements. I believe that you are aware we made other supplemental grants, the particulars of which I shall be happy to give you.

5289. What other provisions did you make?—For instance, with regard to Mr. Mark, the Presbyterian minister of Dunboe, we protected his 10 *l.* for 10 years, and also paid a sum of 200 *l.* down to his presbytery as a parting gift when we left the country in 1871, the fact being that the Presbyterians had been deprived by the withdrawal of the Regium Donum in connection with the disestablishment of the Church in Ireland.

5290. You say you gave 200 *l.* down to Mr. Mark's presbytery?—Yes.

5291. Mr. Mark himself said: "It is correctly stated that they," that is the company, "gave 200 *l.* to the church of which I am minister, and they gave 100 *l.* to the minister of a neighbouring church, but the church of Castlerock, to which they gave an endowment of property of 60 *l.*, is not built on their estate at all, whereas there is a Presbyterian church built on their estate adjoining that one which has never received any endowment except a gift of 100 *l.*"—I will explain that, if I may. To the building fund of the Castlerock Presbyterian Church the company gave 150 *l.* in the autumn of 1870, when we visited the estate, and the idea of selling arose, and then we gave them a further 100 *l.* when we parted from them in 1871. There was no personal interest to be promoted in that case, inasmuch as no Presbyterian clergyman had been appointed or been nominated to receive any donation from the company. With regard to the Episcopal church at Castlerock, which Mr. Mark referred to, he made it rather a sort of grievance that we had given 60 *l.* per annum to the Castlerock Episcopal Church; but I explained to Mr. Mark, and I have pleasure in explaining to you, that it is not a fact that we gave 60 *l.* per annum as a parting gift to the Episcopal Church of Castlerock. We did give 50 *l.* per annum in 1868 together with Sir Hervey Bruce, he being the adjacent landlord. Sir Hervey Bruce agreed that he would charge his estate with 50 *l.* per annum, making 100 *l.* per annum by way of endowment for the new vicar or new church we built at Castlerock, and we built that church for this reason.

5292. When did you build that church?—In 1868; that is before we had any idea of selling the estate. We built that church for this reason, that we wanted to make Castlerock into a watering place, and wanted to encourage villas and residences of that sort; and I suppose most people agree that the best way of making a place for residences of that sort is to build a handsome attractive church and close by a good hotel, which the company proceeded to do.

5293. That was a speculation?—It was done for rather temporal reasons than spiritual ones, I think.

5294. Then was it for temporal or spiritual reasons you gave the Catholic clergyman 10 *l.* per annum?—We gave it him, and always found him a very good sort of man. He ministered to the humbler classes of our tenants, and he always received 10 *l.*, and we always found him a very agreeable and tractable gentleman.

5295. You thought 10 *l.* per annum was a fair recognition of these spiritual and personal services?—Yes. He is a celibate, you know, and the others are not.

5296. Was it solely on the ground of celibacy that he got a less allowance?—I really am not able to define what the reasons were, it is only mere guess work; but the Catholic clergy, to their very great credit, I believe, are accustomed to receive lower emoluments than the clergymen of other sects, and it was supposed the 10 *l.* a year would be sufficient, and he was very thankful for it and never grumbled.

5297. What was the total rental you were drawing from the estate?—£. 6,000 a year.

5298. Gross or net?—Gross.

5299. What was the cost of management?—Well, as far I can charge myself (I observed your question to the previous witness), we took, as near as possible, about 3,000 *l.* a year over to England.

5300. That is to say, that the cost of management, plus contributions, was 3,000 *l.*?—In that cost of management would be included certain improvements which would tend to create a larger capital value for the estate. It is rather ancient history for me, but still I should be happy to go into it. I thought, from the tendency of your questions to the previous witness, I should fulfil your desires by giving it in that way, giving it as 3,000 *l.* a year brought over to England.

5301. I think that is the point. You got 6,000 *l.* from the tenants, and you expended 3,000 *l.* upon exclusively English objects in England?—That is so.

5302. You took half the gross income from these people, and you brought away 3,000 *l.* to be devoted to English objects?—Approximately that is so.

5303. You think it was taking a generous view of the position to give 3,000 *l.* a year for English purposes, and to give 10 *l.* a year to a Catholic clergyman who looked after the interest of your poor people?—Yes, I do. It is a matter of opinion of course, but I doubt very much whether other landlords are in the habit of doing anything like so much.

5304. I only wanted to know what a generous view of the position was; 3,000 *l.* a year has been expended in England?—Approximately.

5305. But it is more than that, surely; there was a certain part of the cost of management expended in England?—I perhaps differ with others, but I do not reckon in that way, because a private landlord does not have any "cost of management in England."

5306. The last witness said, I think that the cost of managing the Fishmongers' Irish estate in England was 800 *l.* a year. I wondered what your loss was corresponding to that?—I should imagine it was not so much. I should say 500 *l.* perhaps.

5307. That makes 3,500 *l.*?—No; 2,500 *l.* plus 500 *l.* equals 3,000 *l.*

5308. You

Chairman—continued.

5308. You included that 800 *l.* in the amount that came to England?—Yes.

5309. It was not the 3,000 *l.* which was paid over to your general account?—It was only subject to deduction for management in England, which I thought was the right way of treating it. I have tried to put it on the ground of a private owner.

5310. In other words 3,000 *l.* was not net surplus paid to the general account, but the 2,600 *l.* would be the net surplus?—That would be so.

5311. Sir Hervey Bruce bought the Clothworkers' Estate, and took it with the honourable understanding to pay for 10 years 242 *l.*, subject to a charge of 50 *l.* for the Episcopal Church?—Of Castlerock.

5312. Was that included?—It was, subject to that as well as 242 *l.*, but the 50 *l.* was a charge in perpetuity. There had been a deed assigning a sum of 50 *l.* out of the Clothworkers' estate, and he took it subject to that charge.

5313. He was to pay 242 *l.* for 10 years, and 50 *l.* for ever?—Yes, that is so.

5314. Then there is the case as to the county court judge. What have you to tell us about that; this was mentioned by Mr. Mark in his evidence?—As Mr. Mark in his evidence said, it is true that Mr. Samuel McCurdy Greer, who afterwards became a county court judge, did build a handsome house at Castlerock as stated. The company gave him a long building lease of his house and grounds, and made the necessary and usual restrictions as to no shop, manufactory, and so forth, in order to uphold and protect the residential character of Castlerock as an aspiring watering place. The farm adjacent was also let to Mr. Greer on lease, but only for 31 years, because it was thought that at the end of that time it would be ripe for building purposes in connection with the project I have named.

5315. If those aspirations bore fruit?—Quite so.

5316. Then there was some contribution made by the Clothworkers' Company to the Church Institution Fund, was not there?—Yes, they made a parting gift to the Presbyterians as I have stated of 500 *l.*, besides the Castlerock Church.

5317. The Castlerock Church was not Presbyterian?—Yes; there is in Castlerock a Presbyterian church and an Episcopal church; but that was not strictly speaking a parting gift; but to the Disestablished Church of Ireland the company gave a parting gift in sympathy with their disendowed position of 1,500 *l.* They distributed it as follows: they gave 500 *l.* to the Killowen Church close by the Clothworkers' Manor House, where the agent lived; 500 *l.* to the Formoyle Church in the mountains, which was built by the company in 1835; 400 *l.* to the Dunboe Church, the advowson of which belonged to the company in the early days of the plantation; and 100 *l.* to Macosquin Church which was only partially on their estate.

5318. That is to say, they gave 1,500 *l.* as a parting gift to the Church of Ireland, which was 1,000 *l.* less than they had been in the habit of expending yearly in England previously; they spent in England every year 2,500 *l.* on English objects, and as a munificent parting gift, and as a generous view of the position, they gave less than one year's annual contribution to English purposes to these great Irish purposes?—If you chose to put it so, but it seems to me the English purpose is the company, which was the owner of the estate.

5319. That may be, but for English purposes?—Certainly.

5320. Whether they were right or not is another matter?—I think they were right.

5321. You know that we have had before us Lord Justice Fitzgibbon, and he gave us some very important and interesting evidence about schools; he told us something about the Coleraine Academical Institution; have you anything to say on that?—The company took a part in the building and establishment of the Coleraine Academical Institution, which was an institution for the secondary education of youths in and about Coleraine, and they instituted there a scholarship which was then known, and it is known now as "The Clothworkers' Scholarship." When they left Ireland they provided for that scholarship by assigning a mortgage debt of 1,000 *l.* which was bearing interest at 3 per cent., and was payable by the Town Commissioners of Coleraine in the matter of the Bann Navigation Works.

5322. Lord Justice Fitzgibbon told the same story that you have done very much. What does Sir Hervey Bruce contribute; Lord Justice Fitzgibbon told us that Sir Hervey Bruce did not contribute?—The scholarship is perpetuated by the 30 *l.* per annum. It is perpetuated by the 1,000 *l.* at 3 per cent., which we assigned to the managers of the school to keep up that scholarship for ever.

5323. Lord Justice Fitzgibbon said you contributed something to the institution. Is the 1,000 *l.* that you are now talking of what you mean?—I imagine he means that we contributed to the building and establishing of it.

5324. He said that on the 4th September 1873 the Clothworkers gave 1,000 *l.*?—Yes.

5325. He refers to anterior contributions?—I suppose so.

5326. With regard to the doles or the subscriptions given for the clothing of the poor, was any arrangement made for continuing these?—For 10 years; that is the 50 *l.*, but in addition to that there were some poor people who were in the habit of receiving 2 *s.* a week, and with regard to those we did not make them part of the arrangements with Sir Hervey Bruce, but we have agreed to pay them for their lives.

5327. You paid pensions. Are those pensions all extinct by now?—There is one, Rachael Williamson, still alive, but nine of them are dead out of the 10.

5328. You looked after your officers and servants left behind?—Yes, we did, very much in the same spirit.

5329. When you say your rental was 8,000 *l.* a year, do you deduct from it county cess, poor rate, and tithe?—No; the county cess and poor rate was a deduction from the 8,000 *l.* I gave you the gross sum.

5330. With

Chairman—continued.

5330. With regard to the sale to Sir Hervey Bruce. How was it you did not offer the land to the tenants?—I will explain that.

5331. The Committee has been told that there was a great indisposition on the part of the Clothworkers to sell to the tenants, and that some eminent clothworker said, the worst thing in the world would be to root the Irish in the soil?—First of all, I think that expression, "rooting in the soil" is only about seven or eight years old in popular phraseology. It may be found in the pages of the historian, but it is only of recent years it has got into the language of the people.

5332. The Clothworkers are surely intimate with the pages of the historian?—In Lecky, and so forth, you may find it.

5333. Is your argument that the statement of Mr. Mark cannot be true because the expression was not known to the Clothworkers?—To some extent it is an argument that can be used, but I have another argument better than that, because I knew Mr. Blossom very well. He was a gentleman who died at the age of 83 two or three years ago, and I only wish he was here to give you his statement of the case: but I will do it for him, inasmuch as I was intimately acquainted with his views on the matter.

5334. Who was he?—A past master of our company.

Mr. John Ellis.

5335. Was he the person who said this?—So Mr. Mark said, but I believe Mr Mark (I know him and respect him) was under a misapprehension.

Chairman.

5336. In short, you think Mr. Mark was in error when he said Mr. Blossom made that remark?—I think he misconceived the tenor of his remarks.

5337. Apart from the remark, was there any indisposition on the part of the Clothworkers to sell to the tenants?—Emphatically no: and if you will allow me I will tell you what occurred in the autumn of 1870, previously to the selling of the estate. My recollection of the matter is very vivid, and I found in looking the other day to the Land Act of 1870, that my recollections of the provisions of that Act were correct. It was as follows: Under the "Bright" clauses of the Act two thirds of the purchase-money was to be advanced to occupying tenants, but there was a provision in the Act also for the sale of estates as a whole, and in the case of a sale of the whole, if four-fifths of the occupying tenants agreed to a sale, there was a provision whereby another purchaser, or other purchasers, not occupying tenants, purchasing one-fifth, the Government would advance them half of the purchase-money as against the two-thirds that they would advance under the same clauses to the occupying tenants. But the company considered that before they arranged with Sir Hervey Bruce. They did look into the question and came to the conclusion, and I think rightly so, as subsequent events have proved, that it would have been perfectly impossible to sell the estate as a whole under the "Bright" clauses of the Act of 1870. The result would have been this, that the better tenants might have purchased, but a good deal of worst property would have remained, and if the company sold at all they intended to sell the estate as a whole. Therefore they came to the conclusion that the "Bright" clauses of the Act of 1870 would not enable them to sell to the tenants as a whole, and therefore it was they returned to Sir Hervey Bruce and negotiated with him.

5338. Sir Hervey Bruce, I suppose, was an adjoining land owner?—He was the owner of land which was then mixed up with the company's, and he was one of the original undertakers. He held his own patrimonial estate on a charge of 5*l*. 8*s*. 8*d*., or some small sum payable to the Irish Society I think. In fact I am sure it was. It was part of the original Clothworkers' proportion. Therefore the two estates coming into the ownership of one man came into a ring fence. Sir Hervey Bruce resides at Downhill, in the middle of the property, and the company believed that, failing sale to the tenants, they were doing the best possible thing by selling to a resident landlord.

5339. You think that selling to a resident landlord was better than an absentee company landlord?—Certainly. We were of that opinion, and still continue of that opinion.

5340. You think that absence is not a good qualification for a landowner in Ireland?—I do not think it is personally, but I am only giving personal evidence now.

5341. I will not go into all these figures about the Land Act of 1870, and the "Bright" clauses, but we were told a very remarkable fact, if it be a fact, and that is that you were offered 165,000*l*. for this estate?—Yes, that is so; and if I may, I will explain the circumstances under which that offer was made.

5342. That is true is it?—£. 175,000 was stated; 25,000*l*. in excess of the price we sold for; but that was no doubt an accidental slip on the part of Mr. Mark. It was 15,000*l*. more, and not 25,000*l*. more.

5343. The fact is that the offer was 165,000*l*.?—That is quite right.

5344. And Mr. Mark was mistaken?—To the extent of 10,000*l*.; after the tenants became aware of the arrangement to sell to Sir Hervey Bruce, Mr. Samuel McCurdy Greer, Mr. Stewart Hunter, Mr. Mark, and two other gentlemen in Coleraine, wrote to me asking to submit an offer on behalf of the tenants generally for the purchase of the estate. I consulted my court, and we came to the conclusion that the contract under letter between the respective agents of Sir Hervey Bruce and the company was such as to make it quite impossible to re-open the question. There might indeed have been a technical question as to the binding nature of the contract, though I do not think there was any question, but still it might have been raised, possibly. They certainly could not have honourably retired, and our advisers were of opinion that specific performance of the contract for sale and purchase might be enforced. Mr. Hunter, Mr. Greer, and Mr. Mark, were informed that the matter was irrevocable, and could not be re-opened, but contemporaneously with that they made an offer of 165,000*l*. I confess I think it was very suspiciously

Chairman—continued.

precisely like 10 per cent. more to tempt Sir Hervey Bruce, but that is only a matter of inference on my part. I do not believe that the tenants would have bought the estate at that figure. I am only stating my own impression.

5345. They would have had to produce what sum?—They would have had to produce a sum of 165,000 *l.*

5346. They would have got two-thirds under the Bright clauses?—No, you could not get two-thirds. If the tenants were to buy they would.

5347. Four-fifths of the tenants?—I will proceed in this way. They would have had to produce more than one-third of 165,000 *l.*; approximately something like 55,000 *l.*

5348. Then how many tenants were there?—I really am not able to charge my memory, but I should be very happy, if you will allow me, to insert that figure afterwards. I think it might have been 300 tenants or more.

5349. You are sure what was in the mind of the company was simply the fact that they had committed themselves to a binding and irrevocable contract for sale and purchase?—That is so, as I have stated before these negotiations with Sir Hervey Bruce the Bright clauses of the 1870 Act were considered.

5350. They took no action upon their view of the Bright clauses?—No, they did not, because we knew perfectly well that it must be perfectly impossible, and it was essential to the conduct of an arrangement, such as that, that we should not make an abortive proposal to the tenants. It would have made the negotiations with Sir Hervey Bruce perfectly impossible.

5351. I do not think I quite understand why they did not resort to the Bright clauses?—Because we believed the condition of the tenants of that estate was such as to make it perfectly impossible. Suppose we take a sanguine view, and suppose that four-fifths would have bought, the remaining one-fifth would have been left on the company's hands.

5352. Your estate would have been broken up?—Entirely.

5353. That was your reason or policy?—It was my own view of the matter, and I believe it was the view held by those in authority at that time.

5354. Did the tenants personally try to press the proposal upon you?—They did after it became known that the sale to Sir Hervey Bruce was arranged. This proposal was then made by them.

5355. They sent a deputation, I think?—They did; I wrote to them before they came to London to try and stop them, and save them a useless errand.

5356. Why did you want to try to stop them?—Because they wrote to me making the proposal, and then I submitted it to my court. They took advice, and I wrote to say that the sale was irrevocable. After that they came over to England. I was very happy to see them personally, but I told them the same thing that I had written by letter, that the circumstances of the case were such as to make it impossible for the company to retire.

Chairman—continued.

5357. Had there been any raising of rent prior to the sale?—None; the last valuation of the estate was in the year 1856.

5358. Was there no raising of rent from 1856 to 1871?—No.

5359. What had been the date of the previous valuation prior to 1856?—As a matter of fact, the idea was that every 20 years the rental should be revised. Sometimes it resulted in a decrease of rent; sometimes it resulted in an increase of rent; but according to the times and seasons. If there were bad times the company reduced the rent. They reduced their rent at the time of the famine, for instance.

5360. But when did they raise it, after the famine. On many Irish estates there was a raising of rent afterwards?—It was let to a middleman up to the year 1841, and the company came into possession of their estate then. The estate at that time was rented at rather more than 7,000 *l.* a year.

5361. £. 7,000 *l.* in 1841. Then in 1856 what was it?—I should think it had been reduced as a matter of arrangement in 1848, the hard times, to something over 5,000 *l.* a year, but I really cannot pledge myself to the exact figures; it was something of that sort, about 6,000 *l.* a year.

5362. Can you tell us what the rental, of what formerly was your estate, is now?—Exactly the same as when we sold; 6,000 *l.*

5363. That is to say, Sir Hervey Bruce draws exactly the same rent as you were drawing in 1870 and 1871?—Yes. In 1876, or thereabouts, not so soon as Mr. Mark supposed, we understand that Sir Hervey Bruce raised his rentals, or some of them, to the extent of about 15 per cent., and by the subsequent action of the Land Court that 15 per cent. has gone away, and has left the estate precisely the same as when we sold it.

5364. Have any of those tenants, formerly your tenants, gone into the Land Court for a reduction?—They have.

5365. With what result?—The result has been to put them back almost precisely, in fact it is exactly, to the same position as they were when we sold; that is to say, the 15 per cent. which Sir Hervey Bruce added in the prosperous times of 1876 has been taken away now that American competition has reduced rents in and out of Ireland.

5366. To-day the rent is about the same as when you parted with it?—Yes.

Sir William Marriott.

5367. Mr. Morley has used the word "obligation"; did the company, while you have been with them, consider there was any obligation, but a moral one, to give subscriptions?—Certainly not; property has its duties as well as rights: and it was in that sense, and in that sense only.

5368. I am afraid those duties are not what you can enforce in a court of law?—Certainly not. They are simply the sort of relations between landlord and tenant which have existed in England, and I hope have also existed in Ireland.

5369. Has anybody tried in a court of law to enforce any obligation?—Certainly not. Never.

5370. Nobody

Sir *William Marriott*—continued.

5370. Nobody has ever tried to suggest, in a court of law, that you have got a trust?—Never.

Colonel *Lewis*.

5371. Did you hear the question I asked the last witness with regard to this Report on the City Livery Companies, and did you hear the quotation I read to him?—Yes, I did.

5372. "Besides the contributions to churches, schools," and so on, "these sums, taken together, amount to a deduction from the rents greatly exceeding the sums commonly contributed to such purposes by private landowners." I think that has been the guiding principle of the Clothworkers' Company?—That is so, and not only in Ireland, but every where else.

5373. That appears to be the view of the Commissioners, and that plainly points to the fact of the relations being the relations of landlord and tenant, and points to no liability to make these contributions?—None.

Mr. *Clancy*.

5374. Did you give any parting gift to the Catholic clergy?—No, we did not. I regret that we did not, but the Catholic clergyman was too modest, I suppose, to ask for any. I was rather surprised when I came to look the matter up, and I found there was none given, but I may say there was no Regium Donum taken away from the Catholics. The reason of our giving the parting gift to the clergy was, in the case of the Episcopal Church, that there had been recent disendowments of the Church of Ireland, for which we sympathised with them, and the withdrawal of the Regium Donum in the case of the Presbyterians.

5375. You did not state what the result of the re-valuation of the estate in 1856 was?—The estate was slightly raised, but not seriously. I think, from recollection, it was some 500 *l.* or 600 *l.*, bringing it up to something like 6,000 *l.* a year.

5376. Have you read the accounts of the annual visitation of the Irish society with regard to the management of your estate?—Do you mean the accounts in the time of the middlemen.

5377. Yes?—I really have not read the visitations of the Irish society except as a casual matter.

5378. I will draw your attention to these two statements; first, with regard to the year 1836, it is stated that neither schools nor places of worship seem to be attended to; the company are not interested in the present prosperity of the estate, nor can they be till it comes into their own hands?—I have no doubt that is substantially true when the estate was held by the middlemen; but then our ideas of morality in 1836 have progressed with the times. The morality of 1880 is not the morality of 1836.

5379. Then there is this statement with regard to 1841: "This property was long in Chancery; during this period several tenants held leases and were correspondingly comfortable; those who did not hold leases were rack-rented and paid the greatest amount that could be obtained from them; no schools erected by landlords are seen; no dispensaries or charitable institutions occurred"; is that correct?—I do not know, and I cannot say; but I suspect that that points to 1836.

5380. That is in 1841?—At the end of 1841 we came into the estate. At that time the estate was rented at 7,000 *l.* per annum, but as soon as we came into possession of the estate we began the same sort of management as I have indicated, though, I believe, we improved as time went on, and we reduced the rents slightly on coming into the estate. We found that the 7,000 *l.* a year was too much, and when bad times came, in the case of individual tenants, the estate was gradually reduced to about 5,300 *l.* or 5,400 *l.* a year, and afterwards it went to 5,500 *l.* a year, but in 1856 it was re-rented at 6,000 *l.* a year, and that was the rent at which we sold in 1871.

5381. Have you any objection to state what you have done with the 5,000 *l.* a year you have carried away to England?—It is impossible for me to say. It has entered into part of the corporate account of the company. It is fused with the other property of the company.

5382. You say it was spent on public objects?—To a great extent, I should say that the Clothworkers' Company certainly spend a very large proportion, not far from three-fourths of their income, on objects which may, I think, fairly be called certainly, if not public, educational character, and so forth. We spend on technical education alone something like 13,000 *l.* a year.

Chairman.

5383. Of this 150,000 *l.*, the lump sum which you got, has a single sovereign gone back to Ireland?—Except what we left in the nature of parting gifts.

Mr. *Lea*.

5384. I think you have told Mr. *Clancy* for what purpose the Clothworkers' Company exists; is it for the encouragement of technical education, and things of that sort?—I should be very pleased to answer that question, but I do not suppose that it is within the scope of this inquiry, is it?

5385. I was going to follow it up by asking if you did not think technical education was as strongly necessary in Ireland as in England?—Yes; but we are the Clothworkers' Company of London in England, not of Ireland.

5386. You obtained 150,000 *l.* for your Irish property, did not you?—Quite so.

5387. Can you tell me what was the rent you received from the middlemen before it came to your hands?—As far as I recollect, I believe the middlemen paid a fine, in the middle of the last century, I think it was, of 28,000 *l.*, and we also received 600 *l.* a year. £. 28,000 was paid by way of fine for the lease for lives which was granted.

5388. What became of that 28,000 *l.*?—Really, I cannot tell you. I imagine it went into the corporate funds of the company.

5389. It was not spent in Ireland?—Not that I am aware of.

5390. You received 600 *l.* a year from the middlemen?—Yes.

5391. When did that conclude?—It went for the three lives; I think it extended for about 60 years, but I cannot be quite positive.

5392. When

Mr. *Lea*—continued.

5392. When did the estate come into your hands?—In 1841.

5393. Then what did you put the rental to?—The rental when we arrived at the possession of the estate was 7,000 *l.* a year, as nearly as possible.

5394. And previous to that time it had been 600 *l.* a year?—It was 600 *l.* a year in the nature of a charge only; you cannot call it a rent. When we let our estate to a middleman on the payment of a fine of 28,000 *l.*, that was in lieu of rental spread over the natural term of years which was included in the three lives.

5395. During the period of this middleman's possession how much did you spend on the estate?—Nothing at all.

5396. The rent was raised from 600 *l.*, with a fine, to 7,000 *l.* without any expenditure on the part of the company?—Yes; but you must look at this, I think, before you argue on. I cannot tell you, I am afraid, but you would have to ask what was the rental of the estate at the time the lease for lives was taken.

5397. £. 600 a year?—Oh no, it was let, say, in 1760, for the sake of argument, for three lives, for a fine of 24,000 *l.* and 600 *l.* a year, which would represent probably 3,000 *l.* a year, or something of that sort, if it was tabled out on the ordinary probabilities.

5398. The 28,000 *l.* came into your London exchequer?—Yes, it did, and was spread over those years. If that was added to the 600 *l.* it would come out to 3,000 *l.*, or something of that sort.

5399. Nothing of that went back to Ireland at all?—Not at all.

5400. That rental of 600 *l.*, plus whatever the 28,000 *l.* was worth, was raised to 7,000 *l.* a year without any expenditure on the part of the company in Ireland?—I cannot say yes or nay. I do not know what the estate was rented at at the time it was leased to the middleman; it may have been rented then at 7,000 *l.* a year for what I know.

5401. Do you think the Clothworkers' Company would have accepted a fine of 28,000 *l.* and a rental of 600 *l.* a year if the rent had been anything like 7,000 *l.* a year?—I do not suppose it would. However, no doubt there was what some gentlemen round this table would call an unearned increment.

5402. Do you know what the rent was before it was let to the middleman?—I really do not.

5403. I think you have told the Chairman sufficient about the reasons you did not sell to the tenants; but are you aware, or do you remember, that in the memorial that was presented to you it was signed by four men on behalf of 166 other tenants?—Yes, I think that is so, and that is the reason why I concluded it was 200. You asked me how many tenants there were, and, remembering the 166, I said I thought 200. I think probably there were more, 250 perhaps.

5404. Would not you have considered that 166 signing a memorial out of about 200 gave a fair chance of the purchase of the whole estate by the tenants?—I do not think so. I thought the difficulty would arise, and I think subsequent legislation has proved it by the fact that each year Parliament has given better terms for the tenants. They found the Bright Clauses in the Act of 1870 were not sufficiently advanced to root the Irish population in the soil, and they were obliged to give better terms, or I presume these sales to tenants never would have been brought about.

5405. The deputation came to London to see the Clothworkers' Company?—They did.

5406. Did they see them?—They saw me but did not see the company.

5407. Could not the company see them?—No; the company never receive deputations, and I wrote to Mr. Mark or Mr. Orser at the time to say that the company did not receive deputations, and that as a matter of fact this sale was irrevocable.

5408. Why do not they receive deputations?—They prefer to have statements made to them in writing, and they do receive deputations in this way, that if there are any points to be cleared up in the matter of a negotiation a committee is formed, and they see one or two people, but it is not convenient to see a party of people. It is embarrassing in many ways that the court of a company, numbering 40 people, should receive another 40 in a deputation. Business is not facilitated by it.

Chairman.

5409. Does not an ordinary English landlord often receive deputations of tenants?—Really I am not an English landlord, and I am afraid I cannot tell you. I daresay it may be so, but our tenants in London are not tenants of the agricultural order. They are tenants of ground rents and so forth, and we do, as a matter of fact, see single tenants, but we do not receive a deputation of tenants.

Mr. *Lea.*

5410. Do not you consider that a deputation of tenants on such an important matter as the sale of the estate ought to have been seen by the Clothworkers' Company?—I do not think so, under the circumstances. It would have been futile to see them. We might, perhaps, have seen them if the irrevocable decision I have mentioned had not been communicated to them.

5411. You had an Irish Committee?—Yes.

5412. How many did that consist of?—We have not now; we did have; I think there were nine.

5413. Would not it have been easy for them to see the deputation?—No doubt they might have seen them, but I think it would have been very futile when the decision had been in advance against them.

5414. Would not it have been courteous, when a deputation came over from Ireland, for the Irish Committee to have seen them?—I thought that I had behaved very courteously in writing to my friends in Ireland, stating that they would only incur a futile journey, and when they arrived in England I explained the matter as patiently and as courteously as I was capable, and I really do not think they at all impugned my courtesy, or that of the company, in the matter.

5415. A deputation came over at one time consisting of a Mr. Lyle and a Mr. Kerr, were they seen by the Clothworkers' Company, or were

Mr. *Lea*—continued.

were they treated as the other deputations?—I heard the evidence of Mr. Mark, but that extended to a time which is not within my historic memory, because I was not clerk to the company at that time. It was about 1846 or 1847, long before I became connected with London or its companies.

5416. Mr. Lyle did come over?—I think he did so.

5417. Mr. Mark has sworn to that; *for that* audacious insult to the company he had notice of ejection, had not he?—I really am not able to tell you. I can look up the matter, probably, although most of our records are gone over to Sir Hervey Bruce. But I looked upon it as rather ancient history, and I did not proceed to the matter, but I will do so if it is required. It was about 1846 or 1847; I really thought so little of it, and it was so long ago to go into old grievances of that sort. I do not believe, from what I know of my company, they would insult anybody.

5418. It is part of that high position they hold to refuse to see deputations?—They have found, on the whole, business is better facilitated by having, in the first instance at all events, a written communication.

Mr. *Lea*—continued.

5419. What leases are your company in the habit of giving to tenants?—In Ireland, I think the building leases were 60 years.

5420. In the case of Judge Carr, what was the length of lease you offered him?—I am not certain, but I have a sort of impression it was 70 years.

5421. Agricultural leases?—There are not many of them; they are far better without leases than with them, and they know it; they did not want leases; they were far better off without them.

5422. You gave grants to schools pretty freely?—I read to you the particulars of those grants; they amounted to 109 *l.* per annum to 11 schools situated at various parts of the estate.

5423. Did you consider how these schools could get on when the Clothworkers left?—Really, no; we considered we had provided for the schoolmasters for the term of 10 years, and afterwards we considered our connection with the estate had ceased, and having taken care of the individuals we considered that we had done our duty.

Monday, 14th July 1890.

MEMBERS PRESENT:

Mr. Clancy.	Mr. Lawson.
Lord Elcho.	Mr. Lea.
Sir John Ellis.	Sir William Marriott.
Mr. John Ellis.	Mr. John Morley.
Mr. T. M. Healy.	Mr. Sexton.
Colonel Laurie.	Sir Richard Temple.

THE RIGHT HONOURABLE JOHN MORLEY, IN THE CHAIR.

Sir OWEN ROBERTS, re-called; and further Examined.

Chairman.

5424. I UNDERSTAND you want to make one or two corrections in the evidence that you gave to the Committee last Friday?—If you will allow me, there are one or two matters I should like to refer to. I said I did not quite remember the number of tenants on the Clothworkers' estate. I mentioned 250 as the number; I find, looking back to the terrier there were a few more than 270. I imagine there would be some double qualifications, but making allowance for that I think I am perfectly safe in saying that there were more than 250. Then another matter I wished to refer to was this; I referred to payments to various clergymen. I have looked at the letter which I wrote to Sir Hervey Bruce on the 10th of February 1881. I find the words were: "Such abatement of interest on mortgage to be in consideration of the continuance by Sir Hervey Bruce (subject to his general discretion) of the payments to the clergy, schoolmasters, &c., as detailed (248 *l.*)," which I gave.

5425. Is there any other correction you wish to make?—There is one other statement I should like to refer to if you will allow me; it is hardly a correction. I spoke of the Clothworkers' estate. The Merchant Taylors had an equitable interest in one-fourth of the estate. Although the Clothworkers were the owners of the estate, one fourth part was payable to the Merchant Taylors as equitable owners.

5426. How did that equitable ownership arise?—By their making a contribution to the 5,000 *l.* when that was originally paid as purchase money.

5427. In the 17th century, you mean?—Yes, in the reign of King James I.

5428. The Merchant Taylors left the management of the estate to the Clothworkers, I understand?—Yes; but the Clothworkers did not receive the whole of the sum I mentioned, viz. 150,000 *l.* from Sir Hervey Bruce, but regard was had to the proportion of the Merchant Taylors. The Merchant Taylors contributed 1,166 *l.* out of the 5,000 *l.* originally paid for the estate.

5429. Do I understand that part was paid to the Merchant Taylors, *pro rata* on the 1,166 *l.* of the 5,000 *l.*?—That is so.

5430. Before the sale, did the Merchant Taylors receive a similar *pro rata* payment annually out of the surplus balance?—That is so.

Mr. Lea.

5431. The Merchant Taylors had an estate of their own in addition to this, had they not?—Yes, they had; but it was sold to Mr. Richardson in or about the year 1730.

Mr. HERBERT CLIFFORD SAUNDERS, Q.C., called in; sworn; and Examined.

Sir William Marriott.

5432. You have been on the Court of the Skinners Company ever since the year 1868, I believe?—I have.

5433. I think you were First Warden of that company in 1872?—Yes.

5434. And you were Master in 1873 and 1874?—Yes, from May 1873 to May 1874.

5435. Some leases fell in about 1872, I think?—Yes; that part of the estate of the Skinners' Company which was called the Pellipar Estate has always from the commencement been held, until 1872, upon leases subject to lives and years; and the last of those leases, which was for three lives and 61 years, fell in upon the death of Mr. Robert Leslie Ogilby in May 1872.

5436. After that lease fell in, what action did the Skinners' Company take with regard to their property?—The company determined immediately that they would not grant the property again upon leases for lives and years, but that, having regard to the increased facility there is for communication between England and Ireland, they would take it into their own management, as the other companies had previously done.

5437. For

Sir William Marriott—continued.

5437. For that purpose did a deputation go to Ireland?—It was not for that purpose that the deputation went to Ireland. We determined upon taking the property into our management, but it was not till the next year that the deputation went over.

5438. A deputation did go over when you were master, I understand?—The first deputation went over in the year I was master.

5439. How many did the deputation consist of?—Five members of the court, if I remember rightly, and the clerk and the surveyor.

5440. As master, did you take considerable pains to look up what the rent had been, and to look into the history of the company?—It was a matter in which I felt a great deal of interest, and I took the greatest pains possible to learn as much as I could of the antecedents of the company, as to the way in which the estate had been acquired, and its past history, so as to enable myself, by knowing something of its history, to learn upon the visit what its requirements were.

5441. Will you give us very shortly the result of what you ascertained upon that point?—I found contemporary evidence that not only the sum of 60,000 *l.* had been spent by the 12 companies originally in planting the estates, but that much larger sums had been paid, probably amounting to 120,000 *l.*, in the course of the history of the companies.

5442. Is that 120,000 *l.* in addition to the 60,000 *l.*, or inclusive?—As far as the minutes of the company go, it would seem as if it was in addition.

Chairman.

5443. You are speaking of all the companies, I understand?—I am speaking now of all the companies. I found a minute in 1627 in which a further sum of 120,000 *l.* was levied upon the companies in respect of the plantation of Ireland. I refreshed my recollection by looking at that minute on Saturday.

Sir William Marriott.

5444. Could we have a copy of that minute?—It is an interesting minute, and I should like to read it if you will allow me. It is not very long; it is dated the 20th of December 1627: "Upon the reading of a precept from the Lord Mayor and Court of Aldermen concerning the levying of 2,820 *l.* assessed upon this company, for their part of 60,000 *l.* to be paid to His Majesty, it was ordered that the wardens should take the weight and value of the plate belonging to the company, and Mr. Warden Highlord and Mr. Hill to consider what land is for the company's own proper use, and not charged with charitable uses, and the whole body of the company to be warned against Saturday following, to be consulted with about the fittest way for the levying of the said 2,820 *l.*" And then there was a minute subsequent to that, dated the 5th July 1628, which mentions the sum of 120,000 *l.* which I referred to: "At this court were read two precepts which were sent to the company from the Right Honourable the Lord Mayor for the levying and providing the sum of 940 *l.*, being the rateable part of 20,000 *l.*, residue of 120,000 *l.* formerly agreed by a Common Council of this City to be paid unto His Majesty upon the sale of lands. Whereupon, notwithstanding the table" (that means the board, as we call it now) "disliked the act of Common Council, divers of the assistants whose names are underwritten, of their own goodwill and love to the company, did offer to lend upon the seal of the House several sums of money (the particulars whereof are subscribed) for the making up of that 940 *l.*, which was accordingly accepted of; and thereupon it is ordered that every person so lending shall have the seal of the House for the security of the repayment of his money at a year's end, with allowance of 8 per centum for the time."

5445. There is another minute bearing upon that, is there not?—There is another minute of the 31st December 1627: "It was at this court ordered, touching the sale of the plate belonging to this company, for the providing out of it part of the 2,820 *l.* assessed by act of Common Council upon this company for their proportion towards the payment of 60,000 *l.* to His Majesty, and that such of the company as will have any of the said plate, which was the gift either of their ancestors or friends, shall have the same upon mortgage for one year. And as for the five cups given by Mr. William Colayne to this company, upon the delivery whereof the company did covenant under the seal of their corporation with his executors to use them yearly for ever at the election of the master and wardens. It is further ordered that the master and wardens for the time being (who have willingly agreed thereunto) shall each of them have one of the said cups, depositing freely so much money as his value shall come unto at five shillings and sixpence the ounce, and the same to keep during their year, and at their going out the succeeding master and wardens to take them for their year, and to pay the former master and wardens their money, and so to pass yearly from master and wardens successively till their money can be paid them. The rest of the plate to be mortgaged for a year. And the master and wardens are desired to take care for providing of the money thereupon. And it is further ordered that Mr. Renter Warden shall disburse out of the moneys in his hands, towards the payment of this 2,820 *l.*, 1,000 *l.* more or less as cause shall require." There is another minute dated the 22nd of December 1627, which I do not think I need read, but I will hand it in. (*The same was handed in.*)

5446. When Dr. Todd gave evidence I think he said that this money was raised by a tax on citizens; is that so?—I believe not, from my reading of the minute. I am bound to say I have only refreshed my memory very cursorily now, but my recollection of it was that the money was all repaid to the individual members from whom it was in the first instance levied.

5447. Repaid by whom?—By the company.

5448. Out of its corporate funds?—Out of its corporate funds, as the minute by such money as was not subject to charitable uses.

5449. Have you any further remark to make upon the ancient history, as I may call it?—I do not know that I have. The books, fortunately, were

Sir *William Marriott*—continued.

were carried in the Fire of London, and are at the disposal of the Committee for the purpose of looking into them if they like. The accounts seem to have been kept in a very methodical way.

5450. Showing the expenditure and receipts, I suppose, from a very early date?—Yes. I was speaking for the account of the repayment of the money, and I believe it also applies to the expenditure and receipts from Ireland.

5451. Now we come on to what your deputation did in 1873. In 1873 you went over to Ireland, did you not?—Yes.

5452. Did you take pains to ascertain the position and the requirements of the estate?—Yes; we took, as we believed, every possible pains. I know it was an excessively busy time.

5453. How long did you spend there?—We were 10 days in Ireland, occupied from morning to night in receiving deputations and seeing people, and driving about from one part of the estate to the other; for it is a scattered estate.

5454. Did you visit all parts of the estate?—We visited all parts of the estate. We saw, I think, clergy of all denominations, and heard their views about things generally as to what was wanted. I may say we did our very best to prove our desire, by liberality on our part, to meet the real requirements of the estate and the wants of the tenantry; and I must say, if I may be allowed to do so, that we were met very warmly and very kindly by the tenantry, and there was a most friendly feeling throughout; indeed, I think I may say that that feeling really prevailed to the present time, so far as regards the relationship between the company and the tenantry. I do not mean to say that there have never been differences as regards individual tenants, but I believe really the relations of landlord and tenant have never been marred by any ill-feeling.

5455. You visited the estate in 1874, did you not?—Yes; I was again one of the deputation in 1874 for carrying out many of the recommendations we had made in 1873.

5456. With regard to the recommendations you made, did the court carry them out in making grants, and so on?—I think the court carried out almost every recommendation we made. I cannot at the moment charge my memory whether any recommendations were not carried out. The court met us entirely in the spirit in which we made the recommendations, with the desire to do everything they could for the benefit of the estate, in which they were as much interested and of which they were as proud as we were.

5457. Were the grants made in capital sums or in annual payments?—They were made in both ways.

5458. Can you give us any details as to that?—Yes. It so happened that just before we came into the estate the Church Act had passed, by which the Church of Ireland was disestablished and disendowed; and among other people who received compensation under that Act were the Skinners' Company, who had three or four advowsons in Ireland, that is to say, the right of presentation to three or four livings. I believe we were the only company who had any advowsons. A sum of money was awarded in respect of those advowsons; that sum was stated by one of the witnesses as being 3,200*l.* paid to the company, but that was not quite correct. A sum of about 5,500*l.* was paid by the Church Commissioners; but, inasmuch as the Act passed while Mr. Ogilby was still tenant of the estate, a portion was paid to him for his life interest.

5459. How much did the company receive?—£. 4,284 was received very soon after we came into possession; it had been waiting apportionment between the late lessee and ourselves.

5460. What was done with that fund?—We determined from the commencement that we would not touch any of that money for our own purposes. We considered that it belonged purely to the Church, that it was Church money. We never, of course, had received any income from advowsons before, and advowsons in England and in Ireland seemed rather questionable matters of property; and we determined that it should be used in the first instance as far as possible for securing that the clergy of the old Church of Ireland, the Episcopal Church, should be continued in all parts of the estate; and, subject to that, for the spiritual requirements of the tenantry of all denominations. I admit we gave the first preference to the clergy of the Church of Ireland; but that was not because we preferred them considered as a church, but because they were the people who were being disendowed, and there was great danger at the time that there might otherwise have been no episcopal ministrations in some of their parishes.

5461. Will you give, or could the clerk give, any details as to what those parishes were?—The clerk will perhaps give that. I have not got them at the moment.

5462. I think a certain sum you gave for vicarage houses and glebe lands?—Yes.

5463. Can you give us the sum?—Yes, I can give you the sum. We gave 2,284*l.* 7*s.* towards the purchase of vicarage houses and glebe lands. The details of that can be given by the clerk.

5464. The clerk will give us any other details?—Yes, he will give what other details are necessary. I may add that in subsequent years we have given money for Presbyterian manses and towards the building the Roman Catholic church, and to meet two or three other demands of the same character, and I think we have never refused any. There is still a small balance of the sum remaining, and we have always accumulated the interest; it is carried to one fund.

5465. I understand you did give to Roman Catholics as well as Presbyterians?—We have drawn no distinction in principle between the one and the other, except that arising from the fact that this money came from the Church of Ireland in the first instance.

5466. What has been your guiding principle; has it been the wants of the neighbourhood?—Yes, the wants of the neighbourhood.

5467. Have the Skinners' Company done anything in the way of planting the estate?—Yes, we have; one of the very first things we recommended was that we should plant in spots where it would either be a protection to the tenants, or where

0.118. X X 2

Sir William Marriott—continued.

where the land was so waste that it could not be used for cultivation. One of the things we did notice, I am bound to say, when we first entered into the estate, was that it was worse in the matter of planting than almost any of the other companies' estates. That, undoubtedly, we attributed to the fact that the leases for lives had not afforded sufficient security or interest to induce planting for posterity. We wanted to remedy that; we appointed a forester, and we planted; and though we had considerable difficulty in arranging with the tenants where it was desirable to plant on any portion of their farms, we generally did succeed in arranging amicably with them in the first instance, and we paid very handsomely indeed for the privilege. The planting was for the benefit of the estate generally, and for the tenants of the particular farms concerned.

5468. How were they off for roads?—One of the main points made to us on the first deputation, and on the second deputation also, was that there was a want of roads, not of main roads but of occupation roads and roads common to two or three farms. We therefore determined to do what we could in the way of improving those farms by means of roads, and we did a great deal, though not quite as much, I admit, as I should like to have seen done, owing to various difficulties.

5469. Did you do anything with regard to railway enterprise?—Yes; that was a matter which also occupied our minds, and seemed to us to be a thing in which we could do a great deal more than the tenants could do for themselves, or than any other landlord could do for them. We were very anxious indeed, as we were without any railway in any part of the estate, to get railway accommodation for them.

5470. Dr. Todd stated that a main railway to Derry, in competition with the Belfast and Northern Counties Railway, would have been the best; what do you say to that?—No doubt for some purposes that is true. If you look at the whole county, and Londonderry particularly, undoubtedly what would have been the best for Ireland would have been to have had a competitive line with the Belfast and Northern Counties Railway from Londonderry. We sketched out upon the map which we prepared at the time, and talked over with the tenantry, and everybody connected with the district, the general line of such a railway, and we left that question very much to the county, advising them that if we could get a main line of railway which would pass through parts of our property it would be the best thing to do. But that would have cost 800,000 l., while the branch line from Newtown-limavady to Dungiven would only cost 60,000 l., and that would bring the railway into the principal town upon the estate; and to make a long story short, after the question had been debated for a long time, it seemed to us, upon the whole, that that was the best thing to do under the circumstances. If we could have found other people to spend the balance of the 800,000 l. upon the main line, that would have been a better thing to do; but it was easier for us to find 20,000 l.

Sir William Marriott—continued.

or 20,000 l. for a line costing 60,000 l. than to apply that sum towards the larger expenditure of 800,000 l. which I have mentioned. We looked in every direction, and we found that there were no other large landowners who would profit by such a railway. It so happened there were few of the city estates that would have been upon the line of the railway, and therefore it was practically impossible to carry out the larger scheme.

5471. You did guarantee a certain sum for a railway from Limavady to Dungiven, did you not?—Yes; we guaranteed a sum of 20,000 l., and 5 per cent. for a branch railway from Dungiven to Limavady.

5472. Was that made?—That railway was made very soon after. It was passed in 1877 or 1878, and made and opened about 1881 or 1882.

5473. Did you pay the 20,000 l. down, or by contributions?—The arrangement was that we should guarantee the interest upon it by which it would be raised in the market, on the principle of the barony guarantees in other parts of Ireland.

5474. You paid 1,000 l. a year, I think?—It amounts to that; 5 per cent. on 20,000 l. would be 1,000 l. a year. The railway never has paid the money, and we have paid the 1,000 l. a year since the commencement.

5475. Are you paying it now?—We are paying it still.

5476. You paid also another sum, I think, in respect of railway enterprise?—Yes; there is another part of the estate on the other side of the mountains which comes down to Draperstown, and joins the Drapers Company's estate. I do not know that it is very material, but this map would help the Committee to understand how scattered the estate is (*handing a map to the Chairman*). You will see there that the Ballynascreen or Draperstown portion of the estate is quite detached. As Dungiven, which is the largest portion of the estate, had got a railway by a drop line from Limavady, we wanted to get a communication for Ballynascreen, which is the poorest part of the estate, and we therefore guaranteed a sum of 4,000 l. towards building a branch railway from Magherafelt to Draperstown. That railway was also constructed, and the money has been paid ever since; for it has not been remunerative.

5477. None of the railways have been remunerative, have they?—I do not think you can very well expect that railways of that kind would be remunerative. They are only branches, which, as we believed, would be very useful indeed for the town, and benefit the town even without their paying money.

Mr. John Ellis.

5478. Have the Drapers Company also property at Ballynascreen?—Yes, they have; we have a very small portion of the town of Draperstown. I do not know that they call their property Ballynascreen, but their property marches with ours there and is bounded by the same boundary. The town of Draperstown mainly belongs to the Drapers Company.

5479. In

Sir William Merriott.

5479. In making these grants, you were guided to a certain extent by your increased rentals, were you not?—Yes; and for the purpose of explaining that, I must go back a little. When we came into our property in 1872, our deputation of 1873 was told on all hands that it was expected everywhere that there would be a re-valuation of the estate; it had not been valued for 40 years.

5480. Dr. Todd says in his evidence that you raised your rents from 5,000 *l.* to 16,000 *l.*; is that so?—Dr. Todd gave his evidence very fairly, and meant, no doubt, to be perfectly accurate; but it is very difficult to keep figures in one's mind, and those figures are not correct. The rents were never 5,000 *l.* and they were never 16,000 *l.* What was the fact was that the tenants had paid more than 11,500 *l.* ever since 1845. Mr. Ogilby had a valuation in 1845, just after the famine year, and the rents had been reduced; he adopted that valuation and reduced the rents to about 11,500 *l.* That was the same rent that was being paid by the tenants in 1872, railway communication having been given in the meantime.

5481. Was there no raising of rents between 1845 and 1872?—No.

5482. Then you had a re-valuation?—Yes, which was fully expected.

5483. What was the result of that re-valuation?—The result of that re-valuation was that Messrs. Brewington and Gale advised they were worth 14,201 *l.*, say 14,200 *l.*, a year.

5484. What did you do upon that?—One or two of the members of the court went over specially for the purpose of meeting the tenants, in order to try and come to a friendly arrangement with representative men, and they succeeded in doing it. We were not ourselves satisfied with the valuation; we thought it was too high.

5485. Instead of taking it at 14,200 *l.*, what was the result?—The result was that we settled amicably with people who professed to be, and I believe were, representative people, for a sum that worked out altogether at 13,100 *l.*

5486. So that the rents were practically raised from 11,500 *l.* to 13,100 *l.*?—Yes, an increase of about 1,600 *l.* a year. In those figures there may be some little discrepancy from what might appear to be the figures; because the Domain House, Pallinar House, had been occupied by old Mr. Ogilby, and it had never formed part of the rental, because he lived in it himself. I should say that the house was on the life of his cousin, who was the last life in the lease. Mr. Ogilby lived after the lease fell in. He was a great invalid, and he was very anxious to live on at Pallinar House, and the company let it to him at 300 *l.* a year (which is an agreed figure); and that is eliminated both from the 11,500 *l.* and the 13,100 *l.*

5487. That makes an increase in the rental of about 1,600 *l.*?—£. 1,500 a year.

5488. You have already accounted for 1,250 *l.* a year, given towards railway enterprise?—Yes. It was mainly owing to the fact that we were in-

Sir William Merriott—continued.

creasing the rents, that we determined to spend that money on those railways. It was not the desire of the Skinners' Company to bring away any more money from Ireland than we had done under the old rental. We believed the rental to be very far below the value of the land (as I believe it was at that time), and we determined that we would guarantee this 25,000 *l.* with a possible charge of 1,250 *l.* a year, as part of the return (if I may say so) for the increased rent. We thought that was a way of giving the tenantry the benefit of it. I think I may say that was the unanimous feeling of the court.

5489. Subsequent to the estate falling into possession, you made a purchase of the shares of some other companies, did you not?—Sir Owen Roberts was describing to you this morning the relative shares of certain companies associated with the Clothworkers. The same system prevailed with us. The money had not all been found originally by the Skinners' Company, but three companies were associated with them in definite proportions ascertained by agreement in the original contributions. All these three companies continued to hold their share in the estate after the time the lease fell in, they were the Bakers', the Stationers', and the Girdlers'. The Bakers' and the Stationers' were anxious to sell their share in the estate, and we were anxious also to have the entire management of it in our own hands; we had taken great interest in it, and we did not at all like the idea of its being referred merely to a joint committee of the three companies. The Bakers' and Stationers' still, if they retained their shares at all, they ought to have a share in the management, which would have meant a large number of our court who knew a good deal about the estate having no share in its management. That was one reason for buying them out. I do not say it was the only reason. We did not think at that time it was a bad thing to invest in property in Ireland, and for that reason among others, we determined to buy them out. We agreed the figure upon the average number of years' purchase, which we found realised in the Encumbered Estates Court, which was about 23 years. I do not mean to say that was the figure it was agreed with them, that we should take it at; we had considerable negotiations with them as to what sum should be given; but a figure was ultimately arrived at which was about the figure that that number of years would give; and where there was some opposition in our court on the ground that we were giving too large a figure, I pointed out that in the Encumbered Estates Court that was the average figure, and what we were giving worked out to that number of years' purchase.

5490. Probably the associated companies asked 25 years, and you suggested 20, and then you both came to 23 years?—I think probably they suggested 26 years.

Mr. John Ellis.

5491. Was that 23 years' purchase of the gross rental?—Of the gross rental. We spent 76,000 *l.* of our own money from England in buying out their proportion of the estate.

Sir William Marriott.

3492. In what year would that be; was it 1876 or 1877?—I think it was 1876; the clerk will give you all these figures accurately. I am almost sure it was 1876; I may say that the Girdlers' Company were anxious to remain shareholders, as it were, in the estate, and they did not want to share in the management, and therefore we did not buy them out. They now hold about 10 or 11 per cent. of the whole estate.

3493. You paid 76,000 *l.* to the Stationers' and Bakers' Companies?—To the Stationers' and Bakers' Companies.

3494. You were also a member of the committee specially appointed by the company to negotiate and carry out the sale of the estate under Lord Ashbourne's Act?—Yes, I was; I served on it throughout.

3495. What year was that?—It began in the autumn of 1886, I think, if I remember rightly; I think our negotiations only began in October 1886, the Act having passed in 1885.

3496. Whom did you employ as your agent for the sale?—We employed Dr. Todd; in fact it was Dr. Todd who first wrote to us about it and told us, if I remember rightly (I have not seen the letter lately), that he believed the tenantry wished to buy. We considered the question, and although we certainly were anxious not to have parted with the estate ourselves for many reasons, yet, believing it was the desire of the tenantry to buy, we unanimously determined that we would give them an opportunity of doing so. May I here add one thing. Very soon after we came into the management of the estate, after the lease fell in, we received a very numerously and influentially signed memorial from the tenantry, begging us not to sell the estate; it had been rumoured that we should do so, in fact we had had offers prior to the lease falling in. I forget the name of the gentleman, but a merchant in Belfast was very anxious to buy the estate, and, as I say, we had a memorial from the tenants begging us not to sell the estate.

3497. Was that in 187[illegible]?—It was in 1872.

3498. You did not sell?—We did not sell.

3499. You did not think of selling?—We certainly should not have sold the whole estate to any one individual. It was the belief that the tenantry wanted to buy and that public policy seemed to demand that the tenantry should have greater fixity than they get in Ireland that induced us to offer to sell.

3500. The statement made by Dr. Todd is that he was not authorised to make any promise of the continuation of the grants after the sale of the estates; is that correct?—Yes, perfectly correct. The question was never mooted. We saw Dr. Todd several times, and he never asked, and he never told us that the tenantry had asked him, and we certainly never gave him any authority to give them any promise at all; in fact we had not made up our own minds. As he said in his evidence, he dealt with everybody by circular, and those circulars were drawn by him and submitted to us and approved.

3501. In another part of the evidence given before this Committee by Archdeacon Hamilton, he said that the company then ceased their contribution to Donaghendy, which he believed was on the estate of the company; is that correct?—Donaghendy is a peculiar case. I am not quite sure whether we did not at one time have a townland there. I was not aware we had until I saw, looking through some books the other day, that there had been a townland there. The reason we gave a grant of a few hundred pounds to Donaghendy was that the son of our own agent was the Vicar of Donaghendy. We saw him once or twice in a friendly way, and we were anxious to do what was right by our agent, and I suppose we were influenced to some extent by the fact that we had a small holding at Donaghendy; but it was only a holding of about 200 *l.* a year, and I had absolutely forgotten that we ever had a farm in it.

3502. Dr. Todd, in his evidence before this Committee, in answer to Question [illegible], says, that the estate was sold at 19 years' purchase; is that correct?—I am sure Dr. Todd did not mean to state anything but what was perfectly accurate, and it is true that in one sense it was arranged at 19 years' purchase; but in every case the tenant was to have one and a-half year's rent allowed. If he had paid it, it was returned in cash, and if it was not paid up, it was allowed for in the sum he paid as purchase money. The sum fixed was therefore 19 years, as correctly stated; but the sum actually paid was 17½, and in many cases 17¼ years.

3503. Dr. Todd also, in answer to Question 3478, said that the statement which he made before Lord Derby's Commission was correct, that the Skinners' was the worst managed estate; do you wish to make any remarks upon that?—He specifically said that in 1863; he did not say it in 1880. Of course opinions may differ. I really do not know a great deal of the other estates (though we took care, the second year the deputation went over, to go to every one of them with introductions to the agents, for the purpose of seeing what they were doing and adopting any plans which seemed to us likely to improve the state of the tenantry), and I am not prepared to say that it may not have been the worst managed estate in 1863; but you will remember we had only come into it in 1873, we were the last company who came into the management of our estate; and I venture to think that no middleman is ever likely to manage an estate as well as the people permanently interested in it. I accept that as Dr. Todd's opinion, but think it is exaggerated. I do not mean to say it was a badly managed estate under Mr. Ogilby, because the tenants applauded Mr. Ogilby to the skies——.

Chairman.

3504. He was the middleman, I presume?—Yes. He lived upon the property and had a very nice house, and was a most liberal landlord. We were told on all hands that he had been most friendly disposed to the tenants, and I think so far as we could see he had managed the estate well; but in matters of planting I quite agree that he had not done what was necessary; and perhaps if he had been permanently interested in the estate, he would have put in more roads, which was the main thing they wanted. He had contributed 800 *l.* towards each of the Church of

Chairman—continued.

Ireland parishes upon the disestablishment, as a help towards their endowment.

3505. With regard to the town buildings in Dungiven which were sold, how were they sold?—The town buildings of Dungiven were sold only upon the ground rent. We have always recognised tenant-right in Dungiven. We have taken great pains to discriminate between the improvements upon the land and the land itself. For instance, generally, I believe the value of land there is put at 2 s. 6 d. a foot frontage; and if we got 2 l. a year, and the man had built a house, we only sold to him at 17½ times 2 l.

3506. Reckoning the whole value of the house as his?—Yes, the whole value of the house belonged to the tenant; he had the tenant-right.

3507. Has tenant-right always existed on your estate?—Tenant-right has always existed on our estate.

3508. That is chiefly in the north of Ireland, I believe?—Yes, mainly in the north of Ireland. We have been most anxious in every way to preserve the tenant-right. Of course I know under the Act as regards agricultural holdings, tenant-right was absolutely secured, and it was not in the power of the landlord to disregard that tenant-right at all; but, as regards the town buildings, the Act did not apply, and we determined from the very earliest moment to recognise the tenant-right in them exactly in the same way as with regard to agricultural holdings.

3509. You have treated the town tenants exactly as agricultural tenants?—Yes; I believe tenant-right has always represented the fair value of the improvements made by the tenants both in agricultural districts and in towns, and the goodwill which existed between the landlords and the tenants. We have never evicted a man from a town building, so far as I am aware.

3510. Can you give us the amount for which the estate sold?—The clerk will give you particulars with regard to that.

3511. Have you sold the whole of it?—No; only two-thirds is sold as yet, and the clerk will tell you what it has sold for.

3512. Has any sum been left for keeping up subscriptions?—No; no sum has been left for keeping up subscriptions. That is a matter which the Court themselves will deal with as demands arise. I may say that I think there are only two cases where we have not determined to go on with the old sums that were given. Where we have entirely sold the estate, I confess I personally thought that everyone would recognise that if a landlord has ceased to have a pecuniary interest in land, he is not bound in the same way to pay subscriptions. But if the people attach so much importance to it, and if we understand that they did, I daresay the Court will be very liberal; because we wish to apply (not that we have any obligation whatever to do so) our surplus income for purposes which are useful to the people, and we have done a great deal, or I will not say a great deal, but a certain amount in Ireland for founding scholarships and things of that kind. What I mean is that we should prefer giving the money for general purposes, rather than appropriating it to any particular part of the property which we once held, and other people now hold. I should prefer myself doing it in that way. But I entirely deny that we have ever recognised any trust whatever of the nature of a legal trust, with regard to whatever donations we have given. All the donations we have given have been simply owing to the recognition of the duties of a good steward with regard to his property, and which every good and liberal landlord must be expected to perform with regard to his property; it is his desire to do what is for the good of his tenantry.

Chairman—continued.

3513. The clerk, I presume, will give us the details as to all these arrangements?—The clerk will give all the details which the Committee wish to have.

3514. Have you anything more to add?—I do not think there is anything more that occurs to me, except an explanation in detail of some of the answers that have been given here. I think the clerk is prepared to give you that. I am of course willing to answer any questions upon any part of the subject that the Committee may wish to put to me.

Mr. Lea.

3515. With regard to the minute which you read, you spoke of 60,000 l. as being in addition to the payment of 20,000 l.?—Would you allow me to ask the clerk one question as to the minutes. (*After consulting the clerk.*) I was not quite sure whether my memory was correct. I see it is not stated on this copy of the minutes that that was with regard to Ireland. It was my recollection that that sum is bearing upon the Irish property, and I understand that is so.

3516. That was the point I was going to ask; you have no recollection as to that, I understand?—I see on the copy that it is not so stated, but I think it is so stated in the minutes. The impression on my mind is that it has reference to the Irish property.

3517. There is not a word about the Irish property on this copy of the minute?—I noticed that for the first time in reading it just now. I had not seen the extract before. I merely desired that it should be taken out of the minutes.

3518. If you do not know that it is in the original, it is no use pursuing it?—The clerk will come into the chair and speak upon that point. He tells me it certainly is; but of course you must not take that upon my authority.

3519. You know nothing, as I understand, beyond this minute which you have handed in?—Except that I have seen the minute in the book, and that that was my impression at the time, and it is my impression still.

3520. Do you mean that it did not refer to Ireland?—No; I think it must refer to Ireland.

3521. Would not the word Ireland be mentioned if it did?—No; it might be by a heading, for instance. Of course, in that kind of minute it would often be by a heading.

3522. If there was such a sum as that, would not it be mentioned in the records of the Irish Society?—I do not know.

3523. Do you know that this money was paid through the Irish Society originally?—I think it must have been, but I am not quite sure.

Mr. Lea—continued.

5524. If this money had been paid through the Irish Society, surely they would have a record of the sum?—I think they must have.

5525. If their records contain nothing about it, we may presume it does, perhaps, belong to England?—That is possible, of course.

5526. I presume your company would not pay more than any of the other companies have paid?—No; I think that is quite certain.

5527. You said that the Merchant Taylors had obtained 76,000l. from your company of your own money?—No, not the Merchant Taylors; the Bakers and Stationers received 76,000l. from us. The Merchant Taylors never had a share in our property.

5528. £.76,000 was paid?—£.76,000 was paid.

5529. I presume, if Parliament were to decide that these are Irish funds, you will expect those companies to refund you the 76,000l.?—I think we should, if they have not spent it.

5530. With regard to Dr. Todd, you said, I think, that you had given him no authority to give any promise with regard to a continuation of the grants?—Yes.

5531. Was the subject mentioned at all in your company?—I do not think it ever was mentioned that I can recollect; that is to say, not as between Dr. Todd and us with regard to any arrangement with the tenants prior to sale. It was mentioned in applications afterwards in one or two cases where it had lapsed by death; that was the general instance. The application was made that we should renew it to the new Presbyterian minister, I think.

5532. Was not it mentioned at the time of the sale?—No. You may perhaps say that this is the time of sale, as it has been going on continuously.

5533. Have you had any memorials with regard to it?—Yes; we did have a memorial as to individual cases.

5534. Was there no general memorial?—I do not think so.

5535. Were you asked to receive any deputation with regard to it?—I think we may have been, but I cannot charge my memory with it.

5536. Did you receive any deputation?—I think not; unless it was during the time of year I am engaged in these Committee rooms, I cannot attend very much in the summer months; but I do not remember any deputation.

5537. You are not aware of any?—I am not aware of any deputation.

5538. Did you not consider it a rather serious matter for districts you were leaving and selling property in, that they should be deprived of all these funds?—No; I cannot say I thought that, because we were losers in selling. We only got three per cent. for our money, and where the tenants paid five per cent. before, they now pay four per cent. to the Government. They were largely the gainers. The land was sold at 17 years' purchase, and therefore 10l. of rent was bought for 170l., upon which they paid four per cent., including the instalments for the repayment of the loan. Therefore they would pay 7l. a year to the Government where they paid 10l. before, and therefore they were gainers of 3l. in every 10l. If they were put in that better position, I should have thought they ought to take upon themselves the duty of landlords if they were landlords.

5539. Had they paid the poor-rate and county cess before?—Upon the re-valuation there was an arrangement under which we paid the county cess and the poor-rate, I think; but I am not sure of that.

5540. Is it not customary for the landlord to pay half the county cess?—I think it was half the county cess that we paid.

5541. If the tenant had to pay the poor-rate and the county cess, ought not that to be considered on the other side?—I may be a little mistaken about that; perhaps you would leave it to the clerk to answer as to that. I am not quite certain whether the county cess was paid by us.

Mr. John Ellis.

5542. When you speak of rental, do you mean the judicial rental?—Yes, the judicial rental; in all cases they were the judicial rentals. I ought perhaps now to say that we were not receiving anything like 15,100l. a year, because the judicial rental had been considerably reduced, and notwithstanding that, we had to pay the amount I have mentioned to the railway companies.

Mr. Lea.

5543. You do not know how much you have expended in donations, subscriptions, and the expenses of the estate?—The clerk has all that. I think all the expenses together were about 5,000l. a year; but the clerk will give that.

5544. Are you aware that you gave some 50l. a year for an intermediate school at Dungiven?—We tried an intermediate school at Dungiven; it was pressed upon us, and we determined to try it. We gave it a very fair experiment for several years, and the numbers dwindled, and there did not seem to be a real demand for it; it was impossible, in fact, to keep a good master there.

5545. You dropped the subscription of 50l., did you not?—Yes, we did.

5546. Then you gave grants to schools?—Yes.

5547. Donaghedy has been referred to, and you said at one time you received a yearly rental of 200l. a year from it?—Yes, I think about that.

5548. Would not it be proper to give 10l. a year to a school there?—Yes, I think it would; but we did not give up the grant till we had sold the property.

5549. Then you gave small sums for provident societies?—Yes.

5550. And you have given up those subscriptions to provident societies, have you not?—I do not think we have, though I think it is probable that would go in accordance with the same principle that we were accepting, which is the English principle and the equitable principle, that when you cease to be landlords you do not continue the moral responsibilities of landlords.

5551. You also gave 5l. a year to the choir fund?—Yes.

5552. The

Mr. *Lea*—continued.

5552. That has also been withdrawn, has it not?—I do not think that is accurate; I do not recollect that it has ever been dropped. We have kept up the great bulk of voluntary subscriptions of that kind to the extent of several hundreds a year.

5553. You think that you have a right to give up those subscriptions?—Certainly; if we are not trustees of our property we have a right to give them up.

5554. Do you think it is worthy of a great City Company's liberality?—Yes, I think so. What I really do think we should have done, and I hope will do even though this question of trust is raised, and it is actually charged against us that we recognise a trust, because we are liberal, what I think we should be inclined to do would be to give for general purposes in Ireland at least as much as we gave before. I am sure there is no feeling of illiberality on the part of the company. When a man dies, and you have entered into an obligation with his successor seemed to us to be the proper time while continuing all vested interests to say that grant will entirely drop, and the tenantry now being themselves landlords will keep that up.

5555. Have you intimated anything of that sort?—No; but what I meant to say is that we have dropped one or two subscriptions upon that principle, I think. Probably the honourable Member, if he was a landlord in Ireland itself, or in England, if he sold the property, would not feel that he had the same claim upon him as he had before.

5556. Do you think you hold your property precisely the same as a landlord in England holds his?—I think we do, except that we are a corporation; that is the only difference I can see. The money was found by us in the first instance for purchasing; we went into it most unwillingly; it was rather forced upon us. It was said to be for the profit of the undertakers; and after incurring all these obligations and receiving a very insufficient return upon our money, just when the profit begins to be apparent, I cannot see that you can impress a trust upon us now.

5557. Do you say the charter was for the profit of the undertakers?—Quite so.

5558. I thought it was for quite a different purpose. I was only asking you with regard to these grants. The Reverend Edward Newland, who is honorary secretary to the Council and Synod of Derry, stated here that you had given 5 *l.* a year to the Provident Fund. I take this merely as a sample.

5559. Then in December 1888 Mr. Newland says he received a letter from the company announcing the cessation of this grant. A letter was then written to the board "drawing their attention to the nature of the fund, and to the fact of the absolute extinction of the fund consequent upon the withdrawal of this 5 *l.*, and stating that the labouring class, who were benefited by it, were utterly unable to make up the deficit," and he "respectfully asked for the re-consideration of this withdrawal," and he says, "I have an official notification of the receipt of the letter, but I have had no answer down with regard to it." The date of his letter was the 30th of May 1889 last year?—Will you tell me when that evidence of Mr. Newland's was given?

5560. On the 28th of July 1889?—He ought to have had an answer by that time certainly.

5561. He also said: "There is another similar provident fund in the parish of Dungiven. That parish has also had notified to it the withdrawal of its grant from the same company, the Skinners' Company." He says he wrote to the company, and up to that date had only received an official notification of the receipt of his letter?—The clerk will be better able to give you the details with regard to that case. I know there are some answers that have been given in previous evidence upon which he wishes to give some evidence.

5562. Then I will pass from that for the present. With regard to the money from the advowsons, as that is a question of figures, I had better reserve it for the clerk?—Yes, as to the exact figures; but I took a great deal of interest in the matter, and I can give you any answers as to principles. The present clerk was not the clerk to the company at that time.

5563. You said you had received 5,000 *l.* from the Church Commissioners. The evidence of Mr. Knowles states it at 5,567 *l.*?—That was given in respect of the estate; but as I have already explained, about 1,400 *l.* or 1,500 *l.* went to Mr. Ogilby, the former lessee, because the advowsons were leased to him with the rest of the property. Therefore, if they had fallen in he would have presented to the living; and, in fact, in one case, he did lose the presentation owing to its falling in between the time of the Church Act passing and the lease falling in.

5564. What has been done with the money?—*L.* 4,294, with interest, has been entirely repaid to Ireland, if one may say so, and it has always been kept as a perfectly separate account. In that case we did look upon it as a moral trust for the spiritual requirements of the estate; for it was not part of property that we should like to deal with as we should with a farm, for instance.

5565. What has become of the other 1,500 *l.*?—About 1,500 *l.* has been given for Presbyterian purposes, and at least 800 *l.* for a Roman Catholic Church, and I fancy that there are a few hundred pounds still awaiting application.

5566. But I thought you considered that the whole fund was received from the sale of the advowsons, and that it belonged, as you said, to the Episcopal Church?—In the first instance it certainly did; but we took a very liberal view in thinking it should be applied for the spiritual requirements of the estate.

5567. Then you do not think that the whole of it belonged to the Episcopal Church of Ireland?—Certainly, it did not belong to it, because it was paid away by the Church Temporalities Commissioners.

5568. But I think you said it morally belonged to them?—I think it morally belonged to the Church of Ireland; but inasmuch as a moral obligation is very different from a legal obligation, and inasmuch as we have given as much money as we thought was absolutely necessary to main-

Mr. *Lea*—continued.

tain spiritual ministration with regard to the Church of Ireland, the company do not think we should be very wrong in giving the Presbyterians something, and the Roman Catholics also. We thought the temper of the times did not demand narrow distinctions in church matters.

3569. You said particularly that the whole of that came from the disestablishment of the Church?—Yes.

3570. Therefore you said it morally belonged to the Episcopal Church?—Yes, and I say so still.

3571. Then surely you never should have given grants from it to the Presbyterians and Roman Catholics?—I say we should have been perfectly within our right in spending it as part of the property of our estate: therefore the moral obligation, so far as that is concerned, is quite satisfied by giving about two-thirds of it; and, in fact, I said what I did rather in answer to complaints that the Presbyterians and Dr. Todd made, that we gave too much instead of too little to the Church of Ireland. I explained that I thought we ought first of all to satisfy the Church of Ireland as to her ministrations for her tenantry, and subject to that, to the spiritual requirements of the tenantry generally.

3572. Have you read Mr. Newland's evidence?—At the time I did, but I have not read it within the last few days.

3573. The answers in his evidence I am referring to are Nos. 451 to 459. Ballynascreen, to which you have already referred, is an extremely poor parish, is it not?—Yes.

3574. Mr. Newland said that most of the population are labourers of the very poorest class; is that so?—No, I should not say that. They are farmers of a very poor class.

3575. He says that their wages in his own neighbourhood range from 5 s. to 8 s. a week, and that they have large families?—I dare say a good many of them, as he says, are labourers; but my recollection is (and I have spent a good many days in Ballynascreen) that there are little farm-houses coming up to the town.

3576. Belonging to Presbyterians?—I should think they were more Roman Catholics; but I did not distinguish very minutely the religious aspect. I think they were the ordinary class of Irish farmers, not labourers.

3577. But I gather you do not know it as a fact, and Mr. Newland clearly states that 46 heads out of 53 families, and they were very poor families, subscribe?—I think that is very likely indeed. I see he says "46 heads of those very poor families subscribe to their utmost power to the sustentation at present." I do not quite remember whether that deals with the Church of Ireland.

3578. He is only dealing with the Church of Ireland. He says there are only three wealthy people in the parish, the Skinners' Company and two local landlords, Mr. O'Neill, who gives 25 *l.*, and Mr. Stevenson, who gives 10 *l.*, and that is the only support that they can expect from local landlords. Then he says, "They are mostly labourers," and then he is asked, "If the aid of the companies is withdrawn what will happen to the parish?" and he says, "The parish of St. Anne's has already you may say collapsed; it has had to be united with another. The parish of Killaloo is similarly circumstanced, and the incumbent says it must collapse if the subscriptions are withdrawn"?—Yes. We have not said that we should withdraw that at all; that part of the property has not been sold mainly; very little of it has been sold.

3579. Having regard to your evidence just now, if you consider you have a right to withdraw these subscriptions when you sell property, the subscriptions probably would be withdrawn?—I suppose that would apply to every Irish landlord who is selling. I am not now drawing a distinction between the company and anybody else: but every Irish landlord when he sells may be assumed to hold, at all events, that there is no obligation upon him to continue his subscriptions. I should not like to see any place fail in keeping up its spiritual ministration from want of subscriptions; I do not think the Skinners' Company would do that. I think there is a considerable distinction between the case where it would fail, and where it would not fail.

3580. There is evidence here given by Mr. Newland of subscriptions withdrawn from schools, of subscriptions withdrawn from provident societies, and of subscriptions recently withdrawn from the Presbyterians of Cumber of 50 *l.* a year, which is fairly *bonâ fide* evidence that you intended to withdraw the subscriptions?—In those particular cases if you say they are withdrawn they probably were withdrawn; I do not remember; but it does not follow that if we were satisfied in any case that the withdrawal would have had the result of depriving the people of the ministrations, we should do so. For instance, with regard to the Presbyterians, we gave a sum there not for the purpose of supporting their ministrations, but, inasmuch as a number of our tenants were Presbyterians, we thought it well to increase the income of the Presbyterian minister. They are stronger on the Ballynascreen portion of the estate than any other denomination, and we never felt that the Presbyterians would be in any way deprived of the ministrations by the withdrawal of our grants. With regard to Ballynascreen, we have given very largely. In addition to the 15 *l.* a year towards the Presbyterians, we gave 500 *l.* or 600 *l.*, if I remember rightly.

3581. Would you view with satisfaction the church being closed and the schools being closed?—Certainly not.

3582. Would you consider that as part of the duties, I will not say the trusts, of your company?—Speaking for myself, most certainly not; and I think I may speak for my colleagues also. If we were satisfied in any particular case that it would have the effect which the witness has thought it would, it would be a very good ground for continuing it as a voluntary donation. The only consideration against that is the argument, if it is to be considered, that we are recognising that we are mere trustees of the estate in every voluntary donation that we give. That may influence the minds of some people. I do not mean to say it would prevent us from making a donation;

Mr. Lea—continued.

a donation; because I hope we have the courage of our convictions, that we are not trustees and should not be deterred on that account.

5583. With regard to dispensaries you also gave subscriptions to dispensary doctors, did you not?—Is that what you alluded to just now as provident societies?

5584. No; that was quite distinct?—We did also give subscriptions for dispensary doctors.

5585. You have withdrawn the grants for the medical officers and dispensaries too, have you not?—I think not generally. I think it is only on the death of the dispensary doctor we determined not to appoint another. Upon that question I do not think the tenants have got the benefit that we thought they would get from dispensary officers; the system has not been so beneficial as we hoped it would be.

5586. If dispensary doctors allege that you withdrew their grants in connection with the withdrawal of the grants to provident societies, and schools and churches, is not that confirmatory of your intention to withdraw altogether?—I have told you generally how it has presented itself to us, rightly or wrongly, that the new landlords could very properly take upon themselves the duties of the old landlords.

5587. With regard to arrears Dr. Todd stated that your estate had the largest arrears of any in the north of Ireland; is that so?—I cannot speak about the other estates. But undoubtedly the late agent was a very old gentleman indeed, when we pensioned off.

Mr. John Ellis.

5588. What was his name?—Mr. Clark, whom we pensioned off in 1869; he had got very lax in his collection of rents; and my experience is that when once the rents are not collected regularly it is almost impossible to recover arrears; therefore at one time we were badly off.

5589. Would you not also consider that it might be in consequence of high rentals?—I do not think they were high rentals at all compared with the other estates and the other property. The reductions made by the Commissioners were not in excess of the reductions made on the other estates. There were reductions made, no doubt. With regard to arrears I do think that the arrears arose more from the fact that there are a certain number of very small holdings which were the result of sub-division at a time the company had nothing to do with it, in which people could not support themselves upon a few potatoes or things of that sort. A widow say, for instance, with three or four acres, could not work her land and could not pay for it; her husband, perhaps, worked elsewhere, and she was really in the position of a labourer's widow. If it were absolutely freehold she could not pay the rent. It afforded her a house and a potato ground; but people could not hope to make a living out of three acres of ground. She would be in no worse position than a man who is in a cottage in a town in England; he cannot expect to make his living out of a cottage; he has to pay so much for maintaining himself there.

5590. With regard to the rental, you say it is 11,800 l., or something over 11,000 l.?—It was.

Mr. John Ellis—continued.

5591. When you began to sell?—No; the clerk will tell you what it was when we began to sell. There had been a drop from 13,100 l., and speaking roughly, I think you are correct in stating that figure; it would bring it to about 11,800 l.; but I do not think I gave that figure.

5592. When you received the estate from the hands of Mr. Ogilby the rent was 3,000 l. a year, was it not?—No; that is a mistake of Dr. Todd's. The rent had been as between the tenants and Mr. Ogilby 11,000 l. a year and upwards ever since the year 1843; the rent of the company was only 1,300 l. a year; Mr. Ogilby paid us 1,300 l. a year.

5593. What was the rental that you received when you first let the estate to Mr. Ogilby?—You mean, I presume, at the beginning of the lease in 1803.

5594. Yes?—£. 1,300 a year; and there had been a fine paid by the tenants; it was only as between the middleman and ourselves.

5595. You received 1,300 l. and a fine?—Yes.

5596. What was it previous to Mr. Ogilby's lease?—I am not sure.

Mr. Clancy.

5597. Was it not 600 l.?—If the honourable Member suggests 500 l., it is possible that that is correct. I do not know how it was as between the middleman and ourselves; the clerk will correct me if I am wrong.

Mr. Lea.

5598. Had you spent any money upon the estate from the time Mr. Ogilby had it till the end of his lease?—No, I do not suppose that we have. We could not afford to do much out of 1,300 l., and it was not necessary that we should. He was the person to spend money upon it.

5599. So far as the company was concerned, the rental was raised from 1,300 l. to 13,000 l., without the company having expended a single shilling upon the estate?—That only affects the relations between Mr. Ogilby and us; it did not affect the tenantry in the slightest degree.

5600. Never mind the tenants; so far as the company is concerned, you received 500 l. before you let to Mr. Ogilby; you received 1,300 l. from Mr. Ogilby in 1803, and onwards, and when you resumed the estate you received a rental of 13,000 l.?—We never actually got more than 10,000 l. or 11,000 l.

5601. In the meantime you had not spent a single shilling on the estate?—That is very likely. Of course, the 500 l. we received up to 1803 was a very poor remuneration for the sum given. For 270 years you may say we never really received interest upon the money, and the profit is only just beginning to come in now.

5602. Is 500 l. a very poor rate of interest upon the 2,800 l. you paid originally?—I beg your pardon; 2,800 l. was not the sum we paid. We paid admittedly 6,000 l. and I believe it turns out more like 18,000 l. We had for many years received only 100 l. a year, and for a long period nothing at all, and up to the commencement of this century never more than 500 l. a year; and considering the difference of the value of money

Mr. *Lea*—continued.

in 1609 and the year 1879, we have made absolutely nothing like an adequate return, and surely the profit of the undertakers, which they have been talking of, has been a long time coming.

5603. Where do you get the words "profit of the undertakers" *from*?—It was in the demands from the Crown to the City forwarded to us pressing us to undertake it. It was to be "Pleasing to Almighty God, honourable to the City, and profitable to the undertakers." You will find that in the year 1609, the profit to the undertakers was not found till the year 1879, and is not so very much now.

5604. I must not examine you upon the charter?—It was not in the charter by the reasons and motives which were the inducement to us.

5605. Was not it really for the civilisation and good government of the province?—That was one purpose, of course. It was that that probably induced the Company to undertake it that pressure was put upon us to begin with, and that it would be for the benefit of the country indirectly; but I do not suppose that they would have undertaken it but for their own profit. It seems just the same kind of mixture of motives as would influence the members of the East African Company at the present time. They go partly for the purpose of the civilisation of the country, but mainly for their own profit, and they would hardly be content perhaps if it were 270 years before they met a profit.

5606. You said that you planted the estate with timber?—Yes.

5607. And that it was very badly off for timber?—It was badly off for timber.

5608. Surely the Irish Society called the attention of the Company to the lack of timber on the estates on more than one occasion?—I think they did; I have seen it stated in evidence here, I think.

5609. I presume it was the Irish Society's duty to look after them?—At one time I believe all timber trees were reserved to the Irish Society, and therefore there was no inducement to spend money in planting till that was released, as I think it was in the last century. Then the Companies had never any control until they came into their estates; but each Company as it came in seems to have planted; for we were very much pleased with the judicious use of the plantations we saw on other Companies' portions, and we determined at all events we would not be wanting, and though we should not get profit out of it for 40 or 50 years, still we would plant.

5610. Do you think the Irish Society was right in pressing that upon the Company?—Certainly; I think planting is a most useful thing.

5611. With regard to the minerals, what is the case with them?—They are all reserved, I think, to the Irish Society.

5612. You have reaped no benefit from them?—We reap no benefit. I do not think there are any minerals on our estate.

5613. Of course there is stone?—Yes, there is stone; and the natives and masons tell us there is plenty of copper and iron upon the estate, but we have not found it.

Mr. *Lea*—continued.

5614. If there is any it belongs to the Irish Society?—I think so.

5615. The Irish Society would have to sign any conveyance of them to the tenants, would they not?—If it is reserved to them the Company would not be consulted I take it; the Society would be the lessors.

Mr. *John Ellis*.

5616. As I understand, you rather suggest that for 270 years there has been no adequate financial return, and latterly the policy has been rather to make up that?—I do not think it has been the policy rather to make that up; but the improved means of communication with Ireland, and more especially the railways and steam transit from England to Ireland, have brought commodities into Ireland that never were there before; and I think we had evidence when we were over in Ireland that if you take the principal articles of produce the tenantry had to sell from their farms, and compare them with what they were in 1857 and 1858, when Griffith's valuation was made, they are double in value. Therefore, that would certainly justify a very large increase in the rental of the farms, whereas in fact the farms were not increased in rental at all between 1858 and 1879 when we were taking that evidence.

5617. Can you give us the year of the fixing of the judicial rent?—It was one or two years after the Act; I was one of a small committee of two with the clerk, who had the arranging with them all; I think it was about 1882 or 1883; it was after the Act of 1881. We agreed, the great mass of them, with the tenantry.

5618. There were agreements out of court in 1882 and 1883?—Some took us into court.

5619. What was the year of the sale agreement?—The first offer of the estate was in 1886; a few agreements were signed that year, but mostly in 1887 and 1888. But here I am speaking subject to correction by the clerk.

5620. You compared the two sums of 7 *l.* and 10 *l.* which the tenants had to pay, and you were suggesting that it was a great advantage to pay 7 *l.* rather than 10 *l.*?—Quite so.

5621. Have you remembered that the 7 *l.* (meaning that figure for the sake of argument) is to be paid for 49 years from 1887, and that the 10 *l.* only had to be paid for 15 years from 1883?—In one sense that is true; it is subject to re-valuation every 15 years; but I think the probability is looking to the future, that rent cannot go down very much.

5622. That is all probability?—It is probability, of course.

5623. The certainty is that the man has to pay 7 *l.* a year for 49 years from 1887?—Yes, and nothing afterwards. On the other hand, he would have to pay 10 *l.*, or whatever figure was settled by the court, not only for 15 years, but 150 or 1,500 years, it may be.

5624. But the certainty is as I have put it?—That is quite right; there may be a re-valuation, and the judicial rent may be fixed differently.

5625. And there might be a reduction?—Yes; and there might be an increase.

5626. Are you not aware that the tendency, since the passing of the Act of 1881, has been for

a fall

Mr. John Ellis—continued.

a fall in the judicial rent; that it is possible that, if those rents, which were fixed in 1882 and 1883, had been fixed in 1887 and 1888, they would have been fixed on a lower scale?—I do not think they would.

5627. Were not they the judicial rent of the Land Commissioners?—There was an Act passed (I forget the exact year) in which every year there is a revaluation for an abatement, and the tendency of the last few years has been rather to put the rents up than down.

5628. Will you take it that that was only of limited application?—Yes; but it applied to our tenantry.

5629. I will not pursue that further, because the tendency of rents under the Land Commissioners' decisions has been on a falling scale, except in the point you called attention to?—I think in the difference between 7 l. and 10 l. you will find ample margin for contingencies.

5630. Is it not a fact that in addition to the 7 l., as the honourable Member has reminded you, the tenants have to bear other payments, which make the 3 l.?—I am not quite sure about the payments. I know at the time we were revaluing there was an arrangement about the county cess, but I cannot charge my memory with it; the clerk will know as to that.

5631. I gather that the clerk will give us all the figures as to the Sessions?—Yes, quite so.

5632. Then, with respect to your visit in 1873, I gather that you found the property, looking at it from an English agricultural point of view, in a bad condition?—I am bound to say it was only my second visit to the north of Ireland, and I did not find the farms like farms in Sussex or Essex; but, comparing them with the other parts of Ireland, I should not say that. Comparing them, for instance, with the south of Ireland, which I knew better from former visits, I should say it was looking well.

5633. At all events, by the year 1882, you had been trying to make up lee way?—Yes. We have not as regards the cultivation of the farms; we have done nothing with regard to that; the custom of the country does not admit of your helping the tenant in the slightest degree in that matter. We did not do anything, simply because it would have been impossible to mix up the interests of the two; because, as that time, you will remember, they had their tenant-right, which we looked at as a separate property, often realising as much, or more than, the freehold. Though, I confess, my first idea, as an Englishman, was to try to encourage the people to farm their lands better, and to keep the fields cleaner. I very soon found it was so contrary to the feelings of the people, that I saw we had much better let them go their own way.

5634. I gather what was done by the company between 1878 and 1882 had no relation to improving the agricultural holdings?—No; except so far as we advanced money for substituting slate roofs for thatch, and offered to lend money for similar purposes.

5635. Did you lend a large amount of money?—Not a large amount; the clerk will tell you what it was. It was a general offer which was not very largely availed of.

5636. What interest did you charge?—It was the intention to charge 5 per cent., but I do not think it was ever paid.

5637. Was anything really done between 1873 and 1882 by the company, with regard to planting and roads on a large scale?—As regards the agricultural parts, I do not know that there was. I do not remember. There may be other matters which do not occur to me at the moment, but I do not remember.

5638. You said you thought that the re-valuation of 14,200 l. was much too high?—We did; not that it was not the value of the farms, but that we thought it was too high a jump to make, and it would create a feeling of dissatisfaction.

5639. You were very anxious, I think, that the tenants should buy if you sold?—Most anxious.

5640. Did that wish on your part originate in what you call the custom of the country, namely, the creation of the agricultural value by the tenants?—Yes, it did in a great measure, owing to the fact that we thought that public opinion on that subject was shown by the memorial to us begging us not to sell to outsiders. Therefore, we determined, I do not mean to say we put the resolution upon the books, but we made up our minds that we never would sell without giving the offer first to the tenantry to buy.

5641. It was dictated by the consideration I have mentioned?—Quite so.

5642. You have found no difficulty in separating the value of what has been created by the tenants, from what you have considered as purely to belong to the company?—None whatever, I think. We always found that the tenant-right sold; we gave perfect freedom of tenant-right sale according to the custom of the estate. I mean to say there were certain conditions upon it which I believe the tenantry thought were to their advantage, and it always sold freely until the recent agitation, and large sums were given. One of the customs of the tenantry was that we should always give preference to a tenant of the estate, and not sell to outsiders if a tenant upon the estate would buy at a fair price. Another custom would be to give preference among the tenants to the one adjoining the holding.

5643. You thought those customs just?—Yes, perfectly so; and we have used our tenantry in every way and had most friendly relations with our tenantry as regards them.

Mr. Clancy.

5644. I think in 1855 the Mercers had a revaluation of their estate, and that a Mr. Saunders was then the valuator; you are not that gentleman?—That was not myself; I am at the bar; he is no relation of mine, and I do not know anything about the gentleman.

5645. You say that when a landlord ceases to have an interest in his estate he is not bound to give the same largesse and donations which he gave when he had an interest in it?—That is the English view of the question.

5646. Your view would be entirely changed, if it was judicially decided or declared by Parliament that you were trustees?—Clearly. I do not say by Parliament; it must be judicially decided.

5647. The thing would be entirely altered if that were the case?—Quite so.

5648. You

Mr. Cleary—continued.

5648. You would have to admit then, that you were acting wrongly in withdrawing your grants?—We have acted upon the belief that we were not trustees.

5649. It all depends in fact, upon whether you are declared by the law or by Parliament to be trustees?—If you will allow me to exclude Parliament, I think I would say, declared by law. If no trust exists, we cannot have a fresh trust declared except by confiscation. Of course Parliament can do whatever it pleases, and if Parliament declares we are trustees they can do so; but that has not been the habit of Parliament.

5650. You would then take a new view of your duties?—Of course we must bow to the decision of Parliament.

5651. You said that you always encouraged tenant-right upon your estate?—Yes: I should say we have if I understand what encouraging it means. We have always given free play to tenant-right; we have never hampered it in the slightest degree that I know of.

5652. Can you produce a document called the Report of the Skinners' Company to the Court of Wardens in 1875?—We have such a report.

5653. May I ask whether it is there suggested that in the case of your company, if the question were litigated, that the Ulster tenant-right custom, though undoubtedly prevalent, does not now find the company as reversioners?—I think we said, that though such an argument was conceivable we entirely brushed it away, because we intended to recognise it; we never have disputed it.

5654. In some of the documents are there not rules recommended?—Yes, I think so.

5655. Of a very stringent character, for the purpose of limiting and gradually destroying the tenant-right?—I do not think so at all; I think the rules I have mentioned now, were the custom of the estate when we came into it.

5656. Are you acquainted with the document which I refer to?—Yes.

5657. Are you able to deny that you there recommended for instance, the prohibition of open free sale?—We certainly do.

5658. Do not you think that that was destructive of tenant-right?—Not at all; we accepted the previous custom of the estate, which was to give the tenants upon the estate the priority. If it had been open free sale.

5659. Do you mean to deny that open free sale was one of the essential elements of tenant-right in the north of Ireland?—I think you will find that the law recognised different customs upon different estates. It was a matter of evidence.

5660. I am referring to the custom upon your estate?—The customs upon our estate have always been, that the tenants upon the property should have the preference over outsiders, and that any tenant on the Pellipar estate should, to a reasonable amount, have the preference over another tenant not immediately adjoining.

5661. Was not it a prohibition of open free sale?—Yes.

5662. The prohibition of open free sale is, as I take it, the destruction of one of the essential elements of tenant-right?—Assuming that tenant-right was an unlimited tenant-right, you would be right, but as the Act of Parliament recognises various customs of tenant-right (and there have been many recognised; not on our estate, but on other estates) it would be a matter of custom: supposing that we had determined that there should be open free sale, it might have been very unfair indeed to the tenants who considered that they had a priority of right of purchase upon the same estate.

5663. But the prohibition would have cut down the value of their interest?—I do not think it would; there is sufficient competition between 1,150 tenants.

5664. But the wider the market, of course, the larger the value they can get?—I do not think that follows beyond certain limits.

5665. Is it open free competition in any ordinary transaction if you are limited to a certain number of customers; is it not better to have it open to the whole world?—It depends upon what a certain number of customers are; in a market, if you have only 400 or 500 people competing for, say, a basket of strawberries, you get as high a price as if you had 50,000 competing.

5666. But that is not so?—I cannot do more than give my opinion.

5667. The tenants on your estate would not be quite sure that they would find purchasers on the estate?—If they could not do so then they could go to outside.

5668. But you recommended a prohibition that would prevent them doing it?—It was a preference to the tenantry upon the estate.

5669. I should like to see that document; I have only a summary of it here?—Perhaps the clerk can give it to me (*the same was handed to the Witness*).

5670. Will you read it?—"Various suggestions as to the manner of dealing with the tenant-right question have presented themselves to the minds of the deputation, gathered from information as to the experience in the management of other and neighbouring estates, and we have been at some pains to satisfy ourselves as to the policy of adopting them. The conclusions at which we have unanimously arrived, and which we have now determined to recommend to the court without a due appreciation of the duty of the Skinners' Company, not only to the several companies interested in the property but also to their tenantry, is as follows: (1st). That no sales by auction of tenant-right shall, except under very special circumstances, be allowed."

5671. That is not confining it to any particular body at all; that is absolutely prohibiting free sale?—Of course, I adopt the honourable Member's statement if he says it is prohibiting free sale; I should not have put that interpretation upon it, but I should rather say it is a prohibition except under certain conditions of sale by auction. I will go on to the next conclusion if you will allow me; "(2nd). That the company shall maintain the right of refusing proposed tenants if for valid reasons considered objectionable." That would apply to a drunkard, for instance, which a certain tenant might have accepted.

5672. You do not put that in?—We say "for valid reasons."

5673. You

Mr. *Clancy*—continued.

5673. You are to be the judge of what are valid tenants?—Yes, somebody must be. It is indifferent to us provided he is a fit tenant. The law recognises distinctly that the landlord is not bound to accept a person who is not a competent tenant. I take drunkenness as one reason, and there might be other reasons why a man should not be a fit tenant, and the law recognises that he must be a fit tenant. Then the next conclusion is "(3rd). That it shall be understood that no one, except a previous tenant of the company, be admitted as an incoming tenant, save under exceptional circumstances."

5674. What is the meaning of that?—That is that preference was given to previous tenants of the company. By a previous tenant it means a tenant on some other part of the estate.

5675. It means that except under exceptional circumstances no outsider is to be entered at all, does it not?—Yes, I say so.

5676. What do you call exceptional circumstances?—In the case no one wanted to buy on the property, or not to buy at the proper price, if the tenant could satisfy us that that was so, we should certainly allow him to go outside. I do not think we ever had an objection on that score.

5677. The tenant might say, "I cannot get a proper price for my holding"?—Then under that rule, if he could not get a proper price, somebody else would be admitted.

5678. That would not be "exceptional circumstances"?—I think it would be; I do not think the case ever arose. I have never found that that in practice has created any difficulty at all. They always got large sums for their holdings.

5679. Will you just state the other condition?—"(4th). That a preference be always given to the tenants whose holdings adjoin a farm, the tenant right of which is about to be sold, so as to secure the enlargement of holdings. (5th). That a form of application for leave to dispose of tenant-right (to be prepared under legal advice) be signed by the out-going tenant, giving all necessary information, and especially the sum at which the tenant-right is proposed to be sold. (6th). That the application to sell be made to the company prior to the transfer being effected; no transfer to be valid without their consent in writing."

5680. Are there any recommendations there with regard to re-valuation?—I do not remember them; there are eight if you will allow me to read them: "(7th). That transfers of tenant-right be sanctioned only subject to any increase of rent which may be determined on, due notice of this liability being before his admission, given to the incoming tenant, who will be required to sign a formal agreement, to hold subject to such liability."

5681. Do you not think that is another restriction on the tenant-right custom?—Not upon the tenant-right custom; because this as we believe correctly represented the tenant-right custom on the estate. It would be a restriction upon absolute free sale. It was only that we were coming into the management of our property, and we were reducing unwritten custom, so to speak, to written custom; we were strangers to the management of the estate at that time.

5682. Yes; but the tenant-right had custom existed?—The tenant-right custom had existed from time immemorial.

5683. Did you ever hear before of a landlord coming into possession, and after some time beginning with a general declaration of what he believed to be the nature of the tenant-right existing on his estate?—If it were a private landlord we should not know what he did; it would be in his own breast; but I should think probably that all the City companies when they came in have done much the same; I should think they probably reduced it into writing for the information of their colleagues.

5684. Have they ever put it in print?—I do not know.

5685. Have you ever heard of a document like that before?—I do not think that I have. I have never heard the contrary.

5686. It appears from that document, if those recommendations represent the existing tenant-right custom on your estate, it would seem that it was a very restricted tenant-right, indeed?—I think our tenant-right was not restricted really in amount; I believe the tenant-right sold at as high a figure upon our estate as upon other estates so far as I have been able to ascertain.

5687. Generally in the face of these recommendations, which you say represent the existing custom upon your estate, you will not deny that it was a restricted form of tenant-right?—It is restricted as compared with absolute free sale, but it was not restricted or reduced by the company beyond what existed, I believe, previously.

5688. You say that this covers the custom upon the estate?—Quite so.

5689. You will not deny that it is a restricted form of tenant-right?—I will not deny that.

5690. In fact it does away with what is understood to be the essential element, namely, the right of free sale?—I am afraid I cannot admit that; because my inquiries all lead me to the belief that every estate had a restriction, of a varying nature, but of the same kind. I have not inquired into every estate, but upon many estates they have them.

5691. You are aware, of course, that when Parliament made that essential change in the Bill of 1870, change of the word "custom" into the word "customs" there was a great outcry in the north of Ireland against it?—That is possible; I do not know that I remember it. The Act certainly does speak of customs as recognising different customs.

5692. It was a contention, was it not, that this change in the Bill sanctioned a variety of evasions of tenant-right that had been made by various landlords and companies in the north of Ireland?—I am not prepared to deny that such statements have been made; I do not remember.

5693. Are you aware that that was the popular view?—I think I have heard so.

5694. Do you know that that is the popular view yet?—Very possibly; I have not heard much about it, I am bound to say.

5695. At all events, you would hardly repeat the answer you gave awhile ago, when you said, in general terms, that you had always taken particular care to keep up the custom of tenant-right?

Mr. *Clancy*—continued.

right?—I think I must repeat the answer now. I believe we always take great pains.

5696. You would answer that you had always taken particular care to obtain a particularly restricted system of tenant-right?—The same restricted tenant-right that prevailed upon the estate before.

5697. You said you had made a bad bargain of the estate, I think?—In the purchase of the shares from the Stationers and Bakers do you mean.

5698. From the tenants, I understand; and that you were now only beginning to reap a profit?—With regard to the original purchase of the estate in 1609, I think, if you take the whole property, the company has made a very bad bargain indeed of the Irish estate.

5699. But you were getting 500 *l.* a-year before you let it to Mr. Ogilby; and when you let it to Mr. Ogilby you got 1,500 *l.*, and a fine of 25,000 *l.*?—Yes.

5700. And you added that 25,000 *l.* to your corporate fund?—I suppose so.

5701. Is not that a liberal payment for what you advanced?—I do not think so. I think the accumulation of the money we had advanced, upon which we had received no interest in the meantime, would have realised a great deal more than that. But I do not know that anyone, at all events with the land laws as they are now, recognises that the money invested three centuries ago is to be calculated as the sum of money now.

5702. I know there has been a change in the value of money?—There has been a change in the value of money, and one of the inducements to landlords to purchase land in preference to other property is, that as time goes on, it does become more valuable. But I do not think this has become as valuable as one would have expected in other cities. If the same money had been put into property in London it would have yielded far more.

5703. That is because of the extraordinary growth of London?—If it had been put into any other property in England it would have yielded far more, I am convinced.

5704. At any rate, it was not the custom in England to take advantage of the improvement of the property periodically to raise the rent?—It always has been. In town holdings no doubt it is done after long periods, the custom being to grant leases, but always at the end of the lease the property, with the improvements upon it, belongs to the landlord.

5705. He having made them?—No. For instance, I am living in a house in London.

5706. I am not talking of town houses?—I was speaking of town houses at the time.

5707. I am speaking of agricultural holdings?—No doubt there is that distinction. In England the custom is for the landlord to put up the agricultural farm buildings.

5708. They go to increase the rent at the end of the term, so that if the value of the property has increased it is not unjust?—But there is always a large element of value which is not the result of the tenant's expenditure, with regard to the improvements he produces.

5709. What is it the result of?—It is the result of general improvements in the country, such as railways and the general advance of the times.

5710. Is not the tenant entitled to some of that?—He is entitled: and I think in Ireland the tenant-right secures that for him.

5711. It does not secure it under your company?—I think so; you will find that the tenant-right very often sold for more than the fee-simple value of the land.

5712. You got 25,000 *l.*, and you raised the rent three times, and at the end of Mr. Ogilby's lease you got a nominal rental of 13,000 *l.*?—£. 11,500, afterwards raised nominally to 13,100 *l.*

5713. That was a considerable sum, was it not?—It was not raised upon the tenants. The tenants had been paying that amount years and years. We only increased it 1,500 *l.* upon the tenants.

5714. Dr. Todd says you increased it by 2,000 *l.* a year?—That was wrong; he did not then know the details of the estate, which he did afterwards. It was increased by 1,500 *l.*, and as I say out of that 1,500 *l.*, 1,250 *l.* was spent upon the railway.

5715. You spoke of the conditions of the farms on your estate; are you aware that it was described in 1838, when you had no connection with it, as the worst managed of all the properties of the companies in Ulster?—I believe it was so stated by the Irish Society; I believe it was owing to a little unpleasantness which occurred between us and them in consequence of litigation; I am not aware that they have changed their opinion, but certainly Mr. Ogilby, who was then responsible, except in planting, had done a great deal for the estate.

Chairman.

5716. All this you had already told us in answer to Sir William Marriott?—Yes, mostly.

Mr. *Clancy.*

5717. You say you have given some money for the cleansing of the streets?—I do not think I mentioned the cleansing of the streets; for the widening of streets and making of roads we have; we spent a good deal in widening the streets of Dungiven.

5718. Certainly, you mentioned something for cleansing the streets?—Very possibly.

5719. Do you think that is a species of grant which ordinary landlords make?—I really do not know; I should not think it was.

Mr. *T. M. Healy.*

5720. I gathered that you stated there was a moral trust with regard to certain religious bodies?—I do not think I mentioned a moral trust.

5721. What was your expression?—I beg your pardon, if it was, of course I must adopt it. It was a moral obligation I should have said.

5722. You withdraw the words "moral trust"?—I do not think we ever speak of a moral obligation as a moral trust. The honourable Member may

Mr. T. M. Healy—continued.

may adopt that phrase if he likes, but that was because it was Church property, as I said.

3723. Will you tell us why you consider it was fair to give the Protestants some of this money?—Because it was necessary almost to secure the ministrations of Episcopal clergymen; I do not think it applies so much to Presbyterians, because there was a large body of Presbyterians, but the Church of Ireland people were in the minority there, they were always accustomed to have their church, and the buildings were there, and unless something was done to repurchase the property which had been disestablished, or of which they had been disendowed, the great likelihood was that the clergy would cease to minister in the churches, and the churches would become derelict.

3724. Why should they not if there was no flock to occupy them?—In all cases they had a flock.

3725. Supposing they had not a flock which could fill the edifice, why should not the edifice fall under the natural law?—That would apply to all denominations.

3726. Why did your society, when you were going away, give one denomination a prop that was not given to the others?—Because, to begin with, we did not think the others required it; they were substantially supported, and I think you would have considered yourself under the circumstances, if a body had been recently disendowed, and you had received money as the result of that disendowment, it would have been rather improper, in the first instance, to hand it over to all the other bodies instead of first seeing that they were properly supported.

3727. What money are you speaking of?—The advowson money.

3728. 1869 is a generation ago?—It was three years before. The money had not actually been paid when we came into the estate; it was in the course of being settled. The amount was settled a year after we came into the estate, and therefore, as soon as ever the money was due, between Mr. Ogilby and ourselves we then determined to set that aside first for meeting the requirements of the Church of Ireland, secondly any surplus for any small requirements generally. We gave the Presbyterians and the Roman Catholics a proportion of it.

3729. Do you think it was calculated to create feelings of pleasantness on the estate when a minority gets a great deal of money, and the majority gets very little?—I think most people would feel that it was only the right and proper thing to do under the circumstances.

3730. You think so?—Yes; and what is more we never had any remonstrances about it. In fact we did not at first have any applications from the Roman Catholics for anything. We never refused them on the ground that they were Roman Catholics, and it was received from the Church of Ireland.

3731. I suppose you have not read the evidence of Father Loughrey last Thursday?—I have not. I met him in Ireland, and a very pleasant and delightful gentleman he was.

3732. Your attention has not been called to his evidence?—If it relates to the question of the house I have heard all about that. That was a very peculiar case with which I think he and everybody must think the company had nothing to do. The former Roman Catholic priest of Dungiven died.

3733. We have had both sides of the statement on that point; we have had Dr. Todd's evidence?—You have had no one witness from the Skinners' Company.

3734. We have had Dr. Todd's evidence. However fair it might be to the Roman Catholics, assuming Dr. Todd's statement to be strictly accurate, that you gave this large grant to the Protestants, and also that you put the Protestant clergyman's property into settlement in trust, why did you sell the Catholic property to a private owner, and why did you make over the Protestant property?—If you will allow me to answer that by traversing the fact we did not sell the Catholic property away from the Catholic Church. It was the private property of a former priest who was our tenant, but it had nothing to do with the Church. He might have sold it at any moment he pleased. He was simply our tenant, and he had an interest in the land.

3735. Why did you, in the case of the Protestants, recognise it to be Church property?—He was not our tenant there. It had formerly belonged to the Church body; we had a sum of money which was given to us in respect of Church property, the advowsons, and this property had to be acquired, and we gave the subscriptions towards purchasing.

3736. Why did you give the Protestants this large sum of money, which has been stated at 350 *l.*, and a donation of 40 *l.* a year, and then cut off the Catholic grant which had hitherto been paid?—We never cut off the Catholic grant.

3737. Here is his statement: "Has that grant of 25 *l.* been stopped?—(*A.*) It has been notified as stopped"; and he had a letter from you notifying that the money would not be continued?—That arises in consequence of the death of the former tenant, and the sale of the property. That is quite apart from the question of the purchase of the glebe for the Rector of Dungiven, which was done in the year 1874 or 1875.

3738. How would you satisfy a jury that it was equitable to cut off entirely a Catholic grant of 25 *l.* a year, and that you are enabled to continue to the Protestants a grant of 350 *l.*, and to continue a donation of 45 *l.* How do you satisfy a jury on the point that that is fair?—I began by saying that I do not think we were bound to do either one or the other, and I do not think, even as a matter of generosity on the part of the company, that any one has a right to complain unless we are actually trustees under a moral obligation. If we are trustees, it seems to me a very extraordinary thing that anybody who has paid a large sum of money for the purpose of profit for himself, but that, of course, is a matter which will be argued before you by counsel. If we are trustees, not only will it apply to that property, but to the rest of our property.

3739. Do you not think it exposes you to depreciation if your Protestants are exceptionally treated

Mr. T. M. Healy—continued.

treated, and the Catholics are not?—I must say we have treated Catholics with great generosity. The whole of that money might have been very fairly held for the Church of Ireland alone. It does seem to me stretching a great point in saying that we hold this available for spiritual requirements, and we will allow the Roman Catholics, who really had no share in it, and the Presbyterians, who had some in finding it, to get the benefit of it.

5740. Would you point out the benefit which has been occasioned to Dungiven. The Catholic grant was continued for one year, that is to say, 25 *l.* a year was given to the Catholics. The priest leased his house and land. The Protestants got a continued grant of 40 *l.* a year, and the rector got 500 *l.*, and the rector's house and property is put in settlement?—You are mixing, or the witness is mixing up things which had no connection with one another, and were very distant in date.

5741. Will you put in your way the manner in which the three religions have been treated?—I will. In 1873 or 1874 a large sum was received for advowson.

5742. Would you please come to the date when you sold your property, and then tell us what you did give each of the three denominations when that property was sold?—If you will not allow me to begin at the beginning I cannot.

5743. You got a large sum in hand from the tenants for your property. Will you start from that date with that sum of money in your hand, how did you treat the three religions?—The only thing is that the 500 *l.* you allude to in putting it in trust was done out of the advowson money; it must be mixed up with it. I will try and leave it out of consideration.

5744. My point is that you should start from the date when you got the cash from the Government; then give your treatment of the three religious bodies?—It was got, not from the Government, but from the Church Temporalities Commissioners, and that was received in the year 1873 or 1874.

Chairman.

5745. I do not see what you gain by going back in this way, and the honourable Member's question is a very plain and definite one, as no one is better able to appreciate than yourself?—I will not go back to it if you do not wish it, but when you talked of the sum received from the Government I thought you meant the advowson.

Sir W. T. Marriott.

5746. The honourable Member meant on the purchase?—I thought you were speaking of the advowson. You mean when we received the money for the sale of the estate. Then we proceeded to deal with the cases which came before us, each on their own merits, and it so happened that a vacancy occurred in the Roman Catholic Church before one occurred in the Church of Ireland, and we dealt with that upon its merits.

Chairman.

5747. A vacancy from the termination of the lease?—From the demise of the former priest. It so happened that Father Tracey died about a year ago, and though I had not remembered the fact, I have no doubt that is a question to be dealt with as to the future trust, and we then thought, which is a question which I need not go back on as I have gone into it very fully before, that having ceased to be landlords the obligation should fall upon the new landlords. Rightly or wrongly that was the determination we came to. There has been no change in the demise, no change in the incumbency of the Church of Ireland there, and the question has not arisen. Individually, as long as the present man lives we should not think of making a change.

5748. That is your answer?—As far as I understand your question that is my answer.

5749. Will you reduce to cash the difference in treatment of the three different bodies. How much in money numbered are the Protestants now getting in Dungiven, how much in money numbered are the Presbyterians getting, and how much in money numbered are the Catholics getting?—The Church of Ireland get the sum I have mentioned.

5750. Can you give us the figure?—I think 40 *l.* a year. I think there are two Presbyterian ministers, but the clerk will be able to tell you.

5751. The Catholics get nothing?—I am not sure whether there is more than one Catholic who ever received anything.

5752. Then as to land, the difference I take it is this, that the rector, in addition to getting his 500 *l.* has had his glebe and land continued?—That is the 500 *l.* for the glebe and land, not in addition to it.

5753. So it is stated?—Then I am afraid it is wrongly stated. We purchased the glebe and the vicarage for the sum of 500 *l.*

5754. What Father Loughrey says at Question 4507 is this: "When the sale took place what was done with regard to the parish priest and with regard to the rectory?—(*A.*) The late rector received, as we are informed, 500 *l.* as a donation or present from the company, and the place was then handed over free to the Church body for the benefit of the incumbent from time to time in years to come"?—That is the 500 *l.*

5755. You state, as I understand, that the 500 *l.* bought it?—Quite so.

5756. Who got the 500 *l.*?—It was paid to the Church body.

5757. Does it not come to the same thing. The Church body then gets the 500 *l.*, and the rector gets the land?—That was the value of the land.

5758. Is it candid therefore to say you did not give the Protestant Church in that district 500 *l.* and their land?—No, I thought it would be most wrong to say we gave 500 *l.* and the land. We gave 500 *l.* for the land.

5759. Who got the 500 *l.*?—It was the then owners of the property who were the Church body. It might have been sold by them in the market to anybody, and then there would have been no land or houses. I am wrong; in that case it was a private owner. I think this was the

Chairman—continued.

the only case in which it was not the Church body; it was his own private property.

5760. Where was the 500 *l.*?—In Canon Ross's pocket.

Mr. T. M. Healy.

5761. Who was Canon Ross?—The former vicar of Dungiven.

5762. Therefore the statement of the reverend Catholic gentleman was perfectly correct that the late rector got his 500 *l.*, and having pocketed his 500 *l.*, then you made over the land free to the Church body for the benefit of the incumbency?—If you will allow me to say his statement is that the late rector received 500 *l.* as a donation. That was not so; it was not a donation to him. He would have sold it to somebody else; he was the private owner of that house; he provided himself with a house in Dungiven, and when he retired, instead of selling it to somebody else, we bought it from him for 500 *l.*

5763. Why did you not do the same with the Catholics. Why when you paid the Catholic property did you not pay the last priest for his house, and then make over his land in trust for his religion?—No application was ever made to us to do that. Would you allow me to say we gave him the land for his church.

5764. He paid you for it?—No, indeed, he did not. We actually gave it at, I think, a nominal rent of 1 *s.*, to secure that it should always be kept for Roman Catholic purposes.

5765. Have the Roman Catholics got that now?—Yes.

5766. You state that?—I state it confidently, they have got that land. I think it was three acres on which their new Roman Catholic church is built.

5767. That was, of course, in years gone by?—It was at the same time that we gave the 500 *l.*

5768. I am dealing with the question of the sale, and I will not allow that to be gone behind, if you will excuse my saying so, to the old donation?—This 500 *l.* is an old donation long before the sale of the estate. If I am to go back to the 500 *l.* for the purchase of the rectory in Dungiven, I think in justice and equity I am entitled to go back to the 500 *l.* for the building of the Roman Catholic church, and I venture to say that if we had known, or any application had been made to us that they wanted a vicarage for the Roman Catholic church in Dungiven, it would have been, I am sure, dealt with fairly. I tell you now that I am convinced that the company would do what is right and proper. We have got some money remaining of the advowson money.

5769. You state that now?—I state that now. I am not the master of the company now, but I will pledge myself to move at the court.

5770. Are you aware of this extraordinary statement, that Father Loughrey applied to you for the vacant manor house, he being compelled to live in a little two-roomed lodging in Dungiven. At Question 4520 he says he lives in lodgings, in a single sitting room and a small bedroom; it is only a small place; there is not much

Mr. T. M. Healy—continued.

choice in the town. (Q.) You applied to the agent, and what did he say?—(A.) The agent told me it could not be rented, but it would be sold, and he advised me to write to the Skinners' estate office, here in London, to ask to have it sold to me; and then I should make the proposal; and I asked them to grant it to me on the most reasonable terms they could, seeing the position in which I was placed. I did not get an answer to that application for some time, and then I was informed, and I suppose justly, that they could not deal, due my writing in some parts of my letter, and the place in the meantime was sold to Mr. Ogilby, a descendant of the late lessee"?—It was agreed to be sold, or offered to be sold, long before any application of that kind was received.

5771. In other words, as I understand, that the Catholic priest had this place for himself as a private house, and you knowing that his successor could get no other place in the town, you made a private bargain behind his back with regard to the manor house?—Not at all. That is not at all, if you will allow me to say so, a correct representation of the fact. The fact was that we knew nothing whatever about any demand on the part of the Roman Catholic body for the acquisition of this land apart from the former priest. The former priest was owner of the property; he signed an agreement in the usual form, as all tenants did. He was merely a tenant of the house. He signed no application for the sale to him, and we agreed to sell to him. He had purchased, or he had taken over the tenant-right from the former priest, and it had been usually done in that way as I understand it; he agreed for it, and in the meantime he died and left this property to his sister. The usual thing, as I understand, would have been for the sister to have sold it to the incoming priest, but she apparently claims that her brother was the owner, as in fact he was, and she does not see her way to sell it to the new priest.

5772. You maintain as a lawyer that you have treated the three denominations on terms of perfect fairness and equality?—Subject to the observation I made as to the advowson money being preferentially given to the Church of Ireland, I do. We have certainly desired to do that. We have given them more than they asked for. The Catholics, I think, were very much surprised.

5773. That would be my own impression?—When we first went over in deputation we had a dinner to which we invited the clergy of all denominations, and in the company there was Father Mooney, whom I remember as a delightful old gentleman, then priest of Dungiven, who sat on my right, and the rector of Dungiven on my left. They all met on the most friendly terms. I do not imagine they expected we could give them any donation, but when we got home we found the feeling of the court, or our own feeling, was to meet them all on the same terms, giving to each according to the needs of each.

5774. The same terms are 40 *l.* a year to one man and 25 *l.* to another?—Because of the previous disendowment of the Church. I will not

Mr. T. M. Healy—continued.

go back on the answers I have already given. We may be right or wrong, but undoubtedly we did consider it was the money of the Church of Ireland, and that we should first allow for that.

5775. What was the money of the Church of Ireland?—The advowson money. I do not want to go back upon it. I do not think the honourable Member was in the room when I gave the answer.

5776. I quite appreciate the point. I understand your point is that this 40 *l.* a year to the present rector will be stopped the day he dies?—Not not I cannot possibly say what they will do.

5777. The fact that you have stopped the Catholic money would be no precedent for stopping the Protestant?—I think it would be a precedent. What I confess I should very much like to see done would be to go back again to the old system if they attach importance to it; but I confess I think probably no one could have thought otherwise than that they would all have recognised that when you ceased to be landlords you ceased to be bound to give the money.

5778. Why did you not stop all the grants?—Because they did not fall in; they did not die.

5779. Does that affect the question when you ceased to be landlord?—Do you not think people might very fairly say, We will not disturb things; a man has been living upon this, and he shall have it as long as he lives, and then after that we shall make fresh arrangements. We have a great many pensioners, and certainly these pensioners I do not think any private landlord would ever think of stopping the pensions of; but as long as they live I am sure we do not.

5780. Let us try the matter on that basis; are we to understand from you that the moment the present incumbents die the whole of this 40 *l.* and 25 *l.* a piece for two Presbyterians will also be stopped?—No, you will not understand that from me. If I have any influence they will not be stopped.

5781. You have stopped them. Had you any influence when the Catholic income was stopped?—No; I had long ceased to be master.

5782. When were you master?—I was master in 1873 and 1874.

5783. Are you still master?—No; I was master when we determined to give these grants. That is, I believe, the reason why I am here today.

5784. You are not at present master?—I am on the court. All I can say is, I should like levelling up better than levelling down. I would rather see all these donations continued, if it was not recognised that we were obliged to do it. The court would feel themselves that it was only right and proper to continue them if there is a strong feeling about it.

5785. Take me as expressing no opinion upon it; I only want to understand it?—I had taken you as expressing a strong feeling.

5786. I am in favour of stopping all the grants, and devoting this money to education?—I am bound to say I should like to see the grants continued, but I am also bound to say there is another way in which it can be done.

5787. If there was a general feeling amongst the people that the better way would be to devote this money to education, would the companies, or your company, do it?—I am sure they would feel that was a better way in some respects. We have done a great deal for education, and it is one of our particular hobbies. I should like very much to see education advanced.

Mr. Sexton.

5788. Can you say generally what proportion of the income was spent?—I should say half.

5789. You were master in 1874?—Yes.

5790. I suppose you remember the proceedings of the court distinctly?—I will not venture to say I remember everything the court did in 1874, but I remember a great deal.

5791. You have been a member of the court ever since?—I have been a member of the court ever since.

5792. Have you attended generally?—Yes, except when my practice before Committees of Parliament here have kept me away.

5793. What is the practice of your court. Do you vote upon each application for a grant?—Yes, we vote upon each application.

5794. Is it necessary for each person in receipt of a grant from you to apply from year to year?—No, I do not think so. There are a good many of these grants that are continued from year to year. All these church grants, I think, are taken as a matter of course, and they are annual grants.

5795. There are two classes of grants; you make one from year to year of your own motion, and others also from year to year, or casually, on application?—Yes.

5796. Upon what principle, if upon any principle, did you proceed in voting these grants?—We took the requirements of every Church of Ireland clergyman, of every Presbyterian minister, and of every Roman Catholic priest into account, what their income was from other sources as far as we were able to ascertain whether they had pew rent, and what necessity there was for giving in each particular case, and we found the greatest necessity at that time was for the Church of Ireland, because of their being disendowed.

5797. I gather then you acted first on this principle, that as between the different communions you endeavoured to be equitable?—We tried to be equitable, I am sure. Equitable does not mean equal; we did not begin by saying, here is 600 *l.* to be divided between them in equal shares. We took the share of each according to its merits.

5798. Taking the very different circumstances into account?—Yes.

5799. Was there any other principle on which you acted in giving or refusing grants?—None whatever among the clergy.

5800. Without regard to the particular denominations, for instance, did you ever consider any relation between their total income and the total of the grant you made?—Generally speaking,

Mr. *Sexton*—continued.

speaking, I think we did. I do not mean to say we gave a percentage.

5801. You said to yourselves "We receive so much and we will give so much"?—No, I do not think I can quite say that; but I think every individual member, in voting, must have taken that into account. If the estates had yielded much less we should have given less in amount.

5802. There was some kind of general relation preserved between the income and the outlay?—Exactly.

5803. Was there ever any deliberate judgment come to as to what that relation ought to be?—No, I do not think so.

5804. How was it arrived at?—In the way I mentioned, by taking out the particular case in all its circumstances. They were all scheduled and carefully gone into. The deputation recommended certain sums, and I think without exception they were adopted by the court. We held a great many meetings. I can say, after coming back from Ireland in trying to do justice, and communicating with all the priests and clergy of every denomination, as far as I can recollect, and learning facts from the agent and otherwise.

5805. In fact, you did not think you had come to the maximum of your grants until you had met the wants of the neighbourhood?—Yes. I may say we went beyond what were the wants, because we found the priests have small wants, and they were apparently very comfortable, as comfortable as a priest requires to be with his simple habits, and they did not apply to us for anything, did not say it was necessary, and we thought giving them something would be a sign of a friendly character, and that we recognised that the Roman Catholics were to us what the Church of Ireland were, I really think we treated the tenantry as tenantry and not as people of any denomination.

5806. Then do I correctly gather that the maximum of these grants was not fixed by any property, but was only limited by your sense of the fair interests of the neighbourhood?—That is so.

5807. Do you represent that as the point of view from which a person considering himself a private owner would calculate his public benefactions?—The consciences of people differ so much that I could not say anything about owners generally. I know some people give a tenth part of their income, and consider that is the proper cost of what they ought to give out of their income for charitable purposes of all kinds, but I think there are very few landlords who give to clergy of all denominations; they generally take those of their own denomination.

5808. What fraction of your income did you give?—I do not say how much we gave, I can not exactly tell you that, but I think that has been given, or Mr. Draper, the clerk, will give you the exact proportion. I think we must have spent more than 3,000 *l.* a year, probably about 3,500 *l.*; I should think we must have spent in one way and another, what with the management, the guarantee for the railway company, and donations.

Chairman.

5809. We are going to have all that afterwards?—Yes.

Mr. *Sexton.*

5810. Did you regard yourselves as private owners or as persons discharging a moral obligation or exercising a trust?—Certainly, in one sense as private owners; that is to say, we considered that we are a corporation, that we had paid for this property just as much as many of the private owners who had acquired properties under the same conditions with the same expenditure at the same time, only they got recompense for it in many cases for giving help to the Crown, and populating a part of Ireland which was then unpeopled. We looked upon ourselves as private owners in that respect, but inasmuch as we were a corporation or a company, and did not have to live upon the income, we considered that we ought to give considerably more than a private owner would do.

5811. In fact that you should only reserve for the Irish themselves so much as you did not consider to be needed by yourselves?—Yes, I think that was so, simply out of the moral obligations which attach to all owners of property, not out of any obligation to do so.

Colonel *Laurie.*

5812. I think you said Dr. Todd acted for you in the sale?—Yes.

5813. Does he act in your case for tenants as purchasers?—Yes, he acted as I understand for both landlord and tenant.

5814. He acted for the purchasers as well as for yourselves?—He acted for the purchasers. He was very friendly with the tenants generally, and had acted constantly for the tenants previously, and we thought, he telling us the tenants wanted to buy, it would be the most friendly way of doing it instead of having two people.

5815. That is not my point; but did he make any objection, acting for the purchaser, to your title?—None whatever.

5816. He made no complaint that it was tainted with a trust at all?—No.

5817. He simply as acting for the purchasers accepted your title?—Yes.

Sir W. T. Marriott.

5818. You are the Clerk of the Skinners' Company, and have been since February 1878?—Yes.

5819. You have prepared a statement of accounts showing the income of the estate belonging to the company, for the 10 years from the 30th April 1877 to the 30th April 1886 inclusive, is not that so?—I think so.

5820. Will you kindly put it in?—They are separate sheets. That is a statement of receipts (*handing in a Paper*).

5821. And you have a statement showing the 10 years' expenditure under five heads?—Yes (*handing in the same*).

5822. Then you have one showing a detailed account of the money received by the company for the advowsons under the Irish Church Disestablishment Act?—Yes, that is the statement with regard to which Mr. Saunders spoke.

5823. The gross income of the company's estate in 1873 was, I think, 11,760 *l.*?—Yes.

5824. In 1877, 13,500 *l.*; is that so?—In round figures it was.

5825. Including the rent of the deanery house, which was 300 *l.*, not included in Mr Ogilby's rental?—Yes.

5826. In 1886, with the Land Act, it was 11,343 *l.*?—Yes.

5827. Were these judicial rents?—With few exceptions.

5828. If necessary, you can give the dates and rentals of all leases since 1811, cannot you?—If desired.

5829. You can produce extracts from the Company's records and minutes, and all that, if they are wanted?—Yes.

5830. Can you state the amount paid to the Skinners' Company for the Land Commission, and show how part of it was absorbed by the purchase from the Stationers' and Bakers' Companies in 1876–77?—I can give them very shortly.

5831. The amount on the Land Commission for cases completed was 134,827 *l.*?—Yes.

5832. From that you deduct one-fifth, being the guarantee deposited?—That is right.

5833. That means 27,131 *l.* That leaves 107,896 *l.*; deducting, for various charges, 17,706 *l.*, that leaves 89,990 *l.* The share paid to the Girdlers' Company was 10,271 *l.*, leaving 79,719 *l.*; amount paid in buying out the Stationers and Bakers in 1876, 76,301 *l.*?—Yes.

5834. Leaving 3,418 *l.*; is that correct?—Yes.

5835. What does that show?—That statement is prepared up to date to show what has been received under Lord Ashbourne's Act for sales completed, and the last line that you have read about buying out the Bakers and Stationers, is by way of showing that the amount of the cash received from these sales by the Skinners' Company might fairly be considered as appropriated towards reimbursing the Skinners' Company for the amount they have paid to the two associated companies, the Bakers and Stationers, in 1876. It is not a statement of account.

Sir W. T. Marriott—continued.

5836. You have got a statement, I think, showing the number and value of the holdings unsold?—Yes, I have. I have not prepared that in such a way as to hand it in. I am prepared to be examined about it if desired.

5837. You can show it if you are cross-examined?—Yes; I have no objection to put it in. The number of holdings on the estate before sale was about 1,257. The number at present unsold is 378. The rental of the unsold part is 3,247 *l.* Up to the date of making up the account the estimated value, if we sell as we have sold to others, is 42,748 *l.*

5838. Has the company come to any decision with regard to selling the residue or not?—They have simply given notice to the tenants that the offer to sell would be considered as withdrawn as from the 1st of April last for a portion of the estate, and I think it was the 1st May for certain other portions.

5839. Why was it withdrawn?—Because there was a slowness on the part of the tenants who had not bought in coming in, and it was thought that the machinery, so to say, for selling had better be stopped; and that the company, for a time, at any rate, had better revert to their original position.

Chairman.

5840. I do not quite see what the slowness of the tenants in coming in had to do with it?—Perhaps I ought to have said, their having ceased altogether to offer. There had not been any offers to buy for some months before. I might add that there was a large number of agreements for sale still before the Land Commission, not completed.

Mr. *T. M. Healy.*

5841. You mean rejected?—No, pardon me.

Mr. Sexton.

5842. Do you mean offers to sell had been before the tenants for a considerable time, and had not led to any action with regard to them?—As regards those that were unsold, but not as regards those that were pending.

Chairman.

5843. What was the occasion of the delay in a pending application?—I do not think I can give you a simple answer.

5844. Give a compound answer?—The case varies. In some cases the division with regard to mountain holdings in common had not been settled, and could not be divided to the satisfaction of the Land Commission.

Sir *W. T. Marriott.*

5845. With regard to the different grants, and continuing them or discontinuing them, has the company come to any resolution about them?—Not generally.

5846. What has been their rule up to now?—You have heard what has been done in two cases of Dungbeady and Lower Cumber.

5847. These

Sir W. T. Marriott—continued.

5847. Those are the only two that have been decided upon?—That is all; but there has been an intimation given to the Catholic Church authorities on the deaths of two Catholic priests, Father Tracey, of Dungiven, and another one, that the company, having sold the estate, might not continue the grants.

5848. With regard to the receipts, are the balances that are annually paid from the company's general corporate fund specially allocated?—No.

5849. They form part of the general fund, but the company do, I think, maintain certain exhibitions in Dublin, do they not?—There are two scholarships for girls at the Alexandra College.

5850. What amount are they?—One 37 l. a year, and the other 31 l.

5851. Have they given to other institutions for educating girls?—Yes; to the Londonderry Ladies Collegiate School, and two others.

5852. Are they all Protestant?—No; the grant was sent to Miss M'Killip, head of the Collegiate School, to be divided amongst three schools. It was left to some advisers of hers as to the way in which it should be appropriated; but there was no denominational preference.

5853. Was any restriction put by the Skinners' Company with regard to denomination?—Certainly not; my impression is that it was called an undenominational gift.

5854. There is something about the Inishowen fishery disaster, what is that?—That has been mentioned in connection with Father Loughrey, when he came over the other day. It reminded me personally that my first knowledge of Father Loughrey was when he applied a few months ago to the company for a grant on the occasion of what was called the Inishowen fishery disaster. There was a serious wreck, and many lives were lost, and the company gave a grant in respect of that.

Chairman.

5855. When was that?—It was the beginning of this year or the end of last.

Sir W. T. Marriott.

5856. What grant did they make?—It was 10 l.

5857. Something has been said about the turbary question on the estate. Have you anything to state about that?—I am prepared to state facts with regard to that if the Committee desire it, and if they do not think that Dr. Todd has satisfied the Committee about it. It is a very important question indeed.

Chairman.

5858. You wash your hands of the turbary?—Yes.

5859. They set up a board of trustees who charge 1 s. to the tenants?—Yes.

5860. Where the charge had previously been 6 d. That was a charge paid to the trustees, and the company had nothing to do with it?—The company do not get the shillings.

Sir W. T. Marriott.

5861. You have no power over it?—No.

5862. About the house occupied by the late parish priest of Dungiven, you recollect what was said about that, and about its now being claimed by his sister. What have you to say about that. That is put forward by Father Loughrey as a grievance?—I can understand it is a grievance amongst the Catholics, but it certainly is not against the company, or ought not to be.

5863. What did the company do?—The house of the priest, for which he paid a rent, was on the list of those given to Dr. Todd, with which list he took offers from the tenants to buy, and amongst those tenants who offered an application was made by Father Tracey, or his representative; I say his representative because I know he was ill.

5864. And they handed it over to her, did they?—Yes. I have brought a copy of the purchase deed in that case. That is a copy of the actual conveyance to Father Tracey. (*The same was handed in.*) Father Tracey's family, as I understand, have not given it up to the Church, but have kept it to themselves.

5865. I understand they have not been able to make an amicable arrangement with Father Tracey's successor?—That is so.

5866. Did you treat Father Tracey in the same way as you treated other clergymen?—Yes; as you heard, the Protestant clergyman is not a paying tenant. I think that was explained by Mr. Saunders.

5867. There is a withdrawal of the grant from Mr. Johnson of Lower Cumber: what have you to say about that?—That was withdrawn when Mr. Johnson became minister there, and the withdrawal was made at that particular date, because there was a change of ministers.

5868. You look upon the money as personal to the minister who was in when you sold?—Different views are to be formed about that. I think the company have looked upon these very much as personal grants.

5869. Also, there is something with regard to the Skinners' Company giving 500 l. to Lower Cumber Church; have you to correct anything with regard to that?—No; 500 l. was given.

5870. You correct the table on Paper 4, page 46, that the Skinners' Company gave 500 l.?—It is not with regard to the amount. The paper handed in by Mr. Dickie is a list of Presbyterian congregations in county Derry; in that there is a misprint. There is a statement of 500 l. being given by the Grocers' Company; I do not know whether the Grocers' Company have given 500 l., but there is not put down 500 l. given by the Skinners' Company, which they certainly did give. There is one other matter there; it is stated on page 3 of that paper, that the number of families in Lower Cumber parish attending the Presbyterian congregation is 812. If desired, I can give the number of families belonging to the Skinners' Estate, but it is not 812.

Chairman.

5871. You are correcting Mr. Dickie's statement?—It is correct on the face of it, but it leads to a wrong inference.

Sir W. T. Marriott.

5672. Father Loughrey stated that properties were treated unequally, especially as to the reservation of minerals; is that correct?—I have no knowledge of it; I have had no opportunity of seeing Father Loughrey's evidence yet.

Mr. T. M. Healy.

5673. You heard it?—I did not hear what he said about that.

Sir W. T. Marriott.

5674. With regard to the Roman Catholics, did you give land at Dungiven for a chapel for them?—Yes.

5675. And also stone from the quarry to build their church?—Yes.

5676. Are there any other grants you would like to mention; have you anything to say, in conclusion, about grants you have given?—No, I have nothing to say about grants.

Mr. Sexton.] I decline to examine the witness on such an account.

Mr. T. M. Healy.] I also decline to examine the witness on such an account.

Mr. Clancy.] I decline to examine the witness.

Mr. John Ellis.

5677. I notice that the payments are made up to a particular date, and the expenditure to a different date; I think that is a most inconvenient form of account, and surely the company can manage better than that; the receipts are made up to November, and the payments are made up to April; it is utterly impossible to examine on such an account?—May I say that the return was prepared before Mr. Tower was examined, and I saw that your request made to him was practically answered in my return, so that I have not altered it since that was made. With regard to the dates of the receipts and expenditure you will find that they really agree. In the first column is the rental or amount receivable for the year ending 1st November 1876; and then the actual receipts and expenditure for the year ending 30th April 1877, and also subsequent years.

Mr. Lea.

5678. Is the part of the estate that you have left the poorest part?—Yes, I think it is.

5679. How many of your tenants had judicial rents fixed, do you know?—Do you mean in court, or out of court?

5680. I mean by the court?—I have tried to ascertain within the last day or two, and as far as I can make out there were only about 100 in court; but I state that subject to closer examination.

Chairman.

5681. Surely you know when judicial rents were fixed upon your property?—The rest were voluntary.

5682. The rest from what?—The remainder, not reckoning the 100, were settled voluntarily.

5683. What was the number?—They were all judicial rents, with very few exceptions indeed.

Mr. Lea.

5684. How many were settled in court, and how many were settled out of court?—I cannot give you the exact figures, but the number of holdings on the estate is something like 1,200, and to my knowledge the rents of about 100 were fixed in the land court. Those rents which were not altered include town holdings, where the tenants hold townparks as well. In some cases there would be duplicates; I will present those figures exactly if it is desired, but I had not anticipated that question.

5685. I want to know how many were settled out of court?—800 or 900 at least.

5686. Is the part of the estate left comprised mostly of those who settled out of court?—Yes, certainly.

5687. Their rents I suppose are rather higher in proportion than those who went into court?—Yes, that is so in proportion to the original rent from which they were reduced; you may take it that the reductions in the Land Court were at a greater rate than those settled out of court. The company did not press for judicial agreements at all, but feeling that the Land Court could be resorted to if the tenant was not willing to come in and settle, they encouraged him to go to the Land Court if he desired.

5688. Were these settled by agreement, and the agreement sanctioned by the Land Court?—Yes, as you know under the Act they are registered in the Land Court.

5689. These are rather higher than those that went into the court and fought out their case?—Yes, I think they were; I can give you an average if you like.

5690. If you have it, I should like to take it?—The reduction was between 20 and 21 per cent. in the land court; the average over the whole estate was less.

5691. What number of years' purchase was given?—In sales going on now.

5692. What number of years' purchase was first paid by the tenant?—I am afraid I do not understand your question.

5693. They are all about 18 years' purchase?—Yes.

5694. All the tenants?—Subject to the qualification which has been given this morning, that there was a year-and-a-half free as a matter of course. A few were sold at a little less.

5695. Did they all buy at the same number of years' purchase?—Subject to a few exceptions.

5696. Those tenants that went into court bought at the same rate as those tenants who did not go into court, but had agreements sanctioned by the court?—Yes, it was 18 times the judicial rent, whether that judicial rent was fixed in court or arrived at out of court.

5697. Is that the reason why this part of the estate is not sold, because the tenants had their agreements fixed out of court?—No, certainly not.

5698. I see one item here is cleansing streets; do you pay for the cleansing of the streets of Dungiven?—Yes, it is a small matter. I have included everything, and I have given every item of account.

5699. Is such an item as that customary for private landlords to pay?—I cannot tell you. I have no knowledge of any other landlord in Ireland. It is a matter of a few pounds.

Chairman.

5700. What was the average per annum of your

Chairman—continued.

your gross receipts during the period covered by this table?—Roughly speaking, the net amount is about 11,000 *l.* a year. Amongst my papers I have one which will give it you. It is 11,057 *l.*

5901. Gross rent received?—Yes.

5902. Have you got the average of your first head, tithe rent, rates and taxes, and insurance?—£. 1,164.

5903. Under the second head of repairs, new works, plantings, roads, loans for improvements and embankments; what you may call permanent improvements?—£. 840.

5904. Then for annual cost of management?—£. 2,310.

5905. What is the average of your contribution to schools, subscriptions, donations, and what I may call public objects?—£. 883.

5906. Railways: that is of course not an annual outlay?—No, because the charge had not begun at the beginning of the 10 years. It is only 408 *l.* at the beginning of the 10 years, but now it is at the rate of 1,250 *l.*

5907. That is a reproductive outlay?—I do not think it is.

5908. It is meant to be reproductive?—Reproductive to whom?

5909. To you?—No.

5910. You have got 1,164 *l.* for the first item, 840 *l.* for the second, 2,310 *l.* for cost of management, and only 883 *l.* for public objects, and your railway expenses are put in too. What was the balance which you handed over to your general account?—£. 5,520, for the two associated companies.

5911. That is to say, you received from this estate 11,057 *l.*, you took 5,520 *l.* to London, and you expended 2,310 *l.* in cost of management. How much of this last item was in London, and much in Ireland?—600 *l.* in London; the remainder in Ireland.

5912. That is to be expended on public objects in Ireland, schools, churches, and subscriptions, 883 *l.* only out of 11,057 *l.*?—That is so.

5913. And though you only gave 883 *l.* for public objects in Ireland, you took over 5,520 *l.* to England for English objects?—General objects of the United Kingdom; it was not reserved to England.

5914. But not to Ireland?—I told the honourable member sometime ago, if you recollect, that amongst the gifts there were certain scholarships in Dublin.

5915. Surely those are included in the 883 *l.*?—Certainly not, I am excluding all that.

5916. What is the good of this account?—I think I can explain. The gift from the Skinners' Company from their general fund to that scholarship in Ireland would be given out of their own corporate funds, and would be a separate matter from the Pellipar Estate account, with regard to which the Girdlers' Company were associated.

5917. Would it be given out of this 5,520 *l.*?—No, not earmarked in that way, but out of the general fund; it is not given out of the 5,520 *l.*

5918. We have to make a deduction from the 5,520 *l.* of sums contributed to exhibitions in Dublin?—If you like.

5919. What I want to get at is a very plain figure; we have found no difficulty in getting at it in the case of the Fishmongers', I cannot see why there should be the least difficulty here; we want to find out the amount you spent for public objects in Ireland as a total, and the amount that was carried to other purposes as distinct from Irish purposes?—I gave that as 5,520 *l.*, and I say that 883 *l.* given to donations in Ireland does not include the Alexandra Scholarship which was mentioned.

5920. Where then in this account is the Alexandra Scholarship?—Not in that account at all; I was not asked for it.

5921. Putting as high as you please the deduction to be made on account of this Alexandra Scholarship, what would you put it at?—I prefer not to deduct it at all.

Mr. John Ellis.

5922. I do submit strongly, as a member of this Committee, that we are entitled to have a business-like statement of the income and expenditure of this company, so far as their Irish estate is concerned, and this is not a business like account when the income ends at a certain date, and the expenditure ends at another date. The discrepancy of date is that one is in November and the other is in April?—I think it is a misunderstanding from the column you are reading from. We have given you the rental up to the 1st November 1885, and we have given you the receipts for that rental for 10 years ending April 1890, that is to say, what accrued due to the 1st November 1885 is included in the receipts we make up to the end of April.

5923. Do you tell me that the receipts and expenditure occur in respect of the same 12 months?—I do.

5924. I understand that the money does come in in the same 12 months?—Yes.

Chairman.

5925. I only want to get clear the item of railway expenditure which you say justly is expended in Ireland; what is the average over this period?—At the commencement, 408 *l.*

Sir W. T. Marriott.

5926. You are paying 1,250 *l.*?—We are paying 1,250 *l.*, but we only began to pay 1,250 *l.* for the last two years of this period of ten.

Chairman.

5927. We cannot go into that. We must confine ourselves for the purpose of any point to the same period. I will go over the figures once more, and then I will leave it. You received 11,057 *l.*; you expended upon permanent improvements, taking an average of this period, 840 *l.* per annum, and 1,164 *l.* you expended in rates, taxes, insurance, and tithes?—Tithe rent-charge is the first.

5928. Cost of management, 2,310 *l.*, 883 *l.* for public objects, 408 *l.* for railways, and 5,520 *l.* plus 600 *l.* for English cost of management, are spent in England; that is to say, supposing it were to be adjudged that there was a trust imposed upon your Irish estates, you would have given 883 *l.* only for the objects of that trust, and you would be giving 5,520 *l.*, six times as much for English objects as against Irish?—Yes, except that I would prefer to state it in the United Kingdom, that is all.

Chairman—continued.

5070. That is to say, out of a rental from Ireland of 11,076 *l.* the objects of the possession of the estate are satisfied, in the opinion of your company, by a payment of 503 *l.*?—I may add that you stated personally the other day that any receipts from any other source than rents should be stated separately, and I have stated it. It is a small amount, [illegible] *l.* a year.

Chairman.] It might be convenient if, after we have heard the Drapers and the Irish Society, we passed on to hear the arguments of counsel, it being of course understood that if any company afterwards thinks it has something to say in reply to anything that has been said, we should be perfectly ready to hear it. It is rather the feeling of the Committee that as next Friday is to be given up to the Irish Society, the Drapers, the Fishmongers, the Grocers, and the Salters, to rebut the case made against them, after that time we might, if you are ready, begin to hear the arguments of counsel.

Dr. *Freshfield.*] On Monday next?

Chairman.] Yes.

Dr. *Freshfield.*] Supposing within those two days you are not able to hear all?

Chairman.] Of course there are the witnesses from Ireland, and we must not detain them beyond Monday. In that case we should not begin to hear counsel until Thursday.

Dr. *Freshfield.*] I do not quite mean that. You named several companies, for instance, the Skinners' Company is now finished; you have got the Drapers' Company and the Irish Society, and I think, if I might be permitted to say so, judging by past experience of the rate of progress, you would not do more than get through those two on Thursday and Friday.

Chairman.] I think, certainly not.

Dr. *Freshfield.*] You would, then, go on with the arguments of counsel on Monday.

Chairman.] That is what I suggest; I wish the companies, whom we have not yet heard, to feel that we have not the least desire to block out any evidence which they might wish to give, and which we might think relevant to our inquiry. It may be, however, that after we have heard counsel we may decide not to hear any more.

Dr. *Freshfield.*] If there is any particular company you would wish to hear, you would perhaps notify it. If we are all ready to go on with the argument of counsel, you would say then any you wanted to hear So-and-so. They are all ready to come if there is any particular person you want.

Colonel *Lawrie.*] The Salters ought to come.

Chairman.] I understand the Drapers are to begin on Thursday. It may be a fond hope, but we hoped that the Drapers will be done with on Thursday.

Dr. *Freshfield.*] The Drapers have been here today.

Sir W. T. Marriott.] Do their witnesses come from Ireland?

Dr. *Freshfield.*] Yes.

Chairman.] We are going to take them first. The Irish Society will take the remainder of Thursday and Friday.

Mr. *Abel Smith.*] Dr. I understand the Grocers' Company need not attend on Thursday?

Chairman.] No, there will be no chance of taking them. We will take the Drapers and the Irish Society alone.

Thursday, 17th July 1890.

MEMBERS PRESENT:

Lord Elcho.	Mr. Lea.
Sir John Ellis.	Sir William Marriott.
Mr. John Ellis.	Mr. John Morley.
Mr. Elton.	Mr. Sexton.
Mr. T. M. Healy.	Sir Richard Temple.

THE RIGHT HONOURABLE JOHN MORLEY, IN THE CHAIR.

SIR HERVEY BRUCE, called in; sworn; and Examined.

Chairman.

5930. You are here, I believe, in consequence of some statements you have read in the evidence given by the Reverend J. Mark?—I may mention that I have not seen the statements in the actual Minutes of Evidence; I only got it from reports in the newspapers, and whether it was correct or not I cannot say.

5931. What was the statement, as you read it, in the paper that you desire to deal with?—I understand from the paper that he had charged me with having entered into an engagement with the Clothworkers' Company, which engagement I have not fulfilled.

5932. You are here, therefore, to maintain before the Committee that you entered into no engagement which you did not fulfil?—Yes.

5933. Will you tell us what was the engagement you entered into with the Clothworkers' Company?—There was no actual binding engagement; there was an understanding that for 10 years I should keep up a certain number of payments, which I think Sir Owen Roberts specified; so that I need not trouble the Committee with them over again.

5934. These were engagements to pay annual sums to certain schools and churches?—Yes.

5935. What induced you to enter into that engagement; what was the consideration in your mind?—There was no consideration in my mind. The Clothworkers' Company wished for that number of years that those things should be paid. What was the inducement in their own minds in connection with the money I was to pay I do not know; but there was nothing specified. There was a different arrangement made on account of the money asked for the property being too large as I thought, and I was to have a rebate upon the money I did not pay them off of a certain sum yearly for a certain number of years.

5936. Mr. Mark does not appear to have charged you with having broken the condition?—Then he was wrongly reported in the local papers, that is all I can say.

5937. I will read you what he says. At Question 403 my honourable friend on my left asked him: "But you understand that the Clothworkers' Company said on the condition that the grant should be continued for 10 years?—(*A.*) Yes. (*Q.*) And it was continued by Sir Hervey Bruce for that time?—(*A.*) Yes, for fully that time." That relates to all these "Endowments to Religion, Education, and Charity." Then he said that you had kept up a large number of subscriptions, but that they had ceased now. That, I suppose, is true?—No, it is not true as to all, because there are several schools to which I still continue to subscribe.

5938. But at all events you are here to say that you fulfilled the bargain that you made with the Clothworkers' Company at the time of the purchase?—It was an honourable understanding, it was not a bargain; and I have more than fulfilled it.

5939. It was not in writing?—No.

5940. There were letters, I suppose?—There were letters.

5941. It was not merely an oral understanding, I suppose?—What Sir Owen Roberts did I do not know. It was a distinct understanding that it was not binding, because Sir Owen Roberts, who was connected with the company, said there might be certain circumstances under which they would not wish it paid.

5942. Can you throw a little light upon another point in the transaction between you and the Clothworkers' Company, which has rather puzzled some members of the Committee. What was the reason, do you suppose, that induced the Clothworkers' Company to accept your offer in preference to the larger offer from their own tenants?—I could not answer that; but before I leave the other subject I might as well state, in my own defence, that although the money has not been continued to be paid exactly in the way originally done by the Clothworkers' Company, I still consider I am paying the amount of money, although in a different way; because I am still giving the money to all the schools but one, and I am giving over 100 *l.* a-year for the clergy, and maintaining the church in the district, and I also gave 500 *l.* as a contribution to the parish, because, with the exception of one, the people are gone

Chairman—continued.

gave to whom the Clothworkers' Company originally gave the money.

5943. Is it fair to ask you whether, although you have discharged this *quasi* legal or honourable obligation to the Clothworkers' Company, you still continue those grants because you feel a moral obligation to the tenants on the estate?—Not at all.

5944. Then why do you do so. I do not put it higher than a moral obligation, you will observe?—I think I should mislead the Committee if I put it that way, because there were some of the people to whom the Clothworkers' Company gave the money who were of the Presbyterian Church. I have given the money to the Episcopalian Church, and I will give you my reasons for doing so.

5945. Have you given to the Presbyterian as well as to the Episcopalian?—No, I have continued to the Episcopalian only.

5946. Giving nothing to the Presbyterians and nothing to the Catholics?—Not now.

5947. In that respect, therefore, your present subscriptions differ from the subscriptions that you paid for 10 years according to your agreement with the Clothworkers' Company?—Yes; but there is a reason for that. Almost all my tenants are Presbyterians and well-to-do, and they got substantial aids under the Act of 1881, that I considered they were able to pay their own clergy; whereas the Episcopalians were much poorer people, and were not able to do so. Having dealt with that special point, I am ready to answer any question that is put to me.

5948. Will you go to that point I put to you just now as to the reason that induced the Clothworkers' Company to take your offer in preference to the larger offer from their own tenants?—I can tell you no more than Sir Owen Roberts upon that point.

5949. Are those all the corrections you wish to make?—Those are all the corrections I wish to make.

Mr. John Glover, called in; sworn; and Examined.

Sir William Marriott.

5950. You are a Solicitor?—Yes.

5951. And you acted as solicitor for the Drapers' Company in Ireland, and were instructed by the company to carry out the sale of their estate to the tenants?—Yes.

5952. What were the terms of sale proposed to the tenants?—The terms of the sale are embodied in a letter written by Mr. Sawyer, the clerk of the company, to a tenant called Mr. Benjamin Hereford, dated the 10th of August 1888.

5953. What are those terms; will you read the letter or put it in?—The letter is in already; it is Paper No. 13 printed in the Appendix. The purchase-money was 18 times the rent. All the arrears of rent to 1st December 1885 were to be paid by the tenants as a condition precedent to carrying out the sale, and the company were to pay the entire cost of the sale. The rent that is mentioned in that letter was the rent, I should tell the Committee, that was settled in the year 1882. Prior to 1882 the company, in the years 1874, 1875, and 1876 had leased off, by leases for 21 years and 31 years, the entire of the estate. In 1882 the tenants complained that the lease rent was high, and the company, yielding to the tenants' complaint, reduced the lease rent by 15 per cent., and they then gave the tenants the option of endorsing upon the lease that reduction or of signing agreement forms as settled by the rules of the Land Act of 1881. A large number of tenants, probably three-fourths of the tenants, accepted the latter alternative, that is to say, they signed forms of agreement on Form No. 23, under the rules of the Act of 1881. By some oversight those agreements were not filed in the Land Commission Office. The company in 1888 were under the impression that these were all judicial rents that had been settled by these agreements in the year 1882, and upon the basis of those rents I was to sell at 18-years' purchase. I understood at the time that they were judicial rents, and except for this oversight of not filing these agreements they were really judicial rents.

Sir William Marriott—continued.

5954. Why did you understand that they were judicial rents?—Because I understood they had signed all those forms. I was told so.

5955. By whom?—By the agent.

5956. What agent?—The agent of the company.

5957. It turned out that it was a mistake?—It turned out that the agreements had not been filed; but I was not aware of it until October 1887.

5958. What was the form?—No. 23, to the rules of the Act of 1881.

Chairman.

5959. I understand that the forms printed in the Appendix Paper are all the forms that were used in the case?—Those are the forms used for the agreements for purchase, but they are not the forms that we used for making the tenants judicial tenants by agreement under the Act of 1881.

5960. Have you got a copy of that form with you?—I could supply that to you; it is printed in the rules. I have not got one here, but I will put in one. As I said, I was not aware till October 1887 that these agreements had not been filed.

Sir William Marriott.

5961. Were those rents higher than the judicial rents would have been, or lower?—The tenants accepted them as for judicial rent.

5962. What did the tenants do when the offer was made to them by you; did they accept or decline?—Before answering that question I would just say another word. As regards those rents which we looked upon as judicial rents, the bulk of the tenants have since held by them, and

paid

Sir William Marriott—continued.

and although the agreements were not filed they look upon themselves as bound by them, that is to say, having signed the forms and they look upon themselves as bound by them. Only 280 out of about 1,050 tenants have availed themselves of the chance, as it were, of the non-filing of these agreements, and have gone into court to fix the rents.

5963. What steps did you take after that to carry out the sale?—The first thing was to issue the letter of Mr. Sawyer.

Chairman.

5964. What date are we at now?—August 1886. The first thing done was to send a copy of that letter of August 1886 to every tenant upon the estate; and in the month of September I took up the division of the estate that is called the Moneymore division. I was not able at that time to take any more in hand. I will hand in to the Committee a summary of the steps I took, with the dates. That will shorten very much my statement. This document gives every step taken from December 1885 till August 1889.

Sir William Marriott.

5965. Can you tell us shortly what the effect of it is?—Yes. The proceedings, as you will see by a glance at this statement, were very long and very intricate.

5966. There was a good deal of correspondence, I presume?—Not only correspondence, but there was making out the title; there was first getting the agreement signed. I will hand to the Committee a copy of the agreement (*handing in the same*).

Chairman.

5967. In fact you went through the usual steps of arranging for sale?—Yes.

Sir William Marriott.

5968. Could you attach blame to any party for the delay?—I thought, and the company think, that the delay was principally owing to the tenants.

Chairman.

5969. How long was the delay?—We were ready to close up in April 1889; or indeed we were ready before that, but the tenants delayed paying in the arrears of rent that were due to the first of November 1885. That was one difficulty.

5970. Could not the company have closed before 1889?—Yes; we could have closed before 1889; but I did not get rulings upon the title till the 20th December 1887, and up to that time I could of course do nothing.

Sir William Marriott.

5971. After that what caused delay?—After that what caused the delay was that the Act of 1887 had passed, and in consequence rules were issued on the 1st January 1888, and the conveyances that we had printed and engrossed, and the maps drawn upon them, were all waste paper. We had to begin them again and get the conveyances recasted and reprinted, and all the work done over again.

Chairman.

5972. What was the provision in the Act of 1887 which made all that necessary?—The provision in the Purchase Act of 1887 was a clause whereby the conveyance was to release the tenant from all rent and arrears of rent. In consequence of the Purchase Act of 1887, the rules of 1885 were abolished and new rules framed.

Sir William Marriott.

5973. Had you any object in delay, or was it the desire of the company to complete?—No; the object was to have it done as expeditiously as possible; not only my object, but my interest was to have it done as expeditiously as possible. But I found (I had not the collection of these arrears myself) that the arrears were not coming in. And another difficulty that the Land Commission put in our way was, that they required the Drapers' Company to get a release from the Irish Society of a clause in their deed of the 4th June 1883; that is a clause in the same form as is inserted in all the conveyances from the Irish Society to all the companies.

5974. It refers to timber and to certain fishing rights and digging?—Yes.

5975. Had the Irish Society to join in the conveyance?—No; but the Land Commission required, in the case of the Drapers' Company, that there should be a deed of release.

5976. Was your title accepted by the Land Commission without the joining in the Irish Society?—Yes; but afterwards that this requisition was put in. That requisition had not been put in in the case of the Salters' or Skinners' or Fishmongers' Companies at all.

5977. It refers to certain timber rights, does it not?—Certain timber rights and certain stone for the use of the plantation.

5978. What was the result of that?—The result of that was that it put one back nine months.

5979. I do not know whether you have read the evidence given by Mr. O'Brien; he made a statement with regard to a Mr. Barefoot and some other tenants; have you read that evidence?—Yes; Mr. Barefoot was the tenant, as you will observe, to whom the communications of the company were sent in 1888, as a representative man. In November 1888 the tenants came to the company's office through some representatives, and they said to the company, "We will not pay you these arrears of rent due to 1st November 1885, for the reason that in the letter of Mr. Sawyer of the 3rd January 1887, you have released us from that; we will pay you no more rent, and we will not pay any interest upon the purchase-money; and we now ask you to carry out your conveyance and we will pay you no more money either on account of rent or on account of interest."

5980. Did the company agree to that?—No; the company said in regard to that, "You are purchasers in possession; you have had the full benefit of the land, and we are entitled to interest upon our purchase-money, and we will charge you only 3¼ per cent.; whereas, if you had been paying to the Land Commission you would have been paying 4 per cent., so that you will be 20 per cent. better off than if you had been

Sir William Marriott—continued.

been paying to the Land Commission." They said, "We will not pay anything;" and the company thereupon issued a writ against Mr. Barefoot as a test case, and the case was tried before Mr. Justice Murphy and a special jury of the city of Dublin.

Chairman.

5981. What was the exact issue between you and Mr. Barefoot; what did you sue him for?—We sued him for rent in the first place, and in the alternative for interest at 3½ per cent. upon his purchase-money.

Sir William Marriott.

5982. Rent, if he chose to act as a tenant, and interest on the purchase-money if he chose to complete the purchase?—Quite so.

5983. What was the result of the action?—It was tried before Mr. Justice Murphy and a special jury, and I have here a shorthand note of the judge's address to the jury if the Committee wish to see it. Perhaps I may extract the parts of it that refer to the answers given by Mr. O'Brien. They are substantially this: that the letters of the 15th August 1866 and the 3rd January 1867 were read to the jury, and handed to the jury, and the jury were asked if those letters released Mr. Barefoot from rent or interest. The company might have taken exception to putting in the letter of January 1867, but they did not. They said, We will have the case tried upon its merits; we raise no technical question upon the matter of evidence. I was examined as a witness, and Mr. Sawyer, the clerk of the company, was examined as a witness, and the jury found that those letters in their opinion did not modify the terms of sale, and that the tenants were bound to pay interest, and they gave a verdict for the company for 3½ per cent. upon the purchase-money.

5984. That was what you claimed?—Yes. The company afterwards forgave Mr. Barefoot one-half of the costs. But it is not a fact that any technical question was raised as to the admissibility of those letters to vary the contract.

5985. Were the terms offered by the Drapers' Company fair and just terms in your opinion, speaking with your knowledge of Ireland?—Practically the terms were 17 years' purchase; because the Drapers' Company charged no rent for 1856, nor interest either. Instead of charging three years' interest as they might have done, they only charged two years and four months' interest at 3½ per cent. So that for the four years 1856, 1857, 1858, and 1859, the company received only two years and four months' interest at 3½ per cent; and the tenants all that time had the entire benefit of the lands. That was giving them practically 17 years' purchase, and two years and four months' interest at 3½ per cent. only.

5986. You have no doubt heard the question raised of there being a trust on the part of the companies?—Yes, I have heard it discussed for 30 years.

5987. It has been stated here by more than one witness that the reason the tenants did not go to law, assuming there to be a trust, was that they had not sufficient money?—I have heard that suggested.

5988. As a matter of fact, do you know that an attempt was made to raise this question about 20 years ago, and legal opinion was taken?—Yes, I do.

5989. The opinion taken, I think, was that of the then Solicitor-General, Sir George Jessel?—Yes; I was the solicitor who came to London with two gentlemen who were a deputation from the Clothworkers' Estate, the late Mr. Taylor, a Member of Parliament, and Mr. Matthews, the chairman of the town of Coleraine. The case was submitted to Sir George Jessel then by me for those gentlemen. I drew up the case, and I submitted the documents myself.

5990. And what was Sir George Jessel's answer?—I have got the case here if the Committee would like to see it.

5991. Could you show it us?—Yes; that is the original document (*handing the same to the honourable Member*).

5992. I will read the questions upon which you desired his opinion. The first question you asked him was, "Whether the Crown, by the Attorney-General, has now the right to interfere in the sale of this property by the Clothworkers' Company, and if so, whether counsel would advise a Bill by way of information at the suit of the Attorney-General to be filed"; and his answer to that was: "I answer this question in the negative"; is that so?—That is quite right.

5993. "Secondly, whether the Clothworkers' Company can appropriate to their own uses in the city of London the entire purchase-money without reserving any portion of it for the public use of the plantations in Ireland"; and his answer was, "I answer this in the affirmative"; is that right?—That is right.

5994. "Thirdly, whether the Clothworkers' Company are trustees for any public general purposes connected with the Plantation of Ulster or any other public purposes in the city of London or the county of Londonderry"; and his answer was "I answer this in the negative"; is that right?—That is right.

5995. And then he states, "I am of opinion that the Clothworkers' Company were in the same position as individual undertakers in the other settled counties, that is, they are ordinary owners in fee-simple, subject only to the reservations expressly mentioned in the conveyance to them, and can therefore, like other owners in fee-simple, sell their own property for their own benefit to whom they please.—*G. Jessel*, Lincoln's Inn, 1st May, 1871"?—That is correct.

5996. And I suppose that prevented any action being brought?—In one sense it did, and in another it did not. We were dissatisfied with that opinion when we came back to Ireland, and we took the opinion of the late Lord Chancellor Law.

5997. What was his opinion?—It was the same as Sir George Jessel's, though I did not show him Sir George Jessel's opinion.

5998. Am I right in saying that the opinions of Sir George Jessel and Mr. Law did prevent you from taking any action?—They did.

5999. Is there anything else you would wish to

Sir William Marriott—continued.

to add before you are examined by other members of the Committee?—Yes. Starting with the check we received in getting the re-conveyance from the Irish Society in July 1888, the Long Vacation was just beginning.

Chairman.

6000. Are you still upon the Moneymore division?—What applies to the Moneymore division up to a certain point will apply to all. Practically, the Moneymore division was what I was working upon up to December 1888. We came to a deadlock in July 1888, until we got the re-conveyance from the Irish Society. At the end of July we were practically into the Long Vacation, and that means it was the 1st of September before I could take any more whatever in carrying on the sales. That carries us to September 1888. I then brought in new conveyances with the Irish Society's release; and in November 1888 we had another series of new rules published by the Land Commission. I had then again to reprint the conveyances; they were printed a second time, as also the maps upon them, in consequence of this new rule; and in December 1888 I got settled for the third time the conveyance to the tenants. That ran me up to December 1888 before I was in a position to ask the company to put their seal to the conveyances. We had then brought in the whole thing; for the Moneymore division was, I may say, absolutely completed in February 1889. I did not know then, but I have since found from inquiry from the Land Commission and from the investigations before this Committee, that on the 12th of February 1889 a petition was presented by 31 tenants from what is called the Ballymacreen and Brackaslievgallon divisions, upon which I had been doing very little, complaining of great harshness on the part of the company.

6001. Do you say they sent you a memorial?—It was not sent to me; they sent it to the Land Commission. I did not know of it at the time, but I will immediately draw the Committee's attention to what the result of it was. Though that memorial was not communicated to the company or to me, nor a copy sent to the company, I saw immediately that everything came to a stand-still, and we were told in that month of February 1889 we must stop the whole proceedings until we explained the delay. We were told that on the 19th of February by the Land Commission. That was seven days after the receipt of the petition, and we knew nothing of the petition at that time. On the 19th February 1889, therefore, the whole thing was absolutely stopped, and Mr. Commissioner Lynch withdrew the advances he had sanctioned in January 1887; that was two years antecedent. Then the whole thing came to a stand-still. Mr. Sawyer, the clerk to the company, and Sir William Conyngham went up on the 3rd of April and saw the Land Commissioners. I was in Dublin at the time, and I understood the Land Commission was going to send down Mr. O'Brien to re-inspect the division of Moneymore, which had been inspected in December 1886 and January 1887, and to inquire after the whole business over again. I saw Mr. O'Brien on the 3rd of April 1889 in his own office, and I said, "If you are coming to Moneymore to re-inspect all these holdings and some of the Brackaslievgallon estate, I wish to tell you that since the company began to sell, some of these tenants, as we think in violation of their written agreements, have been into court and got fair rents fixed, and they have been pressing the company and me now to give them the sale upon those reduced rents. That the company have refused; and I have filled in the agreements for those tenants the same as I have filled them in for all the others, upon the rents settled in 1886, and I have a list ready to hand to you and a schedule showing what has been done with respect to them."

6002. Is that what you told Mr. O'Brien?—That is what I said to Mr. O'Brien in his office. It was arranged that he was either to come to me, or I was to see him during the course of his visit, and if he could not come to me he would write me a letter, and I should go to him. I had this schedule of course prepared at the time this was going on, and as every case occurred I made a note of it. I have a copy of the schedule here, if the Committee would like to look at it. Mr. O'Brien, I understand from Sir William Conyngham, did not call upon him at all, nor did he call upon me nor make any request to me to know, or get any explanation of the statements which he has put in here about several things I should like to refer to.

6003. Could not you have called upon him?—If I had I should not have found him, because he went out early and came in late, and I did not know where to find him; he was to send me a note when I was to see him.

Sir William Marriott.

6004. Have you anything else you wish to add?—The company think they have a right to complain of Mr. O'Brien coming now and making these statements, when he did not give us an opportunity of explaining the matter to him at the time.

6005. He never gave you any opportunity, you say?—He never gave us any opportunity, nor did the Land Commission. Mr. O'Brien came down on the 4th of April, and the report is dated the 12th of April leaving seven or eight days during which he had to inspect 385 holdings.

Chairman.

6006. They were all lying close to each other, were they not?—No; in an area six miles long by two broad.

6007. Do you imply by that that it was impossible for him to inspect them?—Impossible.

6008. What was he inquiring into?—I understand he came to investigate and see whether the Commissioners' security on all these holdings was as good as it was in 1887, when they were inspected by another inspector.

Sir William Marriott.

6009. Would you say that it was a cursory visit?—I say he could not possibly have inspected

Sir William Marriott—continued.

inspected those holdings in that time, nor a tenth of them.

6010. You think it would be physically impossible?—It would be physically impossible. I was going to say that in April immediately after that, Mr. Commissioner Lynch on the 16th of April, without any notice of Mr. O'Brien's report, which was dated the 12th of April, made a ruling rescinding the whole advances that had been formerly sanctioned, and called upon the company to receive neither rent nor interest from that date, and called upon the company to have another new form of conveyance settled in which they released the tenantry absolutely from any claim to rent or interest on foot of judgments, &c.

6011. What did the company do?—The company absolutely declined to do that, and the result was that the sale was practically at an end.

6012. Why did they decline?—They declined because they said Mr. Commissioner Lynch had no right to prevent them receiving interest upon their purchase-money, or arrears of rent that had been stipulated for as a condition precedent to sale.

6013. They held in fact that it was a breach of the agreement?—It was a breach of the agreement. They said, "We have stood to our agreement to our own loss, because we are not getting as much as we might, and we do not think we ought to be treated in this way." They directed me, therefore, to issue letters to the tenants saying that inasmuch as the Land Commissioners had put this requisition upon them they gave them an opportunity of withdrawing from the sale, and they would not yield.

Chairman.

6014. Have we got that letter printed in the Appendix?—Yes, it is Paper, No. 17.

Sir William Marriott.

6015. What happened then?—When the tenants found that the company would not be bullied in that way they immediately got up a memorial to the Land Commission, and they went into the Land Court and begged the Land Commission to let the sale proceed, urging that it would be highly advantageous to them if they did, and a great inconvenience if they did not. The result was that Mr. Commissioner Lynch cancelled his ruling of 16th April 1889, and the whole thing was settled upon the terms we had arranged as it stood in February.

6016. And those are the terms that have been carried out and acted upon?—Those are the terms that have been carried out.

6017. Is there anything more that you wish to state?—I think that is the end of the general statement I wished to make. There are one or two matters I should like to draw attention to in the evidence that has been given. I should like to refer to Questions 1012 and 1013 of Mr. O'Brien's evidence with regard to Mr. Barefoot. As I have explained already, the letters were submitted to the jury in the trial of Barefoot's case, and the company raised no technical objection upon the letters qualifying the contract in any way, but left it absolutely to the jury as to whether the contract had been varied at all.

6018. Is there anything else you wish to add?—I should like to refer to Questions 1032 and 1034, if you please. At Question 1032 Mr. O'Brien said, "There were various remonstrances as to the delay in that particular case." I take it that was the delay in the Barefoot case, but I am not quite certain. There was no delay all round, and therefore there could not be in the Barefoot case, so far as the company was concerned; and so far as I was concerned, I received no remonstrances. Then, with regard to Question 1041, I should like to hand into the Committee a memorial which the tenants presented to Mr. Commissioner Lynch in July 1889. I have here a copy of the memorial presented by the tenants to the Land Commissioners.

Chairman.

6019. We have already got that memorial, I think?—No, it is not printed.

6020. What is the point of this memorial?—It is asking the Commissioner to reconsider his revocation of the advances he had sanctioned before.

Mr. John Ellis.

6021. I understand you are putting this memorial in as representing the company. Did they receive a copy of it?—A copy was furnished to me by the gentleman who handed it to the Land Commission. A copy was served upon the company.

Sir William Marriott.

6022. I will read the memorial, as it is not long: "To the Irish Land Commission.—The memorial of the tenants of the Moneymore Division of the Drapers' Companies Estates respectfully showeth: That your honours having sanctioned an advance from the Public Treasury to enable us to purchase our holdings which we were most anxious to do, and which your honours have intimated that you will withdraw, should the Drapers' Company not agree to certain terms, we request you to consider our position: (1) We affirm that our holdings are ample value as security to the Treasury for the money proposed to be lent to us to buy up the fee-simple from the Drapers' Company, and we are prepared to challenge any investigation upon this point, and beg to say that in most cases the tenant-right of our holdings alone is worth more than the money; (2) The company's claims have, with a few exceptions, been settled and cleared up to the 1st November last without leaving any arrears due, and we feel after doing so that we will be perfectly able to meet the instalments which will accrue to the Government; (3) In reference to the balance of the interest, we believe that if it were left to the goodwill of the Drapers' Company, they will meet us in the same liberal and generous way they did in former times. We therefore pray your honours to allow the sale to proceed without any further delay or difficulty, as we feel that on the whole the sale would be very beneficial to us, and the breaking it off at the present time would not only be a serious disappointment,

Sir William Marriott—continued.

paintment, but disastrous, inasmuch as the Drapers' Company in case the sale falls through are claiming three years' rent, less the interest that has been paid. We are sure that any poor case on the estate may be left in the hands of the Drapers' Company, whom we must always remember as good landlords. And your memorialists will ever pray." In consequence of receiving that memorial, the judgment of Mr. Commissioner Lynch was reversed?—Yes. The company stood indifferent upon that matter. They said "The Land Commissioners having taken that view in this matter, we do not care whether the sale proceeds or not." They asked me to attend when that petition was presented, and I did so, and said I had no instructions either to assist or oppose it.

6023. Is there anything else you wish to add?—There are just one or two matters in the evidence I should like to refer to very shortly. In answer to Question 1041 of Mr. O'Brien's evidence, he refers to three cases where great hardship was, he says, inflicted upon three ladies: Miss Bessie Johnston, Mrs. Crooks, and Miss M'Cullough. I have prepared for the Committee a statement of those three cases, showing how they stood at the time, what money was received from them, and what position they stood in when it was settled, and if you will permit me I will just read one of those cases. Miss Johnston's annual rent was 21 *l.* 5 *s.*; her purchase-money was 385 *l.* for 84 acres 2 roods 34 perches of land. She owed to the 1st November 1885, 63 *l.* 15 *s.*, and she owed interest for two years and four months, 27 *l.* 17 *s.* 8 *d.*; making 91 *l.* 12 *s.* 8 *d.* She paid 66 *l.* 15 *s.*, and the company forgave her 24 *l.* 17 *s.* 8 *d.* It is said by Mr. O'Brien that she was charged very large sums for costs. She was not charged one shilling for costs, the company forgave that.

Chairman.

6024. What do you mean by saying the company forgave her the costs?—The company did not charge it to her.

Sir William Marriott.

6025. Had she to pay any independent costs to any solicitor of her own?—I was coming to that. It is said that she paid 20 *l.* costs for a loan of 83 *l.* That could not be; for the scale of costs for such a loan would be 5 *l.* at the outside.

6026. Did the company charge any costs?—Not a farthing.

Chairman.

6027. You are not contradicting Mr. O'Brien's statement; for Mr. O'Brien says she "borrowed 383 *l.* at 6 per cent., and was involved in 20 *l.* costs in connection with that loan as well"?—That is a misstatement; she did not borrow 383 *l.* at 6 per cent.

6028. Did she borrow any money at any percentage?—Her brother told me she borrowed 63 *l.* She herself was not well, or able to come in, but the brother who transacted the business for her told me that she got a loan of 63 *l.*

Mr. Sexton.

6029. My memory is that there was a mortgage in the case, and there was the cost of the mortgage?—Mr. O'Brien stated there was a mortgage. Her brother, who was acting for her, did not tell me there was a mortgage, nor lead me to infer in any way that there was a mortgage. I understood it was a promissory note given for 63 *l.*

Sir William Marriott.

6030. Did the company sue her on that?—No.

Mr. Sexton.

6031. If there had been a mortgage, those costs would not have been improbable, I presume?—Yes, for a mortgage of 63 *l.* they would have been highly improbable. For a mortgage of 63 *l.* the highest amount charged by the scale would be 5 *l.* No solicitor could make such a charge as 20 *l.* for a mortgage of 63 *l.* The other case is that of Esther Crooks. Mr. O'Brien said that Esther Crook's purchase-money was 311 *l.* But it is not so; her purchase-money is 313 *l.* A point was made upon that at Question 1047, that the 111 *l.* 5 *s.* 10 *d.* that she owed the company was against the rent of the 311 *l.* That was misleading, I think, because the rent that she did owe was 74 *l.* 3 *s.* 6 *d.*; the interest upon the purchase-money for two years and four months was 24 *l.* 1 *s.*; making a total of 98 *l.* 4 *s.* 6 *d.* The company received from her in full 63 *l.* 6 *s.* 10 *d.*, and forgave her the rest. Then the only other case which I will trouble you with is that of Ellen M'Cullough, referred to in the same place. In that case the purchase-money was 189 *l.* She owed, to 1st November 1885, 33 *l.* 3 *s.* for rent, and for two years and four months' interest at 3½ per cent., 14 *l.* 10 *s.* That gave a total for five years of 47 *l.* 13 *s.*: and in lieu of that the company accepted 30 *l.*

Sir William Marriott.

6032. You have mentioned what was the substance of Mr. Law's opinion; could you give us a copy of it?—I have a copy, but I have not the original. The late Mr. Samuel McCurdy Greer had the loan of it from me.

6033. Will you give us the copy, and state what it says?—The same queries were put to Mr. Law as to Sir George Jessel, but he was at the time utterly ignorant that the case had been submitted to Sir George Jessel in London. I told Mr. Law afterwards that it was so. His answers were the same as those of Sir George Jessel, but they were very much more expanded, going into the reasons and grounds for the opinion. I have not got the copy here.

6034. Could you let us have it to-morrow?—I have not got it in London.

6035. Will you let us have it next week?—I have not got the original.

Chairman.

6036. Is yours an authenticated copy?—It is a copy made in my office. I have every reason to believe it is a correct copy.

6037. Where is the original?—The original was lent to the late Samuel McCurdy Greer, who was then member for the county. He is dead,

Chairman—continued.

dead, and I have asked his executors and they cannot find it in his papers.

Sir William Marriott.

6038. Is there any other point you wish to refer to?—I should like to refer to Question 1117. Mr. O'Brien there refers to a case which he thinks was a great hardship upon the tenant. His name is Mallon. If the Committee will permit me I will just give them a statement of what that case was.

Chairman.

6039. Is this the case mentioned in the middle of the answer to Question 1117?—Yes; Mallon's rent was 5 *l.* 3 *s.* The purchase-money was 52 *l.*, his holding being 18 A. 2 R. 3 P. He owed on the 1st of November 1886, 23 *l.* 9 *s.* 8 *d.* for rent, and for costs of a decree taken in April 1887, 2 *l.* 16 *s.* 10 *d.*, making 25 *l.* 5 *s.* 6 *d.*, which is his total indebtedness to the company.

6040. You put that in against Mr. O'Brien's statement that "on the 31st of March 1887 he received an ejectment for 23 *l.* 9 *s.* 8 *d.*" There is some slight discrepancy in the figures?—No, I do not mean that. The figures are the same. The rent owed was 23 *l.* 9 *s.* 8 *d.*, but it would not be upon that that the discrepancy arises. I will show you presently that Mr. O'Brien has either not understood it, or made some mistake. There was a decree taken in April 1887, and in August 1888 Sir William Conyngham, the agent of the company, for the 25 *l.* 16 *s.* 6 *d.* that was due upon the foot of the decree, agreed to accept 19 *l.* 3 *s.* 8 *d.* for the lot; and upon that date, namely, the 20th of August 1888, the tenant paid Sir William Conyngham 10 *l.*, leaving 9 *l.* 3 *s.* 8 *d.* due, and that 9 *l.* 3 *s.* 8 *d.* was returned to me as due. On the 25th of January 1889, Mallon came to my office, and Sir William Conyngham happened to be in at the time, and Sir William Conyngham stated that 9 *l.* 3 *s.* 8 *d.* was the amount due. Mallon said he wished to purchase his holding at the company's terms of 18 years' purchase. I made out a statement of what was due, showing the 9 *l.* 5 *s.* 8 *d.* first, and putting the interest at 3½ for 1887 and 1888, it made his total indebtedness to the company 8 *l.*, and that cleared him of everything till the 1st of November 1888. He said, Sir William Conyngham being present, "I have not the 8 *l.*, but if you will add that 8 *l.* to my purchase-money, I shall be obliged; because I think my farm can bear it very well." I said, "I have no objection, but the Land Commission will have something to say to that by-and-bye; it will be your look out." The agreement was prepared on that date, the 25th of January 1889, putting 8 *l.* to the purchase-money of 92 *l.*, which would make 100 *l.* He signed that agreement, and it is lodged with the Land Commission. After the Land Commission had withdrawn all these advances in April and May 1889, and the company had sent him the letter on the 20th of June 1889, Mallon, on the 29th of February last, came in to me and said: "I could pay in cash that 8 *l.* which you put to my purchase-money, and I will be obliged if you will prepare another agreement and take the 8 *l.* in cash, and allow the purchase-money to remain at 92 *l.*" I said: "I have no objection to do that, but I will not prepare an agreement; I have prepared one, and I will not prepare another. If you will go to a solicitor and get him to prepare an agreement upon those terms, and pay me the 8 *l.* in cash, I will let your purchase-money remain at 92 *l.*" He accordingly went to a solicitor and got an agreement in those terms, and came back with it and paid in the 8 *l.* in cash. I will tell you how the 8 *l.* was made up. As a matter of fact, he paid me 9 *l.* that day, but the 8 *l.* was part of it. The way in which the account given on the 29th of February 1889 was made up, was as follows: Going back to November 1885, the rent due to that date was 2 *l.* 5 *s.* 6 *d.*; from that I took off 17 *s.* 4 *d.*, reducing it to 1 *l.* 8 *s.* 4 *d.*; then I added interest due in 1887, 1888, and 1889, amounting to 7 *l.* 18 *s.*, which made it 9 *l.* 6 *s.* 4 *d.*; and then I deducted poor rates 6 *s.* 4 *d.*, leaving 9 *l.*, making it complete to the 1st of November 1889. He paid the 9 *l.* and signed the agreement, reducing his purchase-money to 92 *l.* The result was that the company have got 10 *l.* and 9 *l.* for seven years' rent.

6041. Still keeping to the Moneymore division, you spoke about Mr. O'Brien being only seven days in examining 340 holdings, and you said that in your opinion that was not one-tenth of time enough. You will remember that he was not there to value for the purpose of giving fair rent, but he was there to see whether there was security for the advances by the Land Commissioners. Do you still think that ten times that time, or 70 days, was necessary to ascertain the validity of the security?—Perhaps ten times is a little more than would be required. I should say 12 holdings in a day would be as much as any inspector could do, if he is to do it fairly to the tenants.

6042. Are you regarding Mr. O'Brien as looking at the holdings for the purpose of fixing fair rent or merely for the purpose of the security?—For the purpose of the security.

6043. How long do you think it would take for an inspector to examine all the holdings which you were prepared to sell?—I should think the Moneymore division would take three weeks to a month.

6044. How long would the other divisions, Ballynascreen and Brackaslievgallion, take?—More; they would take probably two months.

6045. That would be three months in all?—Yes.

6046. Does not that strike you as a very extravagant process?—No.

6047. What is it that Mr. O'Brien is to look at; what is he to find out?—As I understand, the security to the Land Commission is the land.

6048. That is one?—I do not see how an inspector can ascertain that in so short a time. I know the former practice has been to go over field by field of the land, and he could not do that and do more than 12 cases in a day.

6049. Do you say the purchase inspectors go over the holdings field by field?—Yes; they have been doing that all round. I do not see how he could

Chairman—continued.

could advise as to the value of the land as a security unless he did it, because each field will have a different quality of land, and there will be different circumstances in each field with regard to the facility of cultivation.

6030. But he would surely look at other things as well; he would look at the rent and the regularity or otherwise with which the rent was paid, and he would fairly draw his inference. I do not at all accept your view that it is necessary for him to apply what Lord Salisbury called the umbrella test, to dig into the land and find what it was worth. If he found the rent had been paid regularly, and the tenant was in a decently prosperous condition, surely that was one guiding element in considering whether his security was good or not?—That was one element undoubtedly.

Mr. Sexton.

6031. What is sold in these purchases is the landlord's interest in the land, is it not?—Yes, the landlord's interest.

6032. Does not it occur to you that a cursory examination would be sufficient to convince an intelligent person acquainted with land, whether or not the land was sufficient as a security for the purchase-money for the landlord's interest, the two interests being taken together as the security?—The two interests are taken together for the Land Commissioners' security; but I should say, taking the two interests as the value of the land all round, no man could give a fair opinion of what was the value of the land as a security unless he went over it and looked at it very carefully. I should do so myself if I was acting for a mortgagee.

6033. When one interest is sold and you have two interests as security, you do not need so close and searching an examination, do you?—I quite agree as to that. But at the same time, when the Land Commissioners say in some of these cases on the Drapers' Company's Estate, the holding is not security, and the inspection was of such a slight and imperfect kind, then the occasion comes for the landlords to say that they think the inspection has not been satisfactory.

Chairman.

6034. In what sense were you damaged, supposing that this inspection was of a cursory and superficial kind; what harm did it do you?—It did do us harm in this way; we thought it depreciated the value of the estate.

6035. What depreciated it?—Mr. O'Brien goes back to the Land Commission, and he says, This is not security for 380 *l.*, or whatever the price may be.

6036. Did he go back?—Yes, he did; he took 64 cases in the Brackaslievegallion division.

6037. But we are now upon the Moneymore division; it was on the Moneymore division you made that remark upon Mr. O'Brien?—Yes, but he did upon the Moneymore division also.

6038. As regards the Moneymore division, what did he say?—He said in several cases he thought without giving a third instead of a fifth guarantee deposit, the security would not be good.

Chairman—continued.

6039. Pardon me; what he said to the Land Commission was this: "It appears to me that for the protection of the company's security it would be wise to require all outstanding cases to be closed at once, and that all rent, interest, and costs should be released." That is the opinion that he held, and if he had stopped in the Moneymore division six months digging his umbrella into the land, he could not have altered that opinion. Therefore you are mistaken, are you not, in saying that in his report upon the Moneymore division (I will come to the other divisions presently), he said what you suggest; he did not, did he?—Yes, in the Moneymore division he did, after his return.

6040. Will you show me where he does?—It is not in the report.

6041. Then how do you know he did?—I know, because afterwards we had to take up a special lot of cases that Mr. O'Brien reported upon.

6042. Did you ever see his report?—I never saw his report until I saw it printed here.

6043. This report does not bear out what you now say?—That report will not; but the subsequent dealing with individual cases as they came up most certainly will.

6044. I do not see how you are going to prove that. Still keeping to the Moneymore division, I understand you to express a very unfavourable opinion of the new rule of the Land Commission of November 1888, did you not?—I did not express an unfavourable opinion; I said the rule had the effect of making us reprint and re-engross all the conveyances. I did not say whether it was a good or a bad rule.

6045. I understood you to express an opinion against it?—No, certainly not; I only say it has had that effect, and so far as I was professionally concerned it meant about 250 *l.* and the delay.

6066. Apart from Mr. O'Brien's report, Mr. Commissioner Lynch said, in respect of the Moneymore division, that "the company and the tenants are both to blame for the existing deadlock." What is your answer to that?—My answer is that the company were not to blame.

6067. That is a plain answer; but if Mr. Commissioner Lynch said you were, what do you say?—Mr. Commissioner Lynch said we did not bring in the leases. My answer is, that we could not bring in the leases. The tenants had the leases and we called for them to bring them in, time and again, and they did not bring them.

6068. Now what is your answer to this statement in Mr. O'Brien's Report: "There is no doubt, however, that all the tenants have been seriously inconvenienced and immensely irritated by the unexpected payments required, and the legal proceedings by which they were enforced. Many who were badly off before have been very much straitened, inasmuch as they had hoped to relieve their position by accepting the terms of purchase as they understood them. This understanding was based upon verbal statements made by Mr. Glover at several meetings on the estate to which the tenants were summoned by circulars." What is your answer to that?—My answer to that is that I was examined as a witness in Barefoot's case before a special jury in Dublin, and

Chairman—continued.

and that I satisfied the jury that it was not so, and that the tenants were very much better off by paying 3½ per cent. than paying 4 per cent. to the Land Commission.

8069. But that is not the point of Mr. O'Brien's allegation?—Yes; he says they were irritated; I do not know what irritated them.

8070. Do you agree that they were irritated, or do you deny that fact?—I say they should not have been irritated.

8071. You do not deny the fact that they were?—Some of them may have been, and some of them were not certainly.

8072. But some of them were?—Yes; some of them who did not want to pay rent up to 1883, and did not want to pay any interest; they thought they were grievously wronged.

8073. Do you consider the verbal statements which Mr. O'Brien alleges to have been made by you were fully observed?—They were, to the letter.

8074. Mr. O'Brien does not seem to have thought so?—Mr. O'Brien did not know what my verbal statements were.

8075. What were they?—The verbal statements at meetings to which he refers, would be that, say, in 1886, when I was asked, "When do you think the sales will be completed?" I said, "Looking at the way things have been going on before the Land Commission, and the proceedings in the Drapers' Company, I think they should be completed in four months." The tenants said, "That means you will be in default, if you do not complete in four months." I said, "Not you have not paid your rent, and you cannot get in until you do." The Land Commissioners had put a requisition upon me that I could not fulfil in a year and a-half.

8076. Then going on to the other divisions of Ballynascreen and Brackaslievegallion, have you read the printed papers containing Mr. O'Brien's report upon those two divisions?—I have read one report; I suppose it refers to the whole.

8077. Yes, I see it does. Mr. O'Brien says here, that these contracts "appear to me to have been entered into by the tenants under duress and intimidation of the most pronounced character"; what do you say to that?—I say they were not; there was neither duress nor intimidation.

8078. Is it true that some of those contracts were entered into with the sheriff at the door?—No.

8079. No contract was entered into with the sheriff at the door?—No contract was entered into with the sheriff at the door.

8080. Do you think that Mr. Commissioner Lynch was entirely wrong in that passage of his judgment; remember he was giving a solemn authoritative judgment; do you think he was quite wrong when he said, "I conclude, from my examination of these cases, that these contracts were obtained by intimidation and undue influence; that they were entered into under duress." You must feel that a deliberate statement of that kind requires a full answer?—I quite feel the gravity of it; but, if you will allow me to say so, so far as I know he had no evidence upon which to found his judgment, except the report of Mr. O'Brien. He might have brought us into court upon any one of these cases. He might either have called upon the tenants to bring us into court, or the company to bring the tenants and have it investigated in court. We should have been very glad that that should have been done. No application was made to me, and none was made to the company, for any explanation or answer to Mr. O'Brien's report till that judgment was given, and I say now that no duress was exercised, no intimidation was exercised, and if Mr. Commissioner Lynch had given the company the opportunity of coming into court upon these cases, we should have satisfied Mr. Commissioner Lynch that it was not so.

8081. There were arrears owing by those purchasers, were there not?—There were.

8082. Did you say anything to them as to the existence of those arrears?—I did, in every case.

8083. Did you mention the existence of the arrears as a reason why they should purchase?—I did not, nor did I ever think of it.

8084. You kept the two subjects entirely apart?—No, I could not keep them apart.

8085. In what connexion did you mention the two things together?—Allow me to say this: I have taken the cases of the three signatories of the petition to Mr. Commissioner Lynch upon which he founds his judgment.

8086. It would be simpler, I think, if you would answer me my question first, and give the explanation afterwards; you say you talked to the tenants of the two questions together, namely, the purchase and the arrears; in what connexion did you bring them together?—When a tenant came in to me and said, "I want to purchase my holding," the first thing my instructions from the company required me to do, was to say "How much do you owe to November 1883 for rent?" The company's letter said that that was a condition precedent to me dealing with a tenant at all upon purchase. I therefore at once had to say, "How much do you owe to November 1883 for rent?" I then said, "If you have paid the rent to 1883 I can deal with you as if you had been a purchaser from 1883, and I will take interest at 3½ per cent. on the other two years or two-and-a-half years as the case may be; and only on those conditions can I deal with you at all." In that sense the purchase and the arrears of rent came in together, but in that sense only. If he could not do that, all I could say was, "I cannot deal with you on purchase, good or bad; go to the agent."

8087. If the tenant was unable to pay off the arrears, you would not deal with him on any other terms?—I could not.

8088. Then the consequence would be his eviction, I take it?—No.

8089. What was the consequence?—The consequence was that he was remaining a tenant.

8090. With a lot of arrears hanging over his head?—I had nothing to do with that.

8091. I do not say you had; I only want to see how the tenant stood. As I understand he stood in this way, from your account; he owed arrears, and you said to him, "You must pay off the

Chairman—continued.

the arrears, or you cannot purchase"?—"I cannot deal with the purchase if you do not pay them off."

6092. The existence of those arrears left him open to eviction?—Yes; if the company chose.

6093. Therefore, to tell him that was to tell him that if he did not pick up money enough to pay off those arrears he would run a good chance of an ejectment decree or eviction?—I did not say so.

6094. That is true enough; but is not that the effect of it?—He might have inferred that.

6095. I understand, at all events, that what Mr. O'Brien meant when he talked about duress, and what Mr. Commissioner Lynch meant when he said that "these contracts were obtained by intimidation, and that they were entered into under duress," was exactly the state of things which you have very candidly described?—He may or may not have meant that; but what I complained of was that we had no opportunity of explaining——

6096. One minute. You see, at all events, that if the words, "intimidation," and "undue influence," and "duress," are used in the ordinary sense, the transaction which you have described comes within that expression?—Inferentially it may.

6097. And inferentially it evidently did in the mind of Mr. Commissioner Lynch?—In the mind of Mr. Commissioner Lynch I could not say; but he had Mr. O'Brien's report. What I say is, that I think it was unfair to Mr. Commissioner Lynch, to the company, and to me, to draw this conclusion without taking up the cases and bringing us face to face together.

6098. It is not drawing a conclusion; it is a description of a state of facts which you yourself are now admitting; is it not so?—Perhaps you are too able for me in argument.

6099. Nay, I claim no prowess in that line. I do not want to press you?—I know you do not unfairly, but I think it was unfair to me, to a certain extent, on the part of Mr. Commissioner Lynch, to take up these cases, and pass a judgment like that, without asking us to come straight into court, bringing these men face to face with us.

6100. If you had been brought face to face, you would have given the same account of things you have just given to me, I presume?—That state of things might not apply to every individual case. He refers to 64, and I have a tabulated statement here, if the Committee wish to run their eye over it, of the state of things existing in those 64 cases.

6101. That seems a lengthy document: I do not think we can have that put in?—This is a matter upon which I feel a little sore; and, if you would permit me, I will take three cases here, and I may say I take them not by selection.

6102. Three cases out of those 64?—Yes; they happen to be three of the gentlemen who signed the petition to Mr. Lynch in February 1888. They are the cases of Henry O'Neill, Michael Morgan, and James Convery. I cannot put my hand upon the statement of the cases at the moment.

Chairman—continued.

6103. Will you put it in later?—Yes. (*The same was handed in at the conclusion of the sitting.*)

6104. On the other point, as to the preparation of the agreement, I think you had nothing to say to Sir William Marriott in explanation of the irregularity in the preparation of the agreements?—Yes, I have to say this: I have got in my hand a copy of the agreement as settled in the Land Commission of December 1886.

6105. But you see the agreements were alleged to have been irregularly prepared in certain definite particulars; first of all, in the words of Mr. Commissioner Lynch, they were "presented to the Commission in a misleading aspect by the omission or concealment of the judicial rent." What is your answer to that?—My answer to that is, first, that in December 1886 the form of agreement was settled upon which I was acting all round for this estate, not the form of agreement for any other estate.

6106. For all three divisions?—Yes, for all three divisions up to December 1887. This form of agreement covered all the agreements prepared by me to December 1887, and then came the new rules under the Act of 1887. In this form of agreement there is a column headed "Rent paid by tenants," as you will see (*handing in a form*).

6107. But that is not the point, is it?—No, it is not the point; but it is leading up to it. The point did not arise till after the tenants went in, as we say, in violation of their own written agreements in October 1887. 210 of them at the January and April Sessions, 1888, got 200 fair rents, as they call it, fixed. There were then 210 out of the 1,050 tenants who were in that position, that they had gone in and thrown away the agreements, they had signed for judicial tenancies, and had fair rents fixed in court.

Mr. Healy.

6108. Did you take the point in court against them that they were not tenants?—No.

6109. Why did you not contend, when they wished to have a fair rent fixed, that they were not tenants?—We submitted to the Recorder and the Land Commissioners the agreements they had signed in 1883, but which had not been filed in the Land Commission, and we said, these tenants are bound, or if not legally bound, it is a circumstance that you, the Commissioners, and the Recorder are bound to take into consideration as an equitable circumstance.

6110. Have you told the Committee already that they had previously signed agreements for judicial rents?—Yes, I mentioned that before you were in the room, I think.

Chairman.

6111. Still you keep a long way off the point: why you put in a misleading statement of the rent?—I do not think the point has been brought before the Commission in a way that will do fairness to the company. In April 1888, about 200 tenants got judicial rents fixed in face of the agreements by which they were judicial tenants before. Then I had become face-to-face with those 200, who said, "Now the company have offered to sell our holdings at 18 years' purchase

Chairman—continued.

of the rent, we say, that the 18 years is 18 years of the rent fixed yesterday, or the week before, and we ask you to let us purchase upon that rent." I said, "We will do nothing of the kind. When the company offered to sell at 18 years' purchase, it was upon the rents of 1882, which we then thought were judicial rents, and if you do not wish to buy on those terms, we will not sell." They sent a member to the company, and the company said, "We will not sell upon those judicial rents which have just been fixed." Then came the question how I was to fill up the agreement; whether I was to state in that column that there were judicial rents or not. It is laid to my charge that I filled up in that column the rent of 1882, upon which I was selling the estate, and did not put in the column the reduced rent they got fixed in court, say, two or three months before the date of filling that column in. That is the charge that Mr. Commissioner Lynch makes against me. In answer to it I would say I thought the matter very carefully over; I thought that if I put in the judicial rent under the column which is stated in the agreement to be the "rent paid by the tenant," I would be stating what was not true, because those rents were only settled three or four months before the document was prepared, and the tenant had never paid the rent; he had paid the rent of 1882, and we were selling upon the rent of 1882; and if I stated that the rent he paid was the judicial rent, I would have been open to the impeachment by the tenant that I was practising a fraud upon him, by selling him what would have been 20 years of that judicial rent, and not 18 years' purchase.

6112. Did you never think of the duty owed to the Land Commission?—I am coming to that.

6113. That is the point; I am not talking, nor did Mr. Commissioner Lynch, of your attitude to the tenants; it is your breach of the rule of the Land Commissioners; you were misleading them?—I will just deal with that now if you please; I think the Committee will now understand the position I stood in so far as the company and the tenants were concerned, and if you understand that I will now deal with the position I occupied with regard to the Land Commission. It is said that, by the non-insertion of that judicial rent in, say, 43 out of 54 cases, I concealed from the Land Commissioners deliberately and on purpose what was the rent, and the legal rent, at the time that document was signed. I say I did not; I put in the rent that was the rent paid by the tenant, and that is what is stated in the column. It is said that there was a note; that it was a rule of the Land Commissioners that I should have put in the judicial rent; I say there is no rule of the Land Commission that I should put in the judicial rent.

6114. Do you mean to say that you know the rules of the Land Commission better than Mr. Commissioner Lynch?—They are printed rules.

6115. If Mr. Commissioner Lynch says, "This action was a gross breach of our rules," can you expect the Committee to go behind that?—I say there is no rule. I will tell you what Mr. Commissioner Lynch refers to as the rule, but I say it is not a rule.

6116. What do you call it?—He says that, in the margin of the agreement, as printed for other estates, there is a note that if the judicial rent has been fixed it should be so stated; it should be stated there.

6117. Your answers go to this: that Mr. Commissioner Lynch does not understand his own rule, and in his judgment he made a very unjust accusation against you?—No, that is not what I say; I say there is no rule of the Land Commissioners upon the subject.

6118. That Mr. Commissioner Lynch says that there is a rule?—I am explaining what he means by a rule, as he explained it himself, and as Mr. O'Brien has explained it in his evidence; there is a note in the margin of the document in the agreements on other estates.

6119. At any rate, you have now represented to the Committee that this action of yours was owing to the operation of your mind; was that so?—Yes, quite so; the instructions that I had were, that I was not to sell upon the judicial rents.

6120. But you had no direction from your company telling you to put this other rental in the form sent up to the Commissioners?—Nothing, except the general instruction that I was not to sell upon judicial rents.

6121. Whether it was of your own motion or in accordance with the direction of your company, the action you took, at all events, apart from all this matter about the rules, was described by Mr. Commissioner Lynch as a most improper action?—He so described it.

6122. Do you ask the Committee to go behind that, and to believe Mr. Commissioner Lynch was under a delusion?—I cannot say he was under a delusion.

6123. If he was not under a delusion, what is your explanation; I do not want to press you, but I want to have it clear?—I should like you to have it perfectly clear; I have nothing to conceal.

6124. You have made some strong remarks upon Mr. O'Brien's evidence and upon the Land Commissioners; I want to know if you can go beyond this; that you adopted a course of action which the head of the court described as most improper?—I could not restrain him from doing that; but allow me to say that in doing that it is imputed I did so for a purpose.

6125. No, he does not say so; nor does it much concern this Committee; what we want to know is whether you have anything to say in answer to these very strong words, to the effect that your course of action was a most improper one; "It was a course which the solicitors should have refused to follow at the suggestion of their clients, and they should never have allowed tenants, many of them illiterate, to verify these agreements, which it now appears are false in this material respect"; that is very strong language, is it not?—It is. I do not agree with the language.

6126. But you do not give us any reasons for thinking that the language is over coloured; do you deny that the tenants were illiterate?—Some of them were; but it was explained to them in every

Chairman—continued.

every case by the magistrate whom they went before. I explained these formerly myself.

6127. The Committee have now, I presume, heard all you have to say in answer to this language of Mr. Commissioner Lynch, and the Committee must form their own conclusion?—There is just one matter that I wish to mention with regard to that. As I stated at the beginning, when Mr. O'Brien came down in 1889, I had prepared the statement that is before the Committee with regard to these cases. I told Mr. O'Brien what had been going on and what I was prepared to show in that statement that I had prepared, in order to submit along with these agreements for his inspection; all that matter is brought fully out in that statement. I thought that when I was filling in the column with the rent of 1882, if I handed that statement in at the same time I had given every information to the Land Commission that I possibly could.

6128. There is a third defect which Mr. Commissioner Lynch pointed out in your action, and it is this: that you not only exercise undue influence, you not only omitted or concealed the judicial rents, but you also included in the purchase-money arrears and costs of which the tenants held receipts; he complains that the purchase-money was made up in that irregular and indefensible manner; what is your answer to that?—The answer is first that in no case were the costs added.

6129. Were arrears included?—A small part of the arrears was included, and I have a statement here showing in every case what they were. I mean the statement that I had prepared to hand to the Land Commission; that showed in every case what amount of arrears were added and what arrears were forgiven.

6130. You admit then the inclusion of arrears did take place in some cases?—Yes.

6131. You admit that irregularity?—I do not admit it as an irregularity, but as a fact.

6132. Surely it is an irregularity?—No; because in many cases which Mr. Commissioner Lynch has sanctioned, arrears have been added. Mr. Commissioner Lynch has on more than one occasion said he did not mind the arrears being added if the holding was security for the money advanced.

6133. Anyhow Mr. Commissioner Lynch thought it misleading?—At that time he did; but I think he thinks differently now; I know he has said so.

6134. We do not know his mind now; you are not here to give evidence about Mr. Commissioner Lynch's mind?—I am speaking about what I know to be the fact when I say that since that he has sanctioned cases in which arrears have been added.

6135. Do you think he has entirely gone back from the position he lays down here, that "it would be very prejudicial to the operation of the Purchase Acts in the north of Ireland that tenants should think that loans could be obtained under such circumstances" (that is to say, circumstances including arrears and so on) "to stave off the immediate peril of threatened eviction, or that landlords, agents, or solicitors should procure the signature of contracts by such means." Do you think he has gone back from that doctrine?—That is not what I was referring to immediately. What I referred to immediately was the addition of arrears as part of the purchase money.

6136. But he is giving here a reason why the inclusion of arrears is undesirable, because it is prejudicial to the security?—As a rule I do not think it is.

6137. It may prejudice it much or little; but surely you would not contend that it does not prejudice at all?—What I mean is that in the 400 and odd cases that have been sanctioned and passed, and the money paid to the Drapers' Company, I think, if all sums for arrears had been added, it would not in the slightest degree have prejudiced the security.

6138. That is to say the greater the debt the better the security?—I do not put it that way.

6139. It comes to that, does it not?—No. The security was so ample and the margin so good, that a small sum added of a few pounds did not prejudice it in any degree.

Mr. Sexton.

6140. It diminished the margin?—Yes; but the margin was so good in the cases referred to that it could not have possibly touched the value of the security.

Sir William Marriott.

6141. It diminished the margin but it did not make it insecure?—Quite so.

Chairman.

6142. To come to another point; you wrote a letter from Magherafelt on the 20th of June 1889, which you referred to, and which is printed as Appendix Paper, No. 17?—Yes.

6143. In that you say, "For some time past it has been apparent to the company that a number of tenants on these divisions" (that is the Brackaslievegallion and Ballynascreen divisions) "of the estate have combined to withstand the payment of rent, and being determined not to yield to an illegal combination of this kind, the company have been compelled to take proceedings at law in many cases." Have you any evidence at all that there was an illegal combination?—I have.

6144. Mr. O'Brien said, as you are aware, that he did "not think there was anything like a combination among the tenantry." He says, in answer to Question 1101, "They are scattered over a great extent of country; I suppose it is 20 miles from one end of the estate to the other. It is a very rugged and mountainous country; the circumstances of the tenants are such that some are well off and some excessively poor. My impression from conversations with the tenants, from the facts and documents presented to me, would show me that there was nothing like combination." What was your evidence that there was combination?—My evidence that there was combination was that in December 1886 by probably about 180 tenants on the estate the plan of campaign was adopted.

6145. What did they do?—They adopted the plan of campaign.

6146. That is a phrase; what did they actually do?—They held meetings, and appointed trustees,

Chairman—continued.

trustees, and paid in money, if the newspaper reports be correct, which I believe they were.

6147. What money; had they not a right to pay in money if they pleased?—Yes.

6148. The mere payment of money to a fund for any object is not the plan of campaign?—It is called the plan of campaign in the reports of the papers.

6149. We want you to tell us why you thought there was an illegal combination; where is the illegality?—I am not saying it was illegal or legal; I am saying it was a combination.

6150. You said it was an illegal combination in your letter here?—Yes.

6151. Where was the illegality?—The plan of campaign was declared to be illegal, I take it.

6152. First of all you have not shown it was what was called the plan of campaign?—I have a little more to say upon that point; I would rather not do so, but I will say it if you wish. If you do not wish it I will not, because I do not wish to do so.

6153. I do not want to carry it further; you said in that letter that there was an illegal combination, and Mr. O'Brien says there was not?—I say there was. I have other reasons for knowing it.

6154. Was there such evidence before you of the illegality of the combination as to make that a ground for rescinding?—It was one of the grounds upon which the company came to the conclusion that they would rescind.

Mr. *Healy*.

6155. I would like to ask a few questions with regard to the Salters' estate: were you acting for a time for the Salters' estate?—I acted for 17 years as local solicitor for the Salters' Company.

6156. Have you had anything to do with the Mercers' Company's estate?—Yes, I have had a little.

6157. Did you meet *Lord Selborne* on the Mercers' estate?—I did.

6158. What brought Lord Selborne over to Ireland?—Lord Selborne and a deputation of the Mercers' Company came to Ireland in 1867, I think, to settle the rents of the estate for the next 21 years.

6159. Was that in consequence of an enormous increase that was proposed to be put on the Mercers' estate?—There was a revaluation at the time, and the tenants were disputing the amount of the rents that were asked to be put on for the next 21 years.

6160. In other words, Lord Selborne came over to compel the tenants to pay these enormous rents?—I should not like to say that. Lord Selborne stayed at the principal town of the company for two weeks, and ultimately Lord Selborne made a proposition to the solicitors and other representatives of the tenants which they adopted. That proposition did reduce the valuation considerably.

6161. The operation, as I understand, was this; first the company demanded an enormous increase from the tenants; the tenants refused to pay, and Lord Selborne came over and gave some abatement in that enormous increase?—Yes.

6162. Then under the Land Act what became

Mr. *Healy*—continued.

of the rents which were fixed by Lord Selborne?—A great number of tenants went into the Land Court under the Act of 1881, and a good many signed the form of agreements, No. 33 agreement, under the Act of 1881, and ultimately there was a considerable reduction of course.

6163. That is to say the rents Lord Selborne compelled the tenants to pay without protection, the moment the tenants had protection, the Mercers' Company reduced even by agreement?—They were reduced.

6164. We have heard a great deal about benefactions and donations; can you state whether a number of benefactions and donations have been donations to the Irish Church Sustentation Fund, taking first the Mercers' Company?—The Mercers' Company subscribed very largely to the Irish Church Funds, very generously.

6165. Do you know how much?—From memory I cannot say, I know they give very generously to the church; they built the church and have endowed the church, that is to say, they have paid largely into the sustentation fund, and have endowed the rector.

6166. Have they also subscribed to the Emergency Association?—I do not know that.

6167. Or to any of the landlords' associations?—I do not happen to know.

6168. Coming to the Salters' Company, you say you acted as solicitor for the Salters?—Yes.

6169. Did you also act as solicitor for any of the tenants upon the Salters' estate?—No, not until the last two years.

6170. Did you complete the sale, or assist to complete the sale, as between the Salters' tenants and the Salters' Company?—No, I took no part in the sale of the Salters' estate at all.

6171. Do you approve of a solicitor acting for both parties, in a transaction like that for the tenants, and for the company?—No.

6172. You think that the tenants should have the protection of an independent solicitor?—Certainly.

6173. With regard to the Skinners' Company's benefactions, did you hear the evidence given by Mr. Saunders the other day?—Yes, I was in the room when Mr. Saunders was examined. He is a member of the Skinners' Company.

6174. Do you know anything with regard to this question of the purchase of tithe rent-charges; can you explain it to the Committee?—I know that the company's estates paid a large tithe rent-charge prior to the Church Act of 1869, and after the Church Act of 1869 these large sums generally speaking under one of the sections of the Church Act of 1869 became a fixed annual instalment for 52 years, and the purchasing up of those has come to very large sums, for instance the Salters' Company would probably come to 16,000 *l.* and the Drapers would come to 14,000 *l.*

6175. Who got these sums of money?—The first thing was that the rector and curate, or Church officials, got a life estate out of the money.

6176. And then?—Then the balance would go, I suppose, to the good of the country.

6177. How

Mr. *Healy*—continued.

6177. How did the balance go?—I believe the balance is partly now the Church surplus.

6178. And then also figures, I presume, among the benefactions and donations of these companies?—Yes. Of course this was a legal charge under the Act of 1st Victoria, when landlords undertook the payment of tithes, and saddled the tithes upon their estates, in order to put an end to, what was then called, the tithe war.

6179. This tithe business is a purely illusory benefaction, is it not, though it figures among the donations?—The tithe question was a very substantial thing for the Church, and for the members of the Church; they got enormous sums of the money paid under the Act of 1869; enormous sums were paid to persons.

6180. That was a transaction purely between the Episcopal Church and the companies, was it not?—Yes.

6181. The general body of Protestants and Catholics benefited in no way?—They got no benefit.

6182. May I ask, did you read the evidence of the Reverend Father Quinn given here?—No.

6183. He drew a very unfavourable comparison between your company (the Drapers) and the Salters?—I did not read the evidence. In what respect?

6184. He suggested that the Salters' Company had acted liberally in quitting the country, and that the Drapers had acted niggardly?—In the first place, the Drapers have not quitted the country; but I do not think the Salters' Company have acted liberally.

6185. If the Catholic clergyman on the spot thinks the Salters' Company have acted more liberally than the Drapers, and you say the Salters have acted illiberally, what is the conclusion?—I am glad to hear he was pleased.

6186. It is only comparative pleasure?—Yes, quite so; but I should think, if they had quadrupled the Catholic clergyman's grant, he might not have been pleased after all; he had not much to be pleased for.

6187. But he says he got more from the Salters' than from the Drapers' Company?—The Drapers have not finished up yet; there is a good time coming.

6188. I abstain from asking any question as to the Drapers' estate, because I feel it is difficult for me to do so, with the exception of this one question. The evidence Sir William Conyngham gave before the Cowper Commission was, as I understand, that the Brackaghslievegallion division was a poor division, and was far less able to pay 18 years' purchase than the Moneymore division?—I never read his evidence; but I know them for 30 years, professionally from my own knowledge, and a large part of the Brackaghslievegallion division is very good land, and the tenants are very prosperous people.

6189. You do not agree with Sir William Conyngham?—Part of it is poor, and part is not; but, as a whole, it is not poor.

Mr. *John Ellis*.

6190. To take you back to the commencement of your evidence, I want you to explain a little more particularly, if you can, why you, as the solicitor or agent of the company, were not aware that those agreements for sale or judicial rents had not been filed; how came you to be ignorant of that?—It was a matter done by the agent altogether; it did not come into the solicitors' office. The agent had the forms printed, and had them filled in in his own office, and kept them there. I heard from time to time from him that such things had been done; and knowing from him that they had been done, I assumed that the thing was legally completed; but it was no part of my duty to make inquiry, further than a casual conversation to learn that that had been done; it was not my duty to register them, or anything of that sort.

6191. Did it not occur to you, or were not you aware, that possibly negotiations for sale and purchase might come on?—It was not thought at that time. It was in 1885 that the tenants came with a deputation representing all the different parts of the estate, to the Company in London; and, I think, the deputation was repeated.

6192. Then I am to take it from you, that you considered it no part of your business to know what the real rents of the property were?—No. I was handed the rental and I knew that was the rental settled in 1883, with a reduction of 15 per cent., and some had got indorsements upon the lease. I know because I prepared the indorsements upon the lease for any of those that took that course. I did not see the agreements. I knew there were a bundle of agreements.

6193. You did not think it part of your duty to inform yourself as to what had been the action of the tenants as regards the Land Commissioners' rents?—I assumed they were all right from what had passed.

6194. I wish to refer to a statement made by Mr. O'Brien, which perhaps you have not noticed. In his report, dated the 6th of May 1889, at the bottom of page 2 of Appendix Paper, No. 27, he says, "I desire to draw particular attention to the contracts Nos. 2422 and 2323;" and then he draws attention to these particulars, that the first contract purports to have been signed in your presence by a person who has been absent in America for many years; have you any explanation to give as to that?—Yes. That was the case of Patrick Kane; Patrick Kane had been four years in America, and his wife was living upon the land. She came into my office with a letter dated, I think, in December 1884 or 1885 (I have not the exact date here, but I have taken it down upon my books), directing her to come in and sign an agreement to purchase, and authorising her to sign any document that would be necessary to carry that out. I read that letter as an authority, and in fact as a power of attorney from the husband to the wife to do that, and I said to her, "I think this is perfectly good, and you may sign this if you wish." Mr. O'Brien had heard that the husband was in America, and he did not look for this letter, and he referred to that in the report.

6195. But was the name of Patrick Kane appended to that agreement, 2323?—It was. She signed by the authority of this letter, "Patrick Kane," and I thought she was perfectly justified in doing that.

Mr. *John Ellis*—continued.

6196. The woman signed "Patrick Kane;" she did not sign in her own name as, for Patrick Kane?—As the attorney for Patrick Kane.

6197. Did she say "as attorney"?—No; but she had a letter of authority which I regarded as a power of attorney.

6198. Did she put the words "Patrick Kane"?—She did.

6199. Then with regard to the next agreement, what explanation have you to make with regard to that, No. [illegible]?—That is the case of Rose M'Bride. I happened to be from home. She was an old bedridden woman confined to her bed and unable to come out, I understand. I was not present, but I will tell you what I was informed, that the son came in and said, "My mother wants to purchase," and the agreement was either drawn up in the office or by some solicitor, and he took and signed it. Whether he signed "Rose M'Bride" or his own name I cannot tell. I never heard of it, and never thought of it till it was noticed in that report.

6200. Was it signed in your office?—No. It was signed before whoever the magistrate was.

6201. At all events, if it states it was signed "in the presence of A. W. Glover, witness," A. W. Glover was not there as a witness?—I am not A. W. Glover.

6202. Who is A. W. Glover?—He is a son of mine.

6203. Was A. W. Glover present as a witness when this was signed?—I do not know; I believe he was; that is my belief; but I was not in the office at the time, and I did not hear of it or know about it till the matter was challenged in Mr. O'Brien's report.

6204. That is the explanation you desire to give?—Yes.

6205. Then with regard to delay; will you kindly refer a little more particularly than you did in your previous evidence, to the section of the Statute of 1887, which you said required a large amount of work to be done all over again?—I think you will find it is from Section 17 to Section 20 inclusive.

6206. Then you suggest, with reference to the interest charged, that the company charged a lower rate much than the tenant would be paying to the Land Purchase Commission?—Yes.

6207. But you will be aware, of course, that the instalment that they would pay at 4 per cent. would include the purchase instalment?—Yes.

6208. Had you forgotten that?—No; and I do not think the tenants forgot that either.

6209. That is not likely?—They were very well pleased indeed to get 14 years or two years and four months at 3½ per cent., and did not think they were hurt either. I know they did not.

6210. May I suggest to you that the rate of interest, so far as it is interest, and not purchase-instalments, would be about the same?—Yes, the rate of interest would be the same; of course, the redemption would make the difference. The 4 per cent., of course, would have been redemption.

6211. Is it quite fair to suggest that the tenants would be paying less interest to your company than they would be paying to the Land Purchase Commission?—No, not less interest; but paying altogether very much less.

6212. But paying something which was not interest?—If I confused that, I did not intend to do that. That would not be right.

6213. Have you Paper No. [illegible], Mr. Commissioner Lynch's judgment?—Yes.

6214. At the bottom of page 1 he mentions a sum of 6,220 *l.* received in cash from the tenants; can you divide that 6,270 *l.* up into interest, arrears, and costs?—I do not think there were any costs in that.

6215. What would be the proportion of arrears?—The proportion of arrears in that would be (I shall have to give it from memory) about 1,600 *l.*, in round numbers.

6216. Then you mentioned a memorial from the tenants; how did that arise?—I will explain that. The tenants got greatly alarmed at the idea that the purchases were going to be off, when the company said to Mr. Commissioner Lynch, "We will not allow you to dictate to us, and to say we are not to receive rent or interest, and the purchase is now off; if these tenants wish to retire from the purchase we are quite satisfied." They got greatly alarmed at this, and they held meetings over the estate, and they got two or three clergymen to attend these meetings. At these meetings they prepared this memorial and had it adopted, and they sent a deputation to Dublin with this memorial. Prior to going to Dublin they served upon me a copy, to give me notice of what was going on.

6217. Do you suggest, then, that that was entirely spontaneous on the part of the tenants?—Entirely; the company had nothing to do with it.

6218. Who framed the memorial?—I do not know.

6219. You knew nothing about it till you received it?—Till I got the memorial I had nothing to do with it.

6220. Then the expression used in that memorial about the extremely liberal treatment of the tenants by the company arose, I understand from you, spontaneously?—We had nothing whatever to do with it.

6221. In these cases of Johnston, Crosbie, and M'Cullough, that you put in, does the word "rent" there mean judicial rent?—No; there was no judicial rent. That was the rent of 1872.

6222. It does not mean the rent you fixed afterwards?—There was no rent fixed afterwards. As I explained to you, only 260 tenants out of the 1,100 went into court in violation of their agreements.

6223. I see Mrs. Johnston paid 68 *l.* 13 *s.* into court, and she owed in the shape of rent 63 *l.* 15 *s.*?—Yes.

6224. Therefore, you got from her everything she owed in the shape of rent, and a little more; it was only the interest she did not pay?—Yes; but we afterwards made a very large abatement of the amount she owed for the interest; we took a very small sum.

6225. You received every penny, and rather more?—I should think not more.

6226. According

Mr. *John Ellis*—continued.

6226. According to your statement she owed for rent 63 *l.* 15 *s.*, and she paid into court 66 *l.* 15 *s.*; therefore you did receive 3 *l.* more than she owed for rent, according to the statement?—No; in the statement I give her credit for 15 per cent. off after the 1885 rent. I should have mentioned that in 1886 and 1887 the company said: "Notwithstanding we have reduced the rent 15 per cent. all round on the leases, we will give all the tenants who are allowed to pay arrears 15 per cent. more." That was 30 per cent.; and, in making the statement, I give her credit for that additional 15 per cent. I think you will find that would make the difference.

6227. That explanation does not affect the figures; you state that she owed, at the 1st November 1885, 63 *l.* 15 *s.*; you also state she paid into court 66 *l.* 15 *s.*, therefore, she did pay something more than the rent, according to this statement?—My calculation must have been made on giving her allowance of the percentage of the rent.

6228. You mean she did owe more than 63 *l.* 15 *s.*?—She did.

6229. Then to that extent this paper is inaccurate?—I made the reduction of the 15 per cent. She would have legally owed more.

6230. Then I am to take it this paper does not quite disclose all what you consider legal claims against the tenants?—It would have been much more if I had made it out.

Mr. *Lea*.

6231. Have you got that case you submitted to Sir George Jessel there?—Yes.

6232. At whose instance was that taken?—I stated that I think Mr. John Matthews, the chairman, of Coleraine, and Mr. Daniel Taylor.

6233. On behalf of the tenants of the Clothworkers' estate?—They employed me. It stated so on the face of it.

6234. Who employed you?—Mr. Taylor and Mr. Matthews.

6235. Was the opinion taken in consequence of the sale of the Clothworkers' estate?—It was in consequence of the pending sale. The sale was not then completed.

6236. Because the tenants wanted to buy instead of Sir Hervey Bruce?—Quite so.

6237. Was it taken quickly in consequence?—It was; Mr. Taylor and Mr. Matthews came over to London, and I came with them.

6238. What time did you reach London?—I gave this case to Sir George Jessel on 28th April 1871.

6239. When did you receive it back?—He has written a date upon it, 1st May 1871.

6240. Did you see Sir George Jessel with it?—I did, twice, with Mr. Taylor.

6241. How long was it between the two visits?—I saw him on 28th April; that is the day I gave it him, and I handed him all the documents, and he wrote to me a letter, saying that he wished to see me again at his own house. I believe it is contrary to the practice of the English Bar, but I had a letter of introduction from a gentleman in London, and I explained to him the Irish practice was different.

6242. Was it hurriedly, in the morning, that you saw him?—In the evening I saw him on

Mr. *Lea*—continued.

both occasions; I spent two long evenings with him.

6243. Was it the same case that you submitted to Mr. Law?—The same case, copied exactly.

6244. You got up the case?—Yes, I did.

6245. It was in the early days of the movement with regard to the London companies?—There was a good deal of movement before that, but this brought up the question of sale; it was the first for some years that brought up the question of sale; the one preceding that was the Grocers', which was sold in the Landed Estates Court; that was in 1854 or 1856.

6246. Of course, the opinion of counsel depends on the case put before him?—Quite.

6247. How many documents did you put before Sir George Jessel?—He had the whole.

Chairman.

6248. If the Witness will put in the whole case submitted to Sir George Jessel it will save this examination?—This is the whole case, but the documents submitted along with that were the entire proceedings in the Skinners' Company and the Irish Society, a very large book.

Mr. *Lea*.

6249. The case was stated upon eight or 10 documents?—I left with him and he read very carefully the whole of the proceedings in the Skinners' Company and the Irish Society. He had a copy of the deed from the Irish Society, and the Clothworkers' Society.

6250. Were "motives and reasons" put in?—The "motives and reasons" are printed in the proceedings of the Skinners' Company, and the Irish Society. (*The case was handed in*).

6251. When was the case submitted to Mr. Law?—I went back straight to Dublin with that case, and prepared the case and had it submitted. It was in the month of May 1871.

6252. In the same haste?—Yes, there was great pressure to have the opinion immediately of course.

6253. Was Mr. Law in Dublin at the time?—He was.

6254. Who paid for the opinion; was it Mr. Taylor?—Mr. Taylor gave me the money.

6255. Was there a public subscription for it, do you know?—I believe there was a subscription, but whether Mr. Taylor advanced the money I could not say.

6256. The object was, to prevent the sale of the estate away from the Clothworkers' tenants?—Mr. Taylor and Matthews, representing the tenants, offered I think, 25,000 *l.* more to the company.

6257. We know the circumstances?—It was to know when the company refused to sell to them at all, whether they could compel them.

6258. You were acting for the tenants?—I was acting for Mr. Taylor and Mr. Matthews. They were acting on behalf of the tenants.

6259. Then you acted for the Drapers' estate. The Irish Society joined in the title given to the tenants?—They executed a separate deed of release, releasing the timber, stone, and minerals.

Mr. *Lea*—continued.

6260. If the companies were absolute owners in fee, would it be necessary or usual for the Irish Society or anybody else, to join in the conveyance?—That is a mere legal question, which I should think a solicitor could hardly answer. I am afraid my answer on that would be worse than some others.

Mr. *Sexton.*

6261. There is a manifest point of some importance in the question?—Yes, but I do not think a solicitor could answer that.

6262. Could not you say as a solicitor, whether the fact that the Irish Society had to join in the conveyance with the company, does not indicate a peculiar relation of the company to the estate, and not the ordinary relation of an owner?—Mr. Commissioner Lynch thought that they could not give the fee simple without the re-lease.

6263. Then it is a peculiar relation?—It is a very peculiar relation certainly. That is the reason he lectured on it.

Mr. *T. M. Healy.*] It is even stronger than the language of Mr. Commissioner Lynch, who is only a solicitor himself. It was the examiners of titles who were two barristers.

Chairman.] They advised the Land Commissioners they must take this re-lease.

Mr. *T. M. Healy.*] Yes.

Mr. *Lea.*

6264. Coming back for one moment to the opinion of Sir George Jessel and Mr. Law, I think you went into the case of the Skinners' Company and the Irish estate?—Yes.

6265. Do you remember Sir William Follett's opinion with regard to that. I will read the words to you: "I cannot distinguish between one property and the other; if there be a public trust on one there is on the other also"?—That was the Rolls judgment in the Skinners' Company and the Irish Society.

6266. Certainly?—Yes, I remember reading that.

6267. Then Sir William Follett's opinion may be safely put against that of Sir George Jessel or Mr. Law?—Yes.

6268. You are a tenant of the Salters' Company, are not you?—Yes.

6269. Have you ever expressed an opinion with regard to the action of the Salters' Company?—Several times.

6270. Did you write to Mr. Spotswood some years ago?—Yes; I had a long correspondence with Mr. Spotswood some years ago.

6271. Did you charge him, or did you charge the company, with ruining the town of Magherafelt?—I charged him with doing great injury to it by increasing the rents.

6272. And also refusing leases?—Yes.

6273. Did you say to him this: that "The London companies have, one and all, by their refusal to grant perpetuity leases, or for long terms, reduced their towns to petty villages, and prevented merchants from investing money on their estates in the introduction of manufactures?"—Yes; that referred to the Salters' more particularly.

6274. Then did you charge them with manufacturing industries being almost unknown on their estates?—Yes.

6275. "And capital and skilled labour are being transferred to districts where they are beyond the reach of landlords who, being wealthy corporations, non-residents, and uninformed as to the claims, character, and means of their tenants, choose to dictate terms and rules of management?"—Yes; and I told the Salters' Company they were doing themselves and the tenants in Magherafelt a great injury by not giving perpetuity leases, and that the people who had capital went away; I know they did.

6276. Did you tell him also that the Knocklougbrim Flax and Tow Spinning Company, Limited, established on the very borders of their estate, was to have been established at Magherafelt if they had given a long lease?—So it would.

6277. Would the capital of that company then have been 50,000 *l.* to 100,000 *l.*?—Yes, that was the nominal capital.

6278. "But the feeling of insecurity was such that every person shrank from it at first mention." Then did you also say, with regard to the Salters' Company, "I fear the reports from time to time presented to the Court by the deputations who come over here for a few days at midsummer, and who gather information from the few gentlemen who have the honour of dining with them at the Manor House, are not calculated to lead the company to a proper knowledge of either the people or the estate?"—I did, and I thought so.

6279. Did you say: "In any other country, except Ireland, and in any other business or calling of life, the men who by their labour produced such a change, would get the benefit of it to all time"?—I think so.

6280. Did you also say that the inference from the action of the company was, that they intended to charge people on their own outlay?—Yes, so they did.

6281. And you said a good many more things of that sort, and you still believe that is true of the companies?—I do.

6282. Then did you say: "It is painful to mention that the executors of Mr. Adams, who was a faithful public servant here, and held in high esteem, had not, owing to the new rule of the estate, the means of paying his debts, and that his creditors, who had lent him money on faith of the good old custom, had to take 6 *s.* 8 *d.* in the pound on amount due them." Yes, I remember that case.

6283. That was because the Salters' Company destroyed the custom of the estate, his creditors were willing to accept 6 *s.* 8 *d.* in the pound?—Quite so; I know the circumstances and the fact.

6284. You say that, though you are legal agent for the Drapers' Company, and knowing the district and the customs of the district thoroughly?—I say that, knowing the town of Magherafelt for 18 years, and living in it.

6285. So

Mr. T. M. Healy.

6285. Do you say that the tenants on this estate have bought out their own improvements in the town of Magherafelt?—I say they have.

6286. You say they have purchased their own improvements?—The town of Magherafelt was built by the tenants, except a few houses which the Drapers' Company built on the estate. I can tell you my own case.

6287. On the Salters' estate have you purchased your own house?—No, I have not.

6288. Do I understand that you built your own house, and that they are insisting you shall pay for it?—I purchased my own house, and expended 800 *l.* upon it, and gave the company the particulars of that expenditure of 800 *l.*, and notwithstanding that, they raised my rent on notice to quit to 80 *l.*, and ask me to buy on the 80 *l.* now.

6289. They have asked you to purchase your own improvements?—Yes.

Mr. Sexton.

6290. Are you in a position to answer the general question: do you affirm the statements in these letters; do you still adhere to those letters?—I do. There is nothing in those but facts.

6291. Will you put them in?—I have no objection. (*The letters were handed in.*)

Chairman.

6292. Do you know this pamphlet (*handing pamphlet to Witness*)?—Yes.

6293. What is the date of it?—It is dated in 1868.

6294. Was that in any way composed as a sequel to these letters?—No, not as a sequel. You will see at the end of it the correspondence. I think the letters are subsequent to that.

6295. There is a letter here from you?—Yes.

6296. There is nothing in this pamphlet that is now material to the inquiry before the Committee?—No, I think not now.

6297. Have we got the memorial of the Magherafelt people in 1867?—Yes, I think you have. It is printed.

Mr. WILLIAM PHILLIPS SAWYER, sworn; and Examined.

Sir William Marriott.

6298. YOU are the clerk of the Drapers' Company, and have been so for how many years?—Twenty years.

6299.—You are acquainted with the circumstances under which they acquired their Irish estates, and with the system under which it has been managed?—I am.

6300. Have you any return to put in with regard to them?—I have a return here showing how the estate was let previous to 1817, when the company took the management of it into their own hands. On the 7th March 1627 the estate was let to Peter Barker, of Ballylmstren, in the county of Antrim, for a term of 60 years, at a rent of 600 *l.* and on payment of a fine of 340 *l.* This lease was surrendered. On the 23rd March 1633 the estate was let to Sir Joseph Clotworthy for a term of 61 years, at a rent of 800 *l.* The consideration included the surrender of the previous lease. On the 15th August 1644 the estate was let to Mary Clotworthy and others for a term of 48 years, at a rent of 800 *l.* The consideration included the surrender of the previous lease. On the 3rd June 1673 the estate was let to Clotworthy Upton for a term of 46 years from All Saints 1705, at a rent of 800 *l.*; the consideration being 3,000 *l.* On the 24th March 1729 the estate was let to William Rowley for a term of 30 years from All Saints 1751, at a rent of 440 *l.*; the consideration being 1,000 *l.* And on the 13th May 1756 the estate was let to Sir William Rowley for the term of three lives, or 61 years, at a rent of 600 *l.*; the consideration being 6,753 *l.*

6301. Have you any other return to put in?—I have a statement here showing the agricultural rental of the estate in 1817, and the agricultural rental in 1885. The agricultural rental in 1817 was 9,000 *l.*, to which is to be added the tithe, 833 *l.*, making together, 9,833 *l.*, and the agricultural rental in 1885 was 10,830 *l.*

6302. Have you any other return?—I have made out a return in pursuance of what I understood to be the wish expressed by the Chairman of the Committee at the last meeting, of the receipts and expenditure on account of the estate for 15 years from 1875 to 1889 (*same handed in*).

Mr. John Ellis.

6303. Is that arranged under heads?—Under the heads the Chairman named.

Sir William Marriott.

6304. Are those all the returns you have?—Yes.

6305. Can you say what have been the relations between the company and their tenants generally?—Their relations for a very long series of years were most friendly; the rents were most punctually paid and the company had no difficulties with their tenants of any kind.

6306. Have they had any difficulties recently?—During the last few years they have.

3607. With regard to the Roman Catholic tenants, have the company behaved in any way niggardly to them?—The wish of the company has been to treat the tenants with perfect equality, without any regard to religious denominations.

3608. I will not take you now into the questions that Mr. Glover answered, but you heard his evidence with regard to the sale of the land; do you confirm that?—I heard Mr. Glover rather imperfectly, but I think, I may say that I confirm all he said. I should like to allude, if you will allow me to one point, namely, the filling

Sir William Marriott—continued.

up of the agreements, as I fear there may be some misunderstanding in the minds of the Committee with regards to that. There was no consultation between Mr. Glover and the company as regards the mode in which the agreements should be filled up. General instructions were given to Mr. Glover to carry out the sale, but not as regards the filling up of any particular document.

Mr. *Sexton.*

6309. He had no suggestion or authority from you to insert in the agreement of purchase and sale any rent other than the rent actually payable at the time?—None whatever.

Sir William Marriott.

6310. Have you anything else you would like to add?—There are one or two questions I should like to refer to. In answer to Question 1098, Mr. O'Brien states that the Land Commission interfered to prevent the giving by the tenants of the Drapers Company of promissory notes for arrears of rent. I wish to contradict that statement.

Chairman.

6311. Does Mr. O'Brien say that? He is asked, "A number of them gave bills to the company did they not?" and he answers, "The Land Commission were able to stop that proceeding"?—I say the Land Commission did not stop that proceeding.

Mr. *T. M. Healy.*] I think he referred to some other company.

Chairman.

6312. The next question was, "Was there not left over a number of the bills," and he answers, "Not on that estate"?—The impression made on the minds of most people would be that the Land Commission interfered in the case of the Drapers Company's estate.

Mr. *T. M. Healy.*

6313. That was not the impression made on my mind?—As long as it is understood that there was no such interference, I am content.

6314. Mr. O'Brien made it distinctly clear that he was not referring in that respect to the Drapers' Company?—There is one other answer given by Mr. O'Brien, No. 1136. He suggests that the company have declined to give long leases of land in Moneymore. So far as I am aware there has been no such action on the part of the company. In Draperstown they have granted long leases of land, and I believe they would have done so in Moneymore had they been applied to. Then I should like to refer to Question 4736, in the evidence of the Rev. Joseph Quin. Mr. Quin states that the Drapers' Company fixed the purchase-money on the rent instead of on the Government valuation, on the ground that the rent was higher than the valuation. The Government valuation of the lands alone was, I believe in every case lower than the rent; certainly in the aggregate it was from five to six per cent. lower.

Sir William Marriott.

6315. Is there any other point you wish to call attention to?—There is one other point. The Chairman, in his questions to Mr. Glover, seemed to suggest that the company's tenants were forced to buy, in order to relieve themselves of proceedings for the recovery of arrears of rent. It should be stated, that the company offered any tenant who was in arrear in his rent, an opportunity of paying the arrears by instalments, spread over a term of years, or to allow the arrear of rent to remain as a debt on the holding, the tenant paying interest on it at 4 per cent. per annum, so long as he chose to allow the debt to remain.

Chairman.

6316. It was not my suggestion, it was Mr. Commissioner Lynch's assertion?—I rather thought it was your suggestion.

6317. Have you taken out, in your figures for the 15 years, from 1873 to 1888, what the average annual rental was?—I have not dealt with rental, I have dealt with actual receipts on account of rent.

6318. You gave us the rental for 1885, 10,450 *l.*—In my statement I give the actual receipts for each year.

Mr. *Sexton.*

6319. You have not given the rental in your statement?—No; I have not. I can take it out. I draw a distinction between rental and rent received.

Chairman.

6320. I want to have first the gross receipts; second, the cost of management; third, the annual expenditure on permanent improvements; fourth, the amount devoted to public objects in Ireland; and, fifth, the amount transferred to the general account in London. My friend Mr. Healy, I believe, has been appointed one of two arbitrators in connection with difficulties as to arrears, has not he?—Mr. Healy is acting for the tenants.

6321. When was this arbitration agreed to?—About six months ago, I should think.

6322. What was the reference to the arbitrators?—To deal with all questions relating to the arrears of rent.

6323. At that time the reference to arbitration was confined to arrears?—Yes.

6324. It has since then been extended, has not it?—It has not been formally extended, but the company has stated that if the arbitrators wish to call their attention to any particular case in which the terms of sale appear to the arbitrators excessive, they will be happy to consider the case.

6325. Then there has been a kind of extension of the reference submitted to these two gentlemen to the purchase as well as to the arrears?—To that extent there has been an extension of the reference.

6326. Have the arbitrators given any answer yet?—They have not.

6327. What were the points in connection with purchase that were specially submitted?—It was suggested to the company that in the course of the arbitration the arbitrators might meet with cases in which the terms of sale were oppressive

Chairman—continued.

oppressive or hard, and in those cases the company said, if their attention was called to them, they would be happy to consider the recommendation of the arbitrators.

Mr. *Lea*.

6328. When was it decided to refer these cases to the arbitrators?—About a month or six weeks ago, I should think.

6329. At all events, long since this Committee has been sitting?—Well, certainly, since last year, when I presume the Committee first began to sit.

6330. Why did you limit the accounts to 15 years?—I understood the Chairman to say that the accounts should extend over a period of 10 years.

Chairman.

6331. No, you are mistaken there. An account extending over a period of 10 years was submitted to us, and then I said, give us the average of the 10 years, but I never said that was sufficient?—I am quite prepared to put in an account from 1817 down to the present time.

Mr. *Lea*.

6332. The estate has been in your hands since 1817?—Yes, since 1817.

Chairman.

6333. I understand you to say that the agricultural rent in 1817 was 9,033 *l*., and in 1885 only 10,650 *l*.?—Yes.

Mr. *Sexton*.

6334. I suppose, in the meantime, you had suffered reduction under the Land Act. Were you reduced by the Land Act of 1881?—The company reduced their rents voluntarily in 1882. It has been the practice to let the farms on lease, and in 1881 leaseholds were excluded from the Land Act, but in 1882 the company voluntarily made them a reduction of 15 per cent., without regard to leases.

6335. Touching the point raised by the Chairman, he referred to the fact that the rental in 1817 was the lesser sum of 9,000 *l*. Can you give us the maximum figure the rental reached in between that period and this. It would be just before the Land Act of 1881 passed?—I should think in 1875; but you will understand I am only speaking from memory. The actual rental in 1876 was, in round figures, 14,500 *l*. a year. You must deduct from that the rental of the two towns which were producing no rent in 1817, and which have been built by the company. The rents of those two towns were about 2,000 *l*. a year, so that that would bring a maximum agricultural rental of 12,500 *l*. a year.

Chairman.

6336. Then will you put in the figures for the 60 years?—From 1817, or for 60 years?

6337. Sixty years will be sufficient, if you can get them more easily?—I will do so.

Mr. *Lea*.

6338. Sixty years is the fixed time?—The question arises whether it is to be 60 years to 1885, or to the present time. The Drapers' Company's sale began in 1885 or 1886.

Chairman.

6339. Why not put in all the figures from 1807 onward?—The circumstances have changed materially since the holdings began to be sold.

6340. Then will you put them in from 1817 to 1885?—Yes.

Mr. *Lea*.

6341. Did you get a memorial from the tenants, running after this fashion: "To the Worshipful the Drapers' Company. The memorial of the undersigned, humbly showeth, that having learned the disappointment felt on a neighbouring estate by the withdrawal of religious and educational grants subsequent to its sale, we, tenants on your worshipful company's property in County Derry, deeply anxious for the maintenance of religion and education in our midst, beg leave respectfully to approach your company, and to ask that you would kindly inform us what are your intentions with reference to the grants for religious and educational purposes heretofore given for our benefit by your worshipful company, and your memorialists will ever pray"?—I have some recollection of a memorial of that kind being sent.

6342. I have a copy of the names appended to it here, and I should judge, though I have not counted them, that there are something like 200 or 300?—Yes, the memorial I refer to was numerously signed.

6343. What reply was sent to that memorial?—The company have come to no decision whatever with regard to the mode in which they will deal with grants now made for religious, educational, and other charitable purposes on the estate.

6344. In some cases they have dropped continuing these grants?—In the case of grants made to individuals who have died since the sale of the estate has been in progress, the grants have not been paid to their successors. The object of the company being to leave themselves as free as possible from individual interests when they come to deal with the question later on.

6345. If a schoolmaster has changed, his successor is not receiving the grant?—Not at all. In the case of schools the grant has been continued, and is continued to the present day, except in the case of one school at [illegible], which was closed in consequence of the withdrawal of the pupils.

6346. In the case of the dispensaries at Draperstown, there were considerable complaints about them?—The company established dispensaries long before the passing of the Irish Medical Charities Act. They maintained two dispensaries, one in Moneymore and one in Draperstown. I suppose about 15 or 16 years ago the medical officer at Moneymore retired in consequence of great age, and the company gave him a pension. They did not continue their grant to his successor, he being paid under the Medical Charities Act. In the case of Draperstown the medical officer died, and his successor was a gentleman who has been referred to in the evidence, Dr. Hegarty. Dr. Hegarty applied to the Drapers' Company to be allowed to take the house in which his predecessor had lived, but his predecessor's widow pressed the company very strongly to allow her to remain in the house.

Mr. Lea—continued.

Her husband had lived in it a good many years; his father and grandfather had lived in it before him; and the company agreed to allow the widow to remain.

6347. Was this medical gentleman's predecessor in receipt of Poor Law union funds too?—When the Medical Charities Act was passed the company did not stop their grants to the dispensary doctors, so that for a time they were in receipt of payment under the Medical Charities Act, and also from the company.

6348. Would a successor to that gentleman probably purchase the practice with the idea that those grants would be continued?—I think he would be very imprudent to do so without making some inquiries on the point.

6349. It was part of the general scheme, I think I understood, to refuse continuance of those grants until the company had decided what to do with the money?—In the cases of the clergymen who had died since the sales had first started. In all other cases the grants have been continued.

6350. I think I understood you to say, in order that the company may have a free hand?—Exactly so. They do not want to be embarrassed with individual interests when they come to deal with this question later on.

6351. And can withdraw all the money if they wish?—They will deal with it as they think fit, no doubt.

Mr. John Ellis.

6352. Can you give us the reason of the company for enlarging this reference with regard to the purchase?—The company in dealing with the sale had to lay down a general rule to apply to all cases, and they believe that that general rule is a perfectly fair one; but of course amongst a tenantry of 900 or 1,000 strong there may be cases which it would be advisable to treat as exceptional.

6353. You think there may have been some exceptional cases?—There may have been, it is possible.

Mr. T. M. Healy.

6354. I understand you to say that the sales in 1885 and 1886 made a material difference in your accounts. They would naturally?—Naturally.

6355. Therefore I may assume this that you have sold, I may say, the greater portion of your estate?—In value the greater portion has been sold, but not probably in the number of tenants, about half, I think.

6356. Then I may take it after 1885 and 1886. Your rent and receipts naturally might be supposed to decline, from the fact that the payment of rent by the new purchasers would, of course, at once stop short?—The payment of rent by the purchasers stopped short. They subsequently paid interest on the purchase-money, but the company did not receive any purchase-money from the Land Commission for several years after 1885; not I think until last year.

6357. But my point is that the amount you would receive for interest would be a much less sum than you would have previously been receiving as rent?—Very much less.

Mr. T. M. Healy—continued.

6358. Then how do you explain that your receipts in 1888 were 3,789 *l*., and in 1889 they were 17,091 *l*.?—A very considerable sum was paid by purchasing tenants by way of interest on purchase-money in 1889. The purchases were then begun to be concluded, and the tenants paid up the interest on the purchase-money.

6359. They had been previously, I understand, in arrear, and in that year they paid up?—They paid up in order to conclude their purchases.

Mr. Sexton.

6360. Does this current or pending arbitration refer to the whole estate?—The arbitration was only intended to refer to tenants who proposed to purchase their holdings.

6361. And to refer in what sense to those tenants?—A tenant who does not propose to purchase his holding will, it is presumed, remain as a tenant. If he is dissatisfied with his rent he will get a fair rent fixed, and having got it fixed will pay it.

6362. What question did the deed of submission refer to the arbitrators?—It gave the arbitrators full power to deal with all arrears of rent.

6363. Upon the estate?—Yes; I really forget whether in the deed it was mentioned that only those tenants who proposed to purchase were included.

6364. Then in each case there are two elements, first the arrears, and second the question of purchase?—Yes.

6365. Does it not occur to you that the action of the arbitrators upon the question of arrears may be affected by their view of the course to be taken by the company in any particular case upon the question of purchase?—It is possible, but the arbitrators have full power to deal with all arrears irrespective of any other question.

6366. But suppose the arbitrators in any particular case make a proposition or suggestion to you upon the question of purchase in any particular case, does it not occur to you that their expectation that that suggestion will be adopted by you would govern their decision on the question of arrears in the same case?—I presume in such a case the arbitrators would give a provisional decision with regard to arrears; that is to say, that such-and-such an arrangement must be made with regard to arrears, supposing the tenant is allowed to purchase on such-and-such terms. It is a matter entirely within the discretion of the arbitrators.

6367. Is every tenant upon the estate now in a position to suppose that the decision of the arbitrators upon a joint question of arrears and purchase will be respected by the company?—The company have said that if the arbitrators should be of opinion that from exceptional causes the terms of sale should be modified in any particular case, the company will be very happy to consider the suggestion of the arbitrators in the matter.

6368. You must observe that your evidence is putting the two questions on a different footing, and that if the arbitrators come to a decision

so

Mr. Sexton—continued.

on the question of arrears on the faith that their decision on the question of purchase will be accepted, they may find their faith misplaced?—Then the company will, I am sure, give them an opportunity of revising their decision on the question of arrears.

6369. In any particular case in which their decision on the question of purchase might not be accepted?—Certainly.

6370. Do you think the tenants and others concerned may proceed in the general confidence that suggestions upon the question of purchase, as well as decisions on the question of arrears, will be accepted by the company?—The company have so said.

6371. I do not think we have yet had from any witness a specific statement of the purposes for which the London companies generally were founded?—I am not prepared to make a statement on a point so large as that at a moment's notice.

6372. Surely you have all a very clear understanding of it?—I daresay we have, but it is a matter of very ancient history, and I should not like to take upon myself to be the exponent of the views of the companies generally on such a point.

6373. You could not give us an accepted view as to the origin of your own company?—The matter has never been discussed in such a way in my own company as to justify me in attempting to express their corporate view upon it.

6374. Can you say whether it was founded mainly or partly with a view to purposes of public utility?—If you ask my own personal opinion on the point, I should say the evidence does not go to show it was founded mainly with such a view.

6375. What is your view then?—I think it was founded partly for religious, partly for trade, and partly for convivial purposes; so the evidence seems to show.

6376. Those are purposes of public utility and pleasure?—In that way, no doubt.

6377. Conviviality the purpose of pleasure, and religion and trade, the purposes of public utility?—I do not quite understand the nature of the question.

6378. You have given three objects to which you say these companies were devoted, conviviality, religion, and trade. I suggest to you that conviviality is a purpose of pleasure, and that the others are purposes of public utility?—I used the word "trade" rather in the sense of mutual advantage of the people who joined the company. They were traders banded together for their own protection and advantage.

6379. Was it not partly also with a view to the good of the community?—I do not find any evidence of that in the history of the company.

6380. Simply for the benefit of the members?—The mutual benefit of the members.

6381. How many members are there now in your company?—I could only tell you approximately, for the members consist of freemen and liverymen, and we have no record of the freemen; but I should say 1,500 or 1,600.

6382. How many are in the court?—Twenty-five.

6383. In what form, and at what times, do applications relating to your Irish estates come before the court?—They come forward at monthly meetings of the court.

6384. They do not come forward every month but casually?—A monthly meeting is held on a fixed day, and at that monthly meeting all outstanding business is taken up.

6385. Upon what principle do you act in granting or rejecting applications for aid to the public purposes in Ireland?—The company act on the same principle in Ireland as in England. They grant aid to such objects of public usefulness as appear to them to be most in need and deserving of it.

6386. In regard to Ireland they do not govern themselves, for instance, do they, by the consideration that they would not spend more than a certain proportion?—No.

6387. They are governed solely by the merit of the object?—Yes.

6388. Now I notice in this return of yours that whilst the income of your estate appears to have been growing, the grants for public purposes appear to have been diminishing. In the first year you have a gross income of 13,[illegible] l., that is for the year 1875, and on that year expenditure was 9,852 l. The receipts in this account appear to be exhausted. It gives everything you received from the Irish estate?—Yes.

6389. But the expenditure account gives only what you expended in Ireland?—No; it gives the expenditure in England and Ireland. It gives all the expenditure on objects connected with the Irish estate.

6390. Under what heads?—"Public purposes," I think, is the head. I will give you an instance: The Drapers' Company give a subscription of 300 l. a year to the Belfast Technical School. That is included in the statement under the head "public purposes." The Drapers' Company give a scholarship every year to be competed for by Londonderry girls at the Royal University of Ireland matriculation examination; that is included.

6391. Does the column headed "public purposes" include any public purposes in England?—No.

6392. Does the expenditure include any expenditure in England?—No expenditure in England.

6393. Then the expenditure side of the account represents only expenditure in Ireland?—Yes.

6394. The total receipts for the 15 years are 168,000 l. in round figures, and the total expenditure is 101,000 l. That leaves a difference of 67,000 l. on the 16 years, does not it?—Yes.

6395. What happened to that 67,000 l.?—It went into the general funds of the company.

6396. An average of between 4,000 l. and 5,000 l. a year?—Yes, about that.

6397. Was any part of that spent for Irish purposes?—No.

6398. Then we have it that of 168,000 l., about one-third was diverted from Ireland. Now

Mr. Sexton—continued.

as to these public purposes, it is rather curious that when you had an income of 13,100 *l.* you spent 2,100 *l.* out of that; that is about one-sixth of it, for public purposes, and when we come to the year 1889, when you had an income of 17,000 *l.*, you spent 1,250 *l.* that year for public purposes?—You should not speak of this year 1889 as having an income of 17,000 *l.* That was simply the receipts during the year. It included back rents and interest on purchase money.

6399. Taking the column of "public purposes" by itself, you expended such sums as 2,100 *l.*, 2,100 *l.*, and 1,800 *l.* in some of the earlier years of that series; but at the end you have fallen to 1,250 *l.* How is it your sense of the claim of public purposes upon you appears to have become dull in the latter years?—I cannot, at the present moment, compare the expenditure for public purposes in one year with the expenditure in another. It may be in a particular year a large donation might be granted for some special object.

6400. What are these "buildings, works, and improvements;" are they works that confer benefit on particular tenants, or otherwise?—They are building works generally on the estate. Some of these were made for particular tenants, and some for the general benefit of all the tenants. I have included in that heading a payment made by the company for the railway from Magherafelt to Draperstown.

6401. Would I be wrong in assuming these are generally public buildings and works?—I think for the most part they are.

6402. You do not know any case where you have put up on any individual farm buildings or fences?—There have been a good many cases in which the company have either put up or assisted the tenant to put up buildings on the farms; but since the year 1880, the practice has perhaps a little altered.

6403. These buildings and works are mostly such buildings as churches and schools, and market houses, and so on?—Churches and schools are included.

6404. They form substantially the whole of it?—They form a substantial part, I have no doubt, but not substantially the whole of it.

6405. I should like you to give some idea of the proportion which you think individual buildings have been improved out of these sums of money?—I can make a column in the return which I am going to send you of grants to individual tenants, if you wish.

6406. Perhaps you will do that?—That will increase the number of columns.

6407. It is remarkable, I think, that while this column of "buildings, works, and improvements" shows that you spent in the year 1875 4,000 *l.*, and in the year 1883 as much as 9,000 *l.*, and in 1884 1,800 *l.*; that in the years since 1884 they have fallen to these sums: 1885, 700 *l.* in round figures; 1886, 600 *l.*; 1887, 500 *l.*; 1888, 200 *l.*; 1889, 160 *l.*; how is it that the expenditure under this head has shrunk to so very slight a figure?—I really cannot compare the expenditure of one year with another. The circumstances of each year are not sufficiently present to my mind.

6408. But when you find in every year since 1884 that it is a rapidly and consistently decreasing series with reference to this branch of expenditure, you will see it is not a case of an individual year, but apparently a system of contraction?—The company may have been influenced by the fact that in recent years they have been getting no rent, or next to no rent, for a considerable part of the estate.

6409. You mean while the arrears which are now the subject of arbitration are unpaid?—There are very heavy arrears on half the estate at the present moment.

Sir William Fitzwilliam Lenox Conyngham, sworn; and Examined.

Sir William Marriott.

6410. You have been up till recently the agent of the Drapers' Company's estate?—Yes.

6411. You do not now hold that appointment?—I was appointed in April 1883, and resigned in January 1890.

6412. You have been acquainted with the estate and the neighbourhood for a considerable number of years?—All my life.

6413. Has there been any improvement of the condition of the tenants within the period which you have known it?—A very marked improvement.

6414. In the tenancy?—In the tenancy and the country generally.

6415. I will not take you into detail. As landlords, how do you think the Drapers' Company have acted?—Towards their tenantry very liberally.

Mr. T. M. Healy.

6416. Why did you allow such a large arrear to accumulate on the Drapers' estate?—From foolishly trusting in the promises of the tenants.

Mr. T. M. Healy—continued.

6417. Foolishly trusting their promises?—Yes.

6418. Now we have heard a great deal about the existence of the Plan of Campaign on the Drapers' estate?—Yes.

6419. Do you think seriously the Plan of Campaign existed?—It was certainly tried to be established. Two Members of Parliament came down and made speeches, and I was told that it was established, and that money had been paid into the Plan of Campaign office.

6420. Would not you have been very glad, if the tenants had adopted the Plan of Campaign, to take the half year's rent from the Campaign trustees?—At all times I was willing to take half a year's rent from the tenants from the time I was appointed, and such were my instructions from the company.

6421. Is it a fair question to ask when you ceased to be the agent of the Drapers' Company?—On the 17th January 1890, last January, my have

Mr. T. M. Healy—continued.

lease was up, and I resigned. I had resigned previously to that.

6422. You resigned?—Yes.

6423. Would it be excessive to suggest that you felt the difficulty and the impossibility of collecting a great deal of those arrears?—I do not think it was entirely impossible. By giving time I do not think it would be impossible.

6424. Do you remember your evidence before the Cowper Commission?—Yes, I remember being examined.

6425. Do you remember stating the difference in the character of the land between the Brackaslievegallion Division and the Moneymore Division?—I remember being asked a question as to the relative value of the land in those two divisions.

6426. You drew a very marked distinction?—I said there was a very marked difference between the lands, and so there is. Some of the land is equally as good as the other. I could name you one or two townlands in the Brackaslievegallion Division that are quite as good as anything in the Moneymore Division.

6427. You speak generally?—Yes.

6428. Yet the terms of purchase were the same for both?—Yes; but you must recollect that the value of land by Mr. Nolan varied, and I think if you look at my answer to the question before the Cowper Commission, I said, no doubt the quality of land is different, but in Mr. Nolan's valuation he allowed for that. He had made the valuation under which the estate was held when I became agent in 1882.

6429. That is to say, you think that the company took into account, in their rental, the difference in the character of the land?—I do.

6430. It was to be expected, but I gather that your evidence went to this, that the tenants of the Brackaslievegallion Division would be less able to pay a rent even on that valuation than the tenants of the Moneymore Division?—I do not think they would. If I may be permitted I should like to call attention to some portion of Mr. O'Brien's evidence. Mr. O'Brien in one of his answers says he reported himself to me in Moneymore. Now what actually occurred was this: when Mr. O'Brien came down to make that inspection I saw him. I knew him personally before, and I saw him walking about Moneymore, and I went to his hotel and called on him.

Chairman.

6431. You went and saw him?—I called on him at the hotel.

6432. Mr. Glover seemed to say it was impossible to go to Mr. O'Brien?—I found no difficulty. I called on Mr. O'Brien at the hotel. He told me he had come down to inspect the Moneymore Division, and then came on to the Brackaslievegallion Division. I offered him every information in my power. I said to him: "This hotel is a noisy place and not a pleasant one to do business in, I am sure. There is a spare room in my office which is at your disposal at any time you want it, and for any information you may require, the books will be on the spot. I offered to go with him on an inspection, or send the estate overseer, but Mr. O'Brien declined anything, and the only question he asked me for information upon was with regard to the inserting of the old rent instead of the judicial rent which had been fixed in the agreements of sale.

6433. At Question 1261 he is asked: "Did you bring to Mr. Glover's notice that he had put in applications at the wrong rent?" to which he replies: "No; I brought it under the notice of Sir William Conyngham"?—So he did, and I can explain the circumstances. I was leaving home on that day, and walking in Moneymore I saw Mr. O'Brien, who was driving out to the Brackaslievegallion Division, and he stopped and spoke to me. He said, "I have one of these agreements, and that is where you had a judicial rent fixed, and your old rent is in the agreement." I said, "I am quite satisfied that is the right way to put it in, because the base of the agreement for sale was on the old rent, and to insert the judicial rent and then put in 18 years' purchase upon the old rent, would be more misleading than the way you propose to do it."

Mr. Sexton.

6434. Was there anything on the face of the agreement about the number of years' purchase?—No; but it was very well known.

6435. As between the company and the tenants?—Yes. If you look at Mr. Lynch's judgment you will find he states it there, and he knew it was 18 years' purchase on the old rent. Mr. Lynch himself says so.

6436. Does not he say he was misled by the entry in the column, "Rent paid by tenant," of a rent no longer existing?—That is the construction he chose to put upon it.

6437. What other construction could be put upon it?—Simply that it would be equally misleading to put in the price of 18 years' purchase, say of 10 *l.*, when it was a lower rent.

6438. I have pointed out to you that the number of years' purchase was not on the face of the agreement?—Mr. Lynch knew it; and if you look through Mr. O'Brien's evidence you will find he states in one of his answers that the rate of purchase was 22 years' purchase of the fair rent, and bears out my statement.

Chairman.

6439. Have you the references to the questions in Mr. O'Brien's evidence, where he said that because they do not remain in my mind at this moment?—I will try and give them to you.

Mr. Sexton.

6440. Do you contend that it was not misleading to the Land Commission to enter in a column headed "Rent paid by tenant," a rent which had ceased to be the rent payable?—It had not ceased to be the rent payable as regards the agreement to buy.

6441. But at the time when the agreement was made?—I think an explanation might have been asked. That was the only explanation that ever was asked me by Mr. O'Brien.

6442. It was misleading to that extent?—It might be, no doubt, if it was meant to be misleading.

Mr. Sexton—continued.

misleading, but it was never intended in that way.

6443. I am afraid, talking of misleading, you must look at the effect quite as much as the intention?—I am afraid I shall detain you too long in finding the references, but Mr. O'Brien does quote it as 20 years' purchase on the fair rent.

Chairman.

6444. Is there anything else you want to say?—There is only one thing which I do not think has been clearly brought out before the Committee, and that is the circumstances under which the company dealt with the tenants in 1882.

Mr. *T. M. Healy.*

6445. No complaint has been made against you on that point?—I do not think it is understood, but I think it ought to be. In 1882 the greater proportion, or a very large proportion of the tenants on the estate could not take advantage of the Land Act, they being all leaseholders. The company reduced their rents by 13 per cent. all over the estate, giving the tenants the choice to sign agreements to become statutory tenants or to remain leaseholders, with an endorsement on their lease that the rent was to be so reduced.

Mr. *Lea.*

6446. I presume that was done on your recommendation?—No; you are wrong in that. The company had under consideration the reduction of the rent before I was appointed. It was carried out immediately after I was appointed. I think it would be entirely erroneous to say it was done on my recommendation.

6447. You have been unwell for some time?—I had to give up from ill-health.

6448. And for some time past the company has not had the benefit of your assistance?—Nothing could be more kind than the way the company behaved to me. They first gave me six months' leave of absence and leave to report myself when I considered myself able to carry on the work, and then I found that I could not do it. There is one thing on Mr. Quin's evidence I should like to refer to. He refers to an old friend of mine, a Major Miller, who was agent of the Drapers' estate for a great number of years. He died in the year 18[illegible], being then at the very advanced age of [illegible], and I do not think Mr. Quin could have known much about him.

Mr. *T. M. Healy.*

6449. As you have said that, when Rowley Miller died, did not a Presbyterian blacksmith in Moneymore hang out a black flag, having the inscription on it, "Thank God, the tyrant is no more"?—I never heard it, and do not believe it.

Friday, 18th July 1890.

MEMBERS PRESENT:

Sir John Ellis.	Sir William Marriott.
Mr. T. M. Healy.	Mr. John Morley.
Colonel Laurie.	Mr. Sexton.
Mr. Lawson.	Sir Richard Temple.
Mr. Lea.	

THE RIGHT HONOURABLE JOHN MORLEY, IN THE CHAIR.

The Very Reverend ANDREW FERGUSON SMYLY, M.A., sworn; and Examined.

Sir William Marriott.

6450. I BELIEVE you are the Dean of Derry?—Yes.

6451. And you have lived a long time in Derry, but in the north of Ireland?—I have lived almost all my life in the north of Ireland, except during the time of my education in England.

6452. For about how many years have you been living in the north of Ireland?—More or less for 35 years; I have been 34 or 35 years in orders in the diocese of Derry.

6453. Have you during that 34 or 35 years seen much of the action of the Irish Society and the London companies?—At different times I have been in parishes more or less connected with the companies. In 1867 I was in Culmore for two years or so under the Irish Society.

6454. And are you prepared to speak with regard to any of the London companies?—Yes. I was at a parish called Aghadowey, near Coleraine, where I had something to do with the Ironmongers and Mercers, and at Limavady. I was not exactly under the Skinners' Company, but I have received help and kindness from them, and now that I am in Derry I am more or less under the Irish Society.

6455. Could you give us the result of your experience with regard to the dealings of the companies and the Irish Society, with the districts in which they have power or land?—At Culmore, about two miles from Derry, to begin with, when I was there the church was rebuilt that had been left in ruins after the siege; new schools were built, and the company also built a large reservoir for water, for the village was very badly supplied with water.

6456. What company was that?—The Irish Society.

6457. Have you any remarks to make as to the grants they have made?—All I can say is that they were always most generous and kind to me, certainly; and I think also in almost any case fairly brought before them.

6458. I do not know whether you have read the evidence that has been given before this Committee with regard to the management of the Irish Society?—I did not expect to be invited over, and I only read the local newspapers; but I read what appeared in the Derry papers.

Sir William Marriott—continued.

6459. I suppose in the Irish papers the evidence is more fully reported than in the English papers?—Very much more so.

6460. Will you give us your opinion, as founded upon your experience of the administration of the estates by the Irish Society and the other companies?—I should say that their administration, especially of late, has been most beneficial, and, judging from other landlords with whom I have often had to deal in different parishes, I think that they compare very favourably, at any rate.

6461. I do not know whether attention was called to it in the local papers, but some of the witnesses who have been examined have thought it would be advisable to displace the Irish Society, and to place their powers in other hands; what do you say with regard to that?—When I saw that suggestion, I said I hoped it would not be in my day, at all events.

6462. Do you think that would be a change for the better or a change for the worse?—I think it would be a bad change.

6463. Somebody suggested, I think, that the control should be placed in the hands of trustees appointed by the Lord Chancellor?—That would be better than anything connected with the locality; but I do not see why there should be any change from what there is now. If I might make a suggestion, I think if there might be a change perhaps in the period of years of the representation on the Irish Society, I have always felt that the present period was against it.

6464. In what way?—The members are only appointed for two years, and just as a person begins to know the estate, and to take an interest in it, he is moved off, and perhaps he does not come back again for 15 or 20 years, if then.

6465. You think that permanent appointments would be better?—I think appointments for five to seven years would be better. I believe there is always something to be said for a "new broom;" and perhaps if there is an objection with regard to the expense, I would limit the number of the deputation.

Sir William Marriott—continued.

6466. Did you read the evidence of Dr. Todd?—I did.

6467. Do you know Dr. Todd?—Yes, I do.

6468. Have you any remarks to make upon his evidence?—I think the general opinion was that it was rather hard and severe.

6469. Was it in your opinion justified by the facts?—I do not know enough as the background of everything to say exactly; but as regards the statement which I think he made, that the town of Derry had been retarded by the Irish Society, I think certainly of the last few years nothing of that sort could not be said. The growth of Derry during the last four or five years has been something remarkable.

6470. The objection urged against the Irish Society was that they did not grant long enough leases?—I heard of that objection long ago, and of course it was a great objection.

6471. They are now granting leases, are they not?—Certainly. In my own case, with regard to the schools, they are, and, I believe, in other cases too; but I will only speak for what I know.

Mr. Sexton.

6472. Do you profess to be competent to controvert Dr. Todd's evidence upon questions of fact?—I merely speak from my own experience.

Sir William Marriott.

6473. You have lived in the district a longer time than Dr. Todd?—Dr. Todd is a native, too.

6474. But he is a younger man than you, is he not?—Yes.

6475. He has not had 35 years' experience of the district since he came to what I may call years of discretion?—Of course, as I have said, the management now is different from what it was long ago.

6476. When did the management begin to improve?—I think the greatest improvement has been, I hardly like to say it in the presence of Sir Whittaker Ellis, but perhaps I may say that under his management there was great improvement. I remember the Society when Alderman Humphreys was governor.

6477. Was it under Sir Sydney Waterlow that the improvement began?—I was not in Derry then. I was in the county, but not in the city of Derry.

6478. I see you have some papers before you, have you any matters there you wish to refer to?—I understood I was to be asked about some of the smaller grants that were given, and I have just noted down one or two cases here which I could mention. This other is a pamphlet by Sir Whittaker Ellis, with a statement by Mr. Goldwin Smith prefacing it.

6479. May I see it. (*The pamphlet was handed to the honourable Member.*) I see the pamphlet is called "The Lesson from the Government of Ireland." Have you read it?—I read it yesterday evening.

6480. Do you agree with it?—I do.

6481. In all its details?—I think in all its details.

6482. Have you any other matters there you wish to refer to?—The notes I have here are with regard to the smaller grants which I was told I would be asked about, and I could mention the different schools. For instance, the society give to the School of Art in Derry and our own schools, and the Working Men's Institute, and the infirmary, and things like that.

Chairman.

6483. We have had some evidence given by previous witnesses pointing to what they regard as the injudicious distribution of grants; I gather that you are going to show that the distribution of grants has not been injudicious, but judicious?—Yes. Taking, for instance, the school under myself called Creggan School, which in the books of the Irish Society is called the Foundation School; if it had not been for the grants we receive from the Irish Society that school would have been shut up; but in the last two or three years we have been able, acting under the Education Endowment Commissioners, to get a scheme granted for that school. Now with what we get from the Irish Society we are able to have already a flourishing school, although the money was only expended in repairing and fitting it for school purposes last July or August, we have a fairly good school at present.

Sir William Marriott.

6484. Is that owing in a great measure to the expenditure upon that school made by the Irish Society?—We could not have gone on if they had not given us the money. To take another case, that of the School of Art, last year we applied by a memorial to the Irish Society for an increased grant. We were not able to get a permanent master; we had a splendid master, but he went to St. Andrews simply because that was permanent. The Irish Society saw the difficulty, and very kindly gave us a grant of 50*l.*, which enabled us to get a first rate man from Manchester. And the Government have since given us a grant of 750*l.* to put the old town hall into working order for a School of Art, which we could not have done but for the grant that we got last August from the Irish Society.

6485. Have you any other cases of grants?—The infirmary is another case, and my own schools in connection with the cathedral; and they gave a grant of 50*l.* for prizes for the model school; and then for the Working Men's Institute they gave a small grant of 10*l.*, which has enabled us to connect with it a football club and a cricket club, and a recreation ground, which all classes and denominations of Derry can make use of.

6486. Are there any other points you wish to refer to?—They also help us towards Sunday school prizes, and there is the Penny Society which I have noted down here. That is a very old society which was started years and years ago in Ireland, and the Irish Society have very kindly given, for years, a grant of, I think, 40*l.* a year to it. All classes get the benefit of that, and it helps to keep a number of respectable old people out of the workhouse, and give them little comforts in their old age.

6487. On the whole, I may take it, that the result of the Irish Society's management has been beneficial, and not injurious to the places

Sir William Marriott—continued.

places where they have power and property?—Certainly; there is no doubt of late it has been very beneficial. I do not know much about it except for the two years I have referred to, and for the last six and a-half years.

6488. During those years you are satisfied with its government and consider it beneficial?—I do. I think it would be a misfortune if it was altered.

6489. Have you any objection to the way in which they give their grants annually, as it were of their own authority, and not as permanent grants?—Last year when we went to Sir Whitaker Ellis, and asked him to make the grant to the school of art permanent, he said, "I wish you and the deputation to understand that so long as you do well and show spirit in your work, you may look to this; but, of course, it is not permanent, for if it did not succeed we would feel bound to withdraw it." I think that shows care and discrimination, and I think it rather stirs one up to do all one can.

6490. You think that better than a solid endowment, which sometimes leads to lethargy?—I do not exactly know what you would go to endow in Derry; unless you told me what you were going to endow, I do not know that question I would be in a position to answer at all.

6491. Have you anything else to add?—I would like to testify to the kind treatment I have received from the Mercers', Ironmongers' and Skinners' Companies at different times.

6492. In your opinion those three companies have acted liberally as landlords in the way of subscriptions and grants?—I think perhaps the Ironmongers might have been a little more liberal to me, I mean to the parish of Aghadowey, than they were in the old times. Of course I left that parish long ago. But they have been much more liberal since the land troubles came on.

6493. As regards the other company you mentioned, the Mercers, what do you say?—The Mercers has not only been liberal, when I was in their parish, but they also gave me a very handsome donation towards the enlargement and restoration of the cathedral in Derry; and the Skinners' Company also.

6494. Have you any complaints at all to bring against those companies?—Not at all.

Mr. Sexton.

6495. When were you in the parish of Aghadowey?—I was appointed in March 1868.

6496. How long did you remain there?—Eleven years.

6497. What was the company there?—The Ironmongers have a very large portion of the parish, and the Mercers have a smaller portion. Then there were a good number of landlords besides, or at least a small number.

6498. And they made you some grants I understand?—The Ironmongers' Company always gave me 10*l.* a year; and it was that I was alluding to when I said that I thought they might have given a little more. Their yearly grant was 10*l.* They also gave me a grant when I restored the church, but it was the yearly grant I was alluding to.

6499. They maintained that grant as long as you were there?—Yes; they have increased it since I left, as I understand; I do not know it for certain.

Mr. Sexton—continued.

6500. Did you concern yourself at that time to inquire generally into their administration, and consider what their income was, and how much of it they gave to public purposes?—Only with regard to my own grant.

6501. You were satisfied so long as they did not diminish your own grant?—Quite.

6502. Have you any particular experience of the action of the companies as landlords?—Of course, as a clergyman, I would know a great deal of any complaints made, or happiness, or annoyances of the people, and I must say that I never heard the company spoken of in any way but kindly.

6503. We have heard that in some parts of the county the Episcopalian congregation is composed perhaps of the squires and labourers, but not to a great extent of farmers?—I think that would be true.

6504. So that your flock would not be particularly concerned with the society as tenants?—No; but I think in any parish I have ever been in I have known very intimately almost all the people; they would come to me backwards and forwards.

6505. Do you happen to know that the companies, I think without exception, carried out a system of re-valuation every 20 years upon the improvements made by the tenants?—That I could not say anything about.

6506. I think you have said that the Irish Society acted, in your opinion, most generously with any case brought fairly brought before them; I will ask you to define a little. In the first place, what do you mean by a case fairly brought before them?—I mean when a deputation goes to the Irish Society, and tells them exactly how they stand, and what they want. I remember when the grant was given to the waterworks at Coleraine, that I was speaking about just now, the next year I went with a deputation to thank the Irish Society, and a gentleman sitting at the table jumped up and said, "I beg to request that the resolution be put upon the books; I have been here for two years, and I never heard a word of thanks, no matter what we did." I always acted upon that principle; I was thankful for whatever I got, and acknowledged it.

6507. When you bring your mind to consider that this fund is applicable to the benefit of that district, does it occur to you as a good system or a bad system, that the people entitled to benefit by that fund should have no other means of applying to the Society directly, than upon their rare visits to the district?—I think in the case of anything administered by any foreign committee they would have to do the same thing.

6508. I am suggesting to you that the system is fundamentally not the best?—When there is a regular visitation once a year, I do not think people have anything to complain of in that way.

6509. Do not you think some authority having local knowledge and more facility of touch with the locality, would be more likely to administer to its wants more efficiently?—But the

Mr. Sexton—continued.

the Irish Society have an agent and sub-agent there, who are in touch, or can be in touch with everybody.

6510. Do you consider it expedient that the authority should have to depend so much upon individual testimony?—Do you mean individual testimony with regard to the sub-agents?

6511. I mean the agent or sub-agent?—I think that is removed by people going to ask the company, when they are all there together, for different things; questions are then asked by everybody all round the table.

6512. But the occasions of their visits are rare and brief, are they not?—They are once a year.

6513. Do you not consider that a more continual superintendence would be an improvement?—There is local superintendence. The agent is always there, except, perhaps, a month in the year; and I do not know even if he gets that much leave of absence; he is, practically, always there.

6514. A great deal depends upon his individual discretion?—I suppose with any property it would be the same.

6515. Of course, any with property managed by an absentee it is the same?—I beg your pardon; there is a great deal of property where the landlord is resident, and takes a great interest in his property, which is managed in the same way by an agent.

6516. In that case, what I suggest is that the discretion of a liberal resident landlord continually tempers the discretion of the agent, and we want that element in this case?—If you ask me what my treatment under landlords and companies has been, I should say I have certainly been better treated by companies than I have been by landlords.

6517. That brings me to another point; you have said that the Irish Society are most generous by comparison with other landlords; that was your evidence?—Yes. What made me say that was, that for the restoration and enlargement of the cathedral the Irish Society gave at one time, not to me but to the object, 1,000 *l.*, and they very handsomely and kindly afterwards supplemented it by 500 *l.* I doubt whether there is any landlord, perhaps, who could or would have done at all the same thing.

6518. An ordinary landlord is a private owner, who can do what he pleases, without reproach, with the surplus income of his property; but do you apprehend that the Irish Society is a trustee?—Yes; I think they acknowledge that.

6519. Surely that destroys the comparison between the society and a private landowner?—I do not see why it should.

6520. It puts the Irish Society under an obligation from which a private owner is free, does it not?—I think that the private owner is a trustee as much as the Irish Society is.

6521. Are you not aware that the Irish Society themselves admit that the whole of their property is applicable to public uses?—Yes; I know that is the case.

6522. Surely that establishes not a comparison, but a contrast, between the *Irish Society* and a private owner, does it not?—I think a private owner who gives his property, his charities, as we may call them, honestly and fairly, is just as much a trustee as the Irish Society.

6523. I suggest the difference that a private owner has to live upon his income, and the Irish Society has no right to live upon the income of this trust?—I see that perfectly; but I suppose any person that orders his private income fairly, acting honestly before God, will set aside a certain sum for such purposes; some years he may give more to some things and some years less.

6524. Following that idea for a moment, that the Irish Society is bound to administer the income of this property for the public good, let me ask, have you looked into the accounts?—I see the published yearly account in the papers, but I have never seen anything more than is published yearly in the newspapers.

6525. Have you ever put to your own mind these questions: First, whether out of the income of the property a fair or adequate part is absolutely applied to public uses at present; and, secondly, whether the peculiar constitution of the society, and its distance from the district, entails expenditure which might be avoided?—I did say since I came here that I thought the very large deputations might be decreased; and in that way, of course, a saving of expense would follow. I did say that, and I think it.

6526. Have you any personal knowledge of the cost of management of landed property?—To some extent I have.

6527. Would you say that 20 per cent. is too high a rate for the management of property?—With agents to start with, of course, as we all know, there is 5 per cent., and then there are other charges; but I really never put it in that way. Of course, with property that has to be managed with, you might say, two offices, there has to be a little more, or a great deal more, expense than with one office.

6528. Then I should like to ask whether you think that a system which entails two staffs, a staff in London and a staff in Dublin, and which causes law costs by reason of the distance of the principal and so forth, is not a wasteful system, under which a large part of the corpus of the funds goes in expenses instead of going to the public use?—That would apply to a body in Dublin in the same way; and I think, considering everything, it would be better not to have the whole management in Derry. I am perfectly certain the general feeling throughout Derry would be not to have a local body.

6529. Could not they have a body not so distant as Dublin and not so local as Derry, which would have what you may think the minor qualification of being Irish?—I beg to differ from your suggestion that I should look upon anything Irish as of "minor" importance.

6530. I am very glad to hear your disclaimer?—I look upon myself as just as much an Irishman as the honourable Member.

6531. Then you would prefer, naturally, an Irish system?—I will not say that either.

6532. I am putting your professions to the test?—There are Irishmen and Irishmen.

6533. Take any sort of Irishman you please?—I think there is a hard-headedness about Englishmen which is of use to us.

6534. Do

Mr. *Sexton*—continued.

6534. Do you say that, taking even a favourable class of Irishmen, they are soft-headed?—They are not soft-headed, but they have not the experience of Englishmen, and especially of London men.

6535. Do you consider it requires some special experience, which only the British race possesses, to manage a trust estate in Ireland?—No; but they have so much more experience in England than we have. A few years ago Alderman Savory came to Derry, and with his general experience of schools and everything, although he was only in Derry two or three days, he stirred us up and gave us some new ideas, and I hardly meet a deputation from which I do not get "wrinkles," if I may use the term. We have not the knowledge and the experience that London men have.

6536. Surely there are many important trusts, for instance, trusts of the representative church body, and various other trusts of the first importance, which are most capably administered by Irishmen?—There are, but the representative body have had the experience of far more than Ireland.

6537. Suppose you had members of that body appointed trustees of this trust, what would you say?—I think I would be cutting my own throat if I did not say I would be quite willing to submit to the representative body, but they are a body by themselves.

6538. They might form an element in the trust body. I put this question to you broadly; stating that a large part of the income of this trust is at present used up in expenses of management, which could be applied to beneficial public uses if the trust were more economically administered, I put it to you whether an Irish authority, not so local as to be open to jobbery, and yet not remote, would not give you more money for public uses and be more satisfactory?—I would have to answer that question in a roundabout way, for this reason: I do not know, except from what you say, and from seeing it stated in the newspapers, that it does take 20 per cent. at present for expenses of management. It does take 20 per cent.; I think perhaps that might be reduced in many ways. But if you have a body in Dublin there must be more or less expense as well.

6539. It need not be in Dublin?—If it were at Armagh, or anywhere you like, wherever you have two offices there must be double expense.

6540. To come to a conclusion upon the point, would you, if the option were offered to you, adhere to the system by which this Irish trust for Irish uses is managed by a body of commercial gentlemen in London, or would you have a body of Irishmen appointed by the Crown or by the authority of Parliament to manage this trust in the district? That is a simple question?—I do not know that it is a simple question, because if it is to manage people in the district that would imply that the people are district men.

6541. Not necessarily; I say an Irish body?—Then you have the expense of sending the body backwards and forwards.

6542. No?—Then I think I will have to leave my answer as it is.

6543. Supposing you had gentlemen resident in the county of Derry?—If you knew the county of Derry, you would know there are very few resident gentlemen in it.

Chairman.

6544. Do you know how many magistrates there are in the county of Derry?—No.

Mr. *Sexton.*

6545. I should think there are over a 100, are there not?—I think not. The county of Derry is different to almost every other county in Ireland, on account of the large properties held by the companies, and on many of the companies' estates there is only the resident agent.

6546. You said that the distribution of grants by the societies is judicious?—I do not know that I exactly went that far.

6547. That was your language; of course if you wish to correct it you may do so?—Did I say judicious?

6548. That was the word you used; if you wish to substitute another word you may?—Will you tell me in what way you suggest I consider it not judicious, and then I can answer.

6549. I noticed you made a general statement, but supported it only by reference to the grants made to yourself, or grants in which you are directly concerned?—I answer what I know.

6550. But it is necessary to consider the matter in a larger spirit in order to inform the Committee, and to consider the grants as a whole. Let me ask, for instance, whether you consider that the Presbyterians, and your own flock, and the Catholics benefit in a fair proportion?—I cannot give you the amounts, but I know that the Irish Society support Magee College, and the Academy, and different Presbyterian meeting houses and clergy I believe. I see in the newspapers that there are grants for all those objects.

6551. As a witness before the Committee, are you really in a position to say anything more from your own knowledge than that the grants made by the Irish Society to you satisfy yourself?—I am not going to say that others are satisfied. You ask me, do I know from my own knowledge whether other grants are given; I say yes; I know they are given to the Magee College, to the Academy, and to Presbyterian clergymen.

6552. You can scarcely undertake to say that, generally speaking, the grants made bear a just proportion to the relative claims?—Unless I had them all down before me I could not possibly say.

Mr. *Lea.*

6553. I think you said just now that county Derry was deprived of county gentlemen?—I did not say "deprived"; I said there are not very many.

6554. That is because the companies own so much of the county, I understand?—That was the result of it.

6555. And those country gentlemen would probably support charities and schools if they lived there, I presume?—I should hope so.

6556. At one time you lived on the Ironmongers' Estate, I understand?—I was rector of the parish of Aghadowey.

Mr. Lea—continued.

6557. That is on the Ironmongers' Estate?—Yes.

6558. Did they help your church and schools?—Yes; they gave me 10 *l.* a year for the church sustentation.

6559. They have given liberally for the education of the district, have they not?—They have all their schools in their own hands; but they are very liberal to education in that way.

6560. Are you aware that they are selling, or proposing to sell, their estate?—I have seen it in the papers.

6561. Would you not regard the abstraction of all that money from the Ironmongers' Estate to London as a very serious loss to the county?—I think it would be in that way.

6562. Do you not think it would be a great damage to education and religion in the whole district?—I think all the schools on their estates are in their own hands; at least, all that I know of.

Chairman.

6563. I only want to ask you two questions. Have you read the evidence of Lord Justice FitzGibbon before this Committee?—I saw what was reported in the Derry papers; but it was not a very full report.

6564. Did you see enough to perceive that he arrived at a different conclusion to yourself as to local management?—I did; but I thought myself at the time that Lord Justice FitzGibbon had not worked as a poor parson in different parishes.

6565. But he had worked as an Educational Commissioner, had he not?—Yes: but he only had to work as regards money and legal points; he had not to superintend schools and keep them open and work them.

6566. Surely he took the educational point of view as well as the financial?—Certainly.

6567. Are you aware that he said this in his evidence; he was asked (at Question 1409), "As a general result of all that you have said upon the first head of your evidence, namely, the relations of the Irish Society to education in the north of Ireland, I gather that you formed an opinion which was not different from that of the Commissioners of 1854, namely, that if the educational part of the Irish Society's funds were defined and set apart, and placed under the management, as you have just said, of the local bodies, that would be a better arrangement"; and in reply to that question, Lord Justice FitzGibbon said that he and his colleagues did come to that conclusion; he had said in answer to a previous question that he and his colleagues "were quite satisfied that the Irish Society were doing their best to please everybody, with the usual result; we thought the money might probably be more usefully applied if they had left it to the management of the people themselves"?—I think the answer I would give to that is that Lord Justice FitzGibbon was speaking of the larger donations. I do not think the small things I mentioned he would ever have known anything about.

6568. Still the small things you mention, you mention as showing that the Irish Society and the companies did their duty?—Yes.

6569. But then Lord Justice FitzGibbon clearly thought that that duty would be better done if the fund were administered under local management?—What I want you to understand is that I do not think these small cases ever came under Lord Justice FitzGibbon's notice.

6570. They were too small?—Yes.

6571. Then, in fact, your evidence upon this point does not amount to very much?—I do not know in what way you would like to put it; but I presume he was then speaking of Foyle College and the Academy, and perhaps St. Columb's College; but I do not know whether the society give to that or not.

6572. He was speaking of all the more serious destinations of the society's funds?—He was speaking of the larger sums, I presume.

6573. You say you value the management of these funds by gentlemen from London because of their greater experience; how do you expect Irishmen are to get experience in the administration of funds of this kind if they never have the chance of administering them?—It would take some little time for them to learn it.

6574. Must they not begin?—I daresay it would be a very good thing for them to begin; but disestablishment has given us a good deal of experience, and the men now connected with the representative body and other church bodies know very much more about their business now than when they first began.

6575. Then disestablishment has been a good thing?—It has brought out individual labour, and has brought out earnest work amongst the laity.

6576. Does not it occur to you that just as the divorce of the Church from the State was a good thing, as throwing Irishmen rather upon their own resources and widening their experience, so it might be a good thing for the people of Derry (I am not approaching a wider question) if their funds were divorced from the control of gentlemen in London?—It might be, but in the meantime I doubt some of us might be badly off.

Sir John Ellis.

6577. Have you ever acted as a Commissioner, as Lord Justice FitzGibbon was acting?—No.

6578. But has your experience of Commissioners generally been that in all their inquiries their impulse is to take into their own management every institution that comes under their observation?—I am not able to say.

6579. You have not had such a wide experience as I have in that respect?—I could not say anything about that.

6580. And therefore you have not found that to be the result?—In fact I never was before a Commission but the one on education.

6581. As regards the grants, what I understand you really to mean is this: that you are of opinion that these numerous grants diffused amongst voluntary bodies who are exerting themselves in different poor districts, in that portion of Londonderry over which we have influence and control, result in more advantage and usefulness to the poorer classes than would be the case if the money were in some great institution created out of a conglomeration of these funds?—Certainly for working among poorer people, I think it is more beneficial.

6582. You

Sir John Ellis—continued.

6582. You think that the money goes further administered by voluntary bodies than it would be administered by some great institution?—I would like, before I could answer that honestly, to know what kind of institution it would be.

6583. They would have some very fine buildings, no doubt, to begin with?—I know it is a stimulant to many schools and to private undertakings for charitable objects, and tends to the improvement of charities.

6584. You were asked whether, if there was no opportunity of applying to the society (on any business connected with Londonderry, I take it that the honourable Member meant), except on "the rare visits of the society," that was not an inconvenience; you are aware, I suppose, that the society sits every month?—Yes, I know that.

6585. And that any letters or applications of any sort or description are attended to forthwith, and there is no delay?—Yes, I know there is what is called the Irish Committee, which sits once a month in London.

6586. And any application through the agent, specially appointed in Ireland, receives immediate attention?—Certainly.

6587. And the agent there is a man who is quite competent to deal with all matters of detail?—Yes, he is.

6588. Do you know of any other method by which the business of public bodies is generally conducted than through agents, and the meeting of those bodies frequently; that is the usual course, is it not?—I think it is the usual course.

6589. Do you think that the conduct of the agent is not tempered by the action of the society just as much as if there were a resident landlord there?—I think perhaps the agent would be rather more afraid of the company than he would be of a landlord; for if it were a landlord he would only have one to work with.

6590. You think the action of the society is quite equal to that of any resident landlord in tempering the conduct of the agent?—I should think it is even more powerful; because one master, as I say, is much more easily managed than a number.

6591. Do you think the management of a public body such as the Irish Society, which has first to manage its estate and then to administer its funds, is to be compared with the mere receipt of money by an owner, who, when he has once received the money, spends it as he likes?—I do not quite follow what you mean.

6592. Do you think that expenses of management and administration of a public body is to be compared with the mere expense of an owner, who, having received his money, counts nothing in regard to the cost of its administration. I will put it another way; Do you know what the cost of administration of any of the large estates in this country is, such as the estate of the Duke of Sutherland or of the Duke of Bedford?—No, I know nothing about that.

Sir John Ellis—continued.

6593. You do not know what officers they would keep, and how they have a lieutenant general for their manager, and so on?—I know something of the management of some of the estates in Ireland.

6594. Do you think the expenses of the management of the estate, and the administration of the funds which we are dealing with here, are to be compared with the 5 per cent. for collecting rents?—I only put the 5 per cent. as one item, because, of course, there are under agents and bailiffs, and all sorts of things that run up the expenses a good deal; I only put it as one charge.

6595. You do not think it is fair to compare the receipts of rent by a private landowner with the management of a public body such as this?—I do not think it is. You will remember I said 5 per cent. was the first charge; but then there are bailiffs and sub-bailiffs, and all sorts of other charges.

Mr. Sexton.

6596. I do not think you ever heard of 20 per cent. on any Irish estate, did you?—You will remember I said I did not know it was 20 per cent. here, except hearing it from you.

6597. You said you believed that the system of tenure under the Irish Society had been a great inconvenience and injury in the past, but that there had been improvements in recent years; have you made any particular study of the facts in regard to the tenures granted by the Irish Society to their tenants in the town of Derry?—Mixing among the community as I do, I could not help hearing.

6598. But I should like to ascertain whether you have really inquired into the facts specifically?—I have; because at this present time I am building schools for which the Irish Society have very kindly granted me an extended lease.

6599. I have no doubt from what you have said that you have been always kindly treated yourself?—I expect I am not a bit more kindly treated than others.

6600. That is speculation; would you set that against the fact of specific evidence from a professional man like Dr. Todd and other members of the corporation, as to the effect which the refusal of permanent tenures had in checking the development of Derry?—I have heard in old times the complaint was very strongly made; but I can only speak for myself with regard to the lease for schools.

Sir John Ellis.

6601. Are you aware that nine-tenths of the property of the society in Derry was granted on perpetuity leases?—No, I do not know about that.

6602. Then I put it to you, can you answer the question which the honourable Member put just now?—No; I can only speak for myself as to the schools.

The Reverend Robert Ross, D.D., sworn; and Examined.

Sir William Marriott.

6603. I believe you are the ex-Moderator of the Presbyterian General Assembly?—I am not the direct ex-Moderator; the ex-Moderator is the Reverend William Clark; but I have been a moderator a few years ago.

6604. I believe you have lived a great many years in Londonderry?—I have been there 40 years.

6605. You are well acquainted with the general feeling of the Presbyterian body, I think?—Yes.

6606. You have been the pastor, I think, of one of the principal Presbyterian churches in the city of Derry?—It originally was a small congregation, but it has grown to be one of fair dimensions.

6607. How long have you been there?—I have been there 40 years; I was ordained in 1850.

6608. Have you during that 40 years had much experience of, and been brought in contact with, the Irish Society?—I have, repeatedly.

6609. Are you aware of the grants they give to your own particular body; the Presbyterian body?—I am aware of a number of them.

6610. Will you just state what is your opinion of the conduct of affairs by the Irish Society in this district?—My opinion is that the Presbyterian body have never received during the entire history of the plantation their due share of the society's donations in proportion to their numbers.

6611. You think that they ought to have received more?—Yes, in proportion to their numbers. Their numbers at the time of the Siege, according to Mackenzie in his "True Narrative," were as 15 to one; and Leslie, in his answer to Archbishop King in a controversy with regard to the numbers of the different denominations, stated that over the whole of the counties of the plantation not more than one to 50 were Episcopalians.

6612. You think the Episcopalians have been favoured?—I am stating the proportions now. At the present time, according to a recent census, which I have every reason to believe to be correct, the Presbyterians are as three to two of the Episcopalians.

Chairman.

6613. Is that in the city of Derry?—In the city and district. The other proportion which I mentioned of course was over the six counties of the plantation.

Mr. Sexton.

6614. Could you complete the comparison between the creeds and give us the Catholics as well?—I do not happen to know the number of Catholics.

Sir William Marriott.

6615. What is your opinion with regard to the administration of the Irish Society generally?—The administration of the Irish Society in general has been, I believe, productive of a great deal of good in many ways.

6616. Have you anything in which you have had reason to find fault with or criticise them?—No; I personally have not. When any case was presented to them, I am bound to say I have been treated considerately; and especially during the last two governorships, I notice a very decided desire to do the best that the funds will enable them to do for the interests of the community.

6617. I do not know whether you have formed an opinion as to what would be the result of changing the constitution of the Irish Society, and giving over the management to trustees, nominated by the Lord Chancellor of Ireland, or some such person?—I think no man can predict with anything like certainty what would be the result of a change in the constitution of the board of trustees. I think if the Irish Society were changed in this respect, that instead of one-half retiring every year, so that at the end of two years you have practically a new body, a new Irish Society; if, I say, instead of that, one-third retire after a period of seven years, so that you would have two-thirds of the society associated with one-third new members, so that there would be a sufficient number of members acquainted with the wants of the people and capable of administering the funds wisely, I believe it would be a great advantage and greatly for the public benefit.

6618. Have you found any inconvenience from the fact of the Irish Society's headquarters being in London?—No, I am not aware of any. They have a local agent through whom we may communicate, and who is always willing to forward any communication to the Irish Chambers.

6619. With regard to the grants to schools of the Presbyterian body, have they been liberal, in your opinion?—A large number of grants have been made to Presbyterian schools. The Magee College, which is the only university college within the bounds of the plantation, receives at the present time, I believe, about 300*l.* a year from the society; that is to say, they pay the salary of one of the professors and 50*l.* towards the house rents, and they make other donations towards incidental expenses, bringing up their contributions to Magee College to 500*l.* a year, I believe, at the present time.

6620. Are there any other grants you would like to refer to?—There is a grant to the Academic Institution. I do not say that is an exclusively Presbyterian institution, or that Magee College is an exclusively Presbyterian institution, because, though it is mainly founded for the education of candidates for the Presbyterian ministry, yet the classes are open to all denominations, and members of other denominations than the Presbyterian do attend, including some very distinguished students, during the last Session, and young ladies. It is connected with the Royal University as a university college, and consequently those wishing to obtain university distinctions enter Magee College and obtain the advantages of university degrees.

6621. Amongst the Presbyterian body, is there, or is there not, satisfaction as to the way in which the Irish Society manage their affairs?—I have

Sir William Marriott—continued.

I have stated that there is an opinion entertained by the Presbyterians that they have not received their share in proportion to their numbers.

6622. But, assuming that the Presbyterian body are dissatisfied with the amount they receive, as compared with the Episcopal Church, are they dissatisfied in any other respects with regard to the management of the Irish Society?—I am not aware that they are.

6623. Taking the Irish Society as landlords, should you say they are good landlords?—I am hardly in a position to speak as to the relations of the Irish Society to their tenants, living as I do in a city; but so far as my own opinion is concerned, I would not like to see the connection that has subsisted for almost 300 years between the Irish Society and Derry discontinued.

Mr. Lea.

6624. Was there a meeting of the presbytery of Derry in your church lately?—There was.

6625. Was there a wish expressed at the meeting to give evidence before this Committee?—There was.

6626. Did they wish for a return of the grants given to the Presbyterian Church and other churches?—Yes.

6627. Because they felt that the Presbyterian Church had received so much less than their share?—They wished a return, that they might get accurate and reliable information as to whether there was a disparity between the grants which were made to them and those to other denominations.

6628. A strong feeling exists, I believe, that they do not get their fair share?—Precisely.

Sir Richard Temple.

6629. Supposing that the Presbyterians got their fair share of the grants as compared with the Episcopalians, which would you prefer, the Irish Society as it is, or a body of trustees somewhere in Ireland?—With the change in the constitution of the body that I indicate with regard to the tenure of office, I would unhesitatingly prefer the Irish Society.

6630. You would prefer that to any body of trustees in Ireland?—To a local board of trustees.

6631. Whether at Dublin or at Derry?—Yes, whether at Dublin or at Derry.

6632. Do you think that would be the opinion generally of the Presbyterian community?—I am hardly in a position to speak with certainty as to that. I believe there is a diversity of opinion with reference to that point.

Mr. Sexton.

6633. Do you know anything of the companies as distinguished from the Society?—Very little.

6634. I think you said, living in the city, you had but slight knowledge of the relations of the Irish Society to their agrarian tenants?—Not very minute or extensive. Before passing from the question of the grants to schools, if you would permit me, I would like to say that the Irish Society have been rendering a service to the cause of education that it is hard to over-estimate. They are contributing, as I intimated to this university college; they are contributing to four large and very efficient grammar schools substantial aid; they give to our national schools, which are theoretically, at all events, undenominational, substantial aid; they enable the managers of those schools to secure the services of better certificated and more efficient teachers; and in that way a very decided improvement in the education of the community is secured. A large number of national schools receive substantial aid, my own among the number.

Mr. Sexton—continued.

6635. Your evidence then comes to this point: that certain sums of money are applied to uses that you approve of?—Yes.

6636. But have you ever considered the subject at large; have you ever asked yourself whether, starting with the fact that this society has an income of 17,000 *l.* a year, an adequate part of that income is applied to Irish public uses and to the best public uses?—I was not aware of the actual income of the Irish Society until this moment.

6637. Then I understand from you that, hitherto, your view regarding the subject has been to ask yourself whether certain grants, of which you were aware, were good grants, and that you have not gone so far as to consider whether an adequate proportion of the whole income has been devoted to public uses?—Not clearly.

6638. I understand you think your communion have not received their due proportion of the grants?—That is the opinion.

6639. You have held the chief post in the Irish Presbyterian Church yourself, I understand?—I was Moderator of the General Assembly in 1886; I believe that was the year.

6640. The moderator fills the principal post in the church, does he not?—Yes, during the year of office.

6641. It is an annual office?—Yes; he only holds office for one year.

6642. Do you manage the affairs of the Irish Presbyterian Church in Ireland?—The moderator is the chief official.

6643. Do you govern your Church in Ireland?—It is governed by the general assembly; the synods, and the presbyteries.

6644. You do not ask any English body to govern the Irish Presbyterian Church?—No; they govern it themselves.

6645. You would not admit any help from outside, I presume?—We would be very glad of help from the English synod or the Scotch Churches.

6646. But you would not admit outsiders to control your action?—If it was wise and good control, we would.

6647. But you would not let them interfere with your action or the control of your property?—They have never sought to interfere with questions of discipline in our Church.

6648. I presume you cherish the independence of your Church as an Irish institution?—Yes, we do.

6649. Do you really think you could not find in Ireland, or even in Derry, a body of Irishmen perfectly competent to manage this trust for the public

Mr. *Sexton*—continued.

public benefit a body as compared to any body of Englishmen?—I believe there is a very considerable amount of uncertainty as to the possibility of finding a body that would be in a position of sufficient independence of local influence.

6650. That would be entirely a matter of selection, would it not, supposing the Lord Chancellor, for instance, or the House of Commons, nominated the trustees, what would you say?—I might answer that by asking this question: do you suppose any man, even nominated by the Lord Chancellor, would be beyond the reach of that local influence?

6651. I should have supposed it quite possible?—I think you are pretty well aware of the power of local influence everywhere in your own city, and in Derry.

6652. Acting upon local men?—Acting upon local men, men chosen from the locality.

6653. But could not you select men who would be free from that particular influence?—It would be a very serious risk, I have no doubt.

6654. Do you perceive any greater cause why an Irish trust should be managed by Englishmen than that Englishmen should admit a body of Irishmen to come over here and manage their English trusts?—The connection between the Irish Society and Derry, and the whole of the people on the plantation, is of almost three centuries duration, and I do not think it would be a wise thing to imperil or break that connection.

6655. But you are aware our Church sprang out of another Church that had existed a great many centuries, and yet it was thought desirable to reform?—Yes.

6656. The fact that any institution has existed for three centuries is no conclusive reason against reform, if the reform be advisable, is it?—Certainly not, and I have indicated a reform in the constitution of the body.

6657. You would agree with me that the mere fact of something having lasted for some centuries is no reason against change?—I think it is.

6658. It is no reason against a change which is shown to be advisable on other grounds?—It all depends upon the advisability of it.

6659. Antiquity itself is no conclusive reason?—I rather think antiquity is a reason. The fact that it has received the consent of mankind for so long a time is a reason why we should consider carefully before any change is made.

6660. According to that argument the Roman Catholic Church ought still to exist in Ireland, with its old rights and privileges?—Yes, but there may be preponderating reasons why it should not.

6661. Quite so, and I want to suggest to you some preponderating reasons in this case. In the first place is it not inconvenient that trust funds of this magnitude should be administered beyond the sea by persons who very seldom visit the place, and who have next to no local knowledge?—The governor is a permanent official, and I think, practically, the deputy governor is permanent, or almost so, and the local agent is intimately acquainted with the wants of all the people; and I am most uncertain whether the funds could be administered as well by a local body as they have been and are being administered by the Irish Society at the present time.

Mr. *Sexton*—continued.

6662. Allow me to point out in the first place, that the alternative I am suggesting is not a local body, but an Irish body; and secondly, I submit to you you are in error upon a matter of fact that the deputy governor and the governor are not permanent officials?—I meant by permanent that they hold their office for a considerable number of years; I did not exactly know how long.

Sir *John Ellis*.

6663. Perhaps I can clear this up; the governor is elected for life or during good behaviour, and therefore you may consider he is a permanent official?—That is what I thought.

6664. The deputy governor is not a permanent official; he is annually elected, just the same as the moderator of the Presbyterian Church?—I was not sure how that was.

Mr. *Sexton*.

6665. The governor is changed from time to time. Now, you have important questions in relation to property to deal with in connection with the Presbyterian Church in Ireland, have you not?—You mean as regards the investment of commutation capital?

6666. Yes; all these questions are managed by Irishmen, are they not?—Yes; it is managed, I believe, by a body of trustees nominated by the general assembly.

6667. All the trustees being, I presume, Irishmen?—I believe so.

6668. Surely you do not suggest that the general assembly of the Irish Presbyterian Church would nominate Englishmen to manage their Irish property?—No, I do not; I believe they are all Irishmen.

6669. And no doubt they are very well managed; do not you think so?—That is a matter of opinion.

6670. You have an opinion to the contrary, I should think?—There is some property, I believe, that is managed by trustees in connection with the general assembly, and the management has not been satisfactory. I am not referring to the commutation capital; I am thinking of another fund.

6671. Take the three Churches in Ireland; your own, the Episcopalian, and the Roman Catholic Church, all managed by Irishmen. I presume you, as an experienced student of Irish affairs, would say that all these Churches are very capably managed?—Yes, I believe they are.

6672. You would not discover in the management of them any suggestion of superior hardheadedness in the British race; do you not think we have our share of shrewdness in Ireland?—I do think we have.

6673. You said the administration of the Irish Society had been productive of a great deal of good in many ways, and personally you had no fault to find with it. I quite understand that, but might I invite you to come off the personal ground to the public point of view. The question here is not whether a great deal of good has been done. We all recognise that. When you have 17,000*l.* a year to spend for the public use you may do a great deal of good, even though you may mis-spend some of the money. That is not the question. The question is, might not this great

Mr. Sexton—continued.

great income be administered so as to afford a larger measure of public benefit than it at present affords?—I think that is quite possible.

Sir John Ellis.

6674. Upon that I would ask you this: do you think there is any fund at present being administered, either under Government, municipal, or Church auspices, which could not have its management and its usefulness improved?—I am hardly aware of any form of government, ecclesiastical or municipal, that could not be improved.

6675. The connexion between the two cities of London and Londonderry has lasted a good many years, has it not; nearly three centuries?—Almost.

6676. You are acquainted with some of the characteristics of the City of London; you know that they have large estates to manage?—Yes.

6677. And funds to administer?—Yes.

6678. They administer them very much upon the basis upon which their estates are administered in Londonderry; they give largely to charities, and support all beneficent objects and institutions of any kind?—Yes.

6679. Would not you think this great City of London, with its large funds and large experience, was a school from which you might draw men who would be useful as trustees in the administration of your property in Derry?—Yes; I believe it is a school from which perhaps the most qualified trustees to be found anywhere could be drawn, having regard to their experience in the administration of large interests.

6680. Did you ever hear that the great Dr. Johnson once said, he thought the Lord Chancellor might choose every one's wife as well as they choose them for themselves?—No, I never did.

6681. Would you think there is any more fitness in the Lord Chancellor selecting trustees for this purpose than in his choosing men's wives?—I do not believe he is infallible.

6682. I will just ask a question about the Scotch and English Presbyterian Churches. I take it the Irish Presbyterian Church is in full communion with the Scotch and English Churches?—Yes.

6683. And that any assistance or any advice that they would give you you would gladly receive?—Very gladly indeed.

6684. As regards the grants, it has been suggested more than once, indeed a great many times, that it would be better to accumulate these grants into some great fund, rather than diffuse them amongst the voluntary bodies in Londonderry and other districts; do you think as much good would be done by any such individual management?—I entertain the contrary opinion. I believe the large number of schools extends the benefit of education over a much wider area, and that it reaches exactly the portion of the community which the originators of the plantation meant it should reach; and I think a single institution would benefit only a limited portion, and probably not that portion of the community which the plantation was intended to benefit.

Chairman.

6685. I thought the founder of the plantation intended to benefit all the people there, did he not?—Yes, but I was asked what would be the effect of giving it to a single institution.

Sir John Ellis.

6686. A good deal has been made of the question as to whether you have got your share; I apprehend, in this instance, it may be as in other instances; we none of us think we get all that we deserve?—That is true; and I believe the Irish Society at present are endeavouring to render to each portion of the community their share, and in all probability that will be realised.

Mr. ROBERT LYON MOORE, J.P., sworn; and Examined.

Sir John Ellis.

6687. You are a Deputy Lieutenant and Justice of the Peace for the county of Londonderry, I think?—Yes.

6688. And you have served as high sheriff of the county of Londonderry and Donegal?—Yes.

6689. You are the representative lessee of the fisheries of the Bann and Foyle, I believe?—Yes, I am.

6690. Do you know all the transactions in regard to the letting of the fisheries for many years past?—The first lessees that I remember as having anything to do with the fishery were Messrs. McCorkall and Rennie.

6691. Do you recollect the fisheries being let to Messrs. McCorkall and Rennie?—I do not recollect it myself; I have only heard of it; I do not know it of my own knowledge.

6692. Do you know the terms or the rent upon which they held?—I believe it was 6,600 *l.* a year.

6693. How was that letting effected, was it by public tender?—I have always understood so.

Chairman.

6694. When was that?—I believe it was about 1850. I do not remember this, myself.

Sir John Ellis.

6695. It must have been before 1850, I think?—Yes, I think 1850 was the year in which the society kept it in their own hands.

6696. The first thing that you know of your own knowledge was in 1864, when you took it yourself?—Yes, that is the first I know of my own knowledge.

6697. In 1864 were the fisheries put up to public tender?—They were.

6698. Did you then bid, in conjunction with the late Mr. Alexander, 4,625 *l.* a year?—Quite so; in conjunction with others.

6699. Were there many other tenders besides?—I believe there were; I know there were tenders from both Scotland and Ireland.

Sir John Ellis—continued.

6700. Did that lease expire in 1874?—It did.

6701. A new lease was then granted for 21 years?—Quite so.

6702. At an increased rent, the new rent being 3,080 *l.*?—£. 3,080. was the new rent.

6703. Did the Society and the public then believe that there was a valuable oyster fishery there?—Certainly; it was the universal opinion that the oysters were going to be a great success. There had been a number of experiments tried in France, and they were most successful. I visited those beds myself, as did Mr. Alexander, and we were firmly convinced there was a great future for them.

6704. Did that lease contain a provision that you should expend large sums of money in endeavouring to develope the oyster fishery?—It did.

Mr. Sexton.

6705. Was the sum specified?—Yes.

6706. What was the sum?—£. 8,000; it was afterwards reduced to 500 *l.*

Sir John Ellis.

6707. Did you actually spend 8,000 *l.*?—We actually spent 2,500 *l.* There was also an acreage rent of 1 *s.* per acre for every acre occupied to lay oysters upon; there was 6 *d.* an acre for the land which was not occupied, but which we wished reserved in order to increase the beds; and there was also a rent of 20 per cent. upon all oysters sold, payable to the Society.

Mr. Sexton.

6708. On the gross sales?—On the gross sales of all oysters sold.

6709. Was all this in addition to the 3,080 *l.*?—Quite so.

Sir John Ellis.

6710. Did you use your best exertions to establish the oyster fishery?—We did. We believed so thoroughly in it that we went on, though we were disheartened, year after year, until we had spent 2,500 *l.* upon it. We believed thoroughly that we were creating a very large and extensive property, that would not only be beneficial to the lessees and the society, but would give an enormous amount of employment in the district. We laid down two millions of fresh oysters which we imported. We also purchased oysters from various parts of Ireland, and laid the whole of them down, none of which were ever found; they were all sanded up. I cannot say exactly the reason, but I am greatly inclined to think that the sanding up of these came from the scouring of the river which was deposited in that district.

6711. At any rate the experiments failed?—At any rate it failed.

Mr. Sexton.

6712. Do you mean the sewage was deposited there?—No; I mean from the dredgers being emptied there.

Chairman.

6713. You are referring to the harbour dredging?—Quite so.

Sir John Ellis.

6714. At the time the lease was granted, in 1864, there were no drift-nets, were there?—Drift-nets were quite unknown at that time.

6715. How many at present are there using floats at the mouths of the Foyle and Bann?—From 70 to 90 every year.

6716. Of what size?—They are from 500 to 800 yards now.

6717. There is no question of the rights of fishery, is there, from Magilligan Point up to Strabane?—Up to Green Brae the words are, "from the high sea up to Green Brae, Strabane."

6718. That has been thoroughly established, has it not?—I believe there was many years ago a trial between the Sinclair family and the society, but I believe the Society thoroughly established their rights, and there has never been any question of the society's rights that I ever heard of, excepting that in 1865 or 1866 the trawlers were in the habit of trawling in the lough where the salmon lay. We applied for an injunction to the court, and an injunction was granted to restrain them. We then issued licenses to any of them who desired it, under certain restrictions, to fish where the salmon did not lie; it was merely to protect the salmon fishery that that was done.

6719. You have enjoyed it now uninterruptedly since 1854?—Yes, quite so.

6720. If that fishing was allowed between Culmore, between Magilligan Point and Culmore Fort, would the Salmon fishery above be of any value?—None at all.

6721. To come to the next point; you were of course interested in 1874, when the Harbour Commissioners went to Parliament?—We were.

6722. Do you know what the opposition was; the opposition was only on your own account by the Society, was it not?—Not only I think; I think there was also a question as to the compulsory powers which the Board wanted to take.

6723. Do you recognise this report (*handing a paper to the witness*). That I believe was signed by Mr. Alexander, who was your partner?—Yes. That is virtually what was arranged.

6724. Will you tell us what the arrangement was?—As well as I can remember, the Committee of the House of Commons met, and this Bill was opposed because the Harbour Commissioners desired at the time compulsory power to take portions of land on the River Foyle, and they also wanted to erect a training wall which was to extend from a place called the Black Brae. We had at that time entered into the arrangement I have mentioned with the society to lay down oysters, under which we were bound to expend the money I have told you of. This training wall we believed would have had the effect of rendering the arrangement null and void; it would have been perfectly impossible to have cultivated oysters with success, and it would also have had the effect of impounding the fish behind it.

Mr. Sexton.

6725. That so far goes to show that the Irish Society had a very strong motive for opposing the Bill?—Yes; I can explain the whole thing to you so far as that is concerned. The Committee of the House met, and I think it was suggested that

Mr. Sexton—continued.

that this matter could be arranged if we were allowed to postpone it to the next day. The Irish Society, and the Harbour Commissioners, and the fishery lessees met. The fishery lessees withdrew any objection to the Bill so far as they were concerned, provided the work was kept a certain distance under water, and there were certain openings made in it. The Society, I believe, also made an agreement with them (about which I do not know anything), and the opposition was withdrawn.

Sir John Ellis.

6726. You were present on each occasion when the Society was present; all that occurred was that the Society and yourself attended before the Committee of the House of Commons; it was immediately suggested that some arrangement might be made; they retired and appeared before the Committee of the House of Commons the next morning and said that they had completed that arrangement. That was the course pursued, was it not?—That was the course pursued.

6727. There was no reason for any extravagant expenditure caused by you or the Society?—None, that I know of.

Mr. Sexton.

6728. The important point is the suggestion made by a former witness that if it had not been for the sustained opposition of the Irish Society to the Bill, the Bill would have been obtained much more cheaply?—I have told you what the opposition was.

6729. Do you controvert that question?—I have told you what actually occurred; that we met one day, there was a suggestion thrown out by the Committee, and the next day we met the Committee again, and the agreements were entered into.

6730. The opposition up to the time of the agreement was substantially the opposition of the Society, was it not?—I think both the Society and the lessees opposed.

6731. Having a common interest?—I think they opposed in their own interest independently, as far as I remember.

Sir John Ellis.

6732. The Society was represented by counsel, and the junior counsel of the society represented the lessees?—Quite so.

6733. So that it was a common interest?—Yes.

6734. In point of fact the Society only opposed to such an extent as was necessary to protect your interest?—Quite so; their opposition was at once withdrawn when the arrangement was made. That training wall has never been carried out to the present day.

6735. In 1869 there was another application by the Commissioners, and in a like manner it became necessary to again nominally oppose the Bill?—Quite so; that is what occurred.

6736. Was that arrangement made without coming before the Committee of the House of Commons at all?—That I do not actually remember; I thought they did come before the Committee, but I do not remember accurately.

6737. A petition was lodged, but did it come

Sir John Ellis—continued.

before the House?—I do not recollect; I thought it did, but there was an arrangement made, at all events.

6738. There was an agreement come to?—An agreement was come to without very much disputing about it.

6739. You were not put into the witness box in the Committee-room, were you?—No, I think not.

6740. It was a private arrangement altogether before the Commissioners appeared before the Parliamentary Committee?—I do not actually remember whether it was or was not. I can tell you what the arrangement was if you desire.

6741. In point of fact, there was no factious opposition?—There was no factious opposition at all.

6742. It was a friendly arrangement, and the petition was not for the purpose of preventing the Commissioners from attaining their ends?—No; it was simply to protect the property.

6743. To come to an amicable arrangement?—Quite so.

6744. And an amicable arrangement was come to?—Yes.

6745. Without putting the Harbour Commissioners to any lengthened inquiry before the House?—Quite so.

6746. You have been a tenant on the Society's estate for many years, have you not?—I have, as an agricultural tenant.

6747. Can you say from your own knowledge, because you have had a long experience of the dealings of the Society, whether they have ever unfairly asked for rents, or demanded rents for their agricultural property beyond what the tenants were readily able to pay?——

Mr. Sexton.

6748. Before you answer that question, I should like you to consider whether you have personal knowledge that will enable you to answer it?—I will give you my own personal knowledge. In my own personal knowledge I remember four governors of the Irish Society. Under the last three governors I do not think there has been any attempt to impose excessive rents at all; and in reference to Mr. Sexton's question, I may say I have resided all my life in the agricultural district three miles from Derry, and I am intimately acquainted with all the tenantry, I believe. During the time of the late three governors I believe there has been no attempt to enforce exceptional rents.

Sir John Ellis.

6749. When the question was brought before the Society of reducing rents on properties which were under lease to the society in 1886 (that is, prior to the Bill of 1887), is it not the case that they, of their own voluntary will, had a valuation made?—Yes, they did.

6750. They offered the tenants to come in on these terms in 1886?—Yes, I believe it was in 1886. That was Mr. Murphy's valuation, I think.

6751. Did the Society act upon that valuation?—So far as I know, they did.

6752. Did they do so in your own case?—In my own case they did act upon it; but in my

own

Sir John Ellis—continued.

own case, I believe. Mr. Murphy's valuation was higher than my rent; therefore, of course, I got no reduction.

6753. They did not increase it?—They did not increase it.

6754. I may ask you this further question, because I think it is within your knowledge. Did the Society say to their tenants under leases, "We feel that this is an important question, and we should like you to take a specimen case, and let it go to the court, and by that decision we should be prepared to abide, in order to save the trouble and expense of all the tenants going"?—I do not exactly understand your question.

6755. Did not the Society take a test case upon this report of Mr. Murphy's, so that they might have the sanction of the law to the course that they pursued in the reduction of the rents where any reduction was made. Do you not remember that Mr. Babington went into court?—I think you are a little bit confusing two questions. I went into court myself, and so did Mr. Babington; but that was after 1886.

6756. Quite so; that is right?—Mr. Babington and myself met the Society; we wished the society to come to an arrangement with us.

Mr. Sexton.

6757. Who is Mr. Babington?—Another large tenant on the property. Mr. Babington wished certain reductions made for drainage and one thing and another of that kind, and I thought that one of my holdings under the Society was too highly rented; I wished a reduction on that holding. With regard to the other holding, I had no objection to the rent remaining as it was, provided I got clear of an accruing rent of 50 *l.* which was to come into force in 1893. Mr. Babington had an accruing rent coming into force in 1893 also. The Society said we do not feel justified in dealing with you in getting rid of this accruing rent, but we will raise no technical objection and throw no difficulty in your way in going into court. Accordingly Mr. Babington and I went to the court.

Chairman.

6758. When was this?—In the spring of 1888.

Mr. Sexton.

6759. Had not you a right to go under the Act of 1887?—Quite so.

Sir John Ellis.

6760. It was all a consecutive action arising out of our dealings in 1886, was it not?—Yes; we went to the court, and the rents remained exactly the same as they were, except in one case in a small farm where I got a reduction of 4 *l.*

6761. In point of fact the action of the Society was sanctioned by the court, and then we were willing to agree to it?—Quite so.

6762. All we wanted was the sanction of the court to our action?—Yes.

6763. You are sufficiently acquainted with the estate to be able to say that the Society have built a large number of farm-houses and steadings?—A large number.

6764. For the poorer tenants?—Yes.

Sir John Ellis—continued.

6765. And that the Society has also built labourers' cottages?—They built labourers' cottages and they built farms and farm steadings; they squared the fields and did the ditching.

Chairman.

6766. They charged interest, I presume, upon the money?—I think they are charging about 3½ per cent. interest upon the money for the farm steadings.

6767. And on the labourers' cottages?—I do not know. The rents are about 1 *s.* a week.

Mr. Sexton.

6768. Is there any land with the cottages?—Yes, there is a small garden attached to some of them; there are four of them with no land at all. The rent of some is 1 *s.* a week, and of others 1 *s.* 6 *d.* a week. I think it is 1 *s.* 6 *d.* a week for the houses, with land attached to them.

Sir John Ellis.

6769. There is one question with regard to a statement that was made by Dr. Todd at Question 8152, which I want to ask you?—I read Dr. Todd's evidence, and I know what the tenor of Mr. Slade's statement which he referred to is.

6770. He described in a long paragraph the condition of the estate of the Mercers' Company, which he went through.

Mr. Sexton.] That was before this gentleman was here, I should think?

The Witness.] I should think it was.

Sir John Ellis.] Is there any justification for saying that that is an inaccurate description of the present condition of affairs to-day?

Mr. Sexton.] It does not profess to be.

The Witness.] I think the way the question was put to Dr. Todd, as well as I remember it, was this: "Was this a proper description in 1831 of the state of affairs in Ireland at the time?" and he said, I think, he understood it was a correct description of its state in 1602.

Chairman.

6771. Then he was asked, "do you think there has been a very material alteration; would that account be a very great exaggeration of the state of things to-day"? Dr. Todd told you, and chiefly for this reason, that the Land Act of 1881 was imposed and rents were fairly fixed?—Quite so, that was his answer.

Mr. Lea.

6772. It did not touch the Irish Society at all?—I see he says, "I think it is a true account of the period."

Chairman.] That is an historic judgment of his, which may be available or not.

Sir John Ellis.

6773. My main point is, that at the present moment these estates are in a very flourishing condition?—I drove through the Mercers' estate the other day, and it is a perfect pleasure to drive through it. It has an air of contentment and comfort, and the houses certainly were not erected of late years.

6774. They

Sir John Ellis—continued.

6774. They were erected long before 1881?—A long time. It is a pleasure to drive through such an estate; and not only I remarked it, but three gentlemen who were with me.

6775. The legislation of 1881 has not been productive of this?—Not at all.

6776. It must have been long before that?—Long before 1881, I should think.

Mr. Sexton.

6777. Up to 1881, were not the Mercers' tenants and the tenants of the other companies paying rents upon their own improvements?—Really, I could not tell you.

6778. Do not you know that the Act of 1881, by direct operation or by agreements out of court, generally caused reductions of the rent?—Yes; but there have been great changes in agriculture, and therefore it does not follow that the tenants were paying on their own improvements.

6779. As a matter of fact, did not the tenants, before 1881, make the improvements as a rule?—They did.

6780. And was it not the main purpose of the Act of 1881 to free them from paying rent upon their own improvements?—I believe it was.

6781. And that consequence followed?—Yes, I believe so.

6782. Therefore, of course, the Act of 1881 exercised a powerful influence upon their condition?—Certainly; but you see we have northern tenant-right, and northern tenant-right has always been freely allowed, as far as I know, on all those properties; and that seems to meet your question about the improvements, because they could sell that tenant-right, and there were only a few exceptional landlords in the north of Ireland that ever interfered with them.

6783. Surely the Ulster tenant-right was the right of sale?—Quite so.

6784. Was it not quite possible for the landlord, under the Ulster tenant-right, to ask a tenant rent upon his own improvements?—I do not think it often happened.

6785. But it happened?—I have no doubt it did happen occasionally.

Chairman.

6786. Do you think the Act of 1881 was superfluous in the north of Ireland?—No; because there are certain bad landlords in some districts, and therefore I think they should be compelled to do what was right.

Mr. Sexton.

6787. Equitably, of course, the Ulster tenant-right should have controlled the landlord in regard to rent on improvements, but legally it exercised no such control?—There was no legal status.

6788. And the Act of 1881 was required for that purpose?—Yes.

6789. And the pleasant and thriving appearance of an estate is not conclusive proof that the tenants are not paying rents upon what they created?—I think it would, because it would diminish their income.

6790. No doubt it is a question of degree. If the rents were oppressive, of course it would affect the improvements of the estate, but still their improvements might have been rented, and still their estates look well?—It is highly improbable. The rents must have been excessively low if there is an air of comfort about the estate.

Mr. Sexton—continued.

6791. Have you inquired into the history of the subject sufficiently to know that it is the practice of all the companies to re-value every 20 years or so upon the improvements?—I believe they have revalued the property every 20 years. I have heard that.

6792. Does it not follow that at the date of the Land Act there must have been an accumulation of such rent upon improvements?—No, not always, I think; because there was always an allowance made on that. Some landlords, as I have told you, I believe did value the improvements, but the generality of landlords in the North, I believe, did not value the improvements.

6793. There may have been casual allowances at certain seasons?—No, annual use.

6794. Was not the regular system one of rating the improvements?—No, I do not quite agree with you in that, because the full rent was never put upon the land in the North, I believe.

6795. What do you call the full rent?—If you take a farm and put it up to competition, the rent that would be given in competition I would call the full rent. For instance, I can give you an example of my own property. The rent a man paid me was 8 *l.* 3 *s.* This farm was handed over to his son-in-law, and the father went to live with the son-in-law. The son-in-law then, at the father's death, did not think it advantageous to hold it, and he let it to a cousin of his wife's at the sum of 20 *l.* a year. Therefore I call the full rent of that 20 *l.* a year, or what in the open market it would have brought. That man went into the Land Court, as there was a middleman, and he had it reduced to 14 *l.*; but the original landlord was receiving the 8 *l.* 3 *s.*

6796. That was the highest rent they could get anybody to offer?—I could not tell you whether it was the highest rent offered or not.

6797. Would not you say that what we know as "earth hunger" in Ireland, due to the fact that the people have nothing but the land to live on, runs up the rents of land to a point which does not allow subsistence to the tenant?—There is no doubt there is earth hunger in Ireland. The tenant in Ireland has no other idea of investing his money than investing it in land. There are very few manufactories, or anything of that kind, and their only idea is to invest in land.

6798. If there is upon the property a system of terminable leases, and if at the conclusion of each lease you see a new valuation and a raising of the rents, can you come to any other conclusion than that the improvements effected by the labour of the tenant have been used to increase the rent?—There is another element you must take into consideration, and that is prices. If prices had gone up, I presume the rent would be raised without raising it on the tenant's improvements.

Mr. *Sexton*—continued.

6799. Prices fluctuate; they go up and down; but if you find periodical increases at the end of, say, every 20 years, does it not follow that improvements have been rented?—No; I think it depends largely upon prices. If the prices go down, the rent ought to go down; if prices go up, the rent ought to go up.

6800. But if you find an invariable system of heavy increase at the end of every 20 years, coupled with the fact, which is denied by no one, that the improvements are usually made by the tenants, would you quarrel for a moment with the conclusion that the improvements have been rented?—You put it in too general a way, I think, because there is no doubt in some of the companies' estates a great number of improvements were made by the companies themselves; but as a general rule, I say, I believe the tenants have made the improvements.

6801. And they have been rented on them?—No, I do not say that they have been rented on them; I cannot follow you in that, because that abolishes tenant-right.

6802. No; for you have already admitted that the tenant-right only had regard to the sale of the interest, and that the landlord, under the Ulster tenant-right, was as free as elsewhere to raise the rent?—Yes, he was.

6803. That being admitted, then, and the improvements being generally made by the tenant, do you really question that if you find a raising of rents all over the estate at the end of every 20 years, that those increases of rent have been due, at least in a large measure, to the increased value due to the improvements made by the tenant?—I cannot admit that as a general principle.

6804. To what extent do you qualify it?—I am sure there were landlords that did that; but I qualify it by saying there were landlords who did not do that.

6805. You admit that improvements, as a general rule, are made by the tenant?—Yes.

6806. How can you otherwise account for that steady system of increase, except by the conclusion that the improvements have been rented?—Except so far as it is due to change of prices.

6807. Will you take the two elements?—I will tell you what I acknowledge. I acknowledge that if the prices remain in *statu quo*, and if every 20 years there is a valuation made by the landlord, and the rent goes up, that evidently must be an increase of rent on tenants' improvements.

6808. Now, what do you yourself hold from the society?—Two hundred and fifty-two acres, I think it is.

6809. All in your own hands?—Yes.

6810. I understand you are a landlord also?—Yes.

6811. What is your tenure?—I am now a statutory tenant.

6812. What was your tenure when you first became a tenant?—It has been held by my family since before the siege.

6813. What was the rent when you first came into control of it?—I should explain that there were three holdings.

6814. What was the total rent of all the holdings?—I will give you them separately, if you will allow me. There are 119 acres, which I think were subject to 154 *l.* rent. There are 16 acres subject to 14 *l.*; and there are 40 acres subject to, at present, 35 *l.*, but it was 40 *l.*; that is the one on which I said there was 4 *l.* reduction.

6815. What was the rent when you came in?—£. 29 when I came in.

6816. The rents were 154 *l.*, 14 *l.* and 29 *l.* when you came in, making 198 *l.* Were they increased?—No; except in the case of the last one. That was increased from 29 *l.* to 40 *l.*

6817. You sought to obtain a reduction by private negotiation?—Yes.

6818. Did you succeed?—No.

6819. Then you went into the court?—Quite so.

6820. They had no power to stay you?—No; not so far as I am aware.

6821. You were a leaseholder?—I am a leaseholder.

6822. And the Act of 1887 entitled you to go into court?—I believe so.

6823. You owe them no thanks for that?—I do not know. I suppose I owe them no thanks for allowing me to go into court, but I am not sufficient of a lawyer to know whether there were any objections which they might have raised against me in court. They certainly did not raise any. They merely let the court decide the case, and raised no factious opposition in any way to me.

6824. Of course not, you were in your legal right?—I suppose so.

6825. Sir John Whitaker Ellis has told us that Mr. Murphy's valuation, about which he rather praised the society, was in your case higher than your rent?—So I am told.

6826. Was that the case with other tenants?—I do not know.

6827. It may have been higher than the rent in the other cases also?—It may have been for aught I know.

6828. You got a reduction in one case?—In one case, yes.

6829. Now about these fisheries, are you the lessee of all the fisheries owned by the society?—I am one of the lessees.

6830. Joint lessee of all the fisheries?—Yes.

6831. I notice here in the accounts of the society for the year ending February 1889, an entry upon the receipts side: "For fisheries rent, 5,161 *l.* 15 *s.*" Did you pay that?—Yes. I have told you I paid 5 *s.* an acre for the oyster land.

6832. The obligation under your lease for rent is 5,080 *l.*?—Quite so.

6833. When you told us that you paid 1 *s.* an acre for certain other lands, and 6 *d.* for certain other lands, and 50 per cent. on the oyster land, how did those three items only come to 80 *l.*?—As I told you, the oysters were a complete failure. They were all sanded up, I believe.

6834. Then I see, "For rent of Lough Foyle Slobs, 300 *l.*" Had you anything to do with that?—Nothing at all.

6835. When you became the lessee in 1864, was

Mr. Sexton—continued.

was there a public advertisement?—There was, I believe, in the Scotch and Irish papers, and the English too.

6636. Was there a printed form of tender?—There was.

6637. Could you favour us with a copy of that?—No, I could not.

6638. You have not got one?—No.

6639. Were the conditions stated in the form?—As well as I can remember, they were.

6640. Did they say that the highest tender would be accepted?—I do not remember that.

6641. How many tenders were there in 1864?—I do not know.

6642. Was it declared, or was it understood at the time, that the highest tender had been accepted?—I know it was.

6643. It was stated so?—Yes. I know who tendered the next highest; a Scotchman.

6644. That was a 10-years' lease?—Quite so.

6645. And when that expired was the same form of public advertisement repeated?—No, it was not.

6646. What happened then?—I have told you before there was a belief that oyster culture was going to be very successful; that probably there would be a very successful oyster fishery.

6647. This was in 1874?—Yes, about that period. The society asked us whether we would undertake the culture of oysters, and we said we would under certain conditions. We were so convinced that success would attend the cultivation of oysters, that we said we would give the society 20 per cent.; and in order to induce them still more to grant us a lease, we increased our salmon rent.

6648. You increased it from 4,625 *l.* to 5,000 *l.*?—Yes.

6649. And also promised to give 20 per cent. upon the oysters you said?—Yes.

6650. Was it upon these personal negotiations that the new lease was concluded?—It was.

6651. There was no offer to the public of the fisheries?—No.

6652. The lease expired in five years?—It is a lease from 1874 to 1895; 21 years.

Mr. *Lea.*

6653. Is there a contention that at one time the fisheries only extended to Culmore Point?—That is beyond my memory. The trawlers, I have told you, came up and did fish at Culmore Point. We applied for an injunction in Chancery; it was obtained, and then we have since given the fishermen leave to fish for white fish at certain points.

6654. Have there been meetings of fishermen lately in connection with this matter?—Not that I have heard of.

6655. Is there any dissatisfaction amongst the fishermen in consequence of their being prohibited coming up above a certain point?—I think there would be dissatisfaction if you prohibited them, no matter where the limit is. It is a several fishery. Of course it could not have been granted except before Magna Charta. We had a very heavy trial in Coleraine, and the title of the society was proved up to Henry II.

Mr. *Lea*—continued.

6656. With regard to the Mercers' estate, you said you drove through it and saw a number of goodly houses?—A great many houses.

6657. Who erected those houses, generally?—I could not tell you; I do not know.

6658. Would it not be the tenants themselves?—I have no idea at all.

Chairman.

6659. It was a public tender in 1864?—Quite so.

6660. Considering the increased prosperity of the neighbourhood, the advance from 4,600 *l.* to 5,000 *l.* was rather a small advance, was it not?—I may tell you that in 1865 the price of salmon was 10 *d.* a pound in Derry. I cannot tell you what it was in 1874, but at the present time it is 7 *d.* In 1864 there were no drift nets at all. These drift-nets extend across the bay to a very large extent. They are 500 to 600 yards long, as I have told you before, and they capture a very large proportion of the salmon. These nets did not exist in 1864.

6661. Did the use of the drift-nets greatly reduce the cost of the catch?—No.

6662. I do not then follow your point?—It is a public fishery. The public, as I have told you, have 80 to 90 nets now that never were in existence in 1864.

6663. And you feel that the advance from 4,600 *l.* to 5,000 *l.* was a reasonable advance?—Quite so. I am quite sure it was.

6664. But as a man of business, do you not agree that it would have been more satisfactory to the public, and the society administering funds for public purposes, if that arrangement of 1874 had been tested by a public tender?—I have no idea as to whether it would be more satisfactory to the public, which is, I think, the way you put it to me.

6665. The way I put it to you is this: The question of whether 5,000 *l.* was a fair advance upon 4,600 *l.* is a question that would have been more satisfactorily answered if it had been tested in the open market?—More satisfactory to whom?

6666. To the society?—I should say not.

6667. You are aware that the allegation of Mr. Ballantyne is that there was a back stairs influence?—Yes.

6668. That, in short, this was a collusive arrangement?—Quite so. I understand that is Mr. Ballantyne's evidence. It is perfectly untrue. Mr. Ballantyne is completely misled as regards that.

6669. But would it not have been better if that assertion had never been possible; and, it would not have been possible if it had been submitted to open tender?—No; if it had been submitted to open tender it would not have been possible, but the society, I presume, are bound to increase their income as much as possible, and I believe they took the best steps to increase their income with solvent tenants. As I have told you before, the society held these fisheries themselves at a dead loss.

6670. Before 1864?—Before 1864.

Mr. Sexton.

6871. If the witness can really give us any evidence based on personal knowledge on that point, it would be rather important?—I cannot give you personal knowledge.

Colonel *Laurie.*

6872. Were you not bound also to develope the oyster culture by your new lease?—Certainly.

6873. That was part of the consideration, was it?—Yes.

Sir John Ellis.

6874. You spent 2,500 *l.*?—We spent 2,500 *l.* on it.

Chairman.

6875. Then the advance in the rent of the fisheries was more than the difference between 4,600 *l.* and 5,000 *l.* clearly, because you gave an additional consideration?—If there was a sale of the oysters; but you see the oysters never did succeed.

6876. But the chance of a sale of oysters was sufficient to induce you to expend money?—Yes, I see what you mean. Certainly there would have been an income of 20 per cent. on the sale of these oysters added to the society's income.

Colonel *Laurie.*

6877. I think what the Chairman meant was this. In addition to giving the increased rent of 400 *l.* a year, you also expended 2,500 *l.* in oyster culture; is not that so?—Yes.

6878. That shows that the consideration was greater than an additional rent of 400 *l.* a year, because you expended 2,500 *l.*?—Yes.

Chairman.

6879. Is it fair to ask you whether you anticipated that in 1865 there will be a putting-up to public tender?—I do not think it is a question for me to enter into.

6880. Would you like to suggest anything further?—I should like to say that at Question 3956 there is a statement made by Mr. Ballantyne as regards the letting of property in Derry.

6881. It is about Mr. Green?—Quite so.

6882. Now, what do you want to say upon that?—I want to say that I am acquainted with the dealings about that property, and it was let at the time at the price put upon it by the surveyor for the society; I think it is let at one guinea. The adjoining property is let at 1 *l.* a foot, and I think has been let since. The part of it is true which states that Mr. Munn came into the possession of the property; as to the remainder of the answers to the question, I wish to say that it is untrue.

6883. It comes to this, that the fact that Mr. Munn was Mr. Green's father-in-law by his second marriage, was not a deciding consideration in this allotment?—Quite so. Also I can contradict most absolutely the statement there that it was settled by Mr. Green in the way stated. I know that Mr. Munn settled 1,600 *l.* on his daughter.

6884. We do not want to know if he settled, if he did not settle it in that way?—He did not.

Mr. Sexton.

6885. You know that of your own personal knowledge?—Of my own personal knowledge.

Mr. Thomas Bedford Montgomery, sworn; and Examined.

Sir John Ellis.

6886. You are the general agent of the Irish Society?—Yes.

6887. You reside in Londonderry?—Yes.

6888. You have held the office of general agent since 1884?—Yes.

Chairman.

6889. Have you anything to say about the letting of the fisheries?—No.

6890–1. But you can get for us the circumstances of the letting in 1864?—I will endeavour to do so.

Mr. Sexton.] We want a list of the tenders actually received in 1864 for the fisheries; a list of the amounts and the form of tender.

Sir John Ellis.] We will get you every information we can with regard to those transactions.

Sir John Ellis.

6892. You have read the evidence given before this Committee?—I have read some of it.

6893. With reference to perpetuity leases, is it a fact that 9-10ths of the land within the city has been let in perpetuity for many years?—It is.

6894. Was it a fact that the society discontinued to grant these perpetuity leases because they had lost all control over the property, and said it got into very bad repair?—That is my opinion.

6895. And its getting into disrepair and bad order was the reason of their discontinuing to grant perpetuity leases?—Yes.

Mr. Sexton.

6896. How long ago is that?—I think about 1836.

6897. You do not know then?—My recollection of the record is that about 1836 the perpetuity leases were discontinued.

6898. As I understand, Sir John is putting it to you that they were discontinued because of certain condition of repair, but I apprehend you are not in a position to give evidence on that subject?—That is what I have always understood.

Sir John Ellis.

6899. The perpetuity leases that are granted now

Sir John Ellis—continued.

now are granted on certain conditions as to construction of buildings?—Yes.

6900. And in such a manner as will insure proper appropriation of the land?—Yes.

6901. When property has come into the hands of the society, what has been the usual course before dealing with it. Do they obtain the opinion of a valuer?—Yes. Where property comes into the hands of the society, upon which there are good and substantial buildings already standing, the best advice the society can get in regard to the value of the property has been taken; and it has been offered to the occupying tenant on long lease; determinable lease; and in cases where property falls into the hands of the Society in very bad repair, and fit only for rebuilding, it is held on short tenancies until opportunity occurs to let it on building leases, preference being given to the occupying tenants.

6902. As far as you can judge, you think that the granting of perpetuity leases, according to the records of the society, cannot have had anything to do with the impeding of the progress of the prosperity of the city of Londonderry?—I think it threw a great deal of the property into the hands of middlemen, and I do not think that the property in the hands of middlemen has thriven, as can be seen by going through Derry.

6903. The method of the society, you say, is first to get a valuation of their property from a competent valuer, aided with your local experience?—Yes.

6904. And then to offer to the tenants the renewal of their leases upon those terms?—Yes.

6905. And if the tenants do not renew, then the property is put into the public market?—Yes.

6906. That being the case, is there any ground for saying that the rents charged by the society are in any way excessive?—No; not that I am aware of.

6907. There has been a question raised here of the main block of land that came into the hands of this society some two years ago?—You mean in September 1888.

6908. In Shipkey-street?—That was in 1882, I think.

6909. Was it not Shipkey-place, where they proposed to erect baths and washhouses?—That is in Strand-road. In September 1888 that fell in.

6910. Now, is it the fact that tenants along the front of that place desire to remain in their present occupations, only with one exception?—It is the case that they had stated to me.

6911. And they refuse to accept perpetuity leases with a view to rebuilding?—Yes, they requested not to be forced into taking them for the present. But they have told me that rather than be put out they will take them; they will all obtain the society's consent and rebuild their premises, but at the present time they do not wish to do so.

6912. The only reason it is not rebuilt is that the tenant is unable to provide the funds for rebuilding, and the society is unwilling to disturb the tenant?—Just so. And there is one other reason, and that is this, that there is no room for more than four buildings upon the block fronting Strand-road and there are eight tenants in occupation.

0.112.

Sir John Ellis—continued.

6913. Has Mr. Johnson applied for a perpetuity lease with a view to rebuilding?—Yes.

6914. It is impossible to grant that without disturbing the other tenants?—Utterly; he allows so himself.

6915. And is it under consideration between the society and the corporation as to the application of a larger portion of this land for the purpose of baths and wash-houses?—It is.

6916. And except the frontage towards the street which we have just referred to, there is only space for the baths and wash-houses?—That is so.

6917. Is there any great demand in Londonderry for sites for buildings?—No, not for commercial houses.

6918. So that there is no competition that forces prices to any excessive height?—Very little; in fact there is none.

6919. As regards general management of the property of the society, the usual course is for the tenants who may wish to renew, or in any way to change their tenancies, to apply to you?—Yes.

6920. And any applications or requests made by tenants are immediately forwarded by you to the secretary?—Yes.

6921. Is there ever any unreasonable delay in getting an answer?—No, nor any delay in forwarding it.

6922. Do the courts always require a report from you upon all questions that come before them?—Invariably.

6923. And do you make personal inquiries on the spot?—I do.

6924. Both as regards any applications for a renewal, or as regards any application for grants?—Yes, in each case.

6925. You are a Justice of the peace?—I am.

6926. And you have every opportunity on the spot of becoming acquainted with the various institutions with which the society is connected?—I have.

6927. Do you make it your business to observe and watch as to the general working of those institutions?—I do.

6928. And you are in touch with the various authorities who represent those institutions?—I am in frequent communication.

6929. We have heard that a request was made for land upon which to build a temperance hall. Was it a fact that the society were willing to grant it if the user of the hall had been confined to temperance and religious purposes?—That was the fact.

6930. There was also a question raised as to the Roman Catholic Bishop of Derry having applied through Mr. M'Neil for a site for a house for the reception of indigent ladies?—Yes.

6931. Has that application been answered in a proper manner?—Yes.

6932. What is the reason why the matter has not progressed?—The visitation of the Society wrote to the promoters to ask them to come forward and state what they wished, and the promoters declined to do so. Therefore, the matter was not further considered.

6933. Having never intimated to the Society what it is they really want?—No.

6934. Having

Sir John Ellis—continued.

6934. Having written to ask whether the society would give them a grant of land, the society said tentatively, they would do so, but that no further information has been forwarded to the society as to what is wanted?—That is the case.

6935. Now, as to the School of Culmore; a school has just been built there?—The society have built a school, and own a school there; they subsidise a school.

6936. It is open to all denominations?—It is under the National Board; open to all denominations.

6937. Is it ample for all that population there? —Fully so.

6938. Is it the fact that the society either keep any of their grants secret, or take any steps to publish them?—They make the grant, and there is the end of the question.

6939. At Question 6,590 it is stated they keep the Orange grants secret; but in the case of the Catholics, they publish their benevolence by writing to the papers. Now is it the fact that we do keep the Orange grants secret and publish the Catholic grants?—Certainly not, they are all published. The grants are all acknowledged in the public press.

6940. Is that accomplished by the reporters attending at the Government House and getting the information, and then publishing it?—Are you alluding now to what took place at Government House on visitation?

6941. I take it that what is meant there, is that Orange grants are kept secret and Catholic grants are published. But as a matter of fact they are all published in our accounts?—Everything is published.

6942. There is no secrecy in the one with publicity in the other?—They all appear in the papers regularly.

6943. Can you produce a plan, and show us the grant that was made to the Harbour Commissioners?—I can.

Chairman.] What is the object of this?

Sir John Ellis.

6944. The Harbour Commissioners said, or Mr. Hamilton said on their behalf, which I was very much astonished at, that the grants made by the society were worthless. I want to show what the grants were?—The grant in this comprises about 80 acres of ground. The measurements are all set forth in the plan which I now produce.

6945. This is a free grant?—Yes.

6946. There were no perpetuity leases there? —This is all free. This was all slob land.

6947. And this was guaranteed free, and there was also land granted to the railway company?— Yes.

6948. I see on the plan the line of railway at the back of the wharves and quays which were to be constructed?—Yes.

6949. That was granted to the railway, and this was granted to the Harbour Commissioners? —Yes.

6950. Was that the best thing that could be done in the way of forwarding the matter of the harbour and quays?—I think so, decidedly.

Sir John Ellis—continued.

6951. It was a very valuable grant?—Very valuable, and going to be more valuable I should think.

6952. As regards the tenants at the back, was there any reservation that they should have access to the river?—Yes.

6953. But if they used the quays and pier they were to be subject to the dues in the usual way?—Yes.

6954. In addition to this, was the King's Quay absolutely granted by the society to the Harbour Commissioners?—Yes, it was.

6955. And was it a very valuable grant?— Very valuable. I now exhibit a plan of that also.

6956. You exhibit the plans showing the grants made by the society?—Yes.

6957. And you also produce the deeds by which the grants were made?—Yes.

6958. You cannot give me an account of the letting of the fisheries in 1850?—No, I cannot.

6959. You would have to look that up?—I should have to look it up. I am not aware that we have any records in our office.

6960. You have been a land agent all your life, I believe?—A good part of it.

6961. How old are you now?—I am 48.

6962. And from your experience of such a business, do you consider that the society conducts it with as much economy and care as it is possible for a public body to do?—Decidedly; most certainly.

6963. Did you ever have any complaint from the agricultural tenants that they were overrented?—Not since the last Act.

6964. Have they had most of their tenancies settled by arrangement with the society?—Yes; the major part have been settled by mutual consent.

6965. When did you become agent?—At the end of 1884.

Mr. Lea.

6966. With regard to the agricultural tenants have you had many cases in the Land Courts?— Yes, we have certainly.

6967. How many?—I could not tell you exactly. We have had 61; that is to say, that have been listed and gone into court, and heard in court.

6968. Out of how many agricultural tenants? —Out of 138.

6969. What was the average reduction?— The average reduction would be about 20 per cent.

6970. Does that include leaseholds?—Yes; all tenants that have gone into court.

6971. Had you many leaseholds?—Under 61 have gone into court; or rather that hold under judicial leases.

6972. I mean the leaseholders?—I know that is what you mean. Of the original leaseholders that took advantage of the Act of 1887, and that could not take advantage of any Act before that, I think there were 59; I will say about 60.

6973. How many of the statutory tenants?— The remainder between 60 and 138 will be statutory tenants.

6974. I am

Mr. *Lea*—continued.

6974. I am afraid you do not understand my question; how many leaseholders went into court?—I think about 40.

6975. Then there have been some disputes between the Irish Society and the agricultural tenants?—There have been differences.

6976. As to rents?—With regard to rents.

6977. Was there much contention that the Irish Society rented tenants upon their own improvements?—I have never heard that contention advanced in court or out of court. I know as a matter of fact that Mr. Murphy, the valuer, whom the Society appointed to value all their leasehold agricultural estates, had strict orders to exclude all the tenants' improvements in making the valuations, which he did.

6978. Was that the case with Mr. Samuel Osborne: I think he is a large tenant of the Irish Society?—Yes, he is tenant of the Irish Society.

6979. He contended, did not he, that you rented him upon his own improvements?—His was a statutory tenancy.

6980. That was reduced?—By mutual consent.

6981. Without going into court?—Yes; it did not go into court. He has two holdings. One was settled before I became the agent. I really do not know whether that was settled out of court or in court. I think it was settled out of court; but I know his large holding was settled out of court.

6982. You said nine-tenths of the leases were perpetuity leases?—No; I understood you to ask whether nine-tenths of the property of the city of Derry was leased in perpetuity, and I said yes.

6983. How long has that been the case?—Oh, for a hundred years.

6984. Were those given to tenants a hundred years ago?—They were given to the society's lessees.

6985. Then, is it only one-tenth of the property in Derry that is not under perpetuity leases?—That the society owns, because there is a good deal of Derry that the society does not own; Church land and so on.

6986. There are slob lands in the possession of the Irish Society?—Yes.

6987. Do they give perpetuity leases of those?—There are two kinds of slob lands. There are agricultural slob lands, and there are slob lands in the city or about the city, of which you have heard, and which the Harbour Commissioners have had.

6988. We will talk about the city then?—All the land in the city proper has been granted free to the Harbour Commissioners; at least all the foreshore.

6989. Evidence has been given here that you retained the foreshores in your own possession; is that correct?—Yes.

6990. And that this prevented shipbuilding yards for a considerable period?—I cannot admit that. There is a shipbuilding yard at present in full swing, and has been for some years, upon slob land which the society granted to the Harbour Commissioners.

6991. That is Mr. Biggar's?—That is Mr. Biggar's. There is another in process of formation below it.

6992. Mr. Biggar's has been established some three or four years?—Yes; some three or four years.

6993. Do you remember the name of the person who applied to you for a place for shipbuilding some years ago?—I never knew it.

6994. How long have you been the agent?—Since the end of 1884.

6995. It was probably before that time?—Yes.

6996. Do you know what proportion of grants have been given to the Presbyterian Church as compared with the Episcopal Church?—Yes; I can give you a very fair estimate of it. I divide them into two groups; those under Presbyterian or dissenting management, or mainly so, and those under Church of Ireland management, and they are about even; about 1,500 *l.* a year to each. I group the Presbyterians and a few dissenting bodies, who get small grants, into one group, and the society's annual donations to that body amount to about 1,600 *l.* a year.

6997. Does that include the amount given to the Catholics?—No; that is entirely to schools, primary and other schools, under Presbyterian or dissenting management. There are two or three Methodist churches and two Baptist.

6998. Is that the average amount given, or is that only for one year?—That is about the amount given every year so long as they are all in existence.

6999. You say about 1,500 *l.* a year to each?—I say about 1,600 *l.* a year to Presbyterian and dissenting bodies, and 1,500 *l.* a year to the Church of Ireland.

7000. That includes the Magee College?—The Magee College and the Londonderry Academic Institution and the Coleraine Academic Institution, and all the primary schools and Sunday schools.

7001. That includes Coleraine as well as Londonderry?—Yes, I am speaking of the property as a whole.

7002. Have you any detailed statement showing what is given to Presbyterian bodies and what is given to Episcopal Church bodies?—I have statements of each school, but I have not them here. I know the schools that were given to, and I know how much that we gave to them, and I know the management they are under, of course.

7003. Can you tell me the proportion with regard to churches?—I could not tell you the proportion with regard churches. I presume you mean capital sums given to churches.

7004. Yes?—I could not give it to you in proportion, but I could tell you the various grants that have been given from memory. They are, however, so numerous and so various, and are given at all times and seasons, so that I do not know that I can give you an average.

7005. But roughly, about how much?—I do not know how many years back you want me to go.

7006. Can you give me an average roughly of three or four years?—I could not.

7007. I presume the Presbyterian grants are immensely

Mr. *Law*—continued.

immensely less than the last Established Church grants?—They are less certainly; I think I may say that the reason is because an extraordinarily large grant has been given lately to the cathedral, and an extraordinarily large grant has been given towards the renovation of Coleraine Church. For that reason they are larger.

7008. Do you have any connexion with the London companies whose property is in the country?—No.

7009. No communications pass in reference to that property?—No, not as far as I am concerned.

Chairman.

7010. Is it a part of your duty to advise your society as to the distribution of grants?—Yes.

7011. And they take your advice as to so much being given to this school or to that?—Yes.

7012. It is through your eyes, if I may say so, that they see. They look at the recipients of your favour through your eyes?—Yes. They always demand a report from me upon every application that comes before them.

7013. What is the process. Do you make a recommendation to them, or do you submit to them all the applications that you receive?—I make a report, and as a general rule, I recommend what I think ought to be done.

7014. Do you submit applications with your own advice as to preference, or do you say, "I recommend you to give so much and so much"?—I only deal with individual applications as they come before me; I send them forward with a report.

7015. You send on all the applications with a report of your own?—Yes.

7016. And upon that report, I suppose, in nine cases out of 10 they act?—Yes. I should say they do act in a great majority of cases.

7017. Now on the point of the access of tenants to the society, is that perfectly easy always. If any tenant imagines that he has any case to make out before the society, is it very easy for him to get to head-quarters?—It is as simple as possible. My office is open, I may say, daily.

7018. The application goes through you to London?—That is what I was going to say. He makes his application to me, and I immediately forward it.

7019. But is there any difficulty of access for tenants to the society in London?—Not the slightest. Of course you mean through written communications.

7020. No; that is what I do not mean?—I did not quite catch your meaning; because, unless the tenants go there straight, any application a tenant has to make to the Irish Society he makes, as a general rule, through me.

7021. No doubt, as a general rule, he naturally would; but if he were anxious to see the society and state his case, whatever it might be, in his proper person, would there be a difficulty?—He would either have to go to London, or else he would see them at the visitation once a year.

7022. If he went to London would the society see him?—Oh, yes. I know that of my own knowledge.

Chairman—continued.

7023. That does happen?—It does happen, yes.

7024. At the visitation are they easy of access?—To everybody who has any business with them.

7025. One witness, I think it was Sir William Miller, complained of the delay as to bye-laws, caused by the necessity of reference to London. He says that the necessity of submitting bye-laws for the approval and sanction of the Irish Society causes an immense amount of delay in regard to the sanctioning of bye-laws. Now, what sort of delay happens. What is the interval between the submission of a bye-law for the sanction of the society and its ratification by them?—I could hardly tell you exactly, because it is such a long time since any bye-law has been sent forward. If you examine the last bye-law that was sent forward, it was in 1878. But it would come before the first court of the society, and be dealt with in due course, like every other application.

7026. You say the last was in 1878?—Speaking from memory, I think it was 1878.

7027. You mean that in no case has the approval of the Irish Society been sought for a bye-law since 1878?—That is what I have heard.

7028. What is the source of the necessity of getting the approval of the Irish Society; why is it necessary; is it in the charter, or where?—Really I cannot tell you.

Sir John Ellis.] It is in the charter. In 1878 the clerk sent in a new bye-law of the 2nd February, and that we returned to him on the 18th February 1878; that is in 16 days.

Sir William Marriott.] Have there been any new bye-laws, Mr. Patton?

Mr. Patton.] I am instructed there have been none at all since 1878, and the delay then was about a week.

Chairman.

7029. We have heard a good deal of opinion expressed that the cost of management is excessive. I see in Ireland salaries and gratuities amount to 1,8[illegible] *l.*; have you got the items of that?—No.

7030. You have them in your own accounts I suppose?—That is tabulated in London.

7031. Yes, but these are general and incidental expenses in Ireland; the figures must be sent up from Ireland to London?—Yes, so far as regards Ireland, no doubt.

7032. That is all I am talking about. You have in your office all the items of those?—We have sent up the items.

7033. And you have them?—Yes.

7034. And you know them?—Yes, I presume we do.

7035. Then I should like, if you can conveniently, that you should give it rather more in detail as to that first head of expenses in Ireland. It is this: "salaries and gratuities, general agent and

Chairman—continued.

and Deputy Vice Admiral, surveyor, bailiff of Culmore Ford, and lands, &c., and others, 1,899 *l.* 6 *s.* 3 *d.*" Now can you give no more detail. What is the Deputy Vice Admiral for example?—I have the honour to be the Deputy Vice Admiral.

Sir John Ellis.] And I am the Vice Admiral.]

Chairman.

7036. Then "Deputy Vice Admiral" is included with "general agent"?—Yes.

7037. And is the surveyor also the same person?—No, the surveyor is another person.

7038. And the bailiff of Culmore Ford?—Culmore Ford is abolished, but there is a bailiff in Culmore.

7039. I do not want to examine the personality of the bailiff of Culmore, but I want to know exactly what this item of expenditure means. It appears that the Deputy Vice Admiral is a mere title; but what does the bailiff of Culmore do for his money?—It is the bailiff of Culmore, I presume, is meant by "bailiff of Culmore Ford."

7040. Tell me what the bailiff of Culmore does for his money?—He looks over the property.

7041. What is his salary?—His salary, 20 *l.* a year.

7042. What does he do?—He looks over the property and gives me any assistance I want in dealing with tenants.

7043. "And others." Who are the others?—I do not know.

Sir William Marriott.

7044. Now you say that the Deputy Vice Admiral and the general agent go together. What do they get?—£. 800 a year.

7045. "And others"?—The others probably will be the clerk in Londonderry.

7046. How much does he get?—He gets 150 *l.*

Chairman.

7047. Is not this a very loose way of stating the head of expenditure; how much does the surveyor get?—The surveyor gets payment by fees; sometimes it is more, and sometimes it is less.

7048. What is the average?—He might get 100 *l.* a year; very likely more; it is, of course, according to what he does.

7049. Is it not rather surprising that you send up the account to the London office, but that you do not know the details of your own expenditure, of your own office?—I must tell you that that line has not been written by me. I send up the items of expenditure, and then they are tabulated in the London office.

7050. Now then, on the second head of Irish general and incidental expenses, I see, "Visitation expenses, 1888, including costs of entertainments to public bodies and the tenantry." What were these entertainments in the year ending February 1889?—Those were the entertainments that were given by the visitation. There are generally two banquets, one in Coleraine and another in Londonderry.

7051. Do you mean then that two banquets cost 667 *l.*?—Together with the visitation expenses.

7052. What are the visitation expenses?—It would depend entirely upon the number of the visitation coming over.

7053. Hotel bills you mean?—Yes; car hills and so on; there are a great many expenses.

7054. You cannot give us the cost of the entertainments apart from the visitation expenses?—No; I could not. That would also depend upon the number who dine.

7055. You give here, for the information of all whom it may concern, the heads of expenditure, and you give it vaguely; "Visitation expenses, 1888, including costs of entertainments to public bodies and the tenantry." Now, there is some feeling in England, at all events, as to this cost of entertainments on the part of the society. It may be a right feeling, or it may be an excessively jealous feeling. I pass no opinion upon that, but that feeling exists, and we want to know how much money is spent in eating and drinking. Now, you could not have put down "cost of entertainment," unless you knew what it meant. What was the cost of the entertainments?—It might be, perhaps, from 150 to 200 people who dined.

7056. I did not ask you how many people dined, I asked you how much you paid for the entertainment?—We generally got an estimate.

7057. Have you the bill in your office?—Yes.

Sir Richard Temple.] Probably the case is this: the witness does not recollect what the amount was.

Chairman.

7058. If the witness says he has not got it in his memory, and that he has left his memorandum at home, so be it?—Yes, that is the case.

Sir Richard Temple.

7059. I suppose you have got the bills?—The bills have been sent up to London.

7060. But you keep a record of their totals?—Yes, we have a record of what we sent away.

Chairman.

7061. Apart from the expenses of these entertainments to the public bodies and the tenantry, who settles who shall be asked?—There is a general list of parties that I am informed have always been asked; that is to say, the society wish to have their leading tenantry and the representatives of all the leading bodies in the town, and the clergy.

7062. Of all denominations?—Yes, to a certain degree, of all denominations; but with regard to the Roman Catholic clergy, there have been two gentlemen who have always been asked. The Bishop has always been asked, and the President of St. Columbs College.

7063. The Catholic Bishop?—Yes; but the Catholic clergy, so far as I can understand, do not wish to come.

Sir John Ellis.

7064. The question the Chairman put to you was,

Sir John Ellis—continued.

was, are they asked?—Two of them are always asked, but the others are not asked.

Chairman.

7065. You say they are all asked to a certain degree; tell us what proportion of Presbyterians and Episcopalians, on the one hand, are asked, as against the two Catholic gentlemen?—There may be half-a-dozen of each.

7066. That is, there are 12 Presbyterians and Episcopalians against the Bishop of Derry and the President of St. Columbus College?—Yes.

Mr. Lea.

7067. Have annual banquets always been given in Derry?—So far as I know.

7068. And in Coleraine?—Yes, so far as I know.

7069. At one time were not the banquets in Coleraine only held once in seven years?—I do not know. I know that since 1884 they have always been held.

Sir William Marriott.

7070. You said, in answer to the Chairman, that your recommendations were nearly always taken with regard to grants; as a matter of fact, does not the visitation exercise their own judgment with regard to those grants?—Of course they do.

7071. Do not they come in contact with the tenants themselves?—Certainly.

7072. And the tenants see them?—Yes.

7073. Speak to them, and express what they want?—Yes.

7074. I suppose what you put before them are the usual forms that have been granted in former times?—Quite so.

7075. Whose judgment is the guiding principle; their own?—Their own.

7076. There is no obstacle to prevent any of the tenants seeing them?—Oh, no; they have every facility.

7077. And if they have any complaints to make they can make them?—Oh, yes.

Sir William Marriott—continued.

7078. Do they ever make them?—Do you mean complaints of any nature?

7079. Yes?—There have been deputations of tenants in later years in regard to rents.

7080. They do see the members of the Irish Society?—They converse together.

Mr. Healy.

7081. Did you read Father Loughrey's evidence?—I did.

7082. Is that evidence true or false?—I cannot say that I read it all; I had not time.

Chairman.] Dr. Freshfield, I may address you as the representative of the others. We propose on Monday to begin hearing the addresses of counsel, beginning with Mr. Walker, and meeting again on Wednesday, and as many days afterwards as may be necessary; I hope not many. Then, after those arguments are over, we shall be entirely ready to hear all the evidence that any of the City Companies may offer to rebut evidence that has been given, as they think, against them, or we shall ask for any evidence which we may think necessary.

Dr. Freshfield.] I think the feeling is rather to wait for an invitation from you. They do not want to weary you, but, of course, they will all come if they are wanted.

Chairman.] I should think the Salters' probably would like to come. Then there are some accounts that we shall ask to have put in.

Dr. Freshfield.] I do not know whether I am asking the proper person, but it would a very great convenience if you would extend the liberty you have given us, and let us have prints of the speeches of counsel delivered every morning, as if it were a Private Committee sitting on a private Bill. If you will allow me to undertake the arrangement of that, it will save you a great deal of trouble, and save the counsel too.

Monday, 21*st July* 1890.

MEMBERS PRESENT:

Mr. Clancy.	Colonel Lewis.
Lord Elcho.	Mr. Lea.
Sir John Ellis.	Sir William Marriott.
Mr. John Ellis.	Mr. John Morley.
Mr. Elton.	Mr. Sexton.
Mr. Healy.	Sir Richard Temple.

THE RIGHT HONOURABLE JOHN MORLEY, IN THE CHAIR.

Mr. *Walker*, Q.C., Mr. *Gordon*, and Mr. *Charles Dease* appeared as Counsel on behalf of the Beneficiaries in County Derry.

Mr. *George Harris Lea* and Mr. *J. H. Stowe* appeared as Counsel on behalf of numerous interests in the county, including the interests of the Irish Episcopal Church, the General Assembly of the Presbyterian Church, and the various educational interests connected therewith.

Mr. *Latham*, Q.C., Mr. *Hood*, and Mr. *Blakesley*, appeared as Counsel on behalf of the Mercers' and Drapers' Company.

Mr. *Rigby*, Q.C., and Mr. *Hood* appeared as Counsel on behalf of the Skinners' Company.

Mr. *Latham*, Q.C., and Mr. *Blakesley* appeared as Counsel on behalf of the Fishmongers' Company.

Mr. *Latham*, Q.C., and Mr. *Hood* appeared as Counsel for the Salters' Company.

Mr. *Latham*, Q.C., and Mr. *Purcell* appeared as Counsel on behalf of the Grocers' Company.

Mr. *Pollard* appeared as Counsel for the City of London.

Mr. *Romer*, Q.C., and Mr. *Hood* appeared as Counsel for the Irish Society.

Chairman (to Mr. *Walker*.)] I believe you are going to address us first to-day, and perhaps it would save time if I made one or two remarks before you begin. This Committee, as you know, is directed to inquire into the terms of the charters or other instruments by which their estates in Ireland were granted to the Irish Society and to the London companies, and as to the trusts and obligations (if any) attaching to the ownership of such estates. Now so far as the Irish Society is concerned, I think it is hardly necessary, or I may say, not at all necessary, to go beyond the judgment of the House of Lords in the Skinners' case in 1845. It will certainly save time if you and other gentlemen who address us, will be so good as to remember that the judgment of the Master of Rolls, and the final decision of the House of Lords, delivered by Lord Chancellor Lyndhurst, are in the hands of every member of the Committee. Those two judgments are before us; they contain all the facts and arguments, I presume, material to the question of trusts being imposed upon the Irish Society, and I take it that we may report it to the House of Commons as established beyond dispute, that the Irish Society are a body of public officers holding their Irish estates and administering the funds derived from them, subject to certain public trusts and obligations. The case of the 12 companies is different. There we have not got the advantage of a final judicial decision, such as that which makes the position of the Irish Society. In the case of the companies, to which I believe you are going to address yourself, the question is whether, if the Irish Society held its grant subject to trusts, the companies who took from the Irish Society took their estates divested of trusts; Whether the land that was divided in severalty among the twelve companies is legally burdened with the same public obligations and trusts as the House of Lords decided did attach to the possessions of the Irish Society; Whether, in short, if there was a public trust imposed upon one portion of the lands granted by the Crown, the same trusts or corresponding trusts are imposed upon all. The companies who were, and are, the parties in possession are understood to deny that there was any legal limitation on their free beneficial enjoyment of their Irish estates. They have applied to be allowed to press their view upon the Committee by counsel, and I believe there are gentlemen here who will put their case before us. You, Mr. Walker, are here, I believe, to represent parties in Derry who, we understand, insist that the grant of these estates is coupled with certain public purposes and trusts in Ireland independent of the private benefit of the companies, and independent of the destination of the general funds of these companies in England. So much for the scope of the statement we expect from you.

But let me beg you to be kind enough to bear in mind one very important fact, and that is that we are not here as a judicial tribunal appointed to decide the case. It is certainly within our competence, and I daresay the Committee will think fit, to express a view as to the moral

21 *July* 1890.

moral obligations attaching to the estates of the twelve companies. But as regards the legal obligations as to which you are about to address us, the legal construction of the charters and instruments referred to us is clearly a matter for the courts, and it may, perhaps, be found to be enough for this Committee to report to the House that certain views as to the legal obligations alleged to be binding upon the companies were presented to us, and that they were supported by certain general considerations. Therefore, as we are not here to decide a case, we do not desire you to attempt to give us any elaborate or exhaustive legal argument. The arguments in the Skinners' case, if I remember rightly, took 20 days or more, and I may tell you that we hope to be away from here long before 20 days are over. In short, what we wish to hear from you is such a statement of the leading considerations, reasons, and grounds on one side and the other, as will help us at once to lay before the House of Commons, broadly and definitely, and with full justice to all the parties concerned, the two opposed answers to the question into which the House has directed us to inquire. Considering how the scope of your argument is thus limited, and what the Committee conceive to be the objects that we have in view in listening to you, we see no reason why we should not be able to close this week; and I rather entertain the hope that you may be able to state your case in the course of a single day, which, I believe, is not a more disagreeable prospect for you than for us.

Mr. Walker.] Not at all. I am obliged, Sir, for the outline which you have given of the views which the Committee take, and their desire as to the scope of the argument. I will endeavour so far as I can, if proceeding is at all applicable to such a subject, to deal with the different documents to which I shall confine myself, in a popular way, so far as the documents admit of it. I shall, in deference to your views, not go into the citation of cases, or any elaborate argument which might be properly addressed to a legal tribunal, that is, one entirely constituted as such, and shall deal generally with the documents which I think material to the case. With these observations I will proceed at once to the subject in hand.

On the 29th of March 1613, King James I. granted his charter in respect of the then county of Coleraine, with some of the extra portions lying outside Coleraine, which was then for the first time named the county of Londonderry. I shall read some portions of that charter, which is the leading document of title in the case. It commences with the preamble, which is of great importance, and has been considered of great importance by every judge who considered the question. It commences as follows: "Whereas, there can be nothing more kingly than to establish the true Religion of Christ among men hitherto depraved and almost lost in superstition, to strengthen, improve, and cultivate by art and industry countries and lands uncultivated and almost desert, and the same not only to plant with honest citizens and inhabitants, but also to renovate and strengthen them with good statutes and ordinances, whereby they might be more safely defended, not only from the corruption of their morals, but from their intestine and domestic plots and conspiracies, and also from foreign violence. And whereas the province of Ulster, in our realm of Ireland, for many years now past hath grossly erred from the true religion of Christ, and divine grace, and hath abounded with superstition, insomuch that for a long time it hath not only been harassed, torn, and wasted by private and domestic broils, but also by foreign arms; we, deeply and heartily commiserating the wretched state of the said province, have esteemed it to be a work worthy of a Christian Prince, and of our Royal function, to stir up and recall the same province from superstition, rebellion, calamity, and poverty, which heretofore have horribly raged therein, to religion, obedience, strength, and prosperity." The Committee will see that these are all public objects, half political and half national, but all public; upon which great stress has been laid by the judges who dealt with these charters.

It then recites: "And whereas our beloved and faithful subjects the mayor and commonalty and citizens of our City of London, burning with a fervent zeal to promote such our pious intention in this behalf, have laudably undertaken a considerable part of the said plantation in Ulster, below in these presents mentioned" (that is, in other words, the whole county of Londonderry, the city of Derry, and the county of Coleraine), "and in other respects are making progress therein. We, of our especial grace and of our certain science, and mere motion, for us, our heirs and successors, do will." And then it provides that the city of Derry and all that land attached, and all other lands "in or by these presents below given and granted from henceforth, may and shall be united, consolidated, and from henceforth for ever may be one entire county of itself" "distinct and separate from all counties whatsoever within our kingdom of Ireland, to all intents and purposes;" and it is to be "called the county of Londonderry." It then proceeds to incorporate the city of Derry, and attaches to it lands within a circuit of three Irish miles as its liberty. It deals in the same way with the town of Coleraine: and then it provides, as regards what may be properly called for the purposes of this argument, the Irish Society, as follows: "and for the better ordering, directing, and governing all and all manner of things for and concerning the city and citizens of Londonderry, aforesaid, and the aforesaid county of Londonderry and the plantation to be made within the same city and county of Londonderry, and other businesses belonging to the same, we will and grant by these presents for us, our heirs and successors, do ordain and constitute that for ever hereafter there be and shall be six-and-twenty honest and discreet citizens of our City of London," who are to be chosen in the manner mentioned in the charter; "who shall be, and shall be called" (this is their incorporated name) "the Society of the Governor and Assistants London of the new Plantation in Ulster within the Realm of Ireland." They are then incorporated with power to hold lands, and large powers are given to them, and a court is constituted, and it provides that they shall, in the same court or meeting

"there

"have full power and authority to direct, constitute, and ordain all and singular things, which, for or concerning the plantation, supply or establishment, constitution, and government of the aforesaid city of *Londonderry*; and of all other the lands and tenements hereunder in these presents mentioned shall seem to be most profitable and expedient."

Then there follows a great deal in this charter which it is not necessary to call the attention of the Committee to. It proceeds to grant all the subject matters mentioned in the preamble, namely, the entire county of Londonderry, you may call it, as it at present exists, with something more: they are all specifically granted; and it gives them power in a subsequent part of the charter "to make, erect, and ordain one manor of every thousand acres of land by these presents before granted, or of any number exceeding the number of 1,000 acres of land, and so according to such rate so many several manors as they will, so that they make not any manor of a lesser number of acres of land than of the number of 1,000 acres." Then it gives them power "to let to farm so much of the lands, tenements, and hereditaments belonging to such manors, to any person and their assigns to and for such term and terms of years, estate or estates, and for such services and yearly rents to be reserved for and upon the same lands, tenements, and hereditaments, as shall seem best and convenient to the same society of the governor and assistants of London of the new plantation in Ulster aforesaid, and their successors for the time being. To hold of the said society of the governor and assistants of London, of the new plantation in Ulster aforesaid, and their successors, and of their same manor and manors respectively."

Now, at present, that is all I think it is necessary to call your attention to in the charter. I may have to refer to it by-and-by, when I shall very shortly come to deal with the antecedent documents.

Now the considerations upon which that charter is founded are of the greatest importance. They are the public objects in the preamble which I have read. The City of London (that is the city proper) having undertaken the plantation of the city and county of Londonderry, that charter grants all the lands in the County of Londonderry, including those which are held or have been held by the twelve companies to which this discussion principally relates; and you will perceive that the objects that are stated in the preamble are as large as the grant, and pervaded the entire grant and the entire subject-matter. Therefore, these public objects attached to every acre of land held afterwards by the twelve principal companies.

Now I think it will be seen in the course of what preceded that charter that the Irish Society actually only undertook the planting of the city of Derry and the town of Coleraine and the 7,000 acres which were attached to those two towns, the fishings of the Foyle and Bann, where they had the ownership clothed with the trust that was afterwards decided to exist; and it will be seen that the rest of the property, comprising 18,000 acres alive that which the Irish Society undertook and planted, was assigned to the 12 companies to carry out the objects mentioned in the preamble, and that upon them the planting *pro tanto* devolved. Now, on the documents here which I shall call the attention of the Committee to, so far as I consider those documents material, the great question arises whether these 12 companies when they undertook, as I say they undertook, in the place of the Irish Society, the planting of those 17,000 or 16,000 acres (as they are differently mentioned), did they take them free from the public objects and trusts attaching to the subject-matter actually retained by the Irish Society? The scope of those objects, and the duration of them, may be summed up in a few words. Lord Campbell in his judgment in the House of Lords, which the Committee have read, sums them up accurately and definitely in a very few words. He says, in the year 1845, "It seems to me that the objects of the Crown was that public purposes should be attained by the trustees who had the management of these lands, and I am clearly of opinion that the purposes for which the grant was made still continue, and that they are and must ever remain trustees for the public," for those of public purposes. Therefore that public purposes existed then, and that those public purposes are permanent, and exist at the present day, is now beyond reach of controversy.

Chairman.] Of course he was there speaking of the Irish Society?

Mr. Walker.] I know that, Sir; but the point I am making is this: that he was speaking of the position of the Irish Society by reference to the preamble of the charter, and that the preamble of the charter pervades the entire grant, which extended to all the lands, both those retained by the Irish Society and those which ultimately passed into the hands of the 12 companies. Then the question is, does the whole of Derry, the whole of the lands and county of Derry, *plus* the lands retained by the Irish Society, stand free from the obligations of which Lord Campbell speaks?

Now, having just stated the first and leading document in the case, and referred shortly to its purpose and its scope, it will be necessary for me to go back and refer very shortly, and, so far as I can, popularly, to the documents which are antecedent to and leading up to the charter, in order to show the circumstances under which the companies became associated in the undertaking, and the plantation of the county of Londonderry, *alive* that part which the Irish Society took and planted; and then I shall ask this question, which I think is a question going to the root of the whole of this controversy. These deeds which were made to the companies bear date 1617 and 1618; they were made in each of those years; and I would ask in 1617, say when the companies got their grants by the licence of the Crown, and with the consent of the Crown, could they the day after those grants were made, or six months after those grants were made, have divided the proceeds of the property amongst themselves, and applied them for purposes foreign to the county of Londonderry, or purposes beneficial it may be, but for purposes alien to the objects of the charter? If such a proposition as that could hardly bear statement, if they could not be divided as lands of their own amongst them in the year 1613, say before the objects of the charter had been accomplished, then it must be because there were public objects yet unsatisfied attached upon the land in their hands; and if public objects existed then, we have the decision of the House of Lords that those public objects are permanent and endure till to-day, and are just as much in full force now as they were when Lord Campbell spoke of them, in the words I have read, in 1843.

Now, I will run as shortly as I can through those antecedent documents, because it appears to me that they are vital to this controversy. I shall not go into the details of the history of these matters, for the Committee know them better than I do; but we know that in 1609 King James I. wanted to plant, for these great purposes at all events, in a particular manner the county of Londonderry. Londonderry stood, according to the view of the King, in a different position from the other escheated counties which had been escheated by the O'Neill rebellion.

Chairman.] The other five escheated counties were granted to private persons.

Mr. *Walker.*] Yes. As regards Londonderry, I presume, on account of its sea-board, and on account of its facilities for attack and defence, and as stated in the King's own documents, on account of the harbours of the Foyle and Bann, it was more important to deal with Londonderry than with any others of the six escheated counties. But before the King approached the City of Londonderry, as he did next year, he published in 1608, I think the date is, but the date is not very important, what is called "collection of orders and conditions," some of which I find, in what is called "the printed book." The heading is this: "A collection of such orders and conditions as are to be observed by the undertakers upon the distribution and plantation of the escheated lands in Ulster." Those orders and conditions had existence before the negotiations between the city and the Crown; they are orders and conditions, I may say, addressed to all the undertakers, and would include, to a certain extent, the undertakers in the other escheated counties as well.

Chairman.] You mean the private undertakers?

Mr. *Walker.*] Yes. There are one or two passages in those orders and conditions which I will call the attention of the Committee to, avoiding as much as I can even much that might, if I were addressing a legal tribunal, more elaborately go into. To begin with, the preamble is: "Whereas the greatest part of six counties in the province of Ulster, within the realm of Ireland, named Armagh, Tyrone, Coleraine, Donegal, Fermanagh, and Cavan, being escheated and come to the Crown, hath lately been surveyed, and the survey thereof transmitted and presented unto his Majesty, upon view whereof his Majesty of his princely bounty, not respecting his own profit, but the public peace and welfare of that kingdom by the civil plantation of those unreformed and waste countries, is graciously pleased to distribute the said land to such of his subjects, as well of Great Britain as of Ireland, as being of merit and ability, shall seek the same with a mind" (I ask your attention to this because it is important) "not only to benefit themselves, but to do service to the Crown and commonwealth; and forasmuch as many persons being ignorant of the conditions whereupon his Majesty is pleased to grant the said lands, are importunate suitors for greater portions than they are able to plant, intending their private profit only, and not the advancement of the public service, it is thought convenient to declare and publish"; and then follow the rules and ordinances which are to govern the action of the undertakers. There are only two of them to which I draw attention, and they are the last, the fourth and fifth of the general principles which are to be notified to the undertakers of all sorts, and they are these: "That in every the said counties there shall be a convenient number of market towns and corporations erected for the habitation and settling of tradesmen and artificers, and that there shall be one free school, at least, appointed in every county for the education of youth in learning and religion. (5) That there shall be a convenient number of parishes and parish churches, with sufficient incumbents, in every county, and that the parishioners shall pay all their tithes in kind to the incumbents of the said parish churches." You will observe that there are three objects of a most public kind prominently stated there, namely, the advancement of trade by the establishment of market towns, the advancement of education by the establishment of "one free school at least," and the advancement of religion, by reference to which I read to be the sufficiency of incumbents. Now upon that printed book, as we may call it, and as it has been called, I find this commentary by Lord Langdale in his judgment: There are only three or four lines which I will read; he says, "It is plain from these orders and conditions that the King did not merely contemplate the benefit of the persons who should undertake the plantation or colony as it is called in another document, but that he had a great public object in view, and to carry that into effect desired to engage such of his subjects, as well of Great Britain as of Ireland, as being of merit and ability, should seek the lands with a mind not only to benefit themselves but to do service to the Crown and commonwealth." That is the interpretation that has been put upon the earliest of these documents by Lord Langdale.

The next document which has any bearing upon this question was the Commission dated the 21st of July 1609, that the King issued to the Irish deputy of that day, Sir Arthur Chichester, and others, to inquire into the escheated lands; and the only portion of that Commission which I think it necessary to call your attention to is the first direction in it: "That a general care be taken that such orders, conditions, and articles as have been lately published in print, or are to be printed or transmitted, touching the plantation, be observed and put in execution as well by the Commissioners as by the undertakers."

Chairman.] This is not part of the Motives and Reasons, is it?

Mr. *Walker.*] No; it is an earlier document before he addressed the city; it is dated the 21st July

21 *July* 1890.

July 1609. Interpreting, therefore, as I have interpreted, and as Lord Langdale has interpreted the antecedent documents, there is a direction that those objects shall be put in force by all persons entering upon the plantation.

Now the next document bearing upon the case is what has just been referred to by the Chairman, namely, the Motives and Reasons which the King addressed to the city. It is quite evident that the King thought that the county of Londonderry, as it was to be, stood on a peculiar footing, and those Motives and Reasons addressed to the city, strike my mind as being very like the prospectus of a limited company as we should have it now-a-days.

Chairman.] The King being the promoter.

Mr. Walker.] The King being the promoter. It deals in language at all events equal to the occasion, with all the advantages the undertaking would offer. These are Motives and Reasons you will remember "to induce the City of London to undertake the plantation"; and in these Motives and Reasons the King says: "The late ruinated city of Derry situated upon the river of Lough Foyle, navigable with good vessels above the Derry, and one other place at or near the Castle of Coleraine, situate upon the river of Bann, navigable with small vessels only by reason of the bar a little above Coleraine, do seem to be the fittest places for the City of London to plant"; that was the whole area between the Foyle and the Bann. Then he says, "These towns his Majesty may be pleased to grant unto not only corporations with such liberties and privileges for their good government, etc., as shall be convenient, but also the whole territory and county betwixt them, which is above 20 miles in length, bounded by the sea on the north, and the river Bann on the east, and the river of Derry or Lough Foyle on the west, out of which 1,000 acres more may be allotted to each of the towns for their commons, rent free; the rest to be planted with such undertakers as the City of London shall think good for their best profit, paying only for the same the easy rent of the undertakers." I ask your attention to the word "profit" there, because it may be said that in the subsequent documents, where the word profit appears, it contemplated private profit. Here we have, in dealing with the City of London, the word "profit" used; and also we have, by the highest tribunal, an interpretation put upon it showing the status of the City of London and the Irish Society, which was the managing department from that city.

Chairman.] How do you understand the words "Paying only for the same the easy rent of the undertakers"?

Mr. Walker.] I suppose it was a sort of live-and-thrive rent that was contemplated, in which he appears to have been rather disappointed, according to the history of the case. The only other part of these Motives and Reasons that I may mention is that portion of it which refers to the profits which London shall receive by this plantation. It says: "If multitudes of men were employed proportionably to those commodities which might be there by in-dustry attained, many thousands would be set on work to the great service of the King, strength to his realm, advancement of several trades, and benefit of particular persons whose the infinite increasing greatness (that often doth minister occasion of ruin to itself) of this city might not only conveniently spare, but also reap a singular commodity by easing themselves of an insupportable burden which so surcharged all the parts of the city, that one tradesman can scarce live by another, which in all probability would be a means also, and preserve the city from infection, and by consequence the whole kingdom, which of necessity must have recourse thither, which persons pestered or closed up together, can neither otherwise or very hardly avoid." Then he says, "These colonies may be a means to utter infinite commodities from London to furnish the whole north of Ireland which may be transported by means of the rivers of Bann and Lough Foyle into the counties"; and then several counties are mentioned. Therefore the inducements and the profits which the City of London were to derive are national advantages, the advantages resulting from the emigration of thousands who were overcrowding the City of London, the advantages of trade, advantages directly to the City of London, and indirectly to the nation at large.

The result of that was that those Motives and Reasons having been addressed to the city, they were taken into consideration by the Court of Aldermen, and on the 1st of July 1609, occurs for the first time any mention of the several companies of the city. The Court of Aldermen on that day directed that precepts should be sent, that is, it referred to the intimation of the King's "most gracious favour and love to the citizens of London," that is, the Motives and Reasons which he had sent them; and it was ordered that precepts should be sent to all the several companies of this city requiring them shortly, "to assemble together a competent number of the gravest and most substantial men of their several companies, and to consider advisedly" as to what was right to be done "in the undertaking of so worthy and honourable an action." And it appears that the companies, that is the City Companies, took upon themselves to send an answer to the Lords of the Privy Council, the tenour of which is not disclosed, but all we know is that it very much displeased the Privy Council. It apparently would seem to be an answer stating that they did not wish to have anything to do with the project; because on the 18th of July (that is seventeen days afterwards) there appears to have been a meeting of the Court of Aldermen (that is the Court of the City).

Sir William Marriott.] Was that before the Commission, of which I think you said the date was the 21st of July?

Mr. Walker.] Yes. This meeting is three days before that. It appears by the report of this meeting that two precepts had been issued to the companies of the city, and that "by reason of some mistaking of the pleasure of the said honorable Lords, the committees appointed for the several companies, without allowance to the Lord Mayor and Aldermen, had made an answer

21 *July* 1890.

in writing before any conference was had with His Majesty's Council of Ireland, which was ill accepted by the Lords." It does not appear what it was, but at all events they did not like it, and the result was that then, upon that day, the Court of Aldermen incorporated a committee of their own body (not the companies) to confer with the Lords of the Privy Council.

Chairman.] You used the expression, and I see it is used in the report of the company, the Privy Council of Ireland; what does that mean?

Mr. *Walker.*] It says the Privy Council of Ireland, but it could hardly be so, for this reason, that it would appear that on the Sunday after the meeting they went and interviewed the Lords of the Privy Council; I think it would be the English Privy Council. I am informed by my learned friend that the Privy Council of Ireland sat in this country; that would account for it. The Court of Aldermen then nominated a committee of their own, leaving out of view the companies, to confer with the Privy Council, and on the 23rd of July 1609, the Common Council of the City nominated viewers to go to Ireland to consider the project, and to make report to the City. The Common Council and the Court of Aldermen were the two great bodies of the City, I believe; one the legislative, and the other the executive body. It appears that on the 23rd of July 1609, having referred to the antecedent matters, they directed that the City should send viewers; they say "that certain men be chosen, and be sent by us to view the place, and make return unto us, so that if it prove not answerable to that which is reported and profitable for the undertakers, we may be at liberty to leave this undertaking, anything now done, notwithstanding." At the same meeting it appears that a precept was directed to the Master and Wardens of each company, "To require you on Wednesday morning next to assemble in your common hall all the aldermen of your company, and the four committees by you formerly named, and all other the assistants, livery, and men of note of your yeomanry, by especial summons, then and there to understand and be informed by your aldermen and committees the whole proceedings that hath been taken concerning the said honourable intention of plantation, and to make a book of all their names, and to understand every man's answer what he will willingly contribute to the furtherance of so famous a project, to the intent his Majesty may be informed of the readiness of this City in a matter of such great consequence." That was the direction to inquire whether they would willingly contribute. It does not appear they would willingly contribute anything, so far as I can see.

Sir *William Marriott.*] What is the date of the precept?

Mr. *Walker.*] The 23rd of July 1609. Accordingly four men are sent (the names are given but are not material) to view the place for the intended plantation in Ireland. Then it would appear that on the 16th of December 1609 the report of those viewers was presented to the Court of Common Council, and that report set forth various matters under four heads. First, as to the amount of expenditure which they considered desirable; secondly, "What lands and privileges should be demanded"; thirdly, "What things should be performed"; and, fourthly, "How all should be managed and ruled." Now, on the first head, those viewers reported that "though the undertaking somewhat exceeded what was first propounded, yet the sum of money to be expended should only be 15,000 *l.*, and that sum not to be exceeded. And for raising of this sum we hold the fittest course to be by way of companies, and companies by the poll according to the rate of corn set upon every company." I shall in a few moments explain to the Committee what that means. "but some of the inferior companies we thought fit to be spared, yet such as were known able men in those companies, to be set proportionably with men of like ability in other companies. And for this" (that is for the raising of this money in that way) "levy and act to pass in this Court," that is, the Court of Common Council, the city was to do it. Now numbers 2 and 3 really shadow out what was afterwards contained more fully, and with some variations, in the charter, namely, the lands that are to be granted, and privileges to be granted; and in reply to question Number 4, How all shall be managed and ruled; it was reported by the viewers, "that the company be constituted here in London, of persons to be selected for that purpose." This is said to be the city's answer to the report of the viewers, and adopted "as the city's answer to the Lords" of the Privy Council. It appears that when this was presented to the Lords of Privy Council, they thought that 15,000 *l.* was not enough. It is stated at the meeting of the Privy Council of the 22nd November 1609, that when this was presented, "upon reading and examination thereof by their Lordships, though the other points were not excepted unto, yet that whereon was expressed, that the sum of money to be expended was limited only to 15,000 *l.*, and that sum not to be exceeded. This was much disliked by their Lordships, in respect that the clearing of private men's interests in the things offered would be greatly chargeable to His Majesty. And this sum would hardly perform the plantation, being wholly employed that way, therefore the offer tendered to their Lordships was not accepted. That whereupon a new Common Council being called, and they informed hereof, after good deliberation taken, it was this day ordered and agreed by the Right Honourable the Lord Mayor, the Aldermen, his brethren, and the Commons, in this Common Council assembled, and by the authority of the same, that the sum of 5,000 *l.* should be added to their former report, in respect of buying in the private interest and other charges. And so the sum to be expended by the City to be advanced to the sum of 20,000 *l.*, and in all things else their former report to stand."

Chairman.] Was this a promise on the part of the City, do you take it, to expend 15,000 *l.* or ultimately 20,000 *l.*?

Mr. Walker.] Yes; the City was to raise 20,000 *l.*

Chairman]

Chairman.] And to expend it for the purpose of the plantation?

Mr. Walker.] Yes, for the purpose of the plantation. You will find that that was raised from time to time, and became a very much larger sum indeed, and on the 8th January 1609——

Mr. Sexton.] Do not you mean 1610?

Mr. Walker.] No, 1609. In those days you will remember it was the old style, and the year began on the 25th March. It does seem a little out of place, but January and February were the last two months of the year.

Chairman.] It is generally put 1609-10.

Mr. Walker.] Yes. At a meeting of the common council on the 8th January 1609, certain persons were appointed as a committee to consider with conference between themselves and Commissioners appointed by the Lords of the Privy Council, "touching the intended plantation in Ulster, and the said committees before named to take advised care and consideration of all matters whatsoever that to them, in their discretion, shall be thought fit to be propounded, moved, or done on the behalf of this City." Therefore the two bodies that were now to confer were a committee appointed by the Court of Common Council, and a certain deputed body from the Privy Council itself. Then follows the direction about the levy: "And it is further enacted, granted, and agreed by the authority aforesaid" (that is, by the Court of Common Council), "for the better expedition of the said service, that a present taxation be made of the said 20,000 *l.*, and a present levy shall be made of one-fourth part thereof, which 20,000 *l.*, by former acts of Common Council, was, and it is agreed to be expended by this City about the same plantation, and purchasing in, and clearing of all private men's interests by His Majesty in the places demanded by the city. And the said sum of 5,000 *l.* shall be forthwith raised by way of companies of this city, and in companies by the poll according to the rate of corn set upon every company; but some of the inferior companies to be spared, yet such as are known able men in those companies to be set proportionably with men of like ability in other companies, according as in their report of the committees being confirmed by the Common Council is mentioned"; and this sum was to be speedily realised, and the 5,000 *l.* which was to be immediately levied was to be handed over to the Chamberlain of the City; he was the treasurer into whose hands the money was to pass. That being the direction of the Common Council to raise it, it was followed by a precept addressed to the warden and master and assistants of each company, a precept in the same terms substantially as the minute which I have read, referring to the Act of the Common Council. It commanded them "to call a court of assistants, and then to elect such of your company as you shall think fit to join with you, the master and wardens, in the taxing of the said sum of" (then there is a blank left, because this was to be sent to every company), "being one-fourth part thereof, in such manner as in other levies hath been accustomed." Then that precept contains at the foot of it the names of *all* the companies of the City headed by the 12 principal companies to whom the grants were afterwards made, and it specifies the proportion of the principal sum, and the proportion of the 5,000 *l.*, which is to be levied in that manner.

Chairman.] There were then 55 companies in all, 12 principal and 43 minor, were there not?

Mr. Walker.] There were a great many; they all appear at the foot of the precept at all events.

Now, with regard to this money, it would be desirable that I should just recall your attention to the mode in which this money was levied; because it is far from the case that this was a voluntary contribution by the companies, which might strengthen the case of my learned friends on the other side. On the contrary, it was a compulsory impost put upon the companies as a levy; you remember the words "in such manner as in other levies hath been accustomed compulsorily according to the practice that had existed up to that time, and long after the power of the City to levy compulsorily upon its citizens any sum of money that was required. The members of the several city companies and the citizens of London at that time were, in point of fact, convertible terms, and it was only a convenient mode of levying on those citizens that it should be levied by directing a precept for each company to levy it from the individual members of each company, who were the citizens of London.

Chairman.] I do not think you need labour that, because Lord Langdale said explicitly in his judgment,—"that the levies were compulsory is shown by abundant evidence in this case."

Mr. Walker.] Quite so; and you will remember, in the Report upon the City Companies, which is a printed Report of the 28th May 1884, it is referred to by Lord Derby's Commission as a circumstance well known; it is stated in that report that it is "undoubtedly the fact that during the Plantagenet and Tudor periods, and during those of the rebellion, the commonwealth and the restoration, the companies probably, because they constituted a convenient division of the citizens for purposes of taxation, were forced to contribute large sums to the National Exchequer chiefly for the purpose of defraying the expenses of wars, and that under a custom of the City which has long been obsolete, they were at one time bound to lend money to the municipality with which to purchase corn and coals for the poor in times of scarcity." That is the explanation of that phrase, "According to the corn rate." You may therefore start with this: These moneys were levied not as voluntary contributions from the citizens, but as imposts upon the citizens, by machinery which the companies formerly adopted as a convenient process, and just as they would raise money for a foreign war, which was one of the instances quoted here in the argument in this case before Lord Langdale, or the expenses of a Royal Patent, or anything of that kind.

Chairman.]

21 *July* 1890.

Chairman.] Your point is, I suppose, that these were individual contributions and not corporate?

Mr. Walker.] They were not corporate contributions; they did not come from the corporate funds of the city companies, if I may say so; because even then some of these had property of their own. At all events, it is not a corporate payment.

Sir William Marriott.] Did any citizens who were not members of the company pay?

Mr. Walker.] I would rather think that the citizens of London, and members of the company were at that time almost convertible terms, and that when you say it was levied through the citizens of the city, and levied through the companies, you are, in fact, levying it from the citizens, and from the citizens only. That I apprehend is so. It is a curious matter of history that it appears that not only did the city levy this money as city money, to be paid to the Chamberlain, and not as from corporate money of the companies, but it appears that they had also the power of imprisoning people who did not pay, and in respect of this very assessment, in 1610, a Mr. Edward Barne and Thomas Tayle, who were wardens of the Company of Mercers, one of the principal companies, "for that they have not according to divers precepts to them directed by my Lord Mayor, paid to Mr. Chamberlain the second payment assessed on them towards the furnishing of 20,000 *l.* for the plantation in Ireland, are by this court committed prisoners to one of the compters of this city, there to remain during the pleasure of this court." They had not only a very large power, but a very summary mode of exercising it.

Therefore we may start with this, before we approach the most material documents; that the companies did not advance one penny out of the corporate funds, but that the citizens of London advanced it; that the money was paid by the citizens as city money in pursuance of the requisition of the Crown to the city; that it was paid to the Chamberlain of the City, and held by him as such.

Now that was followed by a formal agreement between the King, as represented by the Privy Council and Committees of the Common Council, an agreement of the 30th January 1609. That followed very much the report of the viewers, and shadowed out very much what was afterwards embodied in the charter: "First, it was agreed by the City that the sum of 20,000 *l.* should be levied, whereof 15,000 *l.* was to be expended on the intended plantation, and 5,000 *l.* for the clearing of private men's interests in the things demanded;" and then it provides what was to be done as regards the city of Derry and the town of Coleraine and the attaching portion of land (which was 7,000 acres; I think it was 4,000 to Derry and 3,000 to Coleraine). Then it provided, "That the rest of the territory and the entire county of Coleraine, estimated at 12,000 acres, more or less, undertaken by the city, be cleared from all particular interests except the Bishop and Dean of Derry's inheritance, and except certain portions of land to be assigned under three or four Irish gentlemen at the most then dwelling and settled in the county of Coleraine, who were to be freeholders to the city, and to pay them some small rent;" and then it provided "that the woods and the ground and soil of Glanconkene and Killetragh, extending from the county of Coleraine to Ballinderry, be wholly to the city in perpetuity; the timber trees of these woods to be converted to the furtherance of plantation and all necessary uses within Ireland, and none to be made merchandise;" and then it is provided in large words for the Church patronage being given to the City, and the customs of Derry and Coleraine all privileges, royalties, rights of Admiralty, and so on, should be reserved; and then it provided "That for the purpose of effecting of all things touching and concerning the said plantation and business thereunto belonging, there shall be a company constituted and established within the City of London, which company shall consist of one governor, one deputy for the governor, and four-and-twenty assistants," and of these seven were to be *ex officio* members, and the rest were to be elected in manner provided by this document. And this department of the city were "To treat, debate, resolve, and determine of all matters and causes concerning the business that to them in their discretion shall be thought fit; and also to direct, appoint, and demand what shall be done or performed on behalf of this city touching or concerning the said plantation. And also shall and may give, order, and direction here in England, either by laws or otherwise, into Ireland for the ordering managing and disposing of all things whatsoever concerning the intended plantation or anything belonging to the citizens of London undertaking in that part of Ireland;" and then the moneys were directed to be paid to the Chamberlain of the City, Mr. Cornelius Fiske, and he was to give a receipt for the same.

Chairman.] Then it is the city and not the companies who are undertaking all this?

Mr. Walker.] That is what I want to make clear. That document which I have just read has also received an exposition from Lord Langdale, and I will call your attention to what he says about it. He says, "The city undertook and was to perform. The city was to provide the funds, and the city was to have the profit. The city was set in motion by what has been called the pressure of the Crown or of the Government, and was by its agents the contracting party with the Government with the companies otherwise than as they were involved in or formed part of the general body of the city, the Crown had no negotiations or dealing. The Crown did not, as it seems, concern itself either with the means by which the city was to perform its undertaking, or with the inducements to be held out to individuals further than as such inducements were secured by the general terms of the project and the Motives and Reasons presented to the city. It may reasonably be supposed that when the Court of Common Council, in performance of the contract, found it necessary to exercise a somewhat questionable power of taxation, suggestions of some benefit to result to those upon whom the charge was imposed, would, in some manner, be made. And that

such

such was the case is extremely probable from the nature of the transaction itself, and is apparent from the subsequent proceedings. But in the formal acts at the time the companies are treated as the instruments by which the sums assessed, or the amounts taxed should be levied; and the levies were not made upon any property of the companies, but in companies by the poll. That the levies were compulsory and enforced against reluctant parties by the power of the city is shown by abundant evidence." Therefore that is beyond all question.

The city, therefore, raising the money upon the city, and agreeing with the King, the city undertaking all the lands. The next two documents in the case are those which, introduced for the first time, directly in connection with the lands, the companies of the city, and they are of great importance in the case. The first of them is dated the 14th of January 1610, the 8th of James I.

Chairman.] That is 1610-11?

Mr. Walker.] Yes, I take it to be so. This is the Act of the Common Council, and it is followed by a precept, and this document is extremely important. This is the Act of the Common Council. It is not long and it is material to read it. It is headed "Common Council, 14th January, 8th James I."

Chairman.] That is the first document, what is the other one?

Mr. Walker.] The other one is a precept to the master and wardens of each company following that. The precept is dated the 31st of January 1610. The Act of Common Council is: "And further, it is enacted, granted, and agreed by the authority aforesaid that the governor, deputy, and assistants heretofore established and appointed by Act of Common Councells for the intended plantation in Ulster shall, by virtue hereof, have full power and authority to let all the fishings within the realme of Ireland, specified in itelem articles made and agreed upon betweene the right Honorable the Lords of His Majesty's Privy Council on the one part and those committees, on the behalf of this city on the other part, for the terme of seven yeares to such person or persons, and for such fine or rent as they in their discretions shall think fit and convenient for the most benefit and profite of this city, as they may or can, in regard the fishinge season is now at hand, and the not disposinge of the same in time made breed great losse and detriment to this citie. And further, it is ordered that p'cepts shall forthwith bee sent to ev'y severall companie of the citie to require them to assemble themselves together, and to advise amongst themselves whether they will consent and agree to take and accept of lands in lieu of the monies already by them disbursed or or to be disbursed, towards the sd plantacon, and so to build and plant the same at their owne costs and charges accordinglie, as by the printed book of plantacon is required." Now, I have called the attention of the Committee to the mode in which these moneys were received, and the money acquired. Here is the requisition to the companies to assemble and see whether they would "consent and agree to take and accept of lands in lieu of the monies already by them disbursed towards the sd plantacon, and so to build and plant the same at their owne costs and charges accordinglie, as by the printed book of plantacon is required." I have told you what they were to plant, and this was the requisition contained here. The building and planting having never yet been undertaken by the city, and the companies are required to assemble and consider whether they will accept the land which they are to build and plant at their own cost and charges, in pursuance of the book of plantation.

Chairman.] This is the language of the precept issued in conformity with the Act of the Common Council, as I understand?

Mr. Walker.] I am now reading the language of the Act of Common Council; but you will find that the precept is very much the same. You will find it was to plant; they are to perform this duty according to the obligation of the city, and according to the public purposes designed by the Crown. The precept which follows that is a little fuller, and is not very long; and I consider these two documents important because they are the first which introduced the companies as the corporations building and planting. Remember that they were corporations domiciled in London; corporations which did not contribute anything; corporations which might remain in London just as the city itself, and not corporations which could themselves occupy or fulfil the purposes as private undertakers would. Now the precept is this; it is dated the 31st of January 1610: "Whereas the King's Most Excellent Majesty hath granted unto the city of London, the city of Derry and town of Coleraine, with 7,000 acres of common land thereunto adjoining; and fishing and divers other commodities, privileges and franchises, paying four marks per annum. And whereas the city hath undertaken to disburse in building of houses and fortifications, and for freeing of foreign titles, the sum of 20,000 *l.*; and, whereas, also his Majesty hath further granted to this city divers other lands in the county of Coleraine" (that is the whole of them *ultra* the town lands), "and other undertakers lands to build thereupon" (I ask your attention to this), "which building" (that is by the city) "is to be performed in such manner as is expressed in the printed book now extant; yet with this addition, that they are to have and enjoy the same lands after the Irish measure, being far better than other ordinary undertakers have." The city were to build and plant according to this, and they were to have the benefit. "And for as much as the governors and committees for the plantation in Ireland are now instantly to take care for the letting and disposing of the said lands in the said county of Coleraine, and the said other lands so undertaken" (that is, the whole county), "to be used and managed for the benefit of this city, which would otherwise prove a great hindrance and loss, especially for that the time of the year is now most convenient for the plantation to proceed; yet it is thought fit that the offer of those lands be first made to the several companies of this city, who have and are to to disburse the same, and bear the charges of building before-mentioned. These are therefore to charge and command you that yourselves, together with the assistants and such other of your company as you shall think fitting do forthwith assemble together and advise whether you will accept of a proportion of the same lands according to the quantity of your disbursements to be by you undertaken and managed according to the printed book for plantation." That I say is putting upon the companies the position which the city itself assumed by contract with the Crown, and in a prior part of this precept is stated to be the obligation of the city.

Chairman.] How do you understand the words in the earlier part which you read "to be used and managed for the benefit of this city, which would otherwise prove a great hindrance and loss."?

Mr. *Walker.*] The meaning of that is that they were to do it at once, instantly, to take care for the letting, because, according to the time of year, it required to be done at once; nevertheless they say though the time is pressing we will give the companies this power if they think fit to take it up, in fact to step into the place of the city for those lands which were afterwards allotted to them to be by them undertaken and managed according to the printed book of plantation. That is putting them in the position of the city, and those lands not having been built or planted as recited in this very precept, and the time pressing that they should be built or planted, though the time was pressing, they put the companies in the position of persons to build and plant, according to the printed book of plantation; that is the obligation which in the earlier part of the precept is said to rest upon the city itself according to the printed book of plantation. Therefore the companies are put, according to my view, in the position of the city for building and planting, subject to all the obligations of the city as regards those lands after the townlands of Derry and Coleraine and the 7,000 acres attached to those cities.

The rest of this precept is also of importance: "and that you certify to the said governor and committees in writing under your hands at the Guildhall on or before the 7th day of February next coming, what shall be your full determination therein to the end the business may the sooner be effected," (that is the building and planting), "wherein you are to take advertisement that your company are to pay and bear" (this is also a very important portion of this precept) "their proportion of the charge of the said building, fortifications, and freeing of the tides, whether they accept of the said offer of the lands or no; and also that notwithstanding the acceptance of the lands, you shall likewise still be partakers of all benefits of fishing, with the profits of the towns and other commodities whatsoever." That was one of the passages in the precept which was so strongly relied on in the case of the Skinners' Company; the words "partakers of all benefits of fishing," showing that they had by contract a partnership as it were in the profits. Having put these 12 companies in the position of builders and planters, with the obligation that was to be gathered from the printed book, they say, although we grant you this privilege, or put upon you the burden by reason of what has been done, namely, the mode of levying through the companies, yet you must remember whether you do or do not carry this out or fulfil these obligations, you are to bear and pay all the same.

Now it appears in pursuance of that precept, on the 28th of February 1610, certain of the companies intimated to the city their willingness to accept that which was put upon them. At that time eight of the principal companies directly did so, and 10 of the inferior companies; but that is not material, because ultimately all the companies came into that position, except two, namely, the Coopers and the Brownbakers, who, under a subsequent restriction, forfeited all their rights sooner than pay the annual impost. This precept says, "the Mercers, Grocers," and so on, "have signified their consents in writing to the same governor and assistants" (that is to say, of the city), "to accept of the lands, and to plant upon the same accordingly, as by the printed book of plantation is required." There you have the city accepting the public obligation which the Acts of the Crown required according to the printed book, taking upon themselves all the obligations which the city was not to discharge, but which the companies, by their own consent, were to discharge if they accepted the land.

Chairman.] What do you suppose was the consideration present in the minds of the companies at this stage?

Mr. *Walker.*] I suppose they may have been influenced by this consideration: put yourself in their position, I suppose they thought. Whether we do this or not, we will have to pay all the same; we may as well speculate in this, for we are told by the precept that, whether we take the land or not, we will have to pay all through, not only now, but every subsequent impost; and as the King has said in his Motives and Reasons that this is a profitable undertaking to the city, and would yield them this profit (which is interpreted by the House of Lords to mean profit to the realm and to the public, and not personal profit to the city), we will accept whatever benefits the city will have in these lands, and we might as well do so when we are to bear the burden all the same. Then the precept of the Common Council of the 28th February 1610 goes on: "That the several companies before recited who have made election of lands as aforesaid, shall have severally allotted and set forth unto them (with as much convenient expedition as may be) lands within the county of Coleraine according to their several proportions of money which they have or shall disburse towards the said plantation, and that by lots or such other means as shall be prescribed." Then it provides, "that if those who have signified their denial in accepting lands, or shall not signify their assents within 14 days aforesaid, that the governor and assistants for the time being" (that is of the city as you may call them) "shall have full power and authority, and shall and may forthwith take upon them the letting, managing, and disposing of such lands as shall fall out to be allotted unto them for their proportions so the

best

best benefit and advantage that they may or can;" that is, that the city may or can. Let me put this case. Supposing that the companies, instead of accepting all the 7,000 acres and the fishing, it had happened that only two companies elected to take, or thought they ought to take upon them this burden, and the Irish Society stood in the position of builders or planters to take three-fourths of the lands of the county of Londonderry; if that were so, if they had stood in that position, could it be contended now, after the decision of the House of Lords, that as regards that 8,000 or 10,000 acres, as it might be, that the Irish Society would not be trustees of those for the purposes of the public trust, which was imposed upon them, although you find here in these resolutions of the 28th February 1610, that the intention of the governor and assistants (that is, the intention of the city) was, that as regards all lands which were not accepted, the governor and assistants were to take upon themselves the burden of letting, managing, and disposing "to the best benefit and advantage that they may or can"? We now read those words, "the best benefit and advantage," by the light of the decision of the House of Lords, as meaning the benefit and advantage resulting to the public and the realm. And I say, supposing that event had happened, and it is an accident that it had not happened, and that the land had been retained in the hands of the Irish Society, it would be impossible to contend that the Irish Society would not be in the position of trustees as to all the lands retained in their hands. Now it appears that only two companies, the Coopers and the Haberdashers, adopted that course, and their interest, whatever it might be, merged in that of the city; and for that reason the City of London was made a defendant in this case of the Skinners' Company. Upon these documents, which are very important in this case, of the 14th January 1610, and the 21st January, and the 28th February 1610, we have also the reading of Lord Langdale, of which I will read only a few lines, to which I will ask your attention.

(*Chairman.*] Lord Langdale's Judgment is already before the Committee in print.

Mr. *Walker.*] Lord Langdale's Judgment is reported in 7th Beavan's Reports; and here is what he says referring to those documents which I have mentioned: "From these documents it appears to have been understood that the companies of the city had not previously undertaken the plantation, but that the plantation being undertaken by the city was, in default of other means, to be carried into execution by the society or committee appointed by the city; but that it was thought desirable that the undertaking should be at least in part performed by the incorporated companies, and that the city, having entered into the undertaking, having by their power levied the means of carrying it on, and being actually engaged in carrying it on by their governor and committee or company, offered to each of the incorporated companies an option either to undertake the plantation of a portion of the lands according to the printed book for plantation, or to refer the letting and disposing thereof to the governor and committees." I venture to say that the reading of Lord Langdale upon that is what I have submitted to the Committee; that it is substituting the undertaking by the companies, the city having been the primary person to undertake the building and planting.

(*Chairman.*] Your contention just now was that if the companies had not exercised that option, the land would have been left in the possession, and would ultimately become the Irish Society's, and would therefore, by the Judgment of the House of Lords be subject to these trusts and obligations? That was your point, I understand.

Mr. *Walker.*] Yes. Now, these are the documents in the case, so far as they seem to me material, which preceded that charter of the 29th March 1613. You will remember that the 29th March was the fourth day of that year, and February was the last month of the year. This is a charter, you will remember, to the city. I will not call attention to all the details into it as fully as I would be justified in doing before a legal tribunal under the limitations which have been prescribed by the right honourable Chairman; but you will remember the preamble, and you will remember the words that the City of London had "laudably undertaken a considerable part of the said plantation in Ulster," in the entire of the lands. But that is preceded by the documents which had really substituted, indirectly at any rate, the 12 companies who had elected to take the land for the city, and the obligations imposed upon the city. As I have said, it mentions the Irish Society under the corporate name which is there prescribed. It granted to the society the city of Derry and the town of Coleraine and all the lands in the county, the rivers Bann and Foyle with their fishings, and with the obligation to grant lands for the Bishop and Dean of the Endowed Churches and so forth, and contained a clause which is of some importance about the woods, that the Crown put an obligation upon them, "that all and all manner of trees being, timber growing and being of in and upon the lands of Glenkonkeine and Killetragh, extending from the aforesaid county of Coleraine unto Ballinderry, shall be and for ever hereafter remain only and be converted towards the plantation aforesaid, and the building of houses and edifices, so as aforesaid, to be made, and to be spent towards other necessary uses of our aforesaid realm of Ireland, in the same kingdom, and not for any other cause to be merchandised and sold, anything in these presents to the contrary notwithstanding." It gave them power to create manors with all the rights incident to manors; it gave them all manorial rights, and gave them power to make lettings for such term and terms of years, state or states, and for such services and yearly rents to be reserved for and upon the same lands, tenements, and hereditaments, as shall seem best and convenient." That was to be the mode by which the undertaking was to be made profitable, by lettings, by the persons who should receive the grant, and who should undertake the building and the planting. And it provided for the revenue which would accrue which would represent

21 *July* 1890.

sent the profit, whether public profit or private profit. These tenancies were to be held "of the governor and assistants of London of the new plantation in Ulster aforesaid, and their successors, and of their several manor and manors respectively, to which the said lands, tenements, and hereditaments, so to be granted or demised, do, or shall severally and respectively belong or appertain."

Sir *William Marriott.*] Who were to get the profits of the lettings?

Mr. *Walker.*] The rents were to be received by the persons who let the lands, whether that was a profit in the sense of private profit, to be applied as the person letting thought fit, or was public profit in the sense in which the House of Lords decided, as regards the Irish Society, is, of course, the question here. But you remember what has been decided as regards the Irish Society, that, as regards all lettings in Derry, which are lettings made under this charter, though they are in one sense "profit" received, they are public property under the decision of the House of Lords. The use of the word "profit" determines nothing in the controversy, looking to the sense in which it is used. Under that charter, I submit, the public objects were never accomplished, were never carried into execution before the companies accepted the position put upon them. There was no way of those public objects being accomplished except by the companies standing in the position of the city, and undertaking the burdens cast upon the city; and what those burdens were, and what the objects were, are expressed with all that clearness that might be expected by Lord Lyndhurst, in three or four passages of his judgment, already before the Committee.

Chairman.] Will you give the reference?

Mr. *Walker.*] Clarke and Finnelly, vol. 13, p. 482. The objects of this plantation, and the objects of this grant, are public objects which attach at every step the subject of that grant. That charter having been executed, it appears that on the 30th of April 1613, the money that had already been levied was found to be exhausted; 30,000 *l.* had been already levied, and 10,000 *l.* more was required, and that is directed to be levied by an Act of the Common Council, dated 30th April 1613: "Upon information given to this court by the governor and assistants appointed for the plantation in Ireland, that all the moneys formerly levied towards that charge is altogether issued and expended, and also the sum of 3,000 *l.* more, which they have of late borrowed out of the chamber of London, is likewise almost disbursed; and that a further supply must, of necessity, with all expedition, be made and provided to proceed on in the business. It is, therefore, further enacted, granted, and agreed by the authority aforesaid that a present taxation shall be made of the sum of 10,000 *l.* more, over and above the sum of 30,000 *l.* heretofore by former Acts of Common Council appointed to be taxed and gathered; the same to be employed and expended in and about the said plantation in Ireland. And that the same 10,000 *l.* shall forthwith be taxed, levied, and raised upon all the several companies of this city, according to the late allotment and proportioned, whereby the last sum of 10,000 *l.* was levied and assessed; and shall be paid over before the last day of May next coming unto Mr. Cornelius Fishe, Chamberlain of this city, who by this court is appointed treasurer for the receipt and payment thereof." That shows two things. First, it shows that the building and plantation was in progress, that it was beginning; that it required a large sum of money in order to carry it out, and the companies having then accepted the position which is to be gathered from the documents I have read, the companies are taxed, by compulsory taxation, to provide the further monies for the building and plantation. That was after the date when the companies had accepted the position, which may be an equivocal position, which may be said to be a position carrying with it private profit and not a position of trust; but, whatever the position was, a sum of money was raised in exactly the same way after the companies had accepted the position, by compulsory taxation, for the purpose of carrying on the building and plantation, the burden of which lay upon them. Then it goes on: "It is enacted, granted, and agreed by the authority aforesaid, that every several company of this city shall have their several share and proportion of the said lands, according to the monies by them disbursed; respecting the goodness or badness thereof, the same lands to lie all entirely together and not dispersedly, in several places. At that the same lands shall be proportionate, according to the goodness or badness thereof, with respect to where the land is bad, and allowance be made in the quantity to make it equal in value with that which is better, so that no prejudice (or as little as may be) may happen to any company in the allotting of the said lands, which is afterwards intended to be divided by lots." Then there is a provision as to dividing the lands between the companies, which was carried out.

Chairman.] Do you understand that the city have got possession of the lands yet.

Mr. *Walker.*] I think that appears; it is stated that they have; though they have not got the charter, they must have been working at it.

Chairman.] I do not find any reference to the date at which, or the instrument by which, the lands came into the possession of the city.

Mr. *Walker.*] No; I have not been able to find any document to show that. It appears that on 17th December 1613, the lots were drawn by which the lands are assigned and allotted to the several companies. It is fully described in a minute of the Common Council of that date. They were allotted according to the proportions of taxation that had been put upon them. The Common Council had to divide the obligation of the taxation of 40,000 *l.*, and they divided it into 12 parts of 3,333 *l.* 6 *s.* 8 *d.*, and they ascertained that the 12 principal companies had paid the largest share of the burden, in some cases, I think, in two at all events, the companies exceeded the 3,333 *l.*, and they got, by addition to another company, a portion of the surplus, but where the principal company had not been taxed to the full amount, it

was

was grouped with minor companies, and the allotment was treated as the allotment of the 12. *L.* 3,000 more was directed to be raised on this 17th December 1613. "All the monies formerly levied towards that charge is altogether issued, and that notwithstanding the company had their particular shares of land, which was to be managed by themselves severally, that the general work for the building of the rest of the town and the fortifications was to be done at the general charge, and, therefore, that a further supply must of necessity, with all expedition, be made, and provided to proceed in the business. It is therefore further enacted, granted, and agreed by the authority aforesaid, the present taxation shall be made of the sum of 5,000 *l.* heretofore by former Acts of Common Council appointed to be taxed and gathered; and that the same 5,000 *l.* shall be forthwith taxed, levied, and raised of all the several companies of this city according to the late allotment and proportion, whereby the last sum of 10,000 *l.* was levied and assessed, and shall be paid in before the 1st day of February next coming, unto Mr. Cornelius Fishe, Chamberlain of the City." There again, for the building then in progress the city money, by the same process, was raised for the public objects of the undertaking. It appears that further sums of money were raised that came to about 37,000 *l.* shortly afterwards. The king, it appears, was very much interested in this undertaking and its completion, and it appears that he wrote a letter to the deputy, dated the 30th March 1615, complaining of the slow progress of the works, in which he says, "It is well known to you that if we had intended only, as it seems most of those over-greedily had done, our present profit, we might have converted those large territories to our escheated lands to the great improvement of our Crown there: but we choose rather for the safety of that country, and the civilising of that people, to depart with the inheritance of them at current undervalues, and to make a plantation of them; and since we were merely induced thereunto out of reason of State, we think we may, without any breach of justice, make bold with their rights, who have neglected their duties in a service of so much importance unto us, and by the same law and reason of State, resume into our hands their lands who have failed to perform, according to our original intention, the articles of plantation, and bestow them upon some other men more active and worthy of them than themselves." So you see the way in which the King dealt with these lands, and how he complained of the slow progress made upon them, the developing of them being a public and national work that he was anxious to further; and he contemplates even that he may have to exercise the power of resuming possession of all those lands. Now, the next document in the case is also of extreme importance, it is the license of the Crown that the companies shall hold the land. That license is dated the 30th December 1615.

Chairman.] Were there not two licenses? Was there not a license to alienate as well as a license to hold?

Mr. *Latham.*] It is all the same document.

Mr. *Walker.*] That license is dated the 30th of September 1612. The preamble of this license is of great importance. You will see it is furthering and carrying out what had been agreed between the companies and the city, and giving legal validity, with the consent of the Crown, to what had been arranged between the companies and the city. "James, by the grace of God, &c., to all to whom, &c., forasmuch as we are credibly informed that divers companies, corporations, and fraternities of and within our city of London, within our realm of England, in testimony of their true obedience towards us, and towards the advancing of our earnest desire in the furthering of that worthy work of plantation begun" (you observe the word "begun") "by the Mayor and commonalty and citizens of our said City of London, in the City of Londonderry and town of Coleraine, in our realm of Ireland, and other lands there, have disbursed, expended, and bestowed divers great sums of money for and towards the building, fortifying, planting, strengthening, bettering, and improving the aforesaid city of Derry and town of Coleraine, and some part of other the aforesaid lands, and the said corporation, companies, and fraternities, being willing to proceed in the same work of plantation, do intend so far forth as to them shall seem convenient, to be at further charge for the planting, bettering, and improving of other lands and tenements, in and by certain our letters patents, hereafter mentioned, granted, or intended to be granted, to the Society of the Governor and Assistants, London, of the new plantation in Ulster, in the realm of Ireland, and for their better, more orderly, and speedier proceeding therein, are desirous to have such parts of the said lands as they severally and respectively intend to build on and plant, to be to them severally conveyed by the aforesaid society." That refers to the patent of the 29th March 1613; it refers to the willingness on the part of these companies to proceed in the work of plantation; it refers to the work begun, but in progress, and requiring further expenditure for its completion; and in order to carry out its purpose, the King says, "which by reason that the same companies, corporations, and fraternities, are not enabled to take and hold the same lands and tenements in mortmain, without our special license, could not be performed by the said society, and yet such have been the desires of our said subjects, the said companies and fraternities, as we are informed, to further and promote our zeal towards the same work, that notwithstanding they have not yet any conveyance or assurance of the lands from the said society, they have already, with great alacrity and readiness, begun to build on a great part of the said lands" (that answers the question you put to me): "and have likewise disbursed divers great sums of money for and towards the same." And then he proceeds: "We, therefore, willing, as much as in us lieth, to effect and bring to an end (if so it please God) the said pious and worthy work, and to nourish the happy and hopeful beginning and proceedings aforesaid, begun and prosecuted out of the piety of our said subjects, and to remove, as much as in us lieth, all impediments to that any way may hinder our said subjects in their forward laudable intentions for the performance and

21 *July* 1890.

and finishing of the said plantation, and to the end that they severally may be the better encouraged and enabled to proceed, perfect, and finish the same intended plantation, and in future times reap some gain and benefit of their great travels and expenses, had taken and bestowed therein." And then he grants to the different companies by name "full licence, power, and authority that they and their successors severally and respectfully from time to time, and at all times hereafter, purchase, receive, have, take, and enjoy such, and so many of the counties, countries, baronies, cities, towns, castles, manors, lands, tenements, advowsons, rivers, fishings, rents, tithes, services, possessions, and hereditaments, given or granted, or meant, mentioned, or intended, in or by our Letters Patents, bearing test at Westminster the 29th day of March, in the 11th of our reign of England, France, and Ireland, and of Scotland, the 46th to be given or granted to the said Society of the Governors and Assistants, London, of the new plantation in Ulster, in the kingdom of Ireland, of the gift, grant, feoffment, bargain, sale, assignment, or alienation of the said Society of the Governor and Assistants, London, of the new plantation in Ulster, in the Kingdom of Ireland, and of their successors, or of the gift, grant, bargain, feoffment, sale, confirmation, surrender, or release of any other person or persons whatsoever, bodies politic, and others hereafter to be made as the said Society of the Governor and Assistants, London, of the new plantations in Ulster, in the kingdom of Ireland, and their successors or any other person or persons whatsoever, bodies politic, or others, shall be willing from time to time to give, grant, enfeoff, bargain, sell, convey, assign, alien, confirm, or release" to the several companies. And then in the same document he gives licence to the Irish Society to give and grant the lands to the several companies. There you have the Crown coming in, and by its act, which was necessary in order to carry out what had been done between the city and the companies, giving power to those companies to hold the lands for the purpose of building and plantation; and in order that the plantation might be carried into effect. It is a recognition by the Crown of the companies as joint planters with the Irish Society; it legalises that which otherwise would be illegal.

Sir William Marriott.] What meaning do you attach to these words, "and to the end that they severally may be the better encouraged and enabled to proceed, perfect, and finish the same intended plantation, and in future times reap some gain and benefit of their great travels and expenses had taken and bestowed therein."

Mr. *Walker.*] The meaning I attach to these words is the meaning I attach to the word "profit," profit in the sense of public profit. It is an equivocal word, but you find it coupled with subject matter where it is not private property; and therefore it is perfectly consistent with these grants, in the case of the Irish Society, that it should receive the other signification. That licence being granted on the 29th of September 1616. The next documents in the case are the grants which followed. I need not read them.

Chairman.] You mean the conveyance from the society to the companies.

Mr. *Walker.*] Yes. The only difference between the twelve grants is this, that in five of them a small rent was reserved to the Irish Society, in the other seven there is no rent reserved. They were made in pursuance of that Royal licence given to the Irish Society to make such grants, and the one to the Skinners' Company I may take it as being in the same terms as all the others.

Chairman.] We have two or three before us.

Mr. *Walker.*] They are all the same. The one to the Skinners' Company is dated the 22nd of March 1617.

Chairman.] Do you know whether the rents reserved in five of the conveyances are still paid.

Mr. *Walker.*] That is a matter I do not know. They are very small rents, 17 *s.*, merely nominal rents.

Mr. *Healy.*] Were not there reservations?

Mr. *Walker.*] I will call your attention to this. This grant you may take as a model, for there is no difference except in respect of the rents. It is between the Irish Society and the Skinners' Company, and it witnesses that the Irish Society "as well for and in consideration of a certain competent sum of money to them in hand before the sealing and delivery of these presents by the said master, wardens, and commonalty of the Mystery of the Skinners' Company of London, aforesaid, well and truly paid, whereof they the said society confess and acknowledge the receipt." There was no money passed. That was the form of the conveyances at the time.

Chairman.] You are not going to read the whole conveyance?

Mr. *Walker.*] No. They grant to the Skinners' Company the manor of Pellipar. After the licence was obtained from the Crown, the Irish Society proceeded, in pursuance of their power, to create manors, and they created 12 manors with all manorial rights, and then, the lots having been drawn, the manors having fallen to the respective companies by lot, they make a conveyance accordingly to each company of the particular manor so drawn by lot, and the manor in this case was the manor of Pellipar, and in this grant they grant "all and singular, which lands, tenements, hereditaments and premises aforesaid are contained within the Skinners' proportion. No. 12, according to their lot or division with other companies, and were lately by the said society, by force of, and according to, the King's Majesties Letters Patents to them, in that behalf granted, made, erected, ordained and reduced into a manor to consist of such tenants as in the said Letters Patents is mentioned" (these are the powers to which I have already called attention to the same manors), "and intended to be made a manor as aforesaid, were by the said society, by force and according to the said Letters Patents, named and called by the name of the Manor of Pellipar." Then it proceeds to grant the manor. It springs out of the power conferred

conferred by the patent, and has reference to it. Then there are a number of exceptions. The society, except all the fishing and taking of salmon and eels, in the River Bann. The rent in this case is 17 *l.* 6 *s.* 8 *d.*

"Then they reserve power to the Skinners' Company by the appointment of an agent for the time being, resident in Ulster, for the affairs of the said society, to fell, cut down, take and carry away such, and so many of the timbered trees of the said society, standing, growing, and being nearest and most commodious to the premises aforegranted, as shall be fit and necessary for the building or plantation of any houses, villages, edifices, or buildings within the said manor lands and premises." They reserve special rights in respect of the general purposes of the buildings and plantation; they reserve stone, slate, lime, and other necessary materials. That also is mentioned in the charter. Now, under the grants I have called your attention to, it strikes me that the city companies became associated with the city in a great public work. You must remember that these city companies were all trading corporations; they were not corporations to whom it would be natural to hold lands and work them in Ireland; they are domiciled in England; they are non-resident; they stand in that respect in a position perfectly different from the private undertakers to whom lands would be granted in the other escheated counties.

Chairman.] Do you, or do you not, detect any analogy between the charters granted to the Irish Society and the charter given to the Hudson's Bay Company, or in more recent times, the charter to the North Borneo Company, or the charter to the South African Company; there may be nothing in that, but it occurred to me that there might be an analogy.

Mr. Walker.] It is perfectly possible that you might find a charter giving a plantation in the West Indies or North America, which would have no trust attached to it. But here you start with this: The charter in this case does by virtue of its preamble carry with it a trust, whether those other charters to which you refer do contain a trust or not must depend upon the language of the charters, and until I saw them I could not say whether there was an analogy between those charters and this. Here we start with a charter that is impressed with a public trust. Again there is an obvious distinction between a private undertaker, a person who got a grant of land in Tyrone, and persons whose grant springs out of a contract with the Crown. Here you have a special contract with the Crown, beginning with the document I have called your attention to, and carried on and confirmed by the license of 1613.

Chairman.] Perhaps we may have the point taken up by some other learned counsel as to whether there is an analogy between this charter and charters given, for example, to noblemen and others who founded colonies in what are now the United States. I think we might examine the charter for Maryland, for instance, or Virginia; but do not let me interrupt your argument.

Mr. Walker.] In the first place such a charter, if we had it, would carry with it a public trust of itself, but I rest on the special ground that this does carry a public trust with it.

Mr. Healy.] What were the manorial rights?

Mr. Walker.] They carry with them the right of holding a court, a very large right; the rights of the Crown attached to the manor by the creation of the manor, vest in the person to whom the manor is granted.

Mr. Healy.] Were there any penal powers?

Mr. Walker.] Yes; they had the power of holding a court, and in those days very large powers were vested in the holders of a manor. Now let us see what was the view of the Crown as regards the position of these several grantees, and of the Irish Society. It appears that on the 28th February (10th Charles the First) the Attorney General exhibited an information in the Star Chamber against the City and the Irish Society for the non-performance of their trust. I want to see what the view of the Crown was, the same authority that granted the patent.

Chairman.] You refer to the Star Chamber proceedings in order to show us what the view of the Crown was.

Mr. Walker.] Yes; there was a regular indictment, if we may call it an indictment, against the Irish Society and the city for non-performance of a public trust, and having been cited and having appeared in the Star Chamber, there was a solemn judgment that the patent should be cancelled, and a fine of 17,000 *l.* was imposed upon the city for a breach of its obligations and for non-performance of its duties; it appears that the companies were not made defendants to that suit in the Star Chamber; they did not go so far in their arbitrary career as to condemn a man, not having heard him.

Chairman.] The corporation were defendants.

Mr. Walker.] Yes; and the Irish Society; but at the foot of the proceedings I find: "And whereas the greatest part of the said land are by the said society passed over unto diver companies of the City of London, and by them demised unto their farmers, who are not defendants to this suit, and therefore are not now liable to their Lordships' censures, although in the opinion of the Court they might justly have been censured, if they had been parties to either of the said informations. It is therefore thought fit, and directed by this Court, that if the said companies and their farmers shall not in pursuance of the intention of this sentence, surrender their estates, His Majesty's said Attorney General shall exhibit an information and bring them also to the judgment of this Court."

Mr. Elton.] They gave judgment before the action began?

Mr. Walker.] Yes.

Mr. Healy.] Will you read the material portions of the sentence.

21 *July* 1890.

Mr. *Walker*.] It recites that timber had been sold by the city agents, and applied to purposes not warranted by the charter; and it proceeds: "The Court did declare that the said Society of Governor and Assistants were also fit defendants, and liable to the censure of this Court: for although they have by licence conveyed the several proportions of the said undertaken lands to the 12 great companies, yet they themselves do still retain to themselves the city of Londonderry and the town of Coleraine, and the 7,000 acres, the said woods of Glanconkeine, Killetragh, the castle of Culmore, the fishings and customs, as appears by their own answers and proofs in this Court, and many of the breaches and failures of performance of the Articles of Agreement, were before the lands were passed away to the said Companies." They contended that they were not proper parties to the suit. "Thirdly, the Court is of opinion, and doth declare, that the said Patent according to the tenor and purport of the said warrant, which directed the same should be drawn according to the said 27 articles, nor any covenant therein contained for performance thereof, nor any reference or relation had thereunto, and that without any warrant. And in further abuse of his said Majesty they have made 26 persons by the name of the Society of Governor and Assistants of the new Plantation in Ulster, in the kingdom of Ireland, a body corporate for ever, and have thereby granted unto them and their successors all the said large territories and possessions, together with many large and exorbitant privileges, liberties and franchises: the said warrant directing the said patent to be drawn up to the committees, to be named by the City of London, and not to any such new formed body or corporation, who are not responsible; and by the said Letters Patent they have passed unto the said Society of Governor and Assistants a far greater quantity of land than was proposed or demanded by the committees on behalf of the city or intended by the said 27 articles." And then it declares, "That the mayor and commonalty, and citizens of the City of London and the said society of governor and assistants of the said new plantation have also greatly offended in not performing of their undertakings, for that they did not build the said houses in the city of Derry and Town of Coleraine, by the time limited and agreed upon by the said articles, nor have performed the same fully unto this day as they ought to do by the said articles, and for that they did not in time, according to the 27th Article, nor have as yet, sufficiently built and fortified. By all which means, and by the means of their not keeping a sufficient guard in the said Castle of Culmore, the whole country hath been endangered, and his late and now Majesties were enforced to his and their great charge to maintain garrisons there for defence of the said kingdom. In respect whereof, and of other the failures and non-performances formerly herein mentioned, and of the great destruction of the woods and timber trees there, which is apparently proved to be done by their agents, for whom they must and ought to answer. The whole Court did this day, with one uniform opinion and consent order and judge and decree that the said defendants, the Lord Mayor, commonalty, and citizens of the City of London and the Society of Governor and Assistants of the New Plantation, in Ulster, in the kingdom of Ireland, shall for the offences aforesaid satisfy and pay for a fine to his Majesty's use the sum of 70,000 *l.*; and that the said patent so unduly and surreptitiously obtained to the prejudice and deception of his Majesty as aforesaid, and their estates and interest therein, shall be by them forthwith surrendered up to his Majesty, and shall be brought into this Court here to be cancelled and made void, or otherwise to be disposed of at his Majesty's pleasure." It appears that negotiations commenced with the Crown, and ultimately it went before the House of Commons, the City appealed to the House of Commons, which was then getting to be a power in the country. History repeats itself. The King was heard before the House of Commons, and the city was heard before the House of Commons by Counsel, and a resolution was passed by the House of Commons, affirming everything in favour of the City, and everything against the Crown, and resolving that the patent should not be cancelled, and that, in fact, the City were perfectly right. It appears that then the King made a promise to the City that he would restore the Patent to them. There was a good deal of negotiation about a fine and other things between the Crown and the City, and the King made a promise to restore the Patent, which failed to be carried out by reason of the troubled times that followed. Then, in the time of the Protectorate there was a new charter granted; but when King Charles the 2nd was restored, the course was to wipe out everything that had taken place in the time of the Protectorate, and to treat it as illegal and void. Accordingly, King Charles the 2nd, in a charter dated the 10th of April 1662, after reciting that the former patent had been cancelled, proceeded to re-grant to the Irish Society the lands which had been the subject of the former charter, and that Patent is of some importance in the case, on account of the recital that is in it. It recites the Letters Patent of the 29th of March 1613, and the grant by it to the society of the corporation and the town. It then contains this recital, which I ask your attention to: "And whereas the said Society of the Governor and and Assistants of London of the new plantation in Ulster, within the realm of Ireland, by virtue of a certain licence from our said illustrious grandfather, under the Great Seal of England, bearing date at Westminster, the 30th day of September in the 15th year of his reign over England, France, and Ireland, and over Scotland the 49th, did grant unto the 12 chief companies of our City of London (which have taken upon themselves the greatest part of the burden upon the said plantation) divers great quantities, parcels, and proportions of the said lands, tenements, and hereditaments according to their several disbursements, and did retain in his own hands such part of the same tenements and hereditaments as were not properly divisible for defraying of the charge of the general operation of the said plantation." This is nearly half a century after the charter of 1613; it is after all the documents I have called your attention to; the recital of what occurred is that by virtue of a licence from the Crown,

21 *July* 1890.

Crown, the Irish Society had granted to the 12 chief companies (which had taken upon themselves the greatest part of the burden of the plantation) divers lands, tenements, and hereditaments, but had retained the rest in their own hands, not being properly divisible, certain buildings, hereditaments, and so forth, for defraying the charge of the general operation of the plantation. It then recites: "And whereas the said letters patent were afterwards annulled, abolished, and cancelled in the Court of Chancery" (they are bound by this recital because they take under it), by reason whereof the said Society of the New Plantation, and the said companies of our City of London, and their respective assigns and under-tenants, of all and singular the lands, tenements, and hereditaments, royalties, privileges, franchises, and immunities in the said letters patent mentioned were wholly deprived, and the said Corporation of Londonderry, together with the said Society of the New Plantation, became wholly annulled and invalidated." That is a recital which binds them; they take under it. Then it recites the promise of restitution of King Charles the 1st, and then it says, "And for that it doth manifestly appear to us that the same society of the new plantation and other companies of our City of London have expended very great sums of money in building and planting of the said county of Londonderry and Coleraine. To the intent, therefore, that the said society of the new plantation, or some other such society, by these our letters patent, to be erected and made, and the said companies of our City of London, and their respective assigns, and under tenants may, according to their former several rights and interests therein, be restored to all and singular the county, city, towns, castles, and territories, lands, tenements, royalties, franchises, privileges, and immunities whatsoever, with their and every of their appurtenances so vested in them by force and virtue of the said Letters Patent, and the said several grants by the said society of the new plantation and other companies respectively, theretofore made as fully and beneficially to all intents and purposes as they might have had and enjoyed the same, if no repeal of the said Letters Patent had ever been had or made." It then proceeds to grant the City of Derry and other lands, tenements, and hereditaments.

Chairman.] The drift of all that is, as Lord Lyndhurst said, to replace the parties exactly in their former position, in exactly the same position as if the charter had not been repealed.

Mr. Walker.] Yes; the reason I read the recital is, because it is a statement that binds the parties. Then it proceeds to grant, as Lord Lyndhurst says substantially, though with some variations, the lands in Derry and in Coleraine, exactly as before. It contains the same reservations of trees and timber in the woods for the general purposes of the plantation, and it gives power to create manors. "And so many several manors of such tenements as are hereafter limited to from time to time shall seem convenient to the same society of the governor and assistants, London;" and then "that they may make, erect, and ordain one manor of every 1,000 acres of land by these presents before granted, or of any number exceeding the number of 1,000 acres of land, and so according to such rate, so many several manors as they will; so that they make not any manor of a lesser number of acres of land than of the number of 1,000 acres." Then is given them power to let the land on the same terms as the former charter. I do not think I need read any other portion of the charter to the Committee. Then there are letters from the Crown in 1664 and 1665, which are set out in the appellant's case in the case of the Skinners' Company against the Irish Society, in which the Crown, after these transactions insists on its rights and requires the plantation to be carried on, and the necessary works to be done that were contracted to be done. The only purpose for which I use those letters is this; to shew that all through the action on the part of the Crown was consistent with the interpretation of the charter that was afterwards arrived at, showing that it was a public purpose that the Crown impressed upon the trust; and I do not find any repudiation of that view taken by the Crown, though there were excuses for non-performance and matters of that kind. After the charter of 1662 was granted, there followed it just as before, grants to the 12 companies. They are almost all of the same date; I think all, except one of the 8th of June 1662. Everything that was done before was repeated; I think all the conveyances except the one of the 8th of June 1663, to the 12 principal companies, are precisely in the same form as the grant to the Skinners' Company, from which I read extracts.

Chairman.] Is the new licence identical in words.

Mr. Latham.] No.

Mr. Walker.] I have not seen the new licence. If my learned friend relies on any difference he will call your attention to it. The only difference in these grants by the Irish Society to the companies is this: that they recite the patent, and they recite the former grant and the creation of the manors, and they pretend to re-grant with the same exceptions everything that had been re-granted before. A paper has been put into my hand, dated the 22nd of December 1657, that is, during that period at which the negotiations were going on, when the Crown and the city were quarrelling about their mutual obligations. This paper of that date was handed in, and I understand relied on.

Chairman.] Handed in to this Committee?

Mr. Walker.] Yes, by Mr. Saunders. "At this Court was read the precept from the Lord Mayor and Court of Aldermen concerning the levying of 8,000 *l.*, assessed by act of Common Council upon the company for their part of 60,000 *l.*, being the first payment of 120,000 *l.* granted by the said Common Council to be paid to His Majesty upon the sale of lands in fee-farm from His Majesty to the City of London, in satisfaction as well of the said 120,000 *l.* as of the City's former debts to them due from the late King James, and by the master it was then demanded of the generality of the company then assembled together, what course in their judgment they

thought

21 *July* 1890.

thought fittest for the raising of that proportion of 3,820 *l.*, whether to levy it by the pole or upon sale of the plate belonging to the Hall by disbursement of such money of the company as is in the renter's hands and may well be spared for the time, and by the mortgage of such lands as the company stand seised of and not given to charitable uses. All which being put to the question, the levying of that proportion of 3,820 *l.* by the poll, was by erection of hands utterly denied, and it was by the general consent of the most part of the company condescended unto and thought best that the said proportion of 3,820 *l.* should be levied by sale of the plate belonging to the Hall, disbursements of such money of the company in the renter's hands as may be well spared for the time, and by mortgage of such lands as are the company's, and not given to charitable uses." I understand that it was suggested in the evidence that that gave ground for suggesting that there was some consideration as between the companies and the Crown to give the transaction some new force and validity. I do not find that it has ever been alleged that any money ever passed from the companies to the Crown afterwards; and, so far as I can see, the only consideration that ever existed for these grants which they now hold under was the charter of Charles II.; that there is no consideration for these grants that could give them force or validity, and that they all rest upon transactions I have already referred to. It is possible that in those times, during the negotiations between the Crown and the City, when the fine was imposed, and moneys were to be levied, there may have been some consideration between the companies as to the mode of raising some contingent payment, but I do not see that that was carried out, because we know there was a complete pardon granted by the Crown to the City for its non-performance, and to the Irish Society for its non-performance of its public trust at that time, and I do not find that any money was raised or paid to the Crown. There were also handed in to the Committee certain opinions of Counsel. Counsel's opinions are very much dependent upon the cases submitted to them; and no matter what names may be affixed to those opinions, they still must be governed by the cases submitted, and we know this has been a controversial matter. I know opinions have been given on both sides. I know those opinions have varied, and at the time those opinions were handed in, we know that opinions were obtained from official personages exactly the opposite to those opinions.

Sir William Marriott.] If there are opinions the other way, it would only be fair that they should be handed in.

Mr. Walker.] I know an opinion was given the other way.

Sir William Marriott.] If there are other opinions, the Committee would not object to having them.

Mr. Walker.] All I say is, there are opinions on both sides. Nobody can say the case is not one in which you might not get opinions on one side or the other; but I submit that the case I put is reasonably clear upon the documents. Opinions by Counsel, either on the one side or the other, will not be very much considered by the Committee; the Committee will, no doubt, exercise their own judgment upon any question which appears to them worthy of consideration; I only know that the Solicitor General gave an opinion directly the opposite.

Sir William Marriott.] What Solicitor General?

Mr. Walker.] Mr. Dowse. I would not expect my learned friend's witnesses to proffer unnecessarily opinions the other way; they would naturally put in, quite fairly, opinions which tell for them.

Chairman.] I do not think you need dwell upon this much, because the Committee will judge for themselves as to the value of these opinions.

Mr. Walker.] So I should submit. Now, in the interval between the grant of 1663 and the date of 1832, let us look for some acts of the parties. Acts are evidence, and admissions against the parties. I find on the 24th November 1830, a very remarkable resolution and report of the Irish Society, which I will call the attention of the committee to. It was two years before the filing of the bill, in the case of the Skinners' Company against the Irish Society, and that resolution is as follows: 24th November 1830, "That this Court, in making a dividend, do take the opportunity of assuring the twelve chief companies that the society's constant attention has been devoted to the fulfilment of the important trust confided to them by their charter for the improvement of their plantation in the province of Ulster. That in furtherance of this object, and to recover very valuable rights which have been long usurped, particularly the patronage and right of presentation to a considerable number of advowsons granted to them by their charter, as well as to establish their conservative jurisdiction over the Corporations of Londonderry and Coleraine (the inhabitants of which latter place have earnestly solicited the society to exert their authority for the restoration of their charter and corporate rights), the court have found it necessary to send frequent deputations of their members to Ireland, in order to carry their measures into effect." Then they refer to the expense incurred in making searches for ancient records and documents with reference to these advowsons, and then they say, "that the principal duties incumbent on the society being to establish and endow schools for the benefit of the rising generation, to assist in the erection of places of public worship, and also to promote all charitable institutions for the relief of the poor, the society contributed largely towards the accomplishment of these objects. That the expenditure consequent upon these several obligations, has necessarily and unavoidably intrenched upon the society's funds, and precluded the society from making more frequent dividends." Now there could not be a more full or a more legal definition, or explanation of the duties of the Irish Society than there is contained in these resolutions; they seem themselves to have interpreted the charters as the Courts afterwards interpreted them; they call attention to the fact that they have spent money for education, for religion, and other public purposes, and they excuse themselves on that

21 *July* 1890.

that accounts for not paying larger dividends to the companies. That was relied upon afterwards in the Skinners' case, amongst other documents. Now, a few words as regards the Bill in Chancery; on the 18th July 1832, by the Skinners' Company. I have read the arguments of the learned counsel, who then represented the one side and the other, and I was greatly struck by the arguments of Sir William Follett.

Chairman.] Do you mean his argument in the Court of First Instance.

Mr. Walker.] His argument in the Court of First Instance and also in the Court above. In the Court of First Instance it is more fully reported; I have the shorthand writer's note of Sir William Follett's argument, and I was greatly struck with this. He was arguing against the existence of a Public Trust in the Irish Society, for he was arguing for the Skinners' Company. He said that there was no trust in the Irish Society, but that they held as trustees for the 12 companies, and they were bound to pay everything over to them after satisfying expenses and so on, but his logical mind led him to this conclusion and he pressed it upon the Court that you cannot establish a trust against the Irish Society without coming also to the conclusion that there is a trust attaching upon the twelve companies, because they stand in precisely the same position, and you cannot escape logically from the conclusion that if there is a trust against the Irish Society, therefore, there is a trust against the twelve companies. It struck me that that was a logical proposition from which nobody could escape, and it is my argument entirely in this case that you cannot escape from the position that if it is a trust in the Irish Society, and therefore a trust against the others who are adventurers with them in this plantation, and sharers with them of the burden which is imposed upon them in the way of public duties. Of course, for the purposes of that suit of the Skinners' Company against the Irish Society, it was utterly immaterial whether the Skinners' Company were trustees or not. That suit was to establish that the Irish Society held for them, and they had a right to maintain that suit whether they themselves were trustees or not, because if the Irish Society were trustees for them they held everything they got as trustees for the Skinners' Company and the other twelve companies, and whether the Skinners' Company, when they got their money, were themselves bound to apply it to a public trust, was perfectly immaterial, and therefore that question whether the Skinners' Company was itself a trust, or the other 12 companies were a trust, did not become material in the course of that case, either for decision or argument. It was only an incident, and adverted to in the argument of Sir William Follett, who said that it must logically follow from the argument on behalf of the Irish Society that it would involve the other companies in the position of being trustees also, a position which I admit is perfectly unanswerable. Again, dealing with the acts of the parties here, has there not been in the course of conduct on the part of the 12 companies that which evidences that in their mind, at all events there was a lurking consciousness that they held the position of trustees for this public trust. There has been a course of conduct in making grants for schools, and making grants for education. While they were owners of these estates, it is not disputed, but they made at all events considerable grants for objects which were within the charter, and which appear to me to show that they had a consciousness, but they were bound to do these acts; and when they conveyed away, as they did, or purported to convey away, portions of this estate to purchasers for value, they, as in the case of Sir Hervey Bruce, imposed upon them by the same conveyance the obligation for a period of 10 years to continue the grants which they themselves had theretofore made.

Mr. Latham.] Not an obligation.

Mr. Walker.] At all events it was done; I do not know whether it was by covenant or not. Be that as it may, Sir Hervey Bruce, for a period of 10 years paid grants which theretofore the society had paid, and that evidences to my mind this, that these companies must have had in their mind a shrewd suspicion that they were under some public obligation to make these grants.

Mr. Healy.] Did the Irish Society join in that grant to Sir Hervey Bruce?

Mr. Walker.] I could not tell you.

Mr. Latham.] No.

Mr. Walker.] What the Irish Society have done is of some importance. I think it appears on the Minutes of Evidence that the Irish Society have conveyed, or commuted, or released their rights over mines and minerals and timber.

Mr. Latham.] Not mines and minerals.

Mr. Walker.] But timber; the same observation applies. It is perfectly clear on the decision of the House of Lords, that any rights of timber which the Irish Society had would be covered by the public trust which was established against them; and therefore the Irish Society have actually conveyed away to the grantees a portion of their property which is undoubtedly covered by a public trust, and which, according to the decision of the House of Lords, it would be impossible for them to convey a valid title to, unless the Statute of Limitations came in. I will say a word upon the lapse of time presently. I dare say my learned friends and myself will not differ about that. Any man who holds a charitable estate, provided a trust can be made out from documents of title, holds it upon an express trust; it is not necessary to use the word "trust" to create what is called in law an express trust. You will not find in the whole of the charter of Charles, or the charter of James, the word "trust," yet a trust was created, and fixed upon it. All you have to find out from a legal point of view is that the documents themselves by reading them, and by combining them, furnish evidence that a trust was attached, and that would be in the eye of the law an express trust. Taking the case of the Irish Society or the case of the 12 companies, a trust of that kind

21 *July* 1890.

kind is attached upon them by the documents of title. Then I understand the position of things is this. It would be before the recent Act of Parliament an express trust, and no time would act as a bar as between the trustee, the person who had the trust affixed upon him, and the persons entitled to the benefits of the trust. But by a section of the Real Property Limitation Act, if you convey lands to a purchaser for value, we will take one of these companies, the time would run in favour of him after 20 years had passed, and now after 20 years have passed, but that would not affect the right as against funds which the sellers received. The trust would follow the proceeds of the property, and it might be recovered as against the trustees themselves at any time. It is to be remembered that the last Statute of Limitations of 1888, which enabled as between the trustee and the *cestui que trust*, the Statute of Limitation to be set up contains an express saving as regards the proceeds of trust property which the trustee retains, or which he has converted to his own use or parted with to his own benefit (as the London companies may be said to have done), there is a saving of that right as against the proceeds of trust property which the trustees have in their own hands, or which they have converted to their own use: therefore as regards these it would be no bar at all; some of the companies retain lands still; but six of the companies parted with them far within the period of the Statute of Limitations, and therefore it is not a material consideration in their case, but as regards the others, where the property has been parted with a considerable number of years ago, the proceeds of that trust property are still in the hands of the 12 companies, and provided there is a trust, those proceeds would still be followed in their hands, and could be attached by the parties who had the benefit of the trust, even though the trustees had converted those proceeds to their own use.

Mr. *Latham*.] I may say this, as far as I am concerned, I should not on behalf of the companies raise the Statute of Limitations.

Mr. *Walker*.] My learned friend meets it very fairly, but he would hardly controvert the legal proposition. Therefore the Statute of Limitations is out of the case. The trusts then for which I contend, according to the decision of the House of Lords are still subsisting and permanent. My learned friend would, I think, not dispute this proposition; if you have a trust which is a public trust, or which is a synonym for that a public charitable trust, if it becomes impossible from the failure of the objects to carry out the trust according to the original will of the founder, or according to the intention of the Crown that granted the charter, the Court of Chancery would take hold of the matter, and carry out the trust by analogy to the trust which had become impossible, and settle a scheme, as it is called, in Chancery, to regulate the application of the trust property. But that would hardly be necessary to resort to in this case, because the trusts here are trusts that would endure for ever; the educational and religious trusts still exist in the present day just as much as they did before the making of the harbour and the making of the roads. Anything for the benefit of the county is a public charitable trust. The Committee are probably aware that when the word "charity" is used, it is not necessarily used in the sense of the word "benevolent." Charity in its legal sense means anything that is for the benefit of a county. A trust granted for the benefit of Ireland or the three kingdoms would be a public charitable trust. I need not say in this case the charters treat with objects which are in themselves charitable, being educational, religious, and social, and those are the documents which I think material for the court to consider.

Now these, Sir, are the documents which I think material for the Committee to consider. Having regard to the admonition of the Chairman, I do not think it would be either useful or becoming for me to enter into an elaborate citation of cases, or an exposition of the law, as I might do if I were dealing with this case before a judicial tribunal. Every one of the documents I have called attention to, I consider material, even those which I consider contain passages against me, as well as for me, and, I think, having considered those documents, having considered the circumstances under which this trust was created, we are driven back to the broad proposition with which I started, which lies at the root of the whole of this controversy, namely, can you for any reason sever the position of the 12 companies from the position of the Irish Society, which has been declared to be a trustee? Can you sever the position of the 7,000 acres bound by the trust created by the charter, from the 19,000 acres, so as to make them not bound by the charter? And, again, if the 19,000 acres are not bound by the trusts of the charter, the question comes, what trust does attach upon them? The answer is, there is none; and if so it comes to this, that when the city delegated the position of undertakers, and allowed that position to be undertaken by the 12 companies, and cast upon them the burden of carrying out the plantation, I see no reason in point of fact why those objects might be frustrated the next day, and that in the year 1610, not only the Irish Society but the 12 companies might have sold this property and divided it amongst themselves and applied the proceeds, not within the trust, or for any purposes entirely for the use of the City of London which are wholly foreign to the trusts of the charter.

I therefore would submit to the Committee that the trust is made out, and that the documents to which I have called attention, resting upon the decision of the House of Lords, which is sure ground, established that all these lands stand in the same position.

Sir *William Marriott*.] Before you sit down I should like to ask whether you make any distinction between the Corporation of London and the Irish Society? You have not distinguished between the two.

Mr. *Walker*.] No, Sir; I do not think there is any difference. It was said in argument before Lord Langdale, and before the House of Lords, that there was this difference; it was said the City of London had some visitorial jurisdiction,

jurisdiction, and that was the only jurisdiction that existed; but it is quite immaterial for our purpose whether the trust would be carried out by the undertakers within their visitorial jurisdiction, or in the usual way through the Attorney General, by exhibiting an information; that is merely a question of the mode of carrying it out. The City of London delegated to a department of the city, namely, the Society of the Governors and Assistants, London, of the New Plantation of Ulster, within the realm of Ireland, as they are called, the privileges, powers, and rights which the city had, and except so far as the city itself acquired, as it did in the case of the Coopers and Brown Bakers, any of their rights. I do not see how the City stands in any different position from the Irish Society.

Sir William Marriott.] The City have a controlling influence, as is mentioned in Lord Lyndhurst's Judgment; they have the appointment of the Irish Society.

Mr. *Walker.*] Certainly. There is the appointment of the Irish Society. Of the Irish Society, as I have said, seven are *ex officio* members, and the remaining 19 are elected by the citizens of London, I think.

Sir William Marriott.] There is one other question I should like to ask you before you sit down: the only deed which you quoted was one to the Skinners' Company.

Mr. *Walker.*] Yes.

Sir William Marriott.] Taking that deed, or any deed that can be relied on here, are there any words that you can point to that raise a trust?

Mr. *Walker.*] No; except the incorporation of the patents in them.

Sir William Marriott.] But are there any words in the deed itself that raise a trust?

Mr. *Walker.*] The word "trust" is not used in the deed.

Sir William Marriott.] But is a trust raised by implication?

Mr. *Walker.*] Except by reference to the root of title, out of which the conveyance grew, that is the way I put it. Through the trust you may look back to the antecedent documents, and it is for that reason that I referred back to the antecedent documents anterior to the deeds, to show that they grew out of a transaction which in itself purported to be a public trust; and therefore I would not think that it would be necessary to find in the conveyance itself that which had been before a matter of stipulation.

Sir William Marriott.] Had the company any power to sell their property when it was first handed to them, in your view?

Mr. *Walker.*] If you ask me that question, I would say at once I do not think they had; I think the only title their grantees got was the title conferred by the Statute of Limitations.

Sir William Marriott.] Some of the companies have sold 200 or 300 years ago?

Mr. *Walker.*] I am aware of that, but it does not affect the question of the proceeds.

Sir William Marriott.] They did sell, but you contend they had no right.

Mr. *Walker.*] I do not think they had.

Chairman.] Was there any sale previous to the 19th century?

Dr. *Freshfield.*] The first sale was that of the Haberdashers, in 1675.

Chairman.] Was that to Lord Waterford?

Dr. *Freshfield.*] Yes.

Sir William Marriott (to Mr. *Walker*).] Do you say that Lord Waterford's title is a bad one, seeing that he bought in 1675?

Mr. *Walker.*] No, Sir; I do not say that, but on the contrary. Perhaps I did not make myself clear upon that point. A title got with an express trust attaching in the hands of a purchaser for value may be cured by time. I did not intend to deny that. There is one other observation which I intended to make, but forgot at the moment. The question as to whether these companies, when they got the lands in the way I have mentioned, might, or might not, have a right to have a lien upon them in the same that trustees, as we know, have a lien for everything disbursed for the purpose of the trust, is an unpractical question; for supposing that we were to treat as moneys of the companies the moneys they had disbursed, it is quite an unpractical question now whether a lien exists upon these lands for the purpose of the benefit of the disbursements that have been made, because that lien has been centuries ago satisfied, and therefore it is now not worth considering that question, because they have been repaid over and over again. In an ordinary case, as we know, a trustee has a lien upon trust property for all expenses, but in this case it is immaterial to consider whether they have have that right or not, because, as I say, it has long ago been satisfied.

Sir William Marriott.] Do you go so far as this: assuming that the company have taken so many thousands of pounds a year out of their estate, and have spent a half or a quarter of that money in England, should you say they have a right to do that?

Mr. *Walker.*] I do not think they have any right. I take it you are putting to me that question as the logical consequence of my argument, and I should answer it by saying "No," except that they have the same right as the Irish Society. You will remember that the House of Lords, while they imposed a trust upon the Irish Society, yet said that they had a large discretion; and to the extent that the House of Lords affirmed a discretion on the part of the Irish Society, I apprehend the same discretion exists in the case of the companies.

Sir William Marriott.] All the money spent during the last three centuries beyond the purposes of the trust in England is spent contrary to the terms of the grant, in your view?

21 *July* 1890.

Mr. *Walker.*] I say that the Irish Society and the companies are exactly in the same position.

Sir *William Marriott.*] That is the logical deduction.

Mr. *Walker.*] Yes, according to the decision in the House of Lords.

Sir *William Marriott.*] And you say that any consequences resulting from it are consequences of law; in fact, the starting point for practical purposes is the decision in 1845.

Mr. *Walker.*] Certainly.

Mr. *Healy.*] Would you tell us whether the Irish Land Commission at present requires the Irish Society to join in any conveyances?

Mr. *Walker.*] As I understand, they require them to join in the conveyances of timber.

Chairman.] In sales under the Ashbourne Act?

Mr. *Walker.*] Yes, I am told so.

Mr. *Elton.*] Timber was held on a very peculiar holding, was it not?

Mr. *Walker.*] Yes; there was a reservation for public purposes.

Mr. *Elton.*] It was rather the use of the timber, was it not?

Mr. *Walker.*] I think you will find that they reserved the soil of the woods as well.

Mr. *Elton.*] The ownership of the timber was limited by the limitation of the uses to which it was to be put; and therefore it was not an ordinary conveyance of timber in that case.

Mr. *Walker.*] I apprehend that they gave up the timber, and were therefore required to join in the conveyance.

Mr. *Elton.*] If the companies took over the trusts of the plantation, that is the undertaking of making plantations in Ireland, would it not be their duty to alienate the land to respectable planters, and to sell it?

Mr. *Walker.*] The duty of sub-dividing it, and letting it is one thing.

Mr. *Elton.*] But would that not be by selling?

Mr. *Walker.*] I do not think so; because in that case they would be parting with the land, and you cannot alienate the trust.

Mr. *Elton.*] Surely they did not make a leasehold plantation, but a freehold plantation?

Mr. *Walker.*] They had express power under the charter to let for any terms that they thought fit, and that was the mode of making it profitable for the purpose of having the revenue which the charter gave them; but there is no practical power to alienate the lands generally, and I think, and I would submit to you, as a lawyer, that there would be no implied power of alienation.

Mr. *Elton.*] I only asked you the question in order that you might make your argument clear. Do I understand that they were only to give leasehold estates, and not freehold estates, in your opinion. Are we to understand that all the freehold grants were made through the manorial machinery to which you have referred by the creation of manors?

Mr. *Walker.*] Their leasing power would extend to freehold leases as well as to chattel interests; that is fee-farm leases.

Chairman.] You are clear in your conviction that the public objects of King James I. were not fulfilled by the mere planting of settlers on these devastated provinces?

Mr. *Walker.*] Certainly.

Chairman.] I suppose one reason for concluding that is that the Irish Society was incorporated permanently and not only temporarily?

Mr. *Walker.*] Yes.

Chairman.] Which shows that the objects that King James aimed at were of a permanent nature.

Mr. *Walker.*] They required to have a revenue to carry out the trusts, and the revenue must be obtained by the lettings; they must have tenants in occupation.

Mr. *Healy.*] Amongst any of the documents in the book which you have there before you, is there a copy of the conveyance from the Haberdashers to the Marquis of Waterford in 1675?

Mr. *Walker.*] No; that would be the year after they got their own grant.

Dr. *Freshfield.*] I have asked for that document, Sir, but the Haberdashers' Hall has been twice burned down, partly from a fire in the building itself, and partly from a fire in the neighbouring place, and they could give me no information about it. They gave up all their documents when they sold their estate.

Mr. *Walker.*] We perhaps might get that document in Ireland, having regard to our system of registry there. If these documents are procurable it might be well to have the conveyances of all these lands, if they are available without much trouble.

Sir *Richard Temple.*] Do I understand you to lay great stress on this paper which is printed in the Appendix, entitled, "Licence to hold in Mortmain," dated 30th September 1652.

Mr. *Walker.*] Yes.

Sir *Richard Temple.*] I further understand you to argue that this implies a trust. Now, if so, I draw your attention to the words in line 4, "that worthie worke of plantacon," and those same words are repeated further down, "the same intended plantacon and in future tyme reape some gayne and benefitt of their great travailes, and expences taken and bestowed therein;" would you kindly explain how you interpret these words, "the worthie worke of plantacon."

Mr.

21 *July* 1890.

Mr. *Walker.*] I rely upon the word "plantation," and interpret that by reference to the charter which authorises plantation, and I interpret the charter by the way in which the House of Lords has interpreted it. You are driven back to the word "plantation" to see what the word imported, and it imported everything that the Crown annexed to the plantation.

Sir *Richard Temple.*] What was annexed to the word "plantation" in your opinion?

Mr. *Walker.*] "Plantation" implies building, and all the obligations, the social, national, and political advantages which would follow from the colonisation of Ulster by the new settlers whom the Crown intended to go there.

Sir *Richard Temple.*] You consider that it implies all these public purposes mentioned in the charter of King James 1st?

Mr. *Walker.*] Certainly; that is my argument.

Sir *Richard Temple.*] If so, is it not strange that these public purposes were not repeated in this Scheme itself?

Mr. *Walker.*] I do not think so, because it must be remembered that the document which contained all these public trusts is referred to in it, and that it grew out of the larger title which is there recited; and therefore I do not think it would be necessary to define all the trusts in this document.

Sir *Richard Temple.*] There is no reference to the further charter in this Scheme, is there?

Mr. *Walker.*] Yes, I think there is; I called attention to the words.

Sir *Richard Temple.*] Where are the words you refer to?

Mr. *Walker.*] I think you will find them in the description of the lands. You will there find that they refer to lands granted by Patent of such a date. It is not in the earlier part of the document, but I read it in the portion which I read to the Committee, because it appeared to me of some consequence.

Mr. *Healy.*] With regard to Lord Waterford's Estate, I imagine that when Lord Waterford was making a title before the Land Commission under the Ashbourne Act, he must have produced a copy of this document of which we have been speaking.

Mr. *Walker.*] Yes; I presume you are quite right. I think Lord Waterford's estate was sold under the Encumbered Estates Act, and all these documents of title would be lodged with the Court, and the only thing issued to the purchaser would be the Encumbered Estates Deed, the other documents of title being retained by the Court unless they affect other property?

Mr. *Healy.*] Then you think that that document would still be in the possession of the Court?

Mr. *Walker.*] Yes.

Mr. *Sexton.*] You spoke of the "discretion" of the Irish Society; the word is used in the judgment of the House of Lords, I think; in the administration of the trust. Do you argue that the companies, being, as you say, in an analogous position, their discretion is simply not to devote any part of the income to their private uses, but to the particular uses for which it was given.

Mr. *Walker.*] Certainly. They say they have a large discretion, and that the only power to control that discretion is the power of the Attorney General through an information, and that it is not subject to private trust at all.

Mr. *Sexton.*] But you say the whole of the income ought to be applied to public uses.

Mr. *Walker.*] Yes. For instance such an application as was proved in the case of the Skinners' Company, I apprehend would be as between the Attorney General and the trustees a clear breach of trust, though the Skinners' Company could not complain of it.

Mr. *Sexton.*] Do you argue that the funds of the company are now properly attachable for the purposes of the trusts which you declare to exist in respect of the proceeds of all the sales of land, no matter at what time they were made?

Mr. *Walker.*] That is the legal consequence of my argument.

Mr. *G. H. Lee.*] I appear, Sir——

Chairman.] You will remember what I have already said; that we should only hear you if we thought you were bringing forward matter which has not been dealt with by Mr. Walker.

Mr. *G. H. Lee.*] I quite understand that, Sir.

Chairman.] Do you appear now to argue points which Mr. Walker has neglected.

Mr. *G. H. Lee.*] I should be extremely sorry to suggest that Mr. Walker has neglected anything.

Mr. *Walker.*] I would ask, Sir, on behalf of Mr. Lee, as I know that we are opposed here by two or three members of the English bar, seeing that I have to return to Ireland myself, if anything should occur in the course of their arguments calling for any reply I would ask leave that Mr. Lee might say a word upon the point, if it strikes the Committee as being desirable.

Chairman.] Clearly.

Mr. *G. H. Lee.*] I am extremely obliged to Mr. Walker for his suggestion; but there is one point which I do desire to raise not in any way contradictory of what Mr. Walker has said, but in addition to his argument, and to a certain extent as an argument which does not quite follow from what he has said, but which may take the place perhaps of some part of what he has said. If you would allow me to state very shortly the case as I would desire to put it, you will see in one moment the additional argument which I desire to adduce, which involves the consideration of a certain number of documents which Mr. Walker did not bring forward, and

and which have not been read at present or in any way brought before the Committee. There are a number of letters, in fact there are dealings of the Crown with the companies and with the Irish Society from the time the charters were granted until the date of the Star Chamber Inquiry.

Chairman.] What do these letters show; do they show anything which has not been already shown?

Mr. *G. H. Lea.*] Yes, I think so.

Chairman.] What do they show; do you mean such letters as that of the King to Sir Julius Bodley, and so forth?

Mr. *G. H. Lea.*] No; I mean rather letters from the Crown or the Privy Council to the Common Council, and acts of the Common Council, and further letters from the Crown to the Common Council, and further answers from the Common Council.

Chairman.] You say you are going to refer to them in order to show something; what do they show?

Mr. *G. H. Lea.*] What they show, to put it shortly, is this, to my mind, that if the grantees were entitled to any benefit whatever in respect of their grants their benefit is distinctly limited, and I shall show how it is limited by these letters: that is to say, there are letters here and documents carrying out the original terms of the motives and reasons showing that the easy rents there to be given to the undertakers are construed by the reports of Sir Josiah Bodley and Mr. Pinner's report and other documents which I should like to bring to the Committee's knowledge, and there are these subsequent letters which state, amongst other things, the King's will that the lands be let to the freeholders at 8 *d.* per acre, and to the leaseholders at 1 *s.* an acre, and to the Irish some may be let at 2 *s.* an acre, and there are most distinct limitations as to what the companies who undertake the plantations have the right to do. I consider that these limitations were put upon them by the order and conditions primarily, and I should like to refer to this subsequent correspondence, and these letters and this series of documents as making clear the position which I wish to take in addition to what Mr. Walker has said, and relying upon all the arguments that he has used.

Sir *William Marriott.*] Can you carry it beyond this? If I understand Mr. Walker rightly the only profit that could be got out of the plantation was thinning the population of London by plantation and emigration from London to Ireland and by the encouragement of trade; those are the two definitions of profit as I understand it according to Mr. Walker. Do these letters which you refer to show any other profits.

Mr. *G. H. Lea.*] Yes.

Sir *William Marriott.*] What is the other profit?

Mr. *G. H. Lea.*] My first and primary contention is that which Mr. Walker has put before you, and bearing in mind the instructions of the Committee, I do not repeat that. That no doubt was the profit really intended; but supposing the Committee should consider from any of the words which have been used, particularly the words which were commented on just before Mr. Walker sat down about reapinge oute future gains supposing I say that the Committee, or some Members of the Committee should be disposed to be of the opinion that the companies were intended to reap some future gain, I want to show from those documents, and I think I can show from these documents, that the future gain was of a very limited description, and indeed, it may have been, and I think it will be found if you will look into the figures that it was enough to repay them their advances.

Chairman.] But does that carry us beyond the words in one of the documents as regards easy rents? You are only going to explain what the easy rents meant, as I understand.

Mr. *G. H. Lea.*] If I could show that easy rent is united to certain specific rents, and if I could show that it was the duty of the companies to have let out their lands to freehold tenants, not only at easy rents but that those rents were named specifically, then I have limited the future gain which the companies are entitled to make, and then I think the whole of the surplus is clearly, beyond question, public money.

Chairman.] If we accept the words "easy rents," and if the companies accept the words "easy rents," the fact that the rent charged was 8 *d.*, 9 *d.*, or 1 *s.*, is not very material, that is a subordinate detail.

Mr. *G. H. Lea.*] Of course they may say they have been letting those lands at easy rents all the time. The question is what "easy rents" means.

Chairman.] Surely, if you go into that, you will involve the Committee in what was the comparative value of 1 *s.* in King James the First's time, and what it is now.

Mr. *G. H. Lea.*] With great respect I do not think that would arise; would you just let me say this; the lands were to be let to freeholders at 8 *d.* an acre, and the 8 *d.* would remain just the same; it would be a fee farm rent of 8 *d.*

Chairman.] I do not gather from what you have said that this is a very important position. I do not mean to say that it is unworthy of attention, but it does not seem to me to contribute materially to the general consideration of the legal obligations of the case, which, as I said when the proceedings began to-day, is all that the Committee, not being a legal tribunal, concerns itself with. Therefore I am inclined to recommend you, if you will take my recommendation, to reserve your remarks until you have heard the remarks of the learned gentleman on the other side.

Mr. *G. H. Lea.*] Perhaps I may occupy a few minutes more this afternoon and then do so; because there is another point which I should like just to refer to. I do not know whether my learned friends on the other side have seen these documents,

21 *July* 1890.

documents, but there are a great many documents which have not been referred to yet.

Chairman.] I am aware of that, and I am glad to think it is so.

Mr. *Healy.*] I think it would be much better to hear Mr. Lea in reply.

Mr. *G. H. Lea.*] If you press that upon me, sir, of course I will reserve my remarks till then. I am only anxious to do what the Committee think best, but there are other documents which I rely upon, which I wish to refer to, and which I think should be in the hands of the Committee. If I may be at liberty to refer to them in reply, I am quite willing to reserve my remarks till then.

Chairman.] It appears to me that you might reserve your remarks until the learned gentlemen upon the other side have spoken, and then if the Committee thought there were any points upon which they would wish to hear you, they might ask you to give your answers upon them.

Mr. *Latham.*] And then we should have to ask to be allowed to be heard in reply upon Mr. Lea's reply.

Chairman.] We shall see what course things take.

Mr. *Sexton.*] You say that you wish to refer to one other point; can you state in a sentence what the other point is?

Mr. *G. H. Lea.*] The other point is this: there are a number of documents in the year 1636, which is after the Star Chamber Inquiry. It is difficult to state the point very shortly, and not to refer to the documents at all, but the point is that the companies themselves offered 100,000*l.* to the Crown, if the Crown would convey these lands to them, discharged from all pretences of the articles of plantations and all covenants and claims whatever.

Chairman.] What document is it that you are referring to?

Mr. *G. H. Lea.*] It is the report of the 23rd of January 1636, and there are words here which I think are of the utmost importance.

Chairman.] We will hear what you have to say upon that document; what is the document called?

Mr. *G. H. Lea.*] It is an order of Common Council, and it is printed in the Appendix to the Respondent's case, in the Skinners' Company's case, at page 201.

Chairman (to Mr. *Walker*).] Did you refer to this document?

Mr. *Walker.*] No, I do not think so.

Mr. *G. H. Lea.*] This was after the proceedings in the Star Chamber; I am breaking right into the middle of what I was going to say; but you will remember there was a great question raised of the Woods and Forests. The Woods and Forests were worth (so says the Star Chamber Order), something like half-a-million of money. These Woods and Forests were, contrary to the express wishes and directions of the Crown, cut down by the City or by the companies, and they had the benefit of them in the meantime. That is one of the strongest points made in the Star Chamber Inquiry, and our point made from the beginning, and I say upon the face of that the companies were, and have always been, very well paid, and indeed overpaid, for their outlay. Then after the Star Chamber Report in 1636 comes this very important document: "Whereas by an Order of this Honourable Court of the 24th of May last past, we whose names are subscribed were appointed to meet together and take due and serious consideration of the great and important businesses propounded to the court touching the plantation in Ireland and the fine of 70,000*l.* lately imposed upon this city by a sentence of his Majesty's Court of Star Chamber, and concerning the suit in his Majesty's Court of Exchequer touching the lands conveyed to the city by his Majesty upon the great contract and estates under greenwax upon forfeiture of recognisances, and for non-appearance of jurors and concerning buildings and pretended encroachments made upon the wastes, and also concerning the claim made unto the tithes, lands, and manor of Bleechappleton, and how the matters in question between his Majesty and this city might be compounded and determined, and to certify this court our opinion therein. We do therefore humbly certify to this Honourable Court that according to the said order, we have met several times together and taken due and serious consideration of the premises and of the former passages and proceedings between his Majesty and this city touching the same, and we think it a fit way in our judgments for the compounding and determining of the aforesaid matters between his Majesty and this city (as things now stand), That some persons, committees, may be nominated and authorised by this Honourable Court most humbly in the name of this city to petition his Majesty touching the premises thereby informing his Majestie with the weak and declining estate of the city and citizens thereof, and to treat with such as his Highness shall please to appoint for a conclusion of all matters on that behalf;" and then they say, "we conceive it fit that power be given to those committees by this court to make an humble offer of 100,000*l.* to be paid to his Highness by this city in five years by 20,000*l.* a year, for the compounding and determining of all the said differences, and for his Majesty's gracious grant to be made unto this city of the several matters and things humbly desired by this city." Now we come to the list of things desired by the City of London.

Chairman.] One moment. This document concerns the Irish Society. You are quoting this document to show by the recognition by the Irish Society of trusts and obligations of which they endeavoured to divest themselves, apparently by means of paying a sum of money.

Mr. *G. H. Lea.*] Yes.

Chairman.] But you will remember the existence of trusts and obligations binding the Irish Society is granted since the decision of 1843.

21 *July* 1890.

Mr. *G. H. Lee*.] Yes; but this is as to the whole of the land. This is the report of the Common Council: it says: "At this Common Council was read the Report of divers Aldermen and Commoners, made upon a reference by order of this Honourable Court of the 24th day of May last, the tenour of which report ensueth in these words;" and it is addressed "To the Right Honourable the Lord Mayor of the City of London, and to the Right Worshipful the Aldermen, his Brethren, and the Commons in this Common Council assembled." That is not only the Irish Society.

Colonel *Laurie*.] Who is it that signed that petition that you are reading?

Mr. *G. H. Lee*.] It is not a petition; it is a report of the Court of Common Council.

Colonel *Laurie*.] It has nothing to do with the companies, has it; it is not a petition of the companies.

Mr. *G. H. Lee*.] It concerns the whole of the land.

Mr. *Healy*.] What power had the Court of Common Council to make that offer on behalf of, say, the Skinners' Company.

Mr. *G. H. Lee*.] The whole of the lands were in the hands of the companies, and the companies were ruled by the Common Council.

Mr. *Healy*.] Assuming that offer would have been made, what power had the persons who made the tender to bind the companies?

Mr. *G. H. Lee*.] They were negotiating on behalf of the 12 companies. These negotiations went on for something like two or three years with the consent apparently of both parties.

Chairman.] Surely it was not a negotiation between the companies or anyone on behalf of the companies and the Crown, but it was an Irish Society negotiation.

Mr. *G. H. Lee*.] With great respect I do not think that at that date the Irish Society and the companies were so far dissociated; they were all acting together. Let me refer to number 10 on the list to show exactly what was asked for.

Chairman.] What is your evidence that they were acting together in this transaction?

Mr. *G. H. Lee*.] I will read, if you will allow me, the things desired by the City of London.

Mr. *Sexton*.] This was an attempt, as I understand, to get rid of the sentence imposed upon them by the Star Chamber. It is antecedent to the subsequent charter of King Charles.

Mr. *G. H. Lee*.] Yes.

Mr. *Sexton*.] Did not the subsequent charter of King Charles re-grant all that had been granted in the first instance, and therefore nullify any such proceeding as this previous to the date of the charter.

Mr. *G. H. Lee*.] But this shows the trust which the City themselves considered to attach to their property at this date.

Chairman.] Surely we need not argue that because the House of Lords have settled that once for all.

Mr. *G. H. Lee*.] But this affects the property of the whole of the companies.

Mr. *Healy*.] That is what we want you to show.

Mr. *G. H. Lee*.] This is what they desire——

Chairman.] Will you read us some words showing that the companies were involved as such?

Mr. *G. H. Lee*.] Number 10 is the one I will read, although I should like to read you some others. I may perhaps read the first two or three. The first is, "That the fine in the Star Chamber touching the Irish lands be discharged, and the proceedings in the cause be taken from off the file, that there may not appear a sentence upon record a sentence against the City, the King's Royal Chamber. (2.) That the City may have the Derry, Coleraine, the lands, and other things granted heretofore by his late Majesty in Ireland, secured unto them as their counsel shall advise, by absolute grants, discharged from all pretences of the Articles of Plantation, and all other covenants and claims whatsoever." There, by distinct admission, there were trusts to which the Articles of Plantation were subject.

Colonel *Laurie*.] Let me point out that by the decision of the Star Chamber the claim against the company was that they had not done certain things.

Mr. *G. H. Lee*.] Quite so.

Colonel *Laurie*.] Those were matters from which the City at that time desired relief; they desired relief from the action of the Star Chamber. By the action of the Star Chamber the whole of this charter was forfeited.

Mr. *G. H. Lee*.] Certainly.

Chairman.] I would submit two things to you: in the first place, if this document concerns the Irish Society only, it is superfluous, because the question of a trust in the case of the Irish Society is settled by the House of Lords' Judgment.

Mr. *G. H. Lee*.] Yes.

Chairman.] But, in the second place, if you can show that it affects the companies, even then it does not carry us any further, because matters were all put into order again in 1662.

Mr. *G. H. Lee*.] As to the first point you have put to me, I entirely agree with you, if you will allow me to say so, and I will not say a word about that; but as to the second point, number 10 here says that one thing asked for is "a pardon to the City and companies."

Chairman.] I understand that.

Mr. *G. H. Lee*.] "And the Society for the plantation in Ireland."

Chairman.] Granting that that be so, and that it does affect the companies, all this was put into order afterwards in 1662, and we have to deal with the transactions of 1662, and therefore this particular document of 1636 does not carry us any farther. That is my own view. I do not know what other Members of the Committee may think.

Mr. *G. H. Lea.*] With great submission I would submit that the Charter of 1662 simply put the companies back and the Irish Society back into the position they would have been in if the charter had not been forfeited.

Mr. *Sexton.*] How can it matter what they proposed in 1636 if their position was rehabilitated in 1662?

Mr. *G. H. Lea.*] It matters very much if I can show that in 1636 there were certain trusts to which they were subject then and are subject now, and that they offered 100,000 *l.* to get rid of these trusts.

Mr. *Sexton.*] They wanted to get rid of the strong decree of the Star Chamber.

Mr. *G. H. Lea.*] But they offered 100,000 *l.* if they could get rid of the trusts imposed upon them, and have the lands in absolute fee simple.

Mr. *Elton.*] Was that proposal from the committee accepted by the council?

Mr. *G. H. Lea.*] That proposal was debated for something like three years, and in 1637, one and a half years afterwards, the Recorder made another report, in which he says he was perfectly willing to go on on the terms of paying 100,000 *l.*, but the King asked 125,000 *l.* They were, in fact, making a bargain. The city declined to pay the 125,000 *l.*, but said they were willing, if they could have the land free from the trusts, to pay the 100,000 *l.*

Mr. *Sexton.*] If you can show that in 1636 the city and the companies attached certain meanings to the language of the charter of James that would be important, because it would cast light upon the meaning of the language of the charter. That, I presume, is your argument?

Mr. *G. H. Lea.*] That is my argument.

Colonel *Laurie.*] Not only this charter in connection with the Irish Society, but every charter which the City Companies possessed during the reign of Charles I. was taken away from them; this charter, to which you refer, is only a small part of the charters that were restored to them in the reign of Charles II. You will find that almost every charter that the company acquired was taken away in the reign of Charles I., and very heavy exactions were put upon them, and in the reign of Charles II., the whole of those charters were restored. That is a material historical fact.

Chairman.] I understand that the opinion of the Committee is that you may be able to make a point; will you proceed to make it; will you go on with the document you are dealing with, and bring it to the point?

Mr. *G. H. Lea.*] I have read already the particular points in which they offered to give the 100,000 *l.*, if they may have the lands by an absolute grant, discharged from all the pretences of the Articles of Plantation. What follows is this: In February 1636 the Crown say that they will assent to give them, free from all the trusts of the plantation, if they would pay 120,000 *l.*; you will find that in the respondent's case at page 202.

Mr. *Sexton.*] You say, I so understand, that this refers to the whole of county Derry.

Mr. *G. H. Lea.*] I say it clearly refers to the whole of county Derry beyond question. Then on the 9th March 1637, there was a relation of the recorder expressing willingness on behalf of the City to pay the 100,000 *l.* on behalf of the city upon having the lands so devised. That you will also find in the respondent's case, at page 201. Thus, as you will plainly perceive, there was a bargain going on between the city and the Privy Council. The City said, "If you will let us have all these lands free from these trusts, which we want to get rid of, we will give you 100,000 *l.*" The King said, "No, you must give me 125,000 *l.*" The City said, "No, we will not give you 125,000 *l.*;" and eventually on the 22nd June 1637, these negotiations were ended by the City's paying, not the 70,000 *l.*, which never was paid at all, but 12,000 *l.*, and the King took back the lands, and the fishing and customs; and there are these words which you will find in the respondent's case, at page 203: "This court, well approving of the aforesaid proceedings and offer of the said Committee and rendering all possible thankfulness to His Majesty for his gracious acceptance of the said offer of lands," accepted the offer and paid the 12,000 *l.*, and handed back the lands to His Majesty.

Mr. *Sexton.*] Can you make it appear that the City was acting for the companies at this time, or can you make the companies responsible for what the city did?

Mr. *Healy.*] I presume you can, if you can show that for three years they allowed this statement to be made on their behalf without any repudiation.

Mr. *Latham.*] They were not made on their behalf, so far as I can see.

Mr. *Healy.*] That is a matter of inference.

Mr. *G. H. Lea.*] This is headed "The humble petition of the Mayor and Commonalty and Citizens of the said City of London."

Mr. *Latham.*] That is merely their title.

Mr. *G. H. Lea.*] No doubt they are all members of the companies. Then if you will allow me to refer to another point, to refer to the proceedings of the Star Chamber; the documents show from the beginning to the end, even from the "orders and conditions," that the intention was that British and Irish should be planted on these lands, and one of the grave crimes imputed to them in the Star Chamber action, which I think you have read, which at any rate is printed, is that they did not carry that out, and that is one of the reasons why their lands were forfeited and taken from them. There are a great number of other reasons, but the two mentioned are the fact that they have the woods which

which were of such great value, and had converted them directly contrary to the "Orders and conditions," to uses of merchandise, and had sold them and sent them out of the kingdom, and it is there said that the woods were estimated to be worth something like 350,000 *l.* That is one of the charges laid against them, and it has never been denied that these woods were taken, the woods are gone, and somebody had the benefit of them. Who was there that could have had the benefit except the companies who had then possession and charge of the lands? You will see that my contention is based on this series of letters which you have not allowed me to go through, but which I may venture still to think are of some importance, showing that it was the duty of the companies to plant freeholders on this land. Now, I should like very much to know how far the companies have done that which I maintain, this series of documents shows it was their duty to do. Did the company plant any freeholders at fee farm rents upon the land?

Mr. *Sexton.*] Perhaps there is some misapprehension. That was my question to Mr. Walker, in reply to which he showed that the argument was that there were no freeholders to be planted on the land.

Mr. *G. H. Lee.*] Of course, if they have made the freehold, there is nothing in that point; but I am not aware that any inquiry has been made by this Committee as to how far they have carried out what, as I say, was their duty, and have made their lands freehold.

Chairman.] It would not affect the question we are upon now. The question we are now on is whether the companies are bound by trusts which everybody agrees bind the Irish Society; that is really what we want to get at.

Mr. *G. H. Lee.*] I admit that is a most important point; but all these other points are also of importance to show how they have fulfilled their trusts, and why the lands were taken from them. There are two or three other points which I should like to have taken; one is, that the documents show that the conditions as to alms, and schools, and churches, and educational purposes (and I may remark that I appear here for others who are particularly interested in this question), show that these were intended to be carried out from the commencement by the City companies, and it is a fact that this one thing which they were told to do in the Orders and Conditions, and in the other documents, has, to a very large extent, been done by them. From the beginning they have built churches, they have repaired churches, they have given very large sums for educational purposes.

Chairman.] Mr. Walker dwelt upon this point, when he said that the course of conduct by the companies evinced their consciousness of a trust.

Mr. *G. H. Lee.*] Yes; all I want to point out to you now is that if they now sell their property and take away the proceeds, and leave nothing for these purposes, as they claim to have a right to do, as absolute owners, I say that they are taking the benefit of the grant that was given to them, and at the same time getting rid of the burden which was placed upon them. There was a clear and distinct burden in that respect placed upon them, and I say, in other respects, as to the granting of leases and so on. I put them all on the same ground; there was a burden put upon the companies to do these various things; and I say, so far as the churches and the schools, and these educational matters are concerned, to a certain extent they have done it; and I say they cannot now sell the lands and get rid of the burden which is imposed upon them, in consideration for which the land was given.

There is another point into which I will not go which I might have made, namely, that the companies have shown by their acts, and the manner in which they have dealt with the property, that they considered themselves to a large extent trustees. That has been the subject of an inquiry, and it is not strictly a matter connected with the documents, and therefore I need not trouble you with anything on that point.

I think one of the members of the Committee has suggested that there is very little distinction between the position of the companies, and that of the individual undertakers. Might I just, in attempting to answer that, state what appears to me to be the difference between the position of the companies and that of the other undertakers. In the first place, I say that the companies took, under the document and agreements and charters, which imposed upon them trusts and obligations beyond anything that was imposed upon the other undertakers. In the second place (and I think Mr. Walker dealt with this), time does not run in the case of the companies, as it may, perhaps, have done in the case of the ordinary undertakers. I rely upon the historical evidence, upon the evidence common to all, that the companies took under the Irish Society and the others did not, and that in the one case there is a decision of a legal tribunal, and in the other there is not.

There is one other point which I have not yet dealt with. There are a great many documents which the Committee have not before them, and there is one I should like to refer to, namely, Pinnar's Survey, which I consider a matter of very considerable importance.

Chairman.] As showing what?

Mr. *G. H. Lee.*] As showing the way in which the Crown interfered and looked after these companies after they got the charter.

Chairman.] That argument was put generally before us.

Mr. *G. H. Lee.*] There is similar evidence in support of this, and very strong evidence, that for a series of years, from 1613 to 1632 (the date of the Star Chamber inquiry), there is a long series of documents showing that the Crown took a great interest in this matter, and looked into the way they exercised their powers, and that is directly contrary to the claim of the companies that they are absolute owners of the fee simple.

Chairman.] I think you will do right in calling our attention to the existence of that body of evidence, but it would not be well to go into it if you will make us aware where it can be found if we want to look at it.

31st *July* 1890.

Mr. G. H. Lea.] Perhaps you would like to look at Pynnar's Survey which is to be found in full in Harris's Hibernica; there is a long account given there at page 159 and page 237. It is also referred to in the Concise View.

Chairman.] I was going to ask whether the point was not raised in the Concise View.

Mr. G. H. Lea.] Yes, it is referred to there; but it is given fully in Harris's Hibernica. These are the chief points which I desire to refer to, but there were a great many other points and documents which you have not heard.

Chairman.] When you say "documents," I agree that there may be documents that we have not heard, but are there a great many other points that we have not heard of.

Mr. G. H. Lea.] No, I do not know that there are any more points, but there is a great deal of evidence upon the point.

Chairman.] It would clearly be impossible for a Committee of this kind to exhaust or pretend to exhaust the evidence; we can only get a statement of the points before us. Now as regards this matter of reply, it must be understood in spite of language that may have been incautious, that we do not feel bound to hear a reply. It is only in case there are points raised by the gentlemen who represent the companies and the Irish Society which the Committee may desire to have elucidated; it is only I say on that condition that we shall trouble you, Mr. Lea, to reply. But then Mr. Latham says if Mr. Lea replies, we shall have a reply upon him. We are not pretending here, as is probably evident enough, the methods of a legal tribunal, and I do not think it is at all certain that the Committee will need to hear more than the case presented by the Irish Society and by the City Companies. As to which case should come first, it would appear that the most logical and probably the most convenient order would be to take the Irish Society first.

Mr. Latham.] Since the adjournment in the middle of the day, Sir, some arrangement has been come to rather with the idea that I should address the Committee on behalf of the companies first, and that the Irish Society should follow me if that would be convenient to the Committee. I do not think it makes much difference as to the question of logic. The companies stand on a separate and very distinct footing from the Irish Society, and the Irish Society will take their own course after the companies have been heard.

Chairman.] I confess I do not quite see why the Irish Society wish to be heard at all, because their position has been defined by a judicial decision. But still, we could not refuse them the chance of saying anything if we think fit, when we hear what it is they want to say.

Mr. Latham.] If it is convenient to you, Sir, I would address the Committee at the next meeting, and the Irish Society would follow me.

Chairman.] Very well.

Mr. Healy.] I would like to know whether the Irish Society intend to present any different view to the Committee from that presented in this case, and if not, on what ground they claim to be heard. If they claim to be heard, I think we should know what their view is before we hear the companies' views.

Mr. Sexton.] Perhaps they wish to address themselves to the positive removal of the trusts from their administration.

Chairman.] I have been at a loss all along to know quite why the Irish Society wish to be heard.

Mr. Latham.] I do not appear, Sir, for the Irish Society, and therefore I can hardly say what their arguments are; but I think possibly they might desire to be heard upon the decision of the House of Lords and the Courts below in order to interpret their view of what the decision really was.

Mr. Brady.] As against the House of Lords decision.

Mr. Latham.] No, as against any interpretation that may be put upon it.

Chairman.] Who appears for the Irish Society?

Dr. Freshfield.] Mr. Romer is to appear for them.

Chairman.] Is it not convenient for Mr. Romer to come on Wednesday?

Dr. Freshfield.] I think not.

Mr. Molan.] Having regard to the counsel practising in other courts, we hoped that this Committee would accede to Mr. Latham's proposals to hear the companies' case first. I think that the case of the Irish Society would be shortened by Mr. Latham's exposition upon points which we shall not probably desire to touch upon.

Chairman.] Very well; but remember that Mr. Latham may finish on Wednesday in time for us to hear Mr. Romer.

Mr. Molan.] If you please, Sir.

Mr. Rhodes.] Mr. Rigby will appear also.

Chairman.] For whom does he appear?

Mr. Rhodes.] He appears for the Skinners' Company; we wish him to have an opportunity of saying anything that Mr. Latham might have left unsaid.

Chairman.] That is not very convenient. It was understood that each interest was to be represented by one counsel, and that is one reason why we did not give Mr. Lea as long an innings as he might have wished this afternoon. Mr. Walker was supposed to represent the one side. The companies have their case, and the Irish Society thought that it had a special case to lay before us. I do not think we can hear every individual company unless there are some special features in their case.

31 *July* [illegible].

Mr. Rhodes.] It is only proposed that Mr. Latham and Mr. Rigby should be heard.

Chairman.] But on what principle are we to hear Mr. Rigby that will not commit us to hearing other gentlemen too? If Mr. Rigby likes to present himself here, we will hear what point he intends to raise; but we do not undertake to hear him, and we do not even undertake to hear the Irish Society, unless we think that there is some further point which has not been dealt with in the case of the companies.

Wednesday, 23rd July 1890.

MEMBERS PRESENT:

Lord Elcho.	Mr. Lea.
Sir John Ellis.	Sir William Marriott.
Mr. John Ellis.	Mr. John Morley.
Mr. Elton.	Mr. Sexton.
Mr. Lawson.	Sir Richard Temple.

THE RIGHT HONOURABLE JOHN MORLEY, IN THE CHAIR.

Mr. *T. W. Lea.*] Before Mr. Latham addresses you, I just wish to say one word. There is a document which, I think, should be put in similar to the document which was mentioned just before we rose the other evening, by the honourable Member for Belfast West. It is a lease from the Skinners' Company to one Henry Cary, in the year 1742, and it contains very important covenants, showing what Henry Cary undertook to do, and what the Master and Wardens required him to do. It is to be found in the respondent's case in the House of Lords, page 349.

Mr. *Sexton.*] What point does it establish?

Mr. *T. W. Lea.*] There are a few lines of the covenants which are of importance. The lessee took the estate on the payment of a large fine, at a rent of 500 *l.* a year, and he covenanted to pay to the master and wardens, their successors and assigns, the said yearly rent of 500 *l.*, "and further that he, the said Henry Cary, his heirs and assigns, shall and will, from time to time, and at all times during this demise, observe, perform, and keep, all and singular, the rules, orders, ordinances and directions made, given, or prescribed, or which shall at any time or times hereafter, be made, given, or prescribed in, or by any Act or Acts of Parliament of Great Britain or Ireland, Letters Patent, or acts and regulations of the said society, of the governor and assistants, London, of the new plantation in Ulster, within the realm of Ireland, or their predecessors or successors; and all covenants, articles, and agreements, which have been entered into by the said master and wardens, or their predecessors, or the said governor and assistants, or their predecessors, or any person or persons that have, or hath undertaken on the behalf of the said master and wardens, or governor and assistants or their respective predecessors, or on the part and behalf of the mayor, commonalty, or citizens of London, for or concerning the building or maintaining any houses, or buildings, or preserving trees upon, or sowing, manuring, or improving the said demised premises, or any part thereof, or the securing or planting tenants upon the same, or otherwise concerning the said demised premises, or any part thereof, and of and from all forfeitures, penalties, costs, charges, damages, and expenses whatsoever already incurred, or which may hereafter be incurred for or by reason of the breach, non-observance, or non-performance of the said rules, orders, ordinances, directions, covenants, articles, and agreements, or any of them, and also of and from all taxes, charges, assessments, and impositions whatsoever which now are or at any time or times hereafter may be taxed, charged, assessed, or imposed on the said demised premises, or any part thereof, or on the said yearly rent hereby reserved, or any part thereof, or on the said master and wardens, their successors or assigns for, or in respect of the same premises, and yearly rent or either of them, or any part or parcel of them, or either of them by authority of Parliament or otherwise, howsoever, which now are or at any time hereafter during this present demise shall become due or payable, shall and will, from time to time or at all times hereafter acquit, exonerate, discharge, and keep harmless the said master and wardens of the guild or fraternity aforesaid and of the said governor and assistants, London, of the new plantation in Ulster within the realm of Ireland, and the said mayor or commonalty and citizens of London, and every of them their and every of their successors and assigns, and their and every of their goods, chattels, lands, tenements and hereditaments, or otherwise sufficiently recompense the said master and wardens of the guild or fraternity aforesaid, their successors and assigns for the loss, damage, or hindrance which they thereby or in that behalf shall sustain."

Mr. *Sexton.*] I take the point to be that this lessee in 1742 bound himself to observe any conditions that might be laid down by the Irish Society, though the lease was made by one of the companies.

Mr. *T. W. Lea.*] Exactly.

Sir *William Marriott.*] The lessee undertook to do all that the lessors were obliged to do.

Mr. *T. W. Lea.*] Yes; it showed what the lessors thought they might be obliged to do.

Chairman.] Whatever the lessors were bound to do by covenant, the lessee were equally bound to do, as I understand.

Mr. *T. W. Lea.*] Quite so.

23 *July* 1890.

Mr. Sexton.] Before the learned counsel addresses us, I wish to ask if the Irish Society have handed in the form of tender used for letting the fishings in 1864, and the particulars.

Chairman.] We told them we wanted that; the representative of the Irish Society will understand that we want the form of application and the tender.

Mr. Maton.] It is here.

Chairman.] Is Mr. Watney here?

Dr. Freshfield.] No.

Chairman.] I hope we shall have the pleasure of seeing him again.

Dr. Freshfield.] He has been here every day, but he is not here at this moment.

Chairman.] He must not forget that we want a little account from him. Perhaps you will see that he understands that.

Dr. Freshfield.] We quite understand that.

Mr Latham.] I appear, Sir, for all the City companies who appear here at all; and there are several of them who do appear, except the Skinners' Company, who appear separately. Some of the companies, I think, for example, the Haberdashers, who sold a long time ago, are not before the Committee at all; but I do appear for five or six companies. I do not know that it is material I should give the Committee the names of those for whom I actually appear.

Chairman.] I think you had better give the names.

Mr. Latham.] I appear for the Mercers, who are the leading company; the Salters, the Drapers, the Grocers, the Fishmongers, and the Clothworkers; I think that is all.

Chairman.] You did not mention the Ironmongers, I think.

Dr. Freshfield.] You have not asked them to come, Sir; but if you had, they would be represented by Mr. Latham. You may, in fact, assume that they are represented by Mr. Latham.

Chairman.] Of course, the Ironmongers' Company will understand that we shall desire from them an account of the receipts and payments under the heads I have already given in the case of the other companies.

Dr. Freshfield.] If you remember, Sir, the clerk of the Ironmongers' Company attended before you, and said he was willing to afford you any information you wished. I will tell him what you have said.

Chairman.] Kindly let him understand that we should like to have that account.

Dr. Freshfield.] Yes, Sir.

Mr. Latham.] I had better begin, perhaps, by pointing out the position I occupy as representing these companies, and how I differentiate it from that of others who will appear separately. In the first place the Skinners' Company propose to appear separately before you, if you will hear them, by Mr. Rigby. I do not think, practically, there is much difference between the position of the Skinners' Company and the companies which I represent; but, technically, there is a difference; because the case having been tried between the Skinners' Company and the Irish Society, the Skinners' Company are bound by that decision as a matter of *res judicata* as an estoppel in law, and even if a great mass of evidence were to be discovered at the present time, which would change the position of affairs between the Skinners' Company and the Irish Society, still I apprehend, in a court law, the Skinners' Company would be barred absolutely by the decision that has taken place. So far as I am concerned for the other companies, I am not going to dispute here, before this Committee, that that decision was right; I do not know that I should dispute it before any tribunal, but, certainly, I shall not do so before this Committee; I quite accept the position that the decision in that case is binding upon me as a precedent at any rate; I should not be bound by it as an estoppel; but I am bound by it as a precedent, and I accept the facts stated there, and I accept, I will not say every word of the judgment, because I am not bound to accept that, but all the material reasoning that led to the judgment pronounced in the first place by the court below, and afterwards by the House of Lords.

Then as to the Irish Society I sever myself entirely from the Irish Society. The Irish Society occupies a position, which they will state, if you will allow them, before the Committee, but which is totally different from mine. My position is that whatever trust or trusts or obligations may be imposed upon the Irish Society, or have been imposed upon the Irish Society, by the charters and decisions that have followed them, neither as a matter of fact, nor as a matter of law, nor as a matter of necessary reasonable inference from those decisions, do I stand bound at all. I do not accept the position that because I took lands from the Irish Society, I took those lands subject to any trusts whatever. I demur to the proposition as a universal proposition of law, that a purchaser from trustees is necessarily bound by the trust. That depends upon circumstances. I suppose there is scarcely any property in the kingdom the title to which does not depend at some period within the length of title shown by an ordinary abstract, upon a sale, by persons in some fiduciary relation. The whole question of law, and I may say, the question of morality too, is whether the persons or corporations that sold, were in a position to sell free from the trusts and obligations; and I maintain, whatever may have been the position of the Irish Society in respect of the trusts and obligations they were in a position to sell to me free, and discharged from those trusts and obligations.

Chairman.] When you say that the society were in a position to sell, is "sale" the right word to be used for the transaction between the Irish Society and the companies?

Mr. Latham.] I think the transaction was a transaction of sale, and intended to be a transaction of sale; but I will put it either way, and say

23 *July* 1890.

say that they were either in a position to sell, or in a position under the special circumstances of the case to grant, and to grant free from any trust or obligation.

Chairman.] Then it makes no difference for the substance of your argument whether it was a transaction of sale or whether it was a grant?

Mr. *Latham.*] I think not.

Chairman.] Then your proposition is that they were in a position either to sell or to grant.

Mr. *Latham.*] Yes, either to sell or to grant. Then as to the Corporation of the City of London which I understand propose to present its case before the Committee independently of the Irish Society, I do not think their position touches mine at all. As I understand, they claim some visitorial jurisdiction which they contend is sufficient to deal with these matters, if any reform is necessary; but I do not put their arguments because I do not know them. At any rate, I do not think they touch my case at all.

These, Sir, are the different parties appearing before you, and I hope I have distinguished my position from that of any of the rest.

Perhaps it would be convenient if I give the Committee an outline of the argument I propose to address to them before I discuss documents at all, and then they will see what I am coming to. I propose to commence with the second charter, as being the root of our title, and I propose to put the case in this way: At the date of the second charter, the Crown being fully informed of all the events that had taken place before that time, being fully aware of all the circumstances of the first charter, being aware of the whole alleged misfeasances and infringements with respect to the first charter, being aware of the view that had been taken of the matter by the Star Chamber, by the Court of Chancery, and afterwards the very important view that had been taken of those proceedings by the House of Commons, knowing all those facts, and knowing what, I may say, they might have regarded as their perils, deliberately granted a new charter, and did not guard in any manner whatever by the new charter against the reassertion of the very claims which had been in dispute during the whole period from the date of the first charter. I say the Crown was in a position to know all these matters, and to know its own perils at the time they granted the second charter; and, therefore, I submit by the second charter they established a principle, I will not say a new principle, because it was the position of affairs that had come into existence in the interval between the granting of the first and the granting of the second charter, but I may say the position of affairs which the Crown deliberately recognised by granting the second charter was that the Irish Society should remain in possession of the whole of what we may call the reserved lands and property of various descriptions, and that the Irish Society should hold this property in order to enable them to fulfil various public duties and public trusts of great importance. There were imposed upon the Irish Society by the charter a whole series of duties which were not only temporary, but which I quite admit were permanent. Those duties were to be performed by them; they were to take the property in order to enable them to perform them, and so far as I am concerned I do not care to dispute that this property may have been impressed, and the Committee may come to the conclusion that all the reserved property was impressed, with trusts for public purposes. So far as I am concerned, I repeat, I do not care to dispute that view. You are aware, of course, that in the Skinners' Company's case a claim was set up on behalf of the Irish Society to declare a surplus, and possibly that claim might be asserted at present, notwithstanding the judgment, and the right of the companies might still be asserted to any surplus that might be declared, and deliberately carried over by the Irish Society; but there has been no such surplus for a long time, and I do not care to fight shadows. For my part, I set up no claim to any part of the reserved lands on the interpretation of the second charter; as regards the whole of the reserved lands, I do not care to dispute that proceeds of those lands were intended to be reserved for public duties and public obligations. But I shall endeavour to show that, with respect to the companies, and the land deliberately distributed among the companies, the second charter itself took a totally different line, and that the intention of the charter was to convey, and even that the direct words of the charter did convey, the beneficial interest in this land to the companies. The companies were expressly mentioned in the second charter, in the first charter they were not, but in the second charter they were expressly mentioned; and though the conveyance from the Crown passed the legal estate to the Irish Society, there is on the face of the charter an express indication of the intention of the Crown that the divisible estates should be passed over, and passed over without delay to the companies, and there is no indication whatever in the second charter that any further trust or obligation was intended to be imposed upon this land. I shall argue before the Committee that that is the true interpretation of the charter.

I will then pass on to what happened, without delay, under the charter, coming first of all to the second licence in Mortmain. That second licence in Mortmain, I believe, has never yet been produced before the Committee. It is not, so far as I know, in either of the appendices to the Skinners' case, and I think it has never been produced. We have had it taken out of the Public Record Office, and I propose to place a copy of it before the Committee. I shall indicate to the Committee, by a very short examination of the second licence in Mortmain, that the Crown, precisely in the same manner as in the charter, desired that it should be quite clear that the companies were to take under that licence, and the Irish Society to convey under that licence, free and discharged from any trusts. I shall show to the Committee by the second licence in Mortmain and its variations from the first licence in Mortmain, the same circumstance which I say appears from the variations in the second charter as compared with the first charter, namely, that it was intended that the conveyances to the companies

23 *July* 1890.

panies should be free and discharged from any trusts and obligation whatever. That is the bearing I think of the second licence in Mortmain.

Then I shall proceed to the conveyances under the licence of Mortmain, and refer to the exceptions as having a bearing upon some further matters. And then I think the next material transaction which I shall come to is the transaction in 1779, which has been mentioned already before the Committee, I think, between the Goldsmiths' Company and Lord Shelburne. The Goldsmiths' Company entered into a contract to sell their property to Lord Shelburne in 1779. Lord Shelburne contested the contract; he wished to be off it, and did his best to be off it. A suit was brought by the Goldsmith's Company in Chancery against Lord Shelburne for specific performance. Lord Shelburne fought it step by step, and the Court of Chancery, after having all the documents before them, enforced specific performance of the contract upon him. One requisition made upon the title was that the Irish Society should join, and the Irish Society did join, and ultimately a decree for specific performance was enforced, and the sale was carried into effect by the Goldsmiths' Company as the leading party, and the Irish Society assenting and concurring, to Lord Shelburne. The point, as the Committee will see, of that matter is, that it was the decision of the Court of Chancery, after having all the documents before them, that the Irish Society and the company between them could make a good title enforceable upon a purchaser of part of these divisible lands. I may perhaps here mention that a similar view appears to have been taken recently in the transactions of sale in the Land Commission Court in Ireland in which an independent body, the Land Commissioners, inquired into the titles of some of the companies as regards their divisible lands, and they passed those titles as giving effective freehold titles to the tenants.

Then I shall be bound to refer to the doctrine that has been propounded before the Committee as to the establishment of a trust by the course of dealing; and I may mention at once my argument upon that point, which is a very short one. My argument upon that point is that when you have got admittedly all the documents which concern the matter, you cannot go to the course of dealing to establish a trust inconsistent with those documents; the documents show the title, and the course of dealing is not to be resorted to. But if the course of dealing were resorted to, I still think it would come out very much in favour of the companies. The reason that has been shown as to the course of dealing at present is, that it is consistent, and equally consistent with either of two hypotheses: One is that the companies, as landowners, were generous landowners, making generous grants; and the other is that they were trustees imperfectly discharging certain trusts. You cannot carry the evidence higher than that; and when there are two equally eligible interpretations to be put upon the course of dealing, you can come to no conclusion adverse to the companies upon that point. With regard to the course of dealing, I think it will be only reasonable that I should also call the Committee's attention to the Statute of Frauds, which was passed within a very few years of the date of the second charter, under which you are debarred, in an action at law, at any rate, from establishing a trust, except by a written document.

When I have got to the end of that branch of my argument, I shall hope to have disposed, or, at any rate, I shall have endeavoured to dispose, of the question of trusts in what we understand to be its legal interpretation: that is, a trust enforceable in any court in this country or in Ireland. But in the reference to the Committee there is still a question of "obligation;" and I suppose that the word "obligation" was probably introduced into the reference to the Committee because it was felt that the question of trust was a very definite legal question, and the question of obligation was somewhat wider; and possibly also it may have been thought that parallel with the documents which created the rights to the property, there may have been current a mere matter of contract as between the companies and the Crown, under which, although you cannot affix a trust to the property, you may be able to fasten an obligation upon the companies; and for that purpose I shall have to go back to the earlier documents; because if there be an obligation at all it will be found in the earlier documents. The position I take up as to trusts is to found my title upon the second charter; and from the second charter onwards I cannot find that there was any obligation which could be construed as anything but a trust; that is to say, it was a trust or nothing. But as to the anterior documents, knowing what took place at the time, it is a possible, and I may say a probable, or perhaps even an almost necessary inference from the transactions, that it was understood that certain obligations were imposed upon the undertakers; and I must accept the position that at one time or other the companies became undertakers; it is so stated in Lord Langdale's judgment, and I do not think I can dispute it.

In dealing with the question of obligation, I shall begin with the Orders and Conditions. I notice that my learned friend, Mr. Walker, in dealing with those Orders and Conditions, could only fasten upon two clauses of the Orders and Conditions which he thought helped his case. I shall go through the other clauses, and show the Committee that all those other clauses were necessarily disposed of at a very early period, long before the granting of the second charter. As to the last two clauses in the Orders and Conditions, one was for religious purposes and one was for education, and no doubt these two purposes are continuing purposes up to the present time. It will be impossible to say that for the purposes of religion and education all those duties have been discharged, but I think I shall be able to show, and I think this is one of the matters which I shall be able to conclusively prove to the Committee, that those two clauses were never imposed upon the companies at all. They were imposed upon and accepted by the Crown, and from the time of the Orders and Conditions onwards it was the Crown that undertook the provision for religion and undertook the provision for education.

I shall

21 *July* 1890.

I shall show that upon the interpretation of the document itself, and I shall show it also from what happened immediately afterwards with respect to the direction given by the Crown to their own Commissioners to proceed in that matter, and from the circumstance that schools were founded in accordance with the orders and conditions, and were called Royal Schools, the charge of which was never incumbent upon the companies or the Irish Society at all. I think I shall really have disposed of the orders and conditions, having shown that all these clauses, except those two clauses, were disposed of very early, long before the second charter, and that those two clauses were never binding upon any party except the Crown.

Then I shall have to come to the Motives and Reasons, and I may say as my chief answer to the argument raised upon the Motives and Reasons, I quite accept the position taken by my learned friend Mr. Walker, that the Motives and Reasons were merely a prospectus issued in the first instance by the Crown to induce other parties to come and deal with the plantation; and when you arrive at the articles of agreement immediately afterwards, as I may say, between the Crown and the City of London, you have disposed of the Motives and Reasons altogether. It is like any other document which is a mere negociation; it was absorbed in the subsequent contract.

The agreement, I shall deal with in very much the same manner. As to the agreement, I do not think it can be shown, when you come to look at it, that there were any permanent obligations attaching to the lands at all, or to the persons who were parties to the agreement; but, at any rate, the articles of agreement were dealt with afterwards in the proceedings in the Star Chamber and elsewhere. It was a matter of express complaint that the articles of agreement were not made incumbent upon the City of London or upon the Irish Society, in one form or another by the first charter; it was said that a fraud had been perpetrated by the citizens in getting the charter drawn up, that it did not refer to the articles of agreement. All these proceedings were carried on for some time, and yet, when you get to the second charter, the articles of agreement were no more referred to in the second charter than they were in the first; it being, as I submit, the intention of all parties, the Crown included, that the charter should speak for itself, and not refer to the articles of agreement.

When I have dealt with that I shall practically have dealt with the two branches of the subject, namely, trusts and obligations. As for the question which lies behind to a certain extent, that of moral obligation, I think that will pass very much with the others. I hardly know what the moral obligation in the case of a company or an incorporated body can be. Moral obligations are as various, I suppose, as people's consciences. What I apprehend may be meant by moral obligation would be rather a question of politics than a question for me to argue here; that is to say, it may be thought fit by Parliament at the present period of affairs, having regard to all the events that have happened, I say that it may be thought right and proper or expedient to impose *de novo* upon the companies and the City duties and obligations which have not existed hitherto. That may possibly be what is meant by "moral obligation"; but for myself, I, dealing with what has actually happened in the past, dealing with what has [illegible] ascertainable in it, will, in dealing with the word "obligation," give it a broad and liberal interpretation.

Now, Sir, I trust I have made clear the line upon which my argument will proceed, and I will proceed at once to the charter, subject to this: that before I read the charter, with the view to indicating to the Committee how clearly the facts and the disputes must have been present to the advisers of the Crown at this time, I will refer the Committee to what had happened. I have here an extract from the Journals of the House of Commons, in which there is reported a decision of the House on the subject of the rights of the companies. The companies had petitioned, and the House passed certain Resolutions as the result of that petition.

Chairman.] That is after the decision of the Star Chamber, is it not?

Mr. Latham.] Yes, Sir, I take this, before reading the second charter, simply as indicating that these resolutions must have been present to the minds of the framers of the second charter at the time they framed it, and therefore they must have been fully aware of the claims set up and the claims made by the companies; and I point out that, knowing the claims, they did not provide against them in the second charter.

Chairman.] What is the date of the Resolutions?

Mr. Latham.] They are dated the [illegible] of August 1641.

Chairman.] We have got them before us in Appendix Paper, No. 12.

Mr. Latham.] I did not know that the Committee had it before them. That being so, I can very hastily run through it. "Mr. Whistler reports the case of Londonderry. Resolved upon the Question, that the opinion of this House is, that the citizens of London were solicited and pressed to the undertaking of the plantation of Londonderry." "That the order made in the Court of Star Chamber dated 5° Martii, 8° Caroli, is unlawful both for the matter, persons, and time therein prefixed." "That the King was not deceived in the grant which he made unto the Society of Governor and Assistants of London of the new plantation of Ulster in the Kingdom of Ireland; in particular, not in creating a new corporation" called the Irish Society. Then "That the King did not by that patent grant more lands than was by him intended to be granted; nor was therein deceived. That it doth not appear by sufficient proof that the citizens of London were tied to perform the printed articles." (That was one of the express matters that had been charged against them.) "That admitting the houses were not built, nor the Castle of Culmore repaired, by the time prefixed; yet this is no crime, nor cause for giving damages" (that is not very material in in this matter). "That there is no proof that the

23 *July* 1890.

the Governor, &c., of the new plantation or any of the 12 companies did make any lease to any Popish recusant, nor of any decay of religion there by default of the planters. That there is no proof of any default in the planters for not making a sufficient number of freeholders, nor any article that doth tie them thereunto. That there is not proof that the City of London, or the Governor of the new plantation, have felled any trees in the woods called Glankenkin and Killetragh, contrary to their covenant. That the not conveying of glebe lands to the several incumbents of the several parish churches, in regard they did enjoy the lands, is no crime punishable, nor cause of seizure of their lands. That the breach of covenant (if any such were) is not sufficient cause to forfeit the lands. That the breach of covenant is no crime but triable in ordinary courts of justice." (That is on the footing that the Star Chamber was a criminal tribunal, like a sort of glorified Old Bailey). "That the Court of Star Chamber had no power to examine freehold or inheritance," nor had "any power to examine or determine breach of covenants or trusts. That the sentence upon these two corporations aggregate, no particular person being guilty, it is against law. That in all the proof of this cause there doth not appear matter sufficient to convince the City of London of any crime. That upon the whole matter this sentence in the Star Chamber was unlawful and unjust. That this composition and agreement made with the City upon these terms, in this time of extremity, ought not to bind the City." (That was with regard to the subsequent proceedings in the *scire facias*). "That this House is of opinion that when the King shall be pleased to repay those monies which he hath received upon this composition, and such rents as he hath received by colour of this sentence, that then His Majesty shall be restored to the same state he was in; and the patent thereupon gotten shall be cancelled or surrendered. That the citizens of London and all those against whom the judgment is given in *scire facias* shall be discharged of that judgment. That the opinion of this House is that they think fit that both the citizens of London, and those of the new plantation, and all under-tenants, and all those put out of possession by the sequestration or King's Commissioners, shall be restored to the same state they were in before the sentence in the Star Chamber." Then there was a special reference to the case of Mr. Beresford, to which, perhaps, I need not refer, except as to one piece of information. We have made some little inquiry about the facts, and though I cannot exactly say what happened, apparently the Haberdashers sold before the Star Chamber proceedings, or at least they entered into some agreement for sale with a Mr. Beresford, whose family was afterwards that of the Marquis of Waterford. It was that agreement apparently that was ultimately carried out in the sale at a later date, when they had got effectual possession of the property. It is stated on this Appendix Paper: "That by the Haberdashers being made no parties to the *scire facias*, their estate is not avoided by the judgment." On the proceedings of the *scire facias*, it appears that the Haberdashers were parties, but possibly they may never have been served. I do not exactly know what the story is, and I do not think it much matters. In the same Appendix Paper, the Committee will see that this report is introduced by a statement that the Committee of the House of Commons "had divers times in the House of Parliament heard the same, and the allegations made by the Chile's counsell." You will therefore see that it was not a mere matter proceeded upon hastily; it was a very deliberate resolution arrived at after consideration. It says here, "And that afterwards His Majesty's counsell were likewise heard three or four days." So that both sides were heard before Parliament came to that decision; it was a very deliberate and *quasi* judicial proceeding. That is evidence that when the Crown proceeded to grant the second charter, they knew, as it were, the perils that they were in; that is to say the various claims that were made by the companies; and I submit that if it had been the intention of the Crown to deprive the companies of the absolute right of ownership which they had claimed before, it is reasonable to expect that the Crown, being forewarned and forearmed, would have put such restrictions upon the charter as would have made that matter perfectly clear.

Now I propose to take the Committee to the second charter, and it may be convenient for honourable Members to have copies of the charter before them. (*Copies of the charter were handed to the Committee.*) The charter I am about to deal with is printed in the right hand column. It begins by stating the Grant of King James, and it recites that the grant of the first charter had been "for the considerations therein expressed." That refers to the series of recitals in the first charter as to establishing "the true religion of Christ" (referring to the erring of the Province of Ulster from the true religion), "in so much that for a long time it hath not only been harrowed, torn, and wasted by private and domestic broils, but also by foreign arms; we, deeply and heartily commiserating the wretched state of the said province, have esteemed it to be a work worthy of a Christian Prince, and of our Royal function to stir up and recal the same province from superstition, rebellion, calamity, and poverty, which heretofore have horribly raged therein, to religion, obedience, strength, and prosperity. And whereas our beloved and faithful subjects, the mayor and commonalty and citizens of our City of London, burning with a fragrant zeal to promote such our pious intention in this behalf, have laudably undertaken a considerable part of the said plantation in Ulster." These were the considerations that are referred to in this recital in the second charter. It says that King James "did ordain, constitute, and declare, that the city or town of Derry," and so on, should be called and called by the name of the county of Londonderry, and so forth. I will pass over that. Then lower down, after dealing with the liberties of Coleraine about ten lines from the bottom of the page, it recites that the Crown, by letters patent, "did ordain and constitute a certain number of citizens of our City of London to be one body corporate and politic, that is the Irish Society; and granted to the Irish

Irish Society, "the city, fort, and town of Derry, and the whole Island of Derry, the town of Coleraine, and divers other towns, villages," and so forth, "in such manner and form and with such exceptions, and for and under such several rents services, tenures, reservations, covenants, conditions, and other articles, clauses, and agreements as in the said letters patent are mentioned and comprised, as by the same letters patent more fully appeareth." That is to say, it recites that the original grant was in consideration not only of rent, but of the "covenants," conditions, and other articles which were mentioned in the letters patent themselves, and not covenants to be found or traced in documents outside it. That is the position that the Crown at the period of this charter deliberately accepted, that the original charter was granted for the "covenants, conditions, and other articles," in that charter, and the inference is that there were no other conditions, from the fact of their not being stated.

Then there follows this recital: "That by virtue of a certain license" (that is the first license in Mortmain), the Irish Society "did grant unto the twelve chief companies of our City of London (which had taken upon themselves the greater part of the burthen of the said plantation), divers great quantities, parcels, and proportions of the said lands, tenements, and hereditaments, according to their several disbursements, and did retain in his own hands" (that is the phrase they use, meaning the society; we should say now-a-days "in their own hands") "such part of the same tenements and hereditaments as were not properly devisable" (the word is spelt "devisable," but I believe it is to be treated, and has always been treated, as if it was "divisible"), "for the defraying of the charge of the general operation of the said plantation." That is a very material recital as to the view which the Crown took at that time, which was this: as a matter of fact, in the interval between the first charter and the second charter, this rearrangement had taken place, that a grant had been made by license of the Crown to the twelve companies, expressing no trust and no obligation whatever of the lands which are called divisible lands, using the word, as it is ordinarily meant, as land divided up among separate individuals, and that the Irish Society retained certain parts of these tenements and hereditaments, for what? "For the defraying of the charge of the general operation of the said plantation." That is the argument that I am placing before the Committee; that from the time of the second charter the two sets of lands were distinguished and divided, that the lands which were subject to trusts were the lands which were retained by the Irish Society, and that the rest of the lands were divisible among the companies for their own benefit.

Then the next recital is an interesting recital, because of the way in which it is taken. The recital is, "And whereas the said Letters Patent" (that is the first charter) "were afterwards annulled, repealed, and cancelled in the Court of Chancery, by reason whereof the said society of the new plantation and the said companies of our City of London and their respective assigns" ("assigns" being remarked upon there as well as the companies themselves; so that the companies, even at this early period they were treated as being capable of having assigns), "and under tenants of all and singular the lands, tenements, and hereditaments, royalties, privileges, franchises, and immunities in the said letters patent mentioned were wholly deprived, and the said Corporation of Londonderry with the said society of the said new plantation became wholly annulled and invalidated." Now, I do not want to go into the details about these proceedings. The Star Chamber, I observe, though it was picked up again by my learned friend, Mr. Walker, yesterday, was not recognised by King Charles when he was granting the second charter; but the proceedings in the Court of Chancery were recognised, and it is important that the Committee should not be mistaken as to what those proceedings were. The proceedings were eminently in favour of the companies and in favour of the claim they now make.

(*Chairman.*) In favour of the companies as against whom?

Mr. Latham.] They are in favour of the claim of the companies to enjoy their property absolutely for their own benefit, and under no trusts whatever; and for this reason: The proceeding by *scire facias* was not a proceeding on the equitable side of the Court of Chancery; it was not the proper or even a possible mode of proceeding for enforcing a trust. If at the time the proceedings of *scire facias* were taken, the advisers of the Crown had conceived there was a trust in existence, they would not have taken proceedings in *scire facias*. *Scire facias* is a writ that issues out of the common law side of Chancery; it has nothing whatever to do with trusts and obligations of that nature; it is simply a common law mode of enforcing the right of the Crown to repeal a charter which has been obtained or used improperly; it is a writ still in existence; it is the writ by which what is ordinarily called a patent, may be repealed by the Crown, of its own motion, or through the Attorney General, if the patent has been improperly obtained. If, therefore, there had been at this time we are dealing with, any recognised trust for public purposes, the proceedings would have been on the equitable side of the Court of Chancery for enforcing the trust; and above all, the charter would not have been revoked, because the revocation of the charter would have defeated the trust, and the beneficiaries were not before the Court of Chancery, nor before the Star Chamber, nor were they dealt with by the Court of Chancery, nor was there anybody representing them. Therefore, proceedings by *scire facias* were absolutely inconsistent with proceedings for enforcing a trust at that time.

(*Chairman.*] What would the proceedings have been to enforce a trust?

Mr. Latham.] They would have been by information of the Attorney General in the Court of Chancery in the exercise of its equitable jurisdiction to displace the trustees if necessary, or deprive them of their offices, and to create other trustees to enforce the trust, making the outgoing trustees amenable for misfeasance, and so forth; and although there are heaps of such cases in the books, that was not the course adopted.

adopted. The course adopted was absolutely fatal to the beneficiaries, because it destroyed the charter, and the beneficiaries got nothing; that is to say, the public objects were just as absolutely scored out as if they had never existed.

Then, going on with the recital, there is a reference to King Charles' promise of restitution. We find, at this date, that King Charles II. was anxious to observe the promises made by his royal father, and I do not think there is very much in that promise. Then the next paragraph has a marginal note: "Reason of the present grant" (I merely call the Committee's attention to the marginal note for convenience). "And for that it doth manifestly appear to us that the said society of the new plantation" (that is the Irish Society), "and other companies of the City of London" (that is the companies), "have expended very great sums of money in building and planting of the said county of Londonderry and Coleraine." (You will observe the phrase there is "have expended." Here are the words I was referring to when I spoke at the beginning of my opening of there being something in the nature of a trust imposed). "To the intent therefore that the said society of the new plantation, or some such other society, by these our letters patent, to be created and made" (as a matter of fact the old society was left in a state of extinction, and a new society formed); "and the said companies of our City of London, and their respective assigns" ("assigns," again recognising the right of assigning), "and under tenants may, according to their former several rights and interests therein, be restored to all and singular property so vested in them by force and virtue of the said letters patent, and the said several grants by the said society of the new plantation" (you will observe the restoration was not merely to their position, as it was at the date of the first charter, but the restoration was to their position as it was at the date antecedent to the second charter merely; they were restored to the position they occupied, not only under the charter, but under the subsequent grants) "as fully and beneficially" (I call attention to the word "beneficially"; beneficially is the technical word, and always has been the technical word, ever since the distinction between legal and beneficial interests existed, for conveying the entire equitable interest. The legal interest is not passing at present. They were not being restored by this document to their legal interest; they were being restored to their equitable interest; they took their legal interest under the licence of Mortmain and conveyances to themselves) "to all intents and purposes as they might have had, and enjoyed the same if no repeal of the said letters patent had ever been had or made; and to the intent that there may be a new society made of the new plantation in Ulster aforesaid, consisting of the like number of honest and discreet citizens of our City of London," and so forth, "and that a new incorporation of the said city or town of Derry be constituted." Then I do not flinch from these last words, because these are the words, and, I admit, the only words in the whole recital, which indicate anything to be done in the future whatever, "and for the further and better settling and planting of the said county towns and places with trade and inhabitants." And then the Crown proceeds to grant.

It is one of the objects of the new charter that there should be a "further and better settling and planting." But remember that the Irish Society was being reconstituted, and reconstituted for the express purpose of performing public duties, and had got its area of land allotted to it for that purpose, and with that obligation attached; and, consequently, it was quite proper to say in the recital to the charter that there was a "further and better settling and planting" still contemplated. I should say, also, that the settling and planting was never contemplated to be a matter enforced step by step against anybody. Settling and planting were two words very well understood at that early period. The words are very firmly rooted in our language at the present time. We know what settlers are, and what planters are. The word "planter" is used chiefly in regard to the Southern States of America, and the word "settler" is used chiefly in regard to Australia and Canada; but it comes to very much the same thing; it was simply the sending out of colonists or people to inhabit and live in the country, and carry on the business of planting and settlement; that was a performance of the duties of settling and plantation. I apprehend that that was what the Crown intended by all these early charters for plantation, such as those of Maryland and Virginia, which my learned friend, Mr. Walker, referred to, and Hudson's Bay territory granted about this time to Prince Rupert all over Rupertland, I apprehend that all those charters were in this form, and I presume that was their intention. I apprehend they must have been something like the idea of the old Roman military colonies; that is to say, the intention was that bodies of people should go and cultivate these waste lands. The very fact of their being there would operate to produce the result that the King was desirous of attaining; that is to say, for instance, that the savages should be converted, a particular branch which was more noticeable in the case of South America under the Spanish dominion, or if they were not converted they should be otherwise disposed of, that the land should be brought under cultivation and the country should become prosperous and be of advantage to the people of England who sent out the colonists, as well as the colonists themselves. The intention was that these things should be done, but I apprehend it was never in the contemplation of the Crown to enforce settling and planting, except that if they found that the people who had the lands granted to them simply neglected them, or, as has been suggested, let them to the "mere Irish," that is to say, if they did nothing in the way of setting matters straight, then, probably, the Crown would have thought it time to intervene and say: You are not settling and planting. In the case we are dealing with, however, the settling and planting has been done all along. It has never been in dispute, so far as I know, that the settlers and planters did go out. In fact, the present population of the north of Ireland proves that; they are of Scottish and English name and breed, origin, and habit at the

22 July 1890.

the present time to a very large extent, and that is the result of the planting and settling that took place at this early period.

Chairman.] Before you leave the cases of Maryland and Virginia, have you looked to see whether the wording of those charters is at all like this?

Mr. *Latham*.] I did look. There is a recent publication in America by the librarian of Boston, with which you may be familiar.

Chairman.] Yes.

Mr. *J. H. Stow*.] I have some notes here upon those charters.

Chairman.] We will not interrupt Mr. Latham in his address.

Mr. *Latham*.] I have seen the Hudson's Bay charter, because I may say I advised the Hudson's Bay Company, so that I know about that; but I do not think it helps us here; it is not near enough to help us. The Hudson's Bay Company were given very large jurisdictions and powers; they were a sort of representatives of the Crown for Government and so forth.

Mr. *Lawson*.] I suppose they had the same powers as a Royal chartered company, and more?

Mr. *Latham*.] Yes, the same powers as a Royal chartered company with full power of Government. Many Royal chartered companies have no power of Government whatever. I daresay they were very much the same as the old East India Company.

Mr. *Lawson*.] With the same powers as those in the South African Company's Charter?

Mr. *Latham*.] Yes, or the Borneo Charter, those things are always going on. I do not think there is very much the Committee will learn from a study of those charters, except the broad principle of what was being done at the time.

Mr. *Elton*.] I suppose, of the charters to which the Chairman directed your attention, the one you mention would be the least applicable; in the case of Hudson's Bay it was not intended to transfer a large population to those climates, but it was to be a trading company?

Mr. *Latham*.] Yes. The population there was chiefly ermine and fox.

Mr. *Elton*.] The Massachusetts Charter would be more parallel?

Mr. *Latham*.] Yes; but unfortunately I am not able to find any except the meagrest abstracts from it.

Mr. *Elton*.] The Massachusetts Charter, I think we could obtain, perhaps.

Mr. *J. H. Stow*.] The Pennsylvanian Charter is very much more on all-fours with this.

Chairman.] It is merely a matter of historical interest, and it does not carry us very far.

Mr. *Latham*.] There is a letter bearing upon the meaning of the word "plantation" from King James to Sir Arthur Chichester dated the 25th March 1615, which is printed in the respondent's Appendix at page 400 of the Skinners' case. I do not want to weary the Committee, but there are passages here which I may perhaps read. It says "we have examined, viewed, and reviewed with our own eye every part thereof, and find greatly to our discontentment, the slow progression of that plantation, some few only of our British undertakers, servitors, and natives having as yet proceeded effectually by the accomplishment of such things in all points as are required of them by the articles of the plantation, the rest, and by much the greatest part, having either done nothing at all or so little, or by reason of the slightness thereof to so little purpose, that the work seems rather to us to be forgotten by them, and to perish under their hand than any whit to be advanced by them, some having begun to build and not planted, others begun to plant and not build, and all of them in general retaining the Irish still upon their lands, the avoiding of which was the fundamental reason of that plantation." That is to say that the idea of planting was to supersede the Irish. Then about a dozen lines from the bottom you will see this: "we think we may without any breach of justice make bold with their rights who have neglected their duties in a service of so much importance unto us, and by the same law and reason of state resume into our hands their lands who have failed to perform according to our original intention the articles of plantation, and bestow them upon some other men more active and worthy of them than themselves, and the time is long since expired within which they were bound to have finished to all purposes their plantation, so that we want not just provocation to proceed presently with all rigour against them." The King at that time regarded it not as a continuing duty to go on from generation to generation, but to be done at an early period once for all. He says "yet we are pleased in grace, and that they may be the more inexcusable if they be deficient in their duties hereafter, to assign them a further time which shall be to the last day of August come twelve months, which will be in the year of Our Lord 1616, which we are determined shall be final and peremptory unto them, and at which time we are resolved to seize into our hands the lands of any man whatsoever without respect of persons, whether he be a British undertaker, servitor, or native that shall be found defective in performing any of the articles of the plantation to which he was enjoined." He says, "We require you to give them notice whom it concerns that we do expect full performance in all points of the articles of the plantation by the time above specified. And because we will have no man to pretend ignorance of that which we expect from him in performing the true meaning of the articles of the plantation, we require Sir Josias Bodley" to "signify to the Londoners and every undertaker," their several defects and omissions. So that from these latter passages it appears that the King's view was that the plantation was not a matter to go on throughout centuries; it was a matter for the undertakers to get settlers and tenants, and assign them land if they liked, and see that the plantation was carried out. Then there is a letter in the Calendar of State Papers, dated June the 8th, 1613, which I should like to read, as it is only four lines.

Chairman.] Is not that quoted in the Concise View?

Mr. J. H. Stone.] Yes.

Mr. Latham.] "The King to Chichester. Directs him to afford his best assistance to Captain Raphe Mansfield, an ancient servant, who has given testimony of his zeal to the King's service, and as undertaker in Ulster has shown much forwardness, beyond most of the other undertakers, and has performed all the conditions of the plantation."

Now, I go on again with the charter, and I think I shall not be so long over the remainder of the charter as I have been over the recitals. There is a great deal I need not read; I can follow the marginal notes, "The city of Derry and other granted premises to be the county of Londonderry;" "The city to be called Londonderry;" "Extent of the liberties thereof;" "Extent of the liberties of Coleraine." Then you have the incorporation of the inhabitants of Londonderry, and that they were to have a mayor and commonalty and so on. Then, towards the bottom of page 7, the words of the old charter are copied, and you have a like clause in the new charter, "And so that such laws, ordinances, regulations, and constitutions be certified by the mayor and common council of the city of Londonderry for the time being under the common seal of the same city," "to the Irish Society."

Chairman.] That is the clause, I suppose, under which the bye-laws require their sanction to this day.

Mr. Latham.] Yes, to this day. Then it goes on, "To the intent that the said society;" "may under the common seal of the society, ratify, approve, and confirm such laws, ordinances, regulations, and constitutions;" "within six months next, after the delivery of such certificate," and then they were to be enforced. Those are the clauses as to the constant superintendence and control, which are referred to in the judgments of the Lords in the case of the Skinners' Company and the Irish Society, or some of them at all events; that is why I call your attention to them here, such as the reserving of the bye-laws and so on. Then you come to the appointment of the mayor, and on page 9, the question of the creation of the Irish Society; then on page 10, in the last paragraph, at the bottom of the page, you have this clause: "And that they and their successors for ever" (that is the Irish Society by their own interpretation) "shall be at all future times, persons able and in law capable, to have, purchase, receive, and possess lands, tenements, goods, chattels;" and then follow these other words, "possessions, liberties, privileges, rights, jurisdictions, franchises;" and then, a little lower down you will find that they have power granted to them "to give, grant, demise, and assign lands, tenements, and other hereditaments, goods and chattels;" but it does not go on to say "possessions, privileges, rights, jurisdictions, franchises," which they were not entitled to grant. You will observe therefore, a distinction is drawn between what was in their holding as representatives of the Crown as public servants, and the whole land, the whole being passed over to them: and that there was free liberty to grant anything except their "possessions, liberties, privileges, rights, jurisdictions, and franchises," clearly showing that those were Royal powers which could not be granted; and, of course, the argument which I addressed to the Committee before would come in naturally here, that if the body of trustees had, either on the face of the document in express terms or by necessary implication according to the true interpretation of the document, power to part with their lands by sale or otherwise, and this is not a question of sale only, then the person receiving the land from the trustees is not bound by the trust. Here is an express power.

Then the charter goes into questions of detail which are not material here, and then at page 13, I will call the Committee's attention to this paragraph in the middle of the page: "And further, of our more ample grace," "we do will, and by these presents" "grant that the said persons" (that is the Society) "and their successors from time to time hereafter to be nominated and elected of the same society," "shall and may have full power and authority to convene, assemble, and hold a court" in the City of London or elsewhere, "and in the same court or meeting to do, hear, transact, and determine, all, and all manner of matters and things" "concerning the plantation or government aforesaid, as to them shall seem best and most expedient." Those are what I think Lord Lyndhurst referred to as the extensive or large powers for carrying into effect the intention of the Crown, and these, no doubt, were the powers of the Irish Society which were referred to in the lease to Cary, which was put in by my learned friend, Mr. Law, a little while ago. There were general powers of superintending the plantation, and further powers to "direct, appoint, and ordain" "all and singular things" "concerning the plantation supply establishment, continuation, and government of the said city of Londonderry." Then on page 14, in the first paragraph, their powers were extended "and generally for any other cause matter or thing whatsoever concerning the directing or ordering of the said plantation or concerning any other things whatsoever, which by the true intent of these our letters patent can or ought to be done by them for the better government and rule of the said city of Londonderry and county of Londonderry." Those were local powers exercisable by the Irish Society over the people who were there. They were no doubt magisterial powers of very large extent, and the tenants or occupiers, from time to time, would have to conform to the rules and ordinances of the Irish Society; but, of course, it does not mean that the Irish Society were to have power under this charter to make levies upon people in England for the benefit of that plantation, because that would be extending it beyond all reason. Then you will find at the bottom of page 14 that there is a clause in the old charter which is not in the new charter, and you will find, indeed, a series of clauses omitted, all of which I think are temporary clauses. The first begins by saying the courts shall have power "during the

the term of ten years next and immediately following after the date of these presents" to frame certain laws. The ten years of course had been long passed at the date of the second charter, and either those laws had been made or the necessity for them had been abandoned. I think you will find that a good many of those clauses are not in the second charter.

Mr. *John Ellis*.] Do you suggest that they are all of a temporary character?

Mr. *Latham*.] I am not quite positive, but I think that all which are omitted in the second charter are of a temporary character, or I will not say all, but almost all, for I cannot be quite positive. I think it is very probable, as my learned friend, Mr. Lee, suggests, that some of them were not merely temporary. Then, passing on, you will find a great deal of the old charter is omitted, there is a power of removing officers, and so on.

Chairman.] All this part of the charter you are taking us through affects the Irish Society and its composition and duties only, and not the companies.

Mr. *Latham*.] That is why I am not reading it to the Committee. I do not think it affects us at all. Passing on to page 47 you will see at the bottom of that page, when you come to deal with the exceptions, there are considerable exceptions for ecclesiastical purposes, which may be of importance when I come to deal with the orders and conditions hereafter, because they say that the duty of making provision for religious requirements is cast upon the Crown. You will see that the Crown excepts out of the grant the "rights of patronage of all and singular the churches of Dromore" and so on, and "all lands, tenements, and hereditaments belonging to the Dean of Derry," and "all lands and tenements lately granted to the Archbishop of Armagh and Bishop of Derry." I may mention among all these many exceptions there is no exception in favour of the Crown, of timber, and mines, and minerals. We come to the question of timber, and mines, and minerals, when we come to the dealings between the Irish Society and the companies. Then passing on to page 50, we have there the *habendum*: "To have, hold, and enjoy, the said counties," and so on, and all the premises above granted to the Irish Society, "and their successors for ever": and they were to hold the city of Londonderry and the town of Coleraine with 7,000 acres in free burgage, and the rest of the property they were to hold in free and common socage, and not by knight's service. There is a little bit of history connected with this transaction which is material to notice. The original orders and conditions provided that all the undertakers should hold by knight's service. Knight's service was a tenure which threw very considerable obligations of various kinds, and very heavy liabilities of an uncertain character, upon the tenant holding under the Crown by knight's service; but in the course of the negotiations between the City of London and the Crown, that provision in the orders and conditions was struck out because the Corporation of London would have nothing whatever to do with these uncertain liabilities of tenure, and insisted upon taking their lands in free and common socage, which carries with it, in the absence of any provisions to the contrary, distinctly by common law the right of alienation. It is a right which not only exists by the common law of England, but which exists by statute under the statute of *quia emptores*. The statute of *quia emptores* was a statute of King Edward I. by which it was provided that there should be no new creation of tenure, no sub-infeudation as it was technically called, but it is expressly provided that holders in common socage among others should have the right of alienation.

Then you will observe there are certain covenants put in at the bottom of page 53; and you will find that there are certain covenants in the old charter which are left out in the new. The covenants under the old charter were that the society should "establish, and appoint, and by good and sufficient several conveyances in the law convey to the Bishop of Derry for the time being, and his successors, for the use and behoof of the same bishop and dean, and their successors respectively, four acres of land in the aforesaid Island of Derry, which are and shall be adjoining the tower, called Collumkill Tower; that is to say, to the Bishop of Derry and his successors two acres, and other two acres thereof to the said dean and his successors, to the intent that the same bishop and dean may thereupon build separate houses." That had been imposed originally upon the Irish Society, and it had dropped out in the new charter, apparently having been provided for. Then you will find at the bottom of page 54 there is another very extensive provision in the original charter about religion, which was put in the original charter to compel the Irish Society to convey glebes to the different incumbents, and so to provide for the religious requirements of Ireland. It says: "such and as many acres of glebe land" "as shall be near or approaching to the rate and proportion of 60 acres of land lying in every proportion of land of 1,000 acres lying in every or any parish or precinct within the aforesaid county of Coleraine." So that there were very considerable grants required to be made to incumbents under the original charter, which were no longer required in the new, which carried out the intention of the Crown for religious purposes. Then at the bottom of page 57 you will find a clause as to timber, which says: "for that there will be need that great abundance of timber be had and provided for the planting of the premises and the re-building of houses and edifices within the same, and therefore great care is to be had the timber trees there growing, and which may conveniently and fitly serve towards the plantation of the premises, be not carried out of the said kingdom, or otherwise wasted or spoiled there." Therefore, there is a special provision that the society were to appropriate certain particular timber growing on the lands of Glankonkeine and Killetrough (I may not be accurate in my pronunciation of them), and these were "for ever" to "remain only and be converted towards the plantation aforesaid, and the building of houses and edifices so as aforesaid to be made and to be spent towards other necessary uses of our said

23 *July* 1890.

Realm of Ireland, in the same kingdom, and not for any other cause to be merchandised or sold." You see the effect of this clause is to appropriate certain particular timber for public purposes, and if the whole grant, as was suggested in my learned friend, Mr. Walker's argument, was for public purposes and nothing but public purposes, why should there be inserted this particular clause, allotting the timber of particular lands to public purposes? His argument was that the whole property was appropriated to public purposes. Why then reserve the timber of two particular properties?

Now, there is an important new clause in the new charter at the bottom of page 63. There are, first of all, two clauses on page 64 as to preventing the exportation of hemp and wool, and so forth, and then there is a clause at the bottom of page 63, which I think is material; this is drawing towards the end of the document after the grants had been made: "And further we will and by these presents for us our heirs and successors do covenant and grant to and with the said society," and so forth (meaning the Irish Society), "that we, our heirs and successors for ever hereafter will exonerate, acquit, indemnify, and keep harmless as well the said society," "and their successors, as the said city of Londonderry, and the whole territory and county of Londonderry aforesaid," "of and from all, and all manner of rights, titles, interest, claims, and demands, whatsoever of all and whatsoever persons having, or of right, claiming anything, by, from, or under us, our heirs, or successors of, or in the said City of Londonderry, or in any parcel thereof, or of or in the said territory and county of Londonderry, or in any parcel thereof, or of or in any of the lands, tenements, and other premises abovementioned by these presents to be granted and confirmed; saving the interest and title of the Bishop and Dean of Derry, and their successors respectively for the time being; and saving of certain proportions of land" which had been given to certain Irish gentlemen who were made freeholders. That is a covenant on the part of the Crown to indemnify the Irish Society against any other people's claims. If there were beneficiaries who were specially to be entitled to claim, they must have claimed, and could only claim, under a trust in their favour created by the Crown; and here is a covenant of indemnity by the Crown to protect the Irish Society against them. It is not a mere common form covenant, because immediately afterwards comes the ordinary covenant for quiet enjoyment, but it is an absolute covenant of indemnity.

Chairman.] Do you consider that the quiet enjoyment clause bars out the existence of beneficiaries?

Mr. *Latham.*] I do not think the ordinary quiet enjoyment clause does; but I think that special clause does.

Chairman.] If that had been a good point, would not it have been pleaded in the Skinners' case?

Mr. *Latham.*] I think that observation is just. I do not know whether it was pleaded or argued. I always assent to an argument which I think is a strong one, and I do not see the answer to that. Then there is a clause at the end of the charter at page 96, which says, "And we of our further special grace," and so forth, "do pardon, remise, release, and for ever quit claim to the mayor and commonalty, and citizens of our City of London, and to all and singular companies and bodies politic of the same city, which heretofore purchased any part of the premises in these our Letters Patent, mentioned and granted, or heretofore granted by the said Letters Patent of our said grandfather," all sums of money which they have received "since the death of our illustrious father." That is rather a remarkable use of the word "purchased." The word purchaser may be used in two senses; it may mean either a purchaser for valuable consideration, or it may mean one who takes by purchase, not by transmission of interest; but in either case the companies are treated here as purchasers; that is to say, they must be treated as having taken and acquired by grant, and become legally entitled by grant from the Irish Society, in the capacity of purchasers, and therefore, primâ facie, free from any liabilities whatever. If they took as purchasers, they took for their own benefit; and that is the position that is accepted by the Crown in this charter. Of course it probably refers to the great sum of money they had expended; but either way it comes to the same thing; they took as purchasers, and were consequently owners, and not as trustees.

Chairman.] Do you agree with Mr. Walker that no money ever passed to the Crown; that there was no transaction of purchase with the Crown?

Mr. *Latham.*] The Crown reserved the rents; the Crown treated it as getting rents. The Crown reserved the rents on all the property that it conveyed or granted to the Irish Society. That is where the Crown got the advantage. They got rents, parcel by parcel for the land. They were not very large sums.

Mr. *Elton.*] You mean fee farm rents?

Mr. *Latham.*] I think they were all fee farm rents, that is a continuous rent, not upon lease but reserved as perpetually payable; and they are paid up to the present time.

Chairman.] That is what I wanted to know. How are we to get to know what rents are paid to the Crown now? That has rather escaped us, I think.

Mr. *Latham.*] I think you will find they are no more than the rents that were reserved; they have not altered.

Sir William Marriott.] What do they amount to?

Mr. *Elton.*] Would they be paid to the Crown, or are they sold under the Act?

Mr. *Latham.*] I think they are still paid to the Crown. No, I am told that the City did buy them from the Crown; but they are still paid.

Mr. *Mason.*] It is the first item in the Irish Society's account submitted last year. You will find fied "Permanent payments, Crown rents, &c." Appendix.

Chairman.] Thank you.

Mr. *Latham.*] I am at page 47 of the Appendix of last year, it says, "Permanent payments, Crown rents, &c.: see Account No. 1, page 4, 1,766 *l.*" Now, I propose to pass on to the second licence in Mortmain of the 15th of Charles II., Part II., dated the 7th of April 1663. I do not know whether the Committee have copies of that.

Chairman.] Yes.

Mr. *Latham.*] This is a document which I think will follow out the same line of argument which I have founded upon the charter itself. The King refers to the letters patent of King James, and he says, thereby, he did amongst other things grant to the Irish Society, "incorporated by the same letters patent, the city, fort, and town of Derry, alias Londonderry, town of Coleraine," and so on, lands and hereditaments; and then he goes on to recite, "By virtue of the said letters patent" (that is the previous licence in Mortmain) the Irish Society and the twelve chief companies of London, "who had borne and were to undergo the greatest charge of the said plantations, several great quantities, parcels, and proportions of the said lands, tenements, and hereditaments, according to their respective disbursements." Then he recites that, in consequence of the *scire facias*, they had all gone, and then he recites the new charter, and he recites the intent of the new charter: "To the intent (amongst other things) that the several companies of London who had laid out and disbursed vast sums of money in building and planting the premises, and their respective assigns" (not only they but their assigns, you will observe), "and under-tenants might be reinstated and reinvested in all and singular the castles, manors, lands, tenements, royalties, privileges, and all and singular other the premises with the appurtenances, according to their respective interests therein, as fully and beneficially" (the same word again deliberately inserted), "to all intents and purposes as though no such repeal of the said letters patent of King James had ever been had or made. The which our princely intention cannot legally take effect without our further licence in that behalf." Then there is a grant of the new licence to the intent that they will be willing that the companies "may receive the full benefit of our said gracious intention, and be severally and speedily reinvested and reinstated," and so forth; and "thereby receive some gain and benefit of their great travail and expense taken and bestowed therein;" and he goes on to make the grant of that licence. That you see is very deliberate. It is perfectly clear that he intended that they should receive some gain and benefit; and how anybody can propound such a doctrine as I understood Mr. Walker to be driven to the other day, that the great benefit was the pleasure of spending money upon other people, I cannot conceive.

Sir *William Marriott.*] It was a strong Christian view?

Mr. *Latham.*] A Christian view, no doubt.

Mr. *Elton.*] There seems to be a sort of opposition between the gain and benefit they were to receive, and the great travail and expense they had taken; but according to Mr. Walker they should receive travail and expense for their great travail and expense.

Mr. *Latham.*] Yes; they had incurred travail and expense, and they were to have the gain and benefit: that is, they were to have the property beneficially. And I would remind you here, referring to the old licence in Mortmain, of some very material words in the old licence which now disappear. In the old licence there is a recital that the companies "have disbursed, expended, and bestowed divers great sums of money for and towards the building, fortifying, planting, strengthening, battering, and improving the aforesaid city of Derry and town of Coleraine, and some part of other the foresaid lands and the said corporation, companies, and fraternities, being willing to proceed in the said work of plantation." That is one recital in the first licence, but it is not in the second. That is a very material point, because the inference that I draw from that is, that the Crown were satisfied that the work of plantation had been done, and they were not to proceed further. The old licence goes on that they "do intend so far forth as to them shall seem convenient to be at further charge for the planting, battering, and improving." Those words are gone in the second licence; there is no proposition at all in the second licence that these companies should proceed at all. And again there are the words in the old licence, "for their better, more orderly, and speedier proceeding therein, are desirous to have such parts of the said lands as they are severally and respectively intend to build on and plant to be to them severally conveyed by the foresaid society." That has gone again. So that wherever you come to anything which indicates an intention of doing more, all that is erased from the second licence that was given. At the bottom of the first page of the first licence, when he begins to make the grant, he says: "We therefore, willing so much as in us lieth to effect and bring to end (if it so please God) the said pious and worthy work, and to remove so much as in us lieth all impediments that any way may hinder our said subjects in their aforesaid laudable intentions for the performance and finishing of the said plantation." All that is gone in the second licence, that is to say, it is no longer expressed in the licence, though they must have had this first licence before them, for, when they come to the operative part, they copy it word for word; and yet they drop out any reference to any further obligations or any intentions on the part of the companies. I will ask to be allowed to put in this new licence (*the same was handed in, vide Appendix*); it is not in any of the printed Papers at present. Then there are some variations; but I do not know that they are very material. So much for the licence. Then there followed upon the licence, as I mentioned, the grants. I do not know that I need go into the grants at all.

23 *July* 1890.

Chairman.] When you speak of the grants, do you mean conveyances?

Mr. *Latham.*] At this time they were conveyances by lease and release, as was the fashion at that time. It was no longer a question of feoffment, but there was a lease for six months, and then the release which carried the freehold. There were certain reservations in the grants, to which, perhaps, I had better refer. I do not know whether a sample deed of conveyance has been yet put in by anybody.

Chairman.] Yes, we have three. We have that of the Irish Society to the Salters, for instance.

Mr. *Latham.*] Perhaps I may take Appendix Paper 33, which is the grant to the Mercers. I rather stick to the case of the Mercers, because they are still in possession. I see, however, that Paper 23 is the release in Cromwell's time. I do not refer to that. Paper 19 is the correct one; it is one of 1663. I think the point I was going to call the Committee's attention to here was taken the other day by Mr. Elton, when Mr. Walker was reading this. The point is that the reservation of timber, and the reservation also of minerals, was only a reservation for particular purposes; it was not a general reservation of timber and minerals for all purposes. It was a reservation first of timber trees "to be employed, spent, and converted for, in, and about buildings and other necessary uses within the realm of Ireland;" and in the same manner there was a reservation for the society "to dig and search in the premises afore granted," "for stone, slate, lime, gravel, sand, and other necessary materials," "to be employed and converted in and about buildings in the foresaid county of Londonderry and the Province of Ulster, and not otherwise." It is only a limited right; it is a limited right for the Irish Society to come upon the lands of the Mercers to take their timber and their stone for the purpose of erecting buildings for the public service; and it is material as indicating that it was not anticipated that the companies themselves would be using these materials for the public service; otherwise they would not have taken their property as they did but have left it to the Irish Society. It was because, in the absence of a clause like this, the companies might have dealt with these materials as they thought fit, they put in a right in favour of the Irish Society, upon whom was imposed the obligation of building and planting, to come in to the property they had parted with in order to get the materials for carrying out the public duties. The mines and minerals are now granted; this is only a reservation out of the grant for a particular purpose.

Now, the next point in order, I think, is the lawsuit, to which I referred, for special performance against Lord Shelburne.

The suit was the suit of the Goldsmiths' Company against Lord Shelburne in 1729, folio 366. I have a whole series of the proceedings here, but I will not trouble you with any that are not material to this particular point, and I think the first is the decree on the hearing. I have a spare copy here, which I will hand to the Chairman (*handing in same*).

Mr. *G. H. Lee.*] Where does it come from?

Mr. *Latham.*] From the records of the Record Office. They have been taken out with considerable care from the original documents themselves. We can produce an office copy of these documents if it is desired.

Mr. *G. H. Lee.*] No, that is not necessary.

Mr. *Latham.*] "This cause coming this present day to be heard and debated before the Right Honourable the Lord High Chancellor &c. in the presence of counsel learned on both sides the substance of the plaintiffs' bill appeared to be thus the plaintiffs being seized in fee of the manor of Goldsmiths' Hall in the county of of Londonderry alias Colraine in the province of Ulster and realm of Ireland, leased the same to William Warren Esq., at 900 *l.* per annum for a term which will expire the 1st of November 1730 and on the 7th of February 1728 settled conditions for the disposall thereof to the effect following, viz., that the company would let or sell what estate was conveyed to them by the Irish Society and then was in the occupation of their Tennant Warren by virtue of the said lease, that the fine or purchase-money should be all lawfull money of Great Britain, and paid in Goldsmiths' Hall in London viz., one-third thereof at the time of making the contract one other third at six months then next and the other third part residue thereof on or before 1st day of November 1730 to which day the company would pay interest for each summe of money from the respective times of payment thereof if the purchaser should make default in either of his two last payments he should forfeit to the company his first payment. That a clear yearly rent or rent-charge of 200 *l.* per annum of like money should be reserved payable half-yearly at Goldsmiths' Hall in London.

That the conveyances should be prepared at the charge of the purchaser or by the clerk of the said company and be executed by all parties on or before the 1st of November 1730. That the proposers should sign their proposals and declare their acceptance of the said conditions. That both before and after the said 7th February the plaintiffs caused the said estate to be advertised several times to be disposed of and on the 7th March 1728 the plaintiffs at a Court of Assistants received opened and read divers proposals for the said estate when the defendant the Earl of Shelburne contracted and agreed with the plaintiffs for the purchase of the said estate by contract and agreement under his hand in the words following viz.: I Henry Earl of Shelburne do hereby agree with the wardens and commonalty of the Mystery of Goldsmiths of the City of London to pay to them the sum of 14,000 *l.* of lawfull money of Great Britain for the inheritance of their estate in Ireland subject to a rent-charge of 200 *l.* per annum of like money according to the conditions for the disposall thereof publicly fixed up in their hall. As witness my hand the 7th of March 1728 Shelburne. That at the same time the defendant paid to the plaintiffs 4,700 *l.* being one third of the said purchase money and desired a copy of their minutes upon making the said contract and a copy of the said conditions under their clerk's hand which

was

23 *July* 1890.

were given to him accordingly. That on the 6th of September 1729 the further sum of 4,700 *l.* became due to the plaintiffs for a second payment but the same is not yet paid. Therefore that the said Earl may be decreed" this was the suit "to pay the plaintiffs 4,700 *l.* so due as aforesaid and specifically to perform the said contract with the plaintiffs or that he may release the said contract and his right to the said estate and that the said 4,700 *l.* so paid to the plaintiffs as aforesaid may be retained by them and that they may dispose of the said estate as they think fit is the scope of the Bill whereto the counsel for the defendant by his answer admits that the plaintiffs made such conditions for sale of their estate as aforesaid and caused their said estate to be advertised several times to be disposed of. That he signed such contract for the purchase of the said estate as aforesaid and paid 4,700 *l.* and had a receipt under their clerk's hand. That 1,200 *l.* thereof was the money of Edward Biggs Esq. and that James McCulloch Esq. made proposals to the plaintiff touching the said purchase and signed the same in their books as purchaser of the said estate at 14,100 *l.*"

(*Chairman.*) What is the point of bringing in the names of Biggs and McCulloch?

Mr. *Latham.*] That means that Lord Shelburne thought that Biggs and McCulloch were partners in the purchase and between him and the Goldsmiths' Company the whole burden ought not to be thrown on him. "And thereupon was declared the purchaser, but in regard to the said defendant at the desire of Biggs and McCulloch advanced 3,200 *l.* his name was made use of in the said contract as the purchaser of the said premises, and at their desire he signed the said contract," and then it states that there was an agreement between them which I need not trouble you with.

Then at the top of page 15, "and that Biggs and McCulloch ought to be made parties." Then "Whereupon and upon debate of the matter and hearing the conditions dated the 7th day of February 1728, the agreement signed by the Earl of Shelburne, dated the 7th of March 1728, an indenture tripartite dated 25th March 1729, between the Earl of Shelburne of the first part, the said Biggs of the second part, and the said McCulloch of the third part, and the proofs taken in the said cause read, and what was alleged on both sides his Lordship doth order and decree that it be referred to Mr. John Bennett" (that is one of the masters) "to see whether the company can make a good title to the lands agreed to be purchased by the said Earl by the note of the 7th day of March 1728, and if the company cannot make a good title then the said Earl is to be discharged of the purchase" (an ordinary specific performance decree) "and the company are to repay the 4,700 *l.* together with interest to be computed by the said master, but if the company can make out a good title then it is ordered and declared that the defendant, the Earl of Shelburne, do perfect the purchase according to the said note of the 7th of March 1728, and do make the last two payments of the 1st day of November 1730, at Goldsmiths' Hall, to such person as the company shall appoint, deducting interest thereout for 4,700 *l.* to that day, and that the company do at the same time execute a conveyance, and, if the parties differ about the conveyance, the said master is to settle the the same;" and then comes the next document in the bundle that has been handed in, signed by Mr. J. Bennett, the master to whom the title was referred. "In pursuance of an order made on hearing this cause, bearing date the 1st day of July last, I have been attended by counsel and solicitors on both sides, and in their presence have looked into, and considered of the plaintiffs, the Goldsmiths' Company's title to the land agreed to be purchased by the defendant, the Earl of Shelburne, by his note of the 7th of March 1728, and do conceive that the said plaintiffs, the Goldsmiths' Company can make and convey a good title to the said lands to the said Earl of Shelburne, provided the Society of the Governor and Assistants [of] London of the new plantation in Ulster within the realm of Ireland join in the said conveyance, which I humbly certify and submit to the judgment of this honourable Court." He found a good title; that is to say, if the Irish Society joined, that the Irish Society and the company between them could make a good title. It is clear they could not have made a good title, if there had been a beneficial trust on them for anybody else, or for public purposes.

(*Chairman.*) How does that remark about not making a good title, if it had been subject to trusts apply? Would not that apply to the Irish Society, who are to be parties to this conveyance?

Mr. *Latham.*] I imagine that it is very difficult to ascertain why he required the Irish Society to join. They took no part of the purchase money. We find that from the documents, and from the deed which conveyed, I can only put it, as a conjecture, but I do put it, that they joined, in order to release their particular rights to timber and stone, and so on; that the purchaser said, "I claim to have a free and unfettered title. I find the Irish Society, by the terms of their conveyance, have a reservation to come into my lands to take stone for building purposes, and so forth;" and then what happened was that the Goldsmiths' Company went to the Irish Society and said: "Look here, to save trouble, you join." I suppose they said, "You do not want these particular minerals and so forth, for this particular property; you join." Then they did join, and as you will remember, so then was entered into the deed of indemnity, which has been produced before the Committee, that is to say, a separate form of deed of indemnity to the Irish Society, who had joined at the request of the Goldsmiths' Company, to indemnify them against all consequences of that joining, and that was a natural thing for the Irish Society to ask for, if these were the precise circumstances; but I must admit, I have searched into all the proceedings, and oddly enough, it eludes one at every point.

Mr. *Elton.*] Were the Irish Society under a covenant for further assurance under the original grant?

23 *July* 1890.

Mr. Latham.] Yes; but they reserved their covenant of assurance to Lord Shelburne.

Chairman.] Have you intended to maintain in the earlier part of your argument—perhaps I did not follow you—that timber, and minerals, and the reservations were not impressed with a trust.

Mr. Latham.] I do not think I put it exactly in this way. There was no reservation to the Crown of timber and minerals at all. To the undertakers timber and minerals passed. The reservation of the timber and minerals was to the Irish Society, when the Irish Society came to convey to the companies.

Chairman.] In fact, your argument now, if I do not misapprehend it, is that this transaction shows that the Goldsmiths' Company's estate was not impressed with a trust.

Mr. Latham.] Yes.

Chairman.] But then the Irish Society joined in the conveyance.

Mr. Latham.] Yes.

Chairman.] And you say, as I understand, that your theory is that they joined in order to release the timber, minerals, &c. But if the timber and minerals were impressed with a trust, how could they divest them of it?

Mr. Latham.] I think that is quite possible.

Chairman.] I am only putting it for my own information.

Mr. Latham.] Quite so.

My learned friend tells me it was not timber and minerals, and for this reason, because when you look at that conveyance itself the reservation was still maintained. The timber and minerals were still retained. So that I made a mistake in my conjecture. All that remains is that it was for the purpose of getting a fresh covenant for further assurance from the Irish Society in consideration of the original covenants for further assurance entered into. That is the only thing left.

Sir, I do not wish to weary the Committee by driving the point home. I may merely mention that exceptions were taken to the master's report; the exceptions were argued before the court; various proceedings took place in the somewhat dilatory way in which things took place in Chancery in the old times, but eventually the master's report was confirmed, and the conveyance was carried out in that way, and the decree for specific performance became absolute and the conveyance was made. I need not repeat my argument as to the result of that. It is the finding of a court of competent jurisdiction that the Irish Society and the Goldsmiths' Company between them could make a good title to a purchaser without breach of trust.

Then I need only remind you here of what you have had in evidence, because it relates to the same subject matter, namely, that when the lands of one of the companies were lately sold in Ireland, the Drapers, to the tenants under the special Acts, the title was passed through the office of the Commissioners in Ireland, and that they came to the same result as the Court of Chancery did in 1780, that a good title could be made by those who were selling, and that in effect they must have found there were no trusts. They had all the history before them. The Commissioners were concerned in the matter, and were advancing money to enable tenants to complete their purchase, and it was essential that they should have a good title.

Chairman.] Supposing now the Irish Society which you all admit to hold its property impressed with trusts, were to sell land, I am not sure whether they have any agricultural land, but supposing they sold agricultural land under Lord Ashbourne's Act?

Mr. Sexton.] They have.

Chairman.] If they were to sell under Lord Ashbourne's Act, do you contend that the fact that the Land Commission made an advance upon that purchase and sale is an argument that the Irish Society did not hold under trust.

Mr. Latham.] I can only put it in this form that here is an independent official body who have found they can convey. If they held under trust for public purposes, so that they could not convey, they could not give a good title. The Land Commission is not a tribunal but it is an independent opinion of some value on this subject, and they are gentlemen expressly entrusted to deal with this matter and accustomed to look into titles and examine them for the express purpose of finding whether the titles are good or bad titles. I do not put it higher than that. I may say this because it has reference to an observation that fell from the Chairman at the moment. I take neither one view nor the other as to the Irish Society, but you must remember that the decision in the court was that the Irish Society had a large discretion. It does not follow that because the Irish Society hold all their lands and are also, at the same time, bound to fulfil certain public duties, and that their lands are to enable them to perform those public duties, it does not follow that all those lands are impressed with that public trust, because, as I understand the judgments which I am going to very shortly, the decision distinctly was that there was a large discretion as to what they should spend for public purposes and what they should not. I will not say what the discretion was because it is difficult to find out, and I do not think there is a decision on that subject; but the decision was that it was a discretionary trust and I think the Committee have had some material evidence on this subject from *Lord Justice* FitzGibbon, who said that when they came to deal with this matter of the discretion, it was a kind of will o' the wisp, and it eluded one at every point, and that they could not affix a trust to any property anywhere which would enable them to apply it under the Endowed Schools' Act.

Mr. Sexton.] Mr. Walker's view was that the discretion was a discretion as between various public uses.

Mr. Latham.] That was Mr. Walker's view. I do not wish to argue the Irish Society's case because

because I think it will be for them to argue their own case, and I have enough to do to argue mine.

Sir William Marriott.] Did the Irish Society join in the recent sale by the Drapers' Company?

Mr. *Mason.*] They did not join in the conveyance; they released their rights.

[The Committee adjourned for a short time.]

Mr. *Latham.*] Sir, I now propose to go at once to the decisions in the Skinners' Company's case. I do not think I need trouble the Committee with Lord Cottenham's decision on the interlocutory proceedings.

Chairman.] That was a proceeding for a receiver?

Mr. *Latham.*] Yes; it is not against me so far as I know. It is the same as the rest.

Chairman.] He made one remark which is cited, I think, in the argument of one of the counsel before the House of Lords on page 465 of the 12th Clark and Finnelly.

Mr. *Latham.*] I thought that was the passage you referred to.

Chairman.] I daresay there is nothing to be said about it.

Mr. *Latham.*] I agree with him. I think "The point in question in this case is whether upon the settlement made in the north of Ireland by virtue of the charter of King James I. under which the towns of Londonderry and Coleraine were founded, and a large tract of country granted by the Crown to the city of London, or to the Irish Society, or to the 12 companies, the terms of the grant simply constituted the Irish Society ordinary trustees for the benefit of the companies; or whether the grant was not coupled with certain public purposes and trusts, independently of the private benefit of the companies." I quite assent to that. That is the question; Lord Cottenham's judgment is admirable, clear, and short, but a judgment on an interlocutory application like that is not quite of the same authority as the judgment on the final hearing. I may first of all take Lord Langdale's judgment, which is an authority because it was confirmed by the House of Lords. Lord Langdale's judgment was a very carefully pronounced judgment, and so far as I know there is not a word in Lord Langdale's judgment from which I dissent. In Paper 34 I understand that Lord Langdale's judgment is set out, but on page 6 there is one passage (I have no objection to it whatever), in italics, which is not in italics in the original judgment.

Chairman.] What you object to is the italic printing?

Mr. *Latham.*] Yes.

Chairman.] I do not know what the history of it is.

Mr. *Latham.*] It rather points to a particular point that is against us, and not in our favour.

Chairman.] It is an accident.

Mr. *Latham.*] I have no doubt it is. The Report of the case is in 7th Beavan, p. 593. I do not think I need go into any of the questions on the argument or the previous statement. The fact is the Committee are just as well acquainted with the broad outlines of the facts as the reporter of this case was. The Committee will remember that the Crown were represented in this case, and that the Crown argued that the rents were wholly or primarily devoted to general public objects; and that the Crown had delegated to the Irish Society a discretionary power which the court had no jurisdiction to control. The Crown was represented there by their own legal officers, and must have heard the whole arguments and the whole proceedings in the case, as well as the judgment, and from 1838 to the present time the Crown have never thought fit to take any proceedings to enforce the same doctrines against the companies. They did not assert it in the course of that argument, and after that judgment they have never thought fit to take any proceedings by information or otherwise against the companies. I only mention that as an indication that the Crown do not seem to have drawn that inference from the judgments in the case which is attempted to be drawn now. Lord Langdale says: "There are four distinct parties whose interests or claims have been brought into question. First, the companies of the City of London, for whom the plaintiffs insist that the Irish Society are mere trustees, bound to account to them, and without any right or discretionary power to apply any part of the income of the property vested in them, for any public, charitable, or other purpose." That is the way in which Lord Langdale considered the case of the companies had been brought before him; that the Irish Society were mere trustees bound to account to them without any discretion. Then, secondly, "the Irish Society, who admit that they have no beneficial interest in the property, and that they are trustees for the companies of any surplus which may remain after answering certain public purposes, but claim to have a discretionary power to apply so much of the income as they think fit for those public purposes, without being liable to account for the same to the companies." Then: "thirdly, the City of London, who resist the claim of the plaintiffs, and claim for themselves a species of visitatorial or superintending power, enabling them to control the conduct and proceedings of the Irish Society; and, fourthly; the Attorney General, who, on behalf of the Crown, suggests that the rents and profits are applicable to public purposes." Then he says: "As nothing can be determined as between co-defendants on the present occasion." We were co-defendants. All the companies, except the Skinner's Company who were plaintiffs, were co-defendants, and he guards his judgment against deciding anything as between co-defendants. "As nothing can be determined as between co-defendants on the present occasion, the substantial question in the cause is, whether the Irish Society has, independently of the companies and without being subject to account to them, a discretionary power

to

to apply any part of the rents and profits of the estates vested in them, for purposes which they deem beneficial to the public, with reference to the plantation in Ireland which is mentioned in the Pleadings." "Any part," was the whole point of the story. It was sufficient for the judgment in this case, if the Court could find that the Irish Society had a discretionary power over which no court or tribunal had control, before finding a surplus, to apply any part of their property for public purposes. That is all that was necessary to decide, and all that was decided in this case. "The Irish Society may be answerable to the City of London, or to the companies, as represented or protected by the City of London, or to the Crown, yet, if it is not answerable to the companies severally in this Court;" that is to say, if each company cannot come alone, "the plaintiffs are not entitled to the relief which they ask by this Bill. On the other hand, if the Society had no such discretionary power, as they claim, and are, as trustees, answerable to the companies, severally, for all their receipts and payments, the plaintiffs are entitled to relief; their right has been denied, and accounts have been refused to them." Then he says: "The Irish Society now subsists under a charter of King Charles II., dated the 10th April 1662; that charter was principally, and as to most of its details, founded on a former charter, granted by King James I., on the 29th March 1613, and from the mode in which the case was stated and argued on all sides, it appears to me necessary to consider the circumstances under which the first charter was granted, so far as those circumstances are proved by the evidence in the cause." Then he states that which the Committee knows, that the six counties had come into the possession of the Crown, "and that King James I., being desirous to promote the public peace and welfare of Ireland, by a civil plantation, of what were called 'those unreformed and waste countries,' proposed to induce English and Scotch persons to emigrate thither, and undertake the plantation on certain terms; and for that purpose he caused to be published a collection of such 'orders and conditions,' as were to be observed by the undertakers, upon the distribution and plantation of the lands. It is plain from these 'orders and conditions,' that the King did not merely contemplate the benefit of the persons;" the force of that passage is in the word "merely;" "the king did not merely contemplate the benefit of the persons who should undertake the plantation or colony, as it is called in another document, but he had a great public object in view, and to carry that into effect desired to engage such of his subjects, as well of Great Britain as of Ireland, as, 'being of merit and ability, should seek the lands, with a mind not only to benefit themselves, but to do service to the Crown and commonwealth.'" Then he says it was intended to appoint commissioners, and commissioners were appointed, and that the King became desirous to engage the City of London in the undertaking, caused to be prepared a paper setting forth motives and reasons. Then he says that these motives and reasons "set forth, that His Majesty might be pleased to grant unto those towns, not only corporations with such liberties and privileges for their good government, &c., as might be convenient, but also the whole territory and country between them, which was above twenty miles in length, bounded by the sea on the north," and so on, "out of which 1,000 acres more might be allotted to each of the towns for their commons, rent free; the rest to be planted with such undertakers as the City of London should think good for their best profit, paying only for the same the easy rent of the undertakers." Then that the motives and reasons further set forth that His Majesty might be pleased to grant to those towns the benefits of the customs and licences; and then were specified the land commodities which the north of Ireland produced, the sea commodities and the profits which London should received by the plantation, and the profits which were described were of a public nature affecting the general welfare of the City." Some importance was put on the circumstance, that the profits expressed in the Motives and Reasons were only public profits; but, of course, I do not exclude the orders and conditions which were at the same time before the city when dealing with Motives and Reasons. The Motives and Reasons did not repeat, and it was not necessary for them to repeat, what was in the Orders and Conditions: "These 'Motives and Reasons' were intended to be, and afterwards became, the subject of conference between certain persons authorized to act for the city, and certain members of the King's Council, and precepts were issued by the Lord Mayor to induce the companies of the City of London to appoint persons to act for them; and the first answers having been given and disliked, because given before any conference had with the King's Council for Ireland, persons were afterwards appointed committees for such conference by the city, and such committees had (as is stated in the precept, dated the 24th of July 1609), received such satisfaction." I do not know that I need read through all this. It is a recital of the facts. At the bottom of the paragraph in the middle of page 607, he says: "Under these circumstances, the Court of Aldermen ordered precepts to be sent to the several companies of the City, requiring them to call their companies together, to understand what every particular man would willingly adventure to the same, so that the committees might be fully instructed to give answer to the Council of Ireland, on Friday then next, the 28th. Precepts were accordingly issued. It does not appear, however, that this course was pursued; for an order of the Court of Common Council, dated the 1st of August following, was made, which, without taking notice of any willing adventures, or any offers of contribution, recites that the Privy Council had, theretofore, signified His Majesty's pleasure to divers aldermen and commoners concerning the intended plantation, and that divers aldermen and commoners, elected by that court, had had conference with the Council for Ireland about the same, and then proceeded as follows: 'It is this day, therefore, upon the motion and commandment of the Lords of His Majesty's Privy Council, signified to divers aldermen and commoners of this City, upon Sunday last (the 30th July), at the council table, concluded and agreed that

that, four wise, grave, and discreet citizens of this city should be presently sent to view the place." And then the people were ordered to be sent at the city's charge to Ireland to survey and view the place. "It appears, therefore," and here I quite assent to what Lord Langdale says, "that at this time the King's Government was in treaty with the City of London, to undertake some portion of his plantation, and that the city, before entering into any engagement, proceeded, by commissioners or agents of their own, and at their own expense, to ascertain the facts necessary for their consideration." Still the matter is only in treaty. Then it appears the Commissioners made their Report. "On the 15th December the Report of the committee was made, and it recommended, in substance, that the sum of money to be expended should only be 15,000 l., and that the same should be raised by way of companies, and in companies by the poll, according to the rate of corn set upon every company; but some of the inferior companies were thought fit to be spared." The way, apparently, that peculiar jurisdiction was exercised was that the Court of Common Council of the City of London issued their precept to the companies, and then the companies had their own records of what the contributory quota of each of their members ought to be. They sometimes used their corporate funds, but if they had not got corporate funds they levied a tax, or rather they passed on the levy made by the city to the individuals. What happened was, I think you have it in evidence somewhere, that if a company did not pay its quota the wardens were imprisoned by the city. They did not imprison the individuals who did not produce the money, but they imprisoned the wardens. So that it was treated by the city as a power of levying money on the companies, and in some cases they did imprison also the individuals in default to the company. I apprehend that the companies asked them to and said, "if anybody is to go to prison send those gentlemen who will not pay, instead of the wardens." It was a personal sort of jurisdiction. The companies sometimes left their wardens in prison for some considerable time while they talked the matter over, but ultimately they always redeemed them and got them out, and then, apparently they had the usual festivity to celebrate the occasion: "after this statement as to the sum and the mode of raising it, the committee declared, that the city of Derry and the town of Coleraine should be the places where two cities should be erected; that into Derry 4,000, and into Coleraine 3,000 acres of land should be laid, and that the rest of the territory and county of Coleraine, estimated at 18,000 acres of temporal lands, should be undertaken. Various privileges varying from those mentioned in the first project were proposed to be claimed, and it was suggested that seven years time should be asked for to make such other reasonable demands as time should show to be needful, but could not presently be foreseen. The report then stated what was proposed to be done, and finally suggested that all things should be managed and ruled as follows: It is thought best that a company be constituted here in London, of persons to be selected for that purpose, and corporations to be carried on in the two cities of Derry and Coleraine, but all things concerning this plantation and undertaking to be managed and performed in Ireland, by advice and direction from the company here in London.' The report containing this suggestion, which was the first germ of the Irish Society was approved by the Common Council and Mr. Recorder, and others were appointed to present the same as the city's answer to the Lords of the Council." Then "on the 30th January 1609-10 at a Common Council then held, it was enacted, granted, and agreed, that Sir Thomas Bennett and 22 other persons then named, and the four Commissioners, or viewers, that were sent from the city into Ireland to view the intended place for plantation, should from time to time meet and have conference as well amongst themselves, as with such Commissioners as should be appointed by the Lords of the Council, touching the intended plantation in Ulster; and the said committees, being named, were to take advised care and consideration of all matters whatsoever, that to them, in their discretion, should be thought fit to be propounded, moved, or done on the behalf of the city touching the same plantation as the matter itself, being of that consequence and importance did merit, and Sir Thomas Bennett was appointed to be the president of the said committees." Then it was further enacted, "that a further taxation should be made," and so on. Then in the middle of page 611: "The Lords of the Council and the committees of the city soon afterwards came to an agreement. Articles were drawn up and settled; they bear date, the 28th January 1609-10, and they were approved and allowed by the Court of Common Council on the 30th of the same month, and from the course of proceeding which I have stated, it appears that although it was at one time suggested that individuals should willingly undertake or voluntarily contribute to the undertaking, everything, at length, centered in the city and in the court of common council as representing the city; the city undertook and was to perform; the city was to provide the funds, and the city was to have the profit, and the city was set in motion by what has been called the pressure of the Crown or of the Government, and was by its agents the contracting party with the Government." The Committee will observe that Lord Langdale treats it as providing the funds and taking the profit; that there was to be a profit out of the transaction, even at this early period: "With the companies otherwise than, as they were involved in or formed part of the general body of the city, the Crown had no negotiations or dealing. The Crown did not, as it seems, concern itself, either with the means by which the city was to perform its undertaking, or with the inducements to be held out to individuals (as that would include the companies; " further, than as such inducements were secured by the general terms of the project, and the motives and reasons presented to the city."

Chairman.] Mr. Walker read that passage to us. I do not gather that you draw any inference from it different to his.

Mr. Latham.] I do know that I do. I think it is pretty clear that the companies were not in the

the first transaction regarded at all, but they were in the second.

Chairman.] Do you assent to those words at the close of the paragraph: "That the levies were compulsory, and enforced against reluctant parties by the power of the city, is shown by abundant evidence in this case."

Mr. Latham.] Yes, I do. I do not think that that makes any difference. As a matter of fact, the monies were paid. They were purchasers, and unwilling purchasers, but none the less purchasers. There were plenty of cases of this description in early days. The transaction was forced upon people, but forced upon them, you must remember, in the last branch of the transaction, as it were, as purchasers upon whom a contract has been forced, and who may just at the last moment say, Sooner than go to prison I will accept the position of paying my money, and I pay my money on the expectation of deriving some profit and benefit from it; that is to say, he elects between two unpleasant events which he will undertake. There was no other compulsion. As a matter of fact, they did pay the money. They might have gone to prison, but they did pay the money because they preferred it. In that sense it was only forced upon them because a more disagreeable alternative was presented to them; but I submit that does not prevent their being purchasers, and purchasers for value. I apprehend that the line of argument is directed to this; I do not know whether Mr. Walker put it exactly in that form, that this was in point of fact an exercise of a power of public taxation; that whether the companies had any benefit offered them or not was quite immaterial; that the taxation process must be severed entirely from the process of granting the land; that the taxation would have fallen on them anyhow, and that the grant of lands was merely gratuitous and voluntary on the part of the Crown. I do not know that that makes any difference. It is not as if the matter lay in agreement and promise, and the Crown could say afterwards it was a promise without consideration, and consequently void like voluntary promises are, but the promise was followed by a conveyance, with the concurrence of the Crown, and the whole doctrine of voluntary agreements, and so forth, does not extend to voluntary assignments and conveyances. If I convey my property to A.B. out and out by deed, although there be no consideration expressed in the deed, I cannot get it back again unless I show fraud or some transaction of that sort. He can hold it against me. If I agree with him for nothing, that is *nudum pactum*, and he cannot enforce it against me; but when I have parted with the property, and he has got it, it is just as much his as if I had sold it him. That is the law, and therefore I do not see the force of the suggestion as to whether the contributions were voluntary or not. I do say, as a matter of fact, when it comes to the last pinch of the matter, that it was contract; that is to say, the companies did agree, although under pressure, and under unpleasant pressure, in the event, to say we will pay the money and take the lands; and that is contract.

Chairman.] But then do you take it Lord Langdale, when he speaks of levies, means levying a price?

Mr. Latham.] I think he does. He took it from the whole history of the transaction, and speaks of it as a questionable mode of taxation; but it was the sum that was required, and they levied and increased their levies as time went on to the sum that was wanted. The position that was put before them was this: there will be a lot of money wanted, we cannot fix the amount, and whatever money is wanted you will have to find. That was put upon them by the Crown, and the city had to come, therefore, upon the companies and say: "You have got something to give and something to gain, and we shall find out by degrees what it is." Then the judgment goes on to state that at the same common council it was ordained that there should be a company constituted and established, and that it should consist of such-and-such people; that was the Irish Society. Then: "This enactment or order was the practical adoption, by the City of London, of the suggestion made by the Commissioners in the preceding month of December. This company, as it is called, though it was only a committee of persons appointed by the Court of Common Council, was the Irish Society previously to its incorporation, and may be conveniently distinguished by that name. It proceeded to carry into effect the agreement entered into with the Crown, and the members of the society were so far recognised by the Crown, that applications were made to them in respect of matters relating to the plantation. Thus, by an order of the Common Council, dated the 7th June 1610, it appears that the King's Commissioners for Ireland desired that 2,000 acres of land, agreed by the articles to be passed to the city, should be spared and left out of the intended assurance, to the intent that the same might be otherwise disposed of, and that Alderman Cockaine, the governor, had signified that the company [society], of themselves, had not power to comply with that desire, but that the same was to be done by act of common council," and so on. Then, "on the 14th of January 1610-11, an order made by the court of common council affords the first formal intimation as to the mode in which the companies of the city were to be concerned or interested in the intended plantation. After authorising the society to let the fishings for seven years, for such fine or rent as they should think fit and convenient, for the most benefit and profit of the city, it was ordered that precepts should forthwith be sent to every several company of the city, to require them to assemble themselves together, and to advise amongst themselves whether they would consent and agree to take and accept of lands, in lieu of the monies already by them disbursed, or to be disbursed, towards the said plantation, and so to build and plant the same at their own cost and charges accordingly, as by the printed book of the plantation was required; or else, whether they would refer the letting of the lands there, and the managing of the whole business there, unto the said governor and assistants of the society for the time being; and that every company be required, by the same precept, to deliver their answer in writing on Saturday then next in the forenoon, at the Guild Hall, unto the said governor and assistants, whether of the two said offers they will embrace; to the intent that the said governor and assistants, upon the answer of the several companies of the city, may make a perfect relation to the next court of common council there to be holden, which was appointed to be on Monday next, touching the resolution of the several companies of the said city, to the intent that such further course might then be taken therein as should be thought fit." That was a proposition that the companies should take the lands in lieu of the monies, and I apprehend that that means that if they did not take the lands the City would feel bound at such time as they should be able to repay the monies. They were to take the lands in lieu of the monies. The city offers this: you have paid so many thousands of pounds, will you take your lands and have done with it, subject to the obligations that were still pending, because these were the early days, subject to the obligations of carrying out the settlement and plantation of the colony, or will you have your money back and leave us the lands? Probably they would not have paid the money back at once, but it would have been a debt, though it might have been a bad debt, but that was the proposition.

Chairman.] Do you deny that if the companies had refused to exercise that option of taking the lands, that the lands would then have remained on the hands of the Irish Society subject to trust?

Mr. *Latham.*] They would have remained in the hands of the Irish Society, but I do not think the land was subject to the trust.

Chairman.] You mean that the judgment of the House of Lords, in fact you have already said that to-day, only affected the 7,000 acres that were reserved.

Mr. *Latham.*] Yes.

Chairman.] And did not affect the divisible lands.

Mr. *Latham.*] No; the divisible lands would have been in this position. If they had remained with the Irish Society they would have fallen within the judgment of the House of Lords; that is to say, supposing the Irish Society had never parted with an acre, I think the judgment of the House of Lords would have been and must have been the same.

Mr. *Sexton.*] So far from intending to give the companies back the money they had paid, in case they did not take the lands, did not the city say that even if the companies did not take up the lands they would still have to bear the further charge of digging and planting?

Mr. *Latham.*] Yes, quite right. The city said, "we are under the obligation to the Crown, and have got to provide for it somehow, and you are not going to get off the further contributions you must go on exactly as in the past you have done"; and I submit what they meant was, that where it is a question of lands in lieu of money, those moneys shall remain a debt; and remember, the city did accept that sort of obligation because if the companies did decline to take the lands, the city did take over their interest and become adventurers. With any of those blocks, they paid the out-going companies out of their city funds for the money they had advanced.

Mr. *Sexton.*] I should feel difficulty in seeing how the money already paid can be regarded in the light of purchase, seeing that even if a particular company did not take up any land they were still to bear a further charge.

Mr. *Latham.*] But it would go into account, and the city would pay back.

Mr. *Sexton.*] Where does that appear?

Mr. *Latham.*] That appears in the transactions with the Coopers and Browne Bakers and that is in evidence somewhere. My friend will find it for you. Then the next precept at the bottom of page 616 is: "And for as much as the governors and committees for the plantation in Ireland are now earnestly to take care for the letting and disposing of the lands in the county of Coleraine, and other lands so undertaken, to be used and managed for the benefit of this city, which would otherwise prove a great hindrance and loss, especially for that the time of the year is now most convenient for the plantation to proceed, yet it is thought fit" .

Chairman.] Surely those words imply that the public obligation, whatever it amounted to, lay upon all the lands.

Mr. *Latham.*] The public obligation is planting, on the owners of the lands.

Chairman.] Quite so.

Mr. *Latham.*] I think it did; the obligation of planting. I will call attention to what I deem to be planting.

Chairman.] There is no distinction drawn in those words between the divisible and undivided land.

Mr. *Latham.*] Certainly not, nor could there be at this time. The division has not been provided for yet. It is still in the hands of the Irish Society. They were in negotiation for division, but till the division took place the obligation continued, and I have accepted the position that, so far as the original planting and settlement was concerned, which was a temporary object, as I submit, and for a very short time, all the people who became undertakers became liable to plant and settle, that is to say, it was their duty, and the Crown objected if they did not.

Here is the document about the Coopers and Browne Bakers. I believe it is not in evidence as yet, but it is in the Appellants' Appendix for the Skinners' Company, pages 39 and 40. It is dated 15th September 1615: "Whereas, by Act of Common Councill, made the tenth day of July 1611, it was enacted and agreed that a present taxation should be made of the summe of Ten thousand pounds for a further supply towards the plantation in Ireland over and above the summe of Twenty thousand pounds formerly taxed upon all the several Companies of this Citty, according to the former allotment and proportion,

whereby

whereby the last moyety of the said Twenty thousand pounds was taxed and assessed, and that p'cepts should be then sent forth to all the sev'all Companies of this City not only for the levying of suc the one moyety of the said Ten thousand pounds but also to require ev'y sev'all Company to advise amongst themselves and to certifie in writing at a tyme p'fixed whether they would willingly yield to the said supply of Ten thousand pound's or be contented to lose all such money as they have already disbursed towards the said plantation, and passe ov' their right to such as will undertake the payment for them, and to free them of all other payments hereafter touching the said plantation, and thereupon p'cepts were sent fourth accordingly and the Company of Coopers and Browne Bakers of this City did c'tifie in writing that they were unwilling to yield to the said supply of Ten thousand pounds, but were contented to loose," it is in that sense, "l-o-o-se" is the word, "all such moneys as they had formerly disbursed towards the said plantation. Whereupon it is ordered by this Court that Mr Chamberlain shall disburse and pay all such somes of money as should have been taxed and assessed upon the said Companies of Coopers and Browne Bakers for the supply of the said Ten thousand pounds, and the City to receive all the benefit and profit as well already due as hereafter shall grow due to the said Companyes by the said plantation in Ireland." So that they paid them out.

Mr. Sexton.] Did they give back what they had paid already?

Mr. Latham.] I think so. They were to be paid: "All such sums of money as should have been taxed and assessed upon the said companies of Coopers and Browne Bakers for the supply of the said 10,000 l." That was the agreement; to pass over their right to such, that is to the city, as will undertake the payment for them; that is the payment that was then due, and to free them of all other payments.

Mr. Sexton.] Does not it appear they were relieved from the payment then; apparently in discussion, but they did not get back what they had paid. They got nothing it appears.

Mr. Latham.] I think Mr. Sexton is right, that they did not get back the 10,000 l. What they got was the money that was levied upon them, but not paid.

Mr. Sexton.] Relieved from the pending obligation.

Mr. Latham.] Relieved from the pending obligation and the future payments. They did not get back their share, whatever they had paid of the 10,000 l.

Mr. Sexton.] The word "loose" is "lose" then?

Mr. Latham.] I think it was "lose." At any rate, there it shows the offer of the city. It shows that, notwithstanding, the future obligation might fall to contribute to the payment of the costs, charges, and expenses of the plantations in Ireland, the city undertook, and by that transaction, carried into effect the undertaking to take on itself that burden for the company which declined to go on. They could not let a company out, because that would increase the proportions payable by those who remained in. They were obliged to leave the proportions as they originally stood, because otherwise every company would have complained, and would have said, if somebody goes, that makes our charge the more; that is not fair. What the city did was this: they said, we will take over your liabilities; you remain liable to be assessed, but we take it over, and recoup you, and that was the transaction that took place with the Coopers and Brown Bakers.

Mr. Sexton.] With regard to the future obligations, the Coopers and Brown Bakers found somebody else to take them up.

Mr. Latham.] The city undertook to do it for them, and offered to do it for everybody else, not the Irish Society. Then at page 517 the judgment proceeds: "From these documents it appears to have been understood, that the companies of the city had not previously undertaken the plantation, but that the plantation, being undertaken by the city, was, in default of other means, to be carried into execution by the society, or committee appointed by the city, but that it was thought desirable that the undertaking should be, at least in part, performed by the incorporated companies; and that the city, having entered into the undertaking, having, by their power, levied the means of carrying it on, and being actually engaged in carrying it on, by their governor and committee or company, offered to each of the incorporated companies an option, either to undertake the plantation of a portion of the lands according to the printed book for plantation, or to refer the letting and disposing thereof to the governor and committees. It was an offer (which, by some of the companies, was at this time accepted), to give or allot lands, in lieu of the monies disbursed and to be disbursed towards the plantation; and the companies were informed, that whether they accepted the land or not, they were to pay, and bear their proportions of the charges of buildings, fortifications, and freeing titles, and that, notwithstanding their acceptance of the lands, they should be partakers of all benefits of fishings, with the profits of the towns and other immunities whatsoever."

That is subject, as I have pointed out, to the offers of the city to take over those rights and obligations from them: "After these proceedings the undertaking continued to be carried on by the company or society under the control of the city, the money mentioned was levied." The city advanced moneys to the society, and were afterwards repaid. I do not think there is anything in that. He does not name the companies there when he says, "The undertaking continued to be carried on by the company or the society," that is the Irish Company or Irish Society, "under the control of the city." Then he says: "It is apparent that at this time the companies were understood to have an interest in the sums they had been compelled to pay, and the Court of Common Council was probably understood to have power to declare a forfeiture." That is Lord Langdale's view of the matter, that although

although it had bought a compulsory share, still it was treated as if they had an interest in it to get the money back, or get something for it." During the time to which I have hitherto referred, no charter had been granted, but the city had proceeded on the faith that an assurance of the land would be made to them. The lands are, in the precept of the last day of January 1610–11, mentioned as having been granted, though, in fact, they were not so, and on the 5th of January 1612–13, it was ordered that Mr. William Cockayne, the first governor of the company, should be and continue governor until the assurance from the King unto the city concerning the plantation should be obtained and finished." Then he says that the first charter was obtained, and it recites the King's intention. I need not go through that. Then at page 621 there is Lord Langdale's comment on the charter: "From this statement it is apparent that the Irish Society originated with the city, and that the powers conferred upon it by the charter, though by no means identical with, were suggested by the powers given to it by the order of the 30th January 1610, and it may reasonably be inferred that it was at the request of the City, that the constitution of the society, and the powers to be conferred upon it were considered and granted by the Crown." No doubt it was. It was the result of a considerable amount of negotiation. "But this makes no difference in the effect of the constitution, or in the inferences to be deduced from the powers granted to the society by the charter, and it is, I think, impossible to read and consider the charter without coming to the conclusion that the powers granted to the society were more extensive than, and very different from, any which in the ordinary course of affairs are vested, or would upon this occasion, have been invested, in mere trustees for the benefit of particular undertakers." That is perfectly clear. There were powers of government, and so forth, and all sorts of things like the passing of Orders for the City of London, which could not possibly be transferable or alienable.

Chairman.] Were those words which you laid emphasis upon of franchises, privileges, &c., limited to the 7,000 acres, do you think?

Mr. *Latham.*] I should think not. I am quite willing to answer, but I should like to think first.

Chairman.] That is rather your position.

Mr. *Latham.*] I do not think so. I do not know. When you come to read the powers, they were almost all powers relating to municipal corporations. I do not think those franchises and powers that were granted, could affect the divisible lands, because they were all powers expressly relating to the incorporated bodies of the City of London and Coleraine. I do not think in express terms they were limited to the 7,000 acres. There was a power to create manors, but that was not necessarily a Royal franchise.

Mr. *Sexton.*] Rights of Admiralty over the seashore.

Mr. *Latham.*] Quite so. Lord Langdale goes on to speak of them in this way: "The powers, indeed, are many of them of a public and political nature and considering the charter in connection with the contemporaneous circumstances I think it must have been understood that the powers and estates granted to the Irish Society were given for the public purposes of the plantation, and so far as was consistent with those purposes, for the benefit of the City of London;" there was the benefit.

Chairman.] And these were the purposes.

Mr. *Latham.*] The benefit, so far as was consistent with those purposes, the express purposes. A discretion is vested in the body as to how much was wanted for those purposes, and so far as consistent with the purposes, so far for the benefit of the City of London.

Mr. *Sexton.*] Were not the purposes inexhaustible?

Mr. *Latham.*] Certainly they were not treated as inexhaustible at that time, and I think I shall show when I come to the orders and conditions that they were all exhausted in a short time.

Chairman.] You will deal with them when you come to the end of this part of your argument.

Mr. *Latham.*] When I come to the Orders and Conditions I shall come to what the purposes were. They are not expressed in the charter. It could be granted that the charter did not exhaust public purposes, because purposes in the charter are clearly limited to the society and are offices and functions imposed on the society, and which were not alienable and could not be passed from them to somebody else, as for instance, this question of discretion as to passing laws and ordinances. If there was anything it must be found in the Orders and Conditions. Lord Langdale proceeds: "And independently of the public or general benefits which might accrue from the encouragement or increase of trade with Ireland, and the employment of persons who might be disposed to emigrate thither, and the better government and rule of the city and county of Londonderry, it was intended and understood, that the companies of London were, with the burthen of undertaking the plantation of such lands as might be allotted to them, to receive such benefits as were offered to, and might be realised by other undertakers," that is private undertakers, "on the conditions proposed by the original book for plantation, accompanied by such additional advantages and protection, as were intended to be secured by the power and interest of the City of London, and by the constitution of the Irish Society, and the powers conferred upon it."

Chairman.] Those are important words, "on the conditions proposed by the original book." It is all limited by that.

Mr. *Latham.*] Yes, I think so. We are dealing now with the first charter. The second charter conveyed no intimation whatever as to obligations.

Chairman.] That is true.

Mr. Latham.] But the reason why I have distinguished obligations from trust is that there might have been, and I can conceive the argument being put in that way though the second charters was different from the first charter in cutting away all the previous history and granting afresh; still there may have been concurrently with the subsistence of the second charter the old personal obligation, if I may say so, if there was any, on the society and those who took under them to fulfil the duties of the plantation. I do not think it was put so, but I am dealing as fairly as I can with the Committee in every way that it can be put against me. Then "the companies of London are in no way mentioned in the charter, nor does the Crown appear to have noticed them at the time in any way; but the previous appointment of the society, committees or company, by the Court of Common Council, and the previous proposals and offers made by the society to the companies, as well as the events which soon followed the date of the charter, appear to me to show, that the companies were intended to profit in the way that I have mentioned; and it would further appear, that not the 12 companies only who are mentioned in the order of the 26th February 1610–11, but all the other companies had consented to become undertakers. The charter expressly states, that the society was to have power to make ordinances, on the part and behalf of the City of London, and it does not seem that the society did, under the charter, arrogate any independent authority." Then in April 1613 additional funds were wanting, and so forth, and at the bottom of page 624, he goes on: "By a further order of common council, made on the same day, after reciting that," "In so noble a work so taken to heart by the King, and wherein this city, upon the hopeful success thereof, had already expended and were like further to expend great sums of money, it was generally thought fit (as a matter much importuning the advancement of the said work, as well for the general satisfaction of the several companies of the city who had undertaken the same, as also for accommodating such other affairs and circumstances, as from time to time thereafter should be offered to the further consideration of this court), that some great and worthy magistrate of the city, accompanied by some commoner of special countenance and credit, should be sent into those parts, on the behalf of the city to take exact notice, view, and account of the whole work of plantation, and of every circumstance and thing appertaining thereunto." The city clearly had the satisfaction of the companies in view at that time. Then, at the top of page 626: "This order is remarkable, as showing the great power which, after the charter, the City of London exercised, and contemplated the future exercise of, over the plantation and the affairs thereof, as well as the importance which was, at that time, attached to the satisfaction which should be given to the companies. No doubt seems to have been entertained, that the society, whatever its own powers might be, would act according to the suggestions and views of the city, and that the city, whatever other objects they had to promote, were bound, in duty or in policy, to satisfy the companies. As the necessary expense was not yet defrayed, as the power of the city over the companies afforded the only means of raising the money, and as public and general objects were to be attained, it does not appear difficult to account for the conduct of the several parties." Then it states that full instructions were given; "and the report after stating several abuses and negligences which had occurred, and the proceedings of the commissioners in respect thereof, and stating their opinions that, if it should stand with the liking of the committee, some convenient wall of brick or stone might thereafter be made about the Castle of Coleraine, proceeded as follows: 'Whereas it was generally desired that a division should be made;'" we come to a division here, "'of all the lands, by and amongst the several companies undertaking in this plantation, we have with great travail, first viewed the lands, and carefully inquired after the true value of every Ballibo; and thereupon with great care and pains, and with the assistance and advice of the gentlemen of the country, the City's agents and surveyors proceeded to make an equal division of the land into 12 parts, wherein we have used our best skill and diligence;'" the 12 parts were for the 12 companies; "'and have done the same as equally as possibly we could devise, the form of which division we have here brought you together with the plot of the same. But for the city of Londonderry, and the 4,000 acres there; and the town of Coleraine, and the 3,000 acres appointed to the same, the ferries and the fishings, we are of opinion that a division cannot be fitly made of them, but the rents and profits of them may be divided and go amongst the several companies; and we advise that, upon the division it be provided that, where a proportion of land shall want timber to build with, that the company, to whose share it may fall, may have sufficient timber out of the woods next adjoining, and fitting for that use, to be assigned to them by the City's agents.'" Now that is contemplating a division and contemplating a reservation, and I think here is the first place where we come to the 3,000 and 4,000 acres, and they thought a division of those could not be fitly made, and what the subsequent events indicate, as the reason they thought it was not fit, was that those were the best lands to preserve for the general performance of the trust or obligation, or whatever it was, but that the rents should be divided if there was a surplus. Rents and profits would mean, I apprehend, net rents and profits. Then, "this report was approved by the Common Council. That part of it which related to the division of lands was almost immediately acted upon. That part which states the opinion of the commissioners that the rents and profits of the town lands, ferries, and fishings might be divided, and go amongst the several companies, has naturally been much dwelt upon on behalf of the plaintiffs. What notice may have been taken of it at the time does not now appear, but, in connection with it, we must bear in mind not only that it is in perfect accordance with the precept of the last day of January 1610–11, but also that very considerable and expensive public works were still in progress; that the City was then conceived to have power to levy, compulsorily, all such monies as should be be required; and that some income, of not inconsiderable amount, was at that time derived, or about to be derived from the property not then to be divided. At a time when it was thought that money could be levied by taxation whenever it wanted, the necessity, or even the propriety or prudence of reserving some property producing income to answer the general purposes of the plantation, may not have been suggested; or, if suggested, may have yielded to the greater prudence of holding out prospects of income or profit to those upon whom the burden was imposed by a power which, even if thought lawful, must be considered as arbitrary; and was, according to the evidence in many instances, not obeyed without reluctance on one side, and the application of force on the other." My friend, Mr. Romer is here now. I do not know whether you could indicate the course you intend to pursue.

(*Chairman.*] Mr. Romer is for the Irish Society.

Mr. *Romer.*] Yes, Sir.

Mr. *Latham.*] I thought possibly the Commissioners would be able to give an indication as to the course they would pursue, so that Mr. Romer might know when to be here.

(*Chairman.*] It depends upon you to a great extent.

Mr. *Latham.*] I do not think there is any probability of my finishing my argument before the Committee rise to-day.

(*Chairman.*] Then in any case we should be glad if Mr. Romer would appear here to-morrow, and we will then hear what Mr. Romer wants to say.

Mr. *Romer.*] I shall be very short.

(*Chairman.*] We have had some doubts as to what it was the Irish Society wish to maintain, because we have said we cannot go, naturally and obviously, behind the decision of the House of Lords in 1845.

Mr. *Romer.*] I quite follow that.

Chairman.] Which clearly imposes trusts on the lands held by the Irish Society.

Mr. *Romer.*] Yes, it will be only to try and point out in the view of the Irish Society what their exact legal position is, accepting, of course, the decision in the Skinners' case loyally.

(*Chairman.*] That will be interesting enough, and we will hear that. Do you think you can finish to-day, Mr. Latham?

Mr. *Latham.*] I will try. If I have anything left I shall be able to employ the interval in reducing it to the smallest possible space.

(*Chairman.*] I am not sure, I do not the least wish to interrupt you, that it is necessary to read through all Lord Langdale's judgment. We have it before us in our own print, and I was only wondering whether it would not save you time.

Mr. *Latham.*] I will try and point out the particular passages. It is perfectly true you have it in print, and can refer to it afterwards, but the difficulty is in reading a judgment, if you come to a particular passage it may refer to something that occurred before. I think I can perhaps avoid reading it all. The passage I have just read refers to the reservation of special property. On page 839 he says, "It appears that the companies without waiting for their conveyances, planted and placed divers numbers of British on their proportions of lands, and expended very large sums of money thereon." There Lord Langdale accepts the position that although conveyances had not been granted they had proceeded with the plantation; "but independently of these undertakings, the works which were to be done at the general charge of the city continued to be expensive, and additional sums were levied on the companies." Then he speaks of the license in Mortmain, and six lines down that paragraph he points out that under the license in Mortmain, the conveyance is made absolute; and when Lord Langdale says "absolute" he means absolute, – in some without, and in others with the reservation of rent to the Irish Society. The license for the companies to hold in Mortmain was also a license to the society to convey to them, and it contained a recital, that the companies, in testimony of their true obedience to the Crown, &c., had disbursed, expended, and bestowed divers great sums of money for and towards the building, fortifying, planting, strengthening, and improving the city of Derry and the town of Coleraine," and so forth, "and for speedier proceeding therein were desirous to have conveyances of the land they intended to build on; therefore, and to the end that the several companies might be the better encouraged and enabled to perfect and finish the intended plantation, and in future times reap some gain and benefit of their great travails and expenses taken and bestowed therein,' the licence was granted. The companies of London were thus recognised by the Crown as parties interested in the plantation, as undertakers, and after the conveyances were made, the companies may be considered as entitled to the lands allotted and conveyed to them (subject to the conditions of plantation as to particular lands)," the exact meaning of that parenthesis I am not quite sure of. My first impression was that when he spoke as to particular lands he meant those lands specially reserved for forests, but I think it is possible, and considering it, I think it is probable he means the condition of plantation, and when he uses the phrase "particular lands," he means the land to each particular lot. It comes back to the same thing, that it is the condition of plantation, and the condition of plantation only, "and as respectively entitled to all the profits to arise from those allotments, which (subject to the performance of those conditions) could lawfully be made. The lands not allotted, together with the ferries and fishings, remained vested in the Irish Society, and the City of London, or the Irish Society on its behalf, were bound to the performance of those general and public works, which were among the conditions of plantation; and for the purposes of those general and public works were, or were supposed to be entitled to levy money on the companies for whose satisfaction they, at least, professed themselves to be bound

23 July 1890.

bound to provide." So that the general and public works he treats as the duty, which they clearly were, of the Irish Society and not of the companies.

Chairman.] But does not he say that they were entitled to levy money on the companies?

Mr. *Latham.*] Yes, he does, and no doubt they were supposed to be entitled to levy money on the companies, and he apprehended they would do that, and that the companies were jointly interested in the undertaking.

Mr. *Sexton.*] He says the levying was for the several public works.

Mr. *Latham.*] Yes; and undoubtedly at that time it was supposed the city had the power to levy on them. You will find later in the judgment he drew attention to the difference in the position when the second charter was executed, and that that power to levy was no longer supposed to exist.

Chairman.] But the liability for public works is clearly recognised in these words, though whether exhausted or not by what happened is another question.

Mr. *Latham.*] I agree; I think the Chairman is perfectly right, and that at that time I think we must say that it was supposed if the Irish Society were short of funds for carrying out the public works they might still go on levying. Heavy duties of fortification and so forth were incumbent on them. Then: "About five or six years after the conveyances were made, further complaints were made by the Crown that the conditions of plantation had not been performed. The complaints were laid before the Court of Common Council on the 2nd of June 1624; they principally regarded the general works of the plantation, but in part, the conduct of the plantation of the lands conveyed to the companies." You will find that all through the latter part of this judgment, Lord Langdale distinguishes between the general works and particular works in that sort of way. The general works he always treated as what he said before, as primarily, I put it no higher, incumbent on the Irish Society. "As to the former, answer was made by the Court of Common Council; as to the latter, the subject was made known to the several companies, and, on their part, the Common Council complained that the undertakers had been impeded by monopolies and patents of privilege contrary to the King's Grant. The answer, though approved in the Court of Common Council, was, for alteration in matter of form and works of the like nature, referred to the Irish Society and others who had joined with them in drawing the answer. Not long afterwards, and in the beginning of the reign of Charles I., the King having referred certain matters relating to the plantation to Lords Grandison, Carew, and Chichester, the Chancellor of the Exchequer did, upon their advice, require the City of London to do many things then specified, most of which were general works, but some of them affected the conduct of the companies; the Court of Common Council made answer these requisitions, not only with respect to the general works, but also with respect to the plantation undertaken by the companies; and as to the first demand, which was that a fair new church should be built, they say, that although the work be very chargeable, and that the stocks of all the chief companies of London are already exhausted by means of the plantation, yet, in obedience to His Majesty's pleasure (the work also in itself being pious), they will forthwith give order to make preparation for erecting a fair new church, and will, so soon as conveniently they may, finish and beautify, and adorn the same with seats fit and convenient." You will observe they put it, not only in obedience to His Majesty's pleasure, but also on the object being an object which in those days was considered important and very pious, and they accepted it, not as a duty or obligation, but they said we will do it. Then he comes to the information in the Star Chamber. I am not going into that again, but it is not inconvenient to read it here. He says: "The defendants were charged with the deceitful and undue procuring of the Charter of James, and with wilful breach of the articles agreed upon between the Lords of the Council and the committees appointed by the city on the 28th of January 1609-10, and with the wilful breach of trust which the King had reposed in them. It appears that during the proceedings, it was insisted on by the city that they had nothing to do with the plantation, and that their name was used merely for the transaction of affairs, and for the levying of monies upon the companies for the plantation. This point was overruled, and the court having adjudged that many offences, both of omission and commission, had been committed, inflicted upon the City of London and upon the Irish Society, a fine of 70,000 *l.*, and decreed, that the patent and their estates and interests should be surrendered, and be brought into court to be cancelled, and after reciting that the greatest part of the lands were, by the society, passed over to divers companies of the city, and by them demised to their farmers, who were not defendants to the suit, and therefore not liable to the censure of the court (although in the opinion of the court they might justly have been censured if parties), it was directed, that if the companies and their farmers should not in pursuance of the intention of the sentence, surrender their estates, the Attorney General should exhibit an information, and bring them also to the judgment of the court." That was read to the Committee by Mr. Walker.

Chairman.] "Farmers" means tenants, I suppose.

Mr. *Latham.*] Yes; I think "farmers" means tenants. Then: "This decree, if lawful," as Lord Langdale guards himself by saying, "entitled the Crown to recover not only a fine of 70,000 *l.*, but the possession of all the lands and hereditaments which remained vested in the Irish Society, and it was accompanied by an intimation that these, and also all the lands conveyed to the companies, or demised to the farmers, might be recovered if the Attorney General thought fit to sue from them. Steps were early taken for the execution of the decree, and proceedings were commenced against the 12 companies." It is very important to see what Lord Langdale's view there

23 *July* 1890.

there was, because it affects the real purport of the decision in the Star Chamber. He takes the view, apparently, that the decision of the Star Chamber was not a decision on the merits at all, but that the company and the Crown came to terms as best they could after considerable negotiation by the Crown, because, as appears from the *scire facias* itself, the companies never appeared, and judgment was pronounced in default, because it had been agreed that the lands were to go back. "In these circumstances, a negotiation for money took place between the Crown and the city. The city, pressed by the impending fine and forfeiture, and by other charges made against them, offered a composition of 100,000 *l.* The Crown endeavoured to obtain more, and the city, acting or professing to act only for the companies, and in concurrence with them, offered to give up all the fishings and all the lands held by the society, or by the companies, and all arrears of rent. And at length, after a protracted negotiation, the fine was ultimately compromised, and the city agreed to surrender the lands, fishings, and customs in Ireland, and to pay a sum of 12,000 *l.*, and thereupon proceedings to repeal the Letters Patent were made available by consent or default;" that was the proceedings in Chancery. "But afterwards, in other political circumstances, the city endeavoured to obtain relief from this oppression, and to make available before the House of Commons those arguments which had failed before the Court of Star Chamber; and the House of Commons, then advancing to the ascendancy which it soon afterwards obtained, took upon itself to pass resolutions;" he is not much more complimentary to the House of Commons than he is to the Star Chamber, "declaring its opinion on the judgment of the Star Chamber, and declaring its opinion of the conduct of the city and of the companies respecting the plantation. The proceeding appears to have ended in the King's expressing himself to be willing to restore the plantation to its former footing, and it was proposed to confirm the rights of the companies by Act of Parliament; but civil wars supervened, and it was under the power of Cromwell that the charter and the estates derived under it, were first pretended to be renewed."

Chairman.] I notice that neither the judges here, nor you, say anything about Cromwell, or what he did. There was nothing material I suppose happened.

Mr. Latham.] It is very material, but it is all wiped out afterwards. Cromwell went through exactly the same process as the others did. He granted a fresh charter and a fresh licence in mortmain, and fresh conveyances were made, and a fresh process gone through again by Cromwell. The chief difference between Cromwell's charter and the second charter of the King was that Cromwell does not found it, as you may imagine, on the promise of the King, but founds it on the proceedings of Parliament.

Chairman.] Did the courts ignore all that went on in the protectorate?

Mr. Latham.] Yes, they ignored it absolutely. There was a general Act which wiped away everything that had been done.

Chairman.] In the judgment given in 1663, it was a point of honour not to notice what was done in the protectorate.

Mr. Latham.] Apparently.

Mr. Elton.] There are law reports for that period.

Chairman.] Are they accepted?

Mr. Elton.] Yes. Generally with some slur on the reporter, but still they are quoted and quotable.

Mr. Latham.] They are not frequently in use except in a certain special class of cases with which Mr. Elton is more familiar than I am. Then, "Soon after the Restoration, on the 10th of April 1662, King Charles II. granted the charter, under which the Irish Society now exists, and from which the subsisting titles to the lands and estates thereby granted are derived. This charter recites the charter of James, the grants made by the society, which was constituted under that charter, and that the society retained in its own hands 'such part of the tenements and hereditaments as were not properly divisible for defraying the charge of the general operation of the plantation;' it further recites the repeal of the charter, the promise made by King Charles I. to restore the same, and that it appeared that the society and other companies of the city had expended very great sums of money in building and planting of the county of Londonderry and Coleraine, and then proceeds to express that the present grant was made to the intent that the society, or some other society." Those are the words I read to the Committee out of the charter: "By the present letters patent to be created, and the companies of the City of London and their respective assigns and under tenants might according to their former several rights and interests therein, be restored to all the estates vested in them by force of the former letters patent, and to the intent that there might be a new society of the new plantation in Ulster, and a new incorporation of the City of Derry, and for the further and better settling and planting of the said county towns and places with trade and inhabitants. This grant, therefore, is expressly made for the purpose of restoring the rights derived under the former charter;" he does not say the rights granted by the former charter only, but he uses a wider phrase, namely, "the rights derived under the former charter," which covers the whole of the conveyances, as it clearly means, because it referred to them, "for restoring the rights and interests of the companies of London, and for further and better settling and planting the county, etc., with trade and inhabitants. The lapse of forty-nine years and the change of circumstances made it necessary that there should be some difference between the clauses in the charters of 1613 and 1662, and other differences may have been suggested by former experience, or by the present views and situations of the parties. They are sufficient to show that the charter of Charles was framed with considerable care and attention, and was not a mere transcript of the charter of James. In the charter of James, no mention was made of the companies

companies, but the city and the society acting under the charter of James had made conveyances to the companies, and had levied money for the general purposes of the plantation on the companies, and the intention of the charter of Charles was to restore the Irish Society, and also the companies of the City of London to their former rights; and after making due allowance for all the differences which occur, the charter of Charles appears to me to be substantially, as it was avowedly, a restoration of the charter of James. The two charters are alike in their general purview; in their general object, in the means adopted to carry that object into effect, and in the powers conferred for that purpose." I entirely agree, but subject to the events which occurred subsequently. "Under the new charter, new conveyances were made to the companies, and the Irish Society has ever since continued in the exclusive possession of the town lands, ferries, and fisheries, and has managed or let the same, and received and applied the rents thereof by its own authority. It has applied portions of the rents for purposes alleged to be public or charitable, and has from time to time stated a surplus, to be in its hands, and has paid certain sums, in respect of that surplus, to the twelve companies in equal shares. On one occasion when money was wanting, the society applied, not to the City of London, as in the early period of its history, for further levies, but to the companies for voluntary contributions," the levies had dropped; "and on another occasion, in which it became necessary to make a statement respecting the timber, it represented itself to be entrusted for the companies, and seised of a considerable salmon fishery and other estates in the county of Londonderry, in trust for the companies of the city over and besides the several proportions of lands which had been granted;" that was a special question that was involved in that case which does not really much affect us in this case. "The society, have on other occasions stated themselves to be 'trustees' for the companies, and there is an instance in which one is rather surprised to find them refusing to render any account to the city, and stating themselves to be accountable only to the twelve chief companies of London, to which all the surplus funds under their management not disposed of in the performance of the duties which the charter imposed upon them were regularly transferred and paid"; they had made a mistake in their legal position. "It does not, however, appear to me to be necessary to pursue further the history of the conduct and transactions of the society. The society have vested in them under a Royal charter a very considerable property, in which they have not collectively or individually as members of the society, any beneficial interest, and in respect of which they are invested with great powers, and have important duties to perform, in a sense, therefore, they are trustees." Lord Langdale knew very well what he meant when he said so. The word "trust," is a word a little liable to be abused, and especially when you come to what is called a public trust. Every officer in the army is frequently spoken of as being in a position of public trust, and so he is; but that is not a trust that can be enforced in the Court of Chancery. There is always a little danger in using these words. He says: "in a sense, therefore, they are trustees. The property is part of that which was granted for the purposes of the plantation, and the powers possessed by the society, as well as the duties with which it is charged, have all of them reference to the plantation. Now the objects of the plantation, and the intents and purposes thereof, were of a nature partly public and political, and partly private, regarding only the interests of particular undertakers, whether corporate bodies or individuals. When the Crown treated only with individuals, and made grants to them, it imposed only conditions which were annexed to the enjoyment of the property bestowed, and the rights of the Crown to enforce the conditions constituted the security which it held for the public and political objects which were contemplated." There he is speaking of the Crown dealing with individuals, and the observation applies not only to the companies but to every undertaking throughout the whole of the six counties; and, I suppose, probably if one were to go further in the history of the matter, it would apply equally under other charters and other transactions to nine-tenths of the land of Ireland, the title to all of which was derived under escheats at one time or another, and under processes of plantation either by Elizabeth, or the Stuarts, or the Protector, or King William the Third.

Mr. *Sexton.*] Yes, that is so, certainly; and some of it two or three times escheated.

Mr. *Latham.*] "But when it treated with the City of London, the case seems to have been varied, not by any change in the conditions imposed upon particular undertakers, but by the grant of powers and privileges which could not be bestowed on particular undertakers, and were intended to effect more important objects, to afford special means of enforcing the conditions which affected all, and special encouragements to undertakers, both in their particular character as such, and as members of the City of London, or persons enjoying the protection of the City, or partaking of the benefit of its general prosperity."

Chairman.] You think that Lord Langdale meant to exclude from the words, "of the City of London" the companies?

Mr. *Latham.*] Yes; I think so.

Chairman.] Is he in this passage drawing a distinction between the city and the companies? He is in other places.

Mr. *Latham.*] I think so. He is speaking only of the treaty with the City of London. My friend calls my attention to the previous paragraph, which deals with it: "Now, the objects of the plantation, and the intents and purposes thereof, were of a nature partly public and political, and partly private, regarding only the interests of particular undertakers, whether corporate bodies or individuals." There the companies would be mentioned in the corporate bodies, and then he comes to the treaty with the City of London as a different treaty: "When the Crown treated only with individuals, and made grants to them, it imposed only conditions which

were

were annexed to the enjoyment of the property bestowed, and the right of the Crown to enforce the conditions, constituted the security which it held for the public and political objects which were contemplated. But when it treated with the city of London, the case seems to have been varied, not by any change in the conditions imposed upon particular undertakers, but by the grant of powers and privileges which could not be bestowed on particular undertakers."

Chairman.] Surely the implication is that the burdensome conditions remained, but that the Crown could not grant those powers and privileges?

Mr. Latham.] Powers.

Chairman.] I am only taking the ordinary layman's construction.

Mr. Latham.] I agree, and I think not by any change in the conditions imposed on particular undertakers. What he means is, what he said before about the particular properties undertaken by undertakers; but then he says, on a great body like the City of London they could confer special powers of government, and so forth, which could not be possibly conferred on a trade company.

Chairman.] Undoubtedly, but you do not allow that in those two paragraphs, there is an intention in Lord Langdale's mind to leave all the burdens upon the companies who are particular undertakers, whether as corporate bodies or individuals, but to explain why they could not give them powers and privileges.

Mr. Latham.] I think it is pretty clear; what he means was that there were certain powers and privileges of a costly nature which require considerable expenditure, and so forth, and property which was given to the Irish Society, or reserved to the Irish Society, was liable not only to the conditions of plantation, but liable also to pay for the expenditure on these powers and privileges; that the powers and privileges involved the paying for their exercise. The conditions of plantation were imposed equally on all undertakers, that is the condition of planting, &c., that the broad conditions of plantation and settling was imposed on everybody, but in addition there was imposed on the City of London some special powers and privileges which would involve the expenditure of money.

Mr. G. H. Lee.] The City being one of the corporate bodies.

Mr. Latham.] I think not; "and special arrangements to undertakers, both in their particular characters as such, and as members of the City of London, or persons enjoying the protection of the city, or partaking of the benefit of its general prosperity. The objects were such as affected the general welfare of Ireland and the whole realm; these were the objects of the Crown; such as affected the general welfare of the City of London, these may be considered to have been the objects of the city, and such as affected the particular welfare and interests of the companies or of individual undertakers."

Chairman.] Is not he drawing a distinction between the particular welfare and interests of the companies in this case, and the objects affecting the general welfare of Ireland and the whole realm?

Mr. Latham.] Clearly; he distinguishes the public objects of the charter from the private advantages.

Chairman.] But those public objects lay upon the possessions of the companies.

Mr. Latham.] The public objects lay only upon the Irish Society of the City of London. The planting and settling were a public object in one sense. It was with a view to get Ireland settled and planted that the whole process was undertaken, and in a sense the public objects were imposed on the companies; but it is clear the public objects, in passing the bye-laws of the corporation, and exercising the Admiralty rights, could not be exercised by the companies, but could only be exercised by the Irish Society, and also the expensive burdens undertaken:— "The society emanated from the city, and even after its incorporation by the Crown, appears to have been little, if anything, more than the representative or instrument of the city for the purposes of the plantation. The city had contracted with the Crown to perform the duty, and it was at the suggestion of the city, and as the means, or as their instrument, of performing the same duty, that the society was invested with the property, and with very extensive powers." That is the basis of the judgment. "The mistaken views which the society may have subsequently taken of its own situation and duties (and I think that such mistaken views have been several times taken) do not vary the conclusion to be deduced from the charter, and the circumstances contemporary with the grant of the first charter. The duty to be performed regarded the Crown, and regarded the city, and through the city, the companies," not the companies direct, but through the city the companies.

Chairman.] After the city had disposed of it all, did not the Crown and the companies come face to face?

Mr. Latham.] The city never disposed of it; the Irish Society took the place of the city, and the city were always behind the Irish Society. It did not take the place of the city, because the city were still there, but the city appointed the members of the Irish Society from year to year. The city in that sense are still there, and they exercise the rights, or claim to exercise the rights of visitation. "At and long after the date of the first charter, the city had, or at least was practically considered to have, and really exercised great and extensive powers, not only over the society but over the companies; but the city in its corporate character had no beneficial interest; the money which it had advanced was early repaid."

Chairman.] That is a sentence I do not see any reference to elsewhere; I do not find in any of the other reports and papers when the money was repaid. What is the meaning of "repaid" there; can you throw any light upon that?

Mr.

23 *July* 1890.

Mr. *Latham*.] I think very possibly the repayment means that they took the lands instead of the money; that the grant of the land disposed of the question of the money, and that is means repaid in that sense. I am not aware of any other repayment, or that the city ever got the 60,000 *l.* back.

Chairman.] That may represent it, but I could not see any other construction.

Mr. *Latham*.] I think that is what it must mean. We passed over a document a little while ago in which it referred to the option of taking the money or having the land.

Mr. *Sexton*.] How would the giving of the lands to the companies repay the city?

Mr. *Latham*.] Remember how the City had got the moneys. The City got the moneys from the companies, and the City were in treaty with the Crown, and the Crown had nothing to do with the companies. The Crown said: "You have given your 60,000 *l.*; here is so much land," and the city comes and says to the companies: "The 60,000 *l.* came from you, and we give you the lands." I think that is the explanation. "The money which it had advanced was early repaid, and the power which remained, or which was considered to remain, was, like that of the Society, an entrusted power for the benefit of the plantation and those interested in it. Even after a large part of the territory comprised in the grant had been distributed and conveyed to the companies, much remained to be done for the general purposes of the plantation" "general purposes" being again the phrase he uses, not for the particular purposes of each plot, but the general purposes imposed on the Irish Society, "and that which remained to be done could not be accomplished without expense." This is a very important part of the judgment from my view of the case: "At the time when the power of the city to raise money by taxation was not disputed, it may not have been thought necessary to retain any part of the property as a fund to support the expenses; and it was reported by the Commissioners on the 8th of November 1613, and probably generally understood, that the profits of the undivided hereditaments might be shared among the companies; but in 1662, when the charter of Charles was granted, and the power of the City to levy money on the companies was either no longer claimed, or was subject to very different considerations, it was recited in the charter, that the undivided property was retained to defray the expense of the general operation of the plantation. The expression was borrowed from a petition presented to the House of Commons by the City of London in January 1641, but it has its place in the charter of 1662, and must have weight accordingly." That is that the reserved lands were taken in lieu of the right to levy money."

"It is said, and indeed admitted, that a dividend was made in the year 1623, and if I were at liberty to conjecture, I might perhaps suppose that the demands soon afterwards made on the city, and the difficulty of raising money, led to a conclusion that it was better to reserve the common property for the general purposes of the plantation, than to make division of its whole income, and resort to taxation and levies to defray the expenses which might from time to time be required. It is clear that the general operation of the plantation was not completed at the time when the distribution of lands was made to the companies. It was indeed strongly urged in argument that the general operation, although not then complete, was not long afterwards, or at all events was very long since, completed, and that thereupon, if not before, and in consequence thereof, the society became mere trustees for the companies; but I do not think that this Court has jurisdiction to determine the question whether the general operation of the plantation has been completed or not, and if it had, it does not appear to me that there is any satisfactory evidence on the subject, or anything to show that operations, materially affecting many important objects of the plantation, and requiring expense, may not still have to be performed; and if such should be the case, it does not appear to me that this Court has, on the application of the plaintiffs, jurisdiction to inquire or give directions about such operations. And on the whole, the question is reduced to that which was made on the motion for the payment of money into Court, and for a receiver, whether upon the settlement made in the north of Ireland, by virtue of the charter of King James the First, under which the towns of Londonderry and Coleraine were founded, and a large tract of country granted by the Crown to the Irish Society, the terms of the grant simply constituted the Irish Society ordinary trustees for the benefit of the companies of London, or whether the grant was coupled with certain public purposes and public trusts, independently of the private benefit of the companies." That is as to the grant to the Irish Society, and the whole was granted to the Irish Society. The companies had nothing to do with the first charter. "After having considered the charter of King Charles II. and the charter of King James I., and the several circumstances in evidence in this cause, which preceded and accompanied the grant of the charter of King James, and having read all the documents produced in this cause, to some only of which, though at the expense of so much time, I have but shortly adverted, and having also considered the conduct of the parties under the charter for so long a series of years, I am of opinion that the powers granted to the society, and the trusts reposed in them, were, in part, of a general and public nature, independent of the private benefit of the companies of London, and were intended by the Crown to benefit Ireland and the City of London, by connecting the City of Londonderry and the town of Coleraine, and a considerable Irish district with the City of London, and to promote the general purposes of the plantation, not only by securing the performance of the conditions imposed on ordinary undertakers, but also by the exercise of powers, and the performance of trusts, not within the scope of those conditions. The charter of Charles II. expressly recites, that the property not actually divided was retained for the general operation of the plantation; and considering that the powers given to the Irish Society for the general operation of the plantation were of a general and public or political nature, that the property

remaining

remaining vested in the Society is applicable towards such general operations, and that the companies of London, though interested in any surplus which may remain after the general purposes are answered," he admits it again here, "are not entitled to control the exercise of the powers which are given for general and public purposes. I do not think that this Court has jurisdiction, upon the application of the companies, to determine upon the propriety of the expenditure which has been made. It must not be inferred that I approve of some of the items of expense which were commented upon in the argument. I express no opinion upon the subject, thinking that the Society have a discretion which, though controllable elsewhere, and in another manner, is not to be controlled in this Court upon such a Bill as this."

Chairman.] In short you take it that when the Master of the Rolls said that the property not actually divided, was retained for the general operation of the plantation, you understand those words to mean that the divided property was no longer retained.

Mr. *Latham.*] Yes.

Chairman.] That is read in, as it were. It is possible also to take them in another sense.

Mr. *Latham.*] I think you can hardly avoid it when he goes on to say what he does. It was not his function to decide what the divisible property was.

Chairman.] Quite so.

Mr. *Latham.*] And he is very cautious, but notwithstanding his caution he does say we are interested in a surplus once declared.

Chairman.] However, that is your point. I do not think of arguing it with you.

Mr. *Latham.*] That is my point, and it is the sole point. It was on that view of this judgment that I founded the argument I based on the charter, and my interpretation of the charter and the subsequent proceedings.

Now I think perhaps, having read Lord Langdale's judgment at such length, and having shown so far as I can that Lord Langdale's view was similar to mine, I do not know that I need go through in so much detail the judgment in the House of Lords, because they accept fully the decision of Lord Langdale. The reference to the case in the House of Lords, 10 Clark & Finnelly, p. 476, is where the judgment begins, and again, I do not think I need trouble with any examination of the argument. My friend Mr. Walker seemed to be not quite satisfied with the judgment, and relied a good deal on one of the arguments. It is an entirely new view of treating a legal case to me, and I only know of one argument that was ever regarded as an authority, and that was the famous argument of Sir Samuel Romilly, in Hugenin v. Baseley, which was supposed to state certain equitable doctrines with great force, and which is often referred to; but that is the only argument ever cited in any court of justice as having any authority. Lord Lyndhurst begins with a review of the events, and at page 480 he says that after the first charter was granted there was an application for a licence to hold in mortmain, and then there were the conveyances. In the middle of the page he says: "And the Irish Society from that period to the present have held the Crown lands, both of the city of Derry and of the town of Coleraine, the ferries, and the fisheries, by an absolute title, letting the property, receiving the rents, and employing them entirely, according to their own discretion." He qualifies that a little in the middle of the next page, as I shall show you. That is the actual state of things, and was the actual state of things at the period to which he referred. Then in the middle of page 481: "After the restoration of Charles II., I think in the year 1662, a new charter was granted. That charter recited the promise of Charles I. to restore the charter; and it went on to say that the intention was to replace the parties in their former position, precisely in the same way as if the charter had not been repealed." I have pointed out that the former position was not the former position at the date of the first charter, but the former position at the date of the divided lands. "Then it went on to convey those lands again to the Irish Society, to incorporate the Irish Society, and to carry out the stipulations and conditions of the former charter, as far as they were applicable, in consequence of the lapse of time which had occurred since the grant of the former charter. From that period, as I have before stated, the Irish Society have held possession of the lands and property in question; the different companies have held their lands in severalty." He had said before that the Irish Society held their lands by an absolute title, and dealt with them according to their discretion, and then he says they have exercised their discretion in this way: "The Irish Society have applied the funds for public purposes connected with the plantation, and connected with the affairs of the society. They have applied them for purposes of religion, partly in the building or repairing of churches, of chapels, of public schools, the paying of schoolmasters, building bridges, fortifications, and a variety of other public objects, and after they have satisfied those public objects apparently, according to their own discretion, they have paid over the surplus generally in round sums to the different companies, according to the proportions of their original contributions. Now, the question is this: Under these circumstances, in what situation do the Irish Society stand? Are they trustees for these companies for the private interest and advantage and benefit of those companies; or are they trustees for public objects? If they are trustees for public objects and public purposes, it is quite clear that this suit cannot be maintained; and the sole question therefore, as a general question, is to determine from all the circumstances arising out of these transactions in what character they stand. If they are mere trustees for the private benefit of the companies for their private advantage, then the suit is properly instituted. If, on the other hand, they are trustees for public objects, if they are (if I may say so) public officers, who have important public duties to perform; and if those lands which they hold are applicable to the discharge of those public duties; if they have a discretion as to the extent and manner in which they

they shall apply them, in that case it is quite clear that the suit cannot be maintained in the shape in which it is instituted, at the instance of these companies or of this company, the Skinners' Company." That is exactly the way in which it seems to me the position of the Irish Society ought to be defined, public officers with public duties and with funds applicable to the discharge of those duties. Then he says: "For the purpose of deciding this question, an important question, it is material to consider what was the object of this plantation, and what was the object of this grant. It was a great public object; it was for the purpose of providing for the settlement of this district, which had been laid waste in consequence of the Rebellion; it was to introduce civilisation and order into that district; it was to provide for the establishment there and the maintenance of the Protestant religion. All these were great and important public objects: those are stated to be the objects, much in detail in the different documents that are printed in the Papers on your Lordship's table; these are stated to be the objects in the printed book to which I have referred. In a letter also, directed to Sir Arthur Chichester by the King, in Council, or, I believe, by the King himself personally, those are stated to be the objects of this establishment; they are emphatically stated to be the objects in the preamble to the Charter, to which I have referred. Then he recites that with a view to the objects, and sets out the original charter. Then he says, on page 484, as to the public objects: "That being so, the next question is, what were the powers conferred upon the Irish Society, and what were the duties they had to perform? They had to superintend, order, direct, and manage the whole of this extensive concern;" of course, this was nothing the companies could do; "they were appointed for that object; they had to superintend and govern, and perform, therefore, those duties that were necessary for the purpose of giving effect to the grant, the purposes of the grant being those which I have stated. What, then, were the powers with which they were invested for that purpose? And what were the duties by the charter which they had to perform? For the better ordering, directing, and governing all and all manner of things for and concerning the city and citizens of Londonderry aforesaid, and the aforesaid county of Londonderry, and the plantation to be made within the same city and county of Londonderry, and other businesses belonging to the same we will and grant," &c., "that for ever hereafter there shall be twenty-six honest and discreet citizens of our city," and so on. It is for these purposes that the Irish Society was formed, and, having formed the society, it goes on then; it gives "new power to hold a court, and in the same court and meeting to do, hear, transact, and determine all and all manner of matters and things whatsoever of, for, or concerning the plantation or government aforesaid as to them shall seem best and most expedient; and also in the same court or meeting shall and may have full power and authority to direct, constitute, and ordain for and on the part of the mayor, and commonalty, and citizens of our city of London in our kingdom of England, all and singular, things which for or concerning the plantation, supply, or establishment, continuation, and government of the aforesaid city of Londonderry and of all other the lands and tenements hereunder in these presents mentioned to be granted shall seem to be most profitable and expedient; and also to send orders and directions from this kingdom of England into the said realm of Ireland by letters or otherwise for the ordering, directing, and disposing of all and all manner of matters and things whatsoever of or concerning the said plantation," and so on. And then he concludes by saying, "These, then, are the very extensive and large powers that are given to this society for the purpose of carrying into effect the intentions of the Crown, being these great and important public objects to which I have already called your Lordships' attention."

None of those could have been imposed on the companies, or could belong to the companies in any way. These were great public functions to be performed by public officers.

Chairman.] You are still upon the same proposition, that the imposition of those duties upon the Irish Society is tantamount to a relief of the companies. That is what I am not satisfied of.

Mr. *Latham.*] What would relieve the companies was the reservation of what they considered, and which it appears all the courts considered was necessary, and what they in the exercise of a *bonâ fide* discretion considered to be sufficient to enable them to perform those public duties. Subject to that, they were at liberty to proceed exactly in the same manner as the Court seems to have decided here, that year by year they had a right to divide among the companies surplus income which they carried to general income. The Court seems to have decided that proposition in this very case.

Chairman.] In other words, the view was that there was enough in the 7,000 acres to satisfy all the public objects for which the plantation was created, and the surplus upon the 7,000 acres, the profit on them, and all the divisible lands they could deal with as they thought fit; that is your proposition?

Mr. *Latham.*] That is my proposition.

Mr. *Sexton.*] Has it occurred to you that the 7,000 acres, and the two towns, and the ferries and fishings were not divided because they could not conveniently be divided. The fishings could not be divided; the 7,000 acres were appurtenant to the two towns and could not, therefore, be conveniently divided. When the phrase "not properly divisible" is used as you have used it to-day, might it not be confined to all that could not be conveniently divided, and therefore held by the Society?

Mr. *Latham.*] I think it might be so reserved, but I do not think it makes any difference. If it were the case that those lands and properties were reserved because they could not be conveniently divided, if having reserved, then the Irish Society came to the conclusion that the rents and profits accruing from them were sufficient to discharge their public obligations, still they would be able to divide the residue exactly as they divided the surplus rent.

Mr.

Mr. *Sexton.*] Does that appear to you to hold and include the other proposition, that, therefore, the divided lands were free from the public obligations?

Mr. *Latham.*] I think it includes it in this way, that if they had, then the question would be for them to decide for themselves, subject to no control whatever, except fraud, and putting that aside, if they had a right to dispose year by year of what they did not find to be necessary for the public objects then in the same manner when they have retained that out of the enormous territories which had been conveyed to them, and there was a great deal they did not require and never would require to fulfil all the public objects imposed upon them, then they were at liberty to divide those lands among the companies; and it makes no difference whatever what the reason was for their selecting the 7,000 acres in preference to any others. It is a circumstance that after all is not infrequently occurring in practical business.

When a trading company or a business has found that its assets have increased in value very largely, not by the process of trading or dealing with them, but by what I will call unearned increment, by coming into valuable property; it has happened before now, and will happen over and over again, that the company are advised and well advised that so long as they *bonâ fide* ascertain that the property remaining in their hands, and which they reserve in their hands is equal to their capital as stated in their charter or memorandum of association, or whatever it may be; so long as their capital is intact they are at liberty to divide the residue in specie if they please; but what they do is to sell and divide the proceeds, because they have fulfilled all the obligations imposed upon them by their constitution. They have got their capital, and are obliged to keep it, but they can divide the surplus.

Mr. *Sexton.*] Because a certain part which could not in its nature be divided is kept in one hand, I find it hard to pass from that fact to the inference, that the rest of the property which could be divided was freed from public obligation.

Mr. *Latham.*] I think that is not putting my argument from premise to conclusion in the way I put it. What I say is, that your premise (if I may say so) is an incident and not a necessity. You premise that the land could not be fitly divided, because it was not convenient to be divided; but that is not the circumstance upon which the companies proceeded when they divided the residue of the lands.

Mr. *Sexton.*] The two things might concur.

Mr. *Latham.*] Yes, I admit that they might concur, and I am not at all disposed to insist on the interpretation I have put upon it. Mr. Sexton is perfectly right. I did put the interpretation on those words, "which could not fitly be divided," that that meant those which were most convenient to be reserved, but I do not care what the reason is. I am quite prepared to accept Mr. Sexton's view, that, being fisheries and town lands adjoining towns, there were inconveniences in dividing them. Let us take it so. Still I say that the same circumstances occurred that the Irish Society were satisfied that their reserved lands, for whatever reason reserved, were sufficient to answer the purposes of their public duties and obligations, and therefore they were at liberty to divide the residue; and I say that incidentally at any rate both Lord Langdale and Lord Lyndhurst decided that point, because they say we were interested in the surplus, and that is precisely the same point.

Mr. *John Ellis.*] May I ask whether your argument extends to this, that there is no particular reason why there should have been 7,000 acres? It might so have happened that the condition that you suggest might have been fulfilled by a less amount?

Mr. *Latham.*] It might have happened so.

Mr. *Sexton.*] Do you say the fact that you had an interest in the surplus, when there was any, amounts to an argument that the trusts would have been satisfied by the fact of the existence of a surplus?

Mr. *Latham.*] Yes; I do not think that it would be conclusive. I am only taking the judgment as their Lordships delivered it. This judgment said the Irish Society, and only the Irish Society, were the people to decide whether the trust had been satisfied or not; that if they once decided it as far as the companies were concerned, in dealing with them—I quite admit there may be some other question, but that is the decision—that if they and we have in our discretion come to the conclusion that there is a surplus on the receipts and expenditure of this year 1890, and we carry that balance to the general account, or whatever it may be, I think, according to those judgments, at the present moment, if we were to do that it would be the right of the companies to say that balance from that moment is ours. I think that is what their Lordships say here. They do say that possibly the Irish Society may be called in question by the City of London as visitors, or by the Crown or Attorney General as to whether it is really executing its trust and doing its duty, and if that ever occurs, no doubt, we should not be able to touch the surplus, but that question may possibly arise, even in this very inquiry, whether measures should be taken to make the Irish Society responsible. But remember this, for many years past there has been no surplus, and consequently the question has not arisen. In fact, since the date of the decision in the case of the Irish Society and the Skinners' Company, we have never received a penny. The Irish Society accepted the position that there were great public duties on them to perform and always expended their income, and consequently the question has never arisen, and I take it it never will arise of their taking a surplus to general account. But I do say this, that that discretion once exercised is not a discretion they can go back upon. Take it that there was a yearly surplus, and the Irish Society declared a surplus, and carried it to the general account and divided amongst the companies, and supposing at some future time the Irish Society should be called in question, and a new body created with larger duties to perform—so much

23 *July* 1890.

larger duties, that you could say that in the back years, if these duties had been performed, there would have been no surplus; you could not in any court, and I should suggest not in any reasonable way, go back upon the division which had once been fairly and properly exercised, and not been questioned at the time. I say the same thing about our holding of the lands; that if my contention is right, that the division was made among the companies, *bonâ fide*, loyally, 250 years ago, or whenever it was, and has never been questioned up to the present time, it is not enough now to fix on the Irish Society the back duty that they ought to have done a great deal more than they have done, and that if they had done those larger duties there would have been no surplus, and to say now we will go back and recover from the people amongst whom you have divided your surplus. No court has ever done such a thing. The discretion was exercised, so far as we know, loyally, and was not called in question, but was confirmed by a second charter, and in every possible manner confirmed, and regarded as confirmed, and you cannot go back upon that now by creating legal duties which would exhaust larger revenues.

Chairman.] I do not understand in what sense it can be maintained that the work done by the Irish Society within its own very narrow area was a satisfaction of the general objects of the Crown: in what sense the work done in Coleraine and Londonderry redeemed from superstition, rebellion, &c. land now held by the Mercers, Drapers, and Ironmongers. Outside of this area they do nothing.

Mr. *Latham.*] They do nothing.

Chairman.] Did not the public objects subsist outside such area?

Mr. *Latham.*] I think the public objects were as I have said and have maintained throughout, to settle and to plant with English and Scotch settlers; and that was the process by which the country was to be redeemed from superstition, and so forth.

Chairman.] You maintain that outside the 7,000 acres the King's object was satisfied by merely putting settlers and planters there?

Mr. *Latham.*] Planters and settlers.

Chairman.] And that putting churches, schools, and so forth, was a work of supererogation so far as the King's object went?

Mr *Latham.*] I think so. I think, so far as it was done by the Irish Society, it was a work of supererogation. The Irish Society accepted that view, and they did it.

Chairman.] Why should the public object be geographically limited to the 7,000 acres?

Mr. *Latham.*] I do not think it was.

Chairman.] Then I will put it in another way. Why should there have been a different public object in the 7,000 acres? There you construe the expression "public objects" in its widest sense. It is to include religion, education, and so forth. When you get outside of the 7,000 acres you are content with mere settling and planting. Why is there that difference?

Mr. *Latham.*] You must remember that the public purposes, and objects, and so forth were large public objects and purposes expressly prescribed by each of the charters, and expressly imposed on the Irish Society and not on the companies. That is a prescription and a limitation; and for that purpose, I grant you, in the origin the whole lands were conveyed; but the Irish Society exercised their discretion, and it was under that discretion only they could divide the lands, and they said, "We have enough left to provide for those public duties which are incumbent on us, and we hand over the rest to the companies, severally reminding them as they did, 'You have to observe the conditions as to planting and settling'"; and the second charter says that the duties still remain.

Mr. *Sexton.*] Supposing the whole estate had been conveniently divisible, and supposing there was no such thing as the two towns and the ferries and the fishings that could not be divided, but the whole estate had been conveniently divisible, does it not seem probable that in that case the whole estate would have been divided between the companies? Would you say in that case that the estate would have been relieved of all the trust?

Mr. *Latham.*] There is a second answer to that. I think it would not, but then I think the Irish Society were wise enough to see they had peculiar duties to perform, and if they had parted with the funds that would enable them to perform them they would have to perform them out of their own pockets if they had any, and you remember the second charter deals with the question of the reserved lands, and appropriated the reserved lands then to the performance of public duties.

Mr. *John Ellis.*] When you use the expression "we have enough left," do you mean by that the duties would have been satisfied by a certain corpus of property?

Mr. *Latham.*] I understood the suggestion from Mr. Sexton was this, "if they had found that all the lands could have been conveniently divided, do you say they could have divided the whole, and thus got off the duties?" I say, no, they could not. I say they were bound to perform those duties by the charter, whether they had property or not.

Mr. *Sexton.*] It seems to me difficult to realise that the part of the estate which by its new charter could not be divided, turned out to have been just enough for the public uses.

Mr. *Latham.*] For many years it proved to be in the opinion of the Irish Society, and not only enough, but there was a surplus.

Mr. *Lawson.*] You say if the reserved lands had been sold there would yet have been the liability on the part of the society.

Mr. *Latham.*] Yes.

Mr. *Lawson.*] But what geographical limitation would there have been then?

Mr. *Latham.*] I do not think there is a geographical limitation to the duties of the Irish

23 *July* 1890.

Irish Society. The only way in which it becomes geographical is that I think almost entirely the public duties were restricted to duties connected with the cities of Londonderry and Coleraine. Then I do not know that I have much more to say about this judgment. Then I think I have read the paragraph on page 446. "The next question is, whether these funds are applicable to those objects; with respect to that, no doubt can be entertained; the Irish Society were establishing for the purpose of effecting and superintending these important objects; expense must of necessity have been incurred for those purposes; they had no other funds but the funds arising out of this grant; the grant was given on the condition of these duties being performed, and nobody therefore, reflecting at all on the nature of these transactions, can doubt for a moment that those funds are applicable strictly to those objects." Then, at the bottom of the next page, he goes on, "But the case does not rest there, because, so far as relates to this particular portion of property, the town lands, the fisheries, and the ferries;" that is the 7,000 acres, and the rest. "It is declared expressly in the charter of King Charles the Second, that these funds are applicable to the general operations of the plantations. It is stated in the preamble of that charter, that they were retained for that purpose, and when the Crown states that they were retained for that purpose, it sanctions the application; and when it re-grants the property, it re-grants it subject to that condition, and authorises and directs the application to those objects." Then he speaks with respect to the permanence of those permanent objects, and says, "When it is said that these objects were in a few years accomplished, and that these public trusts ceased, we must look at the charter of Charles the Second as giving at once a denial to that allegation. That charter was published 50 years after the charter of James the First. In that charter it is stated, that the object of the incorporation at that time, in the year 1662, is for the further and better settling and planting of the said country towns and places with trade and inhabitants; so that not only from general reasoning, arising out of the nature of their duty from their constitution, but from the very terms of the charter, it appears that the idea that this was a mere transitory duty, is wholly unfounded; and it appears that at that time there was still much of the same duty remaining to be performed as was required to be performed at the time when the original charter was granted." Then he says, "The conclusion I come to appears to me to be perfectly irresistible; they are public officers." Then in the middle of the next page he says, "If they are public officers, and have in any respect neglected their duty, they are liable to account; but they are not liable to account to the companies. They may be liable to account to the Crown; they may be liable to account for misconduct to the Corporation of the City of London; they are elected by the City of London, they are half of them removed every year. The City of London can exercise a control over them if they misconduct themselves; they can be restrained and kept in order by the authority of the City of London, or by the authority of the Crown, if they are public officers; but they are in no respect, as it appears to me, amenable to the private companies for the manner in which they perform their duties."

Then I do not think there is anything in Lord Campbell's judgment which is very short, except the last passage: "I concur in the opinion that those eminent judges have pronounced. It seems to me that the object of the Crown was, that public purposes should be attained by the trustees who had the management of these lands; and I am clearly of opinion that the purposes for which the grant was made still continue, and that they are and must ever remain trustees for those public purposes." Those lands must have been the lands retained by the Irish Society, because those are the only lands in question.

Mr. *Sexton.*] The question whether the companies were subject to any trust was entirely outside that case.

Mr. *Latham.*] Except so far as I have said, I think it is a necessary inference, from the fact that the Judges said they were entitled to the surplus, or any surplus funds.

Now I come to the last question. I have gone through the documents, and according to my view, there is nothing on the face of the documents from the commencement of the title down to the present day which is sufficient to establish a trust. Then I am told, possibly it may not be on the face of the documents. I take the Charter of Charles the Second as my root of title. I say everything behind me is swept away, and from that date to this there is nothing on the documents which imposes a trust upon me, and I say that if I do not find it on the documents I am entitled to say that it was not intended to be imposed upon me; because there is no case now as there might have been over the original charter, that the Crown had made a blunder and a mistake, which entitled you to hunt amongst other documents. The Crown made no mistake in the time of Charles the Second. They created the rights, and imposed no trust on anybody but the Irish Society for public purposes, and no trust down to the present time has been established against us.

Then it is said we may perhaps find a trust in the course of dealing. Now, what is the course of dealing from which it is suggested you can find a trust. It is said you, the companies, have at intervals, and from year to year, expended considerable sums upon improving the estates in one form or another; you have spent sums not only upon making roads and so forth, which might be really to get a better profit out of them, but you have spent sums of money on divers objects not directly remunerative. You have spent sums of money on schools, churches, and so forth through a great series of years. I think it is put in this way, that it is ever since we came into the management of our properties, because it is rather suggested that we did not do these things in the days when there were middlemen and lessees of the land; but it is suggested from the period when we came into possession of the properties, which

23 *July* 1890.

varies from 1630 down to the present time, we have lavished, and, beyond the measure of ordinary owners of property, spent money upon certain public objects which would come within the four corners of the obligation we propose to put on you, and which do not come within the ordinary duties of owners of property. I think I am stating the case against myself as fairly as it can be stated. It is my desire to do so. I say, where you have got a whole series of documents like this, a complete series of documents, and no suggestion whatever that there is any document not forthcoming or missing, and no suggestion that the question of this trust as it is alleged can come from anywhere but the Crown, and the Crown documents being always accessible through the Crown Office, I say that then you are not in a position, either legally or morally, or in any other way, to interpret a trust out of my course of conduct. You must, in order to create a trust by course of conduct, show that that course of conduct was in pursuance of a trust. At least you must show that; you probably must show a great deal more, but you must show that the person to whom you impute the trust was conscious of the trust that impelled him to do so. How can you show that in the face of the proceedings and the documents from the beginning to the end? I might carry it even a step further. It is not even enough to show that he meant to come under a trust. If, when the circumstances are examined, it is discovered that by the operation of the law there is no trust whatever, he would not be bound by any prescription to apply his money to the same objects he had applied it to, under the impression there was a trust. It would not be enough. There is no prescription that runs in that direction. Then, again, I say, as I pointed out in the earlier part of my address, if conduct is in any way consistent with two courses and two meanings, you have no right to choose one of them, and that one the most onerous upon the person you are attacking, and say we allege that, and throw that burden upon you, and say that this course of action, although you may have been lavish, instead of only being liberal, and I do not think if we have been so it is a matter of which we have any reason to be ashamed if we do not spend anything like a large or a considerable portion of our money in any way, direct or indirect, upon ourselves, if we have as a matter of practice for many years habitually been in the habit of being what I may call generous in disposing of our surplus money for public objects, if we have done that, and if we are owners of land in Ireland, under these circumstances, if we have money coming in from year to year which we do not need, and do not require, but which we can do good with in Ireland, and if thereby we have been somewhat lavish beyond the ordinary course of landowners, that is not enough to impose a trust upon us. That is consistent with our being lavish, as I have said, or if you like, liberal. It is consistent with our doing it because we choose to do it; and it is just as much consistent with that as consistent with what I venture to call the impossible theory that we have been doing it because we thought we were obliged to do it. I say an impossible theory, because the documents I say are not consistent with it; and remember this, that it goes too far. Our conduct as an argument is as good one way as another. The trust that is sought to be imposed upon us is a trust to apply our whole net revenues and profits upon public objects in Ireland. That is the trust which we are supposed to have had knowledge of; but our conduct is absolutely inconsistent with that, because year by year we have carried over at least half of our net income to our own private purposes, and disposed of it in England; and that is in evidence before the Committee. So that as far as our course of conduct is concerned, if it is to be treated as binding upon us in any way, I say it is absolutely inconsistent with the idea that we were obeying the mandates of a trust; we were doing nothing of the sort, but simply disposing of it as we thought fit. Now, I just remind the Committee of this, because it is not immaterial to this branch of the subject, and ought not to be forgotten. I am not disposed to rely upon technicalities, but still I do rely on what is an indication of what Parliament has thought to be important in this matter, of establishing trusts in the early days, when trusts began to come into use. Trusts were not very much in use till Lord Nottingham was Chancellor, in the days of the Stuarts, and the courts and the country became cognisant of the fact that it was very easy to swear someone out of his property, by saying it was in trust for you, and thereupon, just at the very same period as this charter was granted, only three or four years later, the Statute of Frauds was passed, and by the 7th section it is enacted that all declarations or creations of trusts or confidences of any lands, tenements, or hereditaments, shall be manifested and proved by some writing, signed by the party who is by will enabled to declare such trust, or by his last will in writing, or else it shall be utterly void and of none effect. If appearing for the companies I had any reason to be satisfied that there was a lost deed, or something which had imposed a trust upon us, I am certain that the companies would not instruct me to take advantage of the Statute of Frauds; but I do use the Statute of Frauds in this sense, as an indication to the Committee that there is very great harm in relying on that course of argument; that unless you can establish the trust by some writing under the hand of the person to be charged, you are running a very great risk. You certainly will not find, I venture to say, anything in the nature of an acknowledgment in writing of any trust by the companies to dispose of their surplus rents and profits in Ireland. There is nothing of the sort, and I say, therefore, that the course of conduct, in face of the documents and in face of the double interpretation which may be put upon it, entirely breaks down. I will leave that there. I think I have practically disposed of the question of a trust being imposed since the time I take as my root of title.

Mr. *Sexton*.] Before you pass from that, as the reference to the Committee speaks not only of trusts, but of obligations, do you say anything upon the evidence offered by the course of dealing, of the sense of a special obligation?

Mr.

23 *July*, 1890.

Mr. Latham.] So far as I can understand, my observations about the special obligation are precisely the same as I should make about a trust. You must connect the course of dealing with the consciousness, or admission of obligation. The course of dealing in this case is perfectly consistent with its having been voluntary from time to time, from year to year, and from week to week. It is perfectly consistent with that, and in order to prove an obligation out of the course of dealing you want to get a step further.

You must get a course of dealing in pursuance of an obligation not expressed in writing, in which it is obvious that the person who was sought to be charged was conscious of an obligation, and was doing it as an obligation. If the honourable Member is putting it to me as a question of moral obligation, that is another question; but I am speaking now of legal obligation.

Mr. Sexton.] Is "obligation" in your mind synonymous with legal trust?

Mr. Latham.] I think an obligation may be different from a trust in this sense. An obligation may be a personal obligation which would not affect land at all. Through the long process of the jurisdiction of the Court of Equity, the land itself, as well as the owner, is said to be affected by the trust. I can quite imagine the position, and it is the position I shall have to deal with, that there may be concurrently with land absolutely free, a personal obligation upon the original owner of the land, which would not follow the land in any manner, and which would be an obligation on him, that is to say, he may at the same time have entered into a covenant with somebody else that he will perform such and such duties for a long time to come. That covenant may be personally binding on him, though it may not be a trust that would affect the land.

Chairman.] The case of Sir Harvey Bruce would be a case in point; he took his land from the Clothworkers.

Mr. Latham.] He did; he entered into an obligation; he might have entered into a legal obligation, and might have put it in this form. He might have said, I will not bind my land, because I might want to sell it, but I will enter into a covenant with you that I will pay a certain sum to you. He did not do it, but it was left on an honourable understanding. I do not know what Mr. Sexton's view was, or whether he was dealing with a question of an honourable obligation, because that is a different thing.

Mr. Sexton.] I was trying to get at this, whether in your mind there is any room, after you have exploded the notion of a legal trust, for any other kind of obligation.

Mr. Latham.] I think I have during this period, from the time of Charles II., excluded obligation as much as I have excluded trust, that is to say, a trust originating during that time; but what I do admit is that it is conceivable there may be, under the orders and conditions, or in the early part of the proceedings, some obligation or trust imposed upon me which may still be binding on me, or might be deemed to be still binding on me, and that is what I have to deal with.

Mr. Lea.] That is to say, that the 150,000 *l.* which the Clothworkers' Society obtained from the sale of their estate to Sir Harvey Bruce would carry the obligation, if it did not carry the trust.

Mr. Latham.] No, I think if the land was free, the proceeds would be free; but you would equally get at the money if you could fix an obligation on the company by suing them for it and recovering; but if the land is free from trust, the purchase money is free from trust, but the obligation would still remain as a personal obligation.

Mr. Sexton.] Your argument sums it up by saying there is no trust, and therefore no obligation.

Mr. Latham.] No. I admit there might have been, and I think there was an obligation in the early part connected with the orders and conditions, and that is what I want to deal with. I think there was an obligation to settle and plant.

Chairman.] That is the other point you propose to deal with?

Mr. Latham.] Yes; and for that I must go back to the orders and conditions.

Chairman.] Perhaps it would be a convenient point to break off?

Mr. Latham.] Yes. That is a branch of my argument that need not be very long.

Thursday, 24th July 1890.

MEMBERS PRESENT:

Mr. John Ellis.
Mr. Elton.
Colonel Laurie.
Mr. Lawrence.
Mr. Lea.

Sir William Marriott.
Mr. John Morley.
Mr. Sexton.
Sir Richard Temple.

THE RIGHT HONOURABLE JOHN MORLEY, IN THE CHAIR.

Mr. *Latham*.] I propose, Sir, this morning, to go straight to the Orders and Conditions of the 9th of March 1608, and the title: which was read by my learned Mr. Walker, being a "Collection of such Orders and Conditions as are to be observed by the Undertakers upon the distribution and plantation of the escheated lands in Ulster."

Chairman.] We have got copies of this in the Concise View. I do not know whether it is complete there.

Mr. *Latham*.] I am not sure how that is. I ought to observe, about the Concise View, that whatever the Concise View may be it is not the Companies' document; we do not accept it, and it is in no way binding upon us. I really do not know it myself at all, intimately; it may be correct or it may not be; but, at all events, we go to the original documents and not to anything that is set out in the Concise View. The Orders and Conditions are printed in the Appendix to the Skinners' Case. This document was addressed, not to the Companies or the City of London, but it was addressed to anybody who might choose to become an undertaker. It was a collection of general rules to apply to anybody who should come in; and at that time, that is March 1608-9, the City of London was not in contemplation at all, although they were shortly afterwards. The document, as I say, is addressed to any individual who might be disposed to come in. The title of it is a convenient one, but I shall show that the title is not quite complete really. It begins by referring to "the greatest part of six counties." It deals not only with those counties that the Committee have so often heard of connected with the City of London and the Companies, but it deals with the whole six counties; so that whatever obligation and trust you may trace out of these Orders and Conditions would extend not only to the Companies and the Irish Society, but to everybody. It recites that "Whereas the greatest part of six counties in province of Ulster . . . being escheated and come to the Crown . . . His Majesty of his princely bounty" (which rather indicates he was conferring something) "is graciously pleased to distribute the said lands" (that was the intention) "to such of his subjects as well of Great Britain as of Ireland, as, being of merit and ability, shall seek the same, with a mind not only to benefit themselves, but to do service to the Crown and Commonwealth" (I quite accept the position: it was intended to be of service to the Crown and Commonwealth; but in addition to that it is recognised here that there was some benefit to themselves), "and, forasmuch, as many persons being ignorant of the conditions whereupon His Majesty is pleased to grant the said lands are importunate suitors for greater portions than they are able to plant, intending their private profit only, and not the advancement of the public service, it is thought convenient to declare and publish to all His Majesty's subjects the several quantities of the proportions which shall be distributed, the several sorts of undertakers, the manner of allotment, the estates, the rents, the tenures, with other articles"—The subsequent clauses of this document followed this arrangement exactly, and I will take them successively—"with other articles to be observed" (I call attention to this), "as well on His Majesty's behalf, as on behalf of the undertakers." That is to say; this was a document which contained clauses to be found somewhere or other in it, to be observed by His Majesty. Then the first clause is as to the proportions of land to be distributed: "The first and least proportion to contain such and so many of the said parcels as shall make up 1,000 English acres at the least." Those were for the larger undertakers, and that is all I need trouble the Committee about as to that. There were three classes of undertakers, and three quantities of land. A ballibetagh (which is the first) is about 1,000 acres.

Chairman.] One thousand Irish acres?

Mr. *Latham*.] Yes, I think Irish acres. Then the second clause deals with the persons: "The persons of the undertakers of the several proportions shall be of three sorts, viz., first, English or Scottish, as well servitors as others, who are to plant their portions with English or inland Scottish inhabitants."

Chairman.] What do you understand by "servitors"?

Mr. *Latham*.] I believe it means Englishmen who had served in the Army on the Royal side. Then there were, "secondly, servitors in the

Kingdom

24 *July* 1890.

Kingdom of Ireland who may take mere Irish, English, or inland Scottish tenants at their choice. Third, natives of Ireland who are to be made freeholders." It was necessary to make certain freeholders and to utilise the Irish who were willing to serve for that purpose in order to make up the grand juries and to perform certain public duties in the county. It is the first set of undertakers with whom we are chiefly concerned here, that is, those who were to "plant their portions with English or inland Scottish inhabitants." Then it goes on, "His Majesty will reserve unto himself the appointment in what county every undertaker shall have his portion," and in the event the King appointed Derry and Coleraine for the London portion. "But to avoid emulation and controversy which would arise among them if every man should choose the place where he would be planted, His Majesty's pleasure is that the sites or places of their portions in every county shall be distributed by lot." As a matter of fact, in the event the companies did take their several portions by lot, but they took them from the City; the City did not take them by lot; they took directly a large tract of country selected by the Crown; but there was afterwards an allotment, as the Committee know, among the Companies from the City. "Lastly, the several articles ensuing are to be observed as well on His Majesty's behalf as of the several undertakers respectively." So that you see His Majesty was binding himself here.

Chairman.] All through, the word "undertaken" implies the private undertakers as well as the City, I understand?

Mr. *Latham.*] Yes, it must be private undertakers as well as the companies; at that time the companies were not in contemplation at all. Then it goes on: "His Majesty is pleased to grant estates in fee farm to them and their heirs." That deals only with the land. Fee farm of course is a permanent tenure; it may be subject to rent, but it is a permanent tenure. Then the next paragraph is: "They shall yearly yield unto His Majesty for every proportion of 1,000 acres 5 *l.* 6 *s.* 8 *d.* English, and so rateably for the greater proportions, which is after the rate of 4 *s.* 8 *d.* for every 60 acres English." Of course these figures may seem very small at present, but the character of the country at that time must be considered. The preamble to the Charter afterwards indicates what sort of country it was; desolated by war and depopulated as well. Then it goes on: "Every undertaker of so much land as shall amount to the greatest proportion of 2,000 acres or thereabouts shall hold the same by knight's service in capite." That was abandoned afterwards. It ultimately came to the companies, so far as the companies were concerned, and the City, in free socage, because they insisted upon it, but it is just material to notice that circumstance here, because it intimates that although the orders and conditions were published, still there are departures from them, and it is very difficult to say, after the events that happened, that they were not entirely departed from and abrogated by the subsequent documents, which in many respects are inconsistent with them; and this is one instance. The conveyance to the City, and the conveyances to the companies from the City or the Irish Society, were in free socage and not by knight's service; which was a very substantial difference in those days, because the burdens on tenure by knight's service were very various, very great, and very uncertain. There was the liability of wardship, for instance; but in addition to that there were very uncertain liabilities, such as to assist the King at times of war by grants or by actual service, and so on. The incidents of knight's service were very burdensome indeed; so burdensome, that the whole system was abolished in the reign of Charles II. completely.

Mr. *Elton.*] Before the conveyances to the company.

Mr. *Latham.*] Then there is a provision in this clause that "There shall be no wardship upon the first two descents." Then, "Every undertaker of the greatest proportion of 2,000 acres shall, within two years after the date of his Letters Patent, build thereupon a castle with a strong court or bawn about it," and so on. The minor undertakers do not concern us. I merely point out that that was a duty to be performed, if it was to be performed at all, in two years; and presumably it was performed, for there is nothing more about it when we come to deal either with the first or second Charter; by the time of the second Charter, at any rate, it had long passed away and was one of those conditions which had ceased to be binding. Then the clause goes on: "And all the said undertakers shall draw their tenants to build houses for themselves and their families near the principal castle house, or bawn, for their mutual defence and strength, and they shall have sufficient timber by the assignment of such officers as the Lord Deputy and Council of Ireland shall appoint out of His Majesty's woods in that province for the same buildings without paying anything for the same during the said two years, and to that end there shall be a present inhibition to restrain the felling or destruction of the said woods in the meantime for what cause soever." It was contemplated at some future time that the woods might be felled; but that again was an immediate duty that was imposed upon the undertakers in process of settling; they were to build a hall and collect the people around it; that was to be done in two years. Then, "The said undertakers, their heirs and assigns shall have ready in their houses at all times a convenient store of arms." I imagine nothing rests upon that; it is obsolete at the present time at all events. Then, "Every of the said undertakers, English or Scottish, before the end sealing of his Letters Patent shall take the oath of supremacy." That presumably was done; at any rate no complaint was ever made that the oath was not taken. Then the next clause is: "The undertakers, their heirs and assigns, shall not alien or demise their portion or any part thereof to the mere Irish, or to such persons as will not take the oath which the said undertakers are bound to take by the former article, and to that end a proviso shall be inserted in their Letter Patent." The Committee will observe there recognised the right to alien, because it says they shall not

alien

24 *July* 1890.

alien except under certain very limited circumstances. As a matter of fact when you come to the Charter there was no proviso limiting alienation at all in the Charter granted to the Irish Society.

Chairman.] Do you mean the proviso was not inserted in the Letters Patent?

Mr. *Latham.*] It was not inserted. The next clause is: "Every undertaker shall, within two years" (this is, again, a two years' clause), "after the date of his Letters Patent, plant or place a competent number of English or inland Scottish tenants upon his proportion, in such manner as by the Commissioners to be appointed for the establishment of this plantation shall be prescribed." That was in the process of plantation; it was contemplated that the plantation should take place within two years. It is clear, from subsequent documents, that the plantation was not completed within two years, but still it has been completed long before now. The process of sending settlers out, and planting the place, was a process that did take place; and when the second Charter came to be granted, it is clearly accepted that it had been done to the satisfaction of the King, and no provision was inserted in the second Charter to compel them to do any more, except the broad principle that the country should be settled and planted. Then it says: "Every of the said undertakers, for the space of five years" (again the limitation of time) "next after the date of his Letters Patent, shall be resident in person himself upon his portion, or place some other person thereupon, as shall be allowed by the State of England or Ireland." So far as I know there has never been any suggestion that that has not been observed so far as it could be observed by a company. Of course a corporation could not reside; but they have sent people there; their agents have been there almost from the very earliest time, as the correspondence shows, and as the Report of the King's Commissioner shows.

Chairman.] Is it not pretty clear that the intention of Clause 8 was that there should be a person residing there with authority; either the undertaker himself or some other person? What was in the King's mind at that moment, surely, was not a mere agent who was to take his orders from the absentee, was it?

Mr. *Latham.*] I think so. That is what I understand by it. It says, "shall be resident upon the portion, or place some other person thereupon." That is to say, the place was not to be left or neglected, but there was to be somebody there; and there always has been. I do not know if the Committee have had the agents of the companies before them; but they were ready to be examined, at all events, and they could have given evidence upon that.

Chairman.] Yes, we have had evidence from them.

Mr. *Latham.*] Then Clause 10, which is a very material clause, says: "The said undertakers shall not alien their portions during five years next after the date of their Letters Patent." Again you have the limitation of time. After five years, by inference, they might alien.

Mr. *Elton.*] And during the five years they might alien in the manner prescribed in the clause?

Mr. *Latham.*] Yes, even during the five years. It says, they shall not alien during the five years, "but in this manner, viz., one third part in fee farm, another third part for 40 years or under, reserving to themselves the other third part without alienation during the said five years; but after the said five years they shall be at liberty to alien to all persons except the mere Irish, and such persons as will not take the oath." There is, therefore, an express provision in these orders and conditions that the undertakers, after five years, are to be at liberty to alien to all persons except "the mere Irish." Accepting the position that the companies were undertakers (and that they became undertakers I do not dispute), that clause inures to their benefit, and they were therefore at liberty to alien to all persons, except to the mere Irish, and nobody suggests that they did alien to the mere Irish. The mere Irish were of course the natives on the spot. They did alien, and they have aliened up to the present time, and if it is necessary to have an express licence to alien, there it is. Then it goes on: "The said undertakers shall have power to erect manors, to hold courts baron twice every year to create tenures." That they did. "The undertakers shall not demise any part of their lands at will only, but shall make certain estates for years for life in tail or in fee simple." So they did. "No uncertain rent shall be reserved by the said undertakers, but the same shall be expressly set down without reference to the custom of the country, and a proviso shall be inserted in their Letters Patent against cuttings, cosheries, and other Irish exactions upon their tenants." I do not think it has ever been suggested that there has ever been any breach of that clause at all, either in the proceedings of the Star Chamber or since. As a matter of fact, the company have pursued the ordinary rule, and I think it is in evidence before the Committee that they took the lands in the ordinary way, and adopted, perhaps, rather the practice of English than of Irish landowners, and let the land in the ordinary way, on lease, until recently. "The undertakers, their heirs and assigns" (assigns are expressly mentioned here again), "during the space of seven years next ensuing shall have power to transport all commodities." That is simply a power. "It shall be lawful for the said undertakers for the space of five years next ensuing, to send for and to bring into Ireland out of Great Britain, victuals and utensils," and so on. There is nothing in that.

That is the series of clauses concerning the undertakers of the larger plots of land; that is the series of clauses which relates to the duties that were imposed, or intended to be imposed, by the Orders and Conditions upon holders of the nature of the Irish Society and the companies. If any clauses bind them, then I quite admit that those do; but I say you will find nothing whatever in that *fasciculus* of clauses which creates a permanent binding obligation, lasting to the present time, of any sort whatever.

I think I need not trouble the Committee with

24 *July* 1890.

with the next series of clauses, because they relate to servitors in Ireland, which we were not. And then the next series concerns the Irish natives, which we were not.

Then comes the last set of five clauses, and you will observe that this series of clauses bears this as its title, "Certain General Provisions to be notified to the Undertakers of all sorts." I think I shall show the Committee that that notification was intended to include a notification to the undertakers, not only of what they were to do, but still more, what the King intended should be done for their benefit. The first clause is: "That there shall be Commissioners appointed" (that clearly would be part of what the King was going to do) "for the setting forth of the several proportions, and for the ordering and settling of the plantations according to such instructions as shall be given unto them by His Majesty in that behalf." That was the King's affair evidently. The next is: "That all the said undertakers shall by themselves, or by such as the States of England or Ireland shall allow of, attend the said Commissioners in Ireland at or before Midsummer next, to receive such directions touching their plantations as shall be thought fit." I presume they did that; I do not know that anybody says they did not; it was evidently an immediate matter. The third is: "That every undertaker before the ensealing of his letters patent shall enter into bond or recognizance with good sureties to His Majesty's use in the Office of His Majesty's Chief Remembrancer in England or Ireland, or in His Majesty's Exchequer or Chancery in Scotland, or else before two of the Commissioners to be appointed for the plantation to perform the foresaid articles" (you will observe that it says "foresaid articles;" those are what they were to enter into a bond to bind themselves to, that is, the articles that come antecedent to this article) "according to their several distinctions of building, planting, or residence alienation within five years, and making of certain estates to their tenants in this manner, viz.: the undertaker of the greatest proportion to become bound in 400 *l.*," and so forth. That was what they were to bind themselves to do, to observe the foresaid articles." Now come the articles which were not "foresaid articles." Articles 4 and 5, which were relied upon by my learned friend Mr. Walker when he addressed the Committee, as the permanent duties which were imposed upon the undertakers. First of all, Clause 4 says: "That in every of the said counties there shall be a convenient number of market towns and corporations." You will observe that it is not said that the undertakers shall establish them. The establishment of market towns and corporations was a royal function, a matter of royal prerogative. The establishment of market towns and corporations was not within the possibilities of the undertakers. You will remember it was not only the public undertakers, like the Irish Society, but it was also private undertakers who were being addressed in these articles. An ordinary private undertaker could not have established a market town or a corporation. The clause says in every county "there shall be a convenient number of market towns and corporations erected for the habitation and settling of tradesmen and artificers, and that there shall be one free school at least appointed in every county for the education of youth in learning and religion." Now, as to the appointment of free schools, the word "appointment" is a word which does not at any rate obviously address itself to the permanent maintenance by means of an endowment. Recollect what the process of creating free schools at this time was. We know perfectly well from the whole history of the period from the reign of Queen Elizabeth and subsequent reigns, the way in which it was done: it was done almost universally by a charter from the Crown to a particular person. All the great grammar schools, or a great proportion of the grammar schools, in England were created by that process at that time, or about that time, by charters from the Crown.

Mr. *Elton*.] Do not the words "*libera schola*" imply a royal grant?

Mr. *Latham*.] Yes, a grant; but the expression "*libera schola*" does not mean, and cannot mean, a school free from payment.

Mr. *Elton*.] It means, I presume, a school free from the jurisdiction of the ordinary.

Mr. *Latham*.] Probably free from the jurisdiction of the ordinary. Free from the jurisdiction of the bishop, which at that time was a very serious matter; but it no more means that the school was free from payment than a free public-house means a house where you can have beer for nothing. It was not an idea of that sort that was in the mind of the founders in using the word "free" at that time. What was in their mind was that there should be appointed in every county a general provision for education of all sorts and kinds; it is not more than that. You will remember that at this period of English history it never crossed the mind of the wisest Statesman of that period that all the population should be educated. I apprehend that nobody conceived such a thing as that until much more recent times. The utmost that was ever imagined was that there should be in certain districts in every county, or something of that sort, a school to which the capable boys, the boys who really had brains in them and a taste for literature, could resort, and where they could find an education which might raise them. That was the only thing in contemplation at that time; and if it is necessary to produce evidence of that, the Committee will find it in the volumes, which are numerous, of the Report of the Schools Inquiry Commission of 25 years ago.

Mr. *Elton*.] It contains a treatise on Liberæ Scholæ, I remember; I wrote it myself.

Mr. *Latham*.] Yes; I knew the honourable Member would be very familiar with it. There is a particularly interesting charter referred to in the Report of that Commission of the Grammar School of Louth in Lincolnshire, in which is set forth not only the provisions of the charter for that particular grammar school, but by way of recital it sets out what the intention of the King, Edward the Sixth, was in establishing these schools; it sets out that it was the intention that there should be a school to which children could resort if they were competent. That is all that was contemplated in the case of these schools, of which there was to be one appointed in every county here; and I venture to think that the true interpretation of this document is that what the King holds out to the settlers as one of the advantages that they had got to expect in settling here is that the Crown will grant the necessary charters, and I think you will find when I come to another document that they were to provide sufficient endowment to enable a school to exist in each county; but it does not mean that the undertakers were to do it.

Mr. *Elton*.] Would you supply the Chairman with reference to the Commission you have referred to, and the report that has been made, concerning the meaning of the words *liberæ scholæ*; because it seems to be a very relevant matter to the inquiry.

Mr. *John Ellis*.] Upon that point perhaps we might also have before us the Report of the Endowed Schools Committee of 1886.

Mr. *Latham*.] As regards the Schools Inquiry Commission, the first volume which contains the report is, I think, quite sufficient; for it sets forth a summary of the discussion about free schools, with references.

Chairman.] Will you bring this back to its bearing upon the inquiry with which the Committee is at present concerned. I want to follow what its present bearing is. Putting aside this discussion about the meaning of *liberæ scholæ*, what is the exact point of your argument.

Mr. *Latham*.] The phrase in these articles is "free school." As I understand, the argument about these words "free school," and the construction that has been put upon these words in this particular article, is that every undertaker undertook with the Crown that he the undertaker should for all future time see that there should be a sufficient supply of schools for the education of all people who wished to go there, and that they should be free from payment, and that the whole of these things should fall upon the undertakers. The reason why I call the Committee's attention to this particular description of free schools and this dissertation upon it in the Report of the Schools Inquiry Commission, is that they will see from the Report of that Commission what was contemplated by the words "free school" at about this period, and they will see that no such thing was contemplated as permanent endowment and sustentation of the schools by other people, but that that was undertaken by the Crown. As soon as I have dealt with the document I am now upon, I will show the Committee the instruction that the King gave to his own commissioner to see to this matter.

Mr. *Sexton*.] Did the jurisdiction of the ordinary exist in these undeveloped western counties at this time?

Mr. *Latham*.] I daresay it was difficult to assert it; but it was always claimed certainly. There were ordinaries there; there was the Bishop of Derry, as we find, and so on.

Chairman.] Was there a full ecclesiastical organisation at this time?

Mr. *Latham*.] Yes; there was the bishop and the dean, and there was a reservation of land for all the rectors. It may have been a paper system perhaps; I do not know about that; but there it was at any rate.

Mr. *Sexton*.] You say that the meaning of "free school" is, that the school is to be free of that jurisdiction.

Mr. *Latham*.] Free of that jurisdiction; that is the meaning of the expression "free school." The matter is treated in a similar manner in the next clause. It says, "There shall be" (which you will observe is the same phraseology as that used in Clause 4), "a convenient number of parishes and parish churches, with sufficient incumbents in every county, and that the parishioners shall pay all their tithes in kind to the incumbents of said parish churches." You will observe here again, the creation of parishes could not be done by private individuals. It is true that a private individual could have built a parish church, but he could not have created a parish. Then the regulation that hereafter the parishioners shall pay all their tithes in kind to the incumbents, was a matter enforceable by the Crown or by legislation, but not by a private undertaker. I say Clause 5 was a clause incumbent upon the Crown, but it was not part of the duties thrown upon the undertakers. Perhaps I may here remind the Committee that before this Select Committee last year, Canon Babington gave evidence to this effect. You will see in the middle of his answer to Question 568, he says: "Colonel Laurie asked whether the glebes were part of the property of the society. The glebes never were the property of the society at all. When they got the compensation they got it merely for the loss of patronage"; and then he says: "Colonel Laurie asked about the glebes. The glebes did not belong to the companies at any time. The only glebe in these three parishes was in the parish of Banagher, and the glebes were granted distinct from the society's property, by whatever the settlement was in those times." Then at Question 570, he is asked, "The Crown itself reserved glebe lands?" and he said, "It did." That is Canon Babington's evidence. But I think I shall give you even better evidence than that of Mr. Babington; because the next document which I will take the Committee to, is the document referred to by Mr. Walker, "Articles for Instructions for the Plantation of Ulster."

Chairman.] Have you now done with the orders and conditions?

Mr. *Latham*.] Yes, I think so; I have gone rapidly through them, but I do not know that there is anything else to which I need call attention. I have said that all the earlier part is merely temporary and long since performed, and that the two later sections were not incumbent upon the undertakers.

Chairman.] Would you say again what was the effect of that fasciculus of clauses which form the first head of the articles.

Mr.

24 *July* 1890.

Mr. Latham.] I say that all these were merely provisions for planting and settling immediately, and that if they were not carried out in the two years, or the five years, or whatever the time in each case may be, they were carried out within an early time; and long before the second charter was granted, they were accepted as having been sufficiently performed.

Now, the Articles for Instructions for the plantation of Ulster are dated the 21st of July 1609. They are printed in the respondent's appendix, at page 149. The first clause is: "That a general care be taken that such orders, conditions, or articles" (clearly referring to the orders and conditions) "as have been lately published in print, or are to be printed or transmitted, touching the plantation, be observed and put in execution as well by the Commissioners as by the undertakers." That is to say, they were some of those duties, which according to the orders and conditions, were to be put into execution by the Crown Commissioners. Then Clause 3, says: "The omissions and defects in the former survey of the escheated lands in Ulster, either for us or the Church, are to be supplied and amended by new inquisitions, and the ecclesiastical lands to be distinguished from the lands belonging to the Crown." That throws a little light upon how the ecclesiastical part of the government and control was to be arranged. The escheat had not extended to the ecclesiastical lands, and consequently they were still in the hands of the ecclesiastics; whatever lands were ecclesiastic before that time were still in their own hands, and had not escheated to the Crown, and the ecclesiastical lands, under this survey, were to be distinguished from the other lands.

Now, I do not think that I need trouble the Committee with the next few clauses, but I may go on to Clause 9: "The Commissioners are to limit and bound out the precincts of the several parishes." The Committee will remember that the erection of parishes was referred to in the last clause of the Orders and Conditions, to which reference was made. That clause provided "that there shall be a convenient number of parishes and parish churches." This Clause 9 says: "The Commissioners are to limit and bound out the precincts of the several parishes according to their discretions, notwithstanding the limitation of the projects wherein they may observe the ancient limits of the old parishes, so as the same breed, not a greater inconvenience to the plantation, and" (this was for the Commissioners again) "to assign to the incumbents of each parish a glebe after the rate of three score acres for every thousand acres within the parishes in the most convenient places or nearest to the churches." The Commissioners were to find the three score acres, "and, for the more certainty, to give to each glebe a certain name whereby it may be known, and to take order that there be a proviso in the letters patents for passing the glebes to restrain the alienations thereof saving during their incumbency." In the first charter you will remember there was a provision made to this effect; That sixty acres for every thousand should be carved out and handed over, and in the second charter there was no such provision, because it had been done. Then Clause 10 goes on: "It is fit that certain portions be allotted and laid out for towns" (that again is the market towns and corporations referred to in Article 4 of the last chapter of the Orders and Conditions) "in the places mentioned in the project, or in more convenient places as shall seem best to the Commissioners, having regard that the lands be laid as near to the towns as may be." Now we come to the schools in paragraph 11. "The parcels of land which shall be allotted to the college in Dublin" (that seems to have been a further idea; there is nothing about that in the Orders and Conditions) "and to the free schools in the several counties, are to be set out and distinguished by meres and bounds, to the end the same may be accordingly passed by several grants from us." Therefore I say it is as clear as possible upon that document that the intention was that the Crown was to grant the lands for the schools.

Mr. Sexton.] The college in Dublin was, no doubt, Trinity College, Dublin.

Mr. Latham.] Very possibly Trinity College got some property at that time; land was to be allotted for the Dublin College as well as to the schools. Then the clause goes on: "The Commissioners likewise are to set out the quantity of three great proportions lying together in the county of Armagh to be allotted to the said college of Dublin, and six thousand acres to be taken out of the lands omitted in the last survey (if so much shall be found) these to be only of our lands and not of the church land." So that the Crown was going to do all these things. I may just mention that the word "endowment" does not occur in any of these articles whether it was intended or not; but it is clear that the parcels of land are to be given to the schools; and parcels of land means not merely for the site, but a substantial portion of land for the school.

Chairman.] That is to say the rent of the land being the endowment for the school.

Mr. Latham.] Yes, it would practically be an endowment. The word "endowment" is used in the next clause with reference to the hospital, but not in this clause. Now I think I need not trouble about that further. I may mention that there is a considerable body of evidence as to all these matters in the four or five volumes of Irish State Papers, and a good deal of pains has been taken, more by my learned friend Mr. Blakesley than by myself, but at any rate great pains have been taken to take out the references to the material documents, and they have been put into a statement which was prepared for the Clerk of the Fishmongers' Company, but which the Committee, I think, decided that they would not take in evidence. I am not going to trouble the Committee by going through a great mass of documents like that, for it would be wearisome; but the Chairman suggested that a reference of that nature might be regarded by the Committee as bringing the matter before them that there is a body of evidence which we think important. Possibly there may be things in these Papers against us; but we think that in the State Papers, when the whole thing is gone into, and threshed out as it might be in a court of law, there would be many passages that would be evidence of what the exact state of things was at that time.

Chairman.] Could you give us the exact reference to the passage?

Mr. Latham.] There is a very great multitude of documents. I do not know whether you would allow the Fishmongers' document to be put in. That is a document in which the reference to the Papers has been put in with considerable care.

Chairman.] I do not know whether in that case it would not suffice.

Mr. John Ellis.] Perhaps it is only a selected reference.

Mr. Sexton.] A simple reference would be useful, if it was not a document of an argumentative character, founded upon the reference.

Mr. Latham.] I cannot say that this document is not argumentative, and it would not be fair, if it is objected to, to put it in in that form; but if the Committee desire it we could pick out the series of documents, stating only what the documents are, and the page at which they occur, and so forth, just making a list of them.

Chairman.] A list in continuous order we shall value decidedly, and it might be very useful in preparing our Report.

Mr. Sexton.] Indicating the point of each document referred to.

Mr. Latham.] Yes, I think that would be convenient, otherwise you would not know what you were looking for.

Mr. Elton.] Would that include the Carte papers.

Mr. Latham.] The Carte papers we did go into, but I do not think we found much in them that would be of any use to the Committee. We took the Patent and Close Rolls and the Calendar of State Papers. Now I will go to the motives and reasons.

Chairman.] You have done with the Orders and Conditions?

Mr. Latham.] Yes, I have done with them; I think the chief point that was made by my learned friend, Mr. Walker, on the subject of these motives and reasons was in regard to the final paragraph as to "the profits which London shall receive by this plantation." It was in the motives and reasons no doubt that for the first time the Crown approached the City of London, or at all events it is the first formal document in which the Crown approached the City; and no doubt in that last paragraph of this report there are set out various advantages which are, to a very great extent, public matter and not private matters, though in the fourth line the phrase is used "benefit of particular persons" among other things. But what I want to point out to the Committee is that this document must be read with the Orders and Conditions which were issued to all the world; because both documents were sent to the City at the same time, and therefore it was not necessary to put afresh in the motives and reasons all that had been set out in the Orders and Conditions as to making the grants of land and the power of alienation and so forth. That was already in the one document, and it was as a supplement to that document that the motives and reasons were sent; and there, no doubt, the King put forward to the best of his ability the strongest reasons that he could to induce the City of London to undertake the plantation, and to undertake it of course with reference to the orders and conditions. I do not think that I need trouble to go into that document at any great length; it has already been read to the Committee and considered by them.

The motives and reasons, and the Orders and Conditions were followed, as the Committee are aware, by a considerable amount of negotiation, and the negotiation resulted in articles of agreement. Now it is a fair rule of interpretation that when you have got a lot of correspondence as you often have between private parties, and you find that after the correspondence there was some formal agreement arrived at between the parties, you do not go back to the negotiations and say, "These are the terms of the agreement;" but when the parties have arrived at an agreement the negotiations are done with, and what you do not find in the agreement you are entitled to assume the parties intended to abandon or not to perform.

That is really to a very large extent my argument upon all the documents down to the first charter; but I say on this particular point of the motives and reasons, and the Orders and Conditions, that they were superseded by the Articles of Agreement.

Before I leave the motives and reasons, there is a phrase in the motives and reasons, as my learned friend Mr. Rigby reminds me, which has been referred to two or three times. In the third paragraph occur these words: "The rest to be planted with such undertakers as the City of London shall think good for their best profit, paying only for the same the easy rent of the undertakers." The question has been raised as to what that meant; and the interpretation which I put upon it is that the undertakers, and no doubt ultimately the companies, became undertakers, though they were not so at this time; the City of London became the undertaker, and the City of London or the Irish Society, in respect of its undertaking, was to pay the easy rent provided for in the Orders and Conditions; and I suppose as at some time or another the companies became in their turn undertakers, they were also to pay the same easy rent to the Crown and no more. But it does not say that every successive occupant or under tenant, and so forth, was to pay the same easy rent to the undertakers. The undertakers were to pay the easy rent, but they might sub-let or sub-demise the land at any rent they pleased.

Chairman.] How do you then construe the words, "as the City of London shall think good for their best profit;" does that mean for the City of London's best profit or for the undertakers' best profit.

Mr. Latham.] I think it means the City of London's best profit. The companies were not in it, and were not contemplated at this time. These were the motives and reasons to induce the

24 *July* 1890.

the City of London to undertake the plantation. The City of London, therefore, would plant for their own profit, and take the profits; and by the arrangements made of the companies taking over the land became undertakers in lieu of the City.

Chairman.] As to the last paragraph in those motives and reasons, with respect to what Bristol did for the city of Dublin, is there any light to be thrown upon the subject we are inquiring into from that?

Mr. *Latham.*] I do not know. It did occur to me to find out what happened in the case of the city of Bristol but I never followed it up.

Mr. *Ellis.*] Reference is made to that in the first volume of the Report of the Commission on Markets and Tolls, and you will find a little description of what was done about the settlement of Dublin.

Mr. *Latham.*] I mentioned that there were considerable negotiations, and I think it is admitted on all hands that there were in the interval between the motives and reasons and the articles of agreement; but if it is necessary to give evidence of that, a substantial amount of the negotiations will be found in the volumes to which I referred a minute or two ago. As I say, the motives and reasons were superseded by the articles of agreement. And now I will come to the articles of agreement. This was a formal agreement entered into on the 28th January 1610 between the Privy Council on the King's behalf "and the Committees appointed by act of Common Council on behalf of the Mayor and Commonalty of the City of London "concerning a plantation in part of the province of Ulster." The first article is that a sum of 20,000 *l.* should be levied whereof 15,000 *l.* was to be expended on the intended plantation. Then it says that 200 houses should be built at Derry, and that "4,000 acres lying on the Derry side" (this is the first appearance of the 4,000 acres) "next adjacent to the Derry should be laid thereunto. Bog and barren mountains to be no part thereof, but to go as waste for the city, the same to be done by indifferent commissioners." Then the Bishop and Dean of Derry were to have convenient plots of ground for their houses, which they got; that appeared afterwards. "Also that Coleraine should be situated and built on the abbey side, and that 100 houses should be built thereon, and room left for 300 more, and that 3,000 acres of land should be laid thereunto." (That made up the 7,000 acres, which, ultimately, the Irish Society had.) "Then it was agreed the other 3,000 acres to be taken on the other side of the river, otherwise the whole 3,000 acres were agreed to be taken on the abbey side next adjacent to the town of Coleraine." "That the rest of the territory and entire county of Coleraine, estimated at 10,000 acres more or less, undertaken by the City, be cleared from all particular interests, except the Bishop and Dean of Derry's inheritance, and except certain portions of land to be assigned unto three or more Irish gentlemen at the most, then dwelling and settled in the county of Coleraine, who were to be freeholders to the city, and to pay them some small rent, the same portions and rent to be limited by Commissioners, to be indifferently chosen between His Majesty and the City." That was the agreement: That the City should have the grant of the great bulk of the property. It is clear that the freeholders were intended to perform the duties of the grand jury and other county duties; it was necessary to have them for that purpose. Then it says, "That the woods and the ground and soil of Glanconkene and Killetrough extending from the county of Coleraine to Ballinderry be wholly to the City in perpetuity; the timber trees of those woods to be converted to the furtherance of plantation and all necessary uses within Ireland, and none to be made merchandise." Then it proceeds: "That the soil of so much land within and amongst the woods of Glanconkene and Killetrough which stand charged as surveyed lands to be undertaken in like form as the county of Coleraine." It was only the timber as to which there was the restriction, not the freehold of the land. Then, "That the City should have the patronage of all the churches as well within the said city of the Derry and town of Coleraine as in all lands to be undertaken by them. That the 7,000 acres laid to the city of Derry and town of Coleraine should be in fee farm at the rent of 53 *s.* 4 *d.* That the city of Derry and town of Coleraine and 7,000 acres of land to them shall be holden of the King in free burbage." It appears to be mis-spelt there for "burgage" (a mis-spelling which goes on through a good many of the documents.) "That the residue of the county lands and woods and all such lands as were to be undertaken, should be holden of the King in common socage." "That the customs of all goods imported or exported," "the salmon and eel-fishing," should belong to the City, and the City was to have liberty "to transport all prohibited wares;" and the City should have the office of Admiralty, and all royalties and profits belonging thereto, and the liberty of fishing (I am going hurriedly through the articles), and that no flax or hemp was to be carried out of the ports of Derry and Coleraine without license. "That as well the cities and towns as the county of Coleraine be freed from all patents of privileges." That was one of the matters that was in dispute afterwards. "That the City should have the castle of Culmore." "That the liberty of the city of Derry and Coleraine should extend three miles every way." "That the City should have such further liberties to the Derry and Coleraine as upon view of the Charter of London, the cinque ports, and Newcastle-upon-Tyne, or the city of Dublin, should be found fit for those places." "That all particular men's interest in the places about the Derry and county of Coleraine, and in other the undertaking lands be cleared and freed to the City." "That sufficient forces should be maintained at the King's charges for safety of the undertakers for a convenient time." "Then for settling and securing all things touching the said plantation, His Majesty would give his Royal Assent to Acts of Parliament in England, and the like in Ireland to pass. That the City should have time during the term of seven years to make such reasonable demands as time should show to be needful, but could not presently be foreseen." "Lastly, that the City should, with all

all speed, set forward the said plantation in such sort as that there should be 60 houses built in Derry, and 40 houses in Coleraine by the 1st of November then next following, with convenient fortifications, and the rest of the houses with the fortifications should be built, and perfected by the 1st November 1611."

You will see, all through that document, there is no mention of any permanent trust or obligation whatever to be affixed either to any of the Companies, or, at any rate to any of the persons who took under the City, or even to the City itself. I venture to think that when you look at the documents closely, if any permanent obligations existed at all, you must and will, only find them in the charter; you cannot find any permanent duties imposed by any of these preliminary documents. And even if you could find such permanent obligations in any of these preliminary documents, I say that they were swallowed up in the charters; but, as I say, I think you cannot find them there. Then when you get to the charter, the only permanent obligations were obligations laid upon the Irish Society, from which the City Companies were expressly exempted. Alienation was expressly contemplated from the beginning, and expressly authorised in these early documents; and alienation took place. Taking document after document, and coming down to the present time, you never find in any one of them a trust declared. You do not find it in the second charter, which, as I say, is our root of title; you do not find it in the licenses in mortmain; you do not find trusts and obligations declared, or made obligatory upon the Companies in the conveyances to the Companies; and you do not find it in any document down to the present time. Therefore, whether you call it a trust, or an obligation, you cannot fix the Companies with either, at the present time.

Just one or two words in conclusion. I think I am entitled to make this observation, because it has direct reference to this part of the question; and that is as to what sort of issue this inquiry might take. After having heard the parties the Committee will, decide what view they take of the evidence, and of the arguments that have been addressed to them. They may come to the conclusion that we are wrong and that there were trusts, or there were obligations, or trusts and obligations from the first imposed upon the Irish Society and upon the Companies. If the Committee do come to that conclusion, I submit that there is only one proper course to be adopted, and that is that the Committee should report to the House that they have found a *primâ facie* case, and that it is fit and proper that the Attorney General should commence proceedings to establish those trusts and enforce those obligations. In that case we shall have to abide the result of the suit which I do not say we shall enter upon with a light heart, because I apprehend nobody who understands litigation thinks it is ever to be entered upon with a light heart; but we shall endeavour to establish to the satisfaction of a Court of Law what we shall have failed to establish satisfactorily to this Committee.

There is on the other hand, of course, the possibility that the Committee might find that after all there is no real *primâ facie* case of breach of trust or default in obligation whatever. In that case the Committee might either take the line of saying there is an end of the matter, or they might, as I thought was possibly indicated by a question which I observe in the evidence was asked by the Chairman; they might fall back upon Lord Derby's Commission, and say that, whenever the recommendations of Lord Derby's Commission come to be dealt with by Parliament, it would be right and proper, in their opinion, in any new charges and impositions and duties or obligations to be cast upon the Companies, or created for the Companies, these Irish claims should be treated fully and fairly. I think in Mr. Saunders' evidence, it appeared clearly that so far as he was concerned, he was willing personally to use his influence in the Skinners' Company rather in that direction; but at all events, it is obvious that a line of that sort would be the line of least resistance; because if you find against us that there are trusts and obligations, I would ask the Committee to remember that it is a very serious matter. It is a charge against the Companies that for 250 years and more, they, the administrators at the present time, and the administrators during all these 250 years, have misapplied the very large funds that were given them, as trustees for beneficial and public objects, and have taken them for their own profit and advantage, and, in fact, have put them into their own pockets. That is a very serious charge, however gently it may be put, which no public bodies like the City of London Companies can be expected to put up with, without doing their utmost to discharge themselves from it; and consequently as long as that charge is hanging over their heads, they are bound to resist it. But if it is put in the other way, as putting new charges and obligations upon them, that is a matter for Parliament, which would have to be discussed and considered by Parliament, but it casts no reflection upon the Company as administrators.

I think it was suggested that there was a sort of tertium quid or another course that might be adopted by the Committee, but I only mention it to reject it in advance, because I venture to think it is a course that would be contrary to the traditions of Parliament, and I have very little doubt, contrary to the sentiments of the English and Irish gentlemen who form this Committee. This is the sort of suggestion that seems to be adumbrated, that the Committee should in effect come to this sort of conclusion. It is true there is no trust or obligation to be found in the documents; it is true there is no trust or obligation that we can discover from the course of dealing; it is true that so far as the opinions of expert lawyers have come before the Committee, the opinions are one way and one way only, and although those opinions were obtained by people adverse to the Companies, the opinions were in favour of the Companies; it is true that it does not appear that any lawyer of eminence on either side of St. George's Channel has advised that there was a trust or obligation, though the inquiry has been made. The only suggestion on the other side has been that of my learned friend, Mr. Walker, in argument, that the late Baron Dowse

Dowse was said to have expressed some opinion; but that opinion was not produced, it is not in writing, and it is not the sort of opinion upon which the Committee could place much reliance. The suggestion, as I say, is that the Committee should then proceed; although all that is seen we do find to our satisfaction some sort of moral obligation, you may call it, or some sort of something which is akin to a trust, which is not a trust which is not strong enough for me to recommend to Parliament, that the Attorney General should commence a suit against the companies, because probably the Attorney General would be defeated; but we think that we can make out against them a sort of case which will be a sufficient preamble for a new Act of Parliament which shall declare *ex post facto* that in spite of the courts and in spite of opinions, there have been trusts or obligations always upon these companies which ought to be fulfilled.

I venture to think that it is quite impossible for the Committee to take that intermediate course. There are only two lines possible; either there is a trust or obligation, or there is not a trust or obligation; those are the two things. We shall be content if the finding of the Committee is that there is no legal trust or obligation; and the consequences of the finding we must leave to the Committee and Parliament.

Mr. *Rigby*.] I appear, Sir, for the Skinners' Company, the only other company that is separately represented here; and with your permission I should like to offer some observations on their behalf. Of course I do not propose to go with such detail that my learned friend Mr. Latham has gone into the matter.

Chairman.] Will you explain why the Skinners' Company claim a special hearing for themselves; no doubt you have some ground upon which to base your application to be heard separately.

Mr. *Rigby*.] Of course our interests are very large. We were parties to the Skinners' Company's action, and so far as that is concerned, we are absolutely bound by everything in that case, and we rely upon everything that is there decided. We are in a separate position from the rest; we have expended in quite modern times, upon the faith of our title, in the whole some 70,000 *l.* or 80,000 *l.*, in buying up the shares of our co-adventurers, the smaller companies, the Stationers and the Whitebakers. My learned friend Mr. Latham has, no doubt, very well represented the general views of all the companies; but I should like to be permitted, not to go into detail, but to state our view as shortly and concisely as I can upon this question of trust and obligation, and I hope the time will not be wasted if I try to do so.

Chairman.] Very well.

Mr. *Rigby*.] Of course treating the Committee as if it were a court of law, I confine myself entirely to the single question, what in a court of law would be the position of the Skinners' Company; and I confess that that is very much the same, or entirely the same, as the other companies with regard to the lands that were granted to them by charter. I have nothing to do with questions of policy, and I do not propose to say a single syllable about that; I shall only represent our legal title. I am aware that I shall be doing what Mr. Latham has done in detail, in a very short manner; but I hope it will be none the worse for that.

I say that the Skinners' Company are grantees of the Crown of the lands which they hold by virtue of a title accruing in the reign of Charles II. What the intention of the Crown was at that time is to be found from the terms of the charter and the licence to hold in mortmain. Whatever the intentions of the Crown at that time might be they must govern in a court of law. This was 30 years after the original charter; during that interval the charter had been attacked, and for a time successfully attacked in the Star Chamber, and almost every conceivable reason why the charter should not stand had been brought forward; and ultimately by a *scire facias* which was the appropriate remedy for getting rid of the title on the common law side of the Court of Chancery, the title had been got rid of altogether. Then the charter of Charles II. recites that the whole of the lands had got back into the Crown; and at that time, I apprehend, there was no doubt at all that whatever view of the facts the Crown chose to take must be deemed to be the true view. If there were any objection to be taken, it could only be taken legally in one manner. It might be taken again by *scire facias*, by calling upon the grantees to show cause why the Crown grants should not be revoked; but, as a matter of law, until that process had been gone through, all that a court of law could do is to interpret the document to see what the Crown grant means. Knowing that the Committee have had their attention called both to the second licence in mortmain and to the second charter, I shall very briefly recall what the contents of those documents are in the important points.

First of all, the Crown recognises (and, as I say, as a matter of law, what the Crown recognises, as long as the patent stands, is fact) that the companies, of whom I represent one, have taken upon themselves a great burden in reference to the plantations. I say that, so long as the patent stands, that really puts an end to the suggestion that the original companies had not expended monies at all. Granting that, the history shows that the monies had been levied by a sort of power claimed somewhat arbitrarily by the city of London in the form of a tax; yet the Crown, having the property in its hands, chooses, in 1662, to recognise that the expenditure had been expenditure by the companies, and in the very terms of the charter provides that they shall have the same lands that were originally granted to them under the charter of James I. restored to them. It recognises equally that these companies had, and have, a right to assign the property; for it speaks not only of the companies, but of their assigns; and that there may be no doubt at all what is meant, it is coupled with under-tenants, showing, therefore, that they can not only let, but assign the lands that were given to them.

The

24 *July* 1890.

The licence in mortmain plainly points out that the intention of the Crown in granting the charter and in reverting the lands to the Irish Society was that the Irish Society might convey to the companies the very properties that had been conveyed to them before.

Chairman.] If it was to be a conveyance by the Irish Society, how do you make out there was a grant to the companies from the Crown; I am asking for information. The grant from the Crown to the Irish Society I understand.

Mr. Rigby.] Yes, I begin with that of course. That is expressed to be, and by the licence in mortmain is more clearly shewn to be, to the intent that the Irish Society shall forthwith make over to the different companies the identical lands which had been vested in them by virtue of what was done under the first charter.

Chairman.] But you are not direct grantees from the Crown.

Mr. Rigby.] Not direct, certainly.

Chairman.] It is very important of course, because your position in respect to the Irish Society has a very decisive bearing upon the argument whether you took from the Irish Society or took, as I understood you to contend in your opening, directly as grantees from the Crown.

Mr. Rigby.] I do not take as a matter of conveyancing direct as grantee from the Crown, but in substance I contend I do so. I contend that where the Crown by letters patent vests land in a particular corporation to the intent expressed in the letters patent that that corporation shall not retain the lands but pass them on to others, though as a matter of conveyancing I am not a grantee of the Crown but a grantee of a grantee, yet as a matter of construction, and to ascertain what the intent of the Crown over the entire property was, it really makes no difference. Assuming, as I freely admit, that the Irish Society were trustees, I contend, for the question of ascertaining whether a trust of any sort recognisable in law was passed on to the companies as assigns of the Irish Society, I can read the whole documents and read the two together, and ascertain from them that the intention of the Crown was that the property should vest in the companies; and my argument will be that I am free from any trust whatever.

Now I want to point out one matter which perhaps has not been mentioned. I notice that my learned friend Mr. Walker relied, in dealing with the original charter of James I., upon the phrase showing that the Irish Society were authorised to convey such lands as they should be willing to grant, founding upon that that they had discretion. In one sense I agree that they had originally. They were to see that everything was done in a right and proper manner; but I point out that in this second charter when it was fore-ordained by the Crown that the identical lands should be conveyed, the same language is used. The power which is vested in the Irish Society, if you read that alone, is only to grant to the City companies such lands as they (the Irish Society) are willing to grant. But the antecedent recital shows that it was the duty of the Irish Society to re-convey all the lands that had been vested in the company, to the intent that the rights of the company and of the company's assigns, and of the company's under-tenants, should be restored.

Now, as I say, as a mere question of law from that point, the title is an exceedingly simple one. We have only two documents, the charter and the licence to hold in mortmain, that have to be considered; and treating them as existing legal documents which can only be attacked by the process of *scire facias*, by Her Majesty's Attorney General calling upon the holders of the land to shew why the patent should not be revoked and the title to the land resumed; I say that as a matter of construction, there is no ground for affixing any trust whatsoever upon the company. If there be, it must be by means of the words of reference, which would seem to grant to the companies the same title that they had before. I submit that those are mere ordinary words well familiar to conveyancers, that they are to be restored as of their old estate, but that you cannot derive from them any limitation of the estate or interest that is to be vested under the trustees by virtue of the intended grant from the society. If that be so, our case is, I should say, of the very simplest nature. We have only to rely upon that second charter and the grants which are made in strict conformity with the charter. The Mercers' Company have, I think, put in their conveyance. We have a conveyance and reconstruction of the manor of Pellipar, which was the Skinners' Manor, and a grant by appropriate conveyances of the whole of that manor to us. In those grants there is no reference whatever to any trusts; they are exactly grants in the form of one vendor to purchasers upon an ordinary transaction, and no reservation and no implication of any trust. So that we have got to assume that the Irish Society from the first mistook their duty, and that in conveying that manor to the companies, overlooked the most important part of their duty which certainly would have been to bring within the four corners of any conveyance sufficient notice of any trust with which the lands might be affected. Considering this arrangement was the outcome of a great deal of political agitation and a great deal of what had remained of the troubled times before the Long Parliament, that it had to do with what the Long Parliament had determined, we cannot suppose that the matters were not carefully considered, and we are met at the first by the great difficulty that the Irish Society, believing themselves to be carrying out the intentions of the Sovereign, conveyed these lands to us in fee simple without imposing any trust upon us.

Going backwards, if I may go back in history, it is quite impossible; it would be absolutely out of the question in a court of law; that the Attorney-General should come to have these letters patent recalled, on the pretence of any artifice or deceit practised upon the Crown. The revocation of the patent is recited in this patent. All the grounds that ingenuity could suggest in the arbitrary times of the Star Chamber, have been suggested, and were matters of record. The

24 *July* 1890.

The advisers of the Crown knew at the time what objections could be taken; and if they came now to revoke these Letters Patent, they would have a task which I think they would find it exceedingly difficult to make even plausible in a court of law. But if I go back and enquire, I shall submit that it is reasonably plain upon the documents before the Committee, that, not at first, not willingly, but under pressure, and a great deal against their will, the City companies were ultimately brought into this position, that they were undertakers with regard to the plantation; that that was their ultimate position, though, as my learned friend Mr. Latham has pointed out, the original idea with regard to this county of Coleraine, or Londonderry, as it afterwards was undoubtedly, was, that the City of London in some way or other, probably in its corporate capacity, should be undertakers for that particular county, leaving the other counties to be settled by private undertakers. But the motives and reasons when first the City is approached, set forth shortly, because it was not necessary, as they had the other document with them, to do so at length, that the undertakers were to hold such lands as were undertaken by them ultimately, on the easy rent of the undertakers. I will not trouble the Committee by going through the details; they are set forth both in the case before Lord Langdale, and in Lord Lyndhurst's Judgment in the House of Lords. Step by step the suggestion is made to the companies, "Will you come in?" and step by step they do come in as undertakers; and I submit the obligations imposed upon them are obligations of undertakers, and not obligations of a public nature, which certainly were imposed upon the Irish Society.

The argument against me is this: You find here, and undoubtedly you do, recitals in the Letters Patent showing that very great and important public objects were in the purview of the Sovereign at the time. The argument, therefore, is that they must extend to every part of the land that is included in the original grant. I meet that altogether by saying that there is no foundation for it. There I join issue entirely with my learned friend, Mr. Walker, and I say the mere fact that you find in Letters Patent, especially of the date that we are now discussing, those general objects put forward in a very general manner, by no means leads you one step towards the conclusion that all the lands which are the subject of the grant are to be also subject to the trusts.

The Chairman referred to the grants of Virginia and Maryland as being grants made about the same time. I have referred to them, and though I do not know that they are very similar, I think for this purpose they are sufficiently similar to the present case to be the foundation of a fair argument. The Virginia Charter was granted in the year 1606. I am reading from a collection of American Charters which I obtained from the library at Lincoln's Inn, and I will give very shortly indeed the effect of the grant of 1606. There were two companies, one I may call the London Company, and the other the West Country Company, companies of gentlemen, persons of good position, and merchants, who wished to make plantations in Virginia. The King after reciting the application of these gentlemen, "to us that we would vouchsafe to them our licence to make habitation, plantation, and to deduce a colony of sundry of our people into that part of America, commonly called Virginia," "and to that end" (he goes on to say) "we greatly commending and graciously accepting of their desire for the furtherance of so noble a work which may by the providence of Almighty God hereafter tend to the glory of His Divine Majesty in propagating the Christian Religion to such people as yet live in darkness and miserable ignorance of the true knowledge and worship of God, and may in time bring the infidels and savages living in those parts to human civility, and to a settled and quiet government; do by these our Letters Patent, graciously accept and agree to" their desires. Then going on, among the other matters that are agreed to by these Letters Patent, we find towards the end of the charter, that the Crown "does for us, our heirs and successors, by these presents grant and agree to, and with"; and then he introduces the names of the first company of adventurers who were to go to that part of Virginia, "That we, our heirs, and successors, upon petition in that behalf to be made, shall by Letters Patent under the Great Seal of England, give and grant unto such persons, their heirs and assigns, as the council of that colony or the most part of them shall for that purpose nominate and assign, all the lands, tenements, and hereditaments which shall be within the precincts limited for that colony," "to be holden of us, our heirs and successors, as of our manor of East Greenwich, in the county of Kent, in free and common soccage only, and not in capite."

Now, if it were possible to say that the mere recital of these very general public purposes implied a trust as to all the lands, then it might fairly be said under the Virginia Charter that every person who was to get a grant of land under that charter was to be, in some sort, a trustee. Anything further from the real meaning of the Crown, and anything more different from what has been understood to be in practice the meaning of this charter, it would be difficult to conceive. But I say it is a wrong principle to take out a recital and to assume that, because the object is to bring about certain important results, of necessity the trusts can be inferred from that object.

Chairman.] Was it not exactly from a recital of that kind that Lord Langdale and the House of Lords inferred that a trust was meant to exist as regards the Irish Society.

Mr. Rigby.] I thank you, Sir, for that observation, because it brings me at once to what I have to say upon that point, and then I will pass from it. It was from that recital; but now I want to point out the difference between our companies, who are, as we say, the undertakers, and the Irish Society. The Irish Society was a corporation created for the purpose of the charter; it had no independent existence; it was nominated in the first instance as a committee by the City of London, but by the Charter of James I., and again by the restoring Charter of Charles, it was created as a perpetual corporation for the

purposes

purposes of the charter. Our companies existed independently of the charter, long before the charter ever was granted; all of them, I believe, existed for centuries before that. The *Irish Society, ex converso*, from the very first never had or could have, and never claimed, the slightest fraction of beneficial interest in this property, nor any kind of beneficial interest. In the Skinners' case it was treated as a matter of absolute admission that the Irish Society throughout all the time that they had been there, had not, and could not have, a beneficial interest. And why? because no intention to give them a beneficial interest appears anywhere in the charter. They were not created for the purpose of making a profit for themselves; their creation depends upon the charter. You do not find anywhere in the charter that they have other objects, or can have other objects, than those that are to be found in the four corners of the charter. If they had a beneficial interest, where was it to go? it could only be put into the pocket of the corporators, and the corporators of such a grant as this could not for a moment claim anything at all. Of necessity, therefore, they were trustees; that was never questioned at all in the Skinners' case. The only matter that was questioned, and that was then an important one, and is not now unimportant, was as to the nature of the trust upon which they held all the hereditaments that were vested in them; and the argument of the companies, and especially the company I now represent, was this; We can show by a careful examination of these documents that the property that was made over to us was not the whole of the property we were entitled to as undertakers, but that what remained vested in the Irish Society was also ours, though the trusts were not quite clearly declared in the charter; but the lands were ours because we can show outside the charter that the Irish Society only hold them as trustees for us; that is the whole question. Lord Cottenham, when it first came before him, at once, as was said in the House of Lords, seized the point. That it was a trust, everyone took for granted; there could be nothing else but a trust in the case of the society, which only existed for the purposes of the charter. The question was merely whether it was a private trust for the companies, which therefore might be administered by the Court of Chancery, and might be controlled by the Court of Chancery, or whether it partook to such an extent of the nature of a public trust that it was beyond the jurisdiction of the court altogether. The decision was unhesitatingly come to by Lord Cottenham in the first instance, though only dealing with an application for a receiver, and unhesitatingly come to afterwards by Lord Langdale, and by the House of Lords, who adopted and supported Lord Langdale's judgment, that the trust, which confessedly was a trust extending to everything the Irish Society could possibly have, was of the nature of a public trust; and furthermore (and it is important to see how far the decision went), I submit upon all the proceedings it was clearly recognised that if the Irish Society had a surplus after all the public purposes that they were concerned to take care of, had been provided for, that surplus would belong to the companies. The difficulty was, that the companies said, "We can tie you down; we can treat you as private trustees; we therefore can cavil at this or that expense of yours, and cut you down, and so get a surplus;" and they applied that the Irish Society might be deprived of the control of the trust, and that other trustees might be appointed. If it had been a private trust, that would have been quite right, but the test was, that it was a public trust, and nothing else.

Now this is really the point I want to press on the Committee, and let us see whether there is any analogy whatever between the Irish Society and the different companies. First of all, the Irish Society did not provide any of the moneys, at any rate, not in the same way as the companies did. The companies are recognised by the charter as having taken the great burden of expense upon them. The Irish Society of themselves had no money; they had no joint stock; if they provided anything, it must have been through the means of a company, or it may have been through the City of London. I do not care which it was. Of themselves they had no possessions or powers. From the time when the lands were vested in them, undoubtedly they would have the lands which were not divided among the companies, and would hold those lands, and get the revenues and profits of them, and in that sense they would have money; but that would be trust money always. Of their own independent property they had none, for indeed they had no independent existence at all. On the other hand, the companies had, it may be vicariously at first (I care not at all about that), provided the funds. I rely on the view taken by Lord Langdale, that it ultimately was recognised, as certainly it was recognised by Charles II. in his charter, that it was the companies who had provided the funds. Now these companies existed for totally different purposes. They were not concerned any more than other undertakers to deal with the question of Ireland. It was not for the plantation of Ulster that they were called into existence. They were only after great difficulty substituted for the City of London as undertakers, and we say as undertakers, in other counties, and that their obligations are entirely to be treated as those of ordinary undertakers. If I wanted any proof of that, let us see how the property came to be divided among them. I assume that the Charter of Charles was really intended to give an *ex post facto* sanction to what had been done under the Charter of James, but under the Charter of James what took place? The City sent out to Ireland certain persons who made an actual survey of the property there. They came back again. An arrangement was made that each one of the 12 principal companies should have attached to it certain smaller subordinate companies in whom it never was intended that the land should be vested at all; who never at any moment had had any part of the lands vested in them, but who were to be in point of beneficial enjoyment in proportion to the sums which they had subscribed, in precisely the same position as the 12 principal companies. The Committee will remember with what precision the division, which was made after the Charter of James, was carried out. Down to pounds, shillings, and pence the exact

and

24 July 1890.

sum that was attributable to each one of the companies, whether a principal company that was intended to be a grantee, or one of the smaller and subordinate ones, was taken notice of. A few pounds were required to be paid in order to equalise the amounts; those sums were ordered to be paid in no case exceeding 1 l. 6 s. 8 d., down to the smaller one of 6 s. 8 d.; but precisely the same course was adopted as would have been taken had there been a commission to partition these lands into 12 parts. How does that at all fit in with the notion of a trust? Why all that particularity? Why indeed were the companies concerned at all if they were only to be trustees? We had a representative corporation, the Irish Society, fully sufficient to carry out those objects if they had had money. Of course the companies were brought in, because through them and by their aid, money could be got, the Irish Society having no funds. But if they were to be mere trustees, if the money that was received from the companies could be properly described as taxation, and as levied for public purposes, involving no right in the companies to follow the moneys, if that could be said, why the companies at all. And furthermore, why stop with these companies; how can it be explained upon any theory of a subsisting trust, that the companies were grouped together; that each of the 12 had other companies beneficially interested in lands, and that that was done with all the exactitude of a partition, and that everyone of these companies got property exactly proportioned, as far as the ingenuity of man could do it, to the advances which had been made by or for them. It is supposed also that these companies had obligations coincident with the amount of the land. Where comes in the obligation which is imposed upon, say the Stationers, because I represent in my own person, so far as the grant under the charters was concerned, not only the Skinners' Company, but the Stationers' and I think the Girdlers', and the White Bakers. I have purchased from two of them their shares and interests, and it is rather interesting to see upon the evidence of Mr. Saunders how that came about. They wanted to have some share in the management; they never had had any share in the management, and that was not the intention of the grants that were made. The intent was, that the principal companies should take and manage the properties, and no doubt they were trustees in this sense, that so far as the proportion went which belonged to each of the subordinate companies, they were, as they have always held themselves, responsible, and had to account. In that sense, and in that only, were they trustees. Consider how far it was carried. We have the case of the two companies, the Coopers and the Browne Bakers, who, at a critical moment, preferred rather to lose all their advances, and that was taken hold of by Lord Langdale in saying it was clearly recognised there that the companies had still an interest in the moneys they had advanced, but the Coopers and the Browne Bakers refused at that time to make further contributions, and the Corporation of the City of London say, "Either pay this, or forfeit the advantages that you have already obtained." And then came the order that the Chamberlain of the City, when the Coopers and Browne Bakers declined to make the further advance, should make, for the City and on behalf of the City the further advances, and should have all the benefit which the two recalcitrant companies, the Coopers and Browne Bakers, would have had in the plantation. What was the result of that? One of these was under the Ironmongers, as a subordinate company to the Ironmongers, and one was under the Clothworkers. To whom did the Clothworkers from that time, and the Ironmongers account for that share of the profits? Why, to the City of London, and the City of London came, in that indirect manner, into the position of the subordinate companies, and became entitled to their share from the Ironmongers and the Clothworkers, which would otherwise have been paid to the subordinate companies, the Coopers and the Browne Bakers. It was in that capacity that they were made defendants in the Skinners' case, and it was recognised in that case that the City besides any visitorial powers they might have had had a beneficial interest in the estates to the extent of those subordinate companies, the Coopers and the Browne Bakers, that they represented. I present this to the Committee as being altogether inconsistent with the idea that there was any pervading trust, or any prevailing trust at all that extended to the lands that were given in severalty to the different grant companies. It is almost inconceivable that such a scheme should have entered the mind of man; that you should take all that trouble of actual survey if you intended to bring them in as trustees, in order to get the advantage of their administrative power. You would not have gone through this minutely accountancy process of estimating to a farthing what they had done, and imposing upon them just so much trust as corresponded with the moneys they had paid; so that, I say, there is a broad distinction, and I say that Lord Langdale very clearly recognised it throughout the whole of his judgment, which I, for my part, should have read had it not been that I know my friend, Mr. Latham, has insisted upon it before the Committee; but, knowing he has done so, and knowing he has called attention to it, I merely recall to the memory of the Committee that Lord Langdale again and again distinguishes the case of the Irish Society, a society which had no independent existence at all, and which would of necessity be a trustee, from the case of the other companies, which certainly were in a totally different position, both as regards contributions and as regards ability for such contributions, for it appears by these papers that their liability did not cease when the land was conveyed to them, but requisitions were made afterwards and payments were made afterwards, and, so far as my clients are concerned, you will remember that, in 1637, that is years and years after the lands were conveyed to us under the first charter, we were called upon to make a contribution of some 2,700 l., and for that we had to pawn our plate. No doubt, we might have raised it from the members, but, at that time, it was thought better that the joint stock of the company should be made liable. We raised the money upon our plate; we raised it by the balance of cash in our hands; we raised it so far as necessary by mortgage of our other property

24 July 1890.

property not devised to charitable uses. So that when the land was originally granted it was granted to companies who were looked upon as capable and ready to provide the moneys necessary for carrying out the scheme. What resemblance is there to the Irish Society in that? The Irish Society, as I said before, had no money to put down; they had no beneficial interest whatever.

Now I do not think I should be treating the Committee fairly if I merely repeated observations that had been made by my friend Mr. Latham. I do follow him, and adopt his argument; I say, that the orders and conditions (if we take the documents in turn) for the most part concern themselves with matters that must be determined within five or six, or a few years, and in so far as there were in those articles that he referred to any permanent matters looked forward to, they were matters that the Crown had to provide. The condition was to be observed as well by his Majesty as by the undertakers, and then when we come down further, we find that the motives and reasons were simply in the first instance to bring the City of London into the position of undertakers; that all the negotiations which took place, had the effect only of moving from the City of London, to a great extent, the obligations, and the profit at the same time, connected with the undertaking. I do not deny that, as regards the lands that remained vested in them, the Irish Society, though not undertakers to all intents and purposes, were to a great extent undertakers; that is to say, they were bound by the conditions that the Crown imposed upon them, as though they had been undertakers with respect to the preservation of the town of Derry, and keeping the garrison in the castle, and so on. In all these respects, some of the duties that would have been incumbent on the undertakers, are cast upon them, but over and above that, they remained without a fraction of beneficial interest. I do not put forward the Skinners' case as a decision; that would not be fair, because the question was not really raised for the determination of the House of Lords, but in the way in which it was dealt with by Lord Langdale and by everyone concerned, it was treated as plain that the Irish Society must be trustees, and I say on a fair reading of all the documents, it will be found it was treated as equally plain, that although they had unbounded power to spend the money which came into their hands, yet as they had done so, they had not done wrong for the centuries during which they had distributed the money among the companies, but had done right, and if there was any surplus in their hands, that must go to the companies in proportion to their interests. I submit that upon the whole case, there is really no trust and no fair ground upon which a trust can be implied in the companies as distinguished from the Irish Society, and that we have a right to come back again to our root of title, the character and the second licence to hold in mortmain, and to construed the documents, and from the construction of those documents you find nothing more than this, that the companies are to be grantees in fee, with power themselves to assign, a matter inconsistent with a trust altogether. The argument must go to this, that when they got those lands they had no power to assign. If they had power to assign, it follows that they are not trustees. It never could have been contemplated that there was to be a trust which would attach to different parts of the property, even if it had been handed over by the Companies. I submit that there is no evidence of a trust to be found in the charter. I quite agree, as a matter of law, with what my friend Mr. Latham stated, that really everything that was precedent to the first charter must be taken to be negotiation leading up to that; but I say that we may fearlessly go into all that negotiation and find nothing but this, that the Crown recognised that the Companies in their corporate capacity, or by their members, I do not care which, had really been at the great burden and expense of carrying out the objects of the Crown, and, as recompense for that, and as both charters put it, for the purpose that they may hereafter receive some return for their expenditure (I am not giving the words, but the meaning), the grants were to be made to them. If that be so, it is a difficult position indeed to say that the money which came to them as a return for the expense which they had been put to was money which they had no beneficial interest in at all, and which they were not allowed to apply to the same purposes that the ordinary stock of the Companies would properly be applicable to, but that every penny of it could again be seized in their hands and treated precisely as the money in the hands of the Irish Society might have been treated; in short, that they are trustees. I know no position between the two. Either there is a trust or there is not. If there was a trust, then I agree that trust, seeing it must be implied from very wide and general recitals, must be in itself of the widest and most general nature; I can see nothing to restrict it at all. If it is a trust, it is a trust in the hands of the Companies just as it was in the hands of the Irish Society, nothing more and nothing else, that leaves no sort of room for any profit to be derived by the Companies, and that, in truth, leaves no sort of place for giving effect to the avowed and expressed intention both of James and of Charles in granting the charters.

Chairman.] Do you contend, Mr. Rigby, that the whole of the land of the county of Coleraine was not granted for the purposes of the plantation?

Mr. Rigby.] That depends, Sir; it was granted. The whole of the land unquestionably was set apart by the Crown, and taken out of the Crown, being then vested in the Crown for the purposes of the plantation; but then I say one of those purposes was that you should pay and that you should recompense, and make it worth the while of the undertakers, and pay them, in order to do the work; that it was a clear part of the intention of the Crown that all those lands which were fit and proper to be divided (the Committee will remember what my friend Mr. Latham said about the lands divisible, and that there were certain lands recognised as divisible), were undertakers' lands. They are no more and no less for the purposes of the plantation of that county of Londonderry than the undertakers' lands in the other five or six counties are for the purposes of the

24 *July* 1890.

the plantation there. Each and every one of them is needed for the purposes of the plantation. A man does not get 1,000 acres of land at a mere nominal rent simply for his interest, but because it is for the interest of the estate that he should be there as a landowner on easy terms. In that sense, and in no other, do we submit to the Committee, were these lands recognised as properly and fitly divisible among the undertakers, that is to say, the companies, for the purposes of the plantation.

Chairman.] Supposing the companies had refused to accept the lands at the time when they had an option, what would the position of these lands have been in that case?

Mr. *Rigby.*] I apprehend that the purposes of the Crown would have failed altogether. Probably no one else would have been able or desirous to take them up. It is obvious that the Crown, even when making the grant, do not pretend that the company is to make a present profit. It only says that you may in the future time get a return. By an arbitrary exercise both of the prerogative and of the authority of the City, I think that is sufficiently plain now to us, the companies have been turned into unwilling purchasers; and really, as Lord Langdale says, the option was given to them either of losing what had been extracted from them against their will or of taking such return as there might be in the lands. If they had not taken them, and had not expended further sums, we have no means of seeing where the money would have come from. The lands would have lain waste till the present day, or at all events for a long time after that. Obviously here a difficulty arose, and the Crown was under a great difficulty, and from time to time was dissatisfied with the City refusing it, dissatisfied when the companies made terms, almost forcing on them the articles of agreement, and finally giving them these lands, not as a sufficient recompense, but as something in return for the public-spirited work they had done. The Charter refers to the fact that they had gone into possession, and had begun to build, and all that sort of thing, in 1613, when James granted the first Charter. He does not profess to say, I am giving you something worth more than you have paid, but you have been at a heavy burden, and take these lands in order on a future day you may recompense yourselves for the expenditure.

Chairman.] Your theory is that the Irish Society was called into existence in order to satisfy the purposes of plantation in the 7,000 acres.

Mr. *Rigby.*] Yes; and probably I may say more than that. I do not limit myself to that.

Chairman.] If that were your position how would you reconcile it with Lord Lyndhurst's words in the judgment at page 484 of 11 Clark and Finnelly. "The next question is, what were the powers conferred upon the Irish Society, and what were the duties they had to perform? They had to superintend, order, direct, and manage the whole of this extensive concern. They were appointed for that object. They had to superintend and govern, and perform therefore those duties that were necessary for the purposes of giving effect to the grant, the purposes of the grant being those I have stated." Was Lord Lyndhurst there speaking simply, do you take it, of their own 7,000 acres?

Mr. *Rigby.*] I do not think that at all. I think if we went carefully through the Charter we should find there were many more powers than that; but I do say this, that the language of Lord Lyndhurst, with which I have no fault to find at all, is perfectly consistent with my argument. They had the superintending of the granting out of lands among the undertakers. That was obvious. It was left to them according to the first Charter. The Committee will remember that no mention was made of the companies at all in the first Charter, but according to the first Charter the Irish Society were under no obligation to grant lands to anyone whatever if we confine ourselves to the Charter. So that the parting out, the allotting, the apportionment of the land among the undertakers, was part of their duties with regard to that great undertaking. In fact, they were the spring and moving power of the undertaking, but that does not prevent them from properly exercising what was a power given to them among the rest, of alienating altogether the lands which they had. It was pointed out both in the Charter of James and in the license of Mortmain, that power was given to them to alien, and not only to the companies but to other persons. Therefore, they were not to remain in *perpetuity* the owners in fee of the property, but to make it over in fee to someone else.

Chairman.] But with powers and duties of supervision.

Mr. *Rigby.*] We must consider what was the question being agitated there. The question being agitated was not the least what the Irish Society could do towards the company. That question was not the question raised in this action, though incidentally it was dealt with. The question was whether or not the company were beneficiaries in such a sense that they could dictate to the Irish Society, and Lord Lyndhurst says nothing of the sort; this is the supreme authority; this is the authority in which all powers of superintendence and everything else is vested; these are public important trusts which cannot be subject to the supervision even of the High Court of Chancery, and therefore, not of any other court in the kingdom; they are of an indefinite nature and of an important nature; they may be subject to the visitorial powers of the City or the Crown, and in the ultimate resort no doubt the Crown, if the trusts were not carried out, could have a scire *facias* to repeal the patent, as they tried to do in 1640 or about that time.

Chairman.] Do not these words imply in Lord *Lyndhurst's* mind the view that there was a continuing power and duty of superintendence in the Irish Society, and if so, does not that at once distinguish the lands granted to the companies from the other lands to which you have compared them which went to private undertakers? There was no power of supervision over private undertakers.

24 *July* 1890.

Mr. Rigby.] Nor over any private grants of this Irish Society if they choose for their own purpose to grant lands away. Their supervision must be limited by the time when they retained the control of the property. I would ask the Committee to consider carefully that here no question of that kind could possibly have arisen which would have made it prudent or even proper for Lord Lyndhurst to express an opinion upon it. The Skinners' Company come and say we are dealing with the property remaining vested in the Irish Society, and we allege that we are the beneficiaries, and that the Irish Society are mere trustees entitled to do what according to the literal terms of the Charter they are ordered to do; but subject to that extent to account to us for every penny as if they were mere ordinary private trustees. That is the only question, and when Lord Lyndhurst is using the general words he does use there he is no doubt speaking *secundum subjectam materiam*; he is dealing with the property vested in the Irish Society, that was the only subject-matter, and dealing with their powers there, and I submit that there is nothing which is inconsistent with the argument I have now placed before you. I have read over carefully that judgment more than once, and I think you were referring to page 464.

Chairman.] It is the whole of that paragraph I was calling attention to down to the end of 465.

Mr. Rigby.] He says they have to superintend, order, direct, and manage the whole of this extensive concern. That is true literally in the inception of things. They had, every acre of the lands was originally vested in them. They had to arrange and superintend, and decide upon the persons who were to be grantees, although their discretion was very plainly limited, when we come to the heads of agreement, which showed that the intention of the Crown was that the grants should be made to the companies. They were appointed for that object. They had to superintend, and govern, and perform those duties that were necessary for giving effect to the grant. Now it is equally giving effect to the grant to vest lands in fee-simple in the undertakers. The Commissioners of the Crown had to do it in other counties, but here the Irish Society had to do so, for it would be taking a one-sided view of the scheme if you did not remember that the City were invited, and through them the companies to come into the position of undertakers. Then it goes on, "For the better ordering and directing of all, and all manner of things of and concerning the city and citizens of Londonderry." We had nothing to do with that of course. Then for this purpose the Irish Society was formed, and then it goes on and gives them power to hold a court. Those are matters none of which we ever assumed to ourselves at all. If we did we were wrong, and held to be wrong in this case, in so far as we tried to trench upon the powers of the Irish Society. All this is about the City of Londonderry, and then he winds up by saying, "All these are very extensive and large powers that are given to the Society for the purpose of carrying into effect the intention of the Crown."

Chairman.] Will you go on please further, "the intention of the Crown being"——

Mr. Rigby.] "Those great and important public objects to which I have already called your Lordship's attention."

Chairman.] Then, again, on the next page he says, amongst various other things, they had to do, was to provide for the Protestant Establishment, which was not a temporary, but a permanent object, and also support, and take care of that which is closely connected with religion and part of it, the education of the inhabitants of the district.

Mr. Rigby.] That is got from the conclusion. There is nothing in the charter about that.

Chairman.] They are also to perform these public duties of great importance connected with the district, and they are permanent.

Mr. Rigby.] Undoubtedly.

Chairman.] You think all those words are to be limited strictly to the 7,000 acres.

Mr. Rigby.] Not the least. I do not say that, it may be so, I have not gone through the charter for the purpose.

I say the property franchises, rights and privileges, including that of holding courts vested in the Irish Society, must be treated as one whole mass, one *universitas*; and that all those matters as to the power to control the Corporation of Derry, or make bye-laws, or anything of that sort, or hold courts, or superintend education; whatever was vested in them, were vested in them upon public permanent trusts; that is to say, away from and out of the undertakers; but that does not at all indicate, and it would be a total reversal of anything said by Lord Langdale (and Lord Lyndhurst expressly approves of Lord Langdale's judgment) to say that all the lands were subject to those trusts. It would be an unexampled thing, for instance, in an action brought by A. against B., to say that B. is trustee of A., for the judges to turn round and say, on the contrary, the man that you say is trustee is really owner of the lands that are vested in you, and is bound by duties affecting those lands. The whole course of our courts is to confine themselves to the question before them; and these words are perfectly capable of, and are apt and proper words for describing Lord Lyndhurst's view, which was the view of the House of Lords, for it was all adopted as to the whole of the lands vested and remaining in the Irish Society. I do not commit myself to say they have no rights at all outside the 7,000 acres; I say they have immense franchises and powers and privileges, at any rate outside. It may be very well that, as regards the rest of the land, if it all were conveyed away to the companies, they might say that their rights of supervision ceased; but, of course, they had rights; and, not in every case, but in some cases, they reserved rents, and would have the rights of ultimate reversioners; but, so far as Lord Lyndhurst's judgment goes, or, as I venture to think, the nature of the case leads us, there is nothing to

say

24 *July* 1890.

say that they had rights over any property parted with under the Charter down to that time.

The Committee adjourned for a short time.

Mr. Romer.] Now, Sir, as you know, I appear for the Irish Society, and my task is comparatively a light one, for two reasons. In the first place, the Irish Society has not to argue before you the very serious questions which the 12 companies have been obliged to do. There may be, and is, very little doubt as to the true position of the Irish Society, but the Irish Society think it right that they should do their best to lay fully before the Committee what they conceive to be the exact position they occupy legally. The second reason why I should of necessity be very short is this; that I am perfectly aware that all the documents, and the cases which tend to show what the true position of the Irish Society is, are fully before you.

Now about one thing there is no doubt, and that is, that the Irish Society do not claim, and never have claimed, that they hold their estates for their own benefit. In one sense, and in the popular sense, in the sense in which the word is often used by legal as well as non-legal persons, they may be said to be "trustees;" but that word requires a little care in dealing with, because behind it very often lies considerable ambiguity, and it is apt to lead to fallacies. The Irish Society is not a trustee in the sense in which that word is generally and strictly used in the eyes of the courts of law. It is not a trustee for beneficiaries, or for any person who could have called the Irish Society to account in the old Court of Chancery, or in the Chancery Division of the High Court at the present time.

It may be said in one sense, as I have pointed out, to be a trustee, if you use the word in its popular sense, in that it holds its estates not for its own benefit, but for certain purposes. You may say shortly that they hold their estates as trustees, but it is very important to see what their position is. The term "trustees" in its strict sense ought not to be applied to the Irish Society. For example, I would remind you of the somewhat analogous position occupied by the Ecclesiastical Commissioners. I do not suppose that any legal person would say they were strictly trustees. In one sense, and in the popular sense of the term, I agree to some extent they are not trustees, in the strict sense of the term in which that word ought to be used when dealing with it legally. The Irish Society have no *cestui que trusts*, no beneficiaries in this sense. They have no beneficiaries who can call upon them to render accounts, and the importance of their position would be very obvious when you consider if they were in that position what consequences would flow from it. If you had beneficiaries in the ordinary sense of the Irish Society, and the Irish Society were trustees for them, the Irish Society would be bound, whenever called upon to do so, to render accounts to the *cestui que trusts*.

Moreover, a court of justice, that is to say, the Chancery Division of the High Court, might, if called upon to do so, at the instance of the beneficiaries, absolutely say that the trusts, so called, upon which the Irish Society hold their estate, should be administered by the court. Now that, I conceive, no court has the power to do at the instance of any person. What power could be exercised against the Irish Society I will state in a moment, but certainly they are not trustees in the sense that any court would, at the instance of a *cestui que trust*, call upon the Society to render accounts or administer the estate. You will remember in the old days, and that is not so long ago, a Court of Chancery was obliged whenever a beneficiary came forward against trustees strictly so called, to administer that estate. It had no discretion in the matter. That was the state of things in the old days; but it has not been remedied within the last very few years. Now the court will not administer even private trusts, except upon cause shown; but still in the old days, as in the present days, the Irish Society was in this position; that, so far as I am aware, no person or nobody claiming to be their *cestuis que trust*, to use the strict legal phrase, could call upon them to say they would have the estate dealt with or administered by the court; in fact, it is obvious that no court could possibly take on itself to administer the public purposes to which the Irish Society have to devote themselves under the Charter and under the documents regulating its procedure. What is the true position of the Irish Society? The true position is this: it is a public body having cast upon it certain duties, chiefly public, or perhaps they may be described partly as political. I am using the phrase of certain of the judges, and no doubt partly private, public duties in the discharge of which they have an absolute unfettered discretion, so long as they are acting within certain limits; that is to say, in dealing with their estates for the public purposes defined by the Charter, no person, nobody, can interfere with the Irish Society in the exercise of its discretion. Those public purposes are of the widest character. It is difficult to define them; in fact, it is difficult to define them or to collect them together under one single phrase. Perhaps the nearest phrase that would go towards it would be this, that in the first instance they are bound, I think, to apply the income of their estates to the furtherance of the general public objects of the plantation of Ulster. Subject to that, as I think I shall be able to show, they having discharged those objects, if there was a surplus of income in any one year, then they might in their discretion apply that surplus amongst the 12 companies who are represented before you. But all that is a matter of absolute discretion. How they shall best carry out the public purposes of the plantation, using that short phrase, is left entirely to them. What moneys they shall expend on any particular object of those general purposes, is left entirely to them. And although, undoubtedly, I think, if they have fully discharged their general public purposes, and there was a surplus, they could then in the exercise of their power hand over that surplus to the companies, still it is clear that they could not do it till they had discharged, what I may call, their public duties; and, as a matter of fact, you are aware sir, that since the date of that decision in the Skinners' Company's case, the Irish Society never have in fact applied any portion of their income for the private benefit of the City companies. They have

have found, and I have no doubt in future will find, ample scope for the application of the income for the general public purposes, which I have indicated.

Mr. *Sexton*.] They never had a surplus since the Skinners' case.

Mr. *Romer*.] No; in their opinion. I want particularly to dwell, before you, upon two points; first, the large nature of their duties, and that you will not find them, and I think, purposely so, limited or curtailed by any definition in any charter or public document. Bye-and-bye I will call attention and as shortly as possible, to the precise words, and they are very few, which in the Charters of James I. and Charles II. (and they are both alike for this purpose), seem to show what the public purposes are to which the Irish Society ought to devote its estate, and they appear to be purposely put in the most general manner. There is no attempt to limit the Irish Society beyond generally indicating what those objects should be. If you have the Charter before you, there are only five passages that I need call attention to or remind you of in the interests of the Irish Society, and for my purpose it will be sufficient to deal with the Charter of Charles II. On page 3 you will find a recital of the grant by the first Charter to the society and to the companies, and the recital ends in this way: "And whereas the said Society," that is the Irish Society, "by virtue of a certain license from our said illustrious grandfather," bearing date as there stated, "did grant unto the 12 chief companies of our City of London (who had taken upon themselves the greater part of the burthen of the said plantation), divers great quantities, parcels, and proportions of the said lands, tenements, and hereditaments, according to their several disbursements, and did retain in his own hands," that must mean in "their" own hands, "such part of the same tenements and hereditaments as were not properly divisible for the defraying of the charge of the general operation of the said plantation." Those words are very large, and I think passing on you will find there was not any attempt to narrow down or define too strictly as against the Society the objects for which they were to retain the existing lands. Then on the following page there is another recital. It is the end of the recitals as to the reason for the present grant. It commences at the bottom of page 3, and the clause I am reading is at the top of page 4. It is a recital of the reasons for the present grant, that is the charter of Charles II., and amongst the reasons, and the only reasons stated that I need call attention to so far as concerns the Irish Society is this: "And to the intent that there may be a new society made of the new plantation in Ulster aforesaid, consisting of a like number of honest and discreet citizens of our City of London," and so forth, "and for the further and better settling and planting of the said county towns and places with trade and inhabitants." Again, as you will see, a very broad and general statement. Then at page 6, at the bottom, it is stated why the Society (it began in the Charter of James and it is repeated for this purpose in the Charter of Charles) is formed. It is: "For the better ordering, directing, and governing all and all manner of things for and concerning the city and citizens of Londonderry aforesaid, and the aforesaid county of Londonderry and the plantation." Then at page 13, at the bottom, the last clause but one, it states that the Society shall have full power and authority for convening and assembling and holding a court in the Guildhall of the City of London, and so forth: "and in the same court or meeting to do, hear, transact, and determine all and all manner of matters and things whatsoever of, for, or concerning the plantation or government aforesaid, as to them shall seem best and most expedient." Then lower down on the same page in the subsequent clause, full power is given to them to direct appoint and ordain "all and singular things, which for or concerning the plantation, supply, establishment, continuation, and government of the said city of Londonderry, and of all other the lands and tenements hereunder in these presents mentioned to be granted, shall seem to be most profitable and expedient." Then there is but one other reference I need call your attention to in this Charter, and that is in the following page 14, at the top, and this is the clause to which your attention, I know, has been often called. It gives them power "to send orders and directions from this kingdom of England unto the said realm of Ireland, by letters or otherwise, for the ordering, directing, and disposing of all and all manners of matters and things whatsoever of or concerning the same plantation, or the disposition or government thereof. And also for the receipt, ordering, disposing, and laying out of all sums of money now collected and received, or hereafter to be collected and received, and generally for any other cause, matter, or thing whatsoever, concerning the direction or ordering of the said plantation, or concerning any other things whatsoever, which by the true intent of these our letters patent, can or ought to be done by them, for the better government and rule of the said city of Londonderry and county of Londonderry." So far as I am aware, you have in those few phrases that I have read to you the whole that it is necessary for you to consider in the Charter, and indeed in both the Charters, for the purpose of seeing how the public duties of the Irish Society are defined, and what they have to do. Two things are apparent, not only from those Charters, but also from the judgment given in the Skinners' Company's case. First, that within the general limit of regarding as a public purpose the plantation as a whole, and using that in its largest and broadest sense, and the better government and concerning matters which arise therefrom there is no limit to the power and discretion of the Irish Society. As you are aware, from the time of King Charles II. until the present time that discretion has been exercised in the widest possible way, I mean as to the objects, though possibly not as to the places. As to objects, certainly it has been exercised in the widest possible way. I notice it was stated when the appeal was presented to the House of Lords, in the Skinners' Company's case, and I believe accurately stated in the case on appeal, that amongst the purposes to which they had devoted their income were endowing schools, paying schoolmasters, contributing towards the support

support of the Corporation of Londonderry, building or contributing towards the building of churches, chapels, town halls, gaols, quays, bridges, and other public buildings; that they had constantly relieved the distress of the poor and had handed over surplus rents from time to time to the 12 companies in round sums. But within their public purposes, they have always, and I submit, quite rightly taken a broad view of their powers, and the largest possible interpretation of the public purposes to which they have in the first place to devote the rents of their estates, and that I submit was justified by the intentionally wide terms of the Charter, and it was also justified as appears by the judgments in the Skinners' Company's case to certain passages of which I will very shortly call attention. Now, one thing is clear, that from the time of the first foundation of the Irish Society until the present time no person has ventured to attack the Irish Society except the Skinners' Company in that case. No person, no body has ventured to impugn what the Irish Society has done, either in the selection of its objects to which it should devote its rents, or as to the way in which amongst those objects it has apportioned its income. The proceedings of the Irish Society, with the sole exception of the action of the Skinners' Company, have remained unchallenged until this day. The only instance in which the Irish Society was attacked was by the Skinners' Company, and the Skinners' Company as we know failed. So that the only attack which was brought against the Irish Society was dismissed, and from beginning to end, subject to an observation I will make later on upon a passage in the judgment of Lord Langdale, there has been, as far as I am aware, no suggestion but what they have taken a right view of the purposes to which they ought to devote the income of their estates, or as to the method in which they have exercised their discretion, or as to the amounts in which they should distribute that income, though I agree that in a court of law the discretion of the Irish Society could not be challenged by anybody. It could not have been challenged by the Crown; it could not have been challenged by any of the City companies, and as far as I am aware it could not have been challenged by any body or corporation. There is within the Charter an absolutely unlimited discretion vested in them, and so long as they exercise their discretion that discretion cannot be interfered with. Of course there should be no mistake as to the position I am taking up. Should the Irish Society refuse as a public body to discharge its public duties, there are well-known remedies open to the Crown. The Crown might proceed by *scire facias*, or perhaps the more popular and ordinary form would be by writ of mandamus to compel the public body to discharge its duties, and if there had been a clearly gross misappropriation of any portion of the estate not falling within an exercise of discretion on the part of the Irish Society, no doubt the Irish Society could have been attacked for that, and I think it is conclusive proof that the Irish Society never have departed from the public trusts and the public purposes for which they hold their estates; but as I have pointed out, from the earliest times until the present moment, with the single exception of the Skinners' Company's action, no proceeding whatever has been taken against them.

Now, the decision in the Skinners' Company's case by Lord Langdale, I am aware you are fully cognisant of; but I should wish to call attention, just as I called your attention to a few passages only in the Charters, to a few passages in the judgment, which show that I am stating the legal position of the Irish Society. There are very few passages which really concern the Irish Society in this judgment, upon the only points upon which I am addressing the Committee. I, as a lawyer, naturally turn to the report in Beavan, and the first passage I should like to call your attention to is a passage on page 633, but which I am told is at the top of page 5 of your print. Lord Langdale was first referring to the fact that the Irish Society originated with the City; "but," he says, "this makes no difference in the effect of the constitution, or in the inferences to be deduced from the powers granted to the Society by the Charter; and it is, I think, impossible to read and consider the Charter, without coming to the conclusion that the powers granted to the Society were more extensive than and very different from any which, in the ordinary course of affairs, are vested, or would upon this occasion have been vested in mere private trustees for the benefit of particular undertakers. The powers, indeed, are many of them of a public and political nature, and considering the Charter in connexion with the contemporaneous circumstances, I think it must have been understood that the powers and estates granted to the Irish Society were given for the public purposes of the plantation, and, so far as was consistent with those purposes, for the benefit of the City of London." He there was calling attention to what I venture to urge upon the Committee, namely, that we are in a very different position from that of private trustees, and that our powers are of the largest possible character. Then, at page 636 of the report, he calls attention to the fact "Under the new Charter," that is to say, the Charter of Charles the Second, "new conveyances were made to the companies, and," he says, "the Irish Society has ever since continued in the exclusive possession of the town lands, ferries, and fisheries, and has managed or let the same, and received and applied the rents thereof by its own authority." That is to say, with reference to the management of their estates, as well as with regard to the application of its income; again, they have a discretion, and they have power to manage and to deal with those estates unfettered, as far as I can see, by any limitation, subject to this, that they will only deal with them for the public purposes and the private purposes to which they have to apply that income. Then, at the bottom of page 636, he refers to the fact of the Society having paid over surplus rents and income in particular sums to the companies, and refers to it clearly without disapproval, as being a purpose to which, having first complied with the public purposes, the Society were entitled to apply the surplus.

Then again at page 637, after referring to the fact that they are invested with great powers, and have important duties to perform, he says: "In a sense therefore, they are trustees"; and

Lord Langdale, who was an extremely accurate judge, was pointing out there, if I may say so, the distinction I am trying to draw before you to-day, that they are not trustees except in a sense, not trustees in that strict point of view or in the strict sense of the term in which it has been accustomed to use the term in the courts. They are only trustees in a sense such as any public body holding estates, not for their own benefit, might be said conventionally, and even legally for that purpose to hold those estates as trustees. He says: "The property is part of that which was granted for the purposes of the plantation, and the powers possessed by the society as well as the duties with which it is charged, have all of them reference to the plantation." Then he points out what the objects of the plantation were. He says: "Now the objects of the plantation, and the intents and purposes thereof, were of a nature partly public and political, and partly private, regarding only the interests of particular undertakers, whether corporate bodies or individuals." Then again, at page 640 comes that passage which I know has been read to you so often, and I will not repeat it, where he shows what was the only question he had to decide in the Skinner's case. The only question which came before the court in the Skinner's case was this: Is the Irish Society in the position of a trustee to the public companies, and the Skinner's Company as one of the 12? If it had been in that position certain consequences of necessity would have followed. In the first place Lord Langdale would have been bound to make a decree for administration, and would have been bound to have gone into the question, whether or not the Irish Society had exercised its discretion rightly? That was the sole question, and it was decided as we know in this way, that the Irish Society was not a trustee in that sense for any of the public companies, and it was on that ground, and that ground alone, that the action was dismissed as against the society. He again purports to define what the position of the company was in that important clause which commences: "After having considered the Charter of King Charles the Second, and the Charter of King James the First, and the several circumstances in evidence in this Cause, which preceded and accompanied the grant of the Charter of King James, and having read all the documents produced in this Cause, to some only of which, though at the expense of so much time, I have but shortly adverted, and having also considered the conduct of the parties under the Charter for so long a series of years, I am of opinion that the powers granted to the society and the trusts reposed in them, were in part of a general and public nature, independent of the private benefit of the companies of London, and were intended by the Crown to benefit Ireland and the City of London, by connecting the city of Londonderry and the town of Coleraine, and a considerable Irish district with the City of London, and to promote the general purposes of the plantation, not only by securing the performance of the conditions imposed on ordinary undertakers, but also by the exercise of powers and the performance of trusts not within the scope of those conditions." So far as I am aware, I think that that is the very best definition that can be now given of the purposes for which the Irish Society now holds its estate. While I am dealing with that judgment, I would ask permission to say a word with regard to a passage at page 638 of the Judgment, on which, I understand, some observation has been made before the Committee. That was the passage in Lord Langdale's Judgment, where he said that: "Mistaken views, which the society may have subsequently taken of its own situation and duties (and I think that such mistaken views have several times been taken), do not vary the conclusion to be deduced from the charter, and the circumstances contemporary with the grant of the first charter." It is, I think, clear what he was referring to in that part of the judgment. It had been alleged, and was much relied on by the Skinners' Company in their action against the Irish Society, that in some of the old proceedings, especially in some proceedings in 1740, and previously to that time, there had been admissions, or what were relied on as admissions by the Irish Society, or said to have been admissions, that they were in some sense trustees for the Skinners' and the other 12 companies, and it was to that, that Lord Langdale was referring, and to nothing else. As a matter of fact, as far as I am aware, since 1740 or 1741, there has been no transaction or act of the Irish Society which has been, or could be, impeached at all as having been done by them contrary to the true powers which they hold; not one. He was dealing there with some alleged admissions made, as I understand it, certainly before 1740, and which the Skinners' Company had relied on as being admissions that the Irish Society did stand in the position of trustees to the companies, which, of course, we know was an erroneous admission if it had been made.

These matters were, in fact, dealt with in detail by the Irish Society in its case prepared for the appeal to the House of Lords in that case. There, in detail, the Irish Society dealt with these admissions, and dealt with those acts and explained how they came to be made, and then contended, what was supported by Lord Langdale in his Judgment, that even if they had been made erroneously at that time, they could not really affect the true position of the Irish Society, or be used against the Irish Society as tending to take away from that society its true position, and to deprive it of its true rights. They are dealt with at page 37 of the case of the respondents, the Irish Society, on the appeal to the House of Lords, should it be necessary to refer to it in detail. It went into them in detail, and showed exactly how they came to be made. It also dealt with that question which I do not trouble the Committee with, as to the timber and certain proceedings in 1713. I thought I had, but my junior reminds me that, perhaps, I have not sufficiently urged before you this, that, as a matter of right, in the exercise of the discretion of the Irish Society solely, if in any one year it should come to the conclusion that it was not necessary to apply the whole of the rents for the public purposes indicated in the charter, then it could pay the surplus to the 12 companies. That was done, as you are aware, continuously almost up to the time of the decision of the Skinners' case, and was referred to with approval, both by Lord Langdale,

dale, as having been a right application of the surplus, in his judgment, and also in the House of Lords.

Chairman.] You are now upon what point precisely, Mr. Romer?

Mr. Romer.] I am only referring to the purposes for which the Irish Society holds its estates, and how they are bound to apply the rents, and I am pointing out that the first duties cast upon the Irish Society are to apply its rents for the general public purposes which I have already indicated. I was then only pointing out that legally, supposing, in the discretion of the Irish Society, it came to the conclusion that in any one year it had applied all that it properly or reasonably could towards those public purposes, and there was a surplus, that is how it would deal with the surplus. That is all.

Chairman.] Does that carry the Committee further from their point of view. You remember what I indicated in the opening of this stage of the proceedings, that minute examination is not quite what we are here for at this stage.

Mr. Romer.] Certainly. I only wanted, in case it was said, in defining the purposes for which the Irish Society holds its estates. You have not referred to or mentioned at all the fact of the payment of surplus income before the Skinners' case to the twelve companies. I only thought it right that I should refer to it, and state exactly the position that the Irish Society takes up with regard to that.

Sir William Marriott.] Do you maintain that the Irish Society could dispose of any surplus by giving it to the companies if they chose, but that the companies could not compel them?

Mr. Romer.] Exactly; the companies could not compel them.

Chairman.] We know that from the Lords' decision, surely. You need not labour that, because we understand that from the Lords' decision.

Mr. Romer.] Exactly.

Chairman.] And I was very careful to say that in the case of the Irish Society it would be quite unbecoming for this Committee to pretend to go behind the Lords' Judgment, or to open it up in any respect whatever. It is quite enough for us, I mean, as it stands.

Mr. Romer.] There are observations in the Judgment of the House of Lords which are substantially to the same effect as the Judgment of Lord Langdale in the court below. I will say this before I sit down, that you will find in both Judgments a reference of this class, after pointing out that the Irish Society were not accountable to any of the twelve companies, you will find an observation of this kind, both in Lord Langdale's Judgment, and in the Lord Chancellor's (Lord Lyndhurst) Judgment in the House of Lords' case. The Judges said, "The Irish Society, in fact, are not accountable to you; they may be accountable to the Crown or to the Corporation of London," though of necessity, of course, neither Lord Langdale nor the House of Lords could decide that point at all. It was not before them, and there could, of necessity, from the nature of the suit, have been no question arising for the Court's decision between co-defendants. All that Lord Langdale had to decide, and all that the House of Lords had to decide, was, "Are you trustees, so far as concerns the Skinners' case"; and they decided that they are not trustees. All that the learned judges meant by that reference was to leave open that question by saying, "You may be accountable," and that observation is easily explained I think by this. I think the Irish Society could in one sense be made accountable to the Crown. As I am pointing out, supposing, for example, the Irish Society refused to perform it public duties, then as against the Irish Society the Crown would have the same rights as it has against all public bodies who refuse to discharge their duties, and in that case could make it account. So I account for the allusion to the Corporation of London in this wise. So far as I can see, I do not wish to prejudice the question at all, it does not arise, but as far as I can see, the Irish Society are not accountable to the Corporation of London, but in one sense they may be. I do not wish to prejudice the Corporation of London in any way; they may or may not be, but this I do see. I see that in case of misconduct of individual members of the corporation of the Irish Society, the Corporation of London, under the charter has visitorial powers and might remove any members of the Corporation who were not doing their duty. In that sense they could be made accountable to the Corporation of London, but I am not aware how otherwise they could be; and certainly on behalf of the Irish Society, though it is not important for me to dwell upon it any longer, I do not admit any further liability to account. My position is simply this; this is a public body having certain duties cast upon it by charter with regard to its estates, so long as it discharges those duties; it it is accountable to no one, and in discharging the duties, it has a large discretion as to the way in which it should carry out it duties, and an absolute discretion as to the amount in which it should for any special purpose apply its income.

Colonel Lewis.] I want to ask Mr. Latham one question. I think you represent more especially the companies?

Mr. Latham.] Yes.

Colonel Lewis.] It is with reference to a statement made by Mr. G. H. Lea, on pages 359 and 360 of the evidence. On referring to the action of the Star Chamber, he says this: that the woods were sold and sent out of the kingdom. It is there said that they were estimated to be worth something like 450,000 *l.* That is a very large sum. You did not, I think, approach that subject. I am asking you only as counsel?

Mr. Latham.] No, I did not approach that. I omitted it, and neglected it. The allegation was that we had received half a million of money. I will tell you exactly how that is. I have found it out in the proceedings on the *rolls* [illegible] *furtas*. The judgment set out at full length, and the pleadings and proceedings which led up to to the judgment. The Committee will remember the judgment was given by default. Negotiations had taken place before judgment was given between the Crown and the companies, and the companies made up their minds, and the City made up their minds, that they had better let the thing go, and they never appeared at all. The judgment recites the whole of the proceedings up to that time, and among others it recites the various charges which were brought against the companies. Among those charges is this allegation which is recited there; that the Society had cut, it was only the Society, not the companies, in the woods of Glanconkeine and Killetra 500,000 oaks, the value of each being 10s.; 1,000 elms, the value of each being 6s. 8d.; 100,000 ash, the value of each being 5s.; 500,000 oaks, the value of each being 10s.; 1,000 elms, of the value value of 6s. 8d. each; 100,000 ash, at 5s. each, which trees so cut were not converted to the use of the plantation. The sum of half a million has been arrived at by adding up these various trees at the prices mentioned, and so arriving at 550,000*l*. My friend, Mr. Lea, did not put his case high enough, because the allegation was not only that they had cut and sold trees to that extent, but that they had cut and sold trees to that extent every year. Well, I need not say that that is a great deal more than is credible. This was under the old form of pleading. It was really a matter of pleading on a large scale; a stupendous scale. There are many instances of that in old pleadings. It was only a plea and nothing more. If my friend wishes that it should be denied I am quite willing to deny it. We did not cut half a million's worth of timber in Ulster during that period.

Mr. *Sexton*.] Have you cut it in any year?

Mr. *Latham*.] Not in any year.

Mr. *G. H. Lea*.] I said it was so stated in the judgment in the *scire facias*, and it is so stated.

Mr. *Pollard*.] I have the honour to represent the Corporation of the City of London, and I desire to submit a few words to the Committee with reference to something that fell from Mr. Walker as to the position of the City of London.

Chairman.] Nobody has attacked the City, so far as I know. Nobody has impugned the conduct or the position of the City.

Mr. *Pollard*.] Yes; Mr. Walker says that we are in the same position exactly as the Irish Society; and my learned friend, Mr. Romer, before sitting down, has taken upon himself to deny the jurisdiction and controlling authority of the City of London over the Irish Society.

Mr. *Romer*.] No; on the contrary, I said that they had visitorial powers.

Mr. *Pollard*.] Not only has Mr. Walker misrepresented really, I use the word with all respect, but he has misstated the position of the Corporation of the City of London with regard to what trusts or obligations it undertook in the inception of the matter before the Charter of James, and still more what was imposed upon it, if anything, after the Charter of Charles II.

Chairman.] This is an historic inquiry, is not it; I do not think it will help the Committee on its way to knowledge to have a vindication of the duties of the corporation anterior to the Charter of Charles II.

Mr. *Pollard*.] Not at all; but, as far as I can see, the claims put forward by Mr. Walker, on behalf of his clients, or the reason, in fact, of Mr. Walker's presence before the Committee is this. It is founded upon allegations of his as to what were the nature of the original trusts, and what was the nature of the continuing trust, after the grant of the Charter by Charles II.

Mr. *Lawson*.] May I ask whether this is not really outside the reference to the Committee as well. There is no reference whatever to the City of London, beyond that which may be implied in the Irish estates and the City companies.

Chairman.] I confess I do not see quite what the *locus standi* of the City of London is. No doubt reference was made by Mr. Walker to the duty of the Corporation of the City of London, but that was a sort of historic part of his argument, and the general bearing of it was sufficiently dealt with, I should have thought, by Mr. Latham, and afterwards by Mr. Rigby.

Mr. *Pollard*.] They merely confined themselves to the position of the City companies, and did not deal with the position of the Corporation.

Chairman.] That is quite true; but does anybody think either better or worse, in any particular, of the Corporation of London for anything that has gone on in this Committee-room. I cannot imagine that it is so.

Mr. *Pollard*.] Nobody who as yet has addressed the Committee appears to recognise the power which the Corporation undoubtedly have of controlling, and, if any reason should arise, of correcting any misapplication of the funds entrusted to the Irish Society.

Mr. *Sexton*.] That is a question entirely apart from the question as to any trust which the Irish Society may lie under. It is clearly outside the scope of our inquiry.

Mr. *Pollard*.] I am of course in the hands of the Committee; but I should hardly think, with all respect, that any report upon this subject could be perfect without at any rate stating that the Irish Society is controllable in the exercise of its powers of disposal and management of its funds; not with regard to the receipt of the revenue, because the City neither has, nor ever had, the slightest thing to do with the receipt of the revenue. But with regard to the disposal of that revenue, and with regard to the exercise of the vast powers of the Irish Society, the City have, and always have had, a controlling power. They can remove the whole of the members at one swoop if they like, or any of them who are guilty of misconduct in the exercise of their functions as members of the Irish Society.

Chairman.] Is that the proposition which you wish to establish before the Committee?

Mr. *Pollard*.] That is all.

Chairman.] Then even if it be established, that will not affect the object which we are directed

24 *July* 1890.

to inquire into. Granting, for the sake of the argument, that you can establish that proposition demonstrably, it still would not affect the object that we are going to inquire into, and is, therefore, irrelevant.

Mr. *Pollard.*] If that is not called in question by anything that has come before you.

Chairman.] Certainly it is not called in question by any member of the Committee, nor has it been called in question by the representative of the Irish Society.

Mr. *Pollard.*] Yes, with all respect, my friend Mr. Romer, before sitting down, said that their discretion was absolute; there was nobody, neither the Crown nor anybody else, who could control the exercise of that discretion.

Chairman.] Very well; but then whether Mr. Romer was right or wrong in that contention, our Report, whatever it may be, would be exactly the same. We have not got to report upon that point.

Mr. *Pollard.*] As I say, I am entirely in the hands of the Committee.

Chairman.] I think my view is right.

Sir *William Marriott.*] The only way that I can suggest in which Mr. Pollard's argument might be useful, is this: assuming that this Committee were to report against the Irish Society, in what way would the City be affected? If it is affected, of course it has a right to say a word.

Mr. *Pollard.*] If the Irish Society have been guilty of any default in the application of the funds coming from those lands which are, in the words of the charter, retained for the purposes of generally operating the plantation, there might then be some charge underlying that against the City for not having exercised its visitatorial power.

Chairman.] Supposing, for the sake of argument, that this Committee were to recommend, as the Municipal Commission did in 1854, the dissolution of the Irish Society, I want to take an extreme case, and action were taken by Parliament upon our Report, then would be the time for the City to come in and protest against any damage to its rights, and to its position.

Mr. *Pollard.*] The only thing that I would venture to urge upon the Committee, if it is present to the mind of the Committee, is that there was what was called in the argument before the Lords, and which was not dissented from by the Lords, but in fact recognised by the judgment of Lord Lyndhurst, a controlling power and a corrective jurisdiction which still, in fact, remains in the Corporation to control and correct, if need be, whatever may be done by the Irish Society in their conduct in carrying out those large public trusts. The contention of the City is that that still exists. It was originally entrusted to them by the founder, upon whose supposed intentions the parties represented by Mr. Walker come to claim. They are the visiting body of the governing body, as is indicated by the terms of the very grant upon the terms of which Mr. Walker founds his contention.

Mr. *Lawson.*] May I ask whether the extent of that power is the removal of any or all of the members of the society?

Mr. *Pollard.*] Yes, the removal of all or any of them in case of misconduct, and the replacing of proper persons from similar bodies in order to carry out the objects of the society.

Chairman.] Will not it be enough if the Committee take note of your contention? You have told us what your position is as representing the City; we take a note of it, and there it is on record. I do not conceive that it is our business to listen to an argument on the point, or to listen to any further remarks upon it really, because it would not affect the subject of our inquiry.

Mr. *Pollard.*] After that intimation, I feel that it would be only wasting time were I to address you any longer.

Chairman.] I think that is the view of the Committee.

Mr. *Sexton.*] I should like to put one question to the Counsel for the City; I should like to ask whether, when this money was raised by you in the City from the companies for the purposes of plantation, by the poll according to the rate of corn, that was at that time the ordinary or the only mode by which you levied taxation for public purposes in London?

Mr. *Pollard.*] I think that is so, but I think it would be unwise on the part of the Committee to assume that, although the precept recommended that the taxes should be raised by the poll, the money was, in fact, raised in that way; because there is evidence in the documents before the Committee that the money which was contributed by the companies was not raised by the poll, but was in some, if not in many instances, at any rate, raised by the mortgage of properties belonging to the City Companies, and the sale or mortgage of their plate.

Mr. *Sexton.*] But upon the mode as defined in the precept, that was your only way of levying money by taxation in London?

Mr. *Pollard.*] For such purposes, I think so.

Mr. *Sexton.*] I mean if you had to levy money on the citizens, the ordinary and conventional method of levying taxation was on the companies by the poll?

Mr *Pollard.*] By means of the companies, through the companies.

Colonel *Laurie.*] Did the companies contribute the whole of the money for what I may call ordinary domestic purposes?

Mr. *Pollard.*] No, those were raised by rates and taxes.

Colonel *Laurie.*] What we should call now rates and taxes were levied?

M. *Pollard.*] Corporate tolls were levied.

Mr. *Lawson.*] The Corporation has never had any rating power.

Mr. *Pollard.*] They have their metage and weighage.

weighage. You may call it what you like. Whether you call it tolls or rates, there are a great many sums of money which they are entitled to exact, and have exacted from time immemorial, but I think for the purpose to which Mr. Sexton's question refers, that whether it be for giving aid to the Crown in foreign wars, or whatever else it might be, any purpose foreign to the mere internal management of the municipal government of the City itself, such things were raised in the same way as indicated by the precept.

Chairman.] I understand, Mr. Lea, you wish to address the Committee on some point?

Mr. *G. H. Lea.*] I should like to say a few words, if you think right, in reply on the main argument of Mr. Latham.

Chairman.] Not a reply on the main argument: if there is any point, good. That I said from the first the Committee would scarcely be able to have. If there is any point raised which you think was misrepresented, so be it; but general argument, no.

Mr. *G. H. Lea.*] Well, you put me into the difficulty of distinguishing between point and argument.

Chairman.] Any inference I should have said, if you like that better.

Mr. *G. H. Lea.*] I wish to point out what are the words of the second Charter of Charles, upon which the argument was based. I shall not be more than five minutes, if you will give me that time.

Chairman.] Very well.

Mr. *G. H. Lea.*] I understand their contention to be, that this Charter of Charles II. entirely altered the position of matters. It is interpreted by my friend to put the position of the companies upon an entirely new foundation. They stated that from the time that that charter was granted, the companies had held their lands absolutely free from any trusts, whatever they may have done before: and they say that the Irish Society held its own 7,000 acres for the purposes of the Irish Society. I want just to point out how very slender a foundation there is for that argument. The whole foundation is in these words in the recital of the charter, that they did retain in their own hands "such part of the same tenements and hereditaments as were not properly devisable for the defraying of the charge of the general operation of the said plantation." As far as I am aware there are no other words in the whole of that charter which give this new and absolute grant to the companies; and I ask this question: If that had been, as my friend Mr. Latham put it, the leading idea of the new charter, that there was to be from this time forth an absolute division of the lands of the companies from those of the Irish Society, surely there would have been some stronger indication of that fact in some other part of the charter. Now as you go through the charter, the place where you would have expected to find that would be in the *habendum*; but after the grant of, not a part of the premises, but of the whole of the premises, the *habendum* is that the Irish Society shall have, hold, and enjoy the whole of the counties and territories, advantages, and emoluments, and all the other premises granted by the charter, that is, the whole county, "to the only proper use and behoof of the said society, of the governor and assistants, London, of the new plantation in Ulster." So that the whole of these lands are absolutely granted to the Irish Society; and not only is this the case, but the *habendum* is actually divided, and in the first place the 4,000 acres and the 3,000 acres are granted in free burgage to the society; and, secondly, the rest of the lands in the charter are also granted over again to the Irish Society; and there is no indication from the beginning to the end of the charter of the allegation that has been made that this is any new grant and an absolute grant from this time forth to the companies. Not only is that the case, but the actual reasons of the grants are given. You have heard them so often that I will not read them again. The actual reasons of the grants are given in the recitals of the charter, and the reason of the grant was that the parties and the companies might be restored to the lands, and so on, "as fully and beneficially, to all intents and purposes, as they might have had and enjoyed the same, if no repeal of the said letters patent had ever been had or made." This point is dealt with clearly and decidedly by Lord Langdale, so clearly that I should have thought that there could have been no question about it; where he says, that "the intention of the Charter of Charles was to restore the Irish Society, and also the companies of the City of London, to their former rights; and after making due allowance for all the differences which occur, the Charter of Charles appears to me to be substantially, as it is avowedly, a restoration of the Charter of James. The two charters are alike in their general purview, in their intended object, in the means adopted to carry that object into effect, and in the powers conferred for that purpose." So that we have it here, on Lord Langdale's judgment, that one charter was in effect to take the place of the other, and if that is the case, there is no new absolute grant whatever to the companies under this charter. Now, I referred in the opening to a lease granted by the Skinners' Company to Henry Cary, and I think that that is very important at this time. You will remember the statement is, that the City Companies from the time of the charter possessed their property absolutely; but 60 years after the Skinners' Company make a lease to Henry Cary, in which they reserve, in large and important words, which have been already before the Committee, that the lessee is to undertake to obey and abide by all the decisions and orders of the Irish Society, and to fulfil all the conditions of the plantation.

Mr. *Sexton.*] We have already apprehended that point.

Mr. *G. H. Lea.*] Then I will not carry it any further.

Chairman.] I think we have got that.

Mr. *G. H. Lea.*] Then one other point I will make, and that is, that Mr. Latham brought to our

24 July 1890.

our knowledge, almost for the first time, the sale by the Goldsmiths' Company to Lord Shelburne. The point of that case was this: that Chancery would not compel specific performance of the agreement in that case unless the Irish Society joined. We have never said, and we have not contended, that I am aware of,—I do not think Mr. Walker did,—that the Irish Society cannot alienate; but the point is entirely in our favour, as it shows that the Goldsmiths' Company could not alienate, and the Court of Chancery would not compel the Goldsmiths' Company to alienate until the Irish Society joined in the transfer. That was a point I meant to take. There are a great many other similar points, but I do not think the Committee desire to hear me generally, and I think with that I will leave the matter. Do you wish to hear anything, Sir, on the contemporary charters?

Chairman.] No.

Mr. G. H. Lee.] My friend, who is with me, has a lot of information on the contemporary charters.

Chairman.] No, I think not.

LIST OF APPENDIX.

APPENDIX, No. 1.

APPENDIX, No. 2.

APPENDIX, No. 3.

APPENDIX, No. 4.

APPENDIX, No. 5.

APPENDIX, No. 6.

APPENDIX, No. 7.

APPENDIX, No. 8.

APPENDIX, No. 9.

APPENDIX, No. 10.

APPENDIX, No. 11.

APPENDIX, No. 12.

APPENDIX, No. 20.

Paper handed in by the Chairman: PAGE

APPENDIX, No. 21.

Paper handed in by the Chairman:

APPENDIX, No. 22.

Paper handed in by the Chairman:

APPENDIX, No. 23.

Paper handed in by the Chairman:

APPENDIX, No. 24.

Paper handed in by the Chairman:

APPENDIX, No. 25.

Paper handed in by Mr. Latham, Q.C.:

APPENDIX, No. 26.

Paper handed in by Mr. Latham, Q.C., 29 July 1890:

APPENDIX, No. 27.

Paper handed in by the Chairman:

APPENDIX, No. 28.

Paper handed in by the Chairman, 12 June 1890:

APPENDIX, No. 29.

Paper handed in by Mr. J. Glover, 17 July 1890:

APPENDIX, No. 30.

Paper handed in by Dr. R. H. Todd, 20 June 1890:

APPENDIX, No. 82.

Paper handed in by Mr. John Watney, 24 July 1880:

APPENDIX, No. 83.

Paper handed in by the Clerk to the Grocers' Company:

APPENDIX, No. 84.

Paper handed in by Mr. W. P. Sawyer, 17 July 1880:

APPENDIX, No. 85.

Paper handed in by the Clerk to the Fishmongers' Company:

Irish Estate:

APPENDIX, No. 86.

Paper handed in by Mr. E. H. Draper, 14 July 1880:

APPENDIX, No. 87.

Paper handed in by Mr. E. H. Draper, 14 July 1880:

APPENDIX, No. 88.

Paper handed in by the Clerk to the Salters' Company:

APPENDIX, No. 40.

APPENDIX, No. 41.

APPENDIX, No. 42.

APPENDIX, No. 43.

APPENDIX, No. 44.

APPENDIX, No. 45.

APPENDIX, No. 46.

APPENDIX, No. 47.

APPENDIX, No. 48.

APPENDIX, No. 49.

APPENDIX, No. 50.

APPENDIX, No. 51.

APPENDIX, No. 52.

APPENDIX, No. 53.

APPENDIX, No. 54.

APPENDIX.

APPENDIX, No. 1.

PAPER handed in by the Rev. *R. H. F. Dickey*, M.A., 5 June 1882.

To the Worshipful Company of *Skinners*, London.

The Memorial of the Tenants on your Estate, who are Members of the Congregation of Lower Cumber,

Respectfully showeth,—

That memorialists have the closest relationship with the Skinners' Company, their church and manse being both situated on your Irish estate; that more than one-half of the bonâ fide members in connection with the congregation are families residing on the Skinners' Estate, and form a larger body of your tenantry than that which attends any other place of worship on your property.

That memorialists, at a regularly convened meeting in lecture hall of above church, having learned of your intention of making them an exception, in withdrawing your donation of 10 *l.* a year from their congregation, trust that that intention will not be executed.

That memorialists purchased their holdings on the faith that all emoluments and privileges would be continued as hitherto; and that they were, throughout, the most loyal and prompt-paying tenants on any part of your estate.

Memorialists would, therefore, respectfully solicit, and humbly pray your worshipful Company to continue the grant of 10 *l.* a year to the congregation of Lower Cumber.

And memorialists, as in duty bound, will ever pray.

(signed) By over 60 tenants.

APPENDIX, No. 2.

PAPER handed in by the Rev. *R. H. F. Dickey*, M.A., 5 June 1882.

Dear Sir, Dungiven, 2 January 1882.

I HAVE a reply from the Company, and it is to the effect that I am to forward you a cheque for 10 *l.* for the past year (which I now enclose), but to inform you that this grant will not be continued, this payment being final. As you are aware, the Company have sold the portion of their estate on which your congregation reside, and do not intend to continue this donation.

Yours, &c.
(signed) *G. Young.*

Dear Sir, Dungiven, 15 February 1882.

A LETTER from the Skinners' Company, dated the 13th, reached me by the same post as yours. They direct me to say that they are unwilling to reopen the question of the annual grant formerly given, but will transfer the manse and grounds held by the trustees at 1 *l.* a year to them free of rent. This decision may be regarded as final.

Yours, &c.
(signed) *G. L. Young.*

APPENDIX, No. 8.

PAPER handed in by the Rev. *S. H. F. Digby*, M.A., 5 June 1880.

DOCUMENTS relating to the proposed Sale of the Clothworkers' Company, in the County of Londonderry, and the Question of Parliamentary Action in reference to the London Companies and the Irish Society generally.

To the Worshipful Company of Clothworkers, London.

The Memorial of the undersigned Tenants on the Manor of the Worshipful Company of Clothworkers,

Respectfully sheweth,—

That they are informed that your worshipful Company are about to sell your estate in county Londonderry.

That they regret, before offering it to any private individual, your worshipful Company did not give the tenants on your estate the opportunity of purchasing their holdings, under the Irish Land Act of 1870.

That if such opportunity be afforded them, they are prepared, considering the advantages offered to tenants under the said Act, to become purchasers of their own holdings.

Your memorialists therefore pray your worshipful Company to give them such opportunity of purchasing, believing that, if the estate be sold, it will realise a much larger sum if purchased by the tenants than if sold in the manner contemplated.

And your memorialists, as in duty bound, will ever pray.

Presented by the following deputation:—

S. M. Greer.
Stewart Hunter.
John Mark.
James L. Walker.

On behalf of themselves and 150 other tenants on the Clothworkers' Estate.

19 April 1871.

The Deputation also handed the Clerk the following letter:—

"To the Estates Court of the Worshipful Company of Clothworkers, London.

"Gentlemen,

"We, the undersigned, take the liberty of waiting upon you as a deputation from the tenants of your Irish estate to present the accompanying Memorial, largely signed by the tenants, and praying that they may be allowed the opportunity of purchasing from your worshipful Company their respective holdings. If allowed an interview, we are prepared to submit a proposition by which a limited number of your tenants, acting on behalf of all, will undertake to purchase the whole of the manor of Clothworkers, and to give a higher price for it than any private speculator could afford to give, and to do this within a limited time under the Land Act of last Session.

"Hoping that this proposal may be entertained, and that the consequent negotiation may have a favourable result,

"We have the honour to be,
"Your obedient servants,
S. M. Greer.
J. Mark.
Stewart Hunter.
James L. Walker.

"19 April 1871."

Clothworkers' Hall, Mincing-lane, London,
20 April 1871.

Gentlemen,

Referring to the "Memorial" placed in my hands this morning (which will be laid before the Court at its next meeting), and to your request for an interview with the Estates Committee "to submit a proposition by which a limited number of the tenants, acting on behalf of all, will undertake to purchase the whole of the manor of Clothworkers, under the provisions of the Land Act of last Session," I have to repeat the notification already made to Mr. Greer by direction of the Sub-Estates Committee for Irish Affairs (and which it was hoped would have spared you the trouble and expense of a journey to London), that, "after having considered their professional advice, they were of opinion that the arrangements with Sir Harvey Bruce are of such a nature as to preclude the possibility of commencing any further negotiations for the sale of the estate."

Under these circumstances the (Irish) Committee conceived that they would not be justified, having regard to the mutual position, in admitting any proposal on the subject in question.

There will be the monthly meeting of the Estates Committee on Wednesday, when your application will be read, and if you should think it desirable, after receipt of this intimation, I shall be happy to give you their more direct expression of their views.

I have the honour to be, &c.
Owen Roberts, Clerk.

Messrs. S. M. Greer, James L. Walker,
Rev. John Mark, Stewart Hunter.

To the Master and Court of Assistants of the Worshipful Company of Merchant Taylors.

Gentlemen,

We, the undersigned, being a deputation from the tenants on the manor of the Clothworkers, in the county of Londonderry, in which manor, as we understand, your worshipful Company have a substantial interest, take the liberty of waiting upon you to represent to you the anxiety of all the tenants on that estate to purchase their respective holdings. If allowed an interview, we are prepared to submit to you a plan by which a limited number of the more substantial tenants, acting on behalf of all, will undertake to purchase the whole manor of Clothworkers, and to give a higher price for it than any private speculator could afford to give; and to do this within a limited time, under the Land Act of last Session.

Hoping that the proposition will be favourably entertained, and that the [illegible] [illegible] may be [illegible], and that in the meantime you will withhold your assent from any other arrangement.

We have the honour to be,
Your obedient servants,
S. M. Greer.
James L. Walker.
John Hart.
Stewart Hunter.

20 April 1871.

Merchant Taylors' Hall, London, E.C.,
21 April 1871.

Sir,

I am directed by the Master of the Merchant Taylors' Company to acknowledge the receipt of your letter of the 20th instant, and to inform you that he has consulted with his colleagues in the Court of the Company upon the question raised in that communication, and that they fully endorse the opinion which he expressed to you at the personal interview which he had the honour to have with you on Wednesday last, viz., that the arrangements entered into with Sir Harvey Bruce, M.P., as to the sale of the Clothworkers' Manor in Ireland, cannot honourably be disturbed.

I am to add that, under these circumstances, the Master and Wardens of this Company presume that you will not urge the reception of a deputation on the subject.

I have the honour to be, Sir,
Your most obedient servant,
Francis G. Faithful,
Clerk to the Company.

S. M. Greer, Esq.

To Owen Roberts, Esq., Clothworkers' Hall.

Sir,

We beg to acknowledge your communication of the 20th instant, informing us that the Sub-Estates Committee of the Clothworkers' Company were of opinion the arrangements with Sir Harvey Bruce were of such a nature as to preclude the possibility of commencing further negotiations for the sale of the estate.

We assume from your letter that the sale has not been legally completed, and as the Sub-Committee, who seem to have conducted the negotiations with Sir Harvey Bruce, may have unintentionally overlooked the strong [illegible] claims the tenants of the estate have on the Company to buy, or may have been ignorant of the facilities now afforded by the Government to raise the money to carry out the sale,—

We think it right to bring both these matters fully before the Court of the Clothworkers' Company, and the other Companies associated with them, and we feel confident that the equal and equitable claims of the tenants whose forefathers settled on your estate 250 years ago, and by whose industry and loyalty the estate has been improved and preserved for you, will, with the full Court of the Company, overcome any difficulty which the Sub-Committee may have got into by entering into negotiations with Sir Harvey Bruce.

We have made our calculations, and beg to mention that the tenants are prepared to buy at 150,000 *l.*, and we request you will lay this letter before the Estates Committee and on Wednesday first, with the view of bringing the matter before a full Court of the Company.

Your obedient servants,
Stewart Hunter.
John Hart.
James L. Walker.
John Mathers.

24 April 1871.

Sir,

In reference to the communication we addressed to the worshipful the Merchant Taylors' Company on 21st instant, relative to the sale of the Clothworkers' Estate in Ireland, we beg to inform you that we have since then received a communication from the Clerk of the Clothworkers' Company, from which we infer that the sale negotiated by a sub-committee of the Clothworkers, a meeting is called for Wednesday, the 26th, and to ratify the proposed sale.

As we are aware your Company has a large interest in the estate, we think it right to inform you that the tenants are prepared to give 150,000 *l.* for it, and we are sure the members of your Company, who will be called upon to confirm the sale to Sir Harvey Bruce, will not overlook the claims of the tenants, whose forefathers emigrated from England and Scotland and settled the estate with a loyal and peaceable people in times of great trouble and danger, and by whose zeal and industry the Clothworkers' Company's Estate has been so much improved in value since your Company (the Merchant Taylors) sold their estate in 1727 to the Richardson family at 20,000 *l.*

We regret the sub-committee of the Clothworkers' Company seem either to have overlooked these claims, or to have taken it upon themselves to decide upon interests of such vital importance to the tenants without giving them an opportunity of expressing their views, and we trust the Court of the Company will, on fuller consideration of the matter, treat the tenants in a different way.

Your obedient servants,
John Mathers.
Stewart Hunter.
John Hart.
James L. Walker.

To Francis G. Faithful, Esq.,
30, Threadneedle-street, 24 April 1871.

To the Honourable the IRISH SOCIETY, London.

Gentlemen,

We, the undersigned, being a deputation from the tenantry (in the county of Londonderry) of the worshipful Company of Clothworkers, London, and of the Coleraine Town Commissioners, having heard that the said Company are about to dispose of their Irish estate, approach your honourable Society to inquire whether you have any control over the conveyance of said property, and if so, to pray that you may be pleased to withhold your sanction from the sale as contemplated, and use your influence to afford the tenants the opportunity of becoming purchasers of their own holdings under the Irish Land Act of 1870, in accordance with the prayer of their Memorial to the said Clothworkers' Company. We also pray your honourable Society to see that a fair proportion of the purchase-money arising from said sale be allocated to local purposes.

S. M. Greer.
Stewart Hunter.
John Mark.
John Mathews.
James L. Walker.

Dated 21 April 1871.

We also pray.

The Reply of the Honourable the IRISH SOCIETY.

It was resolved that the memorialists be informed that the Society, having referred the Memorial to their law officer, are advised that the Society have no power to exercise any control over the Clothworkers' Company in dealing with their proposition, subject to the exceptions and reservations contained in the grant from the Society to the Company.

Irish Chambers, Guildhall, London, 25 April 1871.

EXTRACT from the MINUTE BOOK of the PROCEEDINGS of the COLERAINE TOWN COMMISSIONERS.

17 April 1871.

THE Commissioners met this day to take into consideration whether any and what action should be taken in reference to the honourable the Irish Society, and to the contemplated sale of the estate of the worshipful Company of Clothworkers in this county.

The Memorial of the tenants on the estate of the Clothworkers' Company to the Premier in reference to the intended sale having been read; it was unanimously resolved:—

That the Commissioners approve of said Memorial, and that a deputation be sent by them to co-operate with the deputation from the tenants on the Clothworkers' Estate to support it, and to urge the necessity of hastening the proposed action of the Government in reference to the honourable the Irish Society and the London Companies, and thereby prevent them from alienating the property which they hold in trust for this locality.

John Mathews, Chairman of Commissioners.
John McKillip, Clerk of Commissioners.

On the 3rd March 1870 a deputation from seven London Companies' estates waited on Mr. Fortescue in London, and presented the following Memorial:—

To the Right Honourable C. P. FORTESCUE, M.P., Chief Secretary for Ireland.

The Memorial of a deputation of the farmers on the estates of the London Companies in the county of Londonderry, in reference to the purchase of the following London Companies' Estates, viz.:—

THE SALTERS.	THE MERCERS.	THE IRONMONGERS.	THE FISHMONGERS.
THE DRAPERS.	THE SKINNERS.	THE CLOTHWORKERS.	THE GROCERS.

We humbly pray you to inquire of the above Companies whether they would be disposed to sell their Irish Estates on the terms in the Irish Land Bill now before Parliament.

Presented 3 March 1870.

At the same time the deputation handed in a written statement, setting forth the grounds on which they sought his aid; amongst others, their rights as settlers under the Articles of Plantation.

The deputation then expressed their fears that these Companies would sell in such a way as not to afford the tenants an opportunity of becoming the purchasers of their holdings.

The action of the Clothworkers' Company, and the statement made to the deputation since they came to London, by a person of high authority among the London Companies, "that all the Companies will now sell their Irish estates," have naturally increased these fears.

APPENDIX, No. 4.

PAPER handed in by the Rev. *R. H. F. Dickey*, M.A., 5 June 1890.

To the Worshipful the Company of Salters, London.

The Memorial of the Tenants on the Company's Estate in the County of Londonderry, Ireland,

Humbly showeth,—

That the undersigned memorialists are each and all tenants on the estate of your worshipful Company.

That the estate of your worshipful Company is part of the lands settled by the Ulster Plantation, and that your memorialists have always possessed, and do still possess, the rights secured by Charter to the tenants of the Plantation.

That the Ulster custom of tenant-right has always existed upon this estate, and that it has always been fully recognised and acted upon, and that, by the Irish Land Act, this custom has been made law, so that the tenant's interest in his farm is now property, recognised and protected by the law of the realm.

That certain rules have been recently introduced into your rent office for the management of this estate which, your memorialists respectfully submit, violate their rights as tenants on the Ulster Plantation, violate the ancient Ulster custom of tenant-right, violate the provisions of the Irish Land Act, and are, in various ways, injurious to the interests and just rights of your memorialists.

That the rules to which your memorialists object are these:—

I. That a tenant cannot sell his tenant-right in his farm until he has first obtained the permission of the landlords.

II. When a farm is sold, the purchasing tenant is required to sign a contract, in which the value of the tenant-right is stated to be a sum not exceeding 10 years' present rent of the farm.

III. When a tenant dies, his son or successor in the farm is required to sign a contract, similar in its terms to the contract signed by a purchasing tenant.

IV. When a new tenancy is created, the tenant is required to sign a contract to pay the whole of the county cess, contrary to the statute, which now provides that the landlord shall pay one-half of this impost.

That memorialists object to these rules for the following reasons, to which others could be added, viz.,—

Memorialists object to the first rule—

That it violates the Ulster custom of tenant-right, now made law by the *Irish Land Act*, by which the tenant enjoys perfect freedom in this matter, and can sell his tenant-right, as he can sell any other portion of his property, whenever it is convenient for himself to do so.

Memorialists object to the second rule—

First.—That the contract which the tenant is required to sign is a complete misrepresentation of facts; it misrepresents the true market value of the tenant-right of the farm, and it misrepresents the price actually paid, which, as your respected agent well knows, is a sum quite different from that stated in the contract and entered on the books of the office.

Second.—That by this rule it was sought to give a fixed value, at least a fixed maximum value, to tenant-right considered as property. This, in the opinion of memorialists, is directly contrary to a principle of political economy now universally acknowledged, namely, that the value of any kind of property which a person proposes to sell ought to be regulated not by law, but by the state of the market. Consequently, the true value of tenant-right can never be a fixed sum, but must vary with the fluctuations of the market, which again depend upon the prosperity or depression of the agricultural interest.

Third.—That by this rule it is sought to place the value of the tenant-right, that is, of the tenant's property, under the arbitrary control of the landlords; for, if the landlords can now absolutely, and at their own will, fix a maximum value of 10 years' rent, why may they not, at any time, in the same [illegible] manner, fix a maximum value of seven years' or of five years' rent? Besides, memorialists do not seek to control the value of the landlords' property; and they consider that the landlords ought not to oppose their claim to obtain the full market value of their tenant-right. The price which ought to be paid for the tenant-right of a farm is a matter which solely concerns the tenants themselves. Properly understood, it in no way affects the landlords' interest, and, therefore, memorialists respectfully submit that the landlords ought not to interfere with it. We know it is frequently said that landlords ought to interfere, and limit the price of tenant-right for the sake of the tenants themselves. This might be a good argument if, in the market, the seller possessed some marked advantage over the buyer; but the contrary is commonly the fact. The advantage is on the side of the buyer, for he is usually under less pressure to buy than the other is to sell. Manifestly, the just and wise course is to give an open market, and leave both parties to take care of themselves. It is also sometimes urged that landlords ought, out of a regard to their own interest, to keep the price of farms low. If the high value of tenant-right on an estate had been found by experience to be, in any shape or form, hurtful to the landlords' interests, we would admit that there was some force in this argument; but experience abundantly proves the very contrary. The high price paid for tenant-right is the best security which landlords can have for the punctual payment of their rents, and the best security also for the good husbandry of their lands. On this point we fearlessly appeal to facts, and we are ready to abide the result, whether the inquiry be confined to Ulster or embrace the whole of Ireland.

Fourth.—

Fourth.—That some of your tenants, upon whom, owing to circumstances, a pressure could be put which the law does not recognise, have complied with this rule and signed the contract. But those who are still free cannot be compelled to sign it, because the law gives to landlords no power to force their tenants to enter into such engagements. One portion of your tenantry are, therefore, put in a much worse position than the others, and that not by the action of the law, but by the exercise of a power which has no sanction of law whatever. The difference thus created between tenant and tenant cannot fail to engender feelings of discord and jealousy, which we would be extremely sorry to see arising on your estate.

Fifth.—That by this rule, especially when taken in connection with the first rule, the tenant, if hereafter he wishes to dispose of his farm, is shut up, no matter what sum he may have actually paid for it, or how much he may have expended during his occupancy upon the improvement of it, to accept the bare sum stated in his contract, viz., ten years of the present rent. In such a case he would obtain redress only by carrying the matter into a court of law, where, we are firmly persuaded, this arrangement would be set aside as both inequitable and illegal. But your memorialists would deeply deplore the necessity which would compel any of them to have to adopt such a course against landlords whose general management of their estate they gladly acknowledge to be both just and considerate.

Sixth.—That the misrepresentation in his contract of the true value of the tenant-right, and the entry in the books of the office of a sum different from the price actually paid, are calculated to place the tenant in a false and most disadvantageous position in regard to any future adjustment of rent. Memorialists, indeed, hold it to be self-evident that the price paid for the tenant-right ought to have nothing whatever to do with the rent to be imposed on the farm. If the tenant has bought the tenant-right of his farm too dear, surely his folly cannot take away the landlord's title to a just and fair rent? If, on the other hand, he has been fortunate enough to make a cheap purchase, can that entitle the landlord to lay upon him an exorbitant rent? But, whilst memorialists hold this to be the clear, just, and equitable principle, yet circumstances can easily be conceived to arise, when the reasons for the present arrangement of the office being forgotten or overlooked, the supposition that the tenant had only paid 10 years' rent for his farm might be allowed to affect his interest very disastrously in the settlement of his rent.

Seventh.—That this rule is useless; because, as has been constantly represented to us by your worthy agent, and as our own experience has hitherto found it, this contract, as a matter of fact, is a dead letter, a mere empty form not acted upon, and not intended to be acted upon to the injury of the tenants. Memorialists would, therefore, respectfully ask what harm can there be in withdrawing the rule? What loss, what injury can it possibly be to your worshipful Company? It may, indeed, be said, if the rule is not acted upon to our injury, why are we so urgent to have it cancelled? We answer, first, it is creating apprehension and fear in the minds of many, and it has a tendency to create and spread among not only the tenants of this estate, but also of surrounding properties, that feeling of uneasiness, discontent, and jealousy of landlords which in time past has been the bane of the South and of the West, and which we would greatly regret to see introduced into Ulster. And, second, that while for the present this contract is treated as a dead letter, as an empty form, yet a time may come, when, as we have before stated, the reasons for this peculiar arrangement being forgotten, and the fact that the price actually paid for the farm is misrepresented in the contract being forgotten also, the dead letter may be converted into a very living reality, and the empty form may be acted upon as a *bonâ fide* compact, to the serious loss and damage of your memorialists or their children.

Memorialists object to the third rule—

That it is open to all the objections urged against the second rule; and that it is even a greater hardship to require the son of a tenant, on his father's decease, to sign such a contract, than it is to require a stranger, who has purchased a farm, to do so.

Memorialists object to the fourth rule—

First.—That, while it is in itself a minor matter, yet it tends to make tenants dissatisfied, and gives the impression that, when the Legislature has made a law favourable to them, landlords are unwilling that they should have the benefit of the law.

Second.—That it places your worshipful Company in an attitude of antagonism and direct resistance to the law of the land. This is surely a most awkward and false position for your worshipful Company to occupy, as you yourselves will admit that it is both the duty and the interest of every honest man and good citizen, and of none more than of landlords, to respect and obey the law.

Lastly.—Memorialists object to all these rules—

That the operation of each and all of them will tend greatly to discourage improving tenants. They will be discouraged from expending either capital or labour upon their farms, or upon improved methods of husbandry, and thus the full and proper development of the resources of the estate will be prevented. The first loss of this will, indeed, fall upon the farmers, but the heaviest loss will, ultimately, fall upon the landlords themselves.

Thus, while memorialists believe that all these rights which they claim from your worshipful Company are guaranteed to them, and protected by law, yet, being sincerely and earnestly desirous to maintain that good understanding and kind feeling, which, in time past, has always existed between you and them, and which ought always to exist between landlord and tenant, and can never be disturbed without great detriment to both, as the sad history of our country only too abundantly proves, they prefer, instead of appealing to any legal tribunal, to bring their grievances in this way by respectful memorial before your worshipful Company. And, knowing that you will rightly interpret their conduct, and that you will both appreciate their motives and cordially reciprocate their feelings, they are fully persuaded their appeal to you will not be in vain.

Memorialists, therefore, pray your worshipful Company to recall the rules referred to; to allow the free sale of farms, according to the ancient Ulster custom, and according to the custom of this estate; and to remove the other grievances complained of in this memorial.

And your memorialists, as in duty bound,

Will ever pray.

APPENDIX, No. 6.

PAPER handed in by the Rev. *R. H. F. Dickey*, M.A., 5 June [illegible].

To the Worshipful the Salters' Company of London.

The Supplemental Memorial of the Tenants of the Town of Magherafelt, in the County of Londonderry.

Respectfully sheweth,

That we have received the reply of your Worshipful Court to our Memorial of the 19th April last.

That without entering into a discussion of the question, whether your Worshipful Company hold the Salters' Estate on conditions of a fiduciary character or not, we beg respectfully to call your attention to the following important considerations:—

1st.—The Honourable the Irish Society have been judicially declared Trustees for the carrying out the Plantation of Ulster, and your Worshipful Company being their Grantees under the Deed of 4th June 1663, cannot be in a better position than those from whom you derive your title.

2nd.—Lord Langdale, Master of the Rolls in 1838, in the case of the Skinners' Company *v.* The Irish Society, says,—"Now the objects of the Plantation and the intent and purposes thereof were of a nature, partly public and political, and partly private;" and again, "I am of opinion that the powers granted to the Society, and the trusts reposed in them were in part of a general and public nature, independent of the private benefits of the Companies of London, and were intended by the Crown to benefit Ireland, and the City of London, &c.

3rd.—That all the facts of the case, the printed Address and Conditions of the Plantation, the King's Commission of Inquiry and Letters, touching the Plantation of Ulster, assume and imply, that the large grant of lands in the County of *Londonderry* made to the Irish Society for a nominal rent, of which rent your Company paid but a small proportion, was accompanied by conditions of a public trust, as the following quotations from the documents to be found in the Appendix to the case of the Skinners' Company *v.* The *Irish Society* in the House of Lords, prove.

In the introductory recital to the Articles of Plantation, it is stated,—

"His Majesty is graciously pleased to distribute the said Lands to his subjects as well of Great Britain as of Ireland, as being of merit and ability shall seek the same, with a mind not only to benefit themselves but to do service to the Crown and Commonwealth; and forasmuch as many persons being ignorant of the conditions whereupon his Majesty is pleased to grant the said Lands are importunate suitors for greater portions than they are able to plant, intending their private profit only and not the advancement of the Public Service, it is thought convenient to declare and publish to all his Majesty's subjects the several quantities of the proportion which shall be distributed, the several sorts of undertakers, manner of allotments, the Estates, the Rents, the Tenure, with other articles to be observed as well on his Majesty's behalf as on behalf of the undertakers."

Articles to be observed by the English and Scotch Undertakers:

No. 12.—"The said undertakers shall not demise any part of their Lands at Will, but shall make certain Estates for years, for life, in tail, or in fee simple."

Articles to be observed by Undertakers of all sorts:

No. 2.—"The Undertakers to enter into a Recognizance to the Crown, with surety, to perform the articles of Plantation."

No. 4.—"That in every of the said Counties there shall be a convenient number of Market Towns and Corporations erected for the habitation and settling of tradesmen and artificers."

4th.—That on the 28th December 1637, the Charter granted by James I. was revoked by him on account of the non-performance of some of the Articles of Plantation by the undertaking Companies.

That we refer to these matters not with a view of arguing any legal question with you, but to remind your Worshipful Company of the circumstances under which the Town of Magherafelt was originally built. That town was built not by you, but by the Settlers on the Estate, who trusted, and on the ample faith of the Tenant-Right Custom existing in the district, invested their capital and created a property valued in the year in 1854 at [illegible] *l.*

Nevertheless your Worshipful Company on coming into direct possession of the property, increased our rents from [illegible] *l.* to [illegible] *l.*, and this you consider as a proof of your indulgence and liberality. Your Memorialists consider it was an act unwarranted by the circumstances, although they were willing to assent to it, and are prepared to abide by it, if no further encroachment on their rights be made.

For your Worshipful Company must have known from the Reports of your Deputations who had regularly visited the Estate from 18[illegible] to 1854, and from the returns made to your Worshipful Court by the Agent of Sir Robert Bateson, during the same period, that the people of the Town of Magherafelt had built the Town by their own capital and labour, and that they had up to 1854 invested in their tenements upwards of [illegible] *l.* of their own money.

On the other hand, your Company never erected on your proportion of the Estates, granted to the Irish Society any town for the habitation and settling of the Tradesmen and Artificers who came over from England and Scotland; but in 17[illegible] you actually abandoned the settlement, leaving the settlers to take care of themselves, and leasing your entire property for the term of 100 years, to the highest and best bidder, for a sum which only averaged [illegible] *l.* per annum.

That after the peaceable, industrious, and loyal settlers had, by their hard toil and unexampled perseverance, under untold difficulties, made your property, without any assistance or encouragement from you, worth [illegible] *l.* per annum, they naturally expected a liberal tenure or compensation for past improvements, and trusted that, with the example of Sir Robert Bateson before you, your Worshipful Company would have endeavoured to carry out the policy which, under your Lessee, produced such satisfactory results.

That your Memorialists have been grievously disappointed in their expectations, inasmuch as your Worshipful Company has enormously increased our rents, and adopted a system of tenure wholly incompatible with the prosperity of the town.

That your Memorialists were surprised to find that your Worshipful Company justified the increase of rent by an *ex parte* Valuation, made by the late County Surveyor, who was wholly incompetent for the task, and who did not enjoy the confidence of the people. That, moreover, your Memorialists were not at the time apprised of the object of his Valuation, nor were the terms for which he thought fit, behind their backs, to set down individual tenants for leases communicated to them until long afterwards; and Memorialists respectfully submit that in the great majority of cases a full consideration was not given by Mr. Gordon to them in considering the length of their interest, as will appear by the following instances:—

Names.	Rent under Sir R. Bateson.	Increased Rent, subject to which Mr. Gordon's Term fixed.	Term fixed by Mr. Gordon.	Purchase Money of Old Premises.	Money Expended.	Date of Expenditure.
	£. s. d.	£. s. d.		£. s. d.	£.	
Mrs. M'Fall - -	3 10 -	10 - -	31 years, from 1st November 1854.	196 - -	1,000	1849
Hugh Walker - -	3 10 -	13 - -	31 years, from 1st November 1854.	Waste ground	1,000	1835
Hugh Wilson - -	4 4 -	13 6 -	21 years, from 1st November 1854.	700 - -	1,000	1854
Robert Cochrane -	3 15 -	9 4 -	No lease, rent now raised to 20 *l.*	100 - -	350	1851
Richard Donnelly -	4 11 -	12 - -	21 years, from 1st November 1854.	100 - -	1,400	1840 to 1845
Geo. Cassidy - -	4 10 -	14 - -	No lease, rent now raised to 48 *l.*	100 - -	800	1841 to 1844

That we are prepared to show to the satisfaction of any respectable Valuator the facts stated in these cases, and numerous similar cases, and we believe no Valuator of any position in the City of London (unacquainted even with our local history and trade) can be found to endorse Mr. Gordon's opinion.

That on your own showing your investment of the sum of [illegible] *l.* from 1850 to 1854, on the same principle as we have by our custom invested our money, and on similar buildings and improvements, does not pay your Worshipful Company 3 per cent.; and assuming this to be true, we respectfully submit that [illegible] years, instead of 21 years, would not exhaust your Worshipful Company's investment.

That in deciding what length of time should in any particular case exhaust the money invested in building and building improvements, regard should be had to the extent of the Town and the trading facilities which the Town affords, and we submit that assuming our views to be correct in this respect, no Lease for a less term than 99 years (which Sir R. Bateson gave) should be offered to any tenant.

That less than 99 years for Building Leases is, as a rule, unusual in small provincial towns, and where the improvements are expected to be made by the tenants alone, as in our case, the Legislature has enabled even tenants for life to grant such terms against the reversion.

That Magherafelt is the only Town in the County of Londonderry, on the Estate of a London Company, which has prospered or exceeded the extent of a petty village, a fact attributable to the wise and sound policy of Sir R. Bateson in granting Leases for 99 years.

That the reason assigned by your Worshipful Company for passing a resolution in May 1854, limiting the price of our tenant-right, namely:—That exorbitant sums were heretofore paid by tenants for dilapidated and ruinous buildings, and that a limitation was necessary for the benefit of the tenant and the protection of the Company's interest, is unfounded, inasmuch as there was no case in which the incoming tenant complained, or in which the Company suffered one shilling of loss, or in which their rights were infringed in any particular by the observance of this old and time-honoured custom.

That on the contrary, this custom as it prevailed until 1854, secured your Worshipful Company your rent and arrears of rent, and generally a large expenditure on improvements by the incoming tenant.

That since your Worshipful Company has adopted this resolution, we find you have made it the means of enforcing additional hardships injurious to the tenant's interests, for when an application has been made to your agent to sell dilapidated and ruinous buildings, you doubled the rent in the first instance, and then permitted the sale, coupling the License to sell with a condition, that the incoming tenant would repair to an extent tantamount to rebuilding.

That such a practice is wholly at variance with the old custom, and tends only to the benefit of your Worshipful Company, and is a practical abolition of our tenant-right.

That we believe it is not the law of Ireland that a tenant from year to year is bound to take such care of his dwelling-house as to prevent it becoming dilapidated and ruinous, and that he is bound only to maintain the premises in fair tenantable condition, due allowance being made for natural deterioration; he is not bound to avert premature decay, nor to efface the foot-prints of time.

That we have seen several instances where your Worshipful Company have purchased old and ruinous tenements (Mrs. Lawrence, Mr. Adams, &c.), and in all such cases you have had to expend a sum equal almost to the cost of a new structure; yet, on your own views of the legal liabilities of your tenants, such improvements would only be repairs, and you would not be at liberty, by your own Resolution, to recognise a claim for extension of Lease, on the ground of such improvements.

That the denial on the part of your Worshipful Company, contained in paragraphs 4 and 5 of your Reply of any knowledge of the terms on which we transferred our interests in our tenements up to 1854, and the statement contained in the same paragraph, that you never gave any promise as to tenant-right, have astonished us more than anything in the whole document.

That your Worshipful Court must have known that Deputations of your Company (Mr. Gillespie, Mr. [illegible], and others) visited the Estate, from 1838 to 1853, and that they were perfectly aware of the nature and extent of our tenant-right custom; and that in pursuance of their instructions returns were made and memorials sent to your Worshipful Court which fully disclosed the custom.

That these deputations were informed of this custom, and encouraged the tenants to continue their improvements and increase the expenditure, and that there are many living witnesses amongst us who can testify to these facts.

That your own acts from 1850 to 1854, in purchasing the interests of a number of tenants in dilapidated and ruinous buildings at full value, implied your previous knowledge of the terms on which tenants transferred their interests, and were naturally regarded as a practical recognition of the custom of tenant-right.

That, therefore, your denial of knowledge of the terms on which we transferred our interests under this

and

tenant-right custom, your denial of giving a promise to respect that custom, and your allegation that you did not abolish that custom, but regulated it by a resolution of your Court, are statements inconsistent with one another, and with your own acts.

That your Worshipful Court must have foreseen the injustice which the resolution of May 1864 would work to those tenants who purchased since 1853, with your knowledge and approval, and who paid their money into your office on faith of the custom, which you have in the most arbitrary manner virtually abolished. One instance out of many will illustrate the statement:—

In 1860, Mr. Glover purchased for [illegible]*l.* a dilapidated and ruinous tenement from Mrs. Hughes, the rent of which was 10*l.*, and paid the purchase-money into your office, there to be handed over to the out-going tenant (first deducting all arrears of rent, &c.). Since 1860, Mr. Glover expended [illegible]*l.* in almost re-building the tenement, and if he now wished to sell he would, under the old custom, be entitled to at least [illegible]*l.* for his interest and improvements, whereas under your regulations of 1864, he could only receive [illegible]*l.* for his tenant-right. An in-coming tenant being accepted on the condition that his rent should be increased to 30*l.* per annum.

That we are not aware of any instance in which long terms have (as you allege) been granted for building leases, and we know that since 1864 no new ground has been taken upon the terms proposed by your Worshipful Court.

That this fact, coupled with others, and particularly with the offers made to you by parties willing to invest capital in the town, provided leases for a reasonable term were granted to them, should convince you that the course you entered on in 1864, and which you have since pursued, is in direct antagonism to the sentiments of the entire community, and are incompatible with the prosperity of the town.

That the opinions and proceedings of your Worshipful Company are also at variance with the opinions and proceedings of the landlords of the most prosperous towns in the United Kingdom, and we respectfully ask your Worshipful Company's next deputation to inspect the neighbouring towns (Ballymena and Cookstown, referred to in our Memorial), and confer with the owners of the property, with a view to remove the obsolete and impolitic opinions heretofore entertained by your Worshipful Court.

That the practice to which you have resorted of serving notices to quit on your tenants, as a preliminary step to increasing their rent, is altogether unknown on any well-managed estate in Ulster.

That in our case the great majority of the inhabitants were served with notices to quit, without being informed of the special object for which the notice was served, and without being consulted as to their willingness or unwillingness to accede to your demands.

That the alleged expenditure of [illegible]*l.* in the town, between 1853 and 1868, and the conditional promises of [illegible]*l.* for future improvements as stated in your reply, are calculated to mislead the public to whom these statements seem to be addressed.

We beg to remind your Worshipful Company of the following matters in reference to these statements:—

1.—No portion of this money was expended on our houses or tenements, and it in no way increased the value of our holdings, nor does it make us more able to pay the proposed increase of rent.

2.—£ [illegible] of this money has been invested by you in new houses, and in purchasing and repairing old ones, which you have let at the highest letting value.

3.—During the same period almost [illegible]*l.* have been invested by ourselves, in purchasing, rebuilding, and repairing houses in the town, for which you now seek to charge us rack rents.

4.—If you gave [illegible]*l.* to assist in building a parish church and parochial schools, you obtained [illegible]*l.* from the Ecclesiastical Commissioners, although you were bound to erect the same at your own expense.

5.—When you gave 1,[illegible]*l.* towards erecting a Presbyterian church, the people subscribed [illegible]*l.* for their share, and they built their own school, at a cost of [illegible]*l.*

6.—You took possession of "Rainey's Charity" house and farm, and built a new charity school, at an expense of [illegible]*l.*, for which you receive a yearly rent-charge of [illegible]*l.* out of lands in the county of Down, purchased with the money of Hugh Rainey, and settled upon a charity "for clothing and putting out to trades the sons of parents who were of good repute and had been reduced to poverty."

7.—You offered us [illegible]*l.* on the condition that we should put the town under the Town's Improvement Act, 1854, and that we would bring water by pipes into the town, sewer and flag the town, according to plans to be furnished by you, the cost of which would exceed [illegible]*l.*

8.—The [illegible]*l.* for assisting to erect Gasworks which would cost us 1,[illegible]*l.* was on condition that the town adopted the Town's Improvement Act, 1854.

9.—The population by the census of 1861 was 1,[illegible], and the Town's Improvement Act could not be adopted unless the population was 1,[illegible], so that your conditions were impossible, and your offers unavailing.

10.—Your offer of 1,000*l.* towards erecting a new Court House, has, we understand, been given on condition that the Grand Jury give up to you the ground of the old Court House and Bridewell (which is rent free for ever), and all the materials of both buildings, and shall give [illegible]*l.* in cash, to be expended on the new Court House. This offer, if accepted, would be a profitable investment for you, but we believe the Grand Jury will not, at the expense of the ratepayers, entertain the project.

That the churches and schools which you have assisted to build may reasonably be expected to supply the wants of the estate for the next century, and considering that you have been in receipt of a rental of [illegible]*l.* a year for the last 13 years, and that for at least 50 years to come, little unproductive outlay will be required, we consider the proposed enormous rise in the town rents unwarranted.

That the expenditure of [illegible]*l.* upon Religious Charities in the town, during 13 years will not appear so munificent, when you remember that you are non-resident landlords, who expend [illegible]*l.* a year in London, and who contribute very little to the wealth of the community which yields this annual sum.

That this unproductive expenditure of [illegible]*l.*, is still further diminished in its apparent magnitude and liberality by the obligation imposed on your Worshipful Company, under the 5th General Article of Plantation, to erect a sufficient number of parish churches.

That the conditions in your leases are equitable in themselves we cannot admit; on the contrary, we submit the following are most inequitable.

The tenant is bound to insure in the joint names of the landlord and tenant, and in case of destruction by fire, to expend the money received from the insurance and all such further sums as may be required to rebuild to the satisfaction of your Worshipful Company.

If the tenant omits to paint, repair, or pay his rent, the lease is forfeited, and the landlord may re-enter the premises, and take possession from the tenant, yet the tenant is not discharged from his liability to the covenants in the lease.

That

That we are still willing to abide the results of an open inquiry, or to refer our claims to indifferent parties who have some knowledge of our customs and local trade, and who would have an opportunity of seeing what we have done.

We, therefore, respectfully pray that your Worshipful Company will re-consider the prayer of our Memorial of 19th April last, with a view to have the grievances complained of redressed.

Read and adopted at a Public Meeting held in the Court House, Magherafelt, on the 4th day of July 1867.

My dear Sir, Salters' Hall, 12 July 1867.

I am directed by the Committee to acknowledge the receipt of the further memorial, and to express their regret at the contents. They consider it utterly useless, even if it were consistent with their position, that they should entertain a controversy with parties, who not only take up the most unreasonable ground of argument, but condescend to statements which are simply the reverse of fact.

They, therefore, desire you to inform the subscribers to the memorial, that the Company have not taken the course they have adopted without the fullest consideration, and it is their firm intention to carry it out.

They regret their consistent and liberal intentions have been, and are so, perversely misinterpreted; and while they are ever prepared to receive any communication from the tenants, couched in a just and becoming spirit, they can take no further notice of a document of the description now [illegible] to them.

I remain, &c.
(signed) *Edward Thompson.*

APPENDIX, No. [illegible]

PAPER handed in by the Rev. *R. H. F. Dickey*, M.A., 9 June 1890.

A.—LIST of PRESBYTERIAN CONGREGATIONS in County *Derry* and County *Tyrone*, which, or part of which, are on LONDON COMPANIES' ESTATES, and GRANTS made by the COMPANIES to MINISTERS.

DRAPERS' COMPANY.

Name of Congregation.	Number of Families.	Annual Grant.	Amount Withdrawn.	Date.
		£. s. d.	£. s. d.	
First Moneymore	164	21 - -	—	—
Draperstown	116	10 10 -	10 10 -	1867
First Magherafelt	204	10 10 -	10 10 -	1860 (?)
Tobermore	140	10 10 -	10 10 -	1864
Ballygoney	75	10 10 -	—	—
Claggan	100	[illegible] - -	[illegible] - -	1865
Orritor	167	10 10 -	10 10 -	1866
First Cookstown	148	10 10 -	10 10 -	1866
Second Cookstown	105	10 10 -	10 10 -	1866
Third Cookstown	185	10 10 -	—	—
Lecumpher	80	10 10 -	10 10 -	1876
Second Moneymore	206	10 10 -	—	—
TOTAL - - -	1,665	134 - -	71 10 -	

CLOTHWORKERS' COMPANY.

Name of Congregation.	Number of Families.	Annual Grant.	Amount Withdrawn.	Date.
		£. s. d.	£. s. d.	
First Dunboe	210	20 - -	20 - -	1865
Castlerock	42	—	—	—
Coleraine, Terrace-row	245	—	—	—
Second Dunboe	110	10 - -	10 - -	1865
TOTAL - - -	707	30 - -	30 - -	

N.B.—On sale of estate to Sir H. Bruce in 1871 endowments were given as follows: First Dunboe, 200 *l.*, Second Dunboe, 100 *l.*, and Castlerock, 100 *l.*

IRONMONGERS' COMPANY.

Name of Congregation.	Number of Families.	Annual Grant.	Amount Withdrawn.	Date.
		£ s. d.	£ s. d.	
Aghadowey - - - - - - -	335	10 - -	—	—
Crossgar - - - - - - - -	78	10 - -	2 - -	1857
First Garvagh - - - - - - -	173	10 - -	3 - -	1857
Second Garvagh - - - - - - -	110	10 - -	6 - -	1857
Third Garvagh - - - - - -	63	10 - -	3 - -	1857
Macosquin - - - - - - -	140	10 - -	6 - -	1857
Moneydig - - - - - - - -	144	10 - -	—	—
Ballylintagh - - - - - - - -	—	10 - -	10 - -	1854
Dromoragh - - - - - - -	160	10 - -	2 - -	1857
TOTAL - - - -	[illegible]	90 - -	35 - -	

SALTERS' COMPANY.

Name of Congregation.	Number of Families.	Annual Grant.	Amount Withdrawn.	Date.
		£ s. d.	£ s. d.	
First Magherafelt - - - - - -	204	20 - -	—	—
Curran - - - - - -	80	—	—	—
Castledawson - - - - - -	250	—	—	—
Saltersland - - - - - -	103	30 - -	—	—
Second Magherafelt - - - - -	65	10 - -	—	—
Lecumpher - - - - - - - -	30	10 - -	—	—
TOTAL - - -	771	70 - -	—	

MERCERS' COMPANY.

Name of Congregation.	Number of Families.	Annual Grant.	Amount Withdrawn.	Date.
		£ s. d.	£ s. d.	
First Kilrea - - - - - - - -	195	25 - -	—	—
Second Kilrea - - - - - - -	85	15 - -	—	—
Swatragh - - - - - - - -	44	20 - -	—	—
Maghera - - - - - - - - -	330	—	—	—
Culnady - - - - - - - - -	75	—	—	—
Moneydig - - - - - - - - -	148	10 - -	10 - -	1859
Churchtown - - - - - - - - -	108	—	—	—
TOTAL - - -	975	70 - -	10 - -	

SKINNERS' COMPANY.

Name of Congregation.	Number of Families.	Annual Grant.	Amount Withdrawn.	Date.
		£. s. d.	£. s. d.	
Dungiven	[illegible]	[illegible] - -	—	—
Scriggan	95	40 - -	—	—
[illegible]	160	10 - -	—	—
Lower Cumber	272	[illegible] - -	20 - -	[illegible]
Upper Cumber	109	[illegible] - -	—	—
[illegible]	163	10 - -	—	—
TOTAL	774	101 - -	20 - -	

FISHMONGERS' COMPANY.

Name of Congregation.	Number of Families.	Annual Grant.	Amount Withdrawn.	Date.
		£. s. d.	£. s. d.	
Ballykelly	378	10 - -	10 - -	1885
Faughanvale	215	10 - -	10 - -	1885
Lower Cumber	223	10 - -	10 - -	1875
Upper Cumber	102	10 - -	10 - -	1884
Drumachose	148	10 - -	10 - -	(?)
Banagher	167	10 - -	10 - -	1885
TOTAL	[illegible]	70 - -	60 - -	

On sale of this estate ministers received three years of their grants as compensation for withdrawal, with the exception of Drumachose, the grant to which had been previously withdrawn.

GROCERS' COMPANY.

Name of Congregation.	Number of Families.	Annual Grant.	Amount Withdrawn.	Date.
		£. s. d.	£. s. d.	
Banagher	157	10 - -	10 - -	1877
Gortnessy	[illegible]	10 - -	10 - -	1877
Faughanvale	215	10 - -	10 - -	1877
Lower Cumber	223	10 - -	10 - -	1877
TOTAL	703	40 - -	40 - -	

SUMMARY.

	Amount of Grant.	Amount Withdrawn.
	£. s. d.	£. s. d.
Drapers	134 - -	28 10 -
Salters	[illegible]	—
Haberdashers	70 - -	30 - -
Clothworkers	30 - -	30 - -
Ironmongers	70 - -	70 - -
Skinners	110 - -	80 - -
Fishmongers	70 - -	70 - -
Grocers	40 - -	40 - -
TOTAL - - - £.	[illegible]	371 10 -

B.—GRANTS made for Building Churches and Manses.

Drapers' Company.—First Moneymore, entirely; Draperstown, entirely; First Moneymore Manse, 84*l.* 5*s.*; Second Moneymore Church, partially; Lecumpher, partially.

Salters' Company.—First Magherafelt Church, 1,200*l.*; Second Magherafelt, 200*l.*

Mercers' Company.—First Kilrea Church, 1,350*l.*; Second Kilrea Church, 51*l.* 10*s.*; Culnady Manse, 100*l.*; Boveedy Church, 80*l.*; Boveedy Manse, 50*l.*

Skinners' Company.—Dungiven Church, 200*l.*; Manse, 200*l.*; Culnady Manse, 10*l.* 10*s.*

Ironmongers' Company.—Macosquin, 5*l.*; Garvagh, 10*l.*; Boveedy, 5*l.*

Grocers' Company.—Lower Cumber Church, 300*l.*; Manse, 100*l.*; Culnady Manse, 52*l.* 10*s.*; Gortnessy, 5*l.*; Faughanvale, 50*l.*

Fishmongers' Company.—Ballykelly Manse, free gift; Ballykelly Church, free gift; Banagher Manse, partially; Faughanvale, 100*l.*

Note.—The Mercers' Company have always refused to give site or lease for manses. There are no manses on the estate. The late Rev. Jas. Dasley, Kilrea, was obliged to build his manse two miles from his church, in consequence of the refusal of company to give him a lease.

C.—GRANTS made to Schools and Colleges.

Drapers.—Intermediate School, Moneymore, 60*l.*; 13 National Schools, 180*l.* annually, of which 25*l.* have been withdrawn. Scholarships and prizes were given to pupils attending schools, but these have ceased.

Salters gave 100*l.* a year to Rainey Intermediate School. This has been reduced to 100*l.*, of which only 60*l.* is available for Rainey School. Grants have been withdrawn from Fair Hill Male, Aughagaskin, and Crabbing National Schools.

Ironmongers give a scholarship of 25*l.* a year to Magee College, Derry, and grants from 10*l.* to 15*l.* to each of 11 Primary Schools under the National Board.

Mercers give 15*l.* a year to each of six Female National Schools, and 20*l.* a year to each of six Male National Schools.

Skinners gave 50*l.* a year to Intermediate School at Dungiven, while it continued, and contribute to five National Schools with seven principal teachers, 40*l.* per annum.

Grocers gave 5*l.* a year to each of the Faughanvale Male and Female National Schools. On withdrawal of these grants in 1877, Company were memorialised that grants might be continued, but receipt of memorial was not even acknowledged. Grants to two other schools, Gortnessy and Eglinton, were continued for seven years by arrangement with purchasers of estate.

Fishmongers built 15 schools on estate and kept them in repair. They introduced the Lancasterian system of education, which was pursued until schools were taken under the National Board. A total annual grant of 180*l.* was made to these schools. This has now been withdrawn.

	£	£	£
[illegible]	[illegible]	None	150
[illegible]	1,404	None	140
[illegible]	None	None	[illegible]
[illegible]	1,500	600	* 100
[illegible]	[illegible]	200	80
[illegible]	None	None	150
[illegible]	1,500	100	(?)
[illegible]	750	None	* 80

* [illegible]

APPENDIX No. 7.

PAPER handed in by the Rev. [illegible], [illegible] July [illegible]

Irish Land Commission, 24 Upper Merrion-street,
Dublin, [illegible] July [illegible].

Sir,

I am directed by the Commissioners to transmit to you the accompanying certified copy of the Deed of Conveyance and Charging Order, dated the [illegible] day of April [illegible], under which you have become proprietor of your holding, subject to the obligation of paying the Annuity specified in the Deed.

The original Deed, which has been duly registered in the Registry of Deeds Office, will remain in the Record Room of this Commission until the Annuity is paid off or redeemed, when it will be handed over to you or to your successors in title.

Your first payment will be due on the 1st day of November [illegible], and must be made within fifteen days from that date. Such payment, as well as your future payments, may be made at any bank in Ireland. A receivable order will be sent to you [illegible] days before each payment becomes due, authorising the bank to receive the same from you, and such receivable order should be presented by you at the bank when making your payment.

	£	s.	d.
The first payment will consist of Interest from the date of Advance to the first Gale Day - - - - - - - - - - - - -	–	–	7
First half-yearly instalment, due 1st November [illegible] - - - - - - -	[illegible]	[illegible]	[illegible]
Total First Payment - - - -	[illegible]	[illegible]	[illegible]

The future payments will consist of the half-yearly instalment of [illegible], no separate charge being made in respect of interest after the first payment. These future payments will, unless redeemed in manner hereinafter mentioned, be payable the 1st day of May and 1st day of November, for [illegible] years, from the 1st day of May [illegible].

You are requested to observe that these payments must be made punctually, and that the Commissioners have no power to make any allowances or abatements whatever, or to enter into any question as to the price or value of your holding, or the circumstances under which you purchased it, or any questions as to boundaries, turbary rights, &c.

Every Annuity, or any portion of it at any time outstanding, may be redeemed by payment to the Land Commission, of a sum equivalent to the then value of such Annuity, or of such portion of it as is sought to be redeemed, such value to be calculated according to the Redemption Table annexed thereto. Thus a borrower of [illegible] can by paying down [illegible] on the day his second half-yearly instalment becomes due clear off the last twenty half-yearly instalments of [illegible] each ([illegible] in all). A present payment of [illegible] will at any time redeem an instalment of [illegible] due 10 years afterwards. Tenant-purchasers can thus invest their savings, small or large, in freeing their holdings from the annuity.

You are also requested to observe that your holding cannot be sub-divided or sub-let without the consent in writing of the Commissioners until all the instalments have been paid off or redeemed.

Every instalment paid or redeemed operates, not merely for the hiring of the land as in the case of rent, but in part payment of the purchase-money, and thereby adds year by year to the present value of your farm until all instalments are paid or redeemed, when the farm will become your absolute property.

Your attention is particularly requested to the annexed extracts from the Land Law (Ireland) Act, [illegible], which refer to your purchase.

I am, &c.
(signed) [illegible],
Solicitor to the Irish Land Commission,
24, Upper Merrion-street, Dublin.

Mr James M'Vey, [illegible], Londonderry.

REDEMPTION TABLE

A Table showing the Amount that will Redeem an Annual Instalment of Four Pounds due after the Expiration of the under-mentioned Number of Complete Years from the Payment of the Redemption Money.

Interval of Years.	Amount of Redemption Money.	Interval of Years.	Amount of Redemption Money.	Interval of Years.	Amount of Redemption Money.	Interval of Years.	Amount of Redemption Money.
	£ s. d.		£ s. d.		£ s. d.		£ s. d.
48	- 19 5	36	1 7 8	24	1 19 5	12	2 16 2
47	1 - -	35	1 8 6	23	2 - 7	11	2 17 10
46	1 - 7	34	1 9 4	22	2 1 10	10	2 19 7
45	1 1 8	33	1 10 2	21	2 3 1	9	3 1 4
44	1 1 10	32	1 11 1	20	2 4 6	8	3 3 2
43	1 2 4	31	1 12 -	19	2 6 -	7	3 5 1
42	1 3 3	30	1 13 -	18	2 7 -	6	3 7 -
41	1 [illegible] 10	29	1 14 -	17	2 9 5	5	3 9 1
40	1 4 7	28	1 15 -	16	2 [illegible] 11	4	3 11 1
39	1 5 4	27	1 16 1	15	2 12 8	3	3 13 3
38	1 6 1	26	1 17 2	14	2 [illegible] 11	2	3 15 5
37	1 6 10	25	1 18 3	13	2 [illegible] 6	1	3 17 9

Extracts from the Land Law (Ireland) Act, 1881.

Sec. [illegible] (1.) As between the Land Commission and the proprietor for the time being of any holding for the purchase of which the Land Commission have advanced money in pursuance of this part of this Act, the following conditions shall be imposed so long as such holding is subject to any charge in respect of an annuity in favour of the Land Commission, that is to say,

(a.) The holding shall not be subdivided or let by such proprietor without the consent of the Land Commission until the whole charge due to the Land Commission has been repaid:

(b.) Where the proprietor subdivides or lets any holding or part of a holding in contravention of the foregoing provisions of this section, the Land Commission may cause the holding to be sold:

(c.) Where the title to the holding is divested from the proprietor by bankruptcy, the Land Commission may cause the holding to be sold:

(d.) Where, on the decease of the proprietor, the holding would by reason of any devise, bequest, intestacy, or otherwise, become subdivided, the Land Commission may require the holding to be sold within twelve months after the death of the proprietor to some one person, and if default is made in selling the same, the Land Commission may cause the same to be sold.

(2.) The Land Commission may cause any holding which under this section they can cause to be sold, or any part of such holding, to be sold by public auction or private contract, and subject to any conditions of sale they may think expedient, and after such notice of the time, place, terms, and conditions of such sale, as they think just and expedient, and the Land Commission may convey such holding to the purchaser in like manner in all respects as if the holding had been vested in the Land Commission.

APPENDIX, No. 8.

PAPER handed in by the Rev. *B. Longley*, 10 July 1890.

This Indenture, made the thirteenth day of April One thousand eight hundred and eighty-eight, between the Corporation of Master and Wardens and Brethren and Sisters of the Guild or Fraternity of Corpus Christi of Skinners of London, otherwise the Master and Wardens of the Guild or Fraternity of the Body of Christ of the Skinners of London, hereinafter called the vendors, of the first part; the Irish Land Commission, hereinafter called the Commission, of the second part; and James M'Vey, of Dungiven, in the county of Londonderry, farmer, hereinafter called the purchaser, of the third part; whereas, the purchaser holds the holding hereinafter described as tenant to the vendors, and the vendors are seised in fee thereof, and of certain other hereditaments subject to a reservation to the governor and assistants, London, of the new plantation in Ulster, their successors and assigns, of all the fishings and taking of salmon and eels and other fish in the Rivers of Bann and Lough Foyle and in all the creeks of the same rivers, or either of them, and in all the ground and soil of the same rivers, or either of them, contained in an indenture of the fifth day of June, One thousand six hundred and sixty-three, and made between the said governor and assistants, London, of the new plantation in Ulster and the vendors (but released and discharged from all other exceptions, reservations, rights, liberties, and privileges whatsoever contained in the said indenture of the fifth day of June, One thousand six hundred and sixty-three), and also subject to the said tenancy, but discharged from the perpetual yearly rent of fourteen pounds six shillings and eightpence, created by the said indenture of the fifth June, One thousand six hundred and sixty-three, under the provisions of an indenture bearing date the twenty-seventh day of May, One thousand eight hundred and eighty-seven; and whereas the purchaser has agreed to purchase the interest of the vendors in the said holding for the sum of One hundred and thirteen pounds, and has applied to the Commission to advance him the said sum of One hundred and thirteen pounds for that purpose, which the Commission has agreed to do under the provisions of the "Purchase of Land (Ireland) Act, 1885," on the terms of such advance being secured by a guarantee deposit as hereinafter provided, the repayment of the said advance with interest, being secured pursuant to the provisions of the "Land Law (Ireland) Act, 1887," by an Order of the Commission endorsed on these presents; and whereas the Commission has, at the request of the purchaser, paid to the vendors the sum of Ninety pounds, and has with the consent of the vendors retained the sum of Twenty-three pounds to satisfy the purposes of a guarantee deposit; now this indenture witnesseth that in consideration of the said sum of Ninety pounds so paid and of the said sum of Twenty-three pounds so retained as aforesaid, the receipt and retention respectively of which said sums, making together the said sum of One hundred and thirteen pounds, the vendors do hereby acknowledge, the vendors as beneficial owners do hereby grant to the purchaser the house and premises in the main street of the town of Dungiven and that part of the lands of Dungiven all in the occupation of the purchaser as such tenant as aforesaid, situate in the barony of Keenaght and county of Londonderry, containing together three acres, one rood, and ten perches, statute measure or thereabouts, excepting and reserving unto the vendors, their successors and assigns, all freestone and beds of freestone, freestone quarries, and pits as well opened as unopened, within, under, or upon the said lands, hereditaments, and premises, and with full right, power, and liberty to the vendors, their successors and assigns, and the agents, workmen, and persons authorised by them, or any of them, at all times to enter upon the said hereditaments and premises, and every part thereof, and with or without horses, carriages, waggons, or carts, and to occupy the surface thereof, and to search for, sink, quarry, open, work, get, raise, draw, make merchantable, and carry away the said freestone, beds of freestone, freestone quarries, and pits, and with full liberty and power to make, construct, erect, and maintain all such quarries, pits, drains, watercourses, roads, buildings, works, machinery, and conveniences, and to remove such stones and rubbish, and generally to do all such other acts and things as may be necessary for the purposes aforesaid, making from time to time compensation to the purchaser, his heirs and assigns, and his and their lessees or tenants, reasonable and adequate compensation for all damage thereby done or occasioned to the said lands, hereditaments, and premises or any buildings thereon.

To hold to the purchaser in fee simple, subject so far as the premises hereby conveyed are affected thereby, to the exception and reservation of all the taking of salmon and eels and other fish in the Rivers Bann and Lough Foyle and in all the creeks and members of the same rivers, and either of them, and of all the ground and soil of the same rivers, or either of them, contained in the said indenture of the fifth day of June, One thousand six hundred and sixty-three, hereinbefore mentioned, but released and discharged from the other reservations, exceptions, and liberties to the said governor and assistants, London, of the new plantation in Ulster in the said indenture contained. And the vendors do hereby, for themselves, their successors and assigns, covenant with the purchaser, his heirs and assigns, that the vendors, their successors and assigns, in exercising the rights, powers, privileges, and liberties hereinbefore reserved, will do as little damage to the surface of the said lands, hereditaments, and premises, and to any buildings thereon, as may be consistent with a fair and *bonâ fide* exercise of the said rights, powers, and privileges, and will make and pay reasonable and adequate compensation for any damage caused to the surface of the said lands, hereditaments, and premises, or to any existing buildings thereon, in the exercise of the said rights, powers, privileges, and liberties. And the vendors do hereby release to the purchaser all arrears of rent due by the purchaser to the vendors out of the said holding up to the date of these presents; in witness whereof the vendors and the Commission have hereunto respectively caused their seals to be affixed, and the purchaser has hereunto set his hand and affixed his seal the day and year first above written.

The Seal of the Vendors was hereunto affixed in presence of
E. H. Draper, Clerk, }
Wm. Bolero, Accountant, } Skinners' Hall.

(SEAL.)

A Memorial hereof was entered in the Registry of Deeds Office, Dublin, at 7 minutes after 9 o'clock, on the 13th day of April 1888, Book 20, No. 97, and the execution hereof and of said Memorial was duly proved.

Fees, 10 s. *J. J. Moran*, A.R.

Office of the Irish Land Commission.

Record No. [illegible]

Before Mr. Commissioner M'Carthy,
Saturday, the [illegible] day of April [illegible].

In the matter of the *Estate* of the Worshipful the Skinners' Company.

Owners of Land

Upon reading the within Deed, the Court doth declare the land comprised in the holding by the said Deed granted, charged pursuant to the provisions of the "Land Law (Ireland) Act, 1887," with the repayment to the Irish Land Commission of the said advance of One hundred and thirteen pounds, by an annuity of Four pounds ten shillings and fourpence for the term of forty-nine years from the first day of May next, payable by equal half-yearly payments on each first day of May and first day of November, the first payment thereof to be made on the first day of November next, and also charged with interest on the said sum of One hundred and thirteen pounds, at the rate of three and one-eighth per cent. from the date hereof, to the first day of May next, and payable with the first instalment of the said annuity.

Henry C. Lynch,
Chief Clerk.

APPENDIX, No. [illegible]

PAPER handed in by the Rev. *E. Loughrey*, 10 July 18[illegible].

This Indenture, made the second day of November One thousand eight hundred and eighty-two, between the Worshipful Company of Skinners, hereinafter called lessors of the one part, and Thomas Gwynne, hereinafter called lessee of the other part: Whereas by agreement dated the sixteenth day of May One thousand eight hundred and seventy-nine, and made between the said Skinners' Company of the one part and the said Thomas Gwynne of the other part, it was agreed that lessee should take the therein and hereinafter described premises situate at Dungiven, and containing twelve perches or thereabouts, and should to the satisfaction of the said lessors, their agents or surveyors, erect, build, and completely finish before the first day of November One thousand eight hundred and eighty, at his own expense, and at an outlay of Two hundred and fifty pounds at least, a good and substantial dwelling house; and whereas the said lessee has built such dwelling-house to the satisfaction of said lessors, now this Indenture witnesseth, that in pursuance of said agreement and in consideration of the rent hereinafter reserved and of the covenants hereinafter contained, and on the part of the said lessee, his executors, administrators, and assigns to be observed and performed, the said lessors do hereby demise unto the said lessee, his executors, administrators, and assigns, all that and those, that dwelling-house and offices so lately built by the said lessee, situate on the north side of Main street, Dungiven, in the county of Londonderry, and as delineated on the map or plan endorsed on these presents, together with all rights, easements, and appurtenances thereto belonging, to have and to hold the premises hereby demised or expressed, so as to be [illegible] the said lessee, his executors, administrators, and assigns, from the first day of November One thousand eight hundred and seventy-nine, for a term of sixty-one years thence next ensuing, yielding and paying during the said term the yearly rent of Three pounds eighteen shillings by equal half-yearly payments on the first day of May and the first day of November in every year, without any deductions for taxes, rates, assessments, or any outgoings whatsoever, landlord's portion of the poor rates only excepted, and the said lessee doth hereby for himself, his heirs, executors, administrators and assigns, covenant with said lessors, their successors and assigns, that he, the said lessee, his executors, administrators, or assigns, will at his or their own cost, at all times during the said term, keep insured the said dwelling-house and offices from loss or damage by fire in the joint names of the lessors and lessee in some [illegible] office or offices to be approved of by lessors, their secretary or surveyor, in a sufficient sum to cover the value of said buildings, and will for that purpose pay all premiums and sums of money payable in respect of such insurance, and will from time to time when required produce to the said lessors the policy of such insurance and the receipt of every such premium and sum of money, and as often as such buildings or any part thereof shall be destroyed or damaged by fire, shall forthwith build or reinstate same under the direction of lessors, their agent or surveyor. And also that he the said lessee, his executors, administrators, and assigns, will at all times during the said term, at his or their cost, well and sufficiently repair, support, amend and keep the said premises hereby demised with all manner of reparations and amendments, and will at the expiration or sooner determination of the said term peaceably and quietly surrender and give up same unto the said lessors, their successors or assigns; and shall also permit the lessors, their surveyor or agent, with or without workmen and others deputed by them to enter into and upon said premises [illegible] in every year during said term to examine the state and condition thereof, and once in every seven years during said term to take an inventory of the fixtures and things to be yielded up at the determination of the said term as aforesaid. And also that the said lessee, his executors, administrators, or assigns, will not at any time during the said term carry on or permit to be carried on any [illegible] trade or unlicensed distillery of spirits. And also will not assign, or underlet, or part with possession of said premises, or any part thereof, without the consent in writing of the lessors or their agent. Provided always, and it is hereby declared between the parties hereto that if the said yearly rent of Three pounds eighteen shillings, or any part thereof, shall be in arrear for the space of twenty-one days next after any of the said days whereon same ought to have been paid as aforesaid after having been duly demanded, or if there shall be any breach of any of the covenants hereinbefore contained on the part of the said lessee, his executors, administrators, or assigns, it shall be lawful for the said lessors or their agent to re-enter on said demised premises and put out the lessee therefrom without prejudice to any claim they may have against lessee, and they the said lessors for themselves, their successors, and assigns do hereby covenant with the said lessee, his executors, administrators, and assigns, that he the said lessee, his executors, administrators, and assigns, paying the said yearly rent of Three pounds eighteen shillings in manner aforesaid, and observing and performing all covenants hereinbefore contained on his or their part to be observed and performed, shall and may peaceably and quietly enjoy said premises during the term hereby granted, without any eviction or disturbance by the said lessors. Provided always that if the said lessors shall at any time during the intended demise desire to resume possession of the whole or any part of the said premises for the purpose of making a new street, road, or any other purpose of a public character, they shall be entitled to do so at the expiration of six calendar months' notice in writing to be given to said lessee, his executors, administrators, or assigns, under the hand of their agent for the time being, whereupon this indenture of lease and the term of years hereby granted, shall as to the whole of said premises, or as the case may be, so far as relates to such part of the premises so resumed, absolutely cease; and in case only a part of the said demised premises shall be so resumed, then a proportionate abatement of rent and compensation shall be made to the said lessee, his executors, administrators, or assigns, by the said lessors, their successors or assigns; and in case the parties cannot agree as to the amount of such abatement, the same shall be determined by the arbitration of two indifferent persons, one to be chosen by each of the parties, or by their umpire, such umpire to be nominated before the said arbitrators shall enter upon the subject of the reference; and in case either parties shall refuse, or shall for the space of one week after notice from the other party, neglect to nominate an arbitrator, the arbitrator of the other party may alone make a final decision; and the said lessee further covenants with the said lessors, that he will in all respects hold and occupy the aforesaid demised premises in accordance with the customs of the [illegible] Estate, and the said lessee further covenants with said lessors that he will not inquire into or question the lessors' title to demise

demise the before described premises. In witness whereof the said Worshipful the Skinners' Company have hereunto affixed their corporate seal, and the said Thomas Grogan has affixed his hand and seal the day and year first hereinbefore written.

Sealed by the said Worshipful Skinners' Company, in presence of
E. Herbert Draper,
Clerk to the Skinners' Company, London.

(Seal.)

Signed, Sealed, and Delivered by said Thomas Grogan, in presence of
James J. Atkinson,
Solicitors' Apprentice, Limavady.
William Gault,
Writing Clerk, Limavady.

Thomas Grogan. (Seal.)

APPENDIX, No. 10.

PAPER handed in by the Chairman.

TRANSLATION OF THE CHARTER OF KING JAMES THE FIRST TO THE IRISH SOCIETY.

Dated the 29th March 1613.

JAMES, by the Grace of God, of England, Scotland, France, and Ireland, King, Defender, &c. To all whom these present letters shall come, greeting. Whereas there can be nothing more kingly than to establish the true religion of Christ among men, hitherto depraved and almost lost in superstition; to strengthen, improve, and cultivate, by art and industry, countries and lands uncultivated and almost desert, and the same not only to plant with honest citizens and inhabitants, but also to renovate and strengthen them with good statutes and ordinances, whereby they might be more safely defended, not only from the corruption of their morals, but from their intestine and domestic plots and conspiracies, and also from foreign violence. And whereas the province of Ulster, in our realm of Ireland, for many years now past hath greatly erred from the true religion of Christ and Divine Grace, and hath abounded with superstition, insomuch that for a long time it hath not only been harassed, torn, and wasted by private and domestic feuds, but also by foreign arms; we, deeply and heartily commiserating the wretched state of the said province, have esteemed it to be a work worthy of a Christian prince, and of our Royal function, to stir up and recall the said province from superstition, rebellion, calamity, and poverty which heretofore have horribly raged therein, to religion, obedience, strength, and prosperity.

And whereas our beloved and faithful subjects, the mayor and commonalty and citizens of our city of London, burning with a fervent and impressive [illegible] such our pious intention in this behalf, have laudably undertaken a considerable part of the said plantation in Ulster, below in these presents mentioned, and in other respects are making progress therein.

We, of our special grace and of our certain science and mere motion, for us, our heirs and successors, do will, ordain, constitute, and declare, that the city or town of Derry, in the province of Ulster, in our realm of Ireland, and all and singular castles, lordships, manors, towns, villages, hamlets, lands, tenements, waters, streams, parts, meadows, pastures, and other territories, and hereditaments whatsoever, below in or by these presents given and granted, and all and singular other castles, lordships, manors, towns, villages, hamlets, lands, tenements, waters and watercourses, rivulets, boundaries, and other territories, islands, lying, and being within the precincts, limits, or circuit of the said castles, lordships, manors, towns, villages, and other the premises in or by these presents below given and granted, from henceforth may and shall be united, consolidated, and from henceforth for ever may be one entire county of itself, distinct and separate from all our counties whatsoever within our kingdom of Ireland, to all intents and purposes, and in as ample manner and form as any other county whatsoever, in our kingdom of England or Ireland, and from henceforth for ever it shall be named, accounted, and called the county of Londonderry, and those all into one entire, free, and distinct county of itself, we do erect, constitute, ordain, and create, by these presents.

And further, of our special grace and certain knowledge, and mere motion, for us, our heirs and successors, we will, ordain, constitute, and declare, that the said city or town of Derry, for ever hereafter be and shall be named and called the city of Londonderry, and that all and singular houses, edifices, lands, tenements, waters, watercourses, and the ground and soil lying and being within the said city of Derry, and within and by the space and circuit of three Irish miles, to be measured and limited from the middle of the said city of Derry, on each and every part of the said city, from henceforth be and shall be within the jurisdiction and liberties of the aforesaid city; and that the said city of Londonderry aforesaid, and the circuits, precincts, limits, bounds, compass, liberties, franchises, and jurisdiction of the same shall, for ever hereafter, extend and spread out, and may extend and spread out, within and through the space and circuit of three Irish miles, to be measured and limited from all and every part of the said city as aforesaid, for ever.

And further we will, ordain, constitute, and declare that all and singular the houses, edifices, lands, tenements, waters and watercourses, ground and soil, situate, lying, and being within the town of Coleraine, in the aforesaid province of Ulster, and within and through the space and circuit of three Irish miles, to be measured and limited from the middle of the said town of Coleraine, and all and every part of the same, from henceforth hereafter may and shall be part and parcel of the aforesaid town of Coleraine, and within the jurisdiction and liberties of the same town of Coleraine, and that the said town of Coleraine, and the circuit, precincts, limits, bounds, compass, liberties, franchises, and jurisdiction of the same town itself, from thenceforth for ever, may extend and spread out, and shall and may extend and spread out, within and through the space and circuit of three Irish miles, to be measured and limited from all and every part of the said town of Coleraine, from henceforth for ever, as aforesaid.

And we do will, grant, establish, ordain, and create that all citizens and inhabitants of the city of Londonderry aforesaid, and they who hereafter shall be citizens and inhabitants of the aforesaid city, and their successors, for ever hereafter, be and shall be by force of these presents a new body, politic and corporate, in deed, fact, and name, by the name of the Mayor and Commonalty and Citizens of the city of Londonderry; and them by the name of the Mayor and Commonalty and Citizens of the city of Londonderry, one new body politic or corporate, in deed, fact, and name, really and fully, for us, our heirs and successors, we do erect, make, ordain, constitute, create, and declare by these presents, and that by that name they shall have perpetual succession, and that they and their successors for ever, by the name of the Mayor and Commonalty and Citizens of the city of Londonderry, be and shall be perpetually in future times persons able, and in law capable to have, purchase, receive, and possess lands, tenements, goods, chattels, rents, reversions, possessions, liberties, privileges, rights, jurisdictions, franchises, and hereditaments of what sort, kind, nature, or quality soever, to them and their successors, in fee and perpetuity, or in any other manner howsoever, and also to give, grant, demise, and assign lands, tenements, and other hereditaments, goods, and chattels, and to do and execute all and singular other acts and things by the name aforesaid; and that they and their successors for ever, by the name of the Mayor and Commonalty and Citizens of the city of Londonderry, may plead and be impleaded, answer and be answered, defend and be defended, in any courts, pleas, and places, and before any judges, justices, and other persons and officers, of us, our heirs and successors, in all pleas, suits, plaints, causes, matters, and demands, of what kind, nature, or form soever, in the same and like manner and form as our other liege people of our kingdoms of England or Ireland (being persons able, and in the law capable) may plead and be impleaded, answer and be answered, defend and be defended, and may have, purchase, receive, possess, give, grant, and demise; and that the aforesaid Mayor and Commonalty and Citizens of the said city of Londonderry

Londonderry aforesaid, and their successors, may, for ever hereafter have a common seal for transacting all business whatsoever, of them and their successors, and that it may be lawful to the same Mayor and Commonalty and Citizens aforesaid, and their successors, at their pleasure, from time to time to break, change, and new make the said seal as to them shall seem best.

And further, we will, and by these presents for us, our heirs and successors, do grant and ordain that for ever hereafter there be and shall be within the city of Londonderry aforesaid, one of the more honest and discreet citizens of the city aforesaid, or of the more honest and discreet inhabitants within the liberties of the same, in form under in these presents mentioned, from time to time to be elected, who shall be and be called the Mayor of the said city.

And that in like manner for ever there be and shall be within the same City, twelve of the more honest and discreet citizens of the City of Londonderry aforesaid, or other inhabitants of the said City or liberty of the same, agreeable to the ordinance hereunder in these presents specified from time to time to be elected, who shall be called the Aldermen of the said city, and shall be of the Common Council of the same City, and that the said Aldermen shall from time to time be assisting and aiding to the Mayor of the said City of Londonderry for the time being in all causes and affairs touching or concerning the same City.

And that in like manner for ever there be and shall be, within the said City of Londonderry, two of the more honest and discreet citizens of the City aforesaid, or of the more honest and discreet inhabitants within the liberties of the same, in form hereunder in these presents mentioned from time to time to be elected, who shall be and be called the Sheriffs of the City of Londonderry aforesaid, and of the aforesaid County of Londonderry.

And that there be and shall be for ever, within the City aforesaid, one of the more discreet citizens of the said City of Londonderry, or of the inhabitants within the liberty of the same City, from time to time in like manner to be elected, who shall be and shall be called the Chamberlain of the said City.

And that in like manner there be and shall be for ever, within the same City of Londonderry twenty-four of the more honest and discreet citizens of the City aforesaid, or of the inhabitants within the liberty of the same, in form hereunder in these presents mentioned from time to time to be elected, who shall be and shall be called Chief Burgesses of the said City, which Chief Burgesses shall be from time to time in like manner assisting and aiding to the Mayor and Aldermen in all affairs and matters of the said City, and touching or concerning the said City and liberties of the same, and shall be of the Common Council of the same City.

And further we will and by these presents for us, our heirs and successors, do grant unto the aforesaid Mayor and Commonalty and Citizens of the city of Londonderry, and their successors, that the Mayor and Common Council of the city of Londonderry aforesaid, for the time being, and their successors, or the greater part of them (whereof we will the Mayor for the time being to be one), upon public summons by the Mayor of the city aforesaid for the time being, or by his precept thereupon to be made, being thereunto assembled, may and shall have full power and authority to establish, constitute, ordain, and make from time to time for ever all reasonable and convenient laws, statutes constitutions, decrees, and ordinances whatsoever in writing, which to them, according to their sound discretions, shall seem good, wholesome, honest, profitable, necessary and requisite, for the good rule and government of the city aforesaid, and of all and singular the officers, ministers, citizens, artificers, inhabitants, residents, and dwellers whatsoever of the city aforesaid, and the liberty of the same for the time being, and also for the rule and government of the markets and fairs within the city of Londonderry aforesaid, and the liberty and limits of the same, and of the people coming or resorting to the said markets and fairs, or any of them, and for declaring in what manner and order the same Mayor and citizens, and all and singular the officers, artificers, and residents of the city aforesaid, and liberties of the same, and their factors, servants, and ministers, in their offices, functions, services, mysteries, arts, and businesses, within the city aforesaid, and liberties of the same for the time being, shall hold, carry, and behave themselves there for the public good, common profit, and good government of the same city and liberty, and of the [illegible] of the same, and for regulating the affairs, causes, and businesses of the city aforesaid, or touching or any ways concerning the citizens, or inhabitants of the same, or the arts, handicrafts, or mysteries in the same city and liberties of the same. And that the Mayor and Common Council of the City aforesaid for the time being, or the major part of them, (whereof we will the Mayor for the time being to be one), as often as they shall appoint, make, ordain, or establish such laws, statutes, regulations, ordinances, and constitutions, in form aforesaid, shall and may make, ordain, limit, provide, and inflict such and the like pains, punishments, penalties, by imprisonment of the body, or by fines and amerciaments, or by either of them, against and upon all delinquents offending against such laws, regulations, ordinances, and constitutions, or any of them, as to the same Mayor and Common Council of the city aforesaid for the time being, or the greater part of them, (whereof we will the Mayor of the said city for the time being to be one), shall seem necessary, fit, convenient, reasonable, and requisite for the better observance of the same laws, ordinances, and constitutions, and the same fines and amerciaments shall and may levy and have, to the use and behoof of the Mayor and Commonalty, and citizens of the city aforesaid, and their successors, without hindrance of us, our heirs and successors, or any of the officers or ministers of us, our heirs and successors, and without any account thereof to be rendered to us, our heirs or successors.

All and singular which laws, ordinances, regulations and constitutions so made as aforesaid, or to be made, we will to be observed under the pains in them to be contained, so that the aforesaid laws, statutes, ordinances, regulations, constitutions, pains, punishments, penalties, imprisonments, fines and amerciaments be reasonable, and not repugnant or contrary to the laws and statutes of our said Realm of Ireland.

And so that such Laws, Ordinances, Regulations, and Constitutions, be certified by the Mayor and Common Council of the aforesaid City of Londonderry aforesaid, for the time being, under the Common Seal of the same City to the Society of the Governor and Assistants, London, of the New Plantation in Ulster aforesaid hereunder in these presents mentioned and named within four months next after the making of such laws, ordinances, regulations, and constitutions.

To the intent that the said Society of the Governor and Assistants, London, of the new plantation in Ulster, or their successors, or the greater part of them, may under the Common Seal of the said Society ratify, approve, and confirm such Laws, Ordinances, Regulations, and Constitutions so as aforesaid made, or any or either of them, within six months next after the delivery of such Certificate to the Governor of the said Society for the time being, or his Deputy, in our Kingdom of England, or else within the same time under the Common Seal of the same Society, shall adjudge and declare such Laws, Ordinances, Regulations, or Constitutions so aforesaid, made or to be made or any of them to be difficult, useless or improper to be observed in the said City of Londonderry and liberties of the same, and we will that immediately after the aforesaid laws, statutes, regulations, ordinances, and constitutions, or any of them shall be approved and confirmed under the Common Seal of the said Society, the same laws, ordinances, statutes, regulations, and constitutions so approved, from henceforth shall be good, valid and effectual, and that the same thenceforth for ever shall be inviolably observed, under the penalties in the same contained.

We will also, that immediately after declaration under the Common Seal of the said Society, that such laws, ordinances, regulations, and constitutions, made or to be made or any of them, are difficult, useless, or improper to be observed in the said city, and liberties, the same laws, ordinances, regulations, and constitutions, so declared under the seal of the said Society, to be difficult, useless, or improper, shall be held and reputed, and from thenceforth shall be repealed and wholly void, and of no force or effect to all intents and purposes, as if the same laws, statutes, ordinances, and constitutions had never been ordained or made.

And for the better execution of our will and grant in this behalf, we have assigned, nominated and made, and by these presents, for us, our heirs, and successors, do assign, nominate, constitute, and make our beloved John Rowley, Gentleman, to become and be the first and present Mayor of the City of Londonderry, aforesaid, we being willing that the said John Rowley be and shall continue in the office of Mayor of the said city, from the making of these presents until the second day of January next, after the date of these presents, and from thence until one other of of the citizens of the same city shall be appointed and sworn in the office of Mayor of the city aforesaid, according to the ordinance and constitution in these presents hereunder expressed and declared. We have also assigned, constituted, nominated, and made, and by these presents, for us, our heirs and successors, do assign, nominate, constitute, and make, our beloved Ralph Bingley, Knight, John Vaughan, John Rowley, Henry Hart, Henry Vaughan, John Baker, Francis White, Henry Sadler, John Wray, William Gage, Jessey Smith and John Baker, Gentlemen, to become and be the first and present Aldermen of the same City of Londonderry, to continue in the same office during their natural lives, unless in the meantime they or any of them shall for any reasonable cause be removed from their offices or places aforesaid, whom for such reasonable cause we will to be removable. We have also assigned, constituted and made, and by these presents for us, our heirs and successors, do assign, nominate, constitute, and make our beloved Richard Griffin and William [illegible], to be the first and present Sheriffs of the said city, and of the said County of Londonderry, to continue in the same office of Sheriffs of the city aforesaid, and County of Londonderry aforesaid, until the aforesaid second day of January next ensuing the date of these presents; and from thenceforth until two others of the citizens of the said city shall be elected, appointed and sworn into the said office of Sheriffs of the City and County of Londonderry aforesaid, according to the ordinance and constitution hereunder in these presents expressed and declared. We have also assigned, constituted, and made, and by these presents, for us, our heirs and successors, do assign, constitute, and make our beloved Robert Goodwyn, Gentleman, to become and be the first and present Chamberlain of the said city, to continue in the same office of Chamberlain until the said second day of January next ensuing the date of these presents, and from thenceforth until one other of the citizens of the said city shall be elected and admitted into the said office of Chamberlain of the said city, according to the ordinance and constitution hereunder in these presents expressed and declared.

We have also assigned, constituted, and made, and by these presents for us, our heirs and successors do assign, nominate, and make our beloved Samuel Calvert, Thomas Dobson, Adam Cottinger, Henry Lovell, William Atkins, Valentine James, William Ironmonger, John Walters, Walter Marlow, Thomas Latham, Roger Price, William Bucker, Thomas Harrard, Richard Ghelby, Richard Middleton, Nicholas Ambrose, Peter Tallen, Thomas Sandy, Richard Jessey, William Whitwell, Francis Southwell, William Raven, Thomas Locke, and Clement Mason, to become and be the first and chief Burgesses of the city aforesaid, to continue in the same office of chief Burgesses of the city aforesaid, during their natural lives, unless in the meantime they or any of them shall for some reasonable cause be removed from that office, which for such reasonable cause we will shall be removable.

And for the better ordering, directing, and governing all and all manner of things, for and concerning the city and suburbs of Londonderry aforesaid, and the aforesaid county of Londonderry, and the plantation to be made within the same city and county of Londonderry, and other [illegible] belonging to the same, we will grant and by these presents for us, our heirs and successors, do ordain and constitute that for ever hereafter there be and shall be six and twenty honest and discreet citizens of our City of London, within our Kingdom of England (in form following to be chosen and appointed), who shall be and shall be called THE SOCIETY OF THE GOVERNOR AND ASSISTANTS, LONDON, OF THE NEW PLANTATION IN ULSTER, WITHIN THE REALM OF IRELAND.

Which said Society in our City of London shall and may be and consist of one Governor, one Deputy of the said Governor, and four and twenty Assistants, of whom we will that the Governor and five Assistants thereof be and shall be Aldermen of the same City of London. And also that the Recorder of our City of London for the time being be and shall be one of the Assistants besides the aforesaid five Aldermen; but that the Deputy of the said Governor, and the rest of the same Assistants be and shall be of the commonalty of our City of London. We will also and by these presents for us, our heirs and successors, do grant that all and singular the citizens of our aforesaid City of London, in our kingdom of England, as well those hereunder in these our letters patent specially and particularly by us nominated, constituted, and appointed to be the said Society of the Governor, Deputy, and Assistants, London, of the new plantation in Ulster within the realm of Ireland as those who hereafter according to the ordinances and provisions hereunder in these presents expressed and limited, shall be chosen and admitted into the same Society and their successors for ever be and by force of these presents shall be one new body corporate and politic, in deed, fact, and name, by the name of the Society of the Governor and Assistants, London, of the new plantation in Ulster, within the realm of Ireland.

And them by the name of the Society of the Governor and Assistants, London, of the new plantation in Ulster within the realm of Ireland, one new body corporate and politic, in deed, form, and name, really, and fully for us, our heirs and successors, we do erect, make, ordain, create, and constitute and declare, by these presents; and that by the same name they shall have perpetual succession.

And that they and their successors for ever, by the name of the Society of the Governor and Assistants of London, of the new plantation in Ulster, within the realm of Ireland, be and shall be, at all future times, persons able and in law capable to have, purchase, receive, and possess lands, tenements, goods, chattels, possessions, liberties, privileges, rights, jurisdictions, franchises, and other hereditaments whatsoever, of what kind, nature, or quality soever they shall be, in our kingdom of England or in our realm of Ireland, or in either of them, to them and their successors in fee and perpetuity or otherwise; and also to give, grant, demise, and assign lands, tenements, and other hereditaments, goods and chattels, and to do and execute all and singular other deeds and things by the name aforesaid. And that they and their successors for ever, by the name of the Society of the Governor and Assistants, London, of the new plantation in Ulster, within the realm of Ireland, may plead and be impleaded, answer and be answered, defend and be defended, in what courts or places soever, and before whatsoever judges, justices, and other persons and officers of us, our heirs and successors, in all pleas, suits, plaints, causes, matters, and demands whatsoever of what kind, nature, or quality soever, in the same manner and form as other of our liege of our kingdom of England, or in our realm of Ireland (being persons able and in law capable), may plead and be impleaded, defend and be defended, answer and be answered, and have, purchase, and receive, possess, give, grant, and demise.

And that the said Society of the Governor and Assistants, London, of the new plantation in Ulster, within the realm of Ireland, and their successors for ever hereafter, may have a Common Seal, to serve for transacting of the causes and business whatsoever of them and their successors; and that it shall and may be lawful to the same Society of the Governor and Assistants, London, of the new plantation in Ulster, within the realm of Ireland, and their successors from time to time, to break, change, and new make the said Seal as to them shall seem best.

We will also, and by these presents for us, our heirs and successors, do grant, constitute, and ordain, that the aforesaid Society of the Governor and Assistants, London, of the new plantation in Ulster, within the realm of Ireland, for ever hereafter, shall be yearly elected and appointed by the Mayor, Aldermen and Commonalty of the said City of London, at the first Common Council to be holden in the same City of London, next after the Feast of the Purification of the Blessed Virgin Mary, at which time the Deputy of the Governor, and twelve of the same persons who shall have been Assistants for the year preceding, shall be removed from that office, and one other Deputy and twelve other Assistants shall be new nominated, supplied, and appointed into the places of the same Deputy and Assistants so as aforesaid, in aid of the Governor and Assistants not removed, for one year next following. And that at the end of that year then next following, such former Assistants who shall have continued in the same office in the said preceding year, shall be in like manner removed, and others in like manner in their places new nominated, supplied, elected, and appointed, and so by an interchangeable course, that twelve of the same Assistants shall be and continue in their places during the term of two years.

And for the better execution of our will in this behalf, we will, and by these presents for us, our heirs and successors, do constitute, ordain, and make our well beloved William Cockayne, Citizen and Alderman of our said City of London, to be the first and present Governor of the same Society, to continue in the same office until the Feast of the Purification of the Blessed Virgin Mary next following, after the date of these presents, and from thence until another shall be elected and admitted into the said office of Governor of the same Society, according to the form and intent aforesaid.

We

We also will, that Martin Bond, citizen and Haberdasher of London, be and shall be Deputy of the same Governor, to continue in the same office, until the Feast of the Purification of the Blessed Virgin Mary next following after the date of these presents, and from thence until one other shall in form aforesaid be elected and appointed, in the room of the said Martin Bond, unto the place or office of Deputy of the Governor of the same Society.

We also will, and by these presents for us, our heirs and successors, do grant, constitute, ordain, and make our beloved Henry Montagu, knight, one of our Serjeants at Law, and Recorder of the City of London aforesaid, Clement Scudamore, John Jolles, knight, John Leman, George Smith, Edward Rotherham, Citizens and Aldermen of London, William Dyos, [illegible] Remembrancer of the same city, Robert Jenkinson, John Gore, Matthias Springham, John Sibley, Merchant Tailors of London; Rowland Heilyn, Adrian Moore, Francis Fuller, [illegible] of London; Morris Abbott, Draper; Greene Heron, Goldsmith; William Greenwell, Robert Middleton, Francis Conell, Skinner; William Freeman, Haberdasher; Nicholas Leek, Ironmonger; James Horton, Vintner; Hugh Morell, Clothworker; and Richard Wesley, Leatherseller; Citizens of London aforesaid, to be the first and present twenty-four Assistants of the Society aforesaid, to continue in the office aforesaid until the Feast of the Purification of the Blessed Virgin Mary next following the date of these presents, and from thence until they, or some of them, shall respectively be removed from that office, according to the ordinance in these presents declared.

And further, we do will, ordain, and constitute, for us, our heirs and successors, that a Common Council in the City of London aforesaid, next after the Feast of the Purification of the Blessed Virgin Mary next after the date of these presents, the nomination and election of the aforesaid Governor, Deputy, and Assistants be and shall be made in form aforesaid, and so from thenceforth yearly from time to time for ever.

And if, and so often as it shall happen, any one or more of the said Society of the Governor and Assistants London, of the new plantation in Ulster, within the realm of Ireland, shall die, or be removed, or depart from his or their office or offices, all which, and every or any of them respectively, not well behaving him or themselves in their offices, we will to be removable and removed at the pleasure of the Mayor and Aldermen, and of the rest of the Common Council of our said City of London, or the greater part of them (whereof we will the Mayor of the said city for the time being to be one), then and so often to supply thereof, one or more, as so many other the citizens of our said City of London as shall be removed from the said Society of the Governor and Assistants London of the new plantation in Ulster, within the realm of Ireland, shall be elected and appointed by the Mayor, Aldermen, and Commonalty of the said City of London, at a Common Council to be holden in the same City of London, next or as soon as conveniently may be, after the death, departure, or removal of such person or persons from the Society aforesaid, or from his office or place in the said Society, into the place or places of him or them so [illegible] happening so to die, depart, or to be removed.

We do also will and grant that after the election of the assistants, so as aforesaid made, the person or persons so nominated and elected (after having severally taken their corporal oaths before the Mayor of the said City of London, for the time being, well and faithfully to and by all things to execute the said office or place), shall, and may have, exercise, and execute that office or place, or places, during the residue of the term respectively limited to his or their predecessor or predecessors, to remain in that office or place, and from thenceforth until one or more other or others shall in like manner be chosen, appointed, and sworn into that office in form above declared, and so often as the case shall happen.

And further of our more ample grace, certain knowledge, and mere motion, we do will and by these presents, for us, our heirs and successors grant, that the said persons above in these presents nominated, elected, or appointed, to be of the number of the said Society of the new plantation in Ulster, within the realm of Ireland, and their successors of the same Society, from time to time hereafter to be nominated and elected, or any nine of them (whereof we will the governor of the Society aforesaid, or the deputy of the same Governor for the time being to be one), shall and may have full power and authority of convening, assembling, and holding a court in the Guildhall of our City of London, or in any other place within the said City of London, so often as to them or that behalf shall seem expedient; and in the same court and meeting, to do, hear, treat, and determine all and all manner of matters and things, whatsoever of, for, or concerning the plantation or government aforesaid, as to them shall seem best and most expedient.

And also in the same court or meeting, shall and may have full power and authority to direct, constitute, and ordain (for and on the part of the Mayor and Commonalty and Citizens of our City of London, in our kingdom of England), all and singular things, which, for or concerning the plantation, supply or establishment, conservation, and government of the aforesaid city of Londonderry, and of all other the lands and tenements, hereunder to these presents mentioned to be granted, shall seem to be most profitable and expedient.

And also to send orders and directions, from this kingdom of England, into the said realm of Ireland, by letters or otherwise, for the ordering, directing, and disposing of all and all manner of matters and things whatsoever, of or concerning the same plantation, or the disposition of government thereof; and also for the receipt, ordering, expending, and laying out of all sums of money now collected and received, or hereafter to be collected and received; and generally any other cause, matter, or thing, whatsoever, concerning the direction or ordering of the plantation aforesaid; or concerning any other things whatsoever, which by the true intent of these our letters patent, can or ought to be done by them, for the better government and rule of the City of Londonderry aforesaid, and the said county of Londonderry aforesaid.

And also in the same courts in form aforesaid, to be holden from time to time, may and shall have power and authority to nominate, make, and constitute such and so many other officers and ministers of the aforesaid Society, as for the [illegible] of the said business, as to them shall seem best and most convenient.

And also in the same courts in form aforesaid, to be holden from time to time, shall and may have full power and authority, for and during the term of two years next and immediately following after the date of these presents, to frame, constitute, ordain, and make laws, statutes, constitutions, decrees, and ordinances, reasonable and convenient, in writing, whatsoever, which to them shall seem to be good, wholesome, honest, useful, necessary, and requisite, according to their sound discretion, for the better rule and government of the aforesaid city of Londonderry, and the liberties of the same, and of all and singular officers, ministers, citizens, artificers, inhabitants, residents, and dwellers whatsoever, within the city aforesaid and the liberties of the same; and also for the better rule and government of the markets and fairs, within the said city of Londonderry, the liberties and limits of the same, and of the people coming to and frequenting the same markets and fairs, or any of them, and for declaring in what manner or order the same Mayor and citizens, and all and singular officers, ministers, artificers, and residents of the aforesaid city of Londonderry and the liberties of the same, and their factors, servants, and ministers, in their offices, functions, ministries, trades, and businesses, within the same city and liberties of the same for the time being, shall hold, carry, and use themselves, for the further public good, common utility, and good rule of the aforesaid city and liberties of the same, and properly to transact the things and causes, in any manner touching or concerning the said city or citizens or inhabitants thereof, or the trades, arts, crafts, or mysteries in the same city and the liberty of the same.

And by these presents, for us, our heirs and successors, we do grant that the aforesaid persons above in these presents nominated and elected, or appointed to be of the number of the Society of the Governor and Assistants of London, of the new plantation in Ulster aforesaid, and their successors, of the same Society from time to time to be nominated and chosen, or any nine of them, of whom we will the Governor of the Society aforesaid, or the deputy of the same Governor for the time being, to be one, so often as such laws, statutes, rights, ordinances, and constitutions shall be framed, made, ordained, or established in form aforesaid, such and the like pains, punishments, and penalties, by imprisonment of the body, or by fines, and amerciaments, or by either of them, therefore, and

upon

upon all delinquents of such rights, ordinances, and constitutions, or any or either of them, as to the same persons above in these presents nominated and elected, or appointed to be of the number of the Society of the Governor and Assistants, of London, of the new plantation in Ulster aforesaid, and their successors, of the same Society, from time to time to be nominated and elected, or any nine of them, of whom we will the Governor of the Society aforesaid, or the deputy of the same Governor for the time being, shall be one, shall seem necessary, opportune, convenient, reasonable, and requisite for the observance of the same laws, ordinances, and constitutions, shall and may make, ordain, limit, provide, and inflict, and the same fines and amerciaments shall and may levy and hold to the use and behoof of the aforesaid Society of the Governor and Assistants, of London, of the new plantation in Ulster, within the realm of Ireland aforesaid, and their successors, without hindrance of us, our heirs, and successors, and of any our officers or ministers, or of any heirs or successors, and without any account to us, our heirs or successors, thereof to be rendered, all and singular which laws, ordinances, rights, and constitutions, so as aforesaid to be made, we will to be observed, made, or done, we will to be observed under the penalties in the same to be contained, so nevertheless, that the aforesaid laws, statutes, ordinances, constitutions, decrees, pains, penalties, imprisonment, fines, and amerciaments be reasonable, and not repugnant nor contrary to the law or statutes of our said kingdom of Ireland.

We will also, and by these presents for us, our heirs and successors, do ordain, constitute, and declare, that whatsoever in such Court or meeting in form aforesaid, to be held, shall be made, decreed, ordained, or determined, be and shall be firm, valid, and effectual for all purposes and intendments, and after the notification of the same in Ulster aforesaid, we will and command, and by these presents, all those things to be inviolably observed there.

We will also, that the Governor of the Society aforesaid, or his deputy for the time being, shall appoint and fix days and times for assembling of the said Society, and shall make, or cause to be made, summonses thereof from time to time, to the same Society.

We also will, and by these presents for us, our heirs and successors, do grant that the Mayor of the city of Londonderry aforesaid, for the time being, and also the Aldermen, Sheriffs, Chamberlain, and chief Burgesses of the same city of Londonderry for the time being, be and shall be called the Common Council of the same city of Londonderry, and every of them, so long as he shall continue in that office or place, be and shall be of the Common Council of the same city of Londonderry.

And we do further will, and by these presents for us, our heirs and successors, grant to the aforesaid Mayor and Commonalty and Citizens of the city of Londonderry aforesaid, and their successors, that the Mayor and Aldermen, and the rest of the Common Council of the city of Londonderry aforesaid, for the time being, or the greater part of them, shall and may from time to time, for the term of ten years next after the date of these presents, have power and authority yearly, and every year, on the second day of January (if it be not Sunday, and if it be Sunday, then on the day next following), in the city of Londonderry aforesaid, to elect and nominate, and they shall and may elect and nominate each and the same person who then at the time of that election shall be Mayor of the same city of Londonderry, or one other of the Aldermen of the same city of Londonderry aforesaid, to be the Mayor of the same city for one whole year then next following, in form hereunder by these presents limited.

And that the name of the aforesaid person so from time to time within the aforesaid space of ten years next following, after the date of these presents, to be nominated and elected for the Mayor for the said city of Londonderry aforesaid, shall be certified and presented from time to time, during the said term of ten years, by the Mayor and others of the Common Council of the said city of Londonderry, under the seal of the Mayoralty there within one month next following such nomination and election to the aforesaid Society of the Governor and Assistants, of London, of the new plantation in Ulster for the time being, to the intent that the same Society of the Governor and Assistants, of London, of the new plantation in Ulster, or the major part of them, of whom the Governor of the same Society or his deputy for the time being, we will to be one, from time to time during the said space of ten years next following the date of these presents shall approve, ratify, and confirm the election and nomination aforesaid within one month after the receipt of the certificate aforesaid, if to the same Society of the Governor and Assistants, of London, of the new plantation in Ulster, or the greater part of them, of whom the aforesaid Governor, or the deputy of the same Governor for the time being, we will to be one, shall seem meet, or the same election, at the will and good pleasure of them, or the greater part of them as aforesaid, within one month as aforesaid, shall reject and as null and make void; and that every one so as aforesaid elected and nominated to be Mayor of the city of Londonderry aforesaid, and by the aforesaid Society of the Governor and Assistants, of London, of the new plantation in Ulster, or the greater part of them, of whom the Governor of the same Society, or his deputy for the time being, we will always to be one, in writing under the common seal of the said Society, from time to time during the said term of ten years next following the date of these presents, approved and confirmed on the feast of the Annunciation of our Lord then next following such nomination, election, and approbation, before the last Mayor, his predecessor, in the presence of such Aldermen and others of the Common Council of the same city of Londonderry aforesaid who shall be then present, shall take as well the oath commonly called the oath of allegiance, as the oath well and faithfully to execute the office of Mayor of the city aforesaid, in and by all things touching that office. And that after such oath so taken, shall and may execute the office of Mayor of the city aforesaid for one whole year then next following, and until another of the Aldermen of the same city of Londonderry aforesaid for the time being shall be in due manner elected, appointed, and sworn to the office of Mayor of the same city of Londonderry, according to the ordinances in these presents expressed and declared.

We will also, and by these presents for us, our heirs and successors, do grant, that so often as it shall happen during the said term of ten years next after the date of these presents, the aforesaid Mayor, Aldermen, and the rest of the Common Council of the same city of Londonderry aforesaid, on the day and place above said, shall not nominate and elect one of the Aldermen of the same city to the office of Mayor of the same city of Londonderry, in manner and form aforesaid, or such nomination and election in form aforesaid specified, from time to time during the said term of ten years next following the date of these presents, shall not certify and present to the Society of the Governor and Assistants, of London, of the new plantation in Ulster, or the greater part of them, of whom the Governor of the Society aforesaid, or his deputy for the time being, we will to be one, shall not approve of the same election, according to the form in these presents above declared, that then and so often as it shall so happen, and within four months then next following, it shall and may be lawful for the aforesaid Society of the Governor and Assistants, of London, of the new plantation in Ulster, within the realm of Ireland aforesaid, or the greater part of them, of whom the Governor or deputy of the same Governor, we will to be one, during the said term of ten years next following after the date of these presents, shall nominate and elect the like, such and the same person, who at the time of such election shall be Mayor of the said city of Londonderry or one other of the Aldermen of our city of Londonderry aforesaid, to be the Mayor of the same city of Londonderry, to continue in the same office until the second day of January then next following, and thenceforth until one other of the Aldermen of the said city shall be in due manner elected, appointed, and sworn to be the Mayor of the same city, according to the ordinances and provisions in these presents declared, and so often as the case shall so happen during the said term of ten years next following after the date of these presents and that he who so as aforesaid shall be elected and nominated to be Mayor of the said city of Londonderry, before he shall be admitted, or take upon himself to execute that office, shall take as well the oath commonly called the oath of allegiance, as the corporal oath, in and by all things well and faithfully to execute that office of Mayor, before the last Mayor, his predecessor, and that after such oath so taken, he shall have and exercise that office until the second day of January then next following, and thenceforth until one other, in form above said, shall be elected, preferred, and sworn into that office of the Mayor of the same city.

And

And further we will, and by these presents for us, our heirs, and successors, do grant to the aforesaid Mayor and Commonalty and Citizens of the city of Londonderry aforesaid, and their successors, that if within the space of ten years next following the date of these presents, it shall happen that the Mayor of the city of Londonderry aforesaid shall at any time within one year after he shall have been appointed and sworn to the office of Mayor of that city die, or from that office be removed, which said Mayor we will to be removed from that office at the pleasure of the Aldermen and the rest of the Common Council of the same city of Londonderry for the time being, or the greater part of them who shall be then present, so that the greater part of the Aldermen of the same city be or shall be then present, or if within the space of ten years next following the date of these presents it shall happen that the person aforesaid nominated or elected to be Mayor of the said city of Londonderry shall happen to die before approbation or rejection, or before oath made and taken, that then and so often it shall and may be lawful for the said Aldermen and the rest of the Common Council of the same city of Londonderry, for the time being as oft as such Mayor shall die, and for the Mayor and Aldermen and the rest of the Common Council of the same city in case such person so nominated and elected to be Mayor of the said city shall die before approbation or rejection or before oath made and taken, to assemble themselves, or the greater part of them, within three days next following such death or removal, in the Common Hall, or other convenient place within the city of Londonderry aforesaid, and there to elect and nominate one other honest and fit man of the Aldermen of the city aforesaid for Mayor, and to be Mayor of the city of Londonderry aforesaid, in the place of him so dying or removed from his office.

And that the name of the said person so from time to time during the said term of ten years next following after the date of these presents to be nominated and elected for Mayor of the said city of Londonderry aforesaid, shall, within 14 days next following such election, be certified and presented from time to time by the Aldermen and the rest of the Common Council of the said city of Londonderry, to the aforesaid Society of the Governor and Assistants of London, of the new plantation in Ulster, for the time being, to the intent that the said Society of the Governor and Assistants of London, of the new plantation in Ulster, or the major part of them, of whom the Governor of the said Society for the time being or his deputy for the time being, we will to be one from time to time during the said term of ten years next following after the date of these presents, shall approve, ratify, and confirm the election and nomination aforesaid, or otherwise the same election and nomination within seven days next after the receipt of such certificate, shall repudiate and frustrate, if to the same Society of the Governor and Assistants of London, of the new plantation in Ulster, or the greater part of them as aforesaid shall seem fit, and that every one so as aforesaid elected and nominated to be Mayor of the city of Londonderry aforesaid, and approved by the aforesaid Society of the Governor and Assistants of London, of the new plantation in Ulster, or the greater part of them, of whom the Governor of the same Society, or the deputy of the same Governor for the time being, from time to time, we will to be one, taking his corporal oath, within sixty days next following such approbation, before such Aldermen or before the Mayor and such Aldermen, as the case may happen and require, and before others of the Common Council of the same city of Londonderry, who shall be then present, rightly, well, and faithfully, in and by all things to execute that office, in and by all things touching that office, shall and may execute the office of Mayor of the city of Londonderry aforesaid, in the place of the same Mayor so dying or removed from his office, or person so nominated or elected and dying during the residue of the same year from thenceforth, until another of the Aldermen of the same city of Londonderry aforesaid, for the time being, shall be in like manner elected, appointed, and sworn to the office of Mayor of the same city of Londonderry, conformable and according to the ordinance in these presents expressed and declared; and if during the said term of ten years next following after the date of these presents, it shall happen that the aforesaid Aldermen and the rest of the Common Council of the said city of Londonderry, in form aforesaid, shall not nominate and elect one of the Aldermen of the same city of Londonderry, in the place of the same Mayor or person nominated and elected to be Mayor so dying or removed from his office, or the name of the aforesaid person so nominated and elected in form aforesaid, shall not be certified and presented, or the aforesaid Society of the Governor and Assistants of London, of the new plantation in Ulster, or the greater part of them, or whom the Governor of the Society aforesaid, or his deputy for the time being, we will to be one, shall not approve the same election according to the ordinance in these presents above declared, that then and so often it shall and may be lawful for the aforesaid Society of the Governor and Assistants of London, of the new plantation in Ulster, or the greater part of them, of whom the Governor of the Society aforesaid, or his deputy for the time being, we will to be one, during the aforesaid term of 10 years next following after the date of these presents, in our same city of London, for this purpose met and assembled, within six months next after such default of election and nomination, or certificate, or after such rejection or non-approval, or after such death of the person so nominated or elected to be Mayor of the said city, to nominate and elect one of the Aldermen of the city of Londonderry aforesaid, to become and be the Mayor of the same city in the place of the Mayor of the same city so dying or removed from his office, or the person so nominated and elected by the Mayor of the said city, to continue in that office during the residue of the same year, from thenceforth until another of the Aldermen of the same city of Londonderry shall be in like manner elected, appointed, and sworn to be Mayor of the same city, according to the ordinance and proviso above declared, and so and so often as the case shall happen during the aforesaid term of 10 years next following after the date of these presents, and that he who shall be so nominated and elected, shall take as well the corporal oath called the oath of allegiance, as the corporal oath before the Aldermen and the rest of the Common Council of the same city of Londonderry, who shall be then present in the case where such Mayor shall die, and before the Mayor and Aldermen, and the rest of the Common Council of the same city of Londonderry, who shall be then present in the case where such person so nominated and elected to be Mayor of the said city, before approbation or rejection, or before the oath made and taken, shall die, in and by all things well and faithfully to execute that office; and after such oath so taken he shall hold and exercise that office during the residue of the same year, and thenceforth until one other in form aforesaid to be elected, appointed, and sworn into the office of Mayor of the same city of Londonderry; but we will, and our intention is, and by these presents, for us, our heirs and successors, do grant unto the aforesaid Mayor and Commonalty and Citizens of the city of Londonderry aforesaid and their successors, that the Mayor, Aldermen, and the rest of the Common Council of the city of Londonderry aforesaid for the time being, or the greater part of them, from time to time forever, after the expiration of 10 years next following after the date of these presents, have power and authority yearly and every year, on the second day of January (if it be not on Sunday), and if it be Sunday then on the day following, in our city of Londonderry, to elect and nominate, and they shall and may elect and nominate such and the same person who then at the time of such election shall be Mayor of the same city of Londonderry, or one other of the Aldermen of the same city of Londonderry, to become and be Mayor of the same city for one whole year in form hereinafter by these presents limited.

And that every one so as aforesaid elected and nominated for the Mayor of the city of Londonderry aforesaid, after the expiration of 10 years next following the date of these presents, shall on the feast day of the Purification of the Blessed Virgin Mary, then next following such nomination and election before the last Mayor his predecessor, in the presence of such Aldermen and others of the Common Council of the same city of Londonderry aforesaid, who shall be then present, take as well the corporal oath commonly called the oath of allegiance, as the corporal oath, rightly, well, and faithfully, in and by all things to execute that office, in and by all things touching that office of the Mayor of the City aforesaid.

And that after such oaths so taken, he shall and may execute the office of Mayor of the city aforesaid for one whole year then next following, and from thence until one other of the Aldermen of the same city of Londonderry aforesaid, for the time being, shall be in due manner elected and sworn to the office of Mayor of the same city of Londonderry, according to the ordinance in these presents expressed and declared.

We will also, and by these presents for us, our heirs and successors, do grant to the aforesaid Mayor and Commonalty and Citizens of the city of Londonderry aforesaid, and their successors, that if the Mayor of the city of Londonderry aforesaid shall happen at any time after the expiration of ten years next following after the date of these presents, within one year after he shall have been appointed and sworn to the office of Mayor of that city tary, to die or to be removed from his office (which Mayor not well behaving himself in that office, we will to be removable at the pleasure of the Aldermen and the rest of the Common Council of the same city of Londonderry for the time being, or the greater part of them who shall be then present, so that the greater part of the Aldermen of the same city be or shall be then present), or if at any time after the expiration of ten years next following after the date of these presents the person so as aforesaid nominated and elected to be Mayor of the aforesaid city of Londonderry shall happen to die before taking his oath, that then and so often it shall and may be lawful for the aforesaid Aldermen and the rest of the Common Council of the same city of Londonderry for the time being, in case when such Mayor shall die, and for the Mayor and Aldermen and the rest of the Common Council of the same city, in case when such person so nominated and elected to be Mayor of the said city shall die before taking his oath, to assemble themselves, or the greater part of them, within three days next following such death or removal, in the Common Hall or other convenient place within the city of Londonderry aforesaid, and there to elect and nominate one honest and fit man of the Aldermen of the city aforesaid for Mayor, and to be Mayor of the city of Londonderry aforesaid in the place of the Mayor so dying or removed from his office.

And that every one so aforesaid nominated and elected for Mayor of the city of Londonderry aforesaid shall [illegible] first take as well the corporal oath, commonly called "the Oath of Allegiance," as the corporal oath, in and by all things rightly, well, and faithfully to execute that office in and by all things touching that office, before such Aldermen, or before the Mayor and such Aldermen as the case shall be and require, and before others of the Common Council of the same city of Londonderry who shall be then present.

And that after the aforesaid oaths so taken, the person so nominated and elected shall and may execute the said office of Mayor of the city of Londonderry aforesaid, in the place of the same Mayor so deceased or removed from his office, or if the person so nominated and elected and dead during the residue of the same year, and from thenceforth until one other of the Aldermen of the same city of Londonderry aforesaid for the time being shall be in due manner elected, appointed, and sworn to the office of Mayor of the same city of Londonderry, according to the ordinances and constitution above in these presents declared.

And further, we will, and by these presents for us, our heirs and successors, do grant to the said Mayor and Commonalty and Citizens of the city of Londonderry aforesaid, and their successors, that the Mayor, Aldermen and the rest of the Common Council of the city of Londonderry aforesaid, for the time being, or the greater part of them, from time to time, during the term of ten years next after the date of these presents, may and shall have authority yearly, and every year, on the second day of January (if it be not Sunday), and if it be Sunday, then on the next day following, in our city of Londonderry aforesaid, to elect and nominate, and that they shall and may elect and nominate two of the more honest and discreet citizens of the city aforesaid or of the inhabitants within the liberty of the same, to become and be Sheriffs of the same city and of all the aforesaid county of Londonderry, for one whole year following.

And that the names of the aforesaid persons so from time to time within the aforesaid space of ten years next following after the date of these presents, to be nominated and chosen for Sheriffs of the same city and county of Londonderry aforesaid, shall be certified and presented from time to time by the Mayor and the rest of the Common Council of the said city of Londonderry, under the Mayoralty seal there, within two months next following such nomination and election to the aforesaid Society of the Governor and Assistants, of London, of the new plantation in Ulster, to the intent that the same Society of the Governor and Assistants, of London, of the new plantation in Ulster for the time being, or the greater part of them, of whom the Governor of the same Society, or his Deputy for the time being, we will to be one, from time to time during the aforesaid space of ten years next following after the date of these presents shall approve, ratify, and confirm the election and nomination aforesaid, within one month next after the receipt of such certificate, or otherwise the same election and nomination within the same time shall repudiate and frustrate, if to the same Society of the Governor and Assistants, of London, of the new plantation in Ulster, or the greater part of them, of whom the Governor of the same Society, or his Deputy for the time being we will to be one, shall seem fit.

And that they so as aforesaid elected and nominated to be Sheriffs of the city of Londonderry aforesaid, and of the said county of Londonderry aforesaid, and approved by the aforesaid Society of the Governor and Assistants of London, of the new plantation in Ulster, or the greater part of them, of whom the Governor of the same Society or his Deputy for the time being, we will to be one; taking their corporal oaths, from the feast of the Annunciation of our Lord, then following such election, nomination, and approbation, before the Mayor of the city of Londonderry aforesaid, for the time being, truly, well, and faithfully to execute that office in and by all things touching that office, and they and each of them shall and may exercise the office of Sheriff of the city of Londonderry aforesaid, and of the said county of Londonderry aforesaid, for one whole year then next following, and from thenceforth until two others of the citizens of the city of Londonderry aforesaid, or of the other inhabitants within the liberties of the same, shall be in due manner elected, appointed, and sworn to that office, according to the ordinances and constitutions in these presents declared.

We will also, and by these presents for us, our heirs and successors, do grant, that if and so often during the aforesaid term of ten years next following after the date of these presents, it shall happen that the aforesaid Mayor and Aldermen and the rest of the Common Council of the said city of Londonderry, aforesaid, on the day and place above said, shall not nominate and choose two of the citizens of the same city, or of the inhabitants within the liberties of the said city, into the office of Sheriff of the same city, and of the said city of Londonderry, or such nomination and election in form above specified, during the said term of ten years next following after the date of these presents, shall not be certified and presented to the aforesaid Society of the Governor and Assistants of London, of the new plantation in Ulster aforesaid, or the greater part of them, of whom the Governor of the Society aforesaid, or his Deputy for the time being, we will to be one, shall reject or not approve the same election, according to the ordinance in these presents above declared, That then and so often it shall and may well be lawful for the aforesaid Society of the Governor and Assistants, of London, of the new plantation in Ulster, for the time being, or the greater part of them, of whom the Governor or his Deputy we will to be one, in our same city of London, for this purpose met and assembled within four months then following during the said term of ten years next following after the date of these presents, to nominate and choose, and that they shall and may nominate and choose two of the citizens of our city of Londonderry, or two of the inhabitants within the liberties of the same, to become and be Sheriffs of the same city of Londonderry aforesaid, and of the aforesaid county of Londonderry aforesaid; and that they so as aforesaid chosen for Sheriffs of the city aforesaid and of the aforesaid county of Londonderry aforesaid, before they shall be admitted to execute that office, taking the corporal oath on the aforesaid feast of the Annunciation of our Lord then next following such nomination and election, before the Mayor of our same city of Londonderry, in and by all things, well, truly, and faithfully to execute that office, shall hold and exercise that office until the second day of January then next following, and thenceforth until two others of the citizens of the city aforesaid, or others of the inhabitants within the liberties of the same, in form aforesaid, shall be elected, appointed, and sworn for Sheriffs of the same city and county of Londonderry aforesaid, and so as often as the case shall so happen, during the said term of ten years next following after the date of these presents.

And further, we will, and by these presents for us, our heirs and successors, do grant to the aforesaid Mayor and Commonalty and Citizens of the city of Londonderry aforesaid, and their successors, That if at any time during the aforesaid space of ten years next following after the date of these presents, it shall happen that the Sheriffs of the aforesaid city of Londonderry, and of the said county of Londonderry aforesaid, or either of them, to die within one year after they shall have been appointed and sworn to the aforesaid office of Sheriffs, or to be removed from that office, which Sheriffs and either of them, not well behaving themselves or himself in the said office we will to be removed and removable at the pleasure of the Mayor and Aldermen, and the rest of the Common Council of the same city of Londonderry for the time being, or the greater part of them

them who shall be then present, so that the major part of the Aldermen of the same city be or shall be then present, or if, during the aforesaid term of ten years next following after the date of these presents, it shall happen that any person or persons so as aforesaid nominated or elected to be Sheriffs of the city aforesaid, and of the aforesaid county of Londonderry, before approbation or rejection, or before oaths made or taken, to die that then and so often it shall and may be lawful for the aforesaid Mayor and the rest of the Common Council of the same city of Londonderry, or the greater part of them, within the space of three days next after such death and [illegible], to assemble themselves, or the greater part of them, in form aforesaid, in the aforesaid city of Londonderry, and there to elect one or two of the citizens of the same city, or of the inhabitants within the liberty of the same, to Sheriff or Sheriffs of the city aforesaid, and of the said county of Londonderry aforesaid, in the place or places of him or them so dead or removed from his or their office, and that during the said term of ten years next following after the date of these presents, the name or names of the aforesaid person or persons so from time to time [illegible] and elected for Sheriff and Sheriffs of the said city and of the said county of Londonderry aforesaid, shall be certified and presented from time to time by the Mayor, Aldermen, and the rest of the Common Council of the said city of Londonderry, within thirty days next following such election, that the same Society of the Governor and Assistants of London, of the new plantation in Ulster, or the greater part of them, of whom the Governor of the same Society, or his deputy, for the time being, we will to be one, from time to time during the said term of ten years next following after the date of these presents, shall approve, ratify, and confirm the election and nomination aforesaid, within seven days after the receipt of such certificate, or otherwise to repudiate and frustrate the same election and nomination within the same time, if to the same Society of the Governor and Assistants of London, of the new plantation in Ulster, or the greater part of them, of whom the Governor of the same Society, or his deputy, for the time being, we will to be one, shall seem fit, and that he or they so elected and nominated to be Sheriff or Sheriffs of the same city and of the said county of Londonderry aforesaid, and approved by the aforesaid Society of the Governor and Assistants, of London, of the new plantation in Ulster, or the greater part of them, of whom the Governor of the same Society, or his deputy, for the time being we will to be one, taking a corporal oath within sixty days then next following such approbation, before the Mayor and such Aldermen and others of the Common Council of the same city of Londonderry who shall then be present, rightly, well, and faithfully to execute that office, shall and may execute the office of Sheriff or Sheriffs of the same city and of the said county of Londonderry aforesaid, in the place or places of him or them so deceased or removed from that office, during the residue of the same year, and from thenceforth until one or two others of the citizens of the same city of Londonderry, or of the inhabitants within the liberties of the same, shall be in due manner elected, appointed, and sworn to the office of Sheriff or Sheriffs of the same city and of the said county of Londonderry aforesaid, according to the ordinance in these presents expressed and declared, and if during the said term of ten years next following after the date of these presents, it shall happen that the aforesaid Mayor and Aldermen, and the rest of the Common Council of the same city of Londonderry, in form aforesaid, shall not nominate and elect one or two of the citizens of the city aforesaid or of the inhabitants within the liberties of the same, to the office of Sheriff or Sheriffs of the same city, and of the same county of Londonderry aforesaid, in the place or places of the same Sheriff or Sheriffs so dead or removed from that office, or the name or names of the person or persons so nominated and elected in form aforesaid, shall not be certified and presented, or the aforesaid Society of the Governor and Assistants, of London, of the new plantation in Ulster, or the greater part of them, of whom the Governor of the Society aforesaid, or his deputy for the time being, we will to be one, shall not approve of the same election, according to the ordinance in these presents above declared, or the person or persons so nominated and elected, before such approbation, or before oath by him or them in form aforesaid taken, shall die, that then and so often during the said term of ten years next following after the date of these presents, it shall and may be lawful for the Society of the Governor and Assistants, of London, of the new plantation in Ulster, or the greater part of them, of whom the Governor, or his deputy, for the time being, we will to be one, in our said city of London for this purpose met and assembled, within three months next after such default of election or nomination, or after such rejection or nonapproval, or after such death, to nominate and elect one or two citizens of the city of Londonderry aforesaid, or of the inhabitants within the liberties of the same, to become and be Sheriff or Sheriffs of the same city, and of the aforesaid county of Londonderry aforesaid, in the place or places of him or them so dead or removed from that office, to exercise in the same office of Sheriff or Sheriffs during the residue of the same year, and thenceforth until one or two others of the citizens of the same city of Londonderry, or of the inhabitants within the liberties of the same, according to the ordinance and provisions above declared, shall be in due manner elected, appointed, and sworn to be Sheriff or Sheriffs of the same city, and of the aforesaid county of Londonderry, and so often as the case shall happen during the aforesaid term of ten years next following after the date of these presents; and that he or they, who so as aforesaid shall be so nominated and elected to be Sheriff or Sheriffs of the city aforesaid, and of the aforesaid county of Londonderry, taking a corporal oath before the Mayor and Aldermen, and the rest of the Common Council of the said city of Londonderry aforesaid, who shall be then present, well and faithfully to execute that office, shall hold and exercise that office during the residue of the same year, and thenceforth until two others in form aforesaid shall be elected, appointed and sworn to the office of Sheriff of the same city, and so of the aforesaid county of Londonderry.

But we will, and our intention is, and by these presents for us, our heirs, and successors, do grant to the aforesaid Mayor and Commonalty, and Citizens of the city of Londonderry aforesaid, and their successors, and the Mayor, Aldermen, and the rest of the Common Council of the city of Londonderry aforesaid, for the time being, or the greater part of them, from time to time for ever, after the expiration of ten years next following after the date of these presents, shall and may have power and authority yearly and every year, on the second day of January, if it be not Sunday, and if it be Sunday, then on the day next following, in our city of Londonderry aforesaid to elect and nominate, and that they shall and may elect and nominate two of the more honest and discreet citizens of the city of Londonderry aforesaid, or of the inhabitants within the liberties of the same, to become and be Sheriffs of the same city, and of the aforesaid county of Londonderry aforesaid, for one whole year following, and that those so as aforesaid elected and nominated for Sheriff of the said city of Londonderry, taking a corporal oath in convenient time after such nomination and election before the Mayor of the city of Londonderry aforesaid for the time being, rightly, well, and faithfully to execute that office in and by all things touching the same, shall and may execute the office of Sheriffs of the city of Londonderry aforesaid, and of the said county of Londonderry aforesaid, for one whole year then next following, and thenceforth, until two others of the citizens of the city of Londonderry aforesaid, or of other inhabitants within the liberties of the same, shall be elected, appointed, and sworn to that office of Sheriffs, shall be in due manner elected, appointed, and sworn to that office of Sheriffs, according to the ordinance in these presents declared.

And also, we will and by these presents for us, our heirs, and successors, do grant to the aforesaid Mayor and Commonalty and Citizens of our city of Londonderry aforesaid, and their successors, that if at any time after the expiration of ten years next following the date of these presents it shall happen the Sheriffs of the said city of Londonderry, and the said county of Londonderry aforesaid, or either of them, to die within one year after they shall have been appointed and sworn to the aforesaid office of Sheriffs, or be removed from that office, which Sheriffs and either of them not well behaving themselves or himself in the said office, we will to be removed and removable at the pleasure of the Mayor and Aldermen, and the rest of the Common Council of the same city of Londonderry, for the time being, or the greater part of them, who shall be then present, so that the greater part of the Aldermen of the same city be, or shall be then present, or if at any time after the expiration of the aforesaid term of ten years next following after the date of these presents it shall happen that any person nominated or elected or to be nominated or elected to be Sheriff of the said city, and the said county of Londonderry aforesaid, die before oath taken, and then so often it shall and may be lawful for the aforesaid Mayor, and the rest of the Common Council of the same city of Londonderry, or the greater part of them, within the space of three days next after such death or removal, to assemble themselves or the greater part of them, in the aforesaid City of Londonderry, and there to elect one or two of the citizens of the same city, or of the inhabitants within the liberties of the same, for Sheriff or Sheriffs of the city aforesaid, and of the said county of Londonderry aforesaid, in the place or places of him or them so deceased or removed from his or their office, and that he or they so nominated and elected for Sheriff or Sheriffs of the same city, and of the said county of Londonderry aforesaid, shall take a corporal oath in convenient time after such election, before the Mayor and such Aldermen and others of the Common Council of the same City of Londonderry who shall be then present, rightly, well, and faithfully to execute that office, and such oath being taken, shall and may execute the office of Sheriff or Sheriffs of the same city and county of Londonderry aforesaid, in the place or places of him or them so deceased or removed from that office during the residue of the same year, and from thenceforth until one or two others of the citizens of the same city of Londonderry, or of the inhabitants within the liberties of the same, shall be in due manner elected, appointed, and sworn to the office of Sheriff or Sheriffs of the same city, and of said county of Londonderry aforesaid, according to the ordinances in these presents expressed and declared, and so as often as the case shall happen.

And further, we will, for us, our heirs and successors, do grant to the aforesaid Mayor and Commonalty and Citizens of the city of Londonderry aforesaid, and their successors, that the aforesaid Aldermen and chief Burgesses in these presents nominated and elected, and either of them, shall take a corporal oath before the Mayor of our city of Londonderry aforesaid, rightly, well, and faithfully in all things to execute their respective offices, and that after such oath so taken, they, and either of them, shall and may hold and exercise the office and offices of Aldermen and Burgesses of that city during their natural lives, and the lives of any of them; and if within the space of two years next following after the date of these presents, any or either of the Aldermen of the city of Londonderry aforesaid shall happen to die, or be removed, or depart from that office (which Aldermen, and any of them not behaving themselves well in that office, we will to be removed and removable at the good pleasure of the Mayor and Aldermen and the rest of the Common Council of the same city or the greater part of them, for the time being), then we will and grant that the Mayor and Aldermen and the rest of the Common Council of the City of Londonderry aforesaid, or the greater part of them (of whom we will the Mayor for the time being to be one), shall and may from time to time elect and appoint in our aforesaid city of Londonderry, within three days next after the death, departure, or removal of such Alderman or Aldermen, one or so many as shall be wanting of the aforesaid number of twelve Aldermen out of the chief Burgesses of the same city of Londonderry, in the place or places of the Alderman or Aldermen so dead, departed, or removed; and that during the said term of two years next following after the date of these presents, the name or names of the aforesaid person or persons so from time to time to be nominated and elected an Alderman or Aldermen of the said city of Londonderry, shall be presented by the Mayor and the rest of the Common Council of the said city of Londonderry, within two months, to the aforesaid Society of the Governor and Assistants, of London, of the new plantation in Ulster, and the rest of the Common Council of the said city, within two months, to the aforesaid Society of the Governor and Assistants, of London, of the new plantation in Ulster, for the time being, to the intent that the same Society of the Governor and Assistants, of London, of the new plantation in Ulster, or the greater part of them, of whom the Governor of the same Society for the time being, or his Deputy, we will to be one, from time to time during the said term of two years next following after the date of these presents, shall approve, ratify, and confirm the election and nomination aforesaid within one month from next after the receipt of such Certificate, or otherwise shall repudiate and frustrate the same election and nomination within the same time, if to the same Society of the Governor and Assistants, of London, of the new plantation in Ulster, or the greater part of them, of whom the Governor of the same Society, or his Deputy for the time being, we will always to be one (as to them shall seem meet), and that every one so as aforesaid elected and nominated to be Alderman of the city of Londonderry aforesaid, and approved by the aforesaid Society of the Governor and Assistants, of London, of the new plantation in Ulster, or the greater part of them, of whom the Governor of the Society aforesaid, or the Deputy of the same Governor for the time being, we will to be one, taking the corporal oath within sixty days then next following such approbation, before the Mayor of the city of Londonderry aforesaid, well and faithfully to execute such office in and by all things touching that office, shall and may hold and exercise and execute the office of Alderman or Aldermen of the city of Londonderry aforesaid, in the place or places of the Alderman or Aldermen so deceased, departed, or removed from that office, for so long time as he or they shall behave well in that office; and if, during the said term of two years next following the date of these presents, it shall happen the aforesaid Mayor and Aldermen, and the rest of the Common Council of the city of Londonderry aforesaid, within the space of three days after the place or places, office or offices of such Alderman or Aldermen of the city aforesaid, by death or removal, or otherwise shall be vacant, shall happen not to nominate and elect, in form aforesaid, one or more of the Chief Burgesses of the same city to the office of Alderman or Aldermen of the city of Londonderry aforesaid in the place or places of the same Alderman or Aldermen so deceased or departed, or removed from that office, or such nomination and election, in form before specified, shall not certify and present the aforesaid Society of the Governor and Assistants, of London, of the new plantation in Ulster, or the greater part of them, of whom the Governor of the same Society, or his Deputy, we will always to be one, at any time during the said term of two years next following after the date of these presents, shall reject, repudiate, or not approve the same elections according to the ordinances in these presents above declared, then and so often during the said term of two years next following, after the date of these presents, shall and may well be lawful for the Society of the Governor and Assistants, of London, of the new plantation in Ulster for the time being or the greater part of them, of whom the Governor, or his Deputy for the time being, we will to be one, for this purpose, met and assembled in our same city of London, within six months next after such defect of election, or nomination, or certificate, or after such rejection or non-approval, to nominate and elect one or more of the Chief Burgesses of the city of Londonderry aforesaid, to become and be Alderman or Aldermen of the same city of Londonderry, in the place or places of the same Alderman or Aldermen so as aforesaid deceased or departed, or removed from that office, to continue in the same office during their natural lives, if they shall so long behave well therein, and so as often as the case shall happen during the said term of two years next following after the date of these presents, and that he or they, after he or they shall so as aforesaid be nominated and elected for Alderman or Aldermen of the city of Londonderry aforesaid, taking a corporal oath before the Mayor of the same city of Londonderry aforesaid, well and faithfully to execute that office, in and by all things touching that office, shall and may hold and exercise that office during their natural lives respectively, if they or any of them respectively shall continue and behave themselves well in that office.

We will nevertheless and our intention is, and by these presents for us, our heirs and successors, we do grant to the aforesaid Mayor and Commonalty and Citizens of the city of Londonderry aforesaid, and their successors, that if after the expiration of two years next following after the date of these presents, it shall happen that any of the Aldermen of the city of Londonderry aforesaid to die or be removed or depart from that office (which Aldermen and every of them not well behaving himself and themselves in that office, we will shall be removable at the good pleasure of the Mayor and Aldermen, and the rest of the Common Council of the same city, or the greater part of them for the time being), then we will, and grant, that after the expiration of two years next following after the date of these presents, the Mayor and Aldermen, and the rest of the Common Council of the city of Londonderry aforesaid, or the greater part of them (of whom we will the Mayor for the time being to be one, shall and may, from time to time, for ever, elect and appoint, in our aforesaid city of Londonderry, within three days next after the death, departure, or removal of such Alderman or Aldermen, one or so many as shall be wanting of the aforesaid number of twelve Aldermen, out of the Chief Burgesses of the same city of Londonderry, in the place or places of the same Alderman or Aldermen so dead, departed, or removed, to continue in the same office during their natural lives) if so long he or they shall well behave in that office.

And that he or they, after they shall have been so as aforesaid nominated and elected to be an Alderman or Aldermen of the city aforesaid, taking a corporal oath before the Mayor of the same city of Londonderry, well and faithfully to execute that office, in and by all things touching the same, and shall and may have and exercise that office during their natural lives respectively, if so long they, and every of them respectively, shall continue and well behave himself or themselves in the said office.

We will also, and by these presents, for us, our heirs and successors, do give and grant to the said Mayor and Commonalty and Citizens of the city of Londonderry aforesaid, and their successors, that if any person who shall be so elected as aforesaid to the office of Mayor, or of an Alderman within the city of Londonderry aforesaid, shall decline and refuse to take upon him the burthen and execution of the office aforesaid, and to discharge the said office to which he shall have been so elected or appointed, that then and so often as such person so elected and appointed shall decline and refuse, the Mayor and the rest of the Common Council of the city of Londonderry aforesaid for the time being, or the greater part of them from time to time, shall and may have by these presents, for ever hereafter, full power and authority to assess, tax, and impose any reasonable pain, penalty, or sum of money upon such persons so elected and appointed, and to be elected and appointed, and so refusing or declining to take upon him the said office of Mayor, or the office of an Alderman of the city of Londonderry aforesaid, or take upon himself the burthen and execution thereof, so that the said pain, fine, penalty, or sum of money do not exceed the sum of two hundred pounds of lawful money of England, to be levied of the goods and chattels of the person so elected and appointed, and to be elected and appointed to the office aforesaid, or either of them, and the burthen and execution thereof as is aforesaid declining and refusing, to the use of the aforesaid Mayor and Commonalty and Citizens of the city of Londonderry aforesaid.

And if such person so elected and appointed to be elected or appointed to the office of Mayor or Alderman of the city of Londonderry aforesaid, shall deny or refuse the burthen and execution thereof as is aforesaid, or to pay, satisfy, or discharge, the said pain, penalty, or sum of money so assessed, taxed, or imposed, or to be imposed, taxed, or assessed upon him at such time or times as the said Mayor and the rest of the Common Council of the city of Londonderry aforesaid, for the time being, or the greater part of them, shall direct or appoint, that then and so often as the case shall happen the said Mayor and the rest of the Common Council of the said city of Londonderry for the time being, and their successors, or the greater part of them, from time to time, shall and may have full power and authority to commit such persons so elected and appointed to be elected and appointed to the office of Mayor and Alderman for the said city of Londonderry, and so as aforesaid declining or refusing the burthen and execution thereof, to the prison or gaol within the same city, there to remain until he shall satisfy or pay the said fine, pain, penalty, or sum of money, so upon him imposed, and so aforesaid taxed, to be imposed, taxed, or assessed.

We will also, and by these presents for us, our heirs and successors, do give and grant to the said Mayor and Commonalty and Citizens of the city of Londonderry aforesaid, and their successors, that if any person who shall be so as aforesaid elected and appointed to the office of Sheriff of the said city and county of Londonderry aforesaid, shall refuse or decline to take upon him the burthen and execution of the office aforesaid, and to execute the office of Sheriffs of the aforesaid city and county of Londonderry aforesaid, to which he shall have been so elected and appointed, that then and so often as the case shall so happen, the Mayor and the rest of the Common Council of the city of Londonderry aforesaid, and their successors for the time being, or the greater part of them, of whom the said Mayor and four Aldermen of the city aforesaid we will to be five, shall and may, from time to time and in future times for ever, have full power and authority to tax and impose any reasonable fine, pain, penalty, or sum of money, upon such person so to be elected or appointed for Sheriff of the city and county of Londonderry aforesaid, and so refusing or declining to take upon him the said office of Sheriff, and the burthen and execution thereof, so that the said fine, pain, penalty, and sum of money, do not exceed the sum of [illegible] marks of lawful money of England, to be levied of the goods and chattels of the said person so elected and appointed and to be elected and appointed to the office of Sheriff aforesaid, and the burthen and execution thereof as is aforesaid declining or refusing, to the use of the aforesaid Mayor and Commonalty and Citizens of the city of Londonderry aforesaid.

And if such persons so elected and appointed, or to be elected and appointed for Sheriff of the aforesaid city and aforesaid county of Londonderry aforesaid, and so as aforesaid refusing or declining to take upon himself and execute the said office and execution thereof so as aforesaid, or refuse to pay, satisfy, or discharge the said fine, pain, penalty, or sum of money so imposed, taxed or assessed, or to be imposed, taxed, or assessed upon him at such time or times as the said Mayor and the rest of the Common Council of the city of Londonderry aforesaid, for the time being, or the greater part of them (of whom the said Mayor and four Aldermen of the said city aforesaid, we will to be five), shall direct or appoint, that then and so often as such case shall happen, the said Mayor and the rest of the Common Council of the city of Londonderry aforesaid, and their successors for the time being, or the greater part of them, of whom the said Mayor and four Aldermen of the city aforesaid we will to be five, from time to time shall and may have full authority and power to commit such person so elected, or to be elected or appointed, and so as aforesaid refusing and declining the burthen and execution thereof, to the prison or gaol within the city aforesaid, there to remain until he shall satisfy or pay the said fine, pain, penalty, or sum of money so upon him taxed, assessed, or imposed, or to be imposed, taxed, or assessed all such fines, pains, penalties, and sums of money as so aforesaid to be imposed, taxed, or assessed, for us, our heirs and successors, we do give and grant to the aforesaid Mayor and Commonalty and Citizens of the city aforesaid and their successors, by these presents; and it shall and may well be lawful for the Mayor and Commonalty and Citizens of the city aforesaid and their successors, to receive, have, and retain to their own proper use and behoof, all such fines, pains, penalties, and sums of money, without any molestation, hindrance, or disturbance of us, our heirs or successors, or any officers or ministers of us, our heirs or successors, and without any account, or any other thing, to us, our heirs or successors, to be therefore yielded, paid, or made.

And further for us, our heirs and successors, we will, and firmly charge and command all such persons as shall be hereafter elected and appointed to the office of Mayor of the city of Londonderry aforesaid, and to the office of Sheriff of the aforesaid city and of the aforesaid county of Londonderry, or either of them, that they and every of them, so long as they shall bear or exercise those offices or either of them, shall abide and inhabit within our city of Londonderry aforesaid, and not elsewhere out of the same city.

And if any or either of the Chief Burgesses nominated in these presents, or any or either of the Chief Burgesses of the aforesaid city of Londonderry, hereafter to be elected, shall die, or be removed from his office (which Chief Burgesses and every of them, respectively, not well behaving in his or their office, we will to be removable at the pleasure of the Mayor and Aldermen, and the rest of the Common Council of the same city, or the greater part of them, for the time being, of whom we will the Mayor of the same city always to be one), then we will and grant that the Mayor and Aldermen and the rest of the Common Council of the city of Londonderry aforesaid, being assembled in any convenient place to be limited and assigned within the same city, according to their sound discretions, or the greater part of them, so assembled (of whom we will the Mayor of the same city to be one), from time to time for ever (so often as the case shall so happen) shall and may elect and appoint one or so many as shall be wanting of the aforesaid number of four-and-twenty Chief Burgesses of the better and more honest citizens of the aforesaid city, or of the inhabitants within the liberties of the same in the place or places of the Chief Burgess or Chief Burgesses so deceased or removed from his or their office from time to time, and that he or they so elected and appointed, may have and exercise the said office to which he or they shall have been so elected and appointed, so long as he or they shall well behave themselves in the said office, having first taken a corporal oath respectively before the Mayor of our city of Londonderry aforesaid, well and faithfully to execute the said office, and this so often as the case shall so happen.

And if it shall happen that the Chamberlain of our city of Londonderry aforesaid shall die or be removed from his office (which Chamberlain not well behaving himself in that office we will to be removable at the good pleasure of the Mayor and the greater part of the Common Council of the city aforesaid for the time being), then we will and grant that the Mayor, Aldermen, and the rest of the Common Council of the city of Londonderry aforesaid, or the greater part of them (whereof the Mayor of the city aforesaid for the time being we will to be one), being to this purpose in like manner assembled in our aforesaid city of Londonderry aforesaid, shall and may from time to time, as often as the case shall so happen, elect and appoint one other of the Chief Burgesses of the city aforesaid, and one of the Aldermen of the same, in the place of the Alderman so happening to die or be removed, and that he so elected and appointed may have and exercise that office so long, and in the same manner and form as by these presents above declared, having first taken his corporal oath well and faithfully to execute that office before the Mayor of the same city, and so as often as the case shall happen.

And further, we will, and by these presents for us, our heirs, and successors, do grant to the aforesaid Mayor and Commonalty and Citizens of the city of Londonderry aforesaid, and their successors, that they and their successors may for ever have in the aforesaid city of Londonderry one honest and discreet man, learned as well in the laws of our kingdom of England as in the laws of our realm of Ireland, in form hereafter in these presents expressed, to be named and appointed, who shall be and be called the Recorder of the city aforesaid.

And we have assigned, constituted, nominated, and made, and by these presents for us, our heirs, and successors do assign, constitute, ordain, and make our beloved George Carey, Esq., to be and become the first and present Recorder of the city of Londonderry aforesaid, to continue in that office during the good pleasure of the Society of the Governor and Assistants, of London, of the new plantation in Ulster; and that the same George Carey, Esquire, before he shall proceed to the execution of the office, shall take as well the corporal oath commonly called the oath of allegiance, as the corporal oath upon the Holy Gospel of God, faithfully to execute that office, as well by all things touching that office, before the Mayor of the city of Londonderry aforesaid; and that after the death or removal of the aforesaid George Carey, which said George Carey we will to be removable from the office of Recorder of the city of Londonderry aforesaid, at the good pleasure of the Society of the Governor and Assistants, of London, of the new plantation in Ulster, and their successors, or the greater part of them, the Mayor, Aldermen, and the rest of the Common Council of the said city for the time being, or the greater part of them for the time being, within two months next after such death or removal, shall and may elect, nominate, and appoint one honest and discreet man, learned in the laws of England, being an Englishman born, from time to time, as often as there shall seem necessary, to be Recorder of the city aforesaid. And that during the term of ten years next following after the date of these presents, the name of the aforesaid person so from time to time to be nominated and elected for Recorder of the city of Londonderry aforesaid, shall be certified and presented by the Mayor, Aldermen, and the rest of the Common Council of the said city of Londonderry, within the forty days next following such election, to the Society of the Governor and Assistants, of London, of the new plantation in Ulster, for the time being, to the intent that the said Society of the Governor and Assistants, of London, of the new plantation in Ulster, or the greater part of them, of whom the Governor of the same Society, or his Deputy for the time being, we will to be one, from time to time, during the said term of ten years next following after the date of these presents, shall approve, ratify, and confirm the election and nomination aforesaid within thirty days next after the receipt of such certificate, or otherwise within the same time shall repudiate and frustrate the same election and nomination, if to the same Society of the Governor and Assistants, of London, of the new plantation in Ulster, or the greater part of them, of whom the Governor of the same Society, or his Deputy, we will to be one, shall think fit. And that he so elected and nominated for Recorder of the city of Londonderry aforesaid, and approved by the aforesaid Society of the Governor and Assistants, of London, of the new plantation in Ulster, or the greater part of them, of whom the Governor of the same Society, or his Deputy, we will to be one, during the said term of ten years next following after the date of these presents, shall take as well the corporal oath commonly called the oath of allegiance, as the corporal oath well and faithfully to execute that office, within sixty days next after such approbation, before the Mayor and such Aldermen and others of the Common Council of the same city of Londonderry aforesaid, who shall be then present, and after oath so taken he shall and may execute the office of Recorder of the same city of Londonderry aforesaid, in the place of the same Recorder so dead, or removed, or departed from his office, so long as he shall behave well therein; and if, during the said term of ten years next following after the date of these presents, it shall happen that the aforesaid Mayor and Aldermen, and the rest of the Common Council of the same city of Londonderry, in form aforesaid, shall not nominate and elect one honest and discreet man learned in the laws of England, being English born, for the office of Recorder of the same city of Londonderry, in the place of the same Recorder so dead, or removed, or departed from his office, or the name of the person so nominated and elected in form aforesaid, shall not be certified and presented, or the aforesaid Society of the Governor and Assistants, of London, of the new plantation in Ulster, or the greater part of them, of whom the Governor of the same Society, or his Deputy for the time being, we will to be one, shall not approve the same election according to the ordinance of these presents above declared, that then and so often it shall and may well be lawful for the Society of the Governor and Assistants, of London, of the new plantation in Ulster, for the time being, or the greater part of them, of whom the Governor of the said Society, or his Deputy for the time being, we will to be one, during the said term of ten years next following after the date of these presents, in our same city of London, for this purpose met and assembled within four months next after such default of election or nomination, or after such default of certificate, or after such rejection, or non-approbation to nominate and elect one other honest and discreet man, learned in the laws, to become and be Recorder of our city of Londonderry aforesaid, in the place of the aforesaid Recorder so dead, removed, or departed from that office, to continue in the same office of Recorder during the good pleasure of the aforesaid Society, and their successors, the aforesaid oaths to be first taken before the Mayor and Aldermen, and the rest of the Common Council of the aforesaid city of Londonderry who shall be then there.

But we will, and our intention is, and by these presents, for us, our heirs and successors, do grant to the aforesaid Mayor and Commonalty and Citizens of the city of Londonderry aforesaid, and their successors, That if and so often as after the expiration of ten years next following after the date of these presents, it shall happen that the Recorder of our aforesaid city of Londonderry for the time being shall die, be removed, or depart from his office, which same Recorder, from the office of Recorder of the city of Londonderry aforesaid, we will to be removable at the good pleasure of the Mayor, Aldermen, and the rest of the Common Council of the city of Londonderry aforesaid, the Mayor, Aldermen, and the rest of the Common Council of the same city, or the greater part of them for the time being, after the death, removal, or departure of such Recorder, shall and may elect, nominate, and appoint one honest and discreet man, learned in the laws of England, being English born, from time to time for ever, after the expiration of ten years next following after the date of these presents, as often as so there shall seem necessary or convenient, to be Recorder of the city in place of the aforesaid Recorder so dead or removed, or departed from his office, to continue in the same office of Recorder during the good pleasure of the Mayor, Aldermen, and of the rest of the Common Council of the city of Londonderry aforesaid, or the greater part of them, the oath aforesaid, commonly called "the oath of allegiance," as the corporal oath well and faithfully to execute that office of Recorder of the said city of Londonderry, as well by all things, to be first taken before the Mayor and Aldermen and the rest of the Common Council of the aforesaid city of Londonderry, who shall be then present.

And also we will, and by these presents for us, our heirs and successors, do grant, that if the Mayor of the aforesaid city of Londonderry aforesaid, or his successors, or the Aldermen and Common Council of the same city, or their successors, or any of them at any time hereafter during the aforesaid term of ten years next following after the date of these presents, shall deny or refuse to give or administer to any person or persons elected and to be elected to become Mayor, Aldermen, or Sheriff, or other officer as aforesaid, respectively by the aforesaid Society of the Governor and Assistants, of London, of the new plantation in Ulster aforesaid, or the major part of them, in the form in these presents mentioned, as well the oath commonly called "the oath of allegiance," as the oath aforesaid, well and faithfully to execute his office, before he shall be admitted to the same office, that then and so often as such denial or refusal shall so happen, the aforesaid Society of the Governor and Assistants, of London, of the new plantation in Ulster, and their successors, or the greater part of them, of whom the Governor of the said Society, or his Deputy for the time being, we will to be one, from time to time during the said term of ten years next following

after

given the date of these presents, shall and may have by these presents, full power and authority to assess, tax, and impose whatsoever reasonable fine, pain, penalty, or sum of money upon such Mayor, Aldermen, and men of the Common Council of the city of Londonderry aforesaid, and any of them so refusing or denying to give and administer the aforesaid oaths respectively, to such person or persons by the aforesaid Society of the Governor and Assistants, of London, of the new plantation in Ulster, or by the greater part of them, by virtue of these presents elected to become Mayor, Aldermen, or other officers as aforesaid, so that such fines, pains, penalties, or sums of money, do not exceed the sum of two hundred pounds; and that the same Society of the Governor and Assistants, of London, of the new plantation in Ulster aforesaid, and their successors, by their ministers and servants hereafter, shall distrain for such fines, and sums of money so imposed, the goods and chattels of such person or persons upon whom such fines shall be taxed, wheresoever they shall be found within our kingdom of England or Ireland, and the said goods and chattels so distrained shall and may retain in their power, until the same Society of the Governor and Assistants, of London, of the new plantation in Ulster aforesaid, from such fines, and sums of money so taxed or imposed, shall be fully satisfied, and if such person or persons upon whom such fines, pains, penalties, or sums of money have been taxed or imposed, shall not pay, discharge, or satisfy, to the same Society of the Governor and Assistants, of London, of the new plantation in Ulster aforesaid, the same fine or sums of money set upon him or them to be assessed and imposed, then it shall and may be lawful thereafter for the same Society of the Governor and Assistants, of London, of the new plantation in Ulster aforesaid, and their successors, within two months next after such goods and chattels shall have been taken and distrained, to sell such goods and chattels so taken and distrained at their pleasure, and that the same Society of the Governor and Assistants, of London, of the new plantation in Ulster aforesaid, and their successors, shall and may, out of the moneys arising therefrom, satisfy and discharge such fines and sums of money, and shall pay, yield, and restore, the residue or surplus of such moneys, and such goods and chattels so taken and distrained, if any should be arising, to such person and persons equally who shall be the proprietor or proprietors of the same goods and chattels so taken and distrained, and that the said Society of the Governor and Assistants, of London, of the new plantation in Ulster aforesaid, and their successors, shall and may have and use any other lawful remedy, by imprisonment or otherwise, for the recovery of such fines and sums of money so taxed and imposed, or to be taxed or imposed, as to them shall seem meet.

And further we will, and by these presents for us, our heirs and successors, do grant to the aforesaid Mayor and Commonalty and Citizens of the city of Londonderry aforesaid, and their successors for ever, from henceforth shall and may have within the city of Londonderry aforesaid, one Sword Bearer who shall be and shall be named the Sword Bearer of the city aforesaid, which said officer called the Sword Bearer of the city aforesaid shall be named, elected and appointed by the Mayor and Aldermen of the city aforesaid, for the time being, and from time to time shall be attendant upon the Mayor of the city aforesaid, for the time being, which said officer called the Sword Bearer shall and may carry and bear everywhere within the city aforesaid, the limits, liberties, and precincts of the same, one sword sheathed before the Mayor of the said city.

And that in like manner he and shall be in the city aforesaid, as officers at the least, and so many and such other officers as from time to time shall seem necessary and expedient to the Mayor and Aldermen of the aforesaid city of Londonderry aforesaid, who shall be and be called the Serjeants at Mace, within the city aforesaid, and the liberty of the same, and shall serve in the courts of the city aforesaid, and for proclamations, arrests, and executions, processes, mandates, and other business belonging to the office of Serjeants at Mace, in the aforesaid city to be executed and performed from time to time, at the will and pleasure of the Mayor and Aldermen of the city aforesaid, which Serjeants at Mace shall be appointed, nominated, and chosen by the Mayor and Aldermen of the city aforesaid, when and as often as it shall seem to the said Mayor convenient and necessary, and shall be attendant from time to time upon the Mayor and Sheriffs of the city aforesaid for the time being.

And that the aforesaid Serjeants at Mace, as is aforesaid to be chosen and nominated, he and shall be in due manner sworn before the Mayor of the city aforesaid for the time being, well and faithfully to execute their office aforesaid, and that after such an oath so taken, they may and ought to execute and perform that office so long as he or they shall well behave him and themselves therein, which same Serjeants at Mace, deputed to carry maces in the city aforesaid, may at their will carry those maces gilded or of silver, and ornamented with the sign of our arms or of others, everywhere within the city aforesaid and the suburbs of the same, and other places belonging to the liberty of the city aforesaid, in attending on us, our heirs or successors, or the Lieutenant, Deputy, or other Governor of our kingdom of Ireland, when we or they shall come or go in or from the same city of Londonderry, and also to proceed with us, or any of ours, or with the said Lieutenant General, Deputy, or Governor of Ireland, in our or their return from the said city, and in the presence of us, our heirs, or successors, and of the said Lieutenant General, Deputy, or other Governor of Ireland, when the said Mayor, Sheriffs, and Aldermen, of the same city, or any of them, shall come to us, our heirs or successors, or to the said Lieutenant General, Deputy, or other Governor of Ireland, upon or without command or warning of us, or any of us, and as often as it shall happen any of the said Serjeants at Mace to be sent to foreign places out of the same city, to execute their offices by command of us, our heirs and successors, or of the Mayor or Sheriffs aforesaid, going and returning publicly as our own Serjeants at Arms attending our person, shall or may, at their pleasure, lawfully, and with impunity, carry their maces, any ordinance or command made to the contrary notwithstanding.

And further for us, our heirs and successors, we do firmly charge and command the aforesaid Mayor and Commonalty and Citizens of the city of Londonderry aforesaid, and their successors, that they, and every of them, do from time to time for ever, well, firmly, and inviolably observe and fulfil these our ordinances and grants according to the true intention of the same, and that all persons offending, or acting contrary to the form and effect of the same ordinances and grants, shall incur and undergo such pains, penalties, forfeitures, and imprisonments, as by any laws or statutes of our kingdom of England or realm of Ireland, or by our prerogative royal may be inflicted and imposed against the contemners and neglecters of our royal commandment in that behalf.

We will also, and by these presents for us, our heirs and successors, do give and grant to the said Society of the Governor and Assistants, London, of the new plantation in Ulster, within the realm of Ireland, and their successors:—

All that the city, fort, and town of Derry, and all edifices and structures thereof, with the appurtenances in the county of the city of Derry aforesaid, and province of Ulster, in our aforesaid realm of Ireland; and also the whole island of Derry, with the appurtenances, and all lands, and the whole ground within the island of Derry aforesaid, in the aforesaid county of the city of Derry, within the province of Ulster, in our aforesaid realm of Ireland.

And also all those lands next adjacent to the aforesaid city or town of Derry, lying and being on or towards the west part of the river of Lough Foyle, containing, by estimation, four thousand acres, besides bog and barren mountains, which said bog and barren mountains may be had and used as waste to the same city belonging, *and the said four thousand acres of land are to be assigned and limited by* [illegible] *Commissioners to be* [illegible] *in that behalf.*

And also all that late abbey, monastery, or religious house of Coleraine, with the appurtenances, in our county of Antrim, within the province of Ulster aforesaid, in our aforesaid realm of Ireland; and the site, circuit, compass and precinct of the same late abbey, monastery, or religious house; and also all lands, tenements, edifices, structures, and other hereditaments lying and being in or within the said site, circuit, and precinct of the said late abbey, with the appurtenances; and all other lands, tenements, and other hereditaments in our aforesaid county of Antrim, to the said late abbey or monastery, or to the chief and convent of the same lately belonging.

And also the town and lands of Coleraine, and all edifices, structures, and [illegible] of the same, with the appurtenances in the aforesaid county of Antrim.

Together with the several other parcels and proportions of land and premises at large set forth in the said Charter.

And also all that our castle and fort of Culmore, otherwise Cullmore, with the appurtenances in our county of Donegall within the province of Ulster aforesaid, and all those lands, tenements, and hereditaments, containing, by estimation, three hundred acres of land, with the said castle and fort now or late occupied, used, or to the same belonging, or reputed, or to be assigned, with the appurtenances to the said castle conveniently adjoining.

And also all that water, creek, river, stream, or rivulet of Bann, from the high sea unto the pool called Lough[illegible], and the ground and soil of the same; and also the rocks and salmon leap there, with the appurtenances; and the whole piscary, fishing, and taking of fishes, as well salmon and eels as all other kind of fishes whatsoever, of, in, or within the aforesaid water, creek, river, stream, or rivulet of Bann and the salmon-leap aforesaid, as well with nets of what kind soever as otherwise howsoever, from the high sea to Lough[illegible] aforesaid, and in, through, and within the whole course of the water within the limits aforesaid, being in the aforesaid counties of Antrim, Coleraine, and Tyrone, and every or any of them.

And the whole water, bay, river, stream, or rivulet of Lough Foyle within the limits aforesaid, and the whole ground and soil thereof, and also the whole piscary, fishing, and taking of fishes, as well salmon and eels as of all other kinds of fishes whatsoever, of, in, or within the water, bay, creek, and river of Lough Foyle, as well with nets of what kind soever, as otherwise howsoever, from the high sea unto the town of Lifford, and unto the utmost flux and reflux of the river of Lough[illegible] aforesaid, and in, through, and within the whole course of the water within the limits aforesaid, being in the county of the city of Derry, and in the counties of Coleraine, Tyrone, and Donegall aforesaid, or in any or more of them within the aforesaid province of Ulster.

And further of our more ample and especial grace and certain knowledge and mere motion, we have given and granted, and by these presents for us, our heirs and successors, do give and grant to the aforesaid Society of the Governor and Assistants, London, of the new plantation in Ulster, and their successors, the advowsons, donations, free dispositions, and rights of patronage of all and singular churches, vicarages, and chapels, of and in the city of Londonderry aforesaid, and of all and singular churches, vicarages, and chapels, of and in the village or town of Coleraine.

And further of our more ample special grace and certain knowledge and mere motion, we have given and granted, and by these presents for us, our heirs and successors, do give and grant to the aforesaid Society of the Governor and Assistants, London, of the new plantation in Ulster, and their successors, the advowsons, donations, free dispositions, and rights of patronage of all and singular the rectories and churches of Tamlaght, [illegible], Tamlaght[illegible], Anlow, [illegible], [illegible], and [illegible], in the barony of Keenaght aforesaid, in our aforesaid county of Coleraine, and also the advowsons, donations, free dispositions, and rights of patronage of all and singular rectories and churches of Dunboe, Temple [illegible], Temple Dersart, [illegible], Cairane, and Killowen, in the barony of Coleraine, in the aforesaid county of Coleraine, and the advowsons, donations, free disposition, and right of patronage of the rectory and the church of [illegible], and all in the aforesaid barony of Armagh, in the said county of Coleraine.

We have also given and granted, and by these presents, for our especial grace, and certain knowledge, and mere motion, do give and grant to the aforesaid Society of the Governor and Assistants, London, of the new plantation in Ulster, and their successors, all and all manner of our ferriages and passages over, upon, and beyond the aforesaid rivers and waters of Lough Foyle and Bann, and each and either of them, with all the profits to the same belonging.

And further of our more ample especial grace, and of our certain knowledge, and mere motion, we have given and granted, and by these presents for us, our heirs and successors, do give and grant to the aforesaid Society of the Governor and Assistants, London, of the new plantation in Ulster, and their successors for ever:—

All that yearly rent or the farm of [illegible] of lawful money of England, issuing or reserved out of, and for all those several balliboes, quarters, and lands, called townlands, lying and being in our aforesaid county of Tyrone, in the aforesaid province of Ulster, in our aforesaid realm of Ireland, that is to say, out of or for all those two balliboes of land, or other lands, called town lands, called [illegible], [illegible], [illegible], Derry, [illegible], Bally[illegible], [illegible], and [illegible], otherwise [illegible], or by whatsoever other name or names the same premises, or any of them, are known, reputed, taken, or called, or may be known, taken, reputed, or called, with their and every of their rights, members, and appurtenances universally, now or late in the tenure, occupation, or possession of Sir Thomas Phillips, Knight, and his assigns.

And also of or for all that castle of Lymavady, with the rights, members, and appurtenances situate, lying, and being in our aforesaid county of Coleraine, in our said realm of Ireland, now or late in the tenure or occupation or possession of Sir Thomas Phillips, Knight, or his assigns.

And also out of or for all the town of Limavaddy, with all its rights, members, and appurtenances universally, in our said county of Coleraine, now or late in the tenure or occupation or possession of the aforesaid Sir Thomas Phillips, Knight, or his assigns.

And also out of or for all those several ballybetaghs, quarters, balliboes, or lands called town-lands, following; that is to say, [illegible], [illegible], [illegible], [illegible], [illegible], [illegible], Derrymore, [illegible], Ballyino, Clane, being one third part of a ballibo of land, or by whatsoever other name or names the same, or any of them, are known, called, reputed, or taken, with all and singular their and every of their rights, members, and appurtenances, lying and being within the ballybetagh or precinct of land of [illegible], within the aforesaid county of Coleraine, now or late in the tenure or occupation or possession of the aforesaid Sir Thomas Phillips, Knight, or his assigns.

And also of or for the whole precincts or quarter of land called [illegible], containing all those balliboes of land called town-lands following; that is to say, [illegible], [illegible], [illegible], with [illegible] otherwise [illegible], with the chapel thereupon erected, or by whatsoever other name or names the same, or any of them are known, called, reputed, or taken, or may be known, called, reputed, or taken, with their and every of their rights, members, and appurtenances universally, situate, lying, and being in the aforesaid county of Coleraine, now or late in the tenure, occupation, or possession of the said Sir Thomas Phillips, Knight.

And also of or for all that precinct or quarter of land of [illegible], lying and being in the ballybetagh of [illegible], containing all those balliboes or lands, called town-lands, following; that is to say, [illegible], otherwise [illegible], [illegible], [illegible], or by whatsoever other names the same or any of them are known, called, reputed, or taken with all and singular their and every of their rights, members, and appurtenances, situate, lying, and being in the aforesaid county of Coleraine, now or late in the tenure, occupation, or possession of the aforesaid Sir Thomas Phillips, Knight, and his assigns.

And also of or for all that ballybetagh of [illegible], otherwise [illegible], containing all those balliboes or parcels of land called town-lands, following; that is to say, [illegible], [illegible], otherwise [illegible], [illegible], [illegible], [illegible], [illegible], otherwise [illegible], [illegible], [illegible], [illegible], otherwise [illegible], [illegible], [illegible], [illegible], [illegible], otherwise [illegible], or by whatsoever other name or names the same or any of them are known, called or reputed, or taken, or may be known, called, reputed, or taken, with their and every of their rights, members, and appurtenances universally, situate, lying, and being in the aforesaid county of Coleraine, now or late in the tenure, occupation, or possession of the aforesaid Sir Thomas Phillips, Knight, or his assigns.

And also of or for all that ballybetagh, or precinct of land of [illegible], containing all those balliboes or lands called townlands following; that is to say, [illegible], [illegible], otherwise [illegible], [illegible], [illegible], [illegible], [illegible], [illegible], [illegible], [illegible], otherwise [illegible], [illegible], otherwise [illegible], [illegible] and [illegible], or by whatsoever other name or names the same premises or any of them are known, called, reputed, or taken, with all and singular their and every of their members and appurtenances, universally situate, lying, and being in the aforesaid county of Coleraine, now or late in the tenure, occupation, or possession of the said Sir Thomas Phillips, Knight, or his assigns, and out of or for the same premises, or any parcel thereof, and other lands, tenements, and hereditaments chargeable with the aforesaid yearly rent of [illegible] aforesaid [illegible] in certain our letters patent sealed with our great seal of England, dated the [illegible] day of December last past, before the date of these presents made to the said Sir Thomas Phillips, Knight, his heirs and assigns.

And also all and all manner of fealty and services of [illegible] reserved out of or for the same premises [illegible] granted, or any parcel thereof, or out of or by any of the said [illegible] or any parcel thereof, and other lands, tenements, and hereditaments, chargeable with the aforesaid annual rent of [illegible] in our said letters patent, reserved and [illegible] to us, our heirs and successors, or by the same letters patent [illegible] to be [illegible].

We have also given and granted, and by these presents for us, our heirs and successors, do give and grant to the aforesaid Society of the Governor and Assistants of London, of the new plantation in Ulster, and their successors, All and singular messuages, mills, houses, edifices, structures, barns, stables, dovehouses, orchards, gardens, lands, tenements, meadows, feedings, pastures, commons, [illegible], glebe lands, [illegible], furzes, heaths, moors, [illegible], woods, underwoods, and trees, and all land, ground, and soil of the same woods, underwoods, and trees, tithes of corn and grain, and of hay, wood, flax, hemp, and lambs, and all other tithes whatsoever, as well great as small, and all oblations, obventions, fruits, profits, waters, [illegible], water courses, fisheries, [illegible], [illegible], [illegible], rents, reversions, and services, rent charges, rents seck, and rents and services as well of free as customary tenants, fee farms, [illegible], knights' fees, wards, marriages, [illegible], [illegible], [illegible], courts leet, courts of view, of frankpledge, perquisites and profits of court leet, and all that [illegible] and view of frankpledge doth appertain, [illegible], waifs, strays, estrays, [illegible] and [illegible], and villeins with their followers, [illegible], and customs of [illegible], fairs, markets, tolls, customs, rights, jurisdictions, franchises, liberties, privileges, profits, commodities, advantages, emoluments, and hereditaments whatsoever, with all their appurtenances, of what kind, nature, or species they be, or by whatsoever names they are known, reputed, taken, or called, situate, lying, and being, growing, renewing, increasing, or arising within the [illegible], towns, villages, hamlets, places, rivers, precincts, limits, [illegible], and [illegible] aforesaid, or in, by, or within any or either of them, or elsewhere [illegible], in the said [illegible], castles, lands, tenements, [illegible], and rivers, and the rest of the premises above by these presents granted, or to them or any of them, or to any part or parcel thereof, in any manner belonging, incident, appendant, or [illegible], or as members, parts, or parcels of the same [illegible], castles, [illegible], lands, tenements, and hereditaments, and of the rest of the premises above by these presents mentioned to be granted, or any of them at any time heretofore had, acknowledged, [illegible], [illegible], or reputed.

And also the reversion and reversions, remainder and remainders, whatsoever, of all and singular the premises above by these presents before granted, or mentioned to be granted, and of every parcel thereof, depending or expectant of, in, or upon any demise or grant, demises or grants, for a term or terms of life, lives, or years, or otherwise of the premises above by these presents above granted, or of any parcel thereof, in any manner made, being of record or not of record.

And also all and singular rents and yearly profits whatsoever, reserved upon whatsoever demise and grant made of or upon the premises by these presents before granted, and of and upon any parcel thereof, being of record or not of record, and the rents and yearly profits of all and singular the same premises above, by these presents before granted, and every parcel thereof.

We have also given and granted, and by these presents for us, our heirs and successors, do give and grant unto the aforesaid Society of the Governor and Assistants of London, of the new plantation in Ulster, and their successors, that they and their successors for ever hereafter shall have, hold, and enjoy, and shall and may have, hold, and enjoy, within the premises above by these presents mentioned to be granted, and within every parcel thereof, as many such and the like courts leet, view of frankpledge, law days, courts baron, hundred courts, county courts, [illegible], and other courts of [illegible] and assay of bread, wine, and beer, chattels waived, goods [illegible], [illegible], chattels of felons and fugitives, [illegible], and of [illegible], [illegible], knights' fees, [illegible], [illegible], [illegible], free warren, and all other rights, jurisdictions, liberties, franchises, customs, privileges, profits, commodities, advantages, emoluments, and hereditaments whatsoever, which, and as many and such and so fully, freely, and wholly, and in as ample manner and form as any abbot, prior, abbess, or prioress of any late monastery, abbey, or priory, or any other or others the aforesaid [illegible], castles, towns, villages, hamlets, waters, rivers, fisheries, lands, tenements, and the rest of the premises, with all their appurtenances, or any of them, or any parcel thereof, heretofore ever had, [illegible] or being thereof seized. As to the same [illegible], castles, towns, villages, hamlets, rivers, waters, fishings, lands, tenements, and other the premises aforesaid, or any of them, or any of them of right belonging or appertaining ever had, used, or enjoyed, or ought to have, hold, use, or enjoy, or might or could hold the same, or any part thereof, by reason or pretence of any charter, gift, grant, or confirmation by us, or any of our progenitors or ancestors, late Kings or Queens of England and Ireland, heretofore had, made, granted, or confirmed, or by reason or pretence of any Act or Acts of Parliament, or by reason or pretence of any lawful prescription, [illegible], heretofore had or used, or otherwise howsoever, by any lawful mode, right, or title whatever, and as fully, freely, and wholly, and in as ample manner and form as we or any of our progenitors or ancestors, late Kings or Queens of England and Ireland, or Kings or Queens, or Lords or Ladies of Ireland, the aforesaid [illegible], lands, tenements, and hereditaments, and the rest of the premises above, by these presents before granted, or any part or parcel thereof, have had, used, or enjoyed, or might or ought to have had and enjoyed.

Further, we also give, and by these presents for us, our heirs and successors, do grant to the aforesaid Society of the Governor and Assistants, London, of the new plantation in Ulster, and their successors, all and singular the premises above by these presents before granted, or mentioned to be granted, with their appurtenances, as fully, freely, and wholly, and in as ample manner and form as all and singular the premises, or any parcel thereof, did come or ought to have come to our hands, or to the hands of any of our progenitors or ancestors, late Kings or Queens of England and Ireland, or Kings or Queens, or Lords or Ladies of Ireland, by reason or pretence of any [illegible] or forfeiture, or by reason or pretence of any dissolution, surrender, or relinquishment of any late monastery, abbey, priory, or hospital, or by reason or pretence of any Act of Parliament, or Acts of Parliament, made in our Kingdom of England or in our realm of Ireland, or by reason of any exchange or purchase, or any gift, grant, or surrender, or by reason of any attainder, or whatsoever other lawful manner, right, or title, have come, or ought to have come, and now be, or ought to be, in our hands.

Except always, notwithstanding, and out of this our grant always reserved all and singular advowsons, donations, free dispositions and rights of patronage of all and singular the churches of Dromachose in the aforesaid barony of [illegible], [illegible], in the barony of Coleraine, and [illegible], in the aforesaid barony of Armagh, and all and singular churches, vicarages, chapels, and other benefices whatsoever, except the advowsons, donations, free dispositions, and rights of patronage, above by these presents mentioned to be granted to the premises by these presents mentioned to be granted, or any parcel thereof, in any manner belonging, appertaining, incident, appendant, or [illegible].

Except also always, and out of this our present grant altogether reserved, all lands, tenements, and hereditaments belonging to the Dean of Derry, and all lands and tenements, commonly called Termon or Erenagh land, and all the Demesne lands of the bishops found in a certain inquisition, bearing date at Limavady, in the aforesaid county of Coleraine, the [illegible] day of August, which was in the year of our Lord one thousand six hundred and nine.

And also except all lands and tenements lately granted to the Archbishop of Armagh and Bishop of Derry, or to either of them; that is to say, all lands and tenements, commonly called Termon or Erenagh lands, and all demesne lands of the bishops found in a certain inquisition, bearing date at Dungannon, in the aforesaid county of Tyrone, the three and twentieth day of August, in the aforesaid year of our Lord one thousand six hundred and nine.

And also except and out of this our present grant always reserved, all that fishery belonging to the Bishop of Derry, in the aforesaid River of Bann, found in the aforesaid inquisition at Coleraine, in the aforesaid county of Coleraine.

And also all that fishery in the aforesaid bay and river of Lough [illegible], belonging to the Bishop and Dean of Derry, found in the aforesaid inquisition of Dungannon, in the aforesaid county of Tyrone.

Except also always and out of this present grant, and these our letters patent, always reserved, all those several

ballibeos,

balliboes, quarters, and lands, called town lands, lying and being in our county of Tyrone, in the province of Ulster aforesaid; that is to say, all those two balliboes of land, or other lands, called town lands, called Mayola, [illegible], [illegible], Derry, [illegible], Ballemeck, [illegible], [illegible], and [illegible], otherwise [illegible], or by whatsoever other name or names the same premises, or any of them, are known, reputed, called, or taken, or may be known, called, reputed, or taken, with all and singular their and every of their rights, members, and appurtenances, late in the tenure, occupation, or possession of Sir Thomas Phillips, Knight, or his assigns.

And also except all that castle of [illegible], with all its members and appurtenances whatsoever, situate, lying, and being in our aforesaid county of Coleraine, in our said realm of Ireland, now in the tenure, possession, or occupation of the aforesaid Sir Thomas Phillips, Knight, or his assigns.

And also except all the town of Limavaddy, with its rights, members, and appurtenances whatsoever, in our said county of Coleraine, now also in the tenure, occupation, or possession of the aforesaid Sir Thomas Phillips, Knight, or his assigns.

And also except all those several ballibetaghs, quarters, balliboes, or lands, called town lands, following; that is to say, [illegible], [illegible], [illegible], [illegible], [illegible], [illegible], Derrymore, [illegible], and [illegible], being one-third part of one balliboe of land, or by whatsoever other name or names the same, or any of them are known, called, or reputed, or may be known, called, or reputed, with all and singular their and every of their rights, members, and appurtenances, lying and being within the ballibetagh or precinct of the land of [illegible], within the aforesaid county of Coleraine, now in the tenure, occupation, or possession of the aforesaid Sir Thomas Phillips, Knight, or his assigns.

And also except the whole precinct or quarter of land called [illegible], containing all those balliboes or lands, called town lands, following; that is to say, Ballymore, [illegible], [illegible], with [illegible], otherwise [illegible], with the chapel thereupon erected, or by whatsoever other name or names the same or any of them are known, called, reputed, or may be known, called, or reputed, with their and every of their rights, members, and appurtenances whatsoever, situate, lying, and being in the aforesaid county of Coleraine, now in the tenure or occupation or possession of the aforesaid Sir Thomas Phillips, Knight, or his assigns.

And also except all that precinct or quarter of land of [illegible], lying and being in the ballibetagh of [illegible], containing all those balliboes or lands called town lands, following; that is to say, [illegible], [illegible], otherwise [illegible], [illegible], [illegible], [illegible], or by whatsoever other name or names the same or either or any of them are known, called, reputed, or taken, or may be known, called, reputed, or taken, with all and singular their and every of their rights, members, and appurtenances, situate, lying, and being in the aforesaid county of Coleraine, now also in the tenure, occupation, or possession of the aforesaid Sir Thomas Phillips, Knight, or his assigns.

And also except all that ballibetagh of [illegible], otherwise [illegible], containing all those balliboes or parcels of land, called town lands, following; that is to say, [illegible], [illegible], otherwise [illegible], [illegible], [illegible], [illegible], [illegible], [illegible], [illegible], otherwise [illegible], [illegible], [illegible], [illegible], [illegible], [illegible], otherwise [illegible], [illegible], [illegible], [illegible], [illegible], otherwise [illegible], or by whatsoever other name or names the same or any of them are known, accepted, reputed, or taken, or may be known, called, reputed, or taken, with their and every of their rights, members, and appurtenances whatsoever situate, lying, and being in the aforesaid county of Coleraine, now in the tenure, occupation, or possession of the aforesaid Sir Thomas Phillips, Knight, or his assigns.

And also except all that ballibetagh or precinct of land of [illegible], containing all those balliboes or lands, called town lands, following: [illegible], [illegible], otherwise [illegible], [illegible], [illegible], [illegible], [illegible], [illegible], [illegible], [illegible], otherwise [illegible], [illegible], otherwise [illegible], [illegible], and [illegible], or by whatsoever other name or names the same premises or any of them are known, called, reputed, or taken, or may be named, called, reputed, or taken, with all and singular their and every of their rights, members, and appurtenances whatsoever, situate, lying, and being in the aforesaid county of Coleraine, now in the tenure, occupation, or possession of the aforesaid Sir Thomas Phillips, Knight, and his assigns, all which premises by these presents before excepted and mentioned to be in the tenure, occupation, or possession of the aforesaid Sir Thomas Phillips, Knight, or his assigns, by letters patent under our great seal, bearing date the thirtieth day of December then last past, before the date of these presents were given and granted, or at least mentioned to be given and granted to the same Sir Thomas Phillips, Knight, his heirs and assigns.

And also except all and singular other lands, tenements, courts leet, liberties, franchises, pre-eminences, jurisdictions, hereditaments, and other things whatsoever, to the same Sir Thomas Phillips, Knight, his heirs and assigns, by the aforesaid letters patent last mentioned, granted, or mentioned to be granted.

To have, hold, and enjoy the aforesaid counties, territories, castles, forts, buildings, manors, towns, villages, hamlets, lands, tenements, meadows, feedings, pastures, woods, underwoods, fisheries, fishings, rivulets and rivers, courts leet, views of frank pledge, courts baron, hundred courts, county courts, advowsons, profits, commodities, advantages, emoluments, and hereditaments, and all and singular other the premises above by these presents granted, or mentioned to be granted, with their rights, members, and appurtenances, universally (except as before excepted) to the aforesaid Society of the Governor and Assistants of London, of the new plantation in Ulster, and their successors, to the only proper use and behoof of the said Society of the Governor and Assistants of London, of the new plantation in Ulster, and their successors for ever.

To hold the aforesaid city of Londonderry, and the four thousand acres, to the same city next adjoining, upon the Derry side, and the aforesaid town of Coleraine, and the three thousand acres of land to the same town of Coleraine next adjoining, of us, our heirs and successors, in free burgage, as of our castle of Dublin, in our realm of Ireland, and not otherwise.

And to hold the rest of the aforesaid castles, buildings, manors, lands, tenements, and all and singular other the premises above by these presents above granted, besides the aforesaid city of Londonderry, and the aforesaid town of Coleraine, and the aforesaid four thousand acres to the same city of Londonderry as aforesaid adjoining, and the aforesaid three thousand acres of land to the same town of Coleraine as aforesaid adjoining, of us, our heirs and successors, as of our castle of Dublin, in our realm of Ireland, by fealty only, in free and common soccage and not in capite, nor by knight's service.

And yielding yearly to us, our heirs and successors, of and for the aforesaid city, fort, and town of Londonderry, and all edifices and structures thereof, with the appurtenances in the aforesaid county of the city of Londonderry, and for the whole of the aforesaid island of Derry, with the appurtenances and all the lands within the island of Derry aforesaid, within the aforesaid county of the city of Derry, within the province of Ulster aforesaid; And for the aforesaid four thousand acres of land next adjoining to the aforesaid city or town of Derry, lying and being on the west part of the river of Loughfoile aforesaid, and of and for the aforesaid bog and barren mountains, which said four thousand acres of land as is aforesaid are to be assigned and limited by indifferent commissioners in that behalf to be authorised. And the aforesaid bog and barren mountains to be assigned as waste to the same city belonging, and of and for the aforesaid late abbey, monastery, or religious house of Coleraine aforesaid, in the aforesaid county of Antrim, and the aforesaid scite, circuit, compass, and precinct of the same late abbey, monastery, or religious house, and all lands, tenements, edifices, structures, and other hereditaments, lying or being in or within the said scite, circuit, compass, and precinct of the said late abbey, with the appurtenances, and all other lands, tenements, and other hereditaments in the aforesaid county of Antrim, to the said late abbey, or to the abbot and convent of the same lately belonging, and for the town and lands of Coleraine aforesaid, and all edifices, structures, and curtilages of the same with the appurtenances, and three thousand acres of land to the same town assigned and adjoining, fifty-three shillings and four pence.

And of and for the aforesaid proportion of land called the great proportion of [illegible], lying in the aforesaid barony or precinct of Coleraine, in the aforesaid county of Coleraine, ten pounds thirteen shillings and four pence.

And of and for the aforesaid proportion of land called the middle proportion of [illegible], lying in the aforesaid barony or precinct of Coleraine, in the county of Coleraine aforesaid, eight pounds.

And

And of and for the aforesaid proportion of land called the small proportion of [illegible], lying in the aforesaid barony or precinct of Coleraine, in the county of Coleraine aforesaid, five pounds nineteen shillings and five pence.

And of and for the aforesaid proportion of land called the small proportion of [illegible], lying in the aforesaid barony or precinct of Coleraine aforesaid, five pounds six shillings and eight pence.

And of and for the aforesaid proportion of land called the small proportion of [illegible], lying in the aforesaid barony or precinct of Coleraine, in the county of Coleraine aforesaid, five pounds six shillings and eight pence.

And of and for the aforesaid proportion of land called the small proportion of [illegible], lying in the aforesaid barony or precinct of Coleraine, in the aforesaid county of Coleraine, five pounds six shillings and eight pence.

And of and for the aforesaid Abbey, Monastery, or religious house of [illegible], with the appurtenances, in the aforesaid barony of Coleraine, and in the county of Coleraine aforesaid, and the site, circuit, compass, and precinct of the same late Abbey, and all lands, tenements, and other hereditaments, above by these presents afore granted, and to the same late Abbey, Monastery, or religious house of [illegible] belonging or appertaining, three pounds and four shillings.

And of and for the aforesaid proportion of land called the great proportion of [illegible], lying in the aforesaid barony or precinct of Keenaght, in the aforesaid county of Coleraine, eleven pounds.

And of and for the aforesaid proportion of land called the middle proportion of [illegible], lying in the aforesaid barony or precinct of Keenaght, in the aforesaid county of Coleraine, eight pounds.

And of and for the aforesaid proportion of land called the middle proportion of [illegible], lying in the aforesaid barony or precinct of Keenaght, in the aforesaid county of Coleraine, eight pounds.

And of and for the aforesaid proportion of land called the small proportion of [illegible], lying in the aforesaid barony or precinct of Keenaght, in the aforesaid county of Coleraine, 5l. 6s. 8d.

And of and for the aforesaid proportion of land called the small proportion of [illegible], lying in the aforesaid barony or precinct of Keenaght, in the aforesaid county of Coleraine, 5l. 6s. 8d.

And of and for the aforesaid proportion of land called the small proportion of [illegible], lying in the aforesaid barony or precinct of Keenaght, in the aforesaid county of Coleraine, 5l. 6s. 8d.

And of and for the aforesaid proportion of land called the great proportion of [illegible], lying in the aforesaid barony or precinct of Annagh, in the aforesaid county of Coleraine, £10 13s. 4d.

And of and for the aforesaid proportion of land called the middle proportion of [illegible], lying in the aforesaid barony or precinct of Annagh, in the aforesaid county of Coleraine, eight pounds.

And of and for the aforesaid proportion of land called the small proportion of [illegible], lying in the aforesaid barony or precinct of Annagh, in the aforesaid county of Coleraine, £5 6s. 8d.

And of and for the aforesaid proportion of land called the small proportion of [illegible], lying in the aforesaid barony or precinct of Annagh, in the aforesaid county of Coleraine, five pounds six shillings and eightpence.

And of and for the aforesaid proportion of land called the small proportion of [illegible], lying in the aforesaid barony or precinct of Annagh aforesaid, in the aforesaid county of Coleraine, £5 6s. 8d.

And of and for the aforesaid proportion of land called the small proportion of [illegible], lying in the aforesaid barony or precinct of Annagh, in the aforesaid county of Coleraine, £5 6s. 8d.

And of and for the aforesaid proportion of land called the small proportion of [illegible], lying in the aforesaid barony or precinct of Annagh aforesaid, in the aforesaid county of Coleraine, £5 6s. 8d.

And of and for the aforesaid villages, hamlets, balliboes, or parcels of land, lying in the aforesaid barony of Annagh, in the aforesaid county of Coleraine; that is to say, the castle and town of [illegible], otherwise [illegible], [illegible], [illegible], [illegible], [illegible], [illegible], [illegible], [illegible], with their sites, members, and appurtenances, containing together by estimation four hundred and twenty acres of land, whether more or less, sixpence.

And of and for all the aforesaid several towns, villages, hamlets, balliboes or parcels of land, lying in the aforesaid barony of Annagh, in the aforesaid county of Coleraine; that is to say, [illegible], [illegible], [illegible], [illegible], with their members and appurtenances, containing together by estimation three hundred acres of land, whether more or less, thirty-two shillings.

And of and for the aforesaid abbey, monastery, or religious house of Dungiven aforesaid, with the appurtenances, and the site, circuit, compass, and precincts of the said late abbey, and all lands, tenements, edifices, structures and other hereditaments, lying and being in or within the said site, circuit, compass, and precinct of the said late abbey, and all the several towns, villages, hamlets, balliboes, or parcels of land, and other premises above by these presents before granted, and to the said late abbey, monastery, or religious house of Dungiven aforesaid, belonging and appertaining, containing together by estimation 300 acres, forty shillings and sixpence.

And of and for the aforesaid proportion of land called the middle proportion of [illegible], being in [illegible], lying in the aforesaid barony of Loughinsholin, in the aforesaid county of Tyrone, eight pounds.

And of and for the aforesaid proportion of land called the small proportion of [illegible] being in [illegible], otherwise [illegible], in the aforesaid barony or precinct of Loughinsholin, in the aforesaid county of Tyrone, five pounds six shillings and eightpence.

And of and for the aforesaid proportion of land called the small proportion of [illegible], being in the territory of [illegible], otherwise [illegible], in the aforesaid barony or precinct of land of Loughinsholin, in the aforesaid county of Tyrone, five pounds six shillings and eightpence.

And of and for the aforesaid proportion of land called the great proportion of land [illegible], being in the territory of [illegible], in the aforesaid barony or precinct of Loughinsholin, in the aforesaid county of Tyrone, £10 13s. 4d.

And of and for the aforesaid proportion of land called the small proportion of [illegible], in the territory of [illegible], in the aforesaid barony or precinct of Loughinsholin, in the aforesaid county of Tyrone, five pounds six shillings and eightpence.

And of and for the aforesaid proportion of land called the small proportion of [illegible], being in the territory of [illegible], in the aforesaid barony or precinct of Loughinsholin, in the aforesaid county of Tyrone, five pounds six shillings and eightpence.

And of and for the aforesaid proportion of land called the small proportion of [illegible], being in [illegible], in the aforesaid barony or precinct of Loughinsholin, in the aforesaid county of Tyrone, five pounds six shillings and eightpence.

And of and for the aforesaid proportion of land called the small proportion of [illegible], being in the territory of [illegible], lying in the barony or precinct of Loughinsholin, in the aforesaid county of Tyrone, five pounds six shillings and eightpence.

And of and for the aforesaid proportion of land called the small proportion of [illegible], being in the territory of [illegible] and [illegible], lying in the barony of Loughinsholin, in the aforesaid county of Tyrone, five pounds six shillings and eightpence.

And of and for the aforesaid parcel or proportion of land called the small proportion of [illegible], lying in the aforesaid barony or precinct of Loughinsholin, in the aforesaid county of Tyrone, forty-four shillings and sixpence.

And of and for the aforesaid towns, villages, hamlets, balliboes, or parcels of land, lying in [illegible], otherwise [illegible], in the aforesaid barony or precinct of Loughinsholin, in the aforesaid county of Tyrone; that is to say, [illegible], [illegible], [illegible], [illegible], [illegible], [illegible], [illegible], and [illegible], with their appurtenances and members, containing together by estimation four hundred and twenty acres of land, whether more or less, forty shillings and sixpence.

And of and for the aforesaid towns, villages, hamlets, balliboes, or parcels of land, lying in the [illegible], otherwise [illegible], in the aforesaid barony or precinct of Loughinsholin, in the county of Tyrone; that is to say, [illegible], [illegible], [illegible], [illegible], [illegible], [illegible], the two [illegible], [illegible], [illegible].

Ballyrowaly, and the third part of the balliboe of Ballydally, with all and singular their and every of their members and appurtenances, containing by estimation five hundred and sixty acres of land, whether more or less, fifty-nine shillings and eightpence.

And of and for the aforesaid proportion of land called the great proportion of Ballyloskin, being in the territory of Tomlagh, in the aforesaid barony or precinct of Loughinsholine, in the aforesaid county of Tyrone, and the aforesaid proportion of land called the small proportion of Loskagh, being in the territory of Killeeragh, otherwise Killetragh, and Tomlagh, in the aforesaid barony or precinct of Loughinsholine, in the same county of Tyrone, forty-four shillings and ninepence of lawful money of England, at the receipt of the Exchequer of us, our heirs and successors of our realm of Ireland aforesaid: that is to say, to the hands of the treasurer, under-treasurer, or our receiver-general of Ireland, for the time being, at the feasts of the Annunciation of the Blessed Virgin Mary and St. Michael the Archangel, by equal portions yearly to be paid for ever for all other rents, services, exactions, and demands whatsoever therefore to be yielded, paid, or made to us, our heirs and successors.

And the aforesaid Society of the Governor and Assistants of London, of the new plantation in Ulster aforesaid, for themselves and their successors, do covenant and grant to and with us, our heirs and successors, by these presents, that the same Society of the Governor and Assistants or their successors, within one year next following after the date of these presents, or sooner if they shall be required in that behalf by the Bishop and Dean of Derry, or either of them for the time being, shall establish and appoint, and by good and sufficient several conveyances in the law convey to the Bishop of Derry for the time being, and his successors, for the use and behoof of the same Bishop and Dean, and their successors respectively, four acres of land in the aforesaid island of Derry, which are and shall be adjoining the tower called Columbkill Tower: that is to say, to the Bishop of Derry and his successors two acres, and other two acres thereof to the said Dean and his successors, to the intent that the same Bishop and Dean may thereupon build separate houses and habitations for them and their successors respectively.

And the aforesaid Society of the Governor and Assistants of London, of the new plantation in Ulster, for themselves and their successors, do covenant and grant to and with us, our heirs and successors, by these presents, that the same Society of the Governor and Assistants, and their successors for ever hereafter, and at their own proper costs and charges, will keep and maintain of, in, and upon the said castle and fort of Culmore, one ward of such and so many men well and sufficiently armed, and such and so many other officers from time to time as may be requisite, necessary, and sufficient for the maintenance, defence, and safe custody of the said castle and fort, and thereof shall acquit, exonerate, indemnify, and keep harmless us, our heirs and successors for ever.

And we will also and command, and the aforesaid Society of the Governor and Assistants, of London, of the new plantation in Ulster aforesaid, for themselves and their successors, do covenant to and with us, our heirs and successors, by these presents, that the same Society of the Governor and Assistants, and their successors, within one year next following after the date of these presents, by sufficient assurances and conveyances in the law, shall give, grant and convey, to all and singular the several incumbents of all and singular churches, vicarages, and chapels, within the several parishes and precincts in the aforesaid county of Coleraine, and the aforesaid barony of Loughinsholin, having cure of souls, and their successors, severally and respectively, such and so many acres of glebe land of the same incumbents respectively, in the several parishes and precincts in the same county of Coleraine, and barony of Loughinsholin aforesaid being, as shall be near or approaching to the rate and proportion of sixty acres of land lying in every proportion of land of 1,000 acres, lying in every or any parish or precinct within the aforesaid county of Coleraine, and the aforesaid barony of Loughinsholin, by the aforesaid Society of the Governor and Assistants, of London, of the new plantation in Ulster, and their successors, above by these presents before granted, and so more or less according to the rate of the greater and lesser proportions, and that the same churches, vicarages, and chapels, and any of them, singly and separately, shall and may be within one year next after the date of these presents, at the costs and charges of the same Society, fully and sufficiently endowed in law with the same glebe lands, according to the rate and proportion aforesaid.

Moreover, we will that the aforesaid glebe lands so far as aforesaid to be conveyed shall be commodious, and conveniently placed, limited, and disposed for the better and more commodious use of the incumbents aforesaid respectively.

We will also and by these presents for us our heirs and successors do grant that the aforesaid lands—so as aforesaid, respectively to be conveyed and assigned in writing and under the common seal of the same Society of the Governor and Assistants, of London, of the new plantation with such grant and endowment of the same lands, as aforesaid, to be made—shall be to the aforesaid churches, vicarages, and chapels respectively, to all intents of law, reputed inseparable and for ever annexed by virtue of the presents to hold the same lands of the said Society and their successors for ever in pure and perpetual alms for all services whatsoever.

Also we give for us, our heirs, and successors, and do grant full licence, faculty, and authority to the aforesaid Society and their successors, that the Governor and Assistants of the same Society, or the major part of them, of whom the Governor for the time being we will to be one, may from time to time and shall freely and lawfully make grants, and against such tenure in pure and perpetual alms, therefore and concerning the aforesaid glebe lands so as aforesaid to be conveyed to the aforesaid incumbents and their successors only, and not otherwise; and the same tenure in pure and perpetual alms to and upon such their conveyances of and for the said glebe lands to be made of the aforesaid Society and their successors for ever to reserve, and that the aforesaid incumbents and their successors, or any of them respectively, immediately after such their conveyances, and any or either of them so as aforesaid made respectively, shall hold, and every of them shall hold such glebe land and conveyances of the same Society and their successors in pure and perpetual alms, according to the tenor and true intention of such their conveyances and assurances, or any or either of them in form aforesaid, in that behalf made, any statute, act, ordinance or provision to the contrary thereof in any wise notwithstanding.

And for that there will be need that great abundance of timber be had and provided, for the planting of the premises, and the rebuilding of houses and edifices within the same, and therefore great care is to be had that the timber trees there growing, and which may conveniently and fitly serve towards the plantation of the premises, be not carried out of the same kingdom, or otherwise wasted or spoiled in the same kingdom:—

We have ordained therefore, and by these presents firmly charge and command the aforesaid Society of the Governor and Assistants, of London, of the new plantation in Ulster, and the same Society, for themselves and their successors, do covenant and grant to and with us, our heirs and successors, by these presents, that all and all manner of trees being timber growing and being of, in, and upon the lands of Glankonkeine and Killetragh, extending from the aforesaid county of Coleraine unto Ballie Derry, shall be and for every hereafter remain only and be converted toward the plantation aforesaid, and the building of houses and edifices so as aforesaid to be made, and to be spent towards other necessary uses of our aforesaid realm of Ireland, in the same kingdom, and not for any other cause to be [illegible] and sold, any thing in these presents to the contrary notwithstanding.

And further, of our more abundant grace, and of our certain knowledge and mere motion, we will, and by these presents for us, our heirs and successors, do grant to the aforesaid Society of the Governor and Assistants, of London, of the new plantation in Ulster aforesaid, and their successors, that we, our heirs and successors, for ever hereafter, yearly and from time to time, shall acquit, exonerate, save harmless, and indemnify, as well the aforesaid Society of the Governor and Assistants, of London, of the new plantation in Ulster, and their successors, as the aforesaid county, territories, castles, manors, forts, lands, tenements, and all and singular other the premises above by these presents granted, or mentioned to be granted, and every parcel thereof (except before excepted), of and from all and all manner of corrodies, rents, fees, services, annuities, pensions, portions, arrearages, and sums of money and charges whatsoever, issuing and to be paid out of or for the premises, or out of or for any parcel thereof, to us, our heirs or successors, or thereupon charged, or to be charged against us, our heirs and successors, saving the rents, tenures, and services above in these presents, to us, our heirs and successors reserved, and saving all arrearages of rent, of all and singular the same premises, if any be due and payable to us by the aforesaid Society only.

We will also, and by these presents, for us, our heirs, and successors, firmly enjoin and command, as well the Treasurer, Chancellor, and Barons of our Exchequer in England and Ireland, and of our heirs and successors whatsoever, for the time being, that they and every of them upon the only showing of these our letters patent, or the inrolment thereof, without any other writ or warrant from us, our heirs and successors, in any manner of wise to be obtained or prosecuted, shall make full, whole, and due allowance, and manifest discharge of and from all and all manner of such corrodies, rents, fees, annuities, pensions, portions, and sums of money, and other charges whatsoever, saving the aforesaid rents, services, tenures, and arrearages of rents aforesaid, and other premises, in these presents as beforesaid reserved, and by the aforesaid Society of the Governor and Assistants, of London, of the new plantation in Ulster, and their successors, payable, to be made or to be performed for the premises, by these presents before granted, or any part or parcel thereof, to us, our heirs or successors, or in any way charged thereupon, towards us, our heirs and successors, charged or to be charged to the aforesaid Society of the Governor and Assistants, of London, of the new plantation in Ulster, and their successors, shall make, and from time to time cause to be made and these our letters patent, or the inrolment of the same, shall be yearly and from time to time sufficient warrant and discharge in that behalf as well to the said Treasurer, Chancellor, and Barons of our Exchequer, and of our heirs and successors for the time being, as to all and every receiver, auditor and other officers and ministers of us, our heirs and successors whatsoever, for the time being, a sufficient warrant and discharge in that behalf.

And further, of our more ample and especial grace, and our certain knowledge and mere motion, we have demised, granted, and to farm letten, and by these presents, for us, our heirs and successors, do grant, demise, and to farm let unto the aforesaid Society of the Governor and Assistants, of London, of the new plantation in Ulster, and their successors, all and all manner of customs, subsidies, tonnages, poundages, and great and small customs, coming, growing, and arising within the city of Londonderry aforesaid, and the liberty of the same, and the said county of Londonderry, and within the town of Coleraine aforesaid, and within the ports and creeks of the same, and every of them, and also within the port of Portrush, and within the aforesaid water of Loughfoyle, and within the aforesaid river of Bann, and within the aforesaid river of Loughswilly, and within the creeks and ports of the same, and every of them for or in respect of all and all manner of goods and merchandises brought to the aforesaid city of Londonderry, and to the aforesaid county of Londonderry, and to the aforesaid town of Coleraine, and ports and creeks of the same, and to and in the aforesaid port of Portrush, and to and in the aforesaid river or water of Loughfoyle, and to and in the aforesaid river or water of Bann, and to and in the aforesaid water or river of Loughswilly, and within the creeks and ports of the same, and every of them from foreign parts beyond the seas for cause of merchandise imported, or out of the same city of Londonderry, or the aforesaid town of Coleraine, and creeks and ports of the same, or of the aforesaid port of Portrush, or out of the aforesaid water of Loughfoyle, or out of the aforesaid river or water of Bann, or out of the aforesaid water or river of Loughswilly, or out of the creeks and ports of the same, and every of them thereafter exported into foreign parts beyond the seas for the purpose of trade.

To hold to the aforesaid Society of the Governor and Assistants, of London, of the new plantation in Ulster, and their successors, from the date of these presents for, and during, and unto the end and term of ninety-nine years from thence next ensuing, and fully to be complete and ended, without impeachment, molestation, or any other thing to be given, and without account therefore to be yielded and made for the same.

Yielding therefore yearly to us, our heirs and successors, [illegible] shillings and [illegible] of lawful money of England at the receipt of the Exchequer of us, our heirs and successors, of our realm of Ireland, or to the hands of the bailiff or receiver of the premises for the time being at the feasts of St. Michael the Archangel and the Annunciation of the blessed Virgin Mary, by equal portions yearly, to be paid during the term aforesaid.

And also we will, and for us, our heirs and successors, do ordain and constitute, that for ever hereafter there be and shall be, within the aforesaid water or river of Loughfoyle, in the aforesaid city of Londonderry, and through and within the liberty of the same city, a sea port, and a port for the application and arrival of ships, boats, and other vessels, and for the lading and unlading of all and all manner of things, wares and merchandises whatsoever, with all and all manner of rights, jurisdictions and free customs, customs' duties, and privileges, belonging, due, or to be due to such a port, and that the same port be and shall be named and called the port of the city of Londonderry aforesaid.

And further, of our more abundant grace, for us, our heirs and successors, we do grant to the aforesaid Society of the Governor and Assistants, of London, of the new plantation in Ulster aforesaid, and to their successors, and by these presents we will, command, and firmly ordain, and expressly do command, that all and singular merchants, mariners, and all other persons whatsoever, bringing any things, wares, or merchandises, into or within the aforesaid waters or rivers of Loughfoyle, or into or within the aforesaid water or river of Loughswilly, or into or within any port, creek, or member of them, or either of them, in any ship, boat, or other vessel whatsoever, from parts beyond the seas on account of trade, and that every ship, boat, and other vessel whatsoever, lading or carrying in any things, merchandises, or wares, and coming and entering into or within the aforesaid water or river of Loughfoyle, or into or within the aforesaid water or river of Loughswilly, or into or within any port, creek, or member of them, or either of them, during the aforesaid term of ninety-nine years, from parts beyond the seas, on account of trade, shall not discharge and unload the same goods, merchandises and wares, or any of them, at any port or ports, place or places, creek or creeks, within the aforesaid water or river of Loughfoyle, or within the aforesaid water or river of Loughswilly, save only at the aforesaid port of the city of Londonderry, without the licence of the aforesaid Society or their officers, in that behalf sufficiently authorized, and at the aforesaid port of the city of Londonderry aforesaid, or in other ports upon such licence as aforesaid, shall pay and satisfy to the aforesaid Society of the Governor and Assistants, of London, of the new plantation in Ulster aforesaid, and to their successors, or to their officers, deputies, and ministers, in that behalf lawfully authorized and constituted, all and all manner of customs, duties, and payments, payable for such ships, boats, and other vessels whatsoever, and for such goods, merchandises, or wares, so brought and discharged or unladen, in or within the water or river of Loughfoyle, or in or within any port, creek, or member of the same, or into or within the aforesaid water or river of Loughswilly, or into or within any port, creek, or member of the same, before they shall go or depart from or out of the same water or river of Loughfoyle, or from or out of the aforesaid water or river of Loughswilly, or from or out of any port, creek, or member of the same, or either of them, upon pain of contempt of our royal commandment, and of the pains due for such contempt, and upon pain of the forfeiture of all such goods, merchandises, and wares exported out of the aforesaid water of Loughfoyle, or out of the aforesaid water or river of Loughswilly, or out of any port, creek, or member of them, or either of them, or the value thereof to the aforesaid Society of the Governor and Assistants, of London, of the new plantation in Ulster, aforesaid, and their successors, during the aforesaid term of ninety-nine years.

We have also given and granted, and by these presents for us, our heirs and successors, do give and grant to the aforesaid Society of the Governor and Assistants, of London, of the new plantation in Ulster, and their successors for ever, the office of Admiral of us, our heirs and successors, and all things which to the Admiralty ought to belong or appertain, on all our coasts or shores of Tirconnell, Coleraine, and county of Londonderry aforesaid, together with all royalties, rights, liberties, profits, privileges, and pre-eminences, to the same office, in any wise belonging or appertaining, incident or appendant, to be exercised by the aforesaid Society of the Governor and Assistants, of London, of the new plantation in Ulster, and their successors, or by their sufficient deputy or deputies, any of our letters patent in that behalf heretofore made or granted in any wise notwithstanding.

We have also given and granted, and by these presents for us, our heirs and successors, do give and grant to the aforesaid Society of the Governor and Assistants, of London, of the new plantation in Ulster, and their successors, all and all manner of wrecks of the sea, of all ships, goods and merchandizes, property belonging to the same Society, or their successors, or to the Mayor, Aldermen, or Citizens of the city of Londonderry aforesaid, or their successors, or to any person or persons being citizens or inhabitants within the city of Londonderry aforesaid, or the liberties of the same, from time to time hereafter happening to be wrecked in Ballyshannon and Coleraine, or on the shores, coasts, ports, and creeks through and between the same places, and also Pheleme, Joanes, and Loggan, and shores, in the places and shores aforesaid, without any forfeiture, or any sum of money, payment, or any other thing therefore to be yielded, paid or made to us, our heirs, successors, or assigns. To the intent nevertheless that every proprietor of the aforesaid ships, boats, or other vessels, or of the aforesaid merchandizes, wares, or other things so wrecked, respectively, shall have and enjoy whatever to himself belongeth of such wrecks. We have also granted, and by these presents for us, our heirs and successors, do give and grant to the aforesaid Society of the Governor and Assistants, of London, of the new plantation in Ulster, and their successors, full licence, power, liberty, faculty, and authority, that they and their successors, and also all the citizens inhabiting the city of Londonderry aforesaid, and the rest of the inhabitants and residents within the aforesaid county of Londonderry, and within the town, places and limits before mentioned to be granted, and every of them for ever hereafter, from time to time, at their will and pleasure may export and transport all and all manner of things, wares, and merchandizes, which by the laws and statutes of the said realm of Ireland are prohibited to be exported, coming, growing, increasing, and renewing of, in, and upon the lands, tenements, and other hereditaments above mentioned, by these presents to be granted without the contradiction or impediment of us, our heirs or successors, or of any of our officers, or ministers, any statute, law, ordinance, prohibition, restraint, or any other thing to the contrary notwithstanding.

We do also command, and by these presents for us, our heirs and successors, do prohibit all and singular other persons whatsoever, that they nor any of them do not export or transport, or cause to be exported or transported, any such things, wares or merchandizes, which by the laws and statutes of the said realm of Ireland, are prohibited to be exported, and coming, growing, and arising of, in, and upon the premises, by these presents before granted, or any of them, into any foreign parts, and beyond the seas out of the said kingdom of Ireland, upon pain of contempt of our royal command, and under such pains, punishments, and forfeitures as by the laws and statutes in that behalf made and to be made, may be inflicted, imposed, and assessed upon such offenders.

We will also, and by these presents for us, our heirs and successors, do grant to the aforesaid Society of the Governor and Assistants, of London, of the new plantation in Ulster, and their successors, and also all their assigns, deputies, ministers, and servants, shall and may have full liberty of fishing, hawking, and fowling, in all the places, lands, tenements, shores, and coasts aforesaid, at their will and pleasure.

And that it shall and may be lawful to and for them, and every of them, to draw and dry their nets, and pack the fishes there taken, upon any parts of the shores and coasts aforesaid where they shall fish, and the salmons and other fishes there taken to take thence and carry away without any impediment, contradiction, or molestation, of us or other, whensoever or wheresoever it shall happen to be done.

And that in like manner they may have the several fishings and fowlings within the city of Londonderry aforesaid, and in all lands and tenements before mentioned to be granted to the aforesaid Society of the Governor and Assistants, of London, of the new plantation in Ulster, and their successors, and in the river or water of Loughfoyle, to the rules of the sea, and in the river or water of Bann to Lough [illegible].

And that the aforesaid Society of the Governor and Assistants, of London, of the new plantation in Ulster, and their successors, may peaceably and quietly have, hold, and enjoy the aforesaid city of Londonderry aforesaid, and all the aforesaid territory and county of Londonderry, and the towns, places, limits, and other the premises above by these presents mentioned to be granted, without any trouble, molestation, expulsion, impediment, or contradiction of us, our heirs or successors, or of any other person or persons (except before excepted), any thing having or of right claiming, or who may have or of right claim, of or in the aforesaid city of Londonderry, or of or in the aforesaid territory and county of Londonderry, or any part thereof, or of or in all and singular the towns, places, and limits before mentioned to be granted, or any parcel of the same.

And that in like manner as well the aforesaid city of Londonderry and town of Coleraine, as the aforesaid county of Londonderry, and the towns, places, and limits, before mentioned to be granted, shall be for ever hereafter preserved or kept indemnified of and from all and all manner of letters patent of privilege heretofore made or granted to any person or persons.

And that we, our heirs or successors, hereafter will not give or grant to any, any such letters patent of privilege to be exercised or used within the aforesaid city of Londonderry, or within the aforesaid county of Londonderry or within the aforesaid town of Coleraine, or within the other lands, tenements, and hereditaments, above in these presents before granted, or in any parcel thereof; and that the same city of Londonderry, and the aforesaid town of Coleraine, and all and singular other the lands, tenements, and hereditaments before granted, and all the men inhabiting and residing within the same tenements, and other the premises before mentioned to be granted for ever hereafter, be and shall be free and quit, for and in respect of the premises before granted, of and from all compositions, impositions, and taxations, which now are or hereafter shall be imposed, taxed, or assessed by any Governor or Governors for the time being, of these parts or of the province of Ulster, or any parcel thereof.

And further we will, and by these presents for us, our heirs and successors, do covenant and grant, to and with the Society of the Governor and Assistants, of London, of the new plantation in Ulster, and their successors, that we, our heirs and successors, will grant to the aforesaid Mayor and Commonalty and Citizens of the city of Londonderry aforesaid, other letters patent, grants, or donations, to them and their successors under our Great Seal of England, or under the Great Seal used in our said realm of Ireland, severally and respectively to be made of such further and more ample privileges, liberties, franchises, immunities, and pre-eminences, as upon consideration of the Charters of London, the Cinque Ports, and Newcastle-upon-Tyne, in our kingdom of England, or of the Charter of the city of Dublin, in the realm of Ireland or of any of them, shall seem to us, our heirs and successors, and shall be deemed from time to time profitable, convenient, and fit to be used in those parts.

And further, of our more abundant special grace and certain knowledge and mere motion, we do covenant and grant to and with the aforesaid Society of the Governor and Assistants, of London, of the new plantation in Ulster, and their successors and for us, our heirs and successors, do give and grant full power and liberty to the aforesaid Society of the Governor and Assistants, of London, of the new plantation in Ulster, and their successors, that they and their successors shall have liberty and time, during the space of seven years next following after the date of these presents, of asking, finding, and having from us, our heirs and successors, such, so many, and any other things and demands, reasonable and convenient, as, when, and which, in time to come, respectively shall seem to us, our heirs and successors, profitable and convenient respectively for the same Society of the Governor and Assistants, of London, of the new plantation in Ulster aforesaid, and their successors, and for the Mayor and Commonalty and Citizens of the city of Londonderry aforesaid, and their successors, and for every of them.

And that we, our heirs and successors, shall and will severally and respectively give and grant to the aforesaid Society of the Governor and Assistants, of London, of the new plantation in Ulster, and their successors, and to the aforesaid Mayor, Commonalty, and citizens of the city of London aforesaid, and their successors, such, so many, and the same rights, liberties, franchises, and other reasonable things as shall seem profitable and convenient respectively for the same Society of the Governor and Assistants, of London, of the new plantation in Ulster, and their successors, and for the aforesaid Mayor and Commonalty and Citizens of the city of Londonderry aforesaid, and their successors.

And further, we will, for us, our heirs and successors, covenant and grant, to and with the aforesaid Society of the Governor and Assistants, of London, of the new plantation in Ulster, and their successors, that we, our heirs and successors, at the proper charges and expenses of us, our heirs and successors, for and during the time that is

or

or shall appear convenient, for the security of the said parts, that we will [illegible], maintain, and retain a sufficient and convenient number of soldiers well armed in the fortresses in the aforesaid province of Ulster, for the defence, protection, and safe keeping of the same, and the people of us, our heirs and successors, there dwelling and residing, and of their goods and chattels: And lastly, we will, and by these presents of our especial grace, certain knowledge, and mere motion, for us, our heirs and successors, covenant and grant to and with the aforesaid Society of the Governor and Assistants, of London, of the new plantation in Ulster, and their successors, that at any parliament or sitting of parliament, of us, our heirs and successors, to be holden within the our kingdom of England; And also at any parliament, or session of parliament, of us, our heirs and successors, to be holden within our realm of Ireland, when it shall be desired by the Society of the Governor and Assistants of London, of the new plantation in Ulster aforesaid, we, our heirs and successors, as well give and grant, and will [illegible] to give and grant our royal and free assent; and consent to any act, bill, or petition, to be exhibited or preferred by the same Society of the Governor and Assistants of London, of the new plantation in Ulster, or their successors, or by any or some of them in the same parliament or session, or either of them, and to be approved and allowed by the Lords Spiritual and Temporal and Commons in such parliament assembled, which may conduce and tend to the establishing, confirmation, and assuring, enjoying, conveying, and granting of all and every or any of the premises to the aforesaid Society of the Governor and Assistants, of London, of the new plantation in Ulster, and their successors, and to the aforesaid Mayor and Commonalty, and Citizens of the City of Londonderry aforesaid, and their successors respectively, may have and hold all and singular the premises above, by these presents before granted, according to the true meaning of these our letters patent.

And further, we will, and of our more abundant and special grace and certain knowledge and mere motion, for us, our heirs, and successors, do give and grant to the aforesaid Society of the Governor and Assistants, of London, of the new plantation in Ulster aforesaid, and their successors, full, free, and lawful power, licence, and authority to make, erect, and ordain, out of and upon the aforesaid lands, tenements, and hereditaments, above by these presents before granted, or any of them, such and so many several manors, of such [illegible] as are hereafter limited, as to the same shall seem convenient to the same Society of the Governor and Assistants, of London, of the new plantation in Ulster aforesaid, and their successors, that is to say—

That they make, erect, and ordain one manor of every thousand acres of land by these presents before granted, or of any number exceeding the number of one thousand acres of land, and so according to such value so many several manors as they will, so that they make not any manor of a lesser number of acres of land than of the number of one thousand acres.

And may appoint and limit to the same several manors such and so many acres of land distinct and several for demesne lands of the said several manors, and of every of them, as shall seem necessary and convenient to the said Society of the Governor and Assistants, of London, of the new plantation in Ulster, and their successors.

And to name and call the same manors by such names as the aforesaid Society of the Governor and Assistants, of London, of the new plantation in Ulster aforesaid, and their successors, shall will.

And further, we grant and give licence to the aforesaid Society of the Governor and Assistants, of London, of the new plantation in Ulster, and their successors, that they and their successors shall and may freely, and without impediment of us, our heirs or successors, grant by copy of Court Roll, or otherwise let to farm, so much of the lands, tenements, and hereditaments, belonging to such manors, to any persons and their assigns, to and for such term and terms of years, estate or estates, and for such services and yearly rents to be reserved for and upon the same lands, tenements, and hereditaments, as shall seem best and convenient to the same Society of the Governor and Assistants, of London, of the new plantation in Ulster aforesaid, and their successors for the time being.

To hold of the said Society of the Governor and Assistants, of London, of the new plantation in Ulster aforesaid, and their successors, and of their same manor and manors respectively, to which the said lands, tenements, and hereditaments so to be granted or demised, do, or shall severally and respectively belong or appertain by suit of Court of the manor aforesaid respectively, to be holden twice by the year or oftener, from three weeks to three weeks, at the will and pleasure of the aforesaid Society of the Governor and Assistants, of London, of the new plantation in Ulster aforesaid, and their successors.

Yielding therefore such and the like rents, sums of money, and other lawful reservations as shall seem best and expedient to the aforesaid Society of the Governor and Assistants of the new plantation in Ulster aforesaid, and their successors. The statute made in the Parliament of our Lord Edward the First, late King of England, our ancestor, in the eighteenth year of his reign, or any law, statute, act, ordinance, or provision whatsoever, to the contrary thereof in anywise notwithstanding.

And further, we will, and by these presents for us, our heirs and successors, do grant and give licence to the aforesaid Society of the Governor and Assistants, of London, of the new plantation in Ulster aforesaid, and their successors, that they and their successors may have and hold, and shall and may have and hold in and within the precincts of the said manors, and every of them respectively, one leet and view of frankpledge of all the tenants of such manors respectively, to be holden twice in the year, and all that to a leet or view of frankpledge doth belong or appertain.

And also shall and may have in and within the bounds of the manors aforesaid, and every of them respectively, one Court Baron, or one Court in the nature of a Court Baron, to enquire, hear, determine, and do all and singular matters and things, and in the same manner and form as in any Court Baron within our aforesaid kingdom of England, or within our said realm of Ireland, ought to be enquired, heard, determined, and done, to be holden before the Steward or Stewards, to be from time to time appointed and constituted by the aforesaid Society of the Governor and Assistants, of London, of the new plantation in Ulster aforesaid, and their successors, and before the suitors of the said manors respectively. And in the same Courts to hold plea of all and singular actions, trespasses, covenants, accounts, contracts, detinues, debts, and demands whatsoever, which in debt or damages shall not exceed the sum of forty shillings sterling, happening or arising in or within the premises before granted, and the limits and bounds of the same.

And that the aforesaid Society of the Governor and Assistants, of London, of the new plantation in Ulster aforesaid, and their successors, shall and may, from time to time, have and take all and singular the profits, perquisites, fines, commodities, advantages, and emoluments, whatsoever belonging or appertaining to such a Court, or by any manner coming or arising therefrom, without account or any other thing therefore in any manner to be yielded, paid, or made to us, our heirs or successors.

We do also give and grant, for us, our heirs and successors, to the aforesaid Society of the Governor and Assistants, of London, of the new plantation in Ulster aforesaid, and their successors, all and all manner of goods, waifs, estrays, deodands, and goods confiscated within the said city and aforesaid county of Londonderry, or within the towns, places, and limits, above by these presents mentioned to be granted, found, or to be found.

And further, being willing to show our more ample grace to the aforesaid Mayor and Commonalty and Citizens of the city of Londonderry aforesaid, of our certain knowledge and mere motion, have granted, and by the tenor of these presents for us, our heirs and successors, do grant to the aforesaid Mayor and Commonalty and Citizens of the city of Londonderry aforesaid, and their successors, shall and may for ever have and hold one Court of Record in any convenient place within the city of Londonderry aforesaid, before the Mayor of the same city for the time being, or the Recorder of the said city for the time being, learned in the laws of Ireland, every day in every week yearly (the Lord's day only excepted), and saving in the several weeks in which the Feasts of the Nativity of our Lord, the Feast of Easter, and the Feast of Pentecost, with their Festivals to them respectively annexed, shall happen, and saving on the Feast or days of the purification of the Blessed Virgin Mary, the Ascension of our Lord, All Saints and All Souls; and also to hear and determine all and all manner of actions, real, personal, and mixed, and other articles and suits whatsoever, of what nature, kind, or species soever they shall be, any manner or wise arising or happening within the city aforesaid, and liberties and precincts of the same, to be levied, affirmed, claimed, commenced, and prosecuted, and due execution to demand in the same, to seek the like, and in so ample manner and form, and as fully, freely, and wholly, and by such and the like process as are respectively used in our Court before the Mayor and Aldermen of our city of London, in our kingdom of England, and in our Court before the Sheriffs of the same city, or either of them, or in our Court in our Hustings in the same city or in any of the said Courts.

And that the Citizens of the city of Londonderry aforesaid, and liberties and precincts of the same, may be impleaded, and plead of and for all causes, matters, and plaints whatsoever, arising or happening within the said city of Londonderry, and the liberties and precincts of the same in our city of Londonderry, in the Court aforesaid.

And that the same Mayor, Commonalty, and Citizens of the city of Londonderry aforesaid may, from and henceforth for ever, have cognizance of all pleas, as well real as personal and mixt, and of other pleas whatsoever of lands and tenements, and concerning lands and tenements being within the city of Londonderry aforesaid and the liberties and precincts of the same, brought and to be brought or moved, in whatsoever of our Courts within our realm of Ireland, be it before us, our heirs and successors, or before the justices of us, our heirs or successors, of the bench, or before the itinerant justices of us, our heirs or successors, assigned or to be assigned to take assizes, juries and certificates whatsoever, or before the barons of the Exchequer, of us, our heirs or successors, or before other justices or other officers of us, our heirs and successors whatsoever, to be moved in the Court aforesaid before the aforesaid Mayor for the time being, or the aforesaid Recorder within the aforesaid city of Londonderry as aforesaid, to be holden upon the only showing of these our present letters patent, or the enrolment thereof, without any writ or writs of allowance thereupon to be prosecuted.

And further, we grant and give license by these presents for us, our heirs and successors, to the aforesaid Mayor and Commonalty and Citizens of the city of Londonderry aforesaid, that the Mayor of the same city of Londonderry aforesaid for the time being, and his successors, and the Recorder of our city aforesaid in our Court aforesaid, to be holden before the said Mayor or Recorder, may have power to correct and punish all and singular officers, clerks, and ministers of that Court, and also all other persons whatsoever, offending in or towards our Court aforesaid, for their contempts, defaults, neglect, or other offences whatsoever, committed in our said Court, by reasonable fine or imprisonment of his or their body or bodies, or by any other lawful ways and means whatsoever.

And if any impannelled and summoned for jurors for the trial of issues shall not appear before the said Mayor of the city of Londonderry aforesaid, or the Recorder in the Court aforesaid, that then such men impannelled and summoned and making default shall forfeit such issues upon them returned, or to be returned in the same and in the like manner and form as those impannelled and summoned in the city of London aforesaid, in our kingdom of England, for the trial of the like issues in the Courts of that city, heretofore have forfeited, or have been accustomed, or ought to forfeit.

And also such issues so forfeited, and to be forfeited, may be levied by the Ministers of the city of Londonderry aforesaid, to the use of the Mayor and Commonalty and Citizens of the same city of Londonderry and their successors.

And further, of our more ample especial grace, certain knowledge, and mere motion, for us, our heirs and successors, we do ordain and constitute that there be, and for ever shall be, a Clerk and a Prothonotary of the Court aforesaid, within the city of Londonderry aforesaid, to write, enter, and insert all and singular pleas, plaints, writs and returns of writs, or bails, bills, declarations, answers, rejoinders, surrejoinders, issues, warrants of attorney, verdicts, judgments, and executions thereof, and all records, processes, and businesses of the same Court, and for keeping the writs, rolls, and records of the same Court, and for this the same clerk may and shall for ever have and take for his labour, industry, and attendance in the execution and exercise of the premises, all and singular such wages, fees, rewards, and profits, as by such clerk or officers in our city of Dublin, in our realm of Ireland, for and in respect of such like businesses, offices, or services there occurring, are taken and received, and not otherwise.

And also, of our especial grace, certain knowledge, and mere motion, for us, our heirs and successors, we do ordain and constitute that there be, and for ever shall be, a Town Clerk for the aforesaid city of Londonderry, and that the same Town Clerk may and shall exercise and execute the same office in as ample manner and form, and shall and may have and take such, so many, the same, and the like privileges, rights, pre-eminences, wages, rewards, fees, profits, emoluments, and advantages as the Town Clerk for our city of London, in our kingdom of England doth exercise his office, and for or in respect or by reason of the same office, doth hold, receive and enjoy, or ought to have, hold, receive, and enjoy.

And further, for us, our heirs and successors, we do ordain and constitute, that the Town Clerk of the city of Londonderry aforesaid for the time being, be, and always shall be, from time to time, Clerk of the Peace of our Crown in the aforesaid county of Londonderry (except the town and liberties of Coleraine aforesaid), and may have and shall have and receive such, so many the same, and the like fees, rewards, profits, and advantages as other Clerks of the Peace of our Crown in our counties in our kingdom of England do or ought to receive or enjoy, which same office of the Clerk and Prothonotary of the Court aforesaid, together with the wages, profits, and emoluments [illegible] appointed thereto, to the said office of Town Clerk of the city of Londonderry aforesaid, by this our present Charter for us, our heirs and successors, we do annex, join, and unite the same office of Town Clerk of the aforesaid city of Londonderry for ever to remain, so that the said office of Clerk and Prothonotary of the Court aforesaid be not by any means withdrawn, divided or separated from the said office of Town Clerk of the aforesaid city of Londonderry.

And further, we will, for us, our heirs and successors, do ordain and constitute the Town Clerk of the city aforesaid, for the time being, and none other, from time to time to be the said Clerk and Prothonotary of the Court aforesaid, and the wages, fees, and profits thereof, to have, receive, perceive, and enjoy by himself or his deputy.

And of our more abundant grace and mere motion, we do by these presents nominate, appoint, ordain, and constitute Robert Goodwin, gentleman, to be the present Clerk and Prothonotary of the Court aforesaid, and the present Town Clerk for the aforesaid city of Londonderry, and also the present Clerk of the Peace, and of our Crown, in our aforesaid county of Londonderry, to hold, occupy, and exercise the offices or places aforesaid to the said Robert Goodwin, by himself, or his sufficient Deputy or Deputies, during the good pleasure of the said Society and their successors, and to have, receive, and take of, in, and for executing the said offices or places aforesaid, the several wages, fees, rewards, emoluments, profits, and advantages severally in these presents above mentioned and appointed.

And further, of our especial grace, certain knowledge, and mere motion, for us, our heirs and successors, we do grant to the aforesaid Mayor and Commonalty and Citizens of the city of Londonderry aforesaid, that the Mayor and Aldermen of the same city, for the time being, or the major part of them, of whom the Mayor of the same city for the time being we will to be one, immediately after the death, or lawful and judicial removal of every such Town Clerk for the aforesaid city of Londonderry for the time being, from the same office, shall and may have full power and authority to nominate, ordain, constitute, grant, and admit one other fit person from time to time for the term of his life, or otherwise, as to the same Mayor and Aldermen shall seem fit, to be Town Clerk of the city of Londonderry aforesaid, and Clerk and Prothonotary of the Court aforesaid, and also Clerk of the Peace and of our Crown, in the aforesaid county of Londonderry, and that after such a nomination, ordination, constitution, grant, and admission by the Mayor and Aldermen of the city of Londonderry aforesaid, for the time being, or the major part of them, of whom the Mayor of the said city, for the time being, we will always to be one, such person so nominated, ordained, constituted, and admitted, may exercise the aforesaid offices of Town Clerk of the said city of Londonderry, Clerk and Prothonotary of the Court aforesaid, and Clerk of the Peace, and of our Crown in our county of Londonderry aforesaid, and shall have and receive of, in, and for exercising the offices, the wages, rewards, fees, profits and emoluments above by these presents appointed and ordained, notwithstanding any statute, act, ordinance, proviso, prohibition, or restriction, in our realm of England or Ireland made or passed, or any other thing, cause, or matter whatsoever.

And further, we will, and by these presents for us, our heirs and successors, do grant to the aforesaid Mayor and

and Commonalty and Citizens of our city of *Londonderry* aforesaid, that all Citizens of the aforesaid city of Londonderry, and liberty of the same (as much as in us is) be for ever quit and free, and all their goods throughout all Ireland, of all tolls, wharfage, murage, anchorage, [illegible], lastage, and of all other tolls and duties whatsoever.

We do also, for us, our heirs and successors, grant to the same Mayor and Commonalty and Citizens of the city of Londonderry aforesaid, [illegible] [illegible] within the city of Londonderry, and the liberties and suburbs of the same.

And further, know ye that we, for us, our heirs and successors, have given and granted, and by this our present Charter confirm to the aforesaid Mayor and Commonalty and Citizens of the city of *Londonderry* aforesaid, the shrievalty of the aforesaid city, and of the said county of *Londonderry* aforesaid, with all things and customs which do, may, or ought to belong to the aforesaid shrievalty within the city and county of Londonderry aforesaid, or within the towns, places, and limits before mentioned, to be granted, by land or water, to have and to hold to them and their successors for ever, and [illegible] of us our heirs and successors, yielding therefore to us, our heirs and successors, ten shillings of lawful money of England at the receipt of the Exchequer of us, our heirs and successors, of Ireland, to be paid at the feast of St. Michael the Archangel, every year for ever.

And we will, and by these presents for us, our heirs and successors, do grant to the aforesaid Mayor and Commonalty and Citizens of the city of Londonderry aforesaid, and their successors, that the Sheriffs of the said city of Londonderry aforesaid, and their successors, shall be from time to time, and at all times from henceforth for ever, Sheriffs as well of the said city as of the aforesaid county of Londonderry.

Wherefore we will, and firmly command, that the aforesaid Mayor and Commonalty and Citizens of the city of Londonderry, and their successors, may for ever, [illegible], hereditarily, freely, quietly, peaceably, and wholly have and hold the aforesaid shrievalty of the aforesaid city, and the aforesaid county of Londonderry aforesaid and other the premises mentioned to be granted, with all things to the aforesaid shrievalty belonging of us, our heirs and successors, by the aforesaid fee farm.

And further, we will, and by these presents for us, our heirs and successors, do grant to the aforesaid Mayor and Commonalty and Citizens of the city of Londonderry aforesaid, and their successors, that no merchant or others may go to meet merchants or other persons coming by land or by water, with their merchandise or victuals towards the city of Londonderry aforesaid, to buy or sell again the same wares or victuals until they shall come to the same city, and have there exposed their wares and victuals to sale, upon pain of such forfeiture and punishment and imprisonment, as by the laws and statutes of the said kingdoms of England or Ireland may or ought to be imposed upon such offenders.

And that every year, in the city of Londonderry aforesaid, as often as need shall be, inquisition shall be made, if any within the liberties of the same city shall use merchandising in that city with the goods of others, which are not or shall not be of the same liberty, avowing the same goods to be their goods against their oath, and contrary to the liberty of the city aforesaid, and they who shall be thereof lawfully convicted as aforesaid, within the liberty of the same city, shall be punished at the will of the Mayor and Aldermen of the city aforesaid.

And that all and singular persons being free of the city aforesaid, and willing to enjoy the liberties and free customs of the same, be in lot and scot, and partake of all charges for the maintaining the state of the same city and liberties of the same, according to their oaths which they shall make when they shall be admitted to that freedom, and he which will not do this shall lose the freedom of the same.

And that all and every person being free of that city, and remaining out of the same city, and by himself or others using merchandising within the said city of Londonderry, and the liberties thereof, so that hereafter shall remain and continue, be in scot and lot with the Commonalty of the same city for their merchandise aforesaid, or otherwise be removed from their freedom.

And that the common seal of the city of Londonderry aforesaid shall remain in the custody of two Aldermen, and two others of the Commonalty of the same city, by the Mayor, Aldermen, and Common Council of the aforesaid city aforesaid to be chosen.

And that the weights and beams concerning merchandises to be weighed between merchants shall remain in the custody of good and sufficient men of the same city expert in that office, and to be chosen thereto by the Mayor, Aldermen, and Common Council of the city aforesaid, to be kept at the pleasure of the Mayor and Aldermen and Common Council of the city of Londonderry aforesaid, and that they be not at all committed to others but such as shall be chosen.

And that the Sheriffs of the aforesaid city, and of the said county of *Londonderry* aforesaid (who for the time being shall be), shall and may by themselves, their officers and ministers, have, take, receive and enjoy reasonable toll, customs and duties to the use of the Mayor and Commonalty and Citizens of the city of Londonderry aforesaid, for all wares, merchandises and other goods brought or imported to the said city of Londonderry, or the liberties of the same, by any person or persons not being citizens and freemen of the same, by water or by land, and for all wares, merchandises, and other goods exported or carried out of the same city of *Londonderry*, and liberties of the same, by any person or persons not being citizens and freemen of the city aforesaid, by land or by water, to and towards the building and erecting of gates and walls for the same city of Londonderry, and for the reparation and maintenance of the same gates and walls of the said city.

Provided always, the said city is included and defended with walls and form, that part excepted which adjoins next to the river of Lough[illegible], with ten years next following after the date of these presents.

And that merchants and others, which are not of the freedom of the city of *Londonderry* aforesaid, shall not sell by retail, any wines or other wares whatsoever, within the same city of Londonderry, the suburbs and liberties, or franchises of the same, upon pain of forfeiture of the things so bought, or the value thereof, to the use of the Mayor and Commonalty and Citizens of the city of *Londonderry* aforesaid.

And also that no person being a foreigner from the freedom of the city aforesaid, shall use or exercise within the same city, liberties, or suburbs of the same, any art, mystery, or manual occupation whatsoever, to make his gain and profit thereof, upon pain of forfeiture of forty shillings for every time wherein such person shall use or exercise within the said city of Londonderry, liberties and suburbs of the same, any art, mystery, or manual occupation as aforesaid.

And that the same forfeitures, be and shall be for ever, to the aforesaid Mayor and Commonalty and Citizens of the said city of Londonderry, and their successors, without any account or other thing therefore to be yielded or made to us, our heirs or successors, and that all the aforesaid forfeitures be from time to time for ever recovered, in the aforesaid Court, within the city of Londonderry aforesaid, for and in the name of the Chamberlain of the same city, for the time being, to the use of the aforesaid Mayor and Commonalty and Citizens of the city aforesaid.

And that brokers of merchandises in the city of Londonderry aforesaid, and liberties of the same, shall be from time to time elected by the Mayor and Aldermen of the city of *Londonderry* aforesaid, and thereupon shall take their oaths before the Mayor and Aldermen of the city aforesaid, well and faithfully to execute their offices.

And that all common boats and other persons resident in the city of Londonderry aforesaid, and the suburbs of the same, although they be not free of the city aforesaid, shall be partakers of all public charges for paving of the places and streets, and cleansing of the city aforesaid, so long as they shall be common boats and residents or [illegible] in the same city, liberties or suburbs of the same, as others such boats in the city and suburbs aforesaid, by reason of their [illegible], shall partake.

And that the goods of the Aldermen of the city of Londonderry aforesaid, shall in all aids, subsidies, and other contributions, happening within the said city, be taxed by men of the city of Londonderry, being thereto lawfully chosen and deputed, as the goods of other citizens of the same city.

Moreover we grant, for us, our heirs and successors, to the Mayor and Commonalty and Citizens of Londonderry aforesaid, and their successors aforesaid, that the Mayor of the city aforesaid, who for the time shall be appointed and named one of the Justices of gaol delivery of the said city, liberties, and suburbs thereof, in every commission to be made to any Justices of gaol delivery to be assigned for the same city, and in every commission thereof to be made, shall be first named.

And that the said Mayor and Commonalty and Citizens of the city of Londonderry aforesaid may have infangthef, outfangthef, and felons' goods of all those that shall be adjudged before them, within the liberties of the aforesaid city of Londonderry aforesaid.

And also we will and grant for us, our heirs and successors, to the aforesaid Mayor and Commonalty and Citizens of the city of Londonderry aforesaid, and their successors, that the clerk of the market of our household of our heirs, or any other officer or minister of us, our heirs or successors hereafter, may not sit within the liberties of the city aforesaid, nor within any town, place or limits before mentioned to be granted, nor may there exercise any office, nor by any means draw any of the citizens of the city aforesaid, nor other inhabitants, nor residents in the other towns, places, and liberties before mentioned to be granted [illegible] out of the liberties of the city of Londonderry aforesaid, for any things arising within the liberty of the same city of Londonderry aforesaid, or within the towns, places, and limits before mentioned to be granted (the towns and liberties of Coleraine excepted).

And that no escheator, nor other hereafter, may exercise the office of escheator within the liberty of the city of Londonderry aforesaid or within the aforesaid county of Londonderry, or within the towns, places, and limits before mentioned to be granted (the towns, liberties, and franchises of Coleraine aforesaid excepted), but that the Mayor of the city aforesaid, for the time being, may exercise the office of escheator within the liberty of the city of Londonderry aforesaid, and within the aforesaid county of Londonderry aforesaid, and the towns, places, and limits before mentioned to be granted (except within the towns, liberties and franchises of Coleraine aforesaid), so that he take his oath faithfully to exercise that office, and therefore answer to us, and our heirs and successors, as he ought.

And that no [illegible], attachment, arrest, distress, or execution, whatsoever, be made by any of the ministers of us, our heirs or successors, whatsoever, by writ or without writ, within the liberty of the aforesaid county of Londonderry, or within any town, place, and limits before mentioned to be granted, unless by the Sheriffs of the county of Londonderry aforesaid, and by the ministers of the city of Londonderry aforesaid.

And that no purveyor, taker, officer, or other minister of us, our heirs or successors, or of any other, may make any prise in the city of Londonderry aforesaid, of the goods of the citizens of the said city, and of other the inhabitants and residents within the same city of Londonderry aforesaid, against their will, unless he shall forthwith make due payment for the same, or have respite at the goodwill of the vendor.

And that no market hereafter be granted by us, our heirs or successors, to any within seven miles compass of the city of Londonderry aforesaid.

And we will and grant, and by this our present charter do confirm, for us, our heirs and successors, to the aforesaid Mayor and Commonalty and Citizens of the city aforesaid and their successors, that hereafter, no merchant, stranger, or foreigner, from the liberties of the city of Londonderry aforesaid, may sell any merchandise within the liberties or suburbs of the said city of Londonderry aforesaid, to any other stranger or foreign merchant, nor any merchant, stranger, or foreigner may buy any merchandise of any other merchant, stranger, or foreigner, within the liberty or suburbs of the said city, upon forfeiture of the same merchandises or value thereof, to the Mayor and Commonalty and Citizens of the city of Londonderry aforesaid.

Further we will, and by this our charter do [illegible] grant, that all manner of wines to be sold in the said city, and also all victuallers, as well fishmongers as others, dwelling in the same city, suburbs, or franchises of the same, and those who shall hereafter come to the said city with victuals, shall be from henceforth under the government and rule of the Mayor and Aldermen aforesaid for the time being.

And moreover of our more abundant grace, we have granted for us, our heirs and successors (so much as in us is), to the same Mayor and Commonalty and Citizens of the city of Londonderry aforesaid and their successors, that they may have the custody of all the gates and postern of the city aforesaid, now erected and built, or hereafter to be erected and built.

And also tronage (that is to say), the weighing of lead, wax, pepper, alum, madder, and such other wares within the city of Londonderry aforesaid, and the liberties of the same, for ever, by themselves, or their sufficient Deputies.

And further, of our more abundant special grace, and of our certain knowledge and mere motion, we have given and granted, and by these presents for us, our heirs and successors, do give and grant to the aforesaid Mayor and Commonalty and Citizens of the city of Londonderry aforesaid, and to their successors, the liberties, franchises, and franchises hereunder written (that is to say), that the Mayor and Recorder of the city of Londonderry aforesaid, who now are, and their successors, Mayors and Recorders of the city of Londonderry aforesaid, for ever, and the three Aldermen who hereafter shall bear the charge of the mayoralty of that city, after they shall leave that mayoralty, and be thereof discharged, so long as they shall remain Aldermen there, and four of the senior Aldermen of the city aforesaid, which next after the date of these presents shall bear and exercise the charge of aldermanship, and have not borne the office of mayoralty in the city aforesaid, and from henceforth so often as it shall happen that there shall not be living four Aldermen of the same city which having not borne the charge of mayoralty in the same city, then and so often so many of the senior Aldermen of the city aforesaid as, together with the Mayor, Recorder, and Aldermen who have borne the office of mayoralty of the city aforesaid, may supply the number of six Justices of the Peace of the city aforesaid, be Conservators of the Peace of us, our heirs and successors, to be conserved and kept within our city aforesaid, and the liberties and suburbs of the same, and to keep and cause to be kept all statutes and ordinances made and to be made, for the good of our peace, and for the conservation of the same, and for the quiet rule and government of our people, our heirs and successors, in all their articles, as well within the city aforesaid, as the liberties and suburbs of the same, according to the force, form, and effect thereof; and to chastise and punish all those whom they shall find offending in the city aforesaid, and liberties and precincts of the same, contrary to the form and effect of the same ordinances and statutes, or any of them, as according to the form of those ordinances and statutes shall come next to be done; and to cause all those that shall use any threats to any of the people of us, our heirs and successors, concerning their body, or burning their houses, to find sufficient security for their peace and good behaviour towards us, our heirs and successors, and all the people of us, our heirs and successors; and if they shall refuse to find such security, then to cause them to be kept safely in the gaol of us, our heirs and successors, of the same city of Londonderry, until they shall find such security.

Also we will and grant that the now Mayor and Recorder, and their successors aforesaid, and such Aldermen as aforesaid, or three of the same Mayor, Recorder, and Aldermen, whereof the said Mayor and Recorder, and their successors aforesaid, we will to be two, be Justices of us, our heirs and successors, to inquire by the oaths of good and lawful men, as well of the city aforesaid, as of the liberties and suburbs of the same, by whom the truth of the fact may be best known, of all manner of murder, felonies, [illegible], witchcrafts, enchantments, sorceries, art magic, trespasses, forestallings, regratings, engrossings, and extortions, whatsoever, and of all and singular other misdeeds and offences, of which Justices of Peace, of us, our heirs and successors, may lawfully, or ought to inquire by whomsoever, or howsoever, within the city aforesaid, or the liberties and suburbs of the same, heretofore done or committed, or which hereafter shall happen to be done or committed, and also of all those which in the city aforesaid, or the liberties and suburbs of the same, shall go, or ride from henceforth, shall presume to go or ride in conventicles, against the peace of us, our heirs and successors, in disturbance of the people of us, our heirs and successors, with armed force.

And also of all those that shall there lie wait to maim or kill the people of us, our heirs or successors, and also of hostlers, and all and singular other persons which have offended or attempted, or hereafter shall presume to offend or attempt in the city aforesaid, and liberties or suburbs of the same, in the abuse of measures and weights, or in the sale of victuals contrary to the form of the ordinances and statutes, or any of them, therefore made for the common profit of our realm of Ireland, and of the people of us, our heirs and successors.

And

And also the office of Clerk of the Market within the aforesaid city of Londonderry, and the liberties of the same, and within the said county of Londonderry and within the aforesaid town, places, and limits before mentioned to be granted, and all and whatsoever doth belong to the office of Clerk of the Market, together with the correcting and punishing all persons there selling bread, wine, beer, and other victuals, with the forfeitures, fines, and amerciaments to be forfeited, and in all other things which there do, and may hereafter there belong to us, our heirs, or successors, to have and exercise the same either by them or [illegible] Deputies.

And that they may in the city aforesaid, and in the aforesaid county of Londonderry aforesaid and in the towns, places, and limits before mentioned to be granted (except in the town and liberty of Coleraine aforesaid) the full execution of all writs whatsoever of us, our heirs and successors, and of all other writs, mandates, precepts, [illegible], and warrants, with the return of the same by their Minister or Deputy, or by their Ministers or Deputies whom they shall choose thereto, so that for ever the Clerk of the Market or household of us, our heirs or successors, or any Sheriffs, escheator, or any other officer or minister of us, our heirs or successors, may by no [illegible] enter or intermeddle, to do anything which doth or may there belong to his or their or any of their office or offices for us, our heirs or successors.

We have also granted to the aforesaid Mayor and Commonalty and Citizens, and their successors, that they may choose all such Under-sheriffs, Clerks, and Bailiffs to the said Sheriffs of the said city and county of Londonderry aforesaid, and of the towns, places, and limits above mentioned to be granted (except the town and liberties of Coleraine aforesaid), for which they will answer as often and when it shall seem meet unto them to be made, elected and chosen, to have, exercise, and occupy those offices, so long as it shall please them, any statute or ordinance made to the contrary in anywise notwithstanding.

Furthermore, seeing it is sufficiently notorious and manifest that they of the city of Londonderry aforesaid, which are called, elected, and taken to the degree of Aldermanship (their manners and merits requiring it), having undergone great charges, costs, and labour, for the time that they make their abode in the same city, diligently attending the public good, and rule and government of the same, and for that cause in the meantime often leaving their possessions and places in the country, therefore they all and every one of them (these things being worthily weighed and considered) may recreate, solace, and divert themselves, and quietly remain and stay in such their houses, places, and possessions, without all fear of [illegible], trouble, or grievance when after such great charge and labour, for cause of recreation and solace, they shall betake themselves thither.

And moreover, of our especial grace we have granted for us, our heirs, and successors, to the aforesaid Mayor and Commonalty and Citizens of the city of Londonderry aforesaid, and their successors, that all they and every of them, which now are Aldermen of the said city, and their successors, there to be Aldermen for the term of their lives, may have the liberty (that is to say), that so long as they shall remain Aldermen there, and shall bear the charge of Aldermanship, they be not put, nor any of them, be put in any assizes, juries, [illegible], recognizances, or inquisitions whatsoever, out of the city of Londonderry aforesaid.

Also we have granted to the same Mayor and Commonalty and Citizens of the city aforesaid, and to their successors for ever, that they may for ever have, hold, and keep within the city of Londonderry, liberties and suburbs of the same, a common Market, to be holden on the Mondays, Wednesdays, Fridays, and Saturdays, in every week throughout the year and also one fair in the city of Londonderry aforesaid, suburbs, and liberties of the same, yearly for ever (that is to say), on the feast of St. Bartholomew the Apostle, and to continue and endure all the said feast, and by eight days next following, together with a Court of Pie Powder, and with all liberties and free customs belonging to such a fair, and that they may there have and hold at the said Court, before their Minister and Deputy, by the said several days, from day to day, from hour to hour, and from time to time, all actions, pleas, and plaints of a Court of Pie Powder, together with all [illegible], attachments, arrests, issues, fines, redemptions, amerciaments, and other rights whatsoever, to the same Court of Pie Powder in any manner belonging or appertaining, without any impeachment, impediment, or trouble of us, our heirs or successors, or of any of our officers or ministers whatsoever.

And also that the same Mayor and Commonalty and Citizens of the city of Londonderry may have in the city and liberties of the same, the view of frankpledge, and all and whatsoever doth belong to the view of frankpledge, together with all [illegible], [illegible], arrests, issues, amerciaments, fines, redemptions, profits, commodities, and other things whatsoever, which may or ought thereof to belong, in any manner to us, our heirs and successors.

And for the improvement of our said city of Londonderry, we do ordain and constitute that for ever hereafter there be and shall be within the same city, a great beam and common balance, for weighing between foreign merchants and the freemen of the city of Londonderry aforesaid, and between foreign merchants; and that for ever hereafter there be and shall be within the same city, the office of keeper of the said great beam and common balance.

And also that for ever hereafter there be and shall be a great balance or weights within the said city of Londonderry, for the weighing of all merchandises of avoirdupois, and of all weights whatsoever, within the said city, liberties and suburbs of the same; and of all spices, wares, and things ponderable, to be weighed in our city of Londonderry aforesaid, liberties and suburbs of the same, and the said office of keeper of the great beam and great balance aforesaid, with all reasonable fees and profits belonging to such office, we do, for us, our heirs and successors, give and grant to the said Mayor and Commonalty and Citizens of Londonderry aforesaid, and their successors, by these presents.

And also we do give and grant to the same Mayor, Commonalty, and Citizens of the aforesaid city of Londonderry, and to their successors, authority and power to make and name, from time to time all and all manner of clerks, porters, servants and ministers of the great beam and balance, and of the [illegible] and weights aforesaid, and to remove the same clerks, porters, servants, and ministers, and every of them, and other or others in his or their place or places to place, put, and constitute, as often as it shall seem expedient to them to have, occupy, and exercise the offices aforesaid, together with the authority and power aforesaid, to the said Mayor and Commonalty and Citizens of the city of Londonderry aforesaid, and to their successors, by themselves, or by their sufficient deputy or deputies for ever, to their proper use and behoof, together with all fees, duties, wages, and profits, reasonable for the doing of the same offices and services, without any account or other thing to be yielded therefore to us, our heirs and successors.

And also for us, our heirs and successors, we do ordain and constitute, that for ever hereafter there be and shall be within our aforesaid city of Londonderry, the offices or occupation of packing all woollen cloth, sheep and calves' skins, vessels of pewter, and all merchandises whatsoever, to be packed, [illegible], piped, barrelled or howsoever [illegible], with the survey of numbering, measuring and weighing of the merchandises aforesaid, and also the oversight of the opening of what merchandises soever [illegible] arriving to the port of [illegible], and going out of the same port, as well by land as by water, within the liberties and franchises of our said city of Londonderry aforesaid and the liberties of the same, as well of the goods of strangers as of denizens whatsoever they have been [illegible].

And that for ever hereafter there be and shall be within the said city of Londonderry the office of packing woollen cloths, sheep, lambs', and calves' skins, with [illegible] and [illegible] of the same skins, and of vessels of pewter and other merchandises, which in the city of Londonderry aforesaid, liberties and suburbs of the same, shall be to be packed, [illegible] or [illegible], or by land to be carried, [illegible], as well the goods of strangers as of denizens. And also of the carriage and portage of all wool, skins, tin, hides, and all other merchandises whatsoever, in the city of Londonderry aforesaid, liberties and suburbs of the same, from the river of Loughfoyle aforesaid unto the houses of strangers, and contrariwise, to the same water of Loughfoyle aforesaid to be carried, or other merchandises, being in any houses, which ought to be carried.

And that for ever hereafter there be and shall be in the city aforesaid, and in the said county of Londonderry (except

(except within the aforesaid town and liberties of Coleraine) the office of [illegible] of what [illegible] and other merchandizes, coming to that city of Londonderry, liberties or suburbs of the same, or within the aforesaid county of Londonderry.

And that [illegible] be and shall be within the aforesaid city and county of Londonderry aforesaid (except within the town and liberties of Coleraine aforesaid) the office of gauger of all and all manner of vessels of all wines whatsoever, and of all other vessels of vinegar, oil, honey, and of all other merchandizes of what nature, kind or form soever [illegible] coming to the said city, and within the said county of Londonderry, except within the aforesaid town and liberties of Coleraine.

And of our more abundant grace, certain knowledge, and mere motion, we do for us, our heirs and successors, by these presents give and grant to the aforesaid Mayor and Commonalty and Citizens of the city of Londonderry aforesaid, and their successors, the offices or occupations of packing of all woollen cloths, sheep skins, calves' skins, vessels of pewter, and of all merchandizes whatsoever to be packed, delivered, [illegible], barrelled or otherwise included, with the oversight of [illegible], [illegible], and weighing of merchandizes, and the oversight of [illegible] whatsoever merchandizes customable arriving at the port of [illegible], and going out of the said port, as well by land as by water, within the liberties and franchises of our city of Londonderry aforesaid and the suburbs of the same, as well of the goods of strangers as of denizens, wheresoever they shall be customed, and the said office of packing of all woollen cloths, sheep skins, lamb skins, and calves' skins, with the [illegible] and [illegible] of the same skins, and of vessels of pewter and other merchandizes, which in the city of Londonderry aforesaid, the liberties and suburbs of the same, shall be customed, packed, [illegible], or [illegible], or by land carried (as well the goods of strangers as of denizens), and also of the carriage and porterage of all wool skins, [illegible], and of all other merchandizes whatsoever, which in the city of Londonderry aforesaid, liberties, and suburbs of the same shall be carried from the water of Loughfoyle aforesaid to the house of strangers and [illegible] to the same water of Loughfoyle aforesaid, and of other merchandizes, being in any house which ought to be carried.

And also the aforesaid office of [illegible] of what [illegible] soever, and of other merchandizes coming to our aforesaid city of Londonderry aforesaid, liberties, and suburbs of the same, or within the aforesaid city of Londonderry (except within the said town and liberties of Coleraine aforesaid), and also the office of Gauger of all and all manner of vessels of all wine whatsoever, and of all other vessels of vinegar, oil, honey, and all merchandizes of what kind, nature, or quality soever they shall be, coming to the said city, and within the said county of Londonderry (except within the aforesaid town and liberties of Coleraine aforesaid).

To have the offices aforesaid, and the several occupations, and every of them, and the disposing, ordering, oversight, and correction of them, and every of them, together with the fees, duties, wages, and profits to such offices and every of them, incident, belonging, or appertaining to the aforesaid Mayor and Commonalty and Citizens of our city of Londonderry aforesaid, and to their successors, to their own proper use and behoof for ever.

And also to exercise and occupy those offices, and every of them by themselves or their sufficient deputies.

We have also given and granted, and by these presents of our more ample special grace and of our certain knowledge and mere motion, for us, our heirs and successors, do give and grant to the same Mayor and Commonalty and Citizens of the aforesaid city, and to their successors, that they and their successors may have authority from time to time to choose such and so many fit persons to be coroners of the city of Londonderry aforesaid, and of the county of Londonderry aforesaid, and towns, places, and limits before mentioned to be granted (except the office of coroner of the town, liberty, and franchises of Coleraine aforesaid), as it shall please the said Mayor, Commonalty, and Citizens, and their successors. And that every person and persons so as aforesaid to be named and elected be and shall be coroner and coroners of us, our heirs and successors, of the said city of Londonderry, and the liberties of the same, and of the said county of Londonderry respectively (except the aforesaid town and liberties of Coleraine aforesaid), and from thenceforth, from time to time, may have and exercise, use and enjoy, that office or offices of coroners, to which they shall be so elected and appointed, during the pleasure of the said Mayor and Commonalty and Citizens of the city aforesaid for the time being, having first taken their corporal oath before the Mayor of the said city of Londonderry for the time being, rightly, well, and faithfully to execute that office; and that the Mayor of that city for the time being, by virtue of these presents, may have and shall have, by virtue of these presents, full power, faculty, and authority, to give and administer such corporal oaths to such person or persons as so aforesaid respectively to be nominated and chosen unto the office of coroner of the said city, and of the said county of Londonderry, truly, well, and faithfully to execute and exercise that office in and by all things to which he or they shall be so chosen and nominated, without any other commission or warrant to be therefore obtained or procured of us, our heirs or successors, so that no other coroner of us, our heirs or successors, may by any means intermeddle within that city and suburbs of the same, in the said county of Londonderry, and the towns, places, and limits before mentioned to be granted (except within the said town and liberties of Coleraine aforesaid).

And further, that the said Mayor and Commonalty and Citizens of the city of Londonderry aforesaid, and their successors, may take and arrest felons, thieves, and other malefactors found in the same city of Londonderry, by themselves, or by their sufficient ministers or deputies constituted in the city aforesaid, and to [illegible] the said premises, and to bring them to our gaol in the said city of Londonderry, there to be safely kept, until by due process of law they be delivered.

And further, of our more abundant grace, certain knowledge, and mere motion, we will, and by these presents for us, our heirs and successors, do grant to the aforesaid Mayor and Commonalty and Citizens of the city of Londonderry aforesaid, and their successors;—

And also by these presents, we do ordain and establish for ever, that there be and shall be in the said city of Londonderry, two Burgesses of the Parliament, of us, our heirs and successors, and that the Mayor and Commonalty and Citizens of the city of Londonderry aforesaid, and their successors, by virtue of any precept, mandate, or process, upon the writ of us, our heirs and successors, for the election of the Burgesses of the Parliament, to them in that behalf duly directed, may and shall have power, authority, and faculty, to choose and nominate two of the most discreet and sufficient citizens and freemen of the said city, for the time being, to be Burgesses of the Parliament of us, our heirs and successors, for the same city, and the Burgesses so elected, at the costs and charges of the said Mayor and Commonalty and Citizens of the said city of Londonderry aforesaid, and their successors, for the time being, to send to our Parliament, and of our heirs and successors, wheresoever it shall then be holden in the same manner and form as in other places, cities, boroughs, or towns, of our realm of Ireland is used and accustomed, which Burgesses so elected and nominated, we will to be present, and to make their stay at the Parliament of us, our heirs and successors, at the costs and charges of the said Mayor and Commonalty and Citizens, for the time being, during the time that such Parliament shall happen to be holden, in the like manner and form as other Burgesses for the Parliament for any other places, cities, boroughs, or towns, within our realm of Ireland, do, or have been accustomed, or ought to do, and which Burgesses in the Parliament of us, our heirs and successors, may as well have their affirmative as negative voices; and the same may make and execute, and all and singular other things do, as other Burgesses of the Parliament of us, and of our heirs and successors, for whatsoever other places, cities, boroughs, or towns, or other place, city, borough, or town whatsoever, have had, done, and executed, or may have, do, and execute, or may enjoy, by any reason or means whatsoever.

And further we have given and granted, and by these presents for us, our heirs and successors, do give and grant to the aforesaid Mayor and Commonalty and Citizens of the city of Londonderry aforesaid, and their successors, and also we do charge, and firmly for us, our heirs and successors, do command all Sheriffs' Officers and Ministers whatsoever of us, our heirs and successors, of our said city of Londonderry, for the time being, to whom any writ or writs for the election of Burgesses for the Parliament, within our said city of Londonderry, at any time hereafter shall be directed, that every such Sheriffs' Officer or Minister to whom any such writ as is aforesaid hereafter shall

 be

[illegible] or their successors to us, our heirs or successors in that behalf to be exhibited and preferred, and upon due examination and certificate of such doubts or defects, in that behalf to be made by the Attorney-General of us, our heirs or successors of our realm of England, for the time being, we, our heirs and successors, will make and grant or cause to be made and granted to the aforesaid Society and their successors other letters patent to be made [illegible] the Great Seal of England, or with the Great Seal of Ireland, with the explanation, amendment, and supply of the same doubts and defects as it shall seem to be requisite and reasonable in that behalf, to us, our heirs and successors.

And for the better giving, granting, assuring, and confirming the same premises to the same Society and their successors, according to the true intention of these letters patent, and the plain signification of the words in these our letters patent contained, anything in these presents to the contrary notwithstanding.

Provided nevertheless, and our intention is, and we by these presents we declare and signify our good pleasure and intention to be, that if we, our heirs and successors, at any time within the term of three years next following, shall make any commission under the Great Seal of Ireland to our Justices, our heirs or successors, assigned or to be assigned for the assizes in the said county of Londonderry, to survey the aforesaid barony of Loughinsholin aforesaid, and all the lands, tenements, and hereditaments whatsoever in the same barony belonging or appertaining, and whereupon the said justices, by such commission authorised, shall return and certify by virtue of their commission, into our Exchequer of Ireland, any survey or inquisition under the seal of those commissioners, and by such inquisition or survey so taken, returned and certified, shall declare that any part or parcel, parts or parcels, of the aforesaid lands, tenements, or hereditaments, by these letters patent above granted, or passed as members of the said barony of Loughinsholin, or as in the same barony belonging or appertaining, is not nor are within the limits, bounds, or precincts of the same barony, that then immediately after such declaration, within the aforesaid term of three years so as aforesaid made by these our letters patent, that such the aforesaid lands, tenements, and hereditaments, so by the commissioners aforesaid, so within the aforesaid term of three years, declared not to be within the limits, bounds, or precincts of the aforesaid barony, shall be and remain altogether void and of no effect in law, any thing in these presents contained to the contrary notwithstanding.

And the aforesaid Society of the Governor and Assistants, of London, of the new plantation in Ulster, within the realm of Ireland, for themselves and their successors, do covenant and grant to and with us, our heirs and successors, by these presents, that they and their successors, all and singular the aforesaid castles, lands, tenements, limits, franchises, and hereditaments aforesaid, above in these presents excepted, and to the aforesaid Thomas Phillips, Knight, his heirs and assigns, by our aforesaid letters patent under our Great Seal of England sealed, bearing date of the present or as aforesaid granted, and also all other castles, lands, tenements, limits, franchises, and hereditaments whatsoever, which by the true intention of the same letters patent, to the same Thomas Phillips, Knight, his heirs and assigns, are to be given and granted or intended to be given and granted to the same Thomas Phillips, Knight, his heirs and assigns, from time to time, within the space of ten years next following, and after the date of these presents, or at any other time or times hereafter within the space of three years afterwards, and when and as often as the said Society shall obtain other letters patent of us, our heirs and successors, for the regranting, reaffirmation, or new granting the aforesaid castles, lands, tenements, and hereditaments, by these presents before granted, or mentioned to be granted, or any of them, at the request of the same Thomas Phillips, Knight, or his assigns, to the proper use and custody of the same Thomas Phillips, his heirs and assigns, shall be conveyed by such reasonable and sufficient conveyance in the law, as by the counsel of the said Thomas Phillips, his heirs and assigns learned in the law, shall be in that respect reasonably devised or advised, any thing in these presents to the contrary thereof notwithstanding, to be held nevertheless of the said Society of the Governor and Assistants and their successors, by the same and the like rents and services as the said Thomas Phillips holdeth the same from us by virtue of the aforesaid letters patent to the same Thomas Phillips, as is aforesaid before made.

And further, we will, and by these presents for us, our heirs and successors, do grant to the said Society of the Governor and Assistants, London, of the new plantation in Ulster aforesaid, and their successors, and to the aforesaid Mayor and Commonalty and Citizens of the City of Londonderry aforesaid and their successors, that these our letters patent, or the enrolment of the same, shall be in and by all things for ever firm, strong, good, sufficient, and effectual in the law against us, our heirs and successors, as well in all our Courts as elsewhere, within our Kingdoms of England and Ireland, without any confirmation, licences, or toleration, in any manner hereafter to be procured or obtained of us, our heirs or successors.

And notwithstanding the ill naming, or ill reciting, or not reciting the aforesaid territories, lands, tenements, advowsons, waters, rivers, fishings, parcels, and other the premises above by these presents before granted, or any of them, or any parcel thereof.

And notwithstanding the not finding of any office or inquisition of the premises, or any parcel thereof, by which our title ought to be found before the making of these our letters patent.

And notwithstanding the misreciting, or not reciting of any demise, or grant made of the premises, or any parcels thereof being of record, or not of record.

And notwithstanding the misnaming, or not naming, or not truly naming any town, hamlet, parish, place, or county in which the premises, or any part thereof, are or is.

And notwithstanding that of the names of the tenants, farmers, or occupiers of the premises, or any parcel thereof, full, true, and certain mention is not made.

And notwithstanding any defect of or in the certainty, or computation, or declaration, or omission of the true yearly value of the premises, or of any parcel thereof, or of the yearly rent reserved for and upon the premises, or of and upon any parcel thereof, expressed and contained in these our letters patent.

And notwithstanding any other defects, in not naming, or not truly naming, any tenant, farmer, or occupier of the premises, or any parcel thereof.

And notwithstanding the statute made in the Parliament of the Lord Henry the 8th, late King of England our Predecessor, the 18th year of his reign.

And notwithstanding any other defects in the not truly and rightly naming of the nature, kind, form, quantity, or quality of the premises, or any parcel thereof.

And notwithstanding any law, statute, provision, ordinance, direction, restraint, or any other thing, cause, or matter whatsoever.

Also we will, and by these presents for us, our heirs and successors, do grant to the aforesaid Society of the Governor and Assistants, London, of the new plantation in Ulster aforesaid, that they may and shall have these our letters patent, in due manner made and sealed under our Great Seal of England, without fine or fee, great or small, in any manner therefore to be yielded, paid or made to us in our hanaper, or elsewhere, to our use.

And that express mention of the annual value, or of the certainty of the premises, or any of them, or of other gifts, or grants by us, or by any of our progenitors or predecessors, made to the aforesaid Society of the Governor and Assistants, of London, of the new plantation in Ulster aforesaid, before this time in these presents particularly set forth, or any statute, act, ordinance, proviso, proclamation, or restraint to the contrary thereof, heretofore had, made, passed, ordained, or provided, or any other thing, cause, or matter whatsoever, in any wise notwithstanding. In witness whereof we have caused these our letters to be made patent.

Provided that the Governor and Assistants, London, of the new plantation in Ulster aforesaid, do inrol, or cause to be inrolled, these our letters patent, in the office of our Remembrancer of the Treasurer of our Exchequer in England, within six months after the date hereof, to the end the same may there remain of record to our use.

Witness myself at Westminster, the twenty-ninth day of March, in the year of our reign of England, France, and Ireland, the 11th, and of Scotland the 46th.

NOTE.

The above translation of the Charter of King James the First is (with the exception of the last paragraph ... on the 46th page) copied from the Charter ... in the book entitled the "... Narrative of the ... Irish Society." In that book there is a blank space left in that particular paragraph. In consequence of the blank the paragraph has been ... from the Latin copy of the Charter in the Public Record Office, ... in the City of London, and the new translation has been ... for that in the book above ... For the information of the Court of the Mercers' Company the actual wording of the ... paragraph in Latin is as follows:—

"[illegible] etiam, ut p presentes p nobis heredibus & successoribus [illegible]
"[illegible] respective conveniend & assignand in scripl & sub sigillo [illegible]
"Societatis Gubernator & assistent London Nove Plantacois [illegible]
"eardem [illegible] respective ad [illegible]
"[illegible] & reputabunt et erunt [illegible] tenore et virtute [illegible]."

APPENDIX, No. 11.

PAPER handed in by the Chairman.

LICENCE TO HOLD IN MORTMAIN.

[illegible]

[illegible] JAMES by the Grace of God &c. To all to whom &c. [illegible] Companies Corporations and Fraternities of and within our Cittie of London in our Realme of England [illegible] works of Plantation [illegible] by the Mayor and Comminaltie and Citizens of our said Citee of London in the Cittie of Derrie and Towne of Coleraine in our Realme of Ireland [illegible]

[illegible]

In witness whereof &c. witness ourself at Westminster the thirtieth day of September.

P BRE DE PRIVATO SIGILLO.

This is a true Copy from the Original Record remaining in the Chapel of the Rolls, having been examined.

HENRY GAWLER

APPENDIX, No. 12.

PAPER handed in by the Chairman.

GRANT to the Company of Mercers, 17th October 1618.

THIS INDENTURE made the Seventeenth daie of October Anno Dni 1618 And in the yeares of the Raigne of or Soveraigne Lord James by the grace of God King of England Scotland ffraunce & Ireland Defendor of the faith etc that is to saie of England ffraunce & Ireland the sixteenth & and of Scotland the two & fiftith Betweene the Societie of the Governor & assistants of London of the new plantacon in Ulster within the realme of Ireland of the one part And the Wardens & Comunaltie of the misterie of the Mercers of the Citty of London of the other part Witnesseth that the said Societie of the Governor & assistants of London of the new plantacon in Ulster within the realme of Ireland As well for & in consideracon of a certaine competent somme of monie to them in hand before the sealing & delivery of theis pntes by the said Wardens & Comunaltie of the misterie of the Mercers aforesaid well and trulie paid whereof they the said Societie confesse & acknowledge the receipt and themselves therewith fully satisfied & contented. And thereof & of every part and parcell thereof do clearlie acquite exonerate & discharge the said Wardens & Comunaltie of the misterie of the Mercers their successors & assignes & every of them by theis pntes as for divers other good and waightie consideracons the said Societie thereunto especially moveing have graunted bargained sould aliened enfeoffed & confirmed And by theis pntes do for & from them the said Societie and their successors fullie clearelie & absolutlie graunt bargaine sell alien enfeoff & confirme unto the said Wardens & Comunaltie of the misterie of the Mercers aforesaid & their successors & assignes for ever all that the mannor of Mercers with the rights members & appurtenances thereof lying & beeing within the Countie of Londonderry within the province of Ulster within the realme of Ireland. That is to saie all that Mannor created & made of & uppon the Ballibos of land called or knowne by the name of Bovead lying and beeing in the Baronie of Colerane in the Countie of Londonderry aforesaid. And of & upon all that Territorie Ballebetoe or porcon of land called or knowne by the name of Mulle Inch within the Countie of Londonderry & province of Ulster aforesaid that is to saie All lands tenements and other hereditaments called or knowne by the names hereafter mentioned or lying and beeing of in or within the severall Townes Villages Hamletts places Ballibos or parcells of land following That is to saie Lanvore beeing one ballibos of land Carnhee beeing one ballibos of land Tawlett beeing one ballibos of land Culdrumn Drum beeing one ballibos of land with all & singular their & every of their rights appurtenances & members And of & uppon all that territorie Ballibettoe or porcon of land called or knowne by the name of Ballina Moina in the Countie of Londonderrie aforesaid That is to saie all lands Tenemts & other hereditaments known or called by the names hereafter mentioned or lying & beeing of in or within the Towne Villag hamlets place Ballibos or parcell of land following That is to saie Mavanaher beeing one ballibos of land with all and singular the rights members & appurtenances thereof And of & upon all that territory ballibettoe or porcon of land called or knowne by the name of Finabe Rushe or Grange in the Countie of Londonderry aforesaid that is to saie All lands Tenemts & other hereditaments knowne or called by the names hereafter mentioned or lying & beeing of in or within the severall townes villages hamletts places Ballibos or parcells of land following That is to saie Clare Letrim being one ballibos of land Leah Leave being one ballibos of land Moyegran being one ballibos of land Killaddy being one ballibos of land Neagena being one ballibos of land Moyknock being one ballibos of land Lisleah being one ballibos of land ffalla Cagey being one ballibos of land Lismegroat being one ballibos of land with all and singuller their and every of their appurtenances & members & also of & uppon all that Territorie Ballibettoe or porcon of land called or knowne by the name of Saroottmona within the Countie of Londonderry aforesaid That is to saie all lands Tenemts & other hereditaments knowne or called by the names hereinafter mentioned or lying & beeing of in or within the severall Townes Villages Hamletts places Ballibos or parcells of land following That is to saie Dromaarrah being one ballibos of land Dillahey being one ballibos of land Moylatroloy being one ballibos of land Crosse Clount being one ballibos of land Oregopola being one ballibos of land Ballymanat being one ballibos of land Larah being one ballibos of land Lisslurin being one ballibos of land with all and singular their and every of their appurtenances & members And also of and uppon all that Territory ballibettoe or porcon of land called or knowne by the name of Ballenleagh within the Countie of Londonderry aforesaid That is to saie all lands Tenemts & other hereditaments knowne or called by the names hereafter mentioned or lying & beeing of in or within the severall townes villages or hamletts places ballibos or parcells of land following that is to saie Dennaher being one ballibos of land Ballelemie being one ballibos of land Teway Ringog being one ballibos of land Carhallen Tubber being one ballibos of land with all and singular theire & every of theire appurtenances & members And also of and uppon all that Territorie Ballibetoe or porčon of land knowne or called by the name of Dunglady in the said Countie of Londonderry within the province of Ulster aforesaid That is to saie all lands tenem^{ts} & other hereditaments knowne or called by the names hereafter menčoned or lying and being of in or within the severall Townes Villages Hamletts places ballibones or parcells of land following that is to saie Moniah Allen being one ballibo of land Daugher' Conwale being one ballibo of land Lismolis being one ballibo of land Bally Kany being one ballibo of land Bally Money being one ballyboe of land Ballino Keely being one ballibo of land Coolnaglee being one ballibo of land Gwotrah being one ballibo of land Gravahan being one ballibo of land Ballenabuber being one ballibo of land Amlord Lane being one ballibo of land Tarrengora being one ballibo of land Drumnik being one ballibo of land Tere Carwell being one ballibo of land Mackab being one ballibo of land Mourcharpan being one ballibo of land Tare being one ballibo of land Knockmeale being one ballibo of land Sletmeale being one ballibo of land Dooglasley being one ballibo of land with all and singular theire & every of their Appurtenñces & Members whatsoever Or by whatsoever other name or names the same lands Tenemen^{ts} & premisses before in theis pñtes severallie or pticularlie named or menčoned as aforesaid or anie of them are called reputed known or taken All and singular wch lands Tenemts hereditaments & premisses aforesaid are contained within the Mercers proporčon number eight according to their lott or division with other Companyes and were latelie by the said Societie by force of & according to the kings Maj^{ts} letters patents to them in that behalf granted made erected ordained and reduced into a mano^{r} to consist of such Tenants as in the said letters patents is menčoned And the same Manno^{r} & all & singular the premisses by the said Societie made or menčoned and intended to be made a Manno^{r} as aforesaid were by the said Societie by force of & according to the said letters patents named and called by the name of the Mano^{r} of Mercers And also the said Societie of the Governo^{r} & Assistants of London of the new plantačon in Ulster within the Realme of Ireland for the considerašon aforesaid have granted bargained sould Aliened enfeoffed & confirmed And by theis pñtes do absolutlie grant bargain sell Alien enfeoffe & confirme unto the said Wardens & Comunaltie of the mystery of the Mercers of the City of London their successors and assignes for ever All and every the rents issues of Court rolles of mill Releifes pains^{s} in name of Releifes fines for Alienačon heriotts forfeitures & all other dutys & pains^{s} and services reserved due or payable by or from the free or other Tenants of the said Mano^{r} And all and singular Messuages houses Barnes cottages bawnes buildings edifices Mills lands Tenem^{ts} Meadowes pastures Comõns Advowsons donačons presentačons oblačons Tithes wastgrounds ffurres heaths Marrishes Moores Bogges Mountaines Mosses Mines Quarryes & Mineralls & Ewres of what nature qualitie or condičon soever they be not being Mines Royall woods underwoods waters watercourses weares fishings fishing places fowling Courts Baron Courts Leete perquisites & proffites of Courts Baron & Courts Leete veiwes of ffranckpledge and all that to veiw of ffranckpledge doth appertaine with free libertie to keep the same Courts goods & chattells waived strayed And all lands goods and chattels of ffellons diodands goods confiscated fferm escheates fforfeitures Releifes herriotts fines amerciamts libertyes priviledges estovers ffaires markets tolls Customes And all other proffits commodities emoluments Royalties & hereditam^{ts} whatsoever of what nature qualitie or condičon soever they be within the said Countie of Londonderry or elsewhere within the said Realme of Ireland to the said Mannore lands Tenements hereditam^{ts} & premisses aforesaid & every or anie of them belonging or in anie wise appertaining or accepted reputed deemed or taken as pt parcell or member of the said mano^{rs} lands & premisses or of or belonging unto the same or anie part thereof And the reverčon and reverčons remainder & remainders rents issues and proffits of all & singular the said manno^{rs} lands & premisses & of every part & pcell thereof And all rents Services dutys & paimts whatsoever respectivlie reserved due & payable by or from all and every the free or other tenants of the said Manno^{r} & other the premisses And also the estate & estates right title interest inheritance pportie claim & demand whatsoever of the said societie of in and to the said manno^{rs} lands & premisses & every pt & pcell thereof Together with all and every the deedes evidences & writings touching or concerning onley the said manno^{rs} lands & premisses or onelie anie part or parcell thereof except neverthelesse and out of theis pnts alwaye reserved unto the said Societie of the Governor & assistants of London of the new plantačon in Ulster within the realme of Ireland their successo^{rs} & Assignes All timber Trees growing or being or that hereafter shall grow or be in or uppon the foresaid pmisses or anie part thereof with free libertie to & for the said Societie their Successors & assignes when & as often as they shall think good to fell cutt down & carry awaie the same & every or anie part thereof And also excepted & reserved to the said Societie theire Successors and assignes free libertie to hawke hunt fishe fowle come go ride carry & re-carry over in through & uppon the said pmisses & every part & parcell thereof at all times convenient And also excepted & out of theis pñts reserved all the fishing & taking of Salmon Eels & other fishes in the Rivers of Banne & Loughfoyle within the province of Ulster aforesaid And in all creeks & members of the same rivers & either of them And all the soile & ground of the said rivers & either of them And also free libertie for the said Societie their successo^{rs} & assignes to digg and search in the premisses aforegranted or any pt thereof except & other then in the houses gardens Orchards Meadows or lands sowne with corn for Stone slate Loame Gravell Sand & other necessary materialls & the same to take & carry awaie to be employed & converted for in & about buildings in the foresaid county & province which premisses in & by theis pñtes excepted or menčoned to be excepted & every of them & every part & pcell of them and every of them the said Wardens & Comunaltie of the Mystery of the Mercers aforesaid for them their successors & assignes do Covenant & grant to & with the said Societie of the Governor & Assistants

Assistants of London of the new plantacon in Ulster in the realme of Ireland their successo[rs] & assignes by theis p[re]ntes That they the said Societie their Successo[rs] Agents servants & assignes shall & maie from time to time at all times hereafter have hold take use carry awaie and enjoy freelie without lett or interrupcon of the said Wardens & Comunaltie of the Mistery of the Mercers of the Cittye of London their Successo[rs] or Assignes To have and to hould the said Mano[r] of Mercers with all & singular other the premisses except before excepted with the rights Members & appurtenances thereof And all & every the said lands tenem[en]ts & hereditam[en]ts & all & singular other the premisses afore hereby graunted bargained & sould or meant menconed or intended to be hereby graunted bargained or sould with their & every of their rights members & Appurtenances & every part & parcell thereof except before excepted Unto the said Wardens & Comunaltie of the Mistery of Mercers of the Cittye of London their Successo[rs] & Assignes for ever to the onelie use & behoof of the said Wardens & Comunaltie of the mistery of the Mercers of the Cittye of London their successo[rs] & assignes for ever Yielding and paying therefore yearlie to the said Societie of the Governo[r] & Assistants of London of the new plantacon in Ulster their Successo[rs] & Assignes the some of Thirteene shillings & foure pence of lawfull current monie of and in England at two feasts or termes of the yeare That is to sai att the feasts of Th'Annunciacon of the blessed Virgin Mary & S[t] Michaell Th'Archangell by even porcons at or in the Chamber of London situate in or neare Guildhall in the Cittye of London in the realm of England And if it shall happen the said yearely rent of Thirteene shillings and foure pence or anie part thereof to be behind & unpaid in part or in all after any Terme of paym[en]t in w[hi]ch it ought to be paid according to the true meaning of theis p[re]ntes That then & so often it shall & maie be lawfull to and for the said Societie of the Governor and Assistants of London of the new plantacon in Ulster their Successo[rs] & Assignes into the p[re]misses afore graunted & every or anie p[ar]cell thereof to enter & distraine & the Distresses so taken to lead chase drive & carry awaie & with them to detain until the foresaid rent so beeing behind & all arrearages (if anie shalbe) according to the true meaning of theis p[re]ntes shall be to them fully satisfied & paid And the said Societie of the Governo[r] & Assistants of London of the new plantacon in Ulster within the realme of Ireland for them & their successo[rs] do covenant promise and grant to & with the said Wardens & Comunaltie of the mistery of the Mercers aforesaid their Successo[rs] & Assignes by theis p[re]ntes that they the said Wardens & Comunaltie of the mistery of the Mercers their Successo[rs] & Assignes paying the rent aforesaid & under the covenants and agreem[en]ts in theis p[re]nts contained shall or maie at all times from henceforth for ever lawfully peaceablie and quietlie have hould occupie possesse & enjoy the said Manno[r] lands Tenem[en]ts hereditam[en]ts & all & singular other the premisses afore hereby graunted bargained & sould or meant menconed or intended to be hereby graunted bargained or sould and every part & parcell thereof with their appurtenances except before excepted & receive p[er]ceive take & enjoy to their owne use and uses for ever all the Rents issues & proffitts thereof as well without any lawfull lett suite trouble molestacon recoverye evicon expulsion or interrupcon of or by the said Societie of the Governor & Assistants of London of the new plantacon aforesaid their Successo[rs] or Assignes or of or by anie other p[er]son or p[er]sons lawfully claiming or to claime by from or under them or anie of them or their or anie of their Act estate means authoritie consent or procurement as also free cleare & freelie & clearlie acquited exonerated & discharged or well & sufficientlie saved & kept harmless by the said Societie their Successo[rs] or Assignes of & from all and singular former bargaines sales gifts graunts leases Alienacons Arrearages of Rents estates charges and encumbrances whatsoever had made committed or done by the said Societie before the sealing & delivery thereof except one Deed made by the said Societie whereby the said Manno[r] is erected made & ordained as aforesaid and except all graunts or estates by Indentures made & graunted or to be made or graunted by the said Societie to severall p[er]sons or freehould tenants of the said Mannor of p[ar]t of the premisses under certaine Rents and Services All and every which Rents dutys & services in the said excepted Indentures heretofore referred shall for & notwithstanding any act or thing made or done or to be made or done by the said Society their successors or Assignes to the Contrary be henceforth yearlie due & payable to the said Wardens and Comunaltie of the mistery of the Mercers their successors & Assignes during the continuance in force of the same graunts & estates respectivelie And further the said Societie of the Governor and Assistants of London of the new plantacon in Ulster within the realme of Ireland for them their Successo[rs] & Assignes do covenant p[ro]mise & grant to and with the said Wardens & Comunaltie of the mistery of the Mercers aforesaid their Successo[rs] & Assignes & every of them by theis p[re]ntes That it shall and maie be lawfull to and for the said Wardens & Comunaltie of the mistery of the Mercers aforesaid their successors & assignes by the appointm[en]t of the generall Agent of the said Societie for the time being resident in Ulster for the affaires of the saide Societie To fell cutt downe take & carry awaie such & so manie of the Timber Trees of the said Societie standing growing & being nearest or most convenient to the p[re]misses aforegraunted as shall be fitt & necessary for the building or plantacon of anie houses villages edifices or buildings within the said Manno[r] lands and premisses AND also that they the said Societie their Successors & Assignes shall & will paie & discharge all rents dutys & other paimts now due & payable or hereafter to be due & payable to the king's most excellent Ma[jes]tie his heires or Successo[rs] for or in respect of the said Manno[r] lands & premisses or anie part thereof or thereof shall save harmless the said Wardens & Comunaltie & their Successors & all the p[re]misses by theis p[re]ntes graunted or intended to be graunted And further that the said Societie their Successors & assignes shall & will from Time to Time & at all Times hereafter for and during the space of Ten yeares upon every reasonable request and at the Costs & Charges in the law of the said Wardens & Comunaltie their Successors and assignes make do execute & p[er]forme all & every such further conveyances & assurances in the law whatsoever bee it by Deed or

Deeds release Confirmacon or otherwise for the further better & more pfect & absolute assurance Conveying & assuring of the said Mano' lands premisses under the rent aforesaid except as before is excepted unto the said Wardens & Comunaltie their Successors & Assignes for ever As by the said Wardens and Comunaltie their Successors or Assignes or their Councell learned shall be reasonablie advised devised & required so as the said Conveyances & Assurances do containe no further Warrantie nor Covenantes for every the premisses then against the said Societie and their Successors onelie AND for the better estating establishing & assuring of the said Manno' lands & premisses & every pt & pcell thereof in unto & upon the said Wardens & Comunaltie of the Mistery of the Mercers aforesaid their Successo^{rs} & Assignes according to the true meaning of theis pñtes The said Society of the Governor & Assistants of London of the new plantacon in Ulster within the realme of Ireland do by theis pñtes constitute ordaine & appoint Tristram Berrisford of Coleraine Esquire & Robert Goodwin of Londonderry gentleman their true & lawfull Attorneys joinctlie & either of them severallie for the said Society & in their name & stead to enter into & uppon the said Manno' & premisses & every or anie pt thereof except before excepted and after entry so made for the said Society and in their name & stead in & uppon the same Mano^{rs} Lands & premisses except before excepted or in or upon anie part thereof in the name of the whole to give & deliver unto the said Wardens & Comunaltie of the mistery of the Mercers aforesaid their Successo^{rs} & Assignes or to their certaine attorney in that behalf authorised full & peaceable possession & Seisin of all & singular the same Manno' lands & premisses & every part thereof except before excepted To hould unto the said Wardens & Coialtie their Successo^{rs} & Assignes according to the forme force & effect of these pñtes ratifying confirming & allowing for good & effectuall in law all & whatsoever the said attorneys joyntlie or either of them severallie shall do in or about the premisses In witnes whereof to the one part of theis pñte Indentures remaining with the said Wardens & Comunaltie of the Mistery of the Mercers of the Cittie of London aforesaid the said Society of the Governo' & Assistants of London of the new plantacon in Ulster in the realme of Ireland have caused their Common Seale to be putt & to the other part thereof remaining with the said Societie the said Wardens & Comunaltie aforesaid have put to their Comon Seale Dated the day & yeare first above written.

The document appears to be signed ex^{d} Jo: Praky Govr By order and authority of the Govr and Committee of London Plantacons in Ireland Samuel Calvert Secretary Ex^{d}.

MEMORANDU That on the fifteenth day of March Anno Dni 1618 and in the Sixteenth yeare of the Raigne of our Soveraigne Lord Kinge James of England ffraunce & Ireland and of Scotland the two and fiftith the w^{th}in named Robert Goodwin for and in the name and stead of the Society of the Governor and assistants of London of the new Plantacon in Ulster within the Realme of Ireland w^{th}in menconed did enter into and upon the Towne Village Hamlette Pines Ballibos or parcell of Lande called Mavanmaher parte of the Mannor of Mercers w^{th}in bargained and after entry so made that is to say the same day & yeare aforesayd the said Robert Goodwin for the said Society and in their name and stead at the Castell or capital Mansion howse situate in and upon Mavanmaher aforesaid in the name of the whole Manor Lands Tente & hereditaments w^{th}in bargained did give and deliver full and peaceable possession and seisin of all and singular the said Mannor Lands Tente and hereditaments w^{th}in bargained and of every parte thereof (except as in w^{th}in excepted) unto Richard Vernon Agent Attorney of the Wardens & Comunalty of the Mistery of the Mercers of the City of of London w^{th}in menconed in the name and stead of the said Wardens and Comunalty and Unto and for the use and behoof of them their Successors and assignes to hould unto the said Wardens and Comunalty their Successors and assignes according to the forme tenor and effecte of the Indenture w^{th}in written wth possession & Seisin so given and delivered as aforesaid was by the said Richard Vernon on the day yeare and at the Castell or capitall Mansion Howse aforesaid received and taken to the use & behoofe aforesaid by virtue and according to a letter of Attorney in that behalf made under the Common Seal of the said Wardens and Comunalty bearing date the twelfth day of January in the yeare abovesaid All wch was done in the presence of us who names are hereunder written.

OLIVER MATHEW CLARKE   WILLIAM PERRY.
ROBERT THORNTON.   THOMAS HUDSON.

The marke of JOHN HUDSON.
The marke of RALPH VERNON.
The marke of DONELL O'QUIN.
The marke of CHARLES WILLIAMS.
The marke of WILLIAM COFTON.
The marke of HUGH O'CURAN.

APPENDIX, No. 13.

PAPER handed in by the *Chairman*.

Grant from the Irish Society to the Ironmongers' Company, dated 7th November, 1618, 16th James the First.

This Indenture, made the seaventh daie of Nvember, Anno Dni. 1618, Stilo Angliæ, and in the yeares of the Raigne of o Soveraigne Lord James, by the Grace of God King of England, Scotland, Fraunce, and Ireland, Defender of the Faith, &c., That is to saie, of England, Fraunce, & Ireland the sixteenth, & of Scotland the two & ffiftieth, Betweene the Societie of the Governour & Assistants of London of the new Plantacon in Ulster, wthin the Kingdome of Ireland, on the one part, and the Maister & Keeps or Wardens & Comunaltie of the mistery or art of Ire Mongers, London, of the other part, Witnesseth that the said Societie of the Govenor & Assistants of London of the new Plantacon in Ulster, wthin the Kingdome Ireland, as well for & in consideration of, a certaine competent somme of monie to them in hand, before the sealling & delivery of theis pntes by the said Maister & Keepers or Wardens & Comunaltie of the misterie or art of Ire Mongers, London, aforesaid, well & truile paid; whereof they, the said Societie, confesse and acknowledge the receipt, and themselves therewth fullie satisfied & contented, and thereof, & of every part & parcell thereof, do clearlie aquite, exonerate, & discharge the said Maister & Keepers or Wardens, their successors and assignes, & every of them, by these pntes, As for divers others good and waightie consideracons them espiallie moveing, Have graunted, bargained, & sould, aliened, enfeoffed, & confirmed, & by theis pntes do for & from them, the said Societie and their successors, fully, clearely, & absolutely graunt, bargaine, sell, alien, enfeoffe, & confirme unto the said Maister & Keeps or Wardens & Comunaltie of the Mistery or art of Ire Mongers, London, aforesaid, & their successors & assignes for ever, All that the Mannor of Lizard, wth the rights, members, & appurtenances thereof lying & being within the County of Londonderry, wthin the province of Ulster, wthin the Realm of Ireland: That is to saie, all that Mannor created and made of & uppon twenty & one Ballibos of the Ballibetaes of Balleas Monie lying in the Barronie of Colerane, wthin the Countie of Londonderry, & of & upon the Ballibos called Garvahey, wthin the said Barronie of Colerane, & of & upon all that Territorie, Ballibettoe, or porcon of land called or knowne by the name of Ath Geme Grange, in the Countie of Londonderry aforesaid; That is to saie, all landes, Tenemts, & other hereditamts, knowne or called by the names hereafter menconed or lying, and being of, in, or wthin the severall Townes, Villages, hamletts, places, ballibos, or parcells of land following, That is to saie, Bally Renh, being one ballibos of land; Bennamore, being one ballibos of land; two third parts of Glaskarl, being two third parts of a ballibos of land; two third parts of Mullamore, being two third parts of a ballibos of land; Ballego Geene, being one ballibos of land; Colerow, being one ballibos of land, wth all & singuler their and every of their appurtenances and Members; And of and upon all that Territorie, Ballibettoe, or porcon of land, called or knowne by the name of Mulla Inch, in the said County of Londonderry aforesaid, That is to saie, all Landes, Tenemts, & other hereditamts, knowne or called by the names hereafter menconed, or lying, & being of, in, or wthin the severall Townes, Villages, Hamletts, places, ballibos, or parcells of land following, That is to saie, Drumtable, being one ballibos of land; Skaltee, being one ballibos of land; Knockduffe, being one ballibos of land; Clonbach, being one ballibos of land; Bnakey, being one ballibos of land; Clarhill, being one ballibos of land; Cloniken, being one ballibos of land; Core Monie, being one ballibos of land; Shaloch, being one ballibos of land; Cleggan, being one ballibos of land; Renske, being one ballibos of land, Mulla Inch, being one ballibos of land; Gortfaddy, being one ballibos of land; Conkerrall, being one ballibos of land; Ringraffe, being one ballibos of land; Condrum, being one ballibos of land; wth all & singuler their & every of their appurtenances & members; And also of & upon all that Territorie, ballibettoe, or porcon of land, called or knowne by the name of Moytalla, wthin the Countie of Londonderry aforesaid, That is to saie, all lands, tenemts, & other hereditamts, called or knowne by the names hereafter menconed, or lying & being of, in, or wthin the severall Townes, Villages, Hamletts, places, ballibos, or parcells of land following, That is to saie, two Cullens, being two ballibos of land, wth all & singuler their and every of their Appurtenances and Members; And also, of & uppon all that Territory, ballibettoe, or porcon of land, called or knowne by the name of Kannakille, in the County of Londonderry aforesaid, that is to saie, all Lands, Tenemts, & other hereditaments, knowne or called by the name hereafter menconed, or lying & being of, in, or wthin the severall Townes, Villages, Hamletts, Places, ballibos, or parcells of land following, that is to saie, Balline Noste, being one ballibos of land; one-fowerth part of Bally Shaslan, being one-fowerth part of a ballibos of land; Ballybrack, being one ballibos of land; Ballielogh, being one ballibos of land; Color, being one ballibos of land; Drum Cram, being one ballibos of land; Bally Willyam, being one

ballibos

ballibos of land; Killrah, beeing one ballibos of land; Kilnagiaffe, beeing one ballibos of land; Ballinachmtah, beeing one ballibos of land; Balline Clan, beeing one ballibos of land; wth all & singuler their & every of their Appurtenances & Members; and also, of & uppon all that Territory, Ballibetton, or porcon of land, called or knowne by the name of Ogovenall, in the said County of Londonderry, wthin the Province of Ulster, aforesaid; That is to saie, all Landes, Tenements, & other hereditamts knowne or called by the names hereafter menconed or lying, & being of, in, or wthin the severall Townes, Villages, Hamletts, places, ballibos, or parcells of land following, that is to saie, Bally Ghagan, beeing one ballibos of land; Bai-bloin, beeing one ballibos of land; Carrowren, beeing one ballibos of land; Tavay Moore, beeing one ballibos of land; Cab, beeing one ballibos of land; Lisball, beeing one ballibos of land; Lisfaloy, beeing one ballibos of land; Taldaffe, beeing one ballibos of land; Lifne Crvoy, beeing one ballibos of land, wth all & singuler their & every of their appertenances & members; And also of & upon all that Territory, Ballibetton, or porcon of land, knowne or called by the name of Ballene Fesigh, in the said County of Londonderry, wthin the province of Ulster aforesaid, That is to saie, all lands, Tenemts, & other hereditamts knowne or called by the names hereafter menconed or lying, and beeing of, in, or wthin the severall Townes, Villages, Hamletts, Places, Ballibos or Parcells of land following, That is to saie, Terkarrin, beeing one Ballibos of land; Gortylagon, beeing one ballibos of land; Makeremoore, beeing one ballibos of land; Coolian, beeing one ballibos of land; Slatanerty, beeing one ballibos of land; Dommaine, beeing one ballibos of land; Brackaloy, beeing one ballibos of land; Colerankean, beeing one ballibos of land, wth all & singuler their & every of their appertenances & Members; And also of & upon all that Territory, Ballibetton, or porcon of land, knowne or called by the name of Farnaltnouan, in the said Countie of Londonderry, wthin the province of Ulster aforesaid, That is to saie, all Lands, Tenemts, & other hereditaments knowne or called by the names hereafter menconed or lying, & beeing of, in, or wthin the severall Townes, Villages, hamletts, places, ballibos, or parcells of land following, that is to saie, Ballimoore, beeing one ballibos of land; Tulanbane, beeing one ballibos of land; Treen Altens, beeing one ballibos of land, wth all & singuler their & every of their appertenances & members whatsoev'. Or by whatsoever other name or names the same landes, tenemts, & premises before in theis pntes severally or pticularly named or menconed as aforesaid, or anie of them are called, reputed, knowne, or taken. All & singuler wch lands, Tenemts, Hereditamts, & premisses aforesaid, are contained wthin the Ire Mongers proporcon, number seven, according to their lots, or devision with other companies, & were lately, by the said Society, by force of & accordinge to the Kings Matis letters patents, to them in that behalf granted, made, erected, ordained, & reduced into a Mannor, to consist of such Tenants as in the said Letters Patents is menconed; And the same Mannor, & all & singuler the premisses by the said Societie made or menconed or intended to be made a Mannor as aforesaid, were by the said Society, by force of & according to the said letters Patents, named & called by the name of the Mannor of the Lizard; And also the said Societie of the Governor & Assistants of London, of the new Plantacon in Ulster, wthin the Realme of Ireland, for the consideracon aforesaid, Have granted, bargained, sould, aliened, enfeoffed, & confirmed, and by theis pntes do absolutelie grannt, bargaine, sell, alien, enfeoffe, & confirme unto the said Maister & Keeps or Wardens & Comltie of the Mistery or Art of Ire Mongers, London, their successors and assignes for ever, all & every the Rents, Suites of Court, suites of mill, releefes, paimts, in the names of Releefes, fines for alienacon, herriotts, & forfeitures, & all other dutyes, paimts, & services reserved, due, or payable by or from the free or other Tenants of the said Mannor, and all & singuler Messuages, Houses, Barnes, Cottages, Bawnes, Buildings, Edifices, Mills, Lands, Tenements, Meadows, Pastures, Commons, Advowsons, Donacons, Presentacons, oblacons, tithes, wast grounds, furzes, heathes, marishes, moores, bogges, mountaines, mines, quarryes, & Mineralls & Ewres of what nature, qualitie, or condicon soever they be, not beeing mines royall, woods, underwoods, waters, watercourses, weares, fishings, fishing places, fowling, courts baron, courts leete, perquisites, and profitts of courts baron and courte leete, viewes of frankpledge, and all that to view of frankpledg doth appertaine, wth free libertie to keepe the same Courts, goods, & chattells waived, strayed, & all lands, goods, and chattells of felons, deodands, goods confiscated, fees, eschetes, forfeitures, reliefes, herriotts, fines, amerciamts, libertyes, privileges, estovers, faires, marketts, tolls, customes, & all other proffitts, commodityes, emolumts, royaltyes, & hereditamts whatsoev', of what nature qualitie or condicon soever they be, wthin the said Countie of Londonderry, or elsewhere wthin the said Realme of Ireland, to the said Mannor, lands, tenemts, hereditamts, & premisses aforesaid, & every or anie of them belonging to or in anie wise appertaining or accepted, reputed, deemed or taken as pt, pcell, or member of the said Mannor, lands, and premisses, or of or belonging unto the same, or anie part thereof; And the reverson & reversons, remainder and remainders, rents, issues, & proffitts of all & singuler the said Mannor, lands, & premisses, & of every part & parcell thereof, And all rents, services, dutyes, & paimts whatsoever, respectivelie reserved, due, and payable by or from all & every the free or other Tenants of the said Mannor, & other the Premisses; And also all the estate & estates, right, title, interest, inheritance, propertie, claime, & demand whatsoever of the said Societie, of, in, & to the said Mannor, lands, & premisses, & every part or pcel thereof, together wth all & every the deedes, evidences, and writings, touching or concerning onelie the said Mannor, lands, & premisses, or onelie anie pt or pcell thereof, Except, neverthelesse, & out of theis pntes, allwaies reserved unto the said Societie of the Governor and Assistants of London of the new plantacon, in Ulster, wth the Realme of Ireland, their successors and assignes; all Timber Trees, growing or beeing, or that hereafter shall grow, or be in, or upon the foresaid premisses, or anie part thereof, wth free libertie to & for the said Societie, their successors & assignes, when & as often as they shall think good to fell, cut downe, and carrie awaie the same, & every or anie part thereof; And also excepted & reserved to the said Societie, their

successors

successors & assignes, free libertie to hawke, hunt, fish, fowle, come, go, ride, carry, & recarry over, in, through, & upon the same premisses, & every part & pcell thereof, by all waies of nell, & at all times convenient; And also excepted, and out of this pnte grant reserved, all the fishing, & taking of Salmons, Eeles, & other Fishes, in the Rivers of Banne & Loughfoile, wthin the Province of Ulster aforesaid, & in all Creekes & members of the same Rivers & either of them; And all the soile and ground of the said rivers & either of them; And also free libertie to & for the said Societie, their successors and assignes, to digg & search in the premisses above granted or anie part thereof, except & other then in the houses, gardens, orchards, meadowes, or lands, sowed wth Corne, for Stone, Slate, Loame, Gravell, Sand, & other necessary materialls, & the same to take & carry awaie to be employed & converted for, in, & about buildings in the foresaid County & province; Which premisses in & by their pnte excepted or mentioned to be excepted, & every of them, & every part & parcell of them, & every of them, the said Maister & Keeps, or Wardens & Comunaltie of the Mistery or Art of Ire Mongers, London, aforesaid, for them, their successors, & assignes, do covenant & graunt to & wth the said Societie of the Governor & assistants of London, of the new plantacon, in Ulster, in the Realme of Ireland, their successors & assignes, by their pntes that they the said Societie, their successors, Agents, Servants, & Assignes, shall, & maie from time to time & at all times hereafter, have, hold, take, use, & carry awaie, & enjoy freelie wthout lett or interrupcon of the said Maister & Keeps, or Wardens & Comunaltie of the mistery or art of Ire Mongers, London, their successors or assignes, To have and to hold the said Mannor of Lizard, wth all & singular other the premisses, except before excepted with the rights, members, & appurtenances thereof, and all & every the said landes, tenemts & hereditamts, & all & singular other the premisses above hereby granted, enfeoffed, bargained, sould, or meant, menconed, or intended to be hereby granted, enfeoffed, bargained, or sould, with their & every of their rights, members, and appurtenances, & every part and pcell thereof, except before excepted unto the said Maister & Keeps, or Wardens, & Comunaltie of the Mistery, or Art of Ire Mongers, London, their Successors & Assignes for ever, To the onely use and behoofe of the said Maister & Keeps, or Wardens & Comunaltie of the Mistery or Art of Ire Mongers, London, their successors & assignes for ever. Yielding and paying therefore yearelie to the said Societie of the Governor & Assistants of London of the new plantacon in Ulster, their Successors & assignes, the somme of Eleven pounds, five shillings & eight-pence, of lawfull & current monie of & in England, at two Feasts or termes of the yeare, that is to saie, at the Feasts of St. Michaell Th Archangell, & the Annunciacon of the Blessed Virgin Mary by even porcons, at or in the Chamber of London, situate in or neare Guildhall, in the Citty of London, in the Realme of England; And if it shall happen the said yearely rent of Eleven pounds, five shillings & eight-pence, or anie pt thereof, to be behind & unpaid in pt or in all after anie terme of paimt, in wch it ought to be paid according to the true meaning of their pntes; That then, & so often, it shall & maie be lawfull to & for the said Societie of the Governor & Assistants of London of the new plantacon in Ulster, their Successors & assignes into the premisses afore granted, & every or anie pcell thereof to enter & distraine, and the distresses so taken, to lead, chase, drive, and carry awaie, & wth them to deteine, untill the foresaid Rent, so being behind, & all arrearages, if anie shal be according to the true meaning of their pntes, shal be to them fullie satisfied & paid; And the said Societie of the Governor & Assistants of London of the new Plantacon in Ulster, wthin the Realme of Ireland, for them, & their Successors, do covenant, promise, & graunt to, & wth the said Maister and Keeps, or Wardens & Comunaltie of the Mistery or Art of Ire mongers, London, aforesaid, their Successors & assignes, by their pntes; That they the said Maister & Keeps, or Wardens and Comunaltie of the Mistery or Art of Ire Mongers, London, aforesaid, their Successors & assignes paying the rent aforesaid, & under the Covenants & agreemts in their pntes contained, shall and maie at all times from henceforth for ever, lawfullie, peaceablie, & quietlie, have, hold, occupie, possesse, & enjoy, the said Mannor, lands, Tenemts, Hereditamts, & all & singular other the premisses afore hereby graunted, bargained, & sould, or meant, menconed, or intended to be hereby granted, bargained, or sould, & every part & pcell thereof, wth their appurtenances except before excepted, & reserved, proper, take & enjoy to their owne use & uses for ever, All the rents, issues, and profitts thereof, as well wthout anie lawfull lett, suite, trouble, molestacon, recovery, evicon, expulsion, or interrupcon of or by the said Societie of the Governor & Assistants of London of the new Plantacon aforesaid, their successors or assignes, or of or by anie other pson or psons lawfully claiming or to claime from, by, or under them or anie of them, or their or anie of their Act, estate, meanes, authoritie, consent, or procuremt; As also free, cleare, & freelie & clearlie acquitted, exonerated, & discharged, or well & sufficientlie saved and kept harmeles by the said Societie, their successors or assignes, of & from all & singular form, bargaines, sales, guifts, grants, leases, alienacons, arrearages of Rents, estates, charges, & incumbrances whatsoever, had made, committed, or done by the said Societie, before the sealing & delivery thereof, Except one deed made by the said Societie, whereby the said Mannor is erected, made, & ordained as aforesaid, & except all grants or estates by Indentures made & granted by the said Societie, to severall psons or freehold Tenants of the said Mannor, of pcell of the premisses under certain rents & services, All & every wch rents, dutyes, & services in the said excepted Indentures heretofore reserved, shall for & notwthstanding anie act or thing made or done or to be made or done by the said Societie, their Successors or Assignes to the contrary, be yearlie due and payable to the said Maister & Keeps or Wardens, their successors and assignes, during the continuance in force of the same grants & estates respectivelie. And further, the said Societie of the Governor & Assistants of London, of the new Plantacon in Ulster, wthin the Realme of Ireland, for them, their successors & assignes do covenant, promise, and graunt to & wth the said Maister & Keeps or Wardens & Comunaltie of the misterie or art of Ire Mongers, London, aforesaid, their Successors & Assignes, & every of them by their pntes, That it shall and maie be lawfull at all time tyme and times hereafter to & for the said Maister & Keeps or Wardens & Cominaltie of the Mistery or art of Ire Mongers, London, aforesaid, their successo^rs and assignes, by the appointm^t of the generall Agent of the said Societie for the time being, resident in Ulster, for the affaires of the said Societie, to fell, cut downe, take, & carrie awaie such & soemanie of the Timber Trees of the said Societie standing, growing, and being nearest or most convenient to the premises afore graunted, as shalbe fitt and necessarie for the building or plantacon of anie houses, villages, edifices, or buildings, w^thin the said Mannor^s, lands, and premises; And also that they the said Societie, their Successo^rs & Assignes shall & will paie & discharge all rents & dutyes & other paiem^ts now due & paiable to the King's Most Excellent Matie his heires, or successo^rs for or in respect of the said Mannor^s, lands and premises, or anie part thereof, shall save harmeles the said Maister & Keeps, or Wardens & their successo^rs & all the premises by theis pates graunted, or intended to be graunted, And further that the said Societie, their successors, & assignes, shall & will from time to time, & at all times hereafter, for & during the space of Ten yeares, uppon every reasonable request, & at the cost & charges in the Law of the said Maister & Keeps, or Wardens, their successo^rs & assignes make, do, execute, & performe, all & every such further conveyances & assurances in the law whatsoever, be it by deed, or deeds, release, confirmacon, or otherwise, for the firmly, better & more [illegible] & absolute assurance, conveying and assuring of the said Mano^rs, lands, and premises, under the rent aforesaid, except as before is excepted unto the said Maister and Keeps, or Wardens, their successo^rs & assignes, for ever, as by the said Maister and Keeps, or Wardens, their successo^rs or assignes, or their Counsell learned shalbe reasonablie advised, devised, & required, so as the same assurances & conveyances do containe no further warrantie, nor covenants, for every the premises than against the said Societie & their successo^rs & all heretofore claiming from, by, or under them, except such estates as are before excepted. And for the better establishing and assuring of the said Mannor^s lands, & premises, & every part and peell thereof, in, unto, & uppon the foresaid Maister & Keeps, & Wardens & Comminaltie, of the Mistery or Art aforesaid, their successo^rs & assignes, according to the true meaning of theis pates, the said Societie of the Governo^r & Assistants of London, of the new plantacon in Ulster, w^thin the Realme of Ireland, do by theis pates constitute, ordaine and appoint, Tristram Berisford, Esquire, & Richard Marter, their true and lawfull attorneyes, joyntlie & either of them severallie for the said Societie, & in their name and stead, to enter into & upon the said Mannor^s & premises, & every or anie part thereof, excepte before excepted, & after entry so made for the said Society, & in their name & stead, in or upon the same Mannor^s, lands, & premises, except before excepted, or in or uppon anie part thereof, in the name of the whole, to give & deliver unto the said Maister & Keeps, or Wardens & Comminaltie of the Mistery or Art of Ire Mongers aforesaid, their successo^rs & assignes, or to their certaine Attorney, or Attorneyes, in that behalf authorised, full and peaceable possession & seisin of all & singular the same Mannor^s, lands, & premises, & every part thereof, except before excepted, To hould unto the said Maister & Keeps, or Wardens, their successors & assignes, according to the forme, force, and effect of theis pates, ratifying, confirming, & allowing for good & effectuall in law, all & whatsoever the said Attorneys joyntlie, or either of them severallie shall do, in or about the premises. In Witness whereof to the one part of theis pates, Indentures remaining wth the said Maister & Keepers, or Wardens & Comminaltie of the Mistery or Art of Ire Mongers, London, aforesaid, the said Societie of the Governo^r & Assistants of London, of the new Plantacon in Ulster, in the Realme of Ireland, have caused their comon seale to be putt & to the other part thereof remaining wth the said Societie, by the said Maister & Keeps, or Wardens, of the Ire Mongers, have putt to their comon seale, Dated the daie & yeare first above written.

By order and authoritie of the
Governor and Committee for
London Plantation in Ireland.

SAMUEL CALVERT, Secretary.

APPENDIX, No. 14.

PAPER handed in by *Mr. H. C. Saunders*, 14 July 18[illegible].

A Court of Assistants and General Assembly of the whole Company, holden at [illegible] Hall, the 22nd day of December 1627.

At this Court was read the precept from the *Lord Mayor* and Court of Aldermen concerning the levying of [illegible]l., assessed by act of Common Council upon the Company for their part of 60,000l., being the first payment of 120,000l., granted by the said Common Council to be paid to his Majesty upon the sale of lands in fee farm from his Majesty to the City of London in satisfaction, as well of the said 120,000l. as of the City's former debts to them due from the late King James. And by the Master it was then demanded of the generality of the Company then assembled together, what course, in their judgement, they thought fittest for the raising of that proportion of [illegible]l., whether to levy it by the pole or upon sale of the plate belonging to the Hall by disbursement of such money of the Company as is in the Renter's hands, and may well be spared for the time, and by the mortgage of such lands as the Company stand seised of and not given to charitable uses. All which being put to the question, the levying of that proportion of [illegible]l. by the pole, was, by erection of hands, utterly denied, and it was by the general consent of the most part of the Company condescended unto and thought best that the said proportion of [illegible]l. should be levied by sale of the plate belonging to the Hall, disbursements of such money of the Company in the Renter's hands as may be well spared for the time, and by mortgage of such lands as are the Company's and not given to charitable uses.

APPENDIX, No. 13.

PAPER handed in by the Chairman.

JUDGMENT of the Star Chamber, 28th February, 10 Charles I.

CAROLUS Dei Grā Angl Scotie Franc & Hibn Rex Fidei Defensor etc. Dilco & Fideli suo Willo Uvedale Mil Clico Concilii nri in Cur Came Stellat vel ejus in ea parte Deputat Salm Quia certiorari Volum^s ex tenore cujusdam Judicii sive Decreti coram nob & Concilio nro in cur nra predict Vicesimo Octavo die Februarii ultimo ptito inter Attorn nrm Gen^alem ex parte nra quer & majorem Cotatem & cives Civitat London & al def facti & redditi quod in Custodia vra remanet vob mandam^s qd tenorem Judicii sive decreti predict cum omib ea tangen nob in Cancellar nram sub Sigillo vro distincte & apte sine dilone mittat & hoc brē T me ipo apud Westm xvj die Marcii Anno R N Decimo

Execucio istius brevis patet in quibusdam certificatibus et Scedulis huic Brevi annexat

M. COAD

Virtute Brevis Excellentissime Majestatis vrae de Certiorand Willo Uvedale Mil Clei Consilii vri Camer Stellat apud Westm vel ejus in ea pte Deputat direct Ego Matheus Coad Deputat dci Willi Uvedale Milit legitime constitutus, incitam Coriam Cancellar vre pd Certiorem reddo quod p scrutatis Rotulis et Recordis vris in Custodia mea existentibz inter alia reperi tenorem cujusd Judicii sive Decreti coram vobis et Consil vro pd in curia vra Camer Stellat pd generat dat xxviij die Febr Anno Regni Car nunc Regis Anglie etc. Decimo Inter Attor R Quer et Major & communitat Civitat London et alios Defendantes cujus quidem Judicii sive Decreti tenorem cum omibus ei tangent insimul Brevi vro de certiorand pd annexat Prout interius de Breve pd mihi precipitur ad dictam curiā vram Cancellar vra pd cu omni obediencia transmittio sub forma verbor sequent (viz)

M. COAD

In Camera Stellata Coram Concilio ibidm Vicesimo Octavo die Februarii Anno Decimo Caroli Regis

This day as before twelve other sitting dayes were wholly spent in the full and deliberate hearing debating and sentencing the matters of the severall Informations exhibited into this Corte the one by Sir Robt. Heath Knt. then his Maties Attorney Genrall against the Right Honoble the Lord Maior Comunaltie and Cittizens of the Cittie of London Tristram Berrisford William Turner Nicholas Leate and Clement Mosse Defties and the other by William Noye Esquire his Maties late Attorney Genrall against the said Lord Maior Comunaltie and Cittizens of the Cittie of London the Societie of Governor and Assistants of London of the newe plantacon in Ulster in the Kingdome of Ireland William Dyce William Turner Tristram Berrisford and Clement Mosse Defties for deceiptfull and undue procuring of Letters Pattents from our late Sov'aigne Lord Kinge James of blessed memory to bee past under the Greate Seale of England of very greate possessions in Ulster in the Kingdom of Ireland with unusual and exorbitant priviledges in many particulars wthout any Warrt. att all and in div'rs other parts not pursuing their Warr' and for wilfull breach of the Articles agreed upon betweene the Right Honble the Lords of his late Maties Most Honble Privie Councell on His Highnes behalfe and Comittees appointed by the Act of Comon Councell on the behalfe of the said Maior and Cominalty of the Cittie of London concerning the plantacon in pte of the said Province of Ulster and for wilfull breach of the trust wch his said late Matie reposed in them in sundry other weightie and important matters touching the said plantacon tending to the apparent hazard and danger of the said Kingdome of Ireland The decay and suppression of God's true religion and the utter rayne of that plantacon the said severall Informations more at large it doth and may appear Uppon full and deliberate hearing whereof it plainly and evidently appeared to this Honoble Corte that whereas his Maties said Kingdome of Ireland having been long infested with the

the rebellions of Shane O'Neale and the Earles of Tirone and Tirconell all or the greatest parte of the Territories and lands of the Province of Ulster in that Kingdome by theire Treasons and Attainders became forfeited and escheated to their late Maties Queene Elizabeth and King James and the same being in the absolute power of his said late Matie Kinge James to dispose of at his good pleasure and Will His Highnes out of his owne pious and princely zeale care and disposicon for the enlargem^t^ of God's Church and establishing of the true religion in those parts wch it p^r^fessed and maintained by the Church of England and for the future settling and p^r^servacon of the peace and safety of the Kingdome wch for many yeares before had bene miserably wasted and torne wth intestine warres and rebellions and to reduce the nations who att that time were rude and rebellious into civillity and due obedience to the Crowne of England to drawe those naturally fertile lands and possions into culture and strengthen the same ag^t^ Forraigne Invasions by makeing and maintaining the Fortes and Fortificacons in convenient places And nothing att all respecting the own p^r^fitt and commoditie that might thereof have beene made and raised wch he might justly have done to the great increase of his revenue did of his owne grace and royall bounty resolve to distribute the premisses and to convey the same for small and easie rents amongst his Sub^ts^ of Greate Brittaine and Ireland who should seeke to take the same under such Condicons and provisions as tended to the Advancement of Religion the hono^r^ of his Matie and the peace and safetie of that Kingdome And to manifest that His Highnes Royal intencon to all his loveinge subiects he caused a publiq Declaracon to be printed heere in London in the yeare of Our Lord God One thousand six hundred and eight Entituled a Collection of such Orders and Condicons as are to be observed by the Undertakers of the Escheated Lands in Ulster in the Kingdome of Ireland whereby his said Matie amongst other things did especially p^r^vide for the planting of those lands wth British Inhabitants or Inland Scotts and that none of the Undertakers should alien their p^r^porcons or any parte thereof to the meere Irish or to any that should refuse the oath of Supremacie Whereuppon many parts of the said p^r^vince of Ulster were undertaken and planted accordingly But that parte of the said province now knowne by the name of the Countie of London Derry lyeinge most northerly and most subject to the Invasions of Forraigne Enimies and to the Rebellions of the natives conteyneing many thousand acres haveing within it divers goodly rivers Loughs Havens and divers greate woods and Tymber Trees of faire and Goodly growth fitt for service being not undertaken to bee planted The Lord Maior Comunaltie and Cittizens of London being persons in whom his late Matie reposed an especiale trust having formerly considered of severall motives sent over out to Ireland by the Lord Deputie Chichester in May One thousand six hundred and nyne to induce them to undertake the plantacon of that parte of the said province & haveing alsoe sent over severall able and judicious persons by theire owne appointment to survey the same lands and findeing the same to answere theire expectacon resolved to become Undertakers & planters thereof And thereupon by Act of Comon Councell did afterwards authorise divers persons of the said Cittie of London to treate and deale wth the Lords of His Maties Most Hono^ble^ Privie Councell for the plantacon thereof and after sev^r^all meetings and propositions made and considered of betweene the said Lords on his Maties behalfe and the said Comittees for the Cittie touching the said plantacon on the eight and twentieth day of January One thousand six hundred and nine in the Seaventh yeare of his said late Majesty's Rayne certaine Articles were drawne and agreed upon betweene the said Lords on his Maties behalfe and the said Comittees appointed by Act of Comon Councell on the behalfe of the said Lord Maior Coialtie and Citizens of the Citie of London and the said Articles were then subscribed by both parties Intituled Articles agreed upon the eight and twentieth day of January One thousand six hundred and nyne betweene The Right Honble the Lords of His Maties Most Honble Privie Councell on the Kings Maties behalfe on the one part and the Comittees appointed by Act of Comon Councell on the behalf of the Maior and Coialty of the Citty of London on the other part concerninge a plantacon in pte of the Province of Ulster in the Kingdome of Ireland wch said Articles were afterwards ratified and confirmed by Act of Comon Councell and on the fifth of August followinge wch was in the yeare One thousand six hundred and tenn A Warrant was drawne and sent to his Maties then Attorney Gen'all by the Right Honble the Earle of Salisbury the Lord Trer of England to drawe a Booke fitt for his Maties signature conteyninge a grant from his Matie to the Comittees to bee named by the Cittie of London of all the Lands Tenements and Hereditaments menconed in a p^r^ticuler annexed to the said Warrant under such rents and provisions as were specified in that particuler and according to the foresaid Articles wch were therewith likewise sent unto him and wth such priviledges Immunities and benefitts as in the said Articles were expressed for all wch there was not one penny consideracon payd or to bee payd unto his said late Matie for his Maties owne use or benefitt but the same proceeded from his meere grace and bountie By collour of which Warrant the said Lord Maior and Cittizens of the Cittie of London in the moneth of March in the Eleaventh yeare of his said late Maties Reigne did unduely procure to be drawne and to passe the Greate Seale of England Letters patents from his said late Matie bearing date the nyne and twentieth day of the said moneth of March One thousand six hundred and thirteene wherein was inserted w^th^out any Warrant att all That his said late Majestie did thereby Graunte Ordaine and Appointe that from thenceforthe for ever there was and should bee chosen twenty six discreete Cittizens of London wch should be called the Societie of Govern^r^ and Assistants of London of the new plantacon of Ulster w^th^in the Kingdome of Ireland and that as well the publiq especially and p^r^ticularly named and appointed by the said Letters patents to the then Societie of the said Governor and Assistants as those wch then after should bee elected of that Societie and theire successors were and from thenceforthe for ever by the said Letters patents should bee one newe body corporate and pollitique in substance deed and name by the name of the Governor and

Assistants of London of the new plantacon of Ulster within the Kingdome of Ireland and by that name to have ppetuall succession and that they and their successors should bee perssons able and capeable to purchase receave and possesse Lands Tenem^ts Goods Chattells and possess liberties privileges Franchises and other Heredittam^ts of what nature kynde or qualitie soever they should bee in England or Ireland or either of them unto them and theire Successors in Fee ppetuitie or otherwise and all and singuler other matters and things to doe and execute by the name aforesaid and by that name to sue and defend in whatsoever Corts and places and before whatsoever Judges Justices and other persons and Officers of his Matie his heirs and successors in all matters whatsoever and should and might have a Comon seale for the doeing of theire affaires and negotiacions and the same to take newe and alter att theire will and pleasure And that the said Societie of Governo^r and assistants should bee elected and chosen yearly by the said Maior Aldermen and Cominaltie at the first Comon Councell next after the Feast of the Purificacon of the Blessed Virgin Mary att wch tyme the Deputie Governor and twelve other psons wch have been Assistants for the yeare before goeing shallbe removed and another Deputie and twelve other Assistants in theire places chosen to bee aydinge to the Governor and Assistants not removed for one yeare then next following And that att the ende of that yeare the first Assistants to bee removed and others chosen in theire places and soe from time to time yeare after yeare soe as twelve of the Assistants should be allowed to continue twoe yeares wch clause as it was w^thout warrant soe the Cort conceived it very p^rjudiciall to his Majestie Moreover it appeareth that in the said Letters pattents the said Lord Maior Cominaltie and Citizens contrary to theire owne Agreement wch was only to have seaven and twentie thousand Acres of good and pfitable land or thereabouts graunted to them besides Boggs and Barren Mountaines Did pcure to bee inserted into the said pattent a Graunte from his said late Majestie unto the said newe Corporacon of Governor and Assistants and their successors and not to the said Maior Cominaltie and Citizens of London who originally contracted with his said late Matie and to whome his late Matie intended the same as clearly appeares both by the Title of the Articles agreed on on theire behalfe and by severall other actes of the Cittie of London Derry the Countie of London Derry and of all the lands therein and together with the towne of Coleraine and all the Landes within the said Countie and Cittie being of farr greater and larger extent and conteineinge about Seaventie thousand acres of good pfitable land more than was intended to bee graunted unto them and for wch there was noe penny rent reserved to His Matie Whereby his Matie hath beene greatly damnified in losse of the rents of above threescore and Tenn thousand acres of Land ever since the First Undertaking of the said plantacon And it likewise further appeared that the said Maior Cominaltie and Citizens of the said Cittie of London and the said Societie of Governo^r and Assistants of the said new plantacon having obtained the said pattent to passe in such sorte as before is expressed wth div^rs other greate and large priviledges Immunities and Freedomes w^thout any covenant therein for the pformance of the said seaven and twentie Articles agreed on And w^thout respect to his Maties intencon when he graunted the same wch was to remove the Natives and to plant the same with Brittish to the end to Civilise the said Country and to establish the true Religion there Albeit they were bound by the printed Articles of Plantacon to plant wth none but English and Inland Scottish and such as had taken the Oath of Supremacy and not alien or demise theire proporcons or anye parte thereof to the meere Irish and that they themselves did att theire first entry uppon the said plantacon understand and took notice that they were bound to plant wth Brittish according to the said printed Articles as appears by twoe sev^rall Acts of Comon Councell made by themselves the one in the moneth of January and the other in February in the yeare One thousand six hundred and tenn Yet neverthelesse they did neglecte and forbeare to remove the Native and plant with Brittish whereof the Lord Chichester then Lord Deputie of Ireland taking notice did by his letters to the Lords of his Maties Privie Councell heere in England Dated the nyne and twentieth of Aprill One thousand six hundred and twelve Declare and make knowne that amonge all the undertakers there none more backwards for sending over of Tenants then the Londone^rs themselves who were best able to accomplish it and that besides theire Workmen they had not then brought over a Man to Inhabite and that theire Ministers there did as hee was credibly advertised recalle backe and constraine many of the natives to staye upon theire Landes that would gladly remove and settle themselves elsewhere out of the Country and that they invited the Irishrie whoe willingly flocke thither out of all other parts of Tirone into the Barronie of Loughenshelyn to inhabit in greater number than had been usually knowne and afterwards his said late Matie King James by his Letter written to the said Lord Deputie of Ireland bearinge date the one and twentieth daye of December One thousand six hundred and twelve did take notice of and found greate faulte wth the slowe progression of the plantacon in those partes for that neither the safetie of the Country nor the planting of Religion and Civilitie amongst those rude and barbarous people wch were the principall motives of that project and wch his said late Matie expected as the onely fruites and retorne of his greate bountie unto the undertakers were then soe waives materially effected His Highnesse esteeming the setting of Religion the introducing of Civillitie order and Governm^t amongst a Barbarous and unsubjected people to bee an act of piety and glory and worthy alwaye of a Christian Prince to endeavour Did thereby comand his Lordp^p that setting aside all favo^r partialitie care or feare to please or displease any man Hee should make a sincere and faithfull narracon what every undertaker ought to doe and what hee had done in pformance thereof And his said late Matie haveing receaved intelligence from Sir Josias Bodley of the Londoners backwardnesse in their said plantacon to quicken and stir them upp to a speedie pformance thereof Did a second tyme write his letter to the said Lord Deputie Chichester bearing date the five and twentieth of March One thousand six hundred

hundred and fifteene therein againe declareing his greate dislike of the slowe progression of the plantacon in those ptes and especially the Undertakers gen'all reteyneing the Irish still upon theire lands the avoyding of wch was the fundamentall reason of that plantacon and gave Commandmt by the Letter that if any faild in the pformance of the Undertaking by the last of August One thousand six hundred and sixteen their pporcon or porcons wherein such omission was should be presently seized and resumed unto his Majs hands and that Notice should be given thereof to all whome it should concerne that his Matie did expect a full pformance in all pointes of the Articles of plantacon with a postscript of his Highnes own handwriting to His Lordshipp in these words vizt: My Lord in this service I expecte that zeale and uprightness from yow that yow will spare noe flesh English nor Scottishe for noe private man's worth is able to counterbalance the perfectuall safetie of a kingdome which this plantacon being well accomplished will procure And afterwards the Right Honorable the Lord Grandison being Lord Deputie of Ireland in August One thousand six hundred and seventeene by direccon of his Matie and the Lords of the Councell in England did write his letter unto the Maior of Derry and the Cittie Agents and Farmors to attend his Lordshipps pleasure and direccon for removeing of the Natives and in further pursuance of his Maties command and direccon did by a Proclamacon printed and published in the said Realme of Ireland in the moneth of October One thousande sixe hundred and Eighteene Declare and Publish his Highnes expresse will and pleasure to bee that all and every the natives or other Irishe Inhabitants dwellinge or residing in or upon any of the said late escheated Lands granted unto Brittish Undertakers within the said province of Ulster should att or before the first day of May next ensuinge the date thereof remove their severall habitacons and dwellings and cleerely depte from the said Lands granted to the Brittishe Undertakers and from thenceforth plant and setle themselves in some other parts of that Kingdome And did by the said Proclamation further charg and command all and every the said Natives and other Irishe Inhabitants their Dwellings or wch then after at any time before the first day of May then next ensuinge should come and dwell in and uppon any of the said Lands granted unto the Brittish Undertakers within the said Province of Ulster that they and every of them should before the said first day of May depte and remove theire severall habitacons and dwellings from the said Undertakers lands to plante and setle themselves and their Families in other place or places and that such natives and Irish Householders as should after the said First day of May p'sume to continue his habitacon uppon any the lands of the Brittish Undertakers contrary to the said proclamacon should paye tenne shillings sterlinge to his Maties use in the name of a Fyne and afterwards by order of the Lords of the Councell in England the profitts of the premises wer ordered to be sequestred for the performance of the plantacon And a Commission awarded out of his Majestys Courte of Chancery in England to the Lord Deputie and other the Lords of his Maties Privie Councell in Ireland to enquire of & certifie the defaults of the Londoners plantacon All wch notwithstandinge the said Defts their Agents and Farmors and such to whom they disposed the said lands did and still doe continue the natives uppon the said plantacon and did contract and undertake to save them harmless from theire fynes and for fower yeares paid the Fynes imposed on them according to the aforesaid proclamacon for not depting from the Brittish Undertakers lands because they would give greate rents for the said Lands than the Brittish were able to make and live upon and did pferre the Irish before the English because they pretended they were more serviceable unto them by wch meanes & by theire excessive raysinge the rent from Fortie shillings and fiftie shillings a Ballibos unto Tenne poundes Twelve pounds & twenty pounds & Thirtie poundes a Ballibos the English were and are much disharted and the Natives doe farre exceede the Brittish uppon some proporcons foure for one uppon some six uppon some Tenne and one some twentie for one whoe keepe footeinge there and give such greate rents though to their undoinge to keepe out the Brittish outs of their hope & expectacon of ayde and assistance from Forraigne parts expectinge the cominge of young Tyrone againe into those parts and divers said Brittish Tennts have beine by them put out from theire said Lands and theire Farmes lett to the native Irishe some for the same and some for lesse Rents then the Brittish did give AND WHEREAS the principall cause and motive wch induced his late Matie to grante the said patent was the reformacon of the superstitious religion and reduceinge the Countrie to the true Religion established and professed in the Church of England the said Defts Agents Farmors and Lessees have and still doe suffer a greate number of beneficed Popish Priests to reside upon the said Plantacon by them undertaken in every Parishe one besides Vagrant Priests Mendicants and Fryers whoe usually say Masse every Sunday and have Masse houses appointed and allowed them for that purpose and the duties and offerings which they take and receave from the Inhabitants there amounts to att least a thousand pounds a year and sev'all Vicars Generall and their Surrogates are alsoe resident uppon the lands of the said Plantacon whoe there exercise Jurisdiccon by authoritie from the Pope of Rome and sev'all popish priests and alsoe Tennts to part of the said lands And it likewise further appeared that whereas the said Maior Comminalty and Cittizens were by the second of the said seaven and twentie Articles to build two hundred houses at the Derry and to leave roome for three hundred more and to laye foure thousand acres of Land thereunto and by the Fourth of the said Articles were to build One hundred houses in Colraine to leave roome for two hundred more and to laye three thousand acres of land thereunto And by the seaven and twentieth of the same Articles were wth all speede to sett forward the said Plantacon in such sorte as that there should be sixtie houses built in the Derry and fortie houses at Colraine by the first daye of November then next followinge with convenient fortificacons and the rest of the houses with the fortificacons to be builte and perfected by the first daye of November wch should be in the yeare of our Lord one thousand sixe hundred and eleven the said Defendtes have fayled in the performance of every of the said pticulars for that in the said Cittie of

Derry there were no Houses att all builte by the said First of November One thousand six hundred and eleven by wch tyme according to the said Article the whole two hundred houses should have been finished neither were the said two hundred houses in the yeare One thousand six hundred twenty eight fully built there according to the Modell agreed on by the Citie in the Guild halle London wch was that every house should containe two Bayes of buildinge sixe and thirtie foot in length twentie foot in breadth but divirse of those houses wch were builte of that length and bredth containing but five or six roomes and havinge but one doore one paire of staires and one Chimney were by the direccon of Alderman Probye and Mr. Springham at their goinge over to viewe the said plantacon by direccon from the Citie made and called two house-e pieces neither was there above twentie houses builte att Coleraine by the said First of November One thousand six hundred and eleven nor in two yeares after nor above three score houses in fourteen yeares after and onely fowerscore in the yeare One thousand six hundred twenty eight and all that tyme not above Five hundred acres of land were layde to the said Towne of Colerayne but not yet assured as by the said Articles itt ought to bee neither was the said Foure thousand acres nor above fifteene hundred acres thereof in the yeare One thousand sixe hundred twenty and foure laide to the Derry and no parte thereof assured and the rest converted to the benefitt of the said Defendts nor any Fortificacons begun to bee mayde eyther att the Derry or Colerayne in divers yeares after the said First of November One thousand six hundred and eleven neither is the said Towne of Coleraine yet otherwise fortified then wth a Mudd wall and the Towne easie to be taken with a very small number of armed Men And whereas by the twentieth of the said seaven and twentie Articles dated in January One thousand six hundred and nyne y^{t} was agreed on his Ma^{ts} behalfe that the said Citie should have the Castle of Culmore and the lands thereunto belonginge in Fee Farme they mainteyninge a sufficient ward of Officers therein the said Defts had fayled in the performance of that likewise although they were bound thereunto by their Covenants in the said Pattent for that in Eight yeares after the said Articles they did not repaire the said Castle and ever since they have had the Custody of the said Castle there hath beene never a Gunner resident there and soe light a guard kept that albeit there is a competent number of Ordinance theire yet many times they lye by the Walles the Carriages being rotten and so weake a guard kept there that the Irishe may make themselves masters of the said Castle when they please there beinge but Tenne Warders usually in paye there and two of them who were for three yeare inrolled as Wardens there were Servants to the Defts Tristram Beresford and lived twenty miles of from the said Castle By reason of all which faylers of the said Defts in not plantinge wth Brittishe and not removinge the Natives nor making such satisfaction as by the said Articles and Patent they should have done his Matie as appeareth by the Proofes was forced to expend Thirtie thousand pounds att the least in mayntenance of Garrisons there for defense of the said Kingdome It likewise further appeared that the said Defts were by the said Pattents to sett forth allott and assure to every incumbent w^{th}in their said plantacon in Frankalmoigne Three score acres of Globe for every one thousand acres w^{th}in every Parishe and that to be done w^{th}in one yeare after the said Pattent sealed at the Charge of the said Citie and that the said lands to be conveniently sett out yet notwithstandinge the said Glebe was not assured unto them until the yeare One thousand six hundred twenty seven and some of them were forced to come over into England here to receive their said Assurances to their great trouble and charge and all of their said Glebes were not assured unto them att the time of the exhibitinge of this Suit and diverse of the said Glebes were inconveniently laid out far distant from their Parish Churches and some out of their Parishes It likewise appeared that in respect the said Defts did not make a competent number of Freeholders in and upon their said plantacon that the Poor Labourers and Leaseholders were forced many times to serve of Juries to their great trouble and charge And that many tymes his Ma^{ts} service for want of freeholders was neglected and hindered And it further appeared that notwithstandinge by the said Seaventh of the said seaven and Twenty Articles dated the eighth and twentieth day of Januarie One thousand six hundred and nyne it was agreed that the woods grounde and soyle of Glankonkeyne and Killetraugh extending from the Countie of Coleraine to Balliinderry should be wholly to the City in perpetuity And that the timber trees of those woods should be converted to the furtherance of plantacon and all necessary uses within Ireland and not to be made Merchandise And a Mandamus contayned in the said Patent to that purpose Yet greate destruccon hath been made of the said woods and great tymber trees in makinge of pipe staves Hogshead staves and clove boards for the Defts Berisford and other the Citie's Agents in the yeares One thousand six hundred and tenne and One thousand six hundred and eleven to a very great number wch were all by him and them transported and made Merchandise And for seaventeene yeares together One hundred thousand pipe staves hogshead staves and Barrell staves were by the direccon of the said Londoners Agents cutt and made out of the said Woods whereof themselves spent and imployed about two and twenty thousand onely for their fishinge & other necessary uses and the rest were transported and twelve boats in one weeke were sent to be loaden with those staves and sent away into Scotland and other places as Merchandise and much of the said woods have beine by the said Defts Berisford and other the Citie Agents consumed in makinge of Iron there for his and theire own uses and soe great destruccon hath beene made of the said Woods that Whereas about Twenty yeares since the woods and trees were so thick that a man could hardly passe through the same A man may now looke through a mile in length by reason of the thinnesse thereof the greatest parte of it being converted to pipe staves Hogshead staves Barrell staves and Clove Boards and much of it transported into Forreigne parts by the Citie's Agents in sev'all shippes at several tymes Uppon Grave and deliberate consideracon of all wch matters the Courte well weighinge and considering the proofes circumstances and allegacons on both sides was of opinion and did declare First that the said Lord Maior Comialtie and Citizens of the Citie of London were fitt Defend^{ts} although it

hath

hath been much insisted and stood upon that the said Lord Maior and Cominaltie had nothinge to doe wth the said plantacon and that their name was used merely for transaccon of affayres and for the levyinge and rayseinge of moneys for the said plantacon uppon the Companies of the Cittie wch could not be done but by Acts of Comon Councell for that it is evident the first treatie touchinge the said plantacon was with the Cittie the Motives sent over out of Ireland was to invite the Cittie to undertake the plantacon the Acts of Comon Councell mentioned the treatie with the Commissioners for Ireland on the behalfe of the Cittie that foure discreet Men of the Cittie should goe into Ireland att the Citties Charge and they to returne an accompte of their s̃vice to the Cittie then another great Committee appointed by Act of Comon Councell to agree of all things on the Citties behalfe touchinge the said plantacon wth the Lords of the Councell on his said late Majts behalfe and their propositions were tendered to the said Lords on the Citties behalfe and allowed of and the very Title of the Articles Dated the eight and twentieth of January One thousand six hundred and nyne shewe the Contract to be theire and by the preamble of the Patent it appeareth that the Maior and Cominaltie of the Cittie of London were the Undertakers of the said Plantacon and therefore they can in no sort to be excused Secondly the Courte did declare that the said Society of Governr and Assistants were also fitt Defendts and lyable to the Censure of this Courte for although they have by Lycence conveyed the severall porcons of the said Undertaken Lands to the twelve great Companies yet they themselves Doe still reteine to themselves the Cittie of Londonderry and the Towne of Coleraine and the seaven thousand acres the said Woods of Glanchonkeine Killitraugh the Castle of Culmore The Fishinge and Customes as appeare by their owne answers and proofes in this Cause and many of the breaches and faylers of performance of the articles of agreement were before the Lands were past away to the said Companies Thirdly the Courte is of opinion and doth declare that the said Pattent according to the tenor and purporte of the said Warrant wch directed the same should be drawne according to the said seaven and twentie Articles nor any Covenants therein contained for pformance thereof nor any reference or relacon had thereunto and that wthout any Warrt And in further abuse of his said Matie they have made six and twentie psons by the name of the Society of Governr and Assistants of the New Plantacon in Ulster in the Kingdome of Ireland a Bodie Corporate for ever and have thereby granted unto them and their Successors all the said large Territories and possessions together wth many larger and exorbitant privileges libties and Franchises the said Warrant directinge the said Patent to be drawne upp to the Comittees to be named by the Cittie of London and not to any such new formed Body or Corporacon whoe are not responsible and by the said Letters Pattents they have past unto the said Society of Governr and Assistants a farre greater quantity of Land then was proposed or demanded by the Comittees on the behalfe of the Cittie or intended by the said 27tie articles to bee past unto them and that they have also highly offended in not planting wth Brittishe as they were bound to doe and in continueing the natives for their owne private gaine and advantage to the great increase and continuance of poverie and danger of the State of that Kingdome Fourthly the Courte did declare that the said Maior Cominaltie and Citizens of the Cittie of London and the said Society of Governr and Assistants of the said Newe Plantacon have also greatly offended in not pformeing of theire undertakings for that they did not build the said Houses in the City of Derry and Towne of Coleraine by the time lymitted and agreed upon by the said Articles nor have pformed the same fully unto this day as they ought to doe by the said Articles and for that they did not in time according to the said fifth Article nor have as yett sufficiently built and fortified By all which meanes and by reason of theire not keepinge a sufficient Guard in the said Castle of Culmore the whole countrie hath beene endangered and his late and nowe Matie were enforced to his and theire great charge to maintaine Garrisons there for defence of the said Kingdome In respect whereof and of other the failer and unperformances formerly herein mencioned and of the greate distruccon of the Woods and Tymber Trees there wch is apparently pved to be done by theire Agents for whome they must and ought to answere The whole Court did this day wth one uniforme opinion and consent Order adjudge and Decree that the said Defts the Lord Maior Cominaltie and Citizens of the Cittie of London and the Societie of Governr and Assistants of the newe plantacon in Ulster in the Kingdome of Ireland shall for theire offences aforesaid satisfie and pay for a Fine to his Matie use the Summe of Three Score and Tenne Thousand pounds and that the said Pattent so unduely and surreptitiously obteyned to the pjudice and deceipte of his Matie as aforesaid and their Estates and interest therein shall bee by them forthwith surrendered up to his Matie and shall be brought into this Court here to be cancelled and made voyde or otherwise to be disposed of att his Maties pleasure And whereas the greatest part of the said lands are by the said Societie passed over unto divers Companies of the City of London and by them demised unto sev'all Farmors whoe are not Defts to this Suite and therefore are not nowe lyable to their Lordps censure Although in the opinion of the Co'te they might justly have been censured if they had been pties to either of the said Informacons It is therefore thought fitt and directed by this Co'te that if the said Companies and their Farmors shall not in pursuance of the intencon of this sentence surrender their Estates his Maties said Attorney shall exhibite an Informacon and bringe them also to the Judgment of this Co'te. And lastly as touchinge the other Defendts Berrisford Clement Mosse Willm Dyos and William Turner Forasmuch as nothing att all was offered to be pved against the said Dyos Turner and Mosse And for that the Co'te was not fully satisfied to convict the said Defendt Berrisford of the offences whereof he stands charged It is therefore ordered that the said Defendants be dismissed and discharged of any further attendance thereabouts hereafter

M COAD

Examined with the Record in the Petty Bag Office in the Court of *Chancery* the eighteenth day of January 1838.

Exd. T. D. HARDY. J. BENTALL.

APPENDIX, No. 16.

PAPER handed in by the Chairman.

(Respondents' Appendix. Pages [illegible].)

Judgment of Scire Facias in Hilary term 13 Charles I.

Whereupon it was adjudged that the letters patent and the inrolment thereof be revoked cancelled and annulled and that all and singular the premises with the appurtenances granted by the aforesaid letters patent to the aforesaid Society of Governor and assistants in London of the new Plantation in Ulster within the realm of Ireland and to their successors be taken and seized into the hands of the Lord the King.

APPENDIX, No. 17.

PAPER handed in by the Chairman.

A grant of Special Pardon to the Mayor Commonalty and Citizens of the City of London.
(Appellants' Appendix. Page [illegible].)

Fourteenth part of Patents in the fourteenth year of the Reign of King Charles.

The King &c. To the High Treasurer of England and to the Commissioners of the Treasury of us our heirs or successors for the time being and also to the Chancellor and Barons of the Exchequer of us our heirs or successors and to all and singular other the Officers and Ministers of us our heirs or successors of the said Court and of the [illegible] there for the time being and to all others to whom these presents shall come greeting. Whereas in our Court of the Star Chamber several bills or informations were heretofore exhibited one of them by Sir Robert Heath Knight our then Attorney General against the Mayor Commonalty and Citizens of the City of London Tristram Beresford William Turner Nicholas Leate and Clement Mosse Defendants and another of them by William Noy Esquire also our late Attorney General against the aforesaid Mayor Commonalty and Citizens of the City of London and the Society of Governor and Assistants of London of the new plantation in Ulster in the Kingdom of Ireland William Dyer William Turner Tristram Beresford and Clement Mosse Defendants for and concerning the [illegible] of certain Letters patent to be made under the Great Seal of England by our late most dear father (of blessed memory) the Lord James late King of England &c. to the said Society of Governor and assistants of large possessions in Ulster aforesaid in the said Kingdom of Ireland with some unusual privileges and in many particulars [illegible] and for other things in the said informations mentioned. And whereas after due and lawful proceedings of the said several informations had in the said Court of our Star Chamber according to the course of the said Court the matters of the said informations came to be heard in our said Court before our Council there on the twenty eighth day of February in the tenth year of our reign and [illegible]

[illegible]

from all prosecutions of any Writs [illegible] [illegible] extents or other process whatsoever against the aforesaid Mayor Commonalty (and Citizens) of the City of London and their successors and the aforesaid Society of Governor and Assistants of London of the new Plantation in Ulster in the Kingdom of Ireland and their successors respectively or against their lands tenements and hereditaments goods or chattels for or in respect of the fine or sum of the aforesaid seventy thousand pounds or any parcel thereof in these presents pardoned released or discharged but also shall from time to time make or cause to be made all such other and further orders [illegible] [illegible] [illegible] of [illegible] and discharges whatsoever as shall be requisite and sufficient for the more full and absolute release discharge and acquittance of the aforesaid Mayor Commonalty and Citizens of the City of London and their successors and of the aforesaid Society of Governor and Assistants of London of the new Plantation in Ulster in the Kingdom of Ireland and their successors respectively and the lands tenements goods and chattels of them and every of them of for or concerning the aforesaid fine or sum above by these our Letters Patent pardoned released acquitted and discharged according to the true intent of these Presents. And these our Letters Patent or the inrolment or exemplification thereof shall be to all and singular persons to whom it shall belong a sufficient warrant and discharge in this behalf. And moreover we will and for us our heirs and successors do by these our Letters Patent grant to the aforesaid Mayor Commonalty and Citizens of the City of London and their successors and to the aforesaid Society of Governor and Assistants of London of the new Plantation in Ulster in the Kingdom of Ireland and their successors that these our Letters Patent or the inrolment or exemplification thereof shall be good firm valid and effectual in the law and shall be construed expounded and allowed in all our Courts and elsewhere strictly against us our heirs and successors and most favourably and beneficially for the aforesaid Mayor Commonalty and Citizens of the City of London and their successors and for the aforesaid Society of Governor and Assistants of London of the new Plantation in Ulster in the Kingdom of Ireland and their successors according to the true intent of these Presents. Notwithstanding the misnaming or not reciting or not rightly naming or reciting the aforesaid several informations or any things or matters in the same mentioned or the order judgment and decree of our said Court in the premises or any other defect uncertainty or imperfection in these our Letters Patent although express mention &c. In witness whereof &c. Witness the King at Westminster the [illegible] day of October.

BY THE KING HIMSELF.

A Special Pardon to the Mayor Commonalty and Citizens of London and the Irish Society and several Companies (Appellants' Appendix. Pages [illegible].)

Twenty fifth part of Patents in the 14th year of the Reign of King Charles.

The King &c To the High Treasurer of England of us our heirs and successors for the time being and to the Commissioners of the Treasury of us our heirs and successors for the time being. And also to the Chancellor Under-treasurer Chamberlains and Barons of the Exchequer and all other the Officers and Ministers of us our heirs and successors of the said Exchequer and to all others to whom these presents shall come greeting. Know ye that we for divers good causes and considerations us hereunto moving and of our especial grace and of our certain knowledge and mere motion have pardoned remitted released and discharged and by these presents for us our heirs and successors do pardon remit release and discharge the Mayor and Commonalty and Citizens of the City of London and their successors and also the Society of Governor and Assistants of London of the new Plantation in Ulster within the Kingdom of Ireland and their successors and also the Wardens and Commonalty of the mystery of Mercers of the City of London and their successors and the Wardens and Commonalty of the Mystery of Grocers of the City of London and their successors and the Master and Wardens and Brethren and Sisters of the Guild or Fraternity of [illegible] Mary the Virgin of the Mystery of Drapers of the City of London and their successors and the Wardens and Commonalty of the Mystery of Fishmongers of the City of London and their successors and the Wardens and Commonalty of the Mystery of Goldsmiths of the City of London and their successors and the Master Wardens and Commonalty of the Mystery of Skinners of London and their successors and the Master and Wardens of Merchant Taylors of the Fraternity of Saint John the Baptist in the City of London and their Successors and the Master and four Wardens of the Fraternity of the art or mystery of the Haberdashers in our City of London and their successors and the Master Wardens and Commonalty of the Art or Mystery of Salters of London and their successors and the Master and Wardens and Commonalty of the mystery or Art of Ironmongers of London and their successors and the Master Wardens and Freemen and Commonalty of the mystery of Vintners of the City of London and their successors and the Master Wardens and Commonalty of Freemen of the Art or Mystery of Clothworkers of the City of London and their successors and the Wardens and Commonalty of the mystery of Dyers of the City of London and their successors and the Master and Wardens and Commonalty of the Mystery or Art of Brewers of the City of London and their successors and the Wardens and Company of the mystery or art of the Leathersellers of the City of London and their successors and the Master Wardens and Commonalty of the mystery of Pewterers of the City of London and [illegible] thereof and their successors and the Master Wardens and Commonalty of the mystery of the Cutlers of London and their successors and the Master Wardens and Commonalty of the mystery of Bakers of London and their successors and the Master Wardens and Commonalty of the mystery of Wax chandlers of the City of London and their successors and the Master Wardens and Commonalty of the mystery of Tallow Chandlers of the City of London and their successors and the Master and Wardens of the art or mystery of Girdlers of London and their successors and the Master and Wardens Brethren and Sisters of the Fraternity or Guild of Saint George of the men of the mystery of the Armourers of the City of London and their successors and the Master Wardens and Commonalty of the art or mystery of Butchers of the City of London and their successors and the Wardens and Commonalty of the mystery or art of Sadlers of the City of London and their successors and the Master Wardens and Commonalty of the mystery of the free men of the Carpenters of the City of London and their successors and the Master Wardens and Commonalty of the mystery of Cordwainers of the City of London and their successors and the Masters or Governors of the mystery and Commonalty of Barbers and Surgeons of London and their successors and the Master Wardens and Company of the Art and mystery of Apothecaries of the City of London and their successors and the Master Wardens and Commonalty of the free men of the art or mystery of Painters called Painter Stainers within the City of London and the suburbs and liberties of the same City and their successors and the Master Wardens and Commonalty of the art or mystery of the Curriers of London and their successors and the Master and Wardens and free men and Brethren of the Company of Masons of the City of London and their successors and the Master Wardens and Commonalty of the free men of the Mystery of Plumbers of the City of London and their successors and the Master and Wardens of the Fraternity or Guild of Saint Julian of Innholders within the City of London and their successors and the Masters Wardens and Commonalty of the mystery of Founders of the City of London and their successors and the Master Wardens and Assistants of the Guild or Fraternity of the Company of Poulterers of London and their successors and the Master Wardens and Commonalty of the free men of the mystery of Coopers of London and the suburbs of the same City and their successors and the Masters or Governors and Commonalty of the mystery of Cooks of the City of London and their successors and the Master and Wardens of the Company of Tilers and Bricklayers of London and their successors and the Master Wardens and Assistants of the Company of the mystery of Bowyers of the City of London and their successors and the Wardens and Company of the art or mystery of the Blacksmiths of London and their successors and the Master Wardens and Commonalty of the faculty of Joiners and Carvers of London and their successors and the Bailiffs and Wardens of the Guild or Company of Weavers of London and their successors and the Master

Master Wardens and Company of Woolmen of London otherwise Wool Packers and their successors and the Master Wardens and Company of Woodmongers of London and their successors and the Master Wardens and Assistants of the Company of Scriveners of the City of London and their successors and the Master Wardens and Commonalty of the mystery of Fruiterers of London and their successors and the Master and Wardens of the Guild or Fraternity of Saint Mary of Plaisterers of London and their successors and the Master Wardens and Commonalty of the mistery of Brown Bakers of London and their successors and the Master and Wardens and Commonalty of the mystery or Art of Upholders of the City of London and their successors and the Master Wardens and Commonalty of the mistery or Art of the Turners of London and their successors and the Master Wardens and Commonalty of the Art or mistery of Glaziers of the City of London and their successors and the Master and Wardens and Commonalty of the mistery or art of Stationers of the City of London and their successors and the Keepers or Wardens and Company of the art or mistery of the Bowyers of the City of London and their successors and the Master Wardens or Free Men of the Fraternity of the Basket Makers of the City of London and the Fraternity of the Fletchers of London and their successors. All and all manner of actions [illegible] nonperformances of any terms and demands of or concerning the planting not planting and building done or to be done by the aforesaid Mayor and Commonalty and Citizens of the City of London and by the Society Governors and Assistants of London of the new plantation in Ulster aforesaid and the Wardens and Commonalty of the mistery of Mercers of the City aforesaid and by the aforesaid other several Companies Guilds or Fraternities before mentioned or any or either of them in and upon the divers certain manors lands and tenements in the Province of Ulster within our Kingdom of Ireland heretofore granted by our most dear father of happy memory the Lord James late King of England to the aforesaid Society Governors and Assistants of London of the new Plantation in Ulster aforesaid. And all and all manner of unlawful receipts perceptions and levies of any sums of money or other things heretofore had or made of any members of the said several Companies Guilds Fraternities or Commonalties before mentioned or of any or either of them respectively for the admission of the said members to the freedoms [illegible] or liveries of the said several Companies Guilds Fraternities or Commonalties respectively or of any or either of them. And all and singular offences crimes violations of the law and faults forfeitures pains and penalties whatsoever by reason of the premises aforesaid or of any or either of them heretofore done committed perpetrated or incurred. And also all and singular their misgovernments in the several Companies Guilds Fraternities and Commonalties aforesaid respectively and all defaults errors and offences in any manner touching or concerning their good rule and government Willing and by these presents for us our heirs and successors strictly enjoining commanding that neither the aforesaid Mayor Commonalty and Citizens of the City of London nor the aforesaid Society Governors and Assistants of London of the new Plantation in Ulster within the Kingdom of Ireland nor their successors nor the Wardens and Commonalty of the mistery of Mercers of the City of London nor their successors (nor the aforesaid several other Companies hereinbefore named) nor the manors lands tenements hereditaments goods or chattels of the aforesaid Mayor and Commonalty and Citizens of the City of London and their successors or of the aforesaid Society Governors and Assistants of London of the new plantation in Ulster aforesaid and their successors or of the aforesaid Wardens and Commonalty of the mistery of Mercers of the City of London nor their successors (or of the aforesaid several other Companies hereinbefore named and their successors) respectively shall at any time or times hereafter be in any wise [illegible] sued vexed molested disturbed [illegible] or in any manner troubled or disquieted for or concerning the premises aforesaid by these presents pardoned remitted released or discharged or mentioned to be pardoned remitted released or discharged as aforesaid. And further we do will and declare our royal pleasure and by these presents for us our heirs and successors strictly enjoining do order and command all and singular Sheriffs Undersheriffs Bailiffs and other persons whatsoever to whom it may belong that if for the aforesaid premises above by these presents pardoned remitted or released or mentioned to be pardoned remitted released or discharged as aforesaid the aforesaid Mayor and Commonalty and Citizens of the City of London or their successors and the aforesaid Society Governors and Assistants of London of the new plantation in Ulster within the Kingdom of Ireland or their successors and the Wardens and Commonalty of the mistery of Mercers of the City of London or their successors and the aforesaid several other Companies hereinbefore named or their successors or any of them or the manors lands tenements hereditaments goods and chattels of them or of any or either of them respectively shall at any time or times hereafter be sued disturbed troubled disquieted seized or [illegible] that then upon the showing of these our letters patent or the inrollment or exemplification thereof they shall be released and restored without any other further Warrant from us our heirs or successors to be in that behalf had procured or obtained Willing and by these presents for us our heirs and successors to be we do order and command and do grant full power and authority to all and singular Justices and Judges of all or any of our Courts at Westminster and also to the Barons of our Exchequer for the time being and to the Judges Justices and [illegible] of any other Courts at Westminster and elsewhere for the time being and to all Earls Sheriffs Bailiffs and other officers of us our heirs and successors whatsoever now or hereafter being that they and every of them respectively shall not only forbear from all prosecution of any Writs [illegible] process [illegible] or other premises whatsoever against the aforesaid Mayor and Commonalty and Citizens of the City of London and their successors and also against the aforesaid Society Governors and Assistants of London of the new plantation in Ulster within the Kingdom of Ireland and their successors and against the Wardens and Commonalty of the Mistery of Mercers of the City of London and their successors (and the aforesaid several other Companies hereinbefore named) and their successors respectively or against the lands tenements hereditaments goods or chattels of them or any of them for or in respect of the premises aforesaid in these presents pardoned released or discharged. But also shall from time to time make or cause to be made all such other and further orders decrees warrants writs of supersedeas and discharges whatsoever as shall be requisite and sufficient for the more full and absolute release discharge and acquittance of the aforesaid Mayor and Commonalty and Citizens of the City of London and their successors and of the aforesaid Society Governors and Assistants of London of the new plantation in Ulster within the Kingdom of Ireland and their successors and of the Wardens and Commonalty of the mistery of Mercers of the City of London and their successors (and of the aforesaid several other Companies hereinbefore named) and their successors respectively and the lands tenements goods and chattels of them and every of them of for or concerning the aforesaid premises by these our letters patent pardoned released acquitted and discharged according to the true intent of these presents and these our letters patent or the inrollment or exemplification thereof shall be to all and singular persons to whom it may belong sufficient warrant and discharge in this behalf. And lastly we will and for us our heirs and successors do by these our letters patent grant to the aforesaid Mayor Commonalty and Citizens of the City of London and their successors and to the aforesaid Society Governors and Assistants of London of the new plantation in Ulster within the Kingdom of Ireland and their successors and to the Wardens and Commonalty of the mistery of Mercers of the City of London and their successors (and to the aforesaid several other Companies hereinbefore named) and their successors and to every and each of them respectively That these our letters patent or the inrollment or exemplification thereof shall be good firm valid and effectual in the law and shall be construed expounded and allowed in all our Courts and elsewhere strictly against us our heirs and successors and most favourably and beneficially for the aforesaid Mayor Commonalty and Citizens of the City of London and their successors and for the aforesaid Society Governors and Assistants of London of the new plantation in Ulster within the Kingdom of Ireland and their successors and for the Wardens and Commonalty of the Mistery of Mercers of the City of London and their successors (and for the aforesaid several other Companies hereinbefore named) and their successors according to the true intent of these presents notwithstanding the not naming or not rightly naming the true names of the aforesaid several Companies Guilds Fraternities and Commonalties or any or either of them and notwithstanding the not naming or not rightly naming or mentioning the aforesaid [illegible] nonperformances of any terms actions or demands of or concerning the plantation in the Province of Ulster within the Kingdom of Ireland by these presents pardoned or or intended to be pardoned. And notwithstanding the not naming or reciting or not rightly and expressly naming or reciting the unlawful receipts perceptions and levies of any sums of money or other things of any members of the aforesaid several Companies Guilds Fraternities or Commonalties for the admission of the said Members to the freedoms [illegible] or liveries of the said Companies respectively by these presents pardoned or intended to be pardoned. And notwithstanding the not reciting or not expressly and particularly reciting or mentioning the offences crimes violations of the law faults forfeitures pains and penalties by the aforesaid several Companies or any or either of them by reason or occasion of the premises done committed perpetrated or incurred and by these presents pardoned and released or intended to be pardoned and released. And notwithstanding the not mentioning or not rightly and expressly mentioning the aforesaid imprisonments of the said several Companies Guilds Fraternities and Commonalties aforesaid or their defaults errors and offences touching or concerning their good rule or government and notwithstanding any other defects uncertainties or imperfections in these our letters patent contained and notwithstanding any statute act ordinance provision or restriction or any other thing cause or matter whatsoever to the contrary thereof in anywise notwithstanding although express mention &c. In witness whereof &c.

Witness The King at Westminster the eighteenth day of October.

BY THE KING HIMSELF.

APPENDIX, No. 18.

PAPER handed in by the *Chairman*.

PETITIONS to PARLIAMENT by the COMPANIES, 11 January, 16th Charles I., 1640–41.

Jn. Wright, No. 39, fo. 164—(Appellants' Appendix, pages 69–81).

COMMON COUNCIL, 11th Jeary, 16th Cha' 1st 1641.

To the Right Hoble the Knights Citizens and Burgesses of the House of Comons in this Parliament assembled.

The humble Petition of the Maior and Cominaltie and Citizens of the City of London in the behalf of themselves and of dyvers Companyes of that City and of Others late having Lands and Tenements in the County of London Derry in the Province of Ulster in the Realme of Ireland.

In all humbly Sheweth: That about July in the Seventh yeare of the reigne of our late Soveraigne Lord King James a proppsicion was made by ye Lords of His said late Maty Privy Councell to ye City of London to undertake the plantacon of divers lands of great extent in the Province of Ulster in the remotest pt of the North of Ireland (at that time deserted by other planters) wch the City at first refused to undertake but upon the pressing importunity of the said Lords that some selected psons from the City might be sent to view the Country and the said Plantacon might be undertaken and upon signification of his said late Mats earnest desire to furthere the said worke and upon tender of large priviledges and immunities to invite them thereunto certaine psons of that City were employed to view the premisses and upon their returne divers Aldren and Comoners were appointed to take into their consideracon how so great a worke might be performed and mony raised for the doing of it by whome it was conceaved that it was fittest to be done by the Companyes of this City and in the Companyes by the Poll and that the said Plantacon should be managed by a Company to be erected for that purpose and that the said Company should take by grant from his said late Matie the said lands to the end they should assign them over to the use and benefit of such from whome the said moneys were to be raised and divers other matters were by them thought meete to be required for the accomplishmt of the said worke wch consideracons being by them presented to the Lords they were by them allowed and approved of and it was required by their Lops that the City should expende but £20,000 whereof £5,000 should goe to cleere ptiuler interests And in January following certen speall Articles were agreed upon betweene the said Lords and the Committee appointed by the said Citie as well concerning 20,000li that should be expended about the said plantacon and in purchasing of private psons interests in the things required as other matters touching the said plantacon the said Comitee absolutely refusing in anywise to be regulated by or to have any relacon to the printed articles or declaracon sett forth and published by his said late Matie for comon and ordinary undertakers in respect they were to build Derry and Coleraine and to search for and find out most of their materialls for building in a naked and wild Country whereupon his said late Mats Surveyor Generall of the Kingdom of Ireland according to a warrant unto him in that behalf directed made a ptiuler of the lands tenements and hereditaments that were to be granted and of the rents to be reserved for the same wch being pfected and returned into England Sr Henry Hobart His Mats then Attorney Generall being a prudent and learned man had warrant from the then lords Thier to drawe a booke to the Comittee to be passed by the Citie of all the lands tenemts and hereditamts menconed in the said ptiuler and before the said graunt was pfected divers lrs were by the said lords sent and directed to ye said Committee appointed by the City to manage the affaires of the said plantacon by the name of ye Governor Deputy and Assistants of London of the new plantacon in Ulster for the yssuing forth of divers great somes of mo: to such persons as were interested in the said lands and also direccons were given by their Lops in theire behalfe by that name unto his Maties said Attorney Generall touching ye said grannt and for that the Corporacon of the said Citie of London never undertooke ye the said plantacon or as to the use of the said Citty disbursed any money thereabouts but their name was only used for the better transaccon of that business and only as a meane to forward the plantacon and raise moneys by and from the severall Companyes and pticular psons as aforesaid wch otherwise could never have been effected the said new Corporacon of the Governor and Assistants of London was erected & to them and their successors were the premisses granted by his Maties lres Patents under the Great Seal of England bearing date the xxixth day of March in the eleaventh yeare of his said late Maties reigne to th' end they might distribute the same to the severall Companies of the said Cittye that had lent and were to undergoe the charge of the said plantacon and in pursuance of the said intencon the said Society did by virtue of a lycense from the said late Matie under the Great Seale of England graunte unto the 12 chief Companyes of London to the use of themselves and of such other Companyes as were joyned wth them sundry great quantities and pcells of the said lands tenemts and hereditamts according to their respective disbursemts and retained in their owne hands such things as were not proply divisable for the defraying of the genrall works of the plantacon in and about which works in hope to have in the future enjoyed some benefitt of their great cost and charge there was expended by the said Societye and the severall Companyes of the said Citty above One hundred and thirtie thousand pounds besides many thousands of pounds expended by their tenntts they having new built the Citie of London Derry and towne of Coleraine and enclosed the City of Derry wth a very fair and strong stone wall rampard wth earth wth gates and bulwarks answerable and built thereon a very faire Church wch cost above 4,000l with a towne house and freeschoole having also made at Coleraine walls and gates wth a large ditch of twenty foote wide having alsoe new built the greatest pte of the castle of Culmore and repayred the other pte thereof and furnished ye said City of Derry and Towne of Coleraigne with arms and munition and the said Castle of Culmore with ordinance armes and municon and built upon the Country lands divers villages forts or bawnes and furnished them alsoe with armes and municon and alsoe new built and repaired fifteen churches upon the Country lands and furnished them with all things needfull and making their wayes passable for draught or otherwise wch before were very dangerous by wch their cost and charges those pts being in former times the most barbarous places of the whole Kingdome became the most civilised of any of the remote parts thereof and the Country able to muster neere upon 3,000 men Brittish well armed and the said Societie and others claiming from them having enjoyed the said lands and premisses during all the residue of the reigne of his said late Matie and untill Hillary Terme in the sixt yeare of the reign of our Most gracious Soveraigne an informacon was then exhibited by Sr Robbert Heath his Maties then Attorney Generall against ye petitioners the Maior and comialtie & citizens of the said Citie of London and against some pticular psons wherein and whereby it was suggested that they had possest themselves of the said lands and taken the profitts before any grannt was made thereof unto them and had a greater quantity of land passed by the said grannt than was intended and that they had by indirect meanes procured ye said grannt to be passed and divers privilidges to be inserted therein for wch the said Attorney Generall that passed the same had noe warrant and that divers other supposed offences had been don and committed by them in and concerning the plantacon for wch cause divers witnesses were examined but before the same was brought to a hearing another informacon was in Hillary terme in the eighth yeare of his now Maties raign exhibited in the said Court against ye petitioners and against the said Societie of the Governors and Assistants of London of the new plantacon in Ulster in the Realme of Ireland and some other pticular psons in wch latter informacon was charged the undue procuring of the said letters patent to be made to the said Societie and for not pforming the lres patent and divers other new charges were inserted and yett ye proofes and depositions taken in the former cause unto wch the said Societie was noe ptie were by order of that Court made use of at the hearing upon the latter informacon. And your Petitioners the Maior and Comialtie of the said City of London who had never anything to doe wth yor sd plantacon otherwise than as aforesaid nor disbursed any moneys or received any benefitt or profitt thereby and the said Societie of Governor and Assistants were by ye sentence of ye said Court in Hilary terme in the tenth yeare of his Maties raigne upon the premisses aforesaid and stand like adjudged to pay 70,000l fine to His Matie and that the said patent being then adjudged to be unduly and surrepticiously obtained to the prjudice and deceipt of his Matie and their estate and interests therein should be by them forthwth surrendered up to his Matie and should be brought into that Court there to be cancelled and made voyd or otherwise disposed of at his Maties pleasure. And it was further declared and ordered that if the said Companyes and their Farmers should not in pursuance of the intencon of that sentence surrender their estate his Maties Attorney Generall should exhibite an informacon to bring them also to judgment. In pursuance of wch part of the said sentence his Maties Attorney Generall in Michas Terme following exhibited a third informacon in the said Court wherein it was recyted that his Maties said Attorney had written severall lres to the 12 Chief Companyes of the said Citie thereby desiring them to surrender unto his Maties hands all such pts of ye premisses as had been conveyed unto them yet the said 12 Companyes and their Farmers and Others confederating wth ye former Defendts had procured to themselves severall Estates and utterly refused to surrender the same into his Maties hands or to bring in their Conveyances to be cancelled as by the declaracon conteyned in the foresaid decree was expressed about which time alsoe a Commission was awarded out of His Maties Court of Exchequer whereby certen Comrs therein named were to enquire of the lands tenemts goods and chattels belonging to to the Corporacon of the said Maior and Cominaltie of the said Citie of London and to the said Societie to the end the same might be extended towards satisfaction of the said fine when proceeded therein accordingly and likewise severall extents were sued out of the said Court and seizures made of divers lands belonging to ye said Citie and to the bridgehouse and which were anciently given for reparacon of the bridge and defraying the publique charges of the said Citie by reason whereof they could make noe new leases and estates, this and divers leases of lands of good value in severall Counties of this Kingdome were extended and exposed to sale the rents and profitts of the said lands and premisses in Ireland were sequestered and divers of the tenants of the lands and houses in and about London to the said Citty apperteyning were commanded to retaine their rents in their hands by reason whereof and of sundry other questions and suits which were sett on foote and prosecuted against the said Corporacon of the Maior and Cominaltie of the said Citie and divers Citizens but principally by reason of the said sentence in Starrchamber tending as the petrs conceaved to the great prejudice and impoverishing not only of the Corporacon of the Maior and Cominaltie of the said Citie but of all the severall Companyes therein they were informed for prevencon thereof not being able to disburse soe greate a summe of money as was required of them to releaste themselves from the penalty of the said sentence and other the premisses and proceedings against them as aforesaid to consent to relinquish their interest in and to the said Yrish lands and to all the arrearages of rents for the same amounting to 20,000li or thereabouts and thereupon a scire facias was brought to repeale the said patent and judgmt was had upon that scire facias by default and the possession of the premisses and divers deeds and evidences concerning the same were taken from the said Companyes wch had the interest therein and had been at such excessive charges about the said plantacon and for which they never had in returne any considerable or competent recompence for forbearance of their money besides the daily care labour and trouble of the Comitties for that plantacon and also the farmers and tents of the said lands who have likewise been at great charges and expences in planting upon the premisses were expelled thence or enforced to make new composicons for pte of their own estates at excessive rates and to forsake the residue and many were then enforced to abandon their dwellings to the great prejudice of the said plantacon and the great impoverishmt of the City of London and the severall Companyes thereof their tents and farmers. Now inasmuch as the proceedings and sentence in ye sd Cause in impeaching and condemning Lres patent whereby soe Great a freehold and inheritance were granted werein your peticoners humbly conceave illegall and irregular and that ye petitioners the Maior and Cominalty and Citizens of the said Citie tho noe parties to any patent or plantacon yett was sentenced and fined at 70,000li upon pretence of breach of trust or Covenantes and for that it was declared that others no pties to the said Suite should if they did not surrender their estates be brought likewise to Judgment and for that the consequence hereof is great in respect of the example and the matter itselfe which much tends to the pjudice of both Kingdomes and reflects upon the honor and justice of His late Matie and his gracious Matie that now is when such solemn Acts and Contracts with soe much advice and upon soe great charge and consideracon done and made shall soe many years after upon pretence of the Kings Attorneys want of sufficient warrant or of his exceeding his warrant of breach of Covenants and other suggestions before declared be made voyd and annulled and soe heavy a fine as 70,000li imposed wthout any respect or consideracon had of soe great expence and of soe difficult a worke pformed in soe remote naked and then in a manner uninhabitable pte of the Country.

Your petrs humbly pray that this matter may receave a full examinacon and hearing and that thereupon such right may be done to the petitioners as in yor great wisdome shall be thought fitt and agreeable to Justice.

And &c.

APPENDIX, No. 19.

PAPER handed in by the *Chairman*.

Jor. 40 *fo.* 4.—Appellants' Appendix, pages 62-63.

COMMON COUNCIL 13th July 1641, 17 Chas 1st

Wright Major

This day Mr Recorder made relacon to this Comon Counsell that the cause of their assembly was touching the peticon wch the City lately pferred to the Comons House of Parlyment concerning the lands in Ireland and that the Committee of the House of Comons thereupon appointed had divers times in the House of Plyament heard the same and the allegacons made by the Cities Councell. And that afterwards his Mats Councell were likewise heard three or foure dayes what they could allege concerning the same and further related that now it is conceaved that the Committee will very shortly determine something therein and in that regards desired the advice of this Courte that in case the said land should be all restored again to this Cittye and that if thereupon some questions or ppositions should be made or asked by the Committee touching any thing to be done or restored to his Maty by the City then what answer to make thereunto.

Whereupon after consideracon had thereof by this Comon Counsell and finding it a matter of great consequence thought fitt and so ordered that the former Comittees wch considered and agreed of the said peticon or such number of them as by the order is menconed shall meete together to-morrow in the afternoone and take into their consideracon what answeare they shall think fitt to give to any ppositions that shall be demanded by the Comittee at ye determynynge of the sayd Cause.

Com. Journ. 20 Aug. 1641.

Mr. Whistler reports the case of Londonderry. *Resolved* upon the Question, That the opinion of this House is,

1. That the Citizens of London were sollicited and pressed to the undertaking of the plantation of Londonderry.

Resolved, &c.

That the copy attested with Mr. Goad's hand is a true copy of the Sentence given in the Star Chamber against the Mayor and Commonalty of the City of London, and the Society of the Governor and Assistants of London of the New Plantation of Ulster in the Kingdom of Ireland.

Resolved, &c.

That the order made in the Court of Star Chamber dated 8° Martii 8° Caroli is unlawful both for the matter, persons, and time, therein prefixed.

Resolved,

4. That this House is of opinion that the King was not deceived in the grant which he made unto the Society of Governor and Assistants of London of the New Plantation of Ulster in the Kingdom of Ireland; in particular, not in creating a new Corporation, called The Society of the Governor and Assistants of London of the new plantation of Ulster in the Kingdom of Ireland.

5. Resolved, That this House is of opinion that the King did not by that patent grant more lands than was by him intended to be granted; nor was therein deceived.

6. That it doth not appear by sufficient proof that the Citizens of London were tied to perform the printed Articles; and consequently not bound to plant with English and Scots; nor restrained from planting with natives.

7. By the 27th Article the City was to build 200 houses in Derry, and 100 at Coleraine by the 1st day of Novr 1611: Admitting the houses were not built nor the Castle of Culmore repaired by the time prefixed; yet this is no crime, nor cause for giving damages, in regard the City had not their patent until the 29th of March 1613.

8. That

8. That there is no proof that the Governor, &c. of the New Plantation or any of the 12 Companies, did make any Lease to any popish recusant, nor of any decay of Religion there by default of the Planters.

9. That there is no proof of any default in the Planters for not making a sufficient number of freeholders; nor any article that doth tie them thereunto.

10. That there is not proof that the City of London, or the Governor of the new plantations, have felled any trees in the woods called Glanconkein and Killetragh, contrary to their covenant.

11. That the not conveying of glebe lands to the several incumbents of the several parish churches, in regard they did enjoy the lands, is no crime punishable, or cause of seizure of their lands.

12. That the breach of covenant (if any such were) is not sufficient cause to forfeit the lands.

13. That the breach of covenant is no crime but triable in ordinary Courts of Justice.

14. That the Court of Star Chamber (while it stood as a Court) had no power to examine Freehold or Inheritance.

15. That the Court of Star Chamber (whilst it stood as a Court) had not any power to examine or determine Breach of Covenants or Trusts.

16. That the Sentence upon these Two Corporations aggregate, no particular person being guilty, it is against Law.

17. That in all the proof of this cause there doth not appear matter sufficient to convince the City of London of any crime.

18. That upon the whole matter this sentence in the Star Chamber was unlawful and unjust.

19. That this Composition and Agreement made with the City upon these terms, in this time of extremity, ought not to bind the City.

20. That this House is of opinion that when the King shall be pleased to repay those monies which he hath received upon this composition, and such rents as he hath received by colour of this Sentence, that then His Majesty shall be restored to the same state he was in, and the Patent thereupon gotten shall be cancelled or surrendered.

21. That the Citizens of London and all those against whom the Judgment is given in the Scire facias shall be discharged of that Judgment.

22. That the opinion of this House is that they think fit that both the Citizens of London and those of the New Plantation, and all undertenants, and all those put out of possession by the Sequestration or King's Commissioners, shall be restored to the same state they were in before the Sentence in the Star Chamber.

The Case of Tristram Beresford, Ralph Freeman, and John Stone.

Resolved, upon the Question, that the Conveyances to Mr. Beresford and the rest of the parties to whom the Conveyances were made are well executed:

That by the Haberdashers being made no parties to the Scire facias their estate is not avoided by the Judgment.

That the opinion of this House is that the sd parties ought to be in the same estate they were in before the issuing of His Majesty's Commission.

Jor. 40 fo. 90.—Appellants' Appendix, page 94.

COMMON COUNCIL 30th Nov 1641, 17 Car. I.

Gurney Maior.

And further Mr Recorder was pleased to intimate to this Comon Councell the Business of London Derry lately voted for the Citty by this Honoble House of Comons and concerninge wch His Matie was graciously pleased at his entrance from Scotland into this Citty to declare his Royall assent to restore it to the Citty and to take the same into their consideracons touching the manner how a Bill may be pferred in Plyament for the confirminge thereof to the Companyes of this Citty. But with all alleged that before any Bill can be pferred there bee many pticulars to bee thought of because the Corporacon is dissolved and besides to consider in whose names to lodge the same either in the Maior and Comalty of London or a select Company and therefore desire them to think of a Committee touching the same.

Whereupon after consideracon had thereof by this Comon Councill It is Ordered and agreed that the same Businesse shall bee referred to the consideracon of the Comittee formerly appointed for matters for the good of the City and fitt to be psented to the Honoble House of Comons and that Sr Nicholas Rayneton Kt shallbee added a Comittee to joyne with them in the place of Sir Xpofer Clethroid Knt deceased.

APPENDIX, No. 20.

PAPER handed in by the *Chairman*.

THE IRISH SOCIETY TO THE WORSHIPFUL COMPANY OF MERCERS.

COUNTERPART RELEASE OF THE MANOR OF MERCERS.—5th *August* 1658.

THIS INDENTURE made the fifth day of August In the yeare of o^r Lord God according to the accompt now used in England One thousand sixehundred fiftie and eight betweene the SOCIETIE OF THE GOVERNOR AND ASSISTANTS OF LONDON of the New Plantation in Ulster in Ireland of the one parte and the WARDENS AND COMINALTIE OF THE MISTERY OF MERCERS OF THE CITTIE OF LONDON of the other parte. WHEREAS King James late King of England by his L̃res Patents under the Great Seale of England bearing date at Westminster the nyne and twentith day of Marche in the eleaventh yeare of his raigne over England Ffrance and Ireland and over Scotland the sixe and ffortith for the consideration therein expressed of his especiall grace certaine knowledge and meere motion Did amongst other things will & graunte ordaine & constitute that there should be from thenceforth twentie and sixe honest and discreete citizens of the Cittie of London in England which should bee and should be called the Societie of the Governo^r and Assistants of London of the New Plantation in Ulster within the realme of Ireland and them into one new bodie corporate and politique in deed fact and name by the name of the Societie of the Governo^r and Assistants of London of the New Plantation in Ulster within the realme of Ireland Did erect make ordeine create constitute and declare AND WHEREAS also the said late King James did in and by the said L̃res Patents give and grant or did mention therein to give and grant unto the said Societie of the Governor and Assistants of London of the New Plantation in Ulster within the realme of Ireland and theire successo^rs divers townes villages hamletts baronies lordshipps manno^rs territories lands tenements rents services woods underwoods liberties powers priviliges franchises jurisdiction heriditaments and divers other things in the said Letters Patents mentioned and contained. AND WHEREAS also the said late King James in and by the said L̃res Patents (amongst other things) Did give and grant unto the said Societie of the Governor and Assistants of London of the New Plantation in Ulster within the realme of Ireland and theire successo^rs ffull free and lawfull power facultie and authoritie to make erect and ordaine out of and uppon the same lands tẽnts and heriditaments in and by the said L̃res Patents granted or aine of them soe manie severall mannors of such tenũte as were in the said L̃res Patents lymitted as from time to time should seeme convenient to the same Societie of the Governor and Assistants of London of the New Plantation in Ulster within the realme of Ireland and theire successo^rs (that is to say) That they might make erect and ordaine one mannor of every thousand acres of land by the said L̃res Patents granted or of anie number exceeding the number of a thousand acres of land and soe according to such rate soe manie severall manno^rs as they would soe that they made not aine manno^r of a lesser number of acres of land than of the number of a thousand acres of land and to appointe and lymitt to the said severall mannors soe manie acres distinct and severed for demeasne lands of the same severall manno^rs and of everie of them as should seeme necessarie and convenient to the said Societie of the Governor and Assistants of London of the New Plantation in Ulster within the realme of Ireland and theire successo^rs and to name and call the said mannors by such names as the said Societie of the Governo^r and Assistants of London of the New Plantation in Ulster within the realme of Ireland and theire successo^rs would or should thinke fitt as by the said Letters Patents relation being thereunto had more at large appeareth. AND WHEREAS the said Societie of the Governor and Assistants of London of the New Plantation in Ulster within the realme of Ireland by virtue power and authoritie of the said L̃res Patents by theire deed or writing sealed with the Common Seale of the said Societie bearing date the fifteenth day of October Anno Dni 1616. And in the yeare of the raigne of the late King James of England Ffrance and Ireland the fourteenth and of Scotland the fiftieth. Did make erect and ordaine of and uppon the lands tẽnts and hereditaments with theire appurtẽnces in the said deed or writing and hereafter

hereafter in theis psts particulerlie named menc̃oned and expressed being parte of the said lands tents hereditaments and p̃misses unto them granted by the said late King James as aforesaid one manno' to consist of such lands as in the said Lres Patents was lymitted. And also did by the said deed or writing appointe and lymite that parte of the said lands and tenements soe by the said deed or writing made and reduced or meant or intended to be made or reduced into a manno' as aforesaid and therein ptiularlie named menc̃oned and expressed should be and should be called and accompted esteemed and taken to be the demeasne lands of the same mano'. And should be and continue parcell of the said mano'. And also did by the said deed or writing name and call the said mannor and all and singuler the lands tents and hereditaments thereby made or intended to be made a manno' by the name of the Manno' of Mercers. And did also lymitt ordaine and appointe divers other matters and things touching and concerning the said mannor in the said deed or writing menc̃oned and expressed As by the said deed or writing due relac̃on being thereunto had more at large it doth and may appeare. And whereas also the said Societe of the Governor and Assistants of London of the New Plantac̃on in Ulster within the realme of Ireland by virtue of the said Lres Patents and of a licence from the said late King James under the then Great Seale of England bearing date at Westminster the thirtith day of September in the thirteenth yeare of his raigne over England ffrance and Ireland and over Scotland the nyne and fortith by theire deed or writing indented sealed with the Comon Seale of the said Societie bearing date the Seaventeenth day of October Anno Dni 1618. And in the yeares of the raigne of the late King James over England ffrance and Ireland the sixteenth and over Scotland the two and fiftith made betweene the said Societe of the Governor and Assistants of London of the New Plantac̃on in Ulster within the realme of Ireland of the one parte and the said Wardens and Comunaltie of the Misterie of Mercers of the Cittie of London of the other parte ffor the considerac̃on in the said last recited deed or writing indented menc̃oned and expressed Did grant bargaine sell aliene enfeoffe and confirme unto the said Wardens and Comunaltie of the Misterie of Mercers aforesaid theire successo's and assignes for ever all that the Mannor of Mercers with the rights members and appurtenances thereof lyeing and being within the Countie of Londonderry within the province of Ulster within the realme of Ireland. And divers lands tents and hereditaments in the said recited deed or writing indented and hereafter in theis presents particularlie named menc̃oned and expressed As by the said last recited deed or writing indented due relacion being thereunto had more at large it doth and may appeare. And whereas afterwards by sentence of the Court of Star Chamb in the tenth yeare of the raigne of the late Kinge Charles uppon severall p̃tences and suggestions It was adjudged that the said Lres Patents of King James and the estates and interests therein should be forthwith surrendered upp unto the said late King Charles & should be brought into that Court there to be cancelled & made voide or otherwise disposed of at the pleasure of the said late King Charles. And whereas a scire facias was afterwards in pursuance of the said sentence brought to repeale the said Lres Patents whereuppon a Judgement was accordingly had in the Court of Chancerie and the said Lres Patents and the enrollment thereof were cancelled and made voide and the possession of the p̃misses taken from the said Societie and Companies of London and others who had the interest therein. And whereas uppon the humble petic̃on of the Maio' and Comunaltie and Cittizens of the Cittie of London on the behalfe of themselves and of divers Companies of that Cittie and of others then having lands and tents in the Countie of Londonderry exhibited in the Highe Court of Pliament uppon full and mature considerac̃on had and taken of the judgement and sentence aforesaid it was on or about the nine and twentith day of August One thousand six hundred fortie and one voted and resolved in Parliament (amongst other things) that uppon the whole matter the foresaid sentence in the Star Chamber was unlawfull and unjust. That the cittizens of London and all those against whome the said Judgement was soe given in the said scire facias should be discharged of that Judgem^t. And that both the cittizens of London and all those of the New Plantac̃on and all undertakers and all those put out of possession should be restored to the same estate they were in before the said sentence in the Star Chamber as by the said votes & resolves of Parliament may appeare. And whereas his Highnes Oliver Lord Protector of the Comonwealth of England Scotland and Ireland and the Dominions thereunto belonging To Thend that the said Societie and Companies of London and theire respective assignes and undertenants according to theire former severall rights and interests therein might be restored to and reinvested in all and singular the counties countries cities townes castles mannors territories lands tenements and hereditaments privilidges and ymunities whatsoev' with theire and every of theire appurtenances as setled and vested in them by force and virtue of the foresaid Lres Patents of King James of the nyne and twentith day of Marche in the eleaventh yeare of his raigne over England ffrance and Ireland and over Scotland the sixe and fortith and of the said licence from the said late King James bearing date the said thirtith day of September in the thirteenth yeare of his raigne over England ffrance and Ireland and over Scotland the nyne and fortith and the severall grants thereuppon by the said Societie and Companies respectively theretofore made as fully and beneficially to all intents and purposes as they might have had and enjoyed the same if the aforesaid sentence in the Star Chamber and proceedings thereuppon in the Chancery had never beine had or made. And to the intent That in Manner as was done and used before such interrupc̃on as aforesaid their might be now a Societie made and erected consisting of the like number of honest and discreete citizens of the Cittie of London as the other Societe consisted of formerly and for other causes and reasons. And of his especiall grace certaine knowledge and meere motion by his Highnes Lres Patents under the Great

Seale

Seale of England bearing date at Westminster the fower and twentith day of Marche in the yeare of or Lord God One thowsand sixe hundred fiftie and sixe. Did will and grant ordain and constitute that theire should be for ever thereafter sixe and twentie honest and discreete citizens of the Cittie of London in England in forme in the said Lres Patents declared to be chosen and appointed which should be and should bee called the Societie of the Governor and Assistants of London of the New Plantacon in Ulster in Ireland. And that the said Societie should be and consist of one Governor and Deputie of the said Governor and of fower and twentie assistants. And that as well those in the said Lres Patents constituted and appointed to be the foresaid Societie of the Governor Deputie and Assistants of London of the New Plantacon in Ulster in Ireland as those which hereafter according to the ordinance and provisions in his Highnes said Lres Patents expressed and lymitted shalbe chosen and admitted into the same Societie and theire successors forever hereafter be and shalbe one new bodie corporate and politique in deed fact and name by the name of the Societie of the Governor and Assistants of London of the New Plantacon in Ulster in Ireland and them by the name of the Societie of the Governor and Assistants of London of the New Plantacon in Ulster in Ireland a new body corporate and politique in deed fact and name really and fully for his Highnes and his successors. Did erect make ordaine create constitute and declare by the said Lres Patents. And whereas also his Highnes the Lord Protector in and by his said Lres Patents did grant and confirme unto the said Societie of the Governor and Assistants of London of the New Plantacon in Ulster in Ireland and to theire successors divers counties countries cities townes villages hamletts manors castles territories lands tents woods fishings powers priviledges & other hereditaments lying and being within the province of Ulster in Ireland menconed in the same Lres Patents. And whereas the said Societie of the Governor and Assistants of London of the New Plantacon in Ulster in Ireland by virtue of the said last-menconed Lres Patents and of the power and authoritie thereby to them given and granted by theire deed or writing sealed with the Common Seale of the said Societie bearing date the thirtieth day of July last past before the date hereof Did make erect and ordaine of and upon the lands and tenements with the appurtences in the said last mencioned deed or writing and hereafter in theis presents particularlie named mencioned and expressed being part of the said lands tenements hereditaments and p'mises wherein they are interested as aforesaid one manor to consist of divers tenants. And did also by the said last menconed deed or writing appointe and lymit that parcell of the said lands and tents soe by the said last menconed deed or writing made and ordained or meant or intended to be made or ordained into a manor as aforesaid and therein particularlie named mencioned and expressed should bee and should be called and accompted esteemed and taken to be the demeasne lands of the said manor and should be and continew parcell of the same. And did also by the said last mencioned deed or writing name and call the said Manor & all and singuler the said lands tents and hereditaments thereby made or intended to be made a manor by the name of the Manor of Mercers. And did also by the said last menconed deed or writing lymitt ordaine and appointe divers other matters and things touching and concerning the said manor as by the said last mencioned deed or writing due relacon being thereunto had more at large it doth and may appeare. And whereas also the said Societie of the Governor and Assistants of London of the New Plantacon in Ulster in Ireland for the reinvesting and restating of the said manor or reputed manor and lands hereafter mencioned in the said Warden and Comunaltie of the Misterie of Mercers of the Cittie of London according to the tenour of the foresaid deed or writing indented bearing date the said seaventeenth day of October Anno Dni 1618 made betweene the said Societie of the Governor and Assistants of London of the new Plantacon in Ulster within the realme of Ireland of the one parte And the said Wardens and Coialtie of the Misterie of Mercers of the Cittie of London of the other parte By theire Indenture of Lease bearing date the fowerth day of this instant moneth of August for the consideracon of the some of Tenn shillings of lawfull money of England to them paid by the said Wardens and Coialtie of the Mistery of Mercers of the Cittie of London Did bargaine and sell unto ye said Wardens and Cominaltie of the Misterie of Mercers aforesaid all that the manor or reputed Manor of Mercers with the rights members and appurtenncs thereof lying and being within the Countie of Londonderry within the province of Ulster in Ireland And all the ballibos of land called or knowen by the name of Boveed lying and being in the Barronie of Colraine in the Countie of Londonderry aforesaid. And all that territory ballibetto or porcon of land called or knowne by the name of Mulle Jnah within the Countie of Londonderrie and province of Ulster aforesaid that is to say All lands tenements and other hereditaments knowne or called by the names hereafter menconed or lyeing and being of in or within the severall townes villages hamletts places ballibos or parcells of land following (that is to say) Lenvore being one ballibos of land Caranro being one ballibos of land Towhat being one ballibos of land Coilvemdrean being one ballibos of land with all and singuler theire and everie of theire rights appurtenncs and members. And also all that territorie ballibetto or porcon of land called or knowne by the name of Ballynasmine in the Countie of Londonderry aforesaid (That is to say) all lands tents and other hereditaments knowne or called by the names hereafter menconed or lyeing or being in or within the townes villages hamletts places ballibos or parcell of land following (that is to say) Mavaneher being one ballibos of land with all and singuler the rights appurtenncs and members thereof. And also all that territorie or ballibetto or porcon of land called or knowne by the name of Inishe Reske or Grange in the Countie of Londonderrie aforesaid (that is to say) all lands tents and other hereditaments knowne or called by the names hereafter menconed or lyeing & being of in or within the severall townes villages hamletts places ballibos or parcells of land following (that is to say) Claraleirum being one ballibos of land Leagh Leave being one ballibos of land Moay

Grar

Crun being one balliboe of land Kilfady being one balliboe of land Nergena being one balliboe of land Moyknock being one balliboe of land Liskeagh being one balliboe of land Ffalle Cogey being one balliboe of land Linnagrott being one balliboe of land with all and singuler theire & everie of theire rights members and appurtenñces And also all that territorie balliboto or porcon of land called or knowne by the name of Ffarest Mone within the Countie of Londonderry aforesaid (that is to say) all lands tents and other hereditaments called or knowne by the names hereafter menconed or lyeing & being of in or within the severall townes villages hamletts places balliboes or parcells of land following (that is to say) Drumnaerrah being one balliboe of land Dillaboy being one balliboe of land Moyhenroloy being one balliboe of land Crum Clonnt being one balliboe of land Creggevela being one balliboe of land Ballymeerot being one balliboe of land Laralt being one balliboe of land Lisnakrin being one balliboe of land with all and singuler theire and everie of theire appurtenñces and members. And also all that territorie balliboto or porcon of land called or knowne by the name of Ballynefeetgh within the Countie of Londonderrie aforesaid (that is to say) all lands tents and other hereditaments knowne or called by the names hereafter menconed or lyeing and being of in or within the severall townes villages hamletts places balliboes or parcells of land following (that is to say) Drumabar being one balliboe of land Ballelerne being one balliboe of land Tawney Kingsey being one balliboe of land Carbullan Tabber being one balliboe of land with all and singuler theire and every of theire rights appurtenñces and members. And also all that territorie balliboto or porcon of land called or knowne by the name of Dungleddie in the said Countie of Londonderrie in the province of Ulster aforesaid (that is to say) All lands tents and other hereditaments called or knowne by the names hereafter menconed or lyeing and being of in or within the severall townes villages hamletts places balliboes or parcells of land following (that is to say) Monlabe Allen being one balliboe of land Daugh in Conway being one balliboe of land Lisnevile being one balliboe of land Ballymany being one balliboe of land Bally Money being one balliboe of land Ballyvekeely being one balliboe of land Cortneglee being one balliboe of land Swotrey being one balliboe of land Ureneban being one balliboe of land Ureneban being one balliboe of land Ballynebohey being one balliboe of land Arsford Laune being one balliboe of land Terenegera being one balliboe of land Drummark being one balliboe of land Terregerwell being one balliboe of land Mackeh being one balliboe of land Moneylarnan being one balliboe of land Tere being one balliboe of land Knockneale being one balliboe of land Sleanmale being one balliboe of land Dungleddy being one balliboe of land with all and singuler theire and everie of theire appurtenñces and members whatsoever or by whatsoever other name or names the same lands tents and pmisses before in theis presents severallie or particulerlie named or menconed as aforesaid or anie of them are called reputed knowne or taken And which are contained within the proporcon of the Companie of Mercers of the Cittie of London number (eight) according to theire lott or division with other Companies And were latelie as is before in theis p'sents menconed by the said Societie of the Governor and Assistants of London of the New Plantacon in Ulster in Ireland made erected ordained and reduced into a mannor And also all and everie the rents arrearages of rents suites of court suites of mill reliefes payments in the name of reliefes fynes for alienacons heriotts forfeitures and all other duties paymentes and services reserved due or payable or which hereafter shalbe reserved or growe due or payable by or from the free or other tennts or reputed tennts of the said manno' or reputed manno' And all & singuler messuages howses barnes cottages Bawnes buildings milnes mills lands tents meadowes pastures comons advowsons donacons p'sentacons obvencons tithes waters groundes furrs heathes marishes moores boggs mountaines mosses mynes quaries and mineralls and everie of what nature qualitie or condicon soever they be not being mynes royall woods underwoods waters watercourses weares fyshings fishing places fowlings Courts Baron Courts Leets pfitts and proffitts of Courts Baron and Courts Leets viewes of ffrankpledge and all that to viewe of ffrankpledge doth apperteyne with free libertie to keepe the same courts goods and chatells waved and strayed and all lands goods and chatells of felons ffelons of themselves and of p'sons put in exigent deodands goods confiscated fees escheats forfeitures reliefes heriotts fynes and amerciaments lyberties priviledges estovers faires marketts tolls customes and all other proffitts comodities emoluments royalties and hereditaments whatsoever of what nature qualitie or condicon soever they be within the said Countie of Londonderrie or elsewhere within Ireland to the said manno' or reputed manno' lands tents hereditaments and pmisses aforesaid and everie or anie of them belonging or in anie wise appertaining or accepted reputed deemed or taken as parte parcell or member of the said manno' or reputed manno' lands and p'misses or of or belonging to the same or anie parte thereof or which had beine at anie time or times assigned or intended to create or make the said manno' or reputed manno' or to be parte parcell incident or appurtenante unto the same in as large and ample manner and forme as the said Societie of the Governo' & Assistants of London of the New Plantacon in Ulster in Ireland had the same Except and nevertheles out of the said Indenture of bargaine and sale alwaies reserved as therein and hereafter in theis pnts is excepted and reserved. To have and to hold to them the said Wardens and Comunaltie of the Misterie of Mercers of the Cittie of London theire successo's and assignes from the day next before the day of the date of the said recited Indenture of bargaine and sale for and during the terme of Sixe monethes from thence next ensueing and fully to be compleate and ended At and for the rent of one peppercorne payable the last day of the said terme if the same should be lawfully demanded as by the said last recited Indenture it doth and may more fullie and at large appeare Which said Indenture of bargaine and sale was made to the said Wardens and Cominaltie of the Misterie of Mercers of the Cittie of London to the intent and purpose that they being thereby possessed and interested of and in the said p'misses for the said terme the freehold and inheritance thereof might be conveyed and assured to them and theire successo^rs to and for the use and behoofe of them the said Wardens and Cōmaltie of the Misterie of Mercers of the Cittie of London theire successo^rs and assignes for ever Now Witness these psents that the said Societie of the Governo^r and Assistants of London of the New Plantacon in Ulster in Ireland for and in consideracon of a competent sume of lawfull money of England to them in hand before then sealing of theise p'sents by the said Wardens and Cōmunaltie of the Misterie of Mercers of the Cittie of London well and trulie paid whereof they the said Societie confesse and acknowledge the receipte and themselves therewith fully satisfied and contented and thereof and of everie parte and parcell thereof Doe clearlie acquit and discharge the said Wardens and Cōmaltie of the Misterie of Mercers aforesaid their successo^rs and assignes and everie of them forev^r by theis p'sents As for divers other good and weightie consideracons the Societie thereunto especially moveing Have granted bargained sold remised released and confirmed And by theis p'sents Doe fully cleerely and absolutely grant bargaine sell remise release and confirm unto the said Wardens and Cōminaltie of the Mistery of Mercers aforesaid theire successors and assignes for ever all that the aforesaid manno^r or reputed Manno^r of Mercers with the rights members and appurtenc̄es thereof. And all and every the said lands tents and hereditaments with theire and everie of theire rights members and appurtenc̄es hereinbefore menconed to be by the said recited Indenture of bargaine and sale to the said Wardens & Cōminaltie of the Misterie of Mercers aforesaid bargained and sold or therein meant menconed or intended to be thereby bargained and sold and every part and parcell thereof. And all the estate & estates right title interest p'pertie claime and demands whatsoever of the said Societie of in & to the same or anie parte or p'cell thereof. Except neverthelesse and out of theis p'sents alwaies reserved to the said Societie of the Governor and Assistants of London of the New Plantacōn in Ulster in Ireland theire successo^rs and assignes All timber trees growing and being or that hereafter shall growe or be in or uppon the aforesaid p'misses or any parte thereof with free libertie too and for the foresaid Societie their successo^rs and assignes when and as often as they shall think meet to fell cut downe and carrie away the same and everie or anie parte thereof. To by employed spent and converted for in and about buildings and other necessarie uses in Ireland and not for anie other cause to be m'chandized or sold And also excepted and reserved to the said Societie of the Governor and Assistants of London of the New Plantacōn in Ulster in Ireland theire successo^rs and assignes free libertie to hawke hunt fishe fowle come goe ride carry and recarrie over in through and uppon the same p'misses and everie parte and parcell thereof at all times convenient And also excepted and out of theis p'sents reserved All the fishing and takeing of Salmon and Eeles and other fishes in the Rivers of Bann and Loughfoile within the Prince of Ulster aforesaid and in all creeks and members of the same rivers and either of them and all the ground and soile of the same rivers and either of them And also free libertie too and for the said Societie of the Governor and Assistants of London of the New Plantacōn in Ulster in Ireland theire successo^rs and assignes to digg and searche in the p'misses aforegranted or anie parte thereof Except and other then in the houses gardens orchards meadowes or lands sowed with corne for stone slate leame gravell sand and other necessarie materialls and the same to take and carrie away to be employed and converted for in and about buildings in the foresaid Countie of Londonderry and province of Ulster and not otherwise. To have and to hold the said manno^r or reputed Manno^r of Mercers with the rights members and appurtenc̄es thereof And all and everie the said lands tents and hereditaments by the said last recited Indenture bargained and sold or therein meant menconed or intended to be thereby bargained & sold with theire and everie of theire rights members and appurtenc̄es and everie parte and parcell thereof (except before excepted) unto the said Wardens and Cōminaltie of the Misterie of Mercers of the Cittie of London their successo^rs and assignes forev^r To the onlie use and behoof of the said Wardens and Cōmaltie of the Misterie of Mercers of the Cittie of London theire successo^rs and assignes for ever Yielding and paying therefore yearlie to the said Societie of the Governor and Assistants of London of the New Plantacōn in Ulster in Ireland theire successo^rs and assignes the sume of thirteene shillings and fower pence of lawfull money of England. Att two feasts or termes in the yeare that is to say at the feaste of Saint Michaell Tharchangell and Thanunciacon of the Blessed Virgien Mary by even and equall porcons att or in the Chamber of London situate in or neere the Guildhall in the said Cittie of London in England. And if it shall happen the said yearlie rent of thirteene shillings and fowerpence or anie part thereof to be behinde or unpaid in parte or in all after anie terme of payment thereof on which it ought to be paid according to the true meaning of theis p'nts That then and soe often it shall and may be lawfull to and for the said Societie of the Governo^r and Assistants of London of the New Plantacon in Ulster in Ireland theire successo^rs & assignes into the p'misses aforegranted and every or any pte thereof to enter & distraine and the distresse soe taken to lead chase drive and carry away & with them to detaine untill the foresaid rent soe being behinde & all arrearages thereof (if anie shall be) be according to the true meaning of theis p'nts fullie satisfied and paid. And the said Wardens and Cōmaltie of the Misterie of Mercers of the Cittie of London for them theire successo^rs and assignes Doe cove'nte & grant to and with the said Societie of the Governo^r and Assistants of London of the New Plantacōn in Ulster in Ireland theire successo^rs and assignes by theis p'nts That they the said Societie theire successo^rs agents servants and assignes shall and may from time to time and at all times hereafter have hold take use carrie away and enjoy freelie all and everie the p'misses by theis p'nts excepted or menconed to be excepted and everie of them and

and every parte and parcell of them & everie of them without the lett or interrupcon of the said Wardens and Coialtie of the Misterie of Mercers of the Cittie of London their successors or assignes To be disposed of & ymployed as in the said excepcon is mentioned and expressed. And the said Societie of the Governor and Assistants of London of the New Plantacon in Ulster in Ireland for them and theire successors Doe covenante promise and grant to and with the said Wardens and Coialtie of the Misterie of Mercers of the Cittie of London theire successors and assignes by these presents That they the said Wardens & Coialtie of the Misterie of Mercers of the Cittie of London their successors & assignes paying the rent foresaid and under the Covenants and agreements in these presents contained shall or may at all times from henceforth for ever lawfullie peaceably and quietlie have hold occupie possesse and enjoy the said mannor or reputed mannor lands tenements hereditaments & all & singular other the premises afore hereby granted bargained sold released & confirmed or meant mentioned or intended to be hereby granted bargained sold released & confirmed and every parte & parcell thereof with theire and everie of theire appurtenances (except before excepted) and receive perceive take and enjoy to theire owne use or uses for ever All the rents yssues & profitts thereof As well without anie lawfull lett suite trouble molestacon recoverie eviction or interrupcon of or by the said Societie of the Governor & Assistants of London of the New Plantacon in Ulster in Ireland theire successors or assignes or of or by any other person or persons lawfully clayming or to claime by from or under them or anie of them theire or anie of theire act estate meanes authoritie consent or procurement and that free and cleer & freelie & clearlie acquitted exonerated & discharged or well & sufficiently saved and kept harmles by ye said Societie theire successors & assignes of and from all & singular former bargaines sales guifts grants leases alienacons arrearages of rent estates charges & incumbrances whatsoever had made comitted or done by ye said Societie of the Governor & Assistants of London of the New Plantacon in Ulster in Ireland before then sealing hereof except the before mentioned deed whereby the said mannor is erected made and ordained as aforesaid and except all grants or estates by Indentures of bargaine & sale or release made & granted by the said Societie of ye Governor & Assistants of London of the New Plantacon in Ulster in Ireland to severall persons or freehold tenntes of ye said mannor or reputed mannor or parcell of ye premises by the nominacon & appointment of the said Wardens & Coialtie of ye Misterie aforesaid under certaine rents & services. All & every which rents duties & services in ye said excepted Indentures reserved shall for & notwithstanding anie act or thing made or done or to be made or done by ye said Societie of ye Governor & Assistants of London of the New Plantacon in Ulster in Ireland theire successors or assignes to the contrarie be henceforth due & payable to the said Wardens & Coialtie of ye Mistery of Mercers theire successors & assignes during ye continewance in force of ye same grants & estates respectivelie. And further the said Societie of ye Governor & Assistants of London of ye New Plantacon in Ulster in Ireland for them theire successors & assignes Doe covenante promise & grant to & with the said Wardens & Coialtie of ye Misterie of Mercers aforesaid theire successors & assignes & ety of them by these pnts. That it shall & may be lawful to & for ye said Wardens & Coialtie of ye Misterie of Mercers aforesaid theire successors & assignes by the appointment of ye Genll Agent of ye said Societie for ye time being resident in Ulster for ye affaires of ye said Societie theire to fall cutt downe take & carrie away such & so manie of ye timber trees of ye said Societie standing growing & being nearest or most convenient to the premises aforegranted as shalbe fitt & necessarie for ye building or plantacon of anie howses villages edifices or buildings within ye said mannor or reputed mannor lands & premises. And also that they ye said Societie theire successors & assignes shall & will pay and discharge All rents duties & other payments now due and payable or hereafter to be due or payable to his Highnes the Lord Protector or his successors for or in respect of ye said mannor or reputed mannor lands & premises or anie parte thereof or thereof shall save harmless ye said Wardens & Coialtie & theire successors & the premises by these presents granted or intended to be granted And further that the said Societie their Successors & assignes shall & will from time to time & at all times hereafter for & during the space of ten yeares now next ensuing upon evry reasonable request & at ye cost & charge in ye lawe of ye said Wardens & Coialtie of ye Misterie of Mercers aforesaid theire successors & assignes make doe execute & performe all & every such further conveyance & assurance in ye law whatsoever be it by Indenture deed or deeds feoffmt release confirmacon or otherwise howsoever for ye further better & more perfect absolute conveyance & assurance conveying and assuring of ye said mannor or reputed mannor lands & premises (except as before excepted or mencioned to be excepted) unto ye said Wardens Coialtie theire successors & assignes for ever. As by ye said Wardens & Coialtie theire successors & assignes or theire counsell learned in ye lawe shalbe reasonably advised or devised & required soe as ye said conveyance & assurance doe containe noe further warrantie nor covenante for enjoyeing ye premises then against the Societie & theire successors onlie. And ye said Wardens and Coialtie of ye Misterie of Mercers of ye Cittie of London for them theire successors & assignes doe covenante promise & grant to & with ye said Societie of the Governor & Assistants of London of ye New Plantacon in Ulster in Ireland theire successors & assignes by these presentes That for securing of ye Englishe interest in those parts of ye said province of Ulster in regard of ye multitude of ye Scottishe nacon now being in ye said province That ye said Wardens & Coialtie of ye Misterie of Mercers aforesaid & their successors or assignes or anie of them shall not & will not make or grant att anie time or times hereafter anie estate or estates in anie ye lands tents or hereditamts to them by these presents granted or mentioned to be granted unto anie person or persons of ye Scottish nacon other than to such persons onlie of that nacon to whom they have formerlie made and granted anie estate or estates

 or

or who have been for divers yeares alreadie past resident & inhabiting uppon the same & are of honest conversacon & well affected to ye p^nt Governm^t without ye speciall licence of his Highnes the Lord Protecto^r of the Comonwealth of England Scotland & Ireland & ye dominions & territories thereunto belonging or his successo^rs in that behalfe first had & obtained. In witnes whereof to ye one p^t of theis p^nts Indentures remayning wth ye said Wardens & Cõialtie of ye Mistery of Mercers aforesaid the sd Societie of ye Governor & Assistants of London of ye New Plantacõn in Ulster in Ireland have caused theire Comon Seale to be put. And to ye other p^te thereof remayning with the said Societie the sd Wardens & Cõmũltie of the Misterie aforesaid have caused theire Comon Seale to be put ye even ye day & yeare first above written.

Exaied. by J^o. GODFREY (L. S.)

Clarke of the Compa of Mercers Lond. & JOHN QUICKE serv^t to Edward Taylor Clarke to ye Society of ye Govern^r & Assistants of London of ye new plant^n in Ulster in Ireland abovesaid.

APPENDIX, No. 21.

PAPER handed in by the *Chairman*.

RELEASE of the MANOR OF MERCERS, 5th June 1663.

THIS INDENTURE made the fifth day of June Anno Dni One thousand six hundred Sixty and three And in the fifteenth yeare of the Reigne of Or Soveraigne Lord Charles the second by the Grace of God King of England Scotland France and Ireland Defender of the Faith etc. BETWEENE the Society of the Governor and Assistants London of the New Plantation in Ulster within the Realme of Ireland of the one part And the Wardens and Cominalty of the Mistery of Mercers of the City of London of the other part WHEREAS King James late King of England by his Letters patents under the great seale of England bearing date at Westminster the Nyne and Twentieth day of March in the eleaventh yeare of his Reigne over England France and Ireland and over Scotland the Sixe and fortith for the consideration therein mentioned Of his especiall grace certaine knowledge and meere motion Did (amongst other things) will and grant ordaine and constitute That there should be from thenceforth Sixe and twenty honest and discreete Citizens of the City of London in England which should be and should be called the Society of the Governor and Assistants London of the New Plantation in Ulster within the Realme of Ireland And them into one New Body Corporate and Politique in Deed fact and Name by the Name of the Society of the Governor and Assistants London of the New Plantation in Ulster within the Realme of Ireland Did erect make Ordaine Create constitute and declare AND WHEREAS ALSO the said late King James Did in and by the said Letters Patents give and grant or did mention therein to give and grant unto the said Society of the Governor and Assistants London of the new plantation in Ulster within the Realme of Ireland and their successors Divers Townes Villages hamletts Barronies Lordshipps Mannors Territories Lands Tenements fishings Rents Services Woods Underwoods Liberties powers priviledges franchises Jurisdictions hereditaments and divers other things in the said Letters Patents mentioned and conteyned AND WHEREAS ALSO the said late King James in and by the said Letters Patents (amongst other things) Did give and grant unto the same Society of the Governor and Assistants London of the New Plantation in Ulster within the Realme of Ireland and their successors full free and lawfull power faculty and authority to make erect and ordaine out of and upon the said lands Tenements and hereditaments in and by the said Letters Patents granted or any of them soe many severall mannors of such Tenants as were in the said Letters Patents lymitted and from time to time should seeme convenient to the said Society and their Successors That is to say That they might make erect and ordaine one Mannor of every Thousand acres of Land by the said Letters Patents granted or of any Number exceeding the Number of One Thousand acres of Land and soe according to such rate soe many severall Mannors as they would See so they made not any mannor of a lesser number of acres of land then of the number of One thousand acres of land And to appointe and limitt to the same severall mannors soe many acres of land distinct and severed for demesne lands of the said severall Mannors and of every of them as should seeme necessary and convenient to the said Society of the Governor and Assistants London of the New Plantation in Ulster within the Realme of Ireland and their Successors And to name and call the said Mannors by such names as the same Society and their Successors would or should think fitt As by the said Letters Patents relation being thereunto had more at large may appeare AND WHEREAS the said Society of the Governor and Assistants London of the new plantation in Ulster within the Realme of Ireland by virtue power and authority of the said Letters Patents by their Deed or Writing sealed with the Common seale of the foresaid Society bearing date the fifteenth day of October Anno Dni One thousand six hundred and Eighteene, and in the yeares of the Reigne of the late King James of England France and Ireland the Sixteenth and of Scotland the Two and fiftith Did make erect and ordaine of and upon the lands tenements and hereditaments with their appurtenances in the said deed or writing and hereafter in these presents particularly named mentioned and expressed being part of the lands Tenements hereditaments and premises Soe to them granted by the said late King James as aforesaid one Mannor to consist of such Tennants as in the said Letters Patents was lymitted And alsoe did by the said Deed or writing appointe and lymitt that parcell of the said lands and Tenements Soe by the said Deed or writing made and reduced or mentioned or intended to be made or reduced into a mannor as aforesaid and therein particularly named mentioned and expressed should be and should be called and accompted esteemed and taken to be the demesne lands of the said Mannor and should be and continue parcell of the said Mannor And also did by the said deed or writing name and call the said Mannor and all and singular the lands Tenements and hereditaments thereby made or intended to be made a Mannor by the name of the Mannor of MERCERS And did alsoe by the said deed or writing lymitt ordaine and appointe Divers other matters and things touching and concerning the said Mannor in the said Deed or writing mentioned and expressed As by the said deed or writing relation being thereunto had more at large it doth and may appeare AND WHEREAS ALSO the same Society of the Governo^r and Assistants London of the new plantac̄on in Ulster within the Realme of Ireland by virtue of the said Letters Patents and of a License from the said late King James under the great seale of England bearing date at Westminster the Thirtith day of September in the thirteenth yeare of his reigne over England ffrance and Ireland and over Scotland the Nyne and fortith By their Deed or Writing Indented bearing date the Seaventeenth day of October One thousand six hundred and Eighteene And in the yeare of the Reigne of the late King James of England ffrance and Ireland the Sixteenth and of Scotland the two and ffiftith made betweene the said then Society of the Governo^r and Assistants London of the new plantac̄on of Ulster within the realme of Ireland of the one part And the Wardens and Comunalty of the Mistery of the Mercers of the City of London of the other part ffor the considerac̄on in the said Deed or writing indented menc̄oned and expressed Did grant bargaine sell aliene enfeoffe and confirme unto the said Wardens and Comunalty of the Mistery of Mercers aforesaid their successo^{rs} and assignes for ever All that the Manno^r of Mercers with the rights members and appurtenances thereof lying and being within the County of Londonderry within the province of Ulster and Realme of Ireland And divers lands tenements and hereditaments in the said recited Deed or writing Indented and hereafter in these p^rsents particularly menc̄oned and expressed As by the said recited deed or writing Indented due relac̄on being thereunto had more at large also it doth and may appeare AND WHEREAS the said Letters Patents were afterwards repealed and cancelled in the high Court of Chancery by reason thereof the said Society and Companies of London and theire respective Assignes and undertennants were wholly deprived of all and every the lands tenements and hereditaments Royalties ffranchises priviledges and Immunities in the said Letters Patents menc̄oned And the said Society of the Governo^r and Assistants London of the new plantac̄on in Ulster within the Realme of Ireland (thereby incorporated and created) became invalid and was disolved AND WHEREAS the late King Charles the ffirst of ever blessed memory In the yeare of O^r Lord One thousand six hundred fforty and one of his princely goodnes to the Maio^r and Comunalty and Citizens of the City of London was pleased to declare his Royall will and pleasure for the restoring back to the said Society and Companies of all and every the lands royaltyes and priviledges in the said Letters Patents menc̄oned and gave his Royall commands for seeing the same accomplished but the late warrs and troubles in the Kingdom of Ireland shortly after breaking forth his princely intention tooke noe effect AND WHEREAS o^r now Soveraigne Lord Charles the Second by the Grace of God of England Scotland ffrance and Ireland King Defender of the ffaith, etc. Uppon the humble petic̄on of severall Companies of the City of London and takeing into his princely considerac̄on the vast sumes of money the foresaid Society and the severall Companies of London had laid out and disbursed in their building and planting the City and County of Londonderry and Towne of Colraine within the Province of Ulster within the Realme of Ireland aforesaid And to the intent that the said Society or some other such Society (to be by his Majesty created and constituted) And the said severall Companies of London and their respective Assignes and Undertennants according to their severall rights and interests therein might be restored and reinvested in and to all and singular the Countyes Countryes Cityes Townes Castles Territories Lands Tenements hereditaments Royaltyes ffranchises priviledges and Immunityes whatsoever with their and every of their appurtenances Soe settled and vested in them by force and virtue of the foresaid Letters Patents of King James bearing date the said Nyne and Twentieth day of March in the Eleventh yeare of his Reigne over England ffrance and Ireland and of Scotland the Nyne and fortith And of the said Licence from the said late King James bearing date the said Thirtith day of September in the Thirteenth yeare of the Reigne of the said late King James over England ffrance and Ireland and over Scotland the Nyne and fortith And the severall grants thereupon by the said Society and Companies Respectively theretofore made As fully and beneficially to all intents and purposes as they might have had and enjoyed the same if noe such repeale of the said Letters Patents had ever beene had or made And to the intent that there might be a new Society made and erected consisting of the like Number of honest and discreete Citizens of the City of London as the other Society consisted of formerly And for divers other causes and reasons And of his especiall grace certaine knowledge and meere moc̄on By his highnes Letters Patents under the great Seale of England bearing date at Westminster the Tenth day of Aprill in the ffowerteenth yeare of his Reigne Did will and grant ordaine and constitute That there should be for ever thereafter Six and Twenty honest and discreete Citizens of the City of London in the Kingdome of England in forme in the said Letters Patents declared to be chosen and appointed which should be and should be called the Society of the Governo^r and Assistants London of the new plantac̄on in Ulster within the Realme of Ireland And that the said Society should bee and consist of one Governo^r one Deputy of the said Governo^r and of fower and Twenty Assistants And that as well those in the said Letters Patents constituted and appointed to be the foresaid Society of the Governo^r and Assistants London of the new plantac̄on in Ulster within the Realme of Ireland As those which hereafter according to the Ordinances and provisions in his Majestye's said Letters Patents expressed and lymited shalbe chosen and admitted into the same Society and their Successo^{rs} for ever hereafter be and shalbe one new body corporate and politique in Deed fact and name by the name of the Society of the Governo^r and Assistants London of the new plantac̄on in Ulster within the Realme of Ireland And them by the name of the Society of the Governo^r and Assistants London of the new plantac̄on in Ulster within the Realme of Ireland a new body corporate and politique in deed fact and name really and fully for his highnes his heires and successo^{rs} Did erect make ordaine create constitute and Declare

Declare by the said Letters Patents AND WHEREAS ALSO his Sacred Majesty King Charles the Second in and by his said Letters Patents did grant and confirme unto the said Society of the Governo^r and Assistants London of the New Plantacon in Ulster within the Realme of Ireland and to their Successo^rs divers Counties Countryes Cittyes Townes Villages hamletts Manno^rs Castles Territories Lands Tenements Woods fishings powers priviledges and other hereditaments lying and being within the Province of Ulster and Realme of Ireland menconed in the said Letters Patents of the Tenth day of Aprill in the said flowerteenth yeare of his reigne. AND WHEREAS the said Society of the Governo^r and Assistants London of the new plantacon in Ulster within the Realme of Ireland by virtue of the said last menconed Letters Patents and of the power and authority thereby to them given and granted by their Deed or writing sealed with the Comon seale of the same Society bearing date the Thirtith day of May last past before the date hereof Did make erect and ordaine of and upon the Lands and Tenements with the appurtenances in the said last menconed deed or writing and hereafter in these p^rsents particularly named menconed and expressed * being part of the * said lands Tenements hereditaments and p^rmisses wherein they are reestated as aforesaid One Manno^r to consist of divers tenements And did alsoe by the said last menconed Deed or writing appointe and lymitt that parcell of the said lands and Tenements See by the said last menconed Deed or writing made and reduced or meant or intended to be made or reduced into a Manno^r as aforesaid and therein particularly menconed and expressed should be and should be called accompted esteemed and taken to be the Demeasne Lands of the said Manno^r and should be and continew parcell of the said Manno^r And did alsoe by the said last menconed deed or writing name and call the said Manno^r and all singular the said lands Tenements and hereditaments thereby made or intended to be made a Manno^r by the name of the Manno^r of Mercers And did alsoe by the said last menconed deed or writing lymitt ordaine and appointe Divers other matters and things touching and concerning the said Manno^r As by the said last menconed deed or writing due relacon being thereunto had It doth and may more at large appeare AND WHEREAS ALSO the said Society of the Governo^r and Assistants London of the new plantacon in Ulster within the Realme of Ireland for the revesting and reestating of the said Manno^r and lands hereafter menconed in the said Wardens and Cominalty of the Mistery of Mercers of the Citty of London aforesaid according to the Tenno^r of the foresaid deed or writing Indented bearing date the said Seaventeenth day of October One thousand sixe hundred and eighteene And in the yeares of the Reigne of the said late King James of England ffrance and Ireland the Sixteenth and of Scotland the two and fiftith made betweene the said then Society of the Governo^r and Assistants London of the new plantacon in Ulster within the realme of Ireland of the one part And the said Wardens and Cominalty of the Mistery of the Mercers of the Citty of London of the other part By theire Indenture of Bargaine and Sale bearing date the flowerth day of this instant month of June ffor the consideracon of the some of Tenn shillings of lawfull money of England to them paid by the said Wardens and Cominalty of the Mistery of the Mercers aforesaid Did bargaine and sell unto the said Wardens and Cominalty of the Mistery of Mercers aforesaid All that the Manno^r or reputed Manno^r of Mercers with the rights members and appurtenances thereof lying and being within the County of Londonderry within the Province of Ulster in the Realme of Ireland. And alsoe all the Ballibos of land called or knowne by the name of Roveed lying and being within the Barrony of Colraine in the County of Londonderry aforesaid AND all that Territory Ballibetto or porcon of land called or knowne by the name of Mulla Jack within the County of Londonderry and Province of Ulster aforesaid (That is to say) All those lands Tenements and other hereditaments knowne or called by the names hereafter menconed or lying or being of in or within the severall Townes Villages hamletts places Ballibooes or parcells of land following (that is to say) Lanvere being one Ballibos of land Carne Roe being one ballibos of land Tawlett being one ballibos of land Caldrum Drean being one ballibos of land with all and singular their and every of their rights appurtenances and Members AND also all that Territory Ballibetto or porcon of land called or knowne by the name of Bally Namoyne in the County of Londonderry aforesaid (That is to say) All lands tenements and other hereditaments called or knowne by the names hereafter menconed or lying and being of in or within the Towne Village hamlett place ballibos or parcell of land following (That is say) Mavanoher being one ballibos of land with all and singular the rights appurtenances and Members thereof. AND also all that Territory Ballibetto or porcon of land called or knowne by the name of Inishe Ronhe or Grange in the County of Londonderry aforesaid that is to say All lands tenements and other hereditaments knowne or called by the names hereafter menconed or lying and being of in or within the severall Townes Villages hamletts places ballibooes or parcells of land following (that is to say) Claraletryn being one ballibos of land Leah Leave being one ballibos of land Mony Gran being one ballibos of land Killeddy being one ballibos of land Nergean being one ballibos of land Moyknock being one ballibos of land Linleah being one ballibos of land Balla Cogey being one ballibos of land Limagroll being one ballibos of land with all and singular their and every of their rights members and appurtenances AND alsoe all that Territory Ballibetto or porcon of land called or knowne by the name of Carnett Mona within the County of Londonderry aforesaid (That is to say) All Lands Tenements and other hereditaments knowne or called by the names hereafter menconed or lying and being of in or within the severall Townes Villages hamletts places ballibooes or parcells of land following (that is to say) Drummerrah being one ballibos of land Dillahey being one ballibos of

* The words between these stars are almost illegible, but we believe they are correct.

of land Moylatraloy being one ballibo of land Crossdowan being one ballibo of land Cregagola being one ballibo of land Ballymenagh being one ballibo of land Larah being one ballibo of land Lissacrin being one ballibo of land with all and singular their and every of their appurtenances and Members AND alsoe all that Territory Ballibetagh or porcon of land called or knowne by the name of Ballinasfreigh within the County of Londonderry aforesaid (That is to say) All lands Tenements and other hereditaments knowne or called by the names hereafter mencioned or lying and being of in or within the severall Townes Villages hamletts places Ballibos or parcells of land following (that is to say) Drumober being one Ballibo of land Ballykenna being one ballibo of land Tawnay Kingogy being one ballibo of land Carbalon Tubber being one ballibo of land with all and singular their and every of their rights appurtenances and Members And alsoe all that Territory Ballibetto or porcon of land knowne or called by the name of Dungiskidy in the said County of Londonderry in the Province of Ulster aforesaid (that is to say) All lands Tenements and other hereditaments knowne or called by the names hereafter mencioned or lying and being of in or within the severall Townes Villages hamletts places Ballibos or parcells of land following (that is to say) Mcknabe Allen being one Ballibo of land Daugh in Conwey being one Ballibo of land Lisnesle being one ballibo of land Bally Nanny being one ballibo of land Bally Money being one ballibo of land Ballyne Keady being one ballibo of land Cindnagloo being one ballibo of land Swearah being one ballibo of land Gronalan being one ballibo of land Ballnebohey being one ballibo of land Amfordlanne being one ballibo of land Terreuegorn being one ballibo of land Drumack being one ballibo of land Tercgarwell being one ballibo of land Mackah being one ballibo of land Mainshurnam being one ballibo of land Ture being one ballibo of land Knockneale being one ballibo of land Glatneale being one ballibo of land Dungiskidy being one ballibo of land with all and singular their and every of their appurtenances and Members whatsoever or by whatsoever other name or names the same lands Tenem^ts^ hereditaments and p'mises before in these p'sents severally or particularly named or menconed as aforesaid or any of them are called reputed knowne or taken and which are conteyned within the proporcon of the Company of Mercers of London Number Eight according to their lott or devision with other Companies And were lately (as is before in these p'sents menconed) by the said Society of the Governo' and Assistants London of the New Plantacon in Ulster within the realme of Ireland made erected ordained and reduced into a Manno' And alsoe all and every the rents suits of Court suits of Mill Reliefs Payments in the name of Reliefs ffynes for Alienacon herriotts forfeitures and all other duties payments and services reserved due or payable or wch hereafter shalbe reserved or growe due or payable by or from the free or other Tennants or reputed Tennants of the said Manno' or reputed Manno' And all and singuler messuages howses Barnes Cottages Bawnes buildings Edifices Mills lands Tenements Meadowes Pastures Comons Advowsons Donacons p'sentacons oblacons Tythes Wast groundes ffurze heathes Marishes Moores boggs Mountaines Mosses Mynes Quarries and Mineralls and Ewers of what nature kinde quality or condicon soever they be (Not being Mines Royall) Woods Underwoods waters watercourses weares fishings fishing places fowling Courts Barron Courts Leete perquisites and proffitts of Courts Barron and Courts Leete Views of ffranckpledge and all that to views of ffranckpledge doth apperteyne with free liberty to keep the said Courts goods and chattles waived and straied and all goods and chattles of ffelons ffelons of themselves and persons put in Exigent Deodands Lands goods confiscated fines Escheats fforfeitures Reliefs heriotts ffynes amerciaments liberties priviledges Estovers ffaires Marketts Tolls Customes and all other proffitts Comodities Emoluments Royalties and hereditaments whatsoever of what nature quallity or condicon soever they bee within the said County of Londonderry or elsewhere within the said Realme of Ireland to the said Manno' or reputed Manno' lands tenements hereditaments and p'mises aforesaid and every or any of them belonging or in anywise apperteyning or accepted reputed deemed or taken as part parcell or Member of the said Manno' or reputed Manno' lands and p'mises or of or belonging unto the same or any part thereof Or which had beine at any tyme assigned or intended to create or make the said Manno' or reputed Manno' or to be part parcell incident or appurtenant unto the said Manno' or reputed Manno' in as large and ample manner as the said Society had the same EXCEPT neverthelesse and out of the said recited Indenture of bargaine and sale alwayes reserved as therein and hereafter in these p'sents is excepted and reserved TO HAVE AND TO HOLD to them the said Wardens and Cominalty of the Mistery of Mercers of the City of London their Successo^rs^ and Assignes from the day next before the day of the date of the said recited Indenture of bargaine and sale for and during the Terme of Six monthes from thence next ensuing and fully to be compleate and ended Att and for the rent of One pepper corne payable the last day of the said terme if the same should be lawfully demanded As by the said last recited Indenture it doth and may more fully and at large appeare WHICH said Indenture of bargaine and sale was made to the said Wardens and Cominalty of the Mistery of Mercers aforesaid to the intent and purpose That they being thereby possessed and interessed of and in the said p'mises for the said terme the ffreehold and Inheritance thereof might be conveyed and assured to them and their successo^rs^ to and for the use and behoofe of the said Wardens and Cominalty of the Mistery of Mercers of the City of London their Successo^rs^ and Assignes for ever NOW WITNES THESE PRESENTS that the said Society of the Governo' and Assistants London of the New Plantacon in Ulster within the realme of Ireland As well for and in consideracon of a competent some of lawfull money of England to them before th'ensealing of these presents by the said Wardens and Cominalty of the Mistery of Mercers aforesaid well and truly paid whereof they the said

and

Society confesse and acknowledge the Receipt and themselves there with fully satisfied and contented And thereof and of every part and parcell thereof Doe clearely acquitt and discharge the said Wardens and Cominalty of the Mistery of Mercers aforesaid their Successo^{rs} and Assignes and every of them by these p'sents As alsoe for divers other good and weighty consideracons the said Society thereunto especially moveing By virtue of the said last menc̃oned Letters Patents and of a license from his Highnes King Charles the second bearing date the seaventh day of Aprill in the said fifteenth yeare of his Reigne and the power and authority thereby given and granted have granted bargained sold remised released and confirmed And by these p'sents doe fully clearely and absolutely grant bargaine sell remise release and confirme unto the said Wardens and Cominalty of the Mistery of Mercers of the City of London their Successo^{rs} and Assignes for ever All that the foresaid Mannor or reputed Manno^r of Mercers with the Rights Members and appurtenances thereof And all and every the said Lands Tenements and hereditaments with their and every of their rights members and appurtenances hereinbefore menc̃oned to be by the said recited Indenture of bargaine and sale to the said Wardens and Cominalty of the Mistery of Mercers aforesaid bargained and sold or therein meant menc̃oned or intended to be thereby bargained and sold and every part and parcell thereof Except neverthelesse and out of these p'sents alwayes reserved unto the said Society of the Governo^r and Assistants London of the New Plantac̃on in Ulster within the Realme of Ireland their Successo^{rs} and Assignes All timber trees growing or being or that hereafter shall growe or bee in or upon the foresaid p'mises or any part thereof with free liberty to and for the said Society their Successo^{rs} and Assignes when and as often as they shall thinke good to fell cutt downe and carry away the same and every or any part thereof To be Imployed spent and converted for in and about buildings and other necessary uses within the Realme of Ireland and not for any other cause to be Merchandized or sold And alsoe excepted and reserved to the said Society of the Governo^r and Assistants London of the New Plantac̃on in Ulster within the Realme of Ireland their Successo^{rs} and Assignes free liberty to hawke hunt fish fowle come goe ride carry and recarry over in through and upon the same p'mises and every part and parcell thereof at all times convenient And alsoe excepted and out of these presents reserved unto the said Society their Successo^{rs} and Assignes All the fishings and takeing of Salmon and Eeles and other fishes in the Rivers of Bann and Loughfoile in the Province of Ulster aforesaid and in all Creekes and Members of the same Rivers and either of them And all the ground and soile of the same Rivers and either of them And alsoe free liberty to and for the said Society their Successo^{rs} and Assignes to digg and search in the p'mises aforegranted or any part thereof (Except and other then in the howses gardens orchards Meadowes or land sowed with Corne) for stone slate lyme gravell sand and other necessary materialls and the same to take and carry away to be Imployed and converted for in and about buildings in the foresaid County of Londonderry and Province of Ulster and not otherwise To HAVE AND TO HOLD the said Manno^r or reputed Manno^r of Mercers with the rights Members and appurtenances thereof And all and every the said lands Tenements and hereditaments by the said last recited Indenture bargained and sold or therein meant menc̃oned or intended to be thereby bargained and sold with their and every of their rights members and appurtenances and every part and parcell thereof (except before excepted) unto the said Wardens and Cominalty of the Mistery of Mercers of the City of London their Successo^{rs} and Assignes for ever To the only proper use and behoofe of the said Wardens and Cominalty of the Mistery of Mercers of the City of London their Successo^{rs} and Assignes for ever YIELDING and paying therefore yearely to the said Society of the Governo^r and Assistants London of the New Plantac̃on in Ulster within the Realme of Ireland their Successo^{rs} and assignes the yearely rent or some of Thirteene shillings and ffower pence of lawfull money of England Att two ffeastes or Termes in the yeare (That is to say) the ffeastes of St. Michaell the Archangell & the Annunc̃acon of the blessed Virgin Mary) by even and equall porc̃ons Att or in the usuall meeting place of the said Society comonly called the Irish Chamber scituate in or neare the Guildhall in the City of London in the Kingdome of England And if it shall happen that the said yearely rent of thirteene shillings and ffower pence or any part thereof to be behinde and unpaid in part or in all after any Terme of payment in which it ought to be paid according to the true meaning of these p'sents That then and soe often it shall and may be lawfull to and for the said Society of the Governo^r and Assistants London of the New Plantac̃on in Ulster within the Realme of Ireland their Successo^{rs} and Assignes into the p'mises afore granted and every or any part thereof to enter and distreyne and the distresse soe taken to lead chase drive and carry away and with them to deteyne untill the foresaid rent soe being behinde and all arrearages thereof (if any) shallbe according to the true intent and meaning of these p'sents to them fully satisfied and paid AND THE SAID Wardens and Cominalty of the Mistery of Mercers aforesaid for them their Successo^{rs} and Assignes doe Covenant and grant to and with the said Society of the Governo^r and Assistants London of the New Plantac̃on in Ulster within the Realme of Ireland their Successo^{rs} and Assignes by these Presents That they the said Society their Successo^{rs} Agents Servants and Assignes Shall and may from time to time and at all times hereafter have hold take use carry away and enjoy freely all and every the p'mises in and by these p'sents before excepted or menc̃oned to be excepted and every of them and every part and parcell of them and every of them without the lett or interrupc̃on of the said Wardens and Cominalty of the Mistery of Mercers aforesaid their Successo^{rs} or Assignes to be disposed of and Imployed as in the before excepc̃ons are menc̃oned and expressed AND THE SAID Society of the Governo^r and Assistants London of the New Plantac̃on in Ulster within the Realme of Ireland for them and their Successo^{rs} doe covenant and grant to and with the said Wardens and Cominalty of the

Mistery of Mercers aforesaid their Successo^rs and Assignes by these p'sents That they the said Wardens and Cominalty of the Mistery of Mercers aforesaid their Successo^rs and Assignes paying the rent aforesaid and under the Covenants and agreements in these p'sents conteyned shall or may at all times from henceforth for ever lawfully peaceably and quietly have hold occupy possesse and enjoy the said Manno^r or reputed Manno^r lands tenements and hereditaments and all and singular other the p'mises afore hereby granted bargained sold released and confirmed or meant mencõned or intended to be hereby granted bargained sold released and confirmed and every part and parcell thereof with their and every of their appurtenances (except before excepted) And receave p'ceave take and enjoy to their owne use and uses for ever all the rents issues and profitts thereof without any lawfull lett suite trouble molestacõn recovery eviccõn expulcõn or interrupcõn of or by the said Society of the Governo^r and Assistants London of the New Plantacõn in Ulster within the Realme of Ireland their Successo^rs or Assignes or of or by any other person or persons Lawfully clayming or to clayme from by or under them or any of them or their or any of their Act estate meanes authority consent or procurement And that free and cleare and freely and clearely acquitted exonerated and discharged Or well and sufficiently saved and kept harmles by the said Society their Successo^rs or Assignes of and from all and singular former bargaines sales guifts grants Leases Alienacõns Arrerages of rents Estates charges & incumbrances whatsoever had made comitted or done by the said Society of the Governo^r and Assistants London of the New Plantacõn in Ulster within the Realme of Ireland before th'ensealing hereof (Except the before mencõned deed whereby the said Manno^r is erected made and ordained as aforesaid) And except all grants or estates by Indentures of bargaine and Sale or release made and granted by the said Society of the Governo^r and Assistants London of the New Plantacõn in Ulster within the Realme of Ireland to severall persons o^r Freehold Tenants or reputed Tennants of the said Manno^r or reputed Manno^r or parcell of the p'mises by the nominacõn and appointment of the said Wardens and Cominalty of the Mistery in of Mercers aforesaid under certaine Rents and services All and every which Rents Duties and services in the said excepted Indentures reserved shall for and notwithstanding any Act or thing made or done or to be made or done by the said Society of the Governo^r and Assistants London of the New Plantacõn in Ulster within the Realme of Ireland their Successo^rs or Assignes to the contrary be henceforth due and payable and paid unto the said Wardens and Cominalty of the Mistery of Mercers aforesaid their Successo^rs and Assignes during the continuance in force of the same grants and estates respectively AND FURTHER the said Society of the Governo^r and Assistants London of the New Plantacõn in Ulster within the Realme of Ireland for them their Successo^rs and Assignes Doe covenant promise and grant to and with the said Wardens and Cominalty of the Mistery of Mercers aforesaid their Successo^rs and Assignes and every of them by these P'sents That it shall and may be lawfull to and for the said Wardens and Cominalty of the Mistery of Mercers aforesaid their Successo^rs and Assignes by the Appointment of the Generall Agents or Agent of the said Society for the time being Resident in Ulster for the affaires of the said Society to fall cutt downe take and carry away such and soe many of the Timber trees of the said Society standing growing and being nearest or most convenient to the p'mises afore granted As shall be fitt and necessary for the building or planting of any howses Villages edifices or buildings within the said Manno^r or reputed Manno^r Lands and P'mises AND ALSO that they the said Society their Successo^rs and Assignes shall and will pay and discharge All rents duties and other payments now due and payable or hereafter to be due or payable to the Kings Majesty his heires or Successo^rs for or in respect of the said Manno^r or reputed Manno^r lands and p'mises or any part thereof Or thereof shall save harmles the said Wardens and Cominalty of the Mistery of Mercers aforesaid and their successo^rs and all the p'mises by these p'sents granted or intended to be granted AND FURTHER that the said Society their Successo^rs and assignes shall and will from time to time and at all times hereafter for and during the space of Tenn yeares now next ensuing upon every reasonable request and at the costs and charges in the Law of the said Wardens and Cominalty of the Mistery of Mercers aforesaid their Successo^rs and Assignes make doe execute and performe All and every such further conveyance and Assurance in the Law whatsoever bee it by Indenture Deed or Deeds ffeoffment Release confirmacõn or otherwise howsoever ffor the further better and more perfect and absolute assurance conveying and assuring of the said Manno^r or reputed Manno^r lands Tenements and p'mises (Except as is before excepted) or mencõned to be excepted unto the said Wardens and Cominalty of the Mistery of Mercers aforesaid their Successo^rs and Assignes for ever As by the said Wardens and Cominalty of the Mistery of Mercers aforesaid their Successo^rs or Assignes or their Councell learned in the Law shalbe reasonably advised or devised and required Soe as the said Conveyances and Assurances Doe conteyne noe ffurther warranty nor covenant for enjoying the p'mises then against the said Society and their Successo^rs only IN WITNES WHEREOF to the one part of these p'sent Indentures the said Society of the Governo^r and Assistants London of the New Plantacõn in Ulster within the Realme of Ireland have caused their Comon Seale to be put And to the other part thereof the said Wardens and Cominalty of the Mistery of Mercers aforesaid have caused their Comon Seale to be put yeoven the day and yeare first above written.

(L. S.)

By order of the said Society
JO. SPRAKELING *Secretary*

APPENDIX, No. 22.

PAPER handed in by the Chairman.

THE IRISH SOCIETY TO THE DRAPERS' COMPANY; RELEASE OF THE MANOR OF DRAPERS.

Dated 5th June 1663, 15th Chas. 2nd.

THIS Indenture, made the Fifth day of June, Anno Domini 1663, And in the fifteenth yeare of the reigne of our Soveraigne Lord Charles the Second, by the Grace of God King of England, Scotland, France, and Ireland, Defender of the Faith, &c. Between the Society of the Governor and Assistants, London, of the New Plantation in Ulster, within the realme of Ireland, of the one part; and the Mr and Wardens, and Brethren and Sisters of the Guild or Fraternity of the blessed Marie the Virgin, of the misterie of the Drapers of the City of London, of the other part. Whereas King James, late King of England, by his Letters Patents under the Great Seale of England, bearing date at Westminster, the Nyne and twentith day of March, in the Eleaventh yeare of his reigne over England, France, and Ireland, and over Scotland the six and fortith, for the considerations therein mentioned, of his especial Grace, certaine knowledge, and meere motion, Did (amongst other things) will and grant, ordaine and constitute That there should bee from thenceforth sixe and twentie honest and discreet Citizens of the Citie of London in England, which should be and should be called the Society of the Governor and Assistants, London, of the New Plantation in Ulster, within the realme of Ireland, and them into one bodie corporate and Politique, in Deed, fact, and name, by the name of the Societie of the Governor and Assistants, London, of the New Plantation in Ulster, within the realme of Ireland, did erect, make, ordaine, create, constitute, and declare. And whereas also the said late King James did by and by the said Letters Patents, give and grant, or did mention therein, to give and grant unto the said Societie of the Governor and Assistants, London, of the New Plantation in Ulster, within the realme of Ireland, and their successors, divers Townes, Villages, hamlets, [illegible], [illegible], [illegible], territories, lands, tenements, fishings, rents, services, woods, underwoods, liberties, powers, priviledges, franchises, jurisdictions, hereditaments, and divers other things in the said Letters Patents mentioned and contained. And whereas also the said late King James, in and by the said Letters Patents (amongst other things) did give and grant unto the same Societie of the Governor and Assistants, London, of the new Plantation in Ulster, within the realme of Ireland, and their successors, full, free, and lawful power, facultie, and authoritie, to make, erect, and ordaine out of and upon the same lands, tenements, and hereditaments, in and by the said Letters Patents granted, or any of them, so many severall Mannors of such [illegible] as were in the said Letters Patents lymitted, as from tyme to tyme should seeme convenient unto the said Societie and their Successors (that is to say) that they might make, erect, and ordaine One Mannor of every thousand acres of land by the said Letters Patents granted, or of any number exceeding the number of One thousand acres of land, and so according to such rate so many severall Mannors as they would, soe that they made not any Mannor of a lesser number of acres of land, than of the number of One thousand acres of land, and to appoint and lymitt to the same severall Mannors, soe many acres of land, distinct and severall for demesne lands of the same severall Mannors and every of them as should seeme convenient and expedient to the said Societie of the Governor and Assistants, London, of the New Plantation in Ulster, within the realme of Ireland, and their successors, and to name and call the said Mannors by such names as the same Societie and their successors would or should think fit, as by the said Letters Patents, relation being thereunto had more at large may appear. And whereas the said Societie of the Governor and Assistants, London, of the New Plantation in Ulster, within the realme of Ireland, by virtue, power, and authoritie of the said Letters Patents, by their Deed or Writing, sealed with the Common Seale of the said Society, bearing date the Eighteenth day of July, Anno Dni One thousand six hundred nineteene, and in the yeares of the reigne of the late King James of England, France, and Ireland the Seventeenth, and of Scotland the Two and fiftieth, did make, erect, and ordaine, of and upon the lands, tenements, and hereditaments, with their appurtenances in the said Deed or Writing, and hereafter in these presents particularly named, mentioned, and expressed, being part of the lands, tenements, hereditaments, and premises, to them granted by the said late King James as aforesaid, One Mannor to consist of such hereditaments as in the said Letters Patents are lymitted, and also did by the said Deed or Writing, appoint, and lymitt that parcell of the said lands and tenements, as by the said Deed or Writing, made and released, or [illegible], or intended to be made or released, into a Mannor as aforesaid, and therein particularly named, mentioned, and expressed, should be and should be called and [illegible], [illegible], and taken to be the Demesne land of the said Mannor, and should be and continue parcell of the said Mannor, and also did by the said deed or writing, name and call the said Mannor and all and singular the lands, tenements, and hereditaments thereby made, or intended to be made a Mannor by the name of ye Mannor of Drapers, and did also by the said Deed or Writing, lymitt, ordaine, and appoint divers other matters and things touching and concerning the said Mannor in the said Deed or Writing mentioned and expressed as by the said Deed or Writing, relation being thereunto had more at large, it doth and may appear. And whereas also the same Societie of the Governor and Assistants, London, of the New Plantation in Ulster within the Realme of Ireland; By virtue of the said Letters Patents and of a Lycense from the said late King James under the Great Seale of England, bearing date at Westminster, the Thirtieth day of September, in the Thirteenth yeare of his Reigne over England, France and Ireland, and over Scotland the Nine and fortieth; By their Deed or Writing indented, sealed with the common Seale of the said then Societie, bearing date the Twentieth day of July, Anno Dni One thousand six hundred nineteene; And in the yeares of the Reigne of the said late King James of England, France, and Ireland, the Seventeenth; and of Scotland the Two and fiftieth made between the sd then Societie of the Governor and Assistants, London, of the New Plantation in Ulster, within the Realme of Ireland, of the one part, and the said Mr and Wardens & Brethren and Sisters of the Guild or Fraternitie of the blessed Marie the Virgin, of the Misterie of the Drapers of the Citie of London, of the other part. For the Consideracons in the said recited Deed or Writing indented, mentioned, and expressed, Did grant, bargain, sell, alien, enfeoff, and confirm unto the said Mr and Wardens and Brethren and Sisters of the Guild or Fraternitie of the Blessed Marie the Virgin of the misterie of the Drapers aforesaid, their Successors, and Assignes for ever, All that the said Mannor of Drapers, with the rights, members and appurtenances thereof, lying and being within the Barony of Loughinsholin, within the County of Londonderrie, als Colraine within the Province of Ulster, within the Realme of Ireland; And divers Lands, Tenements, and Hereditaments, in the said recited Deed or Writing indented, and hereafter in these Presents particularly mentioned and expressed; As by the said recited Deed or Writing indented, due relation being

[illegible]

aforesaid, their Successors and assigns for ever. Now witness these presents, that the said Societie of the Governor and Assistants, London, of the new plantation in Ulster, within the realme of Ireland, as well for and in consideration of a competent summe of lawfull money of England, To them before the ensealing of these Presents by the said Mr and Wardens, and Brethren and Sisters, of the Guilde or fraternity of the blessed Marie the Virgin, of the Misterie of the Drapers aforesaid, well and truly paid; whereof they the said Societie, confess and acknowledge the receipt, and themselves, therewith fully satisfied and contented. And thereof, and of everie part and parcell thereof, doe clearlie acquit and discharge the said M. and Wardens, and Brethren and Sisters of the Guilde or Fraternitie of the Blessed Marie the Virgin, of the Misterie of the Drapers aforesaid, their successors and assigns, and everie of them, by these presents. As also for divers other good and weightie considerations, the said Societie thereunto especially moving; By virtue of the said last mentioned Letters Patents, and of a License from His Highness King Charles the Second, bearing date the seventh day of Aprill, in the said Fifteenth yeare of His Reign, and the power and authoritie thereby given and granted, have granted, bargained, sold, remised, released and confirmed; And by these presents doe fully, clearlie and absolutely, grant, bargaine, sell, remise, release and confirme, unto the said Mr and Wardens, and Brethren and Sisters of the Guilde or Fraternitie of the Blessed Marie the Virgin, of the Misterie of the Drapers of the City of London, their successors and assigns for ever, All that the aforesaid Mannor or reputed Mannor of Drapers, with the rights, members, and appurtenances thereof; And all and everie the said lands, tenements and hereditaments, with their and every of their rights, members and appurtenances hereinbefore mentioned, to be by the said recited Indenture of Bargaine and Sale, to the said Mr and Wardens, and Brethren and Sisters, of the Guilde or Fraternitie of the Blessed Marie the Virgin, of the misterie of the Drapers aforesaid bargained, and sold thereby, granted, mentioned, or intended to be thereby bargained and sold, and everie part and parcell thereof (Excepting nevertheless and out of this present grant, bargaine, and sale always reserved unto the said Societie, and Governor, and Assistants, London, of the New Plantation in Ulster, within the realme of Ireland, their successors and Assigns; All timber, trees, growing or being, or that hereafter shall grow, or be in or upon the aforesaid premisses, or anie part thereof, with free libertie to and for the said Societie, their Successors and assigns, when and as often as they shall think good, fell, cut down, and carry away the same, and everie or anie part thereof, To be employed, spent, and converted, for, in, and about buildings, and other necessary uses within the realme of Ireland, and not for anie other cause to be merchandised or sold; And also excepted & reserved unto the said Societie, their Successors and assigns, free libertie to hawke, hunt, fishe, fowle, come, goe, ride, carry and recarrye, over, in, through and upon the same premises, and everie part and Parcell thereof at all tymes convenient; And also excepted and out of these presents reserved unto the said Societie, their Successors and assigns, All the fishings and taking of Salmon and Eeles and other fishes, in the rivers of Bann and Loughfoyle, within the Province of Ulster aforesaid, and in all Creeks and members of the same Rivers and either of them. And all the Ground and Soile of the same rivers and either of them; And also free libertie to and for the said Societie, their Successors and assigns, to digg and search in the premisses aforegranted, or anie part thereof, Except and other than in the house, Gardens, Orchards, meadowes, or lands sowed with Corne (for Stones, Slate, lyme, gravell, sand and other necessarie materialls, and the same to take and carry away to be employed and converted for, in, and about buildings in the foresaid Countie of Londonderrie and Province of Ulster, and not otherwise. To have and to hold the said Mannor or reputed Mannor of Drapers, with the rights, members, and appurtenances thereof; And all and everie the said lands, tenements, and hereditaments, by the said last recited Indenture, bargained and sold or therein recited, mentioned, or intended to be thereby bargained and sold, with their and everie of their rights, members, and appurtenances, and everie part and parcell thereof (Except before excepted) unto the said M. and Wardens and Brethren and Sisters of the Guilde or Fraternitie of the Blessed Mary the Virgin, of the misterie of the Drapers aforesaid, their Successors and assigns for ever. To the only proper use and behoof of the said Mr and Wardens and Brethren and Sisters of the Guilde or Fraternitie of the blessed Marie the Virgin, of the misterie of the Drapers aforesaid, their Successors and assigns for ever. And the said M. and Wardens and Brethren and Sisters of the Guilde or Fraternitie of the blessed Marie the Virgin, of the misterie of the Drapers aforesaid, for them and their successors, Doe covenant and grant to and with the said Societie of the Governor and Assistants, London, of the New Plantation in Ulster, within the realme of Ireland, their successors and Assigns, by these presents, That they the said Societie, their Successors, Agents, Servants, and Assignes, shall and may from time to time and at all times hereafter have, hold, take, use, carrie away, and enjoy freely, all and everie the premises so and by these presents before excepted or mentioned to be excepted, and everie of them and everie part and parcell of them and everie of them without the lett or interruption of the said Mr and Wardens, and Brethren and Sisters of the Guilde or Fraternitie of the Blessed Marie the Virgin, of the Misterie of the Drapers aforesaid, their successors or assignes, To be disposed of and employed as in the before Exceptions are mentioned and expressed. And the said Societie of the Governor and Assistants, London, of the New Plantation in Ulster, within the realme of Ireland, for them and their Successors, Doe Covenant and grant to and with the said Mr and Wardens, and Brethren and Sisters of the Guilde or Fraternitie of the Blessed Marie the Virgin, of the misterie of the Drapers aforesaid, their successors and assignes, by these presents, That they the said Mr and Wardens, and Brethren and Sisters of the Guilde or Fraternitie of the blessed Marie the Virgin, of the mysterie of the Drapers aforesaid, their successors and assignes under the Covenants and Agreements in these presents contained, shall or may at all times from henceforth for ever, lawfully, peaceably, and quietly have, hold, occupy, possess, and enjoy the said Mannor or reputed Mannor, lands, tenements, and hereditaments, with all & singular other the premisses before hereby granted, bargained, sold, released, and confirmed, or meant, mentioned, or intended to be hereby granted, bargained, sold, released, and confirmed, and everie part and parcell thereof, with their and everie of their appurtenances (Except before excepted) And receive, perceive, take, and enjoy to their own use and uses for ever, All the rents, issues, and profits thereof, without anie lawfull lett, suit, trouble, molestation, recoverie, eviction, expulsion, or interruption, of or by the said Societie of the Governor and Assistants, London, of the New Plantation in Ulster, within the realme of Ireland, their Successors or assignes, or of or by anie other person or persons lawfully claiming or to claim from, by, or under them, or anie of them, or their or anie of their Act, Estate, means, authorities, consent, or procurement. And that free and clear, and freely and clearlie acquitted, exonerated, and discharged, Or well and sufficiently saved and kept harmless by the said Societie, their Successors or assignes, of and from all and singular former bargaines, Sales, Gifts, Grants, Leases, Jointures, arrearages of rents, estates, charges, and incumbrances whatsoever, had, made, committed, or done by the said Societie of the Governor, and Assistants, London, of the New Plantation in Ulster, within the realme of Ireland, before the ensealing hereof (Except the before mentioned Deed), Whereby the said Mannor is erected, made, and ordained as aforesaid; & Except all Grants or Estates by Indentures of Bargaine and Sale, or Releases, made and granted by the said Societie of the Governor and Assistants, London, of the New Plantation in Ulster, within the realme of Ireland, To severall persons or freehold Tenants, or reputed tenants, of the said Mannor or reputed Mannor, or of parcell of the premisses by the consent and appointment of the said M. and Wardens, and Brethren and Sisters, of the Guilde or Fraternitie of the Blessed Mary the Virgin, of the misterie of the Drapers aforesaid, under certain rents and services, All and everie which rents, duties, and services in the said excepted Indentures reserved, shall be and notwithstanding any Acts or things, made or done, or to be made or done, by the said Societie of the Governor and Assistants, London, of the New Plantation in Ulster, within the realme of Ireland, their Successors or assignes to the contrarie, be henceforth due and payable, and paid, to the said Mr and Wardens, and Brethren and Sisters of the Guilde or Fraternitie of the blessed Marie the Virgin, of the misterie of the Drapers aforesaid, their successors and assignes, during the continuance in force of the same Grants and Estates respectivelye. And further, the said Societie of the Governor and Assistants, London, of the New Plantation in Ulster, within the realme of Ireland, for them, their successors and assignes, Doe covenant, promise, and grant, to and with the Mr and Wardens, and Brethren and Sisters, of the Guilde or Fraternitie of the Blessed Marie the Virgin, of the Misterie of the Drapers aforesaid, their successors and assignes, and everie of them, by these presents, that it shall and may be lawfull, to and for the said Mr and Wardens and Brethren and Sisters, of the Guild or Fraternitie of the blessed Marie the Virgin, of the Misterie of the Drapers aforesaid

aforesaid, their successors and assignes, by the appointment of the Generall Agents or Agent of the said Societie for the time being, resident in Ulster, for the affaires of the said Societie, To fell, cut downe, take, and carrie away, such and so much of the Timber Trees of the said Societie, standing, growing, and being in or on the premisses aforegranted as shalbe fitt and necessarie for the building or plantation of such houses, Villages, Edifices, or buildings within the said Mannor, or reputed Mannor, lands, and premises. And also that they, the said Societie, their successors and assignes, shall and will pay and discharge all rents, duties, and other payments now due and payable, or hereafter to be due or payable to the King's Matie, his heires or successors, for or in respect of the said Mannor, or reputed Mannor, lands, and premisses, or some part thereof. Or whereof shall save harmless the said Master and Wardens, and Brethren and Sisters of the Guilde or Fraternitie of the Blessed Marie the Virgen, of the Misterie of the Drapers aforesaid, and their successors. And all the premisses by these presents granted, or intended to be granted. And further, that the said Societie, their Successors and assignes, shall and will, from time to time, and at all times hereafter, for and during the space of Ten yeares next ensuing, upon everie reasonable request, and at the cost and charges in the law of the said Mr and Wardens, and Brethren and Sisters of the Guild or Fraternity of the blessed Marie the Virgin, of the Misterie of the Drapers aforesaid, their successors and assignes, make, doe, execute and performe, all and everie such further Conveyance and Assurance as the law [illegible], bee it by Indenture, Deed or Deeds, Enrollment, release, confirmacon, or otherwise, howsoever, for the further, better, and more perfect and absolute assurance, conveying and assuring of the said Mannor or reputed Mannor, lands, tenements, and premisses (except as is before excepted or mentioned to be excepted) unto the said Corporation of Mr and Wardens, and Brethren and Sisters of the Guilde or Fraternitie of the blessed Marie the Virgen, of the Misterie of the Drapers aforesaid, their successors and assignes for ever; As by the said Mr and Wardens, and Brethren and Sisters of the Guilde or Fraternitie of the blessed Marie the Virgen, of the Misterie of the Drapers aforesaid, their successors or assignes, or their Councell learned in the Law shalbe reasonablie advised or devised and required; Soe as the said Conveyances and Assurances doe conteine no further warrantie or Covenant for enjoying the premisses then against the said Societie and their Successors onelie. In Witness whereof to the one part of these present Indentures, the said Societie of the Governor and Assistants, London, of the new Plantacon in Ulster, within the realme of Ireland, have caused their common Seale to be put, and to the other part thereof the said Mr and Wardens and Brethren and Sisters of the Guilde or Fraternitie of the blessed Marie the Virgen, of the Misterie of the Drapers aforesaid, have caused theire common Seale to be putt, Yeoven, the day and yeare first above written.

By Order of the said Society,
JO. SPRAKELING, Secret:

APPENDIX, No. 23.

PAPER handed in by the *Chairman*.

The Irish Society to the Salters' Company. Release of the Manor of Sal, dated 5th June, 1663, 15th Charles Second.

This Indenture made the 5th day of June, Anno Dni, 1663, and in the 15th year of the reign of our Sovereign Lord Charles the Second, by the Grace of God King of England, Scotland, France, and Ireland, Defend' of the Faith, &c, Between the Society of the Gov' and Assist'ts, London, of the New Plantacon in Ulster, within the Realm of Ireland, of the one part, and the M', Wardens, and Coialty of the Art or Mistery of Salters, London, of the other part. Whereas King James, late King of England, by his Lres Patent under the Great Seal of England, bearing date at Westmin', the nine and twentieth day of March, in the 11th year of his reign over England, France, and Ireland, and over Scotland, the sixth and fortieth, for the consideracons therein menconed of his especiall grace, certain knowledge, and mere mocon, did (amongst other things) will and grant, ordain and constitute, That there should be from thenceforth six and twenty honest and discreet Cittizens of the City of London, in England, which should be and should be called the Society of the Gov' and Assistants, London, of the New Plantacon in Ulster, within the Realm of Ireland, and them into one new Body Corporate and Politick, in deed, fact, and name, by the name of the Society of the Gov' and Assistants, London, of the new Plantacon in Ulster, within the Realm of Ireland, Did erect, make, ordain, create, constitute, and declare, And whereas also the sd late King James Did, in and by the sd Lres Patents, give and grant, or did mencon therein to give and grant unto the sd Society of the Gov' and Assist'ts, London, of the New Plantacon of Ulster, within the Realm of Ireland, and their successors, divers Townes, Villages, Hamletts, Barronies, Lordships, mann'rs, territories, lands, tenem'ts, and fishings, rents, services, woods, underwoods, Kites, powers, priviledges, franchises, jurisdicons, heredit'ts, and divers other things in the sd Lres Patents, menconed and contained. And whereas also the sd late King James, in and by the sd Lres Patents (amongst other things) Did give and grant unto the same Society of the Gov' and Assist'ts, London, of the New Plantacon of Ulster, within the Realm of Ireland, and their successors, full, free, and lawfull power, faculty, and authority, to make, erect, and ordain, out of and upon the same lands, ten'ts, and heredit'ts, in and by the sd Lres Patents granted, or any of them, so many sev'all mann'rs of such Tents as were in the sd Lres Patents limited, as from time to time should seem convenient to the sd Society and their success'rs, (that is to say) that they might make, erect, and ordain, one mann' of every thousand acres of land by the sd Lres Patents, granted, or of any number exceeding the number of one thousand acres of land, and so according to such rate so many sev'all mann'rs as they would, so that they made not any mann' of a lesser number of acres of land than of the number of one thousand acres of land, and to appoint and limitt to the same sev'all mann'rs so many acres of land, distinct and sev'd, for demeasne lands of the sd sev'all mann'rs, and every of them, as should seem necessary and convenient to the sd Society of the Gov' and Assis'ts, London, of the New Plantacon in Ulster, within the Realm of Ireland, and their successors, and to name and call the sd mannors by such names as the same Society and their success'rs would or should think fit, as by the sd Lres Patents, relacon being thereunto had more at large may appear. And whereas the sd Society of the Gov' and Assis'ts, London, of the New Plantacon in Ulster, within the Realm of Ireland, by virtue, power, and authority of the said Lres Patents, by their deed or writing sealed with the Comon Seal of the aforesd Society, bearing date the 10th day of Feb., Anno Dni 1616, and in the years of the reign of the late King James of England, France, and Ireland, the 16th, and of Scotland the two and fiftieth, Did make, erect, and ordain of and upon the lands, ten'ts, and heredit'ts, with their appurtenances, in the said deed or writing, and hereafter in these P'sents p'ticularly named, menconed, and expressed, being part of the lands, ten'ts, heredit'ts, and p'mises so to them granted by the sd late King James as aforesd, one mann' to consist of such ten'ts as in the sd Lres Patents was limited; and also did, by sd deed or writing, appoint and limit That Parll of the sd Lands and ten'ts so by the sd deed or writing made and reduced, or meant or intended to be made or reduced, into a mann' as aforesd, and therein p'ticulary named, menconed.

constitute, & declare, by the sd Lres patents, And whereas, also, his sacred Matie King Charles the Second, in and by his sd Lres patents did grant & confirme unto the sd Society of the Govr & Assistts, London, of the New plantacon in Ulster, within the realm of Ireland, and their successors, divers Counties, Countries, Citties, Townes, Villages, hamletts, mann^rs, Castles, territories, lands, ten^ts, Woods, fishings, powers, privileges, and other hereditamts, lying & being within the province of Ulster, & realm of Ireland, menconed in His Highness sd Letters patents of the 10th day of Aprill, in the sd 14th year of his reign. And whereas the sd Society of the Govr & Assistants, London, of the New plantacon in Ulster, within the realm of Ireland, by virtue of the sd last menconed Lres patents, & of the power & authority thereby to them given, & granted by their Deed or writing sealed with the common Seal of the sd Society, bearing date the 30th day of May last past, before the date hereof, did make, erect, and ordain, of and upon the lands and tents with the appurtenances, in the sd last menconed Deed or Writing, and hereafter in these p'sents particularly named, menconed, and expressed, being part of the sd lands, ten^ts, hereditts, and p'mises, wherein they are restated as aforesd, one Mann^r, to consist of divers tents, and did also by the sd last menconed Deed or Writing appoint and limit that peell of the sd lands and tents, so by the sd last menconed Deed or writing, made and reduced, or menconed, or intended to be made or reduced, into a Mann^r, as aforesd, therein particularly menconed and expressed, should be and should be called accompted, esteemed, and taken to be the demesne lands of the sd Mann^r and should be and continue peell of the sd Manor, and did also by the sd last menconed Deed or writing name and will the sd Mann^r and all and singular the lands, ten^ts, and hereditamts, thereby made or intended to be made a Mannor, by the name of the Mann^r of Sal, and did also by the sd last menconed Deed or writing, limit, ordain, and appoint, diverse other matters and things, touching and concerning the sd Mann^r, as by the sd last menconed Deed or writing, due relacon being thereunto had, it doth and may more fully and at large appear. And whereas also the sd Society of the Govr and Assistts, of the New plantacon in Ulster, within the realm of Ireland, for the vesting and restating of the said Mann^r, or reputed Mann^r, and lands hereafter menconed, in the sd Mr, Wardens, and Cominalty, of the art or mistery of Salters, London, according to the tenor of the afsd Deed or writing indented, bearing date the sd 15th day of Feb, Anno Dni 1618, made between the sd Society of the Govr and Assistts, London, of the New plantacon in Ulster, within the realm of Ireland, of the one part, and the sd Mr, Wardens and Cominalty of the Art or mistery of Salters, London, of the other part, by their Indenture of bargain and Sale, bearing date the 4th of this Inst month of June, for the consideracon of the sume of ten shillings, of lawful money of England, to them paid by the sd Mr, Wardens and Cominalty of the art or mistery of Salters afsd, did bargain and sell unto the sd Mr, Wardens and Cominalty of the art or mistery of Salters, London, all that the Mann^r or reputed Manor of Sal, with the rights, members, and appurtenances thereof, lying and being within the Barrony of Loughinshulin, within the County of Londonderry, within the province of Ulster, within Ireland, and all that territory, Ballibetto, or porcon of land, (as in the Lease,) with all and singular their and every of their appurtenances and members whatsoever, or by whatsoever other name or names the same lands, ten^ts, hereditamts, and p'mises before in these presents sev'ally or particularly named or menconed as afsd, or any of them, are called, reputed, known, or taken, and which are contained within the proporcon of the sd Company of Salters, London, Number 10, according to their Lott or division with other Companys, and were lately, as is before in these p'sents menconed by the sd Society of the Govr and Assistts, London, of the New plantacon in Ulster, within the realm of Ireland, made, erected, ordained, and reduced into a Mann^r; And also all and every the rents, Suites of Court, Suites of Mill, reliefes, payments in the name of reliefes, fines for alienacon, heriotts, forfeitures, and all other duties, payments, and services reserved, due or payable, or which hereafter shall be reserved or grow due or payable, by or from the free or other Tents or reputed Tents of the sd Mann^r or reputed Mann^r, and all and singular messuages, houses, Barns, Cottages, Barrows, buildings, Edifices, Mills, lands, tenemts, meadows, pastures, Comons, arrowances, Dovecotes, p'emisecons, chlanans, tythes, wasteggrounds, Furs, Heaths, Marshes, Moores, Boggs, Mountaines, Mosses, Mynes, Quarries, and Min'alls, and Ewers, of what nature, quallity, or condicon soever they be, (not being Myne Royall,) woods, Underwoods, Waters, Watercourses, weares, fishings, fishing places, fowling, Courts Barron, Courts Leet, perquisites, and profitts of Courts Barron and Courts Leet, Views of frankpledge, and all to view of frankpledge, doth appertain with free Libills to keep the sd Co'ts, Goods, and Chattels wayed and strayed, and all goods and Chattels of fellons, fellons of themselves and of persons put in exigent, Deodands, lands, goods confiscated, fees, Escheates, forfeitures, reliefes, heriotts, fines, am'ciam^ts, Rites, privileges, Estovers, fairs, Marketts, tolls, customs, and all other profitts, commodities, emolum^ts, royalties, and hereditaments whatsoever, of what nature, quallity, or condicon soev^r, they be within the sd County of Londonderry or elsewhere, within the Kingdom of Ireland, to the sd Mann^r or reputed Mann^r, lands, tenem^ts, hereditam^ts, & p'mises afsd, and every or any of them belonging or in anywise appertaining or accepted, reputed, deemed, or taken, as part, peell, or member of the sd Mann^r or reputed Mann^r, lands & p'mises, or of, or belonging unto the same or any part thereof, or which had been at any time assigned or intended, to make or create the sd Mann^r or reputed Mann^r, or to be part, peell, incident or appurtenant unto the sd Mann^r or reputed Mann^r, in as large & ample manner as the sd Society hath the same, except and nevertheless out of the sd recited Indenture of Bargain and Sale, always reserved as therein & hereafter in these p'sents is excepted and reserved; To have and to hold to them the sd Mr, Wardens, and Cominalty of the Art or mystery of Salters, London, their Successors and assignes, from the day next before the day of the date of the said recited Indre of Bargain and Sale, for and during the terme of Six monthes from thence next ensuing, and fully to be compleat and ended, at and for

for the rent of One pepper Corn, payable the last day of the sd terme, if the same should be lawfully demanded as by the sd last recited Indre, it doth and may more fully and at large appear, which sd Indre of Bargain and Sale was made to the sd Mr, Wardens, and Cominalty of the Art or mistery of Salters, London, to the intent and purpose that they being thereby possessd and interested of and in the sd p'mises for the sd Term, the freehold and inheritance thereof, might be conveyed and assured to them and their Successors, to and for the use and behoof of them the sd Mr, Wardens, and Cominalty of the Art or mistery of Salters aforesd, their Succssrs and assignes for ever; Now witness these p'sents, that the said Society of the Gov' and Assist", London, of the New plantacon in Ulster, within the realm of Ireland, for and in consideracon of a competent sume of lawful money of England to them before the ensealing hereof, by the sd Mr, Wardens, and Cominalty of the Art or mistery of Salters aforesd well and truly paid, whereof they the sd society, confess and acknowledge the receipt, and themselves therew'h fully satisfied and contented, and thereof, and every part and parcell thereof, doth hereby acquit and discharge the sd Mr, Wardens, and Cominalty of the Art or Mistery of Salters aforesd, their success'rs and assignes, and evry of them by these p'sents, as for divers other good and weighty consideracons, the said society thereunto especially moving, by virtue of the sd last menconed Lres patents, and of a Lycence from his highness King Charles the Second, bearing date the 7th day of Aprill, in the 15th year of his raign, and the power and authority thereby given and granted, Have granted, bargained, sold, remised, released, and confirmed, and by these presents do fully, clearly, and absolutely grant, bargain, sell, remise, release, and confirm, unto the sd Mr, Wardens, and Cominalty of the Art or Mistery of Salters, London, their success'rs and assignes for ever, All that the foresd mann' or reputed mann' of Sal w'h the rights, members, and app'ts thereof, and all and every the said lands, tenem'ts, and hereditam'ts, with their and every of their rights, members, and app'ts, herinbefore menconed, to be by the sd last recited Indre of Bargain and sale to the sd Mr, Wardens, and Cominalty of the Art or Mistery of Salters afsd, bargained and sold, or therein meant, menconed, or intended, to be thereby bargained and sold, and every p't and parcell thereof, except nevless, and out of these p'sents allways reserved unto the sd Society of the Gov' and Assistants, London, of the new plantacon in Ulster, within the realm of Ireland, their success'rs and assignes, all timber trees, growing or being, or that hereafter shall grow or be, in or upon the aforesaid p'mises, or any part thereof, with free Liberty to and for the sd society, their success'rs and Assignes, when and as often as they shall think good, to fell, cutt down, and carry away the same, and every or any part thereof, to be employed, spent, and converted, for, in, and ab't buildings, and other necessary uses, within the realm of Ireland, and not for any other Cause to be merchandised or sold, And also excepted and reserved to the sd Society, their success'rs and Assns, free liberty to hawke, hunt, fish, fowl, come, go, ride, carry, and recarry, over, in, through, and upon the same premises, and every part and parcell thereof, at all times convenient, and also excepted, and out of these p'sents reserved unto the sd Society, their success'rs and Assns, all the fishing and taking of Salmon and Eeles and other fishes in the rivers of Bann and Loughfoyle, within the province of Ulster aforesd, and in all Creekes and members of the same Rivers, and either of them, and all the ground and soil of the same Rivers and either of them, and also free liberty to and for the sd Society, their success'rs and ass'ns, to digg and search in the premises afore granted, or any part thereof, (Except and other than in the houses, Gardens, Orchards, Meadows, or lands sowed with corn,) for stone, Slate, Lyme, Gravell, sand, and other necessary materialls, and the same to take and carry away, to be employed and converted for, in, and about buildings in the foresd County of Londonderry and province of Ulster, and not otherwise, To have and to hold the sd mann', or reputed mann', of Sal, with the rights, members, and app'ts thereof, and all and every the sd lands, ten'ts, and hereditam'ts, by the sd last recited Indre, bargained and sold, or therein meant, menconed, or intended to be thereby bargained and sold, with their and every of their rights, members, and app'ts, and every part and parcell thereof, (except before excepted), unto the sd Mr, Wardens and Cominalty of the Art or Mistery of Salters, London, their Success'rs and Assns, for ever, To the only proper use and behoofe of the sd Mr, Wardens, and Cominalty, of the Art or Mistery of Salters, London, their success'rs and ass'ns, for ever. And the sd Mr, Wardens, and Cominalty of the Art or Mistery of Salters, aforesd, for them, their success'rs and ass'ns, do covenant and grant to and with the sd Society of the Gov' and Ass'ts, London, of the new plantacon in Ulster, within the realm of Ireland, their success'rs and assns, by these p'sents, That they the sd Society, their success'rs, agents, serv'ts, and ass'ns, shall and may from time to time, and at all times hereafter, have, hold, take, use, carry away, and enjoy freely, all and every the p'mises in and by these p'sents before excepted, or menconed to be excepted, and ev'y of them, and every part and p'cell of them, and every of them w'hout the let or interrupcion of the sd Mr, Wardens, and Cominalty, of the Art or Mistery of Salters aforesd, their success'rs or ass'ns, to be disposed of and employed as in the before excepcions are menconed and expressed, And the sd Society of the Gov' and Assist'ts, London, of the new plantacon in Ulster, within the realm of Ireland, for them and their success'rs, do coven't and grant to and with the sd Mr, Wardens, and Cominalty, of the Art or Mistery of Salters aforesaid, their success'rs and ass'ns by these p'sents That they the sd Mr, Wardens, and Cominalty of the Art or Mistery of Salters aforesd, their success'rs and ass'ns under the Coven'ts and agreem'ts in these presents contained, shall or may at all times from henceforth, for ev' lawfully, peaceably, and quietly have, hold, occupy, possess and enjoy the sd mann' or reputed mann', lands, ten'ts and hereditaments, and all and singular other the p'mises afore hereby granted, bargained, sold, released, and confirmed, or meant, menconed, or intended to be hereby granted, bargained, sold, released and confirmed, and every part and p'cell thereof, with their and every of their app'rts (except before excepted) and receive, perceive, take, and enjoy to their own use and uses for ev' all the rents, issues, and p'fitts thereof, without any

 lawfull

lawfull let, suite, trouble, molestacon, recovery, eviction, expulsion, or interruption of, or by the said Society of the Gov' and Assist^{ts} London, of the plantacon in Ulster, within the realm of Ireland, their success^{rs} or Ass^{ns}, or of or by any other p^{son} or p^{sons}, lawfully claiming or to claim, from, by, or under them or any of them, or their or any of their act, estate, meanes, authority, consent, or procurem^t; And that free, clear, and freely and clearly, acquitted, exonerated, and discharged, or well and sufficiently saved and kept harmless by the s^d Society, their Success^{rs} or Ass^{ns}, of and from all and singular former bargaines, sales, gifts, grants, leases, alienacons, arrearages of rents, estates, charges, and incumbrances whatever had, made, committed, or done by the s^d Society of the Govr, Assist^{ts}, London, of the new plantacon in Ulster, within the realm of Ireland, before the ensealing hereof. (Except the before mentioned Deed, whereby the s^d Mann^r is erected, made and ordained as aforesaid, and except all grants or Estates by Indentures of Bargain and Sale, or Release, made and granted by the s^d Society of the Govr and Assist^{ts}, London, of the new plantacon in Ulster, within the Realm of Ireland, to severall p^{sons} of freehold ten^{ts}, or reputed ten^{ts}, of the s^d mannor or reputed mannor, or of p^{cell} of the p^{mises} by the nominacon and appointm^t of the s^d M^r, Wardens, and Cominalty of the Art or Mistery of Salters afores^d, under certain rents and services, all and every which rents, duties, and Services, in the s^d excepted Indentures reserved, shall for and notwithstanding any Act or thing made or done, or to be made or done, by the s^d Society of the Govr and Assist^{ts}, London, of the new plantacon in Ulster, within the realm of Ireland, their success^{rs} or ass^{ns}, to the contrary, be henceforth due and payable to the s^d M^r, Wardens, and Cominalty of the Art or Mistery of Salters afores^d, their success^{rs} and ass^{ns}, during the continuance in force of the same Grants and Estates respectively. And further, that the s^d Society of the Govr and Assist^{ts}, London, of the New plantacon in Ulster, within the realm of Ireland, for them, their success^{rs}, and Ass^{ns}, do covenant, promise, and grant, to and wth the s^d M^r, Wardens, and Cominalty of the Art or Mistery of Salters afores^d, their success^{rs} and Ass^{ns}, and every of them by these presents, That it shall and may be lawfull to and for the s^d M^r, Wardens, and Cominalty of the Art or Mistery of Salters, London, their Success^{rs} and Ass^{ns}, by the Appointm^t of the Gen^{ll} Agents or Agent of the s^d Society, for the time being, resident in Ulster, for the affairs of the said society, to fell, cutt down, take, and carry away, such, and so many of the Timber Trees of the s^d Society, standing, growing, and being nearest or most convenient to the p^{mises} afore granted as shall be fit and necessary for the building or plantacon of any Houses, Villages, Edifices, or buildings within the s^d mann^r or reputed mann^r, lands, and p^{mises}; And also that they the s^d Society, their success^{rs} and ass^{ns}, shall and will pay and discharge all rents, duties, and other paym^{ts} now due and payable, or hereafter to be due or payable, to the King's Matie, his heirs, or successors, for or in respect of the s^d mann^r or reputed mann^r, lands, and p^{mises}, or any part thereof, or thereof shall save harmless the s^d M^r, Wardens, and Cominalty of the Art or Mistery of Salters afores^d, and their success^{rs}, and all the p^{mises} by these p^{sents} granted or intended to be granted. And further, that the s^d Society, their Success^{rs}, and Ass^{ns} shall and will from time to time, and at all times hereafter, for and during the space of ten years now next ensuing, upon every reasonable request, and at the Costs and Charges in the Law of the s^d M^r, Wardens and Cominalty of the Art or Mistery of Salters, London, their success^{rs}, and ass^{ns}, make, do, execute, and p^{form} all and every such further Conveyance and Assurance in the Law w^{tsoever}, Be it by Indre, Deed or Deeds, Fin^{e}, Release, Confirmacon, or otherwise howsoever, for the further, better, and more p^{fect} and absolute assurance, conveying, and assuring of the s^d mann^r, or reputed mann^r, lands, ten^{ts}, and p^{mises}, (except as is before excepted or mentioned to be excepted,) unto the s^d M^r, Wardens and Cominalty of the Art or Mistery of Salters aforesaid, their Success^{rs}, and Assignes for ever, as by the s^d M^r, Wardens, and Cominalty of the Art or Mistery of Salters afores^d, their Success^{rs}, or Ass^{ns}, or their Counsel learned in Law, shall be reasonably advised or devised, and required, So as the s^d Conveyances and Assurances do conteyne no further warranty nor covenant enjoying the p^{mises} than ag^t the s^d Society and their success^{rs} only. In witness whereof to the one part of these p^{sents} Indres, remaining with the s^d M^r, Wardens and Cominalty of the Art or Mistery of Salters, London, the s^d Society have caused their Common Seal to be put, and to the other part thereof remaining wth the s^d Society the s^d M^r, Wardens and Cominalty have caused their Common Seal to be put, the day and year first above written.

APPENDIX, No. 24.

PAPER handed in by the Chairman.

To all persons to whom these presents shall come the Wardens and Commonalty of the Mistery of Goldsmiths of the City of London Send Greeting Whereas by Indentures of Lease and Release bearing date the 4th and 5th days of June Anno Dni 1663 made or mentioned to be made between the Society of the Governor and Assistants London of the new plantation in Ulster within the Realm of Ireland of the one part and the said Wardens and Comonalty of the Mistery of Goldsmiths of the other part The said Society for the consideration therein mentioned did convey and assure unto the said Wardens and Comonalty and their Successors All that the Mann^r or reputed mann^r of Goldsmiths Hall with the rights members and appurts thereof lying and being within the County of Londonderry alias Colrain within the province of Ulster and Realme of Ireland together with divers lands tenements hereditam^{ts} and premises in the same Indentures or one of them particularly mentioned and expressed except as therein is excepted To hold to them the said Wardens and Comonalty their successors and assigns for ever to the only proper use and behoof of the said Wardens and Comalty of the Mistery of Goldsmiths London their successors and assigns for ever as by the said in part recited Indentures of Lease and Release relation being to them respectively had may more fully and at large appear And whereas upon a representation lately made to the said Society on or about the 31st day of October last at a Court then holden for the said Society by or on behalf of the said Wardens and Comalty setting forth in effect that the said Wardens and Comalty being seised in fee of the said Mann^r of Goldsmiths Hall in Ireland by virtue of the said Indentures of Lease and Release before mentioned and recited had sometime since (vizt) on or about the 7th of March 1728 contracted with the Right Honourable Henry Earle of Shelburne for the sale thereof in consideration of Fourteen thousand one hundred pounds to be paid as in the same Representation mentioned And further setting forth that a suit had been commenced by the said Wardens and Comalty in the High Court of Chancery and a Decree obtained there against the said Earle for a performance of the said Contract by which Decree it was referred to a Mr to examine the said Comp^s Title who had reported that the said Wardens and Comonalty could make a good title to a purchaser provided that the said Society would joyn with them in a conveyance of the premises It was in and by the said Representation finally proposed & requested that the said Society would be pleased to joyn with the said Wardens and Company in a new Convey^e of the premises to the said Earle of Shelburne such as Councell should advise by means whereof the said Company would be enabled to pform the said Contract on their part and speedily reap the benefits thereof And whereas the said Society on due consideration of the said recited representation and the matters therein contained for other reasons inducing them thereunto as mentioned in the minutes or entrys of the said Court holden on the said 31st day of October Did Resolve that they the said Society would at the charge of the said Comp^s do what they reasonably could to enable the said Comp^y effectually to pform the said Contract on their part (being therein Indemnified by the said Comp^y) in such manner as Councell should advise And whereas in pursuance of the said Resolution and other proceedings thereupon since had as may appear likewise by the Minutes and Entrys in the Books of the said Society By a certain Indenture Tripartite bearing date the 31st day of October last past and made or mentioned to be made between the said Wardens and Comonalty and the said Governor and Assistants of the said Society of the first part the said Right Honorable Henry Earle of Shelburne of the second part and George Tomkins Esquire and Robert McConsland Gent of the third part The said Wardens Comalty and at their request and by their direction (testified as therein is mentioned) the said Society for the considerations therein mentioned Did grant bargain sell alien enfeoffe remise release and confirm unto the said Earle and his heirs All that the said Man^r or reputed Man^r of Goldsmiths Hall with the rights members and appurtenances thereof together with divers lands tenements hereditaments and premises in the said last recited Indenture particularly mentioned (except as therein is excepted) To hold to the said Earl his heires and assigns subject to the payment of the rent or yearly sum of £ 200 of lawful money of Great Britain to the said Wardens and Comalty their Successors and Assignes in manner therein mentioned In and by which said last recited Indenture it is covenanted by and on the part of the said Society to and with the said Earle that they the said Society had not nor have not done any act matter or thing whereby or wherewith the premises thereby granted were should or might be impeached charged or incumbered in anywise Except as therein excepted And further that they the said Society would at any time within or during the space of 20 years then next ensuing at the request costs and charges of the said Earle his heirs or assignes make do execute and perform such further Convey^s and assurances in the law of the said man^r and premises thereby granted to the said Earle his and his heirs as by him them or his or their Councell shall be reasonably devised or advised and required and so as such Conveyances or assurances should contain no further Warranty or Cov for enjoying the said premises than therein contained as in and by the hereinbefore in part recited Indenture Tripartite relačon being thereunto had may more fully and at large appear Now these presents witness that in regard the said Society upon the application of or on the behalf of the said Wardens and Coñalty and for the reasons before mentioned have been induced And in consideračon that they the said Society have at the request and by the direčon of the said Wardens and Coñalty become partys unto and have sealed and executed the said Indenture Tripartite as aforesaid They the said Wardens and Coñalty for themselves and their Successors do covenant promise grant and agree to and with the said Society and their successors that they the said Wardens and Coñalty and their successors shall and will from time to time and at all times hereafter save defend keep harmless and indemnified the said Society and their successors and their and every of their lands tenements goods and chattels of from and against all costs charges damages and expenses which they or any of them shall or may pay bear sustain or be put unto for or by reason or means of their becoming partys unto and sealing and executing the said before mentioned and recited Indenture Tripartite and of from and against all or any accon or accons suit or suits at law or in equity to be brought commenced or prosecuted against the said Society or their Successors or whereunto they or any of them may be made partys for touching or concerning the said Indenture or any of the premises therein or thereby granted or conveyed to the said Earl of Shelburne and his heirs or for touching or concerning any matters or thing whatsoever contained in the same recited Indenture Tripartite or relating thereunto In witness whereof the said Wardens and Commonalty have hereunto affixed their Common Seal the 18th day of Decr Anno Domini 1730 And in the fourth year of the Reign of our Sovereign Lord George the Second King of Great Britain &c.

I have perused and approved of this draft on behalf of all the partys

Middle Temple 8 Decr 1730 NATH PIGOT

It being insisted on by the purchaser of the Goldsmiths Compy Estate that he or his Counsell should see the original grant from the Crown to the Irish Society or at least an Office copy thereof in order to know upon what termes or condicons or subject to what rents the Grant was made: The Lord Chancellor on arguing excons Ordered that the purchasers request be complied with and the Society being willing to oblige the Goldsmiths Compy therein provided they may consistently with their Trust for other Companys as well as the Goldsmiths

Q. Whether it be proper for the Irish Society to show the originall Grant or should they refer the partys to the Record

The Grant being on Record to which all persons may have recourse there can be no inconveniance in shewing the original grant and it is proper for them to let it be inspected but not to let it go out of their possession or to suffer it to be copied and the party if he pleases may have a copy from the Record

Nath' Pigot
9th Decr 1730

29 Mar 11 Ja' 1st Lres Pat
9 Sept 1617 Creat' Man'
30 Sept 13 Ja' Lin Mort'
10 Sept 15 Ja' Pleadin'

Lres pat of King Ja' being annulled and ye Society and ye Co' as well as ye Tent' deprived of y' Estates

10 Apl 14 C' on ye pet' of ye Co' this King makes a new Gr'
7 Aug 15 C2 Licen Morter
30 May 1622 Crea Man'
4 and 5 June 1663 Lease and Rel

P Ld Cha Talbot
Mr Lutwiche
Mr Pigot
Mr Ward
Mr Horsman
Mr Green

Con Ld Cha Hardwick
Ld Ch Jn Reeve

Serg' Cheshyre
Mr Peere Will'
Mr Annesley

Lres Pat and Acts Com' Council
Money raised by ye Co.
Licen Mort'
Convey' of 12 pporcions
Premises undivided
Div' 56' p ann
Acco' & Rent' 3 y' to Xmas' 41

APPENDIX, No. [illegible]

PAPER handed in by Mr. [illegible]

LIST of References to the Calendars of State Papers, Ireland, 1608–1610, 1611–1614, and 1615–1625, and to the Calendars of Patent and Close Rolls, Ireland, temp.: James I. and Charles I.

(Stating in continuous order [illegible] the documents are, and indicating the point of each document, and the page at which it occurs, in accordance with the directions of the Committee at p. [illegible] of the printed Minutes of Evidence.)

The intentions of the King appear from his instructions for plantations in divers parts of Ireland, dated [illegible] September, 1605 (Pat. and Cl., Jac. I., pp. [illegible]), and from a commission for [illegible] in Ulster, of [illegible] July, 1608 (Ibid. pp. [illegible]). See also Chichester's notes on the six counties of [illegible] October, 1608 (St. Pap. 1608–10, pp. [illegible]). The report of the Committee of [illegible] December, 1608, contemplated Tyrone alone as the field of operations; Sir John Davys, however, proposed to extend it to all Ulster (St. Pap. 1608–10, p. [illegible]). The King approved of the Tyrone project, and in accordance with Sir John Davys' advice resolved to apply it to the other escheated lands (Ibid. p. [illegible]). Chichester, on [illegible] February, 1608/9, wrote that there were many applicants [illegible] (St. Pap. 1608–10, p. [illegible]).

The prospectus varied at different times. On [illegible] March, 1608/9, Chichester acknowledges the receipt of certain printed books containing the orders and conditions. He hopes for them a better fate than that of "the other" [illegible], and to "perform the conditions," and he criticises the documents, and declares that the time allowed for building is too short, because workmen are too few, and that very few in Ireland will bear any part, for they are all either not able or not content to undergo the conditions (St. Pap. 1608–10, pp. [illegible]). And there is a reference in the State Papers to "two printed books" (Ibid. [illegible]).

The cuttings, coshering, and other Irish exactions referred to in that copy or edition of the Orders and Conditions which has come down to us are described in St. Pap. 1608–1614, pp. [illegible]. An Ulster chief wrote "It is not unknown to your Lordship that the Irish gentry did ever make their followers pursue their only exchequer" (St. Pap. 1611–1614, pp. [illegible]).

And Sir John Davys speaks of the Commissioners having, upon surrender accepted of [illegible] Irish lords and gentlemen, reduced their [illegible], cuttings, and Irish duties of [illegible] to certain rents in money (St. Pap. 1611–1614, pp. [illegible]). And this is mentioned among Chichester's services (Ibid. p. [illegible]).

On the 31st March, 1609, Chichester wrote that no one in Ireland would apply unless some of the conditions were altered; and that "the [illegible]" (St. Pap. 1608–1610, pp. [illegible]). And from a State Paper [illegible] for deferring the plantation till the following spring, it appears that it had been thought fit to mitigate some of the conditions (St. Pap. 1608–1610, p. [illegible]).

The articles for instructions to the Commissioners of the [illegible] June, 1609, were preceded by a different set of instructions, though of the same general character (St. Pap. 1608–10, pp. [illegible]).

On the [illegible] July, 1609, a Commission was appointed to survey the escheated lands in the six counties (St. Pap. 1608–1610, p. [illegible]).

The deputation which the Londoners had agreed to send over to view the land carried with them a letter of recommendation dated the 3rd August, 1609 (Pat. and Cl. Car. I., p. [illegible]). But at the same time the Council sent private instructions to Chichester, directing him to take the best means to encourage the Londoners and to conceal matters of distaste (St. Pap. 1608–1610, pp. [illegible]). On the [illegible] August, 1609, the Commissioners of Survey were at Coleraine, and (as they say) "using their best rhetoric to persuade the Londoners" (St. Pap. 1608–1610, pp. [illegible]). And on the [illegible] September, 1609, Chichester, who was one of the Commissioners of Survey, wrote describing the work performed by the Commissioners; and he states that the Agents of London were with the Commissioners at Coleraine, that their purse and industry would within two or three years improve their property to double value, that they came luckily when the people were more submissive than Chichester had reported, and that nothing should be wanting to continue them in their resolution (St. Pap. 1608–1610, p. [illegible]). And on the [illegible] October, 1609, Chichester writes that the Agents of London have seen everything favourable; and he prays God they prove not like their London women, who [illegible] to-day and loathe to-morrow (St. Pap. 1608–1610, p. [illegible]).

The bargaining between the City and the Government, which resulted in the Agreement of 28th January, 1609–10, took place at three conferences in the Temple, the details of which are set forth in St. Pap. 1608–1610, pp. [illegible].

The conclusion of the agreement was announced to Chichester in a letter of 4th February 1609–10 (St. Pap. 1608–1610, p. [illegible]; Pat. and Cl. Car. I., pp. [illegible]), the receipt of which letter he acknowledges on [illegible] February, 1609–10 (Pat. and Cl., Car. I., p. [illegible]) in which he describes the dearth of workmen.

That the conditions of plantation, whatever they were, applied to the whole of the six counties appears from the grant to Chichester himself of the country of Inishowen (Pat. and Cl., Jac. I., pp. [illegible], and also a grant to Sir John Davys of the [illegible] June, 1610, of the Manor of [illegible] and [illegible], in the barony of [illegible], in the county of Tyrone (Ibid. p. [illegible]), and many other grants of forfeited lands in the counties of Armagh, Cavan, Fermanagh, and Donegal (Ibid. pp. [illegible]). And the Lords informed Sir Oliver Lambert that the Londoners were to plant their lands as other undertakers do, excepting the special privileges expressed in the Articles (St. Pap. 1611–14, p. [illegible]). This document also shows that the obligations of the other undertakers were to be looked for only in the conditions of their patents and in their bonds (Ibid. pp. [illegible]), a point which is further illustrated by the proceedings of the Deputy, who, on [illegible] June, 1612, he asks the direction of the Privy Council to the [illegible] that all the British gained their lands (i.e., obtained their grants) in England, and that "few of their grants are yet transmitted to the Rolls in Ireland, and all their bonds expressing their conditions for building and otherwise were taken in England and Scotland, and never sent to Ireland, so that there is no ground to judge of the breach of such conditions as they stand bound to perform (St. Pap. 1611–1614, p. [illegible]), and on [illegible] August, 1612, acknowledging the receipt of a book containing the [illegible] of the undertakers in Ulster, he adds, "By having them it will be discerned who have failed in their conditions" (Ibid. p. [illegible]). Again in May, 1611, Sir John [illegible] is instructed that undertakers who are [illegible] are to be called on to perform the conditions of the plantation under the [illegible] of their lands (St. Pap. 1611-1614, p. [illegible]). Another document enumerates the "[illegible] of the lands of the undertakers now in [illegible] as well by their lands or patents" (St. Pap. 1611-1614, p. [illegible]); also a similar document (Ibid. pp. [illegible]).

There is a document of 30th November, 1612, which illustrates the King's part in the establishment of free schools (St. Pap. 1611-1614, p. [illegible]). And on 20th Jan., 1613-4, he states that he has already assigned lands in the several counties for the endowment of free schools and the maintenance of schoolmasters (Ibid. pp. [illegible]). On the [illegible] April, 1614, the King informs Chichester that he had selected the Archbishop to distribute the lands reserved in the escheated counties for schools and glebes, and that the lands are accordingly to be conveyed by Royal grant to the Archbishop (St. Pap. 1615-1625, p. [illegible]).

On the [illegible] September, 1616, there was a Royal Commission to assign glebes (Ibid. p. 130), and on the [illegible] June, 1618, Chichester speaks of the lands allotted by the King for the maintenance of free schools (Ibid. p. [illegible]), and there is a recital to the same effect on 12th July, 1623, applying to all the six counties (Pat. & Cl., Car. I., pp. [illegible]).

On the 7th November, 1625, there is mention of a grant by the King for a free school in Fermanagh (Pat. & Cl., Car. I., pp. 72-6), and again on 3rd May, 1626 (Ibid. pp. [illegible]). On the [illegible] July, 1626, the King, taking notice that by the Orders of King James letters patent were to be passed to the incumbents of the several parishes in Ulster, of divers parcels of the escheated lands, directs Falkland to have the same speedily performed (Pat. & Cl., Car. I., pp. 122-3). A similar direction to Falkland to cause the endowments for the free schools to be passed by letters patent to the Archbishop in trust for the schoolmasters (Ibid.).

That there were claimants to the Londoners' estates whom the King was bound by the articles to get rid of, and whose claims interfered with the progress of the plantation in Londonderry, appears from the proceedings of the Temple (St. Pap. 1608-1610, pp. [illegible]) and from Chichester's letter of 1st April, 1610 (St. Pap. 1608-1610, p. [illegible]). And on 29th January, 1610-11, Chichester wrote: "The Agents of London go well forward at "Coleraine, but can do little at the Derry until the difference between them and the new inhabitants be compounded "and the latter satisfied for their titles to the land and houses there" (St. Pap. 1611-1614, p. 1). And on the [illegible] December, 1611, he reported that it was necessary to pay for compositions made and to be made in the behalf of the Londoners and others towards the plantation of which the old inhabitants of the Derry were to have 1,000 marks "[illegible] which they will not deliver possession" (St. Pap. 1611-1614, p. 181). Similarly, Sir T. Caulfeild had to be bought out, as appears from a letter of Chichester to Alderman [illegible] of [illegible] February, 1612 (Pat. and Cl. Car. I., pp. [illegible]). Caulfeild surrendered those lands, "which were claimed by the Londoners as theirs by the "articles of their plantation" before the 12th February 1613 (St. Pap. 1611-1614, p. [illegible]). Caulfeild had strongly protested, and in his protest he claims to have paid dearly for those lands in the charge he was at for buildings (St. Pap. 1611-1614, p. [illegible]). By the 13th May, 1613, Sir T. Phillips had surrendered the lands in his possession claimed by the Londoners, and was to receive compensation from the King (St. Pap. 1611-1614, p. [illegible]). Chichester in vain tried to persuade the Londoners to forego the claim (Ibid. p. [illegible]).

And there are several instances of the King buying out incumbrancers, so that the undertakers might not be troubled with suits at law (St. Pap. 1615-1625, pp. [illegible]).

The workmen whom the Londoners sent over at wages calculated on the presumption of an extraordinary plenty of all things in the place made complaint (St. Pap. 1608-1610, p. [illegible]). The workmen employed by the City are also mentioned in a letter of the Council to Chichester of the [illegible] June, 1610 (St. Pap. 1608-1610, p. [illegible]), though other undertakers had not arrived (Ibid. p. [illegible]).

On the [illegible] August, 1610, there was proclamation made that servitors were to pay a higher rent if they planted with Irish (St. Pap. 1608-1610, p. [illegible]). On the [illegible] Sept., 1610, Davys wrote that if the Irish tenants were to be immediately removed a general dearth would probably ensue; he describes the proceedings taken towards that end, and states that the Londoners at Coleraine were doing better than the Government expected (St. Pap. 1608-1610, pp. [illegible]).

On the [illegible] March, 1611, the Londoners successfully petitioned to be allowed to proceed with their buildings only at Coleraine till they should have finished there, or at least for that summer, but upon the terms that they were to finish all their buildings at Coleraine that year, proceed effectually with preparation of materials at the Derry that year, and fortify the Derry to secure its safety during the following winter (St. Pap. 1611-1614, p. [illegible]).

Under date April 16th, 1611, there is a notice of an exchange made by the Londoners with Sir Thomas Phillips. And because the lands he parted with to the Londoners were for the most part inhabited by natives, he is allowed to have the natives likewise on the lands he takes, as other servitors (St. Pap. 1611-1614, p. [illegible]).

In May, 1611, Sir John Bourchier was instructed to give the Londoners time on certain conditions (St. Pap. 1611-1614, p. [illegible]). He had stated that "experience now tells the undertakers that it will be hard, almost "impossible, for them to perform the work they have undertaken if the natives be all presently removed"; upon which he is instructed to remove the swordmen "as conveniently as may be," with as many of their followers and churls as can be induced to go, and such labourers of the natives as the undertakers are willing to have removed; "but such other natives as the undertakers desire to keep for this year (if the number do seem too great to "be removed at once) that your Lordship may tolerate them for this year" (St. Pap. 1611-14, pp. [illegible]).

A warrant dated the [illegible] August, 1611, for removing the natives, contains a statement of the objects of the plantation which is not identical with that in the Charter of 1613 (St. Pap. 1611-14, p. [illegible]).

In a report of the state of the plantation of Ulster, upon a survey made in the summer of 1611, complaint is made that in the county of Coleraine the Londoners had done nothing towards the performance of the articles of plantation, and sought not to remove the natives, but were building at Derry. Dunalong [illegible] is recommended as the site for a fort, and the Londoners had agreed thereto, but it was on the Bishop's land, and the Bishop requires compensation (St. Pap. 1611-14, pp. 122, [illegible]).

On 1st October, 1611, there is a warrant allowing native labourers to remain upon the proportions of the British undertakers until Mayday next (St. Pap. 1611-14, p. [illegible]).

On [illegible] December, 1611, Chichester expresses a fear that most of the undertakers will prove weak and unable to perform what is fitting, and reports that many have sold their portions, or do little other than receive rent from the natives for their lands without bringing over the families appointed, or doing anything else commendable (St. Pap. 1611-14, p. [illegible]).

There is a project of Sir T. Phillips (St. Pap. 1611-14, pp. [illegible]) for the Londoners' plantation, containing estimated profits on an expenditure of [illegible] (p. [illegible]), showing a profit by rents at [illegible] per acre, to be increased on [illegible] death; and on pp. [illegible] an enumeration of defaults on the part of the Londoners, referring to no obligations but those of the articles, and contemplating their making a profit.

Chichester admitted on the [illegible] February, 1612, that the Londoners had erected houses and been at great charges in Coleraine and Derry (Pat. and Cl., Car. I., pp. [illegible]); but on the [illegible] June, 1612, the Privy Council informed him that though blame ought to be imputed to all the British undertakers, yet they had of late received his information of the negligence of the Londoners in particular in performing their covenants; that they had dealt roundly with them upon that point, representing them in particular their continuing within their several precincts the natives (St. Pap. 1611-1614, p. [illegible]). Then follow the Londoners' answers (Ibid. p. [illegible]), which appear by the replies thereto to have been considered reasonable (Ibid. p. [illegible]). The whole letter is in Pat. and Cl., Car. I., pp. [illegible].

On the [illegible] November, 1612, the Council notice a complaint on the part of the Bishop of Derry, that his predecessor had made a lease at too small a rent, contrary to the conditions of the letters patent, to Rowley, the City's agent (St. Pap. 1611-1614, pp. [illegible]). The Lords thought it defensible (Ibid. p. [illegible]). For this breach of trust Rowley had been dismissed (Ibid. p. [illegible]).

On

On the 23rd December, 1612, the King says he is informed that Cawley had made havoc in the woods against the articles agreed on (St. Pap. 1611–1614, pp. 311–2).

In a proclamation of 26th July, 1613, the King desires that he desires to advance the subjects of the new plantation above those of the rest of the kingdom (Ibid., p. 387).

The King's instructions of 5th June, 1614, direct that as the British undertakers still retain the natives upon their proportions, Chichester is to give orders for the removing of the natives in such manner as shall seem most expedient and as may best stand with the rules of the plantation and the public peace of those places (St. Pap. 1611–14, p. 482).

On the 25th January, 1614–5, the Council inform Chichester that the time is drawing near which was appointed for the removal of the natives from the lands of the Londoners. The Londoners have petitioned to retain them, which is submitted to Chichester's judgment. The Council urge expedition in preparing the Bill for confirmation of the Londoners' Charter, as the Londoners allege that the want of it prevents them from concluding with the several Companies who bear the charge of the plantation (St. Pap. 1615–1625, p. 2).

On the 18th April, 1615, Chichester reported that Coleraine was unsafe, and that he had advised the building of a keep, which the Irish Society promised to do, but had not yet done (Ibid. p. 37).

On the 8th June, 1615, the Council inform Chichester that the Irish Society have been warned of the weakness of Derry and Coleraine, and have promised to strengthen them, but demur to building a fort (St. Pap. 1615–1625, p. 53).

On the 7th March, 1615–6, the Deputy complains that those of Londonderry and Coleraine have not yet set up their gates nor otherwise prepared themselves (Ibid. p. 115).

On the 6th April, 1617, there is a further stay for enforcing the removal of the natives (Ibid. p. 154).

On the 7th May, 1619, the Deputy sends to the Council an account of a re-survey of the plantation, with details of undertakers, servitors, natives, freeholders, leaseholders for life, leaseholders for years, and cottagers. He advises that those that remain in England should send agents authorised to perform their covenants of building and plantation (Ibid. p. 254).

On the 4th April, 1620, there is the grant of a lottery to one Henry Bentley, preceded by a recital of the King's objects: "Forasmuch as the bringing of a lottery in Ireland may greatly tend to the increase of civility," with other purely public objects (St. Pap. 1615–1625, p. 279).

On the 25th February, 1620/1, the Committee for Ireland certify (with reference to a certain petition) that they are against altering the former articles, but would permit the Irish to remain on lease, and would allow them for removing the natives till Mayday, 1622 (Ibid. pp. 322–3).

On the 28th May, 1621, the Deputy considers the conditions of a successful plantation (Ibid. p. 325).

On the 22nd June, 1622, the Lords Justices report as to the plantation of Ulster, that though it be well settled (God be thanked!) and free from the complaints of the natives, yet it has not been so really performed and planted with British as was at first projected and conditioned by the undertakers. These men were petitioners in England, offering for mitigation of their strict covenants a doubling of their rents, which they have again renewed. Having considered of their desire, the Lords Justices have delivered to them a copy of such conditions as they hold fit for them to be tied unto, in case of a new contract or alteration in their patents (St. Pap. 1615–1625, p. 357).

In October, 1622, Sir Thos. Phillips made a survey of Londonderry, showing all that he complained of (St. Pap. 1615–1625, pp. 364–378), and on 3rd June, 1623, his ideas for reformation of abuses in the Ulster plantation. The Londoners objected to the registration of the Irish (Ibid., pp. 411–3).

On the 20th June, 1623, the Irish Church Commissioners recommended that whereas no patents of Church Endowments in Ulster had yet been passed to the clergy it should be done forthwith. And they also speak of the free schools to be erected and endowed in the various late plantations (St. Pap. 1615–1625, pp. 416–7).

On the 1st August, 1623, Falkland answers the complaints made by Sir Thos. Phillips against the Londoners; that they neglect defence, have spoiled the King's woods contrary to their agreement with the King, have neglected to plant with British as they were tied to do, and strive too wickedly to raise their rents. He suggests that the King might forfeit it for failure to plant (St. Pap. 1615–1625, pp. 428–9).

In December, 1623, Sir Thos. Phillips was moving for a commission to inquire into the six counties (St. Pap. 1615–1625, p. 450).

On the 25th January, 1623/4, the Deputy and Council report that they have proclaimed His Majesty's pleasure for the remove of the natives upon the lands where they yet abide in the six escheated counties, until further order (St. Pap. 1615–1625, p. 456).

On the 27th January, 1623/4, a commission was issued to enquire as to the natives in Londonderry (St. Pap. 1615–1625, p. 457). A specimen of the return (for Fermanagh) is given on p. 458.

On the 1st March, 1623/4, Beresford, agent for the Londoners, protested against the inquiry coming into the London plantation, alleging that the Londoners were purchasers not planters (St. Pap. 1615–1625, p. 470).

On the 24th April, 1624, the Deputy reported that he had required the Londoners' agent to accept exchanges in Londonderry; that the Agent said he had no authority, and that the Deputy had ordered Sir John Vaughan to take a sufficient account of the rents (St. Pap. 1615–1625, p. 487), and on the 29th April the Deputy further reported that the Agent had not yet received authority, and that the Deputy found it difficult to levy the rents of his own authority (Ibid., p. 489).

In May, 1624, the Lords made divers demands relating to Londonderry and Coleraine, to which on the 2nd June the Common Council made their answers (St. Pap. 1615–1625, pp. 499–502).

On the 8th June, 1624, Sir T. Phillips said he could prove many omissions on the part of the Londoners, and it was referred to certain Commissioners (St. Pap. 1615–1625, pp. 514–5).

In July, 1624, the Ulster undertakers, being discouraged by threats of forfeiture through provisoes in their patents, asked for more liberally worded patents (St. Pap. 1615–1625, pp. 518–9).

On the 24th September, 1624, the Commissioners to whom Sir T. Phillips' petition had been referred made certain recommendations which the King approved. Sir Thos. Phillips was appointed to see to their execution, with 999*l.* per annum from the Irish Society for damages. The Irish were to be allowed to stay in towns, "and for this favour the Irish Society are to double their rents as other undertakers who have broken their conditions of plantation are to do" (St. Pap. 1615–1625, pp. 537–8).

On the 7th November, 1625, the King mentions a commission to Lord Falkland of the 6th September then last, containing instructions for renewing the undertakers' grants in Ulster, wherein double rents were to be reserved and a fine of 30*l.* upon every 1,000 acres (Pat. & Cl. Car. I., p. 75).

On the 16th August, 1627, a further commission was issued to inquire concerning the Londoners' plantation, with very detailed articles (Pat. & Cl., Car. I., pp. 253–311).

On the 19th October, 1627, the King desires careful execution of the commission of 16th August, 1627, to inquire into abuses and breaches of covenant by the Londoners, and requires an account of the proceedings in the commission by Sir T. Phillips whom he had appointed to negotiate, in the event for the effective prosecution thereof (Pat. & Cl., Car. I., pp. 288–9).

APPENDIX, No. [illegible]

PAPER handed in by Mr. [illegible], [illegible] July [illegible]

LICENCE to hold in Mortmain.

Patent Roll. [illegible] Chas. II. Part [illegible], No. [illegible]

(Transcript.)

[illegible]

Charles the Second, by the grace of God of England, Scotland, France, and Ireland, King, Defender of the Faith, &c. To all to whom these presents shall come, Greeting. Whereas our Royal grandfather, King James, of blessed memory, by his letters patent under the great seal of England, bearing date at Westminster, the twenty-ninth day of March, in the eleventh year of his reign [illegible]

And whereas [illegible]

And whereas [illegible]

We therefore, being willing [illegible]

Mercers of the said Cittie of London, the Wardens and Comminaltie of the Mistery of the Grocery of the said Cittie of London, the Master and Wardens and brethren and sisters of the Guild or Fraternity of the Blessed Mary the Virgin of the Mistery of the Drapers of the said Cittie of London, the Wardens and Comminaltie of the Mistery of the Fishmongers of the said Cittie of London, the Wardens and Comminaltie of the Mistery of Goldsmithes of the said Cittie of London, the Corporation of Masters and Wardens and brethren and sisters of the Guilde or Fraternitie of Corpus Christi of Skinners of the said Cittie of London, the Master and Wardens of the Merchant Taylors of the Fraternitie of St. John Baptist in the said Cittie of London, the Master and fower Wardens of the Fraternitie of the Arte or Mistery of Haberdashers in the said Cittie of London, the Master, Wardens, and Comminaltie of the Arte or Mistery of Salters, London, the Master and Keepers or Wardens and Comminaltie of the Mistery or Arte of Ironmongers, the Master, Wardens, and Freemen and Comminaltie of the Mistery of Vintners of the said Cittie of London, and to the said Master, Wardens, and Comminaltie of Freemen of the Arte or Mistery of Clothworkers of the said Cittie of London, and their successors severally and respectively. To have and to hold to the said Wardens and Comminaltie of the Mistery of the Mercers of the said Cittie of London, the Wardens and Comminaltie of the Mistery of the Grocery of the said Cittie of London, the Master and Wardens and brethren and sisters of the Guild or Fraternitie of the Blessed Mary the Virgin of the Mistery of the Drapers of the said Cittie of London, the Wardens and Comminaltie of the Mistery of the Fishmongers of the said Cittie of London, the Wardens and Comminaltie of the Mistery of Goldsmithes of the said Cittie of London, the Corporation of Master and Wardens and brethren and sisters of the Guild or Fraternitie of Corpus Christi of Skinners of London, the Master and Wardens of the Merchant Taylors of the Fraternitie of St. John Baptist in the said Citty of London, the Master and fower Wardens of the Fraternitie of the Art or Mistery of Haberdashers in the said Citty of London, the Master, Wardens, and Comminaltie of the Art or Mistery of Salters, London, the Master and Keepers or Wardens and Comminaltie of the Mistery or Art of Ironmongers, London, the Master, Wardens, and Freemen and Comminaltie of the Mistery of Vintners of the said Cittie of London, and to the said Master, Wardens, and Comminaltie of Freemen of the said Art or Mistery of Clothworkers of the said Citty of London, and their successors severally and respectively for ever, so that the same premises or any of them be not [illegible] holden of us, our heirs, or successors in capite, nor by Knights service, without lett, impeachment, contradiction, or molestation of us, our heirs, or successors, or of any of our Justices, Escheators, Sheriffes, Baylisses, or other our ministers, or of our heyres or successors whatsoever, and without any inquisition or inquisitions by vertue of anie writte or writts of ad quod dampnum or of any other writte or writts, mandate or mandates, commandement or commandements, of us, our heyres or successors in this behalfe, to be purchased, had, taken, or prosecuted, and without any lycence or lycences of us, our heyres or successors, or warrant or warrants by the said Wardens and Comminaltie of the Mistery of the Mercers of the said Cittie of London, the Wardens and Comminaltie of the Mistery of the Grocery of the said Citty of London, the Master and Wardens and brethren and sisters of the Guild or Fraternitie of the Blessed Mary the Virgin of the Mistery of the Drapers of the said Citty of London, the Wardens and Comminaltie of the Mistery of Fishmongers of the said Cittie of London, the Wardens and Comminaltie of the Mistery of Goldsmithes of the said Cittie of London, the Corporation of the Master and Wardens and brethren and sisters of the Guild or Fraternitie of Corpus Christi of Skinners of London, the Master and Wardens of the Merchant Taylors of the Fraternitie of St. John Baptist in the said Cittie of London, the Master and fower Wardens of the Fraternitie of the Arte or Mistery of Haberdashers in the said Cittie of London, the Master, Wardens, and Comminaltie of the Arte or Mistery of Salters, London, the Master and Keepers or Wardens and Comminaltie of the Mistery or Arte of Ironmongers, London, the Master, Wardens, and Freemen and Comminaltie of the Mistery of Vintners of the said Citty of London, or by the said Master, Wardens and Comminaltie of Freemen of the said Arte or Mistery of Clothworkers of the said Cittie of London, or by every or any of them or their successors severally or respectively in this behalf, for the premises or any of them or them, every or anie of them in this behalf, to be granted or made.

And further, of our more especiall grace, certaine knowledge, and meere motion wee have given and granted, and by these presents for us, our heirs and successors doe give and grant unto the said Society of the Governour and Assistants, London, of the Newe Plantation in Ulster, within the Realme of Ireland, and to their successors, and to all other person and persons, bodyes politicke and corporate whatsoever respectively full and free licence, power, and authoritie to give, grant, enfeoffe, bargaine, sell, assigne, alyen, surrender, release, or confirme unto the said Wardens and Comminaltie of the Mistery of the Mercers of the said Citty of London, the Wardens and Comminaltie of the Mistery of the Grocery of the said Citty of London, the Master and Wardens, and brethren and sisters of the Guild or Fraternitie of the Blessed Mary the Virgin of the Mistery of the Drapers of the said Cittie of London, the Wardens and Comminaltie of the Mistery of Fishmongers of the said Cittie of London, the Wardens and Comminaltie of the Mistery of Goldsmithes of the said Cittie of London, the Corporation of Master and Wardens, and brethren and sisters of the Guilde or Fraternitie of Corpus Christi of Skinners of London, the Master and Wardens of the Merchant Taylors of the Fraternitie of St. John Baptiste in the said Cittie of London, the Master and fower Wardens of the Fraternitie of the Arte or Mistery of Haberdashers in the said Cittie of London, the Master, Wardens, and Comminaltye of the Arte or Mistery of [illegible], London, the Master and Keepers or Wardens and Comminaltie of the Mistery or Arte of Ironmongers, London, the Master, Wardens, and Freemen and Comminaltie of the Mistery of Vintners of the Citty of London, and to the said Master Wardens, and Comminaltie of Freemen of the Arte or Mistery of Clothworkers of the said Cittie of London and their successors severally and respectively, such and soe much of the aforesaid counties, countreys, baronies, cities, townes, castles, lands, tenements and hereditaments whatsoever, given, granted, and confirmed, or meant, mentioned, or intended to be given, granted, or confirmed in or by our said former Letters Patents before in these presents mentioned to the said Society of the Governour and Assistants, London, of the Newe Plantation in Ulster within the Realme of Ireland and their successors or unto other person or persons, bodyes politicke, or corporate or others shall be willing from time to tyme to grant, enfeoffe, bargaine, sell, convey, assigne, alyen, confirme, surrender or release unto the said Wardens and Comminaltye of the Mistery of the Mercers of the said Cittie of London, the Wardens and Comminaltie of the Mistery of the Grocery of the said Citty of London the Master, Wardens and brethren and sisters of the Guild or Fraternity of the Blessed Mary the Virgin of the Mistery of Drapers of the said Cittie of London, the Wardens and Comminaltie of the Mistery of Fishmongers of the said Citty of London, the Wardens and Comminaltie of the said Mistery of Goldsmithes of the said Citty of London, the Corporation of Master and Wardens and brethren and sisters of the Guild or Fraternitie of Corpus Christi of Skinners of London, the Master and Wardens of the Merchant Taylors of the Fraternitie of St. John Baptist in the said Cittie of London, the Master and fower Wardens of the Fraternitie of the Arte or Mistery of Haberdashers in the said Citty of London, the Master, Wardens, and Comminaltie of the said Arte or Mistery of Salters, London, the Master and Keepers or Wardens and Comminaltie of the Mistery or Arte of Ironmongers, London, the Master, Wardens and Freemen and Comminaltie of the Mistery of Vintners of the said Cittie of London, and to the said Master, Wardens and Comminaltie of Freemen of the said Arte or Mistery of Clothworkers of the said Cittie of London and their successors severally and respectively, without lett, impeachment, contradiction or molestation of us, our heyres or successors, or of any of our Justices, Escheators, Sheriffes, Bayliffes, or other, the ministers of us, our heirs or successors, and without anie inquisition or inquisitions or any writt or writts ad quod dampnum, or of any other writte or writtes, mandate or mandates, commandement or commandements of us, our heyres or successors in this behalfe to be had, procured, or obteyned. And for that our desire and pleasure is that the said Society of the Governour and Assistants, London, of the Newe Plantation in Ulster, within the Realme of Ireland, theyr successors and assignes should for ever hereafter quietly and peaceably have, hold, possess, and enjoy the countyes, countreys, baronies, cittyes, townes, villages, lands, tenements, rents, rivers, fishings, hereditaments, and all other things in and by the aforesaid Letters Patents mentioned, named, or intended to be given or granted and confirmed as aforesaid.

We therefore for the more quiett, firme and sure holding and enjoying of the same premises by the said Society, theyr successors and assignes, and for the better strengthening, setling, establishing and confirming of the right, title and interest of the said Society, theyr successors and assignes of, in and to the premises abovementioned of our especiall grace,

grace, certain knowledge, and [illegible] motion, have given and granted, and by these presents for us, our heyres and successors doe give and grant, unto the aforesaid Society of the Governour and Assistants, London, of the Newe Plantation in Ulster within the Realme of Ireland and theyr successors full license, power and authoritie that they and theyr successors may have, take, hold and enjoy the countyes, [illegible], baronyes, [illegible], townes, villages, lands, tenements, [illegible], fishings, customs, liberties, privileges, things and hereditaments whatsoever in or by our said Letters Patents mentioned, meant or intended to be given, granted, or confirmed to the aforesaid Society and every of them of the guift, grant, [illegible], alyenation, surrender, bargayne, sale, confirmation or release of any person or persons, bodyes politique or other whatsoever willing to give, grant, alyen, enfeoffe, surrender, bargayne and sell, confirme or release the same or any part thereof unto the aforesaid [illegible] and theyr successors. To have and to hold the same to the said Society of the Governour and Assistants, London, of the Newe Plantation in Ulster, within the Realme of Ireland, theyr successors and assignes for ever without lett, impeachment, contradiction or molestation of us our heyres or successors or of any our Justices, Escheators, Sheriffes, Bayliffes, or other the ministers of us, our heyres or successors whatsoever, and without any inquisition or inquisitions by vertue of any writt or writts of ad quod dampnum or any other writts or writt, mandate or mandates of us, our heyres or successors in this behalf to be purchased, had, made, taken or prosecuted, and without any lycense or lycenses of us our heyres or successors, or warrant or warrants by the said Society of the Governour and Assistants, London, of the Newe Plantation in Ulster within the Realme of Ireland, or theyr successors in this behalf for the premises or any of them, or any of them in this behalfe to be granted or made.

And further, we doe by these presents, for us, our heyres, and successors, for the reasons and considerations aforesaid, give and grant full power, libertie, lycense, and authoritie unto all and every body and bodyes politique or corporate and theyr successors, and other person and persons whatsoever, from tyme to tyme, and at all tymes hereafter, to give, grant, enfeoffe, alyen, surrender, bargaine, sell, confirme, or release unto the said Society of the Governour and Assistants, London, of the Newe Plantation in Ulster, within the Realme of Ireland, and theyr successors, the countyes, [illegible], baronyes, cittys, townes, villages, lands, tenements, liberties, hereditaments, thing and things whatsoever, in or by our said Letters Patents mentioned, meant, or intended to be given, granted, or confirmed to the aforesaid Society and every or any of them. To have and to hold the same to the said Society of the Governour and Assistants, London, of the New Plantation in Ulster, within the Realme of Ireland, and theyr successors for ever, without lett, impeachment, contradiction, or molestation, of us, our heyres, or successors, or of any our Justices, Escheators, Sheriffes, Bayliffes, or other the ministers or officers of us, our heyres, or successors whatsoever, and without any inquisition or inquisitions, or any wrytt or writtes of ad quod dampnum, or any other writt or writts, mandate or mandates, lycense or lycenses, from us, our heyres, or successors, in this behalf to be had, prosecuted, procured, or obteyned.

And wee will, and by these presents for us, our heyres, and successors do grant to the aforesaid Society of the Governour and Assistants, London, of the Newe Plantation in Ulster, within the Realme of Ireland, and to their successors and to the said Wardens and Comunalty of the Mistery of Mercers of the said City of London, the Wardens and Comunalty of the Mistery of the Grocery of the said Cittie of London, the Master and Wardens and brethren and sisters of the Guild or Fraternity of the Blessed Mary the Virgin of the Mistery of Drapers of the said Cittie of London, the Wardens and Comunalty of the Mistery of Fishmongers of the said Cittie of London, the Wardens and Comunalty of the Mistery of Goldsmithes of the said Citie of London, the said Corporation of the Master and Wardens and brethren and sisters of the Guild or Fraternitie of Corpus Christi of Skinners of London, the Master and Wardens of the Merchant Taylors of the Fraternitie of St. John Baptist in the Cittie of London, the Master and fower Wardens of the Fraternitie of the Arte or Mistery of Haberdashers of the Citie of London, the Master, Wardens, and Comunalty of the Arte or Mystery of Salters, London, the Master and Keepers or Wardens and Comunalty of the Mistery or Arte of Ironmongers, London, the Master, Wardens, and Freemen and Comunalty of the Mistery of Vintners of the said City of London, and to the said Master, Wardens, and Comunalty of the Freemen of the Arte or Mistery of Clothworkers of the said Citie of London, and to their successors, and to all and every other the aforesaid person and persons, bodyes politique and corporate, and others severally and respectively, that these our Letters Patents or the enrollment thereof, and all and every thing and things therein contained, be and shall be taken by all things firm, available, sufficient, and effectuall in the law against us, our heirs, and successors, as well in our courts as elsewhere within our realmes of England and Ireland, Notwithstanding the not true or not right reciting or not expressing of the date of our [illegible] Letters Patents made to the aforesaid Society of the Governour and Assistants, London, of the Newe Plantation in Ulster, within the Realme of Ireland, or not reciting, not mentioning, or not naming the countyes, [illegible], baronyes, cities, castles, mannors, townes, villages, lands, tenements, fishings, [illegible], rents, advowsons, services, customs, liberties, privileges, things, and hereditaments whatsoever, in or by our said Letters Patents mentioned, meant, or intended to be given to the aforesaid Society of the Governour and Assistants, London, of the Newe Plantation in Ulster, within the Realme of Ireland, and every or any of them. And notwithstanding the statute concerning lands and tenements not to be put in mortmaine, or any other statute, act, lawe, ordinance, restraint, cause, or thing whatsoever, made or ordained or to be made or ordained within our Realmes of England or Ireland, or either of them or otherwise, howsoever to the contrary notwithstanding. And this without fine or fee great or small, in our Hanaper or elsewhere to our use, therefore in any kinde to be yielded, paid, or made. Although expresse mention, &c. In witness, &c. Witness the King at Westminster, the [illegible] day of April (A.D. [illegible]).

per breve de privato sigillo

Ex[r] per A. P

APPENDIX, No 27.

PAPER handed in by the Chairman.

The Irish Society's Disclaimer of all Young Trees or Saplins planted or to be planted on any of the respective proportions belonging to the several Chief Companys of London in Ireland, dated 4th August 1741.

THE SOCIETY OF THE GOVERNOUR AND ASSISTANTS London of the New Plantation in Ulster within the Realm of Ireland being sensible not only of the great decay but almost total consumption of the Timber and Woods formerly standing and growing on the several Proportions of Land belonging to the respective twelve Chief Companys of London in Ireland and that there hath been a very great and almost general neglect and disregard for many years past to the planting of young trees either by the said Companys or their Tenants or other persons deriving from or under them for the raising and providing a future Supply and Stock of Timber for the Use and Occasions of the Plantation. And having cause to believe that the chief hindrance and discouragement to the Planting of Young Trees hath arisen and been occasioned by the said Companys or their Tenants or other Persons having or claiming a right to the said Lands being apprehensive that such Young Trees if Planted when they should grow to and become Timber might be claimed by the said Society and disposed of by them in such manner as they should think fit to the prejudice of those by whose care and labour such Trees shall have been planted and preserved. In Order therefore to the removing such Distrusts Apprehensions or discouragements and the giving all possible Encouragement to so useful and beneficial a work as the Planting of Trees on the said Lands which will manifestly conduce not only to the good of the Plantation in particular but to the benefit of the said Kingdom in general as well as to show the Strict regard the Society have to Justice and Equity. And in pursuance of and for the perfecting their said good Intentions therein conformable to a Representation lately made by the said Society to the said Companys and their several Returns testifying their consent and approval thereof. The said Society do hereby declare and agree that all Young Trees or Saplins which have been planted within the space of fifteen years and are now growing or that shall hereafter be planted and grow on any of the said Lands or proportions of the said respective Companys as aforesaid shall not at any time or times hereafter be claimed by the said Society or their successors either when the same shall be or become Timber or otherwise nor shall be disposed of by them to or for the benefit of any of the Estates or proportions of any other of the said Companys their Tenants or other persons deriving or claiming any Estate or Interest under them nor be taken or assigned by the said Society to or for any other use or uses whatsoever but the same shall and may from time to time and at all times hereafter be cut down had and taken by the respective Companys and their several Grantees or Assigns only so as the same be applied and disposed of in the first place for and towards the Buildings and Reparations or other necessary use or uses of their respective Estates holden or derived from the said Society any Exceptions or reservations contained in any Grants or Conveyances heretofore made by the said Society to the said respective Companys or any of them in respect to Timber &c. notwithstanding. In Testimony whereof the said Society have caused their Common Seal to be hereunto affixed the fourth day of August in the Year of our Lord One thousand Seven hundred and forty-one.

APPENDIX, No. [illegible]

PAPER handed in by the *Chairman*, [illegible] June [illegible].

Note.—The Judgment of the House of Lords on Appeal is printed as Appendix, No. I., to the Report of the Commission, [illegible].

THE JUDGMENT of the Right Hon. Lord *Langdale*, Master of the Rolls, in the case of the Skinners' Company *versus* the Honourable the Irish Society,* and others; delivered in his Court, at Westminster Hall, on Monday, [illegible] November 18[illegible].

Lord Langdale.—The plaintiffs in this cause are the Company of the Skinners of the City of London; the defendants are the Society of the Governor and Assistants, London, of the New Plantation in Ulster, within the realm of Ireland, who are usually called the Irish Society; the Company of Mercers, and about forty other companies in the City of London; the Corporation of the City of London, John Thomas Thorpe, Henry Palmer, and Her Majesty's Attorney-General. The Irish Society is a corporate body, possessed of, and entitled to, certain ferries, fisheries, and town lands in Ireland; and the bill prays "that it may be declared, that the plaintiffs, and the other companies who contributed to the expenses of the new plantation in Ulster, are beneficially entitled to the rents and profits of the said ferries, fisheries, and town lands, subject only to certain payments and charges; and that the Irish Society are trustees of the same rents and profits, so subject, for the plaintiffs and the other companies." The bill further prays for an account of such rents and profits, and for a partition of the ferries, fisheries, and town lands between the plaintiffs and the other companies; or (if such partition ought not to be made) for the removal of the Irish Society from being such trustees, and that other trustees may be appointed, or that some other arrangement may be made for securing to the plaintiffs and other companies the due payment of their respective shares of the said rents and profits. The bill also prays for a receiver and injunction, and for further relief.

There are four distinct parties whose interests or claims have been brought into question: First, the companies of the City of London, for whom the plaintiffs insist that the Irish Society are mere trustees for them, bound to account to them, and without any right or discretionary power to apply any part of the income of the property vested in them for any public charitable, or other purpose. Secondly, the Irish Society, who admit that they have no beneficial interest in the property, and that they are trustees for the companies of any surplus which may remain after answering certain public purposes, but claim to have a discretionary power to apply so much of the income as they may think fit for those public purposes without being liable to account for the same to the companies. Thirdly, the City of London, who resist the claim of the plaintiffs, and claim for themselves a species of visitatorial or superintending power entitling them to control the conduct and proceedings of the Irish Society. And, Fourthly, the Attorney General, who on the behalf of the Crown, suggests that the rents and profits are applicable to public purposes.

As nothing can be determined as between co-defendants on the present occasion, the substantial question in the cause is, whether the Irish Society has, independently of the companies, and without being subject to account to them, a discretionary power to apply any part of the rents and profits of the estates vested in them for purposes which they deem beneficial to the public with reference to the Plantation in Ireland, which is mentioned in the pleadings. The Irish Society might be answerable to the City of London, or to the companies, as represented or protected by the City of London, or to the Crown; yet if it is not answerable to the companies severally in this Court, the plaintiffs are not entitled to the relief which they ask by this bill. On the other hand, if the Society have no such discretionary power as they claim, and are as trustees answerable to the companies severally for all their receipts and payments, the plaintiffs are entitled to relief, their right has been denied, and accounts have been refused to them.

The Irish Society now subsists under a charter of King Charles II., dated the 10th of April 1662. That Charter was principally, and as to most of its details, founded on a former charter granted by King James I. on the 29th of March 1613; and from the mode in which the case was stated and argued on all sides, it appears to me necessary to consider the circumstances under which the first charter was granted, so far as those circumstances are proved by the evidence in this cause. And from the evidence, it appears that in the year 1608 the greatest part of the six several counties of Armagh, Tyrone, Coleraine, Donegal, Fermanagh, and Cavan, had by attainder or forfeiture, come into the possession of the Crown, and that King James I., being desirous to promote the public peace and welfare of Ireland by a civil plantation of what were called "those unreformed and waste countries," proposed to induce English and Scotch persons to emigrate thither and undertake the plantation on certain terms; and for that purpose he caused to be published a collection of such orders and conditions as were to be observed by the undertakers upon the distribution and plantation of the lands.

It is plain, from these orders and conditions, that the King did not merely contemplate the benefit of the persons who should undertake the Plantation, or colony as it is called in another document, but that he had a great public object in view, and to carry that into effect, desired to engage such of his subjects, as well of Great Britain as of Ireland, as being of merit and ability should seek the lands with a mind not only to benefit themselves, but to do service to the Crown and Commonwealth; and it was intended to appoint commissioners for setting forth the several proportions of the land, and for the ordering and settling the Plantation according to such instructions as should be given unto them by His Majesty in that behalf; such commissioners were appointed and instructions given to them on the 21st of July 1609; but before that time, the King became desirous to engage the City of London in the undertaking, and caused to be prepared a paper, setting forth "Motives and reasons to induce the City of London to undertake the plantation in the north of Ireland."

These motives and reasons, after suggesting that the ruinated city of Derry and another place, at or near the Castle of Coleraine, seemed to be the fittest places for the City of London to plant, and that the situation was such that the same, especially the Derry, might be made by land almost impregnable, set forth that His Majesty might be pleased to grant unto those towns, not only Corporations with such liberties and privileges for their good government, &c. as might be convenient, but also the whole territory and country between them, which was about twenty miles in length, bounded by the sea on the north, the River Bann on the east, and the River of Derry or Lough Foyle on the west, out of which 1,000 acres there might be allotted to each of the towns for their commons, rent free, the rest to be planted with such undertakers as the City of London should think good for their best profit, paying only for the same the easy rent of the undertakers.

The motives and reasons further set forth that His Majesty might be pleased to grant to those towns the benefit of all the customs of imports and exports for twenty-one years, paying only a rent of 6 *s.* 8 *d.*; and to lay the

* The Irish Society, for [illegible], see page [illegible].

[illegible]

contribute to the Undertaking, every thing at length centered in the City and in the Court of Common Council, as representing the City. The City undertook and was to perform. The City was to provide the funds, and the City was to have the profit. The City was set in motion by what has been called the pressure of the Crown or of the Government, and was by its Agents the contracting party with the Government—with the Companies, otherwise than as they were involved in or formed part of the general body of the City, the Crown had no negotiation or dealing. The Crown did not, as it seems, concern itself either with the means by which the City was to perform its undertaking, or with the inducements to be held out to individuals, further than as such inducements were secured by the general terms of the project, and the matters and customs [illegible] to the City. It may reasonably be supposed, that when the Court of Common Council, in performance of the contract, found it necessary to exercise a somewhat questionable power of taxation, suggestions of some benefit to result to those upon whom the charge was imposed, would in some manner be made. And that such was the case is extremely probable from the nature of the transaction itself, and is apparent, from the subsequent proceedings. But in the formal acts at the time, the Companies are treated as the instruments by which the sums required for the enterprise should be levied; and the levies were not made upon any property of the Companies, but in Companies by the poll. That the levies were compulsory, and enforced against reluctant parties by the power of the City, is shown by abundant evidence in the case.

At the same Common Council by which the agreement was approved and allowed, it was ordained and enacted, "That for the better ordering, directing, and effecting of all things touching and concerning the said Plantation, and the business thereunto belonging, there should be a Company constituted and established within the City of London, which should consist of one Governor, one Deputy to the Governor, and twenty-four Assistants; that the Governor and some of the Assistants should be Aldermen; that Mr. Recorder should be one of the Assistants, and that the Deputy and the rest of the Assistants should be Commoners of the City. And after providing for the continuance of the Company by election at the Court of Common Council, and appointing the present members of the Company, it was enacted and agreed, that the Company should have authority to hold Courts, and in the same to treat and determine of all matters and causes concerning the business that to them, in their discretion, should be thought fit; and also direct, appoint, and determine what should be done or performed on behalf of the City touching the Plantation, and to give orders and directions in England, as in Ireland, for the ordering and disposing of all things concerning the intended Plantation, or any thing belonging to the Citizens of London undertaking in that part of Ireland, as also for the receiving, ordering, disposing, and disbursing of all sums of money that were or should be collected or gathered for that purpose, and generally for any other matter touched or belonging to the business and affairs in Ireland."

This enactment or order was the practical adoption by the City of London of the suggestion made by the Commissioners, in the preceding month of December. This Company, as it is called, though it was only a committee of persons appointed by the Court of Common Council, was the Irish Society, previously to its incorporation, and may be conveniently distinguished by that name. It proceeded to carry into effect the agreement entered into with the Crown; and the Members of the Society were so far recognized by the Crown, that applications were made to them in respect of matters relating to the Plantation. Thus, by an order of the Common Council, dated 7th of June 1610, it appears that the King's Commissioners for Ireland desired that 3,000 acres of land, agreed by the articles to be passed to the City, should be spared and left out of the intended assurance, to the intent that the same might be otherwise disposed of; and that Alderman Cockaine, the Governor, had signified that the Company (Society) of themselves had not power to comply with that desire, but that the same was to be done by act of Common Council; and had proposed the Commissioners to propound the same to the next Court of Common Council then to be holden, which, being done, it was ordered that the intended assurance from his Majesty should be made for the whole quantity, according to the intent of the articles, without omitting the 3,000 acres in question. And again, in July 1610, the King's Irish Commissioners made to the Company or Society four proposals, which were reported to the Common Council, by whom two of the proposals were acceded to, and the other two were rejected, in regard it was conceived, the granting and yielding to them would prove to be very prejudicial to the City, though, upon a subsequent day, one of the rejected proposals was yielded.

On the 11th of January 1610-11, an order made by the Court of Common Council affords the first formal indication as to the mode in which the Companies of the City were to be concerned or interested in the intended Plantation. After authorizing the Society to let the fishings for seven years for such fine or rent as they should think fit and convenient for the most benefit and profit of the City, it was ordered that precepts should forthwith be sent to every several Company of the City to require them to assemble themselves together, and to advise amongst themselves, whether they would consent and agree to take and accept of lands in lieu of the monies already by them disbursed or to be disbursed towards the said Plantation, and so to build and plant the same at their own cost and charges, accordingly as by the printed Book of the Plantation was required, or else whether they would refer the letting of the lands there, and the managing of the whole business there unto the said Governor and Assistants of the Society for the time being; and that every Company be required by the same precept to deliver their answers in writing on Saturday then next, in the forenoon, at the Guildhall, unto the said Governor and Assistants, whether of the two said offers they will embrace, to the intent that the said Governor and Assistants, upon the answer of the several Companies of the City, may make a perfect relation to the next Court of Common Council there to be holden, which was appointed to be upon Monday then next, touching the resolution of the several companies of the said City, to the intent that such further course might then be taken therein as should be thought fit.

In the precept which was issued in pursuance of this order, and which bears date the last day of January 1610-11, it was recited that the King had granted unto the City of London the city of Derry, and town of Coleraine, with 7,000 acres of common land thereunto adjoining, and fishings, and divers other [illegible], privileges, and franchises, paying four marks per annum; and that the City had undertaken to disburse in building of Houses and Fortifications, and for freeing of Foreign Titles, the sum of 20,000 l.; and that also his Majesty had further granted to the City divers other lands in the county of Coleraine, and other undertaken lands, to build thereupon, which building was to be performed in such manner as was expressed in the printed book then extant, yet with this addition, that they were to have and enjoy the same lands after the Irish measure, being far larger than other ordinary undertakers had; and then the precept proceeds as follows:—"Forasmuch as the Governor and Committees for the Plantation in Ireland are now instantly to take care for the letting and disposing of the lands in the county of Coleraine, and of other lands in the county of Coleraine, and the other lands so undertaken to be used and managed for the benefit of this City, which would otherwise prove a great hindrance and loss especially for that the time of the year is now most convenient for the plantation to proceed; yet it is thought fit that the offer of these lands be first made to the several Companies of this City, who have and are to disburse the same, and bear the charges of building before mentioned. These are therefore to charge and command you that yourselves, together with the Assistants and such others of your Company as you shall think fitting, do forthwith assemble together, and advise whether you will accept of a proportion of the same Lands, according to the quantity of your Disbursements, to be by you undertaken and managed according to the printed book for the Plantation, or whether you will refer the letting and disposing thereof to the Governor and Committees; and that you certify to the Governor and Committees, in writing under your hands at the Guildhall, on or before the 7th day of February next coming, what shall be your full determination therein, to the end that the business may the sooner be effected; wherein you are to take advertisement that your Companies are to pay and bear their proportion of the charge of the building, Fortifications and freeing of the Titles, whether they accept of the said offer of the lands or not; and also that, notwithstanding the acceptance of the lands, you shall likewise still be partakers of all benefit of fishing, with the profits of the towns and other [illegible] whatsoever."

In consequence of these proceedings, eight of the principal and two of the inferior companies signified their consent to accept of the lands, to plant upon the same, according to the printed book of Plantation; and the other Companies signified their denial, whereupon it was on the 18th February 1610-11 ordered, that the Companies who consented should have lands allotted to them, and provision was made for the event of the other Companies within a fortnight, and upon further consideration altering their minds, and consenting to accept of lands in lieu of the monies disbursed and to be disbursed by them towards the Plantation in Ireland.

From

From these documents it appears to have been understood that the Companies of the City had not previously undertaken the Plantation, but that the Plantation being undertaken by the City, was in default of other means to be carried into execution by the Society or Committee appointed by the City; but that it was thought desirable that the undertaking should be at least in part performed by the incorporated Companies, and that the City having entered into the undertaking, having by their power levied the means of carrying it on, and being a body engaged in carrying it on by their Governor and Committee or Company, offered to each of the incorporated Companies to [illegible] either to undertake the plantation of a portion of the lands according to the printed book for Plantation, or to refer the letting and [illegible] thereof to the Governor and Committee. It was an offer which by many Companies was at first [illegible] accepted, to give or allot lands in lieu of the monies disbursed and to be disbursed towards the Plantation, and the Companies were informed that whether they accepted the land or not, they were to pay and bear their proportions of the charges of building, [illegible] and [illegible], and that notwithstanding their acceptance of the lands, they should be partakers of benefits of fishings with the profits of the towns and other [illegible] whatsoever.

After these proceedings, the Undertaking continued to be carried on by the Company or Society, under the control of the City, the money needed to be levied; increased taxations and additional levies became necessary and were made. On the credit of these the City advanced monies to the Society, which were afterwards repaid, and the power which the City exercised of commitment was frequently acted upon to compel payment of the Assessments. And it is to be observed, that, by an Order of the Common Council, dated 10th of July 1611 by which an additional taxation of 10,000 *l*., and a present levy of [illegible] *l*. was ordered. The Precept which was then ordered was to require every several Company to assemble and advise among themselves, and thereupon certify to the Governor and Committee of the Plantation, whether they would willingly yield to the supply of [illegible] *l*., or would be content to lose all the money they had already disbursed, and pass over their right thereto to such as would undertake the payment for them, and to free and discharge them of all other payments thereafter touching the Plantation.

It is apparent that at this time the Companies were understood to have no interest in the sums they had been compelled to pay, and the Court of Common Council was probably understood to have power to declare a forfeiture.

During the time to which I have hitherto referred, no Charter had been granted, but the City had proceeded on the faith that an assurance of the lands would be made to them, and the lands are in the precept of the last day of January 1610-11, mentioned as having been granted, though in fact they were not so. And on the [illegible] of January 1612-13, it was Ordered, that Sir, William Cockayne, (the first Governor of the Company), should be Governor, and continue until the Assurance from the King unto the City, concerning the Plantation should be obtained and finished.

The charter of James was obtained soon after the date of this order. It is dated the 29th of March 1613, and after reciting the King's Intention, and that the Mayor, Commonalty, and Citizens of London, had laudably undertaken a considerable part of the Plantation in Ulster, and were making progress therein, proceeds to consolidate the City and Town of Derry, and all the territories and hereditaments thereby granted into one County, to be called the county of Londonderry, to declare that the City of Derry should be called Londonderry, to define the extent of the City of Londonderry and the Town of Coleraine, and to incorporate the Citizens of Londonderry, and to declare that they should have a Mayor, Aldermen, Sheriffs, and a Chamberlain, and the Mayor, Commonalty, and Citizens were empowered to make laws and ordinances, so that such laws and ordinances were certified by the City of Londonderry, under their common seal, to the Society of the Governor and Assistants London of the New Plantation in Ulster after mentioned, within four months after the making of such laws and ordinances, to the intent that the same Society might ratify and confirm such laws and ordinances within six months after the delivery of the certificate, or else within the same time declare the same to be improper, and the laws and ordinances were to be valid when confirmed by the Society, but if declared improper, were to be wholly void.

The Charter then appointed the first Mayor and Aldermen, Sheriffs, Chamberlain, and chief Burgesses, and then proceeded to constitute the Irish Society "For the better ordering, directing, and governing all and all manner of things for and concerning the Citizens and City of Londonderry, and the County of Londonderry, and the Plantation to be made within the same City and County, and other [illegible] belonging to them." And after incorporating the Society, giving them power to purchase, receive, and possess lands, directing the constituency and mode of election, and naming the first members, the Charter provided that the members, or any [illegible] of them (whereof the Governor or his Deputy was to be one) should have full power of assembling and holding a Court, and in the same Court, and meeting to do, hear, treat, and determine all, and all manner of matters and things whatsoever, of, for, or concerning the Plantation or government aforesaid; and also to direct, constitute, and ordain (for and on the part of the City of London in England) all things which for or concerning the plantation, supply, or establishment, conservation and government of the City of Londonderry, and of all other the lands and tenements thereafter granted, should seem to be most profitable and expedient; and also to send orders and directions from England to Ireland for ordering, directing, and disposing of all, and all manner of matters and things whatsoever, of or concerning the same Plantation or the disposition or government thereof; and also for the receipt, ordering, and laying out of all sums of money now collected and received, and generally any other cause, matter, or thing whatsoever concerning the direction or ordering of the Plantation aforesaid, or concerning any other things whatsoever, which, by the true intent of the Charter, could, or ought to be done by them for the better government and rule of the City and County of Londonderry.

The Charter, after giving power to elect officers, and to make ordinances for the Government of Londonderry for ten years, and making many other regulations respecting Londonderry, grants to the Irish Society and their successors the several forts, towns, and lands which are described at great length, and all fealty and services of escuage reserved out of the [illegible] premises, and all knights' fees, wards, marriages, escheats, reliefs, heriots, fines, courts leet, courts of view and frankpledge, hereditaments, and appurtenances to be held as amply as the King had the same with certain exceptions specified. To hold the premises to the only proper use and behoof of the said Society of the Governor and Assistants, and their successors for ever; to hold the City of Londonderry and the 4,000 acres next adjoining upon the Derry side, and the Town of Coleraine and the 3,000 acres to the same adjoining, of the King, in free burgage, as of the Castle of Dublin; and to hold the rest of the premises of the King, as of his Castle of Dublin by fealty only in free and common socage, rendering the rents therein mentioned. And the Society covenanted to convey certain lands to the Bishop and Dean of Derry, within a year, to keep and maintain for ever the Fort of Culmore, to convey certain glebe lands within a year; provision was then made that the timber growing on the lands of Glenkonkeine and Killetragh should for ever after be converted towards the plantation and the building of houses and edifices, to be made as therein mentioned, and to be spent towards other necessary uses for the Kingdom of Ireland in the same Kingdom, and not for any other cause to be merchandised or sold. The Customs were then granted to the Society for ninety-nine years, for a rent of 13 *s*. 4 *d*. The office of admiral was granted for ever in the county or shires of Tyrconnell, Coleraine, and the County of Londonderry, and to these were added various other important powers and privileges.

It is to be observed, that by an order of the 30th of January 1610-11, the Irish Committee, or company as it was called, was made to consist of the Governor, Deputy Governor, and twenty-four Assistants. By an order of the 21st of May 1611, eleven Assistants were added; and by the last appointment, previous to the Charter which was made by the Court of Common Council on the 8th of January 1612-13, the Company consisted of the Governor, Deputy Governor, and thirty-three Assistants. The Charter reduced the Assistants to the original number of twenty-four, but the Governor, the Deputy Governor, and the twenty-four Assistants named in the Charter, were the same Governor, Deputy Governor, and twenty-four of the thirty-three Assistants, chosen by the City in January 1612-13.

From this statement, it is apparent, that the Irish Society originated with the City, and that the powers conferred upon it by the Charter, though by no means identical with, were suggested by the powers given to it by the order of the 28th of January 1610; and it may reasonably be inferred, that it was at the request of the City, that the constitution of the Society, and the powers to be conferred upon it, were considered and granted by the Crown.

But this makes no difference in the effect of the constitution, or in the inferences to be deduced from the powers granted to the Society by the Charter; and it is, I think, impossible to read and consider the Charter, without coming to the conclusion, that the powers granted to the Society were more extensive than, and very different from any which, in the ordinary course of affairs, are vested, or would upon the occasion, have been invested in mere private trustees for the benefit of particular undertakers.

The powers, indeed, are many of them of a public and political nature, and considering the Charter in connexion with the contemporaneous circumstances, I think it must have been understood, that the powers and estates granted to the Irish Society, were given for the public purposes of the Plantation; and so far as was consistent with those purposes, for the benefit of the City of London; and that, independently of the public or general benefits which might accrue from the encouragement or increase of trade with Ireland, and the employment of persons who might be disposed to emigrate thither, and the better government and rule of the City and County of Londonderry, it was intended and understood, that the Companies of London were, with the burden of undertaking the Plantation of such lands as might be allotted to them, to receive such benefits as were offered to and might be realized by other undertakers on the conditions proposed by the original book for plantation, accompanied by such additional advantages and protection as were intended to be secured by the power and interest of the City of London, and by the constitution of the Irish Society, and the powers conferred upon it.

The Companies of London are in no way mentioned in the Charter, nor does the Crown appear to have noticed them at the time in any way: but the previous appointment of the Society, Committee, or Company by the Court of Common Council, and the previous proposals and offers made by the Society to the Companies, as well as events which soon followed the date of the Charter, appear to me to show that the Companies were intended to profit in the way that I have mentioned. And it would further appear, that not the eighteen Companies only who are mentioned in the order of the 28th of February 1610-11, but all the other Companies had consented to become undertakers. The Charter expressly states that the Society was to have power to make ordinances on the part and behalf of the City of London, and it does not seem that the Society did under the Charter arrogate any independent authority.

So early as April 1613, additional funds were wanting, and it became necessary to consider how the division of lands among the Companies was to be effected; and by an order of the Court of Common Council, dated the 15th day of that month, an additional levy of 10,000*l.* was ordered; and it was enacted, that every several Company of the City should have its several share and proportion of the lands according to the manner by them disbursed, respecting the goodness or badness thereof, the same lands to lie all entirely together, and not dispersedly in several places; and that the same lands should be proportioned according to the goodness or badness thereof; with respect that where the land was bad, an allowance should be made in the quantity to make it equal in value to that which was better, so that no prejudice (or as little as might be) might happen to any Company in the allotting of the said lands which were afterwards intended to be divided by lots. And on the signification of the King's pleasure by the Recorder and Governor of the Society, it was, on the 24th of June 1613, ordered that as well certain Walls and Fortifications as also certain Houses at Derry should be raised, made, and builded up together and in such manner and form as the Commissioners appointed for the said Plantation should think fit and direct in that behalf. And by a further order made on the same day, after reciting that in so noble a work, so taken to heart by the King, and wherein the City upon the hopeful success thereof had already expended and were likely to expend great sums of money, it was generally thought fit, as a matter much importing the advancement of the said work, as well for the general satisfaction of the several Companies of the City who had undertaken the same, as also for accommodating such other affairs and circumstances as from time to time thereafter should be offered to the further consideration of that Court (*i.e.* the Court of Common Council,) that some grave and worthy magistrate of the City, accompanied by some commoner of special credit, should be sent into those parts on the behalf of the City, to take exact notice, view, and survey of the whole work of Plantation and of every circumstance and thing appertaining thereunto.

Mr. Alderman Smithes and Matthias Springham were accordingly appointed to go into Ireland, and in the meantime to confer with the Governor, Deputy-Governor, and Assistants of the Irish Society for their better instructions, and to inform themselves of the things necessary to be remembered; and authority was given to them by the Court of Common Council to take an exact notice, view, and survey of the Plantation and of all works and other things done and to be done, and of all disbursements and accounts concerning the same; as also to judge, control, place, displace, dispose, redress, reform, correct, and direct (as far as to them should seem reasonable), all persons employed for the City's use, disbursements, and service in and about the Plantation and generally to do and execute every further act which to them might be thought meet for the better ordering and governing the Plantation and the affairs thereof, to the intent that upon their return and relation of their proceedings, the Court of Common Council might come to such final Resolution touching the Plantation as should be thought fit, and that the charges of the negotiation should be defrayed by the Irish Society out of the general stock of the Plantation.

This order is remarkable as showing the great power which, after the Charter, the City of London exercised and contemplated the future exercise of over the Plantation and the affairs thereof, as well as the importance which was then [illegible] attached to the satisfaction which should be given to the Companies. No doubt seems to have been entertained that the Society, whatever its own powers might be, would act according to the suggestions and views of the City; and that the City, whatever other objects they had to promote, were bound in duty or in policy to satisfy the Companies. As the necessary expense was not yet defrayed, as the power of the City over the Companies afforded the only means of raising the money; and as public and general objects were to be attained, it does not appear difficult to account for the conduct of the several Parties.

Very full instructions appear to have been given to the Commissioners; and on the 8th of November 1613, Mr. Alderman Smithes delivered the report of himself and Mr. Springham, dated 15th of Oct. 1613, to the Court of Common Council; and the Report, after stating several abuses and negligences which had occurred, and the proceedings of the Commissioners in respect thereof, and stating their opinion that, if it should stand with the liking of the City, some convenient Wall of brick or stone might thereafter be made about the Castle of Coleraine, proceeded as follows:—"Whereas it was generally desired that a division should be made of all the lands by and amongst the several Companies undertaking in this Plantation, we have with great travail first viewed the lands, and carefully inquired after the true value of every Ballibo; and thereupon, with great care and pains, and with the assistance and advice of the gentlemen of the Country, the City's Agents and Surveyors proceeded to make an equal division of the land into twelve parts, wherein we have used our best skill and diligence, and have done the same as equally as possibly we could devise, the form of which division we have here brought you together with the plot of the same. But for the City of Londonderry, and the 4,000 acres there; and the town of Coleraine, and the 3,000 acres appointed to the same, the ferries and the fishings, we are of opinion that a division cannot be fitly made of them, but the rents and profits of them may be divided, and go amongst the several Companies; and we advise that, upon the division to be provided that, where a proportion of land shall want timber to build with, then the Company, to whose share it may fall, may have sufficient timber out of the woods next adjoining, and fitting for that use, to be assigned to them by the City's Agents."

This report was approved and allowed by the Common Council. That part of it which related to the division of lands was almost immediately acted upon. That part which states the opinion of the Commissioners that the rents and profits of the town lands, ferries, and fishings, might be divided, and go amongst the several Companies, has naturally been much dwelt upon on behalf of the plaintiffs. What notice may have been taken of it at the time does not very appear, but in connexion with it, we must bear in mind, not only that it is in perfect accordance with the precept of the last day of January 1610-11, but also that very considerable and expensive public works were still in progress:

that

that the City was then conceived to have power to levy, compulsorily, all such sums as should be required; and that each [illegible] of [illegible] inconsiderable amount, was at that time derived, or about to be derived, from the property and then to be divided. At a time when it was thought that money could be levied by taxation whenever it was wanted, the necessity, or even the propriety or prudence of reserving some property producing income to answer the general purposes of the Plantation, may not have been suggested; or if suggested, may have yielded to the greater prudence of holding out prospects of income or profit to those upon whom the levies was imposed, by a power which, even if thought lawful, must have been considered as arbitrary; and was, according to the evidence in many instances not obeyed without reluctance on one side, and the application of force on the other.

A division of the lands by lot was effected under the direction and superintendence of the Court of Common Council, on the 17th of December 1613, and each of the twelve chief Companies had allotted to it so much land as in quantity and value equalled one-twelfth part of the whole of the lands to be divided under an arrangement, by which every Company of the City was to have an interest or share in the divided lands proportioned to the amount of money levied upon it for the purposes of the Plantation. And this being done, an order was immediately made for a further levy, as follows: "After all which done," meaning the allotment, "information was given by the Governor and Assistants of the Irish Society, that all the monies formerly levied towards that charge is altogether spent; and that notwithstanding the Companies had their particular shares of land, which was to be managed by themselves severally; that the general work for the building of the rest of the Towns and Fortifications was to be done at the general charge, and therefore that a further supply must of necessity be made and provided to proceed on the business. And therefore it was enacted, that a present taxation should be made of the further sum of [illegible] *l.*, which was accordingly ordered to be levied and raised of the several Companies of the City. And it was also ordered, that Conveyances should be made of the lands allotted to the several Companies, by the advice of the Recorder, in such manner as the Committees of the Plantation (that is the Irish Society) should think fit.

It appears that the Companies, without waiting for their Conveyances, planted and placed divers numbers of British on their proportions of lands, and expended very large sums of money thereon. But independently of these undertakings, the works which were to be done at the general charge of the City continued to be expensive, and additional sums were levied on the Companies. Complaints were about the same time made on the part of the Crown that the Plantation had not proceeded according to the Conditions, and an intimation was given that the Grant may be resumed. Further time however was given, to the last day of August 1616. The City in the mean time continued its active interference by orders of the Court of Common Council, and employed its own agents; the Irish Society seeming to act rather in its original character of a Committee of the City than as an independent Corporation.

In the year 1618, licence to hold lands in mortmain was granted to the Companies, and in the course of the next or two or three following years licences were granted; and conveyances thereof, and of the allotted lands, were made to the Companies by the Irish Society. The conveyances were absolute; in some without, and in others with the reservation of rent to the Irish Society. The licence for the Companies to hold in mortmain, and also a licence to the Society to convey to them; and it contained a recital that the Companies, in testimony of their true obedience to the Crown, &c., had disbursed, expended, and bestowed divers great sums of money for and towards the building, fortifying, planting, strengthening, and improving the City of Derry, and the Town of Coleraine, and some parts of other lands, and were willing, and intended, so far as to them should seem convenient, to be at further charge for the planting and improving of other lands, and for speedier proceeding therein, were desirous to have conveyances of the land they intended to build on, and therefore, and to the end that the several Companies might be better encouraged and enabled to perfect the intended Plantation and in future time reap some part and benefit of their great charge and expense taken and bestowed therein. The licence was granted, and the Companies of London were then recognised by the Crown as parties interested in the Plantation as Undertakers, and after the conveyances were made, the Companies may be considered as entitled to the lands allotted and conveyed to them, subject to the conditions of plantation, as to particular lands, and as respectively entitled to all the profits to arise from those allotments, which, subject to the performance of those conditions, could be lawfully made. The lands not allotted, together with the Ferries and Fishings remained vested in the Irish Society; and the City of London, or the Irish Society on its behalf, were bound to the performance of those public works which were among the conditions of plantation, and for the purposes of these general and public works were, or were supposed to be, entitled to levy money on the Companies for whose satisfaction they at least professed themselves to be bound to provide.

About five or six years after the Conveyances were made, further complaint was made by the Crown that the conditions of plantation had not been performed. The complaints were laid before the Court of Common Council the 3rd of June 1624. They principally regarded the general works of the Plantation, but in part, the conditions of the Plantation of the lands conveyed to the Companies. As to the former, answer was made by the Court of Common Council; as to the latter, the subject was made known to the several Companies, and on their part the Common Council complained that the Undertakers had been impeded by monopolies and patents of privilege contrary to the King's grant. The answer, though approved in the Court of Common Council, was for alteration in matter of form and words of the like [illegible] referred to the Irish Society, and others who had joined with them in drawing the answer.

Not long afterwards, and in the beginning of the reign of Charles the First, the King having referred certain matters relating to the Plantation to Lords Grandison, Carew, and Chichester, and the Chancellor of the Exchequer, did, upon their advice, require the City of London to do many things there specified, most of which were properly works, but some affected the conduct of the Companies; and the Common Council made answer to these requisitions not only with respect to the general works, but also with respect to the Plantation undertaken by the Companies. And as to the first demand, which was, that a fair new church should be built, they say, that although the work be very chargeable, and that the stocks of all the Chief Companies of London are already exhausted by reason of the Plantation, yet in obedience to His Majesty's pleasure (the work also in itself being pious), they will forthwith give order to make preparations for erecting a fair new church, and will, as soon as conveniently they may, finish, and beautify, and adorn the same with all fit and convenient [illegible].

In the course of a few years afterwards, informations were filed in the Star Chamber against the City of London, the Irish Society, and certain individuals; the defendants were charged with the deceitful and undue procuring of the Charter of James, and with wilful breach of the articles agreed upon between the Lords of the Council and the Committees appointed by the City (on the 28th of January 1609–10) and with the wilful breach of the trust which the King had reposed in them. It appears that during the proceedings, it was insisted on by the City that they had nothing to do with the Plantation, and that their name was used merely for the transaction of affairs, and for the levying of monies upon the Companies for the Plantation. This point was overruled, and the Court having adjudged that many offences, both of omission and commission, had been committed, inflicted upon the City of London, and upon the Irish Society, a fine of 70,000 *l.*, and decreed that the Patent and their estates and interest should be surrendered and be brought into Court to be cancelled. And after reciting that the greatest part of the lands were by the Society passed over to divers Companies of the City, and by them demised to their Farmers, who were not Defendants to the suit, and therefore not liable to the censure of the Court, although in the opinion of the Court they might justly have been censured if parties, it was directed, that if the Companies and their Farmers, should not, in pursuance of the intention of the Sentence, surrender their estates, the Attorney General should exhibit an information and bring them also to the judgment of the Court.

This decree, if lawful, enabled the Crown to recover not only a fine of 70,000 *l.*, but the possession of all the lands and hereditaments which remained vested in the Irish Society, and it was accompanied by an intimation that these, and also all the lands conveyed to the Companies, or demised to their Farmers might be recovered if the Attorney General thought fit to sue from them. Steps were early taken for the execution of the decree, and proceedings were commenced against the Twelve Companies. In these circumstances, a negotiation for money took place between the Crown and the City. The City pressed by the impending fine and forfeiture, and by other charges made against them, offered a composition of 100,000 l. The Crown endeavoured to obtain more, and the City acting or professing to act only for the Companies, and in concurrence with them, offered to give up all the buildings and all the lands held by the Society or by the Companies, and all arrears of rent. And at length, after a protracted negotiation, the fine was ultimately compromised, and the City agreed to surrender the lands, buildings, and customs in Ireland, and to pay a sum of 12,000 l., and the proceedings to repeal the Letters Patent were made available by consent or default. But afterwards, in other political circumstances, the City endeavoured to obtain relief from this oppression, and to make available before the House of Commons those arguments which had failed before the Court of Star Chamber; and the House of Commons, then advancing to the ascendancy which it soon afterwards obtained, took upon itself to pass resolutions declaring its opinion on the judgment of the Star Chamber, and declaring its opinion of the conduct of the City and of the Companies respecting the Plantation. The proceeding appears to have ended in the King expressing himself to be willing to restore the Plantation to its former footing, and it was proposed to confirm the rights of the Companies by Act of Parliament; but civil wars supervened, and it was under the power of Cromwell that the Charter, and the Estates derived under it, were first pretended to be restored.

I have thought it right to refer to these proceedings which were dealt upon in the argument, as affording evidence of facts or conclusions, material to be now considered, and I have read all the documents referred to. But I am of opinion, that allegations and admissions used for the purpose of defence against attempted extortion, under the form of legal proceedings, or for the purpose of obtaining justice irregularly when regularly it could not be had, ought not to be used as evidence of the rights of the parties. If the same allegations are otherwise proved, and undoubtedly some of the allegations now referred to are otherwise proved, regard must be had to such proof. But independently of such other proof, and of fair inference from the facts otherwise proved, I consider, that the allegations and admissions which were made in the Star Chamber, or in the treaty which arose out of the evidence there, or in the proceedings which took place before the House of Commons, ought not in any way to influence my judgment.

Soon after the Restoration, on the 10th of April 1662, King Charles the Second granted the charter under which the Irish Society now exists, and from which the subsisting titles to the Lands and Estates thereby granted are derived. This Charter recites the Charter of James, the Grants made by the Society which was constituted under that Charter, and that the Society retained in its own hands such part of the tenements and hereditaments as were not properly divisible, for defraying the charge of the general operation of the Plantation. It further recites the repeal of the Charter, the promise made by King Charles the First to restore the same, and that it appeared that the Society and other Companies of the City had expended very great sums of money in building and planting of the County of Londonderry and Coleraine; and then proceeds to express, that the present Grant was made to the intent that the Society, or some other Society, by the present letters patent to be created, and the Companies of the City of London, and their respective assigns and under tenants, might, according to their former several rights and interests therein, be restored to all the Estates vested in them by force of the former letters patent, and the Grants by the Society and other Companies respectively theretofore made, as fully to all purposes as they might have had the same if there had been no repeal of the former letters patent, and to the intent that there might be a new Society of the new Plantation in Ulster, and a new incorporation of the City of Derry, and for the further and better settling and planting of the said County, Towns, and Places with trade and inhabitants.

This Charter, therefore, is expressly made for the purpose of restoring the rights derived under the former Charter, for restoring the rights and interests of the Companies of London, and for further and better settling and planting the County, &c., with trade and inhabitants. The lapse of forty-nine years, and the change of circumstances, made it necessary that there should be some differences between the clauses in the Charter of 1613 and the clauses in the Charter of 1662, and other differences may have been suggested by former experience, or by the present views and intentions of the parties. They are sufficient to show, that the Charter of Charles was framed with considerable care and attention, and was not a mere transcript of the Charter of James.

In the Charter of James, no mention was made of the Companies, but the City, and the Society acting under the Charter of James had made Conveyances to the Companies, and had levied money for the general purposes of the Plantation on the Companies; and the intention of the Charter of Charles was to restore the Irish Society, and also the Companies of the City of London, to their former rights; and after making due allowance for all the differences which occur, the Charter of Charles appears to me to be substantially, as it is avowedly, a restoration of the Charter of James. The two Charters are alike in their general purview, in their intended object, in the means adopted to carry that object into effect, and in the powers conferred for that purpose.

Under the new Charter, new Conveyances were made to the Companies, and the Irish Society has ever since continued in the exclusive possession of the town lands, ferries, and fisheries, and has managed or let the same, and received and applied the rents thereof by its own authority. It has applied portions of the rents for purposes alleged to be public or charitable, and has from time to time stated a surplus to be in its hands, and has paid certain sums in respect of that surplus to the twelve Companies in equal shares. On one occasion, when money was wanted, the Society applied, not to the City of London, as in an earlier period of its history for further levies, but to the Companies for voluntary contributions. And on another occasion on which it became necessary to make a statement respecting the tithes, it represented itself to be intrusted for the Companies, and seised of a considerable salmon fishery and other estates in the County of Londonderry in trust for the Companies of the City, over and besides the several proportions of lands which had been granted. The Society have on other occasions stated themselves to be trustees for the Companies; and there is an instance in which one is rather surprised to find them refusing to render any account to the City, and stating themselves to be accountable only to the twelve chief Companies of London, to which all the surplus funds under their management, not disposed of in the performance of the duties which the charter imposed upon them, were regularly transferred and paid.

It does not, however, appear to me to be necessary to pursue further the history of the conduct and transactions of the Society. The Society have vested in them, under a Royal Charter, a very considerable property, in which they have not, collectively or individually, as members of the Society, any beneficial interest, and in respect of which they are invested with great powers, and have important duties to perform. In a sense, therefore, they are trustees. The property is part of that which was granted for the purposes of the Plantation, and the powers possessed by the Society as well as the duties with which it is charged, have all of them reference to the Plantation.

Now the objects of the Plantation, and the motives and purposes thereof, were of a nature partly public and political, and partly private, regarding only the interests of particular Undertakers, whether Corporate bodies or Individuals. When the Crown treated only with Individuals, and made grants to them, it imposed only conditions which were annexed to the enjoyment of the property bestowed; and the right of the Crown to enforce the conditions constituted the security which it held for the public and political objects which were contemplated.

But when it treated with the City of London, the case seems to have been varied, not by any change in the conditions imposed upon particular undertakers, but by the grant of powers and privileges which could not be bestowed on particular undertakers, and were intended to effect more important objects, to afford special means of enforcing the conditions which affected all. And special encouragements to undertakers, both in their particular characters as such and as members of the City of London, or persons enjoying the protection of the City, or partaking of the benefit of its general prosperity. The objects were such as affected the general welfare of Ireland and the whole realm; these were the objects of the Crown. Such as affected the general welfare of the City of London these may be considered to have been the objects of the City; and such as affected the particular welfare and interests of the companies, or of individual undertakers.

The Society emanated from the City, and even after its incorporation by the Crown, appears to have been little, if anything more than the representative or instrument of the City for the purposes of the Plantation. The City had contracted with the Crown to perform the duty, and it was at the suggestion of the City, and as the means or as their instrument of performing the same duty, that the Society was invested with the property and with very extensive [illegible] powers. *The mistaken views which the Society may have subsequently taken of its own situation and duties, (and I think that such mistaken views have several times been taken), do not vary the conclusion to be deduced from the Charter and the [illegible] contemporary with the grant of the first Charter.*

The duty to be performed regarded the Crown and regarded the City, and through the City the Companies. At and long after the date of the first Charter, the City had, or at least was practically considered to have, and really exercised great and extensive powers, not only over the Society, but also over the Companies; but the City, in its corporate character, had no beneficial interest. The money which it had advanced was early repaid, and the power which remained, or which was considered to remain, was like that of the Society, an interested power for the benefit of the Plantation and those concerned in it.

Even after a large part of the territory comprised in the Grant had been distributed and conveyed to the Companies, much remained to be done for the general purposes of the Plantation, and that which remained to be done, could not be accomplished without expense. At the time when the power of the City to raise money by [illegible] was not disputed, it may not have been thought necessary to retain any part of the property as a fund to support this expense; and it was reported by the Commissioners, on the [illegible] November 1613, and probably generally understood, that the profits of the undivided hereditaments ought to be shared among the Companies; but, in 1662, when the Charter of Charles was granted, and the power of the City to levy money on the Companies was either no longer claimed, or was subject to very different considerations, it was recited in the Charter, that the undivided property was retained to defray the expense of the general operations of the Plantation. The expression was borrowed from a petition presented to the House of Commons, by the City of London, in January 1641; but it has its place in the Charter of 1662, and must have weight accordingly.

It is said, and indeed admitted, that a dividend was made in the year [illegible]; and if I were at liberty to conjecture, I might perhaps suppose that the demands [illegible] made on the City, and the difficulty of raising money, led to a conclusion, that it was better to reserve the common property for the general purposes of the Plantation, than to make division of its whole income, and resort to taxation and levies to defray the expenses which might from time to time be required.

It is clear that the general operation of the Plantation was not completed at the time when the distribution of lands was made to the Companies. It was indeed strongly urged in argument that the general operations, although not then complete, was not long afterwards, or at all events, was very long since completed, and that thereupon if not before, and in consequence thereof, the Society became mere trustees for the Companies. But I do not think that the Court has jurisdiction to determine the question whether the general operation of the Plantation has been completed or not, and if it had it does not appear to me that there is any satisfactory evidence on the subject, or anything to show that operations materially affecting many important objects of the Plantation and requiring expense may not still have to be performed; and if such should be the case, it does not appear to me that this Court has, on the application of the plaintiffs, jurisdiction to compel or give directions about such operations.

And, on the whole, the question is reduced to that which was made on the motion for the payment of money into court and for a receiver, "*Whether upon the Settlement made in the North of Ireland by virtue of the Charter of King James I., under which the Towns of Londonderry and Coleraine were founded, and a large tract of country granted by the Crown to the Irish Society, the terms of the Grant simply constituted the Irish Society ordinary Trustees, for the benefit of the Companies of London, or whether the Grant was coupled with certain public purposes and public trusts, independently of the private benefit of the Companies.*"

After having considered the Charter of King Charles the Second, and the Charter of King James the First, and the several circumstances in evidence in this Cause, which preceded and accompanied the Grant of the Charter of King James, and having read all the documents produced in this Cause, to some only of which, though at the expense of so much time I have but shortly adverted, and having also considered the conduct of the parties under the Charter for so long a series of years;—

I am of opinion that the powers granted to the Society and the trusts reposed in them, were in part of a general and public nature, independent of the private benefit of the Companies of London, and were intended by the Crown to benefit Ireland and the City of London, by connecting the City of Londonderry and the Town of Coleraine, and a considerable Irish District with the City of London, and to promote the general purposes of the Plantation, not only by securing the performance of the conditions imposed on ordinary undertakers, but also by the exercise of powers and the performance of trusts not within the scope of those conditions.

The Charter of Charles the Second expressly recites, that the property not actually divided was retained for the general operations of the Plantation; and considering that the powers given to the Irish Society for the general operations of the Plantation were of a general and public or political nature; that the property remaining vested in the Society is applicable towards such general operations; and that the Companies of London, though interested in any surplus which may remain after the general purposes are answered, are not entitled to control the exercise of the powers which are given for general and public purposes;—I do not think that this Court has jurisdiction, upon the application of the Companies, to determine upon the propriety of the expenditure which has been made. It must not be inferred that I approve of some of the items of expense, which were commented upon in the argument. I express no opinion upon the subject, thinking that the Society have a discretion, which though [illegible] elsewhere and in another manner, is not to be controlled in this Court upon such a bill as this.

And upon the whole I think, that the Bill must be dismissed with costs as against the Irish Society, the City of London, and the Attorney General;—without costs as against the other Companies, unless it shall appear that any of the Companies have opposed the claim of the Plaintiffs.

THE HONOURABLE THE SOCIETY OF THE GOVERNOR AND ASSISTANTS, LONDON, OF THE NEW PLANTATION IN ULSTER, (*i.e. the City and County of Londonderry*), FOR THE YEAR 18[illegible]

GOVERNOR:—Sir Matthew Wood, M.P., Alderman.

DEPUTY GOVERNOR.—David Allan, Esq., Deputy.

ASSISTANTS:

The Hon. Charles Ewan Law, M.P., Q.C., Recorder.	Jeremiah Evans, Esq.
Sir Chandler Stephen Bowles, Bart., Alderman.	James Bailey, Esq.
John Humphery, Esq., M.P., Alderman.	Edwin Cuthbert, Esq.
John Atkins, Esq., Alderman.	Thomas Lott, Esq.
Anthony Brown, Esq., Alderman.	John Barwell Abbott, Esq.
Charles Farebrother, Esq., Alderman.	John [illegible], Esq., Deputy.
Henry Francis, Esq.	Edwin Alderman, Esq., Deputy.
John Bowyer, Esq.	[illegible], Esq.
Solomon Bennett, Esq.	Edward [illegible], Esq.
James [illegible], Esq.	John Wheelton, Esq.
William Unthwille Smith, Esq.	John [illegible], Esq., Deputy.
Richard Webb Jupp, Esq.	James [illegible], Esq., Deputy.

SECRETARY:—John [illegible] Davies, Esq.

APPENDIX, No. 23.

PAPER handed in by Mr. *J. Glover*, 17 July 1890.

CASE for Counsel to advise a Deputation of the Tenants of the CLOTHWORKERS' ESTATE in the County of LONDONDERRY, in the Province of ULSTER in IRELAND, before submitting a Memorial to the Right Honourable W. E. GLADSTONE.

Counsel has herewith a copy of a Memorial intended to be submitted, and copies of the correspondence with the Clothworkers Company, and a statement by the Commissioners of Coleraine.

The deputation are advised that the relief they now seek is as much the business of a court of equity as of Parliament, and that the action of the Government in the case will depend very much on the answer to the question whether the Crown has a right to intervene and stay the sale of this estate to Sir Harvey Bruce.

The deputation consider that the Government will look upon the proceeding of the Clothworkers Company in selling the estate without giving any information of it to the tenants, or giving them an offer to purchase under the Land Act of last Session, as an outrage on the Act of Parliament and on public opinion, and that they will be disposed to go the full length they can to arrest the sale.

As the Government probably could not this Session take up this case by way of legislation without dealing with the Irish Society and other London companies generally, the deputation consider that they should ask the Government to file a bill in the Court of Chancery in Ireland, on the information of the Attorney General, disputing the right of the Company to sell these lands and appropriate the purchase money, and praying an injunction.

To ground this application to the Government, this case is submitted to counsel with the following documents and facts.

In 1608 King James I. issued orders and conditions for the plantation of Ulster (see copy sent in large book).

These conditions, it is submitted, attached public trusts to the lands, so far as the Crown is concerned, which are still binding.

By Agreement, dated 28th January 1609, the City of London undertook the plantation of the county of Londonderry (see copy sent).

The lands, the subject of this case, are included in the Charters of James I. and Charles II. to the Irish Society (see copies sent).

From the execution of the Agreement of 1609, until the granting of the first charter in 1613, the King exercised supreme control over the undertakers.

After the Charter of 1613 was granted, the Irish Society, on the 5th June 1618, executed to the Clothworkers a deed of their estate.

Notwithstanding the charter and the deed, the Crown still exercised a close supervision over the Company, under the Articles of Plantation, as will appear by—

The Acts of the Common Council. Pamphlet, 40, 45.

The King's letter to Chichester (copied in pamphlet, pp. 8 and 11).

The Commission to Pynnar, 1618. Pamphlet, p. 14.

The Civil Survey and Down Survey. Pamphlet, p. 18.

The Requisitions of the Privy Council, 9 June 1624, sent.

The Star Chamber Proceedings, 1630 sent.

The letter of Sir Thomas Philips to the King. Pamphlet, p. 36.

The Covenants in the Companies' Leases to their tenants. Pamphlet, p. 44.

The Charter of Charles II. states that the grant was made, among other reasons, "for the further and better settling and planting said county, towns, and places with trade and inhabitants."

The second deed from the Irish Society to the Clothworkers, is dated 4th June 1663 (see copy sent).

The first Deed of Lease from the Crown to the Company is also herewith sent.

The Company leased the estate on 28th January 1770, for a term of years which expired in 1840. Pamphlet, p. 52.

Counsel has herewith the evidence given before the Lords in the case of the Skinners' Company *v.* the Irish Society, in which all the documents relating to the Ulster Plantation are given at length.

This case is fully reported in 12 Clark and Finelly, page 425.

The Attorney General and the Corporation of London were parties to that suit.

Counsel's attention is drawn by marks in the book to the reasons assigned by each party in support of their case, and to the other evidence which it is considered bears on this case.

In that suit the Irish Society were declared trustees for the general and public purposes of the Plantation, and as to any residue after satisfying those public trusts for the companies.

If the Irish Society are still trustees for the public purposes of the Plantation, it is difficult to understand how their grantees can be in a better position.

The companies still assert they purchased these estates and are absolute owners of them discharged of any trust.

The Skinners say as much on the reasons for their case, yet the Corporation of London do not take any such ground.

In the Orders and Conditions of Plantation there is a clause against alienation to mere Irish, or to such as would not take the Oath of Allegiance, No. 7.

The Company since 1840 has expended considerable sums in building and repairing churches and schools, and supporting religion and education on the estate.

They have also given 500*l.* towards the improvement of the navigation of the River Bann.

The Merchant Taylors' Company have some way or other purchased up the rights of the smaller associated companies originally associated with the Clothworkers.

It is said they have an interest to the extent of about one-third.

The

The contract with Sir Harvey Bruce is not, it is believed, yet completed, and in case counsel considers it necessary to serve him with a notice, notice can be done.

Counsel will please advise the Deputation:

1st. Whether the Crown, by the Attorney General, has now the right to interfere in the sale of this property by the Clothworkers' Company, and if so whether counsel would advise a Bill, by way of information, at the suit of the Attorney General, to be filed.

2nd. Whether the Clothworkers' Company can appropriate to their own uses, in the City of London, the entire purchase-money, without reserving any portion of it for the public use of the Plantation in Ireland.

3rd. Whether the Clothworkers' Company are trustees for any public general purpose connected with the Plantation of Ulster, or for any other public purpose in the City of London or the county of Londonderry.

1. I answer this question in the negative.

2. I answer this in the affirmative.

29 April 1871. 3. I answer this in the negative. I am of opinion that the Clothworkers Company were in the same position as individual undertakers in the other settled counties; that is, they are ordinary owners in fee simple, subject only to the reservations expressly contained in the conveyance to them, and can therefore, like other owners of fee simple, sell their own property for their own benefit to whom they please.

G. Jessel.
Linc. Inn, 1 May 1871.

APPENDIX, No. [illegible].

PAPER handed in by Dr. *R. H. Todd*, 20 June 1890.

LIST OF DOCUMENTS.

1. Collection of Orders and Conditions to be observed by Undertakers.
2. Motives and Reasons to induce the City to undertake the Plantation.
3. Order of Corporation to the Companies to meet in the Guildhall and settle as to the Plantation, dated 12th March 1609.

EXTRACTS from Journals of Court of Common Council, &c.:

4. Precept to Companies of 8th July 1609.
5. Precepts of Common Council to Companies, dated 22nd July 1609.
6. Precept to Companies of 24th July 1609.
7. Resolution appointing Viewers, 1st August 1609.
8. Report of Commissioners on Plantation, dated 28th November 1609.
9. Report of Viewers, 2nd December 1609.
10. Order for 5,000 *l.* to buy up private interests.
11. { Act of Common Council directing Taxation, 9th January 1610.
    { Precept of 9th January 1610.
12. Agreement between the Lords of the Privy Council and the City, of 28th January 1610.
13. Order as to Assurance from the Crown to the City of 7th June 1610.
14. Order for Levy of 10th July 1611.
15. Proposals and Demands of King's Commissioners to the City, dated 22nd July 1610.
16. Precepts to Companies to accept proportional share of Lands and have share of Fishings.
17. Order that Companies which had elected to accept Lands should have the same allotted.
18. Order for further Taxation of 20th April 1613.
19. Order for division of Lands among Companies of 17th December 1613.
20. Order for Levy of 11th January 1614.
21. Order for Levy of 13th October 1614.
22. Report of Sir James Berkley as to the Plantation made to the King in 1614.
23. Precepts by Society to Companies in 1615 to make Certificate of the State of their Plantation, and send their Wardens before Society to answer questions touching the same.
24. Letter of the King to Sir Arthur Chichester, dated 18th March 1615.
25. Precepts to Companies directing Method of Plantation, issued in 1616.
26. Order for Alderman Proby and Mr. Springham to go over and direct the affairs of the Plantation, dated 4th May 1616.
27. Duplicate of Grants made by the Irish Society to the Companies' Tenants in 1617.
28. Propositions of Privy Council as to delay and default in carrying out Plantation, and answers of the Common Council, 2nd June 1624.
29. Articles of Privy Council to Governor and Committee as to reformation of Plantation, dated 27th May 1625.
30. Answer of Common Council thereto.

---

31. Charter of James 1st to Irish Society, 29th March 1613.
32. Licenses to Society and the 12 Companies to hold Lands in Mortmain, 30th September 1615.
33. Reports of Sir Thomas Phillips as to the Progress of the Plantation.
34. Letter of Privy Council of England to Lords Justices of Ireland, dated 7th August 1630.
35. Requisition from the Crown to the City to furnish information as to what each Company was doing on its own proportion in promoting the Plantation; and Direction to the Irish Society to call every Company to an examination of its performances.
36. Requisition from Irish Society to Goldsmiths' Company to perform conditions of Plantation.
37. Letter of Charles 1st to Lords Justices of Ireland of 25th July 1631.
38. The Order for the Sequestration of the Society's and Companies' Estates made in 1635, and the Records of Star Chamber Proceedings.
39. Petition from the London Corporation and Irish Society to the King on the Plantation, dated 2nd March [illegible].
40. The Writ of *Scire Facias*, dated 28th December 1637.
41. The Order of the Lord Chancellor made when Cause shown to the Writ of *Scire Facias*.
42. Charles 2nd to Irish Society, 10th April 1662.
43. Indemnity from Haberdashers' Company to Irish Society, dated 8th July 1687.
44. Indemnity from the Goldsmiths' Company to the Society, and Statements by the Company to the Society on 31st October 1730, that they had sold their proportion to the Earl of Shelburne, but were advised they could not make proper conveyance without the Society joining therein. Entry of such representation and order thereon in Irish Society's records.
45. Representation from Society to the 12 Companies as to Salmon, of 12th February 1713.
46. Letter from the Society to the Companies as to Fishery, dated 27th August 17[illegible].
47. Indemnity from the Vintners' Company to the Society of 27th January 1737.
48. Entry of [illegible] of Timber by the Irish Society.
49. The Pleadings and Proceedings in the case of the Skinners' Company and Irish Society, with the several judgments and orders pronounced thereon.
50. Release and Conveyance from Irish Society to the Mercers' Company of 5th June 16[illegible] and the several other deeds of assurance from the Irish Society to the Companies.
51. The Concise View of the Irish Society (a copy of each of the two editions thereof), and particularly the "Conclusion," stated at pages 15[illegible] of the 1842 edition.

APPENDIX, No. 11.

PAPER handed in by Mr. *W[illegible]*, 7 July 18[illegible].

SUMMARY of EXPENDITURE on IRISH ESTATE, from 18[illegible] to 18[illegible], inclusive, and DECENNIAL AVERAGES.

APPENDIX, No. 31.

PAPER handed in by Mr. [illegible], 7 July [illegible].

SUMMARY of Expenditure on Irish Estate, from 1831 to [illegible], inclusive, and Decennial Averages.

	Expenditure, 1831 to 1840.	Average.	Expenditure, 1841 to 1850.	Average.	Expenditure, 1851 to 1860.	Average.
	£. s. d.	£. s. d.	£. s. d.	£. s. d.	£. s. d.	£. s. d.
Abatements	[illegible] 1 –	[illegible]	[illegible] 9 –	3 [illegible] [illegible]	—	—
Agents' Residence	1,[illegible]7 – 7	446 15 –	[illegible]	45 [illegible] 10	[illegible] 11 [illegible]	[illegible]
Agreement Stamps	—	—	—	—	19 10 –	1 19 –
Board of Works	—	—	—	—	[illegible]	[illegible]
Bathing Infirmary	—	—	—	—	10[illegible] 3 3	[illegible]
Compensation to Tenants	[illegible]	[illegible]	1,[illegible] 14 [illegible]	[illegible]	[illegible] 7 [illegible]	[illegible]
Cottages	[illegible] – –	[illegible] – –	[illegible] 5 11	[illegible] 7	1[illegible] 11 –	[illegible]
Dispensary	1,910 3 7	191 – [illegible]	[illegible]	[illegible]	1,[illegible] –	[illegible]
Drainage	—	—	1,[illegible]7 19 7	158 16 11	1,[illegible] 11 9	[illegible] 19 [illegible]
Expenses of Management	11,[illegible] 9 [illegible]	1,1[illegible] 18 11	12,[illegible] 17 [illegible]	1,204 16 9	1[illegible]	1,[illegible] 10 [illegible]
Emigration	1,075 [illegible]	107 11 10	[illegible] 17 5	[illegible] 15 [illegible]	17 4 [illegible]	1 14 [illegible]
[illegible] Road	—	—	—	—	[illegible]	[illegible] 7 7
Incidentals	[illegible]7 15 1	[illegible] 15 [illegible]	3,4[illegible] 3 4	3[illegible] 10 [illegible]	2,[illegible]71 [illegible]	[illegible]
Income Tax	—	—	—	—	[illegible] 4 5	[illegible]
Kilrea Corn Mill	1,[illegible]07 7 1[illegible]	1[illegible]0 14 9	1[illegible] 4 1	15 [illegible] 7	[illegible]	[illegible]
Kilrea New Church	[illegible] –	– [illegible] –	[illegible],0[illegible] 17 [illegible]	[illegible] 7 [illegible]	[illegible]	[illegible]
Kilrea Hotel	—	—	[illegible] 14 [illegible]	[illegible] 9 5	[illegible]	[illegible]
[illegible] Farm	—	—	[illegible]	[illegible]	[illegible] 16 [illegible]	[illegible]
[illegible] Mill	1 4 –	– [illegible] [illegible]	—	—	—	—
Lime Quarry	[illegible] 15 [illegible]	[illegible]	1[illegible] 3	[illegible] 11	7[illegible] 7 [illegible]	[illegible]
Loans	[illegible] – –	[illegible] – –	1,7[illegible] – –	178 10 –	67[illegible] 4 10	[illegible]
Markets	[illegible] 7 11	[illegible] 15 9	74[illegible] – [illegible]	7[illegible] [illegible] –	[illegible] –	[illegible] 1
Mapping and Valuing	1,[illegible] 10 [illegible]	1[illegible] 7 –	—	—	1,[illegible] 7 10	1[illegible] 14 9
Places of Worship	1,[illegible] 1 –	1[illegible] [illegible] 1	2,[illegible] 1[illegible] 1	[illegible] 5	1,[illegible] – –	1[illegible] [illegible] –
Planting and Fencing	1,[illegible] 4 7	1[illegible] – 5	[illegible] –	[illegible]	3[illegible] 17 [illegible]	[illegible]
Police Barracks	401 7 –	[illegible]	11 [illegible] –	1 [illegible]	[illegible] 10	[illegible]
Poor Rates	—	—	[illegible]	[illegible] 10 [illegible]	1,771 [illegible]	177 [illegible]
Portna Flax Mill	—	—	[illegible] 10 [illegible]	[illegible] 13 –	—	—
Presbyterian Meeting House	1,[illegible] 15 [illegible]	1[illegible]	1[illegible] – –	1[illegible] 10 –	—	—
Property purchased	—	—	[illegible]	[illegible] – 10	[illegible]	[illegible] 15 [illegible]
Purchase of Tenant-right	—	—	—	—	—	—
Relief Account	—	—	1,[illegible]	1[illegible] – [illegible]	—	—
Repairs	1,[illegible] 11 [illegible]	1[illegible] 17 [illegible]	[illegible] 1	[illegible] 4 [illegible]	4[illegible]	4[illegible] – [illegible]
Roads and Footpaths	[illegible] 1[illegible]	[illegible] 7	1,7[illegible] 1 [illegible]	173 4 [illegible]	1,[illegible] 11 7	[illegible]
Seed	—	—	[illegible] 1[illegible] –	[illegible] 9 10	—	—
Schools	1,[illegible] [illegible]	144 7 7	[illegible]	[illegible] 17 10	[illegible] 16 1	[illegible] 11 7
Shops	—	—	1,[illegible] 16 7	1[illegible] 5 7	[illegible] 16 1	[illegible] 7
[illegible] Quarry	—	—	[illegible] –	[illegible] 16 10	—	—
Stone Quarry	[illegible] – 9	1 [illegible] –	—	—	—	—
Swatragh Church	—	—	—	—	[illegible] 1 7	[illegible] 1
Tithes	[illegible] 5	[illegible] – 7	[illegible]	[illegible] – [illegible]	[illegible]	[illegible]
[illegible]	1,[illegible] 7	1[illegible] 7	[illegible] 15 9	[illegible] 17 [illegible]	[illegible]	[illegible]
Waterworks	—	—	—	—	1,[illegible] 1 11	14[illegible]
Wharf at [illegible]	[illegible]	[illegible]	—	—	—	—
Deputations	1,47[illegible] 7 [illegible]	14[illegible] 4 [illegible]	—	—	—	—
Tithe Rent-charge purchase	—	—	—	—	—	—
Agents' Offices (building)	—	—	1,[illegible] 1[illegible] [illegible]	—	19 15 6	1 [illegible] [illegible]
Total - - - £.	[illegible] 17 11	—	[illegible],407 16 9	—	[illegible],[illegible]7 1[illegible] 5	—

1	2	3	4	5	6	7	8
—	—	—	—	8 5 1	[illegible] 10 6	—	—
[illegible] 7 [illegible]	43 15 8	[illegible] 12 3	40 17 [illegible]	[illegible] 9 10	1,[illegible] 8 6	141 19 8	15 15 6
210 10 -	81 10 -	[illegible] - -	8 - -	70 17 8	[illegible] 6 6	—	—
8 4 8	- 16 8	—	—	22 19 7	1,148 8 7	—	—
1,510 11 1	151 10 1	1,[illegible] 8 6	145 12 4	131 10 10	9,077 6 7	[illegible] 4 8	95 12 8
[illegible] 16 -	130 17 -	1,3[illegible] 4 1	180 4 4	169 7 5	6,315 11 5	1,049 1 5	115 8 5
14,547 4 -	1,484 11 4	16,473 5 10	1,647 14 7	1,547 11 8	47,577 19 11	9,405 17 8	1,064 4 1
—	—	—	—	[illegible] 10 6	1,501 - 9	—	—
—	—	—	—	10 8 8	[illegible] 15 -	—	—
4,100 14 3	418 6 5	8,003 9 9	365 8 11	845 4 1	17,[illegible] 8 1	9,078 - -	1,100 3 8
2,544 15 -	254 8 6	1,715 6 11	171 11 10	157 10 -	7,[illegible] 8 4	2,[illegible] 10 7	[illegible] 10 -
116 11 8	11 13 1	180 11 -	15 19 1	15 5 4	9,443 18 4	140 18 6	10 15 1
422 3 1	51 4 8	677 10 8	67 15 8	145 10 8	7,[illegible] 8 8	741 8 7	65 2 7
271 8 10	27 1 9	187 14 11	16 15 8	85 1 8	1,[illegible] 1 1	180 12 4	17 15 4
—	—	—	—	18 11 6	620 17 8	—	—
—	—	—	—	- - 5	1 6 -	—	—
704 9 8	10 8 11	—	—	33 9 7	1,654 17 11	—	—
2,036 - -	236 12 -	1,[illegible] 6 8	180 10 6	136 9 -	5,[illegible] 10 1	[illegible] - -	65 11 1
171 7 7	17 8 8	—	—	85 4 8	4,611 6 8	188 17 5	14 8 4
415 2 -	41 10 8	4,626 8 8	465 10 9	170 8 8	8,312 8 8	—	—
1,130 5 -	113 12 6	2,005 14 -	205 11 4	130 7 7	6,070 12 1	1,026 - 1	175 4 5
446 17 11	45 15 8	463 6 6	46 6 4	64 10 11	2,227 7 1	65 6 1	7 6 1
380 10 8	63 17 -	180 17 9	12 19 1	87 17 3	1,046 8 8	436 10 1	36 3 6
1,073 16 8	107 7 7	1,008 5 9	180 6 7	144 16 8	7,840 10 6	1,033 9 4	103 9 11
—	—	—	—	6 10 7	675 10 6	—	—
—	—	—	—	54 7 10	1,719 15 6	—	—
—	—	—	—	30 15 10	1,030 12 2	—	—
—	—	407 8 -	40 14 8	8 8 10	407 8 -	[illegible] 10 -	80 8 4
—	—	—	—	34 17 -	1,280 8 9	—	—
1,030 13 6	103 1 4	1,036 10 -	103 1 -	113 - 10	4,[illegible] 3 7	903 14 11	108 8 10
2,035 16 7	304 17 5	818 3 9	81 6 11	180 3 8	7,826 10 6	305 8 7	35 12 8
—	—	—	—	32 17 11	646 10 -	—	—
6,412 9 -	641 4 10	4,611 19 7	461 8 11	435 1 9	80,[illegible] 19 8	3,857 10 11	385 6 7
7 10 8	- 15 -	—	—	17 8 7	1,[illegible] 8 1	—	—
—	—	—	—	1 8 4	44 9 -	—	—
—	—	—	—	- 6 4	16 - 8	—	—
34 8 -	8 6 7	84 - 8	8 8 -	47 8 6	2,371 8 1	447 8 -	71 13 9
3,807 5 8	380 14 3	841 1 6	84 2 1	448 18 9	15,[illegible] 1 5	—	—
141 6 1	14 9 8	—	—	54 7 4	6,514 9 8	—	—
435 15 9	43 11 9	345 10 7	34 11 -	42 8 1	2,180 4 8	404 6 10	40 10 1
—	—	—	—	4 6 8	131 5 8	—	—
—	—	—	—	80 8 11	1,478 7 5	—	—
—	—	4,410 1 -	441 10 1	80 7 7	4,410 1 -	4,080 14 8	544 8 8
—	—	—	—	86 8 10	1,314 12 -	—	—
63,[illegible] 18 11	—	40,[illegible] 15 8	—			Derry Central Railway 4,404 14 6	438 6

Average Annual Expenditure for [illegible] Years . £. [illegible] 8 8 | £. [illegible] 14 4

Total [illegible] Years, from 18[illegible] to 18[illegible] - - [illegible] 17 -

Total [illegible] Years 18[illegible] to 18[illegible] - - - - [illegible] 15 4

GRAND TOTAL - - £. [illegible] 11 4

[illegible]

APPENDIX, No. 33.

PAPER handed in by the Clerk to the *Grocers'* Company.

STATEMENT.

The last long lease granted by the Grocers Company of their Irish estate was a lease to a certain Thomas Conolly, in the year 1729, for a term of 61 years and two lives, which lease ultimately became vested in David Babington.

In the year 1819 a deputation from the court visited the estate, and on their report the court resolved that it would not be to the interest of the Company to renew the then existing lease, if to relet as a whole at all. The subject was again brought up in the year 1819, and it was then resolved, at the expiration of Conolly's lease, to let as far as possible to the occupiers.

The Company, on taking possession in the autumn of 1823, proceeded to develope and improve the estate; two of the three mills on the estate were repaired, a resident agent was appointed, and orders given for drainage and reclamation work, building of farmhouses and cottages, repairing and building tradesmen's houses at Muff. A sessions and market-house and room for justices' meetings were built at Muff, and a dispensary established. The agent was instructed to buy clover seed and agricultural implements for the poorer tenants.

In the year 1825 a schoolhouse for girls was built at Muff, and a schoolmistress appointed by the Company, who also then commenced a system of subscribing such institutions as the Glendermott Dispensary and the Derry Infirmary. The sum of 100 *l.* was granted to start a charity loan fund institution at Muff, and tenants were encouraged to rebuild their houses; the Company supplying materials.

In 1826 the Company turned their attention to the town of Muff, which was gradually rebuilt, a new school added, and buildings for the accommodation of the constabulary.

The Company's records show a continuous expenditure on the improvement of the estate, in assistance to the tenants, and in supporting the medical and other charities and churches of all denominations.

Appended is a statement of the income and expenditure of the Company in respect of their Irish property from the year 1823, when they took possession, until 1876 (Appendix, Table I.). Table II. of the Appendix gives the amounts of expenditure on management, improvements, and subscriptions, and subscriptions and donations to religious and charitable objects under separate heads between the years 1826 and 1876.

In the year 1873 it was resolved to sell the estate, which was ultimately put into the hands of Messrs. Stewart and Kincaid, of Dublin, on whose advice the tithe was redeemed at a cost of 7,335 *l.*, and the property offered at first in five and subsequently 11 lots.

Messrs. Stewart and Kincaid valued the estate at 150,000 *l.* after redemption of tithe, and the 11 lots were disposed of as follows:—

Lot.	Purchaser.	Price.	Lot.	Purchaser.	Price.
		£.			£.
1 2	W. F. Bigger - - -	22,500	6 7	Davidson - - - - -	41,150
3	S. Stevenson - - -	20,036	8	Tenants - - - - -	12,000
4	G. George (a tenant) - - -	8,167	9 10	W. F. Bigger - - - - -	20,000
5	Tenants - - - - - -	15,700	11	Dr. M'Cutcheon - - - - -	8,000

Several chief rents in respect of what had been native freeholds were sold, and the holding of the Roman Catholic priest, the Presbyterian minister, and Episcopal vicar of Faughanvale were transferred on easy terms to trustees for the benefit of the ministers.

In November 1877 the committee reported the completion of the sale of the estate (about 11,748 acres) for the total sum of 157,551 *l.* 10 *s.*; a piece of bog land only remained to be sold, which being subsequently disposed of for the sum of 300 *l.*, brought the purchase-money up to 157,851 *l.*, after deducting the cost of redeeming the tithe (7,335 *l.*), and expenses of sale (1,707 *l.*), the net result was 148,834 *l.* From this amount also be deducted a further sum of 1,175 *l.* expended in gratuities to church funds, &c., while pensions to the agent, allowances to schools, and doles to the poor have absorbed 5,545 *l.* since that date, and the Company were last year still paying 190 *l.* on the latter account.

The agent reported that at the sale 70 persons, mostly widows and old people incapable of earning a livelihood, were receiving relief out of the funds of the Company in his hands to the extent of 220 *l.* per annum; these allowances were continued by the Company, who, as above stated, are still paying money on this account.

TABLE I.

Date.	Outgoings.	Income.	Amount Remitted to the Company.	Expenditure by the Company in Excess of Receipts.	Date.	Outgoings.	Income.	Amount Remitted to the Company.	Expenditure by the Company in Excess of Receipts.
	£.	£.	£.	£.		£.	£.	£.	£.
1822 -	1,020	1,100	80	—	1850 -	3,620	4,652	1,030	—
1823 -	1,375	2,853	—	1,480	1851 -	3,298	4,819	1,420	—
1824 -	* 11,567	1,738	—	9,794	1852 -	3,467	5,316	1,180	—
1825 -	5,185	5,006	—	291	1853 -	3,572	5,047	1,300	—
1826 -	5,279	4,685	—	697	1854 -	2,495	5,662	2,033	—
1827 -	5,748	6,087	—	721	1855 -	3,934	5,043	2,843	—
1828 -	2,650	4,225	3,578	—	1856 -	3,929	4,991	1,758	—
1829 -	2,920	4,257	1,327	—	1857 -	3,187	5,294	2,040	—
1830 -	3,418	4,025	627	—	1858 -	3,186	4,869	1,822	—
1831 -	3,444	4,251	815	—	1859 -	3,195	5,345	2,300	—
1832 -	3,423	5,241	860	—	1860 -	3,774	5,145	1,880	—
1833 -	1,986	4,580	2,634	—	1861 -	3,020	5,418	2,330	—
1834 -	873	4,530	3,690	—	1862 -	3,441	4,897	1,320	—
1835 -	685	625	—	60	1863 -	4,977	6,770	1,800	—
1836 -	3,480	5,716	2,230	—	1864 -	3,944	5,633	1,770	—
1837 -	3,516	3,997	600	—	1865 -	3,887	5,914	2,025	—
1838 -	3,625	4,778	1,135	—	1866 -	4,004	6,014	2,080	—
1839 -	3,792	6,055	2,313	—	1867 -	3,626	5,795	2,300	—
1840 -	2,949	4,388	1,380	—	1868 -	4,673	5,695	1,970	—
1841 -	2,939	5,440	2,520	—	1869 -	3,565	5,734	2,080	—
1842 -	3,339	5,234	1,750	—	1870 -	3,686	5,864	2,130	—
1843 -	3,080	4,940	1,856	—	1871 -	3,347	5,444	2,250	—
1844 -	3,495	5,209	1,730	—	1872 -	5,449	5,934	4,880	—
1845 -	3,375	4,888	1,480	—	1873 -	3,371	5,938	2,373	—
1846 -	4,084	5,697	1,398	—	1874 -	3,180	5,810	2,440	—
1847 -	4,309	4,818	900	—	1875 -	2,554	4,589	2,358	—
1848 -	3,958	5,127	1,570	—	1876 -	2,525	4,346	1,720	—
1849 -	4,134	6,149	1,030	—					

* This amount includes the sum of 7,000 l. paid to Babington, the Company's late tenant. Nominally, this was in respect of his improvements, but there is no doubt that it included a solatium for his disappointment in not obtaining a renewal of the lease.

TABLE II.

Year.	Agent's Salary, Rates, Taxes, and Management Expenses.	Improvements on Estate, Allowances to Tenants, &c.	Subscriptions and Donations.					Total Outgoings.
			Clergy and Churches.	Schools.	Gifts to the Poor and Charitable Institutions.	Agricultural and other Societies, &c., &c.	Total.	
	£.	£.	£. s.	£. s.	£. s.	£. s.	£. s.	£.
1836 - -	[illegible]	2,0[illegible]	67 10	4[illegible] –	304 10	7[illegible] –	5[illegible] –	3,4[illegible]
1837 - -	[illegible]	2,157	7[illegible] –	27 –	277 –	60 –	4[illegible] –	3,5[illegible]
1838 - -	1,2[illegible]	1,[illegible]	77 –	[illegible] –	19[illegible] –	70 –	[illegible]7 –	3,50[illegible]
1839 - -	1,[illegible]	1,[illegible]	[illegible]0 –	[illegible] 10	[illegible] 10	47 10	[illegible] 10	3,7[illegible]
1840 - -	[illegible]	1,[illegible]7	[illegible] –	[illegible] –	349 10	56 10	[illegible] –	3,3[illegible]
1841 - -	1,0[illegible]	1,[illegible]7	[illegible] –	[illegible] –	1[illegible] –	4[illegible] –	401 –	[illegible]
1842 - -	1,1[illegible]	1,[illegible]	7[illegible] –	102 10	[illegible] –	[illegible] –	474 10	[illegible]
1843 - -	1,0[illegible]	2,[illegible]	7[illegible] –	[illegible] 10	[illegible] –	[illegible] –	[illegible] 10	[illegible]
1844 - -	1,1[illegible]	1,[illegible]7	1[illegible] 10	1[illegible] –	[illegible] –	[illegible] –	[illegible] 10	[illegible]
1845 - -	1,1[illegible]	1,[illegible]1	7[illegible] –	97 10	[illegible]71 10	45 –	4[illegible] –	[illegible]
1846 - -	1,130	2,[illegible]	[illegible] 10	10[illegible] 10	371 –	85 –	67[illegible] –	4,[illegible]
1847 - -	1,[illegible]	2,[illegible]	[illegible] –	[illegible] –	[illegible] –	[illegible] –	77[illegible] –	4,[illegible]
1848 - -	1,040	1,[illegible]	[illegible] –	[illegible] –	[illegible] –	32 10	[illegible] 10	[illegible]
1849 - -	1,[illegible]	1,[illegible]	[illegible] –	[illegible] –	44[illegible] –	4[illegible] –	[illegible] –	4,1[illegible]
1850 - -	1,[illegible]	1,7[illegible]	40 –	10[illegible] –	4[illegible] –	44 –	[illegible] –	3,[illegible]
1851 - -	1,[illegible]	1,[illegible]	65 –	79 10	4[illegible] 10	[illegible] –	[illegible] –	[illegible]
1852 - -	1,1[illegible]	1,[illegible]	[illegible] –	[illegible] 10	[illegible] –	37 –	[illegible] 10	3,[illegible]
1853 - -	1,[illegible]	1,[illegible]	1[illegible] –	7[illegible] –	[illegible] 10	4[illegible] –	613 10	[illegible]
1854 - -	1,1[illegible]	2,018	[illegible] –	7[illegible] –	[illegible] –	[illegible] –	4[illegible] –	[illegible]
1855 - -	1,[illegible]	2,119	[illegible] –	[illegible] –	[illegible] –	7[illegible] –	[illegible] –	[illegible]
1856 - -	1,[illegible]	1,[illegible]	70 –	[illegible] –	[illegible] –	10[illegible] –	[illegible] –	3,[illegible]
1857 - -	1,[illegible]	2,[illegible]	7[illegible] –	71 10	[illegible] –	45 –	47[illegible] 10	3,[illegible]
1858 - -	1,1[illegible]	1,[illegible]	7[illegible] –	7[illegible] 10	[illegible] –	7[illegible] –	[illegible] 10	[illegible]
1859 - -	1,[illegible]	1,537	1[illegible]0 –	63 –	37[illegible] –	7[illegible] –	[illegible] –	[illegible]
1860 - -	1,210	1,[illegible]	1[illegible]0 –	1[illegible]0 –	[illegible] 10	64 –	[illegible] 10	[illegible]
1861 - -	1,[illegible]	1,[illegible]	1[illegible] –	10[illegible] –	[illegible] –	44 –	4[illegible] –	[illegible]
1862 - -	1,[illegible]7	1,4[illegible]	70 –	[illegible] 10	[illegible] 10	4[illegible] –	[illegible] –	3,441
1863 - -	1,[illegible]	2,0[illegible]	[illegible] –	10[illegible] –	[illegible]70 –	50 –	[illegible] –	4,[illegible]
1864 - -	1,[illegible]	1,[illegible]	115 –	10[illegible] –	[illegible] –	5[illegible] –	[illegible] –	[illegible]
1865 - -	1,[illegible]	1,[illegible]	1[illegible] –	[illegible]1 –	4[illegible] –	71 –	7[illegible] –	3,[illegible]
1866 - -	1,[illegible]	1,[illegible]	[illegible]0 –	[illegible] –	494 –	[illegible] –	71[illegible] –	4,0[illegible]
1867 - -	1,[illegible]	1,[illegible]	[illegible] –	[illegible] 10	4[illegible] –	[illegible] 10	[illegible] –	3,[illegible]
1868 - -	1,[illegible]7	2,014	[illegible] –	100 –	[illegible] –	3[illegible] –	7[illegible] –	4,07[illegible]
1869 - -	1,[illegible]	1,[illegible]	70 –	11[illegible] –	41[illegible] –	1[illegible] –	[illegible] –	[illegible]
1870 - -	1,[illegible]	1,7[illegible]	[illegible] –	1[illegible] 10	4[illegible] 10	[illegible] –	[illegible] –	3,[illegible]
1871 - -	1,[illegible]	1,[illegible]70	[illegible] –	[illegible] –	4[illegible] –	[illegible] –	[illegible] –	3,[illegible]47
1872 - -	1,[illegible]	1,4[illegible]	1[illegible] –	[illegible] –	411 –	10 –	[illegible] –	[illegible]
1873 - -	1,[illegible]	1,4[illegible]	[illegible] –	1[illegible] –	4[illegible] –	18 –	[illegible] –	[illegible]
1874 - -	[illegible]	1,[illegible]	100 –	1[illegible] –	407 –	10 –	[illegible] –	[illegible]
1875 - -	[illegible]	1,[illegible]	70 –	1[illegible] –	[illegible] –	[illegible] –	613 –	[illegible]
1876 - -	[illegible]	1,[illegible]	50 –	[illegible] 10	34[illegible] 10	[illegible] –	401 –	[illegible]

[illegible]

[illegible]

[illegible]

[illegible]

RECEIPTS				EXPENDITURE					
Year	[illegible]	Other Receipts	Total	Year	[illegible]	[illegible]	[illegible]	[illegible]	Total
	£ s. d.	£ s. d.	£ s. d.		£ s. d.	£ s. d.	£ s. d.	£ s. d.	£ s. d.
[illegible]	[illegible]	[illegible]	[illegible]	[illegible]	[illegible]	[illegible]	[illegible]	[illegible]	[illegible]
[illegible]	[illegible]	[illegible]	[illegible]	[illegible]	[illegible]	[illegible]	[illegible]	[illegible]	[illegible]
[illegible]	[illegible]	[illegible]	[illegible]	[illegible]	[illegible]	[illegible]	[illegible]	[illegible]	[illegible]
[illegible]	[illegible]	[illegible]	[illegible]	[illegible]	[illegible]	[illegible]	[illegible]	[illegible]	[illegible]
[illegible]	[illegible]	[illegible]	[illegible]	[illegible]	[illegible]	[illegible]	[illegible]	[illegible]	[illegible]
[illegible]	[illegible]	[illegible]	[illegible]	[illegible]	[illegible]	[illegible]	[illegible]	[illegible]	[illegible]
[illegible]	[illegible]	[illegible]	[illegible]	[illegible]	[illegible]	[illegible]	[illegible]	[illegible]	[illegible]
[illegible]	[illegible]	[illegible]	[illegible]	[illegible]	[illegible]	[illegible]	[illegible]	[illegible]	[illegible]
[illegible]	[illegible]	[illegible]	[illegible]	[illegible]	[illegible]	[illegible]	[illegible]	[illegible]	[illegible]
[illegible]	[illegible]	[illegible]	[illegible]	[illegible]	[illegible]	[illegible]	[illegible]	[illegible]	[illegible]
[illegible]	[illegible]	[illegible]	[illegible]	[illegible]	[illegible]	[illegible]	[illegible]	[illegible]	[illegible]
[illegible]	[illegible]	[illegible]	[illegible]	[illegible]	[illegible]	[illegible]	[illegible]	[illegible]	[illegible]
[illegible]	[illegible]	[illegible]	[illegible]	[illegible]	[illegible]	[illegible]	[illegible]	[illegible]	[illegible]
[illegible]	[illegible]	[illegible]	[illegible]	[illegible]	[illegible]	[illegible]	[illegible]	[illegible]	[illegible]
[illegible]	[illegible]	[illegible]	[illegible]	[illegible]	[illegible]	[illegible]	[illegible]	[illegible]	[illegible]
[illegible] £	[illegible]	[illegible]	[illegible]	[illegible] £	[illegible]	[illegible]	[illegible]	[illegible]	[illegible]

APPENDIX, No. 85.

PAPER handed in by the Clerk to the *Fishmongers'* Company.

IRISH ESTATE.

SUMMARY of Expenditure in Ireland and Ballykelly Estate for Eight Years, 1850 to 1857, and Annual Average.

EXPENDITURE.	Eight Years, 1850 to 1857.	TOTAL.	Annual Average.
	£. s. d.	£. s. d.	£. s. d.
Outlay on Estate:			
Ballykelly river, banks, and canal	714 1 6		
Drains, roads, &c.	[illegible] 5 5		
Planting timber and forestry expenses	3,[illegible] 4 7		
Farm buildings	2,[illegible] 1 1		
Ballykelly town parks	783 15 6		
Cultivating [illegible]	[illegible] 13 1		
Gravel, [illegible] and lands	1,[illegible] 7 4		
Quarrying	43 17 1		
Building house for railway station	[illegible] - -		
Repairing houses and estate work	1,[illegible] 17 9		
Compensation to tenants	[illegible] - -		
Salaries	781 18 6	14,[illegible] [illegible] [illegible]	1,[illegible] [illegible] [illegible]
Revenue Charges (a); Expenses of Management (b):			
(a) County cess	[illegible] 1 -		
Poor rate	1,1[illegible] 15 10		
Property tax	1,[illegible] 7 9		
Tithes (£. [illegible] 16. 7.)	[illegible] 11 -		
(b) Agent's house	[illegible] 15 9		
English expenditure for same period (as per Statement)	[illegible] 13 [illegible]		
Salaries	[illegible] 13 [illegible]		
Law expenses	113 [illegible] [illegible]		
Surveying (£. 7,[illegible] 17. 5.)	13 15 4	[illegible] [illegible] [illegible]	[illegible] [illegible] [illegible]
Donations and Subscriptions to Public Objects:			
Donations to ministers and priests	1,[illegible] - -		
General donations	1,[illegible] 11 -		
Relief and pensions	[illegible] 1 10		
Dispensaries and Infirmary	[illegible] 11 5		
Schools	5,[illegible] 12 4		
Planting societies	[illegible] 9 -	11,[illegible] 5 7	1,[illegible] [illegible] [illegible]
TOTAL - - - £.		[illegible] 15 [illegible]	4,[illegible] 14

SUMMARY of Income for Eight Years, 1850 to 1857, and Annual Average.

INCOME.	Eight Years, 1850 to 1857.	Annual Average.
	£. s. d.	£. s. d.
Rent	61,[illegible] 9 [illegible]	7,[illegible] 15 [illegible]
Timber	1,[illegible] 5 -	[illegible] 10 7
Flax mill, threshing mill, &c.	1,[illegible] 14 7	161 14 [illegible]
Town parks	[illegible] 9 [illegible]	[illegible] 16 [illegible]
Mountains	679 10 [illegible]	[illegible] 16 10
Interest and sundries	1,[illegible] - 9	[illegible] - 1
TOTAL - - - £.	67,[illegible] 9 [illegible]	[illegible] 1 [illegible]

Account given in accordance with the Chairman's request, page 217.

N.B.—The bulk of the sales to the tenants was effected during the above eight years, which accounts for the small amount of the net annual revenue.

APPENDIX, No. [illegible].

PAPER handed in by Mr. *E. H. Draper*, [illegible] July 18[illegible].

SKINNERS' COMPANY.

PELLIPAR ESTATE.—RECEIPTS, 10 YEARS 1877–1886.

(Receivable.) Rents due for Year ending	Gross Rental.	Abatements and Allowances.	Net Rents Received.	Market Tolls, Bog Cuttings, Old Trust Interest.	Received in Year ending	TOTAL RECEIPTS.
	£. s. d.	£. s. d.	£. s. d.	£. s. d.		£. s. d.
1 November 1876	11,743 11 10	351 3 10	11,[illegible] 3 [illegible]	1[illegible] 6 10	30 April 1877	11,6[illegible] 10 1
" 1877	10,[illegible] 10 3	[illegible] 7 1	11,[illegible] 10 [illegible]	[illegible] 3 7	" 1878	11,[illegible] 3 [illegible]
" 1878	10,[illegible] 6 [illegible]	440 6 5	11,[illegible] – 11	44 17 6	" 1879	11,[illegible] 18 7
" 1879	13,850 1 6	1,040 5 5	10,146 17 5	64 16 5	" 1880	10,[illegible] 11 10
" 1880	10,857 11 5	[illegible] 5 [illegible]	[illegible] 12 1	[illegible] 6 –	" 1881	9,[illegible] 15 1
" 1881	10,[illegible] 3 10	10[illegible] 17 [illegible]	8,[illegible] 11 11	[illegible] 1 [illegible]	" 1882	8,517 15 7
" 1882	12,[illegible] [illegible] 1	504 14 [illegible]	11,[illegible] 11 7	37 [illegible] 5	" 1883	11,[illegible] 18 10
" 1883	12,674 19 4	7,144 5 6	[illegible] 19 [illegible]	36 [illegible] 9	" 1884	[illegible] 6 6
" 1884	11,464 5 7	[illegible] 2 [illegible]	12,[illegible] 11 6	[illegible] – 11	" 1885	12,1[illegible] 13 5
" 1885	11,846 11 10	550 15 3	8,944 3 [illegible]	126 6 5	" 1886	10,067 10 [illegible]
	1[illegible],1[illegible] 11 [illegible]					
Add, arrears to 1 November 1875	6,[illegible] 9 6					
£.	1[illegible] 13 [illegible]	[illegible] – 6	11[illegible] 13 4	[illegible] 2 5	- - -	111,[illegible] 15 10

PELLIPAR ESTATE.—PAYMENTS, 10 YEARS 1877–1886.

Paid in Year ending	Tithe Rent, Rates and Taxes, Insurance.	[illegible]	[illegible]	Schools, [illegible] and Donations, in connection with the Estate.	Railways.	TOTALS.
	£. s. d.	£. s. d.	£. s. d.	£. s. d.	£. s. d.	£. s. d.
30 April 1877	[illegible] 1 1	4[illegible] 7 –	2,641 [illegible] 1	[illegible] 15 11	—	4,[illegible] 13 [illegible]
" 1878	[illegible] 8	717 15 6	1,[illegible] 3 [illegible]	[illegible] 2 –	1[illegible] 15 6	4,[illegible] 10 [illegible]
" 1879	1,1[illegible] 11 1	[illegible] 15 4	2,[illegible] 9 4	[illegible] 13 10	1[illegible] 13 6	5,[illegible] 5 11
" 1880	1,1[illegible] 10 10	670 [illegible] –	1,[illegible] 17 10	[illegible] 13 [illegible]	—	4,[illegible] 6 10
" 1881	1,179 16 11	[illegible] 11 4	1,[illegible] 16 6	[illegible] 7 [illegible]	—	4,440 6 11
" 1882	1,[illegible] 18 7	[illegible] 12 6	1,[illegible] [illegible] 9	[illegible] 4 4	166 13 4	4,[illegible] 1 6
" 1883	[illegible] 7 10	[illegible] 17 –	2,[illegible] 8 11	[illegible]	116 7 8	5,776 4 9
" 1884	1,670 [illegible] 4	2,1[illegible] 10 [illegible]	2,7[illegible] 13 9	[illegible] 13 [illegible]	9[illegible] 17 9	9,[illegible] 4 [illegible]
" 1885	1,1[illegible] 9 4	[illegible] – [illegible]	2,[illegible] 13 [illegible]	711 13 [illegible]	1,[illegible] – –	5,[illegible]
" 1886	1,[illegible] 4 1	1,151 7 11	[illegible] 14 3	[illegible] –	1,[illegible] – –	7,[illegible] – 6
£.	11,[illegible] – 5	[illegible] 5 6	[illegible] 13 –	[illegible] 9 9	[illegible] 5	[illegible] 15 11

APPENDIX, No. 87.

PAPER handed in by Mr. *E. H. Draper*, 14 July 1882.

SKINNERS COMPANY.

STATEMENT of ADVOWSON'S COMPENSATION ACCOUNT.

	£.	s.	d.	£.	s.	d.
April 1878.—Amount of Companies' proportion	-		-	4,334	10	7
Accrued interest on unapplied balance to 31st December 1880	-		-	1,444	2	3
Valuation, law charges, and law costs	294	13	8			
Grants:						
Dungiven Residence and Glebe	500	-	-			
Lower Cumber and Glebe	630	18	5			
Upper Cumber and Glebe	600	-	-			
Ballinascreen and Glebe	262	19	-			
Banagher and Glebe	300	-	-			
Donaghedy and Glebe	150	-	-			
Learmount and Glebe	300	-	-			
Dungiven Church Yard Wall	107	8	7			
Donaghedy New Church	100	-	-			
Lower Cumber Presbyterian Manse	200	-	-			
Upper Cumber Presbyterian Manse	200	-	-			
Dungiven Presbyterian Manse	200	-	-			
Draperstown Presbyterian Church	50	-	-			
Boveagh Presbyterian Church	50	-	-			
Brackfield Presbyterian Church	100	-	-			
Dungiven Roman Catholic Church	400	-	-			
Upper Cumber Presbyterian Church	105	-	-			
Dungiven Presbyterian Church	300	-	-			
Ballinascreen Church	125	-	-			
Dungiven Rectory House	40	-	-			
[illegible] Roman Catholic Church	75	-	-			
Banagher Roman Catholic Church	100	-	-			
Dungiven Meeting House	20	-	-			
Claudy Presbyterian Manse	10	-	-			
	5,473	14	-			
Balance unapplied	305	7	10			
£.	5,779	1	10	5,779	1	10

SUMMARY FOR SEVERAL DENOMINATIONS.

	£.	s.	d.
Episcopalian	3,195	-	9
Presbyterian	1,655	-	-
Roman Catholic	575	-	-
£.	5,425	-	9

18 June 1880.

APPENDIX No. [illegible]

PAPER handed in by the Clerk to the Salters' Company.

ACCOUNT of the RECEIPTS and EXPENDITURE in connection with the IRISH ESTATE of the SALTERS' COMPANY, from [illegible] May 1853 to 30th June 1889.

RECEIPTS.

YEAR.	Income derived from Rents and other Moneys Received in Ireland.	Sale of Land.	Rainey's School.	Money Borrowed.	Moneys Received in England from Sinking Fund, Invested, &c.
	£ s. d.	£ s. d.	£ s. d.	£ s. d.	£ s. d.
1853-1855 - -	14,[illegible] 3 11	1,000 - -	—	10,[illegible] - -	49 6 8
1855-1856 - - -	15,197 10 0	—	—	—	6,104 13 4
1856-1857 - - -	11,[illegible] 12 3	—	—	6,000 - -	1,863 10 -
1857-1858 - - -	14,763 16 4	—	—	4,[illegible] 9 8	867 10 11
1858-1859 - - -	12,[illegible] 4 8	470 - -	—	—	2,[illegible] 6 7
1859-1860 - - -	13,080 8 9	—	—	3,600 - -	800 - -
1860-1861 - - -	13,920 16 5	—	—	—	17 5 3
1861-1862 - - -	12,866 16 1	—	—	—	1,020 12 4
1862-1863 - - -	11,[illegible] 12 9	—	—	1,500 - -	[illegible] 5 2
1863-1864 - - -	13,805 4 11	—	—	1,450 11 -	—
1864-1865 - - -	13,[illegible] 14 -	—	—	2,500 - -	—
1865-1866 - - -	13,827 13 0	—	—	400 - -	—
1866-1867 - - -	10,843 14 8	—	—	300 - -	—
1867-1868 - - -	13,630 17 4	—	—	300 - -	—
1868-1869 - - -	14,719 19 1	—	146 14 8	—	—
1869-1870 - - -	13,219 2 10	—	157 6 6	700 - -	11 18 7
1870-1871 - - -	16,827 10 4	—	168 4 10	—	1,800 4 7
1871-1872 - - -	11,940 9 8	—	168 15 10	—	2,[illegible] 10 5
1872-1873 - - -	14,176 11 6	—	145 5 9	—	88 10 2
1873-1874 - - -	14,043 8 10	—	—	—	59 11 -
1874-1875 - - -	14,[illegible] 8 8	—	201 11 11	—	1,055 1 1
1875-1876 - - -	15,607 7 4	3,718 8 7	150 16 8	—	—
1876-1877 - - -	14,411 4 7	—	156 9 1	—	66 6 8
1877-1878 - - -	14,230 16 7	—	155 18 10	—	1,370 14 10
1878-1879 - - -	13,443 1 5	—	171 8 3	—	84 10 10
1879-1880 - - -	10,791 7 1	—	180 18 6	—	94 10 10
1880-1881 - - -	13,110 19 -	9 - -	150 - -	—	26 18 1
1881-1882 - - -	14,[illegible] - 6	400 - -	101 5 7	2,[illegible] - -	110 19 6
1882-1883 - - -	12,042 13 0	1,186 - -	190 4 8	—	19 - -
1883-1884 - - -	17,170 8 3	8,[illegible] 15 1	180 15 8	—	1,055 14 11
1884-1885 - - -	14,850 1 8	—	100 8 11	1,600 - -	8,341 11 5
Total Receipts to 30th June 1885 -	[illegible] 6 5	8,[illegible] 4 8	2,[illegible] 8 7	84,943 - 8	34,734 6 9
1885-1886 - - -	8,230 14 5	71,641 18 -	—	—	6 18 1
1886-1887 - - -	4,877 6 8	116,030 4 10	140 9 11	—	6,803 16 -
1887-1888 - - -	8,[illegible] 1 8	2,430 18 5	150 17 4	—	—
1888-1889 - - -	1,[illegible] 19 1	1,443 7 8	—	—	—
TOTAL - - - £.	[illegible] 11 9	[illegible] 9 8	2,[illegible] 9 10	84,943 - 8	[illegible] 10 10

SUMMARY.

	£. s. d.	£. s. d.	£. s. d.
The total income derived from rents and other moneys received in Ireland, was		[illegible] 11 9	
The total received from sales (not including [illegible] l. remaining on guarantee deposit), was		[illegible]	[illegible]
Miscellaneous Receipts, viz.:			
In respect of Ramsay's School		[illegible] 10	
Moneys borrowed		54,843 - 0	
Moneys received in connection with sinking fund		[illegible] 18 10	[illegible] 17 [illegible]
		TOTAL - - - £.	[illegible] 18 9
Charges on estate	50,409 [illegible]		
Interest on loans	15,629 15 5	[illegible] 11 [illegible]	
Loans repaid		54,843 - 0	
Management:			
Ireland	69,875 1 11		
England	31,446 - 7	101,321 2 6	
Improvements		42,684 3 4	
Charitable donations		41,213 15 10	[illegible] - 0
Miscellaneous receipts in connection with sinking fund			[illegible] 10 [illegible]
Distributed amongst associated companies			404,760 - -
		TOTAL - - - £.	[illegible] 18 9

	£.
The average annual income during the [illegible] years, from [illegible] to [illegible] ([illegible]) was	[illegible]
The average charges on estate, including interest on loans, during the same period ([illegible]) was	[illegible]
The average cost of management in Ireland during the same period ([illegible]) was	[illegible]
The average cost of management in England ([illegible]) was	[illegible]
The average amount spent in improvements ($\frac{41841}{[illegible]}$) was	[illegible]
The average amount spent in charitable donations ([illegible]) was	1,077
The average amount distributed amongst the associated companies ([illegible]) including proportion of [illegible] l. received from sales was	[illegible]
£.	[illegible]

APPENDIX, No. [illegible].

PAPER handed in by Mr. [illegible]

STATEMENT of Income and Disbursements of the [illegible] Estates belonging to the [illegible] Company, [illegible] of London, for the Years

	1881.		1882.		1883.		1884.	
	£ s. d.	£ s. d.	£ s. d.	£ s. d.	£ s. d.	£ s. d.	£ s. d.	£ s. d.
BALANCES brought up	—	—	—	[illegible]	—	[illegible]	—	[illegible]
(I.) INCOME	—	[illegible]	—	[illegible]	—	[illegible]	—	[illegible]
DISBURSEMENTS:								
(II.) [illegible]	[illegible]		[illegible]		[illegible]		[illegible]	
(III.) [illegible]	[illegible]		[illegible]		[illegible]		[illegible]	
(IV.) [illegible]	[illegible]		[illegible]		[illegible]		[illegible]	
(V.) [illegible]	[illegible]		[illegible]		[illegible]		[illegible]	
(VI.) [illegible]	—		—		—		—	
Balance carried forward	[illegible]		[illegible]		[illegible]		—	[illegible]
£	[illegible]	[illegible]	[illegible]	[illegible]	[illegible]	[illegible]	[illegible]	[illegible]

DETAILS of above TOTALS.

	1881.		1882.		1883.		1884.	
(I.) [illegible]	—	[illegible]	—	[illegible]	—	[illegible]	—	[illegible]
[illegible]	—	[illegible]	—	[illegible]	—	[illegible]	—	[illegible]
[illegible]	[illegible]	[illegible]	—	[illegible]	—	[illegible]	—	[illegible]
	—	[illegible]	—	[illegible]	[illegible]	[illegible]	—	[illegible]
(II.) [illegible]:								
[illegible]	[illegible]		[illegible]		[illegible]		[illegible]	
[illegible]	[illegible]		[illegible]		[illegible]		[illegible]	
[illegible]	[illegible]		[illegible]		[illegible]		[illegible]	
[illegible]	[illegible]		[illegible]		[illegible]		[illegible]	
[illegible]	[illegible]		[illegible]		[illegible]		[illegible]	
[illegible]	[illegible]		[illegible]		[illegible]		[illegible]	
[illegible]	[illegible]		—		—		—	
[illegible]	—	[illegible]	[illegible]	[illegible]	[illegible]	[illegible]	[illegible]	[illegible]
(III.) [illegible]:								
[illegible]	[illegible]		[illegible]		[illegible]		[illegible]	
[illegible]	[illegible]		[illegible]		[illegible]		[illegible]	
[illegible]	[illegible]		[illegible]		[illegible]		[illegible]	
[illegible]	[illegible]		[illegible]		[illegible]		[illegible]	
[illegible]	[illegible]		[illegible]		[illegible]		[illegible]	
[illegible]	[illegible]		[illegible]		[illegible]		[illegible]	
[illegible]	[illegible]		[illegible]		[illegible]		[illegible]	
[illegible]	[illegible]		[illegible]		[illegible]		[illegible]	
[illegible]	[illegible]		[illegible]		[illegible]		[illegible]	
[illegible]	[illegible]	[illegible]	[illegible]	[illegible]	[illegible]	[illegible]	[illegible]	[illegible]

* [illegible]

APPENDIX, No. [illegible]

PAPER handed in by Mr. [illegible] Esq.

and their Associates the Brewers', Scriveners', Pewterers', Barbers', and Carpenters' Companies, and the [illegible] ending 30th April 18[illegible] to 18[illegible] inclusive.

18[illegible]		1866.		1867.		18[illegible]		18[illegible]		18[illegible]		Average
£ s. d.	£ s. d.	£ s. d.	£ s. d.	£ s. d.	£ s. d.	£ s. d.	£ s. d.	£ s. d.	£ s. d.	£ s. d.	£ s. d.	£ s. d.
[illegible]	—	[illegible]	—	[illegible]	—	—	[illegible]	—	[illegible]	—	[illegible]	—
—	[illegible]	—	[illegible]	—	[illegible]	—	[illegible]	—	[illegible]	—	[illegible]	[illegible]
[illegible]		[illegible]		[illegible]		[illegible]		[illegible]		[illegible]		[illegible]

Numbered I., II., and III.

[illegible]
[illegible]

APPENDIX, No. 41.

PAPER handed in by the *Chairman*, [illegible] June 1890.

IRISH LAND COMMISSIONERS.

RETURN of the Loans (I.) Issued, and (II.) Sanctioned, but not paid under the Purchase of Land (Ireland) Acts, in respect of the Estates of the London Companies in the County of Londonderry, up to the 1st June 1890.

Company's Name.	I. Loans Issued.				II. Loans Sanctioned but not Paid.			
	Number of Loans.	Rental.	Price.	Amount of Loans Issued. (a)	Number of Loans.	Rental.	Price.	Amount of Loans Sanctioned. (b)
		£. s. d.	£.	£.		£. s. d.	£.	£.
The Salters' Company -	[illegible]	14,717 11 10	230,743	230,[illegible]	—	—	—	—
The Fishmongers' Company -	310	7,541 19 9	139,789	132,[illegible]	4	20 - -	[illegible]	[illegible]
The Skinners' Company -	[illegible]	7,[illegible] 5 7	132,125	132,125	75	676 18 -	13,[illegible]	13,[illegible]
The Drapers' Company -	321	6,[illegible] 7 6	[illegible]	[illegible]	94	1,[illegible] 18 5	[illegible]	[illegible]

(a) Where the whole of the purchase-money has not been advanced, the balance was provided by a cash payment by the tenant.

(b) The difference between the price agreed upon and the advance sanctioned is to be provided by cash payments by the tenant.

24, Upper Merrion-street, Dublin,
10 June 1890.

John H. Franks,
Secretary.

APPENDIX No. 42.

PAPER handed in by Mr. *[illegible]*, 19 June [illegible].

COUNTY LONDONDERRY.

ESTATE OF THE DRAPERS COMPANY.

The Brackaghslievegallion division of this estate, comprising about [illegible] acres, lies on the eastern slope of the Slievegallion range of mountains.

The farms referred to in this report are scattered over this division at distances from the village of Moneymore of from two to seven miles; they are, with very few exceptions, situated in the higher part of the district, which is generally steep and rugged, seamed with mountain streams, which cut ravines and glens through the gravel slopes forming the base of the range.

The soil varies; in some places it is a light gravelly loam, in others a stiff clay, interspersed with places of mossy land, steep banks of gravel and clay, while the highest parts are bog, heath, and mountain pasture.

Most of these farms lie at an elevation of between [illegible] and [illegible] feet; they are small in extent, and almost wholly under tillage, oats, potatoes, and flax being the principal crops. They are generally well fenced and well watered; the access to many is steep and bad.

The turbary on this part of the estate is almost exhausted; the want of fuel will be a serious loss to these small farms; many of the tenants procure turf from a great distance; the carriage of coal to the more remote farms would be costly and difficult, and the fireplaces are not adapted to its use.

Nearly all the houses are thatched, and many of them are very bad.

The cattle on these farms are inferior, and badly fed; the tenants, with few exceptions, seem to be poor and struggling.

The poor rates are low, varying from 7*d.* to 10*d.* in the £, according to the electoral division.

I consider the prices in nearly every case are in excess of what it would be prudent to lend.

A very serious consideration arises in connection with these contracts. They appear to me to have been entered into by the tenants under duress and intimidation of the most pronounced character.

In order to answer the Commissioners' queries I examined the rent receipts of the tenants. Very large arrears of rent were due in almost every instance in [illegible], and most of the farms were under eviction when the agreements were signed.

I think it was not unnatural that since [illegible] rents should have been badly paid on small hillside farms so disadvantageously situated as most of these are. The rents were very high, and arrears accumulated to a very large amount.

Suddenly most energetic proceedings for their recovery were instituted; processes and ejectments were served; caretakers' notices were served on the tenants, and decrees placed in the sheriff's hands for execution.

The tenants now hold receipts for rent and interest up to November [illegible], but the amounts stated in these receipts were not paid. The receipts were given in consideration of the tenants signing agreements to buy the farms which were under eviction at the time, and the sums for which receipts were given were included in the prices of the farms, having been added to the prices demanded by the company in the first instance, and refused by the tenants, until they were coerced by the proceedings stated above to sign the agreements.

On the greater number of these farms judicial rents had been fixed by the county court judge before the agreements to buy were signed, but the old rents, not the legal rents, are those stated in the agreements. This fact alone presents the contract to the Commissioners in a very fallacious aspect. The instalments on the purchase-money would in many cases be in excess of the fair rents fixed.

It is possible that some of these judicial rents have not been notified to the Land Commission, but I assume that they were fixed in all cases where I was so informed, as in many instances the tenants produced newspapers giving the reports of the county court judgments.

I refer also to the printed return of judicial rents (C. [illegible]), p. [illegible]; the fair rents for 16 farms in the townland of [illegible] appear there, and correspond with those stated by the tenants. It will be seen that the old rents are those stated in the agreements to buy.

Example.—Application No. [illegible]. Francis [illegible]:

	£	s.	d.
Rent in agreement - - - - - - - - - - - -	6	–	–

This tenant holds two receipts from Messrs. Glover and McGuckin, dated 14th January 18[illegible]. No money having however been paid.

(1.) For 6*l.* 6*s.*, two years' interest on his purchase-money of [illegible]*l.*

(2.) For three years' rent to 1st November 1885 :—

	£ s. d.	£ s. d.
Rent		16 – –
Poor rate	– 10 2	
Abatement	6 14 –	
		7 4 2
		8 15 10
Costs		3 5 3
		£. 12 1 1

Application No. 2,8[illegible]. Hugh McGuckin.

	£ s. d.
Rent by agreement	6 5 –
Price by agreement	[illegible] – –
Judicial rent	5 5 –
Price stated in receipts	116 10 –

Receipts dated [illegible] January 18[illegible] :

(1.) For 7*l.*, two years' interest to 1st November 188[illegible], on 116*l.* 10*s.*

(2.) For three years' rent to 1st November 1885 :—

	£ s. d.
Rent	18 15 –
Abatement	7 16 –
	10 19 –
Costs	3 1 –
	£. 14 – –

The tenants have paid considerable sums by way of costs in connection with these legal proceedings, and they appear to me to be in the most extreme terror of the company's solicitors, Messrs. Glover and McGuckin, of Magherafelt. I was entreated by some not to mention to these gentlemen that they had showed me their receipts or agreements, and in the cases first visited, which I thought were probably exceptions, the tenants refused to let me have their receipts lest I should make any use of them to their injury with Messrs. Glover and McGuckin.

The tenants seem to be, without exception, under the apprehension that if the sale is not carried out they can be sued for the amounts for which they hold receipts, but which they did not really pay.

There are cases on this division where agreements to buy have not yet been signed, because the tenants are not in arrear, and refuse to sign agreements in which the old rents are set out, the real issue being whether they are to pay [illegible] times the old rent or [illegible] times the judicial rent.

My statements as to the legal proceedings, arrears, and the manner in which they were satisfied, can be vouched by the production of the tenants' receipts, and the ejectments served upon them, if the Commissioners so desire. I append the receipts in the case of Application No. 2,5[illegible] as an example.

In one case only is the rent in agreement a judicial rent, viz., Application 2,9[illegible], and this is stated to be a tenancy from year to year, held at this rent since 18[illegible]. The price is [illegible] times the rent.

I conclude from my examination of these cases that these contracts were obtained by intimidation and undue influence; that they were entered into under duress; that they are presented to the Commissioners in a misleading aspect by the omission or concealment of the judicial rents, and by the inclusion in the price of arrears and costs for which the tenants hold receipts.

If the Commissioners are satisfied that the facts are as I have stated, I venture to suggest that they should give publicity to the facts of this case, and their opinion of them. It would be very prejudicial to the operation of the Purchase Acts in the North of Ireland that tenants should think that loans could be obtained under such circumstances to [illegible], or that landlords, agents, or solicitors should procure the signature of contracts by such means.

I desire to draw particular attention to the contracts numbered 2,8[illegible] and 2,9[illegible].

No. 2,8[illegible] purports to have been signed by Patrick Kane, in presence of A. W. Glover. I am informed that Patrick Kane has been in America for the last four years.

No. 2,9[illegible] purports to have been signed by the tenant, Rose M'Bride, in presence of the same witness. Rose M'Bride, the tenant, is an old feeble woman; she informs me that she has been unable to leave her house for a long time, and that it was her son Patrick who signed the agreement, the farm being under ejectment for four years' rent, due to 1888, at the time.

6 May 1889. *Murrough O'Brien.*

APPENDIX, No. [illegible]

PAPER handed in by the Chairman, [illegible] June 18[illegible]

Irish Land Commission, Dublin
[illegible] June 18[illegible]

Sir,

I am directed by the Irish Land Commissioners to acknowledge the receipt of your letter dated the 19th instant and to transmit herewith the enclosed copies of forms of application:—

I.—That directed to be used at the time of Mr. Commissioner Lynch's Judgment of the [illegible] February, 18[illegible].

II.—That now in use.

Rule No. 6 of the 5th December 18[illegible], which is as follows:—

> 6. Agreements between landlord and tenant for the sale and purchase of a holding shall be in Form No. 1, with such variations as may from time to time be directed. All such agreements shall be on stout [illegible] foolscap paper, and endorsed with the record number, title of the matter, county, and tenant's name, and shall be signed by both landlord and tenant or some person acting under a power of attorney on their behalf, and bear an Inland Revenue stamp or stamps to the value of sixpence, which must be cancelled according to law.
>
> No such agreement shall be received after the expiration of two months from the date of the execution thereof by the tenant unless by leave of a Commissioner,

prescribed the use of Form No. 2, on which is a direction as to the statement of the tenant's tenure.

Up to the 1st November 18[illegible], Rule No. 55, which is as follows, relating to the payment of rent on the completion of sale, was in force,—

> 55. Before signing any vesting order or making any advance, the Commissioners shall be satisfied that the tenant's rent up to the last gale day has been paid, satisfied, or released; but the agreement may provide for the payment of interest on the purchase-money pending the completion of the sale:

but in consequence of vendors allowing claims for interest to hang over until after advances had been made, the rule was rescinded, and the following rule was substituted:—

> 1. Before making any advance, the Irish Land Commission shall be satisfied that the tenant's rent up to the gale day immediately preceding the making such advance, and any interest payable upon the purchase-money, over and above one-half year's interest, has been paid, satisfied, or released.

This rule was not made with special reference to the sales of the Drapers' Company, but their sales were pending at the time.

Section 3 of the Land Purchase Amendment Act (30th December 18[illegible]), modified this rule, leaving operative only the part relating to interest.

I am, &c.
(Signed) *John H. Franks.*

W. More Molyneux, Esq.,
House of Commons.

subject to the outgoings in the said Schedule mentioned, at the price of £

which sum is to include all expenses incidental to the purchase. (d)

(e) *The balance of the purchase-money is to be paid as follows:—*

By a Cash Payment by the Tenant to the Landlord of £

By a Mortgage bearing £ per cent. Interest, for £

In case the Irish Land Commission shall sanction the said Advance the said Tenant shall, from the date of this Agreement, discharge all outgoings and pay to the said Landlord Interest at the rate of £ (e) per cent. per annum on his purchase-money or the part thereof remaining unpaid, until the same shall be paid or advanced to or for the benefit of the Landlord, such Interest to be payable half yearly, and the first payment to be made at the expiration of six months from the date hereof, unless the said purchase-money shall have been so previously paid or advanced.

(f) The said [illegible] will when called upon provide a Guarantee Deposit [illegible] being not less than one-fifth of the price of the said Holding.

(g) The Sale shall be carried out by means of a

The lodgment of this Agreement with the Irish Land Commission is to be deemed an application by the Tenant for an advance pursuant to the Land Law (Ireland) Acts, to be repaid by an annuity of £ per cent. for each £100 (and so in proportion for any less sum) for 49 years, commencing from the first succeeding gale-day after making such advance together with interest at the rate of 3¼ per cent. from the date of the advance until such gale-day.

SCHEDULE.—DESCRIPTION OF HOLDING.

County of Townland of

Barony of No. of holding on Map

Nature of Estate which the Landlord offers to sell to his Tenant (x)	Contents of Holding. Statute Measure.	Poor Law Valuation.	Rent Paid by Tenant	Tenure of Tenant. (y)	Annual outgoings (if any) subject to which Holding is to be sold	
	A. R. P.	£ s. d.	£ s. d.			£ s. d.
					Quit or Crown Rent.	
					Tithe rent-charge.	
					Lay Tithe-Rent-rent.	
					Drainage or Land Improvement Charge.	

(x) Whether Fee simple, under Fee farm Grant, or Lease, and if the latter, for what term.

(y) Whether from year to year, or under judicial tenancy, or under Fee-farm Grant (giving the date) or Lease (giving the date) and term.

In case the said Advance shall be refused by the Irish Land Commission this Agreement shall be null and void.

Signature of Landlord,

Postal Address,

Signature of Tenant,

Postal Address,

I have witnessed the said Tenant signing as above (and *I certify the above Application has been read and explained to him in my presence*).

Witness to sign here—

I, the before-named Tenant make oath and say, as follows:—

1. That the particulars stated in the foregoing Schedule are true to the best of my knowledge and belief.

2. I reside on and have in the occupation of the said holding, and paying the rent therefor since the Year 18 and I hold the same as Tenant as in the Schedule stated (and the said (h) is in my possession*).

3. There is not any person in occupation of the said holding as Tenant or otherwise save as mentioned in the following Schedule:—

(*f*) Schedule containing particulars of under tenancies, if any existing on the holding.

Names of the Persons in Occupation as Under Tenants.	Area in Statute Measure.	Rent (if any) Payable by each Occupier.	When Payable.	Tenure.
	A. R. P.	£ s. d.		

4. There is not any charge or incumbrance affecting any interest in the said holding save those specified in the following Schedule:—

Schedule containing particulars of Mortgages, Charges created by decrees of Loans or otherwise, or Charges to the Commissioners of Public Works in Ireland affecting the Tenant's interest in the Holding.

Date.	Name and Address of Incumbrancer.	Particulars of Incumbrance, Mortgage or otherwise.	Principal Sum Due.
			£ s. d.

5. I have not obtained from or (except by this Agreement) applied to the Irish Land Commission for an advance of any sum for the purchase of any land.

If the Deponent be a Marksman the words in italics are to be inserted.

SWORN before me the day of 18
at in the County of
and I know the Deponent, *the same having been first truly read and explained by me to him and he appearing to understand the same.*

Persons to whom communications on behalf of the Landlord are to be addressed:—

Name, Address,

Persons to whom communications on behalf of the Tenant are to be addressed:—

Name, Address,

— II. —

Agreement for Sale between Landlord and Tenant.

COURT OF THE IRISH LAND COMMISSION.

[illegible]

An Agreement made the day of 18
between
of , the Landlord of the holding
described in first part of the Schedule hereto, and
of , the Tenant in occupation of the said holding.

1. In case the Irish Land Commission shall advance the sum of £ to the said Tenant for the purchase of the said holding, the said Landlord will sell and the said Tenant will purchase the same, (*a*)

2. *The balance of the purchase money is to be paid as follows:—*

By a Cash Payment by the Tenant to the Landlord of £.

By a Mortgage bearing £. per Cent. Interest, for £.

3. In case the Irish Land Commission shall sanction the said Advance, the said Tenant shall, from the date of the Agreement, discharge all outgoings and pay to the said Landlord Interest at the rate of £. (*b*) per cent. per annum on his purchase money or the part thereof remaining unpaid, until the same shall be paid or advanced to or for the benefit of the Landlord, such interest to be payable half-yearly, and the first payment to be made at the expiration of six months from the date hereof, unless the said purchase money shall have been so previously paid or advanced.

4. The said will when called upon provide a Guarantee Deposit of £. being not less than one-fifth of the price of the said Holding.

5. The Sale shall be carried out by means of a (*c*)

6. The Lodgment of this Agreement with the Irish Land Commission is to be deemed an application by the tenant for an advance pursuant to the "Land Law (Ireland) Acts," to be repaid by an annuity of £. 4 for each £. 100 (and so in proportion for any less sum) for 49 years, commencing from the first statutory gale day after making such advance, together with interest at the rate of 2½ per cent. from the date of the advance until such gale day.

7. In case the said advance shall be refused by the Irish Land Commission this Agreement shall be null and void.

SCHEDULE.

Insert concise statement of the Estate to be sold by the Landlord to the Tenant: *i.e., either Fee Simple, (or) the interest under Fee-Farm Grant dated the day of 18 , (or) the interest under Lease dated the day of 18, for years.*		*County of* *Barony of*

Reference to Map.	Ordnance Survey Names of Townlands (each on a Separate Line).	Area Statute Measure of the Portion of each Townland to be Sold.	Tenement Valuation.	Rent paid by Tenant.	Tenure of Tenant; whether from Year to Year, or under Judicial Tenancy, or under Fee-Farm Grant (*giving date*), or under Lease (*giving date and term*).
		A. R. P.		£ s. d.	
		First Part.—Description of Holding.			
Second Part.—Additional Land sold under the "Purchase of Land (Ireland) Amendment Act, 1889."					
				N.B.—These lands must not exceed 10 acres contain[illegible] unless the tenement valuation be £. 10 or under. If the lands are not separately valued the apportioned valuation should be given.	

Signature of Landlord,

Postal Address,

Signature of Tenant,

Postal Address,

I have witnessed the said Tenant signing as above (*and I certify the above application has been read and explained to him in my presence*).

Witness to sign here—

I, , the before-named Tenant, make oath and say, as follows:—

1. That the particulars stated in the foregoing Schedule are true to the best of my knowledge and belief.

2. I reside on, and have been in the occupation of the said holding, and paying the rent therefor, since the year 18 , and I hold the same as Tenant as in the said Schedule is stated, (and the said (*d*) is in my possession).

3. There is not any person in occupation of the said holding as Tenant or otherwise save as mentioned in following Schedule:—

Names of the Persons in Occupation as Undertenants or otherwise.	Area in Statute Measure.	Rent (if any) Payable by such Occupiers.	When Payable.	Tenure or Nature of Occupancy.
	a. r. p.	£ s. d.		

If there are no undertenants, fill in the word "none," where applied.

4. There is not any charge or incumbrance affecting my interest in the said holding save those specified in the following Schedule:—

Schedule containing particulars of Mortgages, Charges created by deposit of Lease or otherwise, or Charges in favour of the Commissioners of Public Works in Ireland affecting the Tenant's interest in the Holding:

Date.	Name and Address of Incumbrancer.	Particulars of Incumbrance, Mortgage or otherwise.	Principal Sum Due.
			£ s. d.

If there are no incumbrances fill in the word "none," where applied.

5. I have not obtained from or (except by this Agreement) applied to the Irish Land Commission for an advance of any sum for the purchase of any land.*

* If the tenant has previously applied for any loan write "save a loan of £ ..." giving the particulars.

The words in italics may be struck out unless the Deponent be a Marksman.

† Name by whom.

SWORN before me this day of 18
at
in the County of and I know the Deponent,
the whole of the foregoing Agreement and affidavit having been first read over to
the said
by† *and*
the said *appeared*
perfectly to understand the same, and made h mark thereto in my presence.

If the Tenant wishes to be represented in the Proceedings by a Solicitor, here insert the name and address of such Solicitor:—

Name *Address*

Directions as to the Preparation of the Agreement and Affidavit.

The Agreement and Affidavit must be fairly and accurately prepared, without any blanks, and all clauses not applicable to the case must be struck out, otherwise the agreement cannot be received.

When females are parties to the Agreement they must be described either as "spinster," "widow," or "wife of A.B."

The price, the advance, and the guarantee deposit must be in pounds only.

When it is intended that the Tenant shall bear the costs of his Conveyance or Vesting Order the words "*which sum is to include all expenses incidental to the purchase*" should be struck out.

Clause 1. When additional land is being sold under the "Purchase of Land (Ireland) Amendment Act, 1889," insert at (a) "together with the additional land specified in the second part of the said schedule." Here also insert any rights of grazing, or turbary, or other rights to be included in the sale, which are exercised over lands not included in the Tenant's holding, e.g. "together with such right of grazing and cutting turf as has heretofore been exercised by the said Tenant upon the bog on the lands of *Blackacre* in the possession of the said Landlord; (*or if the bog be demised*) in the occupation of A.B." When the lands sold are held by the Landlord under Fee-Farm Grant or Lease, any exceptions or reservations in such Grant or Lease should be here excepted, though the head rent is to be redeemed. When it is intended that any rights of turbary, or grazing, are to be exercised over the holding by persons other than the Tenant, they should be concisely but specifically preserved; e.g. "subject to the rights of A.B. and C.D., tenants on *Blackacre*, [or] of the remaining tenants upon the lands of *Blackacre*, to cut turf for their own consumption, but not for sale upon the bog on the said holding, [*or if the portion be defined*] upon that part of the said holding coloured brown on the Map, and to such right of entry as is incidental thereto." Also if the holding is to be sold subject to any annual outgoing theretofore paid by the Landlord, the fact should be here specified, *but the redemption of all outgoings will facilitate the sale.*

If the advance is of the whole purchase money strike out Clause 2.

If the advance does not exceed three-fourths of the purchase money strike out Clause 4.

The Agreement must be signed by both Landlord and Tenant or by some person acting under power of attorney. An attorney should sign thus, "A.B. by C.D. acting under power of Attorney." Trustees, or *limited owners selling under the provisions of the "Settled Land Act, 1882," must themselves sign the agreement.*

The person administering the affidavit should not be the Landlord, his agent or solicitor, or the Tenant's Solicitor.

APPENDIX, No. 44.

PAPER handed in by Mr. *Murrough O'Brien.*

Before Mr. Commissioner *Lynch*, 31st day of July 1888.

In the Matter of the Estate of the Drapers' Company. Brackaghreagilliam and Ballynascreen Divisions.

JUDGMENT.

[illegible]

[illegible]

[illegible]

[illegible]

[illegible]

[illegible]

company refused to accede to, and in order to prevent any misunderstanding as to the terms of sale, and having regard to the tenants' convention, it was considered better to insert the rent of [illegible], leaving it open to the company when the inspector came round to explain the matter to him by a statement in the form now used." It was stated voluntarily by Mr. John Glover, when he was examined before me last Friday, that this course was adopted by the direction of the company. I can only say that if this direction was given to the company, it was a most improper one; it was a course which the solicitors should have refused to follow at the suggestion of their client, and that they should never have allowed tenants, many of them illiterate, to verify these agreements, which it now appears are false in this material respect. Assume the case of any ordinary mortgage. The owner of an estate is seeking for a loan, he furnishes a rental to the mortgagee as evidence of value, and he verifies it by a declaration. What would be said if he inserted in that rental, instead of the existing judicial rents, former rents which were 20 or 25 per cent. higher. And this is what was done in the present cases, leaving it to our officer to discover the suppression (or the company to volunteer) the explanation now given. They say they sold at 18 years' purchase on a former rent. In the first place the purchase-money named in many of the agreements is not 18 times the rent, but a great deal more, the figures being now explained by the tacking on of arrears; but in the next place we don't ask to be told the number of years' purchase; 18 years' purchase of one rent might be a very high rate, while 25 years' purchase of another rent might be moderate. What we do require to know is the existing rent, and how it has been created, and the capital sum which the landlord and tenant have mutually agreed upon as the price to be paid by the tenant for the landlord's interest, and it is then for us to satisfy ourselves as to the sufficiency of the security, and it matters not to us the number of years' purchase within which the prices may range, provided the contract be a free one, and that the State has ample security for the money we are asked to advance. I can only say that in my opinion these agreements have been most improperly prepared in violation of our rules, and that they cannot be now regarded as agreements upon which advances might be made.

I turn now to the manner in which the purchase-money in many of the cases was made up, and which the solicitors of the company explain thus; I read from their letter: "The small sums on account of rent added to the purchase-money in a number of cases were added at the request of the tenants in order, as they said, to leave in their hands a larger working capital, and in any case the small sums so added do not, the company believe, affect the security of the Government." I shall give a case taken at random by way of illustration. No. 2014. Rent in agreement, 8*l.* 8*s.*; price in agreement, 157*l.*, that is nearly 18½ years' purchase on the rents. A receipt was given to the tenant for 7*l.*, two years' interest on 113*l.* at 10*s.*, which was entered in the receipt as interest on the purchase-money; a further receipt was given for three years' rent to 1st November 1887, 26*l.* 15*s.*, less 7*l.* 16*s.* abatement, leaving 18*l.* 19*s.*; to this was added 3*l.* 1*s.* 6*d.* costs, making 14*l.* - *s.* 6*d.*, which with 7*l.* for interest makes 21*l.*, which they added to 113*l.* and they produce a purchase-money of 157*l.*, on which the annuity would be 6*l.* 5*s.* 4*d.*, as against a judicial rent of 5*l.* 5*s.* fixed by the county court judge before the agreement was signed.

I am not now discussing the question of sufficiency of security nor the liberality or otherwise of the company in their dealings with their tenants, but assuming that the security was sufficient and that the tenants entered into these contracts freely and voluntarily, knowing their legal obligations and their rights, I say that these unfounded manipulations of facts and figures culminating in the presentation to us of the agreements now before me, and which are the basis of our proceedings, do not commend themselves to my approval.

When these facts came before me I called for further information as to the agreements in the Ballinascreen division; of the circumstances of that estate I know nothing except that it appears that, in 60 out of 152 cases, the same course was adopted as to judicial rents, while in 104 of these arrears of rent or interest or costs were added to the price arranged, and that the company's solicitors are of opinion that a large number of these agreements were signed to delay payment of rent and without any *bona fide* intention of carrying out the purchase. I do not refer to a petition sent to me by about 50 of the tenants represented by Mr Malone, solicitor of Cookstown, and in which

are alleged, nor do I refer to the circular which was issued by the company's solicitor to these tenants and the alternatives therein offered. These are matters which would have to be considered, and proved if the validity of these agreements came to be questioned before me. I have, however, no hesitation in coming to the conclusion that the proper course for me to adopt is to refuse to proceed further on these agreements. I am most anxious that every tenant on the Drapers' Company's Estate who desires to purchase his holding should have every facility from me to purchase, but the agreements to that end, which are the basis of our jurisdiction, must be free from irregularity or taint, and they must be freely and voluntarily entered into. Let the parties here, between this and October, consider their position; let them consult their own solicitors; let them negotiate with the company, whose liberal intentions I do not question, and let new agreements in proper form and approved by their solicitors be signed at such prices as may be arranged, and the sales can then, if we be satisfied as to security, be rapidly closed by proceeding by vesting order and under the 15th Section of the Act, 1887.

We have nothing to say with the [illegible] arrangements as to arrears where they exist. Tenants who have allowed their rents to go into arrear should not seek to use those arrears as a lever to obtain more favourable terms than their thrifty and honest brother tenants who met, to the best of their ability, their just obligations. Uniform rates of purchase as to number of years often produce very inequitable results; each case should be dealt with upon its own merits. There should, on the one hand, be no withholding of rents by the tenants to coerce landlords to sell; nor, on the other, should the existence of arrears which the tenants may be unable to pay, either in the whole or in part, be used by the landlord as a lever to compel the tenant to purchase upon his terms.

The liberal terms upon which Parliament has enabled us to advance the whole purchase-money to tenants leave plenty of room for the adjustment of outstanding obligations which are capable of being met and for the compromise of existing differences. Let the parties on this estate negotiate as landlords and tenants have negotiated in the thousands of cases which we have already closed; let them come to us with a clean bill of health and they will find us prepared to do our part as to any tenants on the Brackaslievegallion division in which there is no irregularity in the form of agreement, and in which we provisionally sanctioned the advance applied for. I shall be prepared to entertain an application on their behalf to have the benefit of my order in the Moneymore division.

APPENDIX, No. 43.

PAPER handed in by the Chairman.

Mr. Commissioner Lynch's Judgment. Moneymore Division.

[illegible]

letters received from the clerk of the company, that they would not be required to pay rent or interest beyond the amount due for rent to 1st November 1885. It is alleged that in August 1886, Mr. Sawyer wrote, that "the terms were to be 18 years' purchase on the rent, all rent to 1st November 1885 to be paid in cash, and no rent to be demanded after that date;" and that in January 1887 he wrote to the effect that, "as the terms were agreed, purchasing tenants will be called upon to pay neither rent nor interest from 1st November 1885."

Subsequently, circulars were sent to the tenants demanding the rents due to 1st November 1886, saying, "your deed cannot be sealed till this rent is paid," but interest was not referred to. I refer to these matters not as in any way impugning the legal right of the company to the interest they had received; these rights were established by judgment of a court of law; but I mention them as showing that the tenants appear to have been unprepared for these demands, which, coming upon them as the accumulated amounts collected at the eleventh hour, have in many instances had to be met by sales of stock necessary for their farms, or by borrowing on short loans at interest. It was in this state of things that I made the ruling of 16th April, which I am now asked to vary. Mr. Venables has put the case of the tenants with great ability, and with moderation and perfect candour; he admitted the great advantages which the Moneymore tenants would obtain by purchasing at the advances we sanctioned; he told us that the great majority of the tenants on his division are thriving and industrious, and he gave instances of the very high rates at which tenants' interests have sold in that district, and the reports which I have received from our inspectors fully confirm his statements. He admits, on the other hand, that there are a good many of those tenants who have been and are in straitened circumstances; these are improvident persons, to be found amongst all classes; but there are others who, through no fault of theirs, were not so well able in the end to battle with adverse seasons and markets, who were in arrear in November 1886, and, who have had to pay those arrears, with costs and interest and who have been crippled by their effort to make these payments, or who have still hanging over them, as appears by this Schedule, the balance of their indebtedness. But Mr. Venables urges upon me the alternative offered by Mr. Glover's circular of 17th June; if the door is closed the completion of these sales might result in ruin to some of these tenants by reverting them to the position of [illegible] tenants for rent with only credit for the payments they had made since May 1887.

While, therefore, I shall make no advance in any case where I believe our security for the punctual payment of the instalments, which under the order I now propose to make would accrue due on the 1st May next, may be weakened, I am prepared to rescind this ruling of 16th April so as to enable those who have paid or are prepared to pay the interest to which the company are entitled, to settle with the company by the 1st October, so as to have their conveyances completed and the advances closed by the 31st October next; their indebtedness to us would in such cases commence from 1st November.

Without, however, casting any doubt upon the admissions of the company in regard of those tenants who are returned in this Schedule as largely in arrear and whose straitened circumstances are known to me and are admitted by the company, as I believe, I shall require that the terms of settlement, whether by remission or payment, in such cases shall be made known to me by the 1st of October, so that I may consider these cases apart from the rest. There are besides, as indicated in our letter of the 4th May to which Mr. Venables referred, some 20 or 25 cases in which, having regard to existing condition of the tenants, I shall require a special deposit as security for the payment of the early instalments, and to this, as I understand, the company are willing to agree.

These Moneymore sales if they are now to go on must be closed before 1st November, and to that end the drafts must be lodged not later than the 1st October, and I shall rely upon Mr. Venables, as acting for the tenants, to see that this order is carried out. He should apprise us of the arrangements, and where there have been deaths or changes of occupancy, make timely provision of the completion of the conveyances in such cases.

I assume, of course, that there are no outstanding claims by the company or their solicitors for costs which are not included in the sums returned as still due by the tenants in this Schedule. If there were such and they have not been already settled, I shall require that the particulars be given to me, so that I may consider such cases with the exceptional ones.

APPENDIX, No. [illegible].

PAPER handed in by Mr. [illegible] [illegible] June [illegible].

COURT OF THE IRISH LAND COMMISSION.

In the matter of the Estate of the Drapers' Company of London - - Owners.

The undersigned and others - - - - - - - - - - - Tenants.

To the Land Purchase Commissioners.

Gentlemen,

We, the undersigned tenants of the Ballynascreen and Brackaghreagh[illegible] portions of the Drapers' Estate, in the county of Londonderry, humbly beg to submit to your consideration the terms of purchase and circumstances under which the tenants of this division have been forced to sign agreements to buy out their holdings from the Drapers' Company. We do this in order that you, as public servants of the Government, may be able while there is yet time to judge of the security the Company are offering you for the enormous advances of cash you are called upon to make to them out of the funds allotted to you for the purposes of the Purchase of Land (Ireland) Acts, 1885–87. We do this also in order that you may have a clear knowledge of the facts, and be able to judge of the probable consequences, before approving of these purchases, and if the tenants, by force of circumstances, which it is very easy to foresee are sure to occur, in the course of a very short time shall not be able to fulfil their obligations to the State, they are not to be told the fault is their own, and that they entered into their engagements voluntarily and with their eyes open, or with a fraudulent intention of never fulfilling them.

In the year 188[illegible] the Drapers' Company offered their estate for sale to the tenants at a price of 1[illegible] years' purchase upon the rental as it then stood, the arrears to be paid up. About one-third of the tenants who live on the flat and fertile lands in the district of Moneymore, and scarcely any of whom were in arrear of rent, then agreed to purchase at the Company's terms. The remaining two-thirds, on whose behalf this petition is humbly presented, and who live in a wild, rugged, mountain district, were all in considerable arrear of rent, averaging from [illegible] to five years, and in a state of extreme poverty.

Their land is not one-fourth the value of that in the Moneymore district, and was rack-rented to an extent which the tenants were absolutely unable to meet. In order to force these tenants on the Draperstown portion of the estate to fall into line with the tenants on the Moneymore division, and buy out on the same terms as others, Messrs. Glover and M'Guskin, solicitors for the Company, issued [illegible] ejectment processes for non-payment of rent against them in the month of October 1887, and in January 188[illegible] and obtained in all these cases decrees; [illegible] of these tenants served notices, under the provisions of the Land Law Act, 1887, to have fair rents fixed before John O. Hallignn, Esq., Q.C., Recorder of Londonderry, and at the time the ejectment decrees were obtained they got an average reduction of [illegible] per cent., and then offered the Company 1[illegible] years' purchase on the judicial rents as fixed by the Recorder. The Drapers' Company refused this offer, and insisted upon selling upon the basis of the old and impossible rents.

In order to coerce the tenants into buying out at the old rents, the law agents for the Company then served upon about [illegible] of the tenants of the Draperstown division notices of eviction, under the seventh section of the Land Act, 1887, and subsequently brought summonses in the petty sessions of Draperstown, and obtained warrants for possession against the greater number of these tenants. Besides these ejectment proceedings, ordinary civil bills for "use and occupation" were issued against all the tenants against whom ejectment decrees had been obtained in October 1887, and ordinary civil bills were also served in January 188[illegible] for the year's rent of 1887. These latter numbered about 1[illegible]0, and there were thus two sets of decrees, with the necessary costs in each, against nearly all the tenants.

In November 188[illegible] the sheriff, with bailiffs, horses, and carts, came out amongst the tenantry, and seized under the ordinary civil bill decrees, and took all the chattels they could obtain from the tenants for the purpose of satisfying them, and in the next month, December 188[illegible], Mr. Glover, solicitor for the Company, came with the sheriff, emergency men, battering ram, and all the other resources of the law, to carry out evictions, after the tenants had been left almost destitute by the execution of the civil bill decrees for rent. The tenants were then driven to one of two alternatives: to sign the agreements to purchase at the terms dictated by the Company, and add the arrears of rent to the purchase-money and pay up all the costs; or leave for the workhouse. Rather than adopt the latter course, they signed the agreements which you are now called upon to approve. They were forced to pay costs, varying in most cases from [illegible] to [illegible], and nearly all the tenants have lost any credit they required to have, and were unable to meet this emergency. Those, however, who could either beg or borrow, by that means strove to bridge over the difficulty, and stave off the day of eviction.

We verily believe that we shall not be able to carry out the contracts made in this manner, and upon these terms. We humbly submit these facts to you, and if you consider the security good enough, and that you are justified under the circumstances in approving of the purchases, then do so. The future will condemn or justify the act.

About [illegible] years ago, before the tenants had any recognised interest in their holdings, the Company were in the habit of advancing sums of money, varying with the value of the holdings, to the tenants for the purposes of making permanent improvements by way of buildings, &c., and the interest upon these advances was charged in the books of the Company, and in the books of the Company alone, as interest, and added to the rent of the tenants' holdings. It appeared from then to this, upon the receipts given to the tenants, as rent, not interest. At the last January quarter sessions, held in Magherafelt, the Company brought, as a test case, against one of these tenants, a process to recover the amount advanced and spent by the tenant upon improving his holding [illegible] years ago. A judicial rent had been fixed in this case about four years ago, and at that time the Company actually relied upon this advance as a reason why the rent should not be reduced. They did not then put it forward as a loan upon which interest had been paid, but when before the Sub-commissioners they treated the advance as money spent by the landlord upon improvements, to the benefit of which the tenant would not be legally entitled. The Commission, the Company, and the tenant recognised the yearly amount payable by the tenant as rent, and upon this basis the Commission fixed the judicial rent. A decree was granted at the quarter sessions, and the decision has been appealed against; but

(signed) Henry O'Neill.
Richard Morgan.
James Connery.
Andrew Hagan.
Ellen Brown.
Patrick Bradley.
Alexander M'Keown.
Peter M'Keown.
Patrick Kennedy.
Patrick M'Gough.
Cortis Cassidy.
John Connery.
Michael Gallagher.
Patrick Hagan.
Patrick Bradley.
James Brown.

John M'Bell.
Pat Connery.
James M'[illegible].
Pat M'Glade.
James Quigley.
James Murphy.
James M'Elhenny.
John Higgins.
Daniel M'Keown.
Thomas Connery.
Patrick M'Keown.
John M'Keown.
James Russell.
Christopher M'Geown.
Bernard M'Williams.

APPENDIX No. [illegible].

PAPER handed in by Mr. M. O'Brien, [illegible] June 18[illegible].

REPORT made as to Cases delayed by Drapers' Company.

County Derry.

ESTATE OF THE DRAPERS' COMPANY.

In compliance with directions in Mr. Commissioner Lynch's Minute of 3rd April 1889, I have visited the farms on the townlands referred to in the schedule.

I find the tenants all most anxious to have the matter closed, and the sales completed without further delay. They are thoroughly discontented, and justly so, it appears to me, at the very long delay which has taken place since they agreed to buy.

1st. Because this has deferred the commencement of their annuities to the Land Commission.

2nd. Because it has led to payments being required from them which (they allege) they were assured they would not have to make; and because these payments were enforced by legal proceedings of which they have had to pay the costs.

The tenants say, and there is a universal concurrence of testimony as to this, that the Company's representative told them that no tenant purchasing would be required to pay rent or interest after the amount due up to November 1885 was satisfied, and that the sale would be completed in a few months after the contracts were signed.

After the decision in one or more test cases writs and processes were issued without notice, and the result is, that most of the tenants have paid, in addition to rent and interest, costs varying from a few shillings up to 4l. or 5l.

Several of the tenants were many years in arrear, and the Company seem to have acted upon no principle except that of taking all they could get without actually dispossessing the tenants.

Since the return of amounts paid since May 1887, and due in May 1889, was made, several tenants have paid the Company, so that the amount now due is much less than what appears on the return.

In many cases the tenants are now clear up to 1st January 1889, but I find that they are quite uncertain whether they are, or will be, liable for any further interest to the Company on completion of the sales. Some tell me that they will pay nothing more except on decrees made against them.

It is not easy to estimate the effect of these payments and proceedings on the financial position of the tenants. Farms may be well cultivated and stocked although the tenants are embarrassed by other debts; while other farms, and badly cultivated, are occupied by persons who have capital which they do not lay out on the land.

Some of the tenants borrowed money to pay the Company; others sold some of their stock; but I see no reason to think that any who were solvent and in comfortable circumstances when they contracted to buy have been made insolvent by their payments to the Company since 1887. Most of the tenants have stock and farm implements; some are wealthy; and, on the whole, this district is as well cultivated as any in Ireland. Some of the farms are models of [illegible].

There is no doubt, however, that all the tenants have been seriously inconvenienced and extremely irritated by the unexpected payments required, and the legal proceedings by which they were enforced. Many who were badly off before have been very much straitened, inasmuch as they had hoped to relieve their position by accepting the terms of purchase, as they understood them.

This understanding was based upon verbal statements made by Mr. Glover at several meetings on the estate, to which the tenants were summoned by circulars. The fact of these statements having been made, and the tenants' view of the matter, are corroborated by letters from Mr. Sawyer, clerk to the Company, which can be produced if required by the Commissioners.

In a letter dated 10th August 1885 Mr. Sawyer stated that the terms were to be 18 times the rent; all rent to 1st November 1885 to be paid in cash; and "no rent to be demanded after that date."

Under date 3rd January 1887 he wrote to one of the tenants, "As the terms now stand purchasing tenants will be called upon to pay neither rent or interest from 1st November 1885. The Company confidently anticipated that many purchases would have been completed before 1st November 1886, but it realises [illegible] several weeks must elapse before any purchase-money is paid to the Company."

In January and November 1887 circulars were sent to the tenants demanding the rents due to 1st November 1886, saying, "Your deed cannot be sealed till this rent is paid." Interest was not referred to.

After such statements and letters it is not to be wondered at that the tenants resisted the payment of interest as inconsistent with their contracts; nor is it surprising that the unexpected payments which they have had to make should have embarrassed those among them who were unprepared for such a demand.

The worst cases of those on the schedule are where the amount now outstanding is large in proportion to the rent. This may be nearly every case be taken as an indication that the tenant is unable to pay; and the enforcement of the Company's demand will materially affect the tenants' ability to pay instalments to the Commissioners.

In those cases where the amount debited to the tenant is small, it is evident that the payment cannot seriously affect the tenant's means, but if it involves further litigation it may do so.

It appears to me that, for the protection of the Company's security, it would be wise to require all outstanding cases to be closed at once, and that all rent, interest, and costs should be released. The long delay has caused infinite discontent, has made the tenants dissatisfied with their purchases, and to a great extent destroyed the pleasure which they would have felt at being converted into freeholders.

Payments are being received daily or weekly by Messrs. Glover and M'Guckin from all who they can get to pay. In fact the tenants have accepted the situation, and are paying up whenever and however they can in order to avoid costs. Those who are supposed to have means to pay are being pressed very hard. Benjamin Boreland, who negotiated the sale for the Company, and persuaded the tenants to give 18 years' purchase instead of the 16 they offered, and who then led them in opposition to the demand for interest, has been served with notice that unless he settles at once the writ against him will be executed forthwith.

Some of the tenants have cash in hand, obtained by selling stock or crop, or by borrowing, which they have promised to pay Messrs. Glover and M'Guckin before the end of the month.

I think that the general appearance of these farms indicates greater prosperity than really exists; they are exclusively devoted to tillage, there being practically no permanent pasture, and grass being grown as a rotation crop. Tillage farming has been for some years far from remunerative, and the appearance of comfort and good cultivation, which is general but not universal (for there are some very poor and wretched homesteads), is to some extent a survival from the times when such farming returned larger profits than it does at present.

I append notes as to details of changes of tenancy, or cases requiring special observation on the several townlands.

19 April 18[illegible] *Murrough O'Brien.*

APPENDIX, No. [illegible]

PAPER handed in by the *Chairman.*

Sir, Magherafelt, [illegible] June 18[illegible].

It has come to the knowledge of the Drapers' Company that a number of tenants on the [illegible] and Ballyna[illegible] Divisions of their Estate, who have applied to the Land Commission under Lord Ashbourne's Acts for advances to purchase their holdings, have, since they signed the applications, made a communication to the Commissioners, in which it is stated that pressure was put upon the tenants to induce them to agree to purchase, and that the holdings are not good security for the advances applied for, and that if the advances are made, the purchasing tenants will be unable to pay the statutory instalments in repayment of them. Of this communication it is only necessary on the part of the Company, at present, to say that it contains many grave misstatements of fact, and that it omits to state many facts very material to the questions raised. The Company will be prepared to reply to it in detail should they have an opportunity of doing so, but in order at once to dispose of the suggestion that they wish to press a sale on any tenant, I am instructed to say that the Company, while they absolutely decline to alter the terms of sale, are prepared to cancel any or all of the Agreements which have been entered into by tenants to purchase their holdings, and that any purchasing tenant who may wish to cancel his agreement can do so by signing the form of letter enclosed and returning it to me by post on or before the 1st July next. As it is not known to the Company by which of the tenants the communication to which I have referred was signed, it has been thought advisable to send this intimation to all purchasing tenants on the [illegible] and Ballyna[illegible] Divisions, although the Company are aware that a very large number of those who have signed are anxious to carry out their agreements. In case you do not return the enclosed letter to me signed by you before the 1st July next, I will assume that you do not wish to recede from your agreement.

The Company desire to take the present opportunity of repeating what has been impressed upon the tenants from the outset of the negotiations, that it is a matter entirely for their discretion whether or not they accept the terms of sale offered to them, but that if they elect to remain tenants, they must be prepared to fulfil the obligations of their tenancies.

For some time past it has been apparent to the Company that a number of tenants on these divisions of the Estate have combined to withhold the payment of rent, and being determined not to yield to an illegal combination of this kind, the Company have been compelled to take proceedings at law in many cases. A majority of the tenants on these divisions now hold at judicial rents, and those who do not can, if they are dissatisfied, apply to the Court for judicial rents, and all who are in arrear for non-judicial rents can obtain time for payment from the Court or by agreement with me on terms settled by the Company.

In the future, therefore, any rent which a tenant may be asked by the Company to pay in respect of his holding will have been fixed, if the tenant has so wished, by a court of law, and the Company trust that those tenants who do not purchase will be prepared to make the payments due from them punctually, and that any further recourse to legal proceedings may be unnecessary.

Yours, &c.
(signed) *J. Glover.*

One-hundred and forty, [illegible], [illegible] January 18[illegible]. [illegible] months in. Nothing done. Commissioners have communicated over and over again. Maps have been provided. Tenants in uncertainty. Number of other cases arranged but not lodged.

Drapers' Company's Estate.

Sir Townland of

In answer to your letter of the [illegible] June 18[illegible], I beg to inform you that I wish to withdraw my application to purchase my holding, under Lord Ashbourne's Act.

Signed

Dated this day of June 18[illegible].

To John Glover, Esq.

APPENDIX, No. [illegible]

PAPER handed in by the Chairman.

Drapers' Company v. Barefoot.

17 December 188[illegible], for Respondent, Mr. [illegible]

Dear Sir, Drapers' Hall, London, E.C., 3 January 1887.

The Drapers' Company have had under consideration your letter of the 12th ultimo. They are sorry that there should still be any difficulty in the way of tenants purchasing their holdings, but they cannot think that they are called upon to make fresh concessions in the matter. As the terms now stand purchasing tenants will be called upon to pay neither rent nor interest from the 1st November 1885. The company confidently anticipated that many purchases would have been completed before the 1st November 1886, but as matters stand, several weeks must yet elapse before any purchase money is paid over to the company. This delay is of course a serious loss to them, and if it continues, may compel them to further consider the terms of sale, but not in the direction which you suggest.

I am, &c.

(signed) W. P. Sawyer, Clerk.

Mr. Benjamin Barefoot,
Annahavil, Moneymore, Co. Derry

Magherafelt, 10th day of March 188[illegible].

Received from Mr. Benjamin Barefoot the sum of 10 *l.* on account of costs of action, Barefoot v. The Drapers' Company.

Glover & (Stamp) *McGuckin*

Magherafelt, 12th day of October 188[illegible].

Received from Mr. Benjamin Barefoot the sum of 7 *l.* 10 *s.* for costs, The Drapers Company v. Barefoot.

Glover & (Stamp) *McGuckin*

APPENDIX, No. [illegible]

PAPER handed in by the Chairman.

Drapers Company v. Barefoot.

17th December 188[illegible], for Plaintiff, Mr. S.

Manor of Drapers.

Sale of the Estate to the Tenants.

Sir, Drapers' Hall, London, E.C., 10 August 188[illegible].

Referring to our interview on the 29th July last, I beg to inform you that the Court of Assistants of the Drapers' Company have had under further consideration the question of the sale of the estate to the tenants, and will modify the terms, as communicated to you by me at the interview, by substituting the payment of one year's rent in cash for the proposed promissory notes, and remitting all rent to purchasing tenants from the 1st November 1885. The terms of sale will therefore stand thus:—

Purchase money, a sum equal to 16 times the rent.

All arrears of rent to the 1st November 1885 to be paid in cash, and no rent to be demanded after that date.

The company to pay the costs of the sale as between them and the tenants.

These terms must be considered as finally and definitely settled so far as the company are concerned, and no further modification will be made in them. They will stand good for one month from this date, and the company will not be bound by them after that date.

I am, &c.

(signed) W. P. Sawyer.

Mr. Benjamin Barefoot,
Annahavil, Moneymore, Co. Derry, Ireland.

APPENDIX, No. 11.

PAPERS handed in by Mr. [illegible], 26 June 1860.

Memorial of 1856.

MEMORIAL of the Corporation of Derry to the Irish Society in 1856.

To the Honourable Society of the Governor and Assistants, London, of the New Plantation in Ulster.

The memorial of the Mayor, Aldermen, and Burgesses of the Borough of Londonderry, in Common Council assembled.

Sheweth—

That your memorialists, as representatives of the citizens of Londonderry, feel it their duty to avail themselves of the present opportunity to bring before your honourable Society a matter of the very greatest importance to the welfare of the city and neighbourhood, and the well-being of the inhabitants, and in which your memorialists hope to have the co-operation of your honourable Society, as being, in common with them, deeply interested in the prosperity of this locality. Your memorialists cannot avoid impressing upon your honourable Society that, notwithstanding the peculiar local advantages enjoyed by the city of Londonderry, situated as it is on the banks of a river navigable for vessels of large tonnage, and in the centre of a country of rich and well-cultivated soil, inhabited by a peaceful, contented, and well-ordered peasantry, it is a fact, which cannot be doubted, concealed, or denied, that this city has not kept pace with others not so advantageously circumstanced. Your memorialists would observe that our tardy progress is not attributable to the absence of enterprise, intelligence, or exertion, nor yet difference in race, on the part of its inhabitants, but, as your memorialists are convinced, and would respectfully impress upon your honourable body, to the want of such a tenure of the land and premises as would secure the tenant and encourage the capitalist to invest their money in substantial and permanent buildings, suitable for manufactories, mills, and residences.

Your memorialists feel that Belfast, the most rising town in Ulster, made its greatest progress towards its present state of prosperity from the time its merchants and other inhabitants obtained leases in perpetuity from the late Lord Donegal. Your memorialists, feeling that the future well-being of this city in no small degree depends upon the tenure which its inhabitants may possess, venture respectfully, but earnestly, to urge upon the attention of your honourable Society, as lords of the soil, this their just and reasonable claim; and would refer your honourable body to the case of Liverpool, where leases have been granted on terms satisfactory to that community. Your memorialists pray your honourable Society to give the subject a serious and favourable consideration; and your honourable Society will be pleased, as one of the results of your first visit to the city of Londonderry, to accede to the wishes of its inhabitants, your tenantry, in this matter, which so materially affects their interests, well-being, and prosperity.

Given under our common seal of the city of Londonderry, this eighteenth day of August, One thousand eight hundred and fifty-six.

COPY of the Memorial of the Tenants of the Town of Magherafelt, in the County of Londonderry.

Respectfully sheweth—

1. That, after your Worshipful Company leased away the entire of your estate, in the county of Londonderry, in 1754, to the grandfather of the present Sir Thomas Bateson, for 800 *l.* per annum, the greater portion of the town of Magherafelt was built entirely by the capital of the tenants, who had previously settled on the estate, under the Articles published in the reign of James I. for the Plantation of Ulster.

2. That Mr. Bateson, disregarding his own private interests, from time to time leased off to the settlers on the estate the building lots on which the town of Magherafelt now stands, for leases varying from [illegible] to 60 years at fair ground rents.

3. That in 1854, when the lease of 1754 expired, and your Worshipful Company entered upon the management of the estate, the value of the tenants' property in the town of Magherafelt was, according to the poor-law valuation, 2,841 *l.*

4. That you then trebled the rents of the town, but confirmed to us at the same time the old and time-honoured custom of the estate to give the tenant full liberty to sell his improvements to the highest bidder.

5. That, in consideration of your leaving the old custom untouched, the town submitted to the increase of rent, though not without murmur and remonstrance.

6. That inasmuch as you continued up to December 1856 to recognise this ancient custom, not only by allowing your tenants to sell to the highest bidder, but by yourselves purchasing, at full market value, the interest of several of your tenants in their holdings, we felt assured that we were safe in continuing to sink our capital and labour in the town, as we had been accustomed to do in times past.

7. That we then learned, with feelings of great alarm, that you had resolved not only again to increase our rents, but to abolish our customary right to sell our property to the highest bidder.

8. That these feelings were deeply intensified in April 1858, by the unexpected service of notices to quit on 66 tenants in the town, including many widows and orphans.

9. That several of us who had very recently spent large sums of money in the purchase of old and ruinous tenements, and in making permanent and valuable improvements thereon, having memorialised your Worshipful Court for relief from our distressing condition, asking such an extension of term as would secure our outlay under the circumstances mentioned in our Memorials, but we have not been able, after repeated petitioning for 18 months, to get any satisfactory replies.

10. That the pressure put upon a number of us who were called upon to accept a nine years' lease, by the threat contained in your Resolution of 11th January 1857, "of dealing with us as tenants from year to year, and increasing

increasing our rents," is inconsistent with the [illegible] promises of your deputations, who had from time to time visited the estate, and the published statements of the Master of your Worshipful Court, on the [illegible] February last, when he declared that "it was the intention of the Salters Company to introduce long leases on their estates."

11. That the prosperity and improvement of the town has been impeded, and the public health of the town imperilled, by your delays in settling our tenures on a liberal and equitable basis.

12. That several neighbouring towns, where perpetuity leases are granted for building purposes, have, within the last [illegible] years, doubled and trebled their population, while Magherafelt has been gradually on the decline.

13. That it is due to your own character, as one of the wealthiest and most charitable corporations of London, and as landlords and undertakers of the Crown of England in Ulster (independent altogether of our claims as peaceable, industrious, and loyal tenants and natives), to endeavour to make the principal town on your estate both prosperous and happy.

14. That notwithstanding the apparent indifference with which memorials from individuals have been treated, we have resolved unanimously to ask you, for the last time, to consider our grievances, not with legal minds, but as [illegible] and honourable gentlemen.

We complain, then, of your interference with our long-established custom of selling our own houses at the highest and best price. First, because you have limited our right to sell to [illegible] years' purchase of the rent. Second, because you have so increased our rents that our marketable interest in the property is completely [illegible].

We complain, that in order to accomplish our submission you have resorted to the notice to quit.

We complain, that your apparent disposition to exact high rents has paralysed trade and improvements in our town, in consequence of which we are less able to pay even the old rents.

We complain, that the term of lease you propose is, in the majority of cases, inadequate to [illegible] of our capital and labour, and in all cases inadequate.

We complain, that your leases contain unreasonable and unusual clauses, unnecessary to protect the landlord's rights.

And lastly, we complain, that on the [illegible] instant you have more than doubled the rent of [illegible] tenants in the town, having previously trebled them in [illegible], and that this is a tax on our own capital, and one which we feel we are quite unable to bear.

That we desire to bring these our grievances before you, divested of all passion, in order that the feelings of distrust and anxiety which now prevail amongst us may be allayed, and our relations for the future settled on a footing that will restore that unbounded confidence and goodwill which for a century existed between us and our former landlords.

We therefore pray that you may be pleased to appoint a deputation of your Worshipful Court to come here, or receive us in London, to settle our tenures and rents, or to leave the settlement of tenures and rents to any two merchants in Ulster; and memorialists will ever pray.

Signed at a public meeting held in the Court-house,
Magherafelt, this 17th April 1867.

The REPLY of the Salters' Company to the Memorial of the Tenants of the Town of Magherafelt, dated 17th April 1867.

(A.) The estate in the county of Derry, held by the Salters and other associated Companies, is their property, unfettered by any conditions of a fiduciary character.

(B.) In the year [illegible], in consideration of the surrender, by the [illegible] family, of a lease granted to them for a term of years which would expire in [illegible], at the rent of [illegible] *l.* per annum, the Company granted a fresh lease for a term of [illegible] years, ending the 1st of May 1853, at the yearly rent of [illegible] *l.* At the expiration of this lease the holdings in the town of Magherafelt yielded the rent of [illegible] *l.* [illegible] *s.* [illegible] *d.* per annum, which rent remained unaltered until November 1853. At that time, in consequence of the survey of the town by two eminent surveyors (one of whom was Mr. Stewart Gordon, the county surveyor), the rent was increased from [illegible] *l.* [illegible] *s.* [illegible] *d.* to [illegible] *l.* [illegible] *s.* [illegible] *d.*, the increased rental, however, bearing no proportion to the valuation of the county surveyor, which amounted to [illegible] *l.* At the same time the poor-law valuation amounted to [illegible] *l.*

(C.) At the time of this survey ample consideration was accorded to those tenants who had not received a full return for money laid out by them on their holdings; and the surveyors were instructed to report such as were deserving of leases on that account; and they accordingly named several such tenants, to most of whom leases were granted, for terms varying from [illegible] to [illegible] years. Since 1853 no general rise in the rental of the town has taken place.

(D.) From 1853 to [illegible] there has been a gradual increase in the rental from [illegible] *l.* [illegible] *s.* [illegible] *d.* to [illegible] *l.* [illegible] *s.* [illegible] *d.*, the increase amounting in [illegible] years to [illegible] *l.*, arising almost entirely from the outlay of the Company during that period of nearly [illegible] *l.* in the erection of new buildings, and in the purchase of tenants' interests; such increase of rent, however, does not pay the Company 3 per cent. interest upon the outlay.

(E.) During the same decennial period upwards of [illegible] *l.* more was expended by the Company in various public improvements in the town, viz., in assisting to build a parish church, a Presbyterian church, parochial and other schools of various denominations, a dispensary, &c.; and a further sum of [illegible] *l.* was expended in rebuilding a grammar school in the town; for this large outlay the Company, of course, obtain no return.

(F.) The gross receipt of rental from the town from [illegible] to [illegible], viz., [illegible] years, has been [illegible] *l.* [illegible] *s.*; and during that period the sum expended by the Company in the town has been [illegible] *l.*, independently of a further sum of [illegible] *l.* in the erection of a manor house and agent's office.

(G.) The Company is further pledged, on certain conditions, to a donation of [illegible] *l.* for water supply to the town and for drainage, and an outlay of [illegible] *l.* towards the introduction of gas; and there has been likewise a promise, within a few weeks, of the donation of [illegible] *l.* towards the erection of a new court-house and bridewell.

Salters' Hall, St. Swithin's-lane,
7 May 1867.

It may be convenient shortly to answer the several paragraphs in the foregoing memorial of the tenants, which has been reprinted for that purpose.

1. This statement has been already answered in the paragraphs A. and B.

2. No lease granted by the Beresford family could extend beyond the period of the lease granted to them by the Company. On the expiration of the building leases, which, it is asserted, were granted, the ground landlord would have been legally entitled to the full rent. It will, however, be seen, by reference to the paragraph C. that consideration was extended to all tenants whose improvements were not then exhausted.

3. It is a fallacious inference that the poor-law valuation is any criterion as to the value of the tenant property. It is simply the yearly value of the fee.

4 and 5. The rents were not increased until 1831, and then augmented only by about [illegible] l., the rents in [illegible] being [illegible] l. [illegible] s. [illegible] d., and in 1855, [illegible] l. 12 s. 7 d. The Company did not at that time know the terms on which the tenants transferred their interests; nor did they ever give any pretence as to tenant-right.

6. By resolution of the Court of Assistants of the Company, in May 1844, it was ordered that the limit of the price paid on the transfer of a holding should not exceed 10 years' purchase; and the agent was directed to make that communication known to the tenants. The exorbitant sums paid by incoming tenants for dilapidated and ruinous buildings induced the Company to adopt this resolution for the benefit of such tenants, and for the protection of the Company's interest.

7. The Company have not abolished, but simply regulated, in accordance with the foregoing resolution, the practice referred to; but it is the intention of the Company to increase the rental of the tenants-at-will, from November 1857, that being the appointed period for the revision of the town rental.

8. It seems to be thought necessary, in practice, that notices to quit should be served on tenants when any alteration in their rents has been determined on.

9. The Company cannot recognise any claim arising from the purchase of old and ruinous tenements, it being the duty of the outgoing tenant to keep and leave them in proper repair. But the Company have ever been and still are willing to make full allowance for permanent and valuable improvements beyond needful repairs. And in every case, when a memorial has been transmitted to the Company through their agent, it has been considered immediately, and the most liberal construction placed thereon; and no delay has occurred in transmitting to the agent the terms proposed in reply to the application.

10. The Company have already agreed to grant leases for 21 years and upwards to a considerable number of their tenants; and it is untrue that the Company ever offered a lease for less than 21 years, the term of nine years referred to being the residue of leases for 21 years offered in 1854. Building leases for long terms have been, and will continue to be, granted in proportion to the amount of money proposed to be laid out, and the character of the building to be erected.

11. The only observation that can be made regarding the improvement and public health of the town is, that the Company, impressed with the importance of efficient sewerage and a supply of good water, had surveys of the town and neighbourhood made, and estimates furnished for accomplishing both these objects, offering to the inhabitants a grant of 2,000 l. towards carrying them into effect; and a further sum of 300 l. was offered towards the introduction of gas into the town. But no advantage has been taken by the tenants of these liberal offers.

12. It is scarcely necessary to point out the irrelevancy of this observation. It surely is not meant to be inferred that the tenants, who for their own benefit settled in Magherafelt, supposed they were to have leases in perpetuity. Such leaseholders would be in effect freeholders, subject to a fixed rent-charge.

In answer to the complaint that the Company's "leases contain unreasonable and unusual clauses, necessary to protect the landlord's rights," the Company reply that the conditions are only such as are equitable in themselves, and customary in leases granted by other Companies.

The Company have ever endeavoured to be mindful of what is becoming in them as members of an important corporation, and as just landlords, just not only to their tenants, but also to themselves and to those Companies whose interest is associated with theirs in the estate; and their dealings with their property in Ireland have ever been regulated by this principle. It is with the utmost regret they have perused the memorial, and observe with surprise the feeling which pervades the whole document.

Salters' Hall, St. Swithin's-lane,
7 May, 1857.

grant of lands in the county of Londonderry made to the Irish Society for a nominal sum, of which sum your Company paid but a small proportion, was accompanied by conditions of a public trust, as the following quotations from the documents to be found in the Appendix to the case of the Skinners' Company *v.* the Irish Society in the House of Lords, prove.

In the introductory recital to the Articles of Plantation, it is stated:—

"His Majesty is graciously pleased to distribute the said lands to his subjects as well of Great "Britain as of Ireland, as being of [illegible] and ability shall seek the same, with a mind not only to "benefit themselves but to do service to the Crown and Commonwealth; and forasmuch as many "persons being ignorant of the conditions whereupon his Majesty is pleased to grant the said lands "are importunate suitors for greater portions than they are able to plant, intending their private "profit only and not the advancement of the public service, it is thought convenient to declare and "publish to all his Majesty's subjects the several quantities of the proportions which shall be distributed, "the several sorts of undertakers, manner of allotment, the estates, the rents, the tenures, with other "articles to be observed as well on his Majesty's behalf as on behalf of the Undertakers."

ARTICLES TO BE OBSERVED BY THE ENGLISH AND SCOTCH UNDERTAKERS:

No. 12.—"The said Undertakers shall not demise any parts of their Lands at Will, but shall "make certain Estates for years, for life, in tail, or in fee-simple."

ARTICLES TO BE OBSERVED BY UNDERTAKERS OF ALL SORTS:

No. 3.—"The Undertakers to enter into a Recognizance to the Crown, with sureties, to perform "the articles of Plantation."

No. 4.—"That in every of the said Counties there shall be a convenient number of Market "Towns and Corporations, erected for the habitation and settling of tradesmen and artificers."

4th.—That on the 28th December 1637 the Charter granted by James I. was revoked by him on account of the non-performance of some of the Articles of Plantation by the undertaking Companies.

That we refer to these matters not with a view of arguing any legal question with you, but to remind your Worshipful Company of the circumstances under which the Town of Magherafelt was originally built. This town was built not by you, but by the Settlers on the Estate, who, trusting, and on the simple faith of the Tenant-Right Custom existing in the district, invested their capital and created a property valued in the year in 1854 at [illegible]*l.*

Nevertheless your Worshipful Company, on coming into direct possession of the property, increased our rents from 307*l.* to 721*l.*; and this you consider as a proof your indulgence and liberality! Your memorialists consider it was an act unwarranted by the circumstances, although they were willing to submit to it, and are prepared to abide by it if no further encroachment on their rights be made.

For your Worshipful Company must have known, from the Reports of your Deputations who had regularly visited the Estate from 1820 to 1854, and from the returns made to your Worshipful Court by the Agent of Sir Robert Bateson, during the same period, that the people of the Town of Magherafelt had built the Town by their own capital and labour, and that they had, up to 1854, invested in their tenements upwards of [illegible]*l.* of their own money.

On the other hand, your Company never erected on your proportion of the Estates, granted to the Irish Society any town for the habitation and settling of the Tradesmen and Artificers who came over from England and Scotland; but in 1734 you actually abandoned the settlement, leaving the settlers to take care of themselves, and leasing your entire property for the term of 120 years, to the highest and best bidder, for a sum which only averaged [illegible]*l.* per annum.

That after the peaceable, industrious, and loyal settlers, had by their hard toil and unexampled perseverance, under untold difficulties, made your property, without any assistance or encouragement from you, worth [illegible]*l.* per annum, they naturally expected a fixed tenure as compensation for past improvements, and trusted that, with the example of Sir Robert Bateson before you, your Worshipful Company would have endeavoured to carry out the policy which, under your lessee, produced such satisfactory results.

That your memorialists have been grievously disappointed in their expectations, inasmuch as your Worshipful Company has enormously increased our rents and adopted a system of tenure wholly incompatible with the prosperity of the town.

That your memorialists were surprised to find that your Worshipful Company justified the increase of rent by an express valuation, made by the late county surveyor, who was wholly incompetent for the task, and who did not enjoy the confidence of the people. That, moreover, your memorialists were not at the time apprised of the object of the valuation, nor were the terms for which he thought fit, behind their backs, to put down individual tenants for leases communicated to them until long afterwards; and memorialists respectfully submit that in the great majority of cases a full consideration was not given by Mr. Gordon to these in measuring the length of their tenures, as will appear by the following instances:—

Names.	Rent under Sir R. Bateson.	Increased Rent, subject to which Mr. Gordon's Term fixed.	Term fixed by Mr. Gordon.	Purchase Money of old Premises.	Money Expended.	Date of Expenditure.
	£. s. d.	£. s. d.		£. s. d.	£.	
Mrs. M'Fall -	5 18 -	19 - -	[illegible] years, from 1st Nov. 1854.	[illegible] - -	1,[illegible]	1840
Hugh Walker -	4 10 -	17 - -	31 years, from 1st Nov. 1854.	Waste Ground	[illegible]	1856
Hugh Wilson -	4 4 -	18 6 -	[illegible] years, from 1st Nov. 1854.	700 - -	1,600	1851
Robert Cochrane -	5 15 -	8 6 -	No lease, rent now raised to 20*l.*	120 - -	[illegible]	1852
Richard Donnelly	4 10 -	12 - -	[illegible] years, from 1st Nov. 1854.	1[illegible] - -	1,[illegible]	1840 to 1848
George Cassidy -	1 10 -	14 - -	No lease, rent now raised to [illegible]*l.*	120 - -	[illegible]	1841 to 1844

That

That [illegible] are prepared to show to the satisfaction of any respectable valuator (the facts stated) [illegible] and [illegible], and we believe no valuator of any position in the city of London (if acquainted with our local history and trade) can be found to endorse Mr. [illegible] opinion.

That on your own showing your investment of the sum of [illegible] l. from 1853 to 1865, on the same principle as we have by our tenants invested our money, and on similar buildings and improvements, does not pay your Worshipful Company 3 per cent.; and assuming this to be true we respectfully submit that [illegible] years, instead of [illegible] years, would not exhaust your Worshipful Company's investment.

That, in deciding what length of time should in any particular case exhaust the money invested in building and building improvements, regard should be had to the extent of the Town and the trading facilities which the Town affords, and we submit that, assuming our views to be correct in this respect, no Lease for a less term than 99 years (which Sir R. Bateson gave) should be offered to any tenant.

That less than 99 years for Building Leases is, as a rule, unusual in small provincial towns, and where the improvements are expected to be made by the tenants alone, as in our case, the Legislature has enabled even tenants for life to grant such terms against the reversion.

That Magherafelt is the only Town in the County of Londonderry, on the Estate of a London Company which has prospered or extended the extent of a [illegible] village, a fact attributable to the wise and sound policy of Sir R. Bateson in granting leases for 99 years.

That the reason assigned by your Worshipful Company for passing a resolution in May 1864, limiting the price of our tenant-right, namely, "That exorbitant sums were heretofore paid by tenants for dilapidated and ruinous buildings, and that a limitation was necessary for the benefit of the tenant and the protection of the Company's interest," is unfounded, inasmuch as there was no case in which the incoming tenant complained, or in which the Company suffered one shilling of loss, or in which their rights were infringed in any particular by the observance of that old and time-honoured custom.

That, on the contrary, this custom, as it prevailed until 1864, secured your Worshipful Company your rent and arrears of rent, and generally a large expenditure on improvements by the incoming tenant.

That since your Worshipful Company has adopted this resolution, we find you have made it the means of enforcing additional burthens injurious to the tenant's interests; for when an application has been made to your Agent to sell dilapidated and ruinous buildings, you declined the sale in the first instance, and then permitted the sale, compelling the tenant to sell with a condition that the incoming tenant would repair to an extent tantamount to rebuilding.

That such a promise is wholly at variance with the old custom, conduces only to the benefit of your Worshipful Company, and is a practical abolition of our tenant-right.

That we believe it is not the law of Ireland that a tenant from year to year is bound to take such care of his dwelling-house as to prevent it becoming dilapidated and ruinous, and that he is bound only to maintain the premises in fair tenantable condition, due allowance being made for natural deterioration; he is not bound to avert premature decay, nor to efface the footprints of time.

That we have seen several instances where your Worshipful Company have purchased old and ruinous tenements (Mrs. Lawrence, Mr. Adams, &c.), and in all such cases you have had to expend a sum equal almost to the cost of a new structure; yet, on your own views of the legal liabilities of your tenants, such improvements would only be repairs, and you would not be at liberty, by your own Resolution, to recognise a claim for extension of Lease on the ground of such improvements.

That the denial on the part of your Worshipful Company, contained in paragraphs 4 and 5 of your Reply, of any knowledge of the terms on which we transferred our interests in our tenements up to 1864, and the statement contained in the same paragraph, that you never gave any promise as to tenant-right, have astonished us more than anything in the whole document.

That your Worshipful Court must have known that Deputations of your Company (Mr. Gillespie, Mr. Hicks and others) visited the Estate, from 1853 to 1863, and that they were perfectly aware of the nature and extent of our tenant-right custom; and that in pursuance of their instructions Returns were made and Memorials sent to your Worshipful Court which fully disclosed the custom.

That these Deputations were informed of the custom and encouraged the tenants to continue their improvements and increase the expenditure, and that there are many living witnesses amongst us who can testify to these facts.

That your own acts from 1853 to 1864, in purchasing the interests of a number of tenants in dilapidated and ruinous buildings at full value, implied your previous knowledge of the terms on which tenants transferred their interests, and were naturally regarded as a practical recognition of the custom of tenant-right.

That, therefore, your denial of knowledge of the terms on which we transferred our interests under this tenant-right custom—your denial of giving a promise to respect that custom—and your allegation that you did not abolish that custom, but regulated it by a resolution of your Court—are statements inconsistent with our position, and with your own acts.

That your Worshipful Court must have foreseen the injustice which the Resolution of May 1864 would work to those tenants who purchased since 1853, with your knowledge and approval, and who paid their money into your office on faith of the custom, which you have in the most arbitrary manner virtually abolished—one instance out of many will illustrate the statement:—

In 1860, Mr. Glover purchased for [illegible] l. a dilapidated and ruinous tenement from Mrs. Hughes, the rent of which was [illegible] l., and paid the purchase-money into your office, there to be handed over to the out-going tenant (first deducting all arrears of rent, &c.). Since 1860, Mr. Glover expended [illegible] l. in almost re-building the tenement, and if he now wished to sell he would, under the old custom, be entitled to at least [illegible] l. for his interest and improvements, whereas under your Regulations of 1864 he could only receive [illegible] l. for his tenant-right. An in-coming tenant being accepted on the condition that his rent should be increased to [illegible] l. per annum.

That we are not aware of any instance in which long terms have (as you allege) been granted for Building Leases, and we know that since 1864 no new ground has been taken upon the Leases proposed by your Worshipful Court.

That this fact coupled with others, and particularly with the offers made to you by parties, willing to invest capital in the Town, provided Leases for a reasonable term were granted to them, should convince you that the course you entered on in 1864, and which you have since pursued, is in direct antagonism to the sentiments of the entire community, and are incompatible with the prosperity of the town.

That

That the opinions and proceedings of your Worshipful Company are also at variance with the opinions and proceedings of the landlords of the most prosperous towns in the United Kingdom, and we respectfully ask your Worshipful Company's next deputation to inspect the neighbouring Towns (Ballymena and Cookstown) referred to in our Memorial and confer with the owners of the property with a view to remove the obsolete and [illegible] opinions heretofore entertained by your Worshipful Court.

That the practice to which you have resorted of serving Notices to Quit on your tenants, as a preliminary step to increasing their rent, is altogether unknown on any well-managed estate in Ulster.

That in our case the great majority of the inhabitants were served with Notices to Quit, without being informed of the special object for which the notices were served, and without being consulted as to their willingness or unwillingness to accede to your demands.

That the alleged expenditure of 16,500*l.* in the Town between 18[illegible] and 18[illegible], and the conditional promises of [illegible]*l.* for future improvements, as stated in your reply are calculated to mislead the public to whom these statements were to be addressed.

We beg to remind your Worshipful Company of the following matters in reference to these statements:—

1.—No portion of this money was expended on our houses or tenements, and it is in no way increased the value of our buildings, nor does it make us more able to pay the proposed increase of rent.

2.—Eight thousand pounds of this money has been invested by you in new houses, and in purchasing and repairing old ones, which you have let at the highest letting value.

3.—During the same period about [illegible]*l.* have been invested by ourselves, in purchasing, rebuilding, and repairing houses in the town, for which you now seek to charge us rack rents.

4.—If you gave [illegible]*l.* to assist in building a parish church and parochial schools, you obtained [illegible]*l.* from the Ecclesiastical Commissioners, although you were bound to erect the same at your own expense.

5.—When you gave 1,[illegible]*l.* towards erecting a Presbyterian Church, the people subscribed [illegible]*l.* for their share, and they built their own school, at a cost of [illegible]*l.*

6.—You took possession of "Rainey's Charity" house and farm, and built a new Charity School, at an expense of 1,[illegible]*l.*, for which you receive a yearly Rent-charge of [illegible]*l.* out of lands in the County of Down, purchased with the money of Hugh Rainey, and entailed upon a charity "for clothing and putting out to trades the sons of parents who were of good repute and had been reduced to poverty."

7.—You offered us 2,[illegible]*l.* on the condition that we would put the Town under the Towns Improvement Act, 18[illegible], and that we would bring water by pipes into the Town, sewer and flag the Town according to plans to be furnished by you, the cost of which would exceed [illegible]*l.*

8.—The [illegible]*l.* for assisting to erect gas-works which would cost us 1,[illegible]*l.* was on condition that the Town adopted the Towns Improvement Act, 18[illegible].

9.—The population by the census of 1861 was 1,[illegible], and the Towns Improvement Act could not be adopted unless the population was 1,[illegible], so that your conditions were impossible, and your offers unavailing.

10.—Your offer of 1,[illegible]*l.* towards erecting a new Court-House has, we understand, been given on condition that the Grand Jury give up to you the ground of the old Court House and Bridewell (which is rent free for ever), and all the materials of both buildings, and shall give [illegible]*l.* in cash, to be expended on the new Court-House. This offer, if accepted, would be a profitable investment for you, but we believe the Grand Jury will not, at the expense of the Ratepayers, entertain the project.

That the Churches and Schools which you have assisted to build may reasonably be expected to supply the wants of the Estate for the next century, and considering that you have been in receipt of a rental of [illegible]*l.* a year for the last [illegible] years, and that for at least [illegible] years to come little appreciable outlay will be required, we consider the proposed excessive rise in the Town rents unwarranted.

That the expenditure of [illegible]*l.* upon Religious Charities in the Town, during 11 years, will not appear so munificent, when you remember that you are non-resident landlords, who expend [illegible]*l.* a year in London, and who contribute very little to the wealth of the community which yields this annual sum.

That this [illegible] expenditure of [illegible]*l.* is still further diminished in its apparent magnitude and liberality by the obligation imposed on your Worshipful Company, under the [illegible] General Article of Plantation, to erect a sufficient number of Parish Churches.

That the conditions in your Leases are equitable in themselves we cannot admit; on the contrary we submit the following are most inequitable:—

The tenant is bound, to insure in the joint names of the landlord and tenant, and in case of destruction by fire, to expend the money received from the insurance and all such further sums as may be required to rebuild to the satisfaction of your Worshipful Company.

If the tenant omits to paint, repair, or pay his rent the lease is forfeited, and the landlord may re-enter the premises, and take possession from the tenant, yet the tenant is not discharged from his liability on the covenants in the lease.

That we are still willing to abide the results of an open inquiry, or to refer our claims to indifferent parties, who have some knowledge of our customs and local trade, and who would have an opportunity of seeing what we have done.

We, therefore, respectfully pray that your Worshipful Company will reconsider the prayer of our Memorial of 18th April 18[illegible], with a view to have the grievances complained of redressed.

Read and adopted at a Public Meeting held in the Court-House,
Magherafelt, on the 4th day of July 18[illegible].

TABLE, showing the Comparative Rental of various Holdings in the Town of *Magherafelt*, under the late Sir Robert Bateson, Bart., and the Marquis of Londonderry, with the increased Rent, charged by the Salters' Company of London, in coming into possession, in the year 1854, and the further increase in 1867; together with the Amount of the Purchase Money of the several Holdings, and the subsequent estimated Expenditure in Buildings.

NAMES.	Rental previous to 1854, under the late Sir R. Bateson, Bart., and the Marquis of Londonderry.	Increased Rent in 1854.	Increased Rent in 1867.	Purchase Money.	Estimated Expenditure in Buildings, &c.
	£. s. d.	£. s. d.	£. s. d.	£.	£.
Mrs. Hall	8 10 –	15 – –	42 – –	Waste Ground	[illegible]
Samuel Porter	8 10 –	5 – –	6 10 –	340	[illegible]
Robert Cochrane	2 15 –	9 5 –	20 – –	120	300
Andrew Allen, No. 3	1 10 –	4 – –	10 – –	Waste Ground	[illegible]
Thomas Johnston	1 8 –	3 – –	6 – –	Waste Ground	110
James Carey	– 19 4	5 – –	9 10 –	165	75
Archibald M'Fall, No. 1	3 2 10	12 9 –	27 – –	300	700
John Steele	5 5 –	9 – –	24 – –	250	[illegible]
James Moran	7 – –	10 10 –	17 10 –	Waste Ground	300
John M'Leveen	1 15 –	4 – –	11 – –	102	300
Logue Caldwell	2 10 –	6 – –	18 – –	181	100
John Tohill	1 8 –	6 – –	4 10 –	35	750
Robert Agnew	1 10 –	4 – –	11 – –	200	104
Dexter Anderson	2 – –	6 12 –	11 – –	170	150
Hugh M'Leveen	1 10 –	3 – –	5 – –	75	300
Owen Richardson	– 13 6	2 – –	5 10 –	65	25
William Thompson	6 – –	14 – –	29 – –	450	1,500
Mrs. Johnston	1 13 4	4 – –	8 – –	70	180
Mrs. M'Callum	5 – –	15 – –	20 – –	600	350
Mrs. John Duncan	8 4 –	18 – –	25 – –	550	800
Hugh M'Aleer	8 10 –	1 10 –	5 – –	78	40
Neil Keith	– 15 –	3 – –	5 – –	60	200
Mrs. Walsh	2 – –	11 – –	17 – –	100	400
John Cassidy	4 10 –	14 – –	43 – –	. .	1,000
William Thompson, jun.	. .	3 – –	7 – –	75	250
James York	4 5 –	7 5 –	17 – –	180	150
James M'Kee	1 7 6	2 10 –	5 – –	60	28
James M'Williams	2 – –	5 – –	8 – –	Waste Ground	250
Andrew M'Guckin	– 11 8	2 – –	3 10 –	Waste Ground	75
Peter Smith	2 – –	4 – –	6 2 –	60	170
William Smith	1 5 –	2 10 –	8 – –	150	80
Robert Crawford	2 – –	5 – –	16 – –	260	150
George Brown	2 2 –	5 – –	12 – –	200	200
James Pollock	2 5 –	5 – –	12 10 –	80	110
William M'Whinney	6 – –	10 – –	15 – –	200	180
Joseph Sumley	1 – –	2 – –	5 – –	80	200
John Graham, No. 1	2 – –	5 – –	15 – –	340	200
Hugh Walker, No. 1	4 – –	8 – –	18 – –	280	100
Mrs. John Duncan	3 – –	6 – –	20 – –	200	–
D. Graham & Sons, No. 1	1 10 –	7 – –	18 – –	200	350
TOTAL . . . £.	87 8 4	283 13 –	668 12 –	5,748	10,590
Andrew Allen, No. 1	2 11 –	2 – –	10 years' lease	800	300
Matthew Lytle	1 10 –	6 – –	8	100	400
Peter O'Connell	2 10 –	5 – –	9	160	250
John Glover	2 10 –	10 – –	9	800	550
John Graham, No. 2	2 17 –	11 – –	11	400	1,200
A. M'Fall, No. 2	5 16 –	13 – –	8	300	1,050
Hugh Walker, No. 2	2 10 –	12 – –	12	Waste Ground	2,000
James Gilmour	2 – –	6 – –	8	700	400
Mrs. James Duncan	7 – –	9 – –	9	Waste Ground	700
Hugh Wilson	4 4 –	11 8 –	9	700	1,000
Mrs. Daley	5 – –	6 – –	9	150	500
Richard Donnelly	4 10 –	12 – –	9	130	1,400
Samuel Darby	3 8 –	10 – –	9	300	150
James Harkness	3 – –	4 – –	21	170	1,200
D. Graham & Sons, No. 2	1 18 –	11 – –	30	505	1,500
William Hastings	2 – –	5 – –	9	394	450
John M'Namara	3 – –	5 – –	10	300	–
Charles M'Kenna	5 10 –	9 – –	10	800	800
Mathew Bowman	2 10 –	4 – –	9	Waste Ground	800
Robert Smith	3 – –	15 – –	Lease	550	1,000
Mrs. Evans	2 – –	10 – –	Lease	Waste Ground	500
TOTAL . . . £.	67 3 –	190 5 –	. .	4,799	15,800

N.B.—A number of important cases are unavoidably withheld, owing to the impossibility of ascertaining the facts in the limited time allowed for the preparation of this Table.

APPENDIX No. [illegible]

PAPER handed in by Mr. *J. [illegible]*, [illegible] July [illegible].

Henry O'Neill, [illegible].

£.	s.	d.	
11	[illegible]	[illegible]	O.R.
[illegible]	15	–	G.V.
11	[illegible]	–	F.R.
[illegible]	[illegible]	7	Instalments.

Purchase-money, [illegible] *l.* [illegible] *s.* for [illegible] A. [illegible] R. 10 P.

He owed to 1st of November [illegible], [illegible] *l.* [illegible] *s.* [illegible] *d.*, for rent, and [illegible] *l.* [illegible] *s.* [illegible] *d.* costs = [illegible] *l.* – *s.* [illegible] *d.*

	£.	s.	d.	£.	s.	d.
January [illegible], [illegible], Cash and Poor-rate	[illegible]	17	–			
Added to purchase	[illegible]	–	–			
Forgiven	[illegible]	[illegible]	[illegible]			
				[illegible]	–	[illegible]

The Land Commission have sanctioned an advance to this tenant in April [illegible] of [illegible] *l.*, although the Company had withdrawn the sale on 1st February [illegible].

Michael [illegible], [illegible].

£.	s.	d.	
[illegible]	[illegible]	[illegible]	O.R.
16	–	–	G.V.
[illegible]	10	–	F.R.
7	[illegible]	[illegible]	Instalments.

Purchase-money, [illegible] *l.* [illegible] *s.* for [illegible] A. [illegible] R. 7 P.

He owed to 1st November [illegible], [illegible] *l.* [illegible] *s.*, for rent, and 10 *s.* costs = [illegible] *l.* [illegible] *s.*

	£.	s.	d.	£.	s.	d.
January [illegible], [illegible], Cash	–					
Added to purchase	16	–	–			
Forgiven	[illegible]	[illegible]	–			
				[illegible]	[illegible]	–

Sir William Conyngham offered to accept [illegible] *l.* [illegible] *s.* in cash in full, and he preferred to add 16 *l.* to the purchase-money.

He has since got a judicial rent fixed at 9 *l.* 10 *s.* At the time he signed the agreement he had no judicial rent fixed.

An ejectment had been taken against him in August [illegible], but Sir William Conyngham settled it, and the case was gone.

James [illegible], [illegible].

£.	s.	d.	
11	[illegible]	–	O.R.
15	15	–	G.V.
[illegible]	17	–	F.R.
[illegible]	[illegible]	–	Instalments.

Purchase-money, [illegible] *l.* for [illegible] A. 1 R. [illegible] P.

He owed to 1st November [illegible] for rent, [illegible] *l.* [illegible] *s.* [illegible] *d.*, and 1 *l.* [illegible] *s.* costs = [illegible] *l.* [illegible] *s.* [illegible] *d.*

	£.	s.	d.	£.	s.	d.
December [illegible], [illegible], Cash	1	[illegible]	–			
Added to purchase	[illegible]	–	–			
Forgiven	[illegible]	10	[illegible]			
				[illegible]	13	[illegible]

This tenant was proceeded against in October [illegible].

APPENDIX, No. 53.

PAPER handed in by Mr. *J. Glover*, 17 July 1865.

Dear Sir, Magherafelt, 22 December 1863.

In reply to the terms offered by the Company for a lease of my holding, I beg to say that to me the terms are astounding. After expending, by purchase and valuable improvements, nearly 800 *l.*, on the faith of a custom long established on the estate, I am told at the end of seven years that I should be doubled in my rent on getting a 31 years' lease.

If this had been told me when I paid 300 *l.* into the company's office, I would not have been their tenant on the terms. There were two circumstances at the time which encouraged me to make the purchase, viz.:—1st, that I knew the company had shortly before purchased Mr. Bryne's place and paid him for his improvements, thereby acknowledging the right of property of their tenants in their own outlay; 2nd, I was told by Mr. Duncan, at the office, before I paid my money, that there was a term of 21 or 31 years granted to Mrs. Hughes' tenements, and I felt assured that the company would not go back of this arrangement.

In the paragraph of the company's letter which you read me, I observed that they were pleased to call my improvements "repairs." You know, and can inform them, that when I got this place it was a perfect ruin, unfit and unsafe for occupation as a dwelling-house. This is well known to every one here. The word "repairs," therefore, when applied to my case, has no meaning unless as a figurative one.

The company have purchased Mr. Lawrence's place on which he never expended any money in improvements, and have laid out a large sum of money on it. If they take mine on easier terms, I shall be very happy to relieve them of tenant right, and pay full value. One thing is certain, that the terms proposed by the company to the town have alarmed us to the utmost and will, if carried out, destroy the little remaining trade and spirit that are amongst us. For the last five or six years the trade and the population of the town have been steadily on the decline, and all is attributable to the feeling of insecurity that exists (and which it appears is now going to be realised) in reference to the tenure of our holdings.

If the company wish the town of Magherafelt to improve and prosper, they must act on the well-recognised and sound principle of Adam Smith:—"Give ample security for the outlay of capital, and leave the rest to private enterprise." The patronage system is radically bad, and won't work in Magherafelt more than in London.

I respectfully beg, therefore, to decline accepting a lease on the terms.

Yours, &c.

A. Spotswood, Esq. (signed) *J. Glover.*

Sir, Magherafelt, 30 March 1864.

Since you read me the extract of the Salters' Company's letter, in reply to mine of the 22nd December last, I have considered their terms, viz.:—To give me a lease for 21 years, from the 1st November 1864, at the present rent. The reply was so curt and illiberal that at first I thought the company had not seen my letter, or had no opportunity of forming an opinion on the merits of the case; and, as the extract stated, it was the reply of a committee, which, I presume, was composed of gentlemen who had not sufficient information on the subject, I beg again to address you, hoping that both my letters may now receive the calm, impartial, and equitable consideration of the entire Court. To this end, and that every individual member of the Court may see the case, and form an opinion for himself, I have taken the liberty of printing both letters, and enclosing you 30 copies, which I beg you will be good enough to forward to the members personally.

Gentlemen who have been in the habit of meeting the deputation of the Court at the Manor House, inform me that the several members of these deputations have uniformly declared the company's wish was to encourage the tenants on the estate, and to make the town of Magherafelt the model for all the London Companies. This, I know, would not be doing much, as the London Companies have one and all, by their refusal to grant perpetuity leases, or for long terms, reduced their towns to petty villages, and prevented merchants from investing money in their estates in the introduction of manufactures. The result is, that on all the London Companies' estates in County Derry manufacturing industry is almost unknown, and capital and skilled labour are being transferred to districts where they are beyond the reach of landlords, who, being wealthy corporations, non-residents, and uninformed as to the claims, character, and means of their tenants, choose to dictate terms and rules of management at the expense of progress and improvement on their estates. You, of your own knowledge, are aware of Mr. Bryne's case (late a tenant on this estate), and who has on a neighbouring property realised a large fortune in the flax and tow spinning trade, and has extended the blessings of honest employment to hundreds of people who must have of necessity emigrated to earn a livelihood. I enclose you also a prospectus of a company (the Knockaloughrim Flax and Tow Spinning Company, Limited) established on the very borders of this estate, in which at least 8,000 *l.* of the capital from this estate will be invested. It was at first contemplated to establish this company for spinning and weaving linens in Magherafelt (which would have been by far the more eligible site) with a capital of 50,000 *l.* to 100,000 *l.*; but the feeling of insecurity was such that every person shrank from it at first mention. I have no doubt the Salters' Company would, if they thoroughly understood the wants and requirements of the people, and the resources of the estate, yield to reason in these respects; but I fear the reports from time to time presented to the court by the deputations who come over here for a few days at Midsummer, and who gather information from the few gentlemen who have the honour of dining with them at the Manor House, are not calculated to lead the company to a proper knowledge of either the people or the estate. This difficulty is greatly increased by the fact that the governing body hold office for so short a time, and that practically the management of the entire affairs rests with the paid officials who have seldom the courage to remonstrate with any rules, however impolitic, prescribed by the company.

About the time I became a tenant on the estate in 1856, there was an unbounded confidence in the liberality and good intentions of the company, and money was readily invested on faith of the [immemorial] custom of the estate; but now that we have been so plainly told that this custom is to be abolished, followed by an immediate rise of rent (whether money has been expended on faith of the custom or not), we see with feelings of surprise and regret that the chief qualification for the management of the estate consists, not in the encouragement of manufactures and trades among the people, but in the ability to increase the company's yearly receipts.

The

The Ulster Tenant Right, so little understood in England and Scotland, is founded on the faith and confidence which the English and Scottish settlers had in the honour and sense of justice of the Plantation undertakers.

These settlers came over here about 250 years ago, under a Royal proclamation, embodied in the Articles of Plantation, extensively circulated in England and Scotland at the time, in one of which they were promised the lands for lives and for long terms of years in the following words:—"The said undertakers shall not demise any part of their lands at will only, but shall make certain estates for years, for life, in tail or in fee simple (see Article 13)." The settlers relied on these Articles and the Royal promises, and at first they must have had great faith in their landlords who seem to have kept faith with them; for, without any security except their honour, they cultivated and planted the lands, selling from time to time, as of right, these improvements to the highest bidder, and at prices almost as high as [illegible]. This course of dealing with the improvements, produced by the labour of the settlers, became a well-recognised custom, and has been, beyond the memory of the oldest man, the established custom of this Estate. It is quite natural and reasonable under the circumstances of the Ulster Plantation, and has, beyond all doubt, mainly contributed to the improvements and prosperous condition of the Northern Counties of Ulster.

The lands of this Estate, containing about 16,000 statute acres, were purchased from the Crown in 1609, for [illegible] l., and without any expenditure or outlay of capital by the company, were in 1860 valued by the Government valuation at a sum considerably above 15,000 l. per annum. If you ask what made these lands so valuable, I answer the *labour* and *capital* of the tenant settlers. This is the key to the Ulster Tenant Right, and by it everything that appears strange to those who are unacquainted with the original condition of the English and Scottish settlers to the practical working of the custom can be easily explained.

In any other country except Ireland, and in any other business or calling in life, the man who by their *labour* produced such a change would get the benefit of it to all time. The British colonies in America, Australia, New Zealand, &c., have had secured to them the lands which they planted. If I had in any of these colonies laid out [illegible] l. of my own money on 1 rood and 17 perches of ground, as I have done in Magherafelt, I would have had the legal right to dispose of or sell it so as to reimburse me for my outlay.

The great bulk of the people on this estate came over from England and Scotland to plant the lands (then wild and uncultivated) under the Plantation Articles of 1609, and their English and Scottish descent can easily be recognised in their manners, morals, and language, to the present day. They have been, under the providence of God, the stronghold of England in this country, both before and since the Union; and, notwithstanding the disadvantages under which they have laboured, continue to be so. I happen to be a descendant of one of these settlers, and I feel that, although as loyal a subject, and as peaceable and hard working a man as any of my forefathers, my landlords are very unlike the London Merchants, who, under great difficulties, undertook the cause of Ireland's civilisation. If I had then expended [illegible] l. in such a small space of ground, paying to your company 16 l. rent, with 4 l. odd for taxes (which with 5 per cent. on my outlay, would make my rent 45 l. per annum), I would have received the protection and encouragement that an industrious and loyal settler deserved. You know the value of loyal and industrious tenantry just now, but our landlords only learn it through the public press. While the south, the west, and the midland counties of Ireland are convulsed, and life and property are secured, not by *the people*, but by the terrors of the law and English bayonets, we have hitherto lived in the security of *our own Tenant Right*, and our loyal attachment to the Constitution of England. At such a time I wonder that, instead of our landlords (London Merchants) voluntarily coming forward and securing to us our rights and property, they are showing, in the most unequivocal way, their determination to confiscate to themselves what our *labour* and *capital* have done. Next to our attachment and love of the English Constitution, our loyalty is secured by the deep and material interests we have in the land. Our labour is in it; our money is in it; destroy that interest and you weaken and impair this loyalty. In my position as a [illegible] in the County, I have the best reasons for saying that the *Land Question* is a deep root of disaffection among the mass of the people, and that nothing short of an equitable settlement of the claims of industrious and loyal tenants can secure the permanent peace of the country. Allay the fears and invigorate the hopes and confidence of the well-disposed and industrious subjects, and sympathy for treason will soon disappear from amongst us.

The Salters' Company are in my opinion labouring under a great fundamental error as to the length of time which will repay outlay of capital in buildings in Magherafelt. A little village of 1,500 inhabitants, placed in the centre of a purely agricultural district of country, without manufacturing industry or commercial enterprise of any kind, is not a place where a speedy return of money can be had. The circulation of money in our banks have never exceeded 20,000 l. per annum, and three-fourths of this circulation is confined to the five months (October to February inclusive). The people in trade manufacture or produce nothing, but merely retail goods bought in England and elsewhere to the farmers in the neighbourhood. The only articles of commerce are the necessaries of life, such as tea and sugar, American bacon, and Indian meal, woollens, and cottons. The demand is, of course, limited to the fixed population of a limited district, and according to the prices of farming produce. The goods are generally sold on credit to meet the custom when farmers have got a return of their crops. Very often the interest on the shopkeeper's account exceeds his profits. As a necessary consequence of the credit system, there is a heavy loss, in the form of bad debts, and the trade is so split up into small shops, with small capital that competition reduces the profits until a person wonders how rent is paid. We have 17 grocers, 21 publicans, seven woollen-drapers, and four retailers of bacon, who almost represent the trade of Magherafelt. Generally speaking, there are little pieces of land to the houses, out of which the people produce, at the lowest cost, potatoes, vegetables, butter, milk, &c., so as to enable them to pay the rent of the town buildings. Under the new regulations, I believe the company refuse to include these holdings or even the gardens by the leases of the tenements, so that their increased rents are to be paid out of the miserable profits which such a trade realises. It was not enough in 1854 when the lease Sir Robert Bateson's and Lord Londonderry's leases expired, to treble the rents of the town, but they must now not only increase these rents (inside twelve years), but strip the town holdings of their little farms.

Sir Robert Bateson and Lord Londonderry leased the tenement I now hold for 41 years, ending November 1853, at 8 l. 15 s. per annum, and same year renewed the lease for 61 years at same rent, making a continuous term of 62 years at 3 l. 15 s. rent. In November 1854, the company came into possession, and immediately raised the rent to 10 l. per annum, and now, after that I have almost rebuilt it within the last seven years, they want me to pay 20 l. a-year rent. I am at a loss to know how the company expect I could pay this rent after such an investment. There are houses in the same street which are in a state of ruin, and no increased rent is asked or paid—it could not be paid. The plain inference is, that the company intend to charge people on their own outlay.

In conversing with gentlemen of experience in England and Scotland, I found they could not understand our complaints about tenant right; but when I pointed out to them some facts touching the matter, they at once saw my case. First. In the County of Londonderry there is a population of 200,000, out of which above 150,000 persons support themselves by farming and by farm labour. Second. The landlords make no improvements, although they periodically increase the rents. Third. The Landlords (a few excepted) reside in England, and, except a small outlay, they expend the rents of the estates there.

The great mass of the people have no idea of anything except a rude and unimproved system of farming. There is no such thing as manufacturing (linen on the old system excepted, and the ordinary tradesmen are superseded by the use of machinery in nearly every branch of business, all of which is invented and sold to us from England and Scotland. A farmer who has three or four sons has no alternative but farming occupation for them, and if he is not able to purchase farms for them they must emigrate to America or Australia. At his death he can only divide his small farm. The idea of sending them out to learn a manufacture or trade is very rare. We have nothing of the kind in the county. The consequence is, that there is a competition for small farms unknown in England or Scotland. The immense manufacturing and trading that is going on there always presents a ready field for the employment of this class at high wages, and the demand for farms is always below the supply.

The

The English and Scotch landlords make all the improvements, and the tenant, instead of investing on the land 10 *l.* the acre as a purchase, as all his capital in his hand to stock and work the farm. His capital is all employed in farming, whereas our capital is generally locked up in the land and in the improvements.

The English and Scotch landlords spend their income on their estates, and by a circulation of the money among the farmers and tradesmen who sell to the landlord for money, they have profits, which, in turn, enable them to educate their families and pay their demands.

I believe some of the members of our Company say our complaints and representations are unreasonable and absurd (they treat them as such at all events), but I ask them to find out in all England or Scotland a county of the population and area of Derry, where there is such a large proportion of the people dependent *solely* on farming, and in which manufacturing industry is in such a backward state? or in what county in England the tenants had invested in dead capital 10 *l.* the acre, upon which they were paying the improved value? or in what county in England there is 120,000 *l.* paid for rents expended out of the county? Unless they can explain this state of things, they should not contradict us. Nothing can be easier, however, than to adduce the strongest proof that such a state of things has existed here for the last 200 years, and still exists. We do not ask favours. We have improved the lands by our own labour and capital, and we say it is unjust in the extreme to make us pay rent for our own improvements at the end of twenty or even ninety-one years. The people here would better their own condition by introducing manufactures if the Company gave them security of perpetuity leases.

I understand it is one of the standing orders of the Company that no leases be granted in perpetuity, and that at the end of twenty-one years at least the full amount of the tenants' improvements will be valued on him, without any allowance for his equity. We all know that in practice they give no such leases. The impolicy and injurious tendency of these rules can easily be comprehended by any person of experience. It applies to the towns much more strongly than to the country. If such an unwise policy had been pursued by the owners of property in Dublin, Belfast, Liverpool, Leeds, Dundee, Edinburgh, Glasgow, &c., none of those cities and towns would ever have attained their present magnitude and commercial importance. It is a strange fact that on all the London Companies' Estates in county Derry there is not a town which ranks above the class of a village. You know of your own knowledge of two neighbouring towns—Ballymena and Cookstown. In both these towns the tenants all got perpetuity leases for building on, and the result is most beneficial. Under Sir Robert Bateson's leases Magherafelt kept pace with them; but since the Company came in our neighbours have had a complete victory.

There is only one other matter which I desire to bring before your notice; that is, the extraordinary form of lease which the Company have got printed for us. The reservations, the penalties, the forfeitures, the vexatious restrictions, and the surrender of all our capital and labour by a special *clause*, confiscating to them all our claims of tenant right, make a lease perfectly valueless. No person could observe and perform them. It is idle for our legislators to tell us that the relation of landlord and tenant is founded on contract. It should have been so when the London Companies got the county of Londonderry, and when the Crown would have protected the tenants' interest—now we have no part in the matter. The contract is all made by the Company. We have no voice in it. Under no circumstances will they allow this form to be altered or a word dispensed with. I have read several of the leases granted by Sir Robert Bateson and Lord Londonderry, which is nearly the same as that granted by the Lord Palmerston on his Irish estates. They contain all that ever can be necessary to protect a landlord. There could be no objection to such a form. It is neither wise nor politic to force on people contracts which cannot be of use to protect the material rights and interests of all concerned. If the Company would only deal with us in the ordinary way so far as the form of the contracts goes, they would do something to relieve us of the dread and terror they have latterly inspired. At all events the system of making the ingenuity of lawyers to be so drawn cannot serve either us or them. I never agreed to take such a lease, and I hope it will not be forced on me, such less a new increase of my rent.

Yours, &c.
(signed) *J. Olver.*

A. Spotswood, Esq.

Sir,

Magherafelt, 20 June 1846.

Notwithstanding the very disheartening answer of the Salters' Company to my Memorial, viz.: a refusal to reconsider my case or (what is most extraordinary), even to allow me an audience in their Court, I take the liberty of writing you another letter on the subject.

The reply of the Salters' Company, which you read to me on 21st instant, satisfies me more than ever that they have had instilled into their minds the most incorrect ideas of the state of their Irish property. I am satisfied that the gentlemen who have the honour of representing the Company in their Court, are honourable and intelligent men; and that if they had not been prejudiced and preoccupied by wrong ideas of what they conceive to be their own interest in the management of their estate here, they would not persist in carrying out a measure which must work a grievous injustice to their tenants.

If I complain that, by a resolution of their Court, made in autumn last, they have swept away a custom of 200 years' standing, upon the faith of which I had invested 700 *l.* odd, and that by this resolution my house and premises, which were in August 1845 worth 800 *l.* in the market, are now worth only 100 *l.*, my complaint is of such a serious kind, that I apprehend all reasonable men will agree with me in saying that I deserved at least their sympathy.

I know this resolution has destroyed 20,000 *l.* of property to the people of Magherafelt, and that I am only one of the individuals affected; but that is no reason why I should not persevere in seeking redress, when I am conscious I have a good case on its own merits.

Since the plan of exterminating our rights to sell our own improvements has been adopted by the Salters' Company they have had means of testing the justice and utility of the system by their own experience.

1st. In 1844, they purchased Mr. Lawrence's place at 400 *l.* and expended 200 *l.* to put it into repair. Before this they were receiving 25 *l.* per annum rent from the tenant, without having invested a penny in it. They are now receiving 55 *l.* per annum from the tenant, viz.: 40 *l.* for the interest of their own money (600 *l.* at 5 per cent.), and 15 *l.* for rent. The result is a loss of 10 *l.* per annum. Mr. Bryan's place is similarly circumstanced.

2nd. They have built six new houses in Church-street at a cost of 220 *l.* each, and they are let at a (rack) rent of 11 *l.* 10 *s.* each, viz.: 10 *l.* 10 *s.* interest of their own outlay, and 1 *l.* for the rent of the ground on which the houses stand. The frontage is about 130 feet, and if let on a perpetuity lease would have brought the Company about 35 *l.* well-secured ground-rent for ever.

3rd. In the case of the late Mr. Adams, they paid to his representatives (first deducting all rent due to themselves) 100 *l.* for a tenement for which he was offered 280 *l.*, and, with an expenditure of [illegible] *l.*, have let it at 20 *l.* per annum. This tenement brought them for ground-rent 3 *l.*, and in the possession of the purchaser referred to would have been put into thorough repair without any expenditure by the Company, at 5 *l.* rent; whereas, after taking interest for their own money, they will now have 5 *l.* for land.

It is painful to mention that the executors of Mr. Adams, who was a faithful public servant here, and held in high esteem, had not, owing to the new rule of the estate, the means of paying his debts, and that his creditors, who had lent him money on faith of the good old custom, had to take 6 *s.* 8 *d.* in the pound on amount due them.

I submit

I submit on these facts the following considerations for the Salters' Company:—

1st. That in all these cases the Company have not, and will never be able to get 5 per cent. for their outlay, and so good a ground-rent as could be obtained on good leases.

2nd. That these rack-rents are not as well secured as rents paid under the old system.

3rd. That in the case of the Church-street new houses they will not be repaid their capital at the end of [illegible] years.

4th. That in the other cases their capital never can be repaid or recovered.

5th. That the marketable price of a house in a village like this is a fallacious principle to proceed upon in fixing a rack-rent.

6th. That, paying a fair ground-rent, 5 per cent., is the largest return which can be reasonably expected for money invested in houses here.

7th. That no tenant can have a fair return for improvements in building houses at the end of 31 years.

8th. That improvements made by the landlord, at the expense of his own capital, is simply an investment of his own money on perpetuity lease.

9th. That the abolition of our customs, as worked, and will work untold injustice to the tenants of the estate, their children, and creditors; and will not in the end enhance the value of the Company's property or increase their rents, except at the expense of their own capital.

These are matters worth the consideration of the Salters' Company, and their application and bearing on my case will be obvious. If the gentlemen who advocate the Company's proceedings, and carry to completion the measure of which I have complained, and still complain so heavily, will only give these matters a kind and generous consideration, I am sure full justice will at once be done me. I believe every member of the Court of the Worshipful Company of Salters would, if he was satisfied in his mind I was right, vote me to-morrow a lease of 999 years.

It is with the strongest feelings of hope that the Salters' Company will, before they have ruined this village, see it to be their interest as well as ours to give us reasonable leases.

That I renew my appeal to them again for a measure of justice; and, believing as I do that I must first convince their minds before I can reach their better feelings, I have referred to the matters in this letter.

There are several other matters which I could (if this letter were not already too long), refer to, in proof of my views, and which I may advert to again.

I reserve my final reply about the taking out of the old lease of 31 years from 1st November 1854, until the Court has had an opportunity of reading this letter, and I hope of re-considering my case.

Yours, &c.

(signed) *J. Glover.*

A. [illegible], Esq.

APPENDIX No. 54.

PAPER handed in by Mr. *E. H. Draper*, 14 July 1890.

Total Advance . . £. 212.	Holding, 2 Townparks.	(Schedule No. 149)
Including Deposit £. 43.	Acreage, 14a 2r 20p.	(Quarries and Fisheries Reserved.)

W. F. Waters, a Commissioner, &c.

THIS INDENTURE made the 23rd day of April One thousand eight hundred and eighty-eight between the Corporation of Master and Wardens and Brethren and Sisters of the Guild or Fraternity of Corpus Christi of Skinners of London, otherwise the Master and Wardens of the Guild or Fraternity of the Body of Christ of the Skinners, London, hereinafter called the Vendors, of the first part; the Irish Land Commission, hereinafter called the Commission, of the second part; and Reverend Michael Tracey of Dungiven, in the county of Londonderry, Farmer, hereinafter called the purchaser, of the third part; whereas, the purchaser holds the holding hereinafter described as tenant to the vendors, and the vendors are seized in fee thereof, and of certain other hereditaments, subject to a reservation to the governor and assistants, London, of the new plantation in Ulster, their successors and assigns, of all the fishings and taking of salmon and eels and other fish in the rivers of Bann and Lough Foyle, and to all the creeks of the same rivers, or either of them, and to all the ground and soil of the same rivers, or either of them, contained in an indenture of the fifth day of June, One thousand six hundred and sixty-three, and made between the said governor and assistants, London, of the new plantation in Ulster, and the vendors (but released and discharged from all other exceptions, reservations, rights, liberties, and privileges whatsoever contained in the said indenture of the fifth day of June One thousand six hundred and sixty-three), and also subject to the said tenancy, but discharged from the perpetual yearly rent of seventy pounds, six shillings, and eightpence, created by the said indenture of the fifth June One thousand six hundred and sixty-three, under the provisions of an indenture bearing date the twenty-seventh day of May, One thousand eight hundred and eighty-seven; and whereas the purchaser has agreed to purchase the interest of the vendors in the said holding for the sum of Two hundred and twelve pounds, and has applied to the Commission to advance him the said sum of two hundred and twelve pounds for that purpose, which the Commission has agreed to do under the provisions of the "Purchase of Land (Ireland) Act, 1885," on the terms of such advance being secured by a guarantee deposit as hereinafter provided, the repayment of the said advance with interest being secured pursuant to the provisions of the "Land Law (Ireland) Act, 1881," by an Order of the Commission endorsed on these presents; and whereas the Commission has, at the request of the purchaser, paid to the vendors the sum of one hundred and sixty-nine pounds, and has with the consent of the vendors retained the sum of forty-three pounds to satisfy the purposes of a guarantee deposit; now this indenture witnesseth that in consideration of the said sum of one hundred and sixty-nine pounds so paid, and of the said sum of forty-three pounds so retained as aforesaid, the receipt and retention respectively of which said sums making together the said sum of two hundred and twelve pounds, the vendors do hereby acknowledge, the vendors as beneficial owners do hereby grant to the purchaser that part of the lands of Dungiven in the occupation of the purchaser as such tenant as aforesaid, situate in the Barony of Keenaght and county of Londonderry, containing fourteen acres two roods and twenty perches statute measure or thereabouts, excepting and reserving unto the vendors, their successors and assigns all freestone and beds of freestone, freestone quarries, and pits, as well opened as unopened, within, under, or upon the said lands, hereditaments, and premises, and with full right, power, and liberty to the vendors, their successors and assigns, and the agents, workmen, and persons authorised by them, or any of them, at all times to enter upon the said hereditaments and premises, and every part thereof, and with or without horses, carriages, waggons or carts, and to occupy the surface thereof, and to search for, sink, quarry, open, work, get, store, dress, make merchantable, and carry away the said freestone, beds of freestone, freestone quarries, and pits, and with full liberty and power to make, construct, erect, and maintain all such quarries, pits, drains, watercourses, roads, buildings, works, machinery, and conveniences, and to remove such stones and rubbish, and generally to do all such other acts and things as may be necessary for the purposes aforesaid, making from time to time nevertheless to the purchaser, his heirs and assigns, and his and their lessees or tenants, reasonable and adequate compensation for all damage thereby done or occasioned to the said lands, hereditaments, and premises or any buildings thereon.

To hold to the purchaser in fee simple, subject so far as the premises hereby conveyed are affected thereby to the exception and reservation of all the taking of salmon and eels and other fish in the rivers Bann and Lough Foyle, and to all the creeks and members of the same rivers, and either of them, and of all the ground and soil of the same rivers, or either of them, contained in the said indenture of the fifth day of June, One thousand six hundred and sixty-three, hereinbefore mentioned, but released and discharged from the other reservations, exceptions, and liberties to the said governor and assistants, London, of the new plantation in Ulster in the said indenture contained. And the vendors do hereby for themselves, their successors and assigns, covenant with the purchaser, his heirs and assigns, that the vendors, their successors and assigns, in exercising the rights, powers, privileges, and liberties hereinbefore reserved, will do as little damage to the surface of the said lands, hereditaments, and premises, and to any buildings thereon, as may be consistent with a fair and bond fide exercise of the said rights, powers and privileges, and will make and pay reasonable and adequate compensation for any damage caused to the surface of the said lands, hereditaments, and premises, or to any existing buildings thereon, in the exercise of the said rights, powers, privileges, and liberties. And the vendors do hereby release to the purchaser all arrears of rent due by the purchaser to the vendors out of the said holding up to the date of these presents. In witness whereof the Vendors and the Commission have hereunto respectively caused their Seals to be affixed, and the purchaser has hereunto set his hand and affixed his Seal the day and year first above written.

The Seal of the Vendors was hereunto affixed in presence of

E. H. Draper, Clerk.
W. Salmon, Accountant.
Skinners' Hall.

(Seal of the Vendors.)

A Memorial hereof was entered in the Registry of Deeds Office, Dublin, at minute after o'clock, on the day of 188 , Book No. , and the indenture hereof and of said Memorial was duly proved. Folio.

(*N.B.*—In the original deed the amounts are written in words in each case.)

Before Mr. Commissioner MacCarthy.

day the day of 188

In the Matter of the Estate of the Worshipful the Skinners' Company,
Owners of Land.

Upon reading the within Deed, the Court doth declare the land comprised in the holding by the said Deed granted, charged pursuant to the provisions of the "Land Law (Ireland) Act, 1887," with the repayment to the Irish Land Commission of the said advance of two hundred and twelve pounds, by an annuity of eight pounds nine shillings and eightpence for the term of forty-nine years from the first day of May next, payable by equal half-yearly payments on each first day of May and first day of November, the first payment thereof to be made on the first day of November next, and also charged with interest on the said sum of two hundred and twelve pounds at the rate of three and one-eighth per cent. from the date hereof, to the first day of May next, and payable with the first instalment of the said annuity.

ANALYSIS OF INDEX.

LIST of the PRINCIPAL HEADINGS in the following INDEX, with the pages at which they may be found.

INDEX.

[*N.B.*—In this Index the Figures following the Names of the Witnesses, and those in the Analysis of Evidence of each Witness, refer to the Questions in the Evidence; and the Figures following *App.* to the Pages in the Appendix.]

A.

ARREARS OF RENTS—continued.

Exceedingly few cases in which the arrears were added by the Fishmongers' Company to the purchase price, the total of the arrears at the time of sale having been 1,700 *l.*; belief that it was known to the Land Commissioners that the arrears were included in the price, *Tease* 5187-5211. 5225, 5226.

Reference to the large arrears of rents on the Skinners' Estate as due partly to the laxity of the late agent of the company, and to the subdivision of holdings, *Saunders* 5587-5589.

Circumstances under which the Drapers' tenants were told by witness that the arrears must be dealt with as a condition of purchase, *Ulster* 6081-6099——Inclusion of a small part of the arrears in the purchase-money; denial that this was an irregularity, or would now be so considered by Mr. Commissioner Lynch, *ib.* 6129-6135——Ample margin as regards security after the addition of a small amount of arrears, *ib.* 6136-6141——Estimate of about 1,500 *l.* secured in cash from certain tenants for arrears due to the Drapers' Company, *ib.* 6414, 6415.

Consideration shown to the Drapers' tenants as to the mode of payment of arrears, *Semper* 6313, 6316——Arbitration now pending in the matter of arrears; special cases of alleged hardship as regards the terms of purchase, *ib.* 6320-6329. 6352, 6353. 6360-6370.

Large accumulation of arrears on the Drapers' Estate through witness having trusted in the tenants' promises to pay, *Sir W. Conyngham* 6416, 6417——Belief that the arrears might be collected if time were allowed, *ib.* 6423.

See also Drapers' Company. Promissory Notes.

Ashbourne Act. Means of so using the Ashbourne Act that, where large arrears exist, it may operate oppressively, *O'Brien* 1276-1280.

See also Arrears of Rents. Land Commission. Sales of Estates.

B.

Bakers' Company (Skinners' Estate). Circumstances under which the Skinners' Company bought up the interests of the Bakers' Company and the Stationers' Company in the estate, paying them 78,000 *l.*, or twenty-two years' purchase of their gross rental, *Saunders* 5489-5491. 5587-5589.

Ballintine, Joseph. (Analysis of his Evidence.)—Witness, who is a Protestant, is a builder and contractor, and the owner of house and land property in Londonderry; is prepared to give evidence upon the management of the Irish Society's property there, 3770-3774. 3858. 3857. 3960. 3961.

Evidence in support of complaint that when land becomes vacant the Society allow it to remain so for years, to the loss of the trust and the rates, and to the inconvenience of traders; statement that there has been no letting to middlemen in witness' time, 3775-3798. 3891-3916. 4013-4015——Instances of the prejudicial effect of the exorbitant head-rents charged by the Society upon business enterprise in Londonderry, 3798-3806. 3858 *et seq.*

Opinion that there has not been any marked improvement in the management of the Society during the last seven years; admission that the leases since 1873 have been granted in perpetuity, 3807-3812. 3917-3920——View of witness that though the Society know less than their local agent they prefer their own judgment to his advice; general feeling that advantages are given by the Society as the result of "backstairs" influence, 3813-3824. 3878-3890. 3955-3977.

Obstruction by the Society to all the improvements that have been proposed by the harbour commissioners, 3825, 3826. 3973-3980——Belief that if the trust had been properly managed for the last thirty-five years the income of the Society would have been doubled; probability that if the letting of the building property and fisheries were thrown into the open market for competition a larger income would be realised, 3826-3846. 3868-3877. 3942-3991. 4016 *et seq.*

Non-objection to the management of the trust, so far as the corporation lands are concerned, being placed in the hands of the Londonderry Corporation, if the remainder be given to local men appointed either by the Government or the Lord Chancellor of Ireland, 3848-3855. 3946-3949. 4008-4010——Entire absence of representation of the Roman Catholics of Londonderry on the corporation, as Mr. O'Neill was elected by favour of the Conservative party; belief that the Catholics would take more interest in the corporation if the franchise were lowered, 3941-3944.

Feeling of the Catholics that it is useless to apply for favours to the Irish Society, the only grant made to them being 125 *l.* a year to St. Columb's College, 3919-3954. 4011.

Ballantine, Joseph. (Analysis of his Evidence)—continued.

4011, 4012——Complaint as to the manner in which the grants of the Society are distributed, the result being, in witness' view, a degrading system of bribery; suggestion that the funds should be devoted to the improvement of the land and the reduction of taxation, 3998–4001. 4018–4029——Grievance of the fishermen that the Lough Foyle Fishery is not free to everybody, 4001–4007.

Ballynascreen Tenants. See *Drapers' Company.*

Bann and Foyle Fisheries. See *Fisheries.*

Bann Navigation. Information respecting a total contribution of 37,140 *l.* by the Irish Society towards the Bann Navigation, *Beales* 2068–2083. 2087. 2104–2117. 2131. 2172.

Barefoot, Mr. See *Drapers' Company.*

Baxter, Aaron. (Analysis of his Evidence.)—Witness is Mayor of Londonderry, in which city he has been fifty years resident; has been a member of the corporation for ten years, 2173–2178.

Statement that the Londonderry Corporation regard the Irish Society as trustees, who are entitled to assist the corporation out of the funds of the trust; belief that this view of the Society is based upon the judgment of the House of Lords in the Skinners' Company's case in 1845; 2178–2186. 2265–2268——Impression of the corporation that some of the expenditure of the Society is rather excessive, 2191–2202. 2269–2271.

Evidence to the effect that the Society contributed 1,289 *l.* to the corporation in the year 1888–89, besides making large annual payments towards public institutions and building improvements in Londonderry and Coleraine, the grant to the schools in Londonderry alone being 2,842 *l.* a year, 2193 2202, 2231–2264——General satisfaction with the manner in which the affairs of the Irish Society are now managed, so far as Londonderry is concerned, the chief complaint formerly having been that perpetuity leases were not granted; opinion that the prosperity of Londonderry would have been more rapid if the leases had been granted thirty or forty years ago, 2173–2178. 2183–2189.

Desirability of greater encouragement being given to persons taking up leases, especially when the lease is granted for manufacturing purposes; belief that the Irish Society would do well if in future they charged lower ground-rents, 2219–2233. 2288–2290——View of the corporation that the surplus funds of the Society every year ought to be devoted to the city of Londonderry and the town of Coleraine, 2234–2237.

Possibility of the trust being better administered by Irish trustees on the spot than, as at present, by a London body who cannot have a good knowledge of local affairs, 2273–2286. 2301–2304——Doubt whether the corporation fairly represents the people of Londonderry, there being only one Roman Catholic member, while about half the population are of that faith, 2290–2300.

Bog Land (Supply of Turf). See *Turbary.* *Waterford Estate.*

Brackaslievegallion Tenants. See *Drapers' Company.*

Broderers' Company. See *Mercers' Company.*

Brown, The Reverend Nathaniel Macauley, D.D. (Analysis of his Evidence.)—Witness is Presbyterian Minister of Limavady, and has been there for more than forty years; he is conversant with the local estates of the London companies, 475–480.

Sale of the Fishmongers' Estate to the tenants shortly before the Ashbourne Act, about fifteen or sixteen years' purchase having been obtained, 481–488. 498. 499——Partial sale of the Skinners' Estate to the tenants, the price realised being about 17½ years' purchase; delay in carrying further sales as the tenants are holding back, 481. 489–497. 500–503. 573–576. 656, 657——Withdrawal of the grants formerly made by the Fishmongers' Company, 498.

Sale of the Haberdashers' Estate nearly two centuries ago, about one-third having been bought by a progenitor of Lord Waterford's family; periodical increase in the rents when tenants' improvements have been made, 508–518. 572, 573——Varying years' purchase obtained when Lord Waterford has sold land in the locality; high price paid by witness for some land in 1871, and by other tenants of Lord Waterford, 513–519. 602–672. 653–654. 658.

Grounds upon which witness considered for a long time that the companies acted more liberally than private landlords in the way of grants to the clergy, schools, &c.; statement, on the other hand, as to the tenants having made all the improvements on the land, whilst the rents were periodically raised, 528–551——Conclusion as to the companies being trustees, and as to their being legally liable for expenditure in respect of religion, education, and other matters, 537, 538. 639–650. 675–689——Very strong feeling created in witness' district by the sale of the companies' estates, and by all the

 purchase-

Report, 1890—*continued.*

C.

Charities.

Charities. Arguments of Mr. Walker, Q.C., on behalf of the receivers of charities in the county of Londonderry, *pp.* 349 *et seq.* —*See also Donations and Grants.*

Charters. Arguments in detail by the different counsel upon the question of the liability of the companies as trustees, so far as the charters impose or imply a trust, *pp.* 350 *et seq.*

Grounds upon which it is contended on the part of the companies that they are not bound under the charters as trustees, *pp.* 361 *et seq.*

Reference by counsel to the Charter of Charles II. as not in any way putting the companies upon a new foundation, *p.* 410.

Translation of the Charter of King James the First to the Irish Society, dated 29th March 1613. *App.* 450–478.

Church Temporalities Commissioners. Grounds for justifying the course adopted by the Skinners' Company in dealing with the fund received from the Church Temporalities Commissioners, and in making payments relatively to Episcopalians, Presbyterians, and Roman Catholics, *Saunders* 5567–5571. 5726–5730. 5772–5775.

Churches and Manses. See *Donations and Grants. Presbyterians. Roman Catholics.*

Clady River. Belief that the reason why the Mercers' Company refused to give a grant towards the drainage of the Clady river was because it was useless to do anything until an obstruction lower down was removed, *Watters* 4338–4351.

CLOTHWORKERS' COMPANY:

1. *As to the Sale of their Estate by the Company to Sir Hervey Bruce.*
2. *Receipts and Expenditure of the Company in respect of the Estate: varying Rental in different Years.*
3. *Question of the Company having held the Estate as Trustees.*
4. *Grants and Donations by the Company, and by Sir Hervey Bruce.*

1. *As to the Sale of their Estate by the Company to Sir Hervey Bruce:*

Evidence in detail in support of the complaint that the Clothworkers' Company sold their estate to Sir Hervey Bruce for 25,000 *l.* less than the tenants would have given, *Mark* 398 *et seq.*——Strong comment upon the refusal of the company to sell to the tenants, one member of the company having said that "it would not be desirable to root the Irish in the soil," *ib.* 388. 400–412. 435. 443–446. 450–470.

Explanatory statement respecting the negotiations for the sale of the Clothworkers' Irish estate to Sir Hervey Bruce in 1871; eventual sale for 150,000 *l.* subject to certain conditions and rebates, *Sir O. Roberts* 5247–5265.

Misapprehension on the part of Mr. Mark in attributing to Mr. Shaw (when on the court of the Clothworkers' Company) a saying that "the worst thing in the world would be to root the Irish in the soil," *Sir O. Roberts* 5331–5336.——Grounds for justifying the sale of the estate to Sir Hervey Bruce, as an adjoining and resident landlord, rather than to the tenants, *ib.* 5317–5326.

Explanation that an offer of 165,000 *l.* (not 175,000 *l.* as stated by Mr. Mark) was made on the part of the tenants, but not till after it was decided to sell to Sir Hervey Bruce; belief, moreover, that it was impracticable for all the tenants to raise the purchase-money, *Sir O. Roberts* 5341–5354. 5403. 5404.

Justification by witness of his action in declining to arrange an interview between a deputation of the tenants which came to London and the Clothworkers' Company; the sale was already irrevocably settled, and he wrote to the deputation asking them not to come over, *Sir O. Roberts* 5354–5356. 5406–5418.——Explanation that there were about 370 tenants on the estate, *ib.* 5414.

Inability of witness to explain why the company accepted his offer for the estate instead of a larger offer on the part of tenants, *Sir H. Bruce* 5942. 5948.

Memorials of tenants, together with correspondence, in 1871, respecting the proposed sale of the Clothworkers' property in the county of Londonderry; desire of the tenants to have the opportunity of becoming purchasers under the Irish Land Act of 1870, *App.* 430–432.

Communications from the Clothworkers' Company and the Irish Society, in April 1871, to the effect that the arrangements for sale to Sir Hervey Bruce cannot be disturbed, *App.* 430, 431.

Case submitted in 1871 for counsel to advise a deputation of the tenants on certain points, *App.* 544, 545.

Opinion of Sir George Jessel that the Crown had not the right to interfere in the sale to Sir Hervey Bruce, *App.* 545.

CLOTHWORKERS' COMPANY—*continued*.

2. *Receipts and Expenditure of the Company in respect of the Estate; varying Rental in different Years*:

Gross rental of 9,000 *l.* a year received by the company, of which about 3,000 *l.* was expended in England, including the cost of management; large expenditure on technical education, *Sir O. Roberts* 5297–5310. 5329. 5381–5386——Very similar rent at present as in 1871; increase and reduction in the meantime, *ib.* 5352–5358.

Statement to the effect that the rental of the estate in 1841, when the company came into possession, was about 7,000 *l.*, that it was considerably reduced in 1848, was slightly raised in 1856, and was 8,000 *l.* at the time of sale, *Sir O. Roberts* 5317–5361. 5375–5380——Explanation as to the rent received by the company from the middleman, who held on lease for three lives till 1841, having been only 600 *l.* a year; fine of 18,000 *l.* paid by him in the first instance, *ib.* 5388–5402.

Statement of receipts and expenditure of the company in respect of their Irish estates in the several years 1841–71, *App.* 564.

3. *Question of the Company having held the Estate as Trustees*:

Grounds upon which it is contended by counsel for the company that they are not in the position of trustees, *pp.* 564 *et seq.*

Opinion of Sir George Jessel, in 1871, that the company are ordinary owners in fee-simple, and can sell their own property for their own benefit to whom they please, *App.* 545.

View of Sir George Jessel that the company could appropriate to their own uses, in the City of London, the entire purchase-money, *App.* 545.

4. *Grants and Donations by the Company, and by Sir Harvey Bruce*:

Statement as regards the sale of the Dunlow Estate by the Clothworkers' Company to Sir Harvey Bruce, and the obligation upon the latter as to continuing the grants made by the company, *Dickey* 82. 163. 186–188——Complaint not only that the estate was sold for 25,000 *l.* less than the tenants would have given but that the rents were largely raised, and that the grants for religious education and charity have been discontinued, though they were kept up for some years by Sir Harvey Bruce as a condition of the purchase, *Mark* 388 *et seq.*

Particulars with reference to the rebate of interest on 75,000 *l.* which remained on mortgage on condition that Sir Harvey Bruce should continue for ten years payments amounting to 228 *l.* a year, which included 90 *l.* to clergymen and 108 *l.* to schoolmasters on different parts of the estate, *Sir O. Roberts* 5050 *et seq.*; 5326–5328.

Examination in detail in justification of the action of the company as regards the stipulation for their donations being kept up for a period of only ten years, though, as a matter of fact, they have been continued beyond that time; denial that there was any legal obligation upon the company in the matter, *Sir O. Roberts* 5176 *et seq.*; 5367–5370. 5421. 5423.

Parting gift of 1,500 *l.* given by the company amongst certain Episcopalian churches, in addition to 900 *l.* to the Presbyterians, *Sir O. Roberts* 5318–5320. 5374. 5383——Accuracy, as regards the Clothworkers' Company, of the statement in the Report on the City Livery Companies as to the liberal contributions by the companies to schools and churches, *ib.* 5371–5373——Explanation as to no parting gift having been given to the Catholic clergy, *ib.* 5374.

Terms of letter from witness to Sir Harvey Bruce as to the latter keeping up, subject to his general discretion, payments to the amount of 241 *l.* a year, *Sir O. Roberts* 5424.

Explanation, with reference to statements by Mr. Mark, that there was no bargain made by witness on his purchase of the Clothworkers' Estate to keep up certain subscriptions, but only an honourable understanding, which he has more than fulfilled, *Sir H. Bruce* 5930–5944.

List of Presbyterian congregations, showing the number of families in each case, the annual grant received by each congregation, and the instances in which withdrawn, with the date, *App.* 439.

See also *Castlerock Presbyterian Church*. *Coleraine*. *Deputations*. *Leases*. *Merchant Taylors' Company*.

Coleraine. Particulars respecting the Irish Society's Free Schools at Coleraine; causes of dissatisfaction with the committee of management, *Lord Justice Fitzgibbon* 1399–1401——Efficiency of the Coleraine Academical Institution, under a mixed governing body;

Coleraine—continued.

body; aid received from the Irish Society and the Clothworkers' Company, *Fitzgibbon* 1003-1007.

Explanation in connection with certain resolutions adopted by the town commissioners and the harbour commissioners recognising the services hitherto discharged by the Irish Society as trustees, and deprecating any change which would prevent a continuance of the same action, *Ervine* 2049-2058. 2098, 2099.

Grants made by the Irish Society for public purposes in Coleraine to the amount of 1,000 *l.* in 1858, 1,000 *l.* in 1877, and 1,500 *l.* in 1883, *Ervine* 2059-2067——Grants made also for religious and educational purposes in Coleraine; large annual grant for the Free Schools, there having been continuous grants ever since 1613, *ib.* 2060-2063. 2089-2094. 2165-2170.

Belief that the people generally of Coleraine are fairly satisfied with the action of the Irish Society in making grants for different local purposes; reference hereon to the franchise on which the town council is elected, *Ervine* 2084-2088. 2118-2125.

View of the bodies represented by witness that the trust funds of the Society should be expended in Coleraine and Derry; apprehended diversion of the funds, *Ervine* 2095-2097. 2100-2103.

Considerable contributions given by the Clothworkers' Company to the Coleraine Academical Institution, *Sir O. Roberts*, 5311-5315.

Motion passed by the Coleraine Town Commissioners in April 1871 in approval of steps being taken by Government in order to prevent the Irish Society and the London companies from alienating the property held in trust for the district of Coleraine, *App.* 432.

See also *Irish Society.*

Combinations of Tenants (Non-payment of Rent). Misapprehension on the part of the Drapers' Company in stating that a number of tenants had combined to withstand payment of rent, *O'Brien* 1100 1101.

Grounds for a statement by witness in a letter of 10th June 1889 that there was an "illegal combination" among a number of tenants of the Ballymacrory and Brackaghlislea division of the Drapers' Estate, *Glover* 6142-6154.

See also *Plan of Campaign.*

Compensation for Improvements. Admission that if a tenant held his land at a nominal rent for a lengthened period that would compensate him in some measure for any outlay he made, *Todd* 3704, 3705.——See also *Improvements. Tenant Right.*

Conyngham, Sir William Fitzwilliam Lenox. (Analysis of his Evidence.)—Witness, who was agent for Drapers' Estate from April 1884 till January 1890, when he resigned, testifies to the marked improvement in the condition of the tenants, and to their liberal treatment by the company, 6410-6415. 6421, 6431. 6447. 6448.

Large accumulation of arrears on the estate through witness having trusted to the tenants' promises to pay, 6416, 6417——Attempt made to establish the Plan of Campaign on the estate, 6418-6420——Belief that the arrears might be collected if time were allowed, 6423——Different character of the land on different parts of the estate, this having been considered in fixing the rents on which the agreements to purchase were based, 6424-6430.

Explanation respecting some conversation between Mr. O'Brien and witness at Moneymore respecting the rent on which the agreements were based; denial that in this matter there was any misleading of the Land Commissioners, or any intention to mislead, 6430-6443——Reduction of rents by 15 per cent. in 1881, but not on witness' recommendation, 6444-6446——Exception taken to some statements reflecting on the character of Major Miller, who was agent of the company for many years, 6445, 6446.

Cooks' Company. See *Mercers' Company.*

Costs (Purchase by Tenants). See *Drapers' Company.*

Information

Dickey, Rev. R. H. F., M.A. (Analysis of his Evidence)—*continued*.

Information as to the enormous increase in the rental of the Salters' Company from their Magherafelt Estate since they leased it about 100 years ago (the Company having eventually sold the property for 440,000 *l.*), whereas all the improvements came from the tenants, 70-100. 121-124. 173-177. 140-243. 289-299.

Complaint as to the companies not only having obtained the highest possible rents from the tenants but having thrown all the rates upon the county and the repairs and improvements upon the tenants; instance in the case of the Drapers' Company, 91-100. 190-116. 154-159. 180-185——Grounds for the statement that the companies have not only failed to encourage industries and manufactures on their property, but have, in effect, discouraged them, 101-108. 150-153. 178-183. 184-213. 228-239.

Comment upon the practice of the companies in acting through agents and deputations, 204-218——Great increase of local interest in the question of grants and subscriptions for educational, religious, and other purposes, it being held that the companies and their successors are bound by the original trusts in these matters, 259-288. 299, 300.

Dispensaries. Amount of support given by the companies to dispensaries, *Dickey* 61-66——Liberal help formerly given by the Drapers' Company to dispensaries, this having been withdrawn; less need for such help since the Poor Law Act, *Wilson* 311-313. 376-384——Explanation respecting the action of the Drapers' Company as regards the support given to dispensaries and medical men, *Sawyer* 6340-6345.

Explanation that the grants by the Mercers' Company to dispensaries have not been withdrawn, but that of the two medical men whom the company induced to settle on the estate, one retired and the other died, and that long ago the Poor Law came into operation; small grant still given to the successor of the doctor who died, *Watney* 4340-4341.

Explanation in connection with the withdrawal of some of the grants given to dispensaries by the Skinners' Company, *Saunders* 5[illegible]-5586.

Documentary Evidence. List of documents required to be furnished to the Committee, *p.* 1——Enumeration of the documents which, in witness' opinion, the Committee ought to have before them, *Todd* 3135, 3136——Paper handed in by Mr. Todd containing a list of the various documents relating to the case of the Irish Society and the several London Companies, *App.* 540.

Quotation by Mr. Walker of extracts from the Charter of March 1613, and from numerous deeds and other documents in support of the conclusion that not only the Irish Society but the several companies hold their estates in county Derry, subject to certain public trusts and obligations, *p.* 334 *et seq.*

Sundry Papers handed in by the Chairman of the Committee, and by counsel, in explanation of the legal position of the Irish Society, and of the several companies, *pp.* 448 *et seq.*

Paper supplied by Mr. Latham, containing a list of references to the Calendars of State Papers, Ireland, and to the Calendars of Patent and Close Rolls, in the years 1603 to 1627, and stating in continuous order what the documents are, and indicating the point of each document, *App.* 549-551.

Donagheady, Vicar of. Explanation as to the Skinners' Company having given a grant of a few hundred pounds to the vicar of Donagheady, *Saunders* 5501.

DONATIONS AND GRANTS (CHURCHES, SCHOOLS, &c.):

Great increase of local interest in the question of grants and subscriptions for educational, religious, and other purposes, it being held that the companies and their successors are bound by the original trusts in these matters, *Dickey* 9-33. 259-288. 299, 300.

Undue preference given, as regards the grants, to Episcopalian members, *Dickey* 34-36. 68-69. 164-167. 299, 300; *Wilson* 331. 354-376; *Ross* 6609-6614. 6824-6826——Injurious effect generally as regards churches and education by the sale of the companies' estates, *Wilson* 311.

Strong objection to the trust funds being conveyed to a religious denomination; recommendation that the successors of the present incumbents be not allowed to have any claim to the grants, which do the public no good, *Todd* 3118. 3180-3184. 3165-3278——Contention that the grants of the Irish Society and companies to schools and churches should be concentrated, as they produce little or no good under the present method of distributing them, *ib.* 3168-3170——Opinion that it is a mistaken policy for the companies to give money to churches instead of to objects by which the whole community would be benefited, *ib.* 3624-3631. 3670, 3677.

Reference to the Report of Lord Derby's Commission in 1884 as testifying to the liberal action of the City Companies in making grants to churches, schools, &c., on their Ulster estates, *Tweed* 6192-6224.

Liberal

Donations and Grants (Churches, Schools, &c.)—continued.

Liberal treatment received by witness from the Ironmongers', Mercers', and Skinners' Companies at different times; reference especially to Aghadowey parish, [illegible] 6491–6505. 6556–6561.

List of Presbyterian congregations, with the annual grants made by the different London Companies, and the grants withdrawn, *App.* 439–441 —— List of grants made by the several companies for churches and manses for Presbyterians, 442.

Statement showing how Presbyterians are treated as compared with Episcopalians, by the different London Companies, *App.* 443.

Summary of expenditure of the Mercers' Company since 1831 in respect of dispensaries, schools, &c., *App.* 548, 549 —— Expenditure of the Mercers' Company in donations and subscriptions in each of the years 1881–89, *ib.* 551.

Summary of the annual donations and subscriptions of the Grocers' Company to clergy and churches, schools, &c., in each of the years 1826–76, *App.* 554.

Annual expenditure of the Drapers' Company for public purposes in each year since 1875, *App.* 555.

Expenditure of the Fishmongers' Company in donations to ministers, schools, &c., in the years 1880–87; total of 11,683 *l.*, *App.* 558.

Expenditure of the Skinners' Company in the years 1877–88 in subscriptions and donations to churches, manses, schools, &c., *App.* 557, 558.

Annual expenditure of the Salters' Company in charitable donations since 1854, *App.* 560.

Statement of expenditure of the Ironmongers' Company in respect of ministers, churches, schools, &c., in the years 1881–90, *App.* 561, 563.

Annual expenditure of the Clothworkers' Company in allowances to clergy, schools, &c.; also, in donations and subscriptions, *App.* 564.

See also Arbor. Clothworkers' Company, 4. *Coleraine. Culmore. Dispensaries. Drapers' Company*, 7. *Education. Fishmongers' Company*, 8. *Foyle College. Haberdashers' Company. Irish Society. Londonderry. Mercers' Company. Pensions. Presbyterians. Private Owners. Rainey School. Roman Catholics. Salters' Company. Skinners' Company. Statute of Limitations. Trusts.*

Draper, Edward Herbert. (Analysis of his Evidence.)—Witness has been clerk to the Skinners' Company since 1875; 5811.

Statement submitted showing the income and expenditure of the company in respect of their Irish estate for ten years, from April 1877 to April 1886 (inclusive); explanation that the rent due or receivable up to 1st November, is included in the receipts up to the following April, 5819–5821. 5877. 5911–5914 —— Gross income from the estate of 11,760 *l.* in 1876, 13,500 *l.* in 1877, and 11,245 *l.* in 1886; judicial rents in nearly all cases, 5823–5827.

Information as to the total receipts from sales through the Land Commission, and the small balance remaining after payments to the Stationers' and Bakers' Companies, &c., 5830–5835 —— Total of 378 holdings still unsold, the rental being 2,147 *l.*, and the estimated value of 42,743 *l.*; 5837, 5838. 5878 —— Cessation of offers by the tenants, so that the unsold portion has been withdrawn from sale for the present, 5838–5844.

Explanation of the action of the company as regards grants; reference especially to the case of the parish priest of Dungiven, and of the clergyman and church of Lower Cumber, 5845–5853. 5862–5876 —— Grant given by the company on the occasion of the Londonderry Fishery disaster, 5854–5856 —— Settlement of questions of turbary, irrespectively of the company, 5857–5861 —— Correction of some inaccuracies in a Paper handed in by Mr. Dickey, 5870, 5871.

Statement to the effect that judicial rents were settled in 800 or 900 cases, either voluntarily or in the Land Court, sixteen years' purchase having been received, less a deduction of one-and-half year's rent, 5878–5897 —— Examination as to the expenditure in Ireland in respect of churches, schools, and other objects, the average for ten years having been 885 *l.*, whilst the average amount applied to general objects in the United Kingdom was 5,820 *l.*; 5900–5901. 5915–5919.

DRAPERS' COMPANY:

1. *Representations in detail by the Inspector for the Land Commission respecting the Proceedings of the Drapers' Company in carrying out the Sale of their Estate; strong Reflections upon the Action of the Company and their Treatment of their Tenants.*
2. *Reports of the Inspector in April and May 1889.*
3. *Petition from Tenants complaining of the higher Terms of Purchase, the excessive Costs, &c.*
4. *Complaint respecting not only the high Terms of Purchase, but the unfair Treatment of Roman Catholic Tenants.*
5. *Explanations in detail on the part of the Company and in Justification or Defence of the Terms of Sale and of their Action generally towards their Tenants.*
6. *Judgments of Mr. Commissioner Lynch upon certain Questions at issue between the Tenants and the Company.*
7. *Grants and Donations, and withdrawal thereof.*
8. *Receipts and Expenditure generally in respect of the Estate.*
9. *Original Deed between the Irish Society and the Company.*
10. *Contention that the Company are under no Obligations as Trustees.*

1. *Representations in detail by the Inspector for the Land Commission respecting the Proceedings of the Drapers' Company in carrying out the Sale of their Estate; strong Reflections upon the Action of the Company and their Treatment of their Tenants:*

Several official visits of witness to the Drapers' Estate, the negotiations for sale having extended over three or four years; complaint by the Land Commission that the sales were delayed in order that the company might first recover arrears of rent and interest, *O'Brien* 990-1008. 1010 *et seq.*—Great anxiety of the tenants on the better land of the estate to purchase their holdings, *ib.* 991.—Desire of the tenants on the poorer lands to purchase, but not at the price asked by the company, *ib.* 992. 1165-1168.

Reference to letters from the clerk of the Drapers' Company in August 1888 and January 1887 to the tenants, stating that no further rent or interest would be demanded after 1st November 1885, *O'Brien* 998-1007.—Complaint as to the litigation, delays, and costs in which the tenants were eventually involved at the instance of the company in order to recover arrears of rent and interest; judgment in favour of the company, the tenants subsequently paying up, as quickly as they could, *ib.* 1008 *et seq.*; 1107-1110. 1310-1315.

Total of about 7,000 *l.* recovered from the tenants on the Moneymore division of the estate for arrears and interest; particular instances of the heavy charges entailed upon tenants in order to provide this sum, *O'Brien* 1014-1018. 1041-1045.

Reference to a judgment by Mr. Commissioner Lynch as showing the view entertained by the Land Commission respecting the action of the company towards their Moneymore tenants, *O'Brien* 1051-1056.

Protracted delay on the part of the company in carrying out the sales on the Ballynascreen and other portions of the estate where the holdings are very small and poor; strong complaint as to the costly litigation and numerous eviction notices meanwhile at the instance of the company, *O'Brien* 1057 *et seq.*—Petition from the foregoing tenants in November 1889 setting forth their grievances against the company, *ib.* 1057-1060.

Personal inquiries by witness on the spot which satisfied him that the petition of the tenants was substantially correct and that many of them had been put under eviction after they had signed agreements to purchase; strong statements in his report to the Commissioners as to the action of the company, *O'Brien* 1061-1067.—Particular instances cited as showing the hard terms exacted by the company and the large increase of the purchase money by including arrears of rent and costs; amount of the judicial or fair rent in these cases, *ib.* 1068-1082. 1117-1122. 1169-1180.

Statement as to an agreement lodged with the Land Commission having represented a rent which was no longer the legal rent; grounds for the opinion that this was practically a fraud on the part of the company, *O'Brien* 1074-1083. 1181-1206.

Judgment of Mr. Commissioner Lynch on 31st July 1889, respecting the cases of tenants on the Ballynascreen and certain other parts of the estate; strong comments upon their treatment by the company, *O'Brien* 1088-1094.—Circular from the company in June 1889 stating that any tenant wishing to cancel his agreement to purchase is at liberty to do so, but that the terms of purchase cannot be altered, *ib.* 1095-1105.

Very slow progress now being made with sales on the estate; undue delay and subsequent expense after agreements to purchase are signed by the tenants before they are lodged with the Land Commission, *O'Brien* 1106-1115.—Revision and increase

DRAPERS' COMPANY—continued.

1. *Representations in detail by the Inspector, &c.*—continued.

of rents by the company from time to time, although the improvements were made by the tenants; widespread grievance on this score in spite of the Ulster tenant right, *O'Brien* 1129–1133. 1757–1762. 1868–1871.

Further statements as to the high rate of purchase money fixed in many instances by the Drapers' Company with reference to the fair rents; that is, more especially by the inclusion of arrears, *O'Brien* 1165–1180. 1319–1680.

Additional evidence respecting the case in which the agreement was misleading as to the amount of the legal costs; reference hereon to several agents who acted locally for the company in these cases, *O'Brien* 1181–1208.

Complaint as to the charge of interest on the purchase money rather than as to the price asked; examination hereon with further reference to certain letters from the company as to the alleged delay after the agreements were signed, *O'Brien* 1211–1222.——Means of ascertaining the judicial rents on the estate irrespectively of information from the company; grounds for complaint however on this score, *ib.* 1246–1251. 1263–1267.——Heavy costs, in some instances further adverted to, these however not resting with the company, *ib.* 1251–1258.

Further evidence as to the protracted and exceptional delay (about three years) between the making of the agreements for sale and their completion in the case of the Moneymore estate; conclusion that delay arose from the action of the company, *O'Brien* 1703–1715. 1841, 1843.

Examination with further reference to the recovery of arrears of rent and of interest from the Moneymore tenants, the Land Commission having come to the conclusion that the delay was protracted for this purpose, *O'Brien* 1716 *et seq.*; 1868.

Grounds for the statement that the interest on the purchase money was claimed up to May 1888 in violation of declarations in letters from the company to the tenants; reference especially to letter of 3rd January 1887, as containing a pledge which was not fulfilled, *O'Brien* 1718–1745. 1836–1875. 1901–1904.

Circumstance of the Commissioners not having been aware of the large amount of arrears claimed by the company, *O'Brien* 1716–1733.——Heavy charges upon the tenants for arrears and interest, the Commissioners having considered, however, that there was sufficient security for their advances to purchasers, *ib.* 1735–1783.

Statement on the subject of the sales in the Moneymore division having been based on the rents in 1880, not judicial rents, *O'Brien* 1764–1769.——Extent to which the company acted in opposition to a requisition by Mr. Commissioner Lynch as to the closing of the accounts with the tenants, *ib.* 1760–1769.

Evidence in detail respecting the action of the Drapers' Company in the matter of fifty-three of the poorer holdings on the Brackaslievegallion division of their estate, in respect of which eighteen years' purchase of the old rent was asked, *O'Brien* 1785–1835.——Large number of ejectments served by the company in the foregoing cases, whilst eventually the terms first offered to them were increased by the addition of rent, interest, or costs, *ib.* 1796–1803.

Circumstance of the judicial rents having been paid long before the agreements were signed in which the old rents were inserted; statement hereon as to the different forms of application or agreement used by the company at different times, *O'Brien* 1804–1808.——Rejection by the Land Commissioners of all the fifty-four cases of applications from the Brackaslievegallion division on the score of insufficient security, *ib.* 1810, 1827.——Inexplicable delays on the part of the company in proceeding with the sales in the foregoing cases; enhanced expense thereby to the tenants, 1828–1835.

Long acquaintance of witness with the Drapers' Estate, whilst he has visited it officially on four occasions, *O'Brien* 1905–1909.——Small holdings and small rents of the poorer class of tenants on part of the estate, some of whom come to England for work as agricultural labourers, *ib.* 1910–1914.——Several respects in which tenants are prejudiced by delays on the part of the company in completing sales, *ib.* 1916. 1927, 1928.

Assertion that in certain cases the judicial rent was fixed before the agreements were signed, *O'Brien* 1916, 1917.——Exceptionally hard treatment of the tenants of the Drapers' Company as compared with those of other companies; reference hereon to the suspension of Mr. Glover, the solicitor to the company, *ib.* 1973–1977.——Statement respecting the amount of expenditure of a public character by the Drapers' Company in former and recent years, respectively, *ib.* 1993–1998.

Letter of 18th May 1889 in which the Commissioners set forth their reasons for refusing loans in respect of the fifty-four holdings on the Brackaslievegallion division of the estate; report previously by witness to the Commission, *O'Brien* 2031–2033.

DRAPERS' COMPANY—continued.

2. *Reports of the Inspector in April and May* 1888:

Report of Mr. Murrough O'Brien, in May 1889, respecting the Brackaslievegallion division of the estate, comprising about 9,000 acres; strong statement therein reflecting upon the administration of the property, the unduly high rents, and the intimidation and undue influence resorted to in order to constrain the tenants to enter into contracts to purchase, *App.* 566, 567.

Report of Mr. Murrough O'Brien, in April 1889, respecting the delay in carrying out the arrangements for the purchase of their holdings by the tenants; blame attributed in this matter to the company, *App.* 579, 580.

3. *Petition from Tenants complaining of the high Terms of Purchase, the excessive Costs, &c.*:

Petition from tenants of the Ballynascreen and Brackaslievegallion divisions to the Irish Land Commissioners in February 1889 complaining of their unduly high rents, of the high rates of purchase, excessive costs, &c., *App.* 577, 578.

4. *Complaint regarding not only the high Terms of Purchase, but the unfair Treatment of Roman Catholic Tenants*:

Circumstance of the poorer tenants of the Drapers' Company on the inferior land being for the most part Roman Catholics, whilst the Protestants are chiefly in the Moneymore division, *O'Brien* 1291–1296.

Sale of the Drapers' Estate on eighteen years' purchase of the rental; less fair basis in this case than in the case of the Salters' Company, *Quinn* 4738–4741——Better land occupied by the Protestant tenants in the Moneymore division than by the Catholic tenants in the Ballynascreen division, whereas the latter were equally required to pay eighteen years' purchase; hardship more especially by reason of the enhanced value through the reclamations and improvements made at the tenants' expense, *ib.* 4741–4766——Pressure put upon the tenants by the Drapers' Company to compel them to buy; this did not apply equally to the Salters' Company, *ib.* 4751–4756.

5. *Explanations in detail on the part of the Company and in Justification or Defence of the Terms of Sale and of their Action generally towards their Tenants*:

Summary of the terms of sale, as set forth in a circular letter from the clerk of the company to the tenants in August 1886; offer to sell at eighteen years' purchase of the judicial rents, *Glover* 5952, 5953, 5963, 5964——Misunderstanding on the part of witness (as solicitor for the company) as to the rents upon which the purchase was based having been all judicial rents, the agreements not having been all signed; small proportion of the tenants who declined on this ground to be bound by the application forms which they had signed, *ib.* 5953–5960. 6111.

Intricate and protracted proceedings before the sales were completed, witness explaining the various causes of delay, and submitting that the difficulties and delays were principally owing to the tenants, *Glover* 5964–5978. 5999 *et seq.*; 6066–6073. 6105——Delay of nine months through the Land Commission having required the company to get a release from the Irish Society of a clause in their deed of 5th June 1663, with respect to timber rights, &c., *ib.* 5973–5979. 5994, 6000. 6059–6063.

Refusal of the tenants (in the person of Mr. Barrison) to pay either the arrears of rent due to 1st November 1885 or any more rent or interest on the purchase-money; subsequent action before Mr. Justice Murphy, in which it was decided that the tenants were bound to pay interest, *Glover* 5979–5984——Explanation that the terms were practically only seventeen years' purchase; reference hereon to the reduced rate of interest charged by the company, *ib.* 5980–5986. 6108–6111.

Considerable delay in completing the sales by the company through the new rules published by the Land Commission in November 1887, *Glover* 6000. 6084, 6085——Ultimate completion of the sales in the Moneymore division in February 1889; *ib.* 6000. 6015, 6016.

Comment upon the action of the Land Commission and of Mr. O'Brien as regards the re-inspection of the Moneymore holdings; very inadequate inspection upon which the latter based his report to the Commissioners, *Glover* 6000–6009. 6041–6063——Subsequent decision of Mr. Commissioner Lynch, releasing the tenants from any payment for rent or interest, *ib.* 6010.

Refusal of the company to follow the ruling of Mr. Commissioner Lynch, the sale having been subsequently completed upon the presentation by the tenants of a memorial to the Land Commission in July 1889; witness reads the memorial, which testifies to the liberal and generous treatment of the tenants by the company, *Glover* 6011–6011.

Drapers' Company—continued.

5. *Explanations in detail on the part of the Company, &c.*—continued.

Explanation in reply to complaint by Mr. O'Brien as to the action of the company in the cases of Miss Johnston, Mrs. Crooks, and Miss M'Cullough (three of their tenants), *Glover* 6023–6031, 6121–6130——Particulars also respecting the case of a tenant named Mallon, witness justifying the action of the company in the matter, *ib.* 6038–6040.

Denial that the tenants generally on the Moneymore division had any cause to be irritated by the action of the company (as stated in Mr. O'Brien's report), or that they were misled by verbal statements made to them by witness, *Glover* 6068–6075——Grounds for denying the accuracy of Mr. O'Brien's report and of Mr. Commissioner Lynch's judgment that the contracts with the tenants in the Ballynascreen and Brackaslievegallion divisions were obtained by intimidation and duress, *ib.* 6076–6103——Complaint that the company were not brought into court upon any one of the cases in which duress was said to have been exercised; Paper submitted containing explanations in these cases, *ib.* 6080, 6095–6103.

Explanations in reply to the charge of Mr. Commissioner Lynch, that "the agreements were presented to the Commission in a misleading form by the omission or concealment of the judicial rent," *Glover* 6104–6117——Inaccuracy of a statement that costs were, in any case, added by the company to the purchase-money, *ib.* 6118.

Dissent from Father Quinn's evidence as to the much more liberal action of the Salters' Company than of the Drapers' Company, *Glover* 6180–6187——Very good land in part of the Brackaslievegallion division, *ib.* 6188, 6189.

Further statement as to witness having been under the erroneous impression that the Moneymore tenants were under judicial rents when first invited to purchase their holdings, *Glover* 6190–6193.

Explanation that Mr. Glover had no authority from the company to have the agreements for sale to the tenants on other than the rents actually payable, *Sawyer* 6308, 6309——Desire of the company to treat their tenants with equality and without regard to religious denominations, *ib.* 6308——Denial that the company have declined to grant long leases of land in Moneymore, *ib.* 6314——Reply to a statement that the company fixed the purchase-money on the rent instead of the Government valuation, *ib.*

Sale of the greater portion of the estate since 1889; large reduction in the rental, *Sawyer* 6334–6350——Total of twenty-five members on the Court of the Drapers' Company, all business relating to the Irish Estate coming before the Court monthly, 6381–6384——Grant of aid in Ireland, as in England, according to the merits and necessities of each case, *ib.* 6385–6387.

Witness, who was agent for Drapers' Estate from April 1882 till January 1890, when he resigned, testifies to the marked improvement on the condition of the tenants and their liberal treatment by the company, *Sir W. Conyngham* 6410–6413, 6421, 6422, 6447, 6448——Different character of the land on different parts of the estate, this having been considered in fixing the rents on which the agreements to purchase were based, *ib.* 6424–6430.

Explanation respecting some conversation between Mr. O'Brien and witness at Moneymore respecting the rent on which the agreements were based; denial that in this matter there was any misleading of the Land Commissioners or any intention to mislead, *Sir W. Conyngham* 6430–6443——Reduction of rents by 15 per cent. in 1882, but not on witness' recommendation, *ib.* 6444–6446.

Exception taken to some statements reflecting on the character of Major Miller, who was agent of the company for many years, *Sir W. Conyngham* 6448, 6449.

Circular letter from the company's agent, in June 1889, with respect to the inaccuracy of certain statements by the tenants, and explaining the course of action to be adopted by the company upon the subject of the purchase of their holdings by the tenants, *App.* 580.

Correspondence and papers in the case of the Drapers' Company *v.* Barefoot, *App.* 581.

6. *Judgments of Mr. Commissioner Lynch upon certain Questions at issue between the Tenants and the Company:*

Judgment of Mr. Commissioner Lynch on 31st July 1889, upon the questions at issue between the Drapers' Company and their tenants on the Brackaslievegallion and Ballynascreen divisions, *App.* 573, 574.

Judgment of Mr. Commissioner Lynch upon the questions at issue between the company and their tenants on the Moneymore division, *App.* 575, 576.

7. *Grant*

DRAPERS' COMPANY—continued.

7. *Grants and Donations, and withdrawal thereof:*

Lengthened residence of witness at Cookstown (Tyrone) close to the Drapers' Estate; long period for which he and his predecessors have received an annual grant of ten guineas from the Company, *Wilson* 301-308 —— Withdrawal of the grant to witness in 1886, grants to other ministers having also been withdrawn; belief that this has been done so that the grantees might not have a vested interest in view of the sale of the estates, *ib.* 305-310.

Several instances of withdrawal or reduction of grants by the Drapers' Company in view of sale of their estate, *Jordan* 835-837. 919-926.

Explanation that the Company have come to no decision on the subject of the continuance of religious and educational grants, *Sawyer* 6341-6345. 6349-6351.

List of Presbyterian congregations, showing the number of families in each case, the annual grant received by each congregation, and the instances in which withdrawn, with the date, *App.* 443.

8. *Receipts and Expenditure generally in respect of the Estate:*

Reference to a return, showing how the Ulster estate of the Company was let, and the rents and fines received, previously to 1817, when the Company took over the management, *Sawyer* 6300-6316 —— Total agricultural rental of 9,893 *l.* in 1817, and of 10,850 *l.* in 1885; increase and reduction at different periods, *ib.* 6301. 6333-6340 —— Return handed in showing the receipts and expenditure for the last fifteen years, *ib.* 6302, 6303. 6317-6319. 6330, 6331.

Explanations respecting the expenditure out of the estate to the effect that out of a total receipt of about 168,000 *l.* since 1875, there has been an expenditure of 101,000 *l.* in Ireland, whilst some 67,000 *l.* went into the general funds of the Company, *Sawyer* 6388-6398.

Statement of receipts and expenditure of the Company in each of the years 1875-89; total of 168,369 *l.* as the receipts, the total expenditure having been 101,586 *l.*; *App.* 855.

Return of the number and amount of leases issued and sanctioned in respect of the estates of the Company, *App.* 865.

9. *Original Deed between the Irish Society and the Company:*

Indenture, in June 1613, made between the Irish Society and the Drapers' Company, *App.* 517-521.

10. *Contention that the Company are under no Obligations as Trustees:*

Argument in detail on the part of counsel for the Company that they are not under legal or other obligations as trustees, *pp.* 584 *et seq.*

See also *Agreements to Purchase. Arbitration. Arrears of Rent. Combinations of Tenants. Delays. Dispensaries. Eviction. Improvements on Estates. McElhatton, James. Moneymore. Plan of Campaign. Roman Catholics. Tenants.*

Dunboe Estate (Clothworkers' Company). See *Clothworkers' Company.*

Dunboe Presbyterian Church. Explanation as to the Clothworkers' Company having given 200 *l.* to the Presbyterian Church at Dunboe, of which Mr. Mark is minister, *Sir O. Roberts* 5888-5891.

Dungiven. Grievance in the sale by the Skinners' Company of houses and land in the town of Dungiven for large sums, although the increased value was all created at the tenants' expense, *Brown* 584-692 —— Subsidence of the strong feeling in Dungiven with regard to the treatment of the tenants by the Skinners' Company on fair rents being fixed and subsequent purchase, *Todd* 3485-3488.

See also *Roman Catholics. Skinners' Company.*

E.

Eccles, William. (Analysis of his Evidence.)—As Town Clerk of Coleraine witness submits resolutions adopted by the Town Commissioners and the Harbour Commissioners recognising the services hitherto discharged by the Irish Society as trustees, and deprecating any change which would prevent a continuance of the same action, 2019-2038. 2098, 2099.

Grants made by the Irish Society for public purposes in Coleraine to the amount of 1,000 *l.* in 1858, 1,000 *l.* in 1877, and 2,500 *l.* in 1883; 2059-2067 —— Grants made also for

Eccles, William. (Analysis of his Evidence)—*continued.*

for religious and educational purposes in Coleraine; large annual grant for the free schools, there having been continuous grants ever since 1813; 2080–2083. 2089–2094. 2163–2170—Information respecting a total contribution of 37,240 *l.* by the Society towards the Bann Navigation, 2081–2083. 2087. 2104–2117. 2171, 2172.

Belief that the people generally of Coleraine are fairly satisfied with the action of the Irish Society in making grants for different local purposes; reference hereon to the franchise on which the Town Council is elected, 2084–2086. 2118–2135—View of the bodies represented by witness that the trust funds of the Society should be expended in Coleraine and Derry; apprehended diversion of the funds, 2095–2097. 2100–2103.

Large expenditure by the Society on visitation expenses, including dinners, respecting which there is some dissatisfaction, 2136–2158. 2162–2164—Chief items making up the income of the Society, the ordinary income being from 17,000 *l.* to 18,000 *l.* a year, 2159–2161.

EDUCATION (GRANTS TO SCHOOLS BY IRISH SOCIETY AND LONDON COMPANIES):

Very few schools in the county of Derry, there being a great neglect of intermediate education on the part of the companies, *Disky* 57. 130–138—Pressing need of aid towards intermediate and technical education, *Brown* 681–684—Expenditure of the Drapers' Company on schools; this has not been considered as affecting the operations of the Land Commission, *O'Brien* 1337, 1338.

Summary of the circumstances under which in October 1888 the Endowed Schools Commissioners visited the Royal Schools and other schools in the north of Ireland in receipt of grants from the Irish Society; that is, in order to determine whether the grants were in the nature of endowments, *Lord Justice FitzGibbon* 1347–1349—Acceptance by the Commissioners as final of the judgment of Lord Lyndhurst in the case of the Skinners' Company *v.* the Irish Society in 1845, which established the existence of a public trust but admitted the right of the Society to increase or decrease the amounts applied from the trust to educational purposes, *ib.* 1349. 1360. 1385–1390. 1411–1413. 1534–1540. 1590–1593. 1610. 1627, 1628.

Reference to the Report in 1858 of the Endowed Schools Commission of 1854 as to the educational grants of the Irish Society "as parts of the trusts of their estates"; recommendation by the Commissioners on the subject of local management of the schools receiving grants from the Society, *Lord Justice FitzGibbon* 1350–1355—Total of 1,501 *l.* given in grants by the Society in 1858 to schools, mainly in the county of Londonderry, *ib.* 1356—Increase from 1,501 *l.* in 1858 to 3,318 *l.* in 1878 in the total educational grants of the Society; reference hereon to the report of the Commission of 1878; *ib.* 1367–1372—Large reduction between 1858 and 1880 in the total number of endowments in the county of Derry, *ib.* 1370–1378—Distinct feature in the case of model national schools that the appointment of teachers rests with the Commissioners instead of with local managers, *ib.* 1401, 1403.

View of the Endowed School Commissioners that it would be a much more satisfactory arrangement if the educational funds of the Irish Society and of the London Companies were defined and were placed under the management of the local bodies; disadvantage through the Society not seeing to the application of the funds, *Lord Justice FitzGibbon* 1404–1409. 1505–1508. 1518–1533—Deprecation of any withdrawal of the educational grants of the Society, *ib.* 1410–1413.

Several grounds upon which it has been contended before the Commissioners that the London Companies were not trustees for educational purposes; reference hereon to the charter and conditions under which their estates were conveyed to them, *Lord Justice FitzGibbon* 1414–1416. 1485–1504. 1585–1589—Summary of the grants and other assistance given by the different companies towards education in various places, *ib.* 1415—Great boon if the Companies set apart more funds for intermediate education under the control of the Commissioners; witness is not prepared to say that there is a legal claim upon them in the matter, *ib.* 1417, 1418. 1485–1504. 1509–1513. 1540.

Complaints before the Commissioners as to the Presbyterians and Roman Catholics not getting a fair share of the educational grants from the Irish Society and London companies, *Lord Justice FitzGibbon* 1514–1516. 1560–1567—Statement on the question of the grants generally having been reduced, *ib.* 1522–1524—Representation in one of the annual Reports of the Commissioners to Parliament as to the serious effect of withdrawal of the grants in the event of the sale of the estates, *ib.* 1541–1545.

Further statement as regards intermediate education to the effect that any available funds are specially wanted in this direction, and that the south and west of Ireland are at a disadvantage as compared with the north, *Lord Justice FitzGibbon* 1554–1561—Division of estates among the London Companies further adverted to, witness not admitting that there is the same educational trust as in the case of the Irish Society, *ib.* 1605–1611. 1631—Inability of witness to state whether there have been any withdrawal of grants since 1858, save in the case of Rainey School, *ib.* 1612, 1613.

Further

EDUCATION (GRANTS TO SCHOOLS, &c.)—continued.

Further evidence as to the amount of support given to intermediate schools, and as to the great need of increased aid, *Lord Justice FitzGibbon* 1604–1606——Special claim of the county of Londonderry in respect of grants from the London companies towards intermediate education, *ib.* 1611, 1682.

Suggestion that if, instead of granting 5*l.* each to a number of schools, the Irish Society gave to one or two good large schools only, the money would be better appropriated, *Sir W. Miller* 2500–2502.

Circumstance of the schools aided by the Irish Society being under the National Board, the teachers, however, being all Protestants, *Loughrey* 2848–2850——Statement as to grants having been withdrawn by the Skinners' Company from Episcopalian and Presbyterian schools as well as from Roman Catholic schools, *ib.* 4871–4891.

Reference to a passage in the Report of the Royal Commission for 1885–86 as representing the views of the Catholics of Derry as to the claim of the district to a continuance of educational grants from the property held by the Irish Society as trustees, *Quinn* 4738, 4769——Great injury as regards schools on the Drapers' Estate if Protestant Schools are alone aided, *ib.* 4801.

Entire approval of grants from the Skinners' Company being devoted to educational purposes; probability that the Company will continue to give liberally in aid of local education, *Saunders* 5516. 5560–5587. 5678–5685. 6754–6811.

Exception taken to certain conclusions of Lord Justice FitzGibbon as to the expediency of an entirely different administration of the educational funds, *Singly* 6563–6580.

Increased benefit to education by distributing grants among a large number of schools instead of combining them in support of one institution, *Ross* 6684, 6685.

Summary of grants made to Presbyterian schools and colleges by the several London companies, *App.* 439–442.

Statement showing, as regards endowments and annual grants respectively, how Presbyterians are treated as compared with Episcopalians by the several London companies, *App.* 448.

See also Coleraine. Donations and Grants. Endowed Schools Commission. Foyle College. Irish Society. Presbyterians. Rainey School. Roman Catholics.

ENDOWED SCHOOLS COMMISSION:

Constitution of the Endowed Schools Commission of 1885 as an executive Commission for framing schemes for endowments, witness being one of the two Judicial Commissioners, and there being three Assistant Commissioners; outline of the procedure, *Lord Justice FitzGibbon* 1339. 1342. 1345. 1346. 1636.

Summary of the views put forward by the Commissioners in their Report to the Chief Secretary for Ireland in November 1886, and in their annual Report in 1887; special stress laid upon the utterly inadequate provision made for intermediate education, *Lord Justice FitzGibbon* 1365. 1368–1383. 1417.

Conclusion of the Commissioners that they could not settle a scheme dealing compulsorily with the grants from the Irish Society without the consent of the latter, *Lord Justice FitzGibbon* 1385, 1387——Schemes framed by the Commissioners for Magee College, the Coleraine and Londonderry Institutions, and for the Royal Schools, *ib.* 1388. 1394.

Action of the Commissioners in defining the districts to which the endowments from the Royal Schools' Estates in Ulster are to be applied, six counties being interested; arrangement as to equal division between Protestants and Roman Catholics, *Lord Justice FitzGibbon* 1540–1548——Obstacle under the Educational Endowments Act to any action of the Commissioners with a view to the capture of fluctuating grants or endowments, *ib.* 1610–1612.

See also Education. Foyle College. Rainey School.

Entertainments (Visitation Expenses). See Irish Society.

Episcopalians. See Church Temporalities Commission. Clothworkers' Company, 4. Donations and Grants. Education. Irish Society. Presbyterians. Roman Catholics. Skinners' Company.

Evictions. Statement as to Mr. Commissioner M'Carthy having decided adversely to the grant of loans where tenants had been placed in possession of farms where there had been evictions, *O'Brien* 1036–1041——Instance of harsh treatment by the Drapers' Company in the case of a tenant named Grant, who was ejected, and whose crops were lost before he was re-instated, *Quinn* 4835–4841.

EXPENDITURE (*LOCAL CLAIMS*):

Grievance locally through the rents being mainly spent in London, the companies being absentee landlords, *Dickey* 68. 146–149. 151——Complaint as to the companies not only having obtained the highest possible rents from the tenants, but having thrown all the rates upon the county, and the repairs and improvements upon the tenants; instance in the case of the Drapers' Company, *ib.* 91–100. 109–116. 154–159. 180–185.

Proposed payment by the companies towards the county cess and the poor rate, as well as towards schools, churches, &c., *Brown* 657. 679–681——Belief that the London companies hold under the same tenure as the Irish Society; strong impression that if the Society expends its money in Derry the companies ought to spend their income where their estates are situated, *Sir W. Miller* 2401–2405. 2474.

Concurrence of witness in the opinion that as the funds derived by the London companies from their London properties are to be expended in London, so the wealth derived from the Irish properties should be expended in Ireland; impossibility of having the matter decided in a court of law, owing to the heavy expense that would be incurred in fighting a powerful company, *Todd* 3119–3134——Contention that the companies ought to spend in Ireland all the money derived from their Irish estates; evidence herein in support of the contention that the companies hold under a trust, *ib.* 3590–3614. 3630–3660. 3678–3684.

Question considered whether the two sums of 60,000 *l.* and 150,000 *l.* were expended by the London companies in Ireland at all; belief that this was so, *Saunders* 5515–5516.

Argument by counsel that the companies, as well as the Irish Society, had only a large discretion as to the expenditure in England of the proceeds of the estates, instead of a right to make such expenditure, pp. 363–386.

Argument on the part of the companies that they are not under any trust binding them as regards expenditure in Ireland, pp. 360 *et seq.*

See also Absenteeism. Clothworkers' Company, 2, 4. *Donations and Grants. Drapers' Companies*, 7, 8. *Education. Entertainments. Fishmongers' Companies*, 2, 3. *Improvements on Estates. Irish Society. Management. Mercers' Company. Private Owners. Trusts.*

F.

Farm Buildings and Improvements. See Improvements on Estates.

FISHERIES:

Attention called to the fact that some adjustment is necessary as regards the Foyle fisheries for the benefit of the poor fishermen who live along the loch, and for the peace of the country, *M'Cormick* 3742. 3749–3751——Grievance of the fishermen that the Lough Foyle fishing is not free to everybody, *Ballantine* 4002–4007——Claim put forward by the Irish Society as regards the fisheries; litigation with the fishermen on the subject, *Hamilton* 4438–4443. 4479. 4480; *Longfoley* 4813–4816. 4818–4832.

Belief that the Bann and Foyle fisheries were formerly let to Messrs. M'Corkell and Rennie by public tender at a rent of 3,500 *l.* a year, *Moore* 6690–6693——Public tender again resorted to in 1864, when Mr. Alexander and witness obtained a lease for ten years at a rent of 4,825 *l.* a year, *ib.* 6698–6700. 6835–6844.

New lease obtained in 1874 for twenty-one years at a rent of 5,080 *l.* a year, and with a condition that the lessees should spend 2,000 *l.* in developing the oyster fishery, and should undertake other industries, *Moore* 6701–6709——Expenditure of 2,500 *l.* by the lessees upon the oyster fishery, which proved an entire failure; probable causes to which owing, *ib.* 6707–6716. 6860–6861——Conclusion as to the Irish Society having a clear title to the fisheries, *ib.* 6717–6720.

Explanation as to the action of the Society and of the fishery lessees in opposing certain clauses in Bills promoted by the Harbour Commissioners in 1874 and 1882; amicable arrangement arrived at, so that the opposition was withdrawn, *Moore* 6721–5746.

Further particulars respecting the increase of rent for the fisheries from 4,825 *l.* to 5,080 *l.* in 1874, there having been no public tender on this occasion, but witness positively denying that there was any collusive arrangement, and asserting that the Society took the best steps for increasing their income from the fisheries, *Moore* 6829–6833. 6845–6855. 6859–6878——Inaccuracy of certain evidence of Mr. Ballantine as regards the fisheries, &c., *ib.* 6867, 6868. 6881–6885——Statement as to the Irish Society having held the fisheries at a dead loss before 1874; *ib.* 6869–6871.

Report, 1890—*continued.*

FISHMONGERS' COMPANY:

1. *Sale of the Company's Estate and Terms of Purchase by the Tenants.*
2. *Administration by the Company; Rental of the Estate and Local Expenditure.*
3. *Grants and Donations; Withdrawal or Commutation thereof.*
4. *Argument that the Company were not in the position of Trustees.*

1. *Sale of the Company's Estate and Terms of Purchase by the Tenants:*

Sale of the Fishmongers' Estate to the tenants shortly before the Ashbourne Act, about fifteen or sixteen years' purchase having been obtained, *Brown* 481–488. 498. 499.

Explanation that the company have sold all their lands in Ireland, having in 1882 first passed a resolution in favour of sale, and having in 1885 eventually decided to offer each tenant his holding at twenty years' purchase of the net rent, *Towse* 4868–4869.

Deduction of 12 per cent. allowed off the purchase-money, in respect of county cess, poor rate, draining and ditching, farm buildings, repairs, &c., a further 8 per cent. having been allowed for possible depreciation and other matters, *Towse* 4880–4885. 5009–5013.

Option of three different modes of purchase given to the tenants; the whole of the tenants (about 400) having practically accepted the terms, *Towse* 4887–4897——Adoption by the great majority of the tenants of the scheme of purchase by means of annual payments, inclusive of sinking fund and interest; main portion of the purchase-money received through the Land Commission, under Lord Ashbourne's Act, *ib.* 4907–4916. 5177–5186——Total of 143,868 *l.* as the purchase-money, less 20,011 *l.* for legal expenses, donations, redemption of tithe, &c., *ib.* 4916–4922. 4991–4994. 5037–5041. 5046–5048.

Evidence to the effect that the company did not get the full value of the estate, some of the farms having since been sold by the purchasers at very enhanced prices, after allowing for the value of the tenant-right, *Towse* 4996–5008. 5240–5244——Due consideration given by the Fishmongers' Company in their settlement with the tenants to the incidence of local burdens, and the liability for religious and educational objects, *ib.* 5235–5238.

2. *Administration by the Company; Rental of the Estate and Local Expenditure:*

Illustration of the exacting character of the administration by the company in the case of some land taken from the tenants and afterwards sold to them, *Brown* 550–561. 781–788——Explanations respecting the total expenditure by the company in Ireland out of their rental (about 10,000 *l.* a year), *ib.* 661–671. 794.

Evidence to the effect that the Fishmongers' Company raised the rents enormously on their estate, two rents that were 8 *l.* 15 *s.* 6 *d.* and 7 *l.* 10 *s.* in 1820 having since become 66 *l.* and 75 *l.*, respectively, *Todd* 3567–3570.

From 1836 till 1887 the company spent on an average about 4,777 *l.* a year in donations and contributions to churches, chapels, schools, &c., and upon general management, *Towse* 4870–4879——Varying size of the holdings from about ten acres to about 150 acres; great variation also in the rent per acre, *ib.* 4898–4906.

Explanation respecting the total rental of the estate and the increase or decrease at different periods since 1820, the gross rental on sale being about 9,800 *l.* as compared with 7,897 *l.* in 1820; reference to special instances of large increase, *Towse* 4939–4962. 4957–4960. 5168–5172. 5217. 5218——Considerable expenditure by the Company in keeping open the canal from Ballykelly to Lough Foyle, which was however quite out of use when the estate was sold, *ib.* 4967–4978.

Explanations in connection with certain returns showing the income and expenditure under different heads, and distinguishing between the amount expended in Ireland and England, respectively, *Towse* 5056–5089. 5219–5234——Average expenditure of about 800 *l.* a year in England on the Irish Estate over and above about 4,700 *l.* spent in Ireland, *ib.* 5082. 5146——Statement on the question of payment of county cess and poor rate by the Company before and since 1872, *ib.* 5127–5140.

Summary of expenditure of the Company in Ireland and England, in respect of their Irish Estate, for the years 1880–87; also, summary of income, *App.* 558.

Return of the number and amount of loans issued and outstanding in respect of the Fishmongers' Estate, *App.* 565.

3. *Grants and Donations; Withdrawal or Commutation thereof:*

Withdrawal of the educational grants formerly made by the Fishmongers' Company, *Brown* 498——Summary of the grants given by the company, those to the clergy having been commuted at three years' purchase, whilst seven schools were left without any compensation, *ib.* 548–558. 560–564. 661–671.

FISHMONGERS' COMPANY—continued.

3. *Grants and Donations, &c.*—continued.

Explanation that on sale of the estate no special provision was made for the continuance of donations to churches, schools, &c., *Towse* 4886——Commutation of the donations to the clergy by a lump payment for three years, *ib.* 4943–4947. 5049. 5050. 5058–5064.

Examination as to the company having discontinued their grants to schools and to churches and as to the grounds upon which witness justifies their action in the matter; reference more especially to the voluntary character of their contributions, and to their large expenditure under these heads before the sale of the estate, *Towse* 5000–5055.

List of Presbyterians in congregations, showing the number of families in each case, the annual grant received by each congregation, and the instances in which withdrawn, with the date, *App.* 441.

Summary of aid given to schools and extent to which withdrawn, *App.* 442——Treatment of Presbyterians as compared with Episcopalians, *ib.* 443.

4. *Argument that the Company were not in the position of Trustees:*

Grounds upon which it is contended by counsel for the company that they were not and are not bound as trustees in respect of their income from the estate, *pp.* 364 *et seq.*

See also Arrears of Rent. Improvements on Estates. Promissory Notes. Tenant Right. Tenants.

FitzGibbon, The Right Honourable Lord Justice. (Analysis of his Evidence.)—Official experience of witness since 1878 in connection with different Commissions on the subject of Education and Educational Endowments in Ireland; he has been engaged in two inquiries into the Ulster endowments, 1339–1344——Constitution of the Endowed Schools Commission of 1885 as an executive Commission for framing schemes for endowments, witness being one of the two Judicial Commissioners and there being three Assistant Commissioners; outline of the procedure, 1339. 1340. 1348. 1346. 1696.

Summary of the circumstances under which in October 1886 the Endowed Schools Commissioners visited the Royal Schools and other schools in the North of Ireland in receipt of grants from the Irish Society; that is, in order to determine whether the grants were in the nature of endowments, 1347–1349——Acceptance by the Commissioners as final of the judgment of Lord Lyndhurst in the case of the Skinners Company *v.* the Irish Society in 1845, which established the existence of a public trust but admitted the right of the Society to increase or decrease the amounts applied from the trust to educational purposes, 1349. 1350. 1385–1390. 1411–1418. 1534–1540. 1580–1603. 1610. 1647, 1648.

Reference to the Report in 1858 of the Endowed Schools Commission of 1854 as to the educational grants of the Irish Society as parts of the trusts of their estates; recommendation by the Commissioners on the subject of local management of the schools receiving grants from the Society, 1350–1355——Total of 1,501 *l.* given in grants by the Society in 1858 to schools, mainly in the county of Londonderry, 1358.

Explanations in detail respecting the case of Foyle College, the grants made thereto by the Irish Society and the London Companies, and the general results shown by the inquiries of the Endowed Schools Commission of 1854 and of the present Commission upon the question of the estates being held in trust for educational purposes, 1359 *et seq.* ——Statement in the Report of 1858 as to the withdrawal of donations from Foyle College by the different London Companies, while the Irish Society had increased their grants to 420 *l.*, having made grants ever since 1613; 1360–1367.

Increase from 1,501 *l.* in 1858 to 3,518 *l.* in 1878 in the total educational grants of the Irish Society; reference hereon to the Report of the Commission of 1878; 1367–1372——Foundation of the Londonderry Academical Institution by voluntary effort, it being under a mixed governing body, 1369——Large reduction between 1858 and 1880 in the total number of endowments in the county of Derry, 1370–1371——Satisfactory working of the arrangement with the present head master of Foyle College, the school being very successful under his charge, 1371–1377.

Contention before the present Commission in 1886 that Foyle College was exempt from the jurisdiction of the Commissioners; also, that the grants made by the Irish Society could be withdrawn at any moment, 1378–1384——Conclusion of the Commissioners that they could not settle a scheme dealing compulsorily with the grants from the Irish Society without the consent of the latter, 1386, 1387.

Summary of the views put forward by the Commissioners in their Report to the Chief Secretary for Ireland in November 1886, and in their Annual Report in 1887; special stress laid upon the utterly inadequate provision made for intermediate education, 1385. 1388–1393. 1427.

FitzGibbon, The Right Hon. Lord Justice. (Analysis of his Evidence)—*continued*.

Schemes framed by the Commissioners for Magee College, the Coleraine and Londonderry Institutions, and for the Royal Schools, 1384, 1394——Explanation as to the Commissioners not having framed a scheme for Foyle College, through the difficulty on financial grounds; particulars herein as to the present income and endowments, 1395-1398——Particulars respecting the Irish Society's Free Schools at Coleraine; causes of dissatisfaction with the committee of management, 1399-1401——Distinct feature in the case of model national schools, that the appointment of teachers rests with the Commissioners instead of with the local managers, 1402, 1403.

View of the Commissioners that it would be a much more satisfactory arrangement if the educational funds of the Irish Society and of the London Companies were defined and were placed under the management of the local bodies; disadvantage through the Society not owing to the application of the funds, 1404-1409. 1499-1508. 1515-1520——Deprecation of any withdrawal of the educational grants of the Society, 1410-1413.

Several grounds upon which it has been contended before the Commissioners that the London Companies were not trustees for educational purposes; reference hereon to the charters and conditions under which their estates were conveyed to them, 1414-1416. 1481-1504. 1584-1589——Summary of the grants and other assistance given by the different companies towards education in various places, 1425——Great boon if the companies set apart more funds for intermediate education, under the control of the Commissioners; witness is not prepared to say that there is a legal claim upon them in the matter, 1427, 1428. 1488-1504. 1509-1513. 1540.

History of the Rainey School at Magherafelt from its foundation in 1707, with explanations in detail as to the governing body, the aid received from the Salters' Company and the claims put forward on the part of the Presbyterians and Roman Catholics, respectively, 1428 *et seq.*——Review of the management and condition of the School from time to time and the several questions and difficulties dealt with by the Commissioners in framing their scheme for the school, with special reference to the action of the Salters' Company and the reduced amount now received from the Company, 1437 *et seq.*; 1637-1645.

Outline of the scheme for Rainey School, as re-cast and finally settled in January 1887; removal of all the objections except those from the Presbyterians, the latter having been overruled when the scheme was before the Privy Council, 1471-1483. 1619-1621——Impossibility of the school being efficiently continued in view of the great reduction in the endowment; grievance as to the superannuation of the head master (Mr. Kincaird), 1484-1487.

Complaints before the Commissioners as to the Presbyterians and Roman Catholics not getting a fair share of the educational grants from the Irish Society and London Companies, 1514-1518. 1560-1567——Statement as to the question of the grants generally having been reduced, 1522-1524——Representations in one of the Annual Reports of the Commissioners to Parliament as to the serious effect of withdrawal of the grants in the event of the sale of the estates, 1541-1548.

Action of the Commissioners in defining the districts to which the endowments from the Royal Schools estates in Ulster are to be applied, six counties being interested; arrangement as to equal division between Protestants and Roman Catholics, 1546-1548——Explanation respecting some 300 acres of land intercepted by the Irish Society from the Royal Free School of Londonderry; much larger sum contributed by the Society to Foyle College than is produced by this land, 1549-1553. 1596-1604.

Further statement as regards intermediate education to the effect that any available funds are specially wanted in this direction, and that the south and west of Ireland are at a disadvantage as compared with the north, 1554-1561——Explanation, in connection with the Rainey School, that there were two market places at Magherafelt but that there was no patent for a market, 1568-1571——Management of the Rainey School further adverted to in reference to the question of the Salters' Company being in the position of trustees, 1572-1583.

Conclusion as to a trust having been imposed upon the Irish Society for local education, though it seemed impossible to fix or set apart any definite amount for Foyle College, 1590-1604. 1610——Division of estates among the London Companies further adverted to, witness not submitting that there is the same educational trust as in the case of the Irish Society, 1605-1611. 1631.

Inability of witness to state whether there have been any withdrawal of grants since 1886, save in the case of Rainey School, 1612, 1613——Voluminous correspondence of the Commissioners in connection with the scheme for Rainey School, 1614——Surrender of the School Fund to the Salters' Company under the scheme as re-cast, 1615.

Obstacle under the Educational Endowments Act to any action of the Commissioners with a view to the capture of diminishing grants or endowments, 1616-1622——Consideration of the extent to which the public interests were represented in the litigation between the Skinners' Company and the Irish Society, the Attorney General having

FitzGibbon, The Right Hon. Lord Justice. (Analysis of his Evidence)—*continued.*

been a party to the proceedings, 1643-1648. 1657-1660——Limited weight attached to certain proceedings in the Star Chamber as regards the question of particular trusts having been attached, or being now attached to the estates of the London Companies and of the Irish Society, 1649-1654.

Inexpediency of the funds of Foyle College being left to the fluctuating discretion of a body in London, 1635——Reason given by the Salters' Company in 1857 for discontinuing their contributions to the Rainey School, that they had sold their estates, 1640-1645.

Explanation as to no Royal free schools having been allowed to the county of Londonderry, Foyle College operating however for the whole county; reference hereon to the withdrawal of the London Companies' grants, 1646-1653——Large support given by the Irish Society to the Academical Institution of Londonderry; scheme framed in this case, 1656.

Further evidence as to the amount of support given to intermediate schools and as to the great need of increased aid, 1659-1662——Efficiency of the Coleraine Academical Institution, under a mixed governing body; aid received from the Irish Society and the Clothworkers' Company, 1663-1667.

Explanations with further reference to the foundation and endowment of the Rainey School, the grants given by the Salters' Company, and the receipts of the company, from the market tolls, 1668-1677——Special claim of the county of Londonderry in respect of grants from the London Companies towards intermediate education, 1681, 1682.

Foyle College. Explanations in detail respecting the case of Foyle College, the grants made thereto by the Irish Society and the London Companies and the general results shown by the inquiries of Endowed Schools Commission of 1854 and of the present Commission upon the question of the estates being held in trust for educational purposes, *Lord Justice FitzGibbon* 1338 *et seq.*

Statement in the Report of the Commissioners in 1858 as to the withdrawal of donations from Foyle College by the different London Companies, whilst the Irish Society had increased their grants to 400 *l.*, having made grants ever since 1813, *Lord Justice FitzGibbon* 1360-1367——Satisfactory working of the arrangement with the present head master of the College, the school being very successful under his charge, *ib.* 1372-1377.

Contention before the Endowed Schools Commission in 1886 that Foyle College was exempt from the jurisdiction of the Commissioners; also, that the grants made by the Irish Society could be withdrawn at any moment, *Lord Justice FitzGibbon* 1378-1384——Explanation as to the Commissioners not having framed a scheme for Foyle College through the difficulty on financial grounds; particulars hereon as to the present income and endowments, *ib.* 1395-1398.

Conclusion as to a trust having been imposed upon the Irish Society for local education, though it seemed impossible to fix or set apart any definite amount for Foyle College, *Lord Justice FitzGibbon* 1597-1602. 1610——Inexpediency of the funds of Foyle College being left to the fluctuating discretion of a body in London, *ib.* 1635.

Foyle Fisheries. See *Fisheries.*

G.

Gaussen, P. C. (Analysis of his Evidence.)—Witness is a member of the Irish bar and is connected with the county of Derry; is conversant with the Salters' Estate, and was counsel for the tenants in regard to the Drapers' Company's sales, 2878-2881.

Submission by witness of a copy of a memorial, dated 1868, from the Mayor and Corporation of Londonderry to the Irish Society complaining of the refusal of the latter to give perpetuity leases, 2882-2885——Memorial, dated the 19th April 1867, from the tenants of the Salters' Estate in Magherafelt to the Salters' Company, complaining of a proposed increase of rent and infringement of the tenant-right custom, handed in by witness; also the Salters' Company's reply thereto claiming that they held the estate unfettered by any fiduciary conditions, 1883-2898.

Statement that the supplemental memorial (also handed in) specifies instances of increase of rent by the Salters' Company, Mrs. M'Fall's rent having been increased from 3 *l.* 19 *s.* to 19 *l.*; belief that Mrs. M'Fall's case is practically typical of the others, 2899-2914——Table showing the comparative rental of the various holdings in Magherafelt before and after 1854, together with purchase money and subsequent estimated expenditure by tenants in buildings, submitted by witness; evidence to the effect that these figures and the condition of the tenants were brought before the House of Commons, 2914-2923.

Unproductive

Gaussen, P. G. (Analysis of his Evidence)—*continued.*

Unproductive result of the expenditure of the Ironmongers' Company on their estate in Derry due to the absence of security of tenure, 3997-3991——Universal impression in the minds of the tenants on the Salters' Estate that the company, when negotiating the sale, gave an assurance that the grants to churches and charities would be continued; statement that, in consequence of an intimation in 1887 that the company would not be responsible for any more grants, several letters from tenants appeared in "The Times" and other papers, the result being that the grants were continued, 3991-3971. 3012-3016.

Evidence in support of the assertion that the Salters' Company put a certain amount of pressure upon the tenants to induce them to buy in 1886, and threatened legal proceedings for the recovery of the rent in one case, 3972-3998. 3004-3011. 3017-3020——Surprise expressed by Lord Ashbourne as to the manner in which the Salters' Company proposed to treat the head master of Bellaghy School, 3991-3101.

Girdlers' Company. Continued interest of the Girdlers' Company in the Skinners' Estate, they are desiring to take part in the management, *Saunders* 5489-5491——The company now hold about 10 or 11 per cent. of the whole estate, *ib.* 5492.

Glover, John. (Analysis of his Evidence.)—Witness, who is a solicitor, acted for the Drapers' Company in the sale of their estate to the tenants, 5950, 5951.

Summary of the terms of sale, as set forth in a circular letter from the clerk of the company to the tenants in August 1886; offer to sell at eighteen years' purchase of the judicial rents, 5951, 5953. 5963. 5964——Misunderstanding on the part of witness as to the rents upon which the purchases are based having been all judicial rents, the agreements not having been all signed; small proportion of the tenants who declined on this ground to be bound by the application forms which they had signed, 5953-5962. 8122.

Intricate and protracted proceedings before the sales were completed, witness explaining the various causes of delay, and submitting that the difficulties and delays were principally owing to the tenants, 5964-5978. 5969 *et seq.*; 6016-6075. 6805——Statement as to Mr. Commissioner Lynch having required the Irish Society to join in the conveyance to the tenants, 5973-5979. 6750-6263.

Refusal of the tenants (in the person of Mr. Barefoot) to pay either the arrears of rent due to 1st November 1885 or any more rent, or interest on the purchase-money; subsequent action before Mr. Justice Murphy in which it was decided that the tenants were bound to pay interest, 5979-5984——Explanation that the terms were practically only seventeen years' purchase; reference herein to the reduced rate of interest charged by the company, 5980-5983. 6806-6812.

Legal opinion obtained in the negative, from the late Sir George Jessel and the late Lord Chancellor Law, upon the question whether the London companies were under a trust in respect of their Ulster Estate, 5986-5998. 6091-6097. 6231-6258. 6264-6267.

Considerable delay in completing the sales by the Drapers' Company through the new rules published by the Land Commission in November 1888; 6000. 6004. 6009——Ultimate completion of the sales in the Moneymore Division in February 1889; 6000. 6019. 6016——Comment upon the action of the Land Commission and of Mr. O'Brien as regards the re-inspection of the Moneymore holdings; very inadequate inspection upon which the latter based his report to the Commission, 6020-6039. 6041-6063——Subsequent decision of Mr. Commissioner Lynch releasing the tenants from any payment for rent or interest, 6018——Refusal of the company to follow the ruling of Mr. Commissioner Lynch, the sale having been subsequently completed upon the presentation by the tenants of a memorial to the Land Commission in July 1889; witness reads this memorial, which testifies to the liberal and generous treatment of the tenants by the company, 6011-6032.

Explanation in reply to complaint by Mr. O'Brien as to the action of the Drapers' Company in the cases of Miss Johnston, Mrs. Crooke, and Miss M'Cullough (three of their tenants), 6053-6091. 8121-8130——Particulars also respecting the case of a tenant named Maher, witness justifying the action of the company in the matter, 6036-6040——Denial that the tenants generally in the Moneymore Division had any cause to be irritated by the action of the company (as stated in Mr. O'Brien's report), or that they were misled by verbal statements made to them by witness, 6068-6075.

Grounds for denying the accuracy of Mr. O'Brien's report, and of Mr. Commissioner Lynch's judgment that the contracts with the tenants in Ballynascreen and Brackaslievgallion Divisions were obtained by intimidation and duress, 6076-61[illegible]——Complaint that the company were not brought into court upon any one of the cases in which duress was said to have been exercised; Paper submitted containing explanations in these

 cases,

Glover, John. (Analysis of his Evidence)—*continued*.

come, 6000, 6095–6103——Circumstances under which the tenants were told by witness that the arrears must be dealt with as a condition of purchase, 6081–6099.

Explanations in reply to the charge of Mr. Commissioner Lynch that "the agreements were presented to the Commission in a misleading form by the omission or concealment of the judicial rent," 6104–6127——Inaccuracy of a statement that costs were in any case added to the purchase money, 6128——Inclusion of a small part of the arrears in the purchase-money; denial that that was an irregularity or would now be so considered by Mr. Commissioner Lynch, 6129–6135——Ample margin as regards security after the addition of a small amount of arrears, 6136–6141.

Grounds for a statement by witness in a letter of 10th June 1889 that there was an "illegal combination" among a number of tenants of the Ballynascreen and Brackaslievgallion divisions, 6142–6162.

Experience of witness for seventeen years as local solicitor for the Salters' Company; explanation hereon as to the abatement, through Lord Selborne, in the large increase of rents proposed in 1867, whilst there was a further reduction under the Act of 1881; 6146–6163, 6168–6177——Very liberal subscriptions by the Mercers' Company to the Irish Church Funds, 6164, 6165——Great benefit to the Church in respect of tithes, under the Church Act of 1869, 6174–6181.

Dissent from Father Quinn's evidence as to the much more liberal action of the Salters' Company than of the Drapers' Company, 6182–6187——Very good land in part of the Brackaslievgallion Division, 6188, 6189.

Further statement as to witness having been under the erroneous impression that the Moneymore tenants were under judicial rents when first invited to purchase their holdings, 6190–6193——Circumstances under which witness considered that the wife of Patrick Kane (absent in America) was entitled to sign an agreement in her name on the strength of a letter from him, 6194–6198——Explanation also as to the son of a tenant named Rose M'Bride having signed an agreement in his mother's name, 6199–6204.

Estimate of about 1,500 *l.* received in cash from certain tenants for arrears, 6214, 6215——Entirely spontaneous character of the memorial from the tenants to the Land Commission in July 1889; 6214–6220.

Examination showing that witness, who is a tenant of the Salters' Company, has written letters charging that company with having ruined the town of Magherafelt by not giving perpetuity leases, and with having compelled tenants who have bought to buy on their own improvements; these letters handed in, 6208–6197——Instance in witness' case of the Salters having included the tenants' improvements in the purchasing price, 6288–6289.

Glover, J. Communications from Mr. Glover to the Salters' Company in December 1885, and March and July 1888, setting forth several grievances as regards the treatment of himself and other tenants in the town of Magherafelt in the matter of rent, expenditure on improvements, &c.; sundry suggestions submitted for the consideration of the company, *App.* 597.

Goldsmiths' Company. Reference by counsel for the companies to certain papers in the case of the Goldsmiths' Company against Lord Shelburne in 1759 as going to prove that the company's estate was not impressed with a trust, *pp.* 372–374.

Reference also to this case as showing that the Goldsmiths' Company had no power to alienate until the Irish Society joined in the transfer, *pp.* 373, 374, 481.

Indenture between the Irish Society and the Goldsmiths' Company, dated 6th December 1791, *App.* 527, 528.

Grocers' Company. Rating of the Grocers' Estate at 6,457 *l.*; sale of portion, but not under the Ashbourne Act, *O'Brien* 984, 985——Belief that the Grocers' Company, who sold their estate in 1871, made some provision with regard to the grants by giving a lump sum to the parish church, *Todd* 3581, 3582.

List of Presbyterian congregations, showing the number of families in each case, the annual grant received from the Grocers' Company by each congregation, and the instances in which withdrawn, with the date, *App.* 441.

Statement handed in by the clerk to the company explanatory generally of the administration of their estate, and of the expenditure under various heads in each year from 1800 to 1876, *App.* 559–614.

H.

Haberdashers' Company. Sale of the Haberdashers' estate nearly two centuries ago, about one-third having been bought by a progenitor of Lord Waterford's family; periodical increase in the rents where tenants' improvements have been made, *Brown* 508-518. 522, 523——Entire discontinuance of the Haberdashers' Company's grants, *ib.* 571, 572.

Statement as to the Haberdashers' Hall having been twice burned down, whilst the Company gave up all their documents relating to their Irish estate when it was sold to Lord Waterford in 1675; *p.* 354.

Hamilton, Edward A. (Analysis of his Evidence.)—Long connection of witness with the Londonderry Port and Harbour Commission, which was incorporated in 1854; 4359, 4360.

Explanatory statement respecting the borrowing powers of the Commissioners, their action in carrying out quays, docks, &c., and in otherwise improving the harbour; enormous development of the port thereby, 4361-4369——Grant conditionally by the Irish Society of the reversionary interest in the lands for the quay and docks; grant also of 1,000 *l.* a year, for seven years from 1854, towards the cost of the works, 4369-4374.

Litigation with the Society respecting the reclamation of slob-land; act eventually obtained by the Harbour Commission at considerable cost through the opposition of the Society, giving them certain powers on this and other points, 4374-4385. 4394, 4395. 4423-4427——Further powers obtained under Act in 1882, under which the shipbuilding yard and extensive dredging have been carried out; cost entailed by this Bill, 4381-4386. 4426-4431.

Statement to the effect that towards a total expenditure of about 136,000 *l.* the Irish Society have contributed little more than 7,000 *l.*; general opinion in the town that the Society have done practically nothing for the Harbour Trust, 4366-4369. 4387-4407——Very small value attached to the grant of the reversion of the land for the quays and docks, 4391. 4418-4421.

Grounds for the conclusion that the Society have acted in a very arbitrary and illiberal manner towards the Harbour Trust; reference hereon to the question of reclamation of the slob-land and the conditions enforced under the arrangement in 1864; 4408-4418. 4476-4478——Great advantage if the rates or dues of the port could be reduced by means of aid from the Irish Society, as by a reduction of the heavy bond debt of the Harbour Trust, which now amounts to 180,000 *l.*; claim upon the Society in the matter, 4432-4437. 4445-4469. 4474. 4476. 4484-4491.

Reference to the local fishery rights claimed by the Society; litigation with the fishermen on the subject, 4438-4443. 4470, 4480——Further statement as to the heavy cost entailed upon the Harbour Commission through the opposition of the Society to the Bills of 1864 and 1882; 4481-4483. 4492-4497.

I.

Improvements on Estates:

Increase in the value of the estates through the tenants' improvements; great mischief in this respect where short leases are given, *Wilson* 339-345——Improvements on the Salters' estate made almost entirely by the tenants, whereas all the increased value has gone to the company and has been taken out of the country, *Jordan* 848, 861-863. 902-910.

Grounds for concluding that the Drapers' Company have not been in the habit of expending money on the improvement of farms or farm buildings, though they have laid out money on plantations, roads, and drains, *O'Brien* 1153-1158. 1257-1263——Increased value of the holdings by reason of tenants' improvements, it being no business of the Land Commissioners to inquire by whom improvements have been made, *ib.* 1650-1609——Universal practice of the country as to repairs and new buildings being carried out at the tenants' expense; exception in so far as the Drapers' Company have spent a very large sum upon the town of Moneymore, *ib.* 1918-1924.

Statement that in most cases the tenants who have made improvements are paying the landlord for them, under the Act of 1881; *Todd* 3346-3348——Statement as to the tenants having made the great bulk of the improvements; reference hereon to the report by Lord Derby's Commission, *ib.* 3440-3445——Reclamation by the tenants at their own expense of 130,000 acres since 1609; estimate that of the estates conveyed to the Commissioners in 1609, which were valued at about three millions, from half to two-thirds had been created by the tenants, *ib.* 3461-3466——Degree of compensation to the tenant for improvements made by him if the land be held at a very low rent, *ib.* 3704. 3705.

1. *Generally*

IRISH SOCIETY—continued.

1. *Generally as to the Administration by the Society, and the Extent and Character of its Expenditure in Ireland:*

Much more liberal action of the Irish Society in recent years than in former times; great improvement if the London companies were equally liberal, *Brown* 675–678.

Impression of the Corporation of Londonderry that some of the expenditure of the Society is rather excessive, *Baxter* 1191–1201. [illegible]——Summary of the grants and other expenditure of the Society in Londonderry, *ib.* [illegible] *et seq.*

Enumeration of some of the items upon which the Irish Society have expended large sums, in Londonderry, Culmore, and Coleraine, under the heading of "Public Improvements, Building Expenditure;" explanation that although Culmore is geographically in Donegal it is included in Derry for taxation purposes, *Sir W. Miller* 1308–1319——Belief that when Sir Charles Lewis denounced the expenditure of the Irish Society in 1878 he was supported by public opinion; existence of a feeling that the cost of management is still excessive, *ib.* [illegible].

Certain amount of dissatisfaction among the agricultural tenants of the Society at their not having got their holdings at reduced rents; complaint of the tenants of the advance in rent on their leases coming to an end, *Sir W. Miller* [illegible]——Opinion that if the expenditure of the Society were cut down the rents could be reduced and the grants increased; impression that there is room for saving being effected in some of the items of expenditure, *ib.* [illegible].

Exhibition of a considerable amount of public spirit by the Irish Society when Sir Sydney Waterlow was Governor, large sums having then been expended on public improvements, *Sir W. Miller* [illegible]——Evidence to the effect that a very large proportion of the funds of the Society is expended in Ireland, *ib.* [illegible]——Beneficial management by the present Governor of the Irish Society, *Magee* 2761.

Evidence to the effect that the management expenses are excessive, and that an improved system of administration is greatly required, *Todd* [illegible]——Unpopularity of the Irish Society in Londonderry; desirability of their being disestablished, as they do no good, *ib.* [illegible]——Grounds for the opinion that the Society have treated their tenants very badly, the latter having had to go to the Land Court to get their rents reduced, *ib.* [illegible].

Opinion that there has not been any marked improvement in the management of the Society during the last seven years; admission that the leases since 1873 have been granted in perpetuity, *Ballintine* [illegible]——View of witness that though the Society know less than their local agent they prefer their own judgment to his advice; general feeling that advantages are given by the Society as the result of "backstairs" influence, *ib.* [illegible].

Belief that if the trust had been properly managed for the last thirty-five years the income of the Society would have been doubled; probability that if the letting of the building property and fisheries were thrown into the open market for competition a large income would be realised, *Ballintine* [illegible] *et seq.*——Complaints as to the manner in which the grants of the Society are distributed, the result being in witness' view a degrading system of bribery; suggestion that the funds should be devoted to the improvement of the land and the reduction of taxation, *ib.* [illegible].

Comment upon the restrictions imposed by the Irish Society on political grounds in respect of a site for a temperance hall, so that the site was not granted, *Langtry* [illegible]——Admission as to the Society having given large grants to Londonderry and Coleraine, *ib.* [illegible].

Very beneficial administration generally by the Irish Society, especially in recent years; witness deprecating any transfer of their functions, *Smyly* [illegible] *et seq.*——Very favourable administration by the Society in comparison with private owners, *ib.* [illegible]——Exception taken to certain evidence of Dr. Todd as unduly severe upon the Society, *ib.* [illegible]——Several instances of the liberal action of the Society in different parts of the diocese of Derry, witness testifying mainly from his personal experience, *ib.* [illegible].

Exceedingly beneficial operation of the Society in many ways; excellent service rendered in the cause of education, *Ross* [illegible]——Probable room for improvement in the system of administration by the Society, as in most other administrations, *ib.* [illegible].

Result of witness' experience as a tenant of the Irish Society, and of the experience of other tenants, that the Society have not demanded excessive rents; reference hereto to some cases brought into the Court, *Moore* [illegible].

Irish Society—continued.

2. *Explanations on the part of the General Agent of the Society:*

Explanation of the action of the Society towards the tenants in Londonderry as regards a block of land in Strand-road, the lease having fallen in; very little competition for same, *Montgomery* 6907-6918——Careful local inquiry by witness in all cases of renewal, &c. upon which the Society require information, *ib.* 6919-6924——Opportunities of witness for becoming conversant with the working of the several institutions with which the Society is connected, *ib.* 6925-6928.

Readiness evinced by the Society to grant a site for a temperance hall, *Montgomery* 6929——Favourable reply given to an application for a site for a house for indigent ladies, *ib.* 6930-6934——The promoters have never intimated what they really want, and have not followed up their application, *ib.* 6932-6934——Publicity of all the grants made by the Society to the different religious bodies, *ib.* 6935-6942.

Result of witness' experience as a land agent that he considers the Irish Society are exceedingly careful and economical in the management of their estate, *Montgomery* 6962——Differences between the Society and some of their tenants as to rents, a considerable number having gone into Court and obtained reductions, *ib.* 6963-6976——Belief that the rents paid by Mr. Samuel Osborne were settled without going into Court, *ib.* 6978-6981.

Grants to the amount of about 1,500 *l.* a year given to Presbyterian and Dissenting schools and colleges, about the same amount being given to those of the Episcopal Church, *Montgomery* 6996-7002——Numerous grants or donations to churches, these being much larger in the case of the Episcopal Church, *ib.* 7003-7007——Advice given by witness to the Society, and usually adopted, as to the grants to be given; judgment exercised by the visitation in the matter, *ib.* 7010-7016. 7070-7073.

Information respecting the expenditure in salaries and gratuities, and the payment to the Deputy Vice Admiral (or general agent), the bailiff of Culmore Ford, the surveyor, and others, *Montgomery* 7029-7049.

3. *Visitation Expenses:*

Large expenditure by the Society on visitation expenses, including dinners, respecting which there is some dissatisfaction, *Keelin* 2136-2158. 2162-2164.

Particulars relative to the visitation expenses of the Society, and the cost of entertainments in Coleraine and Londonderry to public bodies and the tenantry, *Montgomery* 7050-7059——Small number of Roman Catholic clergy invited to the entertainments as compared with Episcopalians and Presbyterians, *ib.* 7061-7066.

4. *Amount at which the Estates are rated:*

Rating of the Irish Society's estates at 11,236 *l.*, *O'Brien* 983, 984.

5. *Income from various Sources; Local Claim thereto:*

Chief items making up the income of the Society, the ordinary income being from 17,500 *l.* to 18,000 *l.* a year, *Keelin* 2149-2161——Main items of 8,881 *l.* from Derry and liberties, and of 3,161 *l.* from fisheries, *ib.* 2160.

Contention that the income of the Society, being derived from Londonderry and Coleraine, should be retained in Derry county, *Baxter* 2034-2037; *Sir W. Miller* 2371-2375. 2611-2614.

6. *Question as to the Society joining in the Conveyances of the London Companies' Estates:*

Statement on the subject of the Irish Society having been required to join in the conveyances from the Drapers' Company to the tenants, *O'Brien* 1003-1007——Inability of witness to say whether any delay was caused by the Society having joined in the conveyance to the Drapers' Company; doubt as to the Society having directly joined in any conveyance under the Land Purchase Act; release only having been given, *Todd* 3401 *et seq.*——Circumstances of the Society not having joined in the conveyance of the estate of the Fishmongers' Company, *Toome* 4981-4982.

7. *Absence of Notice of Sale of the Estate of the Society:*

There has been no notice to the Land Commission respecting any sale of the estate, *O'Brien* 981.

8. *Constitution of the Society:*

Objection to the present system that the members of the Society hold office for much too short a period, and that there are too many members; suggestion that three trustees might be sufficient, *Sir W. Miller* 2356-2358. 2605-2610. 2681-2683.

Irish Society—continued.

8. *Constitution of the Society*—continued.

Improvement if the members of the Society were elected for five or seven years instead of only two years, *Smyly* 6463–6485——Improvement if one-third of the members of the Society did not retire till every seven years, instead of the members being all elected for only two years, *Ross* 6617. 6629. 6636.

Constitution of the Society for the year 1838; *App.* 543.

9. *Question of transfer of Functions from the Society and of Local Administration, as by the Corporation of Londonderry:*

Statement that the Londonderry Corporation regard the Irish Society as trustees who are entitled to assist the Corporation out of the funds of the trust; belief that this view of the Society is based upon the Judgment of the House of Lords in the case of the Skinners' Company, *Baxter* 2178–2180. 2185–2203——Possibility of the trust being better administered by Irish trustees on the spot than, as at present, by a London body who cannot have a good knowledge of local affairs, *ib.* 2178–2182. 2201–2204.

Opinion that there is yet some force left in the recommendation of the Royal Commission of 1854 that the Society should be dissolved, although the administration has been much more liberal towards the township during the last seven years; conclusion that the change is largely due to the personal views of Sir John Whittaker Ellis as Governor, *Miller* 2333–2344. 2413–2472. 2434–2481. 2516–2541. 2577–2583. 2681–2684——Feeling in Londonderry that the relation between the Irish Society and the Corporation is indefensible in principle, and that it causes an immense amount of delay in regard to the sanctioning of bye-laws, *ib.* 2355–2370. 2419–2433.

Doubt as to the advisability of the management of the Society's estate being transferred to local trustees; desire of witness to see the property sold and the money invested in Ireland, *Sir W. Miller* 2424–2428. 2475–2480. 2551 *et seq.*; 2677–2680. 2769–2787.

Conclusion that there is no reason why the trust which is Irish, and for the benefit of Irishmen, should be administered by Englishmen in London; if it were administered locally there would probably be a saving of 2,000 *l.* a year in the expenses, *Sir W. Miller* 2556–2563. 2598–2610.

Grounds for witness' disapproval of the management of the Society's funds being entrusted to local trustees; preference that the estates should be sold rather than the trust transferred, *Magee* 2764–2768. 2817–2845. 2854–2870——Fear that if the Society were abolished some of the funds might be taken from Derry, *ib.* 2871–2877.

Conclusion that the Irish Society is an obsolete body that ought to be dissolved, and that an improved administration is much needed, *Todd* 3091–3103. 3150–3165——Advocacy of a reformed constitution of the Corporation of Londonderry concurrently with a transfer of administration from the Society, *ib.* 3104–3111. 3152–3160.

Non-objection to the administration of that portion of the fund which is applied to general purposes outside the city being in the hands of properly constituted and impartial local trustees; explanation that the word "local" is only intended to apply to the county of Derry, *Todd* 3111–3117. 3161, 3164.

Willingness of witness, if the Irish Society were dissolved, that the funds should be handed over to the Londonderry Corporation; belief that the high franchise is the main reason why there is only one Catholic on the Corporation, *M'Corkell* 3758–3769.

Approval of the management of the trust, so far as the Corporation lands are concerned, being placed in the hands of the Londonderry Corporation if the remainder be given to local men appointed either by the Government or the Lord Chancellor of Ireland, *Dallinstow* 3848–3855. 3946–3949. 4008–4010.

Absence of any material change for the better as regards Derry, under the present governorship of the Irish Society, witness submitting that the Society should clear out altogether, leaving the property to be locally administered, *Loughrey* 4691–4694.

Examination upon the question whether the funds of the Society and their property generally would not be better administered and more economically by a local or county body; advantages attached by witness to the present system of management from London, *Smyly* 6507–6546. 6553–6556. 6563–6591.

Approval generally of the present system of administration by the Society, from London; witness deprecating any change in the direction of a local Irish body, or any severance of the connexion between the Society and the city of Derry, which has lasted for some 300 years, *Ross* 6618–6623. 6629–6631. 6640–6689.

Report, 1890—*continued*.

Irish Society—continued.

10. *Arguments on the part of Counsel as regards the Obligations and Legal Position of the Society:*

Explanation on the part of counsel for the companies that he separates his case entirely from that of the Irish Society, and contends that the former are not bound by any trust which may have been imposed on the latter, *pp.* 360 *et seq.*

Broad distinction on several grounds drawn by counsel for the Skinners' Company between the legal position of that company and of the Irish Society, his contention being that the obligations upon the latter did not apply to the former nor to the companies generally, *pp.* 405 *et seq.*

Explanations by counsel on behalf of the Irish Society as to the powers, duties, and legal position of the Society, and the limited sense in which they are to be considered trustees, though they do not claim to hold their estates for their own benefit, *pp.* 413-417.

Various public purposes to which the Society have applied the rents derived from the estates, *pp.* 413, 414, 417.

Exceptional circumstances under which the Society might be made accountable to the Crown and to the Corporation of London, *p.* 417.

Large discretion claimed for the Society in the discharge of its duties, together with an absolute discretion as to the amount in which it should, for any special purpose, apply its income, *p.* 417.

11. *Documentary Evidence on various Points:*

Translation of the Charter of King James the First, dated 29th March 1613; details therein of the circumstances and conditions of the grant to the Society of the governors and assistants of London of the new Plantation of Ulster, *App.* 464-478.

Copy of judgment of the Star Chamber (10 Charles I.) rescinding the grant to the Irish Society, *App.* 490-496.

Copies of grants of special pardons from Charles the First to the Irish Society and the several London companies, *App.* 496-499.

Petition from the companies to Parliament in 1641 setting forth their claims in connection with their large expenditure in Ulster, *App.* 499-501.

Copy of records of the Common Council in 1641; sundry resolutions in support of the claims of the citizens of London, and in disproof of the order made in the Court of Star Chamber, *App.* 501, 503.

Document, dated 4th August 1741, showing the Irish Society's "disclaimer of all young trees or saplins planted, or to be planted, on any of the respective proportions belonging to the several chief companies of London in Ireland," *App.* 535.

Judgment of Lord Langdale as Master of the Rolls, in November 1838, in the case of the Skinners' Company *versus* the Irish Society, the Mercers' Company, and several other companies; opinion that the powers granted to the Society and the trusts reposed in them were in part of a general and public nature, independent of the private benefit of the companies, *App.* 536-543.

See also *Bann Navigation. Bye Laws. Coleraine. Crown Rents. Culmore. Education. Fisheries. Foyle College. Goldsmiths' Company. Improvements on Estates. Leases. Londonderry. Roman Catholics. Skinners' Company. Tenants. Trusts.*

Ironmongers' Company. Recent division of the Ironmongers' Estate among the several other companies associated with that company as owners; total of 405 tenants on this estate, paying 5,470 *l.* yearly, *O'Brien* 979-982.

Unproductive result of the expenditure of the Ironmongers' Company on their estate in Derry, due to the absence of security of tenure, *Gausen* 4927-4931.

List of Presbyterian congregations, showing the number of families in each case, the annual grant received by each congregation, and the instances in which withdrawn, with the date, *App.* 440.

Copy of grant from the Irish Society to the Ironmongers' Company, dated 7th November 1618; *App.* 485-488.

Statement of income and disbursements of the Irish estates belonging to the Ironmongers' Company and their associates, the Brewers, Scriveners, Pewterers, and Carpenters' Companies, and the Corporation of London, for the years ending 30th April 1881 to 1890, inclusive, *App.* 580, 583.—Details of expenditure under different heads, *ib.*

J.

L.

Report, 1890—*continued.*

LONDONDERRY:

1. *Administration by the Irish Society as regards Leases and Ground Rents; want of Perpetuity of Tenure.*
2. *Action of the Irish Society with reference to the Port and Harbour; Complaints on the part of the Port and Harbour Commission.*
3. *Summary of Grants by the Society in Londonderry.*
4. *Constitution of the Corporation; inadequate Representation of Roman Catholics.*
5. *Claim to Local Expenditure of the Income of the Irish Society.*

1. *Administration by the Irish Society as regards Leases and Ground Rents; want of Perpetuity of Tenure:*

General satisfaction at present with the manner in which the affairs of the Irish Society are managed, so far as Londonderry is concerned, the chief complaint formerly having been that perpetuity leases were not granted; opinion that the prosperity of Londonderry would have been more rapid if the leases had been granted thirty or forty years ago, *Baxter* 2223-2228. 2283-2289——Advocacy of greater facilities, and of more favourable terms with respect to ground-rents in obtaining leases from the Irish Society, especially as regards land for manufacturing purposes, *ib.* 2229-2233. 2238-2250.

Concurrence in the view that if perpetuity leases had been granted by the Society seventy or eighty years ago, Londonderry would probably have been in as good a position now as Belfast, *Sir W. Miller* 2350-2364. 2506-2528. 2584-2597. 2611 *et seq.*

Evidence to the effect that the failure of the Irish Society to grant perpetuity leases before 1770 has had a very bad effect upon the prosperity of Londonderry; statement that the slob lands along the quays are lying waste, waiting for the terminable leases to expire, *Magee* 2746-2703. 2778-1808. 2812-2821——Strong feeling on the part of the citizens in favour of perpetual leases, the church lands, which are granted in perpetuity, being much sought after; opinion that the holders of perpetual leases should be obliged to build, *ib.* 2751-2760. 2807-2811.

Statement as to nine-tenths of the property belonging to the Irish Society having more than 100 years ago been leased in perpetuity; explanation that the ground could not be properly utilised until very lately under the Settled Estates Act on account of the leases being encumbered, *Magee* 2769-2778. 2814-2822. 2865, 2884.

Submission by witness of a copy of a memorial dated 1858 from the Mayor and Corporation of Londonderry to the Irish Society complaining of the refusal of the latter to give perpetuity leases, *Grasam* 2881-2884; *App.* 681.

Refusal of the Irish Society to make grants of the freehold in Londonderry or to give long leases of it; complaint that the nine-tenths of the Society's property alleged to have been given in perpetuity a century ago has been left in the hands of a few private individuals to make or mar the city, *[illegible]* 3429-3436.

Instances of the prejudicial effect of the exorbitant land rents, charged by the Society, upon business enterprise in Londonderry, *Ballantine* 3795-3801. 3848 *et seq.*

Grounds for the statement that the development of Derry has been greatly retarded by the restrictions in the Irish Society's leases, *Langtry* 4637-4641——Great natural advantages of the place, *ib.* 4638.

2. *Action of the Irish Society with reference to the Port and Harbour; Complaints on the part of the Port and Harbour Commission:*

Obstruction by the Society to all the improvements that have been proposed by the Harbour Commissioners, *Ballantine* 3815. 3816. 3973-3983.

Incorporation of the Londonderry Port and Harbour Commission in 1854; *Hamilton* 4359, 4360——Explanatory statement respecting the borrowing powers of the Commissioners, their action in carrying out quays, docks, &c., and in otherwise improving the harbour; enormous development of the port thereby, *ib.* 4361-4369.

Grant conditionally by the Irish Society of the reversionary interest in the land for the quays and docks; grant also of 1,000 *l.* a year for seven years from 1854 towards the costs of the works, *Hamilton* 4369-4374——Litigation with the Society respecting the reclamation of slob land; Act eventually obtained by the Harbour Commission at considerable cost through the opposition of the Society giving them certain powers on this and other points, *ib.* 4374-4386. 4394. 4398. 4423-4427——Further powers obtained under Act in 1882, under which the ship-building yard and extensive dredging have been carried out; cost entailed by this Bill, *ib.* 4381-4386. 4416-4421.

Statement to the effect that towards a total expenditure of about 235,000 *l.* the Irish Society have contributed little more than 7,000 *l.*; general opinion in the town that the Society have done practically nothing for the harbour trust, *Hamilton* 4387-4407. 4366-4369——Very small value attached to the grant of the reversion of the land for the quays and docks, *ib.* 4391. 4418-4421.

Grounds for the conclusion that the Society have acted in a very arbitrary and illiberal manner towards the harbour trust; reference herein to the question of reclama-

Loughrey, The Rev. Edward. (Analysis of his Evidence.)—Considerable experience of witness as parish priest of Dungiven respecting the action of the Skinners' Company and the Irish Society in the city and county of Derry; he represents the views of the Roman Catholic bishop of the diocese, and of tenants on the Skinners' Estate, 4498–4504.

Evidence showing that a marked distinction has been made by the Skinners' Company in their pecuniary treatment of Protestants and Roman Catholics, both on religious and educational grounds, the former community having been dealt with much more liberally than the latter, 4505–4530——Complaint as to the action of the company in respect of the house of the Roman Catholic parish priest of Dungiven and the house of the Protestant rector; more liberal donations also to Church of Ireland and Presbyterian clergy, 4506–4513. 4529. 4530. 4695–4715.

Grievance as regards the increased rents charged to town tenants in 1872 when the Ogilby lease fell in; obstacles to the tenants purchasing under the Ashbourne Act, 4531–4537——Strong comment upon the reservations of royalties, and upon other restrictions in some of the leases on the Skinners' Estate, 4538–4550. 4659–4663——Enhanced value of each holding to the company at the expense of improvements made by the tenants, 4551–4553. 4664——Existence of letters on the part of the company threatening the tenants that they should suffer if they did not purchase, 4553. 4554.

Examination showing in detail the much larger proportionate expenditure of the Irish Society upon Protestant and Presbyterian than upon Roman Catholic cathedrals or other places of religious worship and schools in Derry, 4555–4603——Comment upon the restrictions imposed on political grounds in respect of a site for a temperance hall, so that the site was not granted, 4566–4571. 4656–4658. 4687–4690. 4718–4720.

Personal affront offered by the Society in their mode of addressing the Roman Catholic Bishop of Derry; practical refusal of his application, 4601–4609. 4639–4645. 4683. 4686——Grounds for the statement that the development of Derry has been greatly retarded by the restrictions in the Society's leases, 4607–4612.

Claim put forward by the Irish Society as regards the fisheries; litigation with the fishermen on the subject, 4623–4627. 4628–4633——Dread of tenants as to the renewal of their leases, so that they are afraid to make complaints, 4637——Admission as to the Society having given large grants to Londonderry and Coleraine; reference hereon to the great material advantages of the former, 4633–4638.

Circumstance of the schools aided by the Society being under the National Board, the teachers, however, being all Protestants, 4640–4650——Information respecting portion of the Skinners' Estate not yet sold; opinion that the tenants are on the whole fairly satisfied with the company, 4664–4669——Statement as to grants having been withdrawn by the company from Episcopalian and Presbyterian schools as well as from Roman Catholic schools, 4671–4681.

Equitable claim of the tenants to the enhanced value of the Skinners' Estate given thereto by the tenants, 4680–4684——Absence of any material change for the better as regards Derry, under the present governorship of the Irish Society, witness submitting that the Society should clear out altogether, leaving the property to be locally administered, 4691–4694——Satisfaction to the Roman Catholic body in Derry if all creeds were treated impartially and alike in the matter of grants, 4716. 4717.

Lower Cumber. Memorial of tenants who are members of the congregation of Lower Cumber praying the Skinners' Company to continue the grant of 10 *l.* a year to the congregation, *App.* 429.

Letter on behalf of the company, dated 2nd January 1889, enclosing cheque for 10 *l.* as a final payment, *App.* 429.

Further letter on behalf of the company, dated 15th February 1890, stating that they will transfer to the trustees free of rent the manse and grounds held by them at 1 *l.* a year, *App.* 429.

M.

M'Cormick, William Henry. (Analysis of his Evidence.)—Witness is a magistrate of the city of Londonderry and one of the Roman Catholic residents; speaks on behalf of the Catholics, 3706–3708. 3755–3757.

Statement that the Roman Catholics of Londonderry feel that they, as a body, have been neglected, while the Protestants have been favoured, by the Irish Society; universal conviction that it was useless to ask the Society for anything for the Catholics on account of the terms of the charter, 3709–3740. 3743–3746. 3753. 3754——Desire of the Catholics to see the estate of the Society turned into money, and a portion of the proceeds used for paying off the debts incurred in making the quays, docks, &c., the balance to be divided fairly among all the religious denominations, 3741. 3748.

M'Cormick, William Henry. (Analysis of his Evidence)—*continued*.

Attention called to the fact that some adjustment is necessary as regards the Foyle fisheries, for the benefit of the poor fishermen who live along the loch, and for the peace of the country, 3746. 3749–3751——Willingness of witness, if the Irish Society were dissolved, that the funds should be handed over to the Londonderry Corporation; belief that the high franchise is the main reason why there is only one Catholic on the corporation, 3758–3769.

Magee College. Liberal aid given by the Irish Society to Magee College, *Bass* 6619, 6620.

M'Elhatton, James. Hardship in connection with the issue of writs against J. M'Elhatton, a tenant of the Drapers' Company, for arrears of rent; proceedings in this case for four consecutive years, entailing heavy costs, *Quinn* 4767–4784. 4811–4828.

Magee, Thomas Scholes. (Analysis of his Evidence.)—Witness has been a member of the Corporation of Londonderry for eight years and knows the city well, 2744. 2745.

Evidence to the effect that the failure of the Irish Society to grant perpetuity leases, before 1778 has had a very bad effect upon the prosperity of Londonderry; statement that the slob lands along the quays are lying waste, waiting for the terminable leases to expire, 2746–2763. 2778–2800. 2812–2820——Strong feeling on the part of the citizens in favour of perpetual leases, the church lands, which are granted in perpetuity, being much sought after; opinion that the holders of perpetual leases should be obliged to build, 2754–2760. 2807–2811.

Recognition of the beneficial management by the present Governor of the Irish Society, 2761——Grounds for witness' disapproval of the management of the Society's funds being entrusted to local trustees; preference that the estates should be sold rather than the trust transferred, 2764–2768. 2827–2845. 2854–2870.

Statement as to nine-tenths of the property belonging to the Society having, more than 100 years ago, been leased in perpetuity; explanation that the ground could not be properly valued until very lately, under the Settled Estates Act, on account of the leases being unexpired, 2769–2778. 2814–2822. 2863. 2864——Insufficiency of the representation of Roman Catholics on the Londonderry Corporation, 2838. 2839.

Statement that in the case of renewals of leases, as they fell in, the Society only charged a very small rent, together with a septennial rent and the secretary's fees, 2846–2853——Fear that if the Irish Society were abolished some of the funds might be taken from Derry, 2871–2877.

Magherafelt. Advantage of the long leases given when the town of Magherafelt was built, *O'Brien* 1142–1145.——*See also Salters' Company.*

Management Expenses. Summary of the expenses of management of the Mercers' Company since 1831, in decennial periods, *App.* 548, 549——Total management expenses of the Mercers' Company in each of the years 1881–89; also expenditure under different heads, *ib.* 550, 551.

Summary of the annual management expenses of the Grocers' Company from 1838 to 1876, *App.* 554.

Total amount of the charges of management of the Drapers' Company in each of the years 1875 to 1889, *App.* 555.

Expenses of management of the Fishmongers' Company in the period 1880–87, *App.* 558.

Annual expenditure of the Salters' Company under the head of management in Ireland and England, respectively, since 1864, *App.* 560.

Statement of the cost of management of the Ironmongers' estates in the years 1881–90, *App.* 561, 563.

Annual expenditure of the Clothworkers' Company under the head of management in Ireland in the several years 1841–70, *App.* 564.

See also Agents. Clothworkers' Company. Drapers' Company. Expenditure. Fishmongers' Company. Improvements on Estates. Irish Society. Leases. Londonderry. Private Owners. Salters' Company. Skinners' Company. Trusts.

Mark, The Rev. John. (Analysis of his Evidence.)—Residence of witness on the Clothworkers' Estate for twenty-three years; he is conversant with the circumstances attending the sale of the estate to Sir Harvey Bruce in 1871, 385–388——Complaint that the estate was sold for 25,000 *l.* less than the tenants would have given, that the rents were largely raised, and that the grants for religion, education, and charity have been discontinued, though they were kept up for some years by Sir Harvey Bruce as a condition of the purchase, 388 *et seq.*

Mark, The Rev. John. (Analysis of his Evidence)—*continued.*

Strong comment upon the refusal of the company to sell to the tenants, one member of the company having said that it would not be desirable to root the Irish in the soil, 383. 410–411. 435. 443–445. 446–472 —— Comment also upon the refusal of the company, or their agent, to see deputations in London respecting the former increase of rents and the claims of the Presbyterian body, 398. 400. 446–449.

[illegible] Company. See Mercers' Company.

MERCERS' COMPANY:

Rating of 11,740 *l.* in the case of the Mercers' estate in Derry, no notice of sale having yet been given, *O'Brien* 982, 983.

Reference to the Mercers' Company as the premier London Company of the four associated companies, *Watney* 4033–4036. 4296 —— Submission by witness of a statement giving a short history of the company's dealings with their Irish properties, and including printed copies of the documents of title, *ib.* 4037–4044.

Evidence to the effect that the company have not sold any of their property, except one small freehold in 1812; absence of any representation on the part of the tenants that they wished to buy, *Watney* 4045–4048. 4257–4263 —— Statement that the company did not take any personal part in the management of the estate until 1831 when the long lease fell in; expenditure of 300,000 *l.* since 1831 on the estate; the object having been to benefit the whole property rather than any particular farm, *ib.* 4050–4063. 4070.

Detailed summary handed in, showing the expenditure on the estate; reduction of the annual rental from 10,443 *l.* in 1831 to 9,200 *l.* at the present time, it having been 10,111 *l.* in 1851, and 11,769 *l.* in 1875, *Watney* 4064–4092. 4101–4103. 4178–4183. 4245–4249. 4288–4293. 4832–4834 —— Estimate that the expenses of management amount to about 1,100 *l.* a year, the net rental being about 8,000 *l.* a year; average (during the fifty years) of the expenses, 1,347 *l.*, and of the net rental, 8,000 *l.*, to 10,000 *l.*; *ib.* 4093–4100. 4119–4122. 4184–4188.

Prosperous condition of the estate, there being practically no arrears; occasional complaints from tenants that the rental has been too high, *Watney* 4104–4110. 4118. 4294–4303 —— Belief that two-fifths of the tenants are Roman Catholics, two-fifths Presbyterians, and one-fifth Episcopalians; details of the expenditure of the company on schools, the annual amount being 400 *l.*; *ib.* 4111–4117 —— Information as to the manner in which the accounts of the estate are made up and audited, *ib.* 4123–4136.

Particulars of the rents and fines at each sub-letting of the estate before 1831, showing a great improvement in the value of the property, *Watney* 4137–4150 —— Enumeration of the improvements made by the company since 1831, the last averaging about 5,000 *l.* a year; admission that the agricultural improvements on the holdings have been made by the tenants, *ib.* 4151–4178.

Statement that after payment of the annual expenditure the balance, which is about half of the income from the Irish estate, goes into the general account of the companies; impression that none of that account is expended for Irish uses, *Watney* 4187–4244. 4304–4316. 4351. 4358 —— Evidence to the effect that the building leases given by the company are for ninety-nine years, and that previously they were for sixty-one years, *ib.* 4316–4331 —— Satisfaction of the other associated companies with the manner in which the estate is managed by the Mercers' Company, *ib.* 4313–4349.

Very liberal subscription by the Mercers' Company to the Irish Church funds, *Glover* 6164, 6165 —— Thriving condition of the Mercers' estate, the improvements upon it having been made long before the Act of 1881, *Moore* 6769–6776. 6856–6868.

Argument in detail on the part of counsel for the company that they are not bound as trustees in respect of their estate, pp. 364 *et seq.*

List of Presbyterian congregations, showing the number of families in each case, the annual grant received by each congregation, and the instances in which withdrawn, with the date, *App.* 442.

Copy of the grant from the Irish Society to the company of Mercers, dated 17th October 1618, *App.* 481–484.

Indenture in August 1658 between the Irish Society and the Mercers' Company, being a counterpart release of the Manor of Mercers, *App.* 504–510.

Indenture, as between the Irish Society and the Company, in June 1663, being a release of the Manor of Mercers, *App.* 511–516.

Paper handed in by Mr. Watney containing a summary of expenditure, under various heads, on the Irish estate of the Mercers' Company, in decennial periods from 1831 to 1889; total expenditure of 299,761 *l.* in fifty-nine years, or an average annual expenditure of 5,080 *l.*, *App.* 548, 549. 551.

Mercers' Company—continued.

Statement of receipts from expenditure on the company's estate, showing the amount divisible between the company and the Cooks' Company, Brewers' Company, and Masons' Company, respectively, for the period from 1881 to 1889, *App.* 650.

Detailed statement of receipts from rents, &c., and of expenditure under different heads, for the several years, 1881–89, *App.* 651.

See also Clady River. Dispensaries.

Merchant Taylors' Company. Circumstance of the Merchant Taylors' Company having had an equitable interest in one-fourth of the Clothworkers' estate, so that the whole of the purchase-money did not go to the latter company, *Sir O. Roberts* 5425–5431.

Middlemen. Non-concurrence of witness with the statement that the adoption of perpetual leases would revive to some extent the principle of the middleman; explanation that it is not intended that any estate shall be handed over *en bloc* to one or two men, *Todd* 3108–3115.

Probability that schools, churches, &c., were not largely supported when the Clothworkers' estate was in the hands of a middleman, *Sir O. Roberts* 5376–5380——Prejudicial operation of the system of middlemen under perpetuity leases, *Montgomery* 6901.

Miller, Sir William. (Analysis of his Evidence.)—Witness has been five times Mayor of Londonderry, and holds several official medical positions there; speaks on behalf of his fellow townsmen, 2305–2307. 2570–2572. 2685–2696.

Enumeration of some of the items upon which the Irish Society have expended large sums in Londonderry, Culmore, and Coleraine, under the heading of "Public Improvements, Building Expenses, &c."; explanation that although Culmore is geographically in Donegal, it is included in Derry for taxation purposes, 2308–2319——Belief that when Sir Charles Lewis denounced the expenditure of the Irish Society in 1875 he was supported by public opinion; existence of a feeling that the cost of management is still excessive, 2320–2344. 2364–2371. 2659–2661.

Opinion that there is yet some force left in the recommendation of the Royal Commission of 1854 that the Society should be dissolved, although the administration has been much more liberal towards the tenantry during the last seven years; conclusion that the change is largely due to the personal views of Sir John Whitaker Ellis, 2333–2334. 2413–2423. 2434–2481. 2525–2541. 2541. 2577–2583. 2681–2684——Agreement of witness with the statement that if perpetuity leases had been granted by the Society seventy or eighty years ago Londonderry would probably have been in as good a position as Belfast, 2350–2354. 2306–2525. 2584–2597. 2611 *et seq.*

Feeling in Londonderry that the relation between the Irish Society and the corporation is indefensible in principle, and that it causes an immense amount of delay in regard to the sanctioning of bye-laws, 2355–2370. 2429–2433——Contention that the income of the Society, being derived from Londonderry and Coleraine, should be retained in the county, 2372–2378. 2611–2614.

Certain amount of dissatisfaction among the agricultural tenants of the Society at their not having got their holdings at reduced rents; complaint of the tenants of the advance in rent on their leases coming to an end, 2378–2401. 2406–2412. 2462–2473. 2549–2550. 2671–2676. 2726–2743——Belief that the London companies hold under the same tenure as the Irish Society; strong impression that if the Society spends its money in Derry the companies ought to spend their income where their estates are situated, 2402–2405. 2474.

Doubt as to the advisability of the management of the Society's estates being transferred to local trustees; desire of witness to see the property sold and the money retained in Ireland, 2424–2428. 2475–2480. 2551 *et seq.*; 2677–2680. 2769–2707——Opinion that if the expenditure of the Society were cut down the rents could be reduced and the grants increased; impression that there is room for saving in some of the items of expenditure, 2481–2519.

Suggestion that if, instead of granting 5 *l.* each to a number of schools, the Society gave to one or two good large schools only, the money would be better appropriated, 2500–2509——Approval of steps being taken with a view to the agricultural tenants becoming freeholders, 2541–2548.

Statement that the great objection to the present system is, that the members of the Society hold office for much too short a period, and that there are too many members; suggestion that three trustees might be sufficient, 2556–2558. 2605–2610. 2661–2669——Conclusion that there is no reason why the trust, which is Irish, and for the benefit of Irishmen, should be administered by Englishmen in London; if it were administered locally

Miller, Sir William. (Analysis of his Evidence)—*continued.*
locally there would probably be a saving of 1,000 *l.* a year in the expenses, 1555-1563. 1598-1610.

Concurrence of witness in the opinion that the Catholics are not sufficiently represented in the Londonderry Corporation; belief that they have reason for dissatisfaction with the administration of the Society, from which they have derived no material benefit, 2564-2576. 2697-2699. 2716-2725.——Decided opinion that a system of perpetual leaseholds would be advantageous to Londonderry; probability, however, of such a system preventing an increase in the amount available for public purposes, 1611-1644.

Explanation that the fact that Roman Catholic charities do not figure to any appreciable extent in the accounts of the Society is due to the difficulty experienced by the Society, under their charter, in supporting those charities, 2631-2633. 2710-2716.——Exhibition of a considerable amount of public spirit by the Irish Society when Sir Sydney Waterlow was Governor, large sums having then been expended on public improvements, 1634-1644.——Evidence to the effect that a very large proportion of the funds of the Society is expended in Ireland, 2666-2670. 2708, 2709.

Minerals. Statement that when the Irish Society granted their estates to the companies they retained the minerals, timber, fishing, &c.; opinion that if the Society has parted with any mines to the Drapers' Company it has done so negligently, *Todd* 3407-3418.

Belief that upon sale by the Fishmongers' Company there was no reservation of minerals, *Tower* 4977-4980.——Reservation of all minerals on the Skinners' Estate to the Irish Society, *Saunders* 5811-5815.

Moneymore. Very large outlay by the Drapers' Company in building the village of Moneymore; unsatisfactory results from this expenditure, long leases not having been given, *O'Brien* 1123. 1134-1143. 1831-1841.——Bar to the erection of manufactories in Moneymore through the shortness of the leases granted by the Drapers' Company, *ib.* 1999-2001.——*See also Drapers' Company.*

Montgomery, Thomas Bedford. (Analysis of his Evidence.)—Witness has been general agent of the Irish Society since 1844, 6888-6891. 6981-6985.

Belief that the grant of perpetuity leases was discontinued by the Society about 1836 on account of the bad condition into which the property was allowed to fall, 6893-6898.——Precautions now taken for the proper maintenance of the property when leases are granted, 6899, 6900.——Practice as to the valuation of holdings when leases fall in, a renewal being offered in each case to the occupying tenant; denial that excessive rents are charged, 6901. 6903-6906.

Prejudicial operation of the system of middlemen, under perpetuity leases, 6902.——Explanation of the action of the Society towards the tenants as regards a block of land in Strand-road, the leases having fallen in; very little competition for sites, 6907-6918.——Careful local inquiry by witness in all cases of renewal, &c. upon which the Society require information, 6919-6924.

Opportunities of witness for becoming conversant with the working of the several institutions with which the Society is connected, 6925-6928.——Readiness evinced by the Society to grant a site for a temperance hall, 6929.——Favourable reply given to an application for a site for a home for indigent ladies, 6930-6934.——Funds given by the Society to the school of Culmore, which is undenominational and is ample for the place, 6935-6937.

Publicity of all the grants made by the Society to the different religious bodies, 6938-6942.——Plans produced and explanations thereon showing that the Society have made very valuable grants to the harbour commissioners, 6943-6957. 6987, 6988.

Result of witness' experience as a land agent that he considers the Irish Society are exceedingly careful and economical in the management of their estate, 6958.——Differences between the Society and some of their tenants as to rents, a considerable number having gone into court and obtained reductions, 6959-6976.——Practice not to rent the tenants upon their own improvements, 6977.——Belief that the rents paid by Mr. Samuel Osborne were settled without going into Court, 6978-6981.

Large proportion of the property in the city of Derry which is held on perpetuity leases, 6981-6986.——Dealings of the Society with the slob lands and foreshore without preventing the formation of shipbuilding yards, 6989-6996.

Grants to the amount of about 1,500 *l.* a year given to Presbyterian and Dissenting schools and colleges; about the same amount being given to those of the Episcopal Church, 6998-7001.——Numerous grants or donations to churches, these being much larger in the case of the Episcopal Church, 7003-7007.——Advice given by witness to the Society, and usually adopted, as to the grants to be given; judgment exercised by the witness in the matter, 7010-7016. 7070-7076.

N.

O.

O'Brien, Murrough. (Analysis of his Evidence)—*continued.*

by the Land Commission; additional amounts sanctioned but not yet paid, 969–976. 1156–1158 —— Completion of transactions in respect of 2,186 holdings, the total amount actually paid being 678,302 *l.*; 971–973. 978.

Inability of witness to state the amount or value of the estates in Derry still unsold by the Salters' Company and Drapers' Company, 979. 988, 989 —— Recent division of the Ironmongers' estate among the several other companies associated with that company as owners; total of 405 tenants on this estate, paying 4,470 *l.* yearly, 979–981 —— Rating at 11,740 *l.* in the case of the Mercers' estate in Derry, no notice of sale having yet been given, 982, 983.

Rating of the Irish Society's estates at 11,236 *l.*; there has been no notice of sale, 983, 984. 986 —— Rating of the Grocers' estate at 6,457 *l.*; sale of portion, but not under the Ashbourne Act, 984, 985 —— Rough estimate, based on the rating, of from a million to a million and a-half as the capital value of all the estates, sold under the Act of 1885, or remaining unsold, 986–989. 1159–1164.

Several official visits of witness to the Drapers' estate, the negotiations for sale having extended over three or four years; complaint by the Land Commission that the sales were delayed in order that the company might first recover arrears of rent and interest, 990–1008. 1020 *et seq.* —— Reference to letters from the clerk of the Drapers' Company in August 1886 and January 1887 to the tenants stating that no further rent or interest would be demanded after 1st November 1885, 998–1007 —— Complaint as to the litigation and costs in which the tenants were eventually involved at the instance of the company in order to recover arrears of rent and interest; judgments in favour of the company, the tenants subsequently paying up as quickly as they could, 1005 *et seq.*; 1007–1010.

Repeated efforts made by the Land Commission to induce the Drapers' Company to complete the sales, the delay and the litigation having weakened the security of the Commission for their advances to the tenants; report made by witness to the Commissioners in April 1889 to this effect, 1008. 1014–1040. 1060–1066 —— Total of about 7,600 *l.* recovered from the tenants on the Moneymore division of the estate for arrears and interest; particular instances of the heavy charges entailed upon tenants in order to provide this sum, 1014–1016. 1041–1049.

Reference to a judgment by Mr. Commissioner Lynch as showing the view entertained by the Land Commission respecting the action of the Drapers' Company towards their Moneymore tenants, 1051–1056.

Protracted delay on the part of the company in carrying out the sales on the Ballynascreen and other portions of the estate where the holdings are very small and poor; strong complaint as to the costly litigation and numerous evictions with miserable results at the instance of the company, 1057 *et seq.* —— Petition from the foregoing tenants in November 1889 setting forth their grievances against the company, 1057–1060 —— Personal inquiries by witness on the spot which satisfied him that the petition of the tenants was substantially correct, and that many of them had been put under eviction after they had signed agreements to purchase; strong statements in his report to the Commissioners as to the action of the company, 1061–1067.

Abject terror of the poorer tenants so that they submitted "like sheep" to the terms of the company in order to escape eviction and the workhouse, 1063. 1077–1079 —— Particular instances cited as showing the hard terms exacted by the company and the large increase of the purchase-money by including arrears of rent and costs; amount of the judicial or fair rent in these cases, 1063–1086. 1117–1129. 1169–1180 —— Instance of a tenant sued for arrears of rent, though he has receipts for their payment; high rate of purchase asked in this case, 1063–1074. 1226–1231.

Statement as to an agreement lodged with the Land Commission having represented a rent which was no longer the legal rent; grounds for the opinion that this was practically a fraud on the part of the company, 1074–1083. 1181–1206 —— Judgment of Mr. Commissioner Lynch on 31st July 1889, respecting the cases of tenants on the Ballynascreen and certain other parts of the estate; strong comment upon their treatment by the company, 1088–1094.

Circular from the company to the tenants in June 1889 stating that any tenant wishing to cancel his agreement to purchase is at liberty to do so, but that the terms of purchase cannot be altered, 1095–1105 —— Misapprehension on the part of the company in stating that a number of tenants had combined to withhold payment of rent, 1100–1102.

Very slow progress now being made with sales on the estate; undue delay and enhanced expense after agreements to purchase are signed by the tenants before they are lodged with the Land Commission, 1106–1115 —— Confusion in the minds of the tenants as to what they really owe; great difficulty of witness in ascertaining the actual arrears due, 1116–1122.

O'Brien, Murrough. (Analysis of his Evidence)—*continued.*

Grounds for concluding that the Drapers' Company have not been in the habit of expending money on the improvement of farms or farm buildings, though they have laid out money on plantations, roads, and drains, 1113–1118. 1257–1260——Very large outlay by the company in building the village of Moneymore; unsatisfactory results from this expenditure, long leases not having been given, 1123. 1134–1143. 1232–1242.

Revision and increase of rents from time to time, although the improvements were made by the tenants; widespread grievance on this score in spite of the Ulster tenant-right, 1119–1133. 1257–1262. 1268–1271——Advantage of the long leases given when the town of Magherafelt was built, 1141–1145——Explanation that the advances by the Land Commission are upon the security of the consolidated interest of the landlord and tenant, the interest of the latter in the holding being sometimes very large, 1146–1155. 1243–1248.

Further statement as to the high rate of purchase-money fixed in many instances by the Drapers' Company with reference to the fair rent; that is, more especially by the inclusion of arrears, 1163–1180. 1272–1280——Additional evidence respecting the case in which the agreement was misleading as to the amount of the legal rent; reference hereon to several agents who acted locally for the company in these cases, 1181–1206——Several agents who have acted for the Drapers' Company; reference especially to Sir W. Cunningham and Mr. Glover, 1196–1206. 1316–1334.

Complaint as to the charge of interest on the purchase-money rather than as to the price asked; explanation hereon with further reference to certain letters from the company and the alleged delay after the agreements were signed, 1211–1232——Explanation that arrears were not charged after 1st November 1885, but only interest of purchase-money, 1213–1215.

Means of ascertaining the judicial rents on the Drapers' estate irrespectively of information from the company; grounds for complaint, however, on this score, 1246–1251. 1263–1267——Heavy costs in some instances further adverted to, this, however, not resting with the company, 1255–1256.

Degree of compulsion upon tenants to buy and to allow arrears to be added to the purchase-money, through their liability to ejectment, 1272–1280——Means of so using the Ashbourne Act that, where large arrears exist, it may operate oppressively, 1276–1280.

Statement upon the question of the Land Commission taking steps for preventing arrears being included in the price of purchase; amended form of agreement now adopted at the instance of the Commission with a view to the prevention of abuse in this respect, 1281–1291. 1305. 1306–1309——Circumstance of the poorer tenants of the Drapers' Company, on the interior land, being, for the most part, Roman Catholics, whilst the Protestants are chiefly in the Moneymore division, 1292–1296.

Consideration of the course pursued in requiring tenants to give promissory notes for arrears of rent or interest, the Salters' Company having obtained judgments in one of these cases, 1297–1309——Undue delays, as in the case of the Drapers' Company, further considered, the effect being very costly to the tenants; expediency of the Land Commission expediting completion of agreements and sales in the interests of all parties, 1310–1315.

Poverty and ignorance of many of the tenants on the Drapers' estate, 1335, 1336——Expenditure of the company on schools; this has not been considered as affecting the operations of the Land Commission, 1337, 1338.

[Second Examination.]—Statement to the effect that the terms of sale and the number of years' purchase varied in different cases, 1683–1688——Means of estimating the capital value of the estates unsold by obtaining from the companies the rental still received, 1689–1692. 1696–1698——Substantial interest of several of the companies as owners of agricultural land, 1699–1702.

Further evidence as to the protracted and exceptional delay (about three years) between the making of the agreements for sale and their completion in the case of the Moneymore estate; conclusion that the delay arose from the action of the Drapers' Company, 1703–1718. 1842, 1843——Examination with further reference to the recovery of arrears of rent and of interest from the Moneymore tenants, the Land Commissioner having come to the conclusion that the delay was protracted for this purpose, 1716 *et seq.*; 1868.

Grounds for the statement that interest on the purchase-money was claimed up to May 1889 in violation of declarations in letters from the Drapers' Company to the tenants; reference especially to letter of 3rd January 1887, as containing a pledge which was not fulfilled, 1718–1745. 1836–1875. 1901–1904——Circumstance of the Commissioners not having been aware of the large amount of arrears claimed by the company, 1726–1739——Heavy charges upon the tenants for arrears and interest, the Commissioners

O'Brien, Murrough. (Analysis of his Evidence)—*continued*.

Commissioners having considered, however, that there was sufficient security for their advances to purchasers, 1735–1743.

Statement on the subject of the sales in the Moneymore division having been based on the rents in 1880, not judicial rents, 1754–1759.——Extent to which the company acted in opposition to a requisition by Commissioner Lynch as to the closing of the accounts with the tenants, 1760–1769.

Grounds for the conclusion that it is undesirable to sanction the sales of tenants who may be at variance or in litigation with the Drapers' Company as to arrears, rents, &c. 1770–1771.—— Witness is not aware that the company endeavoured to obtain from the tenants promissory notes for their indebtedness or arrears, 1780–1784. 1871–1878. 1949. 1950.

Evidence in detail respecting the action of the Drapers' Company in the matter of fifty-three of the poorer holdings on the Brackaghslievegallon division of their estate, in respect of which eighteen years' purchase of the old rent was asked, 1785–1795.——Large number of ejectments served by the company in the foregoing cases, whilst eventually the terms first offered to them were increased by the addition of rent, interest, or costs, 1796–1803.—— Circumstance of the judicial rents having been fixed long before the agreements were signed in which the old rents were inserted; statement hereon as to the different forms of application or agreement used by the company at different times, 1804–1815.

Rejection by the Land Commissioners of all the fifty-four cases of applications from the Brackaghslievegallon division on the score of insufficient security, 1816, 1817.——Inexplicable delays on the part of the company in proceeding with the sales in the foregoing cases; enhanced expense thereby to the tenants, 1818–1835.

Explanation that the agreement does not disclose the amount of arrears, and that the Commissioners deal only with the lump sum to be given for the property, 1876–1881. 1915, 1916.—— Doubt when the rule came into operation whereby only six months' interest can be recovered after completion of the sale, 1888, 1889.——Increased value of the holdings by reason of tenants' improvements, it being no business of the Commissioners to inquire by whom improvements have been made, 1890–1895.

Long acquaintance of witness with the Drapers' estate, whilst he has visited it officially on two occasions, 1896–1909.——Small holdings and small rents of the poorer class of tenants on part of the estate, some of whom come to England for work as agricultural labourers, 1910–1914.——Several respects in which tenants are prejudiced by delays on the part of the company in completing sales, 1915. 1917, 1918.

Assertion that in certain cases the judicial rent was fixed before the agreements were signed, 1916, 1917.——Universal practice of the country as to repairs and new buildings being carried out at the tenants' expense; exception in so far as the Drapers' Company have spent a very large sum upon the town of Moneymore, 1918–1924.

Regard had by the Commissioners to the equity of the proceedings, and to the possible exercise of duress before sanctioning loans, 1925, 1926. 2039–2041.——Refusal of advances by the Commissioners in cases where the amount required is unduly increased by the inclusion of arrears, 1925, 1926. 2044–2046.——Total of more than 3,000 applications rejected by the Commissioners, 1926. 2042, 2043.

Further statement as to the probable value of all the estates of the London companies which have been sold under the Land Purchase Acts or otherwise, 1929–1931.——Retention by the Commissioners (or the Treasury) of one-fifth of the purchase-money till, in seventeen and a-half years, it is paid off by the tenants' instalments, 1946–1948.—— Belief as to promissory notes having been taken by the Salters' Company, 1951–1954.——Purchase of the ground-rents of houses on the Salters' estate in Magherafelt by the tenants, the houses having been built by them or their predecessors, 1956–1963.

Many holdings still unsold on the Skinners' estate; opinion that there is no hardship in the tenants being required to buy on the present rental, 1964–1968.——Doubt as to the formation of a syndicate for the purchase of part of the Skinners' estate, 1969–1972.——Exceptionally hard treatment of the tenants of the Drapers' Company as compared with those of other companies; reference hereon to the suspension of Mr. Glover, the solicitor to the company, 1973–1977.

Conclusion as to mountain land on the Drapers' estate having been brought into cultivation by the tenants, 1984, 1985.——Repair of roads on the estate at the cost of the occupiers, 1986–1992.——Amount of expenditure of a public character by the Drapers' Company in former and recent years, respectively, 1993–1998.——Bar to the erection of many houses in Moneymore through the shortness of the leases granted by the company, 1999–2002.

Statement on the subject of the Irish Society having been required to join in the

O'Brien, Murrough. (Analysis of his Evidence)—continued.

conveyances from the Drapers' Company to the tenants, 2023–2027.—Difficulty in arriving at the total value of all the territory originally granted to the City of London, though witness puts it at several millions; ten millions would hardly be an over-estimate, 2028–2026.—Reference to turbary as not now of sufficient value to be used in compulsory purchases by tenants, 2017–2030.

Letter of 16th May 1889 in which the Commissioners set forth their reasons for refusing loans in respect of the fifty-four holdings on the Brackaghslievegallion division of the Drapers' estate; report previously by witness to the Commission, 2031–2033.

Statement as to Mr. Commissioner M'Carthy having decided adversely to the grant of loans where tenants had been placed in possession of farms where there had been evictions, 2036–2041.

P.

Pellipar Estate. See *Skinners' Company.*

Pensions. Continued payment by the Fishmongers' Company of pensions to labourers and others, the amount being about 500 *l.* a year, *Tissar* 4931–4936.

Plan of Campaign. Attempt made to establish the plan of campaign on the estate of the Drapers' Company, *Sir W. Conyngham* 6416–6420.

Planting. Steps taken by the Skinners' Company for the improvement of the estate by planting, which was much needed, *Saunders* 5467. 5504. 5606–5609.—Belief as to the Irish Society having urged the companies to look after the planting, the Skinners' Company having done much in this direction, *ib.* 5066–5810.

Explanation on the part of counsel for the companies that he admits there was an obligation upon them under the original orders and conditions to settle and to plant, p. 356.

Obligations and conditions in the charter granted by James the First to the Irish Society respecting the "Plantation of Ulster," *App.* 450 *et seq.*

Summary of expenditure of the Mercers' Company on planting and fencing, *App.* 548, 549. 551.

Presbyterians. Particulars as to the grants given annually by the companies to Presbyterian ministers in County Derry, the usual amount being 10 *l.* in each case; large reductions and withdrawals from time to time, *Dickey* 17–26. 36–42. 137–143.—Unduly small proportion of grants to Presbyterian bodies, as compared with those to the Episcopalian Church, *ib.* 34, 35. 164–167. 199, 200.

Claims of the Presbyterians in witness' locality as paying three-fourths of the rent in the district; relative population as compared with the Roman Catholics, *Wilson* 321–331. 364–376.—Inadequate grants to Presbyterians as compared with Episcopalians, *ib.* 331. 364–375.—Expediency of Presbyterian and Roman Catholic schools and clergy being at least as well-treated as the Episcopalians, *Brown* 692–696.

Grounds for the opinion that in proportion to their numbers, the Presbyterians in the city and district of Derry have never received their due share of the Society's donations, *Ross* 6508–6514. 6521. 6524–6528. 6538.

List of Presbyterian congregations in the counties of Derry and Tyrone, the number of families in each case, the annual grants received from the several London companies, and the extent to which withdrawn, *App.* 439–442.

Statement showing, as regards endowments and annual grants, respectively, how Presbyterians are treated, as compared with Episcopalians, by the several London companies, *App.* 443.

See also *Clothworkers' Company,* 4. *Donations and Grants.* *Drapers' Company. Dunboe Presbyterian Church.* *Education.* *Irish Society.* *Rainey School. Salters' Company.*

Private Owners. Comparison between the companies and private landlords as regards the support given to schools, charities, public improvements, &c.; instances of the greater liberality of private owners, *Dickey* 67, 68. 164–187. 210–227. 244–250. 289–294.—Grounds upon which witness considered for a long time that the companies acted more liberally than private landlords in the way of grants to the clergy, schools, &c.; statement, on the other hand, as to the tenants having made all the improvements on the land, while the rents were periodically raised, *Brown* 528–551.

Statement that witness still adheres to the opinion he expressed in 1882, that the tenants of the companies are on the average better off, so far as regards the relation of landlord and tenant, than they would have been under private landlords; exercise that

in

Private Owners—continued.

in other respects the country has been somewhat better for the presence of the companies, *Todd* 3137–3158. 3203–3207. 3216–3219. 3323, 3330.

Respects in which the Skinners' Company were actuated, as regards grants, to a more liberal extent than merely as private owners, though they were under no legal obligation to do so much as they did, *Saunders* 5808–5811.

Conclusion that the Irish Society compares very favourably with ordinary Irish landlords; existence of a trust in each case, *Simply* 6480. 6517–6524. 6589–6598.

Promissory Notes (Arrears of Rent). Consideration of the course pursued in requiring tenants to give promissory note for arrears of rent or interest, the Salters' Company having obtained judgment in one of these cases, *O'Brien* 1297–1309.——Witness is not aware that the Drapers' Company endeavoured to obtain from their tenants promissory notes for their indebtedness or arrears, *ib.* 1782–1784. 1881–1885. 1949. 1950.——Further statement as to promissory notes having been taken by the Salters' Company, *ib.* 1951–1955.

Explanation that the taking of promissory notes for arrears was a special advantage given by the Salters' Company to tenants who could not pay cash; probability that if the company were appealed to in the case of a tenant named Badger, they would act leniently towards him, *Todd* 3523–3551.

Reduction of 10 per cent. offered by the Fishmongers' Company for prompt payment of arrears, whilst in two or three cases promissory notes were taken, *Towse* 4960–4966.——Circumstances under which promissory notes were taken by the Fishmongers' Company from some of the tenants for arrears of rent or interest, *ib.* 5210–5221.

Absence of any interference on the part of the Land Commission as regards promissory notes being given by the tenants of the Drapers' Company, *Sawyer* 6310–6315.

Public Works and Improvements. See *Bann Navigation.* *Coleraine.* *Expenditure (Local Claims).* *Fisheries.* *Irish Society.* *Londonderry.* *Railways.*

Purchase by Tenants. See *Agreements to Purchase.* *Arrears of Rent.* *Clothworkers' Company.* *Delays.* *Drapers' Company.* *Evictions.* *Fishmongers' Company.* *Grocers' Company.* *Land Commission.* *Salters' Company.* *Skinners' Company.*

Q.

Quinn, *The Reverend Joseph.* (Analysis of his Evidence.)—Witness, who is a Roman Catholic curate at Magherafelt, is conversant with the estates of the Drapers' and Salters' Companies in South Derry, and is prepared to give evidence respecting the treatment of the Roman Catholics by these Companies, 4721–4725.——He refers to a passage in the Report of the Royal Commission for 1885–86 as representing the views of the Catholics of Derry as to the claim of the district to a continuance of educational grants from the property held by the Irish Society as trustees, 4728, 4729.

Information as to the negotiations respecting the sale of the Salters' estate, the terms varying from nineteen-and-a-half years' purchase of the Government valuation as the maximum, 4730–4740.——Sale of the Drapers' estate at eighteen years' purchase of the rental; less fair basis in this case than in the case of the Salters' Company, 4738–4741.——Better land occupied by the Protestant tenants in the Moneymore division than by the Catholic tenants in the Ballinascreen division, whereas the latter were equally required to pay eighteen years' purchase; hardship more especially by reason of the enhanced value through the reclamations and improvements made at the tenants' expense, 4741–4755.

Pressure put upon the tenants by the Drapers' Company to compel them to buy; this did not apply equally to the Salters' Company, 4751–4755.——Fairness generally of the action of the Salters' Company in carrying out sales, whilst the tenants were more prosperous than on the Drapers' estate, 4756–4766.——Hardship in connection with the issue of writs against J. McElhatton, a tenant of the Drapers' Company, for arrears of rent; proceedings in this case for four consecutive years, entailing heavy costs, 4767–4784. 4811–4828.

Strong comment upon the treatment of Catholics as compared with Protestants by Mr. Rowley Miller as agent of the Drapers' Company, 4769–4771.——Harsh policy carried out on the Salters' estate towards Catholics when Mr. Spottiswoode was agent; great improvement under Sir Henry Cartwright when agent for the Company, 4771–4777. 4788–4780. 4797–4798.——Several illustrations of the partial and illiberal action of the Drapers' Company adversely to the Catholics, as compared with the action of the Salters' Company, 4778–4789. 4806–4807.

Quinn, The Reverend Joseph. (Analysis of his Evidence)—*continued*.

General view of Protestants and Catholics that the companies hold their property in trust for the locality, 4800, 4801——Great injury as regards schools on the Drapers' estate if Protestant schools are alone aided, 4802——Unfair treatment generally of the Catholics on the estates of the London companies, even where the agent is liberal and impartial, 4803, 4804.

View of the people generally that at least a portion of the properties should be retained in trust, 4809, 4810——Statement as to Catholics on the Mercers' estate having been unfairly discriminated against under the late agent, but not since Mr. Watney has been agent, 4879–4833.

[Second Examination.]—Explanation that the terms of purchase of the Salters' Company, though more equitable than the terms of the Drapers' Company, are considered by the people as unfair, 4834——Statement as to a grant of 10 *l.* to a Roman Catholic clergyman by the Drapers' Company having been withdrawn, and as to his having been served with a notice of ejectment as a pressure upon him to purchase his holding, 4834, 4835——Instance of harsh treatment by the Drapers' Company in the case of a tenant named Grant, who was ejected, and whose crops were lost before he was re-instated, 4836–4841.

Further statement as to the unfair treatment of Roman Catholic clergymen generally in the matter of donations, 4841–4844——Explanation that in his former evidence witness did not mean to imply that the Roman Catholics considered the companies to be good landlords because they acted impartially in some respects, 4845–4857.

R.

Railways. Aid given by the Skinners' Company towards a railway, *Brown* 593–598——Contribution of the companies towards the Londonderry Central Railway; contention that the railway is a great blunder, and that the money might have been spent to much greater advantage on a more direct railway, *Todd* 3334–3343——Belief that the Companies have not advanced money towards the railway, but have guaranteed the interest; attention called to the fact that the railway is of little real advantage, owing to its direction, and that it causes the traffic to go to Belfast rather than to Londonderry, *ib.* 3394–3400.

Statement that when a railway is carried into a particular district it has its due influence upon the rents in the locality; complaint that the Irish Society have not taken an active interest in promoting a railway in the centre of Derry, *Todd* 3691–3702.

Particulars as to the branch railways from Dungiven to Limavady and from Magherafelt to Draperstown, both having been aided by a guarantee which is still paid from the Skinners' Company, *Saunders* 5469–5478. 5480–5488——Grants made by the Skinners' Company for railways in view of the increase of the rents, *ib.* 5479. 5488.

Annual expenditure of the Skinners' Company on railways, *App.* 537.

Rainey School:

Particulars respecting the Rainey School at Magherafelt and the payments received from the Salters' Company; grounds for complaint as to the former payment of 160 *l.* having been reduced to 111 *l.*, of which 54 *l.* goes to the Roman Catholics, *Dickey* 53–58. 117–120. 125–136. 160–162——Dissatisfaction with the action of the Salters' Company in respect of the Rainey Schools, *Wilson* 335–336.

Liability of the company as regards the Rainey School till they sold their estate; danger of the school being closed through the reduced aid now received from the company, *Jordan* 604–814. 816. 888–897——Further statement as to the illiberal treatment of the Rainey School with special reference to the case of the head master; strong expression of opinion by Lord Ashbourne on the subject, *ib.* 888–897. 917–934. 954–970.

History of the Rainey School at Magherafelt from its foundation in 1707, with explanations in detail as to the governing body, the aid received from the Salters' Company, and the claims put forward on the part of the Presbyterians and Roman Catholics, respectively, *Lord Justice FitzGibbon* 1418 *et seq.*

Review of the management and condition of the school from time to time, and the several questions and difficulties dealt with by the Land Commissioners in framing their scheme for the school, with special reference to the action of the Salters' Company, and the reduced amount now received from the company, *Lord Justice FitzGibbon* 1437 *et seq.*; 1637–1648.

Outline of the scheme for Rainey School as re-cast and finally settled in January last; removal of all the objections except those from the Presbyterians, the latter having been overruled when the scheme came before the Privy Council, *Lord Justice FitzGibbon* 1474–1483. 1519–1581——Impossibility of the school being efficiently continued in

Rainey School—continued.

in view of the great reduction in the endowment; grievance as to the superannuation of the head master (Mr. Kinnard), *Lord Justice FitzGibbon* 1484-1487.

Explanation, in connection with the Rainey school, that there were two market places at Magherafelt but that there was no patent for a market, *Lord Justice FitzGibbon*, 1568-1572——Management of the school further adverted to in reference to the question of the Salters' Company being in the position of trustees, *ib.* 1573-1583.

Voluminous correspondence of the Lord Commissioners in connection with the scheme for Rainey School, *Lord Justice FitzGibbon* 1614——Surrender of the school land to the Salters' Company under the scheme as proposed, *ib.* 1615——Reason given by the company in 1887 for discontinuing their contributions to the school that they had sold their estates, *ib.* 1640-1645.

Explanation with further reference to the foundation and endowment of the Rainey School, the grants given by the Salters' Company, and the receipts of the company from the market tolls, *Lord Justice FitzGibbon* 1665-1677.

Statement as to Lord Ashbourne having expressed surprise at the manner in which the Salters' Company proposed to treat the head master of Rainey School, *Gleeson* 2997-3001.

Receipts of the Salters' Company in respect of Rainey's School in each year from 1868 to 1888; total of 1,397 *l.*, *App.* 659.

Re-appointment of Committee. Recommended reappointment of Committee at an early date in the next Session of Parliament, *Rep.* iii.

Religious Societies. Address of Mr. George Harris Lea to the Committee on behalf of several religious societies in the county of Londonderry, pp. 347 *et seq.* 410.——*See also* *Donations and Grants. Presbyterians. Roman Catholics.*

Rents. See *Arrears of Rents. Drapers' Company. Expenditure. Fishmongers' Company. Improvements. Irish Society. Londonderry. Magherafelt. Salters' Company. Skinners' Company.*

Roads. Repair of roads on the Drapers' estate at the cost of the occupiers, *O'Brien* 1988-1992——Considerable improvement effected in the roads and streets upon the Skinners' estate, *Saunders* 5468. 5504. 5717-5719.

Summary of expenditure of the Mercers' Company on roads and footpaths, *App.* 546-551.

Annual expenditure of the Ironmongers' Company on roads, *App.* 580, 583.

Roberts, Sir Owen. (Analysis of his Evidence.)—Explanatory statement respecting the negotiations for the sale of the Clothworkers' Irish Estate to Sir Harvey Bruce in 1871; eventual sale for 150,000 *l.*, subject to certain conditions and rebates, 5247-5268——Particulars with reference, more especially to the rebate of interest on 75,000 *l.*, which remained on mortgage, on condition that Sir Harvey Bruce should continue for ten years payments amounting to 242 *l.* a year, which included 90 *l.* to clergymen, and 102 *l.* to schoolmasters on different parts of the estate, 5259 *et seq.*; 5306-5318.

Examination in detail in justification of the action of the company as regards the stipulation for their donations being kept up for a period of only ten years, though, as a matter of fact, they have been continued beyond that time; denial that there was any legal obligation upon the company in the matter, 5276 *et seq.*; 5367-5370. 5411, 5413.

Explanation as to the company having given 100 *l.* to the Presbyterian church at Dunboe, of which Mr. Mark is minister, 5288-5291——Considerable expenditure by the company in connection with the Castlerock Presbyterian Church; perpetual charge of 50 *l.* a year contributed also by Sir Harvey Bruce, 5291-5293. 5311-5313——Reasons for a grant of 10 *l.* a year to a Roman Catholic clergyman on the estate having been considered sufficient, 5294-5296.

Gross rental of 8,000 *l.* a year received by the company, of which about 3,000 *l.* was expended in England, including the cost of management; large expenditure on technical education, 5297-5310. 5369. 5381-5386——Long building lease granted to Mr. Green at Castlerock, subject to certain restrictions, 5314, 5315. 5420——Parting gift of 1,500 *l.* given by the company amongst certain Episcopalian churches, in addition to 300 *l.* to the Presbyterians, 5316-5320. 5374. 5383——Considerable contributions given also to the Coleraine Academical Institution, 5321-5325.

Misapprehension on the part of Mr. Mark in attributing to Mr. Bissett (when on the Court of the Clothworkers' Company) a saying that "the worst thing in the world would be to root the Irish in the soil," 5331-5336——Grounds for justifying the sale of the estate to Sir Harvey Bruce, as an adjoining and resident landlord, rather than to the the tenants, 5337-5358.

Explanation that an offer of 185,000 *l.* (not 175,000 *l.*, as stated by Mr. Mark) was made on the part of the tenants, but not till after it was decided to sell to Sir Harvey

Roberts, Sir Owen. (Analysis of his Evidence)—*continued.*

Bruce; belief moreover that it was impracticable for all the tenants to raise the purchase money, 6341–6354. 6403. 6404——Justification by witness of his action in declining to arrange an interview between a deputation of the tenants, which came to London, and the Clothworkers' Company; the sale was already irrevocably settled, and he wrote to the deputation asking them not to come over, 6354–6358. 6405–6418.

Statement to the effect that the rental of the estate in 1841, when the company came into possession, was about 7,000 *l.*, that it was considerably reduced in 1848, was slightly raised in 1868, and was 6,000 *l.* at the time of sale in 1871; 6367–6381. 6375. 6380——Very similar rent at present as in 1871; increase and reduction in the meantime, 6352–6356——Accuracy as regards the company of the statement in the report on the City Livery Companies as to the liberal contributions by the companies to schools and churches, 6371–6373.

Explanation as to no parting gift having been given to the Catholic clergy, 6374——Probability that schools, churches, &c., were not largely supported when the estate was in the hands of a middleman, 6376–6380——*Statement* as to the rent received by the company from the middleman, who held on lease for three lives till 1841, having been only 600 *l.* a year; fine of 18,000 *l.* paid by him in the first instance, 6387–6401——Practice as to the terms of building leases formerly granted by the company; few agricultural leases, 6419–6421.

[Second Examination.]—Explanation that there were about 370 tenants on the estate, 6419——Terms of letter from witness to Sir Hervey Bruce as to the latter keeping up, subject to his personal discretion, payments to the amount of 140 *l.* a year, 6424.

Circumstance of the Merchant Taylors' Company having had an equitable interest in one-fourth of the Clothworkers' Estate, so that the whole of the purchase-money did not go to the latter company, 6426–6431.

Roman Catholics:

Doubt as to the legal claim of the Roman Catholics to religious grants, though they should share in the secular grants, *Wilson* 369–371.

Explanation that Father Loughrey was not deprived of his house at Dungiven, but that he purchased his holding and then devised it to a relative, *Todd* 3779–3796.

Statement that the Roman Catholics of Londonderry feel that they, as a body, have been neglected, while the Protestants have been favoured, by the Irish Society; universal conviction that it was useless to ask the Society for anything for the Catholics on account of the terms of the charter, *M'Cormick* 3709–3740. 3743–3748. 3753. 3754.

Desire of the Catholics to see the estate of the Society turned into money, and a fraction of the proceeds used for paying off the debts incurred in making the quays, drains, &c., the balance to be divided fairly among all the religious denominations, *M'Cormick* 3741. 3748.

Feeling of the Catholics in Derry that it is useless to apply for favours to the Irish Society, the only grant made to them being 125 *l.* a year to St. Columb's College, *Ballantine*, 3940–3954. 4011, 4012.

Evidence showing that a marked distinction has been made by the Skinners' Company in their pecuniary treatment of Protestants and Roman Catholics, both on religious and educational grounds, the former community having been dealt with much more liberally than the latter, *Loughrey*, 4608–4630.

Complaint as to the action of the Skinners' Company in respect of the house of the Roman Catholic parish priest of Dungiven and the house of the Protestant rector; more liberal donations also to Church of Ireland and Presbyterian clergy, *Loughrey* 4608–4623. 4629. 4630. 4695–4715.

Examination showing in detail the much larger proportionate expenditure of the Irish Society upon Protestant and Presbyterian than upon Roman Catholic cathedrals or other places of religious worship and schools in Derry, *Loughrey* 4585–4603——Personal affront offered by the Irish Society in their mode of addressing the Roman Catholic Bishop of Derry; practical refusal of his application, *ib.* 4604–4608. 4639–4645. 4685, 4686——Satisfaction to the Roman Catholic body in Derry if all creeds were treated impartially and alike in the matter of grants, *ib.* 4716, 4717.

Strong comment upon the treatment of Catholics as compared with Protestants by Mr. Rowley Miller, as agent of the Drapers' Company, *Quinn* 4768–4771——Harsh policy carried out on the Salters' estate towards Catholics when Mr. Spottiswoode was agent; great improvement under Sir Henry Cartwright, when agent for the company, *ib.* 4771–4777. 4781–4786. 4797–4798.

Several illustrations of the partial and illiberal action of the Drapers' Company adversely to the Catholics as compared with the action of the Salters' Company, *Quinn* 4778–4790. 4805–4807——Unfair treatment generally of the Catholics on the estates of the London companies save where the agent is liberal and impartial, *ib.* 4803. 4804——

Statement

Report, 1890—continued.

Roman Catholics—continued.

Treatment as to the Catholics on the Mercers' Estate having been unfairly discriminated against under the late agent, but not since Mr. Wamsy has been agent, *Quinn* 4829-4833.

Complaint as to a grant of 10 *l.* to a Roman Catholic clergyman by the Drapers' Company having been withdrawn, and as to his having been served with a notice of ejectment as a pressure upon him to purchase his holding, *Quinn* 4834, 4835——Further statement as to the unfair treatment of Roman Catholic clergymen generally in the matter of donations, *ib.* 4841-4844——Explanation that witness does not mean to imply that the Roman Catholics considered the companies to be good landlords because they acted impartially in some respects, *ib.* 4845-4867.

Reasons for a grant of 10 *l.* a year to a Roman Catholic clergyman on the Clothworkers' Estate having been considered sufficient, *Sir O. Roberts* 5194-5198.

Consideration of a detailed reply to the evidence of Father Loughrey and other statements respecting the unfair and unequal treatment by the Skinners' Company of the Roman Catholic and Presbyterian clergy of Dungiven as compared with the Protestant clergy; that is, as regards the stoppage or intended stoppage of grants to the former, *Saunders* 5731-5787. 5776-5806.

Reason why witness has continued his payments to the Episcopalian church, but not to the Presbyterian and Roman Catholics, *Sir H. Bruce* 5946-5947.

Explanation that the fact that Roman Catholic charities do not figure to any appreciable extent in the accounts of the Irish Society is due probably to the difficulty experienced by the Society under their charter in supporting these charities, *Sir W. Miller* 2631-2633. 2710-2714.

See also *Clothworkers' Company*, 4. *Donations and Grants*. *Education*. *Entertainments*. *Londonderry*, 4. *Presbyterians*. *Rainey School*.

Ross, The Rev. Robert, D.D. (Analysis of his Evidence.)—Lengthened experience of witness, as a member of the Presbyterian body, in regard to the action of the Irish Society in the City of Derry; he was Moderator of the General Assembly in 1868; 6603-6608. 6630-6641.

Grounds for the opinion that, in proportion to their numbers, the Presbyterians in the City and District of Derry have never received their due share of the Society's donations, 6609-6614. 6621. 6624-6628. 6638——Exceedingly beneficial operation of the Society in many ways; excellent service rendered in the cause of education, 6615. 6616. 6619. 6620. 6634. 6635. 6684.

Improvement if one-third of the members of the Society did not retire till every seven years, instead of the members being all elected for only two years, 6617. 6659-6698—— Approval generally of the present system of administration by the Society, from London, witness deprecating any change in the direction of a local Irish body, or any severance of the connection between the Society and the City of Derry, which has lasted for some 300 years, 6618-6623. 6649-6652. 6641-6663.

Probable room for improvement in the system of administration by the Society, as in most other administrations, 6673. 6674——Increased benefit to education by distributing grants among a large number of schools instead of combining them in support of one institution, 6681, 6683.

Royal Free Schools. Explanation as to no Royal free schools having been allotted to the county of Londonderry, Foyle College operating however for the whole county; reference hereon to the withdrawal of the London Companies' grants, *Lord Justice Fitz-Gibbon* 1846-1853.——*See also Education.*

S.

Sale of Estates. Conclusion as to grants to Presbyterian bodies having been withdrawn in consequence or in view of the sale of the estates, *Dickey* 43-52. 168-172——Very strong feeling created in witness' district by the sale of the companies' estates, and by all the purchase money being taken out of the country, whilst the grants to schools, churches, &c., have been discontinued, as in the case of the Fishmongers' Company, *Brown* 545 *et seq.*

Examination as to the claims now put forward by the tenants and others as against the companies who have sold, in respect of the whole of the money being taken out of the country; definition of what would constitute a fair and just settlement of the matter, *Brown* 624-638. 675-689. 703-709. 725-741——Suggestions as to the basis of the calculation for arriving at a fair valuation or [illegible] of the tenants to be surrendered by the companies; reference hereon to the heavy fines received by them over and above the greatly increased rents, *ib.* 703-718. 728-741.

Report, 1890—*continued*.

Sale of Estates—continued.

Summary of the number of holdings sold, respectively, by the Salters' Company, Fishmongers' Company, Skinners' Company, and Drapers' Company, in the county Derry under the Act of 1885, together with the amount of advances paid in each case by the Land Commission; additional amounts sanctioned but not yet paid, *O'Brien* 969-978. 1156-1158; *App.* 585.

Completion of transactions in respect of 1,188 holdings, the total amount actually paid being 578,302 *l.*; *O'Brien* 971-973. 978——Statement to the effect that the terms of sale and the number of years' purchase varied in different cases, *ib.* 1683-1688.

Universal feeling among the occupiers of the district that the companies' estates should be compulsorily purchased, *Todd* 3163, 3164——Opinion that where the companies have sold the trust property they got a fair market price, *ib.* 3551-3555. 3589, 3590.

See also Agreements of Purchase. Arrears of Rent. Clothworkers' Company. Delays. Drapers' Company. Evictions. Fishmongers' Company. Grocers' Company. Haberdashers' Company. Land Commission. Salters' Company. Skinners' Company.

SALTERS' COMPANY:

1. *Sale of the Magherafelt Estate and Terms of Purchase; Question of Pressure having been put upon the Tenants to Buy.*
2. *Increased Rental and Terms of Purchase through Improvements made or Houses erected at the Expense of the Tenants.*
3. *Memorials from Tenants and Replies by the Company thereto.*
4. *Donations and Grants; Conflicting Evidence respecting their Discontinuance.*
5. *Receipts and Expenditure generally in respect of the Estate.*
6. *Original Conveyance to the Company from the Irish Society.*
7. *Legal Argument as to the Company not being in the position of Trustees.*

1. *Sale of the Magherafelt Estate and Terms of Purchase; Question of Pressure having been put upon the Tenants to Buy:*

Statement on the question of tenants of the Salters' Company having been put under pressure to purchase their holdings; reference hereon to a notice to the tenants, signed by Sir Henry Cartwright, as agent, *Jordan* 877. 885——Impression that the rent of the Salters' Company was about 16,000 *l.*, and that the sales have realised 240,000 *l.*, some property being still left, *ib.* 899-901. 911, 912. 917-918.

Evidence in support of the assertion that the Salters' Company put a certain amount of pressure upon the tenants to induce them to buy in 1886, and threatened legal proceedings for the recovery of the rent in one case, *Gamble* 2972-2998. 3004-3011. 3017-3020.

Presumption that a certain letter, or notice, in which witness is alleged to have threatened proceedings for arrears of rent against unwilling purchasers, must be the notice to tenants who had not carried out their purchases, informing them that a certain time would be allowed them before offers were made to the general public, *Todd* 3057-3062. 3316-3323.

Evidence to the effect that, of the forty holdings remaining unsold in 1884 on the Salters' estate, eight have since been sold; unsuccessful negotiation by witness on behalf of the tenants for the purchase of most of these holdings, *Todd* 3350-3365. 3523 *et seq.*

Statement that the notice to close the sales was issued because witness, on the part of the company, thought that it would be only fair to give the tenants warning that, if they did not purchase, the outside public would be asked; opinion that the tenants were holding out in the hope of getting better terms, *Todd* 3366-3376.

Information as to the negotiation respecting the sale of the Salters' Estate, the terms varying from nineteen-and-a-half years' purchase of the Government valuation as the maximum, *Quinn* 4730-4740——Favourable generally of the action of the Salters' Company in carrying out sales, whilst the tenants were more prosperous than on the Drapers' estate, *ib.* 4758-4765——Explanation that the terms of purchase of the Salters' Company though more equitable than the terms of the Drapers' Company are considered by the people as unfair, *ib.* 4834.

Statement of the number and amount of loans issued through the Irish Land Commissioners in respect of the estates of the company, *App.* 585.

Paper handed in by Mr. Glover containing particulars respecting the terms of purchase in the cases of Henry O'Neill, Michael Morgan, and James Convery, tenants of the company, *App.* 589.

SALTERS' COMPANY—continued.

2. *Increased Rental and Terms of Purchase through Improvements made or Houses erected at the Expense of the Tenants:*

Information as to the enormous increase in the rental of the Salters' Company from their Magherafelt Estate since they leased it about 100 years ago (the company having eventually sold the property for 240,000 *l.*), whereas all the improvements came from the tenants, *Dickey* 70–100. 121–124. 173–177. 241–243. 249–299.

Purchase of the ground-rents of houses on the Salters' Estate in Magherafelt by the tenants, the houses having been built by them or their predecessors, *O'Brien* 1956–1963.

Table submitted showing the comparative rental of the various holdings in Magherafelt before and after 1854, together with the purchase-money and subsequent estimated expenditure by tenants on buildings; evidence to the effect that these figures and the condition of the tenants were brought before the House of Commons, *Gunson* 2914–2923.

Experience of witness for seventeen years as local solicitor for the Salters' Company; explanations hereon as to the abatement, through Lord Selborne, in the large increase of rents proposed in 1867, whilst there was a further reduction under the Act of 1881, *Glover* 6155–6163. 6168–6171.

Examination showing that witness, who is a tenant of the Salters' Company, has written letters charging that company with having ruined the town of Magherafelt by not giving perpetuity leases, and with having compelled tenants who have bought to buy on their own improvements; these letters handed in, *Glover* 6188–6197.

Table showing the comparative rental of various holdings in the town under the late Sir Robert Bateson and the Marquis of Londonderry, with the increased rent charged by the Salters' Company on coming into possession in the year 1854, and the further increase in 1867; together with the amount of the purchase-money of the several holdings and the subsequent estimated expenditure in buildings, *App.* 178.

Letter from Mr. Glover in December 1865, as a tenant of the Salters' Company, complaining strongly of the terms sought to be exacted from him by the company, and referring to his large expenditure on improvements, *App.* 590.

Further letters from Mr. Glover in March and June 1866, in detailed explanation of the grievances urged as regards the company's treatment of himself and other tenants of the company, and submitting an amended course of action in the matter of rents, improvements, &c., *App.* 590–593.

3. *Memorials from Tenants and Replies by the Company thereto:*

Explanations in connection with memorial, dated the 19th April 1867, from the tenants of the Salters' Estate in Magherafelt to the company, complaining of a proposed increase of rent and infringement of the tenant-right custom; also, the company's reply thereto, claiming that they hold the estate unfettered by any fiduciary conditions, *Gunson* 2885–2898.

Statement that the supplemental memorial specifies instances of increase of rent by the Salters' Company, Mrs. M'Fall's rent having been increased from 3 *l.* 19 *s.* to 19 *l.*; belief that Mrs. M'Fall's case is practically typical of the others, *Gunson* 2899–2914.

Memorial of tenants praying that certain rules made by the company may be recalled, objections thereto being submitted in detail; also, that the free sale of farms may be allowed according to the ancient Ulster custom, and the custom of the estate, and that other grievances complained of be removed, *App.* 433, 434.

Supplemental memorial, adopted at Magherafelt, on the 4th July 1867, setting forth in detail the grievances of the tenants on various points and praying for redress, *App.* 435–438.

Letter from the Salters' Company, dated 22nd July 1867, commenting upon the contents of the memorial and the inaccuracy of statements therein, and declaring the intention of the company to abide by the decision already arrived at, *App.* 438.

Memorial of the tenants of the town of Magherafelt, dated 19th April 1867, urging certain grievances upon the Salters' Company, and praying for redress, *App.* 582, 583.

Reply of the Salters' Company, dated 7th May 1867, explaining the action of the company in regard to rents, expenditure on improvements, &c., *App.* 583, 584.

Supplemental memorial of the tenants in July 1867, in further explanation of their grounds of complaint on the score of excessive rents, and of inadequate expenditure by the company in improvements in the town, *App.* 584–587.

SALTERS' COMPANY—continued.

4. *Donations and Grants; Conflicting Evidence respecting their Discontinuance:*

Witness (who is rector of Magherafelt) explains that the Salters' Company have been exceedingly liberal towards his church and to other churches on their estates, and have given considerable help to the various schools and charities; particulars hereon, *Jordan* 793–813. 804—Discontinuance of several grants formerly made by the company to certain schools and to local charities; very strong feeling in the district on the subject, *ib.* 815 *et seq.*

Distinct understanding on the part of purchasers from the Salters' Company that the grants and donations would be continued, it being contended that the agents of the company had so promised; individual declarations to this effect, *Jordan* 830–847. 866–876. 938–941.—Former expenditure of about 600 *l.* a year by the company in respect of the church of Ireland, *ib.* 913–918.

Reference to a letter from witness to the "Times" respecting the refusal of the Salters' Company to receive a deputation; statement therein as to the fatal effect of withdrawing aid from the schools and churches, *Jordan* 948–953.

Universal impression in the minds of the tenants on the Salters' Estate that the company, when negotiating the sale, gave an assurance that the grants to churches and charities would be continued; statement that, in consequence of an intimation in 1887 that the company would not be responsible for any more grants, several letters from tenants appeared in the "Times" and other papers, the result being that the grants were continued, *Gamman* 2999–2991. 3012–3015.

Absolute denial of the statement that witness, along with Sir Henry Cartwright, gave promises to the tenants on the Salters' Company's Estate (in order to induce them to purchase) that the grants to schools and churches should be continued; detailed statement as to what actually took place, the grants not having been mentioned until many of the deeds had been executed, *Todd* 3018–3056. 3116–3131. 3314–3318.

Reiterated denial of the allegation that witness induced the tenants on the Salters' Estate to purchase by promising them a continuance of the grants; reference hereon to the provision made by the company for Rainey School, *Todd* 3456–3468.

List of Presbyterian congregations showing the number of families in each case, the annual grant received by each congregation, and the instances in which withdrawn, with the date, *App.* 440.

5. *Receipts and Expenditure generally in respect of the Estate:*

Account of the annual receipts and expenditure in connection with the Irish Estate of the company from May 1853 to June 1889; *App.* 559.

Annual expenditure under different heads since 1855; *App.* 560.—Summary of receipts and expenditure, *ib.* 561.

6. *Original Conveyance to the Company from the Irish Society:*

Indenture made between the Irish Society and the Salters' Company in June 1663; release of the manor of Sal, *App.* 522–526.

7. *Legal Argument as to the Company not being in the position of Trustees:*

Argument in detail on the part of counsel that the Salters' Company are not bound in any way as trustees, pp. 360 *et seq.*

See also Improvements. Magherafelt. Promissory Notes. Rainey School. Roman Catholics.

Saunders, *Herbert Clifford*, Q.C. (Analysis of his Evidence.)—Witness has been on the Court of the Skinners' Company since 1868; he was First Warden in 1872 and Master in 1873–74; 5431–5434. 5781–5784.

System of leases for lives and years upon which the Pellipar Estate of the company in Ulster was always held, the last of the leases having fallen in in 1872; 5435.—Decision of the company to take the management of the property into its own hands, when the leases fell in; deputation sent to Ireland in 1873 in order to make the necessary arrangements, 5436–5440.

Careful inquiry made by witness, previously to his visit to the company's estate, as to the past history of the property, 5441.—Result of witness' investigations that he ascertained that two sums of 60,000 *l.* and 110,000 *l.*, respectively, were spent by the twelve London companies on their estates in Ulster; minutes of the Skinners' Company of 10th and 31st December 1817 and of 9th July 1818, referring to this expenditure, 5441–5450.—Carefully kept accounts of the company showing the receipts and expenditure from a very early date, 5449. 5450.

Visits paid by the deputation of 1873 to all parts of the Skinners' Estate in order to become thoroughly acquainted with the position and wants of the tenants, 5451–5454.—Excellent relations between the company and their tenants, 5454.—Further deputation

Saunders, Herbert Clifford, Q.C. (Analysis of his Evidence)—*continued*.

tation in 1874, several grants having been made by the company for the benefit of the estate, 5455–5458.

Receipt by the company of a net sum of 4,494 *l.* from the Irish Church Commissioners in respect of these advowsons; administration of this sum for church or spiritual purposes exclusively, 5458–5466. 5563——Statement as to the clergy of the Episcopal Church having been the chief recipients out of the Advowson's Fund on account of their disendowment, though Presbyterians and Roman Catholics have also had donations, 5460–5466.

Steps taken by the company for the improvement of the estate by planting, which was much needed, 5467. 5504. 5606–5609——Considerable improvements effected also in the roads and streets upon the estate, 5468. 5504. 5717–5719.

Particulars as to the branch railways from Dungiven to Limavady and from Magherafelt to Draperstown, both having been aided by a guarantee, which is still paid, from the Skinners' Company, 5469–5478. 5480. 5488——Explanation respecting the rental of the estate in 1844 and 1874, in which latter year there was a re-valuation, and the rents were raised from 11,600 *l.* to 13,180 *l.*, or an increase of 1,500 *l.* a-year; subsequent reduction to about 11,200 *l.*; 5479–5488. 5590–5601. 5638. 5712–5714——Grants made for railways in view of the increase of the rents, 5479. 5488.

Circumstances under which the Skinners' Company bought up the interests of the Bakers' Company and the Stationers' Company in the estate, paying them 76,000 *l.*, or twenty-two years' purchase of their gross rental, 5489–5493. 5617–5619——Continued interest of the Girdlers' Company in the property, they not desiring to take part in the management, 5489. 5497.

Negotiations, through Dr. Todd, in 1888, for the sale of the estate to the tenants under Lord Ashbourne's Act, the terms having been eventually arranged at nineteen years' purchase subject to an allowance of one and a-half year's rent, so that the actual price was only seventeen and a-half years' purchase, 5494–5498. 5501——Numerously signed memorial from the tenants to the company, shortly after the lease fell in, praying the company not to sell the estate; refusal of an offer made by a Belfast merchant, 5498–5499.

Entire withdrawal of any promised continuance of the grants after the sale of the estate, 5500. 5530–5539——Explanation as to the company having given a grant of a few hundred pounds to the Vicar of Dungiveady, 5501——Exception taken to a statement by Dr. Todd, that the Skinners' Estate was the worst managed of all; liberality and popularity of the middleman, Mr. Ogilby, who lived upon the property, 5503. 5504. 5715, 5716.

Explanation that the town holdings in Dungiven were sold only upon the ground-rent, and that the company have always recognised tenant-right in town holdings no less than to agricultural holdings, 5505–5509——One-third of the estate is still unsold, 5510, 5511.

Probability that the company will act liberally in continuing to give subscriptions or donations, though there is no obligation whatever to do so, there being no legal trust, 5512. 5540–5557. 5578–5586——Very few cases in which subscriptions have been discontinued; explanations hereon, 5512. 5543–5561.

Question considered whether the two sums of 60,000 *l.* and 120,000 *l.* were expended by the London Companies in Ireland at all; belief that this was so, 5515–5526——Impression that there was no general memorial from the tenants, nor any deputation from them, respecting the continuance of the subscriptions, 5531–5537——Argument that the company were losers by the sale and that the tenants were considerable gainers, so that the latter as landlords might well have kept up the subscriptions, 5538–5542. 5586. 5612. 5630.

Grounds for justifying the course adopted in dealing with the fund received from the Church Temporalities Commission, and in making payments, relatively, to Episcopalians, Presbyterians, and Roman Catholics, 5562–5571. 5720–5730. 5771–5775——Reply to certain evidence of Mr. Newland as to the withdrawal of subscriptions from churches, schools, &c.; very liberal sums given by the company in Ballynascreen, 5572–5580——Explanations in connection with the withdrawal of some of the grants given to dispensaries, 5583–5586.

Reference to the large arrears of rents on the estate as due partly to the laxity of the late agent of the company and to the sub-division of holdings, 5587–5589——Opinion that the rents were not at all high, 5589——Increase in the rental of the estate further adverted to in connection with the fact that the company spent nothing on the property while it was under lease to Mr. Ogilby, 5590–5601——Exceedingly inadequate return derived during the long period before the company came into possession, though the prospect of profit was one of the inducements to the company to go to Ireland in the first instance, 5598–5605. 5616.

Report, 1890—continued.

Saunders, Herbert Clifford, Q.C. (Analysis of his Evidence)—*continued.*

Belief as to the Irish Society having urged the companies to look after the planting, the Skinners' Company having done much in this direction, 5608-5610——Reservation of all minerals to the Irish Society, 5611-5615.

Ample grounds for justifying the increase of rental and the terms of sale to the tenants with reference to the judicial rents, 5616-5631. 5638——Limited extent to which the company did anything between 1872 and 1882 to improve the property agriculturally, 5632-5637——Anxiety of the company to sell to the tenants rather than to outsiders, the value of the tenant right having always been fully recognised, 5639-5643.

Action of the company as regards donations, &c., in the full belief that they were not trustees, 5645-5650——Examination as to witness' grounds for denying that the company endeavoured to restrict the custom of tenant right on the Pellipar estate, as by the prohibition of open free sale; reference hereon to a report of the company in 1873; 5651-5696.

Further statement as to the rental from the estate, witness submitting that, going back to the original purchase in 1609, the company made a very bad bargain in the matter, 5697-5714.

Consideration of, and detailed reply to, the evidence of Father Loughrey, and other statements respecting the unfair and unequal treatment of the Roman Catholic and Presbyterian clergy of Dungiven as compared with the Protestant clergy; that is, as regards the stoppage, or intended stoppage, of grants to the former, 5731-5787. 5798-5803——Entire approval of grants from the company being devoted to educational purposes, 5784-5787.

Explanation with further reference to the principle on which grants were made, and the proportion of the total rental spent locally upon grants, management, railways, &c., 5788-5811——Respects in which the company were actuated as regards grants in a more liberal sense than merely as private owners, though they were under no legal obligation to do as much as they did, 5808-5811——Circumstance of Dr. Todd, who acted both for the tenants as well as the company, having raised no question about the company being in the position of trustees, 5812-5817.

Sawyer, William Phillips. (Analysis of his Evidence.)—Long experience of witness as Clerk of the Drapers' Company, 6298, 6299.

Reference to a return showing how the Ulster estate of the company was let, and the rents and fines received, previously to 1817, when the company took over the management, 6300, 6331——Total agricultural rental of 9,037 *l.* in 1817 as of 10,850 *l.* in 1885; increase and reduction at different periods, 6301. 6333-6340——Return handed in showing the receipts and expenditure for the last fifteen years, 6302, 6303. 6317-6319. 6330, 6331.

Very harmonious relations between the company and their tenants till within the last few years, 6305, 6306——Desire of the company to treat their tenants with equality and without regard to religious denominations, 6307——Explanation that Mr. Glover had no authority from the company to base the agreements for sale to the tenants on other than the rents actually payable, 6308, 6309——Absence of any interference on the part of the Land Commission as regards promissory notes being given by the tenants, 6310-6313.

Denial that the company have declined to grant long leases of land in Moneymore, 6319——Reply to a statement that the company fixed the purchase money on the rent instead of on the Government valuation, 6314——Consideration shown to the tenants as to the mode of payment of arrears, 6315, 6316——Arbitration now pending in the matter of arrears; recent reference to the arbitrators of any special cases of alleged hardship as regards the terms of purchase, 6320-6329. 6351. 6355. 6360-6370.

Explanation that the company have come to no decision on the subject of the continuance of religious and educational grants, 6341-6345. 6349-6351——Action of the company as regards the support given to dispensaries and medical men, 6346-6348——Sale of the greater portion of the estate since 1885; large reduction in the rental, 6352-6359.

Opinion that the London Companies were originally founded with a view mainly to purposes of trade and for the mutual benefit of their own members, 6371-6382——Total of twenty-five members on the Court of the Drapers' Company, all business relating to the Irish Estate coming before the Court monthly, 6381-6384——Grants of aid in Ireland, as in England, according to the merits and necessities of each case, 6385-6387.

Explanations respecting the expenditure out of the estate to the effect that out of a total receipt of about 191,000 *l.* since 1878 there has been an expenditure of 101,100 *l.* in Ireland, whilst some 89,000 *l.* went into the general funds of the company, 6388-6398——Reduced expenditure on buildings, works, and improvements since 1873, owing probably to the small rent received and the heavy arrears, 6399-6409.

Schools

Report, 1890—continued.

Schools and Colleges. See *Coleraine. Donations and Grants, &c. Education. Endowed Schools Commission. Expenditure (Local Claims). Foyle College. Londonderry Academical Institution. Presbyterians. Rainey School. Roman Catholics. Skinners' Company.*

SKINNERS' COMPANY:

1. *Generally as to the Administration of the Pellipar Estate by the Company since the Expiration of the Leases.*
2. *Rents.*
3. *Sale of portion of the Estate to the Tenants; Terms of Purchase.*
4. *Portion still Unsold.*
5. *Donations and Grants; Extent to which withdrawn.*
6. *Terms of Leases.*
7. *Original Expenditure of the Skinners' Company and other London Companies in respect of their Irish Estates.*
8. *Litigation between the Skinners' Company and the Irish Society; Question of the former being in the position of Trustees.*
9. *Receipts and Expenditure generally.*

1. *Generally as to the Administration of the Pellipar Estate by the Company since the Expiration of the Leases:*

Reference to the Skinners' Company as the worst and most exacting of the London companies, *Brown* 651, 654.

Adherence of witness to the opinion he expressed before Lord Derby's Commission to the effect that the Skinners' Estate was the worst managed estate in the north of Ireland, the tenants being more in arrear on that estate than on any other; statement that the rents in some parts were impossible rents before they were fixed by the Land Court, *Todd* 3478–3484.

System of leases for lives, and years upon which the Pellipar Estate of the company in Ulster was always held, the last of the leases having fallen in in 1873, *Saunders* 5435—Decision of the company to take the management of the property into its own hands, when the leases fell in; deputation sent to Ireland in 1873 in order to make the necessary arrangements, *ib.* 5436–5440—Careful inquiry made by witness previously to his visit to the Company's Estate, as to the past history of the property, *ib.* 5441.

Visits paid by the deputation of 1873 to all parts of the Skinners' Estate in order to become thoroughly acquainted with the position and wants of the tenants, *Saunders* 5451–5454—Excellent relations between the company and their tenants, *ib.* 5454—Further deputation in 1874, several grants having been made by the company for the benefit of the estate, *ib.* 5456–5458.

Exception taken to a statement by Dr. Todd that the Skinners' Estate was the worst managed of all; liberality and popularity of the middleman, Mr. Ogilby, who lived upon the property, *Saunders* 5505. 5574. 5715, 5716.

2. *Rents:*

Grievance as regards the increased rents charged to town tenants in 1872, when the Ogilby leases fell in; obstacles to the tenants purchasing under the Ashbourne Act, *Loughrey* 4531–4537.

Explanation respecting the rental of the estate in 1845 and 1871, in which latter year there was a revaluation and the rents were raised from 11,600 *l.* to 13,100 *l.*, or an increase of 1,500 *l.* a year; subsequent reduction to about 11,900 *l.*, *Saunders* 5479–5482. 5590–5602. 5636. 5712–5714—Opinion that the rents were not at all high, *ib.* 5585.

Increase in the rental of the estate further adverted to in connection with the fact that the company spent nothing on the property whilst it was under lease to Mr. Ogilby, *Saunders* 5598–5601—Exceedingly inadequate return derived during the long period before the company came into possession, though the prospect of profit was one of the inducements to the company to go to Ireland in the first instance, *ib.* 5598–5605. 5616.

Further statement as to the rental from the estate, witness submitting that, going back to the original purchase in 1609, the company made a very bad bargain in the matter, *Saunders* 5697–5714.

Gross income from the estate of 11,780 *l.* in 1872, 13,300 *l.* in 1877, and 11,346 *l.* in 1886; judicial rents in nearly all cases, *Draper* 5813–5817.

3. *Sale of portion of the Estate to the Tenants; Terms of Purchase:*

Practical sale of the Skinners' Estate to the tenants, the price realised being about seventeen and a-half years' purchase; delay in making further sales as the tenants are holding back, *Brown* 481. 485–487. 500–503. 573–576. 656. 657.

Skinners' Company—continued.

3. *Sale of portion of the Estate to the Tenants, &c.*—continued.

Existence of letters on the part of the company threatening the tenants that they would suffer if they did not purchase, *Loughrey* 4553, 4554.

Negotiations through Dr. Todd, in 1886, for the sale of the estate to the tenants under Lord Ashbourne's Act, the terms having been eventually arranged at nineteen years' purchase, subject to an allowance of one and a-half years' rent, so that the actual price was only seventeen and a-half years' purchase, *Saunders* 5414–5418. 5502.

Numerously signed memorial from the tenants to the company shortly after the lease bill in praying the company not to sell the estate; refusal of an offer made by a Belfast merchant, *Saunders* 5498–5499—— Ample grounds for justifying the increase of rental and the terms of sale to the tenants with reference to the judicial rents, *ib.* 5610–5631. 5638.

Information as to the total receipts from sales through the Land Commission, and the small balance remaining after payments to the Stationers' and Bakers' Companies, &c., *Draper* 5830–5835.

Statement to the effect that judicial rents were settled in 800 or 900 cases, either voluntarily or in the Land Court, nineteen years' purchase having been received, less a deduction of one and a-half years' rent, *Draper* 5878–5897.

Indenture made between the Skinners' Company and James M'Vey of Dungiven, showing the terms and conditions of purchase of his holding by the latter, *App.* 446, 447.

Return of the number and amount of loans issued and sanctioned in respect of the estates of the company, *App.* 563.

Deed of sale in April 1886, as between the company and the Rev. Michael Tracey of Dungiven; terms under which an advance is made to the latter by the Irish Land Commission for the purchase of his holding, *App.* 564, 565.

4. *Portion still Unsold:*

Many holdings still unsold on the Skinners' Estate; opinion that there is no hardship in these tenants being required to buy on the present rental, *O'Brien* 1964–1968—— Doubt as to the formation of a syndicate for the purchase of part of the estate, *ib.* 1969–1972.

Information respecting the portion of the estate not yet sold; opinion that the tenants are, on the whole, fairly satisfied with the company, *Loughrey* 4664–4669.

One-third of the estate still unsold, *Saunders* 5510, 5511 —— Total of 376 holdings still unsold, the rental being 2,247 *l.*, and the estimated value 42,743 *l.*, *Draper* 5836. 5878—— Cessation of offers by the tenants, so that the unsold portion has been withdrawn from sale for the present, *ib.* 5838–5844.

5. *Donations and Grants; Extent to which withdrawn:*

Particulars respecting the grants and donations given by the Skinners' Company to the clergy and to schools, these being gradually withdrawn without compensation; short notice of discontinuance in the case of the minister of Lower Cumber, *Brown* 565–570. 576, 577. 581–583. 672. 674 —— Very small aid given to schools by the Skinners' Company, *ib.* 586. 673. 681, 683 —— Statement made by the gentleman who sold for the company that certain payments by the company would be continued, *ib.* 699–702. 719–723. 726, 727.

Assurance that witness never promised on behalf of the Company the continuance of all out-goings, donations, and privileges to the tenants on the Company's estate, in order to induce them to purchase, *Todd* 3060–3069 —— Assertion that if Mr. M'Laughlin states that witness distinctly promised that all emoluments and privileges would be continued by the Skinners' Company as before, and that on that promise the tenants purchased, there must be some mistake, as witness never referred to the grants in the presence of the tenants, *ib.* 3189–3208.

Equitable claim of the district to the enhanced value of the Skinners' Estate given thereto by the tenants, *Loughrey* 4682–4684.

Receipt by the Company of a net sum of 4,894 *l.* from the Irish Church Commissioners in respect of three advowsons; administration of this sum for church or spiritual purposes, exclusively, *Saunders* 5458–5466. 5563 —— Statement as to the clergy of the Episcopal Church having been the chief recipients out of the non-vested fund on account of their disendowment, though Presbyterians and Roman Catholics have also had donations, *ib.* 5460–5465.

Entire disavowal of any promised continuance of the grants after the sale of the estate, *Saunders* 5500. 5530–5532 —— Probability that the Company will act liberally in continuing to give subscriptions or donations, though there is no obligation whatever to

SKINNERS' COMPANY—continued.

5. *Donations and Grants; Extent to which withdrawn*—continued.

to do so, there being no legal trust, *Saunders* 5516. 5530–5537. 5576–5580 —— Very few cases in which subscriptions have been discontinued; explanations hereon, *ib.* 5512. 5543–5551.

Impression that there was no general memorial from the tenants, or any deputation from them, respecting the continuance of the subscriptions, *Saunders* 5531–5537 —— Argument that the Company were losers by the sale and that the tenants were considerable gainers, so that the latter as landlords might well have kept up the subscriptions, *ib.* 5538–5541. 5586. 5620–5631.

Reply to certain evidence of Mr. Newland as to the withdrawal of subscriptions from churches and schools, &c.; very liberal sums given by the Company in Ballymascanlon, *Saunders* 5512–5560 —— Explanation with further reference to the principle on which grants were made and the proportion of the total rental spent locally upon grants, management, railways, &c., *ib.* 5768–5811 —— More liberal action of the Company than of private owners as regards grants, *ib.* 5806–5811.

Explanation of the action of the Company as regards grants; reference especially to the cases of the parish priest of Dungiven and of the clergyman and church of Lower Cumber, *Draper* 5845–5853. 5861–5871.

Further examination as to the expenditure in Ireland in respect of churches, schools, and other objects, the average for ten years having been 683 *l.*, whilst the average amount applied to general objects in the United Kingdom was 5,500 *l.*; *Draper* 5880–5901. 5925–5929.

Memorial of tenants who are members of the congregation of Lower Cumber; reply of the company to the effect that the donation in question will not be continued, *App.* 498.

List of Presbyterian congregations showing the number of families in each case, the annual grant received by each congregation, and the instances in which withdrawn, with the date, *App.* 441.

Statement of Advowson's Composition Account, and of the respective amounts given to Episcopalians, Presbyterians, and Roman Catholics, *App.* 558.

6. *Terms of Leases:*

Indenture made between the company and Thomas Gwynne of Dungiven, showing the terms of lease of certain land and premises to the latter, *App.* 448, 449.

7. *Original Expenditure of the Skinners' Company and other London Companies in respect of their Irish Estates:*

Result of witness' investigations that he ascertained that two sums of 60,000 *l.* and 120,000 *l.* respectively were spent by the twelve London companies on their estates in Ulster; Minutes of the Skinners' Company of 10th and 31st December 1617, and 8th July 1618, referring to this expenditure, *Saunders* 5141–5150.

Resolution adopted at a Court held on 23rd December 1617 as to the mode of raising the sum of 2,800 *l.* assessed upon the company by the Common Council of London, *App.* 489.

8. *Litigation between the Skinners' Company and the Irish Society; Question of the former being in the position of Trustees:*

Consideration of the extent to which the public interests were represented in the litigation between the Skinners' Company and the Irish Society, the Attorney General having been a party to the proceedings, *Lord Justice FitzGibbon* 1613–1648. 1657–1660.

Argument by counsel that the legal proceedings and the decisions in the case of the Skinners' Company go to prove that their estate and the companies' estates generally were not impressed with a trust, though trusts were imposed on the lands held by the Irish Society, pp. 374 *et seq.*

Reliance by counsel upon Lord Langdale's judgment in the House of Lords as supporting the contention that the companies were not under any legal trust, pp. 376 *et seq.*

Argument in detail by counsel on behalf of the Skinners' Company that they were not placed under any legal trust or obligation in respect of their estate, pp. 405 *et seq.*

9. *Receipts and Expenditure generally:*

[illegible] accounts of the company showing the receipts and expenditure from a

Todd, R. H., LL.D. (Analysis of his Evidence)—*continued.*

notice to tenants who had not carried out their purchases, informing them that a certain time would be allowed them before offers were made to the general public, 3057–3079. 3316–3333.

Assurance that witness never promised the continuance of all outgoings, donations and privileges to the tenants on the Skinners' Company's estate, in order to induce them to purchase, 3060–3080——Explanation that after the Skinners' Company transferred the bog to trustees, the latter had to charge 1 s. per tenant for maintenance of the bog; statement that the Company were out of pocket in regard to the bog when they only charged 6 d. each, 3070–3084. 3307–3313.

Suggestion that in all cases of purchase each tenant should be separately represented by his own solicitor, 3085–3090. 3313, 3314——Grounds for the opinion that the Irish Society is an obsolete body that ought to be dissolved; assertion that the management expenses are excessive, 3091–3103. 3159–3165.

Opposition to the transfer of the funds of the Society to the Corporation of Londonderry due to the present Corporation, who do not represent the feeling of the whole city, being averse to the trust fund going into the hands of a new Corporation, probably chiefly Catholic, on a reduced franchive; approval of a new Corporation being entrusted with so much of the fund as belongs to the city, 3104–3111. 3252–3260 ——Non-objection to the administration of that portion of the fund which is applied to general purposes, outside the city, being in the hands of properly-constituted and impartial local trustees; explanation that the word "local" is only intended to apply to the county of Derry, 3111–3117. 3261, 3262.

Strong objection to the trust funds being conveyed to a religious destination; recommendation that the successors of the present incumbents be not allowed to have any claim to the grants, which do the public no good, 3118. 3149–3164. 3265–3278 —— Concurrence of witness in the opinion that as the rents derived by the London Companies from their London properties are to be expended in London, so the wealth derived from their Irish properties should be expended in Ireland; impossibility of having the matter decided in a court of law, owing to the heavy expenses that would be incurred in fighting a powerful company, 3119–3134.

Enumeration of the documents which, in witness' opinion, the Committee ought to have before them, 3135, 3136——Statement that witness still adheres to the opinion he expressed in 1884, that the tenants of the Companies are on the average better off, so far as regards the relation of landlord and tenant, than they would have been under private landlords; assertion that in other respects the country has been somewhat better for the presence of the companies, 3137–3158. 3205–3207. 3318–3319. 3329, 3330.

Belief that the report of the secretary of the Irish Society in 1808, as to the miserable condition of the people on the estates of the Irish Society and London Companies, was a true account; opinion that the Society and Companies were greatly to blame for allowing their land to be let to middlemen, who fleeced the tenants and ruined the country, 3151–3158—— Contention that the grants of the Society and Companies to schools and churches should be concentrated, as they produce little or no good under the present method of distributing them, 3166–3170.

Suggestion that, in the event of the trusts being made over to trustees, the trustees should be appointed by the Lord Chancellor of Ireland or by Parliament; recommendation that there should be three or five of them, 3171–3181. 3185–3187——Assertion that the English and Scotch subjects who accepted King James' offer and planted lands in Ulster, were clearly distinguished from the "Londoners," not being trustees in any sense of the word, 3183–[illegible].

Non-concurrence of witness with the statement that the adoption of perpetual leases would revive to some extent the principle of the middleman; explanation that it is not intended that any estate shall be handed over en bloc to one or two men, 3208–3215.——Universal feeling among the occupiers of the district that the Companies' estates should be compulsorily purchased, 3263, 3264.

Statement that the Rev. Father Loughrey was not deprived of his house at Dungiven, but that he purchased his holding, and then devised it to a relative, 3279–[illegible]——Opinion that the large arrears on the Skinners' estate, which were wiped off by the Arrears Act, were due to prior impossible rents; evidence to the effect that the majority of the tenants on the poor portions of the estate, that were not sold, are Roman Catholics, 3297–3306.

Contribution of the Companies towards the Londonderry Central Railway; contention that the railway is a great blunder, and that the money might have been spent to much greater advantage on a more direct railway, 3334–3345 —— Statement that in most cases the tenants who have made improvements are paying the landlord for them, under the Act of 1881; 3346–3348.

[Second

Todd, R. H., LL.D. (Analysis of his Evidence)—*continued*.

(Second Examination.)—Evidence to the effect that, of the forty holdings remaining unsold in 1884 on the Salters' Estate, eight have since been sold; successful negotiation by witness on behalf of the tenants for the purchase of most of these holdings, 3350–3365. 3373 *et seq*.——Statement that the notice to close the sales was issued because witness thought that it would be only fair to give the tenants warning that if they did not purchase the outside public would be asked; opinion that the tenants were holding out in the hope of getting better terms, 3366–3376.

Explanation that the tenants on the Skinners' Estate are no worse off now that they pay 1 s. each for the management of the bog than they were when they only paid 6 d. each towards it, as they now have an absolute vested right in the whole of the valuable turbary on the estate, 3377–3383.—— Submission by witness of a list of the documents put in by him, 3384, 3386.

Statement that the amounts realised by the sale of the timber on the companies' estates are additional to the purchase-money already mentioned, but are very limited, 3387–3393.—— Belief that the companies have not advanced money towards the railways, but have guaranteed the interest; attention called to the fact that the railway is of little real advantage, owing to its direction, and that it causes the traffic to go to Belfast rather than to Londonderry, 3394–3400.

Inability of witness to say whether any delay was caused by the Irish Society having joined in the conveyance to the Drapers' Company; doubt as to the Society having directly joined in any conveyance under the Land Purchase Act, releases only having been given, 3401 *et seq*.——Statement that when the Irish Society granted their estates to the companies they reserved the timber, minerals, fishing, &c.; opinion that if the Society has parted with any mines to the Drapers' Company it has done so negligently, 3407–3428.

Refusal of the Irish Society to make grants of the foreshore in Londonderry, or to give long leases of it; complaint that the nine-tenths of the Society's property, alleged to have been given in perpetuity a century ago, has been left in the hands of a few private individuals to make or mar the city, 3429–3435.——Disinclination of the tenants to take legal proceedings against the companies in order to recover their rights under the trusts, owing to the heavy expenses that would be incurred by doing so, and to the feeling that it is a question to be dealt with by Parliament, 3436–3439. 3615–3619.

Opinion that had there been any Irishmen on Lord Derby's Commission a more accurate report on the Irish case might have been obtained; non-withdrawal by witness of any of the statements he then made as to the tenants having created the great bulk of the property, 3440–3445.——Increase in the value for taxation purposes and the rental of the Irish estates of the Irish Society and the twelve City companies from 1,800 *l*. and 2,190 *l*. in 1609 and 1635 to 136,000 *l*. and 160,000 *l*. per annum, respectively, in 1889; belief that the companies actually took about 90,000 acres more than were supposed to have been intended by the charters, 3446–3461.

Reclamation by the tenants at their own expense of 130,000 acres since 1609; estimate that of the estates conveyed to the companies in 1609, which were valued at about three millions, from half to two-thirds had been created by the tenants, 3462–3466.—— Prejudicial effect of the refusal of the companies to grant residences in perpetuity to country gentlemen in Derry; tendency of the policy of the companies to induce absenteeism, 3467–3471.

Adherence of witness to the opinion he expressed before Lord Derby's Commission to the effect that the Skinners' Estate was the worst-managed estate in the north of Ireland, the tenants being more in arrear on that estate than on any other; statement that the rents in some parts were impossible rents before they were fixed by the Land Court, 3472–3484.——Subsidence of the strong feeling in Dungiven, with regard to the treatment of the tenants by the Skinners' Company, on fair rents being fixed and subsequent purchase, 3485–3488.

Assertion that there is some mistake on the part of Mr. M'Laughlin if he states that witness distinctly promised that all emoluments and privileges would be continued by the Skinners' Company, as before, and that on that promise the tenants purchased; witness never referred to the grants in the presence of the tenants, 3489–3506.——Evidence to the effect that the Fishmongers' Company raised the rents enormously on their estate, two rents that were 8 *l*. 15 s. 6 d. and 7 *l*. 10 s. in 1860 having since become 56 *l*. and 75 *l*. respectively, 3507–3520.

Belief that the Grocers' Company, who sold their estate in 1871, made some provision with regard to the grants by giving a lump sum to the parish church, 3521, 3522.——Explanation that the taking of promissory notes for arrears was a special advantage given by the Salters' Company to tenants who could not pay cash; probability that if the company were appealed to in the case of Bolger they would act leniently towards him, 3523–3551.

Todd, R. H., LL.D. (Analysis of his Evidence)—*continued*.

Opinion that when the companies sold the trust property they got a fair market price for it, 3551-3555. 3589. 3590.—Reiterated denial of the allegation that witness induced the tenants on the Ballinascreen estate to purchase by promising them a continuance of the grants; reference hereon to the provision made by the company for Rainey School, 3568-3588.

Decided opinion that the companies ought to spend in Ireland all the money derived from their Irish estates; witness further submitting that the companies hold under a trust, 3592-3614. 3631-3660. 3678-3684.—Mistaken policy for the companies to give money to charities instead of to objects by which the whole community would be benefited, 3644-3651. 3675, 3677.

Unpopularity of the Irish Society in Londonderry; desirability of their being extinguished, as they do no good, 3657-3675.—Grounds for the opinion that the Society have treated their tenants very badly, the latter having had to go to the Land Court to get their rents reduced, 3685-3691.

Statement that when a railway is carried into a particular district it has its due influence upon the rents in the locality; complaint that the Society have not taken an active interest in promoting a railway in the county of Derry, 3692-3700.—Admission that if a tenant held his land at a nominal rent for a lengthened period that would compensate him in some measure for any outlay he made, 3704, 3705.

Towse, John Wrench. (Analysis of his Evidence.)—Witness, who is clerk to the Fishmongers' Company, explains that the company have sold all their lands in Ireland, having in 1881 first passed a resolution in favour of sale, and having in 1883 eventually decided to offer to each tenant his holding at twenty years' purchase of the net rent, 4858-4869.—From 1836 till 1887 the company spent, on an average, about 4,777 *l.* a year in donations and contributions to churches, chapels, schools, &c., and upon general management, 4870-4879.

Deduction of ten per cent. allowed off the purchase-money in respect of county cess, poor rate, draining and ditching, farm buildings, repairs, &c., a further 8 per cent. having been allowed for possible depreciation and other matters, 4880-4885. 5109-5113.—No special provision was made for the continuance of donations to churches, schools, &c., 4886.

Option of three different modes of purchase given to the tenants, the whole of the tenants (about 400) having practically accepted the terms, 4887-4897.—Varying size of the holdings from about two acres to about 250 acres; great variation also in the rent per acre, 4898-4906.—Adoption by the great majority of the tenants of the scheme of purchase by means of annual payment inclusive of sinking fund and interest; main portion of the purchase-money received through the Land Commissioners, under Lord Ashbourne's Act, 4907-4918. 5177-5186.

Total of 143,858 *l.* as the purchase-money, less 20,019 *l.* for legal expenses, donations, redemption of tithe, &c., 4918-4929. 4991-4994. 5039-5041. 5047-5048.—Commutation of the donations to the clergy by a lump payment for three years, 4923-4927. 5049, 5050. 5057-5059.—Investigation and approval of the title by the Land Commissioners, 4928-4930.—Continued payment of pensions to labourers and others, the amount being about 300 *l.* a year, 4931-4938.

Explanations respecting the total rental of the Fishmongers' Estate and the increase or decrease at different periods since 1810, the gross rental on sale being about 9,400 *l.* as compared with 7,897 *l.* in 1810; reference to special instances of large increase, 4939-4952. 4957-4960. 5103-5171. 5207, 5208.—Statement as to the company having withdrawn a proposed covenant in the draft leases that there should be no claim for tenant right; legal advice taken on this point, 4953-4956. 5090-5107. 5173-5175.—Reduction of 10 per cent. offered for prompt payment of arrears, which in two or three cases promissory notes were taken, 4960-4964.

Considerable expenditure by the company in keeping open the canal from Ballykelly to Lough Foyle, which was, however, quite out of use when the estate was sold, 4967-4976.—Belief that upon sale there was no reservation of minerals, 4977-4980.—Circumstance of the Irish Society not having joined in the conveyance of the estate, 4981-4988.—Sale, practically, of all the timber, 4989, 4990.

Evidence to the effect that the company did not get the full value of the estate, some of the farms having since been sold by the purchasers at very enhanced prices, after allowing for the value of the tenant-right, 4995-5008. 5140-5141.—Examination as to the company having discontinued their grants to schools and to churches, and as to the grounds upon which witness justifies their action in the matter; reference more especially to the voluntary character of their contributions, and to their large expenditure under these heads before the sale of the estate, 5009-5035.

Explanations in connection with certain returns showing the income and expenditure under different heads, and distinguishing between the amount expended in Ireland and England

Report, 1890—*continued.*

Towse, John Wrench. (Analysis of his Evidence)—*continued.*

England respectively, 5036–5089. 5129–5134——Average expenditure of about 800 *l.* a year in England on the Irish estate, over and above about 4,700 *l.* spent in Ireland, 5141. 5146——Statement on the question of payment of county cess and poor rate by the company before and since 1871; 5127–5149.

Admission as to the tenants having made most of the improvements on the estate, 5176——Exceedingly few cases in which the arrears were added to the purchase price, the total of the arrears at the time of sale having been 1,000 *l.*; belief that it was known to the Land Commissioners that the arrears were included in the prices, 5187–5192. 5195. 5196—— Circumstances under which promissory notes were taken from some of the tenants for arrears of rent or interest, 5210–5221.

Reference to the Report of Lord Derby's Commission in 1884 as testifying to the liberal action of the city companies in making grants to churches, schools, &c., on their Ulster estates, 5222–5224——Due consideration given by the Fishmongers' Company, in their settlement with the tenants, to the incidence of local burdens and the liability for religious and educational objects, 5725–5738——Recognition by the tenants of the careful and equitable spirit in which the scheme of purchase was framed by the company, 5738, 5739.

Trade. Opinion that the London companies were originally founded with a view mainly to purposes of trade and for the mutual benefit of their own members, *Sawyer* 6371–6380.

TRUSTS:

Popular opinion throughout witness' district that the several London companies which hold under the Irish Society are under the same trusts as the Society; recognition of this obligation as regards religion and education, *Hickey* 9–33. 169–179. 300.

Argument that the companies have been under obligations as trustees and that they should not sell their estates and take all the money away from the country without providing for a continuance of the annual grants; belief that there is a legal as well as a moral claim upon them in this respect, *Wilson* 331–361.

Conclusion as to the companies being trustees and as to their being legally liable for expenditure in respect of religious education and other matters, *Brown* 537. 598. 636–651. 675–689——Reasons further given for the conclusion that the companies are trustees and not private landlords, *ib.* 745–781——Duty of the Legislature to secure the execution of the trusts, *ib.* 768.

General feeling of the district that the companies held the estates under trust; reasons for this belief, *Jordan* 848–861. 925–937.

Suggestion that, in the event of the trusts being made over to trustees, the trustees should be appointed by the Lord Chancellor of Ireland, or by Parliament; recommendation that there should be three or five of them, *Todd* 3171–3181. 3185–3187 —— Assertion that the English and Scotch subjects who accepted King James' offer and planted trade in Ulster were clearly distinguished from the "Londoners," not being trustees in any sense of the word, *ib.* 3188–3203.

General view of Protestants and Catholics that the companies hold their property in trust for the locality, *Quinn* 4800, 4801 —— View of the people generally that at least a portion of the properties should be retained in trust, *ib.* 4809, 4810.

Action of the Skinners' Company as regards donations, &c., in the full belief that they were not trustees, *Saunders* 5845–5867——Circumstances of Dr. Todd, who acted both for the tenants as well as the company, having raised no question about the company being in the position of trustees, *ib.* 5819–5817.

Legal opinions obtained in the negative from the late Sir George Jessel and the late Lord Chancellor Law upon the question whether the London companies were under a trust in respect of their Ulster Estate, *Glover* 5988–5998. 6032–6037. 6164–6167.

Reference by the Committee to the judgment of the House of Lords in the Skinners' case in 1845 as establishing beyond dispute that the Irish Society are a body of public officers holding their Irish estates and administering the funds derived from them, subject to certain public trusts and obligations, p. 309.

Distinction drawn by the Committee between the companies and the Irish Society upon the question whether the former took their estates from the latter, subject to the same trusts and obligations as attached to the Society, p. 319.

Argument in detail by Mr. Walker, as counsel on behalf of leaseholders in county Derry, in support of the conclusion that not only the Irish Society but the several City companies hold their estates in the county subject to public trusts and legal obligations, pp. 333 *et seq.*

Statement by counsel as to the word "trust" not appearing in a certain deed of the Skinners' Company, p. 348.

W.

Waterford Estate. Varying years' purchase obtained when Lord Waterford has sold land in the locality; high price paid by witness for some land in 1871, and by other tenants of Lord Waterford, *Brown* 513-575. 601-612. 653-655. 658—Hardship upon the tenants on the Waterford estate in respect of a bog sold as a separate lot instead of being allocated among the holdings, *ib.* 578. 742-744.

See also Haberdashers' Company.

Watney, John. (Analysis of his Evidence.)—Witness has been clerk for fourteen years to the Mercers' Company, which is the premier London Company of the four associated companies, 4033-4036. 4298.

Submission by witness of a statement giving a short history of the company's dealings with their Irish properties, and including printed copies of the documents of title, 4037-4044—Evidence to the effect that the company have not sold any of their property, except one small freehold in 1819; absence of any representation on the part of the tenants that they wished to buy, 4045-4048. 4250-4263.

Statement that the company did not take any personal part in the management of the estate until 1831, when the long lease fell in; expenditure of 300,000 *l.* since 1831 on the estate, the object having been to benefit the whole property, rather than any particular farm, 4050-4063—Detailed summary of the expenditure on the estate handed in; reduction of the annual rental from 10,443 *l.* in 1831 to 9,600 *l.* at the present time, it having been 10,111 *l.* in 1854 and 11,769 *l.* in 1876; 4064-4092. 4101-4103. 4178-4183. 4245-4249. 4286-4293. 4337-4334.

Estimate that the expenses of management amount to about 1,100 *l.* a year, the net rental being about 9,000 *l.* a year; average during the fifty years, of the expenses, 1347 *l.*, and of the net rental, 8,000 *l.* to 10,000 *l.*; 4093-4100. 4110-4127. 4184-4186—Prosperous condition of the estate, there being practically no arrears; occasional complaints from tenants that the rental has been too high, 4104-4110. 4118. 4294-4325.

Belief that two-fifths of the tenants are Roman Catholics, two-fifths Presbyterians, and one-fifth Episcopalians; details of the expenditure of the company on schools, the annual amount being 400 *l.*; 4111-4117—Information as to the manner in which the accounts of the estate are made up and audited, 4123-4136.

Particulars of the rents and fines at each sub-letting of the estate before 1831, showing a great improvement in the value of the property, 4137-4150—Enumeration of the improvements made by the company since 1831, the cost averaging about 6,000 *l.* a year; admission that the agricultural improvements on the holdings have been made by the tenants, 4151-4178.

Statement that after payment of the annual expenditure the balance, which is about half, of the income from the Irish estate goes into the general account of the company; impression that none of that account is expended for Irish uses, 4187-4241. 4284-4285. 4361. 4362—Evidence to the effect that the building leases given by the company are for ninety-nine years, and that previously they were for sixty-one years, 4306-4321.

Belief that the reason why the company refused to give a grant towards the drainage of the Clady river was because it was useless to do anything until an obstruction lower down was removed, 4326-4339—Explanation that the grants to dispensaries have not been withdrawn, but that, of the two medical men whom the company induced to settle on the estate, one retired and the other died, and that long ago the Poor Law came into operation; small grant still given to the successor of the doctor who died, 4340-4349—Satisfaction of the other associated companies with the manner in which the estate is managed by the Mercers' Company, 4343-4349.

Wilson, The Rev. Hamilton Brown, D.D. (Analysis of his Evidence.)—Lengthened residence of witness at Cookstown (Tyrone), close to the Drapers' estate; long period for which he and his predecessors have received an annual grant of ten guineas from the company, 301-305—Withdrawal of the grant to witness in 1886, grants to other ministers having also been withdrawn; belief that this has been done so that the grantees might not have a vested interest in view of the sale of the estates, 306-310.

Decided advantage to the tenants through the sale of the companies' estates, 311—Injurious effect as regards charities and education, 311—Liberal help formerly given by the Drapers' Company to dispensaries, this having been withdrawn; less need for such help since the Poor Law Act, 311-313. 376-384.

Comments upon the refusal of the Skinners' Company to receive a deputation in 1887 prepared to put forward certain claims on the part of the Presbyterian body, 314-321. 324.

—Claims

Report, 1890—*continued.*

Wilson, The Rev. Hamilton Brown, D.D. (Analysis of his Evidence)—*continued.*

——Claims of the Presbyterians as paying three-fourths of the rent in the district; relative population as compared with the Roman Catholics, 321–331. 364–376.

Argument that the companies have been under obligations as trustees, and that they should not sell their estates and take all the money away from the country without providing for a continuance of the annual grants; belief that there is a legal as well as a moral claim upon them in this respect, 331–341——Inadequate grants to Presbyterians as compared with Episcopalians, 331. 364–378.

Dissatisfaction with the action of the Salters' Company in respect of the Balney schools, 335–338——Increase in the value of the estates through the tenants' improvements; great mischief in this respect where short leases are given, 339–345——Doubt as to the legal claim of the Roman Catholics to religious grants, though they should share in the secular grants, 369–371.

Witnesses' Expenses. Particulars thereof; total of 257 *l.* 8 *s.* 6 *d.*; *Rep.* xl.

www.ingramcontent.com/pod-product-compliance
Lightning Source LLC
Chambersburg PA
CBHW022122020426
42334CB00015B/718

* 9 7 8 3 7 4 2 8 1 1 1 3 4 *